Company Law in Context

Company Law in Context

Text and Materials

Second Edition

David Kershaw

London School of Economics

David Kershaw is a Professor of Law at the London School of Economics. He qualified as a solicitor at Herbert Smith and practised corporate law with Wolf Theiss, Vienna and in the Mergers & Acquisitions Group of Shearman & Sterling in New York and London. He holds an LLB from the University of Warwick and an LLM and SJD from Harvard Law School.

OXFORD
UNIVERSITY PRESS

OXFORD
UNIVERSITY PRESS

Great Clarendon Street, Oxford, OX2 6DP,
United Kingdom

Oxford University Press is a department of the University of Oxford.
It furthers the University's objective of excellence in research, scholarship,
and education by publishing worldwide. Oxford is a registered trade mark of
Oxford University Press in the UK and in certain other countries

British Library Cataloguing in Publication Data
Data available

Library of Congress Cataloging in Publication Data
Data available

ISBN 978-0-19-960932-1

Printed in Great Britain by
Ashford Colour Press Ltd, Gosport, Hampshire

For Mum and Dad

■ NEW TO THIS EDITION

Among the new coverage in this edition you will find:

- new discussion of changes to the revised UK Corporate Governance Code and UK Stewardship Code;
- expanded coverage in Chapter 15 (Enforcing Directors' Duties) to cover the case law on the new derivative claim mechanisms;
- discussion of the Supreme Court's decision in *Progress Property Company Ltd v Moorgarth Group Ltd* [2011] 2 BCLC 332 on disguised distributors;
- discussion of the Supreme Court's decision in *Re Paycheck Services 3 Ltd* [2011] 1 BCLC 141 on defacto directors and director liability for unlawful dividends;
- discussion of the effects of *Chandler v Cape Plc* [2011] EWHC 951 QB on group liability;
- and discussion of *O'Donnell v Shanahan* [2009] 2 BCLC 666 on corporate opportunities.

■ PREFACE

Students often view company law as something they have to do in order to get a job in a corporate law firm, to be prepared for working in a corporate law firm, or indeed to assure themselves that they do not want to work in a corporate law firm. The aspiration of this book is to try and persuade more students that company law is not just a useful discipline offering a high return on your intellectual capital investment, but that it is, on its own terms, a fascinating and intellectually rich and challenging area of the law.

The challenge for any teacher of company law is to convey the excitement and enthusiasm that we have for our subject to you, to enable you to discover for yourself the fascination and the intellectual stimulation available from something as apparently immanently dry as company law. In my experience this discovery is not possible for most students without access to the context in which the company and company law operates: the economic and social context within which business activity takes place. This book uses this context to facilitate an advanced understanding of corporate legal concepts, structures, and regulatory choices.

This context is offered in four different ways in the book. First, the book deploys, intermittently, a case study involving the 'Bob's Electronics business': the development of a business from idea, to sole trader, to incorporation, to public limited company. The aim of the case study is to place the student in the shoes of the business actor; to enable the student to empathize with the problems a business person faces in setting up a business and the problems encountered as the company is formed and developed. The context for students comes from the case study, but importantly the case study also aims to encourage you to create your own context as you think about how you would behave in the context described in the case study. Connected to this is a second tool deployed in several chapters of the book to generate context. This is the use of specific assignments for readers after the initial context has been provided but before the substantive law has been engaged. Obviously, for many students short of time and with dates and appointments to keep, it will be far too tempting to skip over the assignments and to plough into the substance. If you can find the time and delay the appointment it would be very beneficial for you to do the assignment; and even more beneficial to talk about these assignments together with your fellow students. The idea of these assignments is to enable you to think from first principles about possible regulatory solutions to the introduced problem and to identify for yourself the policy reasons for and against the identified solutions. These home-made solutions, and the reasons for and against them, provide helpful background for when you engage with the actual legal rules. They enable you to critically engage with the actual legal rules and are invaluable in building confidence when you find that the solutions you create are very similar to the ones actually deployed by UK company law. The third contextual tool is less context than analytical framework: in Part II of the book we make use of a very simple economic framework—the framework of agency problems—to organize the different legal mechanisms which UK company law deploys to control management behaviour. Finally, the fourth element of context is straightforward: where possible the book refers to real world examples—real UK companies and their actual activities.

A further feature of the book, which is not a contextual tool but is used for similar objectives as the above tools, is the use, particularly in Part II of the book on *Corporate Control and Accountability*, of comparative company law. In particular, the book compares UK company law with the company law of the US state of Delaware, which is the most important state for company law in the United States. Why, one might ask, do we need to learn about US company law before we have studied all of UK company law? The reason for using these comparative materials is not that I want students of UK company law to become experts in US company law; rather it is because I believe that comparative law assists students—undergraduate and postgraduate alike—in understanding, as well as enjoying learning about, UK company law. The comparison enables students to see that UK company law involves regulatory choices that are supported by a set of policy justifications and that the UK could, as other jurisdictions do, make different regulatory choices that give different weight to alternative policy considerations. This both facilitates a better understanding of UK company law and gives students confidence to critically evaluate UK company law. This critical vantage point makes learning and teaching company law much more fun. As this is the goal of the comparative engagement it is used in the book to different extents in different areas of company law. It is used when I think it makes a contribution to the above goals.

The book conceives of itself as an advanced undergraduate company text that may also be used for postgraduate company law and corporate governance modules. Unsurprisingly, this understanding of the book structures its form and content. The book consists of the hard copy of the book and two additional chapters that are only available online on the book's web page (www.oxfordtextbooks.co.uk/orc/kershaw2e/). The online chapters are chapters on *Disclosure, Accounting, and Audit*, and *Issuing Shares to the Public*. The hard copy book chapters contain the subject areas which in my view form the basis of a standard undergraduate company law course. The reason for separating these two chapters is simply to ensure that the book is not too big and heavy and that it can be read and carried manageably without injuring your back.

The first edition made the following acknowledgements and thank yous which I would like to repeat with a couple of amendments for helpful contributions from friends and colleagues.

The book is the product of two and half years of hard academic labour; many nights at the computer after our three wonderful children, Jack, Lukas, and Megan, were put to bed. During this time, as always, my wife, Marlies, supported, guided, and inspired my work. I truly could not have done this, or for that matter much else, without her and I am far more indebted and grateful to her than I think she knows.

There are lots of other people that I need to thank. Most importantly, my Mum and Dad. My Mum, Alison, read every single word of this book not once but twice. She is the first person who has read the book cover to cover twice and she may well be the last. Her thoughts and guidance on the book, its structure, its contents, and its punctuation were invaluable. Thank you Mum. My Dad, Bob, the inspiration for Bob's Electronics, didn't read the book and who can blame him, but he was hugely supportive of this project and he fixed our house whilst I was writing this book. Thanks Dad.

Finally, there are lots of family, friends, and colleagues who have made direct and indirect contributions to this book. I could say you know who you are and thank you, but writing a book is not a regular event and this is my first, so I won't take that option. I am enormously grateful, in alphabetical order, to the following people for their comments and contributions to the content, style of, and ideas contained in this book: Adele Barzelay, Erna Braun, Markus Braun, Sylvia Braun, Aaron Callen, Matt Cowie, Suzanne Delrieu, Fabien Delrieu, Julio Faundez, David Kennedy, Duncan Kennedy, Helen Kershaw, Ian Kershaw, Jane Kershaw, Joanne Lythe, Jim Lopez, Imre Moller, Richard Moorhead, Ewan McGaughey, Ronalda Murphy, Ben Peacock, Mike Thurlow, Sheila Tucker, and Edmund Schuster. Many thanks also to Paul Davies, Peter Ramsay, and Charlie Webb for taking the time to talk to me about the book and giving me extremely helpful advice about several issues in the book, and to Demetra Arsalidou, Tom Burns, David Cabrelli, Stuart Cross, Janice Denoncourt, Sandra Frisby, Joanna Gray, Aled Griffiths, Rob Heywood, Paddy Ireland, Patrick Masiyakurima,

Marc Moore, Paul Omar, Harry Rajak, Chris Riley, Lee Roach, Ian Snaith, Mike Varney, and Kevin Wardman for their constructive and thoughtful comments and for their generosity for taking the time to carry out the reviews. Finally I am very grateful to John Carroll, Francesca Griffin, Siân Jenkin, Gareth Malna, Jacqueline Senior, Emma Wilson, and the OUP team for all their encouragement, ideas, and consummate professionalism.

The law is stated as known to me as of December 2011
David Kershaw, 9 January 2012

■ GUIDE TO THE BOOK

There are several features designed to help you make the most of your textbook. This guided tour shows you how to utilise them to reinforce your study and to put company law in context for yourself.

> Before we consider the various available rationales it
> three points:
> • It is not clear that Bob's Electronics, the sole-tra
>   form to protect Bob's personal liability exposure.
>   although not complete protection could be provided
>   contract he enters into the counterparty agrees tha
>   business' assets to satisfy unpaid amounts and not t
>   be some enforcement problems in this regard as a re
>   exclusion clauses in the Unfair Contract Terms Ac
>   tractual exclusions would not address third parties
>   contractual relationship with Bob. However, he ma
>   comfort through significant insurance cover. Of co

Running case study

Running throughout the length of the book, the case study of Bob's Electronics Ltd. forms an integral part of your learning. Examining the life cycle of a business, its practice-orientated approach will encourage you to apply the relevant cases and legislation to real-life scenarios.

> Hypothetical C
>
> After several years of running Bob's Electronics Ltd.
> his house in the south of France. After a lengthy searc
> well-known professional manager, as CEO and sole d
>   Upon Bob's retirement we see that Bob no longer
> managerial services and would be concerned if Marku
> self that could be profitably exploited by Bob's Elect
> have a management and ownership structure that cou
> make value-reducing decisions (such as buying the r
> pany for £2,000,000 even though the return would b

Hypotheticals

Drawing examples from the running case study, these boxes raise numerous points for you to reflect on and allow you to consider the best course of action for each situation.

> ■ *Wilkinson v West Coast Capital* [2005] EWHC 30(
>
> [In this case several investors purchased a company, NGS, th
> operating company (TGS), which ran a retail chain known as '
> structure of NGS was as follows: 40% of the shares were owne
> and his associates; 10% by the founder of the company; 25%
> partnership (West Coast Capital, WCC), in which Sir Tom Hu
> were the only partners; and 25% of the shares were owned
> chief executive officer of NGS. Sir Tom and Mr Gorman were
> Mr Gorman and Mr McMahon were directors of NGS. It was a
> director of NGS.

Extracts from cases, statutes, journals, and newspapers

Primary case and statutory material – together with extracts from journals and newspapers – is consistently interwoven within the text to place important issues and theory in context. Each extract is highlighted within a shaded box to ensure easy reference during study and revision.

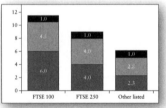

Figures and Tables

Pictorial representation complements the description of key business data and concepts in the text.

Questions and discussion

Questions

1. What does it mean to say that the board's powers in a and undelegated'? Are the powers of a UK board 'origi
2. Are you persuaded by Bainbridge's argument that Del ance right between authority and responsibility? If not
3. What do you think Bainbridge would say about the l *Transactions?*
4. Does Professor Bainbridge overstate the effect on th shareholder instruction rights or more extensive veto a Vodafone/Efficient Capital Structures example set for answer.

In-chapter questions will further your critical engagement with the subject and provide you with ample material to discuss in seminars.

Assignments

Assignment 4

Reread the facts of the Delaware case of *Smith v Van* above.

(1) Applying section 174 of the Companies Act 2006 to t of directors in breach of the duty of care when it ap you find the board liable to compensate the company

(2) If you find the board liable, what losses would the b

(3) In your application of section 174 to the *Van Gorko* hindsight problem. Are you capable of controlling th

These task-based questions will require you to actively apply your knowledge, and craft regulatory solutions to the problems generated by carrying out business activity through the corporate form.

Further reading

Further reading

L. Bebchuk and J Fried, 'Executive Compensation at Fann Incentives, Non-performance Pay, and Camouflage' (2 *Law* 807.

L. Bebchuk and J. Fried, *Pay without Performance: The Compensation* (Harvard University Press, 2006).

B. Cheffins, 'Will Executive Pay Globalise along Ameri *Governance: An International Review* 8.

M.J. Conyon, R.N. Clarke and S.I. Peck, 'Corporate Governa Views from the Top' (1998) 9 *Business Strategy Review*

K. Sheehan, 'Is the Outrage Constraint an Effective Constr

Selected reading recommendations provide you with useful guidance for taking your study even further.

Footnotes

objects amendment cancelled.

In relation to the *ultra vires* rule, over the past century a private, self-ordering response from companies and an i The self-ordering response was to draft exceptionall included every object imaginable and every power imag Such clauses, when well drafted, ensured that companie

⁴ Section 5 Companies Act 1948. Such reasons included for ex economically or efficiently' or 'to enlarge or change the local area Act at www.opsi.gov.uk/ ◍.

Used throughout the text, footnotes elaborate on the discussion within the text, often bringing your attention to useful online sources and material. Where you see the ORC symbol: ◍ go to the Online Resource Centre (www.oxfordtextbooks.co.uk/orc/kershaw2e/) for a detailed web link.

■ GUIDE TO THE ORC

www.oxfordtextbooks.co.uk/orc/kershaw2e/
Company Law in Context is accompanied by an open-access Online Resource
Centre offering ready-to-use teaching and learning resources.

Updates

Ensures you are kept up-to-date with changes to cases
and legislation so that your study is as timely and
relevant as possible.

Annotated web links

The author has carefully selected web links to direct you
to the most useful and reliable online information. This
allows you to be focused and efficient with your research
whilst helping you position your learning within a
contextual framework.

(In addition to the more general, overarching list of
web links, there is also a list of specific web links which
follow up references from individual footnotes).

Interactive ('flashcard') glossary

Test yourself on the complex terminology of company
law with this series of interactive flashcards.

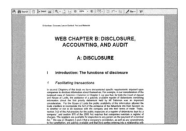

Additional chapters on Disclosure, Accounting and Audit, and Issuing Shares to the Public

The hard copy book chapters contain the subject areas which generally form the basis of a standard undergraduate company law course. These additional online chapters will be of value for students taking postgraduate courses on company law and corporate governance, and as invaluable background reading for undergraduates.

PowerPoint® slides

A suite of diagrams and charts in PowerPoint® has been included, to aid your understanding of challenging cases and concepts.

Video podcast

Meet the author as he introduces the book and sets the scene for your studies.

■ CONTENTS IN BRIEF

CONTENTS IN FULL

PART III CORPORATE FINANCE

PART IV   CREDITOR PROTECTION

■ TABLE OF CASES

Cases and page references in **bold** indicate that the case is discussed in detail with extracts from the judgment

■ TABLE OF LEGISLATION

Page references in **bold** indicate that the text is reproduced in full

Table of Statutory Instruments

■ ACKNOWLEDGEMENTS

Grateful acknowledgement is made to all the authors and publishers of copyright material which appears in this book, and in particular to the following for permission to reprint material from the sources indicated:

Crown copyright material is reproduced under Class Licence Number C2006010631 with the permission of the Controller of OPSI and the Queen's Printer for Scotland. Parliamentary copyright material is reproduced with the permission of the Controller of Her Majesty's Stationery Office on behalf of Parliament.

American Bar Association: extract from H Marsh: 'Are Directors Trustees: Conflicts of Interest and Corporate Morality', 22 *Business Lawyer* 35 (1966).

Behan, Beverly: extract from B Behan: 'Splitting the Chairman and CEO Roles', *BusinessWeek.com* (2008).

Cambridge University Press and the author: extract from J Armour: 'Legal Capital: An Outdated Concept?', 7 *European Business Organization Law Review* 5 (2006). © TMC Asser Press, The Hague, and the contributors, published by Cambridge University Press, reproduced with permission.

Columbia Law Review Association: extract from DW Leebron, 'Limited Liability, Tort Victims and Creditors' 91 *Columbia Law Review* 1565 (1991).

Conyon, Martin and Graham Sadler: table from 'How does UK and US CEO Pay Measure Up', working paper (2005).

Eidenmueller, H, B Grunewald, and U Noack: extract from 'Minimum Capital in the System of Legal Capital', in M Lutter et al (eds) 'Legal Capital in Europe', *European Company and Financial Law Review*, Special Volume 1, 2006.

Financial Reporting Council: extracts from *The Combined Code*. Adapted and reproduced with the kind permission of the Financial Reporting Council. All rights reserved. For further information, please visit www.frc.org.uk or call +44 (0)20 7492 2300.

Financial Times: extracts from T Harford: 'Checks and balances: Burberry is switching jobs from Wales to China. Should the government intervene?', 3 March 2007 in *Weekend Magazine*; R Lambert, 'Buy backs are often doomed to destroy value', 21 August 2011; Stefan Stern: 'Why M&S shareholders should think before they speak', 8 April 2008; and 'Parachute holed: GSK must respond to shareholder concerns on executive pay', 20 May 2003, leader.

Hart Publishing Ltd: extract from R Williams, 'Disqualifying Directors: A Remedy Worse than the Disease', 7 *Journal of Corporate Law Studies* 213 (2007).

Harvard Law Review Association: extracts from S Bainbridge: 'Director Primacy and Shareholder Disempowerment' , 119 *Harvard Law Review* 1735 (2006); H Hansmann, R Kraakman, and R Squire, 'Law and the Rise of the Firm', *199 Harvard Law Review* 1333 (2006); and E Merrick Dodd Jr., 'For Whom are Corporate Managers Trustees', 45 *Harvard Law Review* 1145 (1932).

Harvard University Press: extract from Frank Easterbrook and Daniel R Fischel: *The Economic Structure of Corporate Law* (Harvard University Press, 1991, pp.35–38). Copyright © 1991 by the President and Fellows of Harvard College.

Hughes, Christopher: extract from 'Dash to splash the cash: by using buy-backs companies are taking advantage of low interest rates and cheap borrowing to return money to investors', *Financial Times*, 11 September 2006.

Incorporated Council of Law Reporting: extracts from the Law Reports: Appeal Cases (AC); Chancery (Ch); King's Bench Division (KB); Queen's Bench Division (QB); and Weekly Law Reports (WLR).

Informa Law: extracts from Lloyd's Reports. Reproduced with kind permission of Informa Law & Finance.

International Accounting Standards Committee Foundation: extract from *IAS 24: Related Party Disclosures.*

LexisNexis Australia: extract from the Australian Law Reports.

Marks and Spencer plc: tables from 'Marks and Spencer plc Shareholder Structure (Ordinary shares)', April 2011.

McKinsey & Company: extract from Richard Dobbs and Werner Rehm, 'Debating Point: Are share buybacks a good thing?', *Financial Times*, 28 June 2006.

The New York Times: extract from Milton Friedman, 'The Social Responsibility of Business is to Increase its Profits', 13 September 1970.

New York Stock Exchange Group, Inc.: extract from the *New York Stock Exchange Listed Company Manual*. All rights in the NYSE Listed Company Manual are owned exclusively by NYSE Group, Inc., © 2003-2008 NYSE Group, Inc., All Rights Reserved. For the most recent NYSE publications please visit http://www.nyse.com/.

Northwestern University School of Law: extract from William T Allen, Jack B Jacobs, and Leo E Strine Jr.: 'Realigning the Standard of Review of Director Due Care with Delaware Public Policy: A Critique of Van Gorkom and its Progeny as a Standard of Review Problem', 96 *North Western University Law Review* 449 (2002). Reprinted by special permission of Northwestern University School of Law, *Northwestern University Law Review*.

Oxford University Press: extracts from B Cheffins: Company Law: Theory Structure and Operation (OUP, 1997); R. Kraakman et al: The Anatomy of Corporate Law: A Comparative and Functional Approach (2nd ed, OUP, 2009); and JE Parkinson: Corporate Power and Responsibility (Clarendon Press, 2002).

Oxford University Press Journals: extract from D Kershaw: 'Lost in Translation: Corporate Opportunities in Comparative Perspective', 25 *Oxford Journal of Legal Studies* 603 (2005).

Palmer, James: extract from letter to the *Financial Times*: 'Bill's requirements threaten to make UK law incompatible with practical running of companies', 9 May 2006.

Price Waterhouse Coopers LLC: figures from *Executive Compensation Review of the Year 2009*.

Reed Elsevier (UK) trading as LexisNexis: extracts from *All England Law Reports* (All ER) and *Butterworths' Company Law Cases* (BCLC).

Sweet & Maxwell Ltd: extracts from *All England Law Reports* (All ER); *British Company Cases* (BCC); extracts from Robert Stevens: 'Vicarious Liability or Vicarious Action' 123 *Law Quarterly Review* 30 (2007); D Kershaw, 'Involuntary Creditors and the Case for Accounting Based Distribution Regulation', 2 *Journal of Business Law* 140 (2009); and Marc Moore, ' "A Temple Built on Faulty Foundations": Piercing the Corporate Veil and the Legacy of Salomon v Salomon', *Journal of Business Law* 180 (2006).

University of Chicago Law School: extract from F Easterbrook and D Fischel: 'Limited Liability and the Corporation', 52 *University of Chicago Law Review* 89 (1985).

Vanderbilt Law Review: extract from R Thomas, 'Explaining the International CEO Pay-Gap: Board Capture or Market Driven', 57 *Vanderbilt Law Review* 1171 (2004).

Vodafone Group plc: extracts from the *Articles of Association*.

Wake Forest Law Review: extract from C Elson: 'The Enron Failure and Corporate Governance Reform', 38 *Wake Forest Law Review* 855 (2003).

Washington and Lee Law Review and the author: extract from Stephen M Bainbridge, 'In Defense of the Shareholder Wealth Maximization Norm: A Reply to Professor Green', 50 WASH. & LEE L. REV. 1423 (1993).

Wiley-Blackwell Publishing Ltd: extracts from P Ireland, 'Company Law and the Myth of Shareholder Ownership', 62 Modern Law Review 32-57 (1999), and D Kershaw, 'How the Law Thinks About Corporate Opportunities' , 25 *Legal Studies* 533 (2005).

Wolters Kluwer Law and Business: extracts from Jonathan Rickford et al, 'Reforming Capital: Report of the Interdisciplinary Group on Capital Maintenance', *European Business Law Review* 921 (2004) and Jesse H Choper, John C Coffee, Jr., Ronald J Gilson: *Cases and Materials on Corporations* (6e, Aspen Publishers, 2004).

The Yale Law Journal Company: extract from H Hansmann and R Kraakman, 'Toward Unlimited Shareholder Liability for Corporate Torts', Yale Law Journal 1879 (1991).

Every effort has been made to trace and contact copyright holders prior to going to press but this has not been possible in every case. If notified, the publisher will undertake to rectify any errors or omissions at the earliest opportunity.

PART I
INCORPORATION AND SEPARATE LEGAL PERSONALITY

CHAPTER ONE

AN INTRODUCTION TO THE CONTEXT AND CONSEQUENCES OF INCORPORATION

One of the objectives of this book is to make company law and its accompanying financial jargon accessible and relevant. One way in which the book attempts to further this goal is through the use of a case study, which tracks the development of a business—the Bob's Electronics business—from the initial small-scale attempt to implement a business idea through to the operation of the business as a large company. This case study will provide some context for company law's often difficult to grasp structures and concepts, as well as facilitating a practical understanding of both the economic problems to which company law responds and the problems that the organizational form of the company generates. The context provided by the case study will, along with other contextual tools, enable an advanced engagement with the company law materials set out in the book. Whilst the case study method is very common in other disciplines, such as business administration, it is a relatively unusual approach to legal study and teaching. It is an approach that requires a different type of engagement from the reader than is typical in legal study. It works best if you attempt to place yourself in the shoes of the major players in the case study: what would your concerns be in the situation in question; in what ways could you respond to the specified problems? The responses you have to the case study and the regulatory solutions you would fashion to respond to the identified problems form an invaluable benchmark against which you can engage with and evaluate the actual regulatory solutions discussed in the book.

I BOB'S ELECTRONICS AS A SOLE TRADER

1 The business idea

Bob lives in a small rural village in the Yorkshire Dales, from where he commutes to his job in Leeds. For the past 10 years he has been a successful business development officer in a well-known high street bank, during which time, apart from the periodic unlucky days at the York races, he has been prudent and has managed to save £100,000. He feels that now the time is right to take some risks in his life, to leave his job, and to start his own business.

His time as a business development officer has served him well. He feels confident that he knows a successful business opportunity when he sees one and, as luck would have it, this week he saw that idea. This week he called up Build-to-Order Computers Plc to order a computer that matched precisely the specification he required. The tailoring of consumer products to personal needs and preferences is, Bob is convinced, the name of the contemporary business game. Bob is a confident chap. He thinks there is space in this market for a local, Yorkshire version of a build-to-order computer business. He will take local orders and provide local service: modern technology with local knowledge and a Yorkshire accent. This business will be called 'Bob's Electronics'.

2 The inputs required to run the business

To take orders, build, and deliver computers Bob will require the following inputs/ resources:

- Suppliers:
  - He will need to purchase components to build the computers and will have to contract with suppliers to provide those components.
  - He will need to purchase the equipment and machinery required to build the computers and delivery vans to deliver the computers.
- Employees:
  - He will need to employ people to: take telephone orders; build the computers; deliver the computers; draft contracts; and deal with any maintenance or faults that develop with the computers whilst they are under guarantee.
- Finance:
  - He will need finance in excess of his £100,000 in order to be able to purchase: premises where the business can be operated; equipment to build the computers; office furniture; delivery vans; and an initial inventory of components.
  - He will need to have sufficient funds to enable the business to keep running—to buy more components and pay employees and utility bills etc.—whilst he is waiting to sell the assembled computers or to be paid for the computers that have been sold.

3 Sole trading/sole proprietorship[1]

Bob is wary of lawyers and the fees they charge. He decides to set up Bob's Electronics without taking legal advice about how to set up the business. He is going to run the business as a sole trader. To be a sole trader means that Bob, the individual person, will own all the assets associated with the business and will enter into all contracts related to the business, just as a person owns a house or a car or enters into a contract to buy any product. Bob, the person, owns the components that make the computers. He negotiates and enters into the contracts to provide components, finance, and labour, as well as the contracts with the consumers. He is personally responsible for all legal consequences arising from those contracts and the use of the supplied computers.

In relation to the Bob's Electronics business run as a sole trader, Bob is the common factor in several contractual relationships: with suppliers; with employees; with the providers of finance; and with the customers who purchase this product. In the language of law and economics Bob is a nexus of contracts who brings together various inputs, which, once contracted for, he controls in order to generate an output that is offered to consumers in the computer market place. Bob, as a sole trader, is the simplest type of firm. This firm is represented pictorially in Figure 1.1.

---

[1] The term sole proprietorship is the term that is typically used in the US to refer to what we in the UK typically call a sole trader.

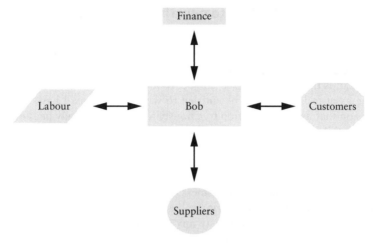

Figure 1.1 *Bob the Firm/Bob as a nexus of contracts*

4 Running Bob's Electronics: decision-making by a sole trader

Bob as a sole trader is the nexus of several contractual relationships that provide the various inputs into the production of customized computers. *He* decides which contracts to enter into: with which suppliers; which possible employees; and which sources of finance. Once he has contracted for these inputs of labour, supplies, and finance, *he* decides how these resources are to be deployed within the sole trader firm. He directs the use of these resources to generate the product: he decides on the range of products which can be offered; which production and distribution methods to deploy; how individual employees will be used and the tasks they are given. Bob is 'an entrepreneur coordinator who directs production'.[2] As the business expands he will delegate more and more of the everyday operational decisions to employees of the business. However, as the 'owner' of the business, he controls the business and may overrule any decision of any employee or agent he disagrees with. He can request and choose to listen to other people's advice, but no one else has a say in the final decision.

A central concern of the law of business organizations is how law and organizational form can assist business persons and entrepreneurs in generating wealth by ensuring that business decisions are made with a view to maximizing the value of the business, which in turn increases the size of our UK wealth-pie. From the perspective of creating wealth in our society, Bob appears to be a good person to make decisions affecting the business. As a sole trader, any business decision he makes affects his personal wealth. A good decision that results in increased sales benefits him as much as it benefits the business of Bob's Electronics. Any decision that results in the business losing or wasting money decreases his personal wealth. Another way of putting this is to say that Bob's business and personal financial interests are *aligned* and we would expect him to make decisions that maximize the value of the business.

Wealth creation is not the only concern that we may have when thinking about how to organize and regulate business activity, although it is unquestionably a very important concern. Indeed, as a sole trader Bob may pursue his non-wealth preferences through the business if those preferences are more important to him than making more money. The key point is that as a sole-trading firm *he* directs production in a way that fulfils *his* preferences. No other person who contracts with Bob-the-firm has any say in how the business is run; how production is directed.

---

[2] R. Coase, 'The Theory of the Firm' (1937) 16 *Economica* 386.

5 What does it mean for Bob to own the business; what is his equity in the business?

People who own businesses as sole traders or who own other assets often say, for example, 'it's my business' or 'it's my house'. Often, however, when they say 'it's my asset' what they mean is that 'it is my asset' subject to all other claims on that asset. That is, 'if I sold the asset today, I would be entitled to what is left once I have discharged all other claims on that asset'. In relation to a house, for example, I may be the legal owner of my house, but if I sold it today I would have to pay back the mortgagee (the bank) the money I borrowed from them to buy the house. What I have is a residual financial interest in the house: what is left when other claimants, who have priority over my claim, have been discharged. Bob as a sole trader has a residual interest in the Bob's Electronics business. If, having run a successful business, he decides he has had enough of running the business but cannot find a buyer for the business, he will pay his suppliers, employees, and providers of finance, and satisfy any customer claims. What remains belongs to Bob. This residual interest is sometimes referred to colloquially as his equity in the business.

6 Investing in Bob's Electronics: an introduction to risk and return

Bob has personal funds of £100,000 which he is willing to invest in the business. However, he is aware that additional finance will be required to set up and run the business. Employees will have to be paid, premises will have to purchased, as will the machinery, equipment, and vehicles necessary to produce and distribute the computers and the components used to make the computers. Some of these funds are required to make long-term investments in the business, such as the purchase of business premises. Other funds are necessary only on a short-term basis, for example to cover the period between buying components and making and selling computers.

There is considerable interest from the local business community in Bob's business idea. He has received offers of finance from varying sources. There are two basic options he has to choose between: should he take a loan from, for example, a bank, or should he fund the business by taking on a co-investor, someone who will share in a portion of the residual interest of the business. If Bob elects to take a loan he will be required to pay interest on the loan as well as paying back the amount of the loan (the 'principal') over a period of time to be agreed with the bank. If he borrows to cover the financing gap between paying for components and being paid for computers it is likely that he will take some sort of overdraft facility whereby he periodically borrows and repays in full variable amounts on a regular basis (this is known as working capital finance). If he borrows money to purchase the premises, the loan may well be paid back over several years (this is referred to here as 'loan capital').

An alternative to borrowing such funds would be to find a co-investor in the business to provide equity capital along with Bob. Such a co-investor would purchase a proportion of the residual interest in the business. This type of investment is referred to generically as an equity investment. The downside of funding the business through debt is that the interest and principal on the loans must be repaid on the specified repayment dates. If the business does not do as well as is hoped and does not generate sufficient cash from sales to repay the loan, this could result in the business having to close down. With a co-equity investment rather than a bank loan, if the business generates cash in excess of its other debts to suppliers and employees etc., the business can still continue. This may be particularly beneficial in the start-up phase for Bob's Electronics as sales may take time to build up. The downside of using equity instead of debt is that this dilutes Bob's **residual interest** in the business and the co-investor may also want to play a role in managing or supervising business actions. With Bob as sole residual interest claimant decision-making and profit distribution is straightforward: he makes the decisions and is entitled to all of the profit/residual interest. If he takes on a co-investor decision-making and profit distribution become more complicated and he will have to agree with the co-investor upon a procedure for addressing these issues.[3]

6.1 Risk and return

Anyone co-investing in or lending to Bob's Electronics will want a return on their equity investment or loan capital; that is, they will want to make money in excess of the original investment. In order to persuade equity investors or the bank to part with their money to enable Bob to pursue his idea, he will have to convince them that investing in the business will provide them with an appropriate return.

What are the factors that an equity investor or a bank would want to take into account to determine whether the return on the proposed investment is sufficient to make the investment? Before reading any further, close this book, and take 15 minutes to think about the types of questions you would have if Bob asked you to finance his project. Would those questions change depending on whether he asked you to lend him money or to be a co-investor?

A central concern for any investor or lender to the Bob's Electronics business will be the risk that the investor or lender will not get the return she expected to get, or even worse will not get all or any of the original investment back. The greater the risk that the investor or lender will lose all or part of her investment, the greater potential return she will demand to compensate her for this risk. If the risk of losing funds is high, but the possible return if the business is successful is low, the investor or lender will not part with her funds.

The extent of the risk is dependent on the probability (the likelihood) that Bob's Electronics will be successful; the likelihood that it will either make or lose money. No investor has a crystal ball; no investor can be sure of what will happen in the future, but investors can attempt to assess the likelihood that the business will succeed and to consider the possible problems it may face. Investors will ask questions such as: what is the market for this product; will the business be able to compete on price with the major competitors in the market; if not, will people be willing to pay more for the service and products that the business will provide; what problems could the business face that could get in the way of success?

In a simple case, having asked these questions and carried out its analysis, a potential equity investor may determine that with a total investment in Bob's Electronics of £200,000, the likelihood of success or the risk of failure can be boiled down to a 50–50 chance of making £1,000,000 and a 50–50 chance of losing everything. If we add a 50% chance of making £1,000,000 (=£500,000) to a 50% of making £0 (=£0) we have £500,000. This sum of £500,000 is the **expected return** of the investment. It is the sum of all possible returns from an investment or a business. Of course, real life is likely to be more complex than a 50–50 probability. There could be, for example, a 90% chance of losing everything, an 8% chance of making £500,000, a 1% chance of making £10,000,000, and a 1% chance of incurring losses of £10,000,000 in excess of the original investment.[4]

---

[3] As Bob and the co-investor would be carrying on a business together for profit they would be doing so through a *general partnership*. If they failed to reach agreement on those terms—explicitly or implicitly—the Partnership Act 1890 would impose rules in this regard. For a brief discussion of partnership see section II.1 of this chapter.

[4] The expected value of this example would be $(90\% \times 0) + (8\% \times 500,000) + (1\% \times 10M) - (1\% \times 10M) = £40,000$. This investment represents a high risk but positive expected value prospect.

As you can see from this example the range of possible profits or losses from an investment can vary dramatically, from substantial profits to losing all the investment and even to negative losses below zero. For example, Bob may invest his £100,000 in the business, but if several of his computers explode and seriously injure customers he may find that he owes them far more in compensation than the sum of his investment and future profits from the business. The greater the variation in possible profits and losses, the greater the risk for the investor. A £100 investment that has a 50% chance of making £200 and a 50% chance of making nothing (i.e. the investor gets her money back) is a lot less risky than a project that has a 50% chance of making £300 and a 50% chance of losing the whole investment. This is what financial economists mean when they say, in finance speak, that risk is a function of the variance of return.

6.2 Risk and the nature of the investment

The nature of the investors' financial contribution to Bob's Electronics will alter the riskiness of that investment and, therefore, the nature of the return that will be required in order to make the investment. Lending to the business is less risky than investing equity capital in the business. If the business is not successful the business will be closed down and its assets sold off to raise as much money as possible. This remaining pool of funds will be used first to pay back the creditors, which could include employees, the government (tax), as well as banks. We discuss later the implications for Bob personally if the business assets are insufficient to pay back the creditors. Anyone investing equity capital in the business will be at the back of the queue when these funds are distributed. In many cases where a business has failed, equity investors will receive nothing or a small percentage of their investment.

Whilst creditors of the company are in front of equity investors in the queue to receive funds following the closure of the business, not all creditors are in the same place in this queue. For our introductory purposes we must note an important distinction between secured and unsecured creditors. Secured creditors would, for example, provide a loan to Bob that is secured on specific business or personal assets, for example: the delivery vehicles; the equipment used to build the computers; or his house (a mortgage). If these secured creditors are not repaid in accordance with the terms of the credit then these assets can be seized by the secured creditor and sold to generate funds to repay them. No other unsecured creditor would have any entitlement to the proceeds from the sale of that asset until the secured creditor in question had been fully repaid—principal and interest. By securing credit in this way the lender's risk is reduced.

6.3 An acceptable return in light of the risk and expected return calculation

Once the investor has made an assessment of the risks associated with, and has calculated the expected return from the project, she needs to determine whether the expected return is sufficient to compensate her for the risks associated with the project. The riskier the project, the higher the return that she will require. The riskier the project, the higher the interest rate a bank will require and the higher the expected return an equity investor will demand. The investor could always invest the money elsewhere. Indeed, there are much less risky ways of investing one's money. Depositing money in a bank and receiving a return equal to their savings rate is not, as we have seen during the recent global banking crisis, risk free, but the risk of losing one's money or of not receiving the agreed return remains low. The investor could instead lend her money to the UK Government where the risk of not getting one's money back is very low, although not, as recent events in the financial markets show us, zero. So if an investor can make a return elsewhere with much less risk than lending to Bob's Electronics, the return offered by Bob will have to be substantially higher if he is going to persuade investors to lend to him.

7 The limitations of sole trading as a way of carrying on a business

As Bob's Electronics grows, Bob finds that carrying out the business as a sole trader generates certain problems for *himself personally* and *for the business*. As we shall see in the next section, the company form offers a solution to these problems.

For Bob *personally*, a primary concern is that his personal wealth and the lifestyle that he has come to enjoy as a result of the success of the business would be threatened if the business fails or he is subject to a major product-related lawsuit, and the business' assets are insufficient to satisfy the creditors or the claimants. The reason his personal wealth is threatened is that as a sole trader Bob is contractually responsible for all the business' obligations and he is the person who would be sued if the business fails to fulfil its contractual obligations or the business' products injure somebody. As he is personally liable for the obligations of the business, the creditors of the business could satisfy their claims against his personal assets, such as his house and car, if the business assets are insufficient to satisfy their claims. This personal problem generates a business problem. Opportunities to develop and expand the business, which are good profit-making opportunities, may be rejected by Bob because, although they are good opportunities, the risk of failure could result in him losing his personal assets. That is, fear of personal liability may make Bob as the manager of the business too wary of risk—too *risk averse*, and only willing to make investments in low risk and lower return opportunities.

A second problem arises from how his business will be divided amongst his three children when he dies. If the business is carried out as a sole tradership, all the inputs that go into making a computer—the micro chips, the keyboards, the labour, the finance—involve either things that are owned by Bob or contractual obligations to provide services to him. If he was to die and if his will provides for his estate to be distributed equally amongst his three children this would involve the distribution of a third of the assets of Bob's Electronics to each of his three children. This creates two problems, a practical problem and a business problem. The practical problem is that each of the business' assets—the components, the warehouse, the delivery vans, etc.—need to be valued and subdivided and then individually transferred to the three children, respectively. This is a difficult and time-consuming problem, although not an insuperable one. The business problem is created by the fact that the assets of the business would then be owned by three separate individuals. If all of his children are a close family unit, and are willing to work together to increase the value of the business, then the business may continue to prosper. However, if, for example, one of Bob's children has a poor relationship with the others, then personal enmities could directly interfere with the operation of the business if that child imposes conditions on, or creates obstacles to, using the business assets which he or she now owns. If the new owners of the business are involved in continual internal negotiations about the use of the business assets then the business will quickly fail.

An additional business problem is that carrying out the business as a sole trader creates a barrier to raising finance for the business and makes such finance, when available, more expensive. There are two reasons for this: one arising from the peculiarities of the English law of security; the other a pure function of the nature of the sole tradership. Consider a scenario in which Bob requires financing to purchase additional warehouse capacity and to expand the fleet of delivery vehicles. The business is generating a considerable amount of cash from computer sales but not enough to fund these purchases outright. Accordingly, he requires additional external finance. He decides to raise this finance from the bank. When approached, the bank will analyse the risk involved in lending funds to Bob's Electronics. The bank's primary concern will be the ability of Bob's Electronics to generate enough free cash flow to repay the loan with interest as agreed. However, a bank will also think ahead and consider its possible future position if the business does not generate sufficient cash to repay the loan with interest. To deal with such a situation the bank will want to take security interests in the business' assets. As noted previously, this means that if the business fails the bank's claim will take priority over other creditors' claims in relation to those secured assets: the assets can be sold and the proceeds used first to repay the bank as secured creditor. When dealing with a sole trader the bank will be able to take security over many of the business' fixed assets such as land, buildings, and machinery. However, many of the business' assets are not fixed. Take, for example, computer components. They will be delivered to the business, used to build computers, which will then be sold on to customers. It would not be practicable for a bank to take a temporary security interest in each component for the time period it remained on the business' premises. As a sole trader there is no legal mechanism to provide the bank with a security interest over all the company's non-fixed assets whilst enabling the sole trader unfettered access to use and dispose of those assets as he chooses. Interestingly, there is such a mechanism available for a company known as a **floating charge**. This security interest floats over all the business assets, both fixed and non-fixed, and only comes into effect on the occurrence of certain events such as the failure to pay back a loan.[5] When it comes into effect—when the charge 'crystallizes'— the bank obtains a security interest over all these assets. The lack of availability of the floating charge to the sole trader reduces the assets that can readily be made available to the bank to secure its position, and, therefore, increases the risk for the bank of doing business with Bob's Electronics. This could lead to a higher interest rate or, if the bank perceives the risk to be too high, a refusal to lend.

A second financing problem arises from the fact that, as the business is run as a sole-trading firm, legally there is no clear distinction between Bob's business assets and his personal assets. He owns the house in which he lives, he also owns the property on which the computers are produced. He enters into a contract to buy a television for his house and he enters into a contract to buy components to build the computers. He incurs debts in his personal life and he incurs debts for the business. This means that there is no clear legally delineated pool of business assets that are separate from his personal assets. In deciding whether or not to lend money to the Bob's Electronics business, the bank must be able to evaluate the risks associated with lending to the business. However, when they lend to Bob's Electronics they are lending to Bob-the-person. The bank's risk in lending to the business is not simply a function of the business' risk; it is also a function of the risks associated with Bob-the-person. If Bob is fond of a trip to the races and is invariably unlucky at the races the bank may find that his creditors from his personal life take steps to recover what they are owed by making claim to certain of the assets used in the business. If the bank has a secured interest in such assets this will not affect their position; however, if a claim is made on unsecured assets it may interrupt and damage the operation of the business. As a sole trader, therefore, Bob's personal habits and peccadilloes represent business risks that any lender would need to be cognizant of. However, whereas the bank has the skills to assess and monitor the risks associated with the business, it is much harder to assess and monitor the risks associated with dealing with Bob-the-person. Given these problems it is likely that as the size of loans required by the business to expand increase either the interest rate attached to such loans will become prohibitively expensive (to reflect the bank's perceived risk) or the bank will refuse to lend above a certain amount.

---

[5] Until a triggering event occurs and the floating charge crystallizes the company has unencumbered access to use those assets—to use, for example, the components in building computers and to sell those computers. See generally, V. Finch, *Corporate Insolvency Law* (2nd edn, 2009).

II INTRODUCTION TO INCORPORATION

Carrying out the Bob's Electronics business through an incorporated company that benefits from limited shareholder liability addresses all of the limitations associated with sole trading identified previously. Before we consider in greater detail, in section III, how the company form resolves these problems, we need first to understand the basics of company formation. If Bob decides to run the business through a company rather than as a sole-trading firm he needs to understand: first, what incorporation options are open to him—what is on the menu of corporate vehicle options from which he might choose; second, once the company type has been selected what then are the procedural steps that must be taken to form the company; and third, once the company is formed how is the sole-trading business transferred into the newly formed company? We address each of these questions in turn.

1 Incorporation options

UK company law offers several types of business organization from which Bob could select. There are two central considerations when determining what type of organization is best suited to the endeavour which the person forming the organization has in mind. First, is the form of business organization a separate legal person; that is, a corporate body which is recognized by law to be a legal person with rights similar to that of a real person, for example, the ability to own property, to enter contracts, to sue and be sued? Secondly, does the form of organization provide that the members—in a company that issues shares the members would be the shareholders—of the organization are responsible for the debts of the organization or are those members shielded in any respect from liability for such debts? In this regard one might distinguish between, on the one hand, the organizational form of a company, which is a separate legal person and typically provides for limited liability so that its shareholder-members are not liable for the debts of the company, and, on the other hand, the business association which we call a partnership, which is not a separate legal person and does not limit its partner-members' liability so that those partners are indeed liable for the debts of the partnership. However, a closer look at the types of business organization in the UK reveals greater complexity which blurs this distinction.

All companies formed in accordance with the UK's primary companies statute, *the Companies Act 2006*,[6] are separate legal persons (bodies corporate) that may, amongst others, own property, enter into contracts, sue, and be sued. However, under the Companies Act 2006 a company can be formed with limited liability[7] or with unlimited liability,[8] whereby the shareholders would be responsible for the debts of the company. To benefit from limited liability the company's constitution must provide that its members' liability is limited.[9] The vast majority of companies benefit from limited liability. The company may be a company limited by shares or by guarantee. The former provides that shareholders are liable to pay only what they agreed to pay for the shares;[10] the latter the amount set out in the guarantee given by the member.[11] Typically companies are limited by shares. Companies limited by guarantee are often used for bodies carrying out quasi-governmental or non-profit functions.[12] Note that the availability of company

---

[6] Following a long reform process in which a major review of English company law was undertaken by the Company Law Review Steering Committee, the Companies Act 2006 was enacted, which replaces the previous Companies Act 1985.

[7] Section 3(1) CA 2006.   [8] Section 3(4) CA 2006.   [9] Section 3 CA 2006.

[10] Section 3(2) CA 2006.   [11] Section 3(3) CA 2006.

[12] For example, the Financial Reporting Council, the UK's accounting regulator is a company limited by guarantee, as is the London School of Economics.

forms other than the company limited by shares is the reason why English company law refers to members, not shareholders. As there are other types of companies that do not have shares, a term broader than 'shareholder' is required. In this book, however, as we are concerned only with companies limited by shares, the terms member and shareholder are used interchangeably.

In relation to companies limited by shares, one must consider a further distinction made by the Companies Act 2006 between public companies[13] and private companies.[14] A public company must have the words public limited company or *Plc* after its name, for example, Marks and Spencer Plc. A private company has to have limited or *Ltd* after its name. Both public and private companies can be formed with only one shareholder.[15] Accordingly, in considering which company form to use to carry out the Bob's Electronics business, Bob could use either type of company.

Some jurisdictions, for example Germany and Austria, have different statutes for public and private companies. This is not an approach taken by the UK. The primary piece of companies legislation in the UK is the Companies Act 2006, which applies to public and private companies. The vast majority of provisions in the Act apply equally to both public and private companies; however, in some contexts which we will encounter during the course of this book, public companies are subject to more onerous regulation.[16] For this reason, most companies formed at the commencement of a business project will be formed as a private company. It is, however, possible for the private company as it grows and develops to convert into a public company.[17] It is also possible for a public company to convert into a private company.[18]

One of the main reasons why private companies convert into public companies is that the original founders of the company wish to issue more shares in the company to a large number of investors either to raise more finance to develop the business or to sell existing shares and realize some of the value that has been created by the business.[19] However, only a public company is allowed to issue shares broadly to the public at large. It follows from this that a company can only list its shares on a stock exchange, such as the Main Market of the London Stock Exchange, if it is a public company. Accordingly, if Bob's Electronics Ltd wishes to issue or sell shares to the public it will need to convert into a Plc. It is noteworthy that although forming or converting into a public company may take place with a view to issuing or selling shares to the public and listing the shares on a stock exchange, in fact a considerable majority of public companies are not listed companies.[20]

By way of contrast with the company form, general partnerships are not separate legal persons—they are merely associations of individuals carrying on business together to make a profit.[21] If Bob had asked his friend Ian to co-invest in the Bob's Electronics project, and Bob and Ian worked together to make the business a success, their business

---

[13] Section 4(2) CA 2006 states that a public company is a company whose certificate of incorporation states that it is a public company and which has complied with additional registration requirements applicable to public companies—see p 15.

[14] Section 4(1) CA 2006 defines a private company as any company that is not a public company.

[15] Section 7(1) CA 2006.

[16] This different regulation is found throughout the Act; however, some of the key regulatory differences are set forth in Part 20 of the 2006 Act.

[17] See sections 89–96 CA 2006 which require, amongst others, shareholder approval by special resolution plus compliance with the minimum capital rules applicable to public companies—see Chapter 19.

[18] Sections 97–101 CA 2006 require shareholder approval by special resolution but also grant rights of objection to shareholders who own 5% of the company's issued shares.

[19] The reasons for issuing shares to the public and the regulation of such issues is addressed in detail in Web Chapter B.

[20] As of 2004, for example, there were 2,600 public companies listed on the London Stock Exchanges Main Market or traded on the London Stock Exchange's Alternative Investment Market. At this time there were 11,700 registered public companies (*Companies in 2003–2004* (DTI, 2004)), cited in B. Pettet, *Company Law* (2nd edn, 2005).

[21] Section 1 Partnership Act 1890.

association would be, in law, a partnership, whether or not they are aware of this fact.[22] As the partnership is not a separate legal person it does not own property; rather 'its' property is owned by its partners as tenants in common. Furthermore, the partners in a general partnership are liable for the debts of the partnership. However, if a partnership is a 'limited partnership' rather than a general partnership it is possible to have limited partners, sometimes colloquially referred to as silent partners, who are not liable for any amount in excess of what they agreed to invest in the partnership.[23] Silent partners lose this protection, however, if they directly undertake to manage or control the partnership business.[24] A limited partnership, whilst not a separate legal person, requires registration with Companies House.[25] A general partnership comes into being without registration.

The separate legal personality and limited liability distinctions between companies and partnerships in the UK has recently been unsettled by the introduction of the limited liability partnership form (an LLP) by the Limited Liability Partnerships Act 2000. This partnership form is both a separate legal person[26] and provides for limited liability for the partners.[27] It is, therefore, probably best to ignore the word 'partnership' to understand this entity. It is really a form of company that is treated as a partnership for tax purposes and is subject to only certain aspects of the detailed regulation of the Companies Act 2006.[28] In one respect this business form resembles a general partnership in that it cannot, in contrast to a public or private company, be formed by one member. At least two partner-members are required to form an LLP.[29]

In this section we have only considered the incorporation options offered by the UK. This is, after all, a book about English company law. However, it is worth noting that as the UK is a member of the European Union, this would enable an entrepreneur such as Bob to form a private or public company in any of the European Member States. He could do this even if his sole intention was to carry out business in the UK.[30] He could form a Dutch company and then carry out business in the UK through what is known as a branch of that Dutch company in the UK. In addition, there are some European Union forms of business association. Most importantly in this regard is the European public company—the *Societas Europaea* (or SE). This corporate form is only available to existing public companies to facilitate cross-border mergers or restructurings.[31] The European Commission has published a proposal to introduce a European private company, an *SPE*, that would be available to entrepreneurs commencing business in any

---

[22] Section 2 Partnership Act providing rules for determining the existence of a partnership.

[23] Limited Partnerships Act 1907.

[24] Section 6 Limited Partnerships Act 1907.

[25] Failure to register the limited partnership will result in it being treated as a general partnership which means the limited partners will lose the benefit of limited liability—section 5 Limited Partnerships Act 1907.

[26] Section 1 Limited Liability Partnerships Act 2000.

[27] Sections 1 and 14 Limited Liability Partnerships Act 2000; Limited Liability Partnerships Regulations 2001, SI 2001/1090.

[28] V. Finch and J. Freedman 'The Limited Liability Partnership: Pick and Mix or Mix-up?' *Journal of Business Law* (September 2002) 475.

[29] Section 2(1) Limited Liability Partnerships Act 2000.

[30] For the relevant European Court of Justice case law supporting this view on the basis of company's freedom of establishment in the European Union see: Case C-212/97 *Centros Ltd v Erhvervsog Selbskapstyrelsen* [1999] ECR I-1459; Case C-208/00 *Ueberseering BV v Nordic Construction Company Baumanagement* GmbH (NCC) [2002] ECR I-9919; Case C-167/01 *Kamer van de Koophandel en Fabrieken voor Amsterdam v Inspire Art Ltd* [2003] ECR I-10155; Case C-210/06 *Cartesio Oktató és Szolgáltató bt* [2008] ECR I-9651.

[31] The European Company form is provided for by EU Council regulation: Council Regulation 2001/2157/EC of 8 October 2001 on the Statute for a European company (SE) 26.11.2001.

European Union Member State.[32] The status of this proposal is currently unclear. These European incorporation options will not be addressed further in this book.

2 Formation basics

For the Bob's Electronics business the UK private company limited by shares would appear to be the most suitable organizational form. Companies limited by shares are the focus of this book. No further consideration will be given to companies limited by guarantee, unlimited companies, or to any partnership form.

So what would Bob have to do to set up a company limited by shares? To incorporate a registered company in England he would have to provide several documents and forms to the Companies Registrar. The Companies Registrar is the chief executive officer of Companies House, the body responsible for registering companies, and for managing and making publicly available the information that is required by law to be provided by companies to Companies House. This information includes, for example, accounting information and information about a company's membership or changes to its constitution.[33]

The person setting up the company, in this case Bob, is known as a subscriber to the company. The forms that must be provided to Companies House include the company's *memorandum of association*, which is simply a document that states that the subscriber or subscribers wish to form a company limited by shares and to take at least one share in the company.[34] Prior to the Companies Act 2006 the memorandum of association was an important constitutional document that contained key identity information about the company, including, for example, whether the members of the company benefited from limited liability, the place of its registered office, and what type of business the company could engage in, known as the objects of the company.[35] With the coming into force of the Companies Act 2006 this is no longer the case. The memorandum of association is now merely a formation document. The implications of this change are discussed in greater detail in Chapter 3. In addition to the memorandum of association, Bob will have to file with Companies House:

- An *Application for Registration*, which contains certain basic information about the company, including: the company's name;[36] its registered office;[37] whether or not the members benefit from limited liability and, if so, whether it is a company limited by shares or guarantee.[38]

- A *Statement of Capital and Initial Shareholdings* containing information about the number of shares issued on formation; the rights attached to those shares; the **nominal value**[39] of those shares; and the number of shares to be taken by each subscriber.[40]

---

[32] See proposed Council Regulation on the Statute for a European private company at http:// ec.europa.eu/ 🌐.

[33] The documents are filed with Companies House (see Part 35 Companies Act 2006). There is a Registrar of Companies for England and Wales, for Scotland, and for Northern Ireland.

[34] Section 8 CA 2006.   [35] Section 2 CA 1985.

[36] This book will not consider the regulation of business names, which is addressed in detail in the Business Names Act 1985. For a thorough consideration of this regulation see P. Davies, *Gower and Davies' Principles of Modern Company Law* (8th edn, Sweet & Maxwell, 2008), 83.

[37] A company's registered office is often not the place where it carries out business. However, the registered office will be the place where, for example, legal process can be delivered to the company— section 86 CA 2006.

[38] Section 9(2) CA 2006.   [39] See section 3 of this chapter.

[40] Sections 9(4) and 10 CA 2006.

- A *Statement of Proposed Officers*[41] of the company which must state who is to be the first director or directors of the company.[42] If the company is a private company it need not have a **company secretary**.[43] If it elects to have one this information must be included in the *Statement of Proposed Officers*. A public company must have a company secretary.[44]

- A *Statement of Compliance* that all the formation requirements of the 2006 Act have been complied with.[45]

In addition to filing the required documents and forms, Bob will have to pay a fee.[46] If the Companies Registrar is satisfied that the forms have been correctly filled in and the requisite fee has been paid[47] then the Companies Registrar will register the company and issue a certificate of incorporation.[48] This certificate of incorporation will contain core identity information about the company, including: its name; its date of incorporation; whether its members benefit from limited liability, and if so whether the company is limited by shares or by guarantee.[49]

If the company is a private limited company it may trade from the date of its incorporation. If the company is a public company it may not trade until the Companies Registrar issues a trading certificate.[50] The trading certificate will be issued when the Companies Registrar receives an additional statement of compliance which states that the company has complied with the minimum allotted share capital obligation which we will consider in detail in Chapter 19.[51]

3 From Bob's Electronics to Bob's Electronics Ltd

Bob delivers to Companies House a memorandum of association together with the other documents outlined previously and the required fee in order to form a private company limited by shares. He is the only subscriber and will be the only member of the company. At the time of formation he decides that the company will only have one £1 share. Under English company law each share must have a nominal value which is a monetary value such as a £1 share or a £10 share.[52] We will revisit this concept in detail later in the book.[53] For now note only that the term 'nominal' bears no real relationship to the actual value of the share. So although the share has a nominal value of £1 in fact you can issue a share to someone for money or money's worth for more than £1. You cannot, however, issue the share for less than the nominal value of the share.[54]

From the moment the certificate of incorporation is issued Bob's Electronics Ltd is a separate legal person with one member-shareholder, who is Bob. At the time it is formed although this company is called Bob's Electronics Ltd it has nothing to do with the Bob's

[41] The term 'officer' is defined in section 1173 to include 'a director, manager or secretary'. Manager here refers to the senior management of the company; secretary to the company secretary.
[42] Section 12 CA 2006.
[43] Section 270 CA 2006. A company secretary—referred to in the 2006 Act simply as 'secretary'—is the person responsible for ensuring that the company's organs—its board and shareholder meetings—comply with the procedures and regulations set forth in the Act and the company's constitution, as well as recording the minutes and resolutions of such organs. See further the Institute of Chartered Secretaries and Administrators at www.icsa.org.uk.
[44] Section 271 CA 2006.
[45] Section 13 CA 2006. The statement of compliance will be signed by either the solicitor who is arranging for the formation of the company or one of the subscribers or proposed directors of the company. See further, Companies House, *Company Formation—GP 1* (2011) at www.companieshouse.gov.uk.
[46] At the time of writing the fee is £40 and £100 for same day service—see www.companieshouse.co.uk.
[47] Section 14 CA 2006.   [48] Section 15(1) CA 2006.   [49] Section 15(2) CA 2006.
[50] Section 761 CA 2006.   [51] Section 762 CA 2006.   [52] Section 542(1) CA 2006.
[53] See Chapter 19.   [54] Section 580 CA 2006.

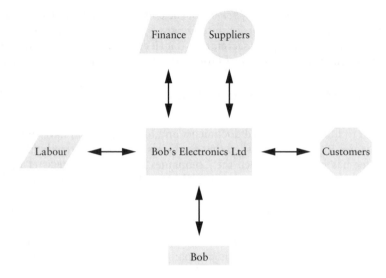

Figure 1.2 *The Effect of Incorporation: Bob's Electronics Ltd as a nexus of contracts*

Electronics business. It is at the moment of its formation a separate legal person, but an empty one. As Bob, as subscriber, paid the nominal value of the one share that has been issued, the company has the grand total of £1 in the bank and no other assets. At the moment of its formation, the company has no activities. In order to get the benefits of the company form for the Bob's Electronics business Bob has to sell his business to the company. That is, Bob and Bob's Electronics Ltd will enter into a contract for the sale and purchase of the business. He will agree to transfer every asset, including real property, intellectual property, components, vehicles, and contracts[55] related to the business to Bob's Electronics Ltd; and in exchange the company will issue shares to him. Bob's Electronics Ltd and Bob, who are formally two separate persons, will agree on a valuation of the transferred assets and the number of shares to be issued by the company in exchange for the assets.

Following the completion of this transaction, Bob's Electronics Ltd will be the owner of all assets associated with the Bob's Electronics business and *from now on*[56] will be the contracting party with all third parties (customers and suppliers etc.) who do business with, what was previously, the sole-trading firm Bob's Electronics. Bob is no longer the owner of the assets of the business; rather he is simply a shareholder of the company, which now owns the business. Being a shareholder gives him two key rights, which we will revisit in much greater detail later in the book. First, shareholders are the **residual interest** right holders. That is, if the business stopped trading tomorrow, sold off all its assets, and paid off all its creditors, whatever is left is for the shareholders. Secondly, a share usually gives the shareholders certain control rights, for example, the ability to vote at shareholder meetings on certain issues, for example, the appointment and removal of directors, or a proposal to alter the terms of the company's constitution.

---

[55] Of course many of these contracts will not be transferable without the consent of the third party contracting with the company, such as the supplier of components.

[56] To the extent that amounts were owed under the contracts between, for example, suppliers and Bob the person, acting as a sole trader, such amounts would have to be paid off by Bob. The obligations under those contracts could only be transferred to Bob's Electronics Ltd with the consent of the third-party supplier.

III THE CONSEQUENCES OF INCORPORATION

Carrying out a business through a company limited by shares addresses all of the limitations identified in section I.7 of this chapter that arise as a result of carrying on a business as a sole trader. In this section we consider in greater detail exactly how the corporate form addresses those problems and how, without the corporate form with separate legal personality and limited shareholder liability, private law would struggle to address those limitations effectively.

1 Separation of personal and business assets: entity shielding

If the Bob's Electronics business is carried out through a company—*Bob's Electronics Ltd*—which has its own separate legal personality, the assets of the business belong to Bob's Electronics Ltd and not to Bob-the-individual, who is now a shareholder in the company. From the perspective of a bank considering making a loan to the company, if it does so it would have a legal relationship with only the company and not with Bob-the-individual. Importantly for the bank's ability to assess the risks of lending money to the business, as Bob's personal creditors have a legal relationship with Bob-the-individual and no legal relationship with the company, such personal creditors would not have direct access to the business' assets to satisfy any unpaid debts, as those assets now belong to a separate legal person—the company. Accordingly, the bank can assess the risks of doing business with the Bob's Electronics business without having to have regard to the risks of doing business with Bob-the-individual. This is what Hansmann, Kraakman, and Squire refer to as 'entity shielding'.

■ **H. Hansmann, R. Kraakman, and R. Squire, 'Law and the Rise of the Firm'** **(2006) 119** *Harvard Law Review* **1333**

A variety of sanctions have been used across history to enforce contracts, including debtor's prison and enslavement. The principal sanction employed by modern legal systems, however, is permitting an unpaid creditor to seize assets owned by the defaulting promisor. When an individual enters into a contract, modern law in effect inserts a **default term**[57] by which the individual pledges all his personal property to bond his performance. A similar legal rule applies to business corporations:[58] unless the contract states otherwise, all assets owned by the corporation bond its obligations. Individuals (or rather, their personal estates) and corporations are thus both examples of legal entities, a term we use to refer to legally distinct pools of assets that provide security to a fluctuating group of creditors and thus can be used to bond an individual's or business firm's contracts.

Special legal rules, which we term rules of asset partitioning, are required to determine which entities bond which contracts, and which assets belong to which entities. Often, the asset partitioning between entities is complete: the creditors of one entity may not levy on assets held by another. But asset partitioning can also be partial, as in the modern general partnership:[59] personal creditors of partners may levy on firm assets, but only if the partnership creditors have first been paid in full. As this example suggests, the separation between the assets of a

[57] A default term is a term that applies to a contract unless the contracting parties specify otherwise.

[58] The words corporation and company can for our purposes be used interchangeably. In the United States companies are usually referred to as corporations. In the UK the term company is typically used.

[59] Types of partnership are discussed briefly at pp 12–13. Note, importantly, that in the UK and the US general partnerships are not separate legal persons.

commercial firm and those of its owners comes in two forms, depending on which set of assets is being shielded from which group of creditors. We label the two forms entity shielding and owner shielding.

A. Entity Shielding as the Foundation of Legal Entities
The term entity shielding refers to rules that protect a firm's assets from the personal creditors of its owners. In modern legal entities, entity shielding takes three forms:

Weak entity shielding grants firm creditors priority over personal creditors in the division of firm assets, meaning that the personal creditors of owners may levy on firm assets, but only if the firm creditors have first been paid in full. As noted, this rule characterizes the modern general partnership.

Strong entity shielding adds a rule of liquidation protection to the protections of weak entity shielding. Liquidation protection restricts the ability of both firm owners and their personal creditors to force the payout of an owner's share of the firm's net assets. The restriction on firm owners is conceptually distinct from the restriction on personal creditors, but, for reasons we will explore, these traits usually come paired. The modern business corporation provides a familiar example of strong entity shielding: not only do corporate creditors enjoy a prior claim to the corporation's assets, but they are also protected from attempts by a shareholder or his personal creditors to liquidate those assets...

B. The Benefits of Entity Shielding
Enabling individuals to organize legally distinct asset pools provides important economic benefits by reducing information costs for prospective lenders and solving problems associated with joint ownership. The first three benefits that we describe here require only priority of claim for firm creditors, and thus are advantages of all forms of entity shielding. The remaining benefits result primarily from liquidation protection, and thus generally arise only in strong entities such as the business corporation.

[1] Lower Creditor Monitoring Costs
All forms of entity shielding reduce creditor monitoring costs by protecting creditors from risks they cannot easily evaluate. We explain this point through use of a historical hypothetical. Imagine a Florentine merchant of the Middle Ages who is a partner in several partnerships. Among these are a wool cloth manufacturing partnership in Florence, a commodity trading partnership in Bruges, and a banking partnership in Rome. Suppose further that the law does not provide entity shielding to partnerships. If the default rule among partners is joint and several liability for partnership debt (which was the case then as now), creditors of the Bruges firm would have the right to levy on all assets owned by the Florentine merchant wherever located, including his shares of the firms in Florence and Rome. Thus, a failure of the trading firm in Bruges to pay its debts would threaten the security available to creditors of the partnerships in both Florence and Rome. And because of our assumption that the partnerships in Florence and Rome lack entity shielding, the claims asserted against them by the creditors of the failed Bruges partnership would be equal in priority to the claims of those partnerships' own creditors. To determine the creditworthiness of the Florence manufacturing firm, a would-be creditor—such as a raw wool supplier selling on credit—would thus need to assess not only that firm's prospects, but also the prospects of the trading firm in Bruges and the banking firm in Rome. But obtaining information about businesses in Bruges and Rome would likely be costly for a creditor in Florence, and a raw wool supplier would likely be in a better position to evaluate a firm in the cloth manufacturing industry than to evaluate firms in the banking or trading industries. In short, without entity shielding, a creditor of a firm is vulnerable to the fortunes of all business and personal affairs of all firm owners, regardless of his capacity to monitor those affairs.

If, however, the partnership in Florence were endowed with entity shielding, even in just the weak form, a would-be creditor of that firm could focus principally on evaluating that firm's own assets and prospects. He would need to be less concerned with the affairs of operations in Rome and Bruges because creditors of those firms would be able to levy on the assets of the partnership in Florence only after he had been paid in full. In short, entity shielding would dedicate the Florence partnership's assets principally to that partnership's own creditors. Although this necessarily distributes value away from the creditors of the Bruges and Rome partnerships, that effect can be offset if those partnerships are also given entity shielding. By this means, all creditors could enjoy a reduction in the cost of appraising the security of their claims, permitting in turn a decrease in each firm's cost of credit. Entity shielding thus promotes specialization, permitting creditors to limit the risks they face to those businesses that they know particularly well or that they can monitor with particular ease...

[2] Protection of Going-Concern Value

When a rule of liquidation protection is added to priority of claim for entity creditors—thereby increasing the degree of entity shielding from weak to strong—further benefits can be realized, perhaps the most important of which is protection of a firm's **going-concern** value.[60] The right to withdraw assets at will can be valuable to an owner of a firm. But the cost of the destruction of going-concern value caused by withdrawal would be spread across all owners, with the consequence that individual owners in a multi-owner firm would face an incentive to exercise the withdrawal right when withdrawal is personally beneficial but socially inefficient. For this reason, firm owners often mutually agree to waive their withdrawal rights for a specified period (as in a partnership for a term) or until a majority of owners votes to liquidate (as in a business corporation). The degree to which the cost of withdrawal is externalized increases with the number of owners, making liquidation protection more valuable as owners become more numerous.

To be fully efficient, the waiver of the withdrawal right must also bind the owners' personal creditors. Otherwise, when an owner defaults on personal debt, that owner's creditors will face the same incentive to force an inefficient liquidation of firm shares...Thus, contemporary entities that provide liquidation protection against owners also provide liquidation protection against creditors. For example, shareholders of a modern business corporation cannot force liquidation of their investments unless they control a majority of shares. This rule also applies to a minority owner's personal creditors, who may—if the owner defaults on personal debts—seize the owner's shares but not the underlying corporate assets. We thus, as indicated above, include liquidation protection against both owners and creditors in our definition of strong entity shielding.

[3] Capital Accumulation and Investment Diversification

By reducing the need for a firm's owners to monitor one another's non-firm financial affairs, entity shielding reduces the costs to owners of bringing on additional equity investors, especially when they are not family, friends, or others who are particularly easy to monitor or trust. Entity shielding thus makes it easier for individuals to make equity investments in multiple firms, and hence to diversify risk.[61] While this is true for all types of entity shielding, it is particularly true for strong entity shielding because of the advantages of liquidation protection.

[4] Transferable Shares

For the same reason that liquidation protection reduces the need for owners to monitor one another's personal affairs, it also reduces the importance of restrictions on who may become an owner, and thus promotes free transferability of shares.

---

[60] Going concern value refers to the fact that companies are often worth more than the sum of their parts: the assets of the company if sold separately would be worth less than if the company were sold as a whole. There may be several reasons for this including the fact that the assets fit together to generate value. Also, much of the company's value may be associated with intangibles such as its reputation in the market place and the good will of its customers and suppliers. This value may only be transferable if the business is sold as a whole.

[61] See section III.2.1.4 of this chapter for an explanation of the benefits of risk diversification.

2 Introduction to limited liability

In the UK the members[62] of a company limited by shares benefit from limited member liability.[63] This means that a member is only liable to pay what he agreed to pay for the shares. Shares may be paid or unpaid. If they are unpaid the shareholder has yet to pay for the shares. Shares may be partly paid, in which case a part of the consideration for the shares has been paid. This means that, unless the shareholders have agreed otherwise, once the shareholder has paid for the shares there will be no mandatory requirement to contribute any additional amount of capital to the company. Even if the company cannot repay its business creditors or satisfy an award of damages against a person injured by the company's products, the shareholders are not required to make any further payment to enable these debts to be satisfied. We find the legal statement of this position in section 74(2)(d) of the Insolvency Act 1986 which provides that when a company is wound up (i.e. its existence comes to an end and its assets sold):

> In the case of a company limited by shares, no contribution is required from any member exceeding the amount (if any) unpaid on the shares in respect of which he is liable as a present or future member.

Under UK company law it is possible to form an unlimited liability company, which means that the company is a separate legal person, but the members of the company remain liable for the debts of the company.[64] In theory there are two ways in which the law could provide for the liability of members for the debts of the company: joint and several liability or pro-rata liability. Under a joint and several liability regime individual members could be held liable for all the debts of the company regardless of the size of their shareholding. Wealthy members of an unlimited liability company would, therefore, be likely targets for a company's liquidator even if those members only have a small shareholding in the company. The alternative approach of pro rata unlimited liability is really a form of limited liability, that is, a member's liability is limited to his proportionate share of the company's debts as determined by his percentage shareholding in the company: a 10% shareholder would be responsible for 10% of the company's debts that are not satisfied by the company's assets. Pursuant to section 74(1) of the Insolvency Act 1986, UK company law adopts the joint and several liability approach for *unlimited* liability companies.

2.1 Why does law provide for limited member liability?

To ask for a rationale for providing limited liability suggests that it gives shareholders protection from types of liability to which they would otherwise be exposed. In the case study, the transformation of Bob's Electronics the sole trader into Bob's Electronics Ltd results in Bob benefiting from limited liability. This simple example where one moves from carrying out the business as a sole trader—where the owner of the company is exposed to personal liability—to carrying on the business through a limited liability company—where the owner of the company is not exposed to personal liability—creates the sense that limited liability protects Bob from liability to which he would have otherwise been exposed. Through the lens of this example a rationale for this shift in liability exposure—from Bob to the business' creditors—seems required.

---

[62] As a reminder, in a company limited by shares the terms member and shareholder can be used interchangeably. There are other types of companies that do not have shares, for example, a company limited by guarantee. As in those cases a member would not be a shareholder, the term member is broader than the term shareholder. In this book, however, we are concerned only with companies limited by shares and, therefore, the terms member and shareholder are interchangeable.

[63] Section 3(1) CA 2006.   [64] Section 3(4) CA 2006.

Before we consider the various available rationales it is worth giving consideration to three points:

- It is not clear that Bob's Electronics, the sole-trading firm, needs the company form to protect Bob's personal liability exposure. Through contract considerable, although not complete, protection could be provided. Bob could require that in every contract he enters into the counterparty agrees that it will only have recourse to the business' assets to satisfy unpaid amounts and not to his personal assets. There may be some enforcement problems in this regard as a result of the regulation of liability exclusion clauses in the Unfair Contract Terms Act 1977. Furthermore, such contractual exclusions would not address third parties injured by products that had no contractual relationship with Bob. However, he may be able to reduce such risk exposure through insurance cover. Of course, insurance cover may not be available for any and all such injuries. Accordingly, although imperfect, through contract he will be able to get significant comfort regarding the exposure of his personal assets to business liabilities. Indeed before the advent of incorporation through registration and limited member liability, many businesses used contract to limit liability exposure for their owners in exactly this way.[65]

- If one takes a different example of share ownership, the imperative to provide a rationale for limited member liability seems less pressing than in the example of Bob's Electronics' transformation from sole-trading firm into Bob's Electronics Ltd. Instead of a small private company, consider a large public company listed on the London Stock Exchange, such as Marks and Spencer Plc. Such a company has many thousands of shareholders. If you buy one ordinary share in the company, say for £4, you purchase certain rights in the company; in particular you have a small percentage residual financial interest and the right to vote one share. As one of many thousands of shareholders, however, your one vote is unlikely to carry much weight. Your position with regard to the running, monitoring, and control of the company is very different to Bob's position in relation to Bob's Electronics Ltd. For such a shareholder, rather then asking what the rationale is for providing that person with the benefit of limited member liability one might ask the opposite question: why should such person's personal assets be exposed to satisfy the debts of the company if the company's assets are insufficient?

- It is not clear that the strength of the rationales considered here apply equally to all types of company. When you read the rationales for limited liability, consider whether there are any types of corporate arrangement to which none of the rationales apply.

2.1.1 Risk-bearing and entrepreneurial activity

In the discussion of the case study in section 1.7, we noted that Bob-the-sole-trader could become risk averse in making decisions, fearful that a decision could backfire and expose himself to the loss of his personal assets. For many people this fear might prevent them from starting or investing in a project at all. If people with ideas are deterred from pursuing or investing in those ideas because of the personal financial risks of doing so, then the economy as whole loses out as those ideas could have generated wealth and jobs. So the first rationale for limited liability is that it facilitates entrepreneurial activity and risk-taking. However, by providing Bob, as member, with limited liability for the debts of the company, the risk of costs of business failure do not disappear, rather they are transferred to other parties, namely, the company's creditors. This is because the assets which were available to them to satisfy their claims have decreased by the value of Bob's personal assets. Limited member liability, therefore, shifts risks from shareholders

---

[65] See further B. Cheffins, *Company Law: Theory Structure and Operation* (OUP, 1997).

to creditors. Many argue that this makes good economic sense because those other creditors are more capable of bearing the risk of loss than Bob is.

■ **B. Cheffins, *Company Law: Theory Structure and Operation* (OUP, 1997), 502**

In important ways limited liability helps to distribute risk away from poor risk bearers in favour of those better positioned to deal with the consequences. People are usually risk averse in the sense that they fear a disastrous loss. Indeed, they typically will forego a greater risk-adjusted return to minimize the likelihood of such an occurrence. An investor who is personally accountable for the debts of a business can be financially ruined if the enterprise fails while heavily in debt. He thus qualifies as a poor risk bearer. The situation will be particularly troubling for an investor who would prefer not to become involved in managerial matters. Under such circumstances he will have no control over the events which expose him to the risk of financial catastrophe. Even an individual who participates actively in day-to-day decision-making has reason to be concerned. Contingencies will inevitably arise over which he has little or no influence. Consequently, he will be uncomfortable with the prospect of facing a loss the magnitude of which he cannot predict.

Limited liability helps to address the concerns of investors since they will know that, in the absence of special circumstances, they will not have to use their personal assets to indemnify creditors. Indeed, survey evidence indicates that for those in charge of small UK companies, the most important reason for incorporating is limited liability.[66] Still, individuals in such enterprises commonly provide personal guarantees for corporate debts. This is, at first glance, a paradox: individuals who attribute substantial weight to limited liability at the same time often waive its benefits. The inconsistency is not as great as it appears. With a personal guarantee a shareholder will be responsible only for what is owed to a single debtor. If the same individual is fully liable for all corporate debts, the amounts involved are less predictable and may be substantially greater.[67]

The fact that limited liability insulates poor risk bearers only tells half of the story. The arrangement will only have a beneficial risk-distribution effect if creditors are better positioned to absorb the losses involved. The evidence suggests that this is the case. An important consideration is that creditors can take precautionary measures when negotiating debt contracts to deal with the burden of limited liability. To start, a lender can always engage in 'screening', which entails acquiring information to determine the probability of default and then refusing to proceed if the risks are too great. Such evaluations occur commonly; they explain in some measure why banks are more willing to lend money to large, well-established enterprises than to small companies. In addition, creditors, being aware of the implications of limited liability, can extract a price concession in exchange for the increased risk imposed upon them. There is little evidence which directly supports the proposition that such an adjustment occurs. In other contexts, however, the rate of return which creditors charge varies in accordance with the risk that there will not be full repayment. For instance, banks charge greater interest rates to high-risk corporate borrowers. Presumably, creditors, when they negotiate terms with debtors, take the impact of limited liability into account in much the same way. Another approach parties lending money

---

[66] A. Hicks et al, *Alternative Company Structures for Small Business* (Certified Accountants Educational Trust, 1995) at 16–17, 27, 64 (though the authors try to downplay the significance of limited liability) and J. Freedman and M. Godwin, 'The Statutory Audit and the Micro Company—An Empirical Investigation' (1993) *JBL* 105 at 112. See also P. Ireland, 'The Rise of the Limited Liability Company' (1984) 12 *International Journal of Society of Law* 239 at 247–9.

[67] Hicks et al, *ibid* at 19 (survey evidence indicating that the top reason operators of small companies value limited liability is 'protection against general business failure') and Company Law Committee, *Minutes of Evidence Taken Before the Company Law Committee*, 1960–1 (Lord Jenkins, chair), (HMSO, 1961) at 863–4. See, in addition, H. Manne, 'Our Two Corporation Systems: Law and Economics', (1967) 53 *Virginia Law Review* 259 at 262.

and extending credit can use is to negotiate terms which improve the likelihood of being repaid what they are owed. Various strategies are available. These include demanding a personal guarantee from those who run the company, taking security against designated assets, curtailing the debtor's capacity to carry out transactions that increase the risk of default and requiring that the company supply information, such as financial statements, which demonstrate continuing creditworthiness.

Some factors other than negotiations with debtor companies serve to ensure that creditors are suitably positioned to deal with burdens of limited liability. One consideration is that many creditors are well-diversified, in the sense that each debt contract has only a small impact on their financial status. A typical lender is thus ordinarily well-suited to absorb the loss associated with the failure of a single business enterprise. Trade creditors will be in this situation because they usually have numerous customers and banks are similarly positioned because they almost invariably lend money to a large number of business enterprises. Lenders who are uncomfortable in a general way with bearing the risks involved with default or are concerned about sustaining a large loss from a particular key customer may have an additional option, which is taking insurance. Suppliers and manufacturers can, for instance, obtain from specialist private insurers cover against losses arising from the insolvency of their customers.

Consider the following extract from *The Times* in 1855 during the passage of the Limited Liability Act 1855 which first introduced limited liability in the UK. Here we see that whilst the relationship between risk-taking and investment is central to the justification of limited member liability, it is less about the entrepreneur and more about allowing 'small people' to participate in the economy as equity investors.

■ *The Times* (27 July 1855), 8

To any unprejudiced observer it must appear, at first sight, a very remarkable thing that there should be any opposition at all to such a measure as the Limited Liability Bill. Why in the world is it so obnoxious, so intolerable, so execrable a thing that a man having, we will say, five hundred pounds, should not be permitted to lend it to a neighbour on the simple and innocent condition of sharing his neighbour's profits, in case of success, and losing no more than his five hundred pounds, in the case of failure? Where is the extravagance, where is the dishonesty, where the peril, where is the un-English character, where is the inevitable loophole for roguery and folly, in such a proposition? In our humble opinion, it may fairly be assumed that, as a general rule, an Englishman who has scraped together five hundred pounds, or even come by it in some less tedious way, will take care of it, if he can, and will not put it into the hands of the first fool, or the first knave, who asks for the use of it. The penalty of losing the money will generally be quite enough to deter the owner from a very wild investment, if there is the opportunity of a better one. Why is it, then, that the proposed liberty of advancing money on the terms just described should be fiercely disputed, on the ground that the money so advanced is not enough, and that the lender must be bound not only to the amount of his advance, but to the whole of his means, every farthing he has in the world, every earthly thing he possesses, and his personal liberty besides? Why this desperate determination to bind a man not only up to the whole of his venture, but to all that he has, body and soul?…

Who are they who insist that in every instance there shall not only be the forfeiture of the sum expressed in the bond, but of everything else the debtor has in the world? We can only answer a simple question, and we answer it only from the columns before us. The honourable members [of Parliament] who make this demand are Mr. Muntz, Mr. Glyn, Mr. W. Brown, Mr. Strutt, Mr. Spooner, Mr. Bass, Mr. J. Forester, Mr. Mitchell, and Mr. Hastie, and then we are told this is not a capitalist question! Why, these are all capitalists.

It does really seem to us a most invidious proceeding that a dozen wealthy men, with great command of capital, and great opportunities of employing it to advantage, should come down to the House. In a body for the purpose of debarring the man with small means from using those small means to the best advantage, except at the risk of everything he has in the world. If it is not a question of capital *versus* labour, these gentlemen are bound to explain why it is that the opposition to the measure in the House is conducted almost exclusively by very large capitalists. We should be, and, indeed, always have been, the very last to encourage any jealousy between capital and labour, or, to speak in plainer language, between the rich and the poor. We shall ever insist, not only on the rights of capital, but on the duty of the Legislature to protect and cherish it from envious and malicious agitation. But we hold it also a matter both of policy and of duty to foster the more humble savings of the poor and increase the opportunities for their use…

No good reason can be assigned why they should not be allowed to advance their money to a neighbour whom they know and whom they trust, on the condition of sharing his profits to the extent of the advance, and no further.

For *The Times*, therefore, in 1855, making limited liability broadly available was not merely about facilitating entrepreneurial activity but also about facilitating the democratization of capitalism: encouraging the less wealthy to fund projects and make investments, where without limited liability they would be wary of doing so.

2.1.2 *Monitoring costs and the transferability of shares*

The justifications set out in this and the following subsections relate to companies that have more than one shareholder, and where not all the shareholders participate in running the company. Bob may, for example, want to realize some of the wealth he has made in building up the business by selling some of his shares. He may continue running the business whilst the other shareholders do not participate in management. Alternatively, as well as selling some of his shares he may decide to appoint a professional manager so that he can have more leisure time. In the extracts from Easterbrook and Fischel in this section, such professional managers are sometimes referred to as agents. As we will see in Chapter 2, in *law* the company is *not* the agent of the shareholders. Nor are directors agents of the shareholders, rather they are members of an organ of the company, the board of directors, and may also act as agents of the company. Economists, however, use the term 'agency' in a looser sense. Where one party is empowered to act in ways that affect another person's well-being or wealth an economist may refer to him as an agent; the person whose well-being is affected is referred to as a principal. This is a theme to which we return at length later in the book (see Chapter 5 'The corporate agency problem'). The extracts that follow use the term 'agent' as an economist would use the term.

■ F. Easterbrook and D. Fischel, 'Limited Liability and the Corporation' (1985) 52 *University of Chicago Law Review* 89

Limited liability decreases the need to monitor. All investors risk losing wealth because of the actions of agents. They could monitor these agents more closely. The more risk they bear, the more they will monitor. But beyond a point more monitoring is not worth the cost. Moreover, specialized risk bearing implies that many investors will have diversified holdings. Only a small portion of their wealth will be invested in any one firm. These diversified[68] investors have neither the expertise nor the incentive to monitor the actions of specialized agents. Limited liability

---

[68] On diversification see section III.2.1.4 of this chapter.

makes diversification and passivity a more rational strategy and so potentially reduces the cost of operating the corporation.

Of course, rational shareholders understand the risk that the managers' acts will cause them loss. They do not meekly accept it. The price they are willing to pay for shares will reflect the risk. Managers therefore find ways to offer assurances to investors without the need for direct monitoring; those who do this best will attract the most capital from investors. Managers who do not implement effective controls increase the discount. As it grows, so does the investors' incentive to incur costs to reduce the divergence of interest between specialized managers and risk bearers. Limited liability reduces these costs. Because investors' potential losses are 'limited' to the amount of their investment as opposed to their entire wealth, they spend less to protect their positions...

Limited liability [also] reduces the costs of monitoring other shareholders. Under a rule exposing equity investors to additional liability, the greater the wealth of other shareholders, the lower the probability that any one shareholder's assets will be needed to pay a judgment. Thus existing shareholders would have incentives to engage in costly monitoring of other shareholders to ensure that they do not transfer assets to others or sell to others with less wealth. Limited liability makes the identity of other shareholders irrelevant and thus avoids these costs.

Easterbrook and Fischel argue that professional managers may act in ways that are detrimental to the interests of shareholders. We shall discuss this problem in detail in Chapter 5. One response of shareholders faced with this problem would be to monitor carefully the managers' actions. Shareholders' incentives to monitor increase as the risks associated with those activities increase. If shareholders in a company are liable for the company's debts to the extent they exceed the company's assets, then they will have strong incentives to monitor management to ensure that they act in ways that reduce the shareholders' exposure to personal liability. Where the unlimited liability rule is joint and several liability—where a wealthy shareholder would cover other poorer shareholder's contributions if those other shareholders have insufficient assets—the shareholders not only have an incentive to monitor the managers but also to monitor fellow shareholders. The reason for this is that if the wealth of one shareholder (shareholder A) decreases, this increases the potential liability exposure of the other shareholders who, if they are asked to cover the unpaid debts of the company, will have to bear shareholder A's contribution if he is no longer in a position to pay. These monitoring costs—monitoring management and monitoring fellow shareholders—however, are not ultimately borne by the shareholder, they are borne by the company because shareholders will reduce the value of what they will pay for the shares according to their calculation of how much the monitoring will cost them. Limited shareholder liability removes any need to engage in such shareholder–shareholder monitoring and reduces the need to engage in shareholder–manager monitoring. Reduced costs of monitoring means that investors will pay more for a company's shares.

If the change in the wealth of one shareholder alters the risks of holding shares in the company for other shareholders, it also means that shareholders will be concerned about the transfer of shares in the company to poorer shareholders. If shares held by shareholder A, who is wealthy, are transferred to investor W, who has no personal assets, the risk of holding shares for shareholders B, C, and D increases. Accordingly, the rational response of shareholders prior to any share transfer is to agree to prevent share transfers without shareholder approval. This would enable the shareholders to vet investor W before consenting to the sale. Limited liability removes this concern and facilitates the free transfer of shares.

Of course these problems are created by only one type of unlimited liability, namely joint and several liability. If the form of unlimited liability was pro rata liability, shareholders would still have strong incentives to monitor management but would not need to monitor fellow shareholders or restrict the transfer of shares, as each individual shareholder's liability exposure for the unsatisfied debts of the company would be determined by the proportion of shares held by that shareholder.

2.1.3 *Managerial efficiency: facilitating the trading of shares and promoting the market for corporate control*

If you want to buy a share in a listed company, for example Marks and Spencer Plc, to find out the price you will have to pay for that share you will have to look at the price at which that share is quoted at any one time on the London Stock Exchange. You might ask: what determines the price of that share? An economist will tell you in general terms that the simple answer to this question is that the value of the share represents a proportion of the future cash flows generated by the company. This is an oversimplification but sufficient for our purposes. Many factors determine how much cash the company will generate in the future: the quality of its products; the market for its products; expectations about general economic conditions. An important factor in this regard is the quality and performance of management. If management is incompetent, lazy, or abuses its position to act in their own interests and not in the interests of wealth generation then the future cash flows will be less than they might have been. From the shareholders' perspective they incur a cost for this type of action: the difference between the actual price of the share and its potential price under better management. Where managers act in their own interests and not in the shareholders' interests any such costs are referred to by economists as agency costs. We will consider these costs in detail in Chapter 5. However, some economists argue that the scope for management to be incompetent or to incur such agency costs is contained by what is called the **market for corporate control.** Here the idea is that if the company would be worth much more under different management then sophisticated and informed investors will buy the shares at a lower price, fire management, and raise the value of the shares by running the company more efficiently. Easterbrook and Fischel argue that limited liability allows the market for corporate control to function.

■ **F. Easterbrook and D. Fischel, 'Limited Liability and the Corporation' (1985) 52** *University of Chicago Law Review* **89**

> By promoting free transfer of shares, limited liability gives managers incentives to act efficiently...So long as shares are tied to votes, poorly run firms will attract new investors who can assemble large blocs at a discount[69] and install new managerial teams. This potential for displacement gives existing managers incentives to operate efficiently in order to keep share prices high.
>
> Although this effect of the takeover mechanism is well known, the relation between take overs and limited liability is not. Limited liability reduces the costs of purchasing shares. Under a rule of limited liability, the value of shares is determined by the present value of the income stream generated by a firm's assets. The identity and wealth of other investors is irrelevant. Shares are fungible; they trade at one price in liquid markets. Under a rule of unlimited liability shares would not be fungible [freely exchangeable]. Their value would be a function of the present value of future cash flows and of the wealth of shareholders. The lack of fungibility would impede their acquisition. An acquiror who wanted to purchase a control block[70] of shares under a rule of unlimited liability might have to negotiate separately with individual

---

[69] Discount here means cheaper than they would be if the company was run by better or less self-serving management.

[70] A control block of shares would be the number of shares required to control the company. Typically this would involve purchasing a minimum of 51% of the voting shares (de jure control); although de

shareholders, paying different prices to each. Worse, the acquiror in corporate control transactions typically is much wealthier than the investors from which it acquires the shares. The anticipated cost of additional capital contributions would be higher to the new holder than the old ones. This may be quite important to a buyer considering the acquisition of a firm in financial trouble, for there would be a decent chance of being required to contribute to satisfy debts if the plan for revitalization of the firm should go awry. Limited liability allows a person to buy a large block without taking any risk of being surcharged, and thus it facilitates beneficial control transactions. A rule that facilitates transfers of control also induces managers to work more effectively to stave off such transfers.

What shareholders are willing to pay for their shares is a function of the risk associated with making the investment. Risk factors would include, amongst others: how likely it is that the company will be successful and generate cash; whether it make losses in excess of assets; if its losses are great whether the investor will have to make any contribution to pay the debts of the company. However, the risks associated with the purchase of shares in a company with *unlimited* liability will vary depending on the wealth of each shareholder—how much she has to lose if the company's losses are considerable. Accordingly, as the risks for shareholders vary because of their personal wealth differences, their valuation of the shares will also vary. This fact makes it difficult for a third party who wishes to buy a controlling stake in the company to acquire ownership of the shares as the price expectations of all the shareholders will vary and the buyer will have to negotiate with them all separately. According to Easterbrook and Fischel, limited liability addresses this problem by taking away the risk factor of the personal wealth of the shareholders. With limited liability the wealth of each of the shareholders and of the buyer becomes irrelevant; shares are freely tradable at one price and third parties can more easily acquire control of badly run companies.

2.1.4 Diversification

The ability of investors to diversify the types of assets which they hold, such as shares or real property, benefits the shareholders because not all their eggs are in one basket. If some investments do badly others may do well, counter-balancing some of the losses from the poorer investments. Sophisticated investors can carefully pick shares in different companies to minimize some of the risks associated with those companies or those industries. For example, a shareholder could buy shares in an oil company and in a plastics company that relies heavily on oil. If the price of oil goes up the value of the oil company goes up and the plastics company goes down and vice versa. The risks associated with changes in the oil price for the shareholder's portfolio of shares are thereby reduced. Not only is this beneficial to investors, it is also beneficial to the company. As diversification enables investors to mitigate or exclude certain types of risk, the risks associated with investing in a particular company are less than they would be if the investor chose only to invest in that company. Less risk means that the investor will not require as high a return for his investment. That means companies selling shares to diversified investors will get a better price for their shares than they would by selling the shares to an undiversified investor. Here Easterbrook and Fischel explain how limited liability facilitates diversification.

facto control could also be obtained with less than majority ownership where some shareholders do not vote.

■ **F. Easterbrook and D. Fischel, 'Limited Liability and the Corporation' (1985) 52 *University of Chicago Law Review* 89**

Limited liability allows more efficient diversification. Investors can minimize risk by owning a diversified portfolio of assets. Firms can raise capital at lower costs because investors need not bear the special risk associated with nondiversified holdings. This is true, though, only under a rule of limited liability or some good substitute. Diversification would increase rather than reduce risk under a rule of unlimited liability. If any one firm went bankrupt, an investor could lose his entire wealth.[71] The rational strategy under unlimited liability, therefore, would be to minimize the number of securities held. As a result, investors would be forced to bear risk that could have been avoided by diversification, and the cost to firms of raising capital would rise...

Limited liability facilitates optimal investment decisions. When investors hold diversified portfolios, managers maximize investors' welfare by investing in any project with a positive net present value. They can accept high-variance ventures (such as the development of new products) without exposing the investors to ruin. Each investor can hedge against the failure of one project by holding stock in other firms. In a world of unlimited liability, though, managers would behave differently. They would reject as 'too risky' some projects with positive **net present values**.[72] Investors would want them to do this because it would be the best way to reduce risks. By definition this would be a social loss, because projects with a positive net present value are beneficial uses of capital.

3 **Managing succession**

When considering the limitations of a sole-trading firm we noted that practical and business problems arose from the transmission of the business to Bob's heirs when he dies. The practical difficulties arose from the actual mechanics of transferring each business asset to his heirs; the business difficulty arose from the fact that different assets would then be owned by different children. If the personal relationships between the children are difficult, then the business assets may become tools in intractable personal battles.

There are, of course, possible private law solutions to this problem.[73] The children themselves could elect to resolve this problem by agreeing that each of the assets transferred to them be held by them all as tenants in common for the purposes of carrying on what would now be a general partnership. However, if the relationship between the children is problematic, one or more of the children may refuse to do this. Alternatively, Bob could himself set up a co-ownership arrangement through the use of the trust mechanism, although this may not be well suited to carrying out a business.

The company form provides a simple solution to these problems. Once brought into being, the company exists in perpetuity until its life is brought to an end, perhaps voluntarily by shareholders such as Bob who no longer want to continue the business

---

[71] Note that Easterbrook and Fischel assume that limited liability involves joint and several liability and not pro rata liability. It is worth considering whether a system of pro rata liability would have as grave an effect on diversification as they suggest here.

[72] The term *net present value* is a term used in corporate finance which refers to a way of calculating the value of a project. Present value distinguishes between the value of an income stream in the future, say in one year's time, and its value today. If you have £1,000 today you could put it in an account in a high street bank and earn say 5% interest so that in a year's time you will have £1,050 not £1,000. Therefore £1,000 today is worth more than £1,000 in a year's time. Accordingly if a project is worth £1,050 in a year's time its current value today is £1,000. Instead of increasing the £1,000 to add interest you discount the £1,050 by what is called a discount rate, which in this case would be 5%.

[73] See J. Getzler and M. Macnair, 'The Firm as an Entity Before the Companies Acts 2006' in P. Brand et al (eds), *Adventures of the Law: Proceedings of the Sixteenth British Legal History Conference* (Dublin, 2003) 267.

or by creditors who have not been paid the amounts the company owes them. When the shareholders of the company die, even a 100% shareholder, the company's assets and the company's business are wholly unaffected. The shares are transmitted to the shareholder's heirs who then become shareholders in the company. There are now no practical problems surrounding the mechanics of transferring business assets and there is no scope for generating hold-up problems in the business that would arise as a result of a sole trader's business assets being transferred to several individuals. This is because the business assets are not part of the shareholder's personal estate; the business assets are owned by a different person—the company—whose life goes on after the death of its shareholder.

Questions

1. What does limited member liability mean?

2. Do we need a rationale for limited liability?

3. Which of these rationales applies to a small private company?

4. Shouldn't the individuals who commence business activity to produce products bear personal responsibility for the debts incurred in making those products and to the individuals who are injured by those products?

5. Which of these rationales applies to a company (a subsidiary company) that is wholly owned by another company (a parent company)?

6. Which of these rationales remains persuasive if joint and several liability is replaced by pro rata liability?

7. Should we make a distinction between the types of company creditor and the application of limited liability—should we distinguish between banks, small business creditors and people who are injured by the company's products?

8. Can contract be used as an effective substitute for limited liability?

9. What is entity shielding and what are its economic benefits?

10. How could one provide Bob's Electronics the sole-trading firm with the benefits of entity shielding without using the company form?

 Online Resource Centre
http://www.oxfordtextbooks.co.uk/orc/kershaw2e/

Visit the Online Resource Centre for additional resources and information available for this chapter, including web links and an interactive flashcard glossary.

CHAPTER TWO

THE ENTITY DOCTRINE

I REALITY AND INCORPORATION

Section 16 of the Companies Act 2006 tells us that the effect of the Companies Registrar registering a company is that the subscribers of the company, in our case Bob as he is the only subscriber, together with any future members of the company are a body corporate. That is, a separate legal person is formed through registration which goes by its chosen name. By forming a company, Bob's Electronics Ltd, and by selling the business to the company in exchange for shares, a *new legal reality* replaces a pre-existing business reality. In a simple case such as Bob's Electronics, from the perspective of a third-party outsider there is little of real substance that has changed, apart from perhaps a sign over the company's warehouse saying Bob's Electronics Ltd, or the name Bob's Electronics Ltd on the company's notepaper or invoices.[1] Bob, as sole trader, had a right to the residual value created by the company; as 100% shareholder he has that same right. As sole trader he controlled and ran the business; as sole director and shareholder of Bob's Electronics Ltd he runs and controls the business. However, from a legal perspective everything has changed and these changes have, as we shall see, *real* effects and distributional consequences.

1 The entity doctrine: *Salomon v Salomon*

Aron Salomon was a leather boot manufacturer in the late nineteenth century whose business was based in Whitechapel, London. Like the case study of Bob's Electronics, Salomon was a sole trader. For whatever reason (it is not completely clear from the case), Salomon decided that he wanted to avail himself of the limited liability company form. Since the Companies Act 1844 it had been possible to incorporate a company by registration; however, it was not until 1855 that the company form was available with limited member liability.[2]

At the end of the nineteenth century the Companies Act of 1862 was the applicable Companies Act. Importantly, this Act required that to form a company there must be seven subscribers to the company. Today under the Companies Act 2006 it is possible to form either a public or a private company with one member, although as recently as the Companies Act 1985 two members were required for a public company.[3] Salomon's legal advisors arranged for the formation of a company named Aron Salomon Ltd. This company had the requisite seven subscribers who were Salomon himself, his wife, and their five children, who each subscribed for one share each. Just like in the Bob's Electronics case study, Salomon the sole trader's leather business was sold to Aron Salomon Ltd.

---

[1] These disclosure requirements are set forth in the Companies (Trading Disclosures) Regulations 2008, as amended, issued pursuant to section 82 CA 2006. These regulations provide for the disclosure of the company's name at its registered office (regulation 3) and other business locations as well as, amongst others, for disclosures on business letters and websites (regulation 7). Sections 83 and 84 of the 2006 Act provide for civil and criminal consequences of non-disclosure.

[2] Limited Liability Act 1855.   [3] Section 7 CA 2006; section 1 CA 1985.

In exchange for the business he received 20,000 shares with a nominal value of £1 and a secured **debenture**. In effect, Aron Salomon Ltd agreed to pay a specified amount to Salomon for his leather business. Part of this payment, in addition to the shares, was to be a cash payment. However, as Aron Salomon Ltd was a brand new company and had no cash to pay to Salomon, Salomon agreed to defer payment. That is Mr Salomon became a creditor to Aron Salomon Ltd. A debenture is a promissory note issued by the debtor (Aron Salomon Ltd), that is a promise to pay the amount specified in the note. Importantly a debenture is a secured promissory note. This meant that Salomon the person had a first priority security interest over the company's assets if the company failed to comply with the terms of the debenture. This meant in effect that if the business failed the first creditor in the repayment queue was Mr Salomon himself.

Following the incorporation of Aron Salomon Ltd and the transfer of the business to it, the business fell on hard times. Apparently, government orders for military boots dried up as strikes in the boot industry meant the government, concerned about supply, distributed their orders amongst several boot manufacturers. The business failed and a liquidator was appointed to realize as much value as possible from the assets in order to repay the creditors. The two main creditor groups were Salomon himself (as debenture holder) and the company's trade creditors, for example, the suppliers of leather and chemicals. However, as Salomon, as the debenture holder, was the sole secured creditor, and as the remaining funds were insufficient to satisfy his secured claim, this meant that all the remaining funds had to be paid to him and that the trade creditors would receive nothing. Had Salomon not incorporated the company he would not, as sole trader, have been entitled to any of these funds. On an action brought by the liquidator, the question for the court was whether Salomon should be allowed to keep these funds by simply changing the legal reality in which the business operated through incorporation, when *in reality* the business and its control remained unaltered.

■ *Broderip v Salomon* [1895] 2 Ch 323 (Court of Appeal)

Vaughan Williams J

This business was Mr. Salomon's business and no one else's; that he chose to employ as agent a limited company; that he is bound to indemnify that agent, the company; and that his agent, the company, has a lien on the assets which overrides his claims. The creditors of the company could, in my opinion, have sued Mr. Salomon. Their right to do so would depend on the circumstances of the case, whether the company was a mere alias of the founder or not. In this case it is clear that the relationship of principal and agent existed between Mr. Salomon and the company.

Lindley LJ

I proceed to examine the legal aspect of this case, which, as I have said, is one of great general importance. There can be no doubt that in this case an attempt has been made to use the machinery of the Companies Act, 1862, for a purpose for which it never was intended. The legislature contemplated the encouragement of trade by enabling a comparatively small number of persons—namely, not less than seven—to carry on business with a limited joint stock or capital, and without the risk of liability beyond the loss of such joint stock or capital. But the legislature never contemplated an extension of limited liability to sole traders or to a fewer number than seven. In truth, the legislature clearly intended to prevent anything of the kind, for s. 48 takes away the privileges conferred by the Act from those members of limited companies who allow such companies to carry on business with less than seven members; and by s. 79 the reduction of the number of members below seven is a ground for winding up the company. Although in the present case there were, and are, seven members, yet it is manifest that six of them are members simply in order to enable the seventh himself to carry on business with limited liability. The object of the whole arrangement is to do the very thing which the legislature intended not to be done; and, ingenious as the scheme is, it cannot have the effect desired so long as the law remains unaltered. This was evidently the view taken by Vaughan Williams J.

The incorporation of the company cannot be disputed. (See s. 18 of the Companies Act, 1862.) Whether by any proceeding in the nature of a scire facias the Court could set aside the certificate of incorporation is a question which has never been considered, and on which I express no opinion; but, be that as it may, in such an action as this the validity of the certificate cannot be impeached. The company must, therefore, be regarded as a corporation, but as a corporation created for an illegitimate purpose. Moreover, there having always been seven members, although six of them hold only one 1l. share each, Mr. Aron Salomon cannot be reached under s. 48, to which I have already alluded. As the company must be recognised as a corporation, I feel a difficulty in saying that the company did not carry on business as a principal, and that the debts and liabilities contracted in its name are not enforceable against it in its corporate capacity. But it does not follow that the order made by Vaughan Williams J. is wrong. A person may carry on business as a principal and incur debts and liabilities as such, and yet be entitled to be indemnified against those debts and liabilities by the person for whose benefit he carries on the business. The company in this case has been regarded by Vaughan Williams J. as the agent of Aron Salomon. I should rather liken the company to a trustee for him—a trustee improperly brought into existence by him to enable him to do what the statute prohibits. It is manifest that the other members of the company have practically no interest in it, and their names have merely been used by Mr. Aron Salomon to enable him to form a company, and to use its name in order to screen himself from liability...In a strict legal sense the business may have to be regarded as the business of the company; but if any jury were asked, Whose business was it? they would say Aron Salomon's, and they would be right, if they meant that the beneficial interest in the business was his. I do not go so far as to say that the creditors of the company could sue him. In my opinion, they can only reach him through the company. Moreover, Mr. Aron Salomon's liability to indemnify the company in this case is, in my view, the legal consequence of the formation of the company in order to attain a result not permitted by law. The liability does not arise simply from the fact that he holds nearly all the shares in the company. A man may do that and yet be under no such liability as Mr. Aron Salomon has come under. His liability rests on the purpose for which he formed the company, on the way he formed it, and on the use which he made of it. There are many small companies which will be quite unaffected by this decision. But there may possibly be some which, like this, are mere devices to enable a man to carry on trade with limited liability, to incur debts in the name of a registered company, and to sweep off the company's assets by means of debentures which he has caused to be issued to himself in order to defeat the claims of those who have been incautious enough to trade with the company without perceiving the trap which he has laid for them.

It is idle to say that persons dealing with companies are protected by s. 43 of the Companies Act, 1862, which requires mortgages of limited companies to be registered, and entitles creditors to inspect the register. It is only when a creditor begins to fear he may not be paid that he thinks of looking at the register; and until a person is a creditor he has no right of inspection. As a matter of fact, persons do not ask to see mortgage registers before they deal with limited companies; and this is perfectly well known to every one acquainted with the actual working of the Companies Acts and the habits of business men. Mr. Aron Salomon and his advisers, who were evidently very shrewd people, were fully alive to this circumstance.

If the legislature thinks it right to extend the principle of limited liability to sole traders it will no doubt do so, with such safeguards, if any, as it may think necessary. But until the law is changed such attempts as these ought to be defeated whenever they are brought to light. They do infinite mischief; they bring into disrepute one of the most useful statutes of modern times, by perverting its legitimate use, and by making it an instrument for cheating honest creditors.

Mr. Aron Salomon's scheme is a device to defraud creditors. We have carefully considered the proper form of order to be made on this appeal, and the order of the Court will be as follows: The Court, being of opinion that the formation of the company, the agreement of August, 1892, and the issue of debentures to Aron Salomon pursuant to such agreement, were a mere scheme to enable him to carry on business in the name of the company with limited liability, contrary to the true intent and meaning of the Companies Act, 1862, and, further, to enable him to obtain a preference over other creditors of the company by procuring a first charge on the assets of the company by means of such debentures, dismiss the appeal of Aron Salomon with costs.

Lopes L J

This is a case of very great importance, and I wish shortly to state my reasons for concurring in the judgment just delivered. I do not propose to restate the facts so fully and clearly detailed by Lindley LJ: I shall content myself with shortly stating the impression they have produced on my mind. The incorporation of the company was perfect—the machinery by which it was formed was in every respect perfect, every detail had been observed; but, notwithstanding, the business was, in truth and in fact, the business of Aron Salomon; he had the beneficial interest in it; the company was a mere nominis umbra, under cover of which he carried on his business as before, securing himself against loss by a limited liability of 1l. per share, all of which shares he practically possessed, and obtaining a priority over the unsecured creditors of the company by the debentures of which he had constituted himself the holder.

It would be lamentable if a scheme like this could not be defeated. If we were to permit it to succeed, we should be authorizing a perversion of the Joint Stock Companies Acts. We should be giving vitality to that which is a myth and a fiction. The transaction is a device to apply the machinery of the Joint Stock Companies Act to a state of things never contemplated by that Act—an ingenious device to obtain the protection of that Act in a way and for objects not authorized by that Act, and in my judgment in a way inconsistent with and opposed to its policy and provisions. It never was intended that the company to be constituted should consist of one substantial person and six mere dummies, the nominees of that person, without any real interest in the company. The Act contemplated the incorporation of seven independent bona fide members, who had a mind and a will of their own, and were not the mere puppets of an individual who, adopting the machinery of the Act, carried on his old business in the same way as before, when he was a sole trader. To legalize such a transaction would be a scandal. But to what relief is the liquidator entitled? In the circumstances of this case it is, in my opinion, competent for the Court to set aside the sale as being a sale from Aron Salomon to himself—a sale which had none of the incidents of a sale, was a fiction, and therefore invalid; or to declare the company to be a trustee for Aron Salomon, whom Aron Salomon, the cestui que trust, was bound to indemnify; or to declare the formation of the company, the agreement of August, 1892, and the issue of the debentures to Aron Salomon pursuant to such agreement, to be merely devices to enable him to carry on business in the name of the company with limited liability, contrary to the true intent and meaning of the Companies Act, 1862, and further, to enable him to obtain a preference over other creditors of the company by obtaining a first charge on the assets of the company by means of such debentures.

Kay L J

It has been argued that all this was a proper and legitimate proceeding under the Joint Stock Companies Acts, and that this result is strictly right and legal; that Salomon wished to trade with limited liability, and the statutes enabled him to do so. It does not matter, it is argued, if the other six signatories of the memorandum were in fact trustees for him. The statutes do not prevent that. I dissent from this view absolutely. The statutes were intended to allow seven or more persons bona fide associated for the purpose of trade to limit their liability under certain conditions and to become a corporation. But they were not intended to legalize a pretended association for the purpose of enabling an individual to carry on his own business with limited liability in the name of a joint stock company.

The question—as was put to counsel during the argument—is, whose was this business in fact after the formation of the company? There really was no attempt to deny that it was the business of Salomon. The pretended sale to the company was an utter fiction. The company had no funds or property whatever except what it took under this alleged sale and £7 payable on the subscrip-tion shares. It borrowed no money. The £10,000 debentures were issued in part of the nominal price. The only security for them was the value of the assets of this business. The company paid nothing to Salomon for the purchase. They had nothing to pay with. There was no pretence of a bargain between the company and Salomon as vendor. There was no independent director to protect the company in the transaction. In truth, there was no purchase and sale at all. The busi-ness remained Salomon's. He carried it on in the name of the company…

Questions

1. Consider what could have been the legislature's intention in requiring a minimum of seven members. Originally under the Limited Liability Act 1855 a minimum of 25 share-holders was the precondition to benefiting from limited liability.

2. Is there any indication from the case extracts that the legislature attempted to define the characteristics of these seven members?

3. How does the Court of Appeal understand the essential characteristics of these seven members? Do you find their position persuasive/workable?

4. Is the Court of Appeal sympathetic to Salomon's creditors? Why is this: should business creditors look after themselves?

5. Vaughan Williams J and the justices in the Court of Appeal seem to find it objectionable that in reality nothing changed in the nature of Salomon's business. They reject attempt-ing to prioritize legal form over the reality of business substance. As Kay LJ put it: 'the business remained Salomon's'. In your view should this be relevant? If not, why not?

6. The Court of Appeal seem at a loss to identify a coherent way of imposing liability upon Salomon. What are the options they identify? Do you find any of them persuasive?

7. Were the Court of Appeal trying to be faithful to the purpose or the spirit of the Companies Act 1862 or did they undermine that purpose? Should judges be concerned with legisla-tive purpose?[4]

■ *Salomon v Salomon* [1897] AC 22 (House of Lords)

Lord Halsbury LC

My Lords, the important question in this case, I am not certain it is *not* the only question, is whether the respondent company was a company at all—whether in truth that artificial creation of the Legislature had been validly constituted in this instance; and in order to determine that question it is necessary to look at what the statute itself has determined in that respect. I have no right to add to the requirements of the statute, nor to take from the requirements thus enacted. The sole guide must be the statute itself.

Now, that there were seven actual living persons who held shares in the company has not been doubted. As to the proportionate amounts held by each I will deal presently; but it is important to observe that this first condition of the statute is satisfied, and it follows as a consequence that it would not be competent to any one—and certainly not to these persons themselves—to deny that they were shareholders.

I must pause here to point out that the statute enacts nothing as to the extent or degree of interest which may be held by each of the seven, or as to the proportion of interest or influence possessed by one or the majority of the share-holders over the others. One share is enough. Still less is it possible to contend that the motive of becoming shareholders or of making them shareholders is a field of inquiry which the statute itself recognises as legitimate. If they are

---

[4] On the contemporary approach to the purposive interpretation of legislation see: *Barclays Mercantile Business Finance Ltd v Mawson* [2004] UKHL 51. On legislative history and statutory interpretation see *Pepper (Inspector of Taxes) v Hart* (HL) [1993] 1 All ER 42.

shareholders, they are shareholders for all purposes; and even if the statute was silent as to the recognition of trusts, I should be prepared to hold that if six of them were the cestuis que trust of the seventh, whatever might be their rights inter se, the statute would have made them shareholders to all intents and purposes with their respective rights and liabilities, and, dealing with them in their relation to the company, the only relations which I believe the law would sanction would be that they were corporators of the corporate body.

I am simply here dealing with the provisions of the statute, and it seems to me to be essential to the artificial creation that the law should recognise only that artificial existence—quite apart from the motives or conduct of individual corporators. In saying this, I do not at all mean to suggest that if it could be established that this provision of the statute to which I am adverting had not been complied with, you could not go behind the certificate of incorporation to shew that a fraud had been committed upon the officer entrusted with the duty of giving the certificate, and that by some proceeding in the nature of scire facias you could not prove the fact that the company had no real legal existence. But short of such proof it seems to me impossible to dispute that once the company is legally incorporated it must be treated like any other independent person with its rights and liabilities appropriate to itself, and that the motives of those who took part in the promotion of the company are absolutely irrelevant in discussing what those rights and liabilities are.

I will for the sake of argument assume the proposition that the Court of Appeal lays down—that the formation of the company was a mere scheme to enable Aron Salomon to carry on business in the name of the company. I am wholly unable to follow the proposition that this was contrary to the true intent and meaning of the Companies Act. I can only find the true intent and meaning of the Act from the Act itself; and the Act appears to me to give a company a legal existence with, as I have said, rights and liabilities of its own, whatever may have been the ideas or schemes of those who brought it into existence.

I observe that the learned judge (Vaughan Williams J.) held that the business was Mr. Salomon's business, and no one else's, and that he chose to employ as agent a limited company; and he proceeded to argue that he was employing that limited company as agent, and that he was bound to indemnify that agent (the company). I confess it seems to me that that very learned judge becomes involved by this argument in a very singular contradiction. Either the limited company was a legal entity or it was not. If it was, the business belonged to it and not to Mr. Salomon. If it was not, there was no person and no thing to be an agent at all; and it is impossible to say at the same time that there is a company and there is not.

Lindley LJ, on the other hand, affirms that there were seven members of the company; but he says it is manifest that six of them were members simply in order to enable the seventh himself to carry on business with limited liability. The object of the whole arrangement is to do the very thing which the Legislature intended not to be done.

It is obvious to inquire where is that intention of the Legislature manifested in the statute. Even if we were at liberty to insert words to manifest that intention, I should have great difficulty in ascertaining what the exact intention thus imputed to the Legislature is, or was. In this particular case it is the members of one family that represent all the shares; but if the supposed intention is not limited to so narrow a proposition as this, that the seven shareholders must not be members of one family, to what extent may influence or authority or intentional purchase of a majority among the shareholders be carried so as to bring it within the supposed prohibition? It is, of course, easy to say that it was contrary to the intention of the Legislature—a proposition which, by reason of its generality, it is difficult to bring to the test; but when one seeks to put as an affirmative proposition what the thing is which the Legislature has prohibited, there is, as it appears to me, an insuperable difficulty in the way of those who seek to insert by construction such a prohibition into the statute.

As one mode of testing the proposition, it would be pertinent to ask whether two or three, or indeed all seven, may constitute the whole of the shareholders? Whether they must be all independent of each other in the sense of each having an independent beneficial interest? And this is a question that cannot be answered by the reply that it is a matter of degree. If the Legislature intended to prohibit something, you ought to know what that something is. All it has said is that one share is sufficient to constitute a shareholder, though the shares may be 100,000 in number. Where am I to get from the statute itself a limitation of that provision that that shareholder must be an independent and beneficially interested person?

My Lords, I find all through the judgment of the Court of Appeal a repetition of the same proposition to which I have already adverted—that the business was the business of Aron Salomon, and that the company is variously described as a myth and a fiction. Lopes LJ says: 'The Act contemplated the incorporation of seven independent bona fide members, who had a mind and a will of their own, and were not the mere puppets of an individual who, adopting the machinery of the Act, carried on his old business in the same way as before, when he was a sole trader'. The words 'seven independent bona fide members with a mind and will of their own, and not the puppets of an individual,' are by construction to be read into the Act. Lopes also said that the company was a mere nominis umbra. Kay LJ says: 'The statutes were intended to allow seven or more persons, bona fide associated for the purpose of trade, to limit their liability under certain conditions and to become a corporation. But they were not intended to legalise a pretended association for the purpose of enabling an individual to carry on his own business with limited liability in the name of a joint stock company'.

My Lords, the learned judges appear to me not to have been absolutely certain in their own minds whether to treat the company as a real thing or not. If it was a real thing; if it had a legal existence, and if consequently the law attributed to it certain rights and liabilities in its constitution as a company, it appears to me to follow as a consequence that it is impossible to deny the validity of the transactions into which it has entered…

My Lords, the truth is that the learned judges have never allowed in their own minds the proposition that the company has a real existence. Then have been struck by what they have considered the inexpediency of permitting one man to be in influence and authority [of] the whole company; and, assuming that such a thing could not have been intended by the Legislature, they have sought various grounds upon which they might insert into the Act some prohibition of such a result. Whether such a result be right or wrong, politic or impolitic, I say, with the utmost deference to the learned judges, that we have nothing to do with that question if this company has been duly constituted by law; and, whatever may be the motives of those who constitute it, I must decline to insert into that Act of Parliament limitations which are not to be found there.

I have dealt with this matter upon the narrow hypothesis propounded by the learned judges below; but it is, I think, only justice to the appellant to say that I see nothing whatever to justify the imputations which are implied in some of the observations made by more than one of the learned judges. The appellant, in my opinion, is not shewn to have done or to have intended to do anything dishonest or unworthy, but to have suffered a great misfortune without any fault of his own.

The result is that I move your Lordships that the judgment appealed from be reversed, but as this is a pauper case, I regret to say it can only be with such costs in this House as are appropriate to that condition of things, and that the cross-appeal be dismissed with costs to the same extent.

Lord Macnaghten

When the trial came on before Vaughan Williams J, the validity of Mr. Broderip's claim was admitted, and it was not disputed that the 20,000 shares were fully paid up. The case presented by the liquidator broke down completely; but the learned judge suggested that the company had a right of indemnity against Mr. Salomon. The signatories of the memorandum of association were, he said, mere nominees of Mr. Salomon—mere dummies. The company was Mr. Salomon in another form. He used the name of the company as an alias. He employed the company as his agent; so the company, he thought, was entitled to indemnity against its principal. The counter-claim was accordingly amended to raise this point; and on the amendment being made the learned judge pronounced an order in accordance with the view he had expressed.

The *order* of the learned judge appears to me to be founded on a misconception of the scope and effect of the Companies Act, 1862. In order to form a company limited by shares, the Act requires that a memorandum of association should be signed by seven persons, who are each to take one share at least. If those conditions are complied with, what can it matter whether the signatories are relations or strangers? There is nothing in the Act requiring that the subscribers to the memorandum should be independent or unconnected, or that they or any one of them should take a substantial interest in the undertaking, or that they should have a mind and will of their own, as one of the learned Lords Justices seems to think, or that there should be anything like a balance of power in the constitution of the company. In almost every company that is formed the statutory number is eked out by clerks or friends, who sign their names at the request of the promoter or promoters without intending to take any further part or interest in the matter.

When the memorandum is duly signed and registered, though there be only seven shares taken, the subscribers are a body corporate 'capable forthwith', to use the words of the enactment, 'of exercising all the functions of an incorporated company'. Those are strong words. The company attains maturity on its birth. There is no period of minority—no interval of incapacity. I cannot understand how a body corporate thus made 'capable' by statute can lose its individuality by issuing the bulk of its capital to one person, whether he be a subscriber to the memorandum or not. The company is at law a different person altogether from the subscribers to the memorandum; and, though it may be that after incorporation the business is precisely the same as it was before, and the same persons are managers, and the same hands receive the profits, the company is not in law the agent of the subscribers or trustee for them. Nor are the subscribers as members liable, in any shape or form, except to the extent and in the manner provided by the Act. That is, I think, the declared intention of the enactment. If the view of the learned judge were sound, it would follow that no common law partnership could register as a company limited by shares without remaining subject to unlimited liability.

Mr. Salomon appealed; but his appeal was dismissed with costs, though the Appellate Court did not entirely accept the view of the Court below. The decision of the Court of Appeal proceeds on a declaration of opinion embodied in the order which has been already read. I must say that I, too, have great difficulty in understanding this declaration. If it only means that Mr. Salomon availed himself to the full of the advantages offered by the Act of 1862, what is there wrong in that? Leave out the words 'contrary to the true intent and meaning of the Companies Act, 1862,' and bear in mind that 'the creditors of the company' are not the creditors of Mr. Salomon, and the declaration is perfectly innocent: it has no sting in it.

In an early case, which in some of its aspects is not unlike the present, the owners of a colliery (to quote the language of Giffard LJ in the Court of Appeal) 'went on working the colliery not very successfully, and then determined to form a limited company in order to avoid incurring further personal liability'. 'It was', adds the Lord Justice, 'the policy of the Companies Act to enable this to be done'. And so he reversed the decision of Malins V.-C., who had expressed an opinion that if the laws of the country sanctioned such a proceeding they were "in a most lamentable state," and had fixed the former owners with liability for the amount of the shares they took in exchange for their property: In re Baglan Hall Colliery Co.

Among the principal reasons which induce persons to form private companies, as is stated very clearly by Mr Palmer in his treatise on the subject, are the desire to avoid the risk of bankruptcy, and the increased facility afforded for borrowing money. By means of a private company, as Mr. Palmer observes, a trade can be carried on with limited liability, and without exposing the persons interested in it in the event of failure to the harsh provisions of the bankruptcy law. A company, too, can raise money on debentures, which an ordinary trader cannot do. Any member of a company, acting in good faith, is as much entitled to take and hold the company's debentures as any outside creditor. Every creditor is entitled to get and to hold the best security the law allows him to take.

If, however, the declaration of the Court of Appeal means that Mr. Salomon acted fraudulently or dishonestly, I must say I can find nothing in the evidence to support such an imputation. The purpose for which Mr. Salomon and the other subscribers to the memorandum were associated was "lawful." The fact that Mr. Salomon raised 5000l. for the company on debentures that belonged to him seems to me strong evidence of his good faith and of his confidence in the company. The unsecured creditors of A. Salomon and Company, Limited, may be entitled to sympathy, but they have only themselves to blame for their misfortunes. They trusted the company, I suppose, because they had long dealt with Mr. Salomon, and he had always paid his way; but they had full notice that they were no longer dealing with an individual, and they must be taken to have been cognisant of the memorandum and of the articles of association. For such a catastrophe as has occurred in this case some would blame the law that allows the creation of a floating charge. But a floating charge is too convenient a form of security to be lightly abolished. I have long thought, and I believe some of your Lordships also think, that the ordinary trade creditors of a trading company ought to have a preferential claim on the assets in liquidation in respect of debts incurred within a certain limited time before the winding-up. But that is not the law at present. Everybody knows that when there is a winding-up debenture-holders generally step in and sweep off everything; and a great scandal it is.

It has become the fashion to call companies of this class 'one man companies'. That is a taking nickname, but it does not help one much in the way of argument. If it is intended to convey the meaning that a company which is under the absolute control of one person is not a company legally incorporated, although the requirements of the Act of 1862 may have been complied with, it is inaccurate and misleading: if it merely means that there is a predominant partner possessing an overwhelming influence and entitled practically to the whole of the profits, there is nothing in that that I can see contrary to the true intention of the Act of 1862, or against public policy, or detrimental to the interests of creditors. If the shares are fully paid up, it cannot matter whether they are in the hands of one or many. If the shares are not fully paid, it is as easy to gauge the solvency of an individual as to estimate the financial ability of a crowd.

One argument was addressed to your Lordships which ought perhaps to be noticed, although it was not the ground of decision in either of the Courts below. It was argued that the agreement for the transfer of the business to the company ought to be set aside, because there was no independent board of directors, and the property was transferred at an overvalue. There are, it seems to me, two answers to that argument. In the first place, the directors did just what they were authorized to do by the memorandum of association. There was no fraud or misrepresentation, and there was nobody deceived. In the second place, the company have put it out of their power to restore the property which was transferred to them. It was said that the assets were sold by an order made in the presence of Mr. Salomon, though not with his consent, which declared that the sale was to be without prejudice to the rights claimed by the company by their counter-claim. I cannot see what difference that makes. The reservation in the order seems to me to be simply nugatory. I am of opinion that the appeal ought to be allowed, and the counter-claim of the company dismissed with costs, both here and below.

One way of understanding the stark difference of opinion between the House of Lords and the Court of Appeal in this case is that the House of Lords were concerned with the literal application of the law—the Companies Act's formal requirements to incorporate a company—whereas the Court of Appeal were concerned that the company form should only be available where *the spirit* of the legislation—in addition to its formal requirements—was complied with. The Court of Appeal observe that the Companies Act 1862 requires seven members to form a company and that if the number of members falls below seven then the company must be wound-up—its life ended. For the Court of Appeal there must be some meaning in the legislature's selection of the number seven rather than the number one: some underlying purpose in choosing seven rather than one. From this legislative election, the Court induces that the Act requires seven 'bona fide' 'independent' members; not one member with six additional dummies or nominees. To allow one person to set up a company in this way and to obtain the benefit of limited liability would be, for the Court of Appeal, an abuse and a 'perversion' of the law.

Lindley LJ apparently remained unconvinced by the House of Lords' position. The 1902 6th edition of Lindley's company law text observes that 'in the opinion of the author such a proceeding was never contemplated by the legislature'.[5]

For the Court of Appeal this manipulation of the formal rules to avoid the spirit of the law is used to the clear detriment of the company's trade creditors. The trade creditors are viewed as victims of a dubious scheme: Mr Salomon 'laid a trap' for the creditors. These *poor creditors* continued to deal with Salomon unaware of the legal implications of the change in their legal position brought about by incorporation and the issue of the secured debenture to Mr Salomon. Whilst Lindley LJ recognizes that in theory the trade creditors could have found out about the secured debenture—and, therefore, could have adjusted the terms on which they did business with Salomon in order to take account of the increased risk that they would not be repaid—he observes that, in practice, traders do not do this, and, therefore, by implication are deserving of the law's protection from such a scheme.

Whilst the policy drivers of the Court of Appeal's position are clear, the legal basis for holding Salomon liable is not. Lindley LJ rejects Vaughan Williams J's reliance on the law of principal and agent. The company, in Lindley LJ's view, exists and owns the assets of the business. How, therefore, could it operate as an agent for a principal that does not own the business? However, although Lindley LJ rejects this approach he does not offer a persuasive account of why Salomon should indemnify the company in order to compensate the trade creditors. He offers an unclear and unelaborated theory of trusteeship. Lopes LJ, on the other hand, appears willing to set aside the original transaction transferring the business into the company. The Court of Appeal, therefore, clearly struggle to find the legal basis to remedy what they view as an abuse of the law.

The House of Lords provides an eloquent and formalistic deconstruction of the Court of Appeal's holding. They dismiss the Court of Appeal's attempt to go beyond the words of the statute and express the intention of the statute. Where, Lord Halsbury asks, is that intention 'manifest'? Lord Macnaghten notes that there is nothing in the Act that requires the members to be 'independent'. For their Lordships, the court's only concern should be whether or not the requirements of that Act have been complied with, and the Act merely required seven shareholders who own one share each. If those requirements have been complied with a company is born and its shareholders benefit from limited liability. Importantly, the House of Lords states clearly that the company that is brought into being is not 'in law the agent of the subscribers': that is, the company is not the agent of the individuals who form the company or who are subsequently members of the company *by reason of the fact of incorporation*.

Lord Halsbury submits that the underlying reason for the Court of Appeal's judgment is that they find it difficult to accept the legal effects of incorporation: that incorporation creates a new legal reality from what many bystanders would view as an unchanged factual reality, namely that Salomon is carrying on his business. Through the House of Lords' lens, if the legislature provides a form through which business can be carried out then those who avail themselves of that form have done nothing wrong and cause no injustice to third parties who do business with the company, even if those third parties' rights are different than they would have been had they contracted with Salomon the sole trader. For the House of Lords, third parties should protect themselves when they do business with a company. They have an opportunity to find out information about the state of the company—its liabilities and secured creditors—and to alter the terms on which they do business with the company in light of that information. If they do not 'they only have themselves to blame for their misfortune'.

---

[5] Note that this edition of the book was revised by Lindley LJ's son, Walter B. Lindley. One presumes this minor act of resistance in relation to one of his father's most famous cases had his father's imprimatur. W.B. Lindley, *A Treatise on the Law of Partnerships considered as a branch of the Law of Partnerships* (Sweet & Maxwell, 1902) 160.

Most contemporary readers find the House of Lords' logic and underlying policy positions very persuasive. Indeed today, when any type of company can be formed with one shareholder and when the corporate form touches every aspect of our lives, it seems odd that a court would read the Companies Act in such a way as to limit access to the corporate form. For these reasons, as well as the eloquent and powerful formalism of the House of Lords' judgment, the Court of Appeal's judgment appears to most contemporary readers as an obvious mistake. It is interesting then to note, as explained in this extract, that the Court of Appeal's position represented the consensus view of the time whilst the House of Lords' judgment represented a radical departure.

■ **R. Grantham, 'The Doctrinal Basis of Company Law' (1998) 57**
Cambridge Law Review **554, 560–1**

[Prior to *Salomon v A Salomon & Co Ltd*] despite the general availability of incorporation the courts persisted with the idea that the company was in essence little more than a large partnership. The conclusion that the members were the proprietors was thus quite logical, while the separate legal personality of the company was neither obvious nor particularly significant. In relation to the creation of the company this meant, first, that it was the members who were incorporated, rather than a new 'person' being created and, secondly, that if there was no genuine association of the members as partners the incorporation was improper. As Sir Frederick Pollock commented in a contemporary note of *Salomon's* case, '[w]hen the founders of company legislation spoke of seven or more persons being "associated", they meant such an association as, without the help of the statute, would have made those persons members of an ordinary partnership.'

Although hidden beneath an ingenuous reliance on the literal wording of the relevant Companies Act, the judgments in the House of Lords represent a fundamental paradigm shift. In holding that the company was properly incorporated, even though Mr. Aron Salomon was the only active member of the business, their Lordships departed from the assumption that had formerly underpinned the law's view of the company. As indicated above, the Companies Act of 1844 was not seen as creating a new form of trading institution. Rather, it took the partnership that was the joint stock form and conferred a separate existence upon it. The existence of a genuine partnership was, therefore, a prerequisite to incorporation, both legally and historically. In holding that the company was properly incorporated the House of Lords thus radically reformulated the corporate concept. It moved the law's paradigm from that of an association of individuals, governed by partnership principles, to something that more closely resembled the old chartered corporation. Incorporation was now to be viewed as the creation of an entity distinct from its members rather than as merely a means for the members to trade as a collective.

Although, as explained by Professor Grantham, the House of Lords' judgment represented a 'fundamental paradigm shift', the judgment was well received by the business community.

■ **Editorial *The Times* (19 November 1896) 9**

The case of '*Broderip v Salomon*', which raised a question of the legality of not a few 'one man' companies, has at last been decided…In commenting last year on the decision in the Court of Appeal we ventured to question the cogency of the reasoning and to complain of the obscurity in which the legal position of the 'one man company' was left. Such doubts and complaints are more than justified by the decision of the House of Lords, which has unanimously reversed the orders of the Court of Appeal and Mr Justice Vaughan Williams. Whether the plaintiff—who, it will be noted, sued in the House of Lords *in forma pauperis*—will be entirely satisfied with the net result is open to doubt. He may feel a little like a patient who, submitting under high surgical advice to an amputation of both legs, is then told on still higher authority that he ought to have lost only one, and at last is informed on the highest authority of all that he need never have lost either.

The reasoning of the Law Lords is very simple. The incorporation of the company was perfect, and could not be impeached. Every requirement of the statute had been complied with, and they find not a particle of evidence of fraud...All the statutory requirements having been complied with, [they] failed to see any reason for describing the transactions impeached as contrary to the true meaning of the Companies Act...

No doubt the scheme which Mr Aron Salomon and his legal advisers had constructed was, however good his intentions, one calculated to do mischief. The 'one-man company' may be, and often is, a snare artfully laid for the unwary. It may be, and often is, a clever trick for defeat-ing creditors—though of this there was no evidence in '*Broderip* v *Salomon*'. It has long been the opinion of many persons of experience that section 6 of the Act of 1862 relative to the formation of companies needs revision—that something more is required than the signature of 'any seven persons'...More than once in our law reports have been brought to light cases in which one or two persons, by getting a memorandum signed by seven clerks and maintaining on the register a certain number of dummy shareholders, traded with limited liability and put themselves out of the reach of the Bankruptcy Act. If ways and means could be found of discriminating between such cases, meriting no protection, and the cases, also very common, in which it is sought to keep in a certain family a long-established business, they would be welcome...Meantime, it is not amiss to remind debenture-holders and other creditors that they cannot complain with much grace if they neglect means of knowledge within their power. How far we have travelled from notions once accepted as to the duty of everybody to use his wits appears from Lord Justice Lindley's half-contemptuous dismissal of the suggestion that the debenture-holders might have found out for themselves the facts as to Mr Salomon's family party. 'It is idle to say that persons dealing with companies are protected by section 43 of the Companies Act, 1862, which requires mortgages of limited companies to be registered, and entitles creditors to inspect the register.' Why 'idle'? There is some force in Lord Watson's reply that the apathy of creditors cannot justify a charge of fraud against those who have provided all the statutory means of information, and that a person who does not take the trouble to consult them must bear the consequences.

Questions

1. After the House of Lords' decision is it possible to question the real existence of a com-pany or to hold its shareholders liable for a company's debts?

2. Do the House of Lords have any sympathy for the creditors? Do you agree with the House of Lords' approach to creditor protection?

3. Would your answer to Question 1 be different if the creditors who lost money were not busi-ness creditors but individuals who had been seriously injured by, for example, leather boots that had been treated with chemicals known to cause serious life-threatening illness?

4. Do you agree with Lord Halsbury's assertion that the Court of Appeal went beyond the ambit of their role as judges by 'inserting into [an] Act of Parliament limitations which are not to be found there'?

5. Do you agree with Lord Halsbury when he says that 'the learned judges appear to me not to have been absolutely certain in their own minds whether to treat the company as a real thing or not'?

2 The implications of separate legal personality

Following incorporation and the transfer of an existing business into the company a new legal reality is created with the original owner of the prior-business often having several different relationships with the company: shareholder, manager, director, employee, or creditor. This new legal reality is created by law but has real, and not always favourable, consequences for the person who created the company. These consequences may appear to many students of company law to be a triumph of legal form over actual substance: legal illusion over reality. Nevertheless, as we shall see, the courts have consistently respected the legal reality created by incorporation and enforced its consequences.[6] In this regard consider the following cases.

■ *Macaura v Northern Assurance Company* [1925] AC 619 (Privy Council)

Lord Buckmaster

The history of the matter can be stated in a few sentences. The appellant upon whose estate the timber in question was originally standing on December 30, 1919, assigned the whole of it to a company known as the Irish Canadian Saw Mills, Ld., the amount to be paid for the timber felled and unfelled being 27,000l., while a further 15,000l. was to be paid for the cost incurred by the appellant in felling the timber that was then down. The total price paid was therefore 42,000l., satisfied by the allotment to the appellant or his nominees of 42,000l. fully paid 1l. shares in the company; no further shares than these were ever issued. The company proceeded with the operations of cutting the timber, and by the end of August, 1921, it had all been felled and sawn up in the saw mills. In the course of these operations the appellant had become the creditor of the company for 19,000l., and beyond this it is stated that the debts of the company were trifling in amount. The timber when cut remained lying on the appellant's land, and on February 22, 1922, the greater part of it was destroyed by fire.

[Following the fire the appellant, Mr Macaura, claimed on the insurance policies in relation to the timber destroyed in the fire. The Northern Assurance Company, however, refused to pay on the grounds that as a shareholder in the company Mr Macaura did not have an insurable interest in the timber that was destroyed by the fire.]

Turning now to his position as shareholder, this must be independent of the extent of his share interest. If he were entitled to insure holding all the shares in the company, each shareholder would be equally entitled, if the shares were all in separate hands. Now, no shareholder has any right to any item of property owned by the company, for he has no legal or equitable interest therein. He is entitled to a share in the profits while the company continues to carry on business and a share in the distribution of the surplus assets when the company is wound up. If he were at liberty to effect an insurance against loss by fire of any item of the company's property, the extent of his insurable interest could only be measured by determining the extent to which his share in the ultimate distribution would be diminished by the loss of the asset—a calculation almost impossible to make. There is no means by which such an interest can be definitely measured and no standard which can be fixed of the loss against which the contract of insurance could be regarded as an indemnity...Neither a simple creditor nor a shareholder in a company has any insurable interest in a particular asset which the company holds.

■ *Lee v Lee's Air Farming Ltd* [1961] AC 12

Mr Lee had formed a company, Lee's Air Farming Ltd. The company provided aerial top dressing services which involved, for example, spraying pesticides over fields by aeroplane. 2,999 shares in the company were held by Mr Lee and 1 share was held by Mr Lee's solicitor. Mr Lee was the sole director of the company. In addition, Mr Lee had entered into an employment relationship with Lee's Air Farming Ltd to provide his services as a pilot. Mr Lee was, therefore, the controlling shareholder, the only director and the only employee. From an outsider's perspective there is one person, Mr Lee,

---

[6] Note that the criminal law has been less willing to enforce the consequences of separate legal personality than the civil law. See, for example, *R v McDonnell* [1966] 1 QB 233, holding that it is not possible for a man to conspire with a company in relation to which he is a sole shareholder.

providing a service. Through incorporation we have two persons: the company and Mr Lee. Mr Lee has three different relationships with the company: director, employee, and shareholder. Unfortunately Mr Lee was killed in a work-related accident. Under New Zealand's Workers Compensation Act 1922 Mr Lee's wife would have been entitled to compensation from the company if Mr Lee classified as a 'worker' under the Act. The court asked could he be a 'worker' for the purposes of this Act when he was also a controlling shareholder and director. The New Zealand Court of Appeal held that he was not. Mrs Lee appealed to the Privy Council.

Lord Morris of Borth-y-Gest

The Court of Appeal recognised that a director of a company may properly enter into a service agreement with his company, but they considered that, in the present case, inasmuch as the deceased was the governing director in whom was vested the full government and control of the company he could not also be a servant of the company. After referring in his judgment to the delegation to the deceased of substantially all the powers of the company, North J. said: 'These powers were moreover delegated to him for life and there remained with the company no power of management whatsoever. One of his first acts was to appoint himself the only pilot of the company...Therefore, he became in effect both employer and worker. True, the contract of employment was between himself and the company...but on him lay the duty both of giving orders and obeying them. In our view, the two offices are clearly incompatible. There could exist no power of control and therefore the relationship of master-servant was not created.'

The substantial question which arises is, as their Lordships think, whether the deceased was a 'worker' within the meaning of the Workers' Compensation Act, 1922, and its amendments. Was he a person who had entered into or worked under a contract of service with an employer? The Court of Appeal thought that his special position as governing director precluded him from being a servant of the company. On this view it is difficult to know what his status and position was when he was performing the arduous and skilful duties of piloting an aeroplane which belonged to the company and when he was carrying out the operation of top-dressing farm lands from the air. He was paid wages for so doing. The company kept a wages book in which these were recorded. The work that was being done was being done at the request of farmers whose contractual rights and obligations were with the company alone. It cannot be suggested that when engaged in the activities above referred to the deceased was discharging his duties as governing director. Their Lordships find it impossible to resist the conclusion that the active aerial operations were performed because the deceased was in some contractual relationship with the company. That relationship came about because the deceased as one legal person was willing to work for and to make a contract with the company which was another legal entity. A contractual relationship could only exist on the basis that there was consensus between two contracting parties. It was never suggested (nor in their Lordships' view could it reasonably have been suggested) that the company was a sham or a mere simulacrum. It is well established that the mere fact that someone is a director of a company is no impediment to his entering into a contract to serve the company. If, then, it be accepted that the respondent company was a legal entity their Lordships see no reason to challenge the validity of any contractual obligations which were created between the company and the deceased. In this connection reference may be made to a passage in the speech of Lord Halsbury L.C. in *Salomon v. Salomon & Co.* 'My Lords, the learned judges appear to me not to have been absolutely certain in their own minds whether to treat the company as a real thing or not. If it was a real thing; if it had a legal existence, and if consequently the law attributed to it certain rights and liabilities in its constitution as a company, it appears to me to follow as a consequence that it is impossible to deny the validity of the transactions into which it has entered'...

Nor in their Lordships' view were any contractual obligations invalidated by the circumstance that the deceased was sole governing director in whom was vested the full government and control of the company. Always assuming that the company was not a sham then the capacity of the company to make a contract with the deceased could not be impugned merely because the deceased was the agent of the company in its negotiation. The deceased might have made a firm contract to serve the company for a fixed period of years. If within such period he had retired from the office of governing director and other directors had been appointed his contract would not have been affected. The circumstance that in his capacity as a shareholder he could control the course of events would not in itself affect the validity of his contractual relationship with the company. When, therefore, it is said that 'one of his first acts was to appoint himself the only pilot of the company,' it must be recognised that the appointment was made by the company, and that it was none the less a valid appointment because it was the deceased himself who acted as the agent of the company in arranging it. In their Lordships' view it is a logical consequence of the decision in *Salomon's* case that one person may function in dual capacities. There is no reason, therefore, to deny the possibility of a contractual relationship being created as between the deceased and the company. If this stage is reached then their lordships see no reason why the range of possible contractual relationships should not include a contract for services, and if the deceased as agent for the company could negotiate a contract for services as between the company and himself there is no reason why a contract of service could not also be negotiated. It is said that therein lies the difficulty, because it is said that the deceased could not both be under the duty of giving orders and also be under the duty of obeying them. But this approach does not give effect to the circumstance that it would be the company and not the deceased that would be giving the orders. Control would remain with the company whoever might be the agent of the company to exercise it. The fact that so long as the deceased continued to be governing director, with amplitude of powers, it would be for him to act as the agent of the company to give the orders does not alter the fact that the company and the deceased were two separate and distinct legal persons. If the deceased had a contract of service with the company then the company had a right of control. The manner of its exercise would not affect or diminish the right to its exercise. But the existence of a right to control cannot be denied if once the reality of the legal existence of the company is recognised. Just as the company and the deceased were separate legal entities so as to permit of contractual relations being established between them, so also were they separate legal entities so as to enable the company to give an order to the deceased...

There appears to be no greater difficulty in holding that a man acting in one capacity can give orders to himself in another capacity than there is in holding that a man acting in one capacity can make a contract with himself in another capacity. The company and the deceased were separate legal entities. The company had the right to decide what contracts for aerial top-dressing it would enter into. The deceased was the agent of the company in making the necessary decisions. Any profits earned would belong to the company and not to the deceased. If the company entered into a contract with a farmer, then it lay within its right and power to direct its chief pilot to perform certain operations. The right to control existed even though it would be for the deceased in his capacity as agent for the company to decide what orders to give. The right to control existed in the company, and an application of the principles of Salomon's case demonstrates that the company was distinct from the deceased. As pointed out above, there might have come a time when the deceased would remain bound contractually to serve the company as chief pilot though he had retired from the office of sole governing director. Their Lordships consider, therefore, that the deceased was a worker and that the question posed in the case stated should be answered in the affirmative.

Both *Macaura v Northern Assurance Co* and *Lee v Lee's Air Farming Ltd* challenge the non-lawyer's notion of good sense. Macaura was the only shareholder who could have instructed the company to transfer the timber back to him at any time, and had he done so prior to the fire he would have had an insurable interest. How can law create an employee from a business that had no employees prior to incorporation and when no other real person apart from Mr Lee was involved in the business after incorporation? The answer is that incorporation creates something that is real: a legal person. The relationships entered into by that legal person are just as real as relationships entered into by real persons. Neither the courts nor the individuals involved in creating the company can challenge the existence of that legal person if it is brought into being having complied with the legislature's prescribed formalities.[7]

Another example of where a non-lawyer's notion of 'good sense' may rub up against the legal reality created by incorporation is in relation to the use by companies—known as parent companies—of wholly owned companies known as subsidiary companies, which are separate legal persons in their own right, to carry out one aspect of what a non-lawyer would view as the 'parent's business'. In this regard consider the following case.

■ *The Gramophone and Typewriter, Ltd v Stanley* [1908] 2 KB 89

The Commissioners for the Inland Revenue brought an action against the Gramophone Typewriter Limited (referred to in the case as the English company) arguing that the company was liable to pay income tax on profits made by a German company in which they held all the shares. These profits had not been distributed to the Gramophone Typewriter Limited.

Cozens-Hardy MR

This is an appeal from the judgment of Walton J, who held that the plaintiff company, whom I shall call the English company, are not liable to pay income tax in respect of 15,000l., part of the profits of a German company, not distributed in the way of dividend or transmitted to England, but written off by the German company in Germany to meet the depreciation of patents...

The German company was established in Germany in 1900 in accordance with German law. It was undoubtedly a company with several shareholders, who brought in considerable capital. One of those shareholders was an English company whose undertaking was subsequently acquired by the present English company. At some date, which is not stated, the English company acquired all the shares of the German company, and I assume in favour of the Crown that this event had happened before the material dates. The fact that an individual by himself or his nominees holds practically all the shares in a company may give him the control of the company in the sense that it may enable him by exercising his voting powers to turn out the directors and to enforce his own views as to policy, but it does not in any way diminish the rights or powers of the directors, or make the property or assets of the company his, as distinct from the corporation's. Nor does it make any difference if he acquires not practically the whole, but absolutely the whole, of the shares. The business of the company does not thereby become his business. He is still entitled to receive dividends on his shares, but no more. I do not doubt that a person in that position may cause such an arrangement to be entered into between himself and the company as will suffice to constitute the company his agent for the purpose of carrying on the business, and thereupon the business will become, for all taxing purposes, his business. Whether this consequence follows is in each case a matter of fact. In the present case I am unable to discover anything in addition to the holding of the shares which in any way supports this conclusion. The German company was not at first, and there is no evidence that it has ever become, a sham company or a mere cloak for the English company. It has its board of management and its board of supervision as required by the German law. Its accounts are made out in accordance with German law. On the other hand the English company has its board of directors, some of whom are on the German board. It has a proper account and balance-sheet, in which its interest in the German company is described accurately as so many shares in the German company, and the gross profits of the German company are in no way brought into the profit and loss account of the English company. Against this the only thing to be said is that the chairman of the English company made a foolish speech in which he treated the gross profits of the German company as profits of the English company, but the dividend declared by the English company did not proceed upon this footing. In my opinion it would be wrong to attribute to the loose and inaccurate language of the chairman a force sufficient to override the formal acts of both the English

---

[7] See *Neufeld v Secretary of State for Business* [2009] EWCA Civ 280 for a recent affirmation of *Lee v Lee's Air Farming Ltd* as a statement of English law.

company and the German company and all the other circumstances of the case. The Crown can, in my opinion, only succeed by making out that the German company was merely the agent of the English company as principal in carrying on the business. Nothing short of this would suffice, and I can see nothing to justify such a conclusion.

Whereas in *Macaura v Northern Assurance Company* it was clarified that the person with complete control over the company has no property interest in the assets used in the company's business *and owned by* the company, here we see the Court of Appeal similarly clarifying that the business of a subsidiary company is not the business of a controlling shareholder (the parent company).

At the end of the extract we read that the Crown could only establish its case by demonstrating that the German company was the agent of the English company. Having recently read the House of Lords judgment in *Salomon* this might seem odd as *Salomon* made it very clear that the company is not the agent of the shareholders. So what is intended here? The holding in *Salomon* is that the relationship between the company and the shareholder body that is created on incorporation is *not* a relationship of principal (shareholders) and agent (company). However, this does not preclude the possibility that a person, who happens to be a shareholder, may instruct the company to act as an agent on his behalf, and that the company accepts this undertaking. This is what is intended when Cozens-Hardy MR says the commissioners must demonstrate that the company is the shareholders' agent.

Consider also the language used by the Court of Appeal of 'sham' and 'cloak'. The court seems to suggest that had the German company been a 'sham' or a 'cloak' then the English company could have been taxed on the German subsidiary's profits. The Court does not provide any indication here as to what are the preconditions for the company being a 'sham' or a 'cloak'. The cases in section II of this chapter look in greater depth at this question of when the separate legal personality of the company may be ignored.

II PIERCING THE CORPORATE VEIL

We have already seen in *Macaura v Northern Assurance Company* and *Lee v Lee Air Farming Ltd* that the effect of incorporating a company creates results that perhaps seem at odds with how things are 'in reality'. The sanctity of separate legal personality following effective incorporation generates effects that may jar with our sense of what is 'really going on' as well as our notions of fairness, responsibility, and good sense. These effects have also, at times, had an impact on the judiciary, resulting in a rich but confused body of case law, which at times appears to respond to the need to balance the entity principle with responsibility or good sense and at others involves the reassertion of the strictness of the entity doctrine as articulated by the House of Lords in *Salomon v Salomon*.

This body of case law is sometimes described under the label lifting the corporate veil or piercing the corporate veil. Piercing the veil is a very visual label: we imagine going through the corporate form to the shareholders, perhaps holding the shareholders to account for the company's debt. However, as we shall see, these cases are not, in the main, about creditors attempting to hold shareholders liable for corporate debts. The ability to do this was dealt a fatal blow by *Salomon v Salomon*. Rather these cases are about circumstances in which we can disregard the separate legal personality of a company and treat it as one with the shareholders of the company. Sometimes these 'disregarding the veil' cases are presented as 'responses to problems generated by limited liability' and are often addressed together with limited liability, which we addressed in

Chapter 1 and will revisit in Chapter 18. However, as we shall see, these cases are not responses to the effects of limited liability, they are responses to the effects of separate legal personality.

For many students and scholars of company law, it is very difficult to make any principled sense of the cases that are presented as 'lifting' or 'piercing' cases. For these students and scholars, the differential impact between the cases of, on the one hand, the entity doctrine and, on the other hand, attempts to do fairness and justice to the facts when the entity doctrine creates unexpected results, have resulted in a set of decisions that do not have any principled thread connecting them. This section suggests that there are, however, coherent ways of categorizing these cases. There are, it is submitted, four categories of cases: first, cases which implicate the identity or nationality of the company that are thought by some commentators to have something to say about when the corporate veil can be disregarded, but in fact have nothing to say about it; secondly, those cases that involve the use of the corporate form to commit a fraud or to evade a person's existing obligations; thirdly, those cases that are concerned with the relationship between a parent company and a subsidiary company that have disregarded the veil where there is no activity taking place within the subsidiary company—this category has three separate incarnations; and fourthly, an inaccurate but intractable category of piercing the veil to do justice to the case.

1 Questions that cannot be answered by incorporation

There are several cases which at first glance appear to be cases that ignore the separate legal personality of the companies by focusing on the nationality of the shareholders rather than of the company. In fact, these cases do not involve any challenge to the separate legal personality of the company, rather they involve certain statutory or common law legal questions that are not capable of being answered with recourse only to the attributes of the company, as a person, that flow from the incorporation of the company. Accordingly, if we are interested in the general principles and rules that guide us in determining when the separate legal personality of the company can be disregarded, these cases are of limited assistance.

■ *Daimler Company, Limited Appellants v Continental Tyre and Rubber Company (Great Britain)*

The Continental Tyre and Rubber Company was an English company whose shares were owned by its German parent company as well as by several individuals who were all German nationals apart from one person who was British. The English company distributed tyres in the UK including to the Daimler Company. After the outbreak of World War I, Continental Tyre requested payment from Daimler for tyres delivered to them. Daimler was willing to pay but was concerned that any payment would contravene the, at the time, common law offence of trading with the enemy. Daimler brought the action to determine whether payment could be made. The case was considered by the Court of Appeal and then appealed to the House of Lords. Extracts from both judgments are set forth here.

■ Court of Appeal [1915] 1 KB 893

Lord Reading CJ
The appellants contend that the plaintiff company must be regarded as an alien enemy notwithstanding that it is a limited liability company, and that as commercial intercourse between persons under the protection of the Crown and persons who are alien enemies is illegal, payment

to the plaintiff company must be illegal. They further contend that the Court should look at the substance and not the technicalities of the matter. If the plaintiff company is to be regarded as an alien enemy the payment would be illegal under the common law and also under paragraph 5, sub-paragraph 1, of the Royal Proclamation relating to Trading with the Enemy issued on September 9, 1914, which forbids payment to or for the benefit of an alien enemy, and is a Proclamation in force within s. 1, sub-s. 2, of the Trading with the Enemy Act, 1914...

It cannot be disputed that the plaintiff company is an entity created by statute. It is a company incorporated under the Companies Acts and therefore is a thing brought into existence by virtue of statutory enactment. At the outbreak of war it was carrying on business in the United Kingdom; it had contracted to supply goods, it delivered them, and until the outbreak of the war it was admittedly entitled to receive payment at the due dates. Has the character of the company changed because on the outbreak of war all the shareholders and directors resided in an enemy country and therefore became alien enemies? Admittedly it was an English company before the war. An English company cannot by reason of these facts cease to be an English company. It remains an English company regardless of the residence of its shareholders or directors either before or after the declaration of war. Indeed it was not argued by Mr. Gore-Browne that the company ceased to be an entity created under English law, but it was argued that the law in time of war and in reference to trading with the enemy should sweep aside this 'technicality' as the entity was described and should treat the company not as an English company but as a German company and therefore as an alien enemy. If the creation and existence of the company could be treated as a mere technicality, there would be considerable force in this argument. It is undoubtedly the policy of the law as administered in our Courts of justice to regard substance and to disregard form. Justice should not be hindered by mere technicality, but substance must not be treated as form or swept aside as technicality because that course might appear convenient in a particular case. The fallacy of the appellants' contention lies in the suggestion that the entity created by statute is or can be treated during the war as a mere form or technicality by reason of the enemy character of its shareholders and directors. A company formed and registered under the Companies Acts has a real existence with rights and liabilities as a separate legal entity. It is a different person altogether from the subscribers to the memorandum or the shareholders on the register (*per* Lord Macnaghten in Salomon v. Salomon & Co.) It cannot be technically an English company and substantially a German company except by the use of inaccurate and misleading language. Once it is validly constituted as an English company it is an artificial creation of the Legislature and it retains its existence for all intents and purposes. It is a living thing with a separate existence which cannot be swept aside as a technicality. It is not a mere name or mask or cloak or device to conceal the identity of persons and it is not suggested that the company was formed for any dishonest or fraudulent purpose. It is a legal body clothed with the form prescribed by the Legislature.

In determining whether a company is an English or foreign corporation no inquiry is made into the share register for the purpose of ascertaining whether the members of the company are English or foreign. Once a corporation has been created in accordance with the requirements of the law it is an English company notwithstanding that all its shareholders may be foreign. Just as a foreign corporation does not become British and cease to be foreign if all its members are subjects of the British Crown (per Lord Macnaghten, Lord Brampton, and Lord Lindley in *Janson v Driefontein Consolidated Mines*). For the appellants' contention to succeed payment to the company must be treated as payment to the shareholders of the company, but a debt due to a company is not a debt due to all or any of its shareholders: *Salomon v. Salomon & Co.* The company and the company alone is the creditor entitled to enforce payment of the debt and empowered to give to the debtor a good and valid discharge. Once this conclusion is reached it follows that payment to the plaintiff company is not payment to the alien enemy shareholders or for their benefit...

It is to be observed that if payment to a company would be payment 'to or for the benefit of an enemy' because all the shareholders are enemies and because payment to the company must be regarded as payment to the shareholders it would seem to follow that payment of a debt to a company which had some enemy shareholders would equally come within the forbidden area. The appellants' answer is that their contention extends at most to those companies in which enemy shareholders are in the majority and in such circumstances as would lead to the conclusion of fact that substantially the company is enemy. Further if this contention were rejected it is urged that when as in the present case all the shareholders and directors are enemies there is no room for doubt as to the fact and a decision in the appellants' favour could be confined to the special facts. There does not appear to be any logical ground for these distinctions. If it were permissible to look behind the existence of the entity and to regard the character of the individual shareholders in order to determine whether or not the payment is 'to or for the benefit of an enemy' the suggested line of demarcation would be wholly arbitrary. If payment to a company with a majority of enemy shareholders is to be regarded as payment to an enemy company, what is the position of the other shareholders? Can it be suggested that the minority consisting of British or neutral shareholders cease to be shareholders in an English company and become members of an enemy corporation?

Buckley LJ (dissenting)

I regret that I am unable to concur in the judgment just delivered. I regard the question as so momentous that I make no apology for stating as clearly as I am able my reasons for arriving at a contrary conclusion.

The artificial legal entity created by incorporation under the Companies Acts is a legal person existing apart from its corporators.[8] This proposition is true without exception, and nothing in this judgment questions the proposition in any way. If there be twelve corporators one of them is not a twelfth or any other part of the corporation. The total number of twelve do not in the aggregate constitute the corporation. On the other hand the corporation cannot exist without corporators. If there are no corporators there can be no corporation. Corporators are essential to the existence of but form no part of the corporation.

The artificial legal person called the corporation has no physical existence. It exists only in contemplation of law. It has neither body, parts, nor passions. It cannot wear weapons nor serve in the wars. It can be neither loyal nor disloyal. It cannot compass treason. It can be neither friend nor enemy. Apart from its corporators it can have neither thoughts, wishes, nor intentions, for it has no mind other than the minds of the corporators. These considerations seem to me essential to bear in mind in determining the present case.

The corporation if it be a British corporation stands in the same position for most purposes as a British subject. For instance as regards rights of ownership of property and the right to protection and assistance by the law. But while it stands for most purposes in the position of a British subject it cannot, I think, be correctly described as a British subject. A subject must, I conceive, be one who can owe and pay allegiance to the King, who can serve the King physically, for instance if he be a male by wearing weapons and serving in the wars, who has a mind and can be either loyal or disloyal to the King. None of these can be predicated of the abstract legal entity. It has no existence at all except in contemplation of law. If these propositions be true, as I think they are, they seem to me to go to the root of the question which has in this case to be determined.

This corporation is one which as a corporation certainly has in law an independent legal existence and that legal person is British. But on the other hand all its directors are Germans resident in Germany. The holders of all its 25,000 shares except one share are Germans resident in Germany. The artificial legal thing is British, resident in England. But all its corporators who can have thoughts, wishes, or intentions are Germans resident in Germany.

The question for determination is whether when all the natural persons who express and give effect to their wishes through the corporation as a legal abstraction are Germans resident in Germany the corporation can sue in this country because those persons who could not sue are

---

[8] The term 'corporators' appears to be being used by Buckley LJ to refer to the members of the company.

as matter of law absorbed in a separate legal person which is British and which (regarding the corporation as a legal person existing apart from and irrespective of its corporators) can sue.

The contractual relations constituted by membership in a corporation under the Companies Acts are singular. The relation between each corporator and the corporation is a contractual relation governed by the statute, involving rights within the corporation, rights against the corporation, and liabilities towards the corporation. Where the corporator is an alien enemy these relations may be vitally affected by a state of war. The motive power of the corporation (which in itself apart from its corporators, or its agents—appointed and authorized through acts done by the corporators—has no life and no power of action) may become paralysed and suspended by the existence of war in a case where every corporator is as an alien enemy under disability as such.

Suppose the case of a corporation sole.[9] A private company may be formed consisting of only two persons. It was much debated a few years ago whether the law should not be so altered as to allow a sole person to incorporate himself as a company with limited liability. Suppose that were the law, and an individual German resident in Germany, an alien enemy in fact, became incorporated here as a British Company, could it be seriously contended that in time of war that alien enemy because he had acquired a legal corporate name and had an artificial legal existence in this country was consequently for the present purpose not an alien enemy? Does it make any difference that there must be two persons, or again does it make a difference that the number is seven or ten? The number of corporators in the present company is six.

Questions

1. What factors do you think are relevant to determining the nationality of a company? Are those factors any different from the factors that might determine whether a company is an 'enemy'?

2. Are the majority and Buckley LJ asking the same question? The majority appear to think that they are having a similar conversation to the one that the House of Lords had with the Court of Appeal in *Salomon v Salomon*.

3. Is Buckley LJ's judgment consistent with the House of Lords' judgment in *Salomon*?

4. Is the Court of Appeal's argument about the inability to draw a line between companies controlled by members who are 'enemies' and companies with minority members who are 'enemies' persuasive?

5. If you were the majority in the Court of Appeal how would you respond to Buckley LJ's argument about the corporation sole with one 'enemy' member?

■ House of Lords [1916] 2 AC 307

Lord Parker Of Waddington

When the action was instituted all the directors of the plaintiff company were Germans resident in Germany. In other words, they were the King's enemies...The principle upon which the judgment under appeal proceeds is that trading with an incorporated company cannot be trading with an enemy where the company is registered in England under the Companies Acts and carries on its business here. Such a company it calls an 'English company', and obviously likens to a natural-born Englishman, and accordingly holds that payment to it of a debt which is due to it, and of money which is its own, cannot be trading with the enemy, be its corporators who they may. The view is that an English company's enemy officers vacate their office on becoming enemies and so affect it no longer, and that its enemy shareholders, being neither its agents nor its principals, never in law affect it at all.

---

[9] A corporation sole is a company with one member, that at the time of this case was not available. Today it is possible to form a public or a private company with only one member: section 7 CA 2006.

My Lords, much of the reasoning by which this principle is supported is quite indisputable. No one can question that a corporation is a legal person distinct from its corporators; that the relation of a shareholder to a company, which is limited by shares, is not in itself the relation of principal and agent or the reverse; that the assets of the company belong to it and the acts of its servants and agents are its acts, while its shareholders, as such, have no property in the assets and no personal responsibility for those acts. The law on the subject is clearly laid down in a passage in Lord Halsbury's judgment in *Salomon v Salomon & Co*: 'I am simply here,' he says, 'dealing with the provisions of the statute, and it seems to me to be essential to the artificial creation that the law should recognise only that artificial existence—quite apart from the motives or conduct of individual corporators…Short of such proof'—i.e., proof in appropriate proceedings that the company had no real legal existence—'it seems to me impossible to dispute that once the company is legally incorporated it must be treated like any other independent person with its rights and liabilities appropriate to itself, and that the motives of those who took part in the formation of the company are absolutely irrelevant in discussing what those rights and liabilities are.' I do not think, however, that it is a necessary corollary of this reasoning to say that the character of its corporators must be irrelevant to the character of the company; and this is crucial, for the rule against trading with the enemy depends upon enemy character.

A natural person, though an English-born subject of His Majesty, may bear an enemy character and be under liability and disability as such by adhering to His Majesty's enemies. If he gives them active aid, he is a traitor; but he may fall far short of that and still be invested with enemy character. If he has what is known in prize law as a commercial domicil among the King's enemies, his merchandise is good prize at sea, just as if it belonged to a subject of the enemy power. Not only actively, but passively, he may bring himself under the same disability. Voluntary residence among the enemy, however passive or pacific he may be, identifies an English subject with His Majesty's foes. I do not think it necessary to cite authority for these well-known propositions, nor do I doubt that, if they had seemed material to the Court of Appeal, they would have been accepted.

How are such rules to be applied to an artificial person, incorporated by forms of law? [Emphasis added]…In the case of an artificial person what is the analogue to voluntary residence among the King's enemies? Its impersonality can hardly put it in a better position than a natural person and lead to its being unaffected by anything equivalent to residence. It is only by a figure of speech that a company can be said to have a nationality or residence at all. If the place of its incorporation under municipal law fixes its residence, then its residence cannot be changed, which is almost a contradiction in terms, and in the case of a company residence must correspond to the birthplace and country of natural allegiance in the case of a living person, and not to residence or commercial domicil. Nevertheless, enemy character depends on these last. It would seem, therefore, logically to follow that, in transferring the application of the rule against trading with the enemy from natural to artificial persons, something more than the mere place or country of registration or incorporation must be looked at.

My Lords, I think that the analogy is to be found in control, an idea which, if not very familiar in law, is of capital importance and is very well understood in commerce and finance. The acts of a company's organs, its directors, managers, secretary, and so forth, functioning within the scope of their authority, are the company's acts and may invest it definitively with enemy character. It seems to me that similarly the character of those who can make and unmake those officers, dictate their conduct mediately or immediately, prescribe their duties and call them to account, may also be material in a question of the enemy character of the company. If not definite and conclusive, it must at least be prima facie relevant, as raising a presumption that those who are purporting to act in the name of the company are, in fact, under the control of those whom it is their interest to satisfy. Certainly I have found no authority to the contrary. Such a view reconciles the positions of natural and artificial persons in this regard, and the opposite view leads to the paradoxical result that the King's enemies, who chance during war to constitute the entire body of corporators in a company registered in England, thereby pass out of the range of legal vision, and, instead, the corporation, which in itself is incapable of loyalty, or enmity, or residence, or of anything but bare existence in contemplation of law and registration under some system of law, takes their place for almost the most important of all purposes, that of being classed among the King's friends or among his foes in time of war.

What is involved in the decision of the Court of Appeal is that, for all purposes to which the character and not merely the rights and powers of an artificial person are material, the person-alities of the natural persons, who are its corporators, are to be ignored. An impassable line is drawn between the one person and the others. When the law is concerned with the artificial person, it is to know nothing of the natural persons who constitute and control it. In questions of property and capacity, of acts done and rights acquired or liabilities assumed thereby, this may be always true. Certainly it is so for the most part. But the character in which property is held, and the character in which the capacity to act is enjoyed and acts are done, are not in pari materia. The latter character is a quality of the company itself, and conditions its capacities and its acts. It is not a mere part of its energies or acquisitions, and if that character must be derivable not from the circumstances of its incorporation which arises once for all, but from qualities of enmity and amity, which are dependent on the chances of peace or war and are attributable only to human beings, I know not from what human beings that character should be derived, in cases where the active conduct of the company's officers has not already decided the matter, if resort is not to be had to the predominant character of its shareholders and corporators.

The Court of Appeal in this case applies the persuasive formalism which we saw in the House of Lords' judgment in *Salomon v Salomon*: the Continental Tyre company is an English company duly created by complying with the formalities of incorporation pursuant to the Companies Act. Lord Reading holds that 'once ... created in accordance with the requirements of the law it is an English corporation notwithstanding that all its shareholders may be foreign'. For the Court of Appeal, to consider the character of the shareholders to determine whether Continental Tyre is an enemy would be to ignore the fact of the company's separate legal personality and the holding in *Salomon v Salomon*. As an English company it cannot, therefore, be an enemy.

For the House of Lords, the legal question of relevance is not one that can be answered by the basic attributes of a company provided by incorporation. The question is: what is the *character* of the company for the purpose of the trading with the enemy prohibi-tion? They note that a real British person can become an enemy by reason of his resi-dence in enemy territory. That real person remains a British citizen but may become an enemy. However, the category of residence does not, the House of Lords hold, assist the court in answering this question in relation to a company because its residence is determined by the country of its incorporation. If incorporation determined enemy character then a company would be in a superior position to a real British person who could, as the court outlined, acquire 'enemy character'. Accordingly, the House of Lords holds that as this question cannot be answered by the fact of incorporation it is necessary to look at other attributes of the company to determine whether it has enemy character. The court finds the relevant attribute in the nationality of the company's controllers: the shareholders who can determine who sits on the board: 'who can make and unmake those officers'.

Accordingly, whilst one could attempt to read *Daimler v Continental Tyre* as set-ting forth criteria on when one can pierce the corporate veil—here the criteria would be control—such a reading is incorrect. Control is used to answer the unusual ques-tion: when does a company have enemy character? Consider now another case that raises some similar issues, and is similarly susceptible to being misinterpreted as a piercing case.

■ *In re FG (Films) Ltd* [1953] 1 WLR 483

The headnote in the case concisely sets forth the facts as follows.

The applicants were incorporated under the Companies Act, 1948, with a capital of £100 in £1 shares, 90 of which were held by one director, J., an American citizen, 10 by the second, who was British, and none by the third, who also was British. The applicants' sole place of business was their registered office, and they did not employ any staff. They agreed to produce a film based on a story the film rights in which [belonged to] an American company of which J. was president, and which agreed to provide the finance and whatever facilities the applicants might require. The film was made in India, and the applicants applied to the Board of Trade to register it as a British film, which the Board of Trade, while admitting that the applicants were a British company as defined in the Act, declined to do on the ground that the applicants were not the 'maker' of the film within the meaning of sections 25 (1) (a) and 44 (1) of the Cinematograph Films Act, 1938.

Vaisey J

The sole question, therefore, which I have to decide is whether the applicants were the 'maker' of the film. This is what they claim to be, but the respondent has decided that they were not and has, on that ground, refused to register the film 'Monsoon' as a British film. The applicants, being aggrieved by that decision, are, in accordance with section 31 of the Act making the present application to the court. In substance, I am asked to reverse the respondent's decision and to say that 'Monsoon' is a British film under the Act.

In section 44 of the Act the expression 'maker' is defined as meaning, 'in relation to a film, the person by whom the arrangements necessary for the making of the film are undertaken...' This is perhaps a strange collocation of words which might in other circumstances give rise to some difficulty of interpretation. 'Undertake' means, I think, 'be responsible for,' especially in the financial sense, but also generally. So far as the present case is concerned, I think that it plainly suggests the following problem: was it the applicants alone who undertook the arrangements necessary for the making of the film, or did they do so in co-operation with some other person, firm or company, reading as including the plural number (in accordance with the Interpretation Act, 1889) the words 'maker,' 'British subject' and 'British company' in section 25 and the words 'maker' and 'person' in the definition? Here the applicants can succeed only if they establish themselves as the sole statutory makers of the film, for, if they were (as may well be the case) one of several makers, the other 'maker' or 'makers' certainly cannot, in the circumstances of this case, be brought within the description of 'British subject' or 'British company.' Their claim is to be, or to have been, the sole exclusive maker of the film.

The applicants have a capital of £100, divided into 100 shares of £1 each, 90 of which are held by the American director and the remaining 10 by a British one. The third director has no shareholding. I now understand that they have no place of business apart from their registered office, and they did not employ any staff. It seems to me to be contrary, not only to all sense and reason, but to the proved and admitted facts of the case, to say or to believe that this insignificant company undertook in any real sense of that word the arrangements for the making of this film. I think that their participation in any such undertaking was so small as to be practically negligible, and that they acted, in so far as they acted at all in the matter, merely as the nominee of and agent for an American company called Film Group Incorporated, which seems (among other things) to have financed the making of the film to the extent of at least £80,000 under the auspices and direction of the said American director, who happened to be its president. The suggestion that this American company and that director were merely agents for the applicants is, to my mind, inconsistent with and contradicted by the evidence, and a mere travesty of the facts, as I understand and hold them to be.

One way of reading this case that may seem attractive if one is thinking about the case through the lens of 'piercing the corporate veil' is that the court looked through the veil of incorporation to determine the company's nationality for the purposes of the Cinematograph Films Act 1938. That is, instead of focusing on the company's nationality, as determined by the place of its incorporation, namely the UK, the court focused on the fact that 90% of its shares were owned by Americans. From this view of the case we might ask the question what justification did the court provide for doing this and one could point to the court's focus on the fact there was no activity being carried on in the company: it had no employees; no place of business. However, this is a strained reading of the case. This is not, as it is sometimes viewed, a piercing case at all. It involves the courts answering a specific legal question arising from the applicable statute, namely: did the company *make* the film? If the company had no place of business and no-employees then it cannot have made anything; rather it could only function in some sort of agency role for the actual makers and financiers of the film. *In re FG Films*, therefore, tells us nothing about the criteria that courts may apply in deciding to disregard the corporate veil.

2 Evading existing obligations

The following cases involve attempts to use the corporate form to avoid existing legal obligations to which the defendants were subject. The question for us to consider is whether or not these cases set out rules according to which the courts will lift the corporate veil, that is ignore the separate legal personality of the company and treat company and shareholder as one.

■ *Gilford Motor Company v Horne* [1933] Ch 935

In *Gilford Motor Company v Horne*, Mr Horne was for a period of time the managing director of the Gilford Motor Company. The business of the company was described by Lord Hanworth MR as follows: the company 'sold motors which were assembled by them, but they were not in fact the actual manufacturers of the whole of the motors thus sold'...Included in Mr Horne's contract as a managing director was a non-solicitation clause that purported to prevent Mr Horne from soliciting customers of the Gilford Motors business. Mr Horne left the company's employ and shortly thereafter set up another company which sold spare parts for Gilford Motor cars. Mr Horne was neither a director nor shareholder of the company. Mr Horne's wife was both a director and shareholder. The court was, however, satisfied that this company was the vehicle for Mr Horne's business. An action was brought by Gilford Motor Company to enforce the non-solicitation covenant. The question for the court was whether this activity was in breach of the non-solicitation provision. The court considered the legality of the non-solicitation provision and decided that it was enforceable against Mr Horne. The court also considered whether it should be enforceable against the company which was the vehicle for Horne's activities. Before reading these extracts let us remind ourselves that the company is a separate legal company, which, in contrast to Mr Horne, was not subject to any agreement not to solicit customers from the Gilford Motor Company.

Lord Hanworth MR

I think the injunction must go against the company...In *Smith v Hancock*[10]...Lindley LJ indicated the rule which ought to be followed by the Court: 'If the evidence admitted of the conclusion that what was being done was a mere cloak or sham, and that in truth the business was being carried on by the wife and Kerr for the defendant, or by the defendant through his wife for Kerr, I certainly should not hesitate to draw that conclusion, and to grant the plaintiff relief accordingly.' I do draw

[10] [1894] 2 Ch 377.

that conclusion; I do hold that the company was 'a mere cloak or sham'; I do hold that it was a mere device for enabling Mr. E. B. Horne to continue to commit breaches of [the non-solicitation clause] and under those circumstances the injunction must go against both defendants.

Romer LJ

In my opinion [the court of first instance] was right...in coming to the conclusion...that this defendant company was formed and was carrying on business merely as cloak or sham for the purpose of enabling the defendant Horne to commit the breach of the covenant that he entered into deliberately with the plaintiffs on the occasion of and as consideration for his employment as managing director.

■ *Jones v Lipman and Another* [1962] 1 WLR 832

In *Jones v Lipman*, Mr Lipman had entered into a sale and purchase contract to sell a freehold property to Mr Jones. However, after having entered the contract, but prior to the completion and transfer to Mr Jones of legal title to the property, Mr Lipman transferred the property to a company which was wholly owned by him and a nominee. Apparently, the purpose of this scheme was to avoid being subject to an order of specific performance to transfer the property to Mr Jones.

Russell J

For the plaintiffs the argument was twofold. First, that specific performance would be ordered against a party to a contract who has it in his power to compel another person to convey the property in question; and that admittedly the first defendant had this power over the defendant company. Second, that specific performance would also, in circumstances such as the present, be ordered against the defendant company. For the first proposition reference was made to *Elliott and H. Elliott (Builders) Ltd. v. Pierson*.[11] In that case resistance to specific performance at the suit of a vendor was grounded on the fact that the property was *vested* in a limited company and not in the vendor. The company, however, was wholly owned and controlled by the vendor, who could compel it to transfer the property, and on this ground the defence to the claim for specific performance failed. It seems to me, not only from dicta of the judge but also on principle, that it necessarily follows that specific performance cannot be resisted by a vendor who, by his absolute ownership and control of a limited company in which the property is vested, is in a position to cause the contract to be completed.

For the second proposition reference was made to *Gilford Motor Co. Ltd. v Horne*. In that case the individual defendant had entered into covenants restricting his trading activities. It caused the defendant company in that case to be formed. This company was under his control and did things which, if they had been done by him, would have been a breach of the covenants. An injunction was granted not only against him but also against the company. In that case...Romer LJ said [the extracts from Romer LJ's judgment set forth above were cited].

Those comments on the relationship between the individual and the company apply even more forcibly to the present case. The defendant company is the creature of the first defendant, a device and a sham, a mask which he holds before his face in an attempt to avoid recognition by the eye of equity. The case cited illustrates that an equitable remedy is rightly to be granted directly against the creature in such circumstances...

The proper order to make is an order on both the defendants specifically to perform the agreement between the plaintiffs and the first defendant, but excepting from the order against the defendant company that part of the agreement which involves the chattels. Accordingly, the court will declare that the contract [to sell the property] ought to be specifically performed as to both the realty and personalty comprised therein by [the company as well as Mr Lipman].

---

[11] [1948] 1 All ER 939.

It is clear that in *Gilford Motor Company v Horne* by granting the injunction against the company controlled by Mr Horne, as well as against Mr Horne himself, and in *Jones v Lipman* by making the order of specific performance against the company controlled by Mr Lipman, as well as against Mr Lipman himself, the courts were ignoring the separate legal personality of these companies. Strictly speaking, the company had nothing to do with the legal obligations to which Horne and Lipman were subject. The obligations were imposed upon the companies in both cases because of their connections to the obligated party. In *Jones v Lipman* the relationship between Lipman and the company was one of controlling shareholder and company. Interestingly, in *Gilford Motors* the relationship was not one of member–company as Horne was neither a member nor director of the company. However, he was viewed by the court as the actual controller of the company. More recently in *Faiza Ben Hasem v Abdulhadi Ali Shayif*,[12] relying on *Gilford Motors* and *Jones v Lipman*, Mr Justice Munby observed that: 'the common theme running through all the cases in which the court has been willing to pierce the veil is that the company was being used by its controller in an attempt to immunise himself from liability for some wrongdoing which existed entirely *dehors* the company'.[13]

One might ask whether it was necessary to subject the companies in these cases to the respective injunctions. Could the objective of ensuring compliance with Lipman's and Horne's existing legal obligations have been achieved without doing this? In *Jones v Lipman* the court clearly states the alternative approach which they endorse: namely, that the remedy of specific performance extends to requiring the person subject to the order to take actions within his power as 100% shareholder to arrange for the transfer of the property. As this would have been sufficient to have provided Mr Jones with a remedy, one wonders why the court thought it necessary to go further and apply the order to the company directly? In *Gilford Motors*, as Mr Horne was not a shareholder he did not formally have the power to instruct the company to take action. However, an injunction imposed upon him to prevent him from being directly or indirectly involved in the solicitation of Gilford Motor Company's clients would have been sufficient to have ensured compliance with his contractual obligation.[14]

The fact that there is an alternative—non-piercing—way of understanding these cases does not mean that we should not analyse them as 'veil-piercing cases'. To what extent, therefore, do these cases provide guidance on the criteria to be applied to determine whether the veil should be pierced? Consider in this regard the language used by the courts. The courts refer to the company as a 'mask' or a 'sham'. A mask is 'a covering worn on or held in front of the face for disguise'.[15] A sham is 'something that is intended to be mistaken for something else, or that is not really what it purports to be'.[16] In *Snook v London and West Riding Investments Ltd*,[17] Lord Diplock defined a sham as follows:

> Acts done or documents executed by the parties to the 'sham' which are intended by them to give to third parties or to the court the appearance of creating between the parties legal rights

---

[12] [2008] EWHC 2380 (Fam).

[13] Meaning 'something outside the ordinary business of the company'—*Antonio Gramsci Shipping Corp v Stepanovs* [2011] EWCH 333 also observing that 'whether dehors the company is ever a very helpful or meaningful expression I do not know'!

[14] In this regard see Lord Cooke of Thorndon, *Turning Points of the Common Law* (1996, Hamlyn Lectures). In this regard see *CMS Dolphin v Simonet* [2001] 2 BCLC 704, taking the approach that eschewed the need to pierce the corporate veil where corporate opportunities were wrongfully diverted to a company by a director in breach of fiduciary duty and where the director owned a significant stake in the transferee company. Laurence Collins J held: 'I do not think that it is necessary to resort to piercing or lifting the corporate veil…the directors are equally liable with the corporate vehicle formed by them to take unlawful advantage of the business opportunities. The reason is that they have jointly participated in the breach of trust.' See also *Antonio Gramsci Shipping Corp v Stepanovs* [2011] EWCH 333 making this point.

[15] *Oxford English Dictionary* (www.oed.com/).

[16] *Oxford English Dictionary* (www.oed.com/).   [17] [1967] 1 All ER 518.

and obligations different from the actual legal rights and obligations (if any) which the parties intended to create.

It is clear why the language of 'mask' and 'sham' is attractive to a court attempting to describe the role of the company in these cases. They are trying to articulate the idea that the company form is being used to conceal illegitimate activity. But the language chosen to do this is misleading.[18] In both *Gilford Motors* and *Jones v Lipman* the relationships created in each case by the incorporation of the companies were real legal relationships; and those relationships were intended to be created. It was the effects of those relationships that were problematic: effective breach of covenant and avoiding completing the sale of the property. The terms 'mask' and 'sham' are singularly unhelpful in trying to identify broader principles for determining when separate legal personality can be ignored. *Gilford Motor Company v Horne* and *Jones v Lipman* are connected in a much more straightforward way: the separate legal personality of the company will be ignored to the extent that the separate legal personality of the company is used to avoid *existing* legal obligations of a member or controller of the company.

3 Agency

The House of Lords made it very clear in *Salomon v Salomon* that the company is not the shareholders' agent by reason of the fact of incorporation. We have also seen in our consideration of the *Gramophone and Typewriter* case that it is possible for a separate relationship of agency to be created between a person who happens to be a shareholder, as principal, and the company, as agent. Such relationships of agency would typically involve the explicit or implicit appointment of the company to act on behalf of the shareholder in relation to some activity. The relationship between the company and the person who is a shareholder would be a contractual relationship of agency governed by the law of agency. If such a separate relationship of agency is created then the person who is the shareholder, as principal, would be liable for the actions of the agent, the company, in contract and in tort provided that the agent is acting within the scope of his actual or apparent authority.[19] This would *not*, however, be an example of piercing the corporate veil. On the contrary, it is an affirmation of a company's separate legal personality that a separate relationship of agency can be created with the company. The liability of the person who happens to be a shareholder (as principal) follows from the relationship of agency, not from disregarding the separate legal personality of the company.

Of course, when considering whether the shareholder could be held liable, a court may well be asked to consider the question of whether there is an agency relationship alongside the question of whether there are any grounds for piercing the corporate veil. The reason for this is that these two approaches may generate the same legal outcome. However, they are legally distinct ways of reaching that outcome. An example of the case where both piercing the corporate veil and the question of agency were considered is the Court of Appeal case of *Adams v Cape Industries*, which, as we shall see in sections 4 and 5 of this chapter, is the leading piercing case. The court in *Adams v Cape*

---

[18] For an example of how the use of this language creates analytical confusion see *Kensington International Ltd v Republic of Congo* [2006] 2 BCLC 296, paras 177–80. See *Yukong Line Ltd of Korea v Rendsberg Investments Corporation of Liberia (No 2)* [1998] 1 WLR 294, expressing doubt about the correct use of the word 'sham' in this context *per* Toulson J; see also *Faiza Ben Hashem v Abdulhadi Ali Shayif* [2008] EWHC 2380 (Fam) where Mr Justice Munby observes 'indeed, I have some difficulty with the very suggestion that a company, so long as it remains on the register of companies, could ever properly be described as a sham in the *Snook* sense'.

[19] On actual and apparent authority see Chapter 4.

Industries found that there was no separate relationship of agency between the parent company and its wholly owned subsidiary. In doing so it focused upon whether the subsidiary had been given authority to act on behalf of and bind the parent.

■ *Adams v Cape Industries Plc* [1990] Ch 433

> **Slade LJ**
> For all the closeness of the relationship between [parent] and [wholly owned subsidiary], strictly defined limits were imposed on the functions which [the subsidiary was] authorised to carry out or did carry out as their representative. First, [the subsidiary] had no general authority to bind [the parent] to any contractual obligation. Second, as counsel for the plaintiffs expressly accepted, there is no evidence that [the subsidiary], whether with or without prior authority from [the parent], ever effected any transaction in such manner that [the parent] thereby became subject to contractual obligations to any person.

If the issue of whether or not there is a distinct relationship of agency between shareholder and company or parent and subsidiary is so clearly distinct from the legal regulation of piercing the corporate veil, one might ask: why then do we address it in this section of the book? The answer to this is that in some cases the terms 'agent' or 'agency relationship' have taken on a very different meaning and significance that is much more akin to the piercing jurisprudence considered in sections 4 and 5 of this chapter. Consider in this regard the following case.

■ *Smith, Stone and Knight Ltd v City of Birmingham* [1939] 4 All ER 116

The claimant company owned certain property that was compulsorily purchased by the City of Birmingham. However, the claimant itself did not carry out business through this property; rather the claimant's subsidiary company carried out business at this address. This created a problem for the claimant as the City of Birmingham would not have to pay compensation for loss of business to the subsidiary company if the subsidiary was the occupier of the premises, but would have to pay compensation to the claimant if the subsidiary occupied the premises as the claimant's agent. Accordingly, in an attempt to obtain compensation, the parent company claimant claimed that the subsidiary company was carrying on the parent company's business as agent.

> **Atkinson J**
> Those being the facts, the [City of Birmingham] rest their contention on *Salomon's* case, and their argument is that the Waste company was a distinct legal entity. It was in occupation of the premises, the business was being carried on in its name and the claimants' only interest in law was that of holders of the shares. It is well settled that the mere fact that a man holds all the shares in a company does not make the business carried on by that company his business, nor does it make the company his agents for the carrying on of the business. That proposition is just as true if the shareholder is itself a limited company. It is also well settled that there may be such an arrangement between the shareholders and a company as will constitute the company the shareholders' agent for the purpose of carrying on the business and make the business the business of the shareholders...
> It seems therefore to be a question of fact in each case, and those cases indicate that the question is whether the subsidiary was carrying on the business as the company's business or as its

own. I have looked at a number of cases—they are all revenue cases[20]—to see what the courts regarded as of importance for determining that question…and I find six points which were deemed relevant for the determination of the question: Who was really carrying on the business? In all the cases, the question was whether the company, an English company here, could be taxed in respect of all the profits made by some other company, a subsidiary company, being carried on elsewhere. The first point was: were the profits treated as the profits of the company?—when I say 'the company' I mean the parent company? Secondly, were the persons conducting the business appointed by the parent company? Thirdly was the company the head and the brain of the trading venture? Fourthly, did the company govern the adventure, decide what should be done and what capital should be embarked on the venture? Fifthly, did the company make the profits by its skill and direction? Sixthly, was the company in effectual and constant control? Now if the judgments in those cases are analysed, it will be found that all those matters were deemed relevant for consideration in determining the main question, and it seems to me that every one of those questions must be answered in favour of the claimants. Indeed, if ever one company can be said to be the agent or employee, or tool or simulacrum of another, I think the Waste company was in this case a legal entity, because that is all it was. There was nothing to prevent the claimants at any moment saying: 'We will carry on this business in our own name.' They had but to paint out the Waste company's name on the premises, change their business paper and form, and the thing would have been done. I am satisfied that the business belonged to the claimants; they were, in my view, the real occupiers of the premises. If either physically or technically the Waste company was in occupation, it was for the purposes of the service it was rendering to the claimants, such occupation was necessary for that service, and I think that those facts would make that occupation in law the occupation of the claimants. An analogous position would be where servants occupy cottages or rooms for the purposes of their business, and it is well settled that if they have to occupy those premises for the purposes of the business, their occupation is the occupation of their principal. I have no doubt the business was the company's business and was being carried on under their direction, and I answer the question in favour of the claimants.

In *Smith, Stone and Knight* the question for the court to consider is the same as the one considered and rejected in *Adams v Cape Industries*, namely: on the facts of the case has a separate relationship of agency been created between parent and subsidiary? However, the court answers this question in a way that is very different than an inquiry into whether a contractual relationship of agency has been created, such as the one we saw in the extract from *Adams*. The court's determination of whether the subsidiary is an agent is answered by asking whether the subsidiary is carrying on its own business or its parent's business. To answer that question the court provides a set of criteria which respond to the question: is the subsidiary doing anything for itself and is there any indication that the company exercises autonomy and self-determination or is it merely a puppet of the parent? Perhaps one might argue that it follows that if a company has no autonomous activity then at the very least it must be the agent of the company that set it up. Whilst the court stresses that the subject companies are independent entities, its analysis goes towards determining whether they behave as one. The approach retains the pretence of respecting the separate legal personality of the company but *in fact* the test of 'agency' here results in disregarding the separate legal identity of the two companies.[21]

---

[20] Atkison J referred to the following cases: *San Paulo Brazilian Ry Co v Carter* [1896] AC 31, *Apthorpe v Peter Schoenhofen Brewery Co Ltd* (1899), 80 LT 395; *Frank Jones Brewing Co v Apthorpe* (1898) 4 Tax Cas 6, *St Louis Breweries v Apthorpe* (1898) 79 LT 551.

[21] For an interesting and very similar use/misuse of the term 'agency' see the well-known New York case of *Walkovszky v Carlton* 223 NE 2d 6 (NY 1966).

The status of this case as authority is somewhat suspect. Whilst several cases have applied the factors referred to in the case, typically they do so without finding a relationship of 'agency'. Other courts have been keen to stress the fact-specific nature of the judgment. In *JH Rayner (Mincing Lane) Ltd v DTI*, Kerr LJ held that the facts of *Smith, Stone and Knight* 'were so unusual that they cannot form any basis of principle'.[22] Other cases, however, have treated the approach in *Smith, Stone and Knight* as applicable law. For example, the Court of Appeal in *Munton Brothers* applied *Smith, Stone and Knight* to pierce the veil between parent and subsidiary companies in relation to a similar fact pattern.[23] What remains of particular interest for us is the fact that this approach to determine 'agency' in *Smith, Stone and Knight* bears considerable similarity to rules that result in the disregarding of the corporate veil in the cases considered in section 4 of this chapter.

4 Single economic unit

We commonly think about, and the media represents, large companies such as Vodafone Plc and Marks and Spencer Plc as *one* company, whatever the range of businesses involved or wherever in the world that business is being carried out. In fact these 'companies' are typically groups of many companies, consisting of a parent company and many subsidiary companies whose shares are owned by the parent company. Although these companies appear in our non-legal everyday world as single units, *in law* these companies are many legal persons, not one legal person.

In this section we ask whether the law recognizes any situations in which the separate legal personality of two group companies can be ignored. Given the holding in *Salomon*, many of you may be wondering why this is deserving of further discussion and a separate section in this book. *Salomon*, you would argue, made it perfectly clear that a registered company is a separate legal person, separate from its incorporators and members. *Salomon* did not say this applied only to companies owned by real persons. Accordingly, there need be no further discussion of this issue in the context of groups of companies. Those of you making this argument have a very strong case and, as we will see, are ultimately vindicated. However, the problems that respect for separate legal personality in the group context has generated has led to pressures to effectively qualify the *Salomon* holding in the group context. Our question here is: in what situations, if any, is it possible to ignore the legal personality of parent and subsidiary companies and treat them as one: as a single economic unit?

■ *DHN Food Distributors v Tower Hamlets LBC* **[1976] 1 WLR 852**

The facts are presented in Lord Denning MR's judgment.

Lord Denning MR
This case might be called the 'Three in one.' Three companies in one. Alternatively, the 'One in three.' One group of three companies. For the moment I will speak of it as 'the firm.' In 1963 at Bow in the east end of London there was a firm of grocery and provision merchants. It

---

[22] [1989] Ch 72. See also *The Government of Sierra Leone v Davenport* [2003] EWHC 2769 (Ch) citing *JH Rayner*. Other cases that hold that the case should be narrowly construed as addressing the application of a particular statute include: *Yukong Lines Ltd Of Korea v Rendsburg Investments Corporation And Others; (The 'Rialto') (No 2)* [1998] 1 Lloyd's Rep 322.

[23] [1983] NI 369. Note that this case could equally be narrowly construed as an application of the relevant statue in question: the Criminal Injuries Acts (Northern Ireland) 1956–1970. Note also that this case also relied on *DHN Food Distributors Ltd v London Borough of Tower Hamlets* [1976] 1 WLR 852, which we consider later and, as we will see, may well be viewed as suspect authority.

imported groceries and provisions and distributed them to shopkeepers. It had a warehouse in Malmesbury Road. The firm had lorries which collected goods from the docks: and distributed them to shopkeepers. Soon afterwards the firm developed a "cash and carry" business. Private individuals came by car. They bought substantial quantities wholesale. They paid for them in cash and carried them away.

Six years later in 1969 Tower Hamlets London Borough Council made a compulsory purchase order. They wanted to acquire the property of the firm, to demolish the warehouse, and to build houses on the site. In February 1970 there was a local inquiry. The firm made strong objection. They said that if the property was taken, it would mean the end of their business. The acquiring authority realised that the firm would lose its business, but they said that the housing requirements took priority and that the firm would receive compensation for any loss...

Now comes the point. It is about compensation. Compensation under the statute is to be made for the value of the land and also compensation for disturbance of the business: see section 5(2) and (6) of the Land Compensation Act 1961. If the firm and its property had all been in one ownership, it would have been entitled to compensation under those two heads: first, the value of the land, which has been assessed in excess of £360,000. Second, compensation for disturbance in having its business closed down. The figure has not yet been assessed. But the firm and its property were not in one ownership. It was owned by three companies. The business was owned by the parent company, D.H.N. Food Distributors Ltd. The land was owned at the time of acquisition by a subsidiary, called Bronze Investments Ltd. The vehicles were owned by another subsidiary, D.H.N. Food Transport Ltd. The parent company D.H.N. held all the shares both in the Bronze company and in the Transport company. The directors were the same in all three companies. As the result of the business having to be closed down, all the three companies are in liquidation.

The question is: what is the effect of the firm being in truth the three companies? The acquiring authority say that the owners of the land were Bronze Investments Ltd., and that company are entitled to the value of the land £360,000. They have actually been paid it. But the acquiring authority say that that company are not entitled to compensation for disturbance because they were not disturbed at all. The authority admit that D.H.N. (who ran the business) and the Transport subsidiary (who owned the vehicles) were greatly disturbed in their business. But the acquiring authority say that those two companies are not entitled to any compensation at all, not even for disturbance, because they had no interest in the land, legal or equitable. They say that in 1970 D.H.N. were only licensees of Bronze, the subsidiary which owned the land: and D.H.N. being licensees only, with no interest in the land, their only claim was under section 20 (1) of the Compulsory Purchase Act 1965. That section says that if a person has no greater interest than a tenant from year to year in the land, then he is only entitled to compensation for that lesser interest. Seeing that a licensee can be turned out on short notice, the compensation payable to D.H.N. would be negligible.

The strange thing about the case is this, that the acquiring authority admit that at any time from February 1970, during the local inquiry and afterwards (right up to the time in October 1970 when the council gave notice to treat) the people running these three companies could have put their house in order so as to make the claim impregnable. All they had to do was to take a very simple step. Being in control of all three companies, they could have arranged for Bronze to convey the land to D.H.N. No stamp duty would be payable because it would be exempt under section 42 of the Finance Act 1930. And D.H.N., being the owners, could also claim compensation for disturbance. So at any time up to October 30, 1970, this group of three companies could have put themselves in an unassailable position to claim not only the value of the land but also compensation for disturbance. But that was not done. The acquiring authority say that, by failing to do it, the group have missed the boat. They are left behind on the quay because of the technical provisions of our company law whereby each of the three companies is in law a separate person. Each of its interests must be considered separately. D.H.N. had no interest in the land. It was only a licensee. So it cannot claim compensation for disturbance.

The President of the Lands Tribunal was asked to determine preliminary points of law. He held that D.H.N. had no interest in the land such as to entitle them to any compensation for disturbance beyond the amount allowed by section 20 of the Act of 1965, which is negligible. D.H.N. appeal to this court...

We all know that in many respects a group of companies are treated together for the purpose of general accounts, balance sheet, and profit and loss account.[24] They are treated as one concern. Professor Gower in *Modern Company Law*, 3rd ed. (1969), p. 216 says:

'there is evidence of a general tendency to ignore the separate legal entities of various companies within a group, and to look instead at the economic entity of the whole group.'

This is especially the case when a parent company owns all the shares of the subsidiaries—so much so that it can control every movement of the subsidiaries. These subsidiaries are bound hand and foot to the parent company and must do just what the parent company says...So here. This group is virtually the same as a partnership in which all the three companies are partners. They should not be treated separately so as to be defeated on a technical point. They should not be deprived of the compensation which should justly be payable for disturbance. The three companies should, for present purposes, be treated as one, and the parent company D.H.N. should be treated as that one. So D.H.N. are entitled to claim compensation accordingly. It was not necessary for them to go through a conveyancing device to get it.

I realise that the President of the Lands Tribunal, in view of previous cases, felt it necessary to decide as he did. But now that the matter has been fully discussed in this court, we must decide differently from him. These companies as a group are entitled to compensation not only for the value of the land, but also compensation for disturbance. I would allow the appeal accordingly.

Goff LJ

In my judgment, this is a case in which one is entitled to look at the realities of the situation and to pierce the corporate veil. I wish to safeguard myself by saying that so far as this ground is concerned, I am relying on the facts of this particular case. I would not at this juncture accept that in every case where one has a group of companies one is entitled to pierce the veil, but in this case the two subsidiaries were both wholly owned; further, they had no separate business operations whatsoever; thirdly, in my judgment, the nature of the question involved is highly relevant, namely, whether the owners of this business have been disturbed in their possession and enjoyment of it.[25]

Shaw LJ

There is the further argument advanced on behalf of the claimants that there was so complete an identity of the different companies comprised in the so-called group that they ought to be regarded for this purpose as a single entity. The completeness of that identity manifested itself in various ways. The directors of D.H.N. were the same as the directors of Bronze; the shareholders of Bronze were the same as in D.H.N., the parent company, and they had a common interest in maintaining on the property concerned the business of the group. If anything were necessary to reinforce the complete identity of commercial interest and personality, clause 6, to which I have referred already, demonstrates it, for D.H.N. undertook the obligation to procure their subsidiary company to make the payment which the bank required to be made.

If each member of the group is regarded as a company in isolation, nobody at all could have claimed compensation in a case which plainly calls for it. Bronze would have had the land but no business to disturb; D.H.N. would have had the business but no interest in the land.

---

[24] As we will see in Web Chapter B companies are required to prepare accounts for the companies and groups of companies are required to provide consolidated accounts, which mean a set of accounts that detail the assets, liabilities, revenues and expenses of the group of companies as a whole.

[25] In support of this position Goff LJ referred to *Harold Holdworth & Co (Wakefield) Ltd v Caddies* [1955] 1 All ER 725; *Scottish Co-operative Wholesale Society Ltd v Meyer* [1958] 3 All ER 66; *Merchandise Transport Ltd v British Transport Commission* [1961] 3 All ER 495.

In this utter identity and community of interest between D.H.N. and Bronze there was no flaw at all. As Bronze did not trade and carried on no business. It had no actual or potential creditors other than its own parent, D.H.N. The directors of that company could at any time they chose have procured the transfer of the legal title from Bronze to itself. Mr. Eyre again conceded that if they had gone through that formal operation the day before the notice to treat was served on October 12, 1970, they would have had a secure claim for compensation for disturbance. Accordingly, they could in law have sought and obtained whatever advantages were derived up to that date from a separation of title and interest between the two companies and still quite legitimately have re-disposed matters right up till October 1970 so as to qualify for compensation. They could not have been criticised, still less prevented, if they had chosen to do so. Yet if the decision of the Lands Tribunal be right, it made all the difference that they had not. Thus no abuse is precluded by disregarding the bonds which bundled D.H.N. and Bronze together in a close and, so far as Bronze was concerned, indissoluble relationship.

Why then should this relationship be ignored in a situation in which to do so does not prevent abuse but would on the contrary result in what appears to be a denial of justice...The President of the Lands Tribunal took a strict legalistic view of the respective positions of the companies concerned. It appears to me that it was too strict in its application to the facts of this case, which are, as I have said, of a very special character, for it ignored the realities of the respective roles which the companies filled. I would allow the appeal.

In *DHN* all of the judges agree on the outcome, but do they agree on the legal basis for the decision? Lord Denning MR, of all the judges, seems to be the most comfortable with the decision to lift the veil. The focus of his analysis appears to be on the complete control by the parent over the subsidiary. The subsidiaries are 'bound hand and foot' to the parent company. His Lordship is also clearly concerned that the legal form of the company in a corporate group context should not get in the way of doing justice to the facts. For Shaw LJ control also seems to be relevant. He refers to the fact that DHN could continue to occupy the premises as long as it chose to do so (because it controlled the subsidiary that owned the land). But for Lord Denning control seems sufficient. This echoes earlier examples of Lord Denning's willingness to pierce the corporate veil, apparently on the basis of control. In *Wallensteiner v Moir*[26] he held that in relation to Liechtenstein companies that were the subject of the case:

I am quite clear that the [Liechtenstein companies] were just the puppets of Dr. Wallersteiner. He controlled their every movement. Each danced to his bidding. He pulled the strings. No one else got within reach of them. Transformed into legal language, they were his agents to do as he commanded. He was the principal behind them. I am of the opinion that the court should pull aside the corporate veil and treat these concerns as being his creatures—for whose doings he should be, and is, responsible.[27]

Goff LJ and Shaw LJ, however, take account of factors other than control. Goff LJ's analysis is brief but focuses in addition to ownership on the fact that there was no business activity in the Bronze subsidiary. This is also relevant for Shaw LJ who refers to the 'utter identity and community of interest between DHN and Bronze' and refers to the fact that Bronze did not trade and had no business or creditors other than its parent. In addition, Shaw LJ also, along with Lord Denning, appears to consider the factor of doing 'justice' to the facts. He views it as relevant where strict adherence to the legal

[26] [1974] 1 WLR 991.
[27] See also Lord Denning's judgment in *Littlewoods Mail Order Stores Ltd v Inland Revenue Commissioners* [1969] 1 WLR 1241.

reality created by incorporation does not generate an abuse of the law but rather results in a 'denial of justice'.[28]

At this stage of our analysis of the legal grounds for piercing the veil in *DHN* we have three options: first, complete control; second, the absence of activity/utter identity of interests; and third, doing justice to the facts of the case. Clearly the notion that control alone could result in disregarding the corporate entity would be completely inconsistent with *Salomon v Salomon*. However, one could argue that the 'absence of activity' or a 'denial of justice to the incorporator where there is no abuse' factors distinguish *Salomon* where such factors were clearly not in issue. Importantly in *DHN*, as in the *Smith, Stone and Knight* case already considered, as well as the following cases, the question of piercing the veil is considered in the context of the parent–subsidiary relationship rather than a straightforward company–individual shareholder relationship such as was the case in *Salomon*. The *DHN* holding may, therefore, be distinguished from the *Salomon* principle and limited in application to parent–subsidiary relationships.

■ *Woolfson v Strathclyde Regional Council* [1978] SC (HL) 90

This case is an appeal to the House of Lords from the Scottish Court of Session. It involves a similar fact pattern to *DHN* involving a compulsory purchase of property where the occupier of the property was not the owner. In this case, however, in contrast to *DHN*, the occupier of the property whose business was disturbed by the compulsory purchase was not the sole shareholder in the company which owned the property which was being compulsorily purchased. In this case, the owner of the property was also the majority shareholder in the occupier.

Lord Keith of Kinkel

A compulsory purchase order made in 1966 by Glasgow Corporation... provided for the acquisition of certain shop premises in St George's Road... Nos. 57 and 59/61 St George's Road were owned by the first-named appellant Solomon Woolfson ('Woolfson') and Nos. 53/55 were owned by the second-named appellant Solfred Holdings Ltd. ('Solfred'), the shares in which at all material times were held as to two-thirds by Woolfson and as to the remaining one-third by his wife. The whole of the shop premises was occupied by a company called M. & L. Campbell (Glasgow) Limited ('Campbell') and used by it for the purpose of its business as costumiers specialising in wedding garments. The issued share capital of Campbell was 1,000 shares, of which 999 were held by Woolfson and one by his wife. Woolfson was sole director of Campbell and he managed the business... His wife also worked for Campbell and provided valuable expertise. Campbell was throughout shown in the valuation roll as occupier of the shop premises, but its occupation was not regulated by lease or any other kind of formal arrangement. Draft leases were at one time prepared, but they were never put into operation... There can be no doubt, and it is not now disputed by the appellants, that Campbell was throughout the occupier of the shop premises and that the business carried on there was that of Campbell.

In these circumstances, the appellants jointly claimed a sum of £80,000 as compensation for the value of the heritage under section 12(2) of the Land Compensation (Scotland) Act 1963 and a further sum of £95,469 in respect of disturbance under section 12(6) of that Act. The Lands Tribunal held... that the appellants had no [right to compensation for disturbance]... The Second Division [of the Court of Session]... affirmed the decision of the Lands Tribunal...

Before the Second Division... the appellants contended that in the circumstances Woolfson, Campbell and Solfred should all be treated as a single entity embodied in Woolfson himself. This followed the refusal by the court to allow Campbell and Mrs Woolfson to be joined as additional claimants in the proceedings. It was argued, with reliance on *D.H.N. Food Distributors Ltd. v. Tower Hamlets London Borough Council,* that the court should set aside the legalistic view that

---

[28] Piercing the veil and justice are considered in greater detail in section II.6 of this chapter.

Woolfson, Solfred and Campbell were each a separate legal *persona*, and concentrate attention upon the 'realities' of the situation, to the effect of finding that Woolfson was the occupier as well as the owner of the whole premises. This argument was rejected by the [lower] court for the reasons given in the opinion of the Lord Justice-Clerk. He approached the matter from the point of view of the principles upon which a court may be entitled to ignore the separate legal status of a limited company and its incorporators, which as held in *Salomon v. Salomon & Co. Ltd* must normally receive full effect in relations between the company and persons dealing with it. He referred to a passage in the judgment of Ormerod LJ in *Tunstall v. Steigmann* 1962 2 Q.B. 593, 601, to the effect that any departure from a strict observance of the principles laid down in *Salomon* has been made to deal with special circumstances when a limited company might well be a facade concealing the true facts. Having examined the facts of the instant case, the Lord Justice-Clerk reached the conclusion that they did not substantiate but negatived the argument advanced in support of the 'unity' proposition and that the decision in the *D.H.N. Food Distributors* case (supra) was distinguishable. It was maintained before this House that the conclusion of the Lord Justice-Clerk was erroneous. In my opinion the conclusion was correct, and I regard as unimpeachable the process of reasoning by which it was reached.

I can see no grounds whatever, upon the facts found in the special case, for treating the company structure as a mere façade, nor do I consider that the *D.H.N. Food Distributors* case (*supra*) is, on a proper analysis, of assistance to the appellants' argument. The position there was that compensation for disturbance was claimed by a group of three limited companies associated in a wholesale grocery business. The parent company, D.H.N., carried on the business in the premises which were the subject of compulsory purchase. These premises were owned by Bronze, which had originally been the wholly owned subsidiary of a bank which had advanced money for the purchase of the premises, but which had later become the wholly owned subsidiary of D.H.N. Bronze had the same directors as D.H.N. and the premises were its only asset. It carried on no activities whatever. The third company, also a wholly owned subsidiary of D.H.N., owned as its only asset the vehicles used in the grocery business, and it too carried on no operations. The compulsory acquisition resulted in the extinction of the grocery business, since no suitable alternative premises could be found. It was held by the Court of Appeal (Lord Denning M.R., Goff and Shaw LL. J.) that the group was entitled to compensation for disturbance as owners of the business. The grounds for the decision [were] that since D.H.N. was in a position to control its subsidiaries in every respect, it was proper to pierce the corporate veil and treat the group as a single economic entity for the purpose of awarding compensation for disturbance...I have some doubts whether in this respect the Court of Appeal properly applied the principle that it is appropriate to pierce the corporate veil only where special circumstances exist indicating that [it] is a mere façade concealing the true facts. Further, the decisions of this *House in Caddies v. Harold Holdsworth &Co. (Wake-field) Ltd.* 1955 S.C. (H.L.) 27 and *Meyer v. Scottish Co-operative Wholesale Society Ltd.* 1958 S.C. (H.L.) 40,[29] which were founded on by Goff LJ in support of this ground of judgment and, as to the first of them, to some extent also by Lord Denning, M.R., do not, with respect, appear to me to be concerned with that principle. But however that may be, I consider the D.H.N. Food case to be clearly distinguishable on its facts from the present case. There the company that owned the land was the wholly owned subsidiary of the company that carried on the business. The latter was in complete control of the situation as respects anything which might affect its business, and there was no one but itself having any kind of interest or right as respects the assets of the subsidiary. Here, on the other hand, the company that carried on the business, Campbell, has no sort of control whatever over the owners of the land, Solfred and Woolfson. Woolfson holds two-thirds only of the shares in Solfred and Solfred has no interest in Campbell. Woolfson cannot be treated as beneficially entitled to the whole share-holding

---

[29] *Meyer v Scottish Co-operative* involved the application of section 210 of the Companies Act 1948 (the now replaced oppression remedy). Lord Keith is clearly correct that the extent to which this case involved piercing it is of no general application but limited only to the application of section 210.

in Campbell, since it is not found that the one share in Campbell held by his wife is held as his nominee. In my opinion there is no basis consonant with principle upon which on the facts of this case the corporate veil can be pierced to the effect of holding Woolfson to be the true owner of Campbell's business or of the assets of Solfred.

The claimant's argument in this case is that the holding in *DHN* is applicable and that the group of companies should be treated as one economic unit that would entitle Mr Woolfson to compensation for disturbance of the business, even though the business was carried out by a separate legal entity (Campbell). The House of Lords holds that *DHN* is inapplicable. Their primary holding in this regard is that on the facts it is distinguishable. The two distinguishing features are: first, that in *DHN* the operational company owned and had complete control over the company who owned the property which was subject to the compulsory purchase order; and secondly, that in *DHN* the parent company had 100% control over the subsidiary, whereas in this case Mr Woolson's wife held one share in Campbell in her own right.

However, not only does the House of Lords distinguish *DHN*, it also casts significant doubt over whether it remains good authority. In doing so it sets out what is today the primary legal framework through which a court determines whether the corporate veil can be pierced. Their Lordships observe that they have doubts as to whether the Court of Appeal in *DHN* properly applied the principle originally articulated by the Court of Appeal in *Tunstall v Steigmann*,[30] that the corporate veil can *only* be pierced '*where special circumstances exist indicating that [the company] is a mere façade concealing the true facts*'. As we have seen, this legal framework did not feature in the reasoning in *DHN*.[31] Perhaps therefore, one might say, it is not surprising that they did not apply it correctly!

In what respect, in the House of Lords' opinion, is the *DHN* decision incompatible with this principle? The House of Lords presents the basis of the decision in *DHN* to be the fact the parent company controlled the subsidiary 'in every respect'. However, as we saw in our analysis the actual holding in *DHN* is more complex than a simple focus on control. In addition the judgment contained 'absence of activity in the subsidiary' and 'denial of justice' factors. The House of Lords provides no guidance on the status of these other considerations. Nevertheless, the House of Lords clearly leaves *DHN* in an unhealthy condition.

Following *Woolfson v Strathclyde* we now have a clear conceptual framework through which to address the question of when the corporate veil can be pierced. The question one has to ask is: whether there are special circumstances indicating that the company in question is a façade concealing the true facts? What then are these special circumstances and what amounts to a façade? Unfortunately, *Woolfson v Strathclyde* provides limited guidance. It tells us that the facts of this case do not fall within the 'façade exception'; but it provides no guidance on what would. We will explore this concept further in section 5. Before we do so, we need to determine whether, after the House of Lords' judgment in *Woolfson v Strathclyde*, there is any life left in the *DHN* single economic unit basis for piercing the corporate veil. The Court of Appeal case of *Adams v Cape Industries Plc*[32] is viewed as the leading case in this regard.

The facts of *Adams v Cape Industries Plc*[33] are exceptionally complicated. Cape Industries Plc was a UK public company operating in the asbestos business in many locations worldwide. One of its mines was owned and operated by a South African

---

[30] [1962] 2 QB 593.
[31] Note that *Tunstall v Steigmann* is in the list of cases referred to in the report of the *DHN* judgment, however, it does not feature in the court's reasoning.
[32] [1990] Ch 433.   [33] [1990] Ch 433.

subsidiary. In the US it had a wholly owned marketing subsidiary called NAAC. This marketing subsidiary arranged for the supply of asbestos from the South African subsidiary to a Texas company which manufactured asbestos-based products. As a result of exposure to asbestos many of the Texas company's employees suffered serious personal injury and in some cases death. These employees sued many of the parties who they viewed as complicit in their injuries, including Cape Industries Plc. The legal proceedings were brought in New York but Cape refused to participate in the proceedings. They argued that the New York courts did not have jurisdiction to hear the case, which means they had no right to hear this case. However, the New York proceedings continued and a substantial award of damages was made against Cape Industries Plc. The claimants attempted to enforce this award in the UK, where the majority of Cape's assets were situated. The question for the UK courts in the enforcement proceeding was: did the New York courts have jurisdiction to hear the case against Cape and make the award of damages? If the answer was 'yes' then the award could be enforced in the UK.

To have jurisdiction over Cape one of two conditions had to be satisfied: either Cape Industries Plc had to have consented to the New York courts having jurisdiction (it was held that they had not), or Cape Industries Plc must have been present, ie they were doing business, in the United States. But Cape Industries Plc did not have any direct operational activities in the United States. Rather it marketed and distributed its product through its wholly owned US subsidiary, NAAC. The question for the Court of Appeal was whether Cape Industries Plc could be deemed present in the United States by reason of the business and operations of its US subsidiary. That is, for the purposes of answering the jurisdiction question, could Cape Industries Plc and its subsidiary be treated as one entity? The Court of Appeal addressed several possible grounds for piercing the veil including the 'single economic unit argument'.

■ Adams v Cape Industries Plc [1990] Ch 433

Slade LJ

The 'single economic unit' argument
There is no general principle that all companies in a group of companies are to be regarded as one. On the contrary, the fundamental principle is that 'each company in a group of companies (a relatively modern concept) is a separate legal entity possessed of separate legal rights and liabilities:' *The Albazero* [1977] AC 774, 807, per Roskill LJ.

It is thus indisputable that each of Cape [and] NAAC...were in law separate legal entities. Mr. Morison did not go so far as to submit that the very fact of the parent–subsidiary relationship existing between Cape and NAAC rendered Cape...present in Illinois. Nevertheless, he submitted that the court will, in appropriate circumstances, ignore the distinction in law between members of a group of companies treating them as one, and that broadly speaking, it will do so whenever it considers that justice so demands. In support of this submission, he referred us to a number of authorities...

[The Court of Appeal referred to several cases including *DHN* in relation to which they quoted the extracts from Lord Denning and Goff LJ previously set forth.]

Principally, in reliance on those authorities and the case next to be mentioned, Mr. Morison submitted that in deciding whether a company had rendered itself subject to the jurisdiction of a foreign court it is entirely reasonable to approach the question by reference to 'commercial reality'. The risk of litigation in a foreign court, in his submission, is part of the price which those who conduct extensive business activities within the territorial jurisdiction of that court properly have to pay...

We have some sympathy with Mr. Morison's submissions in this context. To the layman at least the distinction between the case where a company itself trades in a foreign country and the case where it trades in a foreign country through a subsidiary, whose activities it has full power to control, may seem a slender one. Mr. Morison referred us to *Bulova Watch Co. Inc. v. K. Hattori & Co. Ltd.* (1981) 508 F. Supp 1322, where the United States District Court held that it had jurisdiction over a Japanese corporation which was expanding into a new market by setting up subsidiaries and dealing with competition, both on the theory that the corporation was 'doing business' in New York and under the New York 'long-arm statute'.[34] In the course of his judgment, Weinstein C.J. said: 'these subsidiaries almost by definition are doing for their parent what their parent would otherwise have to do on its own.' It is not surprising that in many cases such as *Holdsworth* [1955] 1 W.L.R. 352, *Scottish Co-operative* [1959] A.C. 324, *Revlon* [1980] F.S.R. 85 and *Commercial Solvents* [1974] E.C.R. 223, the wording of a particular statute or contract has been held to justify the treatment of parent and subsidiary as one unit, at least for some purposes. The relevant parts of the judgments in the D.H.N. case must, we think, likewise be regarded as decisions on the relevant statutory provisions for compensation, even though these parts were somewhat broadly expressed, and the correctness of the decision was doubted by the House of Lords in *Woolfson v. Strathclyde Regional Council*, 1978 S.L.T. 159 in a passage which will be quoted below.

Mr. Morison described the theme of all these cases as being that where legal technicalities would produce injustice in cases involving members of a group of companies, such technicalities should not be allowed to prevail. We do not think that the cases relied on go nearly so far as this. As Sir Godfray submitted, save in cases which turn on the wording of particular statutes or contracts, the court is not free to disregard the principle of *Salomon v. A. Salomon & Co. Ltd.* merely because it considers that justice so requires. Our law, for better or worse, recognises the creation of subsidiary companies, which though in one sense the creatures of their parent companies, will nevertheless under the general law fall to be treated as separate legal entities with all the rights and liabilities which would normally attach to separate legal entities.

In deciding whether a company is present in a foreign country by a subsidiary, which is itself present in that country, the court is entitled, indeed bound, to investigate the relationship between the parent and the subsidiary. In particular, that relationship may be relevant in determining whether the subsidiary was acting as the parent's agent and, if so, on what terms. In *Firestone Tyre and Rubber Co. Ltd. v. Lewellin* [1957] 1 W.L.R. 464 (which was referred to by Scott J.) the House of Lords upheld an assessment to tax on the footing that, on the facts, the business both of the parent and subsidiary were carried on by the subsidiary as agent for the parent. However, there is no presumption of any such agency. There is no presumption that the subsidiary is the parent company's alter ego. In the court below the judge refused an invitation to infer that there existed an agency agreement between Cape and NAAC comparable to that which had previously existed between Cape and Capasco and that refusal is not challenged on this appeal. If a company chooses to arrange the affairs of its group in such a way that the business carried on in a particular foreign country is the business of its subsidiary and not its own, it is, in our judgment, entitled to do so. Neither in this class of case nor in any other class of case is it open to this court to disregard the principle of *Salomon v. A. Salomon & Co. Ltd.* merely because it considers it just so to do.

In support of the single commercial unit argument, Mr. Morison made a number of factual submissions to the following effect: the purpose of NAAC's creation was that it might act as a medium through which goods of the Cape group might be sold. The purpose of the liquidation of NAAC was likewise to protect Cape. Any major policy decisions concerning NAAC were taken by Cape. Cape's control over NAAC did not depend on corporate form. It exercised the same degree of control both before and after the removal of the Cape directors from the NAAC board. The functions of NAAC's directors were formal only. Dr. Gaze effectively controlled its activities. Cape represented NAAC to its customers as its office in the United States of America. In broad terms, it was submitted, Cape ran a single integrated mining division with little regard to corporate formalities as between members of the group in the way in which it carried on its business.

---

[34] Section 301–303 of the New York Civil Practice Law provides for situations in which the New York courts have jurisdiction over non-domiciles (hence 'long arm').

The plaintiffs further submitted in their notice of appeal that NAAC 'did not deal and was not permitted to deal with Egnep or Casap,[35] but had to go through Cape or Capasco'. It seems clear that NAAC, as principal, made direct purchases of raw asbestos from Egnep. On the balance of probabilities, we accept the plaintiffs' submission that it made similar direct purchases from Casap. In referring to the absence of dealing with Egnep or Casap, the plaintiffs were, we understand, intending to submit that as a matter of group policy, which Cape could and did enforce by its power of control over the boards of Egnep, Capasco and NAAC, the transmission of information and orders to or from customers had to be effected and was effected by NAAC through Capasco. We accept that submission. We also accept that the matters referred to in this paragraph lend some broad support to the submission that Cape ran a single integrated mining division with little regard to corporate formalities as between members of the group. However, there has been no challenge to the judge's finding that the corporate forms applicable to NAAC as a separate legal entity were observed.

As to the plaintiffs' other factual submissions in this context we will deal with the purpose of NAAC's creation and existence in considering the 'agency' argument. As to the relationship between Cape and NAAC, it is of the very nature of a parent company-subsidiary relationship that the parent company is in a position, if it wishes, to exercise overall control over the general policy of the subsidiary. The plaintiffs, however, submitted that Cape's control extended to the day-to-day running of NAAC. They challenged the finding of fact made by Scott J. that 'Mr. Morgan was in executive control of NAAC's conduct of its business'. We explore further the facts relative to this finding and to the extent of Cape's control over NAAC's activities in the appendix to this judgment. Our conclusion, shortly stated, is that the finding was justified by the evidence. A degree of overall supervision, and to some extent control, was exercised by Cape over NAAC as is common in the case of any parent–subsidiary relationship—to a large extent through Dr. Gaze. In particular, Cape would indicate to NAAC the maximum level of expenditure which it should incur and would supervise the level of expenses incurred by Mr. Morgan. Mr. Morgan knew that he had to defer in carrying out the business activities of NAAC to the policy requirements of Cape as the controlling shareholders of NAAC. Within these policy limits, such as Cape's requirement that NAAC's orders for asbestos for sale by NAAC in the United States of America be placed through Capasco on behalf of Egnep and Casap, the day-to-day running of NAAC was left to him. There is no challenge to the judge's findings that (a) the corporate financial control exercised by Cape over NAAC in respect of the level of dividends and the level of permitted borrowing was no more and no less than was to be expected in a group of companies such as the Cape group; [and] (b) the annual accounts of NAAC were drawn on the footing that NAAC's business was its own business and there was nothing to suggest that the accounts were drawn on a false footing.

In the light of the set up and operations of the Cape group and of the relationship between Cape/Capasco and NAAC we see the attraction of the approach adopted by Lord Denning M.R. in the D.H.N. case, which Mr. Morison urged us to adopt: 'This group is virtually the same as a partnership in which all the three companies are partners'. In our judgment, however, we have no discretion to reject the distinction between the members of the group as a technical point. We agree with Scott J. that the observations of Robert Goff LJ in Bank of Tokyo Ltd. v. Karoon (Note) [1987] A.C. 45, 64 are apposite:

'[Counsel] suggested beguilingly that it would be technical for us to distinguish between parent and subsidiary company in this context; economically, he said, they were one. But we are concerned not with economics but with law. The distinction between the two is, in law, fundamental and cannot here be bridged'.

If one focuses on the final two paragraphs of this extract there appears to be little scope to rely upon the single economic unit argument. The quoted phrase 'we are concerned with economics not law [and] the distinction between [parent and subsidiary] in

---

[35] These companies were Cape's mining subsidiaries.

law is fundamental' is a firm reaffirmation of the *Salomon* principle requiring that the courts respect the legal reality that is created on incorporation. In addition, the Court of Appeal suggests that the judgment in *DHN* is limited in application to the statutory provisions applicable in that case which provided for compulsory purchase of the property. Slade LJ does, however, acknowledge that the *DHN* holding was more broadly expressed. Furthermore, the Court observes that the House of Lords in *Woolfson v Strathclyde* doubted the correctness of *DHN*.

Oddly, given these observations, there remains on closer inspection an affinity between Slade LJ's judgment and aspects of the *DHN* holding. The attention the Court of Appeal gives to considering whether Cape was involved in the 'day to day running' of NAAC suggests that had Cape in fact been running NAAC then the Court may have treated the two entities as one. The legal principle underpinning this idea of 'day to day running of the subsidiary' is not articulated but would appear consistent with 'utter identity of community and interest' or the 'absence of real activity in the subsidiary'. In this regard, note the attention the Court gives to the financial control over the subsidiary suggests, by implication, that had the level of Cape's financial control over NAAC exceeded what is typical in a parent–subsidiary relationship then this may have made the single economic unit argument available.

In summary, although *Adams v Cape Industries* rejects *DHN* and although it makes a very firm assertion of the *Salomon* principle at the end of extracted judgment, there remains some limited life in the single economic unit argument. However, although formally the argument may still be viable it is in practice very unlikely to be successfully relied upon unless the parent completely ignores the separate existence of the subsidiary.

5 The façade concealing the true facts

We saw in *Woolfson v Strathclyde Regional Council* that the House of Lords considered that there is one circumstance in which the corporate veil can be pierced, namely when there are special circumstances indicating a façade concealing the true facts. However, the House of Lords did not elaborate on the nature of such special circumstances or the meaning of 'façade'. Following *Adams v Cape Industries Plc*, further extracts from which are set out here, it is clear that the 'façade concealing the true facts' test has become the primary reference point for any lawyer investigating whether it is possible to pierce the corporate veil. But what does it mean?

■ *Adams v Cape Industries Plc* [1990] Ch 433

Please read the facts set out in section II.4 of this chapter. Additional factual background is necessary in this regard. During the course of the litigation the Cape Industries Group undertook a reorganization of its US activities apparently aimed at reducing its potential exposure to litigation in the US and the enforcement against it of any US judgments outside of the US. This reorganization involved the liquidation of NAAC, its US subsidiary, which was the focus of the single economic unit analysis. To replace NAAC, Cape arranged for the formation of two additional companies, a US (Illinois) company and a Liechtenstein Company. The Liechtenstein Company, APC, was owned by Cape but the US company, CPC, was now 100% owned by the former chief executive officer of NAAC.

Slade LJ

The 'corporate veil' point
Quite apart from cases where statute or contract permits a broad interpretation to be given to references to members of a group of companies, there is one well-recognised exception to the

rule prohibiting the piercing of 'the corporate veil'. Lord Keith of Kinkel referred to this principle in *Woolfson v. Strathclyde Regional Council*, in the course of a speech with which Lord Wilberforce, Lord Fraser of Tullybelton and Lord Russell of Killowen agreed. With reference to the *DHN* decision, he said:

'I have some doubts whether in this respect the Court of Appeal properly applied the principle that it is appropriate to pierce the corporate veil only where special circumstances exist indicating that it is a mere façade concealing the true facts'.

The only allegation of a façade in the plaintiffs' pleadings was that the formation and use of CPC and AMC in the 'alternative marketing arrangements of 1978 were a device or sham or cloak for grave impropriety on the part of Cape or Capasco, namely to ostensibly remove their assets from the United States of America to avoid liability for asbestos claims whilst at the same time continuing to trade in asbestos there'.

In their notice of appeal (paragraph 2(b)) the plaintiffs referred to their contention made at the trial that CPC 'was set up to replace NAAC in such a way as to disguise the defendants' continued involvement in the marketing of the group's asbestos in the United States of America'. Scott J more or less accepted this contention. He found as a fact:

'the arrangements made regarding NAAC, AMC and CPC were part of one composite arrangement designed to enable Cape asbestos to continue to be sold into the United States while reducing, if not eliminating, the appearance of any involvement therein of Cape or its subsidiaries'.

However, he went on to say...:

'But the question whether CPC's presence in Illinois can, for jurisdiction purposes, be treated as Cape's presence, must, in my view, be answered by considering the nature of the arrangements that were implemented, not the motive behind them. The documentary evidence I have seen has made clear that the senior management of Cape, including Mr. Penna, were very anxious that Cape's connections with CPC and with AMC should not become publicly known. Some of the letters and memoranda have a somewhat conspiratorial flavour to them. But this too, although interesting to notice, is not, in my opinion, relevant to the main question'.

If and so far as the judge intended to say that the motive behind the new arrangements was irrelevant as a matter of law, we would respectfully differ from him. In our judgment, as Mr. Morison submitted, whenever a device or sham or cloak is alleged in cases such as this, the motive of the alleged perpetrator must be legally relevant, and indeed this no doubt is the reason why the question of motive was examined extensively at the trial. The decision in *Jones v. Lipman* referred to below was one case where the proven motive of the individual defendant clearly had a significant effect on the decision of Russell J.

The judge's finding of fact quoted above as to the motives of Cape behind the new arrangements is accepted (no doubt welcomed) by the plaintiffs, so far as it goes. They submit, rightly in our judgment, that any such motives are relevant to the 'corporate veil' point. They further submit that the judge (a) erred in concluding that CPC was an 'independently owned company'; and (b) failed to make a number of findings of fact which are relevant in the context of the 'corporate veil' point.

Mr. Morison has taken us through the arrangements which led to the extinction of NAAC and the emergence of AMC and CPC with care and in considerable detail. The additional facts which the plaintiffs say the judge ought to have found...all relate to these arrangements. It is true that, as the judge said, some of the letters and memoranda have a 'somewhat conspiratorial flavour to them'. Since, contrary to the judge's view, we think motive is relevant in this context, we have thought it right to investigate these contentions in some detail in the appendix.

On analysis, much of the new material does little more than amply support the judge's finding quoted above as to the purpose of the composite arrangement. In this court Mr. Morison made it clear that the plaintiffs were not alleging any unlawful purpose or impropriety on the part of Cape in the sense of any intention to deceive or to do any unlawful act, either in Illinois or in this country. It was, however, asserted for the plaintiffs that AMC and CPC together constituted a façade which concealed the real activities of Cape. We understand that to mean that the purpose of Cape was to conceal, so far as it lawfully could having regard to the requirements of the law in Illinois and this country, any connection of Cape with AMC or CPC...

As to Cape's purpose in making the arrangements for the liquidation of NAAC and the creation of AMC and CPC... The allegation of impropriety was, in our view, rightly abandoned. The inference which we draw from all the evidence was that Cape's intention was to enable sales of asbestos from the South African subsidiaries to continue to be made in the United States while (a) reducing the appearance of any involvement therein of Cape or its subsidiaries, and (b) reducing by any lawful means available to it the risk of any subsidiary or of Cape as parent company being held liable for United States taxation or subject to the jurisdiction of the United States courts, whether state or federal, and the risk of any default judgment by such a court being held to be enforceable in this country...

The question of law which we now have to consider is whether the arrangements regarding NAAC, AMC and CPC made by Cape with the intentions which we have inferred constituted a façade such as to justify the lifting of the corporate veil so as that CPC's and AMC's presence in the United States of America should be treated as the presence of Cape/Capasco for this reason if no other... Assistance on this point is to be found in *Jones v. Lipman*. In that case the first defendant had agreed to sell to the plaintiffs some land. Pending completion the first defendant sold and transferred the land to the defendant company. The evidence showed that this company was at all material times under the complete control of the first defendant. It also showed that the acquisition by him of the company and the transfer of the land to the company had been carried through solely for the purpose of defeating the plaintiff's right to specific performance... Russell J made an order for specific performance against both defendants. He held that specific performance cannot be resisted by a vendor who, by his absolute ownership and control of a limited company in which the property is vested, is in a position to cause the contract to be completed. As to the defendant company, he described it... as being 'the creature of the first defendant, a device and a sham, a mask which he holds before his face in an attempt to avoid recognition by the eye of equity'.

Following *Jones v. Lipman*, we agree with Mr. Morison that, contrary to the judge's view, where a façade is alleged, the motive of the perpetrator may be highly material... From the authorities cited to us we are left with rather sparse guidance as to the principles which should guide the court in determining whether or not the arrangements of a corporate group involve a façade within the meaning of that word as used by the House of Lords in *Woolfson*. We will not attempt a comprehensive definition of those principles.

Our conclusions are these. In our judgment, the interposition of AMC between Cape and CPC was clearly a façade in the relevant sense. Scott J... said it seemed clear that AMC was 'no more than a corporate name' and that he would expect to find, if all the relevant documents were available, that 'AMC acted through employees or officers of either Casap or Egnep'. He rejected... Mr. Morgan's evidence that he understood AMC to be an independent South African trading company, and was satisfied that he knew very well that it was a 'creature of Cape'. 'The seller in CPC's time was, nominally, AMC but in reality still, I think, Egnep or Casap'... In our judgment, however, the revelation of AMC as the creature of Cape does not suffice to enable the plaintiffs to show the presence of Cape/Capasco in the United States of America, since on the judge's undisputed findings, AMC was not in reality carrying on any business in the United States of America.

The relationship between Cape/Capasco and CPC is the crucial factor, since CPC was undoubtedly carrying on business in the United States of America. We have already indicated our acceptance of the judge's findings that CPC was a company independently owned by Mr. Morgan and that the shares therein belonged to him in law and in equity. These findings by themselves make it very difficult to contend that the operation of CPC involved a façade which entitles the court to pierce the corporate veil between CPC and Cape/Capasco and treat them all as one. Is the legal position altered by the facts that Cape's intention, in making the relevant arrangements (as we infer), was to enable sales of asbestos from the South African subsidiaries to be made while (a) reducing if not eliminating the appearance of any involvement therein of Cape or its subsidiaries, and (b) reducing by any lawful means available to it the risk of any subsidiary or of Cape as parent company being held liable for United States taxation or subject to the jurisdiction of the United States courts and the risk of any default judgment by such a court being held to be enforceable in this country?

We think not. Mr. Morison submitted that the court will lift the corporate veil where a defendant by the device of a corporate structure attempts to evade (i) limitations imposed on his conduct by law; (ii) such rights of relief against him as third parties already possess; and (iii) such rights of relief as third parties may in the future acquire. Assuming that the first and second of these three conditions will suffice in law to justify such a course, neither of them apply in the present case. It is not suggested that the arrangements involved any actual or potential illegality or were intended to deprive anyone of their existing rights. Whether or not such a course deserves moral approval, there was nothing illegal as such in Cape arranging its affairs (whether by the use of subsidiaries or otherwise) so as to attract the minimum publicity to its involvement in the sale of Cape asbestos in the United States of America. As to condition (iii), we do not accept as a matter of law that the court is entitled to lift the corporate veil as against a defendant company which is the member of a corporate group merely because the corporate structure has been used so as to ensure that the legal liability (if any) in respect of particular future activities of the group (and correspondingly the risk of enforcement of that liability) will fall on another member of the group rather than the defendant company. Whether or not this is desirable, the right to use a corporate structure in this manner is inherent in our corporate law.[36] Mr. Morison urged on us that the purpose of the operation was in substance that Cape would have the practical benefit of the group's asbestos trade in the United States of America without the risks of tortious liability. This may be so. However, in our judgment, Cape was in law entitled to organise the group's affairs in that manner and (save in the case of AMC to which special considerations apply) to expect that the court would apply the principle of *Salomon v. A. Salomon & Co. Ltd.* in the ordinary way...We reject the 'corporate veil' argument.

Adams v Cape Industries is the leading case in relation to two separate grounds for piercing the corporate veil analysed in this chapter: *the single economic unit* principle and *the façade concealing the true facts* principle. It is somewhat confusing, therefore, that in *Adams* itself, following the submissions made by the claimants in the case, the court distinguishes between treating the companies as a single economic unit and piercing the corporate veil. Perhaps the appropriate way to make sense of this is that the single economic unit argument was a potential basis for piercing the corporate veil, but one that was rejected by the court. The court, therefore, moves to consider the remaining grounds for piercing the veil.

Following the House of Lords decision in *Woolfson*, the Court of Appeal holds that there is one ground pursuant to which the veil can be pierced, namely, '*where special circumstances exist indicating that [the company] is a mere façade concealing the true facts*'. This statement or rule is not particularly helpful for a student trying to understand in what circumstances the courts, at common law, will disregard the corporate veil. What then are these 'special circumstances' and what does it mean to say that a company is a 'façade concealing the true facts'. Unfortunately for the student of company law, the courts have not clearly articulated what they mean by these terms. Indeed, in *Adams*, the Court of Appeal explicitly declines to provide 'a more comprehensive definition of the principles'.

---

[36] Where the future liabilities that are to be avoided arise from dishonest activity which has not taken place at the time the company is formed, even though the corporate form is being used to minimize future liabilities, the courts will pierce the veil: *Raja v Van Hoogstraten* [2006] EWHC 2564 (Ch).

The language of façade reminds us of the language of 'shams' and 'cloaks' which we noticed earlier when reading *Jones v Lipman* and *Gilford Motors*.[37] In those cases, the language of sham and cloak was connected to the use of the corporate form for the illegitimate purpose of evading *existing* obligations. Should we understand 'special circumstances' and 'façade' in these terms? There is some support for this in *Adams* where *Jones v Lipman* is cited with approval for the holding that 'motive' is relevant in the piercing analysis. According to this interpretation there are 'special circumstances indicating that [a company] is a mere façade concealing the true facts' when the corporate form is used to avoid *existing* legal obligations. The courts make it very clear that this would not extend to the use of the corporate form to avoid future, hypothetical obligations and liabilities.[38]

However, this understanding does not do justice to the holding in *Adams v Cape*. You will have noticed that the Court of Appeal did hold that AMC was 'a façade in the relevant sense'. Yet it is also clear from the judgment that AMC was not being used to avoid any existing obligation or liability. Furthermore, the Court noted that there was no impropriety in these arrangements. It follows logically, therefore, that, according to the Court of Appeal in *Adams*, there is more to the special circumstances/façade principle than the avoidance of existing obligations. In *Cape* this seems to be the idea that the company had no independent existence; that is, it was merely a 'corporate name' through which Cape, its parent, acted. Arguably, what is intended is that the company's separate existence was ignored by the parent by failing to observe basic corporate formalities such as appointing directors, holding board meetings, employing persons to carry out the business of subsidiary etc. This, of course, bears a significant family resemblance to the 'single economic unit argument' in *DHN* and the concept of 'agency' in *Smith, Stone and Knight*.

Subsequent case law has rarely considered this second aspect of the special circumstances/façade principle. Only in the first instance judgment, *Re Polly Peck International*, has a post-*Adams* case addressed this basis for piercing the veil. In *Polly Peck* the court found that the company in question was not a 'mere corporate name'. Although the company was used for a single purpose—to raise finance for its parent—it was clear that it was actively involved in raising finance through the issue of its bonds.[39]

In *Ord v Belhaven Pubs*[40] the Court of Appeal held that the Court of Appeal in *Adams* 'were of the view that there must be some impropriety before the corporate veil can be pierced'.[41] This seems correct if one focuses on the evasion of existing obligations line of authority as the concrete articulation of what is meant by the special circumstances/façade principle. Nevertheless, this is inconsistent with the fact that the Court of Appeal in *Adams* held in relation to AMC that it was a 'façade in the relevant sense', even

---

[37] In *Faiza Ben Hashem v Abdulhadi Ali Shayif* [2008] EWHC 2380 *per* Munby J, the court observes that 'down the years a variety of other epithets have been used to express the same concept'.

[38] See *Dadourian Group International Plc v Simms* [2006] EWHC 2973 (Ch) *per* Warren J observing that 'applications of the [façade] principle include *Gilford Motor Co Ltd v Horne*' and referring in this regard to *Jones v Lipman*; in *Re Polly Peck International Plc (in administration) (no 3)* [1996] 1 BCLC 428, *per* Walker J, the court observed that ' "façade" (or "cloak" or "mask") is perhaps most aptly used where one person (individual or corporate) uses a company either in an unconscionable attempt to evade existing obligations'.

[39] *Re Polly Peck International Plc (in administration) (no 3)* [1996] 1 BCLC 428 *per* Walker J: 'the notion that regular sales of large volumes of South African asbestos to an United States purchaser were being effected through a lawyer's office in Vaduz is to my mind of a quite different order of artificiality from the function of PPIF as a single-purpose financial vehicle...In my judgment PPIF was more than a mere façade'. See also *Kensington International Ltd v Republic of Congo* [2005] EXCH 2684 (Comm).

[40] [1998] BCC 607.

[41] See *Faiza Ben Hashem v Abdulhadi Ali Shayif* [2008] EWHC 2380 (Fam) following *Ord* on the question of impropriety.

though, as they held, there was no impropriety. Subsequent cases have focused upon the evasion of existing obligations understanding of the façade principle. In *Trustor AB v Smallbone*, for example, the High Court held that:

> In my judgment the court is entitled to 'pierce the corporate veil' and recognise the receipt of the company as that of the individual(s) in control of it if the company was used as a device or façade to conceal the true facts thereby avoiding or concealing any liability of those individual(s).[42]

6 Doing justice to the facts

We observed in *DHN* that 'doing justice' to the facts was deemed to be a relevant factor for Lord Denning and Shaw LJ in piercing the corporate veil, although, as we saw, the piercing decision in *DHN* was linked to several other factors. There was no indication that 'doing justice' alone would have been sufficient. Nevertheless, in English law there is support for such a proposition. Cases subsequent to both *DHN* and *Woolfson v Strathclyde* have pierced the veil on the basis that to do so was justified by ensuring that justice was done. Most important is the Court of Appeal case of *Re a Company*[43] where Cummings LJ held that 'in our view the cases... show that the court will use its powers to pierce the corporate veil if it is necessary to achieve justice irrespective of the legal efficacy of the corporate structure under consideration'. A closer examination of the facts of *Re a Company* suggests that the case fits clearly within the category of piercing the corporate veil to evade existing obligations. In this case a complex network of companies had been used to siphon assets away from the claimant company's business (the company was in liquidation) once the controller of the business realized that insolvency was imminent. That is, a complex structure of companies was being used to evade the claimant company's *existing obligations* to its creditors.[44]

Nevertheless, whilst it may be the case that the statement in *Re a Company* about piercing to achieve justice is, on closer examination, merely an abstract articulation of the idea that corporate form cannot be used to evade existing obligations, the statement itself has had a broader impact. One can find several lower instance judgments which rely on *Re a Company* to provide a general jurisdiction to pierce the corporate veil where it is necessary to achieve justice.[45]

However, not only is it not clear that *Re a Company* stands for such a general 'justice' jurisdiction, more recent authority suggests that if it does so, then it is incorrect. Most importantly in this regard is Slade LJ's observation in *Adams v Cape Industries*, extracted in section 5, that 'save in cases which turn on the wording of particular statutes

---

[42] [2001] 1 WLR 1177. In *Kensington International Ltd v Republic of Congo* [2006] 2 BCLC 296 Cooke J held that 'the principle [of piercing the corporate veil] is capable of application to a situation where the transactions in question are sham and the companies are utilised for the avoidance of existing liabilities. Unlike Adams, the liabilities of the Congo are not future potential liabilities but existing liabilities under extant judgments'. See also *Antonio Gramsci Shipping Corp v Stepanovs* [2011] EWCH 333 describing the quotation from *Trustor* as a 'seminal passage'.

[43] [1985] BCLC 333.

[44] Justice, as we saw in *DHN*, is often used in this context as an additional, often superfluous, factor in a piercing decision. Arguably this is how 'justice' functioned in *DHN*. See further, for example, *Power Supermarkets Limited v Crumlin Investments Limited* (22 June 1981, unreported, High Court) where Costello J held that 'it seems to me to be well established from these as well as from other authorities... that a court may, if the justice of the case so requires, treat two or more related companies as a single entity so that the business notionally carried on by one will be regarded as the business of the group, or another member of the group, if this conforms to the economic and commercial realities of the situation'.

[45] *Bonotto v Boccaletti* (2001) 4 ITELR 357 9 (Cayman Islands) (this case was also a case involving the use of the corporate form in fraudulent activity); *Creasey v Breachwood Motors Ltd* [1993] BCLC 480 (disapproved of in *Ord v Belhaven Pubs* [1998] BCC 607).

or contracts, the court is not free to disregard the principle of *Salomon v. Salomon* merely because it considers that justice so requires'. Accordingly, *if* the holding in *Re a Company* provides for a broader 'justice-based' approach to piercing then we have two clearly conflicting Court of Appeal judgments. Recent authority has clearly elected to reject the 'justice' approach in favour of the view articulated in *Adams*. In *Trustor AB v Smallbone (No 2)*,[46] for example, Andrew Morritt VC elected to follow *Adams v Cape Industries* in this regard and several subsequent cases have taken Morritt VC's lead.[47] Accordingly, 'justice' is no longer, if it ever was, a basis for piercing the corporate veil.[48]

7 Summary

Given the complexity and volume of the case law in this area it is perhaps useful to summarize where the law stands. Generally speaking, whilst we have seen several examples of piercing the corporate veil on different grounds, the bottom line is that piercing is exceptionally difficult to achieve and will only occur in very rare circumstances.

It is clear that if the corporate form is used to limit a company's possible future liabilities this is legally wholly unproblematic, even though many may view it as morally suspect. A pharmaceutical company that uses a subsidiary company to develop and distribute a high-risk drug, and funds that company primarily through debt with very little in the way of equity investment, will not find itself liable for the debts of the subsidiary that arise as a result of injuries caused to people who use the drug *on the basis that* the subsidiary was set up to avoid parent liability for any such debts. However, it is equally clear that if the corporate form is used to avoid a liability or obligation that *already exists* the courts will pierce the corporate veil to ensure that the liability is met or the obligation performed. Evading existing liabilities appears to be a clear basis for piercing the corporate veil. However, in all the cases in this category it was not at all clear that piercing was necessary to achieve the objective of holding the defendant to the obligation in question.

There also appears to be a second, very limited, basis for piercing the corporate veil. This basis has been articulated using several different concepts: 'agency'; 'single economic unit'; and the 'mere corporate name' branch of the façade category. It has been used, rejected, ignored, and yet remains, intractably, available. It is applicable only in the group context and involves the absence of any activity in the subsidiary company and the failure of a parent company to treat the entity as a separate being; to be respectful of its existence. In this regard, the approach of certain US states may be instructive. Professor Hamilton discussing corporate law in the US, *not in the UK*, argues that:

> While a complete catalogue of dangerous acts is probably impossible to prepare, there appears to be substantial risk that the separate corporate existence will be ignored when business is commenced without the issuance of shares, when shareholder meetings or directors' meetings are not held, or consents are not signed, when decisions are made by shareholders as though they were partners, when shareholders do not sharply distinguish between corporate property and personal property, when corporate funds are used to pay personal expenses, when personal funds are used for corporate expenses without proper accounting, or when complete corporate and financial records are not maintained.[49]

---

[46] [2001] 3 All ER 987; for an earlier similar view see *The Tjaskemolen* [1997] 2 Lloyd's Rep 465.

[47] *Faiza Ben Hashem v Abdulhadi Ali Shayif* [2008] EWHC 2380 (Fam) observing that: 'I take the view that the dicta to that effect [that the veil could be pierced in the interests of justice] of Cumming-Bruce LJ in *In re a Company* [1985] BCLC 333 at pages 337–338, have not survived what the Court of Appeal said in *Cape*'; *Raja v Van Hoogstraten* [2006] EWHC 2564 (Ch); *Re Abacus (CI) Ltd (trustee of the Esteem Settlement)*; *Grupo Torras SA and another v Al Sabah* (2003) 6 ITELR 368 (Jersey).

[48] Interestingly, the UK cases have been very influential in forming the contemporary Irish position that 'justice' is a basis for piercing—see, for example, *Fyffes plc v DCC plc* [2005] IEHC 477.

[49] R. Hamilton, 'The Corporate Entity' (1971) 49 *Texas Law Review* 979.

It is, however, more difficult to articulate the level of activity in the subsidiary that would prevent piercing. In this regard, in attempting to address this question consider the proposition that the corporate entity can be disregarded where the corporate entity is passive and serves no separate corporate purpose other than the avoidance of liability:

■ **M. Moore, '"A Temple Built on Faulty Foundations": Piercing the Corporate Veil and the Legacy of Salomon v Salomon' (March 2006) *Journal of Business Law* 180**

The de facto activity of a company, in relation to the business enterprise of which it is part, is the contingent factor upon which the continuing recognition of that company's legal personality depends…Such a conclusion, though, only serves to conjure up more questions than it does answers. In particular, it must be asked specifically what behaviour on the part of a company will be sufficient to make that company legally active in relation to the business in which it is involved. Surely any company is, strictly speaking, passive in relation to its controlling human agents, given that it is, ultimately, nothing more than an artificial legal device invoked by its incorporators for the preliminary or ultimate purpose of immunising themselves from legal reproach on account of their business liabilities? Carried to its logical extreme, the test that this article proposes would serve to contradict the outcome of even the Salomon case itself, given that A. Salomon & Co. was, in reality, an administrative tool deployed by Mr Salomon partly for this very purpose…

However, this only begs the question: what, then, will serve to make a company legally passive in relation to its [controller] if not the fact of incorporation itself? In answer to this question, it may be suggested that a company should be deemed to be active in relation to the affairs of a business if it exists to promote a genuine purpose of that business. A genuine purpose may be defined, in this context, as a strategy determining the general direction of the business, the existence of which both precedes and also exists independently of the specific activity that gave rise to the dispute at hand. Only when both of these pre-requisites have been satisfied can a corporate entity forming part of a wider business enterprise be classified as formally active in relation to that arrangement as a whole…

[Applying this approach to *Adams v Cape*], NAAC [and AMC one presumes] was ultimately subservient to the specific desire of its incorporator to mitigate the avenues of legal reproach available to the potential victims of Cape Industries' activities. Accordingly, Cape Industries would fail to satisfy a court that NAAC existed to promote a 'genuine ultimate purpose' of its business, thereby justifying a court in disregarding the formally separate legal personality of NAAC relative to Cape. Likewise, in *Gilford Motor Co v Horne*, Mr Horne formed his sham company, J.M. Horne & Co., for the sole purpose of immunising himself from legal reproach under the terms of his restrictive covenant with the plaintiffs. Clearly, therefore, Mr Horne would have failed to satisfy a court that his company existed to serve some wider, longer-term business purpose of his, rendering J.M. Horne & Co. formally passive in relation to Mr Horne's business as a whole. Applying the genuine ultimate purpose rule, therefore, the autonomous legal personality of J.M. Horne & Co. should have been disregarded by the Court of Appeal.

Whilst this is a very strong normative argument, it is clear that the notion of 'genuine business purpose' does not capture the circumstances in which the courts have pierced the veil on the 'mere corporate name' basis. In English law it is clear that using the corporate form to perform a pure liability reduction function, in the absence of any separate corporate purpose, would not result in piercing under this category. This piercing category is less about function and more about the parent's extreme disregard for the separate personality of the subsidiary.

Questions

1. If we are to understand the special circumstances/façade principle through the *Jones v Lipman* and *Gilford Motors* line of authority regarding the evasion of liabilities, what function, if any, is performed by relying upon the language of façade?

2. What would the House of Lords in *Salomon v Salomon* have said about arguments that refer to a properly registered company as a 'façade', 'mask', or 'cloak'?

3. Is the term 'façade' any more useful than 'sham' or 'cloak'?

4. Should the benefits of the corporate form be available to those who fail to respect the fact that it is a separate legal being?

5. Do you think it is possible to formalize the idea that the corporate veil can be disregarded in relation to passive companies ('mere corporate names'). How easy would it be for companies to organize their activities to ensure that they would not fall foul of such a rule?

6. How would you make a case that the only basis for piercing the veil under English corporate law involves the total absence of activity in a subsidiary company and the parent's disregard for its separate existence?

7. How is the term 'agency' used and understood in the piercing cases we have considered?

8. Should there be a general 'justice' jurisdiction for piercing the corporate veil?

9. What would be the implications of holding parent companies liable for the debts, obligations and activities of their subsidiaries?

10. Should the corporate form be disregarded if it does not perform a 'genuine business purpose'?

 Online Resource Centre
http://www.oxfordtextbooks.co.uk/orc/kershaw2e/

Visit the Online Resource Centre for additional resources and information available for this chapter, including web links and an interactive flashcard glossary.

CHAPTER THREE

THE CORPORATE CONSTITUTION/THE MECHANICS OF THE GENERAL MEETING

This chapter addresses two separate, although linked, issues: the nature and function of the corporate constitution and the mechanics of the general meeting. Typically in a company law textbook the mechanics of the general meeting are addressed at a later stage in the book, often at the beginning of the section on corporate governance. There is much to be said for that approach. This book brings forward this section because decision-making by the general meeting is an important factor in subsequent chapters, starting with Chapter 4 on 'Corporate actions'. It is, therefore, helpful for the student of company law to have a good understanding of the basic mechanics of the general meeting earlier rather than later.

A THE CORPORATE CONSTITUTION

I INTRODUCTION

1 What is a constitution and does a company have one?

Any organization, state, or association, whether it has a separate legal personality or not, requires a set of rules that set out what it can do, how it acts, and who has the power and authority to act and to make decisions on its behalf. Those rules could be referred to as rules of association or, more grandly, as a constitution. A state constitution, with which many of you will be familiar, is a body of rules set out in a written document or in conventions and practices that sets forth the powers of the state and the distribution of those powers amongst the different organs of the state. In relation to each organ of a state, the constitution will provide rules regarding: how each organ can act—whether through individuals or collectively—and how power and control over the state apparatus is distributed between these organs. They are, in theory, a set of rules to which the nation state's citizens have implicitly agreed or consented to as the rules that they, or at least a majority of them, believe are the optimal rules of governance. A company, like any other organization or state, requires a set of such constitutional rules. The questions for us in this section are: first, *where* do we find these constitutional rules; and, second, *who* determines what those rules are?

If a company's constitution is the body of rules that govern how a company operates, what it can do, and how it acts, then the constitution of any UK company is found primarily in two places: the Companies Act 2006 and a company's articles of association. The Companies Act 2006 provides for both the basic structural elements of the company and, as we shall see as we progress through this book, provides in many instances specific rules on how a company acts—for example, how it makes a decision to issue shares, or what it can do—for example, in what circumstances it can transfer value to the shareholders. There are two basic structural/organic elements of the company provided by the 2006 Act. First, the Act provides for a body of members (members are shareholders in companies limited by shares). In this regard, section 112 of the Act provides that the initial subscribers of the company are deemed to have agreed to become members of the company and that anyone who agrees subsequently to become a member of the company and is registered in the company's register of members is also a member of the company. The Act also provides for, or at least enables, governance of the company through a delegated power structure, namely delegation to a director of the company or to a board of directors. It provides that a private company will have at least one director and that a public company will have at least two directors.[1]

With regard to the specific regulation of corporate action and decision-making the 701 pages of the Act contain, as one would expect, a litany of rules determining how the company can act and what it can do, including rules on: the issuing and buy-back of shares;[2] the making of distributions of value to shareholders;[3] the removal of directors;[4] and the appointment and removal of auditors.[5] These rules are considered in depth in the subsequent chapters of this book. Perhaps what the new student of company law will find surprising is that in such a large statute providing for the formation and regulation of the company many of the rules required for any organization to function are not set out in the Act. The Act, for example, says nothing explicitly about the distribution of power between the two organs that it provides for—the members and the board; it says little about the procedure for meetings of the members; or how a board is to make decisions or to delegate authority to other agents or committees. These rules are set out in what English company law *in fact* refers to as the *company's constitution*. However, as you will see from the analysis thus far, as compared to how the term 'constitution' is used in relation to nation states, the rules set out in a company's constitution contain only part of the constitution. The company's constitution contains the constitutional rules that are left by the 2006 Act—either explicitly by allowing the company to make a regulatory choice or implicitly by the Act's silence—for the company to decide for itself.

2 The constitutional documents

In the Companies Act 1985, the predecessor to the now in force Companies Act 2006, although the term 'constitution' was used in specific sections[6] it was not generally defined. However, the term was used in company law commentary.[7] Until the Companies Act 2006 there were two documents that formed the constitution of a UK company, whether private or public. These documents were the company's memorandum of association and its articles of association. The memorandum was viewed as the core constitutional document containing core identity/outward-looking information such as: the company's name; what types of business activity the company could engage in (its objects clause); whether the company's members benefited from limited liability; and the company's **authorized share capital**.[8] The articles of association contained primarily internal governance rules providing for the distribution of power between the board and the shareholder body and the procedural rules for board and general meeting action.

The Companies Act 2006 provides the following definition of the company's constitution.

---

[1] Section 154 CA 2006.   [2] See Chapter 17.   [3] See Chapter 19.
[4] See Chapter 6.   [5] See Web Chapter A.   [6] Section 35B CA 1985.
[7] See for example P. Davies, *Gower and Davies' Principles of Modern Company Law* (7th edn, Sweet & Maxwell, 2003).
[8] Section 3 CA 1985.

■ Section 17 CA 2006 A company's constitution

Unless the context otherwise requires, references in the Companies Acts to a company's constitution include—

(a) the company's articles, and

(b) any resolutions and agreements to which Chapter 3 applies (see section 29).[9]

UK company law now provides effectively for a one document constitutional structure. That document is the articles of association. The memorandum of association remains part of English company law; however, it is now merely a formation document that provides that the persons forming a company wish to form the company, that they agree to become members of the company, and that they will take at least one share in the company.[10] The memorandum is no longer part of the company's constitution. For existing companies, section 28 of the Act provides that provisions contained in such memorandums are to be treated as provisions of the company's articles.

If the context requires other documents may be constitutional documents. In this regard the Government's *Explanatory Notes to the 2006 Act* refer to, as an example of another constitutional document, the certificate of incorporation issued upon the formation of the company which sets forth, amongst others, whether the company is a private or a public company. Accordingly, the Act maintains the pre-2006 view that the constitution is about corporate identity as well as governance. However, in most instances, and for our purposes in this book, a reference to the company's constitution will refer to the company's articles of association.

3 The Model Articles of Association

As we have noted, the Companies Act 2006 is silent on very significant issues about how a company acts and functions. It leaves it up to the members of the company to decide on the rules that are to be provided in the constitution. This makes considerable sense: as each company is different and each body of members is different, companies and their members should be allowed to fashion the set of governance rules that is most suitable to them, and that fits with their preferences. However, the power of this rationale for giving members freedom to organize a company's decision-making and action processes as they so choose does not have a natural limit that stops at the boundaries of the areas of activity that the Companies Act 2006 leaves to the corporate constitution to regulate. Why does the Companies Act tell the company what to do in some areas by providing for **mandatory rules** that do not enable the company and its shareholder to do things differently to reflect their preferences, and yet in other areas gives them precisely this freedom of action. This is a question that we will not answer here but it will arise and be addressed at multiple points in our journey through company law in the rest of this book. For now we will note that the answer to the question is found in claims, that we will at the relevant points interrogate, that such rules are necessary to protect the shareholders themselves—perhaps, for example, from the power of management or a large and dominant shareholder—or that, as some regulatory decisions will have effects on other parties that have contractual or other relations

---

[9] Section 29 CA 2006 refers to, amongst others, any special resolution or any resolution agreed to by all the members of the company.

[10] Section 8 CA 2006.

with the company such as the company's creditors, the regulatory decision cannot be left to the shareholders alone.

In the areas of governance left for the company to decide for itself, does the Act leave a blank page for the founding and subsequent members of the company and their lawyers to fill in themselves? For companies and members with significant resources such a blank page would not represent a problem: their lawyers will have drafted constitutions many times before and can pull up a Word file and amend the provisions to suit the needs of the client-company and its members. However, for many small start-up companies providing nothing but a constitutional blank page would represent a significant problem. The founders of such companies may have little understanding of company operations and processes and no money to pay lawyers who would have such an understanding. Such companies may elect to leave the page blank or fill it in with very poorly informed and unworkable rules.

Fortunately for such companies the legislature addresses these problems by providing a set of default articles: articles of association that apply unless the founding or subsequent members decide they do not wish them to apply. Companies may elect to: adopt these default articles in whole; to reject them in whole and draft their own articles from scratch; or to adopt the default rules in part, whereby they apply generally subject to specific different rules that override the corresponding rules in the default articles. These default articles were issued pursuant to powers granted by the Companies Act 2006 to the Secretary of State for Business, Enterprise and Regulatory Reform (BERR)[11] and are known as the 'Model Articles'.

The predecessor model default articles issued under previous Companies Acts were known as Table A Articles. Only one version of Table A Articles was provided for all public and private companies. The Company Law Review recommended that the model default articles could be more responsive than Table A had been to variation in company type.[12] Accordingly, we now have three sets of Model Articles: Model Articles for Private Companies Limited by Shares; Model Articles for Public Companies Limited by Shares; and Model Articles for Companies Limited by Guarantee. Only the Model Articles for Public and Private Companies are of interest to us in this book.

The Model Articles for both Public and Private Companies set out rules in five primary areas: the distribution of power between the board and the shareholder body; board appointment and decision-making; general meeting decision-making; rules on the setting of rights attached to shares, share transfers, and the transmission of shares following the death of a shareholder; and certain rules on the making of dividends and distributions.

The Model Articles are default articles which apply to a company in the absence of contrary intention.[13] However, although these rules are optional they provide an important regulatory function. They do so in two respects. First, they set a benchmark governance standard: a normal approach to specific aspects of governance—although companies may choose to apply a different rule, norms as starting points structure and form variation. Secondly, as the vast majority of companies will not have the time or the funds to consider whether each of the Model Articles' provisions is appropriate for the company's needs, in practice the rules in the Model Articles will apply to, and structure, the governance of the vast majority of UK companies. Accordingly, in our analysis of company law, when considering an area of corporate activity that is left to the articles to regulate, our reference point will be, in the main, the Model Articles for

---

[11] Issued pursuant to a power granted to the Secretary of State by section 19 CA 2006. The Companies Model Articles Regulations 2008 No. 3229, www.bis.gov.uk/ ⬤.

[12] Company Law Review, *Developing the Framework*, para 7.73.

[13] Section 20 CA 2006 provides for the Model Articles application if alternative articles are not registered on the formation of the company or 'in so far as they do not exclude or modify the relevant model articles'.

both Private and Public Companies. Many companies may indeed have opted out from some of those terms but for our purposes we can take it as given that most companies will be subject either to the actual rules set out in the Model Articles or a variation that is closely related to such rules.

Most companies operating in the UK today were not formed pursuant to the Companies Act 2006, but pursuant to earlier versions of the Companies Acts and adopted the corresponding earlier versions of Table A.[14] The introduction of a new set of Model Articles, pursuant to the Companies Act 2006, does not alter the applicability of the earlier versions of Table A to the companies in question. Such companies could, of course, elect to adopt the new Model Articles if they follow the amendment procedure, which is considered below, by replacing Table A with the new Model Articles. Many companies will not elect to do this, preferring to keep the rules they are familiar with. Our reference point in this book, however, will be the new Model Articles, although where relevant we will make reference to Table A to consider in what ways the new Model Articles alter the applicable default rules.

4 Amending the articles of association

It follows clearly from the fact that a company's articles of association may be fashioned as the company thinks fit that the company's original articles adopted upon its formation are not set in stone. As the company develops, grows, and changes it will be necessary to alter aspects of the way in which it is governed to take account of these developments. It will need to change such rules. Accordingly, it is necessary and logical that a company can amend its constitution.

What steps then must be taken by the company to amend its constitution? In this regard there are two issues: first, which corporate organ has the power to alter the constitution; and secondly, what percentage of the votes of the organ in question are required to pass a resolution to amend the constitution? In relation to the first issue, UK company law gives the right to amend the constitution *only* to the shareholder body.[15] In practice, it is likely to be the case that the directors identify a need to alter the rules and propose such a change to the shareholders' general meeting; however, the board of directors itself has *no* voting or approval rights in relation to such an amendment. For a more detailed and comparative discussion of the balance of power issues raised by the distribution of the right to amend the constitution see Chapter 5.

With regard to the question of what percentage of the members votes are required to pass a resolution of the general meeting amending the constitution, there are three obvious candidates: a simple majority vote of the general meeting; a super majority vote; or unanimity. Such thresholds could be applied either to the votes cast at the general meeting or to all of the company's issued voting shares. Here we see a tension between two considerations. On the one hand, given the view already outlined that the company must be able to alter its governance rules to take account of its development and changed circumstances, it is essential that the company can make changes to its constitution easily and quickly. In this regard, it is important that the amendment threshold is not too high. A higher voting threshold is not only more difficult to reach but also facilitates hold-up by smaller shareholders who can block such changes, perhaps because they have separate grievances or demands and wish to use the articles' amendment vote as leverage in relation to those other grievances or demands. Such concerns would suggest that a majority vote rule would be appropriate. One might also argue that in many instances the majority position will have the best interests of the company in mind and, therefore, the resolution should be passed by a majority of those

---

[14] For a list of the various Table As since the introduction of incorporation by registration see: www.companieshouse.gov.uk/ 🌐.

[15] Section 21 CA 2006.

active shareholders interested enough in the company to turn up to or to send a representative to the general meeting.

However, there are several factors that mitigate against such a majority amendment rule. The constitution of a company, like the constitution of a nation state, is a fundamental document that should not be changed lightly. Change to such a document requires a significant consensus of opinion. The US Constitution, for example, can be amended by a proposal approved by two-thirds of both Houses of Congress, which is then put before the States, three-quarters of which must approve of the amendment for it to take effect.[16] A second concern is that the shareholders bought shares in the company on the assumption that a set of rules would apply to the company and some of these rules may be viewed by the shareholder as important to the protection of their interests. This is perhaps a weaker argument when one considers that such shareholders would have also taken into account that the articles could be changed following the applicable amendment rule. However, it certainly could be the case that some shareholders would consider certain terms as a prerequisite to buying shares in the company and that they would only buy the shares if such terms could not be amended.

Accordingly, these considerations suggest that there is a trade-off between flexibility for the company on the one hand and ensuring that changes only take place where there is a clear groundswell of opinion on the other. It also suggests that the company should be able to commit to not changing some provisions at all if they are willing to exchange lack of flexibility for the equity investment of a particular investor.

UK company law provides that the articles can be amended by a special resolution: 75% of the votes cast in general meeting.[17] It is not possible for the company to opt for a smaller majority such as an ordinary resolution: a simple majority of the votes cast in general meeting. The 75% threshold is a mandatory minimum threshold. This contrasts, for example, with a Delaware corporation in the US,[18] where the shareholder voting threshold is a majority of the *issued voting shares*.[19] In Germany the corporate constitution, the *Satzung*, can be amended by a resolution in general meeting which attracts 75% of the votes cast.[20]

With regard to the need for companies to provide specific shareholders with greater security that particular constitutional provisions will not be amended, the 2006 Act allows for a public or private company's constitution to provide for a higher amendment threshold or the specification of other amendment conditions, such as the approval of a particular shareholder.[21] This is known as the 'entrenchment' of the provisions to which such higher thresholds or amendment conditions apply. The special resolution amendment rule is, therefore, a mandatory floor, but not a mandatory ceiling. Such higher thresholds or specific conditions must, however, be provided for on the formation of the company or agreed to by *all* the shareholders of the company. Such higher threshold or specific condition can of course be repealed or amended by the agreement of the members of the company in accordance with the terms of entrenched provision or by a unanimous shareholder vote.[22] Accordingly a provision of the constitution approved by all the members in accordance with section 22 that purports to be 'unamendable' can always be amended by unanimous shareholder agreement.

The Companies Act 2006 provides no other general rules or restrictions on the amendment of the constitution. The common law does, however, subject the exercise of power by the general meeting to limited oversight. Many of the cases that have developed

---

[16] US Constitution, article 5.   [17] Section 21 CA 2006.
[18] On the reasons why a US corporation is a Delaware corporation or a New York corporation rather than a US corporation see pp 212–213.
[19] Section 242(b)(i) (Certificate of incorporation) and section 109 (By-laws) Delaware General Corporation Law. On the constitutional documents of a Delaware company see further Chapter 6 section II.6.
[20] Section 179 German Stock Corporation Law (*Aktiengesetz*).
[21] Section 22 CA 2006.   [22] Section 22(3) CA 2006.

the law in this regard arise from general meeting action to amend the constitution in circumstances that are viewed by minority shareholders as detrimental to their interests. For a detailed discussion of these cases see Chapter 16 on 'Minority shareholder protection'.[23]

II THE LEGAL STATUS OF THE CONSTITUTION: THE CORPORATE CONTRACT

We observed above that shareholders in some instances will view certain constitutional provisions as important, indeed essential, to their interests. Potential investors, before they become shareholders, may be unwilling to invest in a company without the security that such provisions will remain unaltered. Such provisions could, for example: limit the number of shares that can be issued; or provide the shareholder with veto rights over certain transactions, such as those that exceed a value threshold. These rules are valuable to shareholders: they pay for them in the price they pay for the shares.[24] Through this lens, the rules set out in the corporate constitution, including the rules that allow the constitution to be amended, are the contractual terms upon which the shareholders agree to become associated with the company. The corporate constitution is a corporate contract.

In relation to small, **close** companies where the shareholders pay close attention to the terms of the corporate constitution this view of the constitution as a corporate contract appears apposite. But is this contractual view of the constitution as apposite in relation to large companies such as listed companies that may have many shareholders, many of whom own only a small percentage shareholding in the company. Such shareholders obviously do not engage in an archetypal contracting process involving offer, counter-offer, and compromise. Is the constitution appropriately described as a corporate contract in relation to such companies? Some scholars argue that it is. Their view of company law is known as the contractarian view. For these scholars, a company, such as our case study company, Bob's Electronics Plc, is not only a nexus of contracts vis à vis suppliers of components, debt, and labour but also a contractual nexus with the suppliers of equity capital: the shareholders. The terms of the equity contract with shareholders are set out in company law and the corporate constitution. For these scholars, even in large companies there is a contracting-like process. There is not the 'to and fro'/'give and take' of a typical contracting process, but rather an implicit contracting process that comes about by companies offering rules of governance in their constitution, which sophisticated shareholders value when they buy the shares. For these scholars, market pressures to maximize company value in order for managers to maximize their bonus[25] or to ward of potential bidders for the company will pressurize senior managers of companies to offer shareholders constitutional terms that maximize what equity investors will pay for the shares. Where companies do not offer such terms those sophisticated shareholders will pay less for the shares. According to contractarians, therefore, the corporate constitution represents part of (together with company law) the corporate contract—an implicitly negotiated corporate contract. Consider the following extract from the most famous proponents of the contractarian creed.

---

[23] *Allen v Gold Reefs of Africa Ltd* [1900–03] All ER REP 746; *Brown v British Abrasive Wheel Co Ltd* [1918–19] All ER Rep 308; *Sidebottom v Kershaw, Leese and Company Ltd* [1920] 1 Ch 154 (CA); *Dafen Tinplate Company Limited v Llanelly Steel Company* [1920] 2 Ch 124; *Shuttleworth v Cox Bros Ltd* [1927] 2 KB 9 (CA).

[24] On the relationship between price, risk and return see Chapter 1 section I.6.

[25] On the regulation of executive remuneration see Chapter 8.

■ **F.H. Easterbrook and D.R. Fischel, *The Economic Structure of Corporate Law* (1991), 18–19**

> Are terms priced? Provisions in articles…often are picky and obscure. Many are not listed in the **prospectus** of the firms [shares]. Buyers of the original issue [the initial public offering] and in the aftermarket[26] alike may know nothing of the terms in use…They do not consult the *Journal of Financial Economics* before buying. Yet it is unimportant whether knowledge about and effects of the terms is widespread, at least for [listed companies]. The mechanism by which [shares] are valued ensures that the price reflects the terms of governance and operation, just as it reflects the identity of the managers and products of the firms.
>
> The price of [shares] traded in public markets is established by professional investors not by amateurs. These professionals—market makers, arbitrage departments of investment banks, managers of **mutual funds** and **pension funds** [**fund managers**] and others—handle huge sums that they use to purchase undervalued [shares].
>
> If the [share] price is not 'right' in relation to the price it will have in the future, then professionals can make a lot of money. If the terms of corporate provisions and the detail of corporate structure have any effect on investor's welfare, this will be reflected in the profit of the firm and hence the eventual price of the [shares]…
>
> A great deal of data, including evidence that most professionals are unable to beat the market supports the position that prices quickly and accurately reflect public information about firms. Amateur investors then trade at the price the professionals obtain. These amateurs do not need to know anything about corporate governance and the other provisions; the value of these mysterious things is wrapped up in the price established by the professionals. The price reflects the effects of good and bad products. This is yet another example of the ways in which markets transmit the value of information through price, which is more 'informed' than any single participant in the market.

The claim about the pricing of the rules set out in corporate law and corporate constitutions relies on a claim that financial markets that buy and sell shares in listed companies are efficient. What it means to say that such markets are efficient is that as a result of the buying and selling activities of 'professional investors' these markets incorporate into the price of a share the publicly available information about the company, its management, its products, its market place and, importantly for our purposes, the rules that govern the company.[27] In the lengthening shadow of the credit and banking crisis of 2008–2010, it is difficult to accept the proposition that capital markets are efficient. During this period we have seen significant volatility in financial markets and markets appear to have taken a considerable period to incorporate the bad economic news that financial commentators had been pointing to for some time. A sceptic might argue that if markets are not very efficient in relation to economic and financial information, then it is less likely that they are efficient in relation to complex legal rules. Here, however, is not the place for a thorough assessment of whether capital markets effectively value corporate legal rules and corporate constitutions as Easterbrook and Fischel claim. What is noteworthy is that this lens continues to, and will continue to, exercise considerable influence on how scholars view corporate law and the corporate constitution. This view has weathered previous market failures.[28] The extent to which the contractual lens is a

---

[26] The market for shares following the initial public offering.

[27] This is the semi-strong version of market efficiency. See E. Fama, 'Efficient Capital Markets: A Review of Theory and Empirical Work (1970) 25 *Journal of Finance* 383. E. Fama, 'Efficient Capital Markets II' (1991) 46 *Journal of Finance* 1575.

[28] Easterbrook and Fischel's book came out only a few years following another significant market collapse in 1987 which led some economists at the time to cast doubt on the efficiency of capital markets; see, for example, R.J. Shiller, *Market Volatility* (MIT, 1990).

useful lens through which to understand or critique company law will be considered in relation to specific issues throughout the course of the book.

Although corporate law and the corporate constitution of both small and large companies can be viewed, as we have seen, through the lens of contract, how in fact does English law view the legal status of the corporate constitution? Perhaps unsurprisingly it views it in contractual terms. Section 33 provides as follows:

■ Section 33 CA 2006 Effect of company's constitution

(1) The provisions of a company's constitution bind the company and its members to the same extent as if there were covenants on the part of the company[29] and of each member to observe those provisions.

Accordingly, in English company law the constitution has effect *as if* it *were* a contract between the company and the shareholders as well as a contract between the shareholders themselves.[30]

III ENFORCING THE CORPORATE CONTRACT

A contract can be enforced by parties to the contract. If the corporate constitution has effect *as if* it were a contract between the company and the members, then one would expect that the company could enforce the contract against the members, and that the members could enforce the contract against the company. Any failure by any party to observe the terms of the constitution could, one would expect, result in court action to either require compliance with its terms or compensation for loss resulting from non-compliance. Indeed the corporate contract is an enforceable document by the company against its members, the members against the company, and between the members themselves.[31] However, there are generally thought to be two important qualifications to the enforceability of the corporate contract. The first, which we shall argue is not a qualification at all, is that the member can only enforce the contract in his capacity as a member and not in any other capacity. The second is that the member cannot enforce the contract if the non-compliance is deemed to be an internal irregularity rather than a breach of the member's personal contractual rights.

1 Qua member and only qua member?

A contract can only be enforced by the parties who are in privity of contract; third persons who are not parties to the contract cannot enforce the contract. This creates a difficulty in the context of the company where one real person may perform several roles or have several capacities. Consider, for example, Bob's Electronics Ltd, which has several shareholders, including Bob, a board of directors of three individuals, and where Bob is the chief executive officer and director of the company. Bob has three legally distinctive relationships with the company: as shareholder; as director; and as employee. He is, as member, a party to the corporate contract, but he is not as director

---

[29] Prior versions of this provision in predecessor Companies Acts had referred only to the contractual obligations amongst members, however, the constitution was held to be a contract between both the members inter se and between the company and the members: *Hickman v Kent Romney Marsh Sheep-Breeders' Association* [1915] 1 Ch 881.

[30] *Rayfield v Hands* [1958] 2 WLR 851; *Wood v Odessa Waterworks Co* (1889) 42 Ch D 636.

[31] *Ibid*; *Johnson v Lyttle's Iron Agency* (1887) 5 Ch D 687; *Bradford Banking Co v Briggs* (1886) 12 App Cas 29.

or as employee in privity of contract with the company in relation to the constitution.
He could not, therefore, as director or employee, try to enforce the contract. This is the
case even if the corporate contract makes reference to him as director or as employee or
in any other role, for example, as solicitor to the company. If the constitution provides
that Bob shall always be an employee of the company or that he shall always serve as
the solicitor to the company, he cannot enforce the contract as *Bob-the-Employee* or as
Bob-the-Solicitor.[32] One might of course ask why this matters, because although Bob
cannot enforce the contract as director,[33] employee, or solicitor he can enforce the contract as member and can, as a contracting party, demand that the contract is fulfilled
vis à vis those other 'persons' (Bob-the-director-employee-solicitor). After all, if A contracts with B to pay £20 a week to B in exchange for which B will clean C's windows, C
cannot[34] bring suit to enforce B's performance, but A can. From the perspective of the
constitution as a contract this view makes sense. However, when we think about the
constitution *as a constitution* it makes less sense. In this regard we should note that pursuant to section 33 of the 2006 Act the constitution is *not* a contract but is to be treated
as if it were one. As a constitution the articles are designed to distribute and regulate the
exercise of corporate power; they are not designed to address extra-corporate relations
even with individuals who happen also to be members. From such a constitutional perspective it would not make sense for a member to be able to enforce the contract where
it purports to address non-constitutional matters.

One line of authority, however, suggests that whilst the constitution can be enforced
by members it can only be enforced to the extent that it affects their rights as members
(qua members) and not to the extent that it affects their rights in any other capacity.
That is, they cannot require the enforcement of the contract as members if in so doing
they are requesting performance that benefits them in a non-shareholder capacity. The
regularly cited authority for this position is the first instance judgment of *Hickman v
Kent or Romney Marsh Sheepbreeders' Association*,[35] where Astbury J held:

> First, that no article can constitute a contract between the company and a third person; [and] sec-
> ondly, that no right merely purporting to be given by an article to a person, whether a member
> or not, in a capacity other than that of a member, as, for instance, as solicitor, promoter, director,
> can be enforced against the company.

This view has considerable support in UK company law commentary. However, there is
only limited authority that directly follows this holding.[36] There is also authority that

[32] For example *Eley v The Positive Government Security Life Assurance Company, Limited* (1876)
1 Ex D 88 the constitution contained a provision providing that the claimant would be the company's
solicitor. The solicitor was not, on the facts presented in the case, a member of the company but sued
on the basis of the articles when his instruction as solicitor was not continued. The court held that the
articles did not represent an enforceable contract between the solicitor and the company.
[33] Note that in the absence of contrary intention in the contract between a senior manager and the
company, the courts have implied the term in the articles authorizing the appointment and removal
of the manager into the terms of the manager's contract with the company. However, this is clearly
distinct from the ability of the manager or director to enforce the terms of the constitution. See *Read v
Astoria Garage (Streatham) Ltd* [1952] Ch 637.
[34] At common law C cannot bring suit, however she may be able to pursuant to the Contracts (Rights
of Third Parties) Act 1999.
[35] [1915] 1 Ch 881.
[36] For example, *Kanssen v Rialto (West End) Limited* [1944] Ch 154. These *qua member* cases must
be distinguished from cases where it is not possible for a member to enforce the contract because on
the correct interpretation of the provision in question it does not create a right that the member can
enforce. For example, in *Beattie v E & F Beattie Ltd* [1938] Ch 708 the provision of the constitution
in question provided for disputes between members to be referred to arbitration. One of the members
brought suit against a director who was also a member of the company. The director-member applied

provides that a member does have the right to have the corporate contract enforced even where such enforcement confers a benefit on a member in a different capacity. In *Salmon v Quin & Axtens Ltd*[37] the subject company's articles of association provided that the company could only purchase, lease, or sell property with the approval of two specified directors (which we will refer to as directors A and B). A decision to purchase property was made by the board including director A and was confirmed by an ordinary resolution in general meeting.[38] However, director B did not give his consent. Director B was also a member of the company and brought an action to prevent the company from purchasing the property. According to the view already set out that members can only enforce rights set out in the constitution to the extent that the rights relate to their position as members and not in any other capacity, member B would not be in a position to enforce those rights, as the right that was ignored in the decision to purchase the property was director B's veto right. The House of Lords, however, held in favour of member/director B. The Court of Appeal and the House of Lords, in very brief judgments, did not consider the distinction between the rights of members as members or in a separate capacity; rather the constitution was simply treated as an enforceable contract by the parties that entered into it.[39]

However, an alternative reading of this case is available which lends less support to the view that the contract can be enforced by the member regardless of the capacity in which its enforcement benefits the member. This alternative reading is to argue that the right in question although granted to director B was clearly designed to protect the interests of member B and, therefore, that the right was being enforced qua member and not qua director. On this reading, *Salmon v Quin & Axtens Ltd* would only be authority for the proposition that a member can enforce a right in the constitution provided it is connected to his role and position as a member. This would not extend to unconnected 'contractual rights', for example, to be appointed as the company's solicitor. Put differently, the disenfranchisement of director B raised a constitutional matter appropriately enforced by a member, whereas the purported appointment of a member as a solicitor does not. This appears to be the stronger reading of this case; and a reading that is consistent with the *qua member* cases.

2 Internal irregularities versus personal rights

The constitution may be treated *as if* it were a contract between the company and its members individually; however, as we have seen, its primary function is as part of the corporate regulatory jigsaw that determines how power is distributed between a company's organs and how that power can be expressed and exercised. Amongst others, it determines how members operate collectively through the general meeting and the relationship between the general meeting and the other primary organ of the company, the board of directors. That is, the constitution may be treated *as if* it were a contract that creates individual member contractual rights, but in fact, vis á vis members, its primary function is to provide for collective member decision-making procedures and to distribute collective member rights. As right holders are entitled to enforce their rights, arguably it follows that the rights of the collective created by the constitution should be enforced by the collective shareholder body and the individual shareholder rights created by the constitution by the individual shareholders.

---

to have the action stayed and referred to arbitration on the basis of this provision. The court refused to do so. They held that on the interpretation of the provision in question, referral to arbitration was required only when there was a dispute between members, and in this case there was a dispute between a member and a director; the fact that the director was also a member did not alter this position.

[37] [1909] AC 442.

[38] On the effect of the supporting shareholder resolution see pp 200–204.

[39] This view was set forth by Lord Wedderburn in his seminal article 'Shareholder's Rights and the Rule in *Foss v Harbottle*' (1957) *Cambridge Law Journal* 194.

At common law individual members of a company may bring an action to enforce the terms of the constitution where the failure to observe the constitution amounts to a breach of their *personal rights*, but they may not bring an action where the company's failure to comply with the constitution amounts to an *internal irregularity*. An internal irregularity is deemed to be a failure to observe the constitution that should be addressed collectively by a decision of the general meeting. How then do we distinguish between the violation of a 'personal right' and an 'internal irregularity'? In this regard consider the following two cases.

■ *Macdougall v Gardiner* (1875) 1 Ch D 13

The defendant company's articles provided that a vote by poll[40] on the adjournment of the general meeting would be required if requested by five shareholders. The chairman of the company proposed the adjournment of a general meeting upon which a poll was duly requested. The chairman ignored the poll and adjourned the meeting. An action was brought by an individual shareholder effectively requesting that the meeting be reconvened.

James LJ
Everything in this [complaint], as far as I can see, if it is wrong is a wrong to the company, because every meeting that is called must be for some purpose or other—it must be for the purpose of doing or undoing something which is supposed to accrue for the benefit of the company. Whether it ought to have been done, or ought not to have been done, depends upon whether it is for the good of the company it should have been done, or for the good of the company it should not have been done; and, putting aside all illegality on the part of the majority, it is for the company to determine whether it is for the good of the company that the thing should be done, or should not be done, or left unnoticed. I cannot conceive that there is any equity on the part of a shareholder, on behalf of himself and the minority, to say, 'true it is that the majority have a right to determine everything connected with the management of the company, but then we have a right—and every individual has a right—to have a meeting held in strict form in accordance with the articles.' Has a particular individual the right to have it for the purpose of using his power of eloquence to induce the others to listen to him and to take his view? That is an equity which I have never yet heard of in this Court, and I have never known it insisted upon before; that is to say, that this Court is to entertain a bill for the purpose of enabling one particular member of the company to have an opportunity of expressing his opinions *vivâ voce* at a meeting of the shareholders. If so, I do not know why we should not go further, and say, not only must the meeting be held, but the shareholders must stay there to listen to him and to be convinced by him. The truth is, that is only part of the machinery and means by which the internal management is carried on. The whole question comes back to a question of internal management; that is to say, whether the meeting ought or ought not to be held in a particular way, whether the directors ought or ought not to have sanctioned certain proceedings which they are about to sanction, whether one director ought or ought not to be removed, and whether another director ought or ought not to have been appointed. If there is some one managing the affairs of the company who ought not to manage them, and if they are being managed in a way in which they ought not to be managed, the company are the proper persons to complain of that. It seems to me, therefore, that the thing is perfectly plain and obvious, and when the Master of the Rolls had the case before him he immediately pointed it out, and said, 'You have the wrong Plaintiff here—the Plaintiff must be the company.' From the first opening of this case before us, I have never had any doubt in my own mind that this was a bill which, if it was to be sustained at all, could only be sustained by the company...

---

[40] See p 98 for the distinction between a vote by poll and a vote by a show of hands.

Mellish LJ

I am of the same opinion. I think it is a matter of considerable importance rightly to determine this question, whether a suit ought to be brought in the name of the company or in the name of one of the shareholders on behalf of the others. It is not at all a technical question, but it may make a very serious difference in the management of the affairs of the company. The difference is this:—Looking to the nature of these companies, looking at the way in which their articles are formed, and that they are not all lawyers who attend these meetings, nothing can be more likely than that there should be something more or less irregular done at them—some directors may have been irregularly appointed, some directors as irregularly turned out, or something or other may have been done which ought not to have been done according to the proper construction of the articles. Now, if that gives a right to every member of the company to file a bill to have the question decided, then if there happens to be one cantankerous member, or one member who loves litigation, everything of this kind will be litigated; whereas, if the bill must be filed in the name of the company, then, unless there is a majority who really wish for litigation, the litigation will not go on. Therefore, holding that such suits must be brought in the name of the company does certainly greatly tend to stop litigation.

In my opinion, if the thing complained of is a thing which in substance the majority of the company are entitled to do, or if something has been done irregularly which the majority of the company are entitled to do regularly, or if something has been done illegally which the majority of the company are entitled to do legally, there can be no use in having a litigation about it, the ultimate end of which is only that a meeting has to be called, and then ultimately the majority gets its wishes. Is it not better that the rule should be adhered to that if it is a thing which the majority are the masters of, the majority in substance shall be entitled to have their will followed? If it is a matter of that nature, it only comes to this, that the majority are the only persons who can complain that a thing which they are entitled to do has been done irregularly; and that, as I understand it, is what has been decided by the cases of *Mozley v. Alston*[41] and *Foss v. Harbottle*.[42]

■ *Pender v Lushington* (1877) 6 Ch D 70

The company in this case provided for a voting cap that prevented any shareholder from voting more than 100 shares regardless of the number of shares owned by the shareholder. To circumvent this rule Mr Pender transferred shares to certain shareholders ('nominee shareholders'), who formally—as they were recorded on the register of members as members—were members of the company but held the shares on trust for Mr Pender as beneficiary. Aware of this fact, in a general meeting the chairman of the meeting refused to allow these nominee shareholders to vote, arguing that to do so would enable Mr Pender to circumvent the requirements of the articles. Mr Pender together with the nominee shareholders brought an action to restrain the company from acting in accordance with resolutions passed at the meeting (without counting the votes in question).

Jessel MR

This is an action by Mr. Pender for himself. He is a member of the company, and whether he votes with the majority or the minority he is entitled to have his vote recorded—an individual right in respect of which he has a right to sue. That has nothing to do with the question like that raised in *Foss v. Harbottle* and that line of cases. He has a right to say, 'Whether I vote in the majority or minority, you shall record my vote, as that is a right of property belonging to my interest in

---

[41] (1847) 1 Ph 790.

[42] (1843) 2 Hare 461. *Foss v Harbottle* is discussed in much greater detail in Chapter 15, which considers the enforcement of directors' duties.

this company, and if you refuse to record my vote I will institute legal proceedings against you to compel you.' What is the answer to such an action? It seems to me it can be maintained as a matter of substance, and that there is no technical difficulty in maintaining it.

The refusal of the chairman of the general meeting in *Pender v Lushington* to count the votes of the nominee shareholders was a breach of their personal rights to allow their votes to be counted. In *Macdougall v Gardiner*, however, the refusal to allow a vote (by poll) on the adjournment of the general meeting was an internal irregularity[43]—a failure to follow general meeting procedure that could only be challenged if the general meeting itself, *acting as the company*, elected to challenge it.[44] What distinguishes these cases is not clear. One could argue that in *Macdougall v Gardiner*, as in *Pender v Lushington*, the shareholders were denied a right to vote—in this case on the adjournment. Note that, however, in *Macdougall v Gardiner* all shareholders were denied a right to vote; the general meeting was prevented from operating as the constitution provided that it should. In contrast, in *Pender v Lushington* some shareholders were allowed to vote; others were not. Perhaps then the best way of explaining when a shareholder has a right to bring a personal action is when the shareholder has been discriminated against in exercising the rights granted to him through the constitution. Where there is no discrimination and the shareholders as a collective have not been able to vote then an action can only be brought if the general meeting decides to bring an action. Similarly, if an individual shareholder is given a specific right, the violation of that right is enforceable by the shareholder and does not amount to an internal irregularity.[45]

Many commentators are not convinced that the cases offer a coherent account of which infringements of the constitution involve a violation of personal rights and which infringements amount to internal irregularities. Whether or not we can make sense of the distinction, an alternative question is whether it should remain at all. One clear consequence of the rule is that failures to observe the terms of the constitution will often go unsanctioned where non-compliance amounts to an internal irregularity that would require reconvening the general meeting to decide to take action or to rectify the breach. If members were entitled to bring an action, or could credibly threaten to bring an action, in relation to any failure to observe the terms of the constitution, it would increase the likelihood that breaches would be addressed, and thereby decrease the likelihood of breach. '

In this regard the Company Law Review recommended that: 'all obligations imposed by the constitution should be enforceable by individual members both against the

---

[43] *Southern Bank Deposit Bank Ltd v Rider* (1895) 73 LT 374; *Amalgamated Society of Engineers v Jones* (1913) 39 TLR 484; affirming *Macdougall v Gardiner*; see *Burland v Earle* [1902] AC 83.

[44] Note that underpinning the idea of majority rule in *Macdougall v Gardiner* is a presumption that the shareholder meeting acting as the company, on behalf of the company, could themselves bring an action on behalf of the company to enforce the breach or, in the alternative, could instruct the board to take an action to remedy the breach. However, the powers of the general meeting to exercise corporate power (to bring litigation) or to instruct the board to act in a particular way was, and is, a function of the corporate constitution. Many companies of this period did not provide such constitutional rights to their shareholder. See further Chapter 6 pp 200–204 and Chapter 15 pp 596–601.

[45] This would enable the case of *Salmon v Quin & Axtens Limited* [1909] AC 442 to fit within this personal rights/internal irregularities dichotomy. On this point Lord Wedderburn (see note 39) does not agree because the right was vested in director B not in the shareholder himself. For Lord Wedderburn, *Salmon v Quin Axtens* contradicts the internal irregularities approach as it allowed 'member B' to enforce the constitution in relation to what appears to be an internal irregularity: a breach of the constitution that would be enforceable by the shareholder meeting itself. This author is not wholly convinced by that reading. Indeed, the veto right was given to the director but clearly as a means of protecting member B's interests; the right was very closely wedded to member B's rights as a member of the company. The failure to observe the right was, therefore, a violation of the shareholders personal right and not an internal irregularity.

company and other members unless the contrary was provided in the constitution [or] unless the breach in question was trivial or the remedy fruitless'.[46] They observed, as did Mellish LJ in the extract from *Macdougall v Gardiner*, that such a rule runs the risk of an increase in litigation. In some respects encouraging an increase in litigation is precisely the point; however, the concern in this regard is whether such a rule would enable trivial and unnecessary litigation. Given that shareholders run the risk of having to bear the legal costs of unsuccessful action and that in many instances the breach of the constitution will not result in a loss for the shareholders or not one they are entitled to claim for personally,[47] the incentives for shareholders to bring litigation are weak and the likelihood of excessive litigation, therefore, remains low. In any event the Government did not adopt this recommendation. The student of company law must, therefore, continue to struggle with the distinction between enforceable personal rights and internal irregularities that are not enforceable by individual shareholders.

IV SHAREHOLDERS' AGREEMENTS

A company's articles of association and any amendments to the constitution must be filed with Companies House and are made publicly available by Companies House.[48] Any person who has a relationship with the company, or indeed any person who is interested in how a company is governed, can access the constitution through Companies House's WebCHeck online database.[49] Members of companies may not always wish for all the agreements between members regarding how the company will be run and operated to be publicly available. This may simply reflect a desire for privacy regarding the rights that members have in relation to particular companies. However, companies may have good non-privacy based reasons for seeking confidentiality. For example, in relation to a company with very complex decision-making mechanics designed to protect the different interests of several shareholders, a potential contracting party who reads the company's constitution may obtain a negotiating advantage through awareness of the company's internal power dynamics, or, on the other hand, may be wary of entering into negotiations at all with such a company. Such companies would prefer not to have to disclose all their decision-making procedures by placing them in the constitution. An alternative is to place such provisions not in the constitution but in a separate contract entered into between the shareholders which does not have to be publicly disclosed. This agreement is known as a shareholders' agreement. A shareholders' agreement may be between a few or all of the company's shareholders. It is very common for sophisticated shareholders to use shareholders' agreements, particularly where the shareholders are several companies entering into a joint venture.

It is not uncommon, in particular where all the shareholders are parties to the shareholders agreement, for the company also to be a party to the agreement. Where this is the case the legal status of a shareholders' agreement is very similar to the corporate constitution, namely a contract between the shareholders themselves and between the shareholders and the company. Importantly, this contract is not subject to any of the restrictions on enforcement previously outlined. It is a contract that can clearly be enforced by any party to the agreement regardless of whether enforcement affects the members' rights qua member or in another capacity and without regard to the dichotomy

---

[46] Company Law Review, *Final Report*, para 7.34.

[47] If the loss is a 'reflective loss' the shareholder will not be able to claim damages in relation to such loss. See Chapter 15.

[48] Section 18(2) CA 2006 requiring that the original articles are registered with Companies House (unless the Model Articles are adopted) and section 26 CA 2006 requiring that amendments to the articles are filed within 15 days of the amendment.

[49] www.companieshouse.gov.uk/ .

of individually enforceable personal rights and unenforceable internal irregularities. In contrast to the constitution a shareholders' agreement, unless the agreement provides otherwise, cannot be amended without the approval of all the parties to the contract.

An important issue that arises from the use of shareholders' agreements is the inter-relationship between the provisions of the agreement and company law and the corporate constitution respectively. What occurs where a provision in the constitution is contrary to a provision of the shareholders' agreement? What is the status of the agreement when the agreement binds the shareholders to do something that company law provides the company cannot do, or not to do something that company law says the company can always do? For example, as we shall see in Chapter 6, a director of a company can always be removed by an ordinary resolution of shareholders in general meeting without any reason for removal having to be provided.[50] What would the status then be of a term in a shareholders' agreement that bound shareholders never to use their voting power to remove a particular director? These issues were addressed by the House of Lords in *Russell v Northern Bank*.

■ *Russell v Northern Bank Development Corp Ltd* [1992] BCLC 1016

The Tyrone Brick Limited Company (TBL) was owned by its four executive managers (20 shares each) and the Northern Bank Development Corporation (120 shares). All shareholders of the company as well as the company itself[51] entered into a shareholders' agreement (the Agreement), that provided the following provisions:

> '1. The terms of this Agreement shall have precedence between the shareholders over the Articles of Association and the parties agree to do, execute and perform such further acts, deeds, resolutions, consents, documents and things as may be necessary to give effect to this clause. Where the Articles of Association are silent on any matter, the provisions of this Agreement shall operate between the parties. Where there is conflict between the provisions of this Agreement and the Articles of Association the parties hereto shall cooperate where necessary to have the Articles amended from time to time to take account of the provisions of this Agreement and any subsequent consequential changes. Where this Agreement requires any future action to be taken by the Board of Directors or by the members of the company the shareholders as such shareholders or as the parties entitled to nominate the Board of Directors of the Company will co-operate and do all such things as are necessary to implement such future action.
>
> 2. The provisions of this Agreement shall not be amended without the written consent of each of the parties hereto.
>
> 3. No further share capital shall be created or issued in the Company or the rights attaching to the shares already in issue in any way altered (save as is herein set out) or any Share Transfer of the existing Shares permitted, save in the following manner, without the written consent of each of the parties hereto.'

Even though the Agreement provided in clause 3 that the company would not create or issue any further share capital, the company called a general meeting at which a resolution was to be proposed to increase the share capital of the company. One of the shareholders, Mr Russell, brought an action requiring that the other parties to the shareholders' agreement be restrained from voting their shares in favour of the resolution. The first instance court and the Northern Ireland Court of Appeal dismissed the application holding that the provision improperly fettered the powers of the company to raise capital.[52] The claimant appealed to the House of Lords.

---

[50] Section 168 CA 2006.

[51] The company itself failed to execute the agreement but was held to be bound by it.

[52] Art 131 of the Companies (Northern Ireland) Order 1986, SI 1986/1032 providing for the increase of a company's share capital.

Lord Jauncey of Tullichettle

My Lords, while a provision in a company's articles which restricts its statutory power to alter those articles is invalid an agreement dehors the articles between shareholders as to how they shall exercise their voting rights on a resolution to alter the articles is not necessarily so... Shareholders may lawfully agree inter se to exercise their voting rights in a manner which, if it were dictated by the articles, and were thereby binding on the company, would be unlawful.

I turn to examine the agreement in more detail. It appears from the narrative clauses that the agreement was intended to regulate the relationship between the shareholders with regard to the management and control of TBL. Clause 1 provides that the terms of the agreement was intended to regulate the relationship between the shareholders with regard to the management and control of TBL. Clause 1 provides that the terms of the agreement shall have precedence between the shareholders over the articles of association. It further provides that where there is a conflict between the provisions of the agreement and the articles parties shall co-operate where necessary to have the articles amended to take account of the provisions of the agreement. It further provides that no further share capital shall be created or issued in TBL without the written consent of the parties to the agreement. TBL was incorporated under a previous name on 13 July 1979 and the agreement was executed on 14 December of that year. Since that date no attempt has been made to amend the articles for the purposes of clause 1, but I do not find that in anyway surprising because clause 3 affects only existing shareholders and does not purport to bind other persons who may at some future date become shareholders in TBL by allotment or transfer. Clause 3 at least so far as shareholders are concerned constitutes an agreement collateral to the provisions of Regulation 44 of Table A[53] and is, as MacDermott LJ has concluded, neither in substitution for nor in conflict with that regulation...

Turning back to clause 3 of the agreement it appears to me that its purpose was twofold. The shareholders agreed only to exercise their voting powers in relation to the creation or issue of shares in TBL if they and TBL agreed in writing. This agreement is purely personal to the shareholders who executed it and as I have already remarked does not purport to bind future shareholders... TBL on the other hand agreed that its capital would not be increased without the consent of each of the shareholders. This was a clear undertaking by TBL in a formal agreement not to exercise its statutory power for a period which could, certainly on one view of construction, last for as long as any one of the parties to the agreement remained a shareholder and long after the control of TBL had passed to shareholders who were not party to the agreement. As such an undertaking it is, in my view, as obnoxious as if it had been contained in the articles of association and therefore is unenforceable as being contrary to the provisions of article 131 of the Companies (Northern Ireland) Order 1986. TBL's undertaking is, however, independent of and severable from that of the shareholders and there is no reason why the latter should not be enforceable by the shareholders inter se as a personal agreement which in no way fetters TBL in the exercise of its statutory powers.

I would therefore allow the appeal.

The House of Lords held that to the extent that a provision in the shareholders' agreement purports to prevent the company from exercising its available rights the provision is unenforceable. Their Lordships, however, held that as far as the contractual relationship between the shareholders was concerned, as to how they exercise their votes, the contract was enforceable. This would have enabled the claimant to have obtained an injunction preventing the shareholder-parties to the agreement from voting in favour of the resolution in question.[54]

---

[53] Regulation 44 of the applicable Table A provided that: 'The company may from time to time by ordinary resolution increase the share capital by such sum, to be divided into shares of such amount, as the resolution shall prescribe.'

[54] During the course of the proceedings it became apparent that the claimant only wished to obtain a declaration as to the enforceability of the shareholders' agreement and did not actually object to the increase in share capital, accordingly no such injunction was issued.

Questions

1. What is the purpose and function of a constitution?

2. What is the purpose and function of a corporate constitution?

3. What is the difference between a mandatory and a default rule? What is the regulatory policy behind using default rules? How does one determine whether a rule set forth in the Companies Act 2006 is a mandatory or a default rule?

4. Does it make sense to understand the constitution in contractual terms? For all types of company?

5. What is the contractarian understanding of company law and the company's constitution?

6. Is there a tension between the constitution as constitution and constitution as contract? Do the rules on when shareholders can enforce the contract address this tension?

7. What is the legal status of the constitution and who can enforce it?

B THE MECHANICS OF THE GENERAL MEETING

This section of the book aims to provide the student of company law with the basic vocabulary and mechanics of the shareholder meeting. Students may find this section rather technical; however, it is necessary for any student of company law to pay close attention to these basic rules and vocabulary. They represent some of the key building blocks for the rest of the book.

I HOW DO MEMBERS ACT?

1 Resolutions

The Companies Act 2006 provides that the members of a company are: the subscribers to the company's memorandum on formation, as well as any other persons who agree to become a member of the company *and* whose name is entered in the register of members.[55] The 2006 Act also provides for how the members shall act: they act by passing a resolution.

The Act provides that if the company is a private company a resolution may be passed either by passing a written resolution in accordance with the Act; or by passing a resolution in a duly convened members meeting, known as a *general meeting*. If the company is a public company then resolutions may only be passed at a duly convened meeting.[56] There are two types of resolution that can be passed at a shareholder meeting: the ordinary and the special resolution. The ordinary resolution requires a simple majority of the votes cast at the meeting;[57] a special resolution requires 75% of the votes cast.[58] Note, these percentages are of the votes cast, not of all the issued voting shares.

In relation to different types of corporate action, the Act specifies the nature of the resolution that must be passed for the members to act. We saw in Part A of this chapter that a special resolution is required to amend the constitution. Special resolutions are also required, for example, to waive the shareholder's rights to buy a portion of newly issued shares equal to their existing shareholding (pre-emption rights).[59] There are no specified criteria which determine when a resolution should be a special resolution or a less demanding ordinary resolution. However, as we saw in our discussion of amending

---

[55] Section 112 CA 2006.   [56] Section 281 CA 2006.   [57] Section 282 CA 2006.
[58] Section 283 CA 2006.   [59] See further Chapter 17.

the constitution, a special resolution is often associated with the perceived importance of the corporate action in question. Where a shareholder's resolution is required by the Act, but the Act does not specify what type of resolution, the resolution required is an ordinary resolution unless the company's constitution specifies a higher voting threshold.[60]

In order to facilitate decision-making in small private companies without having to call a meeting to pass a resolution, the Act provides for a written resolution procedure for private companies. Importantly, the required voting thresholds for an ordinary or special resolution passed by written resolution are not determined by reference to the votes cast for or against the resolution, but rather by reference to the issued voting shares.[61] The Act provides for a detailed procedure[62] for implementing a written resolution including, amongst others: rules on notification of the proposed resolution by the company to the shareholders;[63] procedures on signifying agreement with the proposed resolution by the shareholders;[64] and the time periods within which the resolution must be passed or lapse.[65]

2 Shareholder meetings

Shareholders in a private company can act through written resolution or by passing a resolution in a duly convened meeting of the shareholders. Note that a written resolution of a private company is treated *as if* it was passed in general meeting.[66] Shareholders in a public company can only act in a shareholder meeting. A shareholders' meeting is known as *the general meeting*. The general meeting is the space where shareholders come together to act. The general meeting is an organ of the company, although it is noteworthy that nowhere in the Act does the Act explicitly provide for the status of the general meeting in such terms.

Public companies are required to hold a general meeting known as an 'annual general meeting' or AGM.[67] Private companies are not required to hold an AGM although they were previously required to do so under the Companies Act 1985.[68] Although AGMs are typically, as their name suggests, held annually, the Act provides some flexibility regarding timing, which may mean that the period between AGMs exceeds 12 months.[69] All other meetings are known simply as general meetings.

Under the Companies Act 1985 a distinction was made between AGMs and extraordinary general meetings, EGMs. The extraordinary nature of these meetings was simply that they were interim meetings held between annual general meetings, which all

---

[60] Section 281(3) CA 2006.

[61] Sections 282(2), 283(2), and 289 CA 2006. Note that it is not possible to use a written resolution to remove a director pursuant to section 168 CA 2006 or an auditor pursuant to section 510 CA 2006 (section 288(2) CA 2006).

[62] Part 13; Chapter 2 CA 2006.   [63] Section 293 CA 2006.

[64] Section 296 CA 2006: the agreement must be set forth in a document sent to the company in hard copy form or electronically.

[65] An acceptance time period may be specified in the company's articles; if none is specified the resolution must be passed in 28 days or it will lapse—section 297 CA 2006. Any agreement signified after lapse is ineffective.

[66] Section 288(5) CA 2006.   [67] Section 336 CA 2006.

[68] Note that a private company that is a 'traded' company must also hold an annual general meeting' (section 336(1A) CA 2006). A traded company is defined in section 360C CA 2006 as a company that is admitted to trading on a regulated market in the EEA. On regulated markets see further Web Chapter B. Note that to be admitted to the Main Market of the London Stock Exchange (a regulated EEA market) the company must be a public company.

[69] The Act provides that the AGM must be held within the six-month period following the anniversary of the company's accounting reference date: section 336(1). A company's accounting reference date is defined in section 391 CA 2006 and is typically a date specified by the company of between 12 and 18 months following the date of its incorporation. Section 391 also sets forth rules for companies incorporated prior to the 2006 Act.

companies were required to hold. Now that AGMs are not required for private companies there may be no AGM that renders the other meetings 'extraordinary'; hence the reference in the 2006 Act to any meeting that is not an AGM as simply a 'general meeting'.

The 2006 Act provides for a set of mandatory rules on the calling of general meetings. Meetings may be called by the directors of their own volition[70] or by directors when required to do so by the requisite percentage of the shareholder body as required by the Act.[71] The rules on when shareholders can demand that the directors call a general meeting are considered in depth in Chapter 6, as they form an important part of the structure of the balance of power between the shareholder body and the board of directors.

The Act provides for a set of core mandatory rules surrounding the procedure for holding meetings. These include rules on: the notice periods necessary for the calling of meetings—generally 14 days and 21 days for a public company's AGM;[72] the contents of the notice of meetings—in essence time, date, and business to be transacted;[73] minimum rules on the number of members that need to attend a meeting for it to be quorate and to be able to act—one for a one-person company, two otherwise;[74] the appointment of a chairman of the meeting;[75] and voting procedures, which are considered in more detail in the next section. These basic rules are supplemented by a company's articles of association. Consult the Model Articles for Public and Private Companies in this regard, which devote several sections to general meeting procedure addressing, amongst others, attendance and speaking at meeting and meeting adjournments.[76]

Finally, the Act also requires that a 'minute'—a written record—of the meeting be kept.[77] This minute must provide a record of the meeting's proceedings which will include a record of the resolutions which were passed at the general meeting. These minutes must be kept by the company for at least 10 years[78] and must be made available for inspection.[79]

3 Voting at general meetings

At a general meeting the proposed resolutions on the agenda will be proposed to the meeting. A discussion of the issues relating to the agenda item will then take place and shareholders will be entitled to speak and voice their views on the agenda item.[80] At some point during the course of the discussion the chairman of the meeting will propose that the matter be put to a vote. There are two ways in which the vote can be effected—either by a show of hands or by a poll. A show of hands is the most efficient way of effecting business. The shareholders, and any person holding a proxy from a shareholder,[81] will vote by raising their hand for or against the proposed resolution, and the number of hands will be counted. As everyone—for voting purposes—only has one hand, regardless of whether a participant at the meeting has one voting share or a million voting shares, on a show of hands each participant has equal voting power.[82] Voting by a show of hands is typically a meeting's default voting arrangement[83] because it is the most effective way of addressing non-contentious agenda items. However, if the

[70] Section 302 CA 2006.   [71] Section 303 CA 2006: 5% of the company's voting capital.
[72] Private companies: section 307(1) CA 2006; public companies: section 307(2) CA 2006.
[73] Section 311 CA 2006.   [74] Section 318 CA 2006.   [75] Section 319 CA 2006.
[76] See, for example, Part 3 of the Model Articles for Public Companies.
[77] Section 355 CA 2006.   [78] Section 355(2) CA 2006.   [79] Section 358 CA 2006.
[80] Articles 29 and 40 of the Model Articles on Public and Private Companies, respectively.
[81] Section 285 CA 2006.   [82] Section 284(2) CA 2006.
[83] For example, article 34 of the Model Articles for Public Companies provides that 'a resolution put to the vote of a general meeting must be decided on a show of hands unless a poll is taken on it in accordance with the articles'.

issue is contentious amongst the shareholder body then the shareholders holding the required majority of voting shares would not find it acceptable that the matter be settled on a show of hands where the number of hands that pass or reject a resolution hold a minority of the voting shares. Clearly, if all a company's business was transacted on a show of hands the votes attached to shares would be worthless and would function only as an entry ticket to the general meeting. Unsurprisingly, therefore, the Companies Act 2006 and the Model Articles provide for a vote by poll, where each vote attached to each share may be cast for or against the resolution.

The Companies Act 2006 protects the shareholders' right to transact business in the general meeting through a poll. Section 321 of the Act renders void any provision in a company's articles of association that purports to deny shareholders a right to demand a poll. There are two exceptions to this rule. A company's constitution may deny the shareholders the right to demand a poll in relation to a vote to elect a chairman of the meeting and in relation to a vote on the adjournment of the meeting. Furthermore, section 321 of the Act protects the right to vote by poll by providing, in effect, mandatory minimum poll calling rules. This means that a poll can always be demanded by either: (1) five shareholders; (2) shareholders holding 10% of the voting capital; or (3) shareholders holding voting shares where the amount **paid-up** on those shares is equal to 10% of the aggregate amount paid-up on the company's shares. A company's articles[84] could provide for more liberal poll-calling rules—such as a lower number of shareholders or a lower percentage of voting shares, but to *the extent to which* a company's articles impose more restrictive rules, the rules are void.

The vote, whether by a show of hands or by a poll, takes place at the meeting. *Only* the participants at the meeting can vote. That does not mean that only shareholders who attend the meeting in person can vote. A member may vote in person or may appoint *a proxy* to vote on his or her behalf. A proxy is a person to whom the shareholder has granted the right to attend and speak at the meeting on the shareholder's behalf and to exercise the votes held by the shareholder.

In large listed companies that have thousands of shareholders, only a small fraction of the shareholder body will actually attend the meeting in person. Most shareholders, if they vote at all, will vote via a proxy. Such shareholders, if they wish, can appoint their own proxies[85] or, as is more typical, will accept the company's offer to appoint a company representative to act as the shareholder's proxy. Large companies typically offer their shareholders several ways of appointing the company-designated person as proxy. Vodafone Plc, for example, offers shareholders the ability to appoint a proxy electronically or by ordinary mail.[86] An appointed proxy may be given the freedom to decide how to vote at the meeting by the shareholder; however, where the company provides for a company designated person to act as a proxy, the shareholder will be asked to indicate how the appointed proxy should cast the vote—for, against, or abstention from each resolution. The form given to shareholders to appoint a proxy with these three options is known as a three-way proxy.[87]

---

[84] Article 36 of the Model Articles for Public Companies provides that a poll may be demanded by: (i) the chairman of the meeting; (ii) the directors; (iii) two or more persons who are entitled to vote; or (iv) one or more persons holding one-tenth or more of the company's voting capital.

[85] Section 324 CA 2006 provides a right to appoint a proxy. If a shareholder appoints her own proxy, obviously the company will need proof that the proxy has been validly granted. Section 327 of the 2006 Act sets forth rules on the minimum amount of time prior to the meeting that a company must receive the proxy documentation in order for the proxy to participate and vote at the meeting.

[86] www.vodafone.com/ ●.

[87] For listed companies the UK Listing Authority's Listing Rules provide that where it provides a proxy form to its shareholders it must be a three-way proxy form (for–against–abstention). Where the shareholder grants a proxy but makes no voting indication the appointed proxy may vote as she sees fit (LR 9.3.6(2) and (4)).

In recent years there has been a strong Government-led drive to encourage shareholders to actually vote, whether in person or by proxy. Historically voting by shareholders in large listed companies has been very low, even where the shares are owned by large **institutional investors** whose portfolio is managed by well-trained and sophisticated **fund managers**. There are several reasons for this apathy which we shall explore in depth in Chapter 6. For now it is worth noting that in recent years voting by shareholders has increased notably. This is viewed in part as a result of governmental pressure to vote, but also as a result of the increasing availability of appointing a proxy electronically.[88]

One of the factors that is often referred to by commentators as *one* of the causes of historically low voter turnout in UK company general meetings is the commonly used practical arrangements for holding and trading shares in listed UK companies. These arrangements result in the legal ownership of the shares being separated from the beneficial ownership. These arrangements and their relationship to how shares are bought and sold in large UK companies are not addressed in any detail in this book. For the leading account and analysis of these rules the reader is referred to Chapter 27 of *Gower and Davies' Principles of Modern Company Law*. For our purposes we restrict ourselves to the following observations. First, shares are often held by a legal **custodian** on behalf of the investor. The legal custodian is the shareholder of record and is the shareholder entered on the company's register of members.[89] As the registered shareholder, the legal custodian is entitled to receive notice of general meetings and to vote the shares, but as the legal and not the beneficial owner of the shares the legal custodian has no interest in the economic well-being of the company or, therefore, in exercising an informed vote.

In order to empower the beneficial owner (the institutional investor) or its representative (the fund manager), the legal custodian could appoint the institutional investor or the fund manager as its proxy with, if necessary, the right to grant a further proxy, and forward all company communications onto the proxy. Whilst in practice this occurred,[90] it was viewed as cumbersome and as creating an obstacle to voting. To address this problem the Companies Act 2006 creates another category of 'voter' apart from member and proxy. Pursuant to section 145 of the Act, a company may in its articles of association permit a member to nominate another person to enjoy and exercise all the specified rights associated with membership. The Act makes this nomination option available to all companies and then provides a set of rights for the nominated person, for example the right to receive copies of company communications to members. These information rights, however, only apply to nominees of listed company shareholders.[91]

II SHAREHOLDER ACTION THROUGH INFORMAL CONSENT

As we have seen, the Companies Act 2006 provides for shareholders to take action through resolutions that are passed in general meeting. Even where the Act provides for written resolutions for private companies, such resolutions are treated *as if* they were passed in general meeting.[92] Pursuant to the Companies Act, therefore, it is not sufficient for the shareholders of a company to agree to a course of action or to say they agree. Such agreement must take place in a general meeting or for a private company through a written resolution which is treated as the product of a de facto general meeting.

---

[88] See *Myners Review of Impediments to Voting UK Shares: Progress One Year On* (2005).

[89] For a more complex overview of the participants in the voting process in listed companies see the *Myners Review of Impediments to Voting UK Shares* (2004) section 2.2.

[90] For an excellent discussion in this regard see R.C. Nolan, 'Indirect Investors: A Greater Say in the Company?' (2003) *Journal of Corporate Law Studies* 73.

[91] The provisions only apply to companies traded on a regulated market such as the London Stock Exchange—sections 146–150 CA 2006.

[92] Section 288(5) CA 2006.

As we have seen, all companies have two primary organs through which they act: the board of directors and the general meeting. In small, **close companies** the same individual persons will be members of both bodies. In some cases the company may only have one director and one shareholder. However, even where the members of both organs are the same individuals, it is important that the formalities of corporate action are still observed: although a meeting of the board of directors may involve the same individual persons as a general meeting, a meeting of the board of directors of the company *is not* a general meeting. Corporate formalities need to be followed to ensure the validity of corporate action. The different organs of the company need to be paid due respect and the *manager–director–members* of the company should not act as if the respective organs did not exist. Following such formalities is not, in practice, a problem, although it may seem a little odd to the uninitiated. It involves clarifying that a meeting is a board meeting or a general meeting before proceeding to consider, pass, and then minute the respective resolution.[93] These formalities should always be followed. This is the advice that a lawyer should always give in the first instance to his corporate client if they ask 'do we really need to follow the formalities of calling a general meeting or a board meeting now?'

However, whilst following the requisite formalities is a reasonable expectation of the members of the company's organs, in practice such formalities may not always be followed. Individuals who set up small companies may simply not understand what it means to follow the formalities associated with corporate action. As far as some such individuals are concerned 'they are the company' and what 'they decide is company action', regardless of whether the requisite meeting is formally called and the discussion and resolutions minuted. Other individuals may be aware of and understand corporate formalities but succumb to shortcuts and bad habits as a result of the pressures of running a small business. The result of this ignorance or of these shortcuts is that the action that the parties think has been taken may not in fact have been taken because the corporate organ in question has not formally taken the action. If, for example, the articles require general meeting approval of any remuneration paid to the board members but the general meeting has not considered or approved of paid remuneration, even though the same individuals who are shareholders sat in a room together *as a board meeting* to award that remuneration, the payment of remuneration is *formally* unlawful. If a director has breached his duty but the shareholders say 'don't worry about it' but do not call a general meeting to formally ratify the breach, then the breach has not formally been ratified and continues *formally* to expose a director to suit. The question for company law is whether, given the likelihood that such poor practice will take place, it should insist upon following formalities and force the parties to bear the consequences of not following formality, or should it recognize that in practice these things will occur and accept some forms of informal decision-making? The latter approach would of course encourage more bad practice but would ensure that legal formality does not generate injustice. As we shall see, the courts have taken the latter approach.

■ *Re Duomatic* [1969] 1 All ER 161

This case involved a challenge by a liquidator of an insolvent company, Duomatic Ltd, to several payments made to directors—Mr Elvins and Mr East—over a two-year period. According to the company's constitution such payments required the approval of the general meeting but no such approval had been given.

---

[93] Where all members of the respective organs are present any notice requirements for the meetings can be waived: *Re Oxted Motor Co* [1921] All ER Rep 646.

Buckley J

Duomatic was incorporated in January 1960, and from about the time when it commenced business its directors were a Mr Elvins...and a Mr East. At that time the issued share capital of the company consisted of 100 ordinary shares and 80,000 non-voting redeemable preference shares, all of £1. The ordinary shares were held as to [98] by Mr Elvins...and as to two by Mr East. The non-voting preference shares were held by some other gentleman whom I will call the preference shareholder...

The affairs of this company seem to have been conducted with extreme informality. There was never any resolution passed determining that any of the directors should receive any remuneration, or at any rate no resolution was ever passed authorising the directors to receive any remuneration in respect of the periods with which I am concerned, which are, the year ended 30 April 1963, the year ended 30 April 1964, and the period from 1 May 1964 to 23 October 1964, when the company went into voluntary liquidation...

It is common ground that none of the sums which I have mentioned were authorised by any resolution of the company in general meeting, nor were they authorised by any resolution of any formally constituted board meeting; but it is said...that the payments were made with the full knowledge and consent of all the holders of voting shares in the company at the relevant times, and he contends that in those circumstances the absence of a formal resolution by the company in duly convened meeting of the company is irrelevant....

In support of the first part of his argument [defendant] counsel...has relied on two authorities. The first was *Re Express Engineering Works, Ltd* ([1920] 1 Ch 466). There five persons formed a private company in which they were the sole shareholders, and they sold to it for £15,000, which was in fact secured by debentures of the company, property which they had, a few days before, acquired for £7,000. The contract for sale to the company and the issue of debentures was carried out at a meeting of the five individuals, who thereupon appointed themselves directors of the company. That meeting was described in the books of the company as a board meeting. The articles forbade any director to vote in respect of any contract or arrangement in which he might be interested; and in a winding-up of the company the liquidator claimed that the issue of the debentures was invalid. In the Court of Appeal it was held, there being no suggestion of fraud, that the company was bound in a matter intra vires by the unanimous agreement of its members...

In *Parker and Cooper Ltd v Reading*, ([1926] Ch 984) the second case relied on by [defendant] counsel..., the directors of a company had created a **debenture** and proceedings were commenced to establish that the debenture and the resolution which authorised its issue and the appointment of a certain **receiver** under it were invalid. The case was tried by Astbury J, who referred to *Re Express Engineering Works*...and himself expressed this view:

> 'Now the view I take of both these decisions is that where the transaction is intra vires and honest, and especially if it is for the benefit of the company, it cannot be upset if the assent of all the corporators is given to it. I do not think it matters in the least whether that assent is given at different times or simultaneously.'

So that the effect of his judgment was to carry the position a little further than it had been carried in the *Express Engineering Works* case, for Astbury J, expressed the view that it was immaterial that the assent of the corporators was obtained at different times, and that it was not necessary that there should be a meeting of them all at which they gave their consent to the particular transaction sought to be upheld. In that case also, as in the *Express Engineering Works* case, no question arose about the position of any shareholders whose shares conferred no right of attending or voting at general meetings of the company.

Counsel for the liquidator in the present application, has contended that, where there has been no formal meeting of the company and reliance is placed on the informal consent of the shareholders, the cases indicate that it is necessary to establish that all shareholders have consented, and he says that as the preference shareholder is not shown to have consented in the present case that requirement is not satisfied and the assent of those shareholders—that is to say,

Mr Elvins and Mr East—who knew about these matters, and who did approve the figures relating to them in the accounts for the year ending 30 April 1963, is of no significance. It seems to me that if it had occurred to Mr Elvins and Mr East, at the time when they were considering the accounts, to take the formal step of constituting themselves a general meeting of the company and passing a formal resolution approving the payment of directors' salaries, that would have made the position of the directors—that is to say, Mr Elvins and Mr Hanley—who received the remuneration, secure, and nobody could thereafter have disputed their right to retain their remuneration. The fact that they did not take that formal step but that they nevertheless did apply their minds to the question of whether the drawings by Mr Elvins and Mr Hanley should be approved, as being on account of remuneration payable to them as directors, seems to me to lead to the conclusion that I ought to regard their consent as being tantamount to a resolution of a general meeting of the company. In other words, I proceed on the basis that where it can be shown that all shareholders who have a right to attend and vote at a general meeting of the company assent to some matter which a general meeting of the company could carry into effect, that assent is as binding as a resolution in general meeting would be. The preference shareholder having shares which conferred on him no right to receive notice of or to attend and vote at a general meeting of the company could be in no worse position if the matter were dealt with informally by agreement between all the shareholders having voting rights than he would be if the shareholders met together in a duly constituted general meeting.

The principle set out in this case has become known as the *Re Duomatic* rule or principle. However, as we see from this extract, it has a longer heritage in English law. The principle is straightforward: provided that all[94] the shareholders have indicated their consent to the action in question then even though a resolution was not passed at a duly convened general meeting the assent of the shareholders will be treated by the courts as a resolution passed in general meeting. This applies not only to approvals required by the constitution, but also to ratifications of breach of duty[95] or statutory required approvals, such as an amendment to the constitution.[96]

There are four aspects of the rules that need to be stressed. First, the consent that is required is the consent of all the shareholders who have the right to attend a general meeting and vote at a general meeting—the non-voting shareholders do not count in this regard. Secondly, regarding the nature of the consent it is clear that informal consent given orally or by implication through conduct is sufficient. However, in *Rolfe v Rolfe*, Newey J held that such consent must involve an 'outward manifestation or acquiescence' by the shareholder and must be objectively verifiable.[97] Thirdly, although such consent could be given by the shareholders at the same time—for example if all

---

[94] *Cane v Jones* [1981] 1 All ER 533, *per* Michael Wheeler QC: 'it is a basic principle of company law that all the corporators, acting together, can do anything which is intra vires the company'. See also *Re Bailey, Hay & Co Ltd* [1971] 3 All ER 693, *per* Brightman J: 'it is established law that a company is bound, in a matter intra vires the company, by the unanimous agreement of all its corporators.'

[95] *Bankgesellschaft Berlin AG (formerly Berliner Bank AG) v Makris* [1999] All ER (D) 56, *per* Cresswell J: 'whether breaches of fiduciary duty are capable of being ratified by ordinary resolution or only by special resolution, they can always be ratified by the consent of all members…the consent of all the members can be given by means of informal meetings—*Gore-Browne* 21.2; *Re Duomatic Ltd* [1969] 2 Ch 365.'

[96] It only applies to approvals given whilst the company is solvent: *Lexi Holdings plc (in administration) v Luqman* [2007] EWHC 2652 (Ch); *West Mercia Safetywear Ltd v Dodd* [1988] BCLC 250; *Precision Dippings Ltd v Precision Dippings Marketing Ltd* [1985] BCLC 385.

[97] [2010] EWHC 244 (Ch). With regard to the objective test Newey J held that: 'in my judgment, there must be material from which an observer could discern or (as in the case of acquiescence) infer assent.' See also *Schofield v Schofield* [2011] EWCA Civ 154 where the Court of Appeal approved of the position articulated by Newey J observing that (*per* Etherton LJ) 'nothing short of unqualified agreement, objectively established, will suffice'.

the shareholders indicated their consent whilst acting as directors in a board meeting—they may also give that consent at different times.[98] Fourthly, the fact that the consent is given in a different capacity—for example in a board meeting—is irrelevant: what matters is that consent was given.[99]

Online Resource Centre
http://www.oxfordtextbooks.co.uk/orc/kershaw2e/

Visit the Online Resource Centre for additional resources and information available for this chapter, including web links and an interactive flashcard glossary.

---

[98] *EIC Services Ltd v Phipps* [2003] EWCH 1507 *per* Neuberger J observing 'whether members of the group give their consent in different ways or at different times does not matter'.

[99] *Multinational Gas and Petrochemical Co v Multinational Gas and Petrochemical Services Ltd* [1983] 2 All ER 563, Dillon LJ observed that: 'it matters not that these meetings were called board meetings, rather than general meetings of the plaintiff...It would equally matter not if the decisions were made by all the shareholders informally and without any meeting at all.'

CHAPTER FOUR

CORPORATE ACTIONS

I INTRODUCTION

An individual person, such as Bob from our case study, is free to set up any type of business as a sole trader provided that he can raise the finance to start the business and that he complies with any applicable external regulations such as obtaining licences where required or complying with health and safety standards. If he sets up Bob's Electronics as a sole trader then Bob, the individual person, is the firm through which the business is conducted. If the business is successful and generates funds, he could, without restriction, decide to invest the generated funds not in the expansion of his build-to-order computer business but in setting up an organic baby food company or a clothing company. There are no limits on Bob-the-individual's/Bob-the-firm's capacity *as a sole trader* to enter into any business area, provided that he complies with the regulatory requirements of that business area.

As a sole trader Bob *is* the nexus of contracts between the inputs of labour, finance, and components, and the outputs of computers sold to customers. In relation to each of these contractual relationships it is Bob, the individual, who agrees to be bound by each contract and, as a sane adult, there are no restrictions upon his ability to bind himself to those contractual obligations. In relation to the obligations created by each contract there is no question that he can incur debt, employ a person or agree to buy property etc.

Contract is at the heart of any business activity. The dominant encounter of any business with law will be with the realm of contract law. The business will, however, throughout its life have other regular and sporadic encounters with other legal realms. If the operation of the business results in injury to customers or others then the business will be faced with claims based on tort law and possibly criminal law. If the products are not compliant with applicable regulatory standards then the business will encounter regulatory agencies who enforce those standards and impose fines. If Bob runs the business as a sole trader then the claims made against the business in tort, or a prosecution for manslaughter, or a regulatory enforcement action will be made against him personally. Clearly Bob, the real person, is capable of committing a tort, or being vicariously liable for his employees' torts, or committing a crime or a regulatory offence.

If the business of Bob's Electronics is carried out through a company rather than as a sole trader then answering the questions about what types of business can be engaged in and how the company acts is more difficult. Whereas an individual such as Bob can enter any business he chooses, is that true for a company? Does the fact that a company is a legal person give it the same flexibility that a real person would have with regard to the types of business it engages in? Questions about how a company acts are even more difficult. A real person has a body and a mind which, tongue in cheek, we might say represents itself: expresses itself; gives its opinion; agrees to be bound; hurts somebody; kills somebody. A company is a legal person not a real person. A company is real and tangible through the things it does—the people it employs; the contracts it enters into—and the things it owns—the office building with its name on the door; the computers with its name on the box. But such tangible facets of a company's existence beg the question: how does it enter into contracts; how does it become the owner of the office building? The company is a legal person that has specified organs through which it acts—the board of directors and the general meeting—but do these organs of the company have the same flexibility and freedom to enter into contracts as a real person would have? And if the company acts through organs and not real persons, is it possible for the company to commit a tort or indeed a crime, areas of regulation which are quintessentially designed to regulate our interaction as individuals?

There are then two questions for us to answer in this chapter. The first question is what is a company, such as Bob's Electronics Ltd, capable of doing: is it restricted, as compared to a real person, in its capacity to do certain things, to enter into certain business areas? If there are such 'capacity restrictions' then where do we find them and what are the legal implications of the company transgressing these restrictions? The second question is: how does the company incur legal obligations—in contract, in tort, and in crime? The first of these questions—the capacity question—will be dealt with in section II; contract, tort, and crime will then be addressed in the subsequent sections.

II CAPACITY

When we ask the question 'what is the company's capacity?' it could be referring to several different things: does a computer company, for example, have the capacity to enter into the business world of organic baby food; or does a company have the capacity to enter in certain contracts, commit certain torts or crimes? In English company law the concept of a 'company's capacity' is used to refer to the former of these two options: the extent to which the company is, or is not, limited in the areas of our life and business worlds in which it can operate.

What a company can or cannot do is set out in a company's constitution. The specific part of the constitution that addresses what type of activity the company can carry out is known as the *objects clause*. Prior to the coming into force of the 2006 Companies Act every company was required to have an objects clause which was set out in the company's memorandum of association.[1] Today, as a UK company has one primary constitutional document, the objects clause would be set out in the articles of association.[2] However, as we shall see, it is no longer necessary to include such a clause in the constitution.

One narrative in the history of UK company law is of the diminishing importance of the objects clause. Upon the introduction of incorporation by registration the idea that the company should have strict limits on the types of activity that it could carry out was considered very important. Underpinning this idea was that exercising power through the corporate form ran certain risks for the public at large and that one of the ways in which the legislature managed these risks was to allow the corporate form to be used for the purposes it said it was going to be used for at the time of incorporation and for no other purposes. Accordingly, the early Companies Acts provided that the objects of the company must be set out in the memorandum and that the objects clause could not be subsequently amended. Lord Hatherley in *Ashbury Railway Carriage and Iron Company Limited v Riche*[3] eloquently explained these restrictions as follows:

> Your Lordships will find throughout the whole of the Act a plain and marked distinction drawn between the interest of the shareholders *inter se*, and the interest which the public have in seeing

---

[1] Section 2(c) CA 1985.

[2] On the transfer of provisions set forth in the memorandum of association into the articles of association under the 2006 Act see p 81.

[3] [1874–80] All ER Rep Ext 2219.

that the terms of the Act are construed in such a manner as to protect them in dealing with companies of this description. The mode of protection adopted seems to have been this: the Legislature said, you may meet altogether, and form yourselves into a company, but in doing that you must tell all who may be disposed to deal with you the objects for which you have been associated...You must state the amount of the capital which you are about to invest in it, and you must state the objects for which you are associated, so that the persons dealing with you will know that they are dealing with persons who can only devote their means to a given class of objects, and who are prohibited from devoting their means to any other purpose. Throughout the Act that purpose is apparent...It is provided that whatever other things you may do in the way of variation, a certain limited power of alteration being given to you, no such power shall you have as to the objects specified in the memorandum of association.

Accordingly, under this legal regime, a company could neither make an investment in any business area outside of its objects clause nor change the objects clause to permit such an investment. If it entered into contracts in an alternative business area beyond its objects those contracts would be void *ab initio*: invalid and unenforceable by either party. Such business activity in areas beyond the objects clause is *ultra vires*—beyond the powers—of the company. As the company did not have the capacity to enter into those contracts the contract never came into existence.

These rules created two problems. First, the rules preventing the alteration of a company's objects increased the costs of doing business where the company wanted to legitimately diversify. To do so would require the setting up and running of a separate company. Secondly, the *ultra vires* rule introduced considerable uncertainty into the business world: if a company entering into a contract did not have the capacity to enter into it then a third party would not be able to enforce the contract if the company failed to perform. This left third parties with the choice of either incurring costs in reading and analysing each counterparty company's constitution or taking some risk that the contract would be unenforceable.

Gradually the law has responded to both of these problems. The endpoint of a long and incremental regulatory reform process, which was finally reached on the enactment of the 2006 Act, is that these restrictions on the company's capacity are no longer of any consequence for third parties and need not be, at the company's election, of any consequence for the company itself. Accordingly, we deal with the developments very briefly.

The first reforms enabled the objects to be amended, however, only for the reasons specified in the Companies Act and only then with a special resolution subject to a right of objection for minority shareholders.[4] The next stage of reform resulted in abolishing the requirement that the amendment must be made for one of the reasons specified in the Act. Amendment could then take place with only a special resolution; however, minority shareholders holding in aggregate 15% of the issued share capital still had the right to bring an action asking the court to cancel the amendment.[5] Today, pursuant to section 21 of the Companies Act 2006, the objects clause can be amended by special resolution and the shareholders do not have a specific right to apply to court to have the objects amendment cancelled.

In relation to the *ultra vires* rule, over the past century there have been two responses: a private, self-ordering response from companies and an incremental legislative response. The self-ordering response was to draft exceptionally broad objects clauses, which

---

[4] Section 5 Companies Act 1948. Such reasons included, for example, 'to carry on its business more economically or efficiently' or 'to enlarge or change the local area of its operation'. See further the 1948 Act at www.opsi.gov.uk/ 🌐.

[5] Sections 4–6 Companies Act 1985.

included every object imaginable and every power imaginable to pursue those objects. Such clauses, when well drafted, ensured that companies could enter any business area whatsoever, and as these clauses were widely used they gave third parties who did not incur the costs of analysing a company's constitution a reasonable amount of comfort that the contract would be enforceable. To get a flavour of such provisions consider the following three paragraphs of Vodafone Plc's objects clause, which consists in total of 24 similar paragraphs.

■ Vodafone Plc's Memorandum of Association[6]

4. *The objects for which the Company is established are:*

(1) To carry on the business of a holding company in all its branches, and for that purpose to acquire and hold for investment shares, stock, debentures and debenture stock, bonds, notes, obligations and securities issued or guaranteed by any company, and debentures, debenture stock, bonds, notes, obligations and securities issued or guaranteed by a government, sovereign ruler, commissioner, public body or authority, supreme, municipal, local or otherwise, whether at home or abroad, and to leave money on deposit or otherwise with any bank or building society, local authority or any other party and to act as and to perform all the functions of a holding company.

(2) To carry on business as dealers in, operators, manufacturers, repairers, designers, developers, importers and exporters of electronic, electrical, mechanical and aeronautical equipment of all types and of parts and accessories thereof and of plant and machinery of all descriptions, and to act as engineers' agents and merchants, and generally to undertake and execute agencies and commissions of any kind.

(3) To purchase, subscribe for, underwrite, take, or otherwise acquire and hold any shares, stock, bonds, options, debentures, debenture stock obligations or securities in or of any company, corporation, public body, supreme, municipal, local or otherwise or of any Government or State and to act as and perform all the functions of a holding company…

The intention is that the objects specified in each paragraph of this Clause, shall except where otherwise expressed in such paragraph, be independent main objects and be in no way limited or restricted by reference to or inference from the terms of any other paragraph.

The courts approved of such provisions even whilst they made a mockery of the supposed function, outlined by Lord Hatherley in the extract from *Ashbury Railway v Riche*, of the objects clause.[7]

The legislative response to the *ultra vires* problem began in the 1970s and was finally completed by the 2006 Act. We are not going to concern ourselves with the intricacies of these incremental changes. There are two simple provisions of the 2006 Act that we need to know in this regard; two provisions that in effect consign the *ultra vires* problem to the legal history books. The first of these provisions was introduced by the Companies Act 1989 and is now set out in section 39(1) of the 2006 Act, which provides that:

The validity of an act done by a company shall not be called into question on the ground of lack of capacity by reason of anything in the company's constitution.

The effect of this provision is that where a company enters into an *ultra vires* transaction the contract is valid and enforceable. This provision overrides the common law rule that the contract would be void. This provision, therefore, abolishes the *ultra vires* rule as far as third parties doing business with the company are concerned. However, to the

---

[6] Vodafone Plc's Memorandum of Association as of 2009.
[7] *Cotman v Brougham* [1918] AC 514.

extent that the directors approve of such *ultra vires* activity they will be in breach of section 171(a) of the Companies Act 2006, which imposes a duty on directors to 'act in accordance with the company's constitution'. If they fail to do so and such failure results in financial loss for the company the directors may be personally liable to the company.

Prior to the introduction of section 39's predecessor—section 35 of the Companies Act 1985—the probability of there being an *ultra vires* contract was very low as the objects clauses of most companies would have been drafted very broadly, as described previously. In practice, *ultra vires* acts and litigation surrounding such acts involved companies that when they were formed did not obtain legal advice on drafting the objects clause and at a later date drifted into another, *ultra vires*, line of business.[8] Companies formed today will not be faced with this problem unless they actively create it for themselves. The reason for this is that section 31(1) of the 2006 Act provides that:

> Unless a company's articles specifically restrict the objects of the company, its objects are unrestricted.

Companies formed pursuant to the 2006 Act have unrestricted articles: they can engage in any business area without restriction. Such companies will only be subject to business area restrictions if the company's founders explicitly provide for such restrictions in the articles or if, subsequently, the shareholders by special resolution elect to impose such restrictions. The vast majority of companies will not do so. For a company with unrestricted objects there is no type of business activity or purpose that is beyond its objects; *in effect* they have the same unlimited capacity as a real person. For those companies that were formed prior to the Companies Act 2006 their constitution will contain an objects clause, as was required pursuant to the Companies Act 1985. For these companies section 39 remains important, as does the requirement that directors observe the restrictions set out in the objects clause if they wish to comply with their duty to act within the terms of the constitution. To benefit from the unrestricted objects clause provided by the 2006 Act existing companies will have to pass a special resolution in general meeting deleting the objects clause in their constitution.

Accordingly, the problems companies have faced in the past with regard to expanding into other business areas and the problems third parties have faced when doing business with companies with restrictive objects clauses need concern the student of company law no more.[9] From the ghosts of company law past one hears a faint cheer.

III CONTRACT AND THE COMPANY

1 Primary and general rules of attribution

How does a legal person that exists only in the contemplation of law, not our corporal world, act. How does that person enter into and become bound by a contract. An excellent analytical framework through which we can consider this question is provided by

---

[8] See, for example, *Re Introductions Ltd* [1970] Ch 199.

[9] To be clear, it is not that there is no scope for the intricacies of the rules regulating what amounts to an *ultra vires* act to rear their heads in a post-2006 Act setting—they could, for example, do so in relation to an action against a director under section 171(a) in a company with restricted articles. However, the probability of such actions being brought is very low and as time progresses will get closer to, although will never reach, zero. The most important of these intricate issues surrounds the conflict between *Re Introductions* [1969] 2 WLR 791 and *Rolled Steel* [1985] 2 WLR 908.

Lord Hoffmann in the Privy Council case of *Meridian Global Funds Management Asia Ltd v Securities Commission*,[10] where he made the following observations.

> Any proposition about a company necessarily involves a reference to a set of rules. A company exists because there is a rule (usually in a statute) which says that a persona ficta shall be deemed to exist and to have certain of the powers, rights and duties of a natural person. But there would be little sense in deeming such a persona ficta to exist unless there were also rules to tell one what acts were to count as acts of the company. It is therefore a necessary part of corporate personality that there should be rules by which acts are attributed to the company. These may be called 'the rules of attribution'.
>
> The company's primary rules of attribution will generally be found in its constitution, typically the articles of association, and will say things such as 'for the purpose of appointing members of the board, a majority vote of the shareholders shall be a decision of the company' or 'the decisions of the board in managing the company's business shall be the decisions of the company'. There are also primary rules of attribution which are not expressly stated in the articles but implied by company law, such as 'the unanimous decision of all the shareholders in a solvent company about anything which the company under its memorandum of association has power to do shall be the decision of the company': see *Multinational Gas and Petrochemical Co v Multinational Gas and Petrochemical Services Ltd*.[11]
>
> These primary rules of attribution are obviously not enough to enable a company to go out into the world and do business. Not every act on behalf of the company could be expected to be the subject of a resolution of the board or a unanimous decision of the shareholders. The company therefore builds upon the primary rules of attribution by using general rules of attribution which are equally available to natural persons, namely, the principles of agency. It will appoint servants and agents whose acts, by a combination of the general principles of agency and the company's primary rules of attribution, count as the acts of the company. And having done so, it will also make itself subject to the general rules by which liability for the acts of others can be attributed to natural persons, such as estoppel or ostensible authority in contract and vicarious liability in tort.

The rules that determine which acts are attributed to the company are referred to by Lord Hoffmann as *rules of attribution*, of which there are two types: *primary rules of attribution* and *general rules of attribution*. The primary rules of attribution are, according to this extract, the rules set out in a company's constitution, together with the statutory and common law rules, which provide that specified decisions of the company's organs are 'decisions of the company'. For example: a decision taken by the shareholders in general meeting in accordance with the constitution is a decision of the company; as would be a unanimous informal decision of the shareholders outside of a general meeting; or a written resolution of a private company passed in accordance with the Companies Act 2006.[12] Furthermore, *per* Lord Hoffmann, a company's constitution typically provides a primary rule of attribution that decisions of the board of directors are decisions of the company.[13]

Reading Lord Hoffmann's judgment one might expect to find in the Model Articles or in the Companies Act 2006 references to particular actions—such as a general meeting

---

[10] [1995] 2 BCLC 116. *Meridian* is addressed in detail at pp 157–61.

[11] [1983] BCLC 461. See Chapter 3 Part B.II and the discussion of *Re Duomatic* [1969] 1 All ER 161.

[12] See further Chapter 3.

[13] Interestingly, however, most companies' articles will not say, as Lord Hoffmann asserts, 'that the decisions of the board are decisions of the company', rather they will provide—as do the Model Articles for Public and Private Companies—that the board is responsible for managing the company's business and in doing so that it may exercise all the powers of the company. Article 3 of the Model Articles for Public and Private companies. For a detailed consideration of the delegation of power to the board see Chapter 6.

decision to appoint directors or a board decision—as being 'decisions of the company'. However, no reference to any particular action being 'a decision of the company' is found anywhere in the Companies Act 2006 or in the Model Articles or its predecessor Table A. Rather a company's constitution and the Companies Act will simply provide what the organs can do and how they do it; for example: the shareholder meeting appoints directors by ordinary resolution[14] and amends the constitution by special resolution;[15] the board must manage the company and will exercise powers of the company by majority vote in a quorate board meeting.[16] It follows by implication from these rules that those decisions are decisions of the company; but the constitutional or statutory rule specifying how the company acts does not provide explicitly that it is 'a decision of the company'. The absence of rules that refer to certain actions being decisions of the company does not mean that there are no primary rules of attribution. What Lord Hoffmann in fact intended by a primary rule of attribution is that an act of *either* (but only) the board or the general meeting taken in accordance with the constitution and applicable law is an act of the company. This is seen more clearly later in the judgment in *Meridian* not extracted earlier,[17] where Lord Hoffmann observes that if liability is dependent on a primary rule of attribution it would require that 'the act giving rise to liability was specifically authorized by a resolution of the board or a unanimous agreement of shareholders', or, one presumes, a decision taken in general meeting.[18]

In addition to these primary rules of attribution there are what Lord Hoffmann refers to as *general rules of attribution*: rules that for the purpose of the contract, tort or crime in question attribute the actions of natural persons, as distinct from actions of the corporate organs, to the company. In relation to contract, these rules are the rules of agency; in relation to tort, which we address in the next section, these are the rules of vicarious liability. These general rules of agency or vicarious liability are not peculiar to the company, they are the rules that are applicable to any person—legal or real—that appoints an agent to act on its behalf or employs a person to perform a service.

In determining whether a company is bound to a particular contract, it is unlikely that the board or the general meeting itself will enter into the contract. Most, if not all, contracts entered into by the company will be contracts entered into by agents of the company not by the organs of the company. As Lord Hoffmann notes it would be impractical for every act of the company to involve a decision of the board or of the general meeting. Even in small companies such a requirement would result in a business grinding to a halt under the weight of internal bureaucracy. However, even in relation to major corporate decisions, such as the sale of a division of the company, where the board considers the transaction and resolves to enter into a contract, the board itself does not directly enter into the contract. Rather the board will authorize a particular management employee to act as the company's agent in negotiating the precise terms of and entering into the contract on the company's behalf. Nevertheless, although the board or general meeting will not itself typically enter into the contract directly, the actions of the primary organs in appointing and authorizing an agent, or making a representation about an agent, are, as we shall see, central to determining whether in fact, according to the general rules of attribution, the company is bound in contract.

---

[14] Articles 17 and 20 of the Model Articles for Private and Public Companies, respectively.

[15] Section 21 CA 2006.

[16] Articles 3, 7 and 11, and 3, 7 and 10 of the Model Articles for Private and Public Companies, respectively.

[17] *Meridian* is considered in greater depth in section V as the facts of the case involve corporate crime.

[18] We will consider later in the chapter rules of attribution that depend on the company's 'directing will and mind'. The person who represents the company's 'directing will and mind' is often said to 'be' the company. Nevertheless, for Lord Hoffmann such a rule is not a primary rule of attribution, rather a special rule of attribution. See further section V of this chapter.

2 The common law of agency: actual authority

As a company grows there is a corresponding increase in the number of agents that can bind the company pursuant to the general rules of attribution. For example, the board of directors of Bob's Electronics Ltd may delegate authority to Bob, as chief executive officer, to act on behalf of the company. He may in turn delegate authority to Alison to run the laptop division of the company, who in turn employs Helen as purchasing manager and delegates authority to Helen to source components for that division. At each stage in the delegation of authority—from the board to Bob, Bob to Alison, Alison to Helen—the board, Bob, and Alison will, or at least should, be careful to specify in writing exactly what authority they are delegating to act as an agent on behalf of the company. At each stage of the delegation the grantor of authority will, ideally, be careful to ensure that the agent's scope of authority is limited to the authority needed to carry out the task he or she has been appointed to carry out. If we take Helen as our example, she will have authority to enter into contracts to buy components and nothing else—she cannot on behalf of the company enter into contracts to sell computers, buy delivery vans, or employ someone. Furthermore, it is likely that the value of component contracts she can enter into will be limited to a value amount to ensure that she does not over-commit the company.

Provided that Bob, Alison, and Helen, as agents with delegated authority, operate within the parameters of the authority delegated to them, the agency law issues are unproblematic. If Helen has authority to enter into contracts to source microchips where the overall value of the contract does not exceed £500,000, and she enters into a contract of a value of £490,000, the contract is binding on the company. The agency law vocabulary we use to describe the reason for this is that Helen has *actual authority* to enter into these transactions. A grant of actual authority involves the *actual* grant of authority from a person or organ who has the authority to delegate such authority. In this example, for Helen to have actual authority there must be no break in the chain of actual authority from the board *as the company*, to Bob, to Alison, and then to Helen. Consider the following explanation of 'actual authority' from Diplock LJ in *Freeman & Lockyer v Buckhurst Park Properties*:[19]

> An 'actual' authority is a legal relationship between principal and agent created by a consensual agreement to which they alone are parties. Its scope is to be ascertained by applying ordinary principles of construction of contracts, including any proper implications from the express words used, the usages of the trade, or the course of business between the parties. To this agreement the contractor is a stranger; he may be totally ignorant of the existence of any authority on the part of the agent. Nevertheless, if the agent does enter into a contract pursuant to the 'actual' authority, it does create contractual rights and liabilities between the principal and the contractor...

Actual authority can be expressly conferred through written or spoken word. This type of actual authority is referred to as *express actual authority*. However, indirect conduct may also confer upon the agent actual authority—this type of actual authority is referred to as *implied actual authority*. Importantly, for both express and implied actual authority the extent to which the agent is empowered to bind the company has nothing do with the third-party contractor; it is purely a question of the terms of the express or implied contract of agency. Clearly, where the grant of actual authority is found in a written document the extent and scope of the grant of authority is easier to determine: it turns on the interpretation of the document. It becomes more difficult where only the spoken word is used to grant authority and more difficult still when the company did not expressly authorize the agent, rather only impliedly authorized the agent through indirect words and conduct. For example, if, extending the example set out on this page, Helen regularly

---

[19] [1964] 1 All ER 630.

exceeds the scope of the actual authority delegated to her and enters into transactions in the value range of £500,000–600,000 and neither Alison or Bob, although aware that she is doing this, question her actions, is this sufficient to give her implied actual authority to enter into such contracts? If when Helen is appointed the extent and scope of her authority is not discussed or set out in any document and she subsequently enters into contracts for orders in excess of £2 million, is the fact of appointing her to her job as purchasing manager sufficient conduct to grant her implied actual authority to enter into such contracts? The leading case in this regard is *Hely-Hutchinson v Brayhead Ltd*.

■ *Hely-Hutchinson v Brayhead Ltd* [1968] 1 QB 549

Mr Richards was the chairman of a public company called Brayhead Ltd. Although he was not the company's managing director, the first instance court concluded that he acted as a de facto managing director and that the board had acquiesced in him so doing. Lord Suirdale, who was the claimant in the action, was the managing director of a struggling electronics company called Perdio Electronics Ltd. Brayhead Ltd was willing to provide financial support to Perdio, which involved taking a significant shareholding in Perdio. At the same time it was agreed that Lord Suirdale would lend money to Perdio but that a condition of making the loan was that Brayhead would guarantee the repayment of that loan and would indemnify Lord Suirdale in relation to a personal guarantee he had given to a bank for Perdio's bank debt. The guarantee and indemnity given by Brayhead were set forth in letters signed by Mr Richards. These attempts to revitalize Perdio's business failed and it went into liquidation. Lord Suirdale claimed from Brayhead pursuant to the guarantee and indemnity that it had given. Brayhead Ltd claimed that Mr Richards did not have authority to give the indemnity and guarantee and that it was unenforceable.

Lord Denning MR

The defence of Brayhead is twofold: First, they say that the letter of indemnity and the letter of guarantee are not binding on the company, because Mr. Richards had no authority, actual or ostensible, to write those letters: and that Lord Suirdale, being himself a director of Brayhead, had notice of that want of authority. So there was no contract by the company. Second, they say that if there was a contract by the company, it is unenforceable by Lord Suirdale because he was a director and had an interest which he did not disclose at any board meeting…

Actual authority may be express or implied. It is *express* when it is given by express words, such as when a board of directors pass a resolution which authorises two of their number to sign cheques. It is *implied* when it is inferred from the conduct of the parties and the circumstances of the case, such as when the board of directors appoint one of their number to be managing director. They thereby impliedly authorise him to do all such things as fall within the usual scope of that office. Actual authority, express or implied, is binding as between the company and the agent, and also as between the company and others, whether they are within the company or outside it…

Apply these principles here. It is plain that Mr. Richards had no express authority to enter into these two contracts on behalf of the company: nor had he any such authority implied from the nature of his office. He had been duly appointed chairman of the company but that office in itself did not carry with it authority to enter into these contracts without the sanction of the board. But I think he had authority implied from the conduct of the parties and the circumstances of the case…The judge finds that Mr. Richards acted as de facto managing director of Brayhead. He was the chief executive who made the final decision on any matter concerning finance. He often committed Brayhead to contracts without the knowledge of the board and reported the matter afterwards.

I think [the judge's] findings carry with it the necessary inference that he had also actual authority, such authority being implied from the circumstance that the board by their conduct over many months had acquiesced in his acting as their chief executive and committing Brayhead Ltd. to contracts without the necessity of sanction from the board.

Lord Denning's judgment suggests that there are two categories of behaviour that could result in there being a grant of implied actual authority. The first is simply the appointment of a person to a particular position that, unless contrary intention is expressed when appointing that person, will give such person the actual authority to bind the company as a person occupying that job would *usually* have.[20] How one goes about determining what is usual for any particular position is not set out in the judgment; we only know that the activities carried out by Mr Richards in this case would not be within the usual scope of a chairman's actual authority. This category of behaviour is sometimes referred to as 'usual authority'—that is, the authority usually associated with the job in question.[21]

One needs, however, to be careful not to overstate the extent to which the act of appointment of a person to a particular position contains an automatic transfer of implied actual authority. Four caveats need to be registered in this regard. First, subsequent case law has not developed this idea of implied actual authority arising from the usual scope of activities of a particular job position. Secondly, implied actual authority/usual authority is perhaps better associated with the more limited idea that once you have granted actual authority there may be some additional—incidental—elements of authority that are necessarily required, and are therefore implied, in order to perform the activities associated with the agent's express actual authority.[22] Thirdly, the generation of implied authority through appointment to a position is inconsistent with other case law dealing with the question of whether there are inherent powers associated with an appointment to the position of managing director, for example, the power to commence litigation. These cases provide that without an express grant of authority directors do not have any power to act on behalf of the company and that the act of appointment alone is insufficient to confer any power.[23] Fourthly, in relation to actual authority—whether express or implied—the grant of authority is the *sole source* of the authority: what is the usual authority for a person operating in that position to have in the industry in question; or what third-party contractors might reasonably expect a person in that position to have, is *irrelevant* to the extent of the authority. Therefore, to the extent that appointment to a position creates implied authority then the conduct in question resulting in the appointment must be capable of being interpreted as also involving a grant of authority; an intention to grant such 'usual authority'. Accordingly, these four factors suggest that the idea that implied actual authority results from the appointment to a particular position, although clearly possible, must be treated with considerable caution.

The second category of behaviour that can lead to a grant of implied actual authority is the acquiescence of a person or organ capable of granting such authority to the actual activities of a director, employee or agent. That is, if the agent acts in ways that assumes greater actual authority than she actually has and the principal's conduct indicates that she is allowed to continue acting in this way then the courts will infer a grant of implied actual authority. The authorities suggest, however, that something more is required from the principal's conduct than merely silent acquiescence. In *Freeman & Lockyer (a firm) v Buckhurst Park Properties*,[24] considered in section 3 of this chapter, Diplock LJ observed that silent acquiescence would be insufficient to confer implied actual authority. What

---

[20] See also *ING Re (UK) v R&V Versicherung AG* [2006] EWHC 1544 acknowledging that 'usual authority' may support a case of implied actual authority (at [125]).

[21] *First Energy (UK) Ltd v Hungarian International Bank Ltd* [1993] BCLC 1409.

[22] For example, in *First Energy (UK) Ltd v Hungarian International Bank Ltd* Steyn LJ observes that 'usual authority...sometimes means that the agent had implied actual authority to perform acts necessarily incidental to the performance of the agency'.

[23] See *Mitchell & Hobbs (UK) Ltd v Mill* [1996] 2 BCLC 102 and *Harold Holdsworth & Co (Wakefield) Ltd v Caddies* [1955] 1 WLR 352. For a discussion of these cases see pp 211–12.

[24] [1964] 1 All ER 630.

is required would be actual 'communication by words or conduct of [the principal's] consent'. In the example set out on page 112—where Helen exceeds the value threshold of her initial grant of authority when entering into contracts yet Alison and Bob, aware that she is doing this, say nothing—Helen would not then have implied actual authority to enter into contracts within the £500,000–£600,000 range. Explicit affirmation of her behaviour through words or conduct would, however, result in a grant of such authority.

3 The common law of agency: apparent authority (sometimes referred to as ostensible authority)

If Helen operates within the parameters of her delegated actual authority (whether express or implied) the company will be bound to contracts she enters into. A problem arises where Helen decides, for whatever reason, to enter into contracts the nature and/ or the terms of which fall outside the actual authority (whether express or implied) which she has been granted. For example, she might enter into a contract for micro-chips the overall value of which is worth £1 million or indeed £50 million; or, given her dissatisfaction with the quality of the stationery she is provided with at work, she may order stationery for the company which has a contract value of £10,000; or, *reductio ab adsurdum*, unhappy with her office space she enters into a contract on behalf of the company for new office space.

The reader's first reaction to these examples might be to say that as she has taken action she was not authorized to take—action beyond the scope of her actual authority as agent—the company cannot and should not be bound by these contracts. From this perspective, the company as a separate legal person was brought into being by the shareholders of the company for particular purposes. Those shareholders carefully devised rules which set out who can bind the company in contract and who can delegate power to act on behalf of the company. If the law failed to give due recognition to those rules and enabled employees, such as Helen in our example, to bind the company, then business persons may be more hesitant to use the corporate form and would certainly be hesitant to put employees in positions of authority at all. However, we also need to consider such contracts from the perspective of the third-party micro-chip manufacturer, stationery provider, and office-space landlord. These parties have entered into contracts which they expect to be honoured. In doing so they may have rejected other opportunities to sell the micro-chips and the stationery or to lease the office space. One response to this would be to say *let the third-party contractor beware*: the seller or landlord in these examples should ensure and require proof that the agent entering into the contract on the company's behalf has the necessary actual authority, and if he fails to verify this and it turns out the company's agent did not have actual authority then he only has himself to blame. The problem with such an approach is that it would throw a considerable amount of sand into the wheels of UK commerce: contracting would become more expensive and time consuming as third-party contractors carefully verified the actual authority credentials of companies' agents. As the cost in terms of time and money of contracting increases, the amount of contracting, and therefore of business activity, will decrease. It is important that legal rules that determine in what circumstances a company's agents can bind it do not impose excessive **transaction costs** on business. However, whilst it may make sense, in the interests of encouraging business activity, that third-party contractors can assume that the company's representative has the power to bind the company, the examples set forth in this section show that there are 'common sense' or 'reasonableness' limits to the legitimacy of such an assumption. It might be reasonable to assume that a purchasing manager of a medium-sized company can enter into a £1 million contract for micro-chips, but it seems less likely that a £10 million contract is reasonable; and the idea of a purchasing manager entering into a new office contract is absurd. The law should provide third-party contractors with security of contract but not in situations where it would be unreasonable to think that the agent in question really had authority to enter into the contract. The law, therefore, needs to strike a balance between the interests of third parties and the interests of the company and its shareholders.

The law of agency attempts to strike this balance through the concept of *apparent authority* (which is sometimes referred to in the cases and the literature as *ostensible authority*). The label 'apparent' is very instructive in understanding what this concept does. Apparent authority in effect provides the 'agent' with authority to enter into the contract where *the company* has acted in a way to suggest to the outside world of third-party contractors—to enable third-party contractors to infer—that the agent has actual authority to bind the company; that is, *because of the company's actions* the agent *appears* to the outside world to have authority. This *appearance* is generated by the act of the company in relation to the agent in question *together with* the reasonable norms and expectations of the business world about the scope and extent of the actual authority that such an agent would be expected to have. The leading authority on the meaning and operation of apparent authority is Diplock LJ's judgment in *Freeman & Lockyer v Buckhurst Park Properties*.

■ Freeman & Lockyer (a firm) v Buckhurst Park Properties [1964] 1 All ER 630

Mr Kapoor, a property developer, identified a development property for sale known as Buckhurst Park Estates. As he did not have sufficient funds to purchase the property alone he brought in a co-investor, Mr Hoon. Mr Kapoor and Mr Hoon formed a company, Buckhurst Park Properties Ltd, in order to purchase Buckhurst Park Estates. Mr Kapoor and Mr Hoon were directors of the company, as were two of their nominees. Following the purchase of the property, initial attempts to resell the property at a profit did not materialize so Mr Kapoor commenced initial steps to develop the property. Mr Kapoor had not, however, been appointed as the managing director of the company although the trial judge found that at all times he had been acting in the role of managing director. In this role he appointed architects to prepare plans for the development of the property and to submit a planning permission application in relation to the property. When the company failed to pay for these services the architects sued the company for payment of their fees. In response, the company claimed that Mr Kapoor had not been authorized to enter into these contracts and had no authority as agent to bind the company, and accordingly, that the company was not obliged to pay.

> *Diplock LJ*
> The county court judge made the following findings of fact: (i) that the plaintiffs intended to contract with [Mr Kapoor] as agent for the defendant company, and not on his own account; (ii) that the board of the defendant company intended that [Mr Kapoor] should do what he could to obtain the best possible price for the estate; (iii) that [Mr Kapoor], although never appointed as managing director, had throughout been acting as such in employing agents and taking other steps to find a purchaser; (iv) that the fact that [Mr Kapoor] was so acting was well known to the board...
>
> The county court judge did not hold (although he might have done) that actual authority had been conferred on [Mr Kapoor] by the board to employ [the architects]. He proceeded on the basis of apparent authority, ie, that the defendant company had so acted as to be estopped from denying [Mr Kapoor]'s authority. This rendered it unnecessary for the judge to enquire whether actual authority to employ agents had been conferred on [Mr Kapoor] by the board to whom the management of the company's business was confided by the articles of association.
>
> I accept that such actual authority could have been conferred by the board without a formal resolution recorded in the minutes...But to confer actual authority would have required not merely the silent acquiescence of the individual members of the board, but the communication by words or conduct of their respective consents to one another and to [Mr Kapoor]...I myself

do not feel that there is adequate material to justify the court in reaching the conclusion of fact (which the county court judge refrained from making) that actual authority to employ agents had been conferred by the board on [Mr Kapoor].

This makes it necessary to enquire into the state of the law as to the ostensible [apparent] authority of officers and servants to enter into contracts on behalf of corporations…We are concerned in the present case with the authority of an agent to create contractual rights and liabilities between his principal and a third party whom I will call 'the contractor'.

It is necessary at the outset to distinguish between an 'actual' authority of an agent on the one hand, and an 'apparent' or 'ostensible' authority on the other. Actual authority and apparent authority are quite independent of one another. Generally they co-exist and coincide, but either may exist without the other and their respective scopes may be different. As I shall endeavour to show, it is on the apparent authority of the agent that the contractor normally relies in the ordinary course of business when entering into contracts…

An 'apparent' or 'ostensible' authority…is a legal relationship between the principal and the contractor created by a representation, made by the principal to the contractor, intended to be and in fact acted on by the contractor, that the agent has authority to enter on behalf of the principal into a contract of a kind within the scope of the 'apparent' authority, so as to render the principal liable to perform any obligations imposed on him by such contract…The representation, when acted on by the contractor by entering into a contract with the agent, operates as an estoppel, preventing the principal from asserting that he is not bound by the contract. It is irrelevant whether the agent had actual authority to enter into the contract.

In ordinary business dealings the contractor at the time of entering into the contract can in the nature of things hardly ever rely on the 'actual' authority of the agent. His information as to the authority must be derived either from the principal or from the agent or from both, for they alone know what the agent's actual authority is. All that the contractor can know is what they tell him, which may or may not be true. In the ultimate analysis he relies either on the representation of the principal, ie, apparent authority, or on the representation of the agent, ie, warranty of authority. The representation which creates 'apparent' authority may take a variety of forms of which the commonest is representation by conduct, ie, by permitting the agent to act in some way in the conduct of the principal's business with other persons. By so doing the principal represents to anyone who becomes aware that the agent is so acting that the agent has authority to enter on behalf of the principal into contracts with other persons of the kind which an agent so acting in the conduct of his principal's business has normally 'actual' authority to enter into.

In applying the law, as I have endeavoured to summarise it, to the case where the principal is not a natural person, but a fictitious person, viz, a corporation, two further factors arising from the legal characteristics of a corporation have to be borne in mind. The first is that the capacity of a corporation is limited by its constitution, ie, in the case of a company incorporated under the Companies Act, by its memorandum and articles of association; the second is that a corporation cannot do any act, and that includes making a representation, except through its agent. Under the doctrine of ultra vires the limitation of the capacity of a corporation by its constitution to do any acts is absolute. This affects the rules as to the 'apparent' authority of an agent of a corporation in two ways. First, no representation can operate to estop the corporation from denying the authority of the agent to do on behalf of the corporation an act which the corporation is not permitted by its constitution to do itself. Secondly, since the conferring of actual authority on an agent is itself an act of the corporation, the capacity to do which is regulated by its constitution, the corporation cannot be estopped from denying that it has conferred on a particular agent authority to do acts which, by its constitution, it is incapable of delegating to that particular agent. To recognise that these are direct consequences of the doctrine of ultra vires is, I think, preferable to saying that a contractor who enters into a contract with a corporation has constructive notice of its constitution, for the expression 'constructive notice' tends to disguise that constructive notice is not a positive, but a negative doctrine, like that of estoppel of which it forms a part. It operates to prevent the contractor from saying that he did not know that the constitution of the corporation rendered a particular act or a particular delegation of authority ultra vires the corporation. It does not entitle him to say that he relied on some unusual provision in the constitution of the corporation, if he did not in fact so rely.

The second characteristic of a corporation, viz, that unlike a natural person it can only make a representation through an agent, has the consequence that, in order to create an estoppel between the corporation and the contractor, the representation as to the authority of the agent which creates his 'apparent' authority must be made by some person or persons who have 'actual' authority from the corporation to make the representation. Such 'actual' authority may be conferred by the constitution of the corporation itself, as, for example, in the case of a company, on the board of directors, or it may be conferred by those who under its constitution have the powers of management on some other person to whom the constitution permits them to delegate authority to make representations of this kind. It follows that, where the agent on whose 'apparent' authority the contractor relies has no 'actual' authority from the corporation to enter into a particular kind of contract with the contractor on behalf of the corporation, the contractor cannot rely on the agent's own representation as to his actual authority. He can rely only on a representation by a person or persons who have actual authority to manage or conduct that part of the business of the corporation to which the contract relates. The commonest form of representation by a principal creating an 'apparent' authority of an agent is by conduct, viz, by permitting the agent to act in the management or conduct of the principal's business. Thus, if in the case of a company the board of directors who have 'actual' authority under the memorandum and articles of association to manage the company's business permit the agent to act in the management or conduct of the company's business, they thereby represent to all persons dealing with such agent that he has authority to enter on behalf of the corporation into contracts of a kind which an agent authorised to do acts of the kind which he is in fact permitted to do normally enters into in the ordinary course of such business. The making of such a representation is itself an act of management of the company's business. Prima facie it falls within the 'actual' authority of the board of directors, and unless the memorandum or articles of the company either make such a contract ultra vires the company or prohibit the delegation of such authority to the agent, the company is estopped from denying to anyone who has entered into a contract with the agent in reliance on such 'apparent' authority that the agent had authority to contract on behalf of the company.

If the foregoing analysis of the relevant law is correct, it can be summarised by stating four conditions which must be fulfilled to entitle a contractor to enforce against a company a contract entered into on behalf of the company by an agent who had no actual authority to do so. It must be shown: (a) that a representation that the agent had authority to enter on behalf of the company into a contract of the kind sought to be enforced was made to the contractor; (b) that such representation was made by a person or persons who had 'actual' authority to manage the business of the company either generally or in respect of those matters to which the contract relates; (c) that he (the contractor) was induced by such representation to enter into the contract, ie, that he in fact relied on it; and (d) that under its memorandum or articles of association the company was not deprived of the capacity either to enter into a contract of the kind sought to be enforced or to delegate authority to enter into a contract of that kind to the agent.

The confusion which, I venture to think, has sometimes crept into the cases is, in my view, due to a failure to distinguish between these four separate conditions, and in particular to keep steadfastly in mind (first) that the only 'actual' authority which is relevant is that of the persons making the representation relied on, and (second) that the memorandum and articles of association of the company are always relevant (whether they are in fact known to the contractor or not) to the questions (i) whether condition (b) is fulfilled, and (ii) whether condition (d) is fulfilled, and (but only if they are in fact known to the contractor) may be relevant (c) as part of the representation on which the contractor relied.

The cases where the contractor's claim failed, viz *J C Houghton & Co v Nothard, Lowe and Wills Ltd*,[25] *Kreditbank Cassel GmbH v Schenkers Ltd*,[26] and the *Rama Corpn*[27] case were all cases where the contract sought to be enforced was not one which a person occupying the position in relation to the company's business, which the contractor knew that the agent occupied, would normally be authorised to enter into on behalf of the company. The conduct of the board of directors in permitting the agent to occupy that position, on which the contractor relied, thus did not of itself amount to a representation that the agent had authority to enter into the contract sought to be enforced, ie, condition (a) was not fulfilled. The contractor, however, in each of these three cases sought to rely on a provision of the articles, giving to the board power to delegate wide authority to the agent, as entitling the contractor to treat the conduct of the board as a representation that the agent had had delegated to him wider powers than those normally exercised by persons occupying the position in relation to the company's business which the agent was in fact permitted by the board to occupy. Since this would involve proving that the representation on which he in fact relied as inducing him to enter into the contract comprised the articles of association of the company as well as the conduct of the board, it would be necessary for him to establish, first, that he knew the contents of the articles (ie, that condition (c) was fulfilled in respect of any representation contained in the articles) and, secondly, that the conduct of the board in the light of that knowledge would be understood by a reasonable man as a representation that the agent had authority to enter into the contract sought to be enforced, ie, that condition (a) was fulfilled...

In the present case the findings of fact by the county court judge are sufficient to satisfy the four conditions, and thus to establish that [Mr Kapoor] had 'apparent' authority to enter into contracts on behalf of the defendant company for their services in connexion with the sale of the company's property, including the obtaining of development permission [with] respect to its use. The judge found that the board knew that [Mr Kapoor] had throughout been acting as managing director in employing agents and taking other steps to find a purchaser. They permitted him to do so, and by such conduct represented that he had authority to enter into contracts of a kind which a managing director or an executive director responsible for finding a purchaser would in the normal course be authorised to enter into on behalf of the defendant company. Condition (a) was thus fulfilled. The articles of association conferred full powers of management on the board. Condition (b) was thus fulfilled. The plaintiffs, finding [Mr Kapoor] acting in relation to the defendant company's property as he was authorised by the board to act, were induced to believe that he was authorised by the defendant company to enter into contracts on behalf of the company for their services in connexion with the sale of the company's property, including the obtaining of development permission with respect to its use. Condition (c) was thus fulfilled. The articles of association, which contained powers for the board to delegate any of the functions of management to a managing director or to a single director, did not deprive the company of capacity to delegate authority to [Mr Kapoor], a director, to enter into contracts of that kind on behalf of the company. Condition (d) was thus fulfilled. I think that the judgment was right, and would dismiss the appeal.

3.1 The structure of the apparent authority doctrine

Diplock LJ's judgment sets forth both the conceptual basis of apparent authority and the criteria that determine when it is generated. He observes that 'apparent authority' operates as an estoppel: the company is estopped, in a suit brought against it by a third-party contractor, from claiming that its 'agent', who purportedly entered into the contract on the company's behalf, did not have actual authority to do so. If the company cannot

[25] [1927] 1 KB 246.   [26] [1927] All ER Rep 421.
[27] *Rama Corpn v Proved Tin and General Investments Ltd* [1952] 1 All ER 554.

make this counterclaim then it has no defence to the contractor's claim and it is forced to comply with the obligations set out in the contract.[28]

The basic structure of apparent authority as set out by Diplock LJ is as follows: a person (the 'agent') will have apparent authority to bind the company where: (1) the company makes a representation in relation to that agent which holds out the agent as actually having actual authority to bind the company although she has not been granted such authority; and (2) the third party who contracts with the agent reasonably relies upon the representation in agreeing to enter into the contract.

Several difficult issues need to be unpackaged from this basic structure of apparent authority in the context of company contracting. First, what types of company behaviour are sufficient to amount to a representation that an 'agent' has authority to act on behalf of the company? Importantly, although *Freeman & Lockyer* provides guidance in this regard, there is no closed list of behavioural categories that can generate such a representation: whether behaviour amounts to such a representation will be judged on a case-by-case basis. For our purposes, however, there are two clear categories of representation: first, appointing someone to a particular position or office, for example appointing a person to the position of 'sales director', 'purchasing manager', or 'finance director'; and second, the company acquiescing to a person acting in a particular way—in this case acting as de facto managing director—would amount to a representation. However, when we look closely at the representation in *Freeman & Lockyer* we see that the architect did not himself see prior acts of acquiescence by the de facto managing director. Accordingly, if it is necessary for the third party to rely on the representation, those acts of acquiescence in *Freeman & Lockyer* were not themselves the representation. The representation here is more abstract than the act of acquiescence: it is that in having previously allowed him to act as a de facto managing director the board has enabled and encouraged him to present himself to the outside world as the managing director.

Such a representation is a necessary but not a sufficient condition to the creation of an agent's apparent authority. Apparent authority is generated *only* if the representation is relied upon by a third-party contractor and *only* to the extent that such reliance is reasonable. From Diplock LJ's discussion of the *Kreditbank Cassel* and *JC Houghton* cases, we see that the questions to be asked in this regard are: first, whether the representation in question would lead a *reasonable man* to infer that the agent had actual authority to act on behalf of the company; and, second, to the reasonable man what the extent of that authority would appear to be.[29] What is reasonable in this regard would depend on, for example: typical purchasing practices in the industry in question; the size of the company; and the nature of the product to be purchased. In *British Bank*

---

[28] On estoppel see, for example, *Hughes v Metropolitan Railway Co.* (1877) 2 App Cas 439; *Morrow v Carty* [1957] NI 174; Cf *W.J. Allen & Co. Ltd v El Nasr Export and Import Co.* [1972] QB 189. See generally M.P. Furmston, *Cheshire, Fifoot & Furmston's Law of Contract* (14th edn, Butterworths, 2001); P. Feltman et al (eds), *Spencer-Bower and Turner: Estoppel by Representation* (4th edn, Lexis, 2003).

[29] Note that the representation could generate apparent authority to act on behalf of, or communicate on behalf of, the company which results in the company becoming bound, even though the representation does not itself support apparent authority for the agent to enter into the transaction on the company's behalf. See *First Energy (UK) Ltd v Hungarian International Bank Ltd* [1993] BCLC 1409 where the court held that an employee had apparent authority to communicate an offer—resulting in the creation of a legally binding contract on acceptance—even though the employee did not himself have apparent authority to authorize or enter into the transaction. See also *Soplex Wholesale Supplies Ltd v Egyptian International Foreign Trade Co, The Raffaella* [1985] 2 Lloyd's Rep 36 at 42 observing that 'if a company confers actual or apparent authority on A to make representations on the company's behalf but no actual authority on A to enter into specific transactions, why should a representation made by A as to his authority not be capable of being...one of the acts of holding out'.

of the Middle East v Sun Life Assurance Co of Canada (UK) Ltd,[30] for example, the House of Lords considered a case in which it was claimed that a branch manager of an insurance company had the apparent authority to make a representation that a junior employee had actual authority to enter into a contract. In deciding that there was no apparent authority the court considered the role and status of branch managers in the insurance industry generally.

With regard to the representation which can create apparent authority, Diplock LJ stresses the importance of the fact that the representation *must come from the company*. The agent cannot himself make the representation by simply claiming to be the company's managing director or forging documents that suggest that he is the managing director of the company or has the actual authority to enter into the contract.[31] Furthermore, the representation must also come from a person or organ that is authorized to make, or is capable of making, the representation. Such a person or organ is a person or organ that itself would have the actual authority to enter into the contract in question or authorize an agent to do so. Accordingly, where the corporate constitution does not empower the board of directors to enter into the transaction in question or where the constitution explicitly limits the authority of particular individuals, for example, the authority of the chief executive officer, then it is not possible for the board of directors or the CEO to make a 'representation' that could create the apparent authority of an agent that exceeds the actual authority of the board or the CEO.

Consider, for example, where the constitution of our case study company Bob's Electronics Ltd provides that the '*board of directors may exercise all the powers of the company provided that it may not enter into or authorize the entering into of any transaction the value of which exceeds £100,000*'. If the board of Bob's Electronics Ltd resolves to appoint Markus as CEO of the company without specifying the extent of his authority then, even if CEOs in the computer business industry typically have authority to enter into contracts worth in excess of £100,000, the appointment does not amount to a representation from the company that can endow Markus the CEO with apparent authority when he enters into a contract the value of which exceeds £100,000. Put simply, the board cannot make a representation capable of generating apparent authority when the board does not itself have the actual authority to enter into the contract. Similarly, if the company had an objects clause saying Bob's Electronics Ltd could only operate in the computer industry and the board was to appoint Jack as chief development officer for a new clothing line of business, such a representation would not amount to a representation for the purpose of creating apparent authority at common law in relation to contracts to source clothing materials and clothes designs because the company does not have the capacity to engage in the clothing business.[32]

This requirement that the person making the representation must have the actual authority to enter into the transaction creates difficulties as a company's organizational structures become more complex. Consider the following example: the board of directors of Bob's Electronics Ltd with unrestricted power and authority appoints Markus as CEO but restricts his authority to enter into contracts worth no more than £20,000. Markus appoints Alison as head of the laptop division of the company and does not impose any restrictions on her authority. Clearly, however, she does not have express or implied actual authority to exceed the £20,000 contract threshold. Nor, however, on a strict reading of Diplock LJ's judgment, would she have apparent authority even where heads of business divisions in the computer industry would typically have actual

---

[30] [1983] BCLC 78. See also *Panorama Developments (Guildford) Ltd v Fidelis Furnishing Fabrics Ltd* [1971] 3 All ER 16 considering the ostensible authority of a 'modern' company secretary.

[31] *Ruben v Great Fingall Consolidated* [1906] AC 439.

[32] Note that section 39 CA 2006, considered in section II of this chapter would operate to prevent incapacity from operating to invalidate this contract. *Rolled Steel Products (Holdings) Ltd v British Steel & Corp* [1985] 3 All ER 52.

authority to enter into contracts worth more than £20,000. Following *Freeman & Lockyer*, Markus himself would have the apparent authority to enter this contract but cannot make a representation that would create apparent authority for Alison, as he does not have the actual authority to enter into the contract. Of course, in *Freeman & Lockyer* this question was not in issue as the representation in question was made by the board. Is such a restrictive reading correct?

There are two ways of viewing Alison as having apparent authority. The first is that a representation can be made by a person with apparent authority, such as Markus in this example, provided that the representation made in relation to Markus was (1) made by an organ or person who would have the actual authority to enter into the transaction, and (2) could reasonably be interpreted as giving Markus the authority to make the representation to the outside world about the authority of Alison. This reading, whilst inconsistent with a literal reading of Diplock LJ's judgment, is supported by subsequent authority. In *British Bank of the Middle East v Sun Life Assurance Co of Canada (UK) Ltd*[33] the question for the House of Lords was whether a branch manager had the apparent authority to make a representation conferring apparent authority on a junior manager. Lord Brandon of Oakbrook concluded that the branch manager did not have apparent authority, although in so doing clearly suggested that had he had apparent authority then he would have been capable of making a representation about the junior employee. Interestingly, Lord Diplock concurred in this judgment. More recently in *ING Re (UK) v R&V Versicherung AG*,[34] at first instance, Toulson J held that the underlying principle in *British Bank of the Middle East* was correct, citing *Bowstead and Reynolds on Agency* (17th edition), that:

> An agent can have apparent authority to make representations as to the authority of other agents, provided that his own authority can finally be traced back to a representation by the principal or to a person with actual authority from the principal to make it.[35]

Perhaps a reading of this situation that would be more faithful to Diplock LJ's position in *Freeman & Lockyer* would be that the representation in question in relation to Alison came not from Markus but from the board in appointing Markus as CEO and in acquiescing to Markus's further delegation of power to the junior member of staff. This would be consistent with the broad reading of Diplock LJ's understanding of 'representation'—a representation is an act that facilitates, whether directly or indirectly, the presentation of a person, whether junior or senior, as having authority to enter into the transaction.

3.2 An alternative lens: the constructive notice doctrine

Through the lens provided by Diplock LJ, representations can only generate apparent authority where the person making the representation would have the actual authority to enter into the transaction itself or to delegate actual authority to an agent to do so. As you will have noticed from the extract in the previous section, Diplock LJ suggests that his approach provides a better lens through which we can understand the limitations

---

[33] [1983] BCLC 78.

[34] [2006] EWHC 1544. See also *Soplex Wholesale Supplies Ltd v Egyptian International Foreign Trade Co, The Raffaella* [1985] 2 Lloyd's Rep 36 (*per* Browne-Wilkinson LJ observing that: 'Suppose a company confers actual or apparent authority on X to make representations and X erroneously represents to a third party that Y has authority to enter into a transaction; why should not such a representation be relied upon as part of the holding out of Y by the company?'

[35] Note that this position follows logically from the view set forth in *First Energy (UK) Ltd v Hungarian International Bank Ltd* [1993] BCLC 1409 discussed at note 29. If a representation can confer apparent authority to communicate an offer it can similarly confer apparent authority to make a representation about another agent.

that the law places on a company organ or agent's ability to create apparent authority than the alternative lens of *constructive notice*. We need, therefore, to understand what this lens of 'constructive notice' is, especially as many commentators and some cases have not heeded Diplock LJ's preference and continue to approach these issues through the lens of constructive notice.

We have seen that reliance by the third-party contractor on the representation made by the company is a key component of the generation of apparent authority. If you rely on a representation you believe it to be accurate and act on the basis of it being accurate. If you know that the representation is not true then it is not possible to rely on it. The third-party contractor who has done his homework may discover that Markus, in the above example,[36] does not have the actual authority to carry out this transaction. If he actually knows this then he cannot rely on the company's representation and, therefore, no apparent authority is created. The doctrine of constructive knowledge provides that for the purposes of determining whether the third-party contractor *knows* that the agent does not have actual authority the contractor is *deemed* to have knowledge of the contents of the company's constitution.[37] In our example, the third party is deemed to have knowledge that the board cannot enter into transactions or authorize Markus to enter into transactions worth more than £100,000. If the third party has deemed knowledge of these limitations then he cannot rely on the representation and apparent authority is not created.

Unless the transaction in question is unusual in nature or large in value most third-party contractors will not read their counterparty-company's constitution. Why would the law, therefore, assume that they had done so? The answer appears to be that during the period following the introduction of incorporation by registration this was indeed the minimum expectation of the courts—a person entering into a contract with a company ought to read the company's constitutional documents; if he does not do so then he must bear the risk that its contents may effect the validity of the contract. The extract in *Royal British Bank v Turquand*, which is set out in sub-section 3.3, is an example of the courts setting forth this expectation.

The effect of Diplock LJ's approach and of the doctrine of constructive notice is the same. The difference between the two approaches is that they focus on a different part of the structure—representation and reliance—of the apparent authority doctrine: Diplock LJ's approach focuses on representation; constructive notice on reliance. Consider, for example, the appointment of a finance director by the board of a company, where the constitution of a company provides that the company may not take on any indebtedness which has a value greater than £100,000, and where the finance director enters into a £200,000 loan on behalf of the company. For Diplock LJ the board of directors cannot make a representation in appointing the finance director that could be relied upon by a third-party contractor to create apparent authority; this is the case even where it would be typical for finance directors of such companies to enter into such contracts. The reason is that the board is not capable of making the representation as it would not be capable itself of entering into the contract; therefore, no apparent authority is created. Through the 'constructive knowledge' lens the focus is not upon the representation but upon reliance—the representation by the board in appointing the finance director is effective but it is not possible to rely on the representation where you know it is not accurate and the third party is deemed to know this as he is deemed to have knowledge of the provisions set out in the constitution. Therefore, apparent authority is not created.[38]

---

[36] See page 121.

[37] *Ernest v Nicholls* (1897) 6 HL Cas 401.

[38] There is lack of clarity as to whether constructive knowledge in such situations prevents the creation of apparent authority or whether it destroys the apparent authority that has already come into existence. See, for example, *Criterion Properties plc v Stratford UK Properties LLC* [2004] 1 WLR

3.3 The indoor management rule

Whilst apparent authority gives third parties comfort that they do not have to establish that the 'agent' actually has the requisite authority, this comfort is subject to the potentially significant limitation that—taking Diplock LJ's preferred approach—if the board itself would not have the actual authority to enter into the transaction in question then it is not capable of making a representation that can confer apparent authority on the agent. The common law has, however, acted to soften the edges of this position. Typically, where a company's constitution restricts the authority of the board of directors or of particular directors or individuals it does not do so absolutely, as in the example in sub-section 3.1, but only subject to the approval of another body or person. So, for example, the restriction set out in the example is more likely to read: *'the board of directors may exercise all the powers of the company provided that it may not enter or authorize entering into any transaction or contract the value of which exceeds £100,000 unless the shareholders in general meeting resolve otherwise'* or *'the managing director of the company cannot enter into a transaction worth more than £50,000 without the approval of the board of directors'*. If the restriction is an absolute restriction then the common law provides no relief. However, if it is a qualified restriction such as in these two examples then, even where that approval has not been granted, for the purposes of determining whether there is apparent authority the law will assume that such approvals have been granted. This rule is known as the *indoor management rule*. The original statement of this rule is found in the case of *Royal British Bank v Turquand*.[39]

■ *Royal British Bank v Turquand* [1843–60] All ER Rep 435

The defendant company's articles of association allowed the company to borrow money with the approval of the general meeting. The directors of the company borrowed £2,000 without general meeting approval. When the bank sued the company for the repayment in accordance with the terms of the loan the company pleaded that the directors had not been authorized by general meeting to borrow the money. The court of first instance held that the debt contract was enforceable.

> *Jervis C J*
>
> I am of opinion that the judgment of the Court of Queen's Bench ought to be affirmed. The [constitution] allows the directors to borrow on bond such sum or sums of money as shall from time to time, by a resolution passed at a general meeting of the company, be authorised to be borrowed...We may now take for granted that the dealings with these companies are not like dealings with other partnerships, and that the parties dealing with them are bound to read the statute and the deed of settlement. But they are not bound to do more. The party here, on reading the deed of settlement, would find, not a prohibition from borrowing, but a permission to do so on certain conditions. Finding that the authority might be made complete by a resolution, he would have a right to infer the fact of a resolution authorising that which on the face of the document appeared to be legitimately done.

1846 observing that 'apparent authority can only be relied on by someone who does not know that the agent has no actual authority'. Nothing rides for us on this distinction and we follow here what this author views as the more logical proposition, namely that it does not come into existence in the absence of effective reliance.

[39] Affirmed by the House of Lords referring to the company's 'indoor management' in *Mahony (Public Officer of National Bank of Ireland) v East Holyford Mining Co Ltd* [1874–80] All ER Rep 427.

Per Jervis CJ, therefore, the law expects a third-party contractor to read the articles of association but does not expect him to find out whether the internal machinery of the company has been put into effect to obtain the correct approvals, authorizations etc. This rule as set out in *Royal British Bank*, clearly fits within the constructive knowledge lens—the knowledge that the third party is deemed to have corresponds to what the courts in the mid-nineteenth century thought it was reasonable for third parties to do—that is, to read the constitutional documents but not to find out whether relevant approvals have been obtained.

This indoor management rule does not fit so neatly into Diplock LJ's 'representation approach' but it can be easily squared: the law will infer that authority has been granted to the organ or person who makes the representation where the constitution provides a mechanism to grant such authority. Lord Simonds put it in *Morris v Kanssen* as follows: 'all things are presumed to be done in due form'.[40] Importantly, however, one cannot rely on the indoor management rule to assume a representation that has not been made, just because it could have been made. A person is not endowed with apparent authority by claiming he is the managing director because the board of directors *could* have appointed him to that position.[41] That would be absurd. An actual representation must be made by an organ or person with the actual authority to make the representation or whose actual authority to make the representation could have been provided by the approval of a specified person or organ of the company.

There are two noteworthy qualifications to the indoor management rule. The first is that a third party cannot rely on the indoor management rule if events surrounding the contract put or should put the third party on notice of a problem with the 'agent's' authority:[42] '[the third-party contractor] cannot presume in his own favour that things are rightly done if inquiries that he ought to make would tell him that they were wrongly done.'[43] The second qualification is that whilst it may be reasonable for a third party to assume that the internal machinery of the company has been put into effect to provide the authority in question, it is not reasonable for an insider such as a director to assume this. In this regard consider the following extract from Lord Simonds in *Morris v Kanssen*, a case in which the plaintiff tried to rely on the indoor management rule to validate an issue of shares to him which was approved by a board of directors, of which he was a member, that had not been properly constituted and therefore had no authority to issue the shares. He argued that the indoor management rule would allow him to assume that the board had been correctly appointed even though it had not.

■ *Morris v Kanssen* [1946] AC 459

Lord Simonds

One of the fundamental maxims of the law is the maxim 'omnia praesumuntur rite esse acta'. It has many applications...The wheels of business will not go smoothly round unless it may be assumed that that is in order which appears to be in order. But the maxim has its proper limits. An ostensible agent cannot bind his principal to that which the principal cannot lawfully do. The directors or acting directors or other officers of a company cannot bind it to a transaction which is ultra vires. Nor is this the only limit to its application. It is a rule designed for the protection of

---

[40] [1946] AC 459. Translated from the Latin maxim used by Lord Simonds: '*omnia praesumuntur rite esse acta*'.

[41] *Ruben v Great Fingall Consolidated* [1906] AC 439.

[42] *B Liggett (Liverpool) Ltd v Barclays Bank, Ltd* [1927] All ER Rep 451; *Rolled Steel Products (Holdings) Ltd v British Steel & Corp* [1985] 3 All ER 52.

[43] *Morris v Kanssen* [1946] AC 459. Note that the Companies Act 2006 provides that, pursuant to section 161, 'the acts of a person acting as a director' are valid even though there was a defect in his appointment, a provision that was originally included in the model articles (see Table B to the Joint Stock Companies Act 1856).

those who are entitled to assume, just because they cannot know, that the person with whom they deal has the authority which he claims. This is clearly shown by the fact that the rule cannot be invoked if the condition is no longer satisfied, that is, if he who would invoke it is put upon his inquiry. He cannot presume in his own favour that things are rightly done if inquiry that he ought to make would tell him that they were wrongly done. What then is the position of the director or acting director who claims to hold the company to a transaction which the company has not, though it might have, authorized? Your Lordships have not in this case to consider what the result might be if such a director had not himself purported to act on behalf of the company in the unauthorized transaction. For here [the plaintiff] was himself purporting to act on behalf of the company in a transaction in which he had no authority. Can he then say that he was entitled to assume that all was in order?... It is the duty of directors, and equally of those who purport to act as directors, to look after the affairs of the company, to see that it acts within its powers and that its transactions are regular and orderly. To admit in their favour a presumption that that is rightly done which they have themselves wrongly done is to encourage ignorance and condone der-eliction from duty. It may be that in some cases, it may be that in this very case, a director is not blameworthy in his unauthorized act. It may be that in such a case some other remedy is open to him, either against the company or against those by whose fraud he was led into this situation, but I cannot admit that there is open to him the remedy of invoking this [indoor management] rule and giving validity to an otherwise invalid transaction. His duty as a director is to know; his interest, when he invokes the rule, is to disclaim knowledge. Such a conflict can be resolved in only one way... [The plaintiff] is not a person who in respect of this transaction comes within the scope of the [indoor management] rule.

Accordingly, when events put the contracting party on notice or if the person contracting with the company is a director of the company it will not be possible for the contracting party to rely on the indoor management rule.[44]

4 The Companies Act 2006 and apparent authority

As in practice any restrictions set out in the constitution on the authority of the board or of specific directors will usually be qualified restrictions that could be lifted with a specified approval, in most cases with the assistance of the indoor management rule the board or the director will be able to make the representation required to generate apparent authority. However, where absolute restrictions upon actual authority are set forth in the constitution—restrictions that are not, for example, subject to the approval of the board or the general meeting—the indoor management rule does not help. The indoor management rule assumes that what can be done has been done; but if it cannot be done then it cannot be done. The common law, therefore, leaves a significant hole of uncertainty for third-party contractors: an absolute restriction could render the contract voidable and unenforceable.

This 'hole' is, however, partially filled by statutory intervention which today is set out in section 40 of the Companies Act 2006. The provision implements the European Union's First Company Law Directive which was issued in 1968 prior to the UK accession to the EU. The relevant provision set out in article 9(2) provides as follows:

---

[44] *Howard v Patent Ivory Manufacturing Co* (1888) 38 Ch D 156. Note that in *Hely-Hutchinson v Brayhead Ltd* [1968] 1 QB 549 the court of first instance relied on apparent authority to uphold the contracts in question even though the plaintiff contractor was a director of the company. This problem arguably explains the Court of Appeal's use of implied actual authority rather than apparent authority which is not dependent on reliance and is not subject to the constructive notice doctrine.

■ First Council Directive 168/151/EEC

The limits on the powers of the organs of the company, arising under the statutes or from a decision of the competent organs, may never be relied on as against third parties, even if they have been disclosed.

Section 40 of the 2006 Act implementing article 9(2), provides as follows:

■ Section 40 CA 2006 Power of directors to bind the company

(1) In favour of a person dealing with a company in good faith, the power of the directors to bind the company, or authorise others to do so, is deemed to be free of any limitation under the company's constitution.

(2) For this purpose—

    (a) a person 'deals with' a company if he is a party to any transaction or other act to which the company is a party,

    (b) a person dealing with a company—

        (i) is not bound to enquire as to any limitation on the powers of the directors to bind the company or authorise others to do so,

        (ii) is presumed to have acted in good faith unless the contrary is proved, and

        (iii) is not to be regarded as acting in bad faith by reason only of his knowing that an act is beyond the powers of the directors under the company's constitution.

(3) The references above to limitations on the directors' powers under the company's constitution include limitations deriving—

    (a) from a resolution of the company or of any class of shareholders, or

    (b) from any agreement between the members of the company or of any class of shareholders.

(4) This section does not affect any right of a member of the company to bring proceedings to restrain the doing of an action that is beyond the powers of the directors.

    But no such proceedings lie in respect of an act to be done in fulfilment of a legal obligation arising from a previous act of the company.

(5) This section does not affect any liability incurred by the directors, or any other person, by reason of the directors' exceeding their powers.

4.1 The effect of section 40

In *Freeman & Lockyer* we saw through the lens provided by Diplock LJ that apparent authority was created through a representation created by an organ or person with actual authority or the power to grant such authority. If the organ or person did not have such actual authority or power then they were incapable of making a representation for the purposes of generating apparent authority. To contextualize the effect of section 40 in this regard consider the following examples:

Hypothetical A

Bob is the 100% shareholder in Bob's Electronics Ltd. Upon his retirement as manager and director he amends the articles so that they provide as follows:

(1) Subject to the articles, the directors are responsible for the management of the company's business, for which purpose they may exercise all the powers of the company.

(2) Subject to the articles, the directors may delegate any of the powers which are conferred on them under the articles to such persons they think fit.

(3) The board of directors does not have authority to enter into contracts worth more than £500,000 or the authority to authorize any directors to enter into such contracts.

(4) Only the Chief Executive Officer acting together with the director appointed as Chief financial officer may enter into any contract for indebtedness with a bank.

(5) Without the approval of the shareholders in general meeting, the board may not authorize the purchase of any real property.

Transaction examples:

(a) Markus, the chief executive officer, acting alone enters into a contract to borrow £600,000 from Risky Business Bank. The board does not explicitly authorize the transaction.

(b) The board authorizes Markus to enter into a contract to sell computers worth £1 million to the London School of Economics.

(c) Markus purchases a piece of land worth £400,000 from Ben on which the company will build a new warehouse facility. Shareholder approval is not obtained.

Transaction examples (a) and (b) involve actions that contravene absolute restrictions set out in the articles.[45] Accordingly, following Diplock LJ's approach to apparent authority, even though the board makes a representation to Risky Business Bank in appointing Markus as chief executive officer, and a representation to the London School of Economics in both appointing Markus and authorizing the sale of computers, and even though, let us assume, it would be common for CEOs of such companies to have the authority to enter into such contracts, as the board itself does not have the actual authority to enter into such contracts these acts by the board do not amount to representations *for the purposes of* the apparent authority doctrine. As these are absolute restrictions the indoor management rule is of no assistance. At common law these contracts would be voidable by the company and would not be enforceable by the counterparties. Example (c), on the other hand, is a qualified restriction which does benefit from the indoor management rule and would be enforceable.

Let us consider examples (a) and (b) in light of the application of section 40 of the 2006 Act. The provision provides that: 'the power of the directors to bind the company, or authorize others to do so, is deemed to be free of any limitation under the company's constitution' provided that the Risky Business Bank and the London School of Economics are 'dealing with the company' and are doing so 'in good faith'. That is, the law deems there to be no limitations on the power of the board to authorize the transactions or to delegate power to Markus to enter into the transactions. That is, section 40(1) dissolves the barrier to the board making a representation which is effective for the purposes of generating apparent authority and it also dissolves the barrier to the board granting actual authority to one of its agents or itself acting with actual authority.[46] This results in Markus having apparent authority to enter into transaction (a) and actual authority to enter into transaction (b).

[45] Transaction (a) contravenes articles 3 and 4; transaction (b) contravenes article 3.
[46] Effectively section 40 creates actual authority in relation to third-party transactions for the purposes of both actual and apparent authority. On its application to both actual and apparent authority see *Criterion Properties Plc v Stratford UK Properties LLC* [2006] BCLC 729 *per* Lord Scott. For an example of its application, see footnote 11 in Chapter 11.

The effect of section 40, therefore, is that *as far as third parties are concerned* the board has the power to manage the company and exercise all the powers of the company. Importantly, this does not affect the requirement to establish the common law requirements of actual or apparent authority but it does mean that the constitution cannot, as far as third parties dealing with the company in good faith are concerned, prevent the board from making a grant of authority or making a representation. In relation to apparent authority, another way of putting this would be to say that this provision abolishes the constructive knowledge doctrine—that third parties are not deemed to have knowledge of the company's constitution or, more accurately perhaps, the constructive notice doctrine continues to apply, but there are, as a result of section 40, no limitations for them to have deemed knowledge of.

Section 40(1)'s predecessor provision referred to the 'board of directors'[47] rather than 'the directors'. This arguably makes no significant change as a restriction on the authority of directors generally or a specific director type, such as CEO or finance director, is in effect also a restriction on the powers of the board of directors. Consider our example where directors who are not the CEO or the chief financial officer can play no role in the incurrence of indebtedness; such a restriction is also a restriction on the board because the board is not empowered to incur indebtedness or to authorize other directors to incur indebtedness.

4.2 Substantive and procedural limitations

The 'limitations' on the power of the board to bind the company or authorize others to do so in our examples in section 4.1 are all substantive limitations: value thresholds and types of contract. A further question is whether the term 'limitations' refers only to such substantive limitations or also to procedural limitations such as 'the board of directors can only act if the board meeting is quorate'. This issue was addressed in *Smith v Henniker-Major & Co*,[48] one of the few cases to directly consider section 40's predecessor provision. In this case the claimant, Mr Smith, was a director and chairman of a company, Saxon Petroleum Developments Ltd (SPDL). The company had certain causes of action against former directors of and the solicitor to the company. A meeting of the board of SPDL was called. At the time there were only two directors, the claimant and another director. However, the second director did not attend the meeting. Believing that he could act alone at the meeting the claimant passed a board resolution to transfer the company's causes of action to the claimant. However, the company's constitution provided that for the board to be quorate at least two directors must be present. The claimant brought proceedings against the company's former directors and former solicitor and the defendants counterclaimed that the transfer of the causes of action to the claimant was invalid. The claimant sought to rely on section 35A of the 1985 Act, the predecessor provision to section 40. This raised two issues of interest for us. First, does the term 'limitation' in what is now section 40(1) of the 2006 Act refer also to procedural limitations such as board quorum requirements and, second, is it possible for a director of the company to rely on section 40? In relation to the first of these questions Robert Walker LJ held as follows:

> In my judgment the irreducible minimum, if section [40] is to be engaged, is a genuine decision taken by a person or persons who can on substantial grounds claim to be the board of directors acting as such, even if the proceedings of the board are marred by procedural irregularities of a more or less serious character. This is not a precise test and it would have to be worked out on a case by case basis. But the essential distinction is between nullity (or non-event) and procedural

---

[47] Section 35A CA 1985. No explanation is given of this amendment in the explanatory notes.
[48] [2003] Ch 182.

> irregularity... If an outsider had been negotiating in good faith with the company, believing that the draft contract was to be approved at a board meeting, Mr Smith's one-man meeting... would in my view have passed the test and attracted protection under [section 40].

Carnwarth LJ, however, dissented on this point:

> I do not, with respect to Robert Walker LJ, think that this problem can be solved by the suggested distinction between 'nullity' and 'procedural irregularity'. The problem is illustrated by this case. By what criterion is it to be said that Mr Smith's decision to constitute himself as a board of the company is to be treated as a mere procedural irregularity, rather than a nullity? He had no more authority to take a decision in the name of the company than the office-boy. To an outsider, of course, such a document, emanating from the chairman, could reasonably have been assumed to have more validity than a similar document signed by the office-boy. Yet, viewed under the company's constitution, the decision had no validity of any kind; it was a nullity.

In *Ford v Polymer Vision Ltd*,[49] Blackburne J followed Robert Walker LJ in holding that procedural irregularities—involving the failure to give notice to two of the four board members and the holding of the board meeting in the UK, which was contrary to the articles—fell within the ambit of section 40's 'limitations' on the powers of the directors. Supporting his holding in this regard Blackburne J observed that:

> It is difficult to think of any policy reasons why, in favour of a third party, (an 'outsider' in contrast to, say, a director) either of the defects should not be within the purview of section 40 and every good reason why they should, not least, in the case of the first defect, the difficulty of knowing who might be entitled to notice and whether notice had been given.

With respect, it is submitted that Carnwarth LJ's position that section 40 should not apply to procedural irregularities is correct. The meaning and application of section 40 is a function of statutory interpretation not a function of policy. Nor, as outlined later, is it necessary to stretch the meaning of section 40 in this way to achieve these policy goals.

Section 40 is concerned with the effects of the constitution on the power and authority of the board to enter into contracts, to authorize an agent to enter into a contract, or to make representations about the authority of an agent. A procedural restriction such as a quorum requirement does not affect the powers of the board rather it is one of the conditions that determines how the board exercises the power that has been delegated to it. A procedural pre-requisite is not a 'limitation' on the power of the board, rather it sets forth the means by which the board exercises power. Section 40 of the Act, therefore, does not cure any failure to observe procedural requirements.

As far as third parties are concerned, however, the inapplicability of section 40 to such procedural irregularities is of little consequence as such a procedural failure would be cured by the indoor management rule: 'all things are presumed to be done in due form.' Certainly in *Morris v Kanssan*[50] the court was of the view that the indoor management rule would have operated in relation to defectively appointed directors had the person relying on the indoor management rule not been an insider. As the 'being put on notice of inquiry' and 'insider' qualifications to the indoor management rule show us, this rule is not without limitation, its availability being dependent on the circumstances and the reasonableness of the assumption by the third party that everything that appears in order is in order. However, the irregularities in both *Smith v Henniker Major* and *Ford v Polymer Vision* would appear to fall within the purview of the rule.

---

[49] [2009] 2 BCLC 160.   [50] [1946] AC 459.

It is also important here not to be confused by Robert Walker LJ's statement that for section 40 to apply a genuine decision needs to be taken by the board. However, for section 40 to apply this decision *need not be*, although it may be as it was in *Smith v Henniker-Major*, a board decision to explicitly authorize the transaction in question or grant authority to an agent to enter into the transaction in question. Remember that the starting point is with the requirements of apparent authority: what is required is that the board make a representation which could be specific in relation to the transaction in question or a general pre-transaction representation about the agent's authority—for example, in appointing a person to a particular position. Section 40 comes into effect to nullify any limitation in the constitution that prevents the board making a representation that is effective for the purposes of generating apparent authority. For example, in transaction (a) in *Hypothetical A* on page 128, section 40(1) enables the board's general representation in appointing the chief executive officer to generate the apparent authority of the CEO, provided that the third-party contractor relies on the representation and it would be reasonable for a third-party contractor to assume that a CEO would have the authority to enter into such contracts.

4.3 The preconditions to the application of section 40

The availability of section 40(1) is dependent on the relationship between the third-party contractor and the company amounting to 'a person dealing with the company' and that such dealing is in 'good faith'. The remainder of section 40 provides, amongst others, a little flesh on these prerequisites.

The first prerequisite is that the third party be a 'person' as understood by the section. No definition of person is provided. One context arises in which this meaning of person is problematic: namely whether a director of the company is a person who, provided she complies with the other prerequisites of the section, can benefit from this section. The answer to this question is provided by section 41 of the Act, which explicitly regulates transactions entered into with directors where 'its validity depends on section 40'.[51] By implication, therefore, section 40 is available to directors; however, section 41 renders the availability of section 40 of no consequence. The reason for this is that section 41(2) reasserts that such a transaction is voidable and that any such director is liable to account for any profit made to the company and indemnify the company for any loss resulting from the transaction.[52]

Section 40(2) provides that 'a person "deals with" a company if he is a party to any transaction or other act to which the company is a party'. However, the terms used to explain 'dealing' generates logical circularity: in cases where section 40(1) is needed to enforce a transaction there is no enforceable transaction unless the third party contractor is 'dealing with the company'; yet dealing with the company depends on a person being a party to a transaction. To make sense of this definition 'transaction' must be read broadly to mean a 'purported transaction' or 'an arrangement that would be a transaction *but for* the constitutional restriction that vitiates apparent authority and which section 40(1) is required to remedy'.[53]

---

[51] Note that section 41's predecessor provision in the 1985 Act did not explicitly refer to section 35A and therefore such a clear reading was not possible. The leading case in this regard under the 1985 Act was *Smith v Henniker-Major* the facts of which have already been set forth. In this case the Court of Appeal held that the director/chairman could not benefit from the section, however, the court focused in reaching its judgment on the fact that he was not only a director but also the chairman, which appeared to leave some space to argue that a director who was not the chairman could be 'a person' who could benefit from section 35A of the 1985 Act.

[52] Section 41(3) CA 2006. This provision also applies to 'connected persons' (section 41(7)) which is defined in section 252 CA 2006. For a discussion of connected persons see p 502.

[53] *TCB Ltd v Gray* [1986] 1 All ER 587 where in relation to the interpretative conundrum created by this provision the court observed that 'the section is dealing with purported actions by a company which, having regard to its internal documents, may be a nullity'.

Section 40 also provides some assistance in determining whether the third-party contractor dealing with the company is doing so in good faith. First of all there is a presumption of good faith unless the contrary is proved by the party seeking a determination that the contract is voidable. Secondly, the third party will not be deemed to be acting in bad faith simply because the third-party contractor actually knows that the 'agent' does not have actual authority. Note this is not that the third party has simply been provided with the constitution, it goes further than that: namely that good faith is not lost *just because* the third party has received the constitution and has read and understood the limitations on the agent's authority. This strikes most students of company law as odd. If a third party is aware that the agent has no authority yet enters into a contract and then attempts to enforce it, such duplicity would appear to be an obvious example of bad faith. However, it is important to note that the Act does not exclude consideration of this fact in considering the person's 'good faith', but there must be other evidence of bad faith in addition to this for the court to determine that the third party was not acting in good faith. Furthermore, as pursuant to section 40(2)(b)(i) the third-party contractor is not required to inquire as to whether the constitution contains any limits on the board's authority, the good faith of the third party cannot be impeached even when events put the third party on notice that there may be an authority problem. The section does not, however, inform us how a court should determine whether a person has acted in good faith. Some guidance in this regard is obtained from *Barclays Bank Ltd v TOSG Trust Fund Ltd*,[54] where Norse J clarified that the term 'good faith' in section 40's predecessor—section 9(1) of the European Communities Act 1972 which implemented article 9(1) of the First Council Directive extracted previously[55]—was a subjective standard requiring that the third-party contractor act genuinely and honestly:

> A person who acts in good faith will sometimes, perhaps often, act in a manner which can also be described as being reasonable. But I emphatically refute the suggestion, if such it is, that reasonableness is a necessary ingredient of good faith. That would require the introduction of an objective standard into a subjective concept and it would be contrary to everything which the law has always understood of that concept. In my judgment a person acts in good faith if he acts genuinely and honestly in the circumstances of the case.

4.4 Shareholder action in relation to unauthorized transactions

In relation to any proposed contract that the board or an agent of the company is considering entering into where the directors are not empowered either to enter into the transaction or to authorize an agent to enter into the transaction, the Act provides that the shareholders have a right to petition the court to order the directors or the agent not to enter into the proposed transaction.[56] However, the shareholders have no right to challenge a transaction that has been entered into which, although beyond the powers of the directors, benefits from the combination of apparent authority and section 40.

Where the board or the directors enter into transactions or authorize the entering into transactions in excess of their power and authority, the directors in question are in breach of their duty set out in section 171(a) to act in accordance with the company's constitution. Such directors are exposed to suit from the company, or by the shareholders derivatively[57] on behalf of the company, where such a breach causes loss to the company. Section 40(5) clarifies that the application of section 40(1) has no effect on such liability.

---

[54] [1984] BCLC 1.   [55] See pp 127.   [56] Section 40(4) CA 2006.
[57] See Chapter 15 on the enforcement of directors' duties.

Questions

1. How does one determine the extent of a grant of implied actual authority?

2. Why is silent acquiescence not sufficient to grant an agent implied actual authority?

3. How does implied actual authority differ from apparent authority?

4. What does Diplock LJ understand by the notion of 'a representation' by the company about an agent?

5. Would silent acquiescence amount to a representation for the purpose of the apparent authority doctrine?

6. What is the policy justification for providing that a company's constitution can restrict the making of a representation by the board for the purpose of the apparent authority doctrine?

7. Does an agent always have to have actual authority to be able to enter into the contract in question in order to make a representation about a junior/sub agent for the purpose of the apparent authority doctrine?

8. Why does Diplock LJ's representation approach not require the doctrine of constructive knowledge?

9. Does section 40 work with/facilitate the operation of the apparent authority doctrine or does it work on a stand-alone basis?

10. How often in practice do you think it is necessary to rely on section 40?

11. Does section 40 apply to the procedures with which the board must comply in order to make an effective decision?

IV TORT AND THE COMPANY[58]

1 Attributing tortious acts to the company

A company through the combined actions of its organs, employees, and agents produces products, provides services, and makes claims and representations about those products and services. Such products, services, claims, and representations may result in physical or economic injury and loss to parties who have entered into contracts with the company as well as third parties who are not in privity of contract with the company. The question for us in this section is: in what circumstances is the company liable in tort for the injuries caused to both contracting parties and non-contracting parties?

1.1 Vicarious liability

Simply stated the company will be liable if either the organs of the company or its agents and employees acting within the course of their agency or employment commit the tort in question; that is, if their actions fall within the criteria of relevance that determine liability in tort. This simple position can be set out within the framework provided by Lord Hoffmann in *Meridian Global Funds Management Asia Ltd v Securities Commission*[59] of the primary and general rules of attribution. If the corporate organ, acting *as the company*, acts in ways which fall within the criteria of relevance for the tort in question then the company will be liable as a result of the primary rules of attribution. It will, of course, be very unusual for a corporate organ itself to have committed the act that results in tort liability. For example, the board of directors may have authorized the production of the product in question, but will rarely have anything to do with the

---

[58] I am particularly grateful to Charlie Webb and Ewan McGaughley for their thoughts and advice on the issues raised in this section. The usual disclaimer applies.

[59] [1995] 2 BCLC 116.

negligent act that rendered the product dangerous or with the negligent driving by the company's delivery person that injured a pedestrian. Accordingly, whilst in theory the company may be liable as a result of the acts of its organs and the primary rules of attribution, in practice this will very rarely occur.

Typically a company will be liable in tort as a result of the general rules of attribution, which in tort involves the application of the doctrine of vicarious liability. Traditionally, vicarious liability has been understood to impose liability on the company where its *agent or employee commits* a tortious act in the ordinary course of the agent's or employee's agency or employment. As we have seen, at common law the ability of a company to enter into contracts may be limited by the terms of the constitution: the types of business activity the company can engage in (its objects); or restrictions on the authority of the company's organs or its agents to act on behalf of the company. In theory one could extend to torts the logic of constitutional restraints on actions that we encounter in relation to contracts. This logic would proceed as follows: the company's ability to act is determined by the constitution, as the constitution does not permit illegal or tortious acts the company is not capable of committing a tort. Such a position would be perverse and is not taken by English law.[60] The terms of the constitution have no bearing on the company's tort liability, whether primary or vicarious.[61]

In relation to vicarious liability, the central question is how to determine when an agent or employee is acting within the course of his agency or employment. A considerable body of complex case law has arisen from attempts to answer this question.[62] Here we deal with the concept with relative brevity. Reference is made to the leading texts on tort law for a fuller exposition.[63] The modern approach taken to this question is set out in the House of Lords judgment in *Dubai Aluminium v Salaam*, a case involving the question of a law firm's vicarious liability for the actions of one of its partners.

■ *Dubai Aluminium Company Ltd v Salaam* [2003] IRLR 608

Lord Nicholls of Birkenhead

Vicarious liability is concerned with the responsibility of the firm to other persons for wrongful acts done by a partner while acting in the ordinary course of the partnership business or with the authority of his co-partners. At first sight this might seem something of a contradiction in terms. Partners do not usually agree with each other to commit wrongful acts. Partners are not normally authorised to engage in wrongful conduct. Indeed, if vicarious liability of a firm for acts done by a partner acting in the ordinary course of the business of the firm were confined to acts authorised in every particular, the reach of vicarious liability would be short indeed. Especially would this be so with dishonesty and other intentional wrongdoing, as distinct from negligence. Similarly restricted would be the vicarious responsibility of employers for wrongful acts done by employees in the course of their employment. Like considerations apply to vicarious liability for employees.

---

[60] Professor Davies observes in this regard that 'it would seem perverse to give the company an advantage (i.e. escape from the doctrine of vicarious liability) which it would not have, had it conducted the business in a lawful way'. P. Davies, *Gower and Davies' Principles of Modern Company Law* (8th edn, Sweet & Maxwell, 2008), 179.

[61] In *Campbell v Paddington* [1911] 1 KB 869 the High Court held that a company could be held liable in tort.

[62] See, for example, the development of the case law on 'unauthorized acts' and 'unauthorized modes': *Plumb v The Manchester, Sheffield and Lincolnshire Railway Co* (1873) LR 8 CP 148; *Rose v Plenty* [1976] 1 WLR 141.

[63] See generally S. Deakin, A. Johnston and B. Markesinis, *Markesinis and Deakin's Tort Law* (OUP, 2007); J. Fleming, *Law of Torts* (9th edn, Law Book Company, 1998) G. Williams, 'Vicarious Liability: Tort of the Master or of the Servant?' (1956) 72 *LQR* 522; P. Atiyah, *Vicarious Liability in the Law of Torts* (Butterworths, 1967); P. Atiyah, 'Personal Injuries in the Twenty-First Century: Thinking the Unthinkable' in P. Birks (ed.), *Wrongs and Remedies in the Twenty-First Century* (OUP, 1996).

Take the present case. The essence of the claim advanced by Dubai Aluminium against Mr Amhurst is that he and Mr Salaam engaged in a criminal conspiracy to defraud Dubai Aluminium. Mr Amhurst drafted the consultancy agreement and other agreements in further-ance of this conspiracy. Needless to say, Mr Amhurst had no authority from his partners to con-duct himself in this manner. Nor is there any question of conduct of this nature being part of the ordinary course of the business of the Amhurst firm. Mr Amhurst had authority to draft commer-cial agreements. He had no authority to draft a commercial agreement for the dishonest purpose of furthering a criminal conspiracy.

However, this latter fact does not of itself mean that the firm is exempt from liability for his wrongful conduct. Whether an act or omission was done in the ordinary course of a firm's business cannot be decided simply by considering whether the partner was authorised by his co-partners to do the very act he did. The reason for this lies in the legal policy underlying vicari-ous liability. The underlying legal policy is based on the recognition that carrying on a business enterprise necessarily involves risks to others. It involves the risk that others will be harmed by wrongful acts committed by the agents through whom the business is carried on. When those risks ripen into loss, it is just that the business should be responsible for compensating the person who has been wronged.

This policy reason dictates that liability for agents should not be strictly confined to acts done with the employer's authority. Negligence can be expected to occur from time to time. Everyone makes mistakes at times. Additionally, it is a fact of life, and therefore to be expected by those who carry on businesses, that sometimes their agents may exceed the bounds of their authority or even defy express instructions. It is fair to allocate risk of losses thus arising to the businesses rather than leave those wronged with the sole remedy, of doubtful value, against the individual employee who committed the wrong. To this end, the law has given the concept of 'ordinary course of employment' an extended scope.

If, then, authority is not the touchstone, what is? Lord Denning MR once said that on this question the cases are baffling: see *Morris v C W Martin & Sons Ltd* [1966] 1 QB 716, 724. Perhaps the best general answer is that the wrongful conduct must be so closely connected with acts the partner or employee was authorised to do that, for the purpose of the liability of the firm or the employer to third parties, the wrongful conduct may fairly and properly be regarded as done by the partner while acting in the ordinary course of the firm's business or the employee's employ-ment. Lord Millett said as much in *Lister v Hesley Hall Ltd* [2001] IRLR 472; 484. So did Lord Steyn. McLachlin J said, in *Bazley v Curry* (1999) 174 DLR (4th) 45, 62: 'the policy purposes underlying the imposition of vicarious liability on employers are served only where the wrong is so connected with the employment that it can be said that the employer has introduced the risk of the wrong (and is thereby fairly and usefully charged with its management and minimisation)'.

To the same effect is Professor Atiyah's monograph *Vicarious Liability in the Law of Torts*, (1967): 'The master ought to be liable for all those torts which *can fairly be regarded* as reasonably inci-dental risks to the type of business he carried on' [emphasis added by Lord Nicholls].

In these formulations the phrases 'may fairly and properly be regarded', 'can be said', and 'can fairly be regarded' betoken a value judgment by the court. The conclusion is a conclusion of law, based on primary facts, rather than a simple question of fact.

This 'close connection' test focuses attention in the right direction. But it affords no guidance on the type or degree of connection which will normally be regarded as sufficiently close to prompt the legal conclusion that the risk of the wrongful act occurring, and any loss flowing from the wrongful act, should fall on the firm or employer rather than the third party who was wronged. It provides no clear assistance on when, to use Professor Fleming's phraseology, an incident is to be regarded as sufficiently work-related, as distinct from personal: see Fleming, *The Law of Torts*, 9th edn (1998), p. 427. Again, the well-known dictum of Lord Dunedin in *Plumb v Cobden Flour Mills Co Ltd* [1914] AC 62, 67, draws a distinction between prohibitions which limit the sphere of employment and those which only deal with conduct within the sphere of employ-ment. This leaves open how to recognise the one from the other.

> This lack of precision is inevitable, given the infinite range of circumstances where the issue arises. The crucial feature or features, either producing or negativing vicarious liability, vary widely from one case or type of case to the next. Essentially the court makes an evaluative judgment in each case, having regard to all the circumstances and, importantly, having regard also to the assistance provided by previous court decisions. In this field the latter form of assistance is particularly valuable…Historically the courts have been less ready to find vicarious liability in cases of employee dishonesty than in cases of negligence.

For Lord Nicholls, following the House of Lords judgment in *Lister v Hesley Hall Ltd*,[64] the determination of whether an employee is acting within the course of his agency or employment hinges upon whether what was done was so 'closely connected' to what he was authorized to do that a court would fairly view the act in question as amounting to an act carried out in the ordinary course of the company's business. As his Lordship recognizes, this approach provides only limited guidance for the court, which in practice has considerable discretion to make 'an evaluative judgment in each case'.[65]

1.2 Vicarious liability or vicarious attribution?

Traditionally it has been assumed that a precondition to a company's vicarious liability was that a tort has been committed by the company's agent or employee in question acting in the course of his agency or employment. That is, vicarious liability was a mechanism of transferring (jointly and severally) liability to the company: the company assumed liability for the tort but did not *itself* commit the tort. As liability for someone else's actions was being assumed by the company, commentators have focused much of their energies on searching for policy justifications for holding the company liable—to justify the assumption of another person's liability. Such justifications are not considered in depth here but include, for example: 'where the benefits lie so must the burdens'; the company made the commission of the act possible and therefore must bear responsibility for the loss; to deter company wrongdoing; or justifications based upon the efficient distribution of the risk of loss as suggested by Lord Nicholl's judgment in *Dubai Aluminium Company Ltd v Salaam*.

It follows from this view of the doctrine of vicarious liability that if no tort is committed by the agent or employee then no tort can be committed by the company.[66] This view of the effect of the doctrine of vicarious liability creates a problem where if the action taken by an agent or employee were treated as having been taken by the company itself it would amount to the commission of a tort by the company; however, in fact no tort has been committed by the agent or employee herself. In such circumstances, according to the logic of vicarious liability no one, neither the agent nor the company, would be liable for the tort. This problem arises particularly in relation to the tort of negligent misstatement where, as we shall discuss in greater detail in section IV.3, the agent is unlikely to have assumed personal responsibility for the inaccurate or misleading information and typically, therefore, will not be liable.

To address this conceptual anomaly, it is submitted that a better view of the effect of the doctrine of vicarious liability is the view set out recently by Professor Robert Stevens

---

[64] [2001] IRLR 472.

[65] For a more recent example of the application of this approach see *Brinks Global Service Inc v Igrox Ltd* [2011] IRLR 343, finding that an employee's theft was within the course of his employment.

[66] *Staveley Iron and Chemical Co. Ltd v Jones* [1956] AC 627. *Markesinis and Deakin's Tort Law* observes that 'this requirement seems obvious since vicarious liability is, by definition, imposed on one person for the wrongdoing of another' (S. Deakin, A. Johnston and B. Markesinis, *Markesinis and Deakin's Tort Law* (OUP, 2003), 582.

that the doctrine provides not for the assumption of an agent's or employee's liability by the company but for the *attribution* of the agent's or employee's actions *to* the company and, therefore, the commission of the tort *by* the company. It follows from this that there is no need for a special justification for imposition of liability on the company, as the company itself committed the tort. For a fuller exposition of this recharacterization of the doctrine consider the following extract:

■ Robert Stevens, 'Vicarious Liability or Vicarious Action' (2007) 123 *LQR* 30

If an employee carelessly runs over a pedestrian in the course of his employment, his employer will also be liable. Is what is attributed to the employer the actions of the employee or the employee's liability for the harm he has caused? In most cases, including this simple example, it makes no difference as the employer will be liable on either view.

At one time it was the dominant view that what was attributed was the employee's action (e.g. *Middleton v Fowler* (1699) 1 Salk. 282, per Holt C.J.; *Ackworth v Kempe* (1778) 1 Dougl. 40 at 42, per Lord Mansfield), and this was reflected in the maxim, *qui facit per alium facit per se* ('he who acts through another, acts himself'). Current orthodoxy rejects this approach and torts textbooks describe it as fictional. The (modern) language of 'vicarious liability' presupposes that what is being imputed is liability for the harm and not the act itself. Although none of the policy justifications for the attribution of an employee's liability to that of his employer is convincing,[67] the only modern-day supporter of the view that what is attributed is the employee's action was Glanville Williams.[68]

The House of Lords in *Majrowski v Guy's & St Thomas's NHS Trust* [2006] UKHL 34; [2006] 3 W.L.R. 125 endorsed the orthodox position…Unfortunately, orthodoxy is wrong and Glanville Williams was right. The significance of the distinction between the two approaches, and which is correct, can be demonstrated in a number of ways. [Four] will be given here…

[First], the liability of corporate bodies for misfeasance demonstrates that rules for the attribution of words and actions are indispensable. It is tempting to think of a company as a physical person which acts in the same way as a natural person. Of course, this is not so. Corporations are legal constructs and do not exist in the physical world. When we refer to the conduct of a corporation, this is a form of shorthand for the acts of a corporation's human agents, usually its employees. A corporation's liability for actions where this does not correspond with any liability imposed upon an employee, is always based upon the attribution to it of the acts of natural persons (e.g. *Williams v Natural Life Health Foods Ltd* [1998] 1 W.L.R. 830).[69]

[Secondly], the attribution of an employee's acts to an employer may result in the commission of a tort by the employer even though the same acts do not amount to a tort by the employee. The employer is liable despite the absence of any corresponding liability on the employee. In *Broom v Morgan* [1953] 1 Q.B. 597 the claimant and her husband were employed by the defendant to run a public house. The wife was carelessly injured by the husband during the course of his employment. At the time no husband or wife was entitled to sue the other for a tort. Despite this the Court of Appeal held the employer liable for her injuries as a result of their employee's carelessness. If we see the rule of attribution as concerned with the defendant's acts, this is correct. If we see the rule of attribution as concerned with the attribution of liability for the wrong, we are forced to say that the husband did commit a tort but that he had a procedural immunity which his employer did not possess. The procedural immunity view is difficult to maintain. After divorce one spouse could not sue the other for a tort committed during marriage, which indicates that the immunity is substantive rather than procedural.

---

[67] Professor Stevens cites in this regard: P.S. Atiyah, 'Personal Injuries in the Twenty-First Century: Thinking the Unthinkable' in P. Birks (ed.), *Wrongs and Remedies in the Twenty-First Century* (Clarendon Press,1996), 16.

[68] G. Williams, 'Vicarious Liability: Tort of the Master or of the Servant?' (1956) 72 *LQR* 522.

[69] See section 3 'Liability of directors and officers for acts undertaken on behalf of the company' for a detailed discussion of *Williams v Natural Foods*.

[Thirdly], where the duty is personal to the employee so that the same acts by someone else would not amount to the commission of a wrong, the attribution of the acts to the employer do not amount to a wrong by the employer…If an employee voluntarily assumes personal responsibility to another, without assuming responsibility on behalf of his employer, the employer cannot be liable for the breach of such an undertaking. Although rarely of this kind, some statutes impose a duty upon employees which is personal to them so that the attribution of the employee's acts to their employer will not amount to the commission of a tort by the employer. In *Darling Island Stevedoring & Lighterage v Long* (1957) 97 C.L.R. 36 a statutory duty was imposed on the 'person in charge' of loading and unloading a ship, but not upon his employer. The defendant's employee was in breach of this statutory duty and was liable in tort to the claimant. The claimant sought to hold the defendant vicariously liable. The High Court of Australia held the employer not liable. The best explanation is that provided by Kitto J. Whilst the employee's acts could be attributed to his employer, as the duty was only upon the employee the employer was not liable…

[Fourthly], where a defendant is vicariously liable for the acts of another, where he seeks to bring a contribution claim against another wrongdoer he is treated as the person who has committed the wrong, and not as an innocent party held liable for the wrong of someone else. A strong case illustrating the point is the decision of the House of Lords in *Dubai Aluminium Co Ltd v Salaam* [2002] UKHL 48; [2003] 2 A.C. 366. The claimants alleged that they were victims of a fraudulent scheme. Claims were settled against a number of defendants. One of the fraudsters was a partner in a firm of solicitors. The wrongful action of the fraudulent partner was attributed to his co-partners who were wholly innocent. The innocent partners sought a contribution from the other defendants. In assessing the appropriate contribution to be made, Rix J. at first instance allowed the innocence of the partners to be a relevant factor counting in their favour [1999] 1 Lloyd's Rep. 415 at 472. On appeal, both the Court of Appeal and the House of Lords, Lord Nicholls delivering the leading speech, rejected this approach. The partners had the serious wrongdoing of the dishonest partner attributed to them for all relevant purposes, not just the imposition of liability. Only as between themselves and the dishonest partner could the partners to whom his actions were attributed rely upon their personal lack of blame.[70]

Once it is accepted that the common law has rules for the attribution of action, and that these rules are of wider significance than the question of whether an employer should be liable for the losses caused by an employee's tort, the justifications commonly proffered for 'vicarious liability' need to be re-examined. These justifications seek to explain a rule which does not reflect the law.

Professor Stevens presents a compelling account of vicarious 'liability' as a rule of attribution providing for the attribution of the wrongdoer's acts, not his liability to the company. If this view is correct it follows that the question of relevance for the company is whether—given the attribution of those acts—the company has committed the tort in question. This does not exclude the possibility that the agent or employee in question may himself—individually—have committed the tort in question, but the company's liability is not dependent on the existence of the individual agent's or employee's liability.

2 Directors as the embodiment of the company: the identification doctrine

Lord Hoffmann in *Meridian*, when making a distinction between primary and general rules of attribution, views the primary rules of attribution as the rules that provide that certain actions are the *acts of the company*. This contrasts with actions that are *attributed to* the company. However, there is also long-standing authority for viewing certain acts of directors outside of the board meeting as *acts of the company*, rather than as acts

[70] See further *Stone & Rolls Ltd (in liquidation) v Moore Stephens* [2008] EWCA Civ 644.

of agents attributed to the company. Many of these cases address statutory and common law criminal rules; however, the approach to attribution is equally available to corporate tortuous liability.[71] In *Tesco Stores v Nattrass*,[72] a case dealing with Tesco's liability pursuant to the Trade Descriptions Act 1968, Lord Reid made the following observations in this regard:

> A living person has a mind which can have knowledge or intention or be negligent and he has hands to carry out his intentions. A corporation has none of these: it must act through living persons, though not always one or the same person. Then the person who acts is not speaking or acting for the company. He is acting as the company and his mind which directs his acts is the mind of the company. There is no question of the company being vicariously liable. He is not acting as a servant, representative, agent or delegate. He is an embodiment of the company or, one could say, he hears and speaks through the persona of the company, within his appropriate sphere, and his mind is the mind of the company. If it is a guilty mind then that guilt is the guilt of the company. It must be a question of law whether, once the facts have been ascertained, a person in doing particular things is to be regarded as the company or merely as the company's servant or agent. In that case any liability of the company can only be a statutory or vicarious liability.
>
> [The persons who are the embodiment of the company are those individuals who] represent the directing mind and will of the company, and control what it does. I think that is right for this reason. Normally the board of directors, the managing director and perhaps other superior officers of a company carry out the functions of management and speak and act as the company. Their subordinates do not. They carry out orders from above and it can make no difference that they are given some measure of discretion. But the board of directors may delegate some part of their functions of management giving to their delegate full discretion to act independently of instructions from them. I see no difficulty in holding that they have thereby put such a delegate in their place so that within the scope of the delegation he can act as the company. It may not always be easy to draw the line but there are cases in which the line must be drawn.

This approach views the actions of the company's 'directing will and mind'[73] as the actions of the company. Accordingly, where a director when carrying out company business commits a tort, the company is liable in tort not as a result of vicarious liability or attribution but because the director embodies the company. This approach is known as the identification doctrine.

This approach appears to cut across Lord Hoffmann's framework of primary and general rules of attribution. It does not involve a primary rule of attribution but does involve the company itself acting, rather than the act of an agent being attributed to the company. The identification doctrine is only applicable to the acts of directors and the most senior members of management such as the CEO. Importantly, this approach seems to suggest a third category of ways in which directors can act in relation to the company[74] and a third way in which a tort can be committed by the company through its directors or senior management of the company—in addition to acting as members of the board of directors or as agents of the company—namely as the physical embodiment of the company.

---

[71] For an example of its application in the context of tort law see *Trevor Ivory Ltd v Anderson* [1992] 2 NZLR 517.

[72] [1972] AC 153, 170.

[73] The phrase 'directing will in mind' was originally set forth in the House of Lords case *Lennard's Carrying Co Ltd v Asiatic Petroleum Co Ltd* [1915] AC at 713, a civil case concerning the Merchant Shipping Act 1894. See also *Bolton (Engineering) Co Ltd v T J Graham & Sons Ltd* [1957] 1 QB 159.

[74] The exact legal status of the directors in this regard is somewhat opaque—they are not acting as member of the board and therefore appear to be agents, yet they are viewed here as the physical embodiment of the company. In the New Zealand case of *Trevor Ivory Ltd v Anderson* [1992] 2 NZLR 517, Hardie Boys J observed in this regard that 'in that sense they are certainly agents; but in the popular rather than the strictly legal sense of the word. It is not the case that they are always agents in the legal sense.'

3 Liability of directors and officers for acts undertaken on behalf of the company

If the actions of the company's 'directing will and mind' are not attributed to the company but rather are the acts of the company because those individuals embody the company, then it is, arguably, logical that only the company has committed the tort, as the director as an individual person *has not acted*; he has only acted as the physical embodiment of the company rather than in an individual capacity as its agent. According to this logic, a consequence of the separate legal personality of the company is that in certain circumstances the individual director acting on behalf of the company is relieved of personal liability for his actions because those actions are the actions of the company rather than his actions that are attributed to the company: 'the special treatment of directors thus arises because the tortious act is not that of the director, but of the company itself'.[75] If this is correct then not only does company law shield shareholders from liability for the debts of the company, but it also shields directors from personal liability for their actions that they would otherwise have. Professors Grantham and Rickett have argued strongly that this position is supported by sound policy justifications. They observe that:

> While on occasion there may be sound policy reasons why liability should be imposed on directors personally for torts committed in the course of operating the company, *prima facie*, company law doctrines must necessarily be accorded primacy. While such a claim may seem imperialistic, such primacy is inherent in the very nature of company law. The primary purpose of the set of rules which makes up company law is to ensure that principles of law generally applicable, such as those of torts, are applied to a different and non-natural entity in a particular manner, which usually means that the scope of their application is limited. Thus, although, necessarily, a director may be the actual tortfeasor or the individual responsible for a contract, the company law regime modifies the normal consequences of the director's actions, precisely to ensure that responsibility for, and the legal consequences of, the tortious conduct or contractual undertaking are not sheeted home to the individual. Where the company law regime applies, its essential function is to identify a different entity as the tortfeasor or contractor. To refuse to accept that these general principles are modified is not only to deny the primacy inherent in the rules of company law, but in a sense it is to deny the company's very existence.[76]

From this viewpoint, the determination of whether the director is liable for the actions in question is not answered by asking if he has committed the tort—he could not have done so as his actions were only those of the company. Rather liability, if any, is a function of the company law rules that police the company's separate legal personality.

It is important to remind ourselves, however, that this view of the role of company law in shielding directors from liabilities is the logical product of the identification doctrine approach to attribution already set forth. If directors when they act other than as members of the board of directors are acting only as company agents whose actions are attributed to the company and form the basis for an assessment of the directors' personal liability as well as the liability of the company, then the idea that the directors act *as* the company and not as individuals does not arise. From this viewpoint the question of whether the director is liable is a straightforward application of tort law: has the director as an individual agent committed the tort?

The issue of director liability in tort for actions carried out on behalf of the company was considered in two recent House of Lords' judgments.

---

[75] R. Grantham and C. Rickett, 'Directors' Tortious Liability: Contract, Tort or Company Law?' (1999) 62 *MLR* 133.
[76] *Ibid.*

■ *Williams v Natural Life Health Foods Ltd* [1998] 2 All ER 577

In 1983 Richard Mistlin set up a natural health food shop in Salisbury. In 1986 he arranged for the formation of Natural Life Health Foods Ltd in order to franchise the business concept. Franchising involves the licensing of intellectual property rights, such as the right to use the name 'Natural Life Health Foods', as well as the provision of advice on running the business and the use of the group of stores as a whole to purchase supplies, thereby benefiting from the group's superior purchasing power as compared to individual stores. The company's sole director, 'sole'[77] shareholder, and managing director was Mr Mistlin. The company employed three other individuals. In 1987 Mr Williams requested information about the health food franchise and was provided by one of the company's employees—not Mr Mistlin—with a company brochure. The company brochure contained estimated financial projections for a Natural Life Health Food Store. Mr Williams subsequently purchased a franchise from the company to set up a shop in Rugby. Unfortunately, the shop in Rugby was not successful, generating income far below what the company brochure had projected. Mr Williams sued the company for negligent provision of advice. However, the company itself had fallen on hard times and had been wound up and dissolved. On finding out about the company's position, Mr Williams added Mr Mistlin as a defendant and discontinued the action against the company.

Lord Steyn

My Lords, the principal question on this appeal is whether a director of a franchisor company is personally liable to franchisees for loss which they suffered as a result of negligent advice given to them by the franchisor company. At first instance Langley J ([1996] 1 BCLC 288) answered that question in the affirmative. By a majority, the Court of Appeal ([1997] 1 BCLC 131) upheld this conclusion and dismissed an appeal...Only one issue was canvassed in the Court of Appeal, namely whether the judge was entitled to find that Mr Mistlin was personally liable to the plaintiffs on the basis of an assumption of responsibility. A majority (Hirst and Waite LJJ) upheld the judge's conclusion and dismissed the appeal (see [1997] 1 BCLC 131)...Waite LJ said (at 154):

'...where representations are made negligently by a company so as to attract tortious liability under the principle of *Hedley Byrne*, the primary liability is that of the corporate representor. In the vast majority of cases it is also the sole liability. The law does, however, recognise a category of case in which a director of the representor will be fixed with personal liability for the negligent misstatement. It is a rare category, and a severely restricted one. If that were not so, representees could set at naught the protection which limited liability is designed to confer on those who incorporate their business activities. The mesh is kept fine by the stringency of the question which the law requires to be asked: do the circumstances, when viewed as a whole, involve an assumption by the director of personal responsibility for the impugned statement?'...

The theory of the extended **Hedley Byrne** *principle*

It is clear, and accepted by counsel on both sides, that the governing principles are stated in the leading speech of Lord Goff of Chieveley in *Henderson v Merrett Syndicates Ltd* [1994] 3 All ER 506...[where] applying *Hedley Byrne*, it was made clear that:

'reliance upon [the assumption of responsibility] by the other party will be necessary to establish a cause of action (because otherwise the negligence will have no causative effect)...' (See [1994] 3 All ER 506 at 520, [1995] 2 AC 145 at 180.)

It will be recalled that Waite LJ took the view that in the context of directors of companies the general principle must not 'set at naught' the protection of limited liability...It is clear what [he] meant. What matters is not that the liability of the shareholders of a company is limited but that a company is a separate entity, distinct from its directors, servants or other agents. The trader

---

[77] The claimant's wife was also a shareholder of a nominal number of shares.

who incorporates a company to which he transfers his business creates a legal person on whose behalf he may afterwards act as director. For present purposes, his position is the same as if he had sold his business to another individual and agreed to act on his behalf. Thus the issue in this case is not peculiar to companies. Whether the principal is a company or a natural person, someone acting on his behalf may incur personal liability in tort as well as imposing vicarious or attributed liability upon his principal. But in order to establish personal liability under the principle of *Hedley Byrne*, which requires the existence of a special relationship between plaintiff and tortfeasor, it is not sufficient that there should have been a special relationship with the principal. There must have been an assumption of responsibility such as to create a special relationship with the director or employee himself.

The practical application of the extended Hedley Byrne *principle*

Not surprisingly, opposing counsel approached the application of the principle of assumption of risk from different perspectives. Counsel for the plaintiffs concentrated in his argument on the pivotal role of Mr Mistlin in the affairs of the company. Counsel for Mr Mistlin concentrated on the absence of direct dealings between the plaintiffs and Mr Mistlin…The touchstone of liability is not the state of mind of the defendant. An objective test [must be applied which] means that the primary focus must be on things said or done by the defendant or on his behalf in dealings with the plaintiff. Obviously, the impact of what a defendant says or does must be judged in the light of the relevant contextual scene. Subject to this qualification, the primary focus must be on exchanges (in which term I include statements and conduct) which cross the line between the defendant and the plaintiff. Sometimes such an issue arises in a simple bilateral relationship. In the present case a triangular position is under consideration: the prospective franchisees, the franchisor company, and the director. In such a case where the personal liability of the director is in question, the internal arrangements between a director and his company cannot be the foundation of a director's personal liability in tort. The inquiry must be whether the director, or anybody on his behalf, conveyed directly or indirectly to the prospective franchisees that the director assumed personal responsibility towards the prospective franchisees. An example of such a case being established is *Fairline Shipping Corp v Adamson* [1974] 2 All ER 967, [1975] QB 180. The plaintiffs sued the defendant, a director of a warehousing company, for the negligent storage of perishable goods. The contract was between the plaintiff and the company. But Kerr J (later Kerr LJ) held that the director was personally liable. That conclusion was possible because the director wrote to the customer, and rendered an invoice, creating the clear impression that he was personally answerable for the services. If he had chosen to write on company notepaper, and rendered an invoice on behalf of the company, the necessary factual foundation for finding an assumption of risk would have been absent…

That brings me to reliance by the plaintiff upon the assumption of personal responsibility. If reliance is not proved, it is not established that the assumption of personal responsibility had causative effect. In his Hamlyn Lecture Lord Cooke of Thorndon…emphasised in the context of an issue of personal liability of a company's employee the distinction between 'mere reliance in fact and *reasonable* reliance on the employee's pocket-book'…This reasoning is instructive. The test is not simply reliance in fact. The test is whether the plaintiff could *reasonably* rely on an assumption of personal responsibility by the individual who performed the services on behalf of the company…

Applying the principle to the facts

Mr Mistlin owned and controlled the company. The company held itself out as having the expertise to provide reliable advice to franchisees. The brochure made clear that this expertise derived from Mr Mistlin's experience in the operation of the Salisbury shop. In my view these circumstances were insufficient to make Mr Mistlin personally liable to the plaintiffs. Stripped to essentials, the reasons of Langley J, the reasons of the majority in the Court of Appeal and the arguments of counsel for the plaintiffs can be considered under two headings. First, it is said that the terms of the brochure, and in particular its description of the role of Mr Mistlin, are sufficient to amount to an assumption of responsibility by Mr Mistlin. In his dissenting judgment [in the Court of Appeal's judgment] ([1997] 1 BCLC 131 at 156) Sir Patrick Russell rightly pointed out that in a small one-man company 'the managing director will almost inevitably be the one possessed of qualities essential to the functioning of the company'. By itself this factor does not convey that the managing director is willing to be personally answerable to the customers of the company. Secondly, great emphasis was placed on the fact that it was made clear to the franchisees that Mr Mistlin's expertise derived from his experience in running the Salisbury shop for his own account. Hirst LJ summarised the point by saying that 'the relevant knowledge and experience was entirely his qua Mr Mistlin, and not his qua director'. The point will simply not bear the weight put on it. Postulate a food expert who over ten years gains experience in advising customers on his own account. Then he incorporates his business as a company and he so advises his customers. Surely, it cannot be right to say that in the new situation his earlier experience on his own account is indicative of an assumption of personal responsibility towards his customers. In the present case there were no personal dealings between Mr Mistlin and the plaintiffs. There were no exchanges or conduct crossing the line which could have conveyed to the plaintiffs that Mr Mistlin was willing to assume personal responsibility to them. Contrary to the submissions of counsel for the plaintiffs, I am also satisfied that there was not even evidence that the plaintiffs believed that Mr Mistlin was undertaking personal responsibility to them. Certainly, there was nothing in the circumstances to show that the plaintiffs could reasonably have looked to Mr Mistlin for indemnification of any loss. For these reasons I would reject the principal argument of counsel for the plaintiffs....[and] would allow the appeal.

The first point to note about this case, which makes us all feel better as students of company law, is that even senior judges get confused about the implications of incorporation. The Court of Appeal noted their concern that holding Mr Mistlin liable would challenge the bedrock of limited member liability. But, as the House of Lords clarify, the issue in question does not involve limited liability but the potential liability of the company's agent, its managing director. The fact that he is the same real person as the company's controlling shareholder does not mean that any liability imposed upon him as a director lifts the corporate veil and holds the shareholders liable for the company's debts. However, as Lord Steyn observes, 'we know what was meant': the corporate form enables a person to 'avoid' liability for wrongs committed in the course of carrying out a business, that *had he carried out the business as a sole trader* he would have been liable for himself; holding the director liable for the debts of a one-person company would vitiate that benefit.

In this case the legal questions of relevance are: first, whether the company has committed a tort; and second, whether Mr Mistlin himself has committed a tort or was liable for the company's tort. The former question lapsed upon the claimants finding out that the company had been dissolved. According to *Williams v Natural Health Foods*, the question of whether Mr Mistlin is liable is answered by determining whether Mr Mistlin had assumed personal responsibility for the misstatement vis à vis the claimant. As the court observes, this is not determined by applying a subjective test— whether the defendant considered himself to be taking personal responsibility for the misstatement—but rather through the application of an objective test, that is, whether a reasonable person would view the defendant's actions as involving an assumption of personal responsibility. In this regard, it is clear that in relation to any company—a one-man company or a widely held company—it is very unlikely that the company's agent will be deemed to have assumed personal responsibility for the statements or claims that that person makes where such person does so clearly in her capacity as an agent of the company—on the company's letterhead; the company email address; a company brochure; on the company telephone; or in a company meeting, wherever that is held. The possibility of assumption of responsibility diminishes significantly where there is no personal contact or direct communication between the agent and the claimant. However, even where there is such contact such assumption remains highly unlikely where the context of the engagement is a corporate one.

It is possible to view the holding in *Williams* in two ways. One way is that the requirement of the assumption of personal responsibility by the director is a company law requirement applicable to determine whether a director is liable for the tort in question in relation to which the company is liable. That is, as the company commits a tort through its directors as the embodiment of the company, the director himself is not liable unless he takes certain additional steps to render him liable, namely, an additional assumption of personal responsibility.[78]

This view of the role of company law in shielding its senior agents from liability has been forcefully critiqued by Professors Campbell and Armour. They refer to this approach as the 'distribution heresy'. In their view, the correct way of understanding *Williams v Natural Health Foods Ltd* is that a director's liability is a question not of company law but of tort law as applied to *any* agent. According to this view the assumption of responsibility requirement is a core element of the tort of negligent misstatement. It follows, therefore, that 'when the civil liability of a corporate agent is called in question the only relevant enquiry is whether the elements of the civil wrong are proved against the agent'.[79]

In a subsequent case, *Standard Chartered Bank v Pakistan National Shipping Corporation*, the Court of Appeal adopted the former position, whilst the House of Lords corrected them by reaffirming the understanding that a director's liability is a function of the application of the law of tort and unaffected by company law.

■ Standard Chartered Bank v Pakistan National Shipping Corporation

It is typical in a cross-border sale of goods for the sale to be supported by a letter of credit from a bank. A letter of credit is effectively an agreement by a bank to pay the amount due for the goods on the presentation of shipping documents to the bank, including most importantly a bill of lading. A bill of lading is a document given by the shipping company transporting the goods which confirms that the goods have been placed on the vessel. Often letter of credit transactions involve several banks: the 'issuing bank'—the local bank of the buyer that issues the letter of credit—and the 'confirming bank' which confirms the letter of credit issued by the issuing bank and provides for the direct payment to the seller. In this case, the seller of goods, Oakprime Ltd, agreed to sell bitumen to a Vietnamese company. The sale was supported by a letter of credit confirmed by Standard Chartered Bank. As a condition of the letter of credit the goods had to be shipped at the latest by 25 October. However, Oakprime was only able to arrange shipment at a later date. The managing director of Oakprime Ltd, Mr Mehra, persuaded the shipping company, Pakistan National Shipping Company, to backdate the bill of lading to 25 October. Based on this fraudulent document Standard Chartered, as confirming bank, paid the amounts due on the letter of credit. However, on discovering irregularities with the documents the issuing bank, a Vietnamese bank, refused to pay the amounts Standard Chartered claimed were owed to it. It was clear in this regard that the company had acted fraudulently and was liable to Standard Chartered for the tort of deceit. The question for the court was whether Mr Mehra was personally liable to Standard Chartered. At first instance the court found that both Oakprime and Mr Mehra personally were liable in the tort of deceit. Mr Mehra appealed.

---

[78] See, for example, Grantham and Rickett, note 75.

[79] N. Campbell and J. Armour, 'Demystifying the Corporate Liability of Civil Agents' (2003) 62 *Cambridge Law Journal* 290.

■ Court of Appeal [2000] 1 Lloyd's Rep 218

Aldous LJ

In my view the representations were made by Oakprime and all the evidence points to the conclusion that SCB relied upon them as being representations by Oakprime.

Since *Salomon v. Salomon Co. Ltd.* [1897] A.C. 22, companies have been recognized as separate legal entities to their shareholders, their directors and their employees. Leaving aside certain cases, not applicable in this case, where it has been held permissible to lift the corporate veil e.g. where the company is a mere façade, directors or employees acting as such will only be liable for tortious acts committed during the course of their employment in three circumstances.

First, if a director or an employee himself commits the tort he will be liable. An example is the lorry driver who is involved in an accident in the course of his employment. Although Mr. Mehra was the person who was responsible for making the misrepresentations, he did not commit the deceit himself. For reasons I have already stated the representations were made by Oakprime and not by him. Further, SCB relied upon them as representations by Oakprime and not as representations by Mr. Mehra.

The second way that a director or an employee will become liable is a branch of the first. A director or an employee may, when carrying out his duties for the company, assume a personal liability. An example where personal liability was assumed was *Fairline Shipping Corporation v. Adamson*, [1974] 1 Lloyd's Rep. 133; [1975] Q.B. 180. A different conclusion was reached in *Trevor Ivory Ltd. v. Anderson*, [1992] 2 N.Z.L.R. 517. What amounts to such an assumption will depend upon the facts of the particular case. Guidance as to how to decide whether such an assumption took place can be obtained from *Williams v. Natural Life Health Foods Ltd*...[In that case], Lord Steyn had in mind that the cause of action relied on was negligence. However the principles stated are applicable to other torts, in particular to deceit. There must be an assumption of responsibility such as to create a special relationship by the plaintiff with the director or employee himself. Whether that exists is to be judged objectively with the primary focus on things said and done by the director or employee. It is necessary to enquire whether the director conveyed directly or indirectly to the plaintiff that he assumed a personal responsibility towards the plaintiff.

In the present case, Mr. Mehra, by his actions or statements never led SCB to believe he was assuming personal responsibility for the misrepresentations. SCB believed they were dealing with Oakprime. It follows that Mr. Mehra cannot be held liable on this ground.

The third ground of liability arises when the director does not carry out the tortious act himself nor does he assume liability for it, but he procures and induces another, the company, to commit the tort. A person who procures and induces another to commit a tort becomes a joint tortfeasor (see *Unilever Plc. v. Gillette (U.K.) Ltd.*, [1989] R.P.C. 583 and *Molnlycke A.B. v Procter & Gamble Ltd.*, [1992] R.P.C. 583). There is no reason why a director of a company should be in any different position to a third party and therefore it is possible that a director can be capable of becoming a joint tortfeasor by procuring and inducing the company, for which he works, to carry out a tortious act...

I would allow the appeal by Mr. Mehra.

■ House of Lords [2003] 1 Lloyd's Rep 227

Lord Hoffmann

My Lords, I come...to the question of whether Mr Mehra was liable for his deceit. To put the question in this way may seem tendentious but I do not think that it is unfair. Mr Mehra says, and the Court of Appeal accepted, that he committed no deceit because he made the representation on behalf of Oakprime and it was relied upon as a representation by Oakprime. That is true but seems to me irrelevant. Mr Mehra made a fraudulent misrepresentation intending SCB to rely upon it and SCB did rely upon it. The fact that by virtue of the law of agency his representation and the knowledge with which he made it would also be attributed to Oakprime would be of interest in an action against Oakprime. But that cannot detract from the fact that they were his representation and his knowledge. He was the only human being involved in making the representation to SCB (apart from administrative assistance like someone to type the letter and carry the papers round to the bank). It is true that SCB relied upon Mr Mehra's representation being attributable to Oakprime because it was the beneficiary under the credit. But they also relied upon it being Mr Mehra's representation, because otherwise there could have been no representation and no attribution.

The Court of Appeal appear to have based their conclusion upon the decision of your Lordships' House in *Williams v Natural Life Health Foods Ltd* [1998] 2 All ER 577. That was an action for damages for negligent misrepresentation. My noble and learned friend, Lord Steyn, pointed out that in such a case liability depended upon an assumption of responsibility by the defendant. As Lord Devlin said in *Hedley Byrne & Co Ltd v Heller & Partners* [1964] AC 465, [1963] 2 All ER 575, 530 of the former report, the basis of liability is analogous to contract. And just as an agent can contract on behalf of another without incurring personal liability, so an agent can assume responsibility on behalf of another for the purposes of the *Hedley Byrne* rule without assuming personal responsibility. Their Lordships decided that on the facts of the case, the agent had not assumed any personal responsibility.

This reasoning cannot in my opinion apply to liability for fraud. No one can escape liability for his fraud by saying 'I wish to make it clear that I am committing this fraud on behalf of someone else and I am not to be personally liable'. Sir Anthony Evans framed the question ([2000] 1 Lloyd's Rep 218, 230) as being 'whether the director may be held liable for the company's tort'. But Mr Mehra was not being sued for the company's tort. He was being sued for his own tort and all the elements of that tort were proved against him. Having put the question in the way he did, Sir Anthony answered it by saying that the fact that Mr Mehra was a director did not in itself make him liable. That of course is true. He is liable not because he was a director but because he committed a fraud.

Both Sir Anthony Evans and Aldous LJ treated the *Williams* case [1998] 2 All ER 577 as being based upon the separate legal personality of a company. Aldous LJ referred ([2000] Lloyd's Rep 218, 233) to *Salomon v A Salomon & Co Ltd* [1897] AC 22. But my noble and learned friend, Lord Steyn, made it clear that the decision had nothing to do with company law. It was an application of the law of principal and agent to the requirement of assumption of responsibility under the *Hedley Byrne* principle. Lord Steyn said it would have made no difference if Mr Williams's principal had been a natural person. So one may test the matter by asking whether, if Mr Mehra had been acting as manager for the owner of the business who lived in the south of France and had made a fraudulent representation within the scope of his employment, he could escape personal liability by saying that it must have been perfectly clear that he was not being fraudulent on his own behalf but exclusively on behalf of his employer.

I would therefore allow the appeal against Mr Mehra.

Lord Hoffmann's judgment settles the score very clearly. The liability of a director for a tort depends upon whether or not his actions fall within the criteria of relevance for the tort in question. In *Williams v Natural Health Foods Ltd* the consideration of the assumption of responsibility was not, as the Court of Appeal in *Standard Chartered Back v Pakistan National Shipping Corporation* saw it, an element of company law to be applied in relation to all torts committed by the company, but rather an element of the tort of negligent misstatement. As the assumption of responsibility is not a component of the tort of deceit it had no role to play in considering Mr Mehra's liability.

This approach also allows us to make sense of the rules referred to in Aldous LJ's judgment regarding the liability of directors for tortious acts they procure or induce.[80] Through Lord Hoffmann's framework this is an application of the rules of tort law that apply to anyone who procures or induces a tort.[81] If one follows the Court of Appeal's reasoning an absurd anomaly is generated—the director would be liable for the deceit procured by him of a junior employee but not his own deceit unless he personally assumed responsibility for that deceit. Lord Hoffmann's assertion that director liability in this regard has nothing to do with company law saves us from having to account for such an anomaly.

4 Group liability in tort

In Chapter 2 we learnt that in English law a company is a separate legal person and that it is only in a very limited set of circumstances that the separate legal personality of the company will be disregarded. We also saw that respect for the separate personality of the company extends to the group company context where subsidiary companies are owned and controlled by parent companies. This was most apparent in *Adams v Cape Industries Plc*[82] where, for the purposes of determining whether under English law the New York courts had jurisdiction over Cape Plc, the parent company was deemed not to be present in the United States by reason of its subsidiary's US presence.

In *Adams v Cape Industries* the central question was whether a judgment against Cape Industries Plc could be enforced in the UK. The New York judgment found that *pursuant to New York law* Cape Industries Plc was liable in tort for the claimant's personal injuries. What the claimants in *Adams v Cape Industries* did not do, however, was sue Cape Industries Plc in the UK pursuant to English tort law. But could they have done so? Perhaps intuitively, with Chapter 2 fresh in our minds, we might say that to do so would violate the separate legal personality of the parent: the parent did not sell asbestos to the company whose use of asbestos injured its employees—the South African subsidiary did so.[83] This intuition would not, however, be correct. We have seen in this chapter that a company can be liable in tort. Tort law regulates responsibility for harms suffered even where there is no direct contractual relationship between the party injured and the party held responsible. If a parent owes and breaches a duty of care to a person who is *also* owed a duty of care by the subsidiary, the parent's and subsidiary's separate legal personality remain clearly intact. However, although a parent's liability in tort does not directly affect the separate legal personality of a company or shareholders' limited liability, clearly tort law here has the potential to undermine some of the benefits of limited liability. An expansive approach to the parent's duty of care would, if breached, impose *parallel* liability on the parent in relation to the same loss that the subsidiary is also liable for. Although this would *not* involve imposing liability on the parent for some of the debts of the subsidiary the effect would be *as if* it was.

The question for us here is whether, and in what circumstances, tort law imposes a duty of care on the parent in relation to individuals whose primary relationship with the group is with the subsidiary—either because they have a contractual relationship

---

[80] *Rainham Chemical Works Ltd v Belvedere Fish Guano Co Ltd* [1921] 2 AC 465, 476, *per* Lord Buckmaster: 'prima facie a managing director is not liable for tortious acts done by servants of the company unless he himself is privy to the acts, that is to say unless he ordered or procured the acts to be done.' See also *Performing Rights Society Ltd v Ciryl Theatrical Syndicate Ltd* [1924] 1 KB 1; C *Evans v Spritebrand Ltd* [1985] 1 WLR 317. The attempt to tailor the doctrine to the company context, and make it more difficult to apply to directors in *Whitehorse Distillers Ltd v Gregson Associates Ltd* [1984] RPC 61 was disapproved of in *C Evans v Spriteband*.

[81] Campbell and Armour, note 79; *CBS Songs Ltd v Amstrad Consumer Electronics Plc* [1988] AC 1013.

[82] [1990] Ch 433.

[83] See pp 67–8 for a summary of the facts in *Adams v Cape Industries Plc*.

with the subsidiary, for example, the subsidiary's employees or customers, or because they were injured by a product produced or service provided by the subsidiary. Consider these two recent and thought-provoking cases addressing these issues.

■ *Newton-Sealey v ArmorGroup Services Ltd* [2008] EWHC 233

This case involved an action for summary judgment in relation to claims brought by an employee of a subsidiary company (AG (Jersey)) against the parent (AG plc) and a sister company (AG (UK)) for damages for personal injury suffered in the course of his employment as a security guard in Iraq. The claimant had entered into a contract of employment with AG (Jersey). However, the contract contained wide exemption clauses for liability for personal injury which apparently were enforceable in Jersey although they would not have been enforceable in the UK. The claimant sued the UK parent and sister companies in contract and tort. The contractual claims were rejected by the court and concern us no further here. The claimant claimed that AG plc and AG (UK) owed him a duty of care. He argued that although he signed a contract with AG (Jersey) he was given the impression that he was dealing with, and would be employed by, the Group: the interview was in London; it was conducted by an AG (UK) employee working for the Group; he was not told in the interview that he would be employed by the Jersey company; his initial deployment orders in Iraq were on AG (UK) letterhead; and AG (UK) took responsibility for deployment in Iraq. The contractual relationship between AG (Jersey) and AG plc was also relied upon by the claimant. AG (UK) had significant contractual control over AG (Jersey), for example, AG (UK) had approval rights in relation to the recruitment of personnel provided to the Group by AG (Jersey), and AG (UK) could instruct AG (Jersey) to terminate an employee's employment. Note, as the case involves an application for summary judgment the judge is concerned only with whether or not there is 'no real prospect of success' of the claim and not with the final determination of the whether AG (UK) and AG plc are liable.

Cranston J

This case raises the issue of liability within a corporate group. It is sometimes described as an issue of enterprise liability. Persons deal with a business, as in this case an international business, and do not necessarily distinguish between its different corporate members. From their point of view they are dealing with the enterprise as a whole. Something goes wrong and they seek to hold the group liable through its most convenient member or members. They are then met with the argument that as a matter of law each member of the group is quite distinct, that their dealings were with one member of the group only, and that other parts of the group have no legal responsibility to them. The context in which this issue arises here is a claim for personal injuries against three members of a corporate group.

The duty of care

The Claimant contends that AG (UK) and AG plc owed duties of care equivalent to those owed by his employer, AG (Jersey)... The issue fought out in the present action was the very existence of those duties of care although at trial it will be necessary not only to establish those duties but also their breach and causation between that and the loss suffered by the Claimant. The Claimant submits that he has a real prospect of establishing a duty of care on the part of AG (UK) and AG plc...

The fundamental issue is whether the law imposes on AG (UK) and AG plc a duty of care. It is not enough to establish a duty of care in general. What is demanded is a duty of care on their part in relation to the kind of damage which the Claimant says he sustained. To put it another way, the issue is whether the relationship between the Claimant and these two members of the ArmorGroup imposed on them a duty to take care to avoid or prevent the injuries the Claimant has in fact experienced. Mr Dingemans QC for the Claimant submitted that I should approach the question by applying the threefold test in *Caparo Industries plc* v *Dickman* [1990] 2 AC 605—was the loss reasonably foreseeable, were the Claimant and AG (UK) and AG plc in a relationship of proximity and was it fair, just and reasonable that those companies should owe a duty of care to the Claimant? Mr Maskrey QC for the Defendants, submitted that the better approach was to ask whether the two companies had voluntarily assumed a responsibility to the Claimant to guard against the injury or loss for which he now claims. I would not anticipate it making any difference to the outcome which approach is adopted. In my judgment there is a real prospect of the Claimant succeeding, either by establishing reasonable foreseeability by AG (UK) and AG plc and the proximate relationship between it and the Claimant demanded by the *Caparo* approach, or the special type of relationship between the two sides necessary for a duty of care based on a voluntary assumption of responsibility approach.

The special relationship demanded both by the *Caparo* approach, and the voluntary assumption of responsibility approach, began with the Claimant's initial interview. That took place at the head office of AG (UK) and AG plc. Although there is a dispute as to what happened and was said at the interview, there is a two page written summary, produced by the Head of Human Resources of AG (UK) and the group, as confirmation of what the Claimant and the other recruits were to be told at their oral briefing ('Pre Selection Briefing—Human Resources'). It deals with the position, primarily, of the ArmorGroup as a whole. The first paragraph, 'Background to the Company' is about AG (UK) and mentions its ownership by the holding company, AG plc. The only mention of the Jersey company is under para 7, 'Insurance', namely, 'Details of Service Agreement/employer—AG Jersey'.

The document 'ArmorGroup Corporation Information Summary', given to the Claimant during the recruitment briefing, continues in the same vein. It does not mention the Jersey company at all, although it includes a list of subsidiaries including AG (UK). ArmorGroup is said to be headquartered in London and wholly owned by Armor Holdings Inc, a New York listed public corporation. Its corporate policy is said to be to apply certain listed principles, globally. AG (UK) is said to be the cornerstone of the ArmorGroup's risk management business. Its uniqueness stems from its global footprint 'coupled with high calibre operational personnel on the ground'. On the next page the 'Specialist Security Capabilities' are set out, including specialist manpower and guard for management. In sum, the Claimant was given a clear indication from this document that he was dealing with ArmorGroup, acting primarily through AG (UK). Whatever the position with his contract of employment, the presentation of material was strongly suggestive of a special relationship with the group as a whole, acting through AG (UK).

Once the Claimant arrived in the Middle East he was given what was called 'Initial Deployment Orders'. As already mentioned this contains a list of security personnel in Iraq and details of their deployment. It is on notepaper of ArmorGroup AG (UK). The Claimant was briefed by an employee of AG (UK), as indicated earlier. All this is against a background…[in] which…AG (UK) undertakes to be responsible for the deployment of personnel in Iraq…

As with many corporate groups those at the top of ArmorGroup did not draw clear distinctions between the activities of its different corporate members…In presenting itself to the world, however, and in their day to day activities the ArmorGroup executives adopted a broader perspective. It was the group as a whole they were concerned with and they were not constantly alive to the nice distinctions drawn by lawyers.

I cannot see any basis for concluding that ArmorGroup security personnel, in particular the Claimant, entered into contractual relations with other members of the ArmorGroup…As in other areas, however, the law of negligence may impose liability when contract fails. The issue is simple, at base, are these other members of the group under a duty of care? In other words, despite a person having contractual relations with only one member of a corporate group, the question to be answered is whether other corporate members have acted in such a way as to be under a duty of care to him. That turns on an analysis of whether the Claimant's loss was reasonably foreseeable by these other corporate members, whether they and the Claimant were in a relationship of proximity, and whether it would be fair, just and reasonable for them to owe such a duty of care. Alternatively, did they have a specific responsibility to take care of the Claimant,

> one identifying principle of which is whether there is a special relationship based on an assumption of responsibility by the other members of the group to the Claimant. Either way, in my judgment, there is a real prospect of the Claimant establishing that those other members of the corporate group owed him a duty of care.

In *Caparo Industries Plc v Dickman*[84] Lord Roskill observed that 'phrases such as "foreseeability", "proximity", "neighbourhood", "just and reasonable", "fairness", 'voluntary acceptance of risk", or "voluntary assumption of responsibility" will be found used from time to time in the different cases. But, as your Lordships have said, such phrases are not precise definitions. At best they are but labels or phrases descriptive of the very different factual situations which can exist in particular cases and which must be carefully examined in each case before it can be pragmatically determined whether a duty of care exists'.[85] What then is it about the actions and behaviour of AG plc and AG (UK) that justify the attribution of the labels 'voluntary assumption of responsibility' or 'relationship of proximity' in this case?

The dominant consideration for Cranston J was the fact that an impression was created by the AG Group that the claimant was dealing with the Group and would be employed by the Group rather than by AG (Jersey). With regard to the broader implications of the case, it is noteworthy that such an impression is one that would be held by many employees working for group companies that actively promote group identity and culture. Indeed it is an impression that is arguably necessary and unavoidable for the smooth and effective working of a group of companies—in order to ensure that all entities and employees work towards Group targets and objectives.

Important open questions remain from the case. First, to what extent could a parent prevent the generation of such a duty of care by providing clarification to the employee about which group company will be the employer, as well as providing the employee with the reasons for using this entity and explaining to him any material consequences of being employed by this company? In this case there is a sense that the AG Group, through the use of the Jersey subsidiary, is surreptitiously gaining reduced liability exposure that the employee was not aware of and which, had he been aware of it, may well have affected his decision to accept such a dangerous undertaking. Would such a clarification prevent the generation of a duty of care whilst enabling parental involvement/interference in the subsidiary's activities? If so, parent companies may be able to easily manage the additional liability exposure threatened by this judgment.

The second open question is to what extent could this approach be used in relation to customers of the subsidiary entity? Clearly, many such customers will also operate under the impression—actively promoted by the group—that they are purchasing something from the group. Would such an active promotion of group identity be sufficient to create a duty of care to consumers physically injured[86] by the subsidiary company's products or is a closer connection and actual communication between parent employees and the customer (such as those which took place between AG (UK) and the claimant) required to generate the required degree of proximity?

---

[84] [1990] 2 AC 605.   [85] *Ibid* at 628.

[86] Note that it is clear that we are only concerned with physical injury. Tort liability for economic loss is very limited generally and the possible tort liability of the parent for economic loss of a person whose primary relationship with the subsidiary is highly unlikely—see generally *Murphy v Brentwood District Council* [1991] 1 AC 398; *Caparo Industries v Dickman* [1990] 2 AC 605.

■ *Chandler v Cape Plc* [2011] EWHC 951 (QB)

The claimant had been an employee of Cape Building Products Ltd (Cape Products) which was a wholly owned subsidiary of Cape Plc. As a result of his exposure to asbestos in the course of his employment the claimant contracted asbestosis. However, at the time the action was brought Cape Products no longer existed and, furthermore, during the period of the claimant's employment Cape Products had no insurance policy that would cover asbestosis claims. The claimant brought an action against Cape Plc arguing that the parent company owed a duty of care in relation to injuries suffered by Cape Product's employees arising from asbestos exposure. Cape Plc rejected this claim but accepted that if the court found that it owed the claimant a duty of care that it had acted negligently and would be in breach of that duty.

The court considered in detail the relationship between Cape and Cape Products. It observed that Cape Plc exerted considerable governance and operational control over Cape Products. The court observed that for considerable periods the two companies had the same board of directors and that the parent company effectively directed and controlled Cape Products' operational decisions. Furthermore, the court observed that the parent was closely involved in the health and safety practices of the Group as a whole, including the appointment of Group Medical officers. The court made the following factual findings:

'In the light of the contemporaneous and later documents discussed above there can be little doubt that the Defendant exercised control over some of the activities of Cape Products from the time that it came into existence and through the period during which the Claimant was one of its employees…It does not seem to me, however, that the Claimant's case stands or falls simply upon whether he can establish that the Defendant controlled all the activities of Cape Products. It is enough, in my judgment, if he can establish that the Defendant either controlled or took overall responsibility for the measures adopted by Cape Products to protect its employees against harm from asbestos exposure. I will explain why in the next section of my judgment.

'On the basis of the whole of the evidence adduced before me I reach the following conclusions on balance of probability. First, throughout the period of the Claimant's employment with Cape Products the Defendant employed a doctor as a Group Medical Adviser. He was responsible for the health and welfare of all the employees within the group of companies of which the Defendant was a parent…Second, during the same period, the Defendant employed a Chief Chemist or Chief Scientist…involved in seeking out ways of suppressing dust from the time…. Third, [one of the Chief Medical officers]…was, in effect, involved in an investigation of a case of a person who had contracted an asbestos related disease at the factory at Uxbridge…[Fourth] many aspects of the production process (particularly that which involved substantial expenditure) was discussed and authorised by the Defendant's board. As and when it felt it appropriate the Defendant did control what Cape Products was doing.'

Wyn Williams J

Essentially, my task is to apply [Lord Bridges' three-stage test set forth in *Caparo Industries plc v Dickman*] to the facts of this case. Before doing so, however, it is necessary to dispel certain possible misunderstandings which might arise in cases of this type or upon a cursory reading of this judgment. First, the fact that the Claimant was owed a duty of care by Cape Products does not prevent such a duty arising between the Claimant and other parties. No doubt, the fact that a duty situation exists between the Claimant and his employer is a factor to be taken into account when deciding whether another party owes the Claimant such a duty. But, to repeat, the existence of the duty between the Claimant and his employer cannot preclude another person being fixed with a duty of care. Second, the fact that Cape Products was a subsidiary of the Defendant or part of a group of companies of which the Defendant was the parent cannot mean by itself that the Defendant owes a duty to the employees of Cape Products. So much is clear from *Adams and others v Cape Industries plc and another.* Equally, the fact that Cape Products was a separate legal entity from the Defendant cannot preclude the duty arising. Third, this case has not been presented on the basis that Cape Products was a sham—nothing more than a veil for the activities of the Defendant. Accordingly, this is not a case in which it would be appropriate to 'pierce the corporate veil'.

It is commonly the case that injured workmen suffer their injuries as a consequence of the negligent acts or omissions of more than one legally identifiable party[87]...Mr Feeny [counsel for the defendant] acknowledges the possibility that the Defendant could assume a duty to the Claimant; he submits, however, that there can be no general duty upon the Defendant to prevent an independent third party from causing harm to the Claimant. Mr Feeny submits that special or exceptional circumstances needed to exist before a duty could be imposed upon the Defendant to prevent harm to him from asbestos exposure which was caused by the negligence and/or breach of statutory duty of Cape Products.

It is true that generally the law imposes no duty upon a party to prevent a third party from causing damage to another. That emerges clearly from *Smith v Littlewoods Organisation Ltd* [1987] AC 241. However, that same case makes it clear that there are exceptions to the general rule. In his speech Lord Goff identified the circumstances in which a duty might arise. They were:

a) where there was a special relationship between the Defendant and Claimant based on an assumption of responsibility by the Defendant;

b) where there is a special relationship between the Defendant and the third party based on control by the Defendant;

c) where the Defendant is responsible for a state of danger which may be exploited by a third party; and

d) where the Defendant is responsible for property which may be used by a third party to cause damage.

Mr Weir QC submits that if it is necessary to show that special or exceptional circumstances exist in the instant case that can be done. He submits that there was a special relationship between the Defendant and the Claimant based upon the Defendant's assumption of responsibility for safeguarding the Claimant against illness from exposure to asbestos; alternatively, the Defendant had the ultimate control of those measures which were taken to protect the Claimant from the risk of exposure to asbestos.

I end my discussion of the parties' submissions upon the law where I began. I must apply the three-stage test in *Caparo*. I must do so in the factual context that I have outlined in the preceding section of this judgment. On the basis of the evidence adduced before me I am satisfied that the Defendant had actual knowledge of the Claimant's working conditions...Asbestolux was produced in a building which had no sides. Dust was permitted to escape without any real regard for the consequences. This was no failure in day-to-day management; this was a systemic failure of which the Defendant was fully aware.

The risk of an asbestos related disease from exposure to asbestos dust was obvious. Mr Feeny does not suggest otherwise. There can be no doubt that the Defendant should have foreseen the risk of injury to the Claimant. As I have said that is admitted.

The Defendant employed a scientific officer and a medical officer who were responsible, between them, for health and safety issues relating to all the employees within the group of companies of which the Defendant was parent. On the basis of the evidence as a whole it was the Defendant, not the individual subsidiary companies, which dictated policy in relation to health and safety issues insofar as the Defendant's core business impacted upon health and safety. The Defendant retained responsibility for ensuring that its own employees and those of

---

[87] Citing *Connolly v The RTZ Corporation plc* (first instance, unreported QBD 4 December 1998): 'if the situation is that an employer has entirely handed over responsibility for devising, installing and operating the various safety precautions required of an employer to an independent contractor, then that contractor may owe a duty to the individual employee which is virtually coterminous with that of the employer himself. That is not to say that the employer, by so handing over such responsibility, will necessarily escape his own liability to his employee.'

its subsidiaries were not exposed to the risk of harm through exposure to asbestos. In reaching that conclusion I do not intend to imply that the subsidiaries, themselves, had no part to play—certainly in the implementation of relevant policy. However, the evidence persuades me that the Defendant retained overall responsibility. At any stage it could have intervened and Cape Products would have bowed to its intervention. On that basis, in my judgment, the Claimant has established a sufficient degree of proximity between the Defendant and himself. At para 27 of the skeleton argument submitted on behalf of the Claimant the suggestion is made that in this case the degree of proximity between the Defendant and Claimant is central to the analysis of whether, on the facts, a duty of care was owed. I agree. The facts I have found proved in this case persuade me that proximity is established.

No argument was advanced to me by Mr Feeny that if foreseeability and proximity were established nonetheless it was not fair, just and reasonable for a duty to exist. Had such an argument been advanced I would have rejected it. By the late 1950s it was clear to the Defendant that exposure to asbestos brought with it very significant risk of very damaging and life threatening illness. I can think of no basis upon which it would be proper to conclude in those circumstances that it would not be just or reasonable to impose a duty of care upon an organisation like the Defendant.

In my judgment the three-stage test for the imposition of a duty of care is satisfied in this case. Accordingly, the Claimant succeeds in his claim.

In *Smith v Littlewoods Organization Ltd*,[88] a case of some importance to Wyn Williams J's judgment in *Chandler v Cape*, Lord Goff observes that there is a 'general perception that we ought not to be held responsible in law for the deliberate wrongdoings of others'. It is this principle, he observes, that drives tort law's resistance, absent 'special circumstances',[89] to acknowledging a duty of care to prevent another person from causing harm. In this case we have two separate legal persons—the subsidiary and the parent. Wyn Williams J finds that the 'special circumstances' factors identified by Lord Goff in *Smith v Littlewoods* are fulfilled here and, therefore, that Cape Plc had a duty to prevent Cape Products from causing harm to the claimant.

The judgment could be read more expansively than this. Wyn Williams J's conclusions about the duty of care do not appear to be restricted to the duty to prevent another from causing harm. Indeed the discussion about a duty to prevent another from causing harm reads almost as an interlude to a discussion about a general duty of care. The latter part of the judgment suggests that due to its actions and the resulting proximity between it and the claimant, Cape Plc was *itself* under a duty to care to prevent risk of harm to the claimant and his fellow employees. However, in this author's view the case should be read as applying only to a duty to prevent a third party from harming another. As the courts have recently stressed, foreseeability of physical harm is not a sufficient basis on which to found a duty of care.[90] There must be a relationship of proximity between the two parties—requiring a connection between the two parties beyond the fact that's one's actions can have the effect of injuring another. In *Newton-Sealy* this was clearly established through the impression that was actively created that the defendant was dealing with parent and sister companies. The facts as presented in *Chandler v Cape* do not appear to establish such a relationship of proximity between Cape Plc and the defendant.

As Wyn Williams J observes, Lord Goff identifies factors that are indicative of special circumstances that would generate a duty to take care to prevent a person from harming another. The four factors ((a)–(d)) are set forth in the extract of the judgment. Only (a) and (b) are relevant considerations. With regard to factor (c), a finding that Cape Plc

---

[88] [1987] AC 241. [89] *Ibid* Lord Goff at 272.
[90] *Mitchell v Glasgow City Council* [2009] UKHL 11 para 19.

was responsible for creation of the risk would ignore the separate legal personality of the two entities and this case is not, as Wyn Williams J correctly holds, a piercing the veil case. Although Cape Plc may exert control and influence over Cape Products they did not create the risk; that risk was created by the factory that was owned and run by the subsidiary—to say that that risk was created by the parent is to see all subsidiaries as mere creatures of the parent and not as separate entities in of themselves. Factor (d) does not apply as the property used to cause the harm was owned by the subsidiary.

Factor (a) is of central importance. Although, as noted previously, in *Caparo* the House of Lords observed that the 'assumption of responsibility' concept is merely a label which is applied following the identification of circumstances which support the imposition of the duty of care, here we see that the notion of assumption of responsibility has its own independent legal significance. The act of actually assuming responsibility for activities that, if negligently performed, can result in harm to an individual may result in the imposition of a duty of care to prevent another person from causing harm. In *Chandler v Cape*, the court found that Cape Plc had assumed responsibility for the health and safety of Cape Products' employees.

Factor (b) involving the control over the party who commits the wrong is also relevant. Wyn Williams J finds that Cape Plc controlled Cape Products in relation to the steps taken to prevent harm to employees. It is important to note here that corporate control—understood as the ability of a controlling shareholder to control the general meeting and appoint and remove the board—does *not* fall within this understanding of 'control'.[91] 'Control' here requires actual control over the subsidiary's activities, or part thereof, which caused the harm—the theoretical ability to exercise such control simply because a person is a controlling shareholder is not sufficient in the absence of active control. For Wyn Williams J 'control' and 'assumption of responsibility' cover the same ground: the parent's control over/responsibility for an area that was of crucial importance to the well-being of Cape Product's employees. One could say that the parent in this case rested control over and responsibility for these health issues away from the subsidiary and as a result a duty of care to prevent the subsidiary from causing harm was created.

As in *Newton-Sealy*, open questions remain about the extent to which this holding affects parent–subsidiary relations more generally. Business factors which generate risks for a group of companies as a whole will necessarily result in direction and involvement by the parent in its subsidiaries' activities. Indeed, the failure of a parent's board of directors to take some responsibility for risk controls over the group as a whole could, in theory, amount to a violation of certain of their director's duties, which we consider in Chapters 9 to 14. It may, therefore, not be possible to operate a group of companies without such parental involvement and responsibility in relation to the core risks that could, foreseeably, result in harm to third parties as a direct result of the subsidiary's activities. Accordingly, making the imposition of a duty dependent on the understanding of control and responsibility set forth in *Chandler v Cape* would impose a duty of care on most, if not all, parents to prevent subsidiaries acting in ways that foreseeably cause harm to others—from employees to customers—in those areas where the parent takes the lead in defining and implementing group policy.

If it is the parent's lead role in a particular risk area that is the primary driver of the imposition of a duty of care, an open question remains as to whether a duty would be imposed if the parent provided only guidance and recommendations to the subsidiary in relation to the areas of risk rather than imposing (formally or informally) required actions as well as group structures—such as a group risk officer—that overlapped the separate legal personalities of the parent and subsidiary entities.

[91] For an alternative view see on this point see: E. McGaughey, 'Donoghue v Salomon in the High Court' (2011) 4 *Journal of Personal Injury Law* 249.

A final caveat needs also to be noted about whether higher courts will follow this ruling.[92] Whilst the control and assumption of responsibility may create the proximity required under the *Caparo* three-stage test to create a duty of care to prevent the subsidiary from causing harm, it is unclear that the courts will continue to hold that it is fair, just, and reasonable to do so under the third *Caparo* pillar. Whilst on the facts of this case alone it is clear that the imposition of liability would be 'fair and reasonable', in this category higher courts have taken account of the broader policy implications of imposing a duty of care. Consider, for example, *Mitchell v Glasgow City Council* where the House of Lords held that it would not be fair and reasonable to impose liability on a Council for failing to warn a tenant of the danger of injury from the tenant's neighbour as a result of eviction proceedings.[93] A central concern for the House of Lords in reaching its conclusion was that such a duty could result in landlords being less willing to deal with problematic tenants. We live in a world in which boards of directors of parent companies are often berated and sued for failing to control the activities of management and more junior employees. We have seen this recently in the context of banking failures, major oil spills, and rogue bank traders.[94] If the imposition on parents of a duty of care would result in parents taking less active control over these broader group risks then the courts may consider that it would not be 'fair and reasonable' to impose a duty of care on the parent.

Questions

1. How does a company commit a tort?
2. What does it mean to understand the vicarious liability rule as a rule of vicarious attribution of actions?
3. Why, if at all, does it matter if we understand the vicarious liability doctrine as a rule of vicarious liability or of vicarious attribution of actions?
4. Are directors protected by company law from the commission of torts?
5. In what ways can you imagine that a company would be liable in tort as a result of its primary rules of attribution?
6. In what circumstances if any can a parent company be liable in tort to parties who deal with a subsidiary company?
7. Does liability in tort for the parent in relation to individuals who also have a claim against the subsidiary for the same loss ignore the separate legal personality of the two companies?
8. Is it 'fair and reasonable' to impose liability on the parent for the physical injuries caused by subsidiary companies?

V CRIME AND THE COMPANY

There are two questions for us to address in this section. The first and primary question is: how does a company commit a crime; what are the rules of attribution that determine when a company is liable for a crime? The second question, to which only limited attention will be given, is: what are the benefits of using the criminal law to regulate corporate activity? As the company is not a real person it cannot be subject to the primary deterrent used to enforce criminal law, namely, incarceration. Why use the criminal law vis à vis a company instead of a civil law fine or sanction; what additional deterrent, if any, is generated by using the criminal law rather than relying only on a civil sanction?

---

[92] During the final proof stage of this book the Court of Appeal affirmed the first instance judgement. Unfortunately, at this stage in the book's process we cannot discuss the case in any detail. It should be noted that Lady Justice Arden's judgement is arguably more expansive than Wyn Williams J's judgement ([2012] EWCA CIV 525). The basis for a duty of care for Lady Justice Arden in this context is: (1) foreseeability of harm; (2) subsidiary reliance on the parent in respect of the unsafe practices; and (3) parental intervention in this respect. The concerns about the imposition of a duty on the parent noted above still stand.   [93] [2009] UKHL 11, at para 28.

[94] 'UBS Chief resigns over rogue trader affair' 24 September 2011, *Financial Times*; 'Hayward's end just first step for BP' 26 July 2010, *Financial Times*.

1 Attributing crimes to companies: special rules of attribution

With regard to types of criminal offence a distinction is often made between regulatory offences which typically provide for strict liability, and the statutory and common law offences which require, as an element of the offence, proof of a state of mind or compliance with a behavioural standard on the part of the accused. Regulatory offences may be directly or indirectly applicable to companies. There are many examples from the Companies Act 2006 of the imposition of criminal liability directly on companies for the failure to observe the requirements of the Act. These include, for example: the failure of a company to observe an order issued by the Secretary of State requiring the company to change its name;[95] the failure by a company to comply with regulations issued in relation to disclosures about its name and other information about the company;[96] the failure to comply with the inspection rules for the register of members;[97] or the provision by a company of prohibited financial assistance.[98] Outside of the companies legislation there are multiple examples of regulatory offences imposing criminal liability on companies. However, typically, the offence will regulate the activities of 'persons', which would include companies as legal persons. For example, the Health and Safety at Work Act 1974 provides that an employer commits an offence[99] if he contravenes his duty 'to conduct his undertaking in such a way as to ensure, so far as is reasonably practicable, that persons not in his employment who may be affected thereby are not thereby exposed to risks to their health or safety'. The Trade Descriptions Act 1968 provides that any person who applies a false trade description to a good is guilty of an offence. As most business activity takes place through companies, in the vast majority of cases these offences are committed by companies.

In many instances regulatory offences impose criminal liability strictly on the failure to perform an act. For example, if a document has to be filed within a set time period and it is not filed, an offence is committed by the company. However, in relation to both regulatory offences and other criminal offences, committing the offence in question may require the attribution to the company of a state of mind such as: whether the company knew of the circumstances in question; intended something to happen; or was reckless about its occurrence. Alternatively, the offence may provide that the benchmark for determining criminal liability is whether a standard of behaviour was complied with, such as taking reasonable precautions or not acting with gross negligence.

To attribute such a state of mind or behaviour to the company necessarily requires that the states of mind of real people or the behaviour of real people (directors, employees, agents) be attributed to the company. However, the statute or the cases setting forth the regulatory or other criminal offences will usually just refer to the company—where the offence relates directly to the company—or to 'a person' to whom the offence is applicable. Such statutes and cases do not typically provide clear guidance on whose actions—the actions of which real people connected to the company—are relevant to attributing the state of mind or behaviour in question to the company. In such circumstances how do we determine which real person's actions count for the purpose of determining whether the company is criminally liable? To use Lord Hoffmann's framework, what, if any, are the general rules of attribution in relation to such criminal offences?

In 1944 a UK court held for the first time that a company could be liable for a criminal offence that required proof of a state of mind. The case in question was *DPP v Kent & Sussex Contractors Ltd*[100] where the company defendant was being prosecuted in relation to its purported breach of statutory rules[101] relating to post-Second World War petrol rationing.

---

[95] Sections 67 and 68; and sections 75 and 76 CA 2006.   [96] Sections 82–84 CA 2006.
[97] Section 114 CA 2006.
[98] Section 680 CA 2006. The rules on financial assistance will be considered in detail in Chapter 17.
[99] Section 33 CA 2006.   [100] [1944] KB 146.
[101] Defence (General) Regulations 1939, SI 1939/927, regs 82(1)(c), 82(2); Motor Fuel Rationing (No 3) Order 1941, SR & O 1941/1592.

DPP v Kent & Sussex Contractors Ltd is typically presented in company law commentary as the beginning of the general application of the identification doctrine[102] to criminal law cases where the offence in question requires a particular state of mind or sets forth a behavioural standard as the basis for liability.[103] Indeed Viscount Caldecote CJ held that 'the officers are the company' for the purposes of determining the state of mind in question. It is worth noting, however, that two of the three judgments took a more flexible view of which agents of the company could attribute to the company the requisite state of mind.[104] Furthermore, with regard to the general application of the identification doctrine to criminal law, it is worth remembering that this case involved the application of a particular statutory provision. This observation is of particular relevance when we consider in detail the *Meridian* case. It is doubtful that the identification doctrine was ever the general rule of attribution for crimes requiring proof of a state of mind in English company law. After *Meridian* there is no doubt that it is not.

■ *Meridian Global Funds Management Asia Ltd v Securities Commission* [1995] 3 All ER 918

The case involved the attempted takeover of a New Zealand company, Euro National Corp Ltd (ENC), by a syndicate of bidders including Meridian Global Funds Management (Asia) Ltd (Meridian). Acting on behalf of Meridian, two of its investment banking employees, Koo and Ng, purchased shares in ENC amounting to 49% of the issued shares in the company. New Zealand Securities Laws require the disclosure of a share position in a listed company, when the shareholder becomes a 'substantial security holder' which is defined as owning 5% or more of the shares. However Meridian failed to disclose that interest. The reason for this was that Koo and Ng wished to conceal the transaction from their superiors. Failure to comply with these provisions can result in enforcement action being brought by the New Zealand Securities Commission and the imposition of fines on the parties breaching the provision. An action was brought against Koo and Ng individually but also against the company. The question of whether the company knew that it was a substantial security holder was deemed central to the determination of whether Meridian was in breach of the disclosure obligations. The court of first instance held that Meridian knew that it had become a 'substantial property holder' and was in breach of the disclosure obligations. In this regard, the first instance judge, Heron J, attributed their knowledge as employees of Meridian to the company for the purposes of determining whether it complied with the disclosure obligations. Meridian appealed.

Lord Hoffmann

Heron J held that Meridian knew...that it was a 'substantial security holder' in ENC...He arrived at this conclusion by attributing to Meridian the knowledge of Koo and Ng, who undoubtedly knew all the relevant facts. He did not go into the juridical basis for this attribution in any detail. It seemed obvious to him that if Koo and Ng had authority to enter into the transaction, their knowledge that they had done so should be attributed to Meridian. It had therefore been in

---

[102] Note that this case did not in fact refer to the *Lennard's Carrying Co* case which, as we saw, first coined the phrase 'directing mind and will' in a civil law context. The idea deployed in Viscount Caldecote CJ's judgment is, however, closely akin to the 'directing mind and will' idea.

[103] B. Pettet, *Company Law* (2nd edn, Longman, 2005), 30; *Gower and Davies*, 186; *Sealy and Worthington*, 152. See also *El Ajou v Dollar Land Holdings plc* [1994] 2 All ER 685, a case addressing knowing receipt where Nourse LJ observed that 'this doctrine, sometimes known as the alter ego doctrine, has been developed, with no divergence of approach, in both criminal and civil jurisdictions, the authorities in each being cited indifferently in the other'.

[104] MacNaughton J in *DPP v Kent & Sussex Contractors Ltd* held that: 'if the responsible agent of a company, acting within the scope of his authority, puts forward on its behalf a document which he knows to be false and by which he intends to deceive, I apprehend that, according to the authorities that my Lord has cited, his knowledge and intention must be imputed to the company.'

breach of its duty to [disclose]…The [New Zealand] Court of Appeal affirmed the decision of Heron J on somewhat different grounds. It decided that Koo's knowledge should be attributed to Meridian because he was the 'directing mind and will' of the company…By leave of the Court of Appeal, Meridian now appeals to their Lordships' Board. It says that its only directing mind and will was that of its board…but not Koo…

The phrase 'directing mind and will' comes of course from the celebrated speech of Viscount Haldane LC in *Lennard's Carrying Co Ltd v Asiatic Petroleum Co Ltd* [1915] AC 705. But their Lordships think that there has been some misunderstanding of the true principle upon which that case was decided. It may be helpful to start by stating the nature of the problem in a case like this and then come back to *Lennard's* case later.

Any statement about what a company has or has not done, or can or cannot do, is necessarily a reference to the rules of attribution (primary and general) as they apply to that company. Judges sometimes say that a company 'as such' cannot do anything; it must act by servants or agents. This may seem an unexceptionable, even banal remark. And of course the meaning is usually perfectly clear. But a reference to a company 'as such' might suggest that there is something out there called the company of which one can meaningfully say that it can or cannot do something. There is in fact no such thing as the company as such, no 'ding an sich', only the applicable rules. To say that a company cannot do something means only that there is no one whose doing of that act would, under the applicable rules of attribution, count as an act of the company.

The company's primary rules of attribution together with the general principles of agency, vicarious liability and so forth are usually sufficient to enable one to determine its rights and obligations. In exceptional cases, however, they will not provide an answer. This will be the case when a rule of law, either expressly or by implication, excludes attribution on the basis of the general principles of agency or vicarious liability. For example, a rule may be stated in language primarily applicable to a natural person and require some act or state of mind on the part of that person 'himself', as opposed to his servants or agents. This is generally true of rules of the criminal law, which ordinarily impose liability only for the actus reus and mens rea of the defendant himself. How is such a rule to be applied to a company?

One possibility is that the court may come to the conclusion that the rule was not intended to apply to companies at all; for example, a law which created an offence for which the only penalty was community service. Another possibility is that the court might interpret the law as meaning that it could apply to a company only on the basis of its primary rules of attribution, ie if the act giving rise to liability was specifically authorised by a resolution of the board or a unanimous agreement of the shareholders. But there will be many cases in which neither of these solutions is satisfactory; in which the court considers that the law was intended to apply to companies and that, although it excludes ordinary vicarious liability, insistence on the primary rules of attribution would in practice defeat that intention. In such a case, the court must fashion a special rule of attribution for the particular substantive rule. This is always a matter of interpretation: given that it was intended to apply to a company, how was it intended to apply? Whose act (or knowledge, or state of mind) was *for this purpose* intended to count as the act etc of the company? One finds the answer to this question by applying the usual canons of interpretation, taking into account the language of the rule (if it is a statute) and its content and policy.

The fact that the rule of attribution is a matter of interpretation or construction of the relevant substantive rule is shown by the contrast between two decisions of the House of Lords, *Tesco Supermarkets Ltd v Nattrass* [1971] 2 All ER 127, [1972] AC 153 and *Re Supply of Ready Mixed Concrete (No 2), Director General of Fair Trading v Pioneer Concrete (UK) Ltd* [1995] 1 All ER 135, [1995] 1 AC 456. In the *Tesco* case the question involved the construction of a provision of the Trade Descriptions Act 1968. Tesco were prosecuted under s 11(2) for displaying a notice that goods were 'being offered at a price less than that at which they were in fact being offered…' Its supermarket in Northwich had advertised that it was selling certain packets of washing powder at the reduced price of 2s 11d, but a customer who asked for one was told he would have to pay the normal price of 3s 11d. This happened because the shop manager had negligently failed to notice that he had run out of the specially marked low-price packets. Section 24(1) provided a defence for a shopowner who could prove that the commission of the offence was caused by 'another person' and that:

'he took all reasonable precautions and exercised all due diligence to avoid the commission of such an offence by himself or any person under his control.'

The company was able to show that it owned hundreds of shops and that the board had instituted systems of supervision and training which amounted, on its part, to taking reasonable precautions and exercising all due diligence to avoid the commission of such offences in its shops. The question was: whose precautions counted as those of the company? If it was the board, then the defence was made out. If they had to include those of the manager, then it failed.

The House of Lords held that the precautions taken by the board were sufficient for the purposes of s 24(1) to count as precautions taken by the company and that the manager's negligence was not attributable to the company. It did so by examining the purpose of s 24(1) in providing a defence to what would otherwise have been an absolute offence: it was intended to give effect to 'a policy of consumer protection which does have a rational and moral justification' ([1971] 2 All ER 127 at 151, [1972] AC 153 at 194–195 per Lord Diplock). This led to the conclusion that the acts and defaults of the manager were not intended to be attributed to the company. As Lord Diplock said ([1971] 2 All ER 127 at 158, [1972] AC 153 at 203):

'It may be a reasonable step for an employer to instruct a superior servant to supervise the activities of inferior servants whose physical acts may in the absence of supervision result in that being done which it is sought to prevent. This is not to delegate the employer's duty to exercise all due diligence; it is to perform it. To treat the duty of an employer to exercise due diligence as unperformed unless due diligence was also exercised by all his servants to whom he had reasonably given all proper instructions and upon whom he could reasonably rely to carry them out, would be to render the defence of due diligence nugatory and so thwart the clear intention of Parliament in providing it.'

On the other hand, in the *Ready Mixed Concrete* case a restrictive arrangement in breach of an undertaking by a company to the Restrictive Practices Court was made by executives of the company acting within the scope of their employment. The board knew nothing of the arrangement; it had in fact given instructions to the company's employees that they were not to make such arrangements. But the House of Lords held that for the purposes of deciding whether the company was in contempt, the act and state of mind of an employee who entered into an arrangement in the course of his employment should be attributed to the company. This attribution rule was derived from a construction of the undertaking against the background of the Restrictive Trade Practices Act 1976: such undertakings by corporations would be worth little if the company could avoid liability for what its employees had actually done on the ground that the board did not know about it. As Lord Templeman said, an uncritical transposition of the *Tesco* construction:

'would allow a company to enjoy the benefit of restrictions outlawed by Parliament and the benefit of arrangements prohibited by the courts provided that the restrictions were accepted and implemented and the arrangements were negotiated by one or more employees who had been forbidden to do so by some superior employee identified in argument as a member of the "higher management" of the company or by one or more directors of the company identified in argument as "the guiding will" of the company.'

Against this background of general principle, their Lordships can return to Viscount Haldane. In the *Lennard's* case the substantive provision for which an attribution rule had to be devised was s 502 of the Merchant Shipping Act 1894, which provided a shipowner with a defence to a claim for the loss of cargo put on board his ship if he could show that the casualty happened 'without his actual fault or privity'. The cargo had been destroyed by a fire caused by the unseaworthy condition of the ship's boilers. The language of s 502 excludes vicarious liability; it is clear that in the case of an individual owner, only his own fault or privity can defeat the statutory protection. How is this rule to be applied to a company? Viscount Haldane rejected the possibility that it did not apply to companies at all or (which would have come to the same thing) that it required fault or privity attributable under the company's primary rules. Instead, guided by the language and purpose of the section, he looked for the person whose functions in the company, in relation to the cause of the casualty, were the same as those to be expected of the individual shipowner to whom the language primarily applied. Who in the company was responsible for monitoring the condition of the ship, receiving the reports of the master and ship's agents, authorising repairs etc? This person was Mr Lennard, whom Viscount Haldane described as the 'directing mind and will' of the company. It was therefore his fault or privity which s 502 attributed to the company.

Because Lennard's Carrying Co Ltd does not seem to have done anything except own ships, there was no need to distinguish between the person who fulfilled the function of running the company's business in general and the person whose functions corresponded, in relation to the cause of the casualty, to those of an individual owner of a ship. They were one and the same person. It was this coincidence which left Viscount Haldane's speech open to the interpretation that he was expounding a general metaphysic of companies. In *H L Bolton (Engineering) Co Ltd v T J Graham & Sons Ltd* [1956] 3 All ER 624 Denning LJ certainly regarded it as a generalisation about companies 'as such' when, in an equally well-known passage, he likened a company to a human body:

> 'They have a brain and a nerve centre which controls what they do. They also have hands which hold the tools and act in accordance with directions from the centre.'

But this anthropomorphism, by the very power of the image, distracts attention from the purpose for which Viscount Haldane said he was using the notion of directing mind and will, namely to apply the attribution rule derived from s 502 to the particular defendant in the case:

> 'For if Mr. Lennard was the directing mind of the company, then his action must, unless a corporation is not to be liable at all, have been an action which was the action of the company itself *within the meaning of s. 502.*' [Lord Hoffmann's emphasis]

…Once it is appreciated that the question is one of construction rather than metaphysics, the answer in this case seems to their Lordships to be as straightforward as it did to Heron J. The policy of [New Zealand Securities Amendment Act 1988] is to compel, in fast-moving markets, the immediate disclosure of the identity of persons who become substantial security holders in public issuers. Notice must be given as soon as that person knows that he has become a substantial security holder. In the case of a corporate security holder, what rule should be implied as to the person whose knowledge for this purpose is to count as the knowledge of the company? Surely the person who, with the authority of the company, acquired the relevant interest. Otherwise the policy of the Act would be defeated. Companies would be able to allow employees to acquire interests on their behalf which made them substantial security holders but would not have to report them until the board or someone else in senior management got to know about it. This would put a premium on the board paying as little attention as possible to what its investment managers were doing. Their Lordships would therefore hold that upon the true construction of [the statute], the company knows that it has become a substantial security holder when that is known to the person who had authority to do the deal. It is then obliged to [disclose its shareholder in accordance with the Act]. The fact that Koo did the deal for a corrupt purpose and did not give such notice because he did not want his employers to find out cannot in their Lordships' view affect the attribution of knowledge and the consequent duty to notify…

But their Lordships would wish to guard themselves against being understood to mean that whenever a servant of a company has authority to do an act on its behalf, knowledge of that act will for all purposes be attributed to the company. It is a question of construction in each case as to whether the particular rule requires that the knowledge that an act has been done, or the state of mind with which it was done, should be attributed to the company. Sometimes, as in the *Ready Mixed Concrete* case and this case, it will be appropriate…On the other hand, the fact that a company's employee is authorised to drive a lorry does not in itself lead to the conclusion that if he kills someone by reckless driving, the company will be guilty of manslaughter. There is no inconsistency. Each is an example of an attribution rule for a particular purpose, tailored as it always must be to the terms and policies of the substantive rule…

Their Lordships will humbly advise Her Majesty that the appeal should be dismissed.

The New Zealand Court of Appeal whilst affirming the lower court's judgment does so on a very different basis. For the Court of Appeal, as the question of company liability involves a question of state of mind—did the company *know* it had crossed the 5% disclosure threshold—this is answered by asking whether the company's 'directing will and mind' *knew* that the threshold had been crossed. As we have already discussed, and as we see from Lord Hoffmann's judgment, this approach has a long pedigree in English law. Indeed, in applying the identification doctrine to the issue of whether Meridian knew that it was required to disclose its shareholding in ENC, the court was adopting a widely held view at the time that 'if the offence required proof of a mental element...then the identification principle applied'.[105] However, according to Lord Hoffmann, the Court of Appeal's mistake is to assume that in relation to *any* state of mind question in the criminal context the rule of attribution is necessarily the 'directing will and mind' rule. This rule may well be the applicable rule in relation to some statutory or common law crimes; however, whether it is applicable is a function of the interpretation of the statute or the common law rules creating the offence.[106] Accordingly, the 'directing mind and will' rule is not *the* rule of attribution in relation to determining whether a company has the requisite state of mind or complies with the applicable behavioural standard, but rather one possible *special* rule of attribution depending on the statute or cases creating the offence.

For Lord Hoffmann it is the identification doctrine's anthropomorphic effects—giving human attributes of 'will' and 'mind' to the company—that have led courts and commentators to mistake the identification doctrine as *the rule of attribution* when it is only one of several, offence-dependent, rules of attribution. This anthropomorphism distracts us from the fact that the rule was first introduced in the *Lennard's Carrying Co* case as a statement of the rule of attribution arising from the application of the statute in question—the Merchant Shipping Act 1894—to a company.

Accordingly, depending on the offence in question—even those offences that require a specific state of mind or determine liability through the application of a behavioural standard—the rule of attribution determining a company's criminal liability may, amongst others, be: strict liability; vicarious liability in relation to any of its employees—requiring that those employees have the requisite state of mind or fail to comply with the behavioural standard; or require that the individuals who represent the company's 'directing mind and will' have such a state of mind or fail to comply with such a standard.

We see that different offences generate different rules of attribution when we compare *Tesco v Nattrass*,[107] discussed by Lord Hoffmann in *Meridian*, with a more recent Court of Appeal case *R v British Steel Ltd*,[108] which concerned the application of section 3 of the Health and Safety at Work Act 1974. In *Tesco v Nattrass* the question whether Tesco had taken sufficient precautions to prevent a breach of the Trade Descriptions Act 1968 was answered by looking at how its senior management had behaved—the steps that they had taken to ensure that employees did not breach the 1968 Act. In *R v British Steel Plc* an employee of British Steel had failed to supervise certain activities properly which resulted in the death of a sub-contractor. Section 3(1) of the 1974 act provides that 'it shall be the duty of every employer to conduct his undertaking in such a way as to ensure, so far as is reasonably practicable, that persons not in his employment who may be affected thereby are not thereby exposed to risks to their

---

[105] C. Wells, *Corporations and Criminal Responsibility* (2nd edn, OUP, 2001), 101; see generally chapter 5 where Professor Wells considers the development of different approaches to attributing criminal liability to the company.

[106] Applying this principle see the Court of Appeal judgment in *Jafari-Fini v Skillglass Ltd* [2007] EWCA Civ 261 and Lord Hoffmann's recent judgment in *Lebon v Aqua Salt Co Ltd* [2009] UKPC 2 (Privy Council).

[107] [1972] AC 153.   [108] [1995] 1 WLR 1356.

health or safety'. The question for the court was whether the actions of senior members of management to put in place sound policies and practices to ensure the safety of the workplace amounted to doing everything 'reasonably practicable' to ensure the sub-contractor was not exposed to risks to their health and safety. Alternatively, did the failure of the company's employee to supervise the sub-contractor effectively mean that the company had not done everything 'reasonably practicable'? Counsel for *British Steel* argued that *Tesco v Natrass* supported their claim that the company was not liable if the company's 'directing will and mind' had taken the reasonable care to prevent such activities happening. The Court of Appeal forcefully rejected this position in a judgment that fits very clearly within Lord Hoffmann's approach in *Meridian*. In rejecting British Steel's position, the Court of Appeal made the following observation:

> If it be accepted that Parliament considered it necessary for the protection of public health and safety to impose, subject to the defence of reasonable practicability, absolute criminal liability, it would drive a juggernaut through the legislative scheme if corporate employers could avoid criminal liability where the potentially harmful event is committed by someone who is not the directing mind of the company. After all...is framed to achieve a result, namely that persons not employed are not exposed to risks to their health and safety by the conduct of the undertaking. If we accept British Steel's submission, it would be particularly easy for large industrial companies, engaged in multifarious hazardous operations, to escape liability on the basis that the company through its 'directing mind' or senior management was not involved. That would emasculate the legislation.

When we juxtapose *Tesco v Nattrass* and *R v British Steel Ltd* we see clearly that the question of which company actors, and their requisite state of mind or behaviour, are relevant to determining whether the company is criminally liable is clearly a function of the offence in question and the statute or cases that are the source of the offence.

Accordingly, in summary, although Lord Hoffmann does not say this, in contrast to contracts and torts where we see general rules of attribution, in relation to crimes attributed to the company there is *no* general rule of attribution but only special, offence-dependent, rules of attribution. As there is no general rule of attribution, any criminal offence, no matter how serious or trivial, could be attributed to the company through any rule of attribution. Given this, an important question for the student of company law is: how do the courts go about determining the applicable rule of attribution? Clearly, in many instances the statute itself may render this process clear and straightforward. However, what about those statutory and common law offences where little guidance is available. In such circumstances, is it possible to identify any rules of interpretation that are applied by the courts in fashioning the appropriate rule of attribution?

Two factors appear to be of particular importance in this regard: first, the identification of the objective of the offence in question; and, second, a consideration of the effect on fulfilling that objective of the rule of attribution. In *Tesco v Nattrass*, in deciding that the defences of 'reasonable precautions' applied to the actions of senior management rather than the actions of junior managers and employees, Lord Reid observed that:

> If I look to the purpose and apparent intention of Parliament in enacting this defence I think that it was plainly intended to make a just and reasonable distinction between the employer who is wholly blameless and ought to be acquitted and the employer who was in some way at fault, leaving it to the employer to prove that he was in no way to blame.

As we have seen from the extract in *R v British Steel Plc* the court observed that a 'directing mind and will approach' would have 'emasculated the legislation' and, accordingly, it did not fit with the offence in question. In *Tesco Stores v Brent*,[109] the offence in question

---

[109] [1993] 2 All ER 718.

involved the sale of certain videos to minors. In applying a rule
all employees, the court observed that it would be 'absurd to su.
manage a vast company would have any knowledge or any inform.
a casual purchaser of a video film'.

2 Corporate manslaughter

The rule of attribution applicable to an offence in question determines
that the company will be held criminally liable for the offence. It is clea
actions, behaviour, and state of mind of any of the company's employees are   ͺputed
to the company then the company is much more likely to be found liable for the crime in
question than if the rule of attribution rule is the 'directing will and mind' rule, which
would require a demonstration that the very senior members of the company's board or
management failed to behave as the offence requires or had the requisite state of mind.
Indeed, in relation to many offences the application of the 'directing will and mind' rule
is likely to reduce to zero the probability of the company being held liable. One such
offence which, as we shall see, has generated a considerable amount of debate resulting
ultimately in reform is the offence of common law manslaughter.

Unfortunately serious injury and death caused by business activity, whether to those
individuals who work for the business or third parties who encounter business activities, is not uncommon. In 2002–3, for example, 226 people were killed in the UK in
work-related accidents.[110] Whilst many of these deaths may have arisen from unforeseeable accidents, many may well have been avoided if more care had been taken. Indeed,
according to research by the Health and Safety Executive[111] 70–80% of workplace
deaths are preventable.[112] In this regard consider the following extract from the Law
Commission's report on the law of manslaughter which details some of the more recent
and high profile cases in which corporate activity has resulted in multiple deaths.[113]

> On 18 November 1987 a fire of catastrophic proportions occurred in the King's Cross under-
> ground station, claiming the lives of 31 people. In his report on the fire, Mr Desmond Fennell QC
> (as he then was) was critical of London Underground for not guarding against the unpredictabil-
> ity of the fire, and also because no one person was charged with overall responsibility.
>
> In July 1988, the Piper Alpha oil platform disaster in the North Sea caused 167 deaths. In a pub-
> lic inquiry, conducted by Lord Cullen, which also served in effect as an inquest, serious criticism
> was directed at the platform operator, holding it responsible for the deaths.
>
> On 12 December 1988, the Clapham rail crash caused 35 deaths and nearly 500 injuries when
> three rush-hour trains collided after a signal breakdown. In his report, Mr Anthony Hidden QC
> (as he then was) was very critical of British Rail, whose 'concern for safety was permitted to
> co-exist with working practices which…were positively dangerous…the evidence showed the
> reality of [their] failure to carry that concern through into action'. Further, 'the errors go much
> wider and higher in the organisation than merely to remain at the hands of those who were
> working that day', and the report lists 16 serious relevant errors.

The question that arises from death caused by corporate activity is whether the company can be held liable for crimes related to killing, namely murder and manslaughter.
As the mandatory sentence for murder is life imprisonment a company cannot commit

---

[110] Health and Safety Commission Press Release (C065: 0319 November 2003).

[111] The Health and Safety Executive is the regulatory body responsible for enforcing the Health and
Safety at Work etc. Act 1974.

[112] Reported by Wells, note 104, at 9.

[113] The Law Commission, *Legislating the Criminal Code: Involuntary Manslaughter* (Law Com No
237).

clearly it cannot go to jail. However, manslaughter, the involuntary killing individual as a result of the gross negligence[114] of the accused, can be punished by ne or incarceration and, formally at least, could be committed by a company.

In 1990 an action was brought against P&O Ferries Ltd accusing the company of corporate manslaughter in relation to the Zeebrugge ferry disaster in 1986, where a ferry capsized as a result of the failure to correctly secure the ship's bow doors before sailing. 193 people lost their lives. Turner J dismissed the case against the company. In doing so, however, he clarified that a company could be held liable for manslaughter. He held that 'where a corporation, through the controlling mind of one of its agents, does an act which fulfils the prerequisites of the crime of manslaughter, it is properly indictable for the crime of manslaughter'.[115] This holding specified first, that the company could only be guilty of manslaughter if one of its agents was guilty of manslaughter, and, second, that such an agent must be part of the company's directing will and mind—i.e. the applicable rule of attribution for common law manslaughter was the identification doctrine.

It was thought by some commentators that the Privy Council's decision in *Meridian* could result in a loosening of this rule of attribution as applied to manslaughter.[116] In fact *Meridian* had nothing specific to say about manslaughter. Shortly thereafter the Court of Appeal, following a reference by the Attorney-General seeking clarity on the law of manslaughter as applied to companies, confirmed that the applicable rule of attribution was the 'directing mind and will' rule. They observed that: 'the identification principle remains the only basis in common law for corporate liability for gross negligence manslaughter'. The Court of Appeal also confirmed that 'unless an identified individual's conduct, characterizable as gross criminal negligence, can be attributed to the company the company is not, in the present state of the common law, liable for manslaughter'.[117]

In none of the major events referred to previously has there been any conviction of a company for common law manslaughter. The reason for this is found in a combination of: the nature of corporate activity; the fact that *one* individual corporate agent must have committed manslaughter; and the 'directing mind and will' rule of attribution. Whatever the rule of attribution—whether vicarious liability or the identification doctrine—holding a company liable for manslaughter is far more problematic than holding an individual liable for manslaughter. In relation to the individual who drives his car at speed through a pedestrian area killing a pedestrian, the court has to ask whether the individual's actions amounted to gross negligence that resulted in the death of the individual. Deaths arising from corporate activity involve more complex causal patterns. Although we may look at a series of events that led up to the deaths in question with incredulity at the level of organizational incompetence, the gross negligence that can be seen from our 'bird's eye' view of the company's actions is unlikely to have been committed by one person, but rather by several persons: the persons who failed to write a policy on the opening and closing of a ferry door; the training team that failed to make clear the correct procedures for closing the door; the ferry employee who made a mistake which led to the doors not closing; the ship's administration that failed to ensure there were clearly marked exits and sufficient safety vessels.[118] If manslaughter requires the commission of an act of manslaughter by a specific individual in order to

---

[114] Evidence of mens rea (state of mind) although relevant is not necessary to convict a person of manslaughter/involuntary killing. What must be demonstrated is that the accused's 'gross negligence' resulted in the death in question: see *R v Adomako* [1994] 3 All ER 79.

[115] *R v P & O European Ferries (Dover) Ltd* (1990) 93 Cr App R 72 at 84.

[116] Wells, note 104.

[117] *Attorney-General's Reference (No 2 of 1999)* [2000] 2 BCLC 257.

[118] These points are speculative and not directly based on the *Herald of Free Enterprise* disaster.

be attributed to the company then many deaths arising from company activity will be unable to be attributed to the company.

As noted, the rule of attribution at common law is the 'directing mind and will' rule. Such a rule clearly lowers the probability even further that a company will be found to be liable for corporate manslaughter. In large organizations, although the board and senior management may make significant errors—for example decisions on safety of the produced products or safety procedures—these failures will typically not amount to gross negligence that caused the death in question. The death will typically have arisen as a result of the additional failings of several other front-line junior employees. That is, if the actors who matter to the determination of whether a company is guilty of manslaughter are the senior members of staff, who are remote from the front-line operations of the company, then such companies are unlikely to be held liable for common law manslaughter. Of course, in small organizations where the senior members of management are also front-line employees, then the possibility of holding such companies liable for manslaughter increases.[119]

A strong public and media view developed that it is appropriate for companies who are responsible for tragic events such as those referred to previously to be held liable for corporate manslaughter, and that if the common law regime inhibited this then reform was necessary.[120] One might, of course, ask what is to be gained from subjecting companies to such an offence when the only formal sanction is a fine and when large fines can be imposed for breach of regulatory criminal offences such as section 3(1) of the Health and Safety at Work Act 1974. One answer to this challenge is the deterrent effect of the reputational impact of a corporate criminal manslaughter conviction. Such a conviction might significantly affect customers' willingness to buy the company's products, or suppliers' and finance providers' willingness to do business with the company. Arguably the potential for reputational damage would operate as a significant incentive to companies to ensure that they take all steps necessary to prevent the occurrence of business-related deaths.

Reform options run alongside the two problems identified previously: (1) provide that corporate manslaughter can be committed by the acts of several individuals acting on behalf of the business—this is sometimes referred to as the theory of aggregation which is an approach taken in several US states;[121] and (2) provide that the acts and states of mind of more junior employees will be attributed to the company for the purposes of determining whether the company has committed manslaughter. Reform options, however, have the potential to undermine the rationale set out previously for applying corporate manslaughter to companies in the first place: namely that the company's desire to avoid reputational damage encourages safe practices. If reform makes it too easy to hold a company liable for manslaughter then the reputational effect of holding a company liable for manslaughter may be diminished if a conviction is not viewed by the public as such a strong signal of bad behaviour. Similarly, if reform was to result in a vicarious liability rule of attribution, which meant that companies who took all policy steps possible to diminish the possibility of death caused by business activities could still be

---

[119] The only successful prosecutions for corporate manslaughter are in relation to such close 'one man' companies—*R v Kite and others* (1994) *Independent*, 9 December and *R v Jackson Transport* (1996) (referred to in Wells, note 104, at 107).

[120] See, for example, the reaction to the failure of the manslaughter charges brought against Balfour Beatty Plc and its senior executives in relation to the Hatfield train derailment in October 2000 which resulted in four people losing their lives and 70 being injured—see Mark Milner, 'Judge dismisses Hatfield rail manslaughter charges: Failure of case will increase pressure for change in law': *Guardian* (15 July 2005).

[121] See generally Wells, note 104. Aggregation was rejected in *R v HM Coroner for East Kent Ex p Spooner* (1989) 88 Cr App R 10; confirmed by the Courts of Appeal in *Attorney General's Reference (No 2 of 1999)* [2000] 2 BCLC 257, as well as by the Scottish courts in *Transco Plc v HM Advocate (No 1)* [2004] SLT 41.

held liable for manslaughter when an employee committed manslaughter, then the reputational effect of a manslaughter conviction would be diminished as the public came to realize that 'good companies' may be found liable 'through no fault of their own'.[122]

The process of reform was a lengthy one which we do not have the space to consider in detail here. It culminated in the Corporate Manslaughter and Corporate Homicide Act 2007. The Act abolishes the application of common law manslaughter to companies[123] and sets forth the following new offence of corporate manslaughter:

■ Corporate Manslaughter and Corporate Homicide Act 2007

Section 1. The offence

(1) An organisation to which this section applies is guilty of an offence if the way in which its activities are managed or organised—

    (a) causes a person's death, and

    (b) amounts to a gross breach of a relevant duty of care owed by the organisation to the deceased.

(2) The organisations to which this section applies are—

    (a) a corporation;

    (b) a department or other body listed in Schedule 1;

    (c) a police force;

    (d) a partnership, or a trade union or employers' association, that is an employer.

(3) An organisation is guilty of an offence under this section only if the way in which its activities are managed or organised by its senior management is a substantial element in the breach referred to in subsection (1).

(4) For the purposes of this Act—

    (a) 'relevant duty of care' has the meaning given by section 2, read with sections 3 to 7;

    (b) a breach of a duty of care by an organisation is a 'gross' breach if the conduct alleged to amount to a breach of that duty falls far below what can reasonably be expected of the organisation in the circumstances;

    (c) 'senior management', in relation to an organisation, means the persons who play significant roles in—

        (i) the making of decisions about how the whole or a substantial part of its activities are to be managed or organised, or

        (ii) the actual managing or organising of the whole or a substantial part of those activities.

(5) The offence under this section is called—

    (a) corporate manslaughter, in so far as it is an offence under the law of England and Wales or Northern Ireland;

    (b) corporate homicide, in so far as it is an offence under the law of Scotland.

(6) An organisation that is guilty of corporate manslaughter or corporate homicide is liable on conviction on indictment to a fine.

The offence of corporate manslaughter reflects common law manslaughter in requiring a gross breach of duty that causes the death in question. However, in important respects

---

[122] Hybrid options that would mitigate such effects would involve a vicarious rule of attribution coupled with a defence—sometimes called a due diligence defence—that would provide the company with a defence where they had put in place reasonable precautions to prevent death and injury.

[123] Section 20 Corporate Manslaughter and Corporate Homicide Act 2007.

the Act alters the common law of manslaughter as well as the corporate rules of attribution applicable to manslaughter. Of particular importance in this regard is subsection (3) which provides that the company is guilty of corporate manslaughter where 'the way in which its activities are managed or organised by its senior management' amounts to a *substantial element* in the gross breach of the duty of care. Whereas the common law required the commission of the act of manslaughter by an individual (senior management) agent of the company, this provision appears to contemplate an element of aggregation.[124] That is, the actions of different members of senior management which of themselves would not amount a gross breach of duty may be aggregated together for the purposes of determining whether there has been a gross breach of duty. This change makes it easier to hold a company liable for corporate manslaughter.

In relation to the rules of attribution the Act adopts an approach similar to but clearly less demanding than the 'directing mind and will'/identification doctrine approach. Whereas the identification doctrine required that the gross negligence causing the death in question be committed by a person who operated at the very top of the corporate hierarchy, the Act refers to senior participants in the company's management but not necessarily only those at the very top of the managerial hierarchy.

Pursuant to the Act, 'senior management' includes not only senior managers for the 'whole' of the organization but also for a 'substantial part of its activities', suggesting that senior managers of important divisions of a company would fall within the definition of senior management. Subsections (4)(c)(i) and (ii) make it clear that 'senior management' refers to both the board of directors making decisions about the delegation of authority and appointment of managers (subparagraph (i)) as well as the actual senior managers themselves (subparagraph (ii)). In summary, although the rules of attribution in relation to the new offence of corporate manslaughter remain demanding, the increased range of managers whose actions can result in the company being liable in manslaughter increases the likelihood of companies being liable for the statutory offence of corporate manslaughter as compared to common law manslaughter. However, to date the only reported case in which a conviction for corporate manslaughter pursuant to the Corporate Manslaughter Act involved a small 'one-man band' company where the director, manager, and controlling shareholder was the same person. It is noteworthy that the facts of the case would appear to have supported a conviction for corporate manslaughter under the common law had it been applicable.[125]

As outlined previously, under the Act it is now possible that the company could be liable for corporate manslaughter when no one individual member of the company's senior management could be held individually liable for manslaughter. This change in the law in turn raises the possibility of reversing the logic of common law liability for manslaughter: instead of from the guilty individual to the company, from the guilty company to the individual senior manager who could be said to have aided and abetted the offence. This option was firmly rejected by the Government. Section 18 of the Act provides that:

■ Corporate Manslaughter and Corporate Homicide Act 2007

Section 18. No individual liability

(1) An individual cannot be guilty of aiding, abetting, counselling or procuring the commission of an offence of corporate manslaughter.

(2) An individual cannot be guilty of aiding, abetting, counselling or procuring, or being art and part in, the commission of an offence of corporate homicide.

---

[124] D. Ormerod and R. Taylor, 'The Corporate Manslaughter and Corporate Homicide Act 2007: Legislative Comment' (2008) *Criminal Law Review* 589 describing the Act as introducing an element of 'qualified aggregation'.

[125] *R v Cotswold Geotechnical (Holdings) Ltd* [2011] All ER (D) 100.

Questions

1. Is there a general rule of attribution for criminal offences?

2. What is the status of the directing will and mind rule as it applies to criminal offences?

3. How does one determine what is the applicable rule of attribution in relation to a particular crime?

4. Does the Corporate Manslaughter and Corporate Homicide Act 2007 make it easier for a company to be found liable for manslaughter?

5. What, if any, are the implications of making a corporate manslaughter conviction easier?

6. Does it make sense in your view to use the criminal law to regulate companies? If so, why?

 Online Resource Centre
http://www.oxfordtextbooks.co.uk/orc/kershaw2e/

Visit the Online Resource Centre for additional resources and information available for this chapter, including web links and an interactive flashcard glossary.

PART II

CORPORATE CONTROL
AND ACCOUNTABILITY

CHAPTER FIVE

THE CORPORATE AGENCY PROBLEM

| THE PROBLEM OF NON-ALIGNED INTERESTS

In our hypothetical case study of the Bob's Electronics business we have traced the development of the business from the business idea, to the commencement of the business as a sole trading firm, to the incorporation of a private limited company. In Bob's Electronics Ltd, Bob is the sole shareholder and the sole director of the company. Bob as the senior manager of the company is also an employee of the company. Traditionally the senior manager of the company who is also a director of the company is called in the UK the Managing Director or MD. Today, especially for public companies, the American term Chief Executive Officer or CEO is the commonly used term.

Necessarily, as Bob is both director, CEO and sole shareholder in Bob's Electronics Ltd, the interests of the company's director, senior manager and shareholder—with regard to what the company does, how corporate power is used and how the company performs—are the same: the interests of director, manager and shareholder are *fully and unavoidably aligned*. If he pays himself £20,000 in wages this reduces company profits by £20,000 and reduces the funds available to pay a dividend to himself as shareholder. Bob as a shareholder loses out by this decision but as a director he benefits to an equal extent. It is irrelevant to Bob-the-individual whether he gets the funds as a result of his position as director or as shareholder.[1]

As his interests are aligned it would never make sense for Bob to make a decision on behalf of the company that *increased* his wealth as a director by less than it *decreased* his wealth as a shareholder. What would be an example of such a decision? Consider the following hypothetical.

Hypothetical A

Bob's Electronics Ltd has been very profitable and currently has £2 million in the bank. Bob as director and senior manager has two options with regard to how to use these funds. First, he has been made aware of a business that is for sale in a related area: build-to-order stereo systems. His analysis suggests that this business will generate an annual return of 4%; that is £80,000 a year. The second option would be to return the funds to the shareholder, Bob, by a dividend. If these funds were deposited in a high street bank they would generate an annual return of 6%. Accordingly, it makes economic sense to return the funds to Bob. You might ask why would a director of a company faced with such a decision ever be tempted to take the first option and buy the related business for £2 million when there is no business case to do this? One answer would be that the bigger the company the better managers feel about themselves and the higher their social standing in the business and broader community. Bigger companies may be good for managers' egos and they may also be good for their bank balance: the more people and

---

[1] This ignores, for simplicity's sake, the personal tax consequences for Bob of receiving payments as dividends or salary.

assets under your management the better case you may have for a higher salary. But of course as Bob the director is also the sole shareholder, he would never elect to buy the related build-to-order stereo business. To do so would be to effectively throw away some of his personal wealth.

Let us now complicate the management and ownership arrangements of Bob's Electronics Ltd to consider the implications of, and problems that arise when, Bob manages and runs the business as CEO but where he is not the sole owner of the company. Consider the following hypothetical.

Hypothetical B

Bob's Electronics Ltd has been very successful and Bob believes that it has a very bright future. He wishes to control and continue running the business and receive the lion's share of its future capital growth. However, he believes that he ought to have the personal trappings of a 'man in his position'. A house in the south of France and his own helicopter are a must. However, although he receives a high and regular salary as CEO this is insufficient to finance such large personal investments. In order to finance his personal life he must sell some of his shares.

Bob decides to sell 25% of his shares to Ian to obtain the required funds. Ian agrees to play no role in the management of the company. Let us consider the effect of this sale of 25% of the company on the incentives that Bob has as a shareholder and as a director. Take the simple example of management salary. It is no longer the case that if Bob pays himself less as a manager he receives an equivalent amount more as a shareholder; or if he pays himself more as a manager he receives an equivalent amount less as a shareholder. If the board decides to pay Bob £20,000 more then Bob's personal wealth will increase by £20,000. If Bob does not receive this pay rise then: Bob's Electronics Ltd will be £20,000 better off; the value of Bob's shareholding will be £15,000 higher (75% of £20,000); and his personal wealth £5,000 lower than had he received the pay rise. Bob would, therefore, prefer a salary increase of £20,000. Indeed from this perspective the more the company pays Bob the better off he is.

We can certainly imagine other contexts in which this conflict could become more problematic in financial terms, for example, where Bob identifies a new business opportunity related to the Bob's Electronics business which it is estimated will generate £10 million in five years from a £2 million investment. If Bob exploits this opportunity himself he will make £8 million in five years. If Bob's Electronics Ltd exploits the opportunity his personal wealth will only increase by £6 million (as a 75% shareholder in Bob's Electronics Ltd).

Consider further the earlier example where Bob as a director has a choice between using the company's spare cash to purchase a business or to return the funds to the shareholders. On these facts it is unlikely that the additional benefits Bob could receive by running a bigger company would outweigh the financial loss he would incur as a shareholder by using the funds in this way. There remains, therefore, on the facts of this hypothetical a significant alignment of interests between Bob the director and Bob the shareholder.

As Bob's Electronics Ltd evolves the nature of this problem (that the interests of the managers and the directors may not be aligned with the interests of all shareholders) changes. Consider the following development.

Hypothetical C

After several years of running Bob's Electronics Ltd, Bob decides it's time to retire to his house in the south of France. After a lengthy search he decides to employ Markus, a well-known professional manager, as CEO and sole director.

Upon Bob's retirement we see that Bob no longer has any interest in overpaying for managerial services and would be concerned if Markus exploited opportunities for himself that could be profitably exploited by Bob's Electronics Ltd. Furthermore, we now have a management and ownership structure that could encourage Markus the CEO to make value-reducing decisions (such as buying the related build-to-order stereo company for £2 million even though the return would be less than putting the money in a high street bank) if he thinks that such decisions benefit him personally.

In *Hypothetical C*, the interests of the CEO and the shareholders are not aligned in relation to decisions made by Markus the CEO on behalf of Bob's Electronics which benefit Markus personally but destroy value for Bob and Ian as shareholders. However, although we can imagine situations, as set forth in the hypothetical examples, where the interests of senior managers and shareholders are not aligned, in practice with this type of ownership arrangement it seems very unlikely that Markus the CEO will have much room to make such decisions that benefit him personally and yet destroy value for the shareholders. As substantial owners of the company, Bob and Ian have considerable incentives to pay attention and to monitor Markus's performance and to keep themselves up to date and informed on the company and the industry. Any indication that Markus the CEO is making decisions to benefit himself could lead to greater controls over his decision-making authority or could result in him losing his job. Markus's room to exploit the power and authority he has been granted as CEO and sole director for his own benefit is, therefore, constrained by ownership arrangements that give the two shareholders in Bob's Electronics Ltd strong incentives to pay attention.

We can see from *Hypothetical C* that although there is potential for Markus the CEO to abuse his discretion he is prevented from doing so by the presence of large shareholders: shareholders that have a significant personal stake in the company and who, therefore, have good incentives to pay close attention to Markus's activities and performance and to discipline him where he acts in his own and not the company's interests. Now we need to consider what happens as ownership arrangements change. Consider the following development in the case study.

Hypothetical D

Bob decides that the appointment of Markus the CEO did not sufficiently relieve him of the burden of being involved with Bob's Electronics Ltd. Because so much of his wealth is tied up with the business he is forced to pay regular attention to its activities. He also wishes to turn the paper fortune of holding shares in Bob's Electronics Ltd into cash by selling his shares.

One option would be to sell his 75% holding to someone willing to buy all the shares from him. There may, however, not be so many investors willing to take such a large position in one company. As discussed in Chapter 1, the risk associated with a person's investment portfolio can be reduced by diversifying the investments. If one invests a large portion of one's assets in one company then effective diversification may no longer be possible. Also investors may be wary of buying such a large block of shares for fear that it would be difficult to sell it themselves.

Of course there may be other companies in the industry that would be interested in buying Bob's Electronics Ltd and combining it with their existing business. Such purchases would be of considerable interest to Bob. However, if no such purchasers are available another option for Bob would be to sell his shares to the public. That is, sell the shares to many investors who purchase only a small percentage of the shares. Bob could do this by selling his shares as part of an initial public offering (**IPO**) (i.e., the first public offering of shares). To make such an offer of the shares Bob's Electronics Ltd would have to be converted into a public company. This is a relatively straightforward process which, pursuant to sections 90–96 of the Companies Act 2006, requires: that the shareholders in general meeting pass a special resolution supporting the conversion; and, following such a resolution, the re-registration of the company as a public company. We will look at the regulation of offering shares to the public in Web Chapter B. Here we are concerned with the effects of a significant change in the ownership arrangements in Bob's Electronics Plc.

Let us assume that both Bob and Ian sell all their shares in the initial public offering of shares. For Bob's Electronics Plc this means the company is now owned by several hundreds, if not thousands of shareholders, who each may only hold a small percentage of the company's shares. A company with such a shareholder base is often referred to as being **widely-held**. Following the IPO, Markus remains the CEO of the company.

Markus the CEO's incentives to use the power and discretion delegated to him are unaltered as compared to those in *Hypothetical C*. Markus may, in relation to certain types of decision such as the exploitation of new business opportunities or the use of the corporate funds to expand the business, have conflicting interests. This may be clear and brazen in the case of his personal exploitation of an opportunity that the company would be interested in exploiting but less clear in relation to business decisions such as the expansion of the business.

The difference, following Bob and Ian's exit from the business, is that there is no longer a major shareholder of the company. Previously Bob and Ian had a significant investment in the company which meant that they had a significant interest in paying close attention to Markus's behaviour and performance. The important question here is whether the smaller shareholders in the widely-held Bob's Electronics Plc have similar incentives to monitor and pay attention.

There appear to be two problems here. Consider the position of Sue, a shareholder who owns 1% of Bob's Electronics Plc. She is obviously concerned that the company is run to maximize the value of her shares. Even though she only owns 1% of the company this may still be worth a significant amount of money: if Bob's Electronics Plc is worth £1 billion (which in finance speak we would call market capitalization) then her shares are worth £10 million. Simply looking at the financial value of her shares one might think that it would make sense for her to monitor carefully Markus the CEO's activities and decisions. However, monitoring and paying attention costs money. For example: in order to fully understand Bob's Electronics Plc's financial statements she may need to employ an accountant; to understand and critically evaluate its strategy she may need to employ a business consultant. But even if she is sufficiently financially and business literate to do these things herself, most importantly for Sue is that her time may literally be her money. The time spent monitoring Bob's Electronics Plc could have been spent making money through other investments or running her own businesses etc. These costs are what economists call **opportunity costs**. In addition to these costs, Sue would be aware that in addition to monitoring Markus and understanding the business, she would have to persuade her fellow shareholders to act with her. The foul cries of a 1% shareholder are likely to fall on very deaf CEO ears. If Sue acts alone Markus is unlikely to be shaking in his CEO boots. She would need other shareholders to join forces to control management's actions. There are, however, substantial opportunity costs of time and effort involved in persuading other shareholders to join forces and these costs expand exponentially when you need to convince many shareholders in order to have a group that is powerful enough to effect change. These are the **costs of collective action**.

Assume, for example, that the value of Bob's Electronics would increase by £10 million if she paid attention to his activities and decisions. Assume also that the costs of paying attention and acting including direct costs, her own opportunity costs and the costs of collective action are £300,000. On these initial figures one might think that monitoring makes sense. But remember she only owns 1% of the company, so the £10 million saved is only worth £100,000 to her. So although the company and the shareholder body as a whole would benefit from her activities, as someone who is rationally interested in increasing her wealth *she would do nothing*. The legal economic literature often refers to shareholders like Sue as being **rationally apathetic**. Other small shareholders will have similar incentives to Sue and will do nothing as well. All would hope that someone would do something and that they can **free ride** on someone else's effort and good will. But all those small shareholders who are rational wealth maximizers will do nothing. This is what is often referred to in the context of company law as the **collective action problem**.

This means that although Markus the CEO has personal interests that may conflict with the shareholders' interests when Bob's Electronics becomes a widely-held company there is, according to the above analysis, no one to pay attention and monitor. In a widely-held company therefore the scope for Markus the CEO to act in his own interests is considerably greater than it was when Bob and Ian were the only shareholders.

II THE LANGUAGE OF ECONOMIC AGENCY COSTS

1 The economist's view of the principal–agent problem

We have already seen from the above general analysis that if our concern is to ensure that those who run the company should make decisions that aim to increase the value of the company then problems are generated when those who run the company do not themselves own the company. Those problems are exacerbated if the shareholder body has poor incentives to monitor and sanction managerial misbehaviour. We need to provide some conceptual clarity to the problems we have analysed. This clarity is provided in the corporate legal world by the economic analysis of agency problems.

Before looking at the economic analysis of agency problems we need to register a strong caveat in relation to the use of the vocabulary of *agency*. We saw in Chapter 2 in our analysis of the separate legal personality of the company and the House of Lords' decision in *Salomon v Salomon* that the company is *not simply by reason of incorporation the agent of a shareholder-principal*. Of course, although the company is not in law the agent of the shareholders, the shareholders are **residual interest holders** in the company: that is, if the company ceased trading they would have a claim to all the company's assets once all creditors have been repaid. Furthermore, as we shall see in Chapter 10, in English company law commercial companies should be run in the interests of the shareholder body, which is generally understood to mean maximizing long-term shareholder value. The company's assets, therefore, should be deployed with the goal of maximizing the value of the shareholders' residual interest. Through this lens, the company looks like a type of agent: a body acting on behalf of another group: the shareholders. Economists, unconcerned themselves with legal niceties, look at the relationship between management and the shareholders as one example of what they call the **principal–agent problem**.

In Part II of the book, in our analysis of *Corporate Control and Accountability* we will use the language of agency as used by economists. You must remember to hold the legal and economic understandings of agency separate. As we shall see, the economic account of the agency problem is a very useful way of understanding legal rules that regulate the company, but you must not allow the use of this economic terminology to cloud the very basic legal observation that *in law the company is not by reason of incorporation the shareholders' agent.*

■ **R. Kraakman et al, *The Anatomy of Corporate Law: A Comparative and Functional Approach* (2nd edn, OUP, 2009) 35–36**

For readers unfamiliar with the jargon of economists, an 'agency problem'—in the most general sense of the term—arises whenever the welfare of one party, termed the 'principal,' depends on actions taken by another party, termed the 'agent.' The problem lies in motivating the agent to act in the principal's interest rather than simply in the agent's own interest. Viewed in these broad terms, agency problems arise in a broad range of contexts that go well beyond those that would formally be classified as agency relationships by lawyers.

In particular, almost any contractual relationship, in which one party (the 'agent') promises to perform to another (the 'principal'), is potentially subject to an agency problem. The core of the difficulty is that, because the agent commonly has better information than does the principal about the relevant facts, the principal cannot easily assure himself that the agent's performance is precisely what was promised. As a consequence the agent has an incentive to act opportunistically,[2] skimping on the quality of his performance, or even diverting to himself some of what was promised to the principal. This means in turn that the value of the agent's performance will be reduced, either directly or because, to assure the quality of the agent's performance the principal must engage in costly monitoring of the agent. The greater the complexity of the tasks undertaken by the agent, and the greater the discretion the agent must be given, the larger these 'agency costs' are likely to be...

Three generic agency problems arise in business firms. The first involves the conflict between the firm's owners and its hired managers. Here the owners are the principals and the managers are the agents. The problem lies in assuring that the managers are responsive to the owner's interests rather than pursuing their own personal interests. The second agency problem involves the conflict between, on the one hand, owners who possess the majority or controlling interest in the firm and, on the other hand, the minority or non-controlling owners. Here the non-controlling owners can be thought of principals and the controlling owners as the agents, and the difficulty lies in assuring that the former are not expropriated by the latter. While this problem is most conspicuous in tensions between majority and minority shareholders, it appears whenever some subset of a firm's owners can control decisions affecting the class of owners as a whole. Thus if minority shareholders enjoy veto rights in relation to particular decisions, it can give rise to a species of this second agency problem...The third agency problem involves the conflict between the firm itself - including, particularly, its owners—and the other parties with whom the firm contracts, such as creditors, employees and customers. Here the difficulty lies in assuring that the firm, as agent, does not behave opportunistically towards these various other principals such as by expropriating creditors, exploiting workers, or misleading customers.

We see from this extract that for an economist there is an agency problem whenever 'the welfare of one party...is dependent on actions taken by another party'. As Kraakman et al observe, there are different types of agency problem in the context of a business

---

[2] The authors use the term 'opportunism' here, following the usage of Oliver Williamson, to refer to self-interested behaviour that involves some element of deception, misrepresentation, or bad faith (O. Williamson, *The Economic Institutions of Capitalism* (Free Press, 1985)).

firm such as a company: between managers[3] (agent) and shareholders (principal); controlling shareholders (agent) and minority shareholders (principal); and between the company (agent) and other stakeholders such as employees (principal). The primary concern addressed in Chapters 5 to 15 of the book is the agency problem between managers and shareholders. We shall call this the **managerial agency problem**. Other agency problems such as those between controlling shareholders and minority shareholders (which we also saw in *Hypothetical B*) and those between the company and creditors are addressed in Chapters 16, and 18 and 19, respectively.

Kraakman et al label the costs that are incurred when managers act in their own interests to the detriment of the shareholders' interests as agency costs. However, these costs do not necessarily represent value that is taken away from shareholders. Contractarian scholarship, which we introduced in Chapter 3,[4] would argue that when shareholders buy shares in a company they assess the scope that managers have to act in ways that incur managerial agency costs and reduce the price they are willing to pay for the shares accordingly. If this is correct then these costs are reflected in the reduced value of the shares and make it more costly for the company to raise equity finance. However, if such costs are not taken account of by shareholders when they buy the shares then the incurrence of such costs represents a real transfer of value from shareholders to managers.

2 Managerial agency cost categories

We have already seen several examples of potential agency costs in the analysis of the Bob's Electronics Ltd/Plc *Hypotheticals*. It is helpful, however, to provide a more detailed, although not exhaustive, list of agency cost types. Not only does this help us understand what is meant by agency costs but, in addition, as we shall see in this Part II of the book, legal strategies and solutions to the managerial agency problem are responsive to particular agency cost types.

There are two agency cost categories. The first category involves behaviour and business decisions that *directly transfer value* to managers. The second category involves behaviour and business decisions that provide *indirect* financial and psychological benefits, but do not involve an immediate transfer of wealth to the senior manager/director.

2.1 Direct transfers of value

– *Self-dealing.* If a manager enters into a transaction with the company there is a risk that the terms of that contract will benefit the manager at the company's expense. If the company overpays for an asset sold to it by the manager or the manager purchases a company asset for less than it is worth, value is transferred directly into the manager's pocket. This value transfer is an agency cost. If the company loans the manager money at a zero interest rate this is an agency cost as the interest it could have obtained by depositing the funds in a bank is effectively transferred into the manager's pocket.

– *Senior management remuneration.* Remuneration is really an example of self-dealing: it is a transaction for employment services between the manager and the company. If a manager arranges for remuneration which is above the market rate this is an agency cost. Remuneration commands a sub-category of its own and receives specific regulatory attention.

– *Business opportunities.* Managers during their employment and as a result of the position they hold will come across potential new business opportunities. If an

---

[3] The term 'manager' is used here to refer to the senior management of the company, which are referred to later in the book as executive directors.

[4] See p 86.

opportunity identified by the manager would be valuable to the company but the manager decides to exploit the opportunity personally then the value generated by the project is transferred directly to the manager himself. This lost value for the company is an agency cost.

2.2 Indirect agency costs

- *Shirking and incompetence.* Managers as agents are employed to generate value. This requires that they give the company their full attention and that they work hard in the interests of the company. Managers who shirk their responsibilities— who are lazy and do not pay attention, spend too much time on the golf course or in the bar and not enough time at work—destroy value. This lost value is an agency cost.

- *Perquisites.* Many of us are affected by what society classifies as distinctive, valuable, or important and feel better about ourselves if we possess items that, in society's view, distinguish us. An obvious example of such an item would be the car we drive or perhaps how we fly: economy, business, first class, or private jet. Business persons are no different in this regard. Typically, they would rather drive a BMW 7 series than a Ford Mondeo; they would rather fly first class than economy and, if possible would prefer to fly on a company jet. These items provide managers with an indirect financial benefit: the most expensive BMW 7 series costs much more than the most expensive Ford Mondeo; a manager who is provided with a BMW is, therefore, provided with an indirect salary enhancement as compared to one who is provided with a Ford Mondeo. In addition, there are psychological benefits that the manager may receive by driving the BMW rather than the Ford Mondeo: recognition from friends and strangers which comes from driving a symbol of success. But such symbols cost the company money. If the car has no business function, then shareholders would prefer to pay as little as possible for the car. If first class provides adequate comfort for the executive then they would not wish to incur the considerable additional expenditure of buying a company jet. There may be, it should not be forgotten, good reasons to provide a manager with a BMW—you want to attract high quality staff; it is important that when an executive arrives at a customer's offices that he arrives in style—and good reasons to provide a private jet—executives should not waste their time in queues at Heathrow Airport; a corporate jet allows an executive's time to be utilized productively. However, these reasons may not be good enough to justify the incurrence of the expenditure. Where the reason that drives the decision is the indirect financial or psychological benefit of the manager then agency costs are incurred. A real life and extreme example highlights the problem of perquisites. In this case the former CEO of Tyco International Inc, a US company, was accused of misusing corporate funds as follows:

■ **A. Hill and A. Michaels, 'Paw taste condemns Kozlowski: Report says Tyco bought $15,000 dog umbrella stand for chief's apartment' (18 September 2002)** *Financial Times*

The scandal over corporate plundering by top US executives plumbed new depths of extravagance and dubious taste yesterday when it was revealed that Tyco spent $15,000 (£9,700) of shareholders' money on a dog [shaped] umbrella stand.

The stand was acquired for the apartment on New York's Fifth Avenue used exclusively by Dennis Kozlowski, the conglomerate's former chairman. Other household essentials included a $6,000 shower curtain, a $1,650 notebook and a gilt wastepaper basket priced at $2,200.

The inventory of excess was disclosed in a report by the company which found that its funds were used to decorate the apartment 'with appointments and furnishings lacking any legitimate business justification'.

– *Hubris and corporate funds.* We saw in our discussion of the Bob's Electronics *Hypotheticals* that managers may be tempted to use corporate funds for projects that have poor returns relative to the returns that the shareholders could obtain if the funds were distributed to them. The motivation for investing in such projects may not be to generate value for the business but rather to expand the size of the business: the assets under management; the number of employees controlled by management. The benefits for management are twofold: first, managers might feel better about themselves (more important and more powerful) the larger the company they run and control; and, secondly, there may be indirect financial benefits as managers may legitimately claim they should be paid more the more responsibility that they have and the more work they have to do.

III PRIVATE AND REGULATORY RESPONSES TO MANAGERIAL AGENCY COSTS

1 Shareholder responses to the managerial agency problem

Kraakman et al in the extract set out in section II.1 suggest that there are two options available to principals (in the economic use of the term) such as shareholders to respond to the possibility that an agent may act in his own interests to the detriment of the principal. The first option would be to reduce what the principal is willing to pay. The second would be to monitor the agent's actions to ensure that he does not misbehave and to sanction him if he does.

The first of these options would mean that shareholders, rationally aware of the scope for management to incur agency costs, would simply reduce what they are willing to pay for the shares to take account of an estimate of these costs. If you wish to buy a car but the seller is unwilling or incapable of credibly promising that the mileage on the speedometer is correct, then you would either significantly reduce what you are willing to pay (to take account of your assessment of the risk that the speedometer is inaccurate) or, if the risk is too high, you would refuse to buy the car. Buying shares involves a similar process. A rational shareholder would discount the value he is willing to pay for the shares of the company in question to take account of the probability that agency costs will be incurred. If a share would be worth £10 under management that could guarantee that they would not incur any agency costs, it will be worth £8 if shareholders estimate that management will incur agency costs worth £2 a share.

The second of Kraakman et al's options to address an agency problem is the monitoring of the agent by the principal. As we saw in our analysis of the Bob's Electronics *Hypotheticals*, an important consideration in determining the extent to which management can incur agency costs is the ownership structure of the company. We saw in the analysis of *Hypothetical C* that with Bob and Ian as the only shareholders it was unlikely that Markus the CEO would have much room to act opportunistically for his own benefit. However, we also saw in *Hypothetical D* that when the company became a widely-held company owned by many shareholders the freedom for Markus to act opportunistically increased dramatically because individual shareholders who are rationally apathetic would not monitor and discipline Markus's transgressions.

Accordingly, to understand the actual extent of the managerial agency cost problem in UK companies to which UK company law must respond, we need to understand the ownership structure of UK companies.

The vast majority of UK companies by number are small private companies with only, at most, a handful of shareholders. The scope for agency costs in those companies is limited for the reasons explained in *Hypothetical C*. In relation to the UK's large listed companies, such as Marks and Spencer Plc, Vodafone Plc, or BP Plc, it is commonly thought that in the UK the shares in these companies are widely-held with many hundreds, if not thousands, of shareholders, any of whom only own a relatively small percentage shareholding and who, therefore, are subject to the rational apathy and collective action problems analysed in *Hypothetical D*. If this is correct then there is considerable scope for managers to incur agency costs in large UK companies. However, as has become increasingly clear in recent years, this view of the ownership structure of UK companies is inaccurate, although, as we shall see, the assumption of rational apathy may not be.

In the past half century the ownership of the shares of UK companies has changed dramatically.[5] We have seen a significant shift in the ownership of 'UK plc' from shareholders who are known as **retail investors** to **institutional investors**. Retail investors are individual investors who directly invest their own funds to buy shares. Even wealthy retail investors rarely have sufficient capital to buy anything other than a small fraction of a listed company's issued shares. Whilst retail investors are still an important part of the investor landscape in the UK, their percentage shareholding in UK companies has decreased dramatically over the past few decades.[6] Retail investors have been replaced by UK and foreign institutional investors. The institutional investors include: insurance companies who invest insurance premiums paid to them to insure, for example, cars or houses; pension funds that invest the sums paid to them by employers and employees to provide employees with an income when they retire; and mutual funds that provide individuals with a way to invest in shares which is mediated by professional investors, by buying shares in the mutual fund which then uses those funds to invest in the capital markets. Today institutional investors own approximately 80% of the shares of listed UK companies.[7] Furthermore, whilst it is not the norm in relation to each investment made by an institutional investor, it is not unusual for an institutional investor to hold more than 5% of a listed company's issued shares. In this regard, consider the share ownership structure of Marks and Spencer Plc as set out in its 2011 **Annual Report** (see Table 5.1),[8] a company which at the time of writing had a market capitalization of approximately £5 billion.[9]

This data reveals that as of April 2011 Marks and Spencer Plc has 210,811 shareholders, with a significant number—202,200—of retail shareholders. These retail investors, however, own comparatively few shares: 18% retail investor ownership as against

[5] For an account of the evolution of UK share ownership see B. Cheffins, 'Dividends as a Substitute for Corporate Law: The Separation of Ownership and Control in the United Kingdom' (2006) 63 *Washington and Lee Law Review* 1273; B. Cheffins, *Corporate Ownership and Control: British Business Transformed* (OUP, 2008); and B. Cheffins, 'The Stewardship's Code Achilles Heel' (2010) 73 *MLR* 985.

[6] Cheffins, 'Dividends as a Substitute' *ibid*.

[7] See Office of National Statistics, *Share Ownership Survey 2008* (2010) 1 (available at: www.ons.gov.uk/ons/rel/pnfc1/share-ownership-share-register-survey-report/2008/index.html). Note that in recent years the Office for National Statistics have documented an increasing shift towards foreign institutional ownership of UK companies and away from domestic institutional ownership. As of 1990 foreign institutional ownership amounted to 11.8% of UK shares; by 2008 the figure stood at 41.5%. By way of contrast, as of 1990 the percentage of shares owned by UK pension funds stood at 31.7% of UK shares, by 2008 the figure had been reduced to 12.5% of UK shares (see *ibid* at 4).

[8] Marks and Spencer Plc Annual Report 2008 (available at: http://corporate.marksandspencer.com/).

[9] At the time of writing (7 October 2011) Marks and Spencer Plc had a market capitalization of £5.16 billion.

82% institutional investor ownership;[10] 74% of the company's **ordinary shares** are owned by only 0.08%[11] of the shareholders by number. Elsewhere in Marks and Spencer Plc's 2011 Annual Report the company reveals that there are five shareholders with a greater than 3% shareholding: 6.57%; 5.09%; 4.81%; 3.99%; 3.01%.[12] In practice, however, the potential voting power of these shares is considerably greater than their aggregate 23.5% as not all the company's shareholders vote in person or in proxy at a Marks and Spencer Plc general meeting. At the 2011 AGM only 59.5% of the shares were voted.[13] This would have given these five shareholders approximately 40% of the *votes cast*. Coordinating a group of five shareholders would not involve significant collective action costs. Accordingly, if real economic benefits can be generated through active monitoring by these shareholders and if the costs of monitoring could be shared between them, then it seems highly plausible that it would be rational for these shareholders to monitor rather than be apathetic.

Table 5.1 *Marks and Spencer Plc Shareholder Structure (Ordinary shares) as of April 2011*

Analysis of share register
Ordinary shares
As at 2 April 2011, there were 210,811 holders of ordinary shares whose shareholdings are analysed below.

	Number of holdings	Percentage of total shareholders	Number of ordinary shares	Percentage of ordinary shares
Range				
1–500	106,294	50.42	20,940,524	1.32
501–1,000	41,998	19.92	31,415,804	1.98
1,001–2,000	32,201	15.27	46,127,764	2.91
2,001–5,000	21,565	10.23	66,141,629	4.17
5,001–10,000	5,556	2.64	38,530,292	2.43
10,001–100,000	2,587	1.23	59,709,860	3.77
100,001–1,000,000	440	0.21	144,481,595	9.12
1,000,001–HIGHEST	170	0.08	1,177,516,414	74.30
Total	210,811	100.00	1,584,863,882	100.00

Many private investors hold their shares through nominee companies, therefore the percentage of private holders is much higher than that shown – we estimate approximately 30%.

	Number of holdings	Percentage of total shareholders	Number of ordinary shares	Percentage of ordinary shares
Holders				
Private	202,200	95.92	285,522,151	18.02
Institutional and Corporate	8,611	4.08	1,299,341,731	81.99
Total	210,811	100.00	1,584,863,882	100.00

[10] This compares with figures of 21% and 79% as of 2008 (see Marks and Spencer Plc Annual Report 2008 (available at: http://corporate.marksandspencer.com/).
[11] This compares with 72% owned by 0.9% of the shareholder base as of 2008 *ibid*.
[12] *Ibid*, 35. This data is sourced from a slightly different date—23 May 2011—than the ordinary share ownership structure data. Note that three of the shareholders in this list of five large shareholders were the three largest shareholders as 6 May 2008 which shows that many large shareholders remain shareholders in the company for a long period of time.
[13] See http://corporate.marksandspencer.com/investors/press_releases/poll_result_for_2011_agm.

Compare this data with information on Vodafone Plc's shareholder structure taken from its 2011 Annual Report. Vodafone has a similar ownership structure involving a large number of retail shareholders and a limited number of investors owning most of the shares in the company.[14] However, according to Vodafone's Annual report it only had two shareholders with a greater than 3% shareholding: one owned 6.00% of the shares and the other 3.59%. Clearly for the shareholders in Vodafone Plc the potential rational apathy and collective action problems are more significant than they appear to be for Marks and Spencer's major shareholders. However, if one makes the reasonable assumption that there are several other shareholders with between 2–3% of the shares[15] then the top 10 shareholders in Vodafone are likely to represent, in aggregate, a significant block of shares, possibly in the region of 30% of the voting shares. Note, however, that the voter turnout at Vodafone's annual general meeting is significantly higher than at Marks and Spencer's, amounting to 69% of the voting shares at the 2011 general meeting. The bigger turnout renders control by a small group of shareholders at Vodafone more difficult than at Marks and Spencer. Nevertheless, for Vodafone Plc, and particularly for Marks and Spencer Plc, the rational apathy and collective action problems are not as significant as has been traditionally assumed. However, that is not to say the costs of collective action are negligible—the costs of coordinating 10 shareholders with different interests and investment profiles should not be understated.

If these ownership structures are at all representative of large UK listed companies, which available evidence suggests that they are,[16] then one might reasonably expect UK institutional investors to be playing an active and effective role in monitoring management and keeping in check managerial agency costs. We do not have the space here to explore this issue in detail, however, in short this expectation would be largely *incorrect*. We will see during the course of our analysis of UK corporate governance—particularly in Chapters 7 and 8 when we consider board composition and compensation—examples of institutional shareholder activity with a very public profile. There is also a widely held belief that institutional investors engage in a considerable amount of informal, behind the scenes, monitoring and disciplining of managers. However, the empirical evidence in support of this claim that institutional investors actively monitor, either publicly or informally, is weak.[17]

In the main even large institutional investors do not monitor and do not coordinate with each other to share the costs of monitoring and activism. There are several reasons for this which have been explored in the literature.[18] Most important in this regard is the way in which institutional investment funds are managed. A pension fund, for example, will not manage the fund itself. Instead the pension fund will employ a financial expert called a **fund manager** to make the investment decisions. Individual fund managers who work at these fund manager companies will typically be responsible for investing in many tens if not hundreds of companies. Accordingly, the individual fund managers who actually makes the decision to purchase 5% of a listed company's shares simply

---

[14] Vodafone Annual Report 2011, 134 (www.vodafone.com/ ●).

[15] The Annual Reports do not disclose less than 3% shareholders. Pursuant to the Disclosure and Transparency Rules issued by the UK Listing Authority, shareholders who cross the 3% ownership threshold must disclose this fact to the company (DTR 5).

[16] See F. Barca and M. Becht, *The Control of Corporate Europe* (OUP, 2002), ch 10; B. Black and J. Coffee, 'Hail Britannia? Institutional Investor Behaviour under Limited Regulation' (1994) 92 *Michigan Law Review* 1997, detailing the fact that control of listed UK companies can be obtained with relatively few shareholders.

[17] See Black and Coffee, *ibid*, and the important work of G. Stapledon, *Institutional Shareholders and Corporate Governance* (OUP, 1996). However, in both studies the evidence of informal monitoring is based on interviews with the informal monitors themselves—the institutional investors. A limited set of pilot interviews carried out by this author in preparation for a project on institutional investor activism with non-institutional participants suggests such formal and informal activism is the exception to a rule of passivity.

[18] See Black and Coffee, *ibid* and Stapledon, *ibid*.

do not have the time or resources to: monitor effectively the companies in which they make those investments; actively respond to problematic behaviour by management; and coordinate monitoring activity with other fund managers.[19]

Furthermore, the fee arrangements according to which fund managers are remunerated do not typically provide fund managers with strong incentives to actively monitor the companies in which they invest, even when it would be rational from the institutional investor's perspective to do so.[20] Fund managers are typically paid according to the total value of the funds which they manage and invest—typically they are paid a fee of approximately 2% of the asset value of the fund which they manage. To understand why fee arrangements dampen the fund managers' incentives to monitor consider the following example:

> A fund manager has £1 billion from a pension fund under management. Active monitoring at one of the companies in which it has a significant holding of shares would generate a £1 million return for the pension fund. From the pension fund's perspective such monitoring would be rational as the costs of activism for the pension fund would be £500,000 (that is, the active monitoring would result in a total return of £500,000 for the fund). However, is it rational for the fund manager to be active in this case? His fee based on the assets under management would be £20 million without the activism and £10,000 more (2% of £500,000) with the activism; i.e. a fee increase of 0.0005%. Given the opportunities that might be missed as a result of the time spent by the fund manager in actively monitoring the company in question it seems unlikely that in many instances activism makes sense for fund managers.

Accordingly, for the fund managers who manage the wealth of the institutional investors they are also rationally apathetic with regard to the monitoring of companies in which they invest. Therefore, an assumption of large-scale rational apathy on the part of shareholders in large UK companies is a reasonable one.[21] This may be a function of, in some companies, widely-held ownership and collective action problems, and in others a function of the capacity and remuneration arrangements of the fund managers who manage the wealth of the institutional investors. This book will use the term 'rational apathy' to refer to the effects of *either* the incentives for small percentage shareholders to be active in widely-held companies *or* the effects of institutional investors investing through fund managers.

As a result of the ongoing financial crisis, politicians and regulators have begun to pay closer regard to the inactivity of institutional shareholders. Questions were asked in the

---

[19] One of the author's ongoing projects is to produce a contemporary study of institutional shareholder activism. In this regard a limited number of interviews to date have been carried out. In one interview a former fund manager of a major UK fund management company observed that he and two other junior colleagues had been responsible for the 250 small listed companies; in this regard he observed that 'the idea that I could spend more than four hours a year on a company was laughable'.

[20] Of course in many instances the fund manager's **opportunity costs** of activism will render the activism irrational even if the benefits of acting in relation to the particular company exceed the costs. The opportunity costs of acting are the losses incurred as a result of spending time on the activism rather than looking at other investment opportunities or being attentive to other aspects of a fund manager's portfolio.

[21] In recent years we have seen in the UK and elsewhere an increase in shareholder activism by investment vehicles called hedge funds. Interestingly, these Hedge Funds have very different fee arrangements, including, typically, 20% of amounts generated above a specified return in addition to a 'funds under management' fee of typically 2%. The development and importance of such activism in the UK has only been subject to a limited amount of research and, unfortunately, there is no space to consider this issue here. For those interested in these developments see: W. Bratton, 'Hedge Funds and Governance Targets' (2006) Georgetown Law and Economics Research Paper No 928689 available at SSRN: http://papers.ssrn.com/; Becht et al, 'Returns to Shareholder Activism Evidence from a Clinical Study of the Hermes U.K. Focus Fund' (December 2006) ECGI—Finance Working Paper No 138/2006 available at SSRN: http://papers.ssrn.com/; Brav et al, 'Hedge Fund Activism, Corporate Governance and Firm Performance' (2006) ECGI Working Paper; A. Klein and E. Zur, 'Hedge Fund Activism' (September 2006); AAA 2007 Financial Accounting & Reporting Section (FARS) Meeting Paper available at SSRN: http://papers.ssrn.com/.

initial autopsy of the 2007–2009 financial crisis about the failure of institutional shareholders to question what—with the benefit of hindsight—we now see as banks' excessive and systemically dangerous risk taking.[22] As a result of the crisis, the Government asked Sir David Walker to carry out a review of the governance of banks and financial institutions. As part of this review Sir David considered the actions, and inactivity, of institutional shareholders prior to the crisis.[23] His primary recommendation in this regard was that the Financial Reporting Council (FRC)—the UK's accounting and actuary regulator, which also has responsibility for the UK's Corporate Governance Code[24]—should take control over what was previously a self-regulatory code of best practice for institutional shareholders: *The Responsibilities of Institutional Shareholders And Agents—Statement of Principles*, maintained by the Institutional Shareholders Committee (ISC).[25] The Government accepted these recommendations resulting in this code of best practice being adopted and amended by the FRC. The Code and is now known as the UK Stewardship Code.

The Stewardship Code provides a *light touch* set of principles for 'firms that manage assets of behalf of institutional shareholders'[26] with regard to the monitoring of companies in which they own shares. The Code is a *comply or explain* code.[27] This means that fund managers who have been designated 'authorized persons'[28] by the Financial Services Authority are required to disclose whether they comply with the Stewardship Code.[29] If they do not do so then they must disclose their alternative investment strategy. With regard to fund managers who are not FSA authorized persons, the Code represents merely a set of best practice guidelines. The Code's core principles are as follows:

The Stewardship Code (FRC, 2010)

The Principles of the Code

Institutional investors should:

- Publicly disclose their policy on how they will discharge their stewardship responsibilities.
- Have a robust policy on managing conflicts of interest in relation to stewardship and this policy should be publicly disclosed.
- Monitor their investee companies.
- Establish clear guidelines on when and how they will escalate their activities as a method of protecting and enhancing shareholder value.
- Be willing to act collectively with other investors where appropriate.
- Have a clear policy on voting and disclosure of voting activity.
- Report periodically on their stewardship and voting activities.

---

[22] Lord Myners, a business minister in the last Labour administration, described institutional shareholders as 'absentee landlords'. See 'Myners hits at "landlord shareholders"' (22 April 2009) *Financial Times*.

[23] *A Review of Corporate Governance in UK Banks and Other Financial Industry Entities: Final Recommendations* (2009) available at: http://webarchive.nationalarchives.gov.uk/+/http://www.hm-treasury.gov.uk/d/walker_review_261109.pdf ◎.

[24] See Chapter 7.

[25] The ISC is a group of trade associations which represent institutional investors. It consists of the Association of British Insurers, the Investment Management Association and the National Association of Pension Funds.

[26] The UK Stewardship Code (FRC, 2010) at 2. The term 'institutional shareholders' is used here; it appears to refer to the ultimate institutional investors, such as pension funds, working together with their fund managers to reach a decision as to whether to engage with managers.

[27] For further discussion of the *comply or explain* regulatory technique see Chapter 7.

[28] Under section 19 of the Financial Services and Markets Act 2000 a person who carried out a regulated activity such as fund management must be authorized by the Financial Services Authority (FSA) to carry out this activity.

[29] FSA, *Conduct of Business Sourcebook*, Rule 2.2.3 requiring that the firm disclose on its website 'the nature of its commitment to the Financial Reporting Council's Stewardship Code'.

The Code provides additional guidance on how these investors can act in accordance with these principles.[30] For example, in relation to the first principle the Code recommends that fund managers disclose their policy on how they will monitor firms and their strategy on intervening in a portfolio firm.[31]

Many have expressed doubts that this Stewardship Code will result in an increase in fund manager monitoring.[32] Not least because, as noted earlier, the Code will not have to be considered by the many foreign institutional investors/fund managers who are not FSA authorized persons and who own and manage an increasing, and significant, percentage of shares in UK companies.[33] Furthermore, aside from this important practical concern, the nature of the Stewardship Code means that its effect is likely to be moderate at best. Even for those fund managers subject to the *comply or explain* obligation, the Code is merely a regulatory plea for involvement, together with some limited guidance for those that decide to engage. The Code observes, for example, that: 'institutional shareholders are free to choose whether or not to engage [with company management] but their choice should be a considered one based on their investment approach'. The Code provides neither a stick nor a carrot to actively monitor. Accordingly, it is most unlikely that the practical and economic drivers of fund manager apathy discussed earlier will be counterbalanced by a code of this nature.

The fact that the Stewardship Code is likely to be ineffectual does not mean that regulators should act more aggressively to force institutional investors to be active by, for example, regulating fund manager remuneration in order to incentivize active monitoring or limiting the number of companies that a fund manager can have in its portfolio in order to address the practical difficulties identified. The state of empirical research is such that we do not know at present whether greater shareholder activism in the UK will reap rewards in excess of the increased cost of activism.[34] Until we do, we should be very wary of regulating for shareholder activism. In the absence of such regulation, students of this book can feel comfortable about adopting an assumption that the shareholders in widely-held UK companies are rationally apathetic.

2 Regulatory responses to the managerial agency problem

One option for a regulator, given the problem of managerial agency costs identified, would be to do nothing. We could say shareholders are rational people capable of looking after themselves and they will discount the value of what they are willing to pay according to their estimate of potential managerial misbehaviour. Those managers who want to increase share value will take action or impose restraints upon themselves to convince shareholders that they will not misbehave and, if convinced, shareholders will pay more for the shares. From this perspective, persons with sufficient funds to invest in shares are capable of looking after themselves and if they fail to do so then that is their own fault and they will quickly learn to pay more attention to the next investment. This approach would leave it to the market place to resolve the problem itself.

There are several potential difficulties with this approach. First, do we think that all investors, even financially sophisticated ones such as fund managers, are capable of and have the time to assess the likelihood that, and the extent to which, management of a particular company will incur agency costs? If not, a regulator with a paternalistic inclination might be tempted to step in to protect shareholders and to try and prevent managerial misbehaviour through regulation. Another difficulty with the market-oriented or private-ordering approach might be that if shareholders become too distrustful it will be difficult for even the best and most upstanding of management

---

[30] *Ibid* at 5–9.   [31] *Ibid*: Guidance to Principle 1, p 5.
[32] B. Cheffins, 'The Stewardship's Code Achilles Heal' (2010) 73 *MLR* 985.
[33] See note 7.   [34] See literature set forth in note 21.

to convince shareholders that they will not misbehave. If this happens then all managers, good and bad, would find it more costly to sell shares to investors (increasing companies' cost of capital) making running businesses more expensive. This type of problem—where it is difficult for buyers to distinguish between a good and bad product and so they refuse to pay more than the price of a bad product—is referred to by economists as a market for lemons.[35] If there is a risk of there being such a market for shares it may benefit all companies for the state as regulator to impose certain types of regulation on companies designed to reduce managerial agency costs.

However, as we saw in Chapter 3, the available regulatory choices are not just between *either* mandating legal rules on how to run and organize the company *or* doing nothing at all and allowing the parties to sort it out themselves through private ordering. A third option is to provide regulatory assumptions or guidance: rules that are applicable unless a company elects for the rule not to apply. These rules are available if the company wishes for them to apply, but they allow the company to make a different rule choice if the company would prefer a different rule. These types of rule are known as **default rules**, that is they only apply in default of or in the absence of a different choice.

The landscape of our analysis in this section should be coming into focus. Where companies have rationally apathetic shareholders—either *in fact* because the company is widely held or *in practice* due to the fund management arrangements through which institutional investors make their investments—we cannot rely on shareholders to monitor and to constrain the incurrence of managerial agency costs. Law and regulation is, therefore, an important component in limiting the ability of management to incur agency costs. The legal and regulatory strategies used to regulate managers need not, however, be provided by the state imposing mandatory rules on companies. In some instances they will be provided by the state in either mandatory or default form; in others they will be provided by the company themselves. We are interested in this Part of the book in the nature of the regulatory strategies that respond to and mitigate the managerial agency problem, and we are also interested in the form that such regulatory strategies take: are they, or indeed should they be, state-provided mandatory or default rules; or are they, or should they be, provided by the company themselves?

The approach to this area of company law that considers legal strategies to control or mitigate agency problems is most comprehensibly outlined in the seminal comparative corporate law text *The Anatomy of Corporate Law*.[36] This book adopts the structure of *The Anatomy*'s approach but uses different, although overlapping, categories to organize these legal and non-legal strategies. The strategy categories provide a road map for this Part II of the book. These categories are set out here. They are each subject to detailed analysis in the remainder of this Part II.

- *Structuring the balance of power between the board, management and the shareholder body.* As we have seen, for investors to obtain the benefit of carrying out business activity through the corporate form authority must be relinquished to the board of directors and to managers. The question for this legal strategy is: in what areas of corporate administration and activity, *if any*, should shareholders retain power and to what extent, if any, does the retention of power ensure that managers act in the company's interests and not in their own. The balance of power is addressed in the next chapter.

- *Regulating board composition.* The analysis just set out, as is typical of theoretical discussions of the agency problem, presents the problem as between the manager agent and shareholder principle. It typically fails to account for the role of the

---

[35] G. Akerlof, 'The Market for Lemons' (1970) 84 *Quarterly Journal of Economics* 488.
[36] See R. Kraakman et al, *The Anatomy of Corporate Law: A Comparative and Functional Approach* (2nd edn, OUP, 2009).

board of directors in controlling managers' activities. Part of the reason for this is that, absent the type of regulation discussed in this section, it is assumed that the board becomes a puppet of managers' intentions and desires. The question of relevance here is: how can we make the board of directors an effective control mechanism? In particular, this legal strategy asks who/what types of person should sit on the board of directors to make it effective; should management sit on the board of directors; should all decisions be made by the board as a whole or should certain decisions be made by certain types of directors. This legal strategy focuses on the *structure and composition of the board.*

- *Regulating remuneration.* Remuneration of senior management although connected to composition and structure questions is really a separate strategy involving two elements addressed in Chapter 8: first, how to ensure that remuneration can be used to control agency problems by aligning the personal (wealth) interests of management with the company's interests in generating value; and, secondly, how to ensure that remuneration does not in of itself become an agency cost with management being overpaid for their services as a result of the power which they yield.

- *Behavioural standards/duties imposed on the directors.* If a person (as principal) decides to allow her assets to be managed and invested by an expert investor or manager (the agent), that person would have certain behavioural expectations of the agent. These behavioural obligations are crystallized in UK company law in the form of directors' duties owed to the company. These duties are analysed in Chapters 9–14.

- *Enforcing behavioural standards.* If the behavioural standards are to be effective in ensuring that the directors behave appropriately it will be necessary to provide mechanisms of enforcing those standards. Chapter 15 will consider the enforcement options in relation to the standards. Here the primary question for analysis is how to ensure enforcement when the directors who may have breached the duties are the individuals who decide whether the company should enforce the duties (against themselves!). We will ask to what extent should shareholders have a say in the enforcement process, and what, if any, are the problems that arise from giving them a role in this process.

- *Market mechanisms.* There are several market places within which companies, directors and managers operate. We have seen several of these in our analysis thus far. Companies sell products in product markets; companies must access the capital markets to raise finance for their activities; managers compete in the market for managerial services. There is also a market for the control of companies: the 'market for corporate control'.[37] Companies whose shares trade for less than they would trade for under different management are exposed to being taken over by individuals or other companies who can acquire a controlling interest in the company's shares. Managers who are the subject of successful takeovers may and often do lose their jobs.

- These markets all operate to constrain agency costs. If you behave badly it may be difficult to get another job; so you restrict your bad behaviour. If a manager incurs high agency costs then capital may become too expensive making the company less competitive and exposing the company to a takeover bid which could result in the manager losing his job and finding himself back in a market for managerial services which will now be sceptical about his abilities. These market constraints are non-legal constraints, but in several ways law plays a very important role in facilitating

---

[37] The first edition of this book contained a Web Chapter on the *Market for Corporate Control.* This chapter is no longer part of this book but part of an expanded look at the takeover regulation in D. Kershaw, *Principles of Takeover Regulation* (OUP, forthcoming 2013).

these market constraints, whether through the regulation of the information made available to the market (Web Chapter A on disclosure and accounting) or through the explicit regulation of the market itself.

IV **THE PROBLEM OF AUTHORITY**

As should now be clear, this Part of the book on *Corporate Control and Accountability* is primarily concerned with restricting the ability of managers who are given discretion to run the company from abusing that discretion to benefit themselves personally. We are concerned with the legal strategies that are deployed to regulate this managerial agency problem. However, there is a danger contained within this viewpoint that we need to be aware of. Excessive focus on how to control and constrain abuses of discretion—how to ensure managers behave responsibly—may distract us from giving due regard to a fundamental, if somewhat obvious, observation. The agency cost problem is a product of the corporate form that allows assets to be managed by professional managers for the benefit of those who have funds to invest but do not have the skills, the time or the inclination to manage. The limited liability company with separate legal personality is without doubt one of the most important inventions of the modern age. Without it the UK as a nation would be a lot poorer than it is today. To enable value to be created through the corporate form we must give management the freedom and authority to make decisions and to make them quickly; to devise a business strategy and to implement that strategy. A manager that has to negotiate with the owners of a firm prior to making any decision which would be binding on the company would not be a successful manager. Giving authority and discretion to managers is a prerequisite to value creation through the corporate form.

Whilst we need to ensure that managers do not abuse their discretion, if in the quest for ensuring that management behave responsibly we deny management sufficient authority and discretionary freedom to do their job then we may destroy more value than the agency costs that are saved. Accordingly, when analysing and critiquing the legal strategies deployed by UK company law to regulate the managerial agency problem we must always bear in mind that company law must strike the right balance between reducing agency costs and giving managers freedom to act; the right balance between *responsibility and authority*. Consider Professor Kenneth Arrow, Nobel Laureate, in this regard.

■ Kenneth J. Arrow, *The Limits of Organization* (1974) Fels Lectures on Public Policy Analysis 77

> To serve its functions, responsibility must be capable of correcting errors but should not be such as to destroy the genuine values of authority. Clearly, a sufficiently strict and continuous organ of responsibility can easily amount to denial of authority. If every decision of A is to be reviewed by B, then all we have really is a shift in the locus of authority from A to B and hence no solution to the original problem. To maintain the value of authority, it would appear that responsibility must be intermittent.

 Online Resource Centre
http://www.oxfordtextbooks.co.uk/orc/kershaw2e/

Visit the Online Resource Centre for additional resources and information available for this chapter, including web links and an interactive flashcard glossary.

CHAPTER SIX

THE BALANCE OF POWER BETWEEN THE BOARD, MANAGEMENT, AND THE SHAREHOLDER BODY

I INTRODUCTION

Let us return to our case study of Bob's Electronics Ltd to set the scene for our analysis of the legal regulation of the distribution of power between the board of directors and the shareholder body.

Following the incorporation of the Bob's Electronics business into Bob's Electronics Ltd when Bob is the sole director, manager and shareholder, questions about the balance of power would be of little concern to Bob as *Bob-the-person*—through his three guises of manager, director, and shareholder—wields absolute control. It is of little concern to him whether that power is exercised through his position as manager, director or shareholder. His only concern with regard to his authority and the exercise of corporate powers will be to ensure that he pays due regard to the company's constitutional requirements when acting as a manager, a director or a shareholder to ensure that actions taken as manager, director, or shareholder are valid and enforceable.[1]

However, if Bob decided to keep his shares but to retire from both his position as a manager and as a director of the company then questions about how power within the company is distributed between the board and the shareholder body would be of acute concern to Bob. Assume, for example, that he wishes to retire and no longer wants to have an operational role in the company. He wishes to employ *Markus the CEO* to run the business profitably. Markus, somewhat unusually when the manager is not a shareholder but usefully for the purposes of our initial analysis in this section, will be the sole manager and director of the company. In such circumstances what would Bob's concerns be in deciding how to distribute power between the shareholder body (currently himself) and the board and management (Markus)?

There are two primary areas of concern for Bob given the above fact pattern: first, who, as between the board, management and the shareholder body, has the power to make decisions (and what type of decisions) on behalf of the company; and second, what are the rules that determine how Markus is appointed as a director and as a manager, and what are the rules determining how and in what circumstances he can be removed as a director and/or as a manager? We address each of these issues in turn in sections II and III.

II DECISION RIGHTS

1 Who should make corporate decisions?

In this section we are interested in how the power and authority to make decisions on behalf of the company is distributed between senior management, the board, and the

---

[1] On the effect of informal unanimous shareholder decisions see *Re Duomatic* [1969] 1 ALL ER 161 and its progeny discussed in Chapter 3 B II.

shareholder body. Decision types would range from, for example: employing persons (from a cleaner to the chief executive officer); to entering into contracts with third parties (from buying stationery to selling all of the company's assets); to issuing shares in the company. The power to make business decisions could, *in theory*, be given directly to senior management alone, the board of directors alone, or the shareholders alone; or it could be shared by, for example, giving the board decision-making authority subject to approval by the shareholder body or to being overruled by the shareholder body. Different decision types could, *in theory*, be given to different organs or persons.

In our case study, Bob is retiring as the CEO of Bob's Electronics Ltd and clearly does not want to make, or have to give his approval for, all of these decisions; rather he intends to employ Markus the CEO to make the bulk of these decisions. Not only does he want to relieve himself of the burden of decision-making, he also recognizes that Markus the CEO must be given a certain degree of freedom to act in order to be successful. Bob may, of course, want to retain the right to re-assert himself in the operational side of the business if unhappy with particular decisions or decision-making by Markus the CEO generally. He may therefore wish to retain the right to overrule Markus's decisions (to the extent that that is possible, provided that the company has incurred no legal obligation) or the general right to instruct Markus to take a specific action, for example to sell, or to reject an offer for, an asset. We shall refer to such a right as an **instruction right**. There may also be decision types or areas of business activity where, following Markus's decision, Bob will not want the decision to be put into effect until he gives his approval as shareholder. We shall refer to these rights as **veto** or **approval rights**.

An important question in relation to veto or approval rights is what are the criteria by which one determines the specific decision-types or areas where decision-making power should be retained by or shared with the shareholder body? From our analysis in Chapter 5 it is clear that a primary concern for Bob following the appointment of Markus the CEO would be the possible incurrence of **managerial agency costs** as a result of Markus using the power delegated to him for his own benefit. One basis for determining the decision-types in relation to which shareholders should retain or share corporate power would be the scope for the incurrence of agency costs as a result of those decisions. However, there are many decisions that could result in the incurrence of agency costs. We saw that the former CEO of Tyco International Inc spent $15,000 on a dog-shaped umbrella stand with company funds. This is clearly an agency cost but it is unlikely to be a decision-type in relation to which shareholders, including a 100% shareholder such as Bob, would wish to retain decision-making power. If Bob was to review such decisions the benefits of appointing professional management would be lost as managerial authority collapses at the behest of responsibility. Agency costs alone, therefore, do not provide a useful criterion for determining the decision areas where shareholders should retain power. Perhaps, therefore, we might wish to focus on areas where the agency cost problem is significant, for example, in relation to large self-dealing transactions or corporate opportunities.

A second factor that may be relevant to determining which decision-types should be retained or shared with Bob as shareholder would be those decisions that could fundamentally alter his shareholder relationship to the company: decisions that affect him as a shareholder as contrasted with the business decisions taken by the company in carrying out its activities. Decision-types such as the issuing of shares or the merger of a company with another company would fall into this category.

A third category of decision in relation to which Bob may wish to retain decision-making power would be decisions that are so significant or have such grave implications for the future of the firm that they ought to be retained by the shareholder body or shared by the board and the shareholder body. Bob might not wish to be involved in anything that could be described as the day-to-day running of the company, but may wish to get involved in periodic, significant decisions such as the purchase or sale of a very large asset.

Assignment

Take 15 minutes to think about what types of decision rights you would wish to give to the board; and what types of decision rights (approval/veto rights or initiation/instruction rights) you would wish to give to the shareholder body.

The decision rights structure that you have identified from the assignment is likely to be tailored to the fact pattern identified: Bob retires but retains 100% of the shares. It is also likely to be tailored to the knowledge you have about Bob: he is a successful entrepreneur who created and ran the Bob's Electronics business for several years. That is, the decision rights that we think should be retained by the shareholders may vary according to the nature of the shareholder body, in particular the *capacity* of the shareholders to make informed decisions and the *incentives* for the shareholders to make an informed decision. If Bob, for example, after appointing Markus the CEO intends to transfer the shares in Bob's Electronics Ltd to his son David and he is aware that David is poorly informed about everything, has very strong opinions, and never hesitates to make decisions, but invariably makes very bad decisions, then the distribution of power that Bob would like to craft prior to his retirement and the transfer of shares to David would look very different from the one that you crafted in the assignment. The appropriate or optimal distribution of power in companies is, therefore, likely to vary according to the specific attributes of the company, including, most importantly, the attributes of the shareholder body. Developing this line of thought, does it make sense for companies that are widely-held to retain any type of shareholder decision-making power? According to our analysis in Chapter 5 of the rational apathy problems in widely-held companies, even where there is significant institutional investor presence, shareholders in listed UK companies are unlikely to have the correct incentives to pay attention to company activities or to inform themselves properly when asked to make a decision. Does this consideration mean that such shareholders should have no decision rights or does it simply affect the types of decision rights it makes sense for them to have?

2 The basic distribution of decision-making power in UK company law

Perhaps surprisingly for a statute that is 955 pages long,[2] the Companies Act 2006 makes no *general statement* about the powers of the board of directors. The board of directors is not provided with any authority to make decisions by the Companies Act 2006. The Act provides that a private company is required to have at least one director and a public company at least two directors,[3] but it says nothing about what these directors are empowered to do. Nor does the Act provide any general statement about the authority or powers of the shareholder body. In UK company law the general distribution of decision-making power is set out as a **default rule** in, prior to the 2006 Act, **Table A** Articles and henceforth in the **Model Articles** for public and private companies.

The fact that it is left to the articles to determine the distribution of decision-making power between the board and the shareholder body tells us that in UK company law the originating power of the company is located in the shareholder body acting in general meeting. The articles are default terms that can *only* be altered by the shareholder body by special resolution,[4] which means that any powers given to the board by the articles are powers that could be retained by the shareholder body. If no powers are granted to the board through the articles, the board would be powerless and the company could

---

[2] Including the schedules to the Act.   [3] Section 154 CA 2006.   [4] Section 21 CA 2006.

only act through the shareholder body. In UK company law it is the shareholder body that empowers the board of directors.

2.1 The default distribution of decision-making power

Table A Articles 70, 71, and 72 provided for a default distribution of power to the directors as follows.

■ Table A Articles of Association

Powers of directors
70. Subject to the provisions of the Act, the memorandum and the articles and to any directions given by special resolution, the business of the company shall be managed by the directors who may exercise all the powers of the company. No alteration of the memorandum or articles and no such direction shall invalidate any prior act of the directors which would have been valid if that alteration had not been made or that direction had not been given. The powers given by this regulation shall not be limited by any special power given to the directors by the articles and a meeting of directors at which a quorum is present may exercise all powers exercisable by the directors.

71. The directors may, by power of attorney or otherwise, appoint any person to be the agent of the company for such purposes and on such conditions as they determine, including authority for the agent to delegate all or any of his powers.

72. The directors may delegate any of their powers to any committee consisting of one or more directors. They may also delegate to any managing director or any director holding any other executive office such of their powers as they consider desirable to be exercised by him. Any such delegation may be made subject to any conditions the directors may impose, and either collaterally with or to the exclusion of their own powers and may be revoked or altered. Subject to any such conditions, the proceedings of a committee with two or more members shall be governed by the articles regulating the proceedings of directors so far as they are capable of applying.

Under the 2006 Act, although there are two sets of Model Articles for public and private companies, the provision dealing with the powers of directors are identical and are set out in articles 3–5 in both sets of Model Articles.

■ Model Articles for Public Companies/Model Article for Private Companies Limited by Shares

Directors' powers and responsibilities

Directors' general authority
3. Subject to the articles, the directors are responsible for the management of the company's business, for which purpose they may exercise all the powers of the company.

Members' reserve power
4(1) The members may, by special resolution, direct the directors to take, or refrain from taking, specified action.
  (2) No such special resolution invalidates anything which the directors have already done.

Directors may delegate
5(1) Subject to the articles, the directors may delegate any of the powers which are conferred on them under the articles—
  (a) to such persons or committee;

(b) by such means (including by power of attorney);

(c) to such an extent;

(d) in relation to such matters or territories; and

(e) on such conditions or subject to such restrictions,

as they think fit.

(2) If the directors so specify, any such delegation may authorise further delegation of the directors' powers by any person to whom they are delegated.

(3) The directors may revoke any delegation in whole or part, or alter its terms.

The provisions set out in Table A and the Model Articles provide for an identical default distribution of power. Article 3 of the Model Articles provides that directors are responsible for the management of the business[5] and that they may exercise *all* the powers of the company. Such authority is made subject to any other provisions of the articles. Article 4 provides the shareholder body with an instruction right; that is, the shareholder body retains the power to tell the board what to do by passing a special resolution. The Model Articles in this respect are clearer than Table A was about the power this gives to shareholders: shareholders may require either positive action by the board or restrain them from taking action. Table A referred only to 'directions given by special resolution', although it is clear that such directions could require either positive action or block a course of action.

As was the case under article 70 of Table A, Article 4 of the Model Articles recognizes that if the directors have already acted then the shareholder resolution does not invalidate the board's action. To the extent that the board has acted itself or through its agents to bind the company then clearly the company is legally bound and a contrary shareholder instruction could not alter the legal effect of that transaction. However, this limitation on the shareholder instruction right goes further than this: it does not affect the validity of anything *the board* has done, regardless of whether this has resulted in the company becoming legally bound or not. To understand this point consider the following, perhaps contrived, example: if the directors have resolved to enter into a contract to sell a significant asset and have authorized the CEO to enter into that contract on the company's behalf then, even if the contract has not been signed and the company at the time the special resolution is passed is not legally bound to sell the asset, the authorized CEO may still go ahead and bind the company without being in breach of the articles until the board withdraws that authorization. This default provision does *not*, therefore, give shareholders a right to overrule positive decisions (to do something) made by the board, only to tell them what to do going forward, to the extent that is possible in accordance with the company's binding obligations. This would include instructing the board to reconvene and to withdraw an authorization to enter into a contract, which the board could be expected to do quickly following the instruction. Another example would be instructing the board to sell an asset which it has refused to sell.

As Table A applied to all companies inevitably this meant that the default provision may have been more suitable for one type of company. Indeed, the Company Law Review Steering Committee in recommending a different set of articles for public and private companies was concerned that many of Table A's provisions were designed with public companies in mind.[6] In this regard, one might think that an instruction right is more suitable for a private company like Bob's Electronics Ltd where Bob has retired

---

[5] See Chapter 7 on the board being responsible for the management rather than managing the company.

[6] Company Law Review Final Report, paras 4.13–4.16. See also *Developing the Framework*, paras 7.70–7.85.

but is very capable of making informed decisions and using these rights effectively. In a listed company one would have thought that the shareholders would rarely have the capacity and information to engage in operational decisions or, for the reasons considered in Chapter 5, the incentive to use this instruction right at all. Indeed, anecdotal evidence from practice suggests that in relation to widely-held companies this right is very rarely deployed (for a rare example of its use see the discussion of Vodafone/Efficient Capital Structures in section 2.2). Nevertheless, the legislature has retained this right for both public and private companies in the respective versions of the Model Articles. Furthermore, a shareholder instruction provision is found in many public companies' articles, even where those articles have been carefully adapted to a company's needs. Consider, for example, the *Directors' Powers* provision of Vodafone Plc's articles.

■ Vodafone PLC's Articles of Association[7]

Directors' Powers

107 *The directors' management powers*
107.1 The Company's business will be managed by the directors. They can use all the Company's powers except where the Articles, or the Companies Acts, provide that powers can only be used by the shareholders voting to do so at a General Meeting. The general management powers under this Article are not limited in any way by specific powers given to the directors by other Articles.
107.2 The directors are, however, *subject to*:

* the provisions of the Companies Acts;

* the requirements of these Articles; and

* any other requirements (whether or not consistent with these Articles) which are approved by the shareholders by passing a *special resolution* at a General Meeting.

However, if any change is made to these Articles or if the shareholders approve a requirement relating to something which the directors have already done which was within their powers, this will not invalidate any prior act of the directors which would otherwise have been valid.

One might argue that there are still good reasons for retaining this right for public companies even if currently it is used rarely by the shareholder body. First, its presence as a default rule provides a guideline or a reminder of the ultimate location of power in a UK company, whether public or private. Secondly, the future is unpredictable and we cannot foresee possible situations in which the right may become useful to counteract an unforeseen abuse of board power.

2.2 Exercising instruction rights

As we have seen, the Model Articles and the articles of most UK companies provide instruction rights. However, in order to be able to exercise those rights the shareholders need to meet in a shareholder meeting. As we have seen, public companies are required to hold an annual general meeting (AGM).[8] To facilitate shareholder action—such as the exercise of instruction rights—in relation to public company AGMs,[9] the Act provides that in certain circumstances shareholder's proposed resolutions must be included

---

[7] As of 10 October 2011 (www.vodafone.com/content/dam/vodafone/investors/corporate_governance/ vgplc_articles_2010_agm.pdf ●).
[8] Section 336 CA 2006. Private traded companies must also hold an AGM (section 336(1A) CA 2006).
[9] As we saw in Chapter 3 only public companies are required to call AGMs.

in the AGM agenda and notice of those resolutions must be given by the company to other shareholders.

■ **Section 338 CA 2006**

Public companies: members' power to require circulation of resolutions for AGMs

(1) The members of a public company may require the company to give, to members of the company entitled to receive notice of the next annual general meeting, notice of a resolution which may properly be moved and is intended to be moved at that meeting.

(2) A resolution may properly be moved at an annual general meeting unless—

(a) it would, if passed, be ineffective (whether by reason of inconsistency with any enactment or the company's constitution or otherwise),

(b) it is defamatory of any person, or

(c) it is frivolous or vexatious.

(3) A company is required to give notice of a resolution once it has received requests that it do so from—

(a) members representing at least 5% of the total voting rights of all the members who have a right to vote on the resolution at the annual general meeting to which the requests relate (excluding any voting rights attached to any shares in the company held as treasury shares), or

(b) at least 100 members who have a right to vote on the resolution at the annual general meeting to which the requests relate and hold shares in the company on which there has been paid up an average sum, per member, of at least £100.[10]

However, if shareholders had to wait for the next annual general meeting to exercise the instruction right then the right would, in effect, be unexercisable for most of the year. If, for example, the company had an offer to sell an asset to a third party which the board refused to sell but which the shareholder body thought should be sold, if the annual general meeting is six months away then in all likelihood the buyer will no longer be available by the time the meeting is held. In the interim, the shareholders could ask the board to convene a meeting, but if the board is not required to do so and the shareholders want to take action that the board refuses to take then in all likelihood the board will refuse to call the meeting. The effectiveness of a shareholder instruction right is, therefore, dependent upon the ability of shareholders to require that the board call a general meeting in between annual general meetings. Section 303–305 of the 2006 Act set out the situations in which shareholders can require that a general meeting is held.

■ **Section 303 Members' power to require directors to call general meeting**

(1) The members of a company may require the directors to call a general meeting of the company.

(2) The directors are required to call a general meeting once the company has received requests to do so from—

(a) members representing at least 5% of such of the paid-up capital of the company as carries the right of voting at general meetings of the company (excluding any paid-up capital held as treasury shares); or

---

[10] Section 338A CA 2006 provides a corresponding right for traded companies, which would include a private company where its shares are traded on an EEA regulated market. See further Chapter 3 note 68.

(b) in the case of a company not having a share capital, members who represent at least 5% of the total voting rights of all the members having a right to vote at general meetings...

(4) A request—

(a) must state the general nature of the business to be dealt with at the meeting, and

(b) may include the text of a resolution that may properly be moved and is intended to be moved at the meeting.

(5) A resolution may properly be moved at a meeting unless—

(a) it would, if passed, be ineffective (whether by reason of inconsistency with any enactment or the company's constitution or otherwise),

(b) it is defamatory of any person, or

(c) it is frivolous or vexatious...

■ Section 304 Directors' duty to call meetings required by members

(1) Directors required under section 303 to call a general meeting of the company must call a meeting—

(a) within 21 days from the date on which they become subject to the requirement, and

(b) to be held on a date not more than 28 days after the date of the notice convening the meeting...

■ Section 305 Power of members to call meeting at company's expense

(1) If the directors—

(a) are required under section 303 to call a meeting, and

(b) do not do so in accordance with section 304, the members who requested the meeting, or any of them representing more than one half of the total voting rights of all of them, may themselves call a general meeting.

(2) Where the requests received by the company included the text of a resolution intended to be moved at the meeting, the notice of the meeting must include notice of the resolution...

(6) Any reasonable expenses incurred by the members requesting the meeting by reason of the failure of the directors duly to call a meeting must be reimbursed by the company...

These sections empower shareholders representing 5% of the paid-up share capital of the company to require that the directors call a shareholder meeting at any time. This would include a single shareholder holding 5% of the paid-up shares, but also a group of shareholders who in aggregate hold this percentage of shares. Where, following such a shareholder request, the directors fail to call a meeting, the requisitioning shareholders can call a meeting themselves. The reasonable expenses paid by the shareholders to convene the meeting are borne by the company. This means that if a shareholder or shareholder group wishes to call a meeting they will not be deterred by the costs of holding a meeting. It should be noted that these are mandatory rules that cannot be waived or altered by a company's articles of association. Accordingly, not only do the shareholders in most UK companies have the right to instruct the board to take action; UK company law also ensures that if the shareholders wish to exercise their rights then they can meet in order to do so.

Shareholders, or a shareholder group, who themselves do not have sufficient votes to pass a resolution, must persuade their fellow shareholders to exercise the instruction rights. In a widely-held company, however, most shareholders are unlikely to turn up to the shareholder meeting—whether an AGM or an interim general meeting—to discuss and be persuaded by the active shareholder to take action. Accordingly the active shareholder will be well advised to contact the other shareholders in advance of the meeting to share their thoughts and ask for their support in the vote. Such support, if given, could involve turning up to the meeting to vote in support of the resolution, or, as is more likely, granting the active shareholder a **proxy** to vote the shares on the supporting shareholder's behalf.[11]

In theory the shareholders could contact the members directly themselves. Every company is required to keep a register of members which contains details of the members' names and addresses as well as details of the members' shareholdings.[12] Members are allowed to inspect the register free of charge and, for a fee, to obtain copies of the register.[13] With this information to hand the other shareholders could then be contacted directly by the active shareholder. The Companies Act 2006, however, offers a simpler option in this regard.

■ Section 314 Members' power to require circulation of statements

(1) The members of a company may require the company to circulate, to members of the company entitled to receive notice of a general meeting, a statement of not more than 1,000 words with respect to—

(a) a matter referred to in a proposed resolution to be dealt with at that meeting, or

(b) other business to be dealt with at that meeting.

(2) A company is required to circulate a statement once it has received requests to do so from—

(a) members representing at least 5% of the total voting rights of all the members who have a relevant right to vote (excluding any voting rights attached to any shares in the company held as treasury shares), or

(b) at least 100 members who have a relevant right to vote and hold shares in the company on which there has been paid up an average sum, per member, of at least £100...

Section 314 simplifies the process of shareholder–shareholder communication by providing that the company will circulate communications of up to 1,000 words. Of course, the 1,000-word limitation imposes constraints on the effectiveness of this mechanism. Other shareholders may not be willing to support shareholder action on the basis of a very brief outline of the reasons for action. If more detailed communication is required shareholders will have to do this themselves. However, note that an additional incentive to use the section 314 mechanism is that in relation to business to be conducted at a public company's annual general meeting the costs of circulating the statement are borne by the company. In relation to all other meetings the costs will be borne by the members who require the resolution to be circulated.[14]

In practice the use of this provision is very rare. However, as the following example shows, even in relation to public companies it is sometimes used. In relation to Vodafone Plc's 2007 AGM one of its shareholders—an investment fund called Efficient Capital Structures—relying on sections 338 and 314 CA 2006, placed a resolution

---

[11] Section 324 CA 2006 providing a right to appoint a proxy. See further Chapter 3, p 99 on proxy voting.   [12] Section 113 CA 2006.
[13] Section 116 CA 2006. Non-members are also allowed to inspect on the payment of a fee. The company must either permit inspection or apply for a court order that the inspection request is not for a 'proper purpose' (section 117 CA 2006).   [14] Section 316 Companies Act 2006.

on the agenda to increase shareholder instruction rights by amending the constitution to render them exercisable with only an ordinary resolution rather than a special resolution. Resolutions were also proposed in relation to Vodafone's business and financial strategy. The following letter was distributed to shareholders by the company on Efficient Capital Structures behalf.[15]

■ Message from the Chairman of Efficient Capital Structures [ECS][16]

6th June 2007

Dear Fellow Shareholder,

REQUISITION OF RESOLUTIONS AT THE ANNUAL GENERAL MEETING OF VODAFONE TO REORGANISE THE CAPITAL STRUCTURE, CREATE AND ISSUE TO SHAREHOLDERS SHARES REPRESENTING THE INVESTMENT IN VERIZON WIRELESS AND INTEREST-BEARING BONDS

This letter contains very important information about four resolutions which we, as your fellow shareholders, have required the company to put to you at the Annual General Meeting on 24th July.
  ECS as a shareholder in Vodafone considers that Vodafone shares:

- Have performed poorly over recent years—the share price today is no higher than it was in January 2002 since when the FTSE 100 index has risen by 28%
- Do not reflect the real underlying value the company.

We believe there are two main obstacles to the shares reaching a price that reflects the real value of Vodafone:

1. THE PASSIVE INVESTMENT IN VERIZON WIRELESS—A STRANDED ASSET WITHIN VODAFONE
Vodafone has a valuable 45% investment in Verizon Wireless—a successful fast growing US business. This is a passive investment which we believe brings no commercial benefit to Vodafone. The investment is 'buried' within Vodafone's Emerging Markets division, preventing the market from valuing it directly.
  There are sound commercial reasons why this passive investment should be separated from Vodafone's controlled activities, which use incompatible technologies. [To do this ECS recommended that Verizon be placed in a separate company and new shares in that company be issued to existing shareholders. The shares that would be issued are referred to in this letter as *Tracking Shares*.]
  The resolutions you are voting on permit Vodafone to put in place an efficient structure to maximise the benefit to shareholders from its investment in Verizon Wireless.

2. UNDER-USED BALANCE SHEET
The Company has slow profits growth but, like a utility company, strong and consistent cash flow. Consequently it has the capacity to increase significantly its borrowings which would enable it to issue **bonds**, paying interest at market rates, to shareholders.
  …

THE RESOLUTIONS
A. The first 'Special' Resolution seeks to amend the Company's Articles of Association to enable shareholders to direct management by ordinary resolution.

---

[15] I am grateful to Marc Moore for suggesting that I use this example.
[16] For the full letter see www.ft.com (http://ftalphaville.ft.com/blog/2007/06/07/5042/the-vodafone-letter-to-shareholders/ ☻)

B. The first 'Ordinary' Resolution allows shareholders to vote in favour of receiving Tracking shares or new holding company shares in respect of Vodafone's holding in Verizon Wireless...

C. The second 'Ordinary' Resolution allows shareholders to vote in favour of receiving Vodafone bonds.

D. The second 'Special' Resolution seeks to protect the borrowing capacity of the Company by putting a ceiling on the amount that the company can spend on acquisitions in any one year without seeking shareholder approval.

...

What you should do: Vote to increase shareholder value by voting FOR each of the Special and Ordinary Resolutions

Yours sincerely,
Glenn Cooper
Chairman
Efficient Capital Structures

Questions and discussion

- Efficient Capital Structures received only limited support from Vodafone shareholders and from the financial press for their proposals. The company firmly rejected the proposals. The *Financial Times* noted 'with Vodafone's management already executing what is basically a sound strategy, this latest call looks like little more than a distraction'.[17]

■ **A. Parker, 'Vodafone sees off rebel investor'** *Financial Times* **(24 July 2007)**

A clear majority of Vodafone investors on Tuesday backed management in rejecting a rebel shareholder's call for the mobile phone operator to gear up and spin off its minority stake in Verizon Wireless, the US mobile group.

Based on initial proxy returns—which do not include all votes cast at Vodafone's annual meeting on Tuesday—the activist investor, Efficient Capital Structures, looked as though it had failed to attract the votes or abstentions of investors holding more than 10 per cent of Vodafone's shares.

Earlier, ECS, which is backed by John Mayo, former deputy chief executive of Marconi, claimed it had won the argument in favour of Vodafone changing strategy on its 45 per cent stake in Verizon Wireless.

Glenn Cooper, chairman of ECS, said he expected the investor group to retain its small stake in Vodafone because it believed it would see an increase in value from a new strategy. He claimed Vodafone's efforts to defeat the ECS resolution, during discussions with investors, meant the UK group would have to change its strategy on Verizon Wireless, possibly within a year...[18]

- If you were a passive **retail investor** who received such a letter would you be willing to question the board's strategy and vote in favour of a change on the basis of a one-page letter? In response, you might decide to acquire additional information to make your mind up. Whilst some of this information may be difficult for an average shareholder to acquire and understand the market place does provide shareholders with some relatively cost-free assistance. For example, simply reading the opinion sections of the *Financial Times,* such as LEX or Lombard, may be of assistance in this regard. In addition, there are organizations that provide shareholders with some assistance by providing a

---

[17] Vodafone Rebels, LEX, *Financial Times* (8 June 2007).
[18] As of writing (12 October 2011) the strategy remains in place.

recommendation themselves. These include, for example, Pirc[19] and ISS (Institutional Shareholder Services). But if you were this retail investor with a—from your personal perspective—substantial stake in the company, even with this extra information to hand, would you be willing to join hands with Efficient Capital Structures?

- Fund managers acting on behalf of institutional investors are likely to have a much better understanding of the company that is the subject of a shareholder instruction resolution than a retail investor would have. Furthermore, fund managers may have access to other industry and firm expertise within the fund management company to assist them in making a decision. They would also be in a position to call up and speak to both the active investor, as well as the subject company's senior management, in order to obtain a thorough understand of the proposal and its merits. The rejection of the Efficient Capital Structures proposal by Vodafone's institutional investor base may, therefore, be subject to several differing interpretations. The first is that the fund managers studied the proposal, became informed about the proposal, and decided the proposal was weak; had it been a better proposal they may well have supported it. The second interpretation is that although fund managers have the capacity to make an informed decision, in fact because of the time and remuneration constraints of being a fund manager (discussed in Chapter 5) they are no more likely to make an active informed decision than is a retail investor. The default position of an inactive and uninformed investor will be to support management. The third interpretation is that although the fund managers are informed and sophisticated they would very rarely attempt to second-guess management, because making such decisions is, in most fund managers' view, what managers have been employed to do. According to this interpretation, even if fund managers are informed and the case for supporting the resolution appears to be very strong such fund managers would not support it as their strong default position is that, on balance, management is more likely to be right.

- If the majority of the shareholder body is highly unlikely to support a shareholder instruction resolution whether for reasons of rational apathy or deference to the board, what is the point of making this right available? Is there a case to be made that this instruction right may be abused by small shareholders, resulting in managers spending their time on dealing with these shareholders and not focusing on doing what they were employed to do, namely running the business?

- In what ways, if at all, does this example make you question some of the arguments made about the rational apathy of shareholders in large public companies?

2.3 The enforcement of the distribution of power

As we have seen, in UK company law corporate power is originally located with the shareholder body. The shareholder body delegates power to the board and by altering the articles of association the shareholders may alter that initial distribution. Intuitively, one might think that, as the shareholders are the ultimate holders of power in the company, a majority of the shareholders should be able to tell the board what to do regardless of what is set forth in the articles. This *inaccurate* intuition has led to several cases involving attempts by shareholders to circumvent the original distribution of power to the board as set out in what is today Articles 3 and 4 of the Model Articles of Association. The outcome of these cases clarifies that although the shareholder body may be the original source of power, the articles of association provide for an enforceable contractual distribution of power. The courts have enforced this contractual distribution of power, making it clear that if the distribution of power is to be altered then it can only be altered in accordance with the rules providing for the amendment of the articles.

---

[19] For the Pirc recommendation on Efficient Capital Structures proposal see 'Pirc Call to Vodafone Investors' P. Stafford, *Financial Times* (12 July 2007) recommending rejection of ECS proposals, although recommending abstention on the tracking stock.

■ *Automatic Self-Cleansing Filter Syndicate Company, Limited v Cuninghame* [1906] 2 Ch 34 (Court of Appeal)

The headnote to the case sets forth the facts as follows]: A company had power under its memorandum of association to sell its [business] to another company…By its articles of association the general management and control of the company were vested in the directors, subject to such regulations as might from time to time be made by extraordinary resolution, and, in particular, the directors were empowered to sell or otherwise deal with any property of the company on such terms as they might think fit. At a general meeting of the company a resolution was passed by a simple majority of the shareholders for the sale of the company's assets on certain terms to a new company formed for the purpose of acquiring them, and directing the directors to carry the sale into effect. The directors, being of the opinion that a sale on those terms was not for the benefit of the company, declined to carry the sale into effect.

The articles of the company provided for the distribution of decision making authority as follows:

> 'The management of the business and the control of the company shall be vested in the directors, who, in addition to the powers and authorities by these presents expressly conferred upon them, may exercise all such powers and do all such acts and things as may be exercised or done by the company, and are not hereby or by statute expressly directed or required to be exercised or done by the company in general meeting; but subject nevertheless to the provisions of the statutes and of these presents, and to such regulations, not being inconsistent with these presents, as may from time to time be made by extraordinary resolution, but no regulation shall invalidate any prior act of the directors which would have been valid if such regulation had not been made.'

Note that this distribution of power does not contain a right of instruction by extraordinary resolution (i.e. 75% of the vote at a shareholder meeting) rather it provides for articles (alternatively referred to as 'regulations') to be altered by what we would call today a special resolution. Powers have been delegated to the board subject to no instruction right and the question the court is called upon to answer is whether a majority of the shareholders, as the ultimate power holders in the company, have an implied reservation of authority such that they can instruct the directors by simple majority to sell the business.

> #### Cozens-Hardy LJ
>
> It is somewhat remarkable that in the year 1906 this interesting and important question of company law should for the first time arise for decision, and it is perhaps necessary to go back to the root principle which governs these cases under the Companies Act 1862. It has been decided that the articles of association are a contract between the members of the company inter se…We must therefore consider what is the relevant contract which these shareholders have entered into, and that contract, of course, is to be found in the memorandum and articles…It seems to me that the shareholders have by their express contract mutually stipulated that their common affairs should be managed by certain directors to be appointed by the shareholders in the manner described by other articles, such directors being liable to be removed only by special resolution.[20] If you once get a stipulation of that kind in a contract made between the parties, what right is there to interfere with the contract, apart, of course, from any misconduct on the part of the directors? There is no such misconduct in the present case. Is there any analogy which supports the case of the plaintiffs? I think not. It seems to me the analogy is all the other way. Take the case of an ordinary partnership. If in an ordinary partnership there is a stipulation in the partnership deed that the partnership business shall be managed by one of the partners, it would be plain that in the absence of misconduct,

---

[20] As we shall see in section III of this chapter, UK company law now contains a mandatory rule providing for removal of directors by ordinary resolution (section 168 CA 2006).

> or in the absence of circumstances involving the total dissolution of the partnership, the majority of the partners would have no right to apply to the Court to restrain him or to interfere with the management of the partnership business. I would refer to what is said in *Lindley on Partnership*, 7th ed: 'Where, however, the partner complained of has by agreement been constituted the active managing partner, the Court will not interfere with him unless a strong case be made out against him'; that is to say, unless there is some case of fraud or misconduct to justify the interference of the Court. Nor is this doctrine limited to a case of co-partners. It is not a peculiar incident of co-partnership: it applies equally to cases of co-ownership…You are dealing here, as in the case of a partnership, with parties having individual rights as to which there are mutual stipulations for their common benefit, and when you once get that, it seems to me that there is no ground for saying that the mere majority can put an end to the express stipulations contained in the bargain which they have made. Still less can that be so when you find in the contract itself provisions which shew an intention that the powers conferred upon the directors can only be varied by extraordinary resolution, that is to say, by a three-fourths majority at one meeting…I cannot see anything in principle to justify the contention that the directors are bound to comply with the votes or the resolutions of a simple majority at an ordinary meeting of the shareholders.

The Court of Appeal focuses upon the contractual distribution of power as set forth in the constitutional documents. Cozens-Hardy LJ refers to the 'express contract' and the shareholders' 'mutual stipulations'. The Court sees its role here as enforcing the terms of the agreement.

A degree of confusion in this area of the law stems from the use of the word 'regulation' in the provision of the articles distributing power to the directors. In *Automatic Self-Cleansing* (and in the pre-1985 Companies Acts' Table A Articles) the 'directors' powers' article provided for an exception from the delegation of management powers to the board for 'such *regulations*, not being inconsistent with these presents, as may from time to time be made by extraordinary resolution'. In *Automatic* the court operates under the implicit assumption that the word 'regulations' means 'articles' and that, accordingly, no instruction right has been reserved for the shareholder body. In other cases, however, litigants have argued that the word 'regulation' means 'resolution' rather than 'article' so that this article contains an instruction right by extraordinary resolution.

In *Quin & Axtens Limited v Salmon*[21] the company in question had articles very similar to those set out in *Automatic Self-Cleansing* whereby the business of the company was to be managed by the directors, who were empowered to exercise all the powers of the company 'subject to such regulations (being not inconsistent with the provisions of the articles) as may be prescribed by the company in general meeting'. The articles of the company also contained a provision that any board resolution to acquire or let property would require the approval of Director A and Director B in order to be effective. The board, however, passed a resolution relating to the acquisition and lease of premises without the approval of Director B and the shareholders subsequently passed an ordinary resolution to the same effect. On an action brought by the shareholder-director B, Lord Loreburn, the Lord Chancellor held as follows:

> The only question of substance to my mind is the third contention of [shareholder's counsel], when he said that the word 'regulations' as employed in article [distributing power to the board of directors] includes at all events, if it is not equivalent to, directions whether general or particular as to the transaction of the business of the company. Now it may be a question for argument, but for my own part I should require a great deal of argument to satisfy me that the word 'regulations' in this article does not mean the same thing as articles, having regard to the language of the first of these articles of association. But, whether that be so or not, it seems to me that the regulations or resolutions which have been passed are of themselves inconsistent with the provisions of these articles, and therefore this appeal fails.

---

[21] [1909] AC 442.

Lord Loreburn was unimpressed by, although does not unequivocally reject, the argument that shareholders reserved an instruction right through the articles because 'regulation' means 'shareholder resolution'. In any event, he considers such a resolution to be inconsistent with the articles which gave Directors A and B a veto right over acquisitions and lettings of property. The House of Lords enforces the contractual distribution of power between the board and the shareholder body. Indirectly, the House of Lords also enforces the distribution of power between the shareholder body. In close companies it is common practice for veto powers to be granted to every shareholder by requiring approval of all shareholders to undertake certain actions, such as the purchase of real property. It is also common practice where the shareholders and directors are the same individuals to use the board as the body where the veto is exercised. Had the House of Lords allowed the shareholders to overrule this distribution of power giving Director B a veto, it would have allowed the majority of shareholders to change the terms of the original distribution of power between the board and the shareholders, and also indirectly between the shareholders themselves, without complying with the mechanism to effect such a change, namely by changing the articles by special resolution.

In *John Shaw v Shaw & Shaw*[22] the Court of Appeal considered the enforceability of an instruction by the shareholders passed by ordinary resolution in general meeting for the directors to discontinue litigation the board had commenced against some of its own directors. The company had articles very similar to those set out in *Quin & Axtens* with a proviso relating to 'regulations' made by the shareholders in a general meeting. Greer LJ held that:

> I think the judge was also right in refusing to give effect to the resolution of the meeting of the shareholders requiring the chairman to instruct the company's solicitors not to proceed further with the action. A company is an entity distinct alike from its shareholders and its directors. Some of its powers may, according to its articles, be exercised by directors, certain other powers may be reserved for the shareholders in general meeting. If powers of management are vested in the directors, they and they alone can exercise these powers. The only way in which the general body of the shareholders can control the exercise of the powers vested by the articles in the directors is by altering their articles, or, if opportunity arises under the articles, by refusing to re-elect the directors of whose actions they disapprove. They cannot themselves usurp the powers which by the articles are vested in the directors any more than the directors can usurp the powers vested by the articles in the general body of shareholders.

Whilst Greer LJ does not explicitly address the meaning of the word 'regulation', his judgment is consistent with the word being understood in terms of 'article' rather than shareholder resolution. That is, this distribution of power gave authority to the board to manage the business of the company subject only to a change in the articles.[23] Again the Court enforces the distribution of power 'vested in the directors' through the articles.[24]

In summary, therefore, we see from this analysis of these cases that the courts treat the distribution of power as a matter of contract, which the courts will enforce. Furthermore, in relation to the default term provided by the pre-1985 Table A articles, whilst the courts always recognized that shareholders by amending the articles of association *could* reserve management powers to themselves, under the actual articles

---

[22] [1935] 2 KB 113.

[23] In Slesser LJ's judgment in this case he provides explicitly that 'Lord Loreburn's dictum in *Quin & Axtens case* is correct that the words "regulations" and "articles" in the articles in that case, which were substantially similar to the present article 95, mean the same thing'.

[24] For a more recent case dealing with company litigation and the shareholder meeting see *Breckland Group Holdings v London and Suffolk Properties* [1989] BCLC 100 where in relation to an article very similar to the one in *John Shaw v Shaw & Shaw*, Harman J held that the article 'confides the management of the business to the directors and in such a case it is not for the general meeting to interfere'.

addressed in these cases there was no instruction power whether by special or ordinary resolution. Accordingly, the introduction in the Table A articles issued pursuant to the Companies Act 1985 of a default instruction right exercisable by special resolution represented a change in the default rule that shifted the default balance of power toward the shareholder body.

3 Shareholder veto and approval rights

In the assignment at the beginning of this section II you considered the types of decision rights that the shareholder in our case study might wish to retain in the form of an exclusive power to exercise a decision or a veto or approval right in relation to a board decision. We asked what criteria one could use to identify decision rights that might be appropriately reserved to the shareholder body. With your list of types of shareholder decision rights to hand, let us now analyse shareholder veto or approval rights in greater depth and consider in what areas UK company law reserves such rights to shareholders.

■ R. Kraakman et al, *The Anatomy of Corporate Law: A Comparative and Functional Approach* (OUP, 2004)

Corporate law seldom limits board discretion *unless* corporate actions share at least one (and usually three) of the following characteristics: (1) they are large relative to the value of the company; (2) they require broad gauge,[25] investment like judgements that shareholders are arguably equipped to make; and (3) they create a possible conflict of interest for directors even if this conflict does not rise to the level of a self-dealing transaction. We begin by exploring why these features might bear on whether it is useful to cabin the board's discretion

Consider first the size of corporate action. At first glance it is not obvious why size should matter to board discretion. One might suppose that if the board's expertise is critical in ordinary business decisions, it is even more so for decisions that involve very large stakes for the company. The response to this point, however, is that the relative size of the corporate action also increases the value of any legal intervention that increases the quality of the company's decision making. To take the classic example, given that shareholders meetings to authorise corporate transactions are costly, they are more likely to be efficient (if they are efficient at all) for large transactions than for small ones.

After size, the second characteristic that is often associated with 'significant' corporate actions is a decision requiring broad, *investment-like* judgement rather than narrow or firm specific expertise. The logic is straightforward. Legal constraints are unlikely to improve on board (and top management) decision making about matters requiring deep expert knowledge, such as the merits of a particular investment opportunity. However, legal checks on board discretion might well make sense when the board proposes an investment-like action to sell or merge the company—or to buy another large company for that matter.

Finally, the third characteristic of corporate actions that is often associated with constraints on board discretion is a risk of self-interested decision making by the board. Low-powered conflicts of interests frequently dog major transactions, even where there is no evidence of self-dealing or a similar high powered conflict on the part of the board. For example, directors and officers who negotiate to sell their companies enter a 'final period' or 'end game', which compromises their incentives to pursue shareholder interest. Either they negotiate their own severance agreement, or they negotiate their new employment contract—with the acquirer rather than their own [company].

[25] 'Broad gauge' here means general investment decisions, not requiring insider knowledge of a business.

Stepping back, then, all corporate actions that are large, investment-like, and potentially self-interested are candidates for shareholder approval or other constraints on unfettered board decision-making. Nevertheless, which corporate actions are 'significant' and how they are regulated varies among jurisdictions.

3.1 Significant transactions: who is best placed to make a decision?

Kraakman et al identify three different characteristics of corporate actions which typically require shareholder approval: the size of the corporate action; where the decision involves an investment type decision; and where the decision involves conflicts of interests. Is it clear, however, from their analysis why size of the corporate action should justify shareholder involvement? The cost of the shareholder meeting as compared to the value of the corporate action proposed to be taken is raised as one justification, although it appears to be an ancillary one: 'at least shareholder involvement is not significantly costly as compared to the value of the action'. Perhaps we might feel that shareholder involvement in large-scale decisions is intuitively appropriate: the bigger the decision the more important it is for shareholders (the 'owners' of the company) to have a say. If, taking the case study as an example, the CEO of Bob's Electronics PLC wishes to sell the company's build-to-order laptop business to another company and this part of the business accounts for 75% of the company's revenues, then shouldn't the 'owners' of the company have a say before the board agrees to this?

Responding to this one might say that the key concern is not about the size of the corporate action itself, but whether the size of the corporate action affects the capability of the potential decision-makers (the board and/or the shareholder body) to make a decision. As you have seen already, and will be repeated in several other parts of this book, the determination of who is the better decision-maker depends on:

- the capability and knowledge of the decision-maker;
- the decision-maker's incentives to pay attention to the decision at hand; and
- her incentives to make a decision that is in the best interests of the company, which for the time being, we shall assume is in the interests of shareholder value.

In this regard consider the following observations:

- Do shareholders have incentives to pay attention? Whether the company is a close company with only a few shareholders or a widely-held company with many shareholders, all shareholders' incentives to pay attention will increase if the transaction value is a considerable proportion of company value. In the example just given, by selling the laptop business Bob's Electronics Plc is selling 75% of its value. The incentive to pay attention, therefore, even for small percentage shareholders, is a strong one.

- Who is more capable of making a decision? Who is better informed about the market place; whether this sale price is a good price; how the sale affects the company's long-term strategy? Logically one would think that this would be the management and the board: those individuals who have an intimate knowledge of the business and its potential. If Bob's Electronics Plc had one shareholder, Bob, who previously ran the company, Bob would be just as capable of making a decision as Markus the CEO. If Bob's Electronics Plc is widely-held then we might consider Markus the CEO to have a clear capability advantage over shareholders. One should not, however, underestimate the sophistication and talent of shareholders in widely-held companies *once those shareholders have a good incentive to pay attention*. As we have seen, many of these shareholders are institutional investors, such as pension funds or large insurance companies, who employ highly trained and highly paid fund managers to manage their investment. These individuals may well have an in-depth knowledge of the business and the industry and, if they do not, will have ready access to other individuals with such company and industry knowledge. Nevertheless, this sophistication and understanding is unlikely to match the capability of management who have the advantage of working full-time in the company and the industry.

- Thus far in our analysis, the arguments for giving shareholders decision rights in relation to significant transactions, such as the sale of substantial parts of the business, seem weak unless you think that shareholders are on average as capable of making these decisions as managers. However, an additional important consideration in determining whether we think that managers are better decision-makers is our assessment of the likelihood that managers would act in their own interests rather than the shareholders' interests. Kraakman et al, in the extract set out previously, note that conflicts of interests of themselves may be a ground to give the shareholders a veto or approval right. However, do large transactions *just because they are large*, raise conflict issues? If the transaction involves the purchase of an asset, then shareholders may be legitimately concerned that the motivating factor for the decision to buy the asset is not maximizing shareholder value but rather hubris: the desire to run a bigger company to obtain direct psychic[26] and, indirectly financial benefits.[27] The regulatory question here is whether this type of agency cost problem is one that is so serious (and cannot be controlled by the other mechanisms we look at in this Part II of the book) that we need to involve arguably less capable decision-makers (shareholders) in the decision-making process. If, on the other hand, the transaction involves a sale of the assets then there is no apparent conflict. There is no concern about hubris and no reason why a manager would not be incentivized to obtain the best price.[28]

3.2 UK significant transaction regulation

In the absence of any direct conflict of interest for directors in relation to the transaction in question—such as where they are also the buyer or the seller, or have direct or indirect connections with the buyer or the seller (see further Chapter 13)—the Companies Act 2006 provides no specific reservation of power for shareholders in relation to significant transactions. As we have seen, under the Model Articles the shareholders, by special resolution could tell the board to sell or not to sell the asset. In many private companies, however, the articles will be amended to provide for shareholder approval where transactions exceed a specified value threshold.

In relation to listed public companies there is an additional layer of regulation that does provide for approval/veto rights in relation to significant transactions. In order to list shares on the Main Market[29] of the London Stock Exchange a company must comply with the Listing Rules issued by the **United Kingdom Listing Authority**.[30] The

---

[26] One might feel like a more important person if one manages a bigger company.

[27] Managers of bigger companies may have a case to get paid more because they are responsible for the management of more assets.

[28] This would not hold if the manager was interested in being employed by the buyer to manage the assets. In such a situation the manager may trade off asset value for personal benefits from his new employer.

[29] The Main Market is the UK's primary 'regulated market'. On 'regulated markets' see further Web Chapter B.

[30] At the time of writing the UKLA is part of the Financial Services Authority. The Conservative–Liberal Coalition Government has announced that the FSA will be disbanded and its functions transferred to existing and newly formed regulatory bodies. The UKLA will be transferred to the Consumer Protection and Markets Authority. These changes will not be effected until the end of 2012.

Listing Rules make a distinction between a 'standard listing' and a 'premium listing'.[31] Shares that are listed with a standard listing must comply with the minimum standards set forth in the EU Prospectus Directive,[32] The Transparency Directive,[33] and the Market Abuse Directive.[34] Shares that are listed with a premium listing are subject to more onerous rules. Certain of these rules, which we consider here and in other chapters of the book,[35] provide important investor protections and accordingly are viewed favourably by investors. It is expected that the vast majority of UK companies listed on the Main Market of the London Stock Exchange will retain a premium listing.[36] Listing Rule 10 addresses 'Significant Transactions' and applies to premium listings.[37] It divides business transactions into three categories: Class 1, Class 2, and Class 3. Class 1 transactions are transactions that, according to the application of several tests,[38] amount to 25% of the value of the company; Class 2 transactions are transactions that amount to between 5% and 25% of the value of the company; and Class 3 transactions are transactions that are worth less than 5% of the company and where the company issues securities.[39] For our purposes, Class 1 transactions are particularly noteworthy, because if the threshold is crossed the Listing Rules require that shareholder approval (ordinary resolution) is obtained prior to completing the transaction. In relation to a Class 1 transaction the Listing Rules also require the provision of detailed information to shareholders regarding the transaction.[40] The requirement for the company to proactively provide shareholders with information lowers the costs for shareholders of acting and making an informed decision.[41] Class 2 and 3 transactions do not require shareholder approval; rather they only require that information about the transaction is disclosed to the shareholders.

Questions

1. Who do you think is better placed to make a business decision: the board or the shareholders?

2. Why, if at all, does your answer vary depending on the make up of the shareholder body?

3. Does your answer to question 1 vary depending on the nature of the transaction in question?

4. Does the size of the transaction make any difference to your analysis of questions 1 and 2?

[31] UKLA Listing Rule (LR) 1.5. Note that the distinction between a standard listing and a premium listing was introduced in April 2010. Prior to this date all UK companies with shares listed on the Main Market had to comply with all the Listing Rules. Non-UK companies could make what was known as a secondary listing which subjected the company only to the EU minimum standards. The primary objective of this change was to attract UK companies to the Main Market who do not wish to be subject to more onerous rules than the minimum rules set forth in the EU Directives. See further: *A Review of the Structure of the Listing Regime* (FSA, 2008) *Listing Regime Review 10/2* (FSA, 2010).

[32] Directive 2003/71/EC.　　　[33] Directive 2004/109/EC.　　　[34] Directive 2003/6/EC.

[35] See Chapters 13 and 16 considering LR 11 *Related Party Transactions*.

[36] Note only premium listed companies are eligible for the FTSE index series including the FTSE 100 (www.londonstockexchange.com/companies-and-advisors/main-market/companies/primary-and-secondary-listing/listing-categories.htm). UK Companies can convert to a standard listing by following the procedure set forth in LR 5.4A which requires, among others, a resolution of the shareholders in general meeting passed by 75% of the holders of the shares (LR 5.4A.4). Given the typical shareholder turnout at general meetings of UK companies (see Chapter 5) it would be difficult for a UK company to effect such a conversion 👃.

[37] LR 10.1.1.

[38] There are four such tests: the gross assets test; the profits test; the consideration test; and the gross capital test. See Listing Rule 10 Annex 1.

[39] LR 10.2.2.

[40] For the information that must be contained in a *Class 1 Circular* sent to shareholders see Listing Rule 13.4.

[41] Note that the FSA has the power to waive the Class 1 approval requirements for a company in severe financial difficulty (see LR 10.8.1).

5. If size of transaction matters, how big should the transaction be to warrant a shareholder approval/veto requirement?

6. Is the Class 1 threshold of 25% too low or too high?

3.3 Other shareholder approval rights in UK company law

In both the introductory analysis for this chapter and in the extract from Kraakman et al it is suggested that concerns about managerial conflicts of interests and agency costs are central considerations in deciding whether shareholders ought to retain decision-making authority. The regulatory logic here is clear. If one cannot trust management to make a decision that is in the company's interests, and if the decision in question that is made in the interests of management could result in significant detriment to the company, then an alternative, less conflicted, decision-maker is required. Although the shareholders may be comparatively weaker in terms of their capability for making a decision as well as their incentives to make an informed decision, in some instances a weak and uninformed decision-maker may be better than a conflicted one.

In UK company law we see shareholders retaining decision-making authority through statute, case law and the UKLA's listing rules in decision areas that appear to raise acute agency problems arising from a direct conflict of interests (**direct agency costs**). Most importantly this would include:

- the common law position on authorizing the taking of corporate opportunities (see Chapter 14);

- authorizing the taking of corporate opportunities in public companies under the Companies Act 2006 (default rule) (see Chapter 14);

- self-dealing transactions between the director and the company where the value of the transaction exceeds £100,000 or 10% of the value of the shares (see Chapter 13);

- self-dealing transactions in listed companies in all but *de minimis* transactions (see Chapter 13);

- granting loans to directors (see Chapter 13);

- granting of certain types of remuneration and service contracts that exceed two years (see Chapter 8).

We also see shareholder decision-rights being deployed to regulate the agency problem that arises from a dominant shareholder abusing his power to the detriment of the minority shareholders. This would include, for example:

- ratification of breach of duty excluding the votes of any shareholders that are connected to the wrongdoing director (see Chapters 15 and 16);

- disinterested shareholder approval in relation to related-party transactions between the company and a substantial shareholder (see Chapter 16).

We also see shareholders retaining veto rights in relation to decisions that have the ability to change the shareholder's relationship with the company. Some of these decision-types could also be explained through the agency cost lens. However, it is submitted that an alternative lens has greater explanatory power for explaining why shareholder approval rights are deployed, namely that these decisions affect the shareholders as shareholders. Such approval rights include:

- end game decisions such as the decision to approve a merger (which is effected in the UK through what is known as a scheme of arrangement);[42]

---

[42] See sections 895–899 CA 2006.

- the decision to end the life of the company by winding up the company;
- fundamental company decisions such as changing the company's constitutional documents (see Chapter 3 and section II.4 of this chapter);
- agreeing to issue shares; and share buy-backs, whether a general buy-back or selective buy-backs from specific shareholders (see Chapter 17).

Here is not the place to deal with these areas of law which, as previously indicated, will be subject to detailed analysis in the chapters that follow. It is worth noting, however, that UK company law makes significant use of shareholder approval rights—much greater use than other jurisdictions such as Germany and the leading US corporate law state of Delaware, which are considered in outline in sections 6 and 7 of part II of this chapter.

4 Changing the distribution of power

The articles of association provide for the distribution of power to the board by the shareholder body. The Model Articles provide for the default distribution of power in the UK. Shareholders unhappy with the way in which management is behaving may wish to change this balance of power to reserve powers for themselves in addition to existing mandatory veto rights provided by company law. An important part of the understanding of the balance of power between the board and the shareholder body is, therefore, the ease with which shareholders can, in theory and in practice, alter the articles of association and, therefore, the balance of power in their favour. In this regard, three factors are relevant to determine how easy it is to change the articles of association.

- First, can shareholders acting alone, that is without a supporting board resolution change the articles of association? If board approval was also required to change the distribution of power this would give the board a veto over any changes to the original distribution of power.
- Second, can the shareholders, acting alone, call a shareholder meeting to pass a resolution changing the articles of association? In order to exercise their rights shareholders have to convene a general meeting. *If* shareholders were required to wait for an AGM[43] in order to act this would substantially compromise their power in relation to pressing corporate actions and business decisions.
- Third, what is the threshold vote required to change the articles of association: an ordinary resolution or a special resolution? The higher the threshold the more difficult it is to change the articles.

We have seen already in our discussion of the corporate constitution that shareholders acting alone have the power to change the articles of association by special resolution.[44] We have seen also that, pursuant to sections 303–305 of the Companies Act 2006, 5% of the shareholder body can require that a shareholder meeting is called. Accordingly, in theory, UK company law provides shareholders with all the legal authority necessary to change the distribution of power by changing the articles. It provides UK shareholders not only with the right to assert their authority but the means by which to do so. As one might expect given our analysis of the rational apathy problem afflicting large UK companies, if one sees shareholders using these rights it is in the context of close companies. It is very rare to see a change in the articles initiated by the shareholders

---

[43] As discussed in Chapter 3, private companies (unless they are 'traded companies') are no longer required to hold annual general meetings. Public companies are required to hold such meetings.
[44] Section 21 CA 2006.

themselves in widely-held companies. Note, however, that in the Efficient Capital Structures/Vodafone example considered previously, Efficient Capital Structures were also proposing a change to the articles.

5 The formal distribution of power between the board and management

Just as the Companies Act 2006 has nothing to say about the powers of the board, it also has nothing to say about the powers to be delegated to the management of the company. The Model Articles of Association also have little to say on this issue. Article 5 of the Model Articles provides the board with a general power to delegate their authority to 'persons' on such terms 'as they think fit'. The board has the power to appoint management and to delegate to managers such powers as they deem appropriate. The Model Articles also empower the board to revoke this delegation which could involve altering the terms of the delegation or, more radically, replacing management. This differs marginally from the Model Articles' predecessor, Table A, which referred in article 72 explicitly to the board's power to delegate powers to a 'managing director' as well as other directors holding executive office. This power of delegation and revocation aside, the Model Articles have nothing more to say about the powers of senior management. Nor, in practice, do companies' articles elaborate on such managerial powers. Consider again Vodafone Plc's articles in this regard:

■ **Vodafone Plc's Articles of Association**[45]

82 Appointing directors to various posts

82.1 The directors can appoint any director as chairman, or a deputy chairman, or to any executive position on which they decide. So far as the Companies Acts allow, they can decide on how long these appointments will be for, and on their terms. *Subject to* the terms of any contract with the Company, they can also vary or end these appointments.

82.2 A director will automatically stop being chairman, deputy chairman, managing director, deputy managing director, joint managing director or assistant managing director if he is no longer a director. Other executive appointments will only stop if the contract or resolution appointing the director to a post says so. If a director's appointment ends because of this Article, this does not prejudice any claim for breach of contract against the Company which may otherwise apply.

82.3 The directors can delegate to a director appointed to an executive post any of the powers which they jointly have as directors. These powers can be delegated on such terms and conditions as decided by the directors either in parallel with, or in place of, the powers of the directors acting as a board. The directors can change the basis on which these powers are given or withdraw them from the executive.

The responsibilities and powers delegated to executive management are, therefore, a matter of board discretion. The extent of the delegation is typically not made public. Nor does the law imply any inherent responsibilities and powers merely by virtue of being appointed to a specific executive office such as managing director or chief executive officer.

---

[45] As of 11 October 2011 (www.vodafone.com/content/dam/vodafone/investors/corporate_governance/vgplc_articles_2010_agm.pdf ☻).

■ *Harold Holdsworth & Co (Wakefield) Ltd v Caddies* [1955] 1 WLR 352

The appellant company (the 'Parent') purchased the whole of the share capital of a textile company. Mr Holdsworth became managing director of the textile company. At a later date he became managing director of the Parent. The agreement appointing him gave the Parent's board discretion to alter his responsibilities. At a later date following a falling out with the board, the board directed him to confine his activities to the subsidiary textile company. Mr Holdsworth sued for breach of contract. On the face of the agreement between the Parent and Mr Holdsworth the board appeared to be empowered to direct the managing director to focus his activities on the textile subsidiary. However, the lower court held that there are inherent responsibilities associated with that position which impose limitations on the extent to which the board can alter those responsibilities.

Earl Jowit

By an agreement between the [Parent] and [Mr Holdsworth] dated April 1, 1949, which was to operate as from October 1, 1948, [Mr Holdsworth] was appointed managing director of the Parent…Clause 1 of that agreement was in the following terms:

'a managing director of the company and as such managing director he shall perform the duties and exercise the powers in relation to the business of the company and the businesses…of its existing subsidiary companies…which may from time to time be assigned to or vested in him by the board of directors of the company.'

…

Differences of opinion arose between Mr Holdsworth and his fellow directors of the [Parent] and culminated in the passing of a resolution by the [Parent's] board in the following terms: 'The board decided that the managing director confine his attentions to British Textile Manufacturing Co. Ld. Only…'

[Mr Holdsworth] regarded this resolution as a repudiation of the agreement and by letter of June 19, 1950, intimated to the [Parent] that as they had so repudiated the agreement he regarded himself as no longer bound to give, and intimated that he would not give, his services to the [Parent].

[Mr Holdsworth] brought his action against the [Parent], as defenders…The first question raised before us was therefore whether in the light of the averments as to surrounding circumstances…the passing of the resolution constituted a breach of the contract…My Lords I am clearly of the opinion that the resolution did not constitute any breach of the agreement. I think that upon the true construction of clause 1 of the agreement of 1949 [Mr Holdsworth] was to perform such duties and exercise such powers in relation to the business of the appellants and to perform such duties and exercise such powers in relation to the business of the textile company and the other subsidiaries as might from time to time be vested in him by the [Parent's] board. In directing [Mr Holdsworth] on May 10, 1950, to confine his attention to the textile company the board of the [Parent] were, in my opinion, merely exercising the right given to them by the agreement.

The Lord President took a different view because he considered that the appointment of managing director was:

'a well recognised title in company administration, carrying responsibilities of a familiar nature and involving sundry obligations and liabilities under the Companies Act. The pursuer was not appointed to perform such duties, if any, as the board might assign to him.'

The Lord President, having formed this view, no doubt considered that the resolution which called upon the respondent to devote his whole time to the affairs of the textile company prevented him from carrying out those responsibilities, obligations and liabilities which on this view he had the right to perform for the [Parent] by virtue of his office as their managing director. My Lords, with the greatest respect for the Lord President, I do not think that [Mr Holdsworth] by the mere fact that he was appointed managing director of the [Parent] had any responsibilities,

> obligations or liabilities which would prevent the [Parent] ordering him to devote his full time to a subsidiary: and I am of the opinion that the [Parent] had by clause 1 of the agreement expressly preserved their right to call upon the [Mr Holdsworth] to devote his time to the affairs of the textile company if they judged this course desirable. I think the action should have been dismissed without proof, and accordingly I would allow the appeal.

More recently in *Mitchell & Hobbs (UK) Ltd v Mill*[46] the High Court revisited the issue of a managing director's powers. In this case a managing director of the company had commenced litigation against the **company secretary** without obtaining board approval to commence the litigation. The court held that the managing director did not have the authority to commence litigation in the absence of a specific delegation of authority by the board to the managing director. In the absence of such a delegation the authority was retained by the board.[47]

> [Counsel for Mr Radford, who was the managing director] submitted that [the managing director's] capacity as managing director imbued him with powers over and above those enjoyed by a non-managing director, notwithstanding that there was no evidence that any powers had been delegated to Mr Radford as managing director. He submitted to me that a managing director, ex virtute officii, had the power to institute proceedings. I do not find that in any way a matter which the articles in Table A provide for. The managing director of a company is not under the articles given any powers over and above other directors in relation to the business of the company. As I say and as [article] 72 makes clear, in a particular case the managing director may have powers over and above those enjoyed by his co-directors *because they may have delegated those powers to him* and, if they have done, so be it. There being in the present case no such delegation, in my view, [article] 72 does not assist the plaintiff company. It is for these reasons that I hold…that these proceedings were instituted without authority.

6 Decision rights in the US

To contextualize the balance of power in UK companies it is helpful to look at how other jurisdictions address the distribution of power between the board, management and the shareholder body. Comparative analysis is an important tool for allowing us to see that the balance of power struck in UK company law between the board and shareholder body is a regulatory choice,[48] which represents a point on the continuum between authority and responsibility. This section takes the United States and Germany as our comparative benchmarks.

6.1 Corporate law in the US

As this is the first juncture at which we will give detailed consideration to corporate law in the United States, a few introductory words are necessary. The US has a system

---

[46] [1996] 2 BCLC 102.

[47] For more recent affirmation of this position see *Smith v Butler* [2011] EWHC 2301 (Ch) *per* Judge Behrens observing that 'the powers of the managing director depend…on the articles'. Affirmed by the Court of Appeal: [2012] All ER (Ch) 136. See also *Fusion Interactive Communications Solutions Ltd v Venture Investment Placement Ltd* [2005] EWHC 736 affirming *Mitchell & Hobbs*.

[48] This is not to suggest that the position adopted by the UK or other jurisdictions represents a conscious decision by regulators or judges about the nature and extent of the trade-off between authority and responsibility. The evolution of corporate law is clearly as much more complex process. See generally, D. Kershaw, 'The Path of Corporate Fiduciary Law' (2012) *New York University Journal of Law and Business* (forthcoming). What is intended here is that as it stands today the balance of power set forth in UK company law represents a regulatory choice.

of federalized government in which many matters are not regulated by the Federal Government but are regulated individually by the 50 US State Governments. Company law in the US (typically referred to as corporate law) is one such area. Although there are several areas of regulation that affect companies that are provided for by Federal legislation,[49] the sphere of company law with which we are concerned in Part II of this book is regulated exclusively by the States.

This means that if, in our case study, Bob had decided to incorporate a company in the US he would have 50 separate jurisdictions to choose from with 50 different regimes of corporate law. Each State is interested in attracting Bob to incorporate in their State as there would be certain taxes payable to them (known as franchise taxes) if he chose to incorporate the business in their State.[50] This means that States are in competition with each other to attract Bob's Electronics and other incorporations. This process is known as charter competition. The legal rules that they offer and corporate services they can provide, for example a skilled corporate judiciary, would be factors in Bob's decision as to where to incorporate.

It is widely accepted that Delaware is the winner in this corporate law competition for incorporations. Over 50% of the biggest US companies are incorporated in Delaware even though the State of Delaware only has a population of 900,000 people in a nation of 300 million. Delaware has the most sophisticated and most developed corporate law in the US.[51] Accordingly, in this book the primary, although not the exclusive, US corporate legal reference point will be Delaware law.

The company law statute in Delaware is entitled the Delaware General Corporation Law. A Delaware company, known as a corporation, has two constitutional documents. The two documents are the certificate of incorporation and the by-laws. The certificate of incorporation contains, amongst others, fundamental company information such as its name, the nature of its business, and the number of shares it can issue.[52] The by-laws typically contain the internal governance machinery such as procedures for holding board and shareholder meetings. The split between these two documents is similar, although not identical, to the split between the memorandum of association and the articles of association in *pre-2006* UK company law. A corporation formed in Delaware will take the suffix Inc (for incorporated) or Corp (for corporation) rather than the UK suffixes of Ltd and Plc.

6.2 The distribution of decision rights in Delaware law

In the UK, the board's authority is distributed to it by the shareholders through the provisions of the articles of association. In the absence of any article distributing power to the board, the board would have no power to do anything. In contrast, in a Delaware corporation the board's authority to manage the corporation is provided by the Delaware General Corporation Law. That is, the authority of the board to exercise the powers of the company is provided by statute. The statute, not the shareholders, empowers the board.[53] The relevant provision is set out in section 141(a).

---

[49] Most importantly, the US Securities Act 1933 and the US Securities Exchange Act 1934.

[50] Companies pay franchise taxes to the state of incorporation, which in Delaware, for example, is calculated according to the number of a company's authorized shares. As of writing the minimum tax payable is $350 and the maximum tax payable is $180,000 (http://corp.delaware.gov/frtax.shtml).

[51] Critics of Delaware corporate law argue that in its desire to attract incorporations its law has a bias in favour of managers. See further, D. Kershaw, 'Lost in Translation: Corporate Opportunities in Comparative Perspective' (2005) 25 *Oxford Journal of Legal Studies* 603 (in support of this position) and D. Kershaw, 'The Path of Corporate Fiduciary Law' (2012) *New York University Journal of Law and Business* (forthcoming) (expressing scepticism about this view).

[52] Section 102(a) Delaware General Corporation Law.

[53] The board's power, accordingly, is said to be 'original and undelegated'.

■ Delaware General Corporation Law

Section 141(a) Board of directors; powers

(a) The business and affairs of every corporation organized under this [Act] shall be managed by or under the direction of a board of directors, except as may be otherwise provided in this chapter or in its certificate of incorporation. If any such provision is made in the certificate of incorporation, the powers and duties conferred or imposed upon the board of directors by this chapter shall be exercised or performed to such extent and by such person or persons as shall be provided in the certificate of incorporation.

One question that arises in relation to this provision is whether or not it is a default provision. That is, the power to manage is given to the board by section 141(a) but can the constitution change this provision and give some of the power back to the shareholders? The provision provides 'except as provided in this [Act] or in its certificate of incorporation' which suggests that the shareholders could retain certain powers by altering the certificate of incorporation. However, some commentators, for example Professor Bebchuk of Harvard Law School, have argued that the subsequent sentence of this section 141(a) suggests that what the certificate of incorporation can provide for is to delegate director-like responsibilities to another person, who we might call a substitute director, and that it does not allow the certificate of incorporation to give shareholders a general instruction right in their role as shareholders.[54] Whether or not this is the correct interpretation of the section, in practice one does not see amendments to this provision.

However, even if, contrary to Professor Bebchuk's opinion, such rights can be reserved through amending the certificate of incorporation, it is important to note that the default position is set in favour of the board: the shareholders would have to take such instruction rights back from the board; rather than, as in the UK, the shareholders having to give up the default instruction right provided by the Model Articles. The balance of power in Delaware tilts clearly towards the board.

6.3 Delaware companies: veto rights in significant value transactions

In contrast to the UK Companies Act 2006, the Delaware General Corporation Law does provide for shareholder approval rights in relation to one type of significant transaction, namely, the sale (not the purchase) of assets which amount to 'all or substantially all'[55] of the assets of the company. The resolution approving the sale must by passed by a majority of the issued voting shares not merely the votes cast at the shareholder meeting. No percentage value threshold is provided; however, the courts have interpreted 'all or substantially all' to involve a sale of assets which is 'quantitatively vital to the operation of the corporation, *and* is out of the ordinary and substantially affects the existence and purpose of the corporation'.[56] Although no percentage threshold has been set by the courts, typically this involves transactions worth in excess of 50% of the value of the company, although shareholder approval has been held to be required in cases where the value was less than 50%.[57]

---

[54] L. Bebchuk, 'The Case for Increasing Shareholder Power' (2005) 118 *Harvard Law Review* 833, 890.

[55] Section 271 Delaware General Corporation Law.

[56] *Gimbel v Signal Cos.*, Del Ch, 316 A 2d 599, 606 (1974).

[57] See *Katz v Bregman*, Del Ch, 431 A 2d 1274 (1981) where approval was held to be required under section 271 DGCL in relation to the sale of a subsidiary that was worth 51% by value of the company and produced 44% of the group's revenues.

However, beyond this provision there is no further shareholder approval right in relation to significant transactions provided by Delaware corporate law. Nor is there any additional shareholder approval requirement such as that found in UKLA's Listing Rule 10 for those companies that are traded on US stock exchanges such as the New York Stock Exchange. Accordingly, for listed companies, UK significant transaction regulation with its 25% value threshold is far more intrusive into board managerial authority than US regulation.

6.4 Delaware companies: other shareholder approval rights

As in the context of UK law, detailed discussion of specific approval rights for shareholders in the areas which raise agency problems arising from direct or indirect conflicts will be deferred to subsequent chapters. It is worth noting here, by way of brief comparison, that the use of shareholder veto rights as a tool to regulate agency problems is less common in the US than in the UK. For example, shareholders do not have rights of approval in relation to share issues, and direct conflicts of interest are typically dealt with through board approval or court review rather than shareholder approval. In relation to changes in the company's constitutional documents shareholder approval rights are provided in relation to changes in the certificate of incorporation (see further section 6.6) but, typically, the board can amend the company's by-laws acting alone.[58] In other areas, for example 'life-changing' corporate decisions such as mergers, as in the UK shareholder approval is required.[59]

6.5 Delaware companies: the distribution of power between the board and management

As in the UK, Delaware General Corporation Law empowers the board to appoint and to delegate powers to executive directors.[60] Beyond this the statute is silent.

6.6 Delaware companies: amending the distribution of power

Assuming that the distribution of power could be altered to provide shareholders in a Delaware corporation with instruction rights, how easy would it be for shareholders to amend the certificate of incorporation to change the balance of power between the board and the shareholder body? Whereas in the UK, as we have seen, it is possible for shareholders to force an interim shareholder meeting to be convened and to alter the articles by special resolution at that meeting, in Delaware there are several obstacles to such a course of action.

In order to change the certificate of incorporation Delaware law requires not only a shareholder vote but also a board resolution proposing the amendment.[61] The shareholder resolution must be passed by a majority of the issued shares. Accordingly, without board support to amend the certificate of incorporation the shareholders cannot

---

[58] While the power to amend the by-laws is originally located with the shareholder body, the certificate can provide that the directors have the power to amend or repeal the by-laws (section 109 Delaware General Corporation Law). It is very common for corporations to provide this power to the board—see *Kurz v Holbrook* 989 A.2d 140 (2010) observing that 'the charters of Delaware corporations routinely grant this authority to the board'; see also D. Ferreira, D. Kershaw, T. Kirchmaier and E. Schuster: 'After The Crisis: Is there a Case Against Shareholder Empowerment?' (on file with the authors, forthcoming 2012).

[59] See Section 251 Delaware General Corporation Law.

[60] Sections 141(2) and 142 Delaware General Corporation Law.

[61] Section 242(b) Delaware General Corporation Law.

amend the certificate. Furthermore, shareholders are only empowered to insist that the board calls an interim shareholder meeting or to call one themselves *if* the constitutional documents (the certificate or the by-laws) allow them to do so.[62] Many companies have no provision in this regard or explicitly exclude such an option in the certificate of incorporation.[63]

7 Decision rights in German corporate law

German corporate law provides, as in the UK, for two types of company: a private limited liability company (GmbH) and a public company (AG). However, in contrast to the UK it provides two different statutes for each of the companies, a Limited Liability Company Act (*GmbH-Gesetz*)[64] and a Stock Corporation Act (*Aktiengesetz*) respectively. For the purposes of this brief comparative excursion we will look only at the public company: the *Aktiengesellschaft* (AG).

The sources of regulation for a German public company are similar in structure to current UK sources with a detailed corporate statute combined with a single constitutional document called a *Satzung*. German public companies take the suffix AG (for *Aktiengesellschaft*).

By way of introduction, in German public companies instead of a single board of directors there are two board tiers: a management board (*Vorstand*) and supervisory board (*Aufsichtsrat*). The management board consists only of senior management including the CEO and other senior officers such as the chief financial officer. The supervisory board consists of non-managerial members including both outside directors who do not work at the firm but also employees and union representatives.

7.1 Management board and supervisory board decision rights

In contrast to UK company law, the powers of the directors of the company are set out in the German Stock Corporation Act. As under Delaware corporate law, it is a statute not the shareholder body which empowers the respective boards.

Importantly and distinctively, the German Stock Corporation Act sets forth separately the powers of executive directors (the management board) and the supervisory directors (the supervisory board). The management board, the members of which are appointed by the supervisory board,[65] may consist of one or more members. Siemens AG, one of the largest German companies, for example, has a management board of 11 members; whereas Aixtron AG, a smaller listed company, has a management board of three members. Whereas UK company law leaves it up to the board, in taking 'responsibility' for the management of the company, to determine the powers of senior management (the executive directors), the German Stock Corporation Act directly empowers senior management *as a group* acting together as a management board.

---

[62] Section 211(d) Delaware General Corporation Law.

[63] See D. Ferreira, D. Kershaw, T. Kirchmaier and E. Schuster: 'After The Crisis: Is there a Case Against Shareholder Empowerment?' (on file with the authors, forthcoming 2012).

[64] Note that Delaware also has a Limited Liability Company statute. However, this provides for a vehicle that is more akin to incorporated partnership than a corporation and is not subject to analysis in this book—see Delaware Limited Liability Company Act. Limited Liability Companies formed under this Act are not the US counterpart to a UK private limited company or a GmbH. The corporation regulated by the Delaware General Corporation Law is the counterpart to both the UK's private and public company and Germany GmbH and AG.

[65] Section 84 German Stock Corporation law.

■ German Stock Corporation Act

> *Section 76*
>
> (1) The management board has sole responsibility for the management of the company.[66]

These powers of the company are not delegated by the shareholders to the management board or by the supervisory board to the management board, they are provided directly to managers by statute. Nor are the rights to manage the company and to exercise corporate powers in this regard shared with the supervisory board. These different boards have different responsibilities and powers that they exclusively exercise.

The supervisory board does not have a general power to interfere in the management of the company. The supervisory board does not have *general powers* of instruction. This contrasts sharply with the board of a UK public company which, although it delegates authority to management, may alter the terms of that delegation at any time and may—in theory although rarely in practice—directly involve itself in operational decisions. Uwe Hueffer, a leading commentator on German corporate law, argues that section 76 is the central provision of the German Stock Corporation Act. For Hueffer, the management board is the decision-making centre of the company.[67]

The Stock Corporation Act provides that the supervisory board's general responsibility is to supervise the managers of the business.[68] In addition, the Act provides that the supervisory board has specific responsibilities and/or decision rights in a specific range of areas including, for example, the power to appoint and to remove management;[69] examination of the annual accounts and the dividend recommendation;[70] and co-decision-making power with management in relation to the terms of a share issue.[71] In addition, the supervisory board can itself by supervisory board action reserve the power to veto certain types of business decision.[72] The *Satzung* (the articles) can also provide for the supervisory board to have approval/veto rights in relation to certain pre-specified business actions.[73] In practice in German public companies the business decision approval rights typically adopted by or given to the supervisory board are limited although they will vary depending on the nature and size of the company. Such rights could include, for example, the sale of real property and the incurrence of bank debt and giving of guarantees.[74]

Thus far the analysis of the distribution of power in a German public company has focused of the *legislative* provision of power to the supervisory and management boards. What of decision rights for shareholders in German companies? It is clear from section 76 of the German Stock Corporation Act already discussed that the management of the company is entrusted to the management board. This delegation of power is not a default delegation that can be changed by the company's constitution in order to *to empower the shareholder body*. Although the constitution can be used to pass decision-making authority to the supervisory board by increasing the decisions that require supervisory board approval, it cannot be used to give shareholders an instruction right similar to

---

[66] Translation from 'Der Vorstand hat unter eigener Verantwortung die Gesellschaft zu leiten'.
[67] U. Hueffer, *Aktiengesetz* (7th edn, 2006) (C.H. Beck), 384–5.
[68] Section 111 German Stock Corporation Act.
[69] Section 84 German Stock Corporation Act.   [70] Section 171 German Stock Corporation Act.
[71] Section 204 German Stock Corporation Act.
[72] Section 111(4) German Stock Corporation Act.
[73] Section 111(4) German Stock Corporation Act.
[74] J. Boehm, *Der Einfluss der Banken auf Grossunternehmen* [*The Influence of Banks on Large Enterprise*] (Steuer-und Wirtschaftsverlag, 1992), 171–2.

that provided to UK shareholders under Model Article 4. Indeed, the German Stock Corporation Act makes this explicitly clear by providing pursuant to section 119(2) of the Act that 'the shareholder body can only make management decisions when asked to do so by the management board', that is, when *management decides* to give the shareholder body decision making authority.

7.2 Significant transaction and other shareholder approval rights in German law

The German Stock Corporation Act does not provide for shareholder approval rights in relation to significant transactions. An interesting and somewhat controversial issue in German corporate law surrounds the issue of whether, although not stated in the Stock Corporation Act, shareholders should have approval rights in relation to very significant transactions. In the famous *Holzmüller* case[75] the highest Federal Court (*Bundesgerichtshof*) held that the transfer of significant company assets to a subsidiary company (amounting to approximately 80% by value of the company) required shareholder approval. The court held that the management board is under a duty to submit a transaction to the shareholders for approval when the transaction would have the effect of interfering 'so substantially with the rights of the members and their financial interests that the board cannot reasonably assume that it may take a decision in its own right and without participation of the general meeting'. The precise parameters of the approval requirement remain unclear and we are not in a position to explore them here.[76] More recent jurisprudence of the German courts has clarified that *Holzmüller*-approval rights are exceptional and should be strictly construed.[77]

With regard to other veto rights, the Stock Corporation Act provides a non-exhaustive list of decision rights for the shareholder body, including: the appointment of auditors; approval of payments to members of the management and supervisory boards; and measures relating to the raising of capital and the issue of shares.[78] This list can be added to by the articles; however, such rights cannot invade the sphere of managerial authority given to the management board by the Act.[79]

Questions

1. What is the source of board authority in UK company law?
2. What is the source of management authority in UK company law?
3. What rights does article 4 of the Model Articles of Association give shareholders?
4. Do you think it makes sense to provide shareholders with instruction rights? For private companies? For public companies?
5. Should such rights if provided by the legislature be default or mandatory rights?
6. From the analysis thus far, do you think that UK company law is shareholder or director friendly? What examples would you cite in support of your argument?
7. What is the source of board authority in Delaware and German corporate law?

---

[75] BGHZ (Federal Court of Justice) 83, 122.

[76] For a further analysis of the *Holzmüller* decision see C. Gerner-Beuerle, D. Kershaw, M. Solinas, 'Is the Board Neutrality Rule Trivial? Amnesia about Corporate Law in European Takeover Regulation' (2011) 22 *European Business Law Review* 559–622;

[77] *Gelatine* BGHZ 159, 30; *Macrotron* BGHZ 153; see further, M. Loebbe, 'Corporate Groups: Competences of the Shareholders' Meeting and Minority Protection—the German Federal Court of Justice's recent *Gelatine* and *Macrotron* Cases Redefine the *Holzmüller* Doctrine' (2004) 5 *German Law Journal* 1057. T. Liebscher, 'Ungeschriebene Hauptversammlungszuständigkeiten im Lichte von Holzmüller, Macrotron und Gelatine' (2005) 34 *Zeitschrift für Unternehmens- und Gesellschaftsrecht (ZGR)* 1, 24.

[78] Section 119 German Stock Corporation Act.   [79] See *Hueffer*, 604–16.

8. What is the source of managerial authority in Delaware and German corporate law?

9. Does it make any difference whether the board is empowered through a company law statute or through the articles of association?

10. Does it make any difference whether management is empowered through a company law statute or through the delegation of authority from the board?

III APPOINTMENT AND REMOVAL

1 Appointment and removal rights in theory

In the first part of our hypothetical case study, Bob had decided to keep his shares in Bob's Electronics Ltd, but to retire from his operational role and to appoint Markus the CEO as sole director and chief executive officer. As we have seen in section II, the board of directors has the power under the Model Articles of Association to appoint and remove management. In his role as director Markus will, therefore, be appointing himself as chief executive officer. What happens if Bob becomes dissatisfied with Markus's performance as chief executive officer. If Bob decides that Markus needs to be replaced as CEO he cannot (as a shareholder in a company with Model Articles) do this directly, as the board appoints and removes management. Bob would clearly, therefore, want the power to remove Markus as a director. Bob could then appoint a new director and that director could remove Markus from his position as CEO. In theory such a removal right could provide for Markus the Director's removal at any time and for any reason or for no reason. In the context of this example, where Bob is the 100% shareholder, such a right would be a very powerful disincentive for Markus to abuse his delegated powers: if he performs badly or behaves opportunistically and gets caught, he will lose his job.

At the same time, however, Bob is aware that he wants to encourage Markus to exercise the authority he has been given to form and implement the company's strategy in order to generate value. In this regard, Bob will be aware that Markus will want a degree of job security. Fear of losing one's job and the benefits the job brings may make the decision-maker too careful about the decisions he makes; too risk averse. Without any sense of job security Markus may avoid the risky decisions because if those good decisions turn out badly he may lose his job. However, Bob may want Markus as manager to take such risks and, had Bob been the manager, he would have taken those risks himself. So assuming Bob can design the removal and appointment rights as he chooses, Bob will need to take into account both Bob's desire to hold Markus accountable for his performance, but also the need to ensure that these rules themselves do not hinder Markus's performance.

Assignment

Take 15 minutes to think about the following questions:

- What should be the term of Markus's appointment as director?

- During his term in office on what basis (grounds), if any, should it be possible to remove Markus from his position as a director?

- Would your answer to these questions vary depending on whether the company is Bob's Electronics Ltd owned only by Bob or Bob's Electronics Plc which is widely-held?

As should now be clear, when thinking about the design of a rule, we need to incorporate the context within which that rule will apply. Most importantly for us we need to consider how a change in the company's ownership arrangements affects the considerations we have just identified in the context of Bob's Electronics Ltd with a single shareholder. If Bob sells his shares to the public, so that Bob's Electronics Plc is a widely-held company, many of the company's shareholders will suffer from significant rational apathy and collective action problems. As we have seen, even if institutional shareholders take significant stakes in the company, thereby reducing the costs of collective action, the fund managers responsible for making the investment decisions typically remain inactive. What are the consequences of this shareholder inactivity for the design of the director's term in office and the director removal and appointment rights?

First, one might question whether such rules are of any consequence at all in the widely-held context. One might argue that if shareholders pay little attention to company activities then in practice shareholders will not exercise any removal rights given to them even if dissatisfied with managerial performance. Nor will they involve themselves in the director appointment process when the term of a director's term in office comes to an end. This means that in practice the board of directors will nominate individuals to replace the retiring directors at the end of their tenure. Shareholders will either not vote or will vote according to the board of directors recommendation by filling out the **proxy form** sent to them by the board of directors in favour of the board's nomination. In practice, therefore, where you have rationally apathetic shareholders, the board appoints itself and shareholders do not make use of their removal rights.

Although there is much to commend this argument we need to be careful not to caricature the extent of shareholder *inactivity* in widely-held UK companies. If board and managerial failure goes too far then apathy and collective action problems may be overcome; fund managers may feel compelled to take an active stance. By giving shareholders in widely-held companies removal rights directors know that at some level of incompetence or self-serving opportunistic behaviour the shareholder removal rights may be exercised. Accordingly, directors of widely-held companies with shareholder removal rights would have less room to incur agency costs than directors of widely-held companies where the shareholders have no removal rights, where, for example, the board formally (and not just in practice) appoint new members to replace retiring directors.[80] It is also worth noting in relation to the design of removal rights that there are arguably positive effects of rational shareholder apathy. The reduced likelihood that shareholders will exercise any rights given to them may allow directors to feel sufficiently secure in their jobs even when shareholders are given strong removal rights.

2 Appointment and removal rights in UK company law

2.1 Appointment

The Companies Act 2006 has little to say about the method of appointing directors. Pursuant to section 160 it requires only that for public companies two or more directors cannot be elected by a single resolution. So if Bob, Alison, and Markus are nominated to the board of directors, the general meeting cannot appoint them by one vote, rather it must do so by a vote on each appointment individually. The reason for this is clear: if a majority of shareholders want to vote for Bob and Alison but not for Markus and if there is only one vote they will be pressurized to vote for all three or nobody will be elected. This rule can be waived but only by a shareholder resolution that is agreed without any votes being cast against the proposal.[81]

---

[80] The Dutch 'structure regime', which has now been abolished used to provide for such a mechanism. In this regard, see Kraakman et al, *The Anatomy of Corporate Law* (1st edn, OUP, 2004), 36.
[81] Section 160(1) CA 2006.

A company's articles of association typically provide for the appointment of directors. Both Model Articles for private[82] and public companies[83] provide that directors may be appointed by a simple majority of the votes cast at the meeting or by a decision of the directors themselves. The Model Articles for Private Companies do not specify a term of office. A person appointed to be a director of a private company with model articles would, therefore, be appointed until he is removed or resigns.[84] The Model Articles for Public Companies adopts the position of its predecessor Table A Articles. For those directors appointed by the shareholder body, article 21 provides for the retirement of a third of the board of directors at each annual general meeting. Effectively, therefore, this provides each director with a three-year term. Such boards are referred to as classified or staggered boards. At the end of this term the director may be reappointed. Until recently most UK companies provided such staggered three-year terms for their directors. However, as a result of recent changes to the UK's Corporate Governance Code (which we consider in depth in Chapter 7) the Code now recommends that listed companies that form part of the FTSE 350 index[85] provide for the retirement and re-election of directors on a yearly basis.[86] Previously, consistent with the Model Articles, the Corporate Governance Code had recommended three-year staggered terms.[87] The stated motivation for this change was to increase the accountability of directors to shareholders by giving shareholders a more regular opportunity to signal disapproval than they have when a board is classified.[88] As we will discuss in depth in Chapter 7, this Corporate Governance Code is a *comply or explain* code, which means that a company may elect to ignore the recommendation and explain to its shareholders why it has done so. Companies will report on this provision for the first time in 2012, at which point we will see whether companies elect to follow this recommendation. Note also that pursuant to the Model Articles any director appointed by the board of directors must retire at the following annual general meeting.[89]

2.2 Removal

Whether or not UK directors of public companies are provided with three-year or one-year terms, their term in office may be brought to an end at any time before the term expires. The shareholders' right to remove the directors is set forth in section 168 of the 2006 Act.

■ Section 168 CA 2006 Resolution to remove director

(1) A company may by ordinary resolution at a meeting remove a director before the expiration of his period of office, notwithstanding anything in any agreement between it and him.

---

[82] Article 17 of the Model Articles for Private Companies Limited by Shares.

[83] Article 20 of the Model Article for Public Companies.

[84] Articles 17 and 18 of the Model Articles for Private Companies Limited by Shares. Providing also that a director will cease to be a director on the occurrence of certain events including personal bankruptcy or mental incapacity. The corresponding provisions in the Model Article for Public Companies on bankruptcy and incapacity are set forth in article 22.

[85] The FTSE 350 Index is an index of the largest 350 companies by market capitalization (the number of shares multiplied by the price of the shares) who have a primary listing on the London Stock Exchange.

[86] Provision B.7.1 UK Corporate Governance Code (FRC, 2010).

[87] Provision A.7.1 Combined Code (FRC, 2008) (prior to the 2010 iteration of the Code the Corporate Governance Code was known as the Combined Code).

[88] *Review of Combined Code: Final Report* (FRC, 2009) Para. 3.24 .

[89] Article 21(2) Model Article for Public Companies.

Section 168 is a very simple provision. It provides that a director may be removed at a shareholder meeting by an ordinary shareholder resolution. At any shareholder meeting called during any point in the director's tenure he can be removed by a simple majority of the votes cast at that meeting. The section does not require that a reason be given to remove the director. This is sometimes referred to as 'without cause' removal, as the shareholders do not have to give any reason or a cause to remove him. A director of a UK company does not, therefore, have any formal security of tenure.

The only protection that the Companies Act 2006 provides a director is to require that if shareholders intend to propose a resolution to remove a director that they give the company (and thereby the director[90]) 28 days notice of the intention to move such a resolution.[91] This is known as special notice.[92] The Act also allows the director to require the company to circulate to the shareholders representations he wishes to make in relation to his proposed removal and to be heard at the meeting where his removal is proposed.[93]

The Model Articles do not provide for the effect on a senior manager's position (such as Markus the CEO in our case study) of being removed from his position as a director. In most instances if an executive director is removed as a director either his employment contract will provide for its termination or his removal from his management role by the board will follow shortly thereafter. Many companies provide in their articles for the immediate termination of certain executive positions if removed as a director. For example, Vodafone Plc's articles provide that a 'director will automatically stop being chairman, deputy chairman, managing director, deputy managing director, joint managing director or assistant managing director if he is no longer a director'.[94] The removal of a director and his contemporaneous or subsequent removal as management employee will not affect any claim the manager has for compensation for breach of his employment contract by the company.[95] If a manager has one year of his contract remaining without any provision for a shorter notice period he will be entitled to one year's salary to compensate him for breach of contract.[96]

As we discussed in relation to altering the balance of power between the board and the shareholder body, the effectiveness of a shareholder right is dependent not only on the provision of that right, it is also dependent upon the ease with which shareholders can exercise such a right. UK company law, as we have seen, provides mandatory rules to enable 5% of the shareholder body to call a meeting.[97] Accordingly, shareholders willing to act can at any time require that a shareholder meeting be held at which a simple majority of the votes cast, in person or by proxy, can remove any or all of the directors.

The question for scholars of UK corporate governance is whether such a removal right for shareholders provides for an optimal balance between managerial accountability and authority. Formally at least UK executive directors have no security of tenure. As employees (managers) they will have a contract of employment with the firm that in most cases will provide for compensation for loss of office. As noted, the 2006 Act makes it clear that their removal from office does not affect their contractual rights to

---

[90] Section 169 CA 2006.   [91] Section 168(2) CA 2006.   [92] Section 312 CA 2006.

[93] Section 169 CA 2006. See *Monnington v Easier* [2006] BCLC on the use of special notice to circumvent shareholders' intentions by the incumbent director's resignation and the appointment by the board of a new director within the 28-day notice period prior to the meeting.

[94] Article 82.2 Vodafone Plc's articles of association (/www.vodafone.com/content/dam/vodafone/investors/corporate_governance/vgplc_articles_2010_agm.pdf 🌐).

[95] Section 168(5) Companies Act 2006. See also *Southern Foundaries v Shirlaw* [1939] 2 All ER 113. If an executive director has no service contract or that contract does not set forth a contract term and a notice period, and the articles of the company provide for the termination of the managerial position on the removal from office, then termination of the management position does not amount to a breach of contract: *Read v Astoria Garage (Streatham) Ltd* [1952] 1 All ER 922.

[96] See Chapter 8 for a more detailed consideration of payments to directors following removal.

[97] Sections 303–305 CA 2006; see pp 195–6.

compensation. However, such compensation may not fully compensate managers for the financial and non-financial benefits of office. The question then is whether the insecurity of tenure created by section 168 is likely to lead to more risk-averse decision-making or, whether in widely-held companies shareholder apathy gives directors sufficient security of tenure because they take comfort from the fact that the removal rights will not readily be exercised. In regard to this balance between authority and responsibility, it is again helpful to see how other jurisdictions approach the removal question. Prior to doing so, however, one final issue regarding section 168 needs to be resolved, namely: is the removal right a mandatory rule or can it be adjusted by a company's constitution?

2.2.1 Is section 168 a mandatory rule?

Section 168's predecessor was section 303 of the Companies Act 1985. The provision provided as follows:

■ Section 303 CA 1985

> A company may by ordinary resolution remove a director before the expiration of his term. A company may by ordinary resolution remove a director before the expiration of his period in office, notwithstanding anything in its articles or in any agreement between it and him.

It is clear from the final sentence of section 303 that it is a mandatory rule. A rule in the articles of association or in an agreement between the director and the company which provides that a director shall serve as long as he wishes to or as long as he lives would be unenforceable, as would any attempt to say that the director can only be removed if he performs poorly or acts in bad faith. Section 168, however, is not quite so clear: it refers only to 'notwithstanding anything in any agreement between it and him'. The absence in section 168 to a reference to 'notwithstanding anything in the articles' creates an interpretative problem. Read alongside section 303 of the 1985 Act, the drafting of section 168 suggests that the removal right no longer explicitly overrides contrary intention in the articles. Such an interpretation, however, is incorrect: the rule remains a mandatory rule that cannot be contracted out of by the articles. The reason for the deletion of reference to the articles was, as stated in the parliamentary record, that the Government felt that it was unnecessary to include these words 'as the articles may not override the requirements set out in the [Act]'.[98] That is, a provision is a mandatory rule unless it *explicitly* gives the company authority to opt out of the rule.

With regard to the mandatory application of section 168, however, consider the House of Lords decision in *Bushell v Faith* which addresses section 168's predecessor provision in the Companies Act 1948.

■ *Bushell v Faith* [1970] AC 1099 (House of Lords)

The facts are stated in Lord Upjohn's judgment.

> **Lord Upjohn (with whom the majority of Law Lords agreed)**
> My Lords, this appeal raises a question of some importance to those concerned with the niceties of company law, and the relevant facts, which are not in dispute, can be very shortly stated. The respondent company Bush Court (Southgate) Ltd (a formal party to the proceedings) was incorporated on 19 September 1960, and at all material times had an issued capital of 300 fully paid-up shares of £1 each held as to 100 shares each by a brother and his two sisters namely the appellant Mrs Bushell, the respondent Mr Faith and their sister Dr Kathleen Bayne.

---

[98] Lord Sainsbury of Turville, Hansard, 9 May 2006.

The respondent was a director but his conduct as such displeased his sisters who requisitioned a general meeting of the company which was held on 22 November 1968, when a resolution was proposed as an ordinary resolution to remove him from his office as director. On a show of hands the resolution was passed, as the sisters voted for the resolution; so the brother demanded a poll and the whole issue is how votes should be counted on the poll having regard to special [article] 9 of the company's articles of association.

The company adopted Table A [articles promulgated under the Companies Act 1948] with variations which are immaterial for present purposes. The relevant articles of Table A are:

'2. Without prejudice to any special rights previously conferred on the holders of any existing shares or class of shares, any share in the company may be issued with such preferred, deferred or other special rights or such restrictions, whether in regard to dividend, voting, return of capital or otherwise as the company may from time to time by ordinary resolution determine.

'62. Subject to any rights or restrictions for the time being attached to any class or classes of shares, on a show of hands every member present in person shall have one vote, and on a poll every member shall have one vote for each share of which he is the holder.'

Special [article] 9 is as follows:

'In the event of a Resolution being proposed at any General Meeting of the Company for the removal from office of any Director, any shares held by that Director shall on a poll in respect of such Resolution carry the right to three votes per share and regulation 62 of [the articles] shall be construed accordingly.'

Article 96 of Table A, which empowers a company to remove a director by ordinary resolution is excluded by the articles of the company so that the appellant relies on the mandatory terms of s 184(1) of the Companies Act 1948,[99] which so far as relevant is in these terms:

'A company may by ordinary resolution remove a director before the expiration of his period of office, notwithstanding anything in its articles or in any agreement between it and him…'

It is not in doubt that the requirements of sub-s (2) have been satisfied. So the whole question is whether special [article] 9 is valid and applicable, in which case the resolution was rejected by 300 votes to 200, or whether that article must be treated as overridden by s 184 and therefore void, in which case the resolution was passed by 200 votes to 100. So to test this matter the appellant began an action for a declaration that the respondent was removed from office as a director by the resolution of 22 November 1968, and moved the court for an interlocutory injunction restraining him from acting as a director. This motion comes by way of appeal before your Lordships.

The appellant argues that special [article] 9 is directed to frustrating the whole object and purpose of s 184 so that it can never operate where there is such a special article and the director in fact becomes irremovable. So she argues that, having regard to the clear words 'notwithstanding anything in its articles' in s 184, special [article] 9 must be rejected and treated as void. The learned judge, Ungoed Thomas J, so held. He said: 'It would make a mockery of the law if the courts were to hold that in such a case a director was to be irremovable', and later he concluded his judgment by saying: 'A resolution under article 9 is therefore not in my view an ordinary resolution within s 184. The [appellant] succeeds in the application.'

The respondent appealed, and the Court of Appeal ([1969] 1 All ER 1002, [1969] 2 WLR 1067) (Harman, Russell and Karminski LJJ) allowed the appeal. Harman LJ ([1969] 1 All ER at 1004, [1969] 2 WLR at 1070) did so on the simple ground that the 1948 Act did not prevent certain shares or classes of shares having special voting rights attached to them and on certain occasions. He could find nothing in the 1948 Act which prohibited the giving of special voting rights to the shares of a director who finds his position attacked…

---

[99] The predecessor section 168 of the Companies Act 2006.

My Lords, when construing an Act of Parliament it is a canon of construction that its provisions must be construed in the light of the mischief which the Act was designed to meet. In this case the mischief was well known; it was a common practice, especially in the case of private companies, to provide in the articles that a director should be irremovable or only removable by an extraordinary resolution; in the former case the articles would have to be altered by special resolution before the director could be removed and of course in either case a three-quarters majority would be required. In many cases this would be impossible, so the Act provided that notwithstanding anything in the articles an ordinary resolution would suffice to remove a director. That was the mischief which the section set out to remedy; to make a director removable by virtue of an ordinary resolution instead of an extraordinary resolution or making it necessary to alter the articles...

An ordinary resolution is in the first place passed by a bare majority on a show of hands by the members entitled to vote who are present personally or by proxy and on such a vote each member has one vote regardless of his shareholding. If a poll is demanded then for an ordinary resolution still only a bare majority of votes is required. But whether a share or class of shares has any vote on the matter and, if so, what is its voting power on the resolution in question depends entirely on the voting rights attached to that share or class of shares by the articles of association.

I venture to think that Ungoed Thomas J overlooked the importance of [article] 2 of Table A which gives to the company a completely unfettered right to attach to any share or class of shares special voting rights on a poll or to restrict those rights as the company may think fit. Thus, it is commonplace that a company may and frequently does preclude preference shareholders from voting unless their dividends are in arrears or their class rights are directly affected. It is equally commonplace that particular shares may be issued with specially loaded voting rights which ensure that in all resolutions put before the shareholders in general meeting the holder of those particular shares can always be sure of carrying the day, aye or no, as the holder pleases.

Counsel for the appellant felt, quite rightly, constrained to admit that if an article provided that the respondent's shares should, on every occasion when a resolution was for consideration by a general meeting of the company, carry three votes such a provision would be valid on all such occasions including any occasion when the general meeting was considering a resolution for his removal under s 184.

My Lords, I cannot see any difference between that case and the present case where special voting rights are conferred only when there is a resolution for the removal of a director under s 184. Each case is an exercise of the unfettered right of the company under [article] 2 whereby '...any share in the company may be issued with such...special rights...in regard to...voting...as the company may from time to time by ordinary resolution determine.'

Parliament has never sought to fetter the right of the company to issue a share with such rights or restrictions as it may think fit. There is no fetter which compels the company to make the voting rights or restrictions of general application and it seems to me clear that such rights or restrictions can be attached to special circumstances and to particular types of resolution. This makes no mockery of s 184; all that Parliament was seeking to do thereby was to make an ordinary resolution sufficient to remove a director. Had Parliament desired to go further and enact that every share entitled to vote should be deprived of its special rights under the articles it should have said so in plain terms by making the vote on a poll one vote one share. Then, what about shares which had no voting rights under the articles? Should not Parliament give them a vote when considering this completely artificial form of ordinary resolution? Suppose there had here been some preference shares in the name of the respondent's wife, which under the articles had in the circumstances no vote; why in justice should her voice be excluded from consideration in this artificial vote? I only raise this purely hypothetical case to show the great difficulty of trying to do justice by legislation in a matter which has always been left to the corporators themselves to decide.

I agree entirely with the judgment of the Court of Appeal ([1969] 1 All ER 1002, [1969] 2 WLR 1067), and would dismiss this appeal.

Lord Morris of Borth-y-Gest (dissenting)

My Lords, it is provided by s 184(1) of the Companies Act 1948 that a company may by ordinary resolution remove a director before the expiration of his period of office. The company may do so notwithstanding anything to the contrary in its articles. So if an article provided that a director was irremovable he could nevertheless be removed if an ordinary resolution to that effect was passed. So also if an article provided that a director could only be removed by a resolution carried by a majority greater than a simple majority he would nevertheless be removed if a resolution was passed by a simple majority.

Some shares may, however, carry greater voting power than others. On a resolution to remove a director shares will therefore carry the voting power that they possess. But this does not, in my view, warrant a device such as special [article] 9 introduces. Its unconcealed effect is to make a director irremovable. If the question is posed whether the shares of the respondent possess any added voting weight the answer must be that they possess none whatsoever beyond, if valid, an ad hoc weight for the special purpose of circumventing s 184. If special [article] 9 were writ large it would set out that a director is not to be removed against his will and that in order to achieve this and to thwart the express provision of s 184 the voting power of any director threatened with removal is to be deemed to be greater than it actually is. The learned judge thought that to sanction this would be to make a mockery of the law. I think so also. I would allow the appeal.

The House of Lords decision does not question that it is *not possible* to explicitly opt out of the shareholder removal right provided by the Companies Act. It is clear to all of the Law Lords that section 168 (as it now is) is a mandatory rule. However, a majority of their Lordships are unwilling to allow the mandatory nature of the rule to invalidate additional voting power given to shareholders conditional upon an attempt to remove a shareholder as a director. This seems difficult to square with the mandatory nature of the rule; in effect, allowing for such weighted voting rights renders section 168 a default rule. For Lord Morris it 'made a mockery of this rule'. The argument made by Lord Upjohn is that it is an acceptable practice, which the Companies Act does not prohibit, to attach different voting rights to different shares. The existence of multiple voting rights does not affect, per Lord Upjohn, the removal vote: an ordinary resolution is required to remove a director; the question of whether those votes are available is determined by the voting rights attached to the shares. In this case in the vote to remove Mr Faith as a director, Mr Faith as a shareholder held shares with three votes per share and could outvote his sister shareholders.

Although the use of different classes of shares with different voting rights is more common in continental Europe than it is in the UK, it is not uncommon in UK companies. A company could, for example, issue Class A shares with five votes a share, Class B shares with one vote a share, and Class C shares with no vote. Lord Upjohn is sensitive to the fact that if the weighted voting rights provided in this case were held to be illegal then what would be the implications for other shares with variable voting rights. What of, for example, a director who held Class A shares with five votes a share in any vote (rather than just a removal vote)? Would a director-shareholder lose his voting power in relation to a vote to remove a director simply because he happened to be a director? On the other hand, there seems to be something objectionable about the design of voting rights that explicitly undermine the mandatory rule. Is it really so difficult to distinguish between the conditional voting rights in *Bushell v Faith* and shares with multiple voting rights which are applicable in all circumstances and are not tailored to evade the statutory removal right?

Some commentators[100] have argued that the reach of the *Bushell v Faith* case is limited and most likely only applies to small close companies where parties such as Mr Faith have an expectation that they will play a role in the company's management so long as they remain a shareholder in the company. Support for this position is found in Lord Donovan's judgment, with whom Lord Guest agreed, who held that:

> There are many small companies which are conducted in practice as though they were little more than partnerships, particularly family companies running a family business; and it is, unfortunately, sometimes necessary to provide some safeguard against family quarrels having their repercussions in the boardroom.

For the other Law Lords in the majority, however, this was not a factor of relevance. For Lord Reid, who focused on similar considerations to Lord Upjohn, the basis for allowing the weighted voting rights is equally applicable to the widely-held public company as it is to the small private company.

In addition to using weighted voting rights as a mechanism for protecting a director from the section 168 removal right, UK company law allows shareholders to enter into an agreement relating to how they will vote their shares even if such agreement would be unenforceable if its terms were incorporated into the articles.[101] This would allow shareholders to contract not to vote to remove particular directors. Obviously, given the number of shareholders in a widely-held company, such agreements are only practical in close companies with a limited number of shareholders.

Question and discussion

1. Do you think shareholders should be required to have a good reason (a 'cause') to remove a director before the expiry of his term in office?

2. Draft a *with*-cause removal right: how would you specify the types of reason that would justify removal?

3. How, if at all, would a 'with cause' removal requirement affect director behaviour?

4. Do you think section 168 should be a mandatory rule? What are the justifications for making it a mandatory rule? Put differently, what is the justification for depriving shareholders of the freedom to decide to give directors greater security of tenure by weakening their removal rights? Many of us may consider such a decision foolhardy, but why would we want to deny shareholders that option if they think it is in the company's best interests? This argument in favour of shareholder freedom seems particularly pertinent in the context of close private companies when shareholders would be involved and informed in making this decision. Why do we force such shareholders to go through the process of providing contingent weighted voting rights such as those provided in *Bushell v Faith*?

   In the context of widely-held companies there are two policy concerns in making the removal rule a default rule. First, would shareholders buying the shares in a company with 'with cause' or no removal rights during the director's term actually pay attention to or understand the rule before buying the shares? Secondly, if shareholders in widely-held companies are rationally inattentive would there be a risk that directors could propose a change in the removal right by amending the articles which the shareholders

---

[100] P. Davies, *Gower and Davies' Principles of Modern Company Law* (8th edn, Sweet & Maxwell, 2008), 390–1.

[101] *Russell v Northern Bank Development Corporation Ltd* [1992] 1 WLR 588. Lord Jauncey of Tullichettle interprets the House of Lords decision in *Welton v Saffery* [1897] AC 299 as holding that 'shareholders may lawfully agree inter se to exercise their voting rights in a manner which, if it were dictated by the articles, and were thereby binding on the company would be unlawful'. See further Chapter 3.

would blindly approve? In relation to the first of these policy concerns, do you think the state should be in the business of paternalistically protecting investors in shares, particularly when most of these investors are institutional investors who employ professionals to make their investment decisions? Is this a type of purchase decision where we can fairly say *caveat emptor*: let the buyer beware? In relation to the second of these policy concerns, evidence from the US in particular suggests that where attempts are made to change the articles to reduce the strength of the shareholder removal right, shareholders in widely held companies pay attention and resist.[102]

3 Removal rights in comparative perspective

3.1 Removal rights in the US

In Delaware corporate law there are two default positions in relation to the rights given to shareholders to remove directors from office. The default rule that applies depends on whether the company has a classified board. As we previously noted, a board is classified or staggered when the directors' terms of office are staggered over different, usually three-year, time periods.

■ Section 141(k) Delaware General Corporation Law

(k) Any director or the entire board of directors may be removed, with or without cause, by the holders of a majority of the shares then entitled to vote at an election of directors, except as follows:

　(1) Unless the certificate of incorporation otherwise provides, in the case of a corporation whose board is classified…shareholders may effect such removal only for cause…

Section 141(k) Delaware General Corporation Law provides that if a company does not have a classified board, so that the whole board has a one-year term and is subject to re-election at each annual general meeting, then the removal right is a 'with or without cause' removal right identical to the removal right set forth in section 168 of the Companies Act 2006.[103] That is, the directors can be removed during the course of their term in office without the shareholders having to specify any reason as to why they are being removed. Of course in order to remove the directors in-between annual general meetings the shareholders would have to be able to convene an interim meeting. As noted already, the shareholders would only have this right in a Delaware corporation if

---

[102] Details of such shareholder activism are set forth in M. Klausner, 'Institutional Investors, Private Equity and Anti-takeover Protection at the IPO Stage' (2003) 152 *University of Pennsylvania Law Review* 755, 760 noting that '59% [of the survey respondents] consistently vote against management proposals to adopt classified boards, and 65% vote in favour of shareholder proposals to repeal classified boards'. See section III.3 of this chapter on the effect of a classified board on director removal rights in Delaware companies.

[103] Until 1967 the Delaware General Corporation Law contained no provision dealing with director removal. The 1967 amendments to the statute provided only that a director would hold office until 'his successor is elected' or 'until his earlier resignation or removal'. Section 141(k) was added by amendments to the statute made in 1974. The common law position applicable prior to these amendments was that the director had a vested right in serving his term and could only therefore be removed for cause: *Roven v Cotter* 547 A 2d 603 (Del Ch 1988); *Kurz v Holbrook* 989 A 2d 140 (2010).

it is explicitly granted to them in the **certificate of incorporation** or the by-laws which in many companies it is not.[104]

If, however, the company has a classified board then the default rule is that the directors can only be removed 'for cause'. It is a default rule as the certificate of incorporation can be amended to provide for 'without cause' removal even where the company has a classified board. In practice, a considerable number of large Delaware companies have classified boards providing for 'with cause' removal.[105]

In order to determine the nature of the removal right which shareholders have when there is a classified board we need to understand what 'for cause' means. How badly does a director have to behave or perform to give the shareholders 'cause' to remove him? The question of the meaning of 'for cause' in the Delaware statute has received relatively limited judicial attention. The leading case, decided prior to the introduction of section 141,[106] is *Ralph Campbell v Loew's Incorporated*[107] where the court held that deliberate obstruction of corporate business would amount to 'cause'.[108] The court gave other examples of 'cause' such as disclosing corporate secrets or embezzling funds. These examples suggest that a director's misbehaviour must involve a form of impropriety to provide cause for his removal. Poor corporate performance alone would not amount to 'cause'.

If the shareholders of a Delaware company are unhappy with management's performance and they wish to replace management but the board refuses to do so, if the company has a typical classified board—with three classes of directors and a 'for cause' removal right—then the shareholders will have to wait for two successive AGMs before they can replace a majority of the board with new directors who will then remove management. Director and management tenure in a Delaware corporation is, therefore, significantly more secure than in the UK.

3.2 Removal rights in Germany

The German Stock Corporation Act provides that the directors of a supervisory board may be given up to a five-year term.[109] German public companies typically provide supervisory board directors with such five-year terms.[110] However, the Stock Corporation Act provides, as a mandatory rule, that at any time during the five-year period the directors appointed by the shareholders[111] may be removed by the shareholders. The majority required to remove the directors is a default of 75% of the votes cast at the meeting.[112]

[104] Section 211(d) Delaware General Corporation Law. Whilst the shareholders acting alone could amend the by-laws to include such a right, they cannot do so if the certificate explicitly excludes such a right (section 109(b) providing that the by-laws can contain any provision *not* inconsistent with the certificate). See further D. Ferreira, D. Kershaw, T. Kirchmaier and E. Schuster: 'After The Crisis: Is there a Case Against Shareholder Empowerment?' (on file with the author, 2012).

[105] See L. Bebchuk, A. Choen and A. Ferrell, 'What Matters in Corporate Governance' (2009) 22 *Review of Financial Studies* 783. Although note that in many non-Delaware financial companies with staggered boards it is not unusual to provide for with cause removal—See Ferriera, Kershaw, Kirchmaier and Schuster, *ibid*.

[106] This provision was introduced in 1967.   [107] 134 A 2d 565 (Del 1957).

[108] The case also provides that if a director is to be removed for cause the director must receive adequate notice of the charges and an opportunity to rebut them. See further *Bossier v Connell* WL 12785 (Del Ch 1986).

[109] Section 102 German Stock Corporation Act.

[110] See, for example, Siemens AG's *Satzung*, para 11(2).

[111] Section 103 German Stock Corporation Act. German law provides that, depending on the size of the company, a certain number of the supervisory board seats are reserved for employees and union representatives: Codetermination Act (*Mitbestimmung-gesetz*) 1976. For a review of these rules see D. Kershaw, 'No End in Sight for the History of Corporate Law: The Case of Employee Participation in Corporate Governance' (2002) *Journal of Corporate Law Studies* 34, 73.

[112] Section 103 German Stock Corporation Act.

The articles may increase or decrease this voting threshold.[113] Typically the articles of most German companies do not alter this threshold.[114]

How easy is it for German shareholders to call a shareholder meeting to exercise these rights? Section 122 of the Stock Corporation Act provides that the management board must call a shareholder meeting when they receive a written demand from shareholders representing 5% of the issued shares of the company setting forth the basis for and purpose of the meeting. This provision allows the articles to elect a lower percentage, although typically this provision is unaltered by the articles.

Removal of supervisory board members by shareholders, although not requiring any reason or cause, is more difficult than under section 168 of the Companies Act 2006 because the number of votes required to remove a director is higher. Furthermore, in our analysis of UK removal rights we saw that an executive director if removed as a director was also removed as a manager either automatically pursuant to the articles or by board action following the appointment of new directors. In German company law if shareholders are dissatisfied with management and the supervisory board refuses to replace them then the shareholders may elect to change the shareholder representatives[115] on the supervisory board. Such a change will, however, have no automatic effect on the managerial appointments, as members of the management board are not supervisory board members. Furthermore, under German company law the new members of the supervisory board, who may be more willing to do the shareholders' bidding, do not have unrestricted discretion to replace management. The new members of the supervisory board would only have the right to remove management if they have an 'important reason' (*ein wichtiger Grund*)[116] to do so. This 'important reason' is a threshold somewhat below impropriety, including, for example, lack of managerial capacity or a vote of no confidence by the shareholder body. In any event, in practice it seems that management can be removed and although they may have a claim that there was no 'important reason', these claims are typically settled after lengthy proceedings. Accordingly, even if there is no 'important reason' executive management can be removed if the company is willing to pay any damages awarded to management.[117]

IV SHAREHOLDER VERSUS DIRECTOR PRIMACY

German corporate law along with Delaware corporate law provides significantly more director- and management-friendly removal regulation than the UK. Similarly, German and Delaware corporate law provide a balance of decision-making power that leans towards the management board and the board of directors, respectively, both in the form in which the board is empowered (through statute rather than through shareholder delegation) and in the substantive division of authority between the board and the shareholder body. We might say therefore that UK company law with its clear tilt towards shareholder authority is an example of a *shareholder primacy* system of corporate governance, and Delaware law and German corporate law are *director* or *managerial primacy* systems of corporate governance.

With regard to the German director primacy classification, however, one important contextual factor needs to be taken into account here when looking at German law as a comparison. German public companies typically have a large shareholder who because of the size of its shareholding has good incentives to pay attention and to act

---

[113] *Ibid.*   [114] See, for example, Siemens AG's *Satzung.*
[115] See note 111 on employee supervisory board membership—co-determination.
[116] Section 84(3) German Stock Corporation Act.
[117] M. Peltzer and A.G. Hickinbotham, *German Stock Corporation and Co-determination Act* (O. Schmidt, 1999), 13.

to discipline management.[118] Accordingly, in large companies in the United Kingdom, the United States, and Germany we have: the United Kingdom with strong shareholder rights but weak incentives for shareholders to use those rights; Germany with weaker shareholder rights but strong incentives for the shareholders to use them; and the United States with weak shareholder rights and weak incentives to use the rights available to them. Taking into account the context of ownership arrangements in the United Kingdom, Germany, and the United States there appears to be a different policy election made by the United States as compared with the United Kingdom and Germany, namely the benefits of authority outweigh the increased scope for agency costs.[119]

■ **S. Bainbridge, 'Director Primacy and Shareholder Disempowerment' (2006) 119** *Harvard Law Review* **1735**

All organizations must have some mechanism for aggregating the preferences of the organization's constituencies and converting them into collective decisions. As Professor Kenneth Arrow explains, such mechanisms fall on a spectrum between 'consensus' and 'authority.' Authority-based decision making structures, which are characterized by a central agency empowered to make decisions binding on the firm as a whole, tend to arise when the firm's constituencies face information asymmetries and have differing interests. Because the corporation demonstrably satisfies those conditions, vesting the power of fiat in a central decision-maker is the essential characteristic of its governance...

It is fair to assume that shareholders come to the corporation with wealth maximization as their goal, but once uncertainty is introduced it would be surprising if shareholder opinions did not differ on how to maximize share value. Shareholder investment time horizons are likely to vary from short-term speculation to long-term buy-and-hold strategies, which is likely to result in disagreements about corporate strategy. Likewise, shareholders in different tax brackets are likely to disagree about such matters as dividend policy, as are shareholders who are divided over the merits of allowing management to invest the firm's free cash flow in new projects...

Shareholders lack incentives to gather the information necessary to participate actively in decision making. A rational shareholder will expend the effort necessary to make informed decisions only if the expected benefits outweigh the costs. Given the length and complexity of [information about a company] the **opportunity cost** entailed in making informed decisions is significant. In contrast, the expected benefits of becoming informed are quite low, as most shareholders' holdings are too small to have significant effects on the vote's outcome. Accordingly, corporate shareholders are rationally apathetic.

Given these conditions, it would be surprising if a modern public corporation's governance arrangements attempted to make use of consensus-based decision making anywhere except perhaps within the central decision making body. Instead, it is 'cheaper and more efficient to transmit all the pieces of information once to a central place' and to have the central office 'make

---

[118] M. Faccio and L. Lang, 'The Ultimate Ownership of Western Corporations' (2002) 65 *Journal of Financial Economics* 365, finding that in 64% of German companies a family owns 20% or more of the shares in the company as compared to 23% in the UK.

[119] A policy election with a bias towards authority is only one available explanation for the different approaches to the balance of power in the UK and Delaware. It seems improbable that this variation represents different conscious policy elections in these jurisdictions. Perhaps more likely it that the 'policy election' is an *ex-post* rationalization for a system of corporate law that is the product of historical contingency and/or economic and interest group pressures. In this regard explanations, that we do not have space here to explore, include possible managerial bias generated by regulatory competition in the United States (see section 6.1 of this chapter and note 51). Note, however, that many of these differences have a historical pedigree dating back to the very first corporate statutes in both jurisdictions. See, for example, *Hoyt v Thompson*, 5 NY 322 (1859). In this regard see D. Kershaw, 'The Path of Corporate Fiduciary Law' (2012) *New York University Journal of Law and Business* (forthcoming) arguing that the different 19th-century conceptions of the corporation in the UK and US have significant explanatory force in explaining corporate legal variation between the US and the UK.

the collective decision and transmit it rather than retransmit all the information on which the decision is based.'[120]

Where then is the corporation's central office located? The Delaware Code, like the corporate law of virtually every other state, gives us a clear answer: the corporation's 'business and affairs...shall be managed by or under the direction of a board of directors.' Hence, as an early New York decision put it, the board's powers are 'original and undelegated.'[121]

To be sure, the separation of ownership and control creates the principal-agent problem...Associated with the shareholders' purchase of the residual claim on the corporation's assets and profits is an obligation on the part of the board of directors and managers to maximize shareholder wealth. Given human nature, however, it would be surprising indeed if directors did not sometimes shirk or self-deal. Consequently, much of corporate law is best understood as a mechanism for constraining agency costs.

A single-minded focus on agency costs, however...can easily lead one into error. Boards of directors are subject to a pervasive network of accountability mechanisms that are more or less independent of shareholder oversight. The capital and product markets, the internal and external employment markets, and the market for corporate control all constrain [agency costs]...These incentive structures induce directors to behave generally in ways consistent with shareholder wealth maximization.

An even more important consideration, however, is that agency costs are the inexorable consequence of placing ultimate decision making authority in the hands of someone other than the shareholders. That we choose not to eliminate agency costs by eliminating the board's power of fiat suggests that vesting discretion in directors' hands has substantial virtues. A complete theory of corporate governance thus requires balancing the virtues of discretionary fiat against the need to ensure that such power is used to further the interests of shareholders...

My principal argument against expansive shareholder voting rights now should be apparent. Active investor involvement in corporate decision making seems likely to disrupt the very mechanism that makes the widely held public corporation practicable: namely, the centralization of essentially non-reviewable decision making authority in the board of directors. The chief economic virtue of the public corporation is not that it permits the aggregation of large capital pools, as some have suggested, but rather that it provides a hierarchical decision making structure well-suited to the problem of operating a large business enterprise with numerous employees, managers, shareholders, creditors, and other constituencies. In such an enterprise, someone must be in charge: 'Under conditions of widely dispersed information and the need for speed in decisions, authoritative control at the tactical level is essential for success.'[122]

Calls to facilitate greater shareholder activism necessarily contemplate that institutions will review board decisions, step in when board performance falters, and exercise voting control to effect a change in policy or personnel...Giving investors the power of review differs little from giving them the power to make board decisions in the first place. Even if investors are not inclined to micromanage portfolio corporations, vesting them with the power to review board decisions inevitably shifts some portion of the board's authority to them. This remains true even if the review entails only major decisions. GM's [General Motors] board, after all, no more micromanages GM than would a coalition of activist institutional investors, but it is still in charge.

In response, [commentators] may ask why shareholders have voting rights at all. In the purest form of an authority-based decision making structure, all decisions would be made by a single, central body—here, the board of directors. Thus, if authority were corporate law's sole value, shareholders likely would have no voice in corporate decision making. As we have seen, however, authority is not corporate law's only value. In the nexus of contracts model, shareholders have certain contractual rights, which include the requirement that directors maximize shareholder wealth as their principal decision making norm. Like many intra-corporate contracts, however,

---

[120] Kenneth J. Arrow, *The Limits of Organization* (Norton, 1974), 68–70.
[121] *Manson v Curtis*, 119 NE 559, 562 (NY 1918).
[122] Kenneth J. Arrow, *The Limits of Organization* 68–70 (Norton, 1974), 69.

the shareholder wealth maximization norm does not easily lend itself to judicial enforcement except in especially provocative situations. Instead, it is enforced indirectly through a complex and varied set of extrajudicial accountability mechanisms, of which shareholder voting is one.

Like the other accountability mechanisms discussed above, shareholder voting must be constrained in order to preserve the value of authority. As Arrow explains: 'To maintain the value of authority, it would appear that [accountability] must be intermittent. This could be periodic; [or] it could take the form of what is termed "management by exception," in which authority and its decisions are reviewed only when performance is sufficiently degraded from expectations…'[123]

Accordingly, shareholder voting is properly understood not as a primary component of the corporate decision making structure, but rather as an accountability device of last resort, to be used sparingly, at most.

In sum, because corporation lawmakers apparently recognize the significant value of fiat within the corporation, they have not lightly interfered with boards' decision making authority in the name of accountability. To the contrary, throughout corporation law, preservation of managerial discretion is the default presumption. Because the separation of ownership and control mandated by U.S. corporate law effects just such a presumption, by constraining shareholders both from reviewing most board decisions and from substituting their judgment for that of the board, this separation has a strong efficiency justification.

Questions

1. What does it mean to say that the board's powers in a Delaware company are 'original and undelegated'? Are the powers of a UK board 'original and undelegated'?

2. Are you persuaded by Bainbridge's argument that Delaware company law gets the balance right between authority and responsibility? If not why not?

3. What do you think Bainbridge would say about the UK's *Listing Rule 10: Significant Transactions*?

4. Does Professor Bainbridge overstate the effect on the board's authority of providing shareholder instruction rights or more extensive veto and approval rights? Consider the Vodafone/Efficient Capital Structures example set forth above when considering your answer.

 Online Resource Centre
http://www.oxfordtextbooks.co.uk/orc/kershaw2e/

Visit the Online Resource Centre for additional resources and information available for this chapter, including web links and an interactive flashcard glossary.

---

[123] *Ibid*, 78.

CHAPTER SEVEN

BOARD COMPOSITION AND STRUCTURE REGULATION

I INTRODUCTION TO BOARD FUNCTION AND COMPOSITION

1 The core functions of the board

In the previous chapter we looked at the distribution of power in a UK company and saw that UK companies have a single or unitary board of directors, which is the central repository of corporate power. Whilst the original power and authority to act on behalf of the company is located in the shareholder body acting in general meeting, shareholders invariably delegate this power to the board, subject to certain constitutional and statutory reservations of power. But what do we expect the board of directors to do with this power and authority? That is, what is the role and function of the board of directors in a UK company?

The Companies Act 2006 tells us nothing about the function of the board; nor have any of the Act's predecessors. Limited guidance in this regard is, however, provided by the Model Articles. Before looking at the Model Articles we should consider first the Model Articles' predecessor, Table A, which structures the board's powers and function in the vast majority of existing UK companies.[1] With regard to board function, Table A provides first, that 'the business of the company shall be managed by the directors who may exercise all the powers of the company'[2] and, second, that the board may delegate 'any of their powers' to 'any managing director or any director holding any other executive office'.[3]

In Table A's instruction to the board to manage and its permission to delegate there is a fundamental conflict. On the one hand, if the board is to actively manage the company or perform any management functions then the senior managers of the company must necessarily be members of the board: how could a board manage without the company's senior managers? Accordingly, Table A provides that the power to delegate power is a power to delegate to individuals who are directors, and not to senior members of management who are not directors. On the other hand, the notion of delegation of authority contains within it the idea that the *delegator* and the recipient of the delegation, the *delegatee*, are not the same person, or controlled by the same person. One would expect from the idea of delegation that the delegator of power delegates power to the delegatee and then monitors the exercise of the power—and withdraws that power when, in the view of the delegator, it is being exercised poorly. To comply with the idea that the delegator of power and the delegatee of power are separate persons, board members would not be senior managers.

The Model Articles of Association for Public and Private Companies issued pursuant to the Companies Act 2006 make slight but important changes to the functions of the

---

[1] See pp 192–3 for the relevant extracts from Table A and the Model Articles.
[2] Article 70, Table 70.   [3] Article 72, Table A.

board[4] as compared to Table A Articles. Instead of providing that the 'company shall be managed by the directors' it provides that 'the directors are responsible for the management of the company's business, for which purpose they may exercise all the powers of the company'. No longer, according to the Model Articles, do directors *manage the company*, rather they are *responsible for* the management of the company. Clearly, however, this change does not strip the board of its formal management function. To be responsible for management and to be able to exercise all the powers of the company means that the board retains the ability to manage. In addition, the scope of the power to delegate authority in the Model Articles is significantly expanded beyond Table A's executive directors to 'any person [the board] thinks fit'.[5] This amendment removes the default presumption contained in the Table A Articles, discussed earlier, that senior managers will be directors. In practice, this will remain the case because the board in a company with Model Articles retains a management function and will need some senior managers to perform this function. It is clear, however, that these two changes in the new Model Articles represent a subtle change in the functions of the unitary board: away from the management function and towards the delegation and monitoring function. This, as we shall see, fits with a modern tendency in the UK to stress the delegation and monitoring function of the board over its managerial function.[6]

Accordingly, simply taking the functions set out in the Table A Articles and the Model Articles for Public and Private Companies, one would expect a board of directors to consist of non-managerial directors—typically referred to as non-executive directors—and management directors—typically referred to as executive directors. However, for small close companies this would not be the case. In these companies the boards' management and delegation functions will both be performed solely by the managers to whom power is delegated. Whilst this perhaps appears odd to the uninitiated, it raises few concerns: the interests of those exercising power (management and the board) are typically identical to the interests of those they serve (the shareholders) as they are the same real persons. These companies are not the concern of this chapter. Here we are concerned with large, widely-held companies, such as the majority of UK listed companies, where ownership and control are separated and where we would indeed expect to see a board capable of fulfilling both the management and delegation and monitoring functions to consist of a mix of executive and non-executive directors.

Composition and structure regulation which is the focus of this chapter is about how, as best as possible, to resolve the conflict between the management and the delegation and monitoring functions of the unitary board in widely-held companies: how to organize board membership and the roles of different members to ensure that the boards of such companies perform both of these functions effectively. In essence this boils down to two questions: first, what for a the unitary board of a widely-held company is the appropriate number of, and what are the appropriate board roles that should be given to, the non-executive and executive directors; and second, what are the appropriate set of characteristics and skills of those directors, in particularly of the non-executive directors.

---

[4] The change is identical for public and private companies. See article 3 of both the Model Articles for Public Companies and the Model Articles for Private Companies.

[5] Article 5 of both the Model Articles for Public Companies and the Model Articles for Private Companies.

[6] We should be wary of overstating the effect of these changes. We need to remind ourselves that these rules are model default articles not mandatory rules. Many companies, particularly larger companies, have altered their articles from the Table A form to take account of the evolving function of the board and the needs of the particular company. Vodafone Plc's articles, for example, provide for delegation to any 'manager of the company' (article 109.2 www.vodafone.com/content/dam/vodafone/investors/corporate_governance/vgplc_articles_2010_agm.pdf ❿); however, its articles continue to require that 'the company's business *will be managed* by the directors' (emphasis added) (article 107.1).

2 The board's managerial role and the number of executive directors

In practice the board of directors of all companies—large and small, **close** and widely-held—will delegate significant managerial powers to full-time managers. The vast majority of management decisions, therefore, will take place outside of the board-room with no requirement to refer the matter in question to the board. However, certain actions are required by statute to be exercised by the board; certain matters will require board action pursuant to the company's constitution; and the board may retain some decision-types for board action when they delegate power to senior management.

When the board is required to make a decision the board exercises managerial power. Typically, the smaller the company the more decisions are reserved to the board and the more the board exercises managerial power. In small companies, for example, the board is often used as a control mechanism to ensure that all parties can participate in what the shareholders, when they agreed the terms of the constitution, considered would be important management decisions. For example, in small companies the board may need to approve of any transactions or investments over a specified value threshold. In these companies board meetings will be frequent and if necessary are easy to arrange at short notice. Many, if not all, of the directors will work at the company or be in regular and close contact with the company. However, as the company, and the volume of transac-tions the company enters into, expands it becomes impracticable for the board to be involved in ordinary course, everyday business decisions. As the company grows the managerial role of the board necessarily shrinks. The boards of larger companies will discuss and approve the company's strategy but will only be involved in management decisions that are very significant—such as a new major investment or the sale of one of its divisions—or that they are required by statute to be involved in, such as the issuing[7] of or buy back of shares,[8] or a capital reduction.[9] Accordingly, whilst the board of a large company plays a less significant managerial role than the board of a small com-pany, it will nevertheless have an important managerial function.

When thinking about the composition of the board of directors—the make-up of the members of the board—we could say that the importance of the function determines the number of—or weighting given to—executive or non-executive directors. Here we are discussing the management function, so one could say that, as the board gets larger and the management function shrinks, the board of a large company should have fewer execu-tive directors. However, as we have seen, whilst the management function of the large company board necessarily shrinks it still exists and is of considerable importance in rela-tion to less common but very significant decisions. The board needs managerial input to make good decisions when it is required to make a decision. There is, therefore, no neces-sary inverse relationship between the shrinkage in the board management function as the company grows and the number of senior managers who should sit on the board.

In order to answer the question of how many managers should sit on the board, we must look at this question in a different way. In relation to the management decisions that are taken by the board in a large company it is clear that the executive direc-tors will be more informed about the reasons for taking these decisions and whether those reasons are good enough to support these decisions. In practice, the non-execu-tive directors may be able to raise questions and to challenge the proposed action, but in most instances the executive directors' preferred course of action will be put into effect. Accordingly, most of the time these 'board management decisions' are in real-ity made outside the boardroom by executive managers in their office, over coffee, or through email exchange. We will consider later, when discussing the characteristics of

---

[7] See Chapter 17.   [8] See Chapter 17.   [9] See Chapter 19.

the non-executive director how, if at all, we can ensure that the non-executive directors play an active and valuable role in these managerial decisions.

However, whilst the deliberative process of the board *in session* will not in most instances alter the course of action recommended by the executive directors—it will in most cases affirm the informal decision made by the executive directors—it is noteworthy that the composition of the board of directors *may* have a significant impact on this informal management decision-making process. This is because the number of *executive* directors who sit on the board alters the power dynamic of the informal decision-making process which takes place between senior management prior to the board's consideration of the issue. If the only executive manager to sit on the board is the chief executive officer then other senior managers, who would have no right to attend, speak, and vote at the board meeting on a proposal, are significantly disempowered in the executive decision-making process. Consider the following hypothetical which explores this point.

Hypothetical A

Bob and Billy are the chief executive officer and chief operating officer (COO) of Bob's Electronics Plc, respectively. As part of his role as COO, Billy is responsible for managing the development and design of new computers. This role is central to the future success of the company; if new products do not respond to the development of consumer demand and expectation, the company's sales will fall.

Bob and Billy fundamentally disagree on the future direction of the laptop computer sales market and, therefore, on the company's business strategy. Bob thinks the future successful product for the company is low-specification small and light computers that are very cheap and appeal to young children who can put the computers in their school bags, but it is not too disastrous if the computer is damaged or stolen. Billy, however, thinks that the company's resources should be put into tablet computers for family use which, although not high specification, are much more expensive than the sorts of computers Bob has in mind.

For our purposes it does not matter who is right; what is important to understand is how the managerial decision-making process about this issue may be, in part, a function of whether or not Billy, in addition to Bob, is a member of the board. If Billy is a board member he has direct and readily available access to fellow board members outside of the board meeting with whom he can raise issues and concerns about Bob and the development of the business. He will know these members personally from the numerous board meetings they both attended. If he is a board member he has the ability, in theory, to express dissent about Bob's strategic view at the board meeting. Whilst he may typically be reticent to express a dissenting view, the option remains open to him. Such dissent could undermine Bob's attempt to obtain board approval for his strategy and could sow seeds of doubt with the board about his performance as CEO. Bob is aware of this and would want to stop any attempts by Billy to undermine him and his strategy through informal contacts with board members or through formal dissent at a board meeting. This knowledge may alter Bob's receptiveness to Billy's idea, his willingness to compromise on this conflict, or to trade Billy's concession on this issue for Bob's concession on a different matter.

If Billy is not a board member his negotiating power in this regard is undermined. Of course, even if he is not a board member he can approach board members; however, he may not know these members well personally and some board members may view this approach as inappropriate. Although he may be invited to attend board meetings as an observer and informant, his ability to speak and contribute may not be the same as it would be if he was a member of the board.

Of course, the extent to which the appointment of Billy as a director could affect the power dynamics of management will be dependent on many factors, including, for example, the personalities of Bob, Billy, and the other board members, as well as the culture and dynamics of the company's board meeting. The point of this hypothetical is to give an example of how the decision to make Billy an executive director as well as a senior manager has *the potential* to affect such management decision dynamics.

Accordingly, the important question here is not how many senior managers must sit on the board to perform the board's management function but rather how many and which executives do you want to empower in management's shadow board decision-making process. The preferred course will vary depending on the company, the personalities of the management, and the managerial preferences of shareholders. On the one hand, by weighting managerial power in the hands of the CEO and making him the only executive director, one would ensure that the CEO's vision and strategy could be clearly implemented and that the CEO has to spend less time in internal political battles and negotiations about decisions and strategy. On the other hand, weighting too much power in the CEO means that there may be no effective check on his power and his ideas by other senior managers. The trade-off here is between clear authority and implementation and ensuring an effective check on the company's direction and strategy.

In summary our analysis of the management function of the board in larger companies does not lead to a clear conclusion about the extent to which managers should be directors. Two key factors need to be kept in mind in this regard: first, although the managerial role of the board in large companies is very limited, the board is still required to make some important managerial decisions, which suggests that a significant managerial board presence is important; and secondly, we need to bear in mind that the number of managers who are appointed directors could significantly affect the managerial decision-making dynamics of the company.

Assignment 1

In light of the above analysis consider how many senior managers should serve on the Bob's Electronics Plc board from the following choices. Prepare reasons for the number and identity of your chosen board members.

- Bob, who is the chief executive officer of the company;
- Jane, who is the finance director of the company—responsible for capital structure of the company—how much of the companies activities should be funded by debt or by equity—as well as the production of the company's financial information;
- Billy, who is the chief operating officer—responsible for managing the development, design and manufacture of the computers;
- Fabian, who is head of sales and marketing—responsible for the sales team and for marketing the product;
- Ben, who is the chief information officer—responsible for all information technology including the company's website and online sales processing;
- Erna, who is the head of component supplies—responsible for sourcing the required components to build the computers;
- Suzanne, head of distribution—responsible for the distribution and delivery of the ordered products throughout the UK.

3 The function, number, and characteristics of non-executive directors

As we have already established, one of the board's two core functions is to appoint management to whom the board delegates significant corporate power. It follows from the act of delegation that if the managers do not meet the performance and behavioural expectations that the board has of them, then the board should act to replace them. In order to determine whether those behavioural and performance expectations have been met, the board needs to monitor the managers' activities and performance. Given that it would make no sense to talk about the executive directors monitoring the performance of themselves and disciplining or firing themselves if they failed to achieve the expectations they had—of themselves!—when we consider the delegation and monitoring function of the board, we mean the delegation and monitoring function of the outside, non-executive directors.

More concretely the non-executive directors' delegation and monitoring function involves, *in theory*, the following roles and activities:

- selecting and appointing the senior management of the company;
- monitoring the performance of management and replacing management where management fails to perform to the board's expectations;
- ensuring that internal management and information systems and controls are in place within the company to ensure that accurate information about the company is produced. The reliability of this information is central to the board's ability to assess management's performance (on internal controls see further Chapter 12);
- ensuring the integrity of the auditing process of the company's financial statements; ensuring that the financial information that is produced is informative and reliable for investors but also that it provides a reliable basis for the board to assess management's performance (on the auditing of financial statements see further Web Chapter A);
- setting executive director pay (see further Chapter 8);
- monitoring compliance with directors' duties and obligations; this would include, for example, ensuring that any self-dealing transactions comply with obligations set out in the Companies Act 2006 and the Listing Rules; or determining whether to authorize the taking of a corporate opportunity in accordance with section 175 (on self-dealing and corporate opportunities see further Chapters 13 and 14, respectively). The non-executive directors in this regard are a key mechanism of controlling and sanctioning managerial agency costs;
- initiating legal action against directors or former directors who have breached these obligations (see further Chapter 15);
- controlling the search for and nomination of new directors to the company so that appointed directors will not be grateful or beholden to executive directors so that those directors can effectively and independently perform their functions.

For many years in legal academic circles there has been, and still remains today, a considerable degree of scepticism regarding the ability of the board to perform these functions. Commentators on company law and corporate governance—and this book is certainly guilty of this as well—often talk about the managerial agency problem in **widely-held** companies as if the board did not exist or as if the board was simply the handmaiden of management—the executive directors.

The traditional view was that the non-executive directors did not act as an effective check on management. There were several reasons for this. First, executive directors often played a significant role in nominating and therefore appointing the non-executive directors. The shareholders in widely-held company typically had little to say about this process. Rational apathy problems meant that the shareholders did not involve them-selves in the board nomination process and that they typically voted to rubber stamp the board's nomination. Accordingly, such non-executive directors were grateful to and felt beholden to the executive directors, as it was the executive directors who effec-tively brought them onto the board by recommending to the previous board that they should be nominated to the board. Secondly, the non-executive directors were often well known to the executive directors, as friends, former colleagues, or family members. So not only were they grateful for the appointment, but bonds of collegiality, friendship, or family meant that their loyalties might first be to the executive directors and not to the interests of the company. Thirdly, these non-executive directors typically had no or a very small equity interest in the company and, although they would receive a salary for their board membership and meeting attendance, they had no significant economic interest in the company that would incentivize them to spend significant resources of time and effort to understand the company and to monitor closely the executive direc-tors' activities. These factors, coupled with an overwhelming knowledge advantage of the executive full-time directors about the company, its strategy, industry etc., meant that the prevailing view was that non-executive directors did little apart from rubber stamping what their 'paymaster' executive directors told them to do.

Accordingly, from this critical point of view, although formally UK company law provides that the shareholders in general meeting appoint the board and that the board appoints, monitors, and removes management, in practice this was subverted so that the managers effectively appointed the board and the board appointed management; that is, management appointed itself. In this view, therefore, the board and management are dissolved into each other. The board is no longer a mechanism for controlling manage-ment and reducing managerial agency costs. It becomes part of the managerial agency problem not part of the solution.

The question for us in this *Introduction to board function and composition* is what could be done in terms of regulating how the board activities are organized (the struc-ture of the board) and who is allowed to serve as a non-executive director of the board (the composition of the board) in order to revitalize the board's delegation and monitor-ing function? In this regard consider the following assignment. Please give some thought to this assignment before reading further.

Assignment 2

In light of the criticisms set forth above regarding the ineffectiveness of non-executive direc-tors, what regulatory steps would you recommend to revitalize the effectiveness of non-executive directors in their delegation and monitoring function. In particular what would your regulatory response be to the following questions (prepare reasons to support your conclusions):

- What is the ideal number of board members for a board to have?
- Given your response, how many executive directors should be allowed to serve on the board?
- How many non-executive directors should serve on the board?
- What characteristics or relationships would exclude individuals from serving on a board?
- What, if any, functions of the board should be reserved solely for non-executive directors and why?

Over the past 20 years in response to several waves of corporate scandals and failures in the UK and elsewhere in the world—most recently the banking failures resulting from the global financial crisis—regulators have focused their attention on how to make the delegation and monitoring function of large company boards more effective; how to ensure that the board operates as a real check on the executive directors of the board. The resulting regulation is referred to here as *board structure and composition regulation*. The UK is widely and correctly seen as a leader and innovator in this regard.

There are five central themes that organize the current regulatory debate about board structure and composition regulation:

- How many non-executive directors should serve on the board?
- How independent from the executive directors do the non-executive directors need to be?
- What areas of board activity should be controlled by or dealt with solely by the non-executive directors?
- To what extent does the gender composition of the board matter for effective governance and to what extent should we be concerned about the gender make-up of UK boards regardless of the governance implications, if any, of board diversity?
- Should the position of chair of the board meeting itself be held by the chief executive officer or by a non-executive director, and if the latter should such non-executive director be independent?

We consider each of these themes in turn below. Before doing so, however, we need to register a factor that must not be forgotten as we turn our focus to the question of how to make the board's delegation and monitoring function work. Non-executive directors remain members of the board in all respects; they are not there only to perform the delegation and monitoring function; they are there to perform the board management function as well. For non-executive directors there are two aspects to this function: first, making informed management decisions when required to do so; and, second, non-executive directors bring skills, experience, and contacts to the board which are available to assist senior management: to give the executive directors the benefit of their advice and experience when they request or need it; and to make use of their pool of business, political, and regulatory contacts for the company's benefit. We will refer to this aspect of the non-executive's management function as their *advisory function* to distinguish it from the decision-making part of the management function. Some commentators argue that this advisory function is the most important contribution made to companies by non-executive directors. Professor Ghoshal, for example, has argued that:[10]

> The primary role of the board is to add value to the company by providing important business connections, wise counsel and strategic guidance to senior executives. Of course, the board has a monitoring and control role, but that is secondary to the coaching and support role.

Accordingly, when thinking about how to make the board's delegation and monitoring function work effectively we need to take account of any impact the proposed solutions may have on the non-executives' ability to effectively perform their managerial decision-making and advisory functions.

3.1 How many non-executive directors?

Three key factors determine how many non-executive directors sit on the board. The first is a determination of the balance and importance of the board's delegation and monitoring function versus its management function. The second is how many—in number or percentage terms—non-executive directors are necessary to enable the non-executive directors to perform the roles given to them and to have sufficient weight and influence in the boardroom. The third is the optimal size of the board.

---

[10] S. Ghoshal, 'Boardrooms need advisors not policeman' *Financial Times* (8 September 2003).

The first consideration regarding the management function of the board has already been considered. With regard to the second consideration, the concern is twofold. First, you need enough non-executives to be able to perform the functions given to the non-executive directors. The position of non-executive director is a part-time position and although remunerated, the remuneration is not that high (relatively) for many of the high-earning individuals that act as non-executives.[11] There is, therefore, only so much time that they will be willing to devote to board service. Secondly, part-time outsiders may feel uncomfortable about asking difficult questions of executive management; they will not want to feel like a lone troublemaker nor wish to look stupid in the face of the executive directors' considerable company-specific knowledge. They may therefore prefer to keep quiet rather than ask questions. One response to this is to ensure that there are enough non-executive members of the board to ensure that the non-executives do not feel overwhelmed or intimidated by the executive directors; so that the non-executive directors feel that the executive directors answer to them. This notion that numbers may embolden the non-executive directors to carry out their delegation and monitoring function effectively makes some sense. Weight of numbers alone, however, provides no guarantee that non-executives will be more assertive and demanding and more willing to ask difficult questions. Indeed, we need to be aware that too many non-executives may in fact undermine the monitoring function if it reduces the number of executive directors on the board who might offer alternative informed opinions about the issues being considered by the board. A board of 10 directors with only one executive director, the CEO, may be a perfect recipe for management control of the board.

The third consideration that a regulator needs to consider when specifying the number of non-executive directors who should sit on the board is the size of the board. The more people that are responsible for making a decision, the more difficult it is to make a decision. The more people on a decision-making body the more scope for disagreement; the more scope for different people with different interests and priorities to pursue different agendas, to 'hold up' the board from acting by refusing to do 'X' unless everyone else agrees to 'Y' as well. Whilst the board should have enough members to perform its functions effectively, it should not have too many members or it will become a slow and cumbersome decision-maker. Different companies of course will have different needs and requirements and, therefore, optimal board size will vary considerably. Generally speaking, in the UK market traditionally a board size of between 10 to 12 members has been the norm,[12] although very successful companies have as many as 20 members, and of late board size appears to be increasing.[13]

As the optimal board size for a company varies, it is unlikely that regulation will specify a particular number of non-executive directors to serve on a board; a more effective way of regulating for non-executive director membership would be to require a specific proportion of non-executive directors: for example, a third, a half, or three-quarters. As we shall see, this is a more typical approach to board composition regulation.

If a regulator does not wish to inhibit companies from having effective boards tailored to the company's circumstances it is indirectly constrained in its preferred proportion of non-executive directors by the number of executive directors whom it is deemed necessary to perform the management function. If a large company board was

---

[11] See further section IV of chapter 8.

[12] Research by Deloitte for the Walker Review Of Corporate Governance in UK Banks and Other Financial Industry Entities (available at: http://webarchive.nationalarchives.gov.uk/+/http://www.hm-treasury.gov.uk/d/walker_review_261109.pdf ●) found that as of 2007 the average board size was 10 members (at para 3.1).

[13] For example the board of HSBC Holdings Plc has 18 board members at the time of writing. At the time of writing, Vodafone Plc has a board of 15 members (from 11 in 2008); Marks and Spencer Plc has a board of 14 members (from 11 in 2008); BP Plc has a board of 15 members; WPP plc has a board of 16 members.

required to have three-quarters of its board members to be non-executive directors and yet it considered it necessary to have eight executive members in order to perform the board's management function, then the board would need to consist of 32 members, which is likely to be an unwieldy and ineffective board. Even if the required proportion of non-executive directors was reduced to a half, this would still require a board of 16 members. Accordingly, if on average the optimal board size is considered to be around 10 to 12 members,[14] for those companies that wish to have a significant management presence on the board any regulation that requires more than half of the board members to be non-executive directors would hinder the formation of an effective board. Optimal board size constraints appear, therefore, to place an *upper limit* on any generally applicable non-executive board membership requirement at around, at most, half of the board.

3.2 The independence of the non-executive directors

As noted, one of the long-standing concerns about the effectiveness of non-executive directors has been that they were connected to senior management in ways that made them in the first instance loyal to management rather than to the company. Such directors were not therefore independent of management.

There are several ways in which such ties to management could compromise a non-executive director's independence. Most obviously this could include: family connections; bonds of long-standing friendship with the executive directors; previous employment at the company; or prior or continuing business relations where, for example, a non-executive director owns, is employed by, or serves on the board of another firm which provides services or products to the company. Other less direct ways in which independence can be compromised include: cross-directorships—where the non-executive director of Company A is an executive director of Company B, where the CEO of Company A is a non-executive director; membership of the same societies, clubs, churches, or religions of the executive directors; or the making of charitable donations by the company to the non-executive directors 'pet' charities and 'good causes'.

Recent corporate failures in the US have highlighted how the apparent independence of the board can easily and subtly be subverted. Consider, for example, the case of Enron, which was one of the most successful and apparently innovative companies of the 1990s. For five years in a row the US business publication *Fortune* magazine awarded Enron the title of most innovative company. In August of 2000 its share price traded at $90 a share, but by December of the same year the company had entered bankruptcy proceedings and its shares traded at 40 cents a share. What went wrong and what were the multiple causes of its failure were the subject of forensic business and academic analysis.[15] One of the several causal factors which this analysis identified was that although Enron had 13 apparently independent non-executive directors on a board of 15 members, various relationships between the 'independent' directors and the company rendered the directors' independence more façade than reality. Consider the following extract.

---

[14] See generally, T. Eisenberg, S. Sungren and M. Wells, 'Larger Board Size and Decreasing Firm Value in Small Firms' (1998) 48 *Journal of Financial Economics* 35; D. Yermack, 'Higher Market Valuation of Companies with a Small Board Of Directors' (1996) 40 *Journal of Financial Economics* 185.

[15] For an excellent analysis of these causes see W. Bratton, 'Enron and Dark Side of Shareholder Value' (2002) 76 *Tulane Law Review* 1275.

■ C. Elson, 'The Enron Failure and Corporate Governance Reform' (2003) 38 *Wake Forest Law Review* 855

Various aspects of the relationships between the Enron directors, the company, and its management may have reduced the directors' independence. Independence may have been partially compromised by the long tenure of many of the directors and the substantial fees they received for board service. When directors serve for extended periods of time, they may become too comfortable and entrenched. The biggest risk involved with long-tenured directors is that they may become more accepting of management's activities and less likely to fully perform the management monitoring function. A number of Enron's directors had served on the board for fifteen years or longer. These directors may have become more trusting of management because of the long-term relationships they had developed over the years with that team. Additionally, the Enron directors were extraordinarily well compensated for their services, receiving over $350,000 per year worth of stock options—substantially above the normal levels. Such large fees may make preservation of one's position, linked closely to acquiescence to management, a dominating concern.

More importantly, though, than the independence compromising problems of tenure or compensation, some board members did not appreciate the severity of the company's condition perhaps because of the linkages to management created by consulting fees paid in addition to standard director compensation. Indeed, Lord John Wakeham, John A. Urquhart, and Charles Walker each received significant consulting fees beyond their normal board pay.[16] Any sort of significant financial tie to a company other than a director's long-term equity stake is problematic. When a director accepts a consulting fee, he or she becomes a part of the company's management team; immediately there is a conflict between acting as a manager and monitoring the managers. The roles of director and consultant cannot be combined. It may be difficult for a director to exercise independent judgment vis-à-vis management's decisions if that board member feels that he or she is part of the management team or seeks to preserve the flow of consulting fees by acquiescing in management's decisions.

If a company wants a consultant, it should hire a consultant; if it wants a director, it should hire a director. Directors are already expected as part of their ordinary responsibilities to contribute their perspectives on company issues when necessary as they are paid a substantial fee to be available to management. Additionally, in other instances, business relationships existed between directors and Enron. For example, Herbert Winokur was concurrently an Enron director and a member of the Board of the National Tank Company, which recorded over $2.5 million in revenue from sales to Enron subsidiaries.

In addition to consulting fees and other financial relationships, various charitable donations and political contributions created relationships between management and the Board that may have weakened the independence and objectivity of certain Enron directors. Enron board members Charles LeMaistre and John Mendelsohn both served as presidents of the M.D. Anderson Cancer Center, which received a $1.5 million pledge from Enron in 1993 and donations from Kenneth Lay and Enron totaling nearly $600,000 over five years. The George Mason University Mercatus Center, which employs Enron board member Wendy Gramm, was the recipient of more than $50,000 in donations from Enron and the Lay Foundation. She had an additional financial connection to the company: Her husband, former chairman of the Senate Banking Committee, Senator Phil Gramm, has been called 'one of Congress' biggest recipients of Enron campaign donations.' All told, at least eight 'outside' directors had significant direct or indirect financial relationships with the company. These relationships likely diminished objectivity and consequently the ability of the directors to have appreciated the severity of the red flags before them...

---

[16] Elson: 'In 2000, Wakeham and Urquhart received $72,000 and $493,000, respectively, solely for consulting services. Enron paid more than $70,000 to two firms partially owned by Walker for tax consulting and government relation services. For over ten years, Enron was a major contributor of up to $50,000 annually to the American Council for Capital Formation—a non-profit corporation chaired by Walker.'

In summary, the Enron Board's failure to live by a key element of acceptable corporate governance—independence—fostered an environment where objectivity was compromised. The relationships the directors had with company management created a comfort level in them vis-à-vis management that made it possible for them to simply explain away or miss completely the various warning signs before them. Their independence deficit did not necessarily make them bad actors, only much less sensitive ones. This is why independence and the objectivity it brings is so critical to effective management oversight.

The regulatory response in relation to these independence concerns is, in theory, straightforward: prohibit directors from serving as non-executive directors if they have any such business or personal connections to the company or the executive directors which compromises their independence. However, as is clear from this analysis and extract, the list of ways in which independence can be compromised is very long and within each category of family, business connections, friendship etc. there are very broad and very narrow readings of those categories. Is, for example, a non-executive director's independence compromised where she is the sister of the CEO; his niece, his second cousin once removed? One might argue that the longer the list and the broader the reading of each category, the more independent the non-executive director and the better for the governance of UK companies. However, excessive independence comes at a cost. It is not always easy to find non-executive directors who are willing to sit on a company's board and who are capable of bringing something to the board in terms of relevant knowledge, experience, and business contacts. There may be individuals who could make a significant contribution to the management and advisory functions of the board who would be able to serve on a more narrow definition of independence but are excluded on a broader definition. The broader the definition of independence, therefore, the more individuals you exclude from the pool of potential candidates to serve on the board. Excluding such individuals could damage the company. The regulatory balance between independence and ensuring a deep pool of knowledgeable and skilled non-executive director talent is not, therefore, an easy one to strike.

This problem has been recently highlighted in relation to the governance of banks as a result of the ongoing credit crisis. It has been argued by some observers that one of the reasons for recent bank failures is the fact that many banks' non-executive directors, although independent, had minimal experience, or understanding, of the banking world.[17] In a review of Bank Governance by Sir David Walker commissioned by the UK Government in the immediate aftermath of the crisis, the concern that boards of banks had become populated with independent directors who had limited understanding of the financial services industry[18] led Sir David to stress the importance of non-executive knowledge and understanding of the banking industry.[19] This concern clearly applies beyond the banking industry. Wholly independent directors who do not understand the company's

---

[17] See, for example, Kirchmaier arguing that 'it is often rare to find people with a background in banking or financial services on boards of banks; it is not uncommon that the only non-executive directors with banking experience are former executives of that bank': T. Kirchmaier, 'Inject Governance, and Not Just Cash: Some Thoughts on the Governance of Banks' (27 October 2008), available at SSRN: http://papers.ssrn.com/ 🌐. See also D. Ferreira, T. Kirchmaier, and D. Metzger, Boards of Banks (2010) EGGI Finance Working Paper No 289/2010.

[18] Whilst this was a clear failing in relation to some failed banks (e.g. HBOS plc), it was a not a failing in all of these banks (e.g. RBS plc)—See the Financial Services Authority report on *The Failure of the Royal Bank of Scotland* (FSA, 2011) available at: www.fsa.gov.uk/pages/Library/Other_publications/Miscellaneous/2011/rbs.shtml 🌐 providing a salutary lesson that well crafted, knowledgeable and independent boards can fail.

[19] Walker Review Of Corporate Governance in UK Banks and Other Financial Industry Entities (available at: http://webarchive.nationalarchives.gov.uk/ + http://www.hm-treasury.gov.uk/d/walker_review_261109.pdf) at 3.7–3.15.

business are unlikely to be able to monitor and discipline management effectively. A too demanding definition of independence could, therefore, result in ineffective boards.

3.3 Board activity to be controlled by the non-executive directors

There are three aspects of board activity that are core to the delegation and monitoring function: first, the activity that fundamentally affects the independence of the non-executive directors: the nomination to the general meeting of persons to serve as non-executive directors; secondly, the monitoring of executive directors' conflicts of interest in areas where there is significant potential for the incurrence of managerial agency costs: in particular in relation to remuneration, self-dealing transactions, and corporate opportunities; and thirdly, controlling the processes that produce information about the company, for example financial statements upon which the directors, shareholders, and other investors rely.

As shareholders in widely-held companies are subject to rational apathy problems, the nomination of a person to serve as a board member rarely comes from the shareholders themselves. The board nominates a person and that nomination is invariably approved by the shareholders in general meeting. Clearly if the non-executives are nominated and elected to the board following a recruitment process in which management has played a significant role, such directors are likely to be grateful to management for providing them with a prestigious position and a source of income. People are rarely wholly independent when asked to monitor, judge and sanction those individuals to whom they are grateful. Accordingly, it is necessary to de-couple the process of nomination and appointment of non-executive directors from the executive directors' control and influence. One way to do this is give this role to a committee—a nomination committee—consisting solely of, or majority controlled by, non-executive directors whose recommendation *must* be accepted by the board. From an independence perspective the committee would consist only of non-executive directors. However, in terms of deciding who would be an appropriate person to serve as a non-executive director, the senior managers of the company will have opinions that may be invaluable for finding good candidates. If the regulator considers such input to be necessary then majority non-executive control of the committee may be the preferred option. If, however, the regulator feels that such concerns are overstated and that, in any event, informal management soundings can be taken by the non-executive directors then the regulator will give sole control to the non-executive directors. Importantly, even if a nomination committee consists only of non-executive directors, management will still play an important informal role in identifying and recommending candidates. Accordingly, even with a nomination committee consisting of wholly independent non-executive directors, a newly appointed non-executive director will to some extent owe his position to the executive directors.

A second core aspect of the monitoring function is to ensure that individual directors do not use their power to benefit themselves financially; that is, to prevent direct managerial agency costs. Clearly all directors, not just non-executive directors, can abuse their position and power in a self-serving manner. However, the concern is greater in relation to executive directors than non-executive directors. As we have seen, such directors are likely to wield greater influence on the board due to both their knowledge advantages and the possible feelings of indebtedness, gratitude, and loyalty that non-executive directors may have toward them. Furthermore, executive directors will be faced with greater temptation than the non-executive directors: their personal wealth is dependent on the remuneration paid to them by the company; they may have a greater ability to steer business towards their other business interests or family members' business interests; and in the course of doing their job they will regularly identify business opportunities that may be of interest to the company.

The final core aspect of the delegation and monitoring function is to ensure that the information that is required by investors to understand the financial performance of the company and the information that the non-executive directors need to assess management's performance is comprehensive, transparent, and reliable. Executive directors are aware that their jobs and, as we shall see later in Chapter 8, their remuneration are linked to this financial information. This creates an incentive for them to massage the financial information to create a rosier financial picture of the company. Furthermore, as the company's **financial statements** are verified (audited) by independent external auditors,[20] management is also incentivized to place similar pressure on outside auditors to accept management's preferred presentation of the financial information. We shall consider this problem in depth in Web Chapter A. For now, note that the effectiveness of the non-executive directors' delegation and monitoring function is dependent upon ensuring that: the company's information and internal control systems are sound; internally staff members can express concerns to non-executive directors about the financial statements and inappropriate management pressure to massage those statements; and that the external audit process is protected from such managerial pressure. An obvious regulatory response to these concerns would be to give ultimate control over the production of financial information, the audit process, and the assurance of satisfactory internal controls to a committee of non-executive directors. Such a committee is in most jurisdictions referred to as an audit committee.

As was the case with the nomination committee, in thinking about the make-up of the audit committee there are other considerations that need to be taken into account other than the non-executive director's independence from the executive directors. Financial statements are highly technical, requiring a thorough understanding of the company's business as well as the applicable accounting standards[21] that determine how the company's transactions are recorded in the accounts. Part-time non-executive directors are unlikely to have the level of understanding of the business that may be required to cast an informed and objective eye over the financial statements. Whilst executive directors may have such an understanding, to include them as members of the audit committee significantly undermines the core monitoring function of the committee. Nevertheless, it is clear that, even with an audit committee consisting solely of non-executive directors, the executive directors and other senior management closely involved in the financial statement process—for example, the chief financial officer and chief accounting officer—will need to work closely with the members of the audit committee.

Furthermore, in addition to understanding the company's business, to be effective the non-executive members of the audit committee will need to be able to understand the accounting issues involved in the production of the financial statements. Applying accounting standards is often more of an art than a science:[22] there may be several ways of interpreting and applying the applicable standards resulting in different (more or less positive) presentations of the financial statements. Audit members that find these issues difficult to follow and understand will take the lead from those who do not—either more informed non-executive directors or management themselves. Accordingly, to the extent that there is a significant imbalance between the financial and accounting skill set of the non-executive members of the audit committee and senior management, the audit committee is unlikely to fulfil its monitoring function effectively in this regard.

---

[20] We look in detail at the audit process in Web Chapter A.
[21] For an explanation of accounting standards see further Web Chapter A.
[22] See further Web Chapter A.

3.4 Gender diversity on boards

Women make up 46% of the active economic workforce in the UK yet they make up only 12% of directorships of FTSE 100 companies and only 15% of non-executive directorships. In 2008 women made up only 11% of new directorship appointments.[23] Two questions are raised by these statistics. First, what is the cause of low female representation? Is it systematic indirect discrimination, whereby capable women are excluded because they do not fit the cultural profile of a non-executive director of a major UK company, whatever that may be? Does the UK non-executive community have 'club-like' characteristics which operates to exclude women or, more benignly, to over-identify suitable men rather than women as new appointments? Or is the low level of women on boards simply a function of the limited supply of senior female candidates? Such supply problems could be explained again through the lens of discrimination and cultural barriers or, alternatively, through the lens of lifestyle choices made by women, which mean that career progression is truncated as women limit their own ambitions to find a balance between their role as mum and as business woman. The second question raised by these statistics is what are the consequences of low female board representation for the operation and success of UK companies, and therefore for the success of the UK economy? Would companies be run differently, and more effectively, with a greater female presence on UK boards because of character traits that are said to be more dominant amongst women than men?[24] Or would the presence of women make no difference at all because one cannot count on gender stereotypes being realized in the women and men chosen to sit on boards?

Unsurprisingly, the answers to these questions are contentious and unclear. Here we can only introduce the debate. A recent UK Government-commissioned report into women on boards carried out by Lord Davies concluded that there were informal cultural barriers to female progression up the corporate ladder, including into the non-executive board room, and concluded that UK companies were missing out on female perspectives and voices that would make the board more effective. The report also concluded that there was some economic evidence to support the case for more women on boards.

■ Lord Davies' Report on Women on Boards

The female executive pipeline challenge[25]
The low number of women on boards is in part a symptom of insufficient numbers emerging at the top of the management structure and the under-representation of women in senior management generally. However, Cranfield School of Management research has identified a pipeline of 677 women on the corporate boards and executive committees of all FTSE 350 companies, not counting the 116 women on FTSE 100 boards...

This leaking pipeline may be partially explained by the level of female attrition from the UK workforce. Male and female graduate entry into the workforce is relatively equal. This equality is maintained at junior management positions but then suffers a marked drop at senior management levels. The reasons for this drop are complex, and relate to factors such as lack of access to flexible working arrangements, difficulties in achieving work-life balance or disillusionment at a lack of career progression...

Barriers to success
Over the course of this review it has become clear that there are many women who are ready to serve on corporate boards, but complex barriers and challenges stand in their way.

---

[23] Lord Davies' Report on *Women on Boards* available at: www.bis.gov.uk/assets/biscore/business-law/docs/w/11–745-women-on-boards.pdf ✪ (hereafter 'Women on Boards').

[24] See generally, C. Gilligan, *In A Different Voice* (Harvard, 1982).

[25] Extract from pages 15–16 of Women on Boards.

Many consultation respondents told us that women with corporate experience were frequently overlooked for development opportunities and that there were differences in the way that men and women were mentored and sponsored, which gave men the edge over their female peers. Others cited gender behavioural traits as a key issue, whereby women tend to undervalue their own skills, achievements and experiences. Also, the relatively low number of successful female role models often compounds stereotypes and reinforces perceived difficulties in rising up the corporate ladder. Meanwhile, there is a perception that the many women in leadership positions in academia, the arts, the media, the civil service or professional services are often overlooked because they do not have specific corporate experience and Chairmen fear that they will not understand corporate issues or corporate board governance.

Our consultation found that the informal networks influential in board appointments, the lack of transparency around selection criteria and the way in which executive search firms operate, were together considered to make up a significant barrier to women reaching boards.

Improving performance[26]

There is a body of research which demonstrates how the appointment of female directors can improve a company's performance. Female directors enhance board independence.[27] Better decision-making is assumed to occur as a result of directors having a range of experiences and backgrounds. Women take their non-executive director roles more seriously, preparing more conscientiously for meetings.[28] Women ask the awkward questions more often, decisions are less likely to be nodded through and so are likely to be better. Boards are often criticized for having similar board members, with similar backgrounds, education and networks. Such homogeneity among directors is more likely to produce 'group-think'...

A more recent non-academic study conducted by an asset management firm in the UK looked at those companies with a threshold of at least 20% female representation across FTSE-listed boards. They found that operational and share price performance was significantly higher at one and three year averages for those companies with women making up over 20% of board members than those with lower female representation.[29]

The correlation between strong business performance and women's participation in management is striking. Studies have shown that where governance is weak, female directors exercise strong oversight, can have a 'positive, value-relevant impact' on the company, and that a gender-balanced board is more likely to pay attention to managing and controlling risk. A Leeds University Business School study showed that having at least one female director on the board appears to cut a company's chances of going bust by 20% and that having two or three female directors lowered the chances of bankruptcy even further.[30]

The views set forth in the Davies' Report on the economic implications of the low representation of women on boards are not universally shared. Adams and Ferreira, for example, find in a US study that although women directors attend more meetings and improve male directors' attendance, 'the average effect of gender diversity on firm performance' is negative.[31] Consider further the observations of *Financial Times* columnist Lucy Kellaway.

[26] Extract from pages 8–9 of Women on Boards.

[27] N. Fondas, and S. Sassalos, 'A Different Voice in the Boardroom: How the Presence of Women Directors Affects Board. Influence over Management' (2000) 12 *Global Focus* 13.

[28] D. Izraeli, 'Women Directors in Israel' in R. Burke and M. Mattis (eds), *Women on Corporate Boards of Directors: International Challenges and Opportunities* (Kluwer Academic Publishers, 2000), 75–96.

[29] M. Bhogaita, *Companies with a better track record of promoting women deliver superior investment performance* (New Model Advisor, 2011).

[30] N. Wilson, 'Women in the boardroom help companies succeed' *The Times* (19 March 2009).

[31] R. Adams and D. Ferreira, 'Women and the Boardroom and their Impact on Governance and Performance' (2009) 94 *Journal of Financial Economics* 291.

■ Lucy Kellaway 'Female quotas would target the wrong women' *Financial Times* (27 February 2011)

But from a business point of view, the obsession with women on boards seems all wrong. The two of us [Ms Kellaway is a non-executive director of a UK listed company which has two women on the board], by virtue of our sex, have had no tangible effect on shareholder value in our four years in the job. That's not because we are seen as token women to whom no one listens. It is because the role of the non-exec is an odd one. We grapple with corporate governance and try to give sound advice and guard against calamity. But we don't run the company. At least in good times, I sometimes think we are less important than the women on the phones in the call-centres. They are the ones who are actually making the money.

The hot debate should not be about boardroom quotas versus voluntary codes of conduct. It shouldn't be about the boardroom at all—or at least not about the non-executives. What matters are the women on the staff, and making sure that the good ones get to the top. Whether there are one, two or three female non-execs who pitch up a few times a year for board meetings strikes me as a peculiar thing to get into such a stew about.

A while ago I asked the men who were on our board in its earlier, all male days, how much difference it made having two women around. They hummed and hawed for a bit and said that we approached things in a slightly different way. And that we were a good example to the women lower down in the company.

I'm not sure about either point. It is, of course, vital that board members don't all jump to identical conclusions about everything. But in my experience, gender is less important than profession: a male journalist and a male accountant probably take more sharply opposing positions on business issues than do, say, a male and a female accountant.

And as for the role model thing, that's even more doubtful. In my day job as a journalist, I'm not remotely inspired by the one female non-exec on the board of Pearson (which owns the FT). In fact, I've just had to Google her to find out her name. But the fact that our chief executive is a woman is another matter altogether: I do find that inspiring, in an abstract kind of way.

Equally, I don't kid myself that my own inanely grinning face in the annual report is a good example to the bright, ambitious women working in the company on whose board I serve. I'm happy to say that there are rather a lot of them, and they were doing rather well long before I came along.

Not only is the fuss over women non-execs beside the point, it may end up being counter-productive. Many of the news stories last week named and shamed the companies with no women on their boards. Now all these companies need do to stop such stories is ship in a couple of vaguely plausible female non-execs—which is an awful lot easier than changing anything important—such as how they treat their women managers.

3.5 Chairing the board of directors

The final board structure and composition theme for us to consider is which director should be responsible for organizing board activity and process. Every board has a chairman.[32] The chairman, working together with the company secretary, is typically responsible for board meeting schedules,[33] setting the agenda for the board meeting and providing the relevant information to other directors for the meeting. Where a board vote is deadlocked the chairman, pursuant to most companies' articles, will be given a casting vote.[34] The primary issue in this regard is who should perform the role of the chairman. More specifically there are two issues. First, should the role of chairman be

---

[32] While clearly every board chair is not male, the term chairman is used in the debate in a gender neutral—albeit clearly gendered!—fashion. This section adopts this terminology.

[33] Note that whilst in practice the chairman will typically call a board meeting, under most companies' articles any director has the power to call a board meeting.

[34] Article 13 of the Model Articles for Public Companies.

given to the chief executive officer or should it be performed by a non-executive director? Secondly, if the role of chairman is to be given to a non-executive director does that non-executive director need to be independent?

This is one of the most contentious issues in structure and composition regulation. In the next part of this chapter we shall see that different jurisdictions take very different positions. The debate's terms, however, are straightforward. Those in favour of separating the roles of chairman and CEO argue that if the CEO is allowed to control the board process this undermines the effectiveness of the delegation and monitoring function. Issues that are central to the effective performance of that function may be left off the board agenda or sidelined; the information provided for the board meeting may be consciously or unconsciously biased in favour of management's preferred outcome. For proponents of separating these roles, separation is essential for ensuring that the board acts as an effective check on senior management power. There are, however, strong arguments against separation. In particular, those opposed to separation argue that giving the control over board process to a part-timer means the board can become distracted from the key issues that are central to the company's success. The chief executive officer knows better than any other person which issues need to be addressed and dealt with by the board in order to effectively implement the company's strategy. In response, one could argue that a part-time chairman will of course consult with the CEO about key board issues; indeed he would be wholly ineffectual without such input. A further concern is that the chairman may as 'chairman of the board of directors' feel publicly responsible for the company's performance simply because he is one of the two figureheads of the company and, as a result, attempt to interfere in the operational realm of the executive directors. Such interference could undermine the formation and implementation of the company's strategy: a 'too many cooks spoil the broth' concern.

The arguments previously set out do not resolve this issue. Whilst in the UK most business people, investors, and commentators support separation of these roles, in the US the majority position is opposed to separation. We will look in section III at some of the empirical evidence on the relationship between company performance and the separation of roles. For now, however, it is important to note that the drivers behind these opposing positions are the different weightings given by proponents and opponents to: on the one hand, giving authority to management to create value through the efficient implementation of strategy; and on the other, the effectiveness of the board's delegation and monitoring function.

Assignment 3

You have been given the task of designing a corporate governance code for UK listed companies. How will you respond to the following questions? To the extent that there is any overlap with previous assignments, consider whether the analysis in section 3 alters your previous answers.

- How many non-executive directors should serve on the board of a listed company/what percentage of the board's members should be non-executive directors?
- Should all the non-executive directors be independent?
- Provide a definition of independence.
- What functions of the board should be solely or majority controlled by the board?
- In relation to the above functions explain the reasons why you choose sole non-executive control or majority non-executive control.
- Should there be quotas for female representation on boards?

- What level of financial expertise would you expect of the members of an audit committee?
- Should the role of chairman and CEO be performed by separate persons or can they both be performed by the CEO?
- Are your rules mandatory rules or default rules and why?

II BOARD STRUCTURE AND COMPOSITION REGULATION: THE CORPORATE GOVERNANCE CODE

The Companies Act 2006 provides minimal regulation of the composition and the structure of the board. Section 154 of the 2006 Act provides that a private company must have at least one director and that a public company must have at least two directors, thereby requiring that a public company has a board of directors. Section 157 of the Act specifies that a director must be at least 16 years old. The Act does not distinguish between non-executive directors and executive directors, let alone require a certain number or percentage of non-executive directors. The chairman of the board of directors is mentioned only once in the whole Act in relation to the authentication by the chairman of board minutes.[35] The Act says nothing about board function and does not in any way allocate particular board functions to particular directors apart from the approval by disinterested directors of the taking of corporate opportunities.[36]

As we have seen, the Model Articles provide for the dual management and delegation functions of a unitary board. In addition, the Model Articles provide rules on board processes—in particular, quorum and voting. However, they do not provide **default rules** for the composition and the structure of the board. Indeed for private or public companies that are *not listed* on the London Stock Exchange there is, apart from the provisions already mentioned, no composition and structure regulation either in mandatory or default form.

For premium listed companies,[37] however, there is a significant body of composition and structure regulation. This is found in what is now called the 'UK Corporate Governance Code', which is a corporate governance code maintained and periodically revised by the UK's Financial Reporting Council (FRC), which, in addition to maintaining the Corporate Governance Code, is the UK's primary accountancy and actuary regulator. Prior to 2010, the UK Corporate Governance Code was known as the Combined Code.

The Corporate Governance Code is a relatively recent regulatory innovation. Following several auditing and corporate scandals in the late 1990s, the *Institute of Chartered Accountants for England and Wales* sponsored the Cadbury Committee, under the chairmanship of Sir Adrian Cadbury, to consider the 'financial aspects of corporate governance in the UK'.[38] The recommendations that emanated from the Cadbury Committee were, however, more wide-ranging in terms of composition and structure regulation than one might have expected from a committee whose mandate was to focus on the financial aspects of governance. During the 1990s there were other governance committees which looked at executive remuneration (the Greenbury Committee) and the

---

[35] Section 249 CA 2006.

[36] See further Chapter 14.

[37] On the difference between a premium and a standard listing see Chapter 6. Premium listed companies may be both UK and non-UK incorporated companies.

[38] Report of the Committee on the Financial Aspects of Corporate Governance 1992, available at www.ecgi.org/ 🌐.

development of a sound system of company internal controls (the Turnbull Committee). The guidance from all these committees was subsequently combined into the Combined Code. The Combined Code has since been subject to revision and review on several occasions, most notably resulting from a review of the Code by the Hampel Committee which reported in 1998[39] and, following the collapse of Enron and WorldCom in the US, by the *Higgs Review of the Role and Effectiveness of Non-executive Directors*[40] in 2003 and the *Smith Report on Audit Committees* also in 2003.[41] The most recent review and revision of the Combined Code took place in the aftermath of the Credit Crisis in 2009–10, and resulted in some substantial revisions to the Code as well as the renaming of the Code as the 'UK Corporate Governance Code'. This most recent review process also resulted in the publication of additional guidance, which is not part of the Code, on board effectiveness.[42] This review was influenced by several of the findings of Sir David Walker in his review on *Governance in UK Banks and other Financial Industry Entities*.[43]

The Corporate Governance Code applies to premium listed companies.[44] It sets forth a set of abstract governance principles known as the 'Main Principles' and then provides best practice guidance on the implementation of those principles known as 'Code Provisions'. The Principles and Provisions address five areas of governance: board leadership; board effectiveness; board accountability; remuneration; and relations with shareholders. The Code is an example of principles-based regulation — the principles take precedence over more specific rule-based guidance. The Listing Rules do not provide directly that companies must comply with the Main Principles, but Listing Rule 9.8.6(5) does so indirectly by requiring a statement from premium listed companies explaining how they have applied the Main Principles. However, a statement from the company as to how it has applied the principles which from an objective bystander's perspective indicates that the principles have not been complied with would not breach this Listing Rule 9.8.6(5).

In relation to the Code Provisions the Corporate Governance Code does not provide a mandatory code of rules, rather the Provisions provide a set of specific recommendations about board composition and structure which the company *either* has to comply with *or*, if it does not comply, explain in its annual report why it does not comply. The UKLA's Listing Rule 9.8.6(6) requires that listed UK companies must either *comply* with the provisions set forth in the Code or *explain the failure to comply*. Accordingly, there is a *mandatory rule* to *either* comply with the Code Provisions or explain why the company has not done so; but the option of explaining non-compliance makes the specific governance guidelines optional rules. Failure to either comply with the Provisions or explain non-compliance is a breach of the Listing Rules which could result in sanctions imposed by the Financial Services Authority, ranging from de-listing to a fine.[45] To date there has been no enforcement action taken by the Financial Services Authority in relation to any breach of the comply and explain obligation.

---

[39] Available at www.ecgi.org/ 🌐.

[40] Available at www.berr.gov.uk/ 🌐.

[41] See ORC for this report. Following the banking crisis of 2007–2009, in March 2009 the FRC announced a review of the Code. The consultation period in this regard will end in 2009.

[42] Financial Reporting Council, Guidance on Board Effectiveness (FRC, 2011).

[43] Walker Review of Corporate Governance in UK Banks and Other Financial Industry Entities (available at: http://webarchive.nationalarchives.gov.uk/ + http://www.hm-treasury.gov.uk/d/walker_review_261109.pdf 🌐).

[44] UK Corporate Governance Code, Governance and the Code para 6. Whilst our concern here is only with UK premium listed companies, in fact the Code applies to non-UK companies with a premium listing.

[45] On possible sanctions for failing to comply with the Listing Rules see Web Chapter B.

The rationale for a comply and explain code is clear: not all companies are the same and, therefore, not all companies have the same governance needs; *one size does not fit all*. For example, as we have seen in relation to the size of the board, some companies will need more executive directors on the board than others, and if there is a mandatory percentage of non-executive directors this could render some company boards too large and, therefore, ineffectual. Shareholders of some companies may prefer a board driven by the managerial preferences of the CEO; others will be more concerned to check CEO power by separating the roles of chairman and CEO. Nevertheless, although companies may have different needs, the specific governance recommendations in the Corporate Governance Code set out a best practice expectation, which one would expect most firms to follow. They represent a benchmark of best practice that should not be readily departed from without a good reason to do so. However, if there is such a good reason then companies should feel free to depart from the Code's recommendations, provided that they explain to their shareholders the reasons for the departure. In this regard, the FRC has made it clear that compliance with the code should not be viewed as a mandatory box-ticking exercise. The Corporate Governance Code itself explains the *comply and explain* idea as follows:

■ Corporate Governance Code, Comply or Explain

1. The 'comply or explain' approach is the trademark of corporate governance in the UK. It has been in operation since the Code's beginnings and is the foundation of the Code's flexibility. It is strongly supported by both companies and shareholders and has been widely admired and imitated internationally.

2. The Code is not a rigid set of rules. It consists of principles (main and supporting) and provisions. The Listing Rules require companies to apply the Main Principles and report to shareholders on how they have done so.[46] The principles are the core of the Code and the way in which they are applied should be the central question for a board as it determines how it is to operate according to the Code.

3. It is recognized that an alternative to following a provision may be justified in particular circumstances if good governance can be achieved by other means. A condition of doing so is that the reasons for it should be explained clearly and carefully to shareholders, who may wish to discuss the position with the company and whose voting intentions may be influenced as a result. In providing an explanation, the company should aim to illustrate how its actual practices are both consistent with the principle to which the particular provision relates and contribute to good governance.

4. In their responses to explanations, shareholders should pay due regard to companies' individual circumstances and bear in mind, in particular, the size and complexity of the company and the nature of the risks and challenges it faces. Whilst shareholders have every right to challenge companies' explanations if they are unconvincing, they should not be evaluated in a mechanistic way and departures from the Code should not be automatically treated as breaches. Shareholders should be careful to respond to the statements from companies in a manner that supports the 'comply or explain' process and bearing in mind the purpose of good corporate governance. They should put their views to the company and both parties should be prepared to discuss the position.

---

[46] See earlier on whether the Listing Rules actually require companies to 'apply' the Main Principles'.

5. Smaller listed companies, in particular those new to listing, may judge that some of the pro-visions are disproportionate or less relevant in their case. Some of the provisions do not apply to companies below the FTSE 350. Such companies may nonetheless consider that it would be appropriate to adopt the approach in the Code and they are encouraged to do so. Externally managed investment companies typically have a different board structure which may affect the relevance of particular provisions; the Association of Investment Companies' Corporate Governance Code and Guide can assist them in meeting their obligations under the Code.

6. Satisfactory engagement between company boards and investors is crucial to the health of the UK's corporate governance regime. Companies and shareholders both have responsi-bility for ensuring that 'comply or explain' remains an effective alternative to a rules-based system.

Clearly, making compliance with the governance rules optional runs the risk that listed companies may ignore the recommendations and continue to operate with poor governance arrangements, giving weak and unpersuasive reasons for non-compliance. In some jurisdictions, such board structure and composition rules are not optional.[47] For example, companies listed on the New York Stock Exchange (NYSE) must comply with the governance requirements set out in the NYSE Listing Manual.[48] However, although an optional best practice code runs some risk that companies will not comply, in the UK compliance levels with the Corporate Governance Code are exceptionally high, although where there is non-compliance the explanations for non-compliance are often weak and pro forma.[49] Indeed the Financial Reporting Council is less concerned with non-compliance than it is with a possible culture of box-ticking: that is, complying with the Code in order to be seen to be complying rather than giving serious thought to whether the recommendations are actually suitable for the company.[50] If companies are of the view that their scope to depart from the Code is limited because, for example, institutional shareholders and the media will have knee-jerk responses to non-compliance—namely, that it must be bad[51]—then, although regulators may comfort themselves with the claim that if the guidelines are too onerous or have negative side-effects for particular companies then those companies need not comply, in practice for such companies these optional best-practice guidelines creep towards mandatory-rule status.

1 The role, number, and independence of non-executive directors

1.1 The role and number of non-executive directors

The Code provides a limited degree of guidance on the role of non-executive directors. As we have observed, the articles of most UK companies delegate to the board both

---

[47] It is noteworthy, however, that the trend is clearly towards comply and explain governance rules and not mandatory rules. See, for example, the comply and explain code introduced in Germany in 2002. In Germany, the comply and explain obligation is set forth in the corporate statute (section 162 German Stock Corporation Law).

[48] See the New York Stock Exchange's Listing Manual, para 303A.00 Corporate Governance Standards.

[49] For empirical evidence documenting high and increasing compliance levels see S. Arcot and V. Bruno, 'In Letter but Not Spirit: An Analysis of Corporate Governance in the UK' at http://papers.ssrn.com/ 🌐; and I. McNeil, 'Comply or Explain: Market Discipline and Non-Compliance with the Combined Code' (2006) *Corporate Governance: An International Review* 486.

[50] See the Code's explanation of the Comply or Explain approach extracted at 254, stressing that shareholders should not evaluate compliance in a mechanistic way.

[51] Such knee-jerk responses are considered further in section II.4 of this chapter.

a management and the delegation and monitoring function. Whilst non-executive directors logically take sole responsibility for the latter, they also retain a management function. In practice, they do not involve themselves in the operational running of the company, but will periodically make important management decisions. The Corporate Governance Code acknowledges both functions but places clear emphasis on the delegation and monitoring function. Main and Supporting Principles A.4 provide:[52]

Main Principle
As part of their role as members of a unitary board, non-executive directors should constructively challenge and help develop proposals on strategy.

Supporting Principle
Non-executive directors should scrutinize the performance of management in meeting agreed goals and objectives and monitor the reporting of performance. They should satisfy themselves on the integrity of financial information and that financial controls and systems of risk management are robust and defensible. They are responsible for determining appropriate levels of remuneration of executive directors and have a prime role in appointing and, where necessary, removing executive directors, and in succession planning.

Prior to the introduction of board composition regulation in the 1990s, the typical board of a UK company was majority controlled by executive directors. In the absence of composition regulation, executive directors dominated listed UK companies. This contrasted sharply with the US where there was some, although limited, pre-1990s composition regulation and where typically outside non-executive directors numerically dominated the board. In this regard a study by Dayha, McConell and Travlos[53] observed that:

During 1988, for only 21 companies of the Financial Times 500 did outside directors comprise a majority of the board and, when boards are ranked according to the fraction of outside board members, outsiders comprised only 27 percent of the [average][54] board's membership…In comparison, outsiders comprised a majority of the board for 387 of the [US] **Fortune 500** companies. Furthermore, for the [average] board of the Fortune 500 companies, outside directors comprised 81 percent of the membership.

The original recommendation of the Cadbury Committee on the number of non-executive directors was that each company should have a minimum of three non-executive directors, two of which had to meet the Code's independence guidelines.[55] This relatively modest recommendation for a non-executive presence on the board is perhaps unsurprising given the traditionally low level of non-executive representation on UK listed company boards.

During the course of the 1990s the recommended number of non-executive directors set out in the Corporate Governance Code continued to rise. The specific number recommendation was replaced by a percentage recommendation of not less than one-third of the board following amendments to the Code proposed by the Hampel Committee in 1998. The Code recommended that a majority of this 'one-third' should meet the Code's independence guidelines.[56] It is also noteworthy that during the course of the

---

[52] See further FRC Guidance on Board Effectiveness (FRC, 2011) paras 1.2, 1.18–1.23
[53] J. Dayha, J. McConnell and N. Travlos, 'The Cadbury Committee, Corporate Performance, and Top Management Turnover' (2002) 57 *Journal of Finance* 461.
[54] Median board membership.
[55] Paragraph 4.11 of the Cadbury Report.
[56] See, for example, Provision A.3.2 of the 2000 Combined Code.

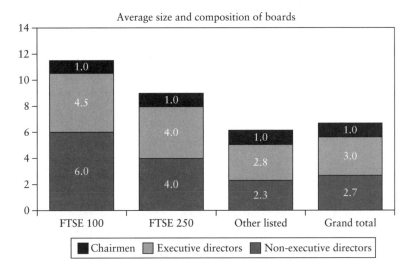

Figure 7.1 *The executive and non-executive director make-up of listed companies in 2002*

1990s boards of listed companies increased non-executive representation by above the recommended one-third level, so that by the time of the Higgs review in 2003 the majority of **FTSE 100** companies had a majority of non-executive directors. Consider Figure 7.1 taken from the Higgs Review detailing the executive and non-executive director make-up of listed companies in 2002.[57]

The Higgs Review recommended that at least half the members of a listed company board should be non-executive directors and that *all* of them should comply with the independence requirements of the Code. This recommendation is now set forth in provision B.1.2 of the Corporate Governance Code which provides that:

> Except for smaller companies,[58] at least half the board, excluding the chairman, should comprise non-executive directors determined by the board to be independent. A smaller company should have at least two independent non-executive directors.

If the chairman is also a non-executive director who complies with the Code's independence requirements then a majority of the board of a Code-compliant company will consist of independent non-executive directors.

1.2 The definition of independence

The increase in the recommended percentage of non-executive directors reflects an increasing tendency to see the listed board's primary function as the delegation and monitoring function. This view is also reflected in the increasing breadth of the Code's definition of independence. Compare the independence requirements in the original Cadbury Code and in the Corporate Governance Code 2010, both of which follow.

---

[57] Higgs Review, n 31, 18.

[58] A smaller company is defined by the Corporate Governance Code to be a company that falls outside of the FTSE 350 (Corporate Governance Code (2010), note 6 to B.1.2).

■ *Report of the Committee on the Financial Aspects of Corporate Governance (1992), para 4.12*

> An essential quality which non-executive directors should bring to the board's deliberations is that of independence of judgment. We recommend that the majority of non-executives on a board should be independent of the company. This means that apart from their directors' fees and shareholdings, they should be independent of management and free from any business or other relationship which could materially interfere with the exercise of their independent judgment. It is for the board to decide in particular cases whether this definition is met. Information about the relevant interests of directors should be disclosed in the Directors' Report.

■ *Corporate Governance Code (2010) B.1.1*

> The board should identify in the annual report each non-executive director it considers to be independent. The board should determine whether the director is independent in character and judgment and whether there are relationships or circumstances which are likely to affect, or could appear to affect, the director's judgment. The board should state its reasons if it determines that a director is independent notwithstanding the existence of relationships or circumstances which may appear relevant to its determination, including if the director:
>
> - has been an employee of the company or group within the last five years
>
> - has, or has had within the last three years, a material business relationship with the company either directly, or as a partner, shareholder, director or senior employee of a body that has such a relationship with the company;
>
> - has received or receives additional remuneration from the company apart from a director's fee, participates in the company's share option or a performance-related pay scheme, or is a member of the company's pension scheme;
>
> - has close family ties with any of the company's advisers, directors or senior employees;
>
> - holds cross-directorships or has significant links with other directors through involvement in other companies or bodies;
>
> - represents a significant shareholder; or
>
> - has served on the board for more than nine years from the date of their first election.

The Corporate Governance Code requires that the board should consider the independence—in character and judgment—of each director. In effect, the Code sets out a list of relationships that formally would disqualify a person from being 'independent'. However, the Code provides a 'safety-valve' where a director, although viewed as independent by the board, does have one or more of the relationships set out in Provision B.1.1. In such circumstances the board may still deem him to be independent but must provide reasons why they view him as independent. Strictly speaking, if the board still views a director as independent in spite of the existence of one of the relationships set out in B.1.1 then this does not amount to a failure to comply with the Code that requires an explanation for non-compliance—as opposed to an explanation of why the director is in fact independent. Such a non-compliance explanation would only be required where the board does not deem a non-executive director to be independent but still wishes to nominate him.

The independence criteria set out in Provision B.1.1 are ongoing requirements; they do not only apply at the time of appointment. The board is required to consider the independence of each director every year. If any of the relationships set out in Provision B.1.1 develop after appointment, such directors will no longer be independent, unless the board deems them to be independent in spite of the relationship.

The relationships and circumstances which compromise independence are very broadly drafted. For example, no employee of the company within the past five years can qualify as independent nor can a director who (from his perspective, not the company's) has had a material[59] business relationship with the company. The director cannot receive any additional remuneration from the company apart from his director's fee. Participation in the company's share option scheme renders the director not independent, thereby preventing share options from being used to compensate non-executive directors, unless an explanation for why using options would not affect independence is given by the board. The provision deems directors holding cross-directorships not to be independent, as are those directors who have 'significant links' with the company's other directors, which could include, for example, a separate business or not-for profit venture undertaken with another director.

Unsurprisingly, the provision provides that close family ties with the company's directors, management, and advisors compromises independence but does not specify the precise relationships which would be 'close family ties'. Arguably, this enables the independence provision to adjust flexibly to the myriad of family relations that exist in the real world: a director may not have a close family relationship with her husband from whom she has been separated for 10 years but not divorced, but may have a close family relationship with a distant cousin with whom she was brought up in the same household.

The final two categories in Provision B.1.1 are worthy of attention. The provision provides that a director is not independent if he represents a significant shareholder. A 'significant shareholder' is not defined in the Code, but some guidance in this regard may be taken from the definition of 'substantial shareholder' in the Listing Rules regulation of related party transactions,[60] which is a shareholder with 10% or more of a company's voting shares.[61] Providing that representatives of significant shareholders are not independent is somewhat surprising if one views the primary function of non-executive directors to be to control managerial agency costs, and when one of the problems of making non-executive directors effective is that they do not have a big enough stake in the company to invest time and effort in monitoring and disciplining management. A non-executive director who represents a significant shareholder would, however, have precisely those incentives. Why then discourage[62] the appointment of such directors by deeming them not to be independent? The reason is that the Corporate Governance Code's concern in this regard is not the managerial agency problem but rather the **controlling shareholder agency problem**, where a controlling shareholder abuses her power and influence to benefit herself but to the detriment of the minority shareholders. From this viewpoint the role of the independent non-executive director is to monitor

[59] Materiality is not defined by the Code.

[60] On related party transactions see Chapter 16.

[61] Listing Rule 11.1.4. Note that several terms we have encountered in the Corporate Governance Code have not been defined—'material'; 'close family ties'; 'significant shareholder'. The objective in not defining these terms is to provide for greater flexibility in capturing circumstances and relationships that in fact problematize independence; to ensure that the terms used are interpreted and applied in a way that captures the spirit of independence—(email from Mr C. Hodge of the FRC to the author confirming this; on file with the author). This contrasts sharply with the approach taken by the NYSE Listing Manual (section 303A.00) that gives detailed guidance on the application of the mandatory corporate governance rules. Arguably because of the non-mandatory nature of the Corporate Governance Code and the absence of any enforcement action by the FSA for explanation failures, companies do not feel concerned that there are any enforcement consequences of non-compliance, and therefore can live with the uncertainty created by these non-defined terms. Where the rules are mandatory and breach may incur consequences, companies would, it is submitted, wish to see more definitional detail than is currently provided by the Code.

[62] They are discouraged only to the extent that if half the board should consist of independent non-executive directors then the more non-independent directors the larger and more ineffective the board.

executive activity to ensure that not only are managerial agency costs minimized but also that executive directors do not collude with significant shareholders and their board representatives to the disadvantage of minority shareholders.[63] This concern is particularly acute where, because of the voting power of the significant shareholders, the executive directors feel that keeping their jobs requires keeping favour with the significant shareholder. Furthermore, in relation to the audit monitoring function of non-executive directors it is clear that significant shareholders may share some of the executive directors' skewed incentives to present the financial statements in a more favourable light,[64] for example, during a period when she is considering selling her shares and where good financial news will increase the share price.

Provision B.1.1 also provides that a director who has served for more than nine years will not be deemed to be independent (unless the board decides otherwise). The idea of this provision is that over time as the relationships between the non-executive directors and executive directors develop those relationships will become cosier and bonds of friendship and fidelity to the board team will build up, compromising the independence which the non-executive director had at the time of his appointment. Professor Elson argued in the extract set out earlier that this was one of the problems that developed on the Enron board. The countervailing argument is that one of the primary problems with independent non-executive directors is that they understand little about the company and its industry and it takes time to develop the necessary knowledge and experience to be effective. By setting a time-period of service beyond which a non-executive director will no longer be independent deprives the company of precisely the types of directors the company wants: informed and independent. If a regulator decides to impose such a time limit the decision as to where to draw the time limit is obviously somewhat arbitrary. The Corporate Governance Code draws the line at nine years.[65]

2 The independence–knowledge trade-off

The previous discussion about the trade-off between director independence and knowledge raised by a non-executive director's length of service leads us more generally onto the two primary problems with independence. The first of these is how to ensure that non-executive directors are informed enough not only to monitor effectively but also to contribute to the board's management function. The 'number of non-executive directors' and the 'definition of independence' issues are concerned with making the board's delegation and monitoring function effective. However, we must not forget—as there is a tendency to do when focusing on composition and structure issues—that an independent non-executive director is a director with the same general power and authority as any other director,[66] and that all directors acting together with one vote each[67] are required to perform all the functions of the board, which includes being responsible for the management of the company. As we have seen, although the

---

[63] On the ways in which majority shareholder can act to the detriment of minority shareholders see Chapter 16.

[64] See further Web Chapter A.

[65] The Higgs Review recommended two terms of three years, which was extended to nine by the FRC following lobbying by business groups. See A. Parker, T. Tassell and A. Jones, 'Higgs Report Concessions Mooted After Backlash By Business' *Financial Times* (8 May 2003).

[66] This point refers to general powers rather than any specific powers that have been delegated to any directors.

[67] Most company articles provide for one vote per director, although they could provide for multiple votes for certain directors or, as is often the case, provide for veto rights in relation to particular decisions for particular directors. The Model Articles for Public Companies provides for one vote per director (article 12(2)) and an extra vote for the chairman of the board if there is a deadlock (article 13).

management function of a listed company board is, due to pragmatic constraints, necessarily limited, it is not irrelevant. Given some of the significant management decisions that a board of a listed company will be required to make, it would clearly be problematic to have a board full of members who do not know very much about the company or its industry.[68] Such members would not be in a position to make an informed contribution to the management function and would necessarily need to rely upon and defer to the executive managers' preferred position. Furthermore, returning to the delegation and monitoring function, an independent director that struggles to understand the company's business will find herself increasingly deferential to management and hesitant to ask any questions that could reveal to other directors her lack of knowledge and understanding.

The broader the definition of independence the more difficult it becomes to find individuals who are willing to serve on the board who know and understand the company and its industry. If the definition of independence results in a shallow pool of available non-executive talent then the selected non-executive directors may struggle to perform their management functions effectively: to make, where required, informed management decisions and to provide valuable advice and counsel to management. The Corporate Governance Code provides in Main Principle B1 that boards 'should have the appropriate balance of skills, experience, independence and knowledge'. Nevertheless, the Code's broad definition of independence elevates the importance of independence over knowledge and takes a risk that the pool of advisory talent will continue to be deep enough. Of course companies that are of the view that the pool of independent board talent with industry knowledge is not deep enough could elect not to comply with the Code and explain the reasons for not doing so. Indeed Sir David Walker in his review of the Governance of Banks stressed the importance of this option for banks, particularly in relation to former employees that do not comply with the five-year rule or existing directors who have been with the company for more than nine years.[69]

The Code also acknowledges the importance of knowledgeable non-executives in its recommendation that non-executives receive a thorough induction to the company[70] and continually update their knowledge and familiarity with the company.[71] The Code provides that 'the chairman should ensure that new directors receive a full, formal and tailored induction on joining the board'. One might legitimately, however, harbour reservations about whether inductions and updates can really address any knowledge deficit.

It is worth noting in this regard that the independence standard in the UK is broader than in other jurisdictions. Consider, for example, the mandatory independence standard for New York Stock Exchange listed companies, which must have a majority of independent directors.[72]

---

[68] As previously noted, some commentators have identified the limited knowledge and experience of banking of the non-executive directors of failed UK banks as one of the causal factors for the current crisis. Whether this is correct clearly requires further investigation.

[69] Walker Review, Final Report (see note 43), at 3.3 and 3.9 observing that 'it cannot be regarded as a satisfactory outcome that the experience of many [Bank] executives is effectively excluded from the industry because they are unable to serve on the boards of the entities from which they retire and will commonly in practice understandably, be reluctant to serve on the boards of entities with which they were in keen competition in their former executive roles.'

[70] UK Corporate Governance Code (2010), B.4 Main Principle. See also FRC, Guidance on Board Effectiveness (FRC, 2011) paras 1.18–1.19.

[71] *Ibid* B.4 Supporting Principle.

[72] New York Stock Exchange Listing Manual, 3.03.A.01 Independent Directors.

■ *New York Stock Exchange Listed Company Manual, 303.A.02 Independence Tests*

(a) No director qualifies as 'independent' unless the board of directors affirmatively determines that the director has no material relationship with the listed company (either directly or as a partner, shareholder or officer of an organization that has a relationship with the company).[73]

(b) In addition, a director is not independent if:

(i) The director is, or has been within the last three years, an employee of the listed company, or an immediate family member is, or has been within the last three years, an executive officer, of the listed company.

(ii) The director has received, or has an immediate family member who has received, during any twelve-month period within the last three years, more than $120,000 in direct compensation from the listed company, other than director and committee fees and pension or other forms of deferred compensation for prior service (provided such compensation is not contingent in any way on continued service).

(iii) (A) The director is a current partner or employee of a firm that is the listed company's internal or external auditor; (B) the director has an immediate family member who is a current partner of such a firm; (C) the director has an immediate family member who is a current employee of such a firm and personally works on the listed company's audit; or (D) the director or an immediate family member was within the last three years a partner or employee of such a firm and personally worked on the listed company's audit within that time.

(iv) The director or an immediate family member is, or has been within the last three years, employed as an executive officer of another company where any of the listed company's present executive officers at the same time serves or served on that company's compensation committee.

(v) The director is a current employee, or an immediate family member is a current executive officer, of a company that has made payments to, or received payments from, the listed company for property or services in an amount which, in any of the last three fiscal years, exceeds the greater of $1 million, or 2% of such other company's consolidated gross revenues.

Whilst the NYSE has had composition rules and independence standards for audit committees since 1978,[74] it only introduced general board composition rules in 2002 following the Enron and WorldCom scandals. Its Listed Company Manual now requires a majority of independent directors.[75] Without considering the NYSE rules in considerable detail, it is clear that its independence tests are much narrower than those set out in the Corporate Governance Code. For example, the Corporate Governance Code has a

---

[73] Note that the specific independence rules in (b) supplement the general principle-based requirement in (a) that the board certify the independence of each member of the board. The commentary to (a) makes it clear that relationships other than those specified in the independence tests may compromise independence.

[74] Requiring an audit committee of independent members. For a brief history of the early development of the role of audit committees for NYSE listed companies see M. Metz, 'Inside the Audit Committee' *Internal Auditor* (October 1993).

[75] NYSE Listing Manual, 303A.01 Independent Directors. Interestingly, whilst listed companies in the US have not had to comply with composition rules until recently, traditionally US company boards have consisted of many more non-executive directors than UK boards prior to composition regulation. In 1988, for example, outside directors made up a majority of boards in 387 of Fortune 500 companies (data from J. Dayha, J. McConnell and N. Travlos, 'The Cadbury Committee, Corporate Performance, and Top Management Turnover' (2002) 57 *Journal of Finance* 461, 462).

five-year bar on former employment, the NYSE three years. Pursuant to the Corporate Governance Code the non-executive directors can receive no additional remuneration if they are to retain their independent status, under the NYSE listing manual such directors can receive up to $120,000. Particularly noteworthy is the absence of two of the contentious provisions in the Corporate Governance Code, namely representing a significant shareholder and board service in excess of nine years' service.[76]

One explanation of the NYSE's more flexible approach to 'independence' is that it reflects a different weighting given to the concern about having a deep pool of non-executive directors who can effectively perform their management and advisory function: a regulatory preference that leans more towards authority than we see in the UK's Corporate Governance Code. An alternative explanation is that if mandatory rules are imposed, as they are pursuant the NYSE's Listing Manual, then the regulator needs to be wary about being too prescriptive. As the Corporate Governance Code is a comply and explain code and as a UK company board can deem a director to be independent even if he does not comply with all the independence tests, this provides the UK regulator with greater scope to be demanding in the knowledge that companies are not barred from appointing a top-class non-executive who does not fully comply with the independence tests. This position holds provided that UK companies are willing, where necessary, to deploy the 'safety valves' that the Corporate Governance Code formally gives them. If this latter explanation explains the difference between these two approaches to 'independence' then we see that the regulatory technique which is deployed—comply and explain versus mandatory rules—may affect the regulator's choice of substantive rule. This also means that if in practice comply and explain rules are treated as mandatory rules then the substantive rules may be inapposite.

3 The structure of the board and the roles of the non-executive director

3.1 The Corporate Governance Code's committee structure

The Corporate Governance Code recommends that premium listed companies have three committees: a nomination committee; a remuneration committee; and an audit committee. It does not recommend a committee of non-executive directors for addressing executive directors' direct conflicts of interest apart from in relation to executive remuneration.

In relation to the nomination committee, Provision B.2.1 of the Code provides that:

> There should be a nomination committee which should lead the process for board appointments and make recommendations to the board. A majority of members of the nomination committee should be independent non-executive directors. The chairman or an independent non-executive director should chair the committee, but the chairman should not chair the nomination committee when it is dealing with the appointment of a successor to the chairmanship.

Typically, therefore, UK listed company nomination committees will be chaired by the company's chairman, which, as we shall see, is typically a different person than the CEO.[77] The CEO in practice is not normally a member of the remuneration committee. But note that although the underlying idea of a nomination committee is to ensure that

---

[76] The commentary to the rules notes explicitly that 'as the concern is independence from management, the Exchange does not view ownership of even a significant amount of stock, by itself, as a bar to an independence finding' (subparagraph (a)).

[77] Note that, whilst it is unusual, in some UK companies both the chairman and the CEO will serve on the nomination committee. This is Code compliant if the committee is expanded to five or more

the board does not feel beholden to executive management, the CEO is not prevented by the Code from serving on the nomination committee. Take HBOS Plc, for example, which, before its collapse and purchase by Lloyds TSB Plc, had a Code compliant nomination committee of six members including both the Chairman and the CEO.[78] Note, further, that the role of the nomination committee is to search for possible directors and make a nomination recommendation to the board; such nomination will then be put forward to the shareholders in general meeting. In theory, the board could reject the nomination committee's recommendation, although such a step would be highly unusual.

In relation to the remuneration committee, Provisions D.2.1 and D.2.2 provide that:

> **D.2.1** The board should establish a remuneration committee of at least three, or in the case of smaller companies two, independent non-executive directors. In addition the company chairman may also be a member of, but not chair, the committee if he or she was considered independent on appointment as chairman. The remuneration committee should make available its terms of reference, explaining its role and the authority delegated to it by the board. Where remuneration consultants are appointed, a statement should be made available of whether they have any other connection with the company.
>
> **D.2.2** The remuneration committee should have delegated responsibility for setting remuneration for all executive directors and the chairman, including pension rights and any compensation payments. The committee should also recommend and monitor the level and structure of remuneration for senior management. The definition of 'senior management' for this purpose should be determined by the board but should normally include the first layer of management below board level.

The Code provides for a typical remuneration committee of up to four members—three independent non-executive directors and the chairman of the board, who may be a member if independent on appointment but may not chair the committee. Note that in contrast to the nomination committee, the Code recommends that the remuneration committee should have 'delegated responsibility for setting remuneration' rather than making a recommendation to the board. We will consider the effectiveness of the remuneration committees in greater detail in Chapter 8.

In relation to the audit committee, Provision C.3.1 of the Code provides that:

> The board should establish an audit committee of at least three, or in the case of smaller companies two, independent non-executive directors. In smaller companies the company chairman may be a member of, but not chair, the committee in addition to the independent non-executive directors, provided he or she was considered independent on appointment as chairman. The board should satisfy itself that at least one member of the audit committee has recent and relevant financial experience.

The audit committee is, therefore, in large companies wholly independent, although in small companies[79] the chairman may also serve as a member of the committee provided he was independent on his appointment. With regard to the financial expertise of the members of the committee, the Code requires only that one member of the committee has 'recent and relevant financial experience'. We look in detail at the role and effectiveness

members with three or more independent directors. See, for example, HBOS Plc's committee structure prior to 2009.

[78] See HBOS Plc Annual Report and Accounts 2006 at 97.

[79] A smaller company is defined by the Corporate Governance Code to be a company that falls outside of the FTSE 350 (Corporate Governance Code (2010), note 6 to B.12).

of the audit committee in Web Chapter A, which considers the governance role of the audit process.

3.2 A comparative note on NYSE committee structure

The New York Stock Exchange's Corporate Governance Rules set out in the NYSE Listing Manual provide for a nomination committee, a remuneration committee, and an audit committee.[80] The NYSE Listing Manual does not provide for how many members each committee should consist of, although in relation to audit committees it requires a minimum of three members. It provides further that all committees must consist *entirely* of independent members.

One further point in relation to the financial expertise of audit committees. Whereas the Corporate Governance Code requires only one audit committee member who has recent and relevant financial experience, the NYSE Listing Rules require that:

> Each member of the audit committee must be financially literate, as such qualification is interpreted by the listed company's board in its business judgment, or must become financially literate within a reasonable period of time after his or her appointment to the audit committee. In addition, at least one member of the audit committee must have accounting or related financial management expertise, as the listed company's board interprets such qualification in its business judgment.[81]

4 Separation of chairman and CEO

4.1 The Corporate Governance Code's separation recommendation

Prior to the introduction of composition and structure regulation in the UK, whilst it was not unusual for the roles of CEO and chairman to be split between different persons, in most UK companies the CEO was also the chairman. In 1988, for example, the CEO also acted as chairman of the board in 328 of the UK's top 500 companies.[82] The Cadbury Committee recommended that 'given the importance and particular nature of the chairman's role, it should in principle be separate from that of the chief executive'. The Committee expressed concern that 'if the two roles are combined in one person, it represents a considerable concentration of power'.

The effect of the Cadbury Committee guidance was to bring about a notable shift towards the separation of the roles of chairman and CEO. By the time of the Higgs Review approximately 90% of listed companies had a separate chairman and CEO.[83] Today the Corporate Governance Code provides a clear statement that these roles should be performed by different persons. Provision A.2.1 provides that 'the roles of chairman and chief executive should not be exercised by the same individual'.[84]

The Corporate Governance Code views the separate chairman as having three primary functions: first, leadership of the board including controlling the board agenda

---

[80] The rules on audit committee composition are set out in Rule 10A-3 issued pursuant to the Securities and Exchange Act 1934, as amended by the Sarbanes-Oxley Act. The NYSE Listing Manual provides directly that audit committees should comply with Rule 10A-3 (Listing Manuel Rule 303A.06).

[81] Commentary to NYSE Listing Manual Rule 303.A.07(a).

[82] J. Dayha, J. McConnell and N. Travlos, 'The Cadbury Committee, Corporate Performance, and Top Management Turnover' (2002) 57 *Journal of Finance* 461, 462.

[83] See Higgs Review, para 5.3.

[84] Until the Higgs Review the Combined Code provided that: 'A decision to combine the posts of chairman and chief executive officer in one person should be publicly justified' (Combined Code 2000, A.2.1).

and meeting process; secondly, ensuring that the non-executive directors are informed and effective; and, thirdly, ensuring good communications with shareholders.[85] The Code provides as follows:

A.3 *Main Principle*

The chairman is responsible for leadership of the board and ensuring its effectiveness on all aspects of its role.

A.3 *Supporting Principle*

The chairman is responsible for setting the board's agenda and ensuring that adequate time is available for discussion of all agenda items, in particular strategic issues. The chairman should also promote a culture of openness and debate by facilitating the effective contribution of non-executive directors in particular and ensuring constructive relations between executive and non-executive directors. The chairman is responsible for ensuring that the directors receive accurate, timely and clear information. The chairman should ensure effective communication with shareholders.

E.1 *Supporting Principle*

Whilst recognizing that most shareholder contact is with the chief executive and finance director, the chairman should ensure that all directors are made aware of their major shareholders' issues and concerns.

E.1.1 *Code Provision*

The chairman should ensure that the views of shareholders are communicated to the board as a whole. The chairman should discuss governance and strategy with major shareholders.

In our general discussion about the advantages and disadvantages of different persons performing the roles of CEO and chairman, we noted that one of the key concerns about splitting these roles was that the CEO would not be able to clearly and efficiently implement his strategy if the chairman of the board overstepped the boundaries of his role and sought to become involved in the management of the business. The Corporate Governance Code is sensitive to this concern and recommends that 'the division of responsibilities between the chairman and chief executive should be clearly established, set out in writing and agreed by the board'.[86]

This 'too many cooks spoil the broth' concern led to a more controversial proposal by the Higgs Review, namely that a retiring CEO should not become the chairman of the board and that the chairman should satisfy the Code's independence criteria at the time of appointment. The Higgs Review noted in this regard that 'having been responsible for the day-to-day running of the company and with the detailed knowledge of it that this brings, such a chairman can sometimes find it difficult in practice to make room for a new chief executive'. However, this proposal created something of a furore in the UK's business community. Many business leaders argued that the company benefited from retaining the knowledge base of the outgoing CEO within the company by making him the chairman of the board on retirement.[87] Whether these objections to the proposal were driven by the potential loss of an expected career path or reflected legitimate concerns is difficult to parse from the debate. However, it is important to note that the idea of an independent chairman put forward by the Higgs Review was not motivated

---

[85] See further FRC, Guidance on Board Effectiveness (FRC, 2011) at 1.4–1.8.

[86] UK Corporate Governance Code (2010) A.2.1. See also A.2 Main Principle.

[87] The Walker Review (see note 43) added weight to these objections by noting in the context of his discussion of the executive director knowledge deficit that 'it is also noteworthy that bank boards where the previous CEO became chairman appear to have performed relatively well both over a longer period and in the recent crisis phase' (at para 3.9).

by concerns about effective monitoring—as is the concern with independence in relation to non-executive directors—rather independence in relation to the chairman was viewed as a way of making the chairman weaker, to ensure that the new CEO could get on with his job.[88] In spite of the objections, the proposal was adopted by the Corporate Governance Code, although amended to take some account of businesses' concerns. The Code now provides that:[89]

> The chairman should on appointment meet the independence criteria set out in B.1.1 below. A chief executive should not go on to be chairman of the same company. If exceptionally a board decides that a chief executive should become chairman, the board should consult major shareholders in advance and should set out its reasons to shareholders at the time of the appointment and in the next annual report.

With regard to the separation of CEO and chairman of the board as well as the appointment of an outgoing CEO to the position of chairman, work by Kirchmaier and Owen, extracted here, casts an interesting light on current UK business opinion on these issues. Their findings are based on interviews with a selection of chairmen from UK FTSE 350 companies.

■ **T. Kirchmaier and G. Owen, 'The Changing Role Of The Chairman: Impact of Corporate Governance Reform in the UK 1995–2005 on Role, Board Composition and Appointment' (2008) 9 *European Business Organisation Law Review* 187**

The chairman/chief executive split
Overall, we found strong but not unanimous support for splitting the roles of chairman and chief executive. It was thought that the tasks of running the board and running the company had become more complex, and more different from each other; it was unlikely that one person would have both sets of skills, or would have sufficient time to do both jobs well.

In what circumstances does the chief executive become chairman?
Only two of the chairmen we interviewed envisaged the possibility that they would be succeeded by their current chief executive, and most of them were emphatic that such transfers should be ruled out. There was, however, a recognition that in some complex and highly regulated sectors—banking, for example, or some high-technology industries—there was a case for retaining the specialist knowledge which the chief executive had built up; subject to other conditions being satisfied (notably an agreed division of roles between chairman and chief executive), that knowledge could be used in the chairman role.

The chairman/chief executive relationship
The effectiveness of the board depends crucially on the relationship between the chairman and chief executive. These two people need to be complementary in skills, experience and personality, and there needs to be total clarity about their roles. Most of the chairmen we interviewed were operating with written job descriptions agreed with the chief executive and approved by the board.

Is the chairman executive or non-executive, and what does independence mean?
A number of our interviewees questioned whether the distinction between executive and non-executive chairmen was helpful or meaningful, and there was also some unease about the word 'independent'. The chairman should not be a detached monitor, but fully committed to the success of the business…

---

[88] *Higg's Review of the Role and Effectiveness of Non-Executive Directors* (2003) para. 5.6.
[89] UK Corporate Governance Code (2010), A.3.1.

Appointing a new chairman

The qualities which chairmen look for in their successor generally include: experience of bottom-line accountability in some form, probably as chief executive or finance director of a quoted company; a track record of making good appointments; experience as an effective outside director of other quoted companies; a feel for the company's business (though not necessarily direct experience of the industry) and an understanding of its culture; and complementarity with the chief executive. The majority view among our interviewees was that, wherever possible, a new chairman should be appointed from among the existing non-executive directors.

Whilst Kirchmaier and Owen found 'strong but not unanimous support for splitting the roles of chairman and chief executive' some commentators have expressed concern that amongst the UK's institutional shareholder and financial media circles that splitting of roles of CEO and chairman is a religion and that most explanations that companies might give for combining the roles in one person are unlikely to receive a favourable hearing. This position is unaltered by recent high-profile banking failures where the bank had a separate chairman and CEO.[90] That is, although the Corporate Governance Code is a comply and explain code, in practice the non-compliance and explanation option in relation to this issue is likely to receive such resistance by institutional shareholders and the financial media that only the hardiest of boards and CEOs will be willing to brave the storm. For most boards, therefore, the Code's separation recommendation will be viewed effectively as a mandatory requirement. A recent example in this regard is the case of Marks and Spencer Plc who in 2008 announced that it would temporarily combine the roles of CEO and chairman by appointing its CEO as executive chairman. Institutional shareholders and much of the media[91] were singularly unimpressed. Consider, for example, the following extract:

■ **K. Burgess, E. Rigby and T. Braithwaite, 'Investor fury at M&S role for Rose'** *Financial Times* **(11 March 2008)**

Marks and Spencer was last night facing an investor backlash after it announced plans to elevate Sir Stuart Rose to executive chairman in clear defiance of the UK's corporate governance code.

Legal & General Investment Management, M&S's second largest shareholder, said the announcement was 'unwelcome', as a broader base of leading shareholders voiced their anger at the move, which reflects the problem the retailer has in choosing Sir Stuart's successor.

'As set out in the Combined Code, we believe strongly in the separation of the roles of chairman and chief executive, believing that this provides a much-needed balance in the boardroom and prevents potentially damaging concentration of power,' said Mark Burgess, head of equities at Legal & General Investment Management.

'This is a very retrograde step,' said another investor. The Association of British Insurers said shareholders were pressing for further explanation. Many big investors complained they were informed of the radical changes only yesterday.

M&S said it had taken the decision to promote Sir Stuart to the post of executive chairman, effective from June…

---

[90] A. Hill, 'RBS Shows Governance is a Work in Progress' *Financial Times* (12 December 2011), observing that an independent chair remains 'a fulcrum of good governance'. See FSA report on the failure of RBS at note 18.

[91] See, for example, LEX *Financial Times* (8 July 2008), arguing against the combination of roles and pointing out by analogy and somewhat melodramatically that 'historians argue persuasively that Europe lurched into the first world war partly because power was concentrated in one leader in Austria-Hungary, Germany and Russia'.

Yesterday Sir Stuart defended the move, insisting that just under 30 per cent of the shareholding base contacted by the company were broadly comfortable with the arrangement…

He argued that he now had '38–40 months' to find a successor, rather than just a year. The change in his role is part of a wider shake-up that will bring a handful of rising stars on to the executive committee. 'I will be fishing below the board and we will see who grows big and strong,' said Sir Stuart.

Lord Burns, the outgoing chairman, said this was the best solution as it kept Sir Stuart on board while creating space for new executives to flex their muscles. 'Stuart has the unique skills to continue the challenge of making M&S a world-class leader, and to develop future leaders for the business,' he said.

But shareholders and analysts yesterday complained the company had failed to manage Sir Stuart's succession effectively.

For a critical viewpoint on investors' reactions to the proposed combination of roles at Marks and Spencer Plc and what those reactions tell us about investors willingness to countenance non-compliance with the separation recommendation, consider the following extract:

■ S. Stern, 'Why M&S shareholders should think before they speak' *Financial Times* (8 April 2008)

Dear Shareholder,

You have asked me to explain my outburst of a few days ago, when I threw down my copy of the Financial Times and declared, to no one in particular: 'Why don't some of these shareholders just shut up?!' I am now writing to provide some detail of my deliberations prior to making that outburst.

We have been told in recent days that the proposed changes in the Marks and Spencer boardroom are 'in breach' of the UK's Combined Code on corporate governance.

Apparently the English word 'or' as in 'comply or explain', has lost its meaning. M&S has, slowly and in stages, provided an explanation. You may not like that explanation. But its move does not necessarily constitute a breach of anything.

Board directors at the company have effectively been dismissed as weak and spineless. Richard Buxton, head of UK equities at Schroders, said the appointment of Sir Stuart Rose as executive chairman would mean 'there isn't going to be any realistic questioning' of the strategy he might choose to set.

Who makes up this lily-livered crew that sits alongside Sir Stuart? Among the non-executives there is Steven Holliday, chief executive of the National Grid. Well, there's a real softie, pushover industry for you. I bet the regulators rub their hands with glee when he enters the room. Mr Holliday did 19 years at Exxon, by the way. The wimp. Another M&S non-exec is Jeremy Darroch, chief executive of BSkyB. Obviously, the way to get to the top of a Murdoch-chaired company is to keep your head down and never express a view on anything. Sir Stuart should see him off without breaking sweat. And as for those key executive directors at M&S—Kate Bostock (clothing), Steven Esom (food) and Ian Dyson (finance and operations)—clearly they will all now sit idly by with no regard to their future, and let Sir Stuart lead the company full speed ahead on to the rocks. Rarely has power been so unfettered.

You will, I trust, forgive this note of sarcasm. But the sound and fury of the past few days now has to be challenged.

What on earth [are we to make] of Peter Chambers, Legal and General Investment Management's chief executive, who said last week: 'We believe we have a moral responsibility to uphold corporate ethics in the UK, and believe that the bellwether companies in the UK share this responsibility to uphold the highest standards of corporate governance…Top FTSE companies ought to adhere to the code rather than go down the 'comply or explain' route.'

> Dear Shareholder, most managers are not knaves. They just want their businesses to do better. What is immoral, or unethical, about the Rose-led turnround of M&S? The 'highest standards of corporate governance' will not be achieved through the unthinking compliance with codes…
>
> Dear Shareholder, there is a time to speak up, but also, assuredly, a time to shut up. In their rush to read the main points of the Combined Code, some shareholders have forgotten about point seven from the Code's preamble:[92] 'Pay due regard to companies' individual circumstances and bear in mind in particular the size and complexity of the company and the nature of the risks and challenges it faces. While shareholders have every right to challenge companies' explanations if they are unconvincing, they should not be evaluated in a mechanistic way, and departures from the code should not be automatically treated as breaches.'
>
> Yours faithfully,
> stefan.stern@ft.com

4.2 A comparative US note on separation of chairman and CEO roles

In 1988, in 387 of the US **Fortune 500** companies the CEO performed the role of chairman of the board. In 2008, in 377 of the **S&P 500** companies the CEO performed the role of chairman of the board.[93] The sea change in the separation of the roles of CEO and chairman that took place in the 1990s in the UK has not taken place in the US. Nor is it likely to. What has taken place in the US over the past 20 years is the introduction of what are called lead or presiding directors.[94] There is no specific requirement in the NYSE Listing Manual for such directors; however, the vast majority of US listed companies have a lead or presiding director.[95] The precise function of a lead or presiding director varies from company to company, however, the general view being that such a director operates as a counterbalance to a CEO/chairman by marshalling the collective strength of the non-executive directors. However, it is also clear that in some companies the lead or presiding director plays a 'chairman-light' role by, for example, being responsible for discussing and setting the board agenda with the CEO/chairman and ensuring that adequate information is provided by management for the board meetings. In this regard consider the following extract from General Motors Inc's *Corporate Governance Guidelines* on the role of its presiding director.

■ General Motors Inc, *Corporate Governance Guidelines*[96]

The Role of the Lead Director
At any time when the Chairman is not an independent director as described in Guideline 11, the Board will designate a Lead Director, elected by and from the independent directors of the Board. The Lead Director will have the duties assigned by the Board, which may include:

- Chairing executive sessions of non-management directors;

- Developing agendas for executive sessions of the Board in consultation with the Chairman and other Board members;

---

[92] This is now set forth in the Corporate Governance Code's section on Comply or Explain, extracted at 254.

[93] See ORC for a report on the statistics produced in this regard by the Corporate Library.

[94] The two terms are used interchangeably.

[95] As of 2005 95% of S&P 500 boards had a lead or presiding director (Spencer Stuart, A Closer Look at Lead and Presiding Directors—see ORC for further information).

[96] http://investor.gm.com/corporate-governance/docs/CG%20Guidelines_03%2015%2011%20 (Final).pdf .

- Leading the non-management directors in the annual evaluation of the performance of the Chairman and CEO and communicating that evaluation to him and management succession plans;

- Reviewing Board meeting agendas, schedules, materials recommended by the Chairman for concurrence;

- Serving as liaison between non-management directors and the Chairman (although all non-management directors have direct and complete access to the Chairman at any time that they deem necessary or appropriate); and

- Serving as the Board's liaison for consultation and communication with major stockholders.

Whilst, as can be seen from this extract, a lead director performs, informally, some of the functions of a non-executive chairman, there is less concern that a lead director will overstep the ambit of her function and interfere with the operational management of the company. The lead director's role is organizational and advisory. As a lead director rather than the chairman she will not feel that she is the public face of the company with particular responsibility for its performance. Furthermore, she has, as compared with the chairman of the board, more limited formal control over board processes which she can use to overreach her given role. However, whilst a lead director is less likely to create a 'too many cooks spoil the broth' problem the informal and advisory role may not sufficiently empower the lead director to operate as a real counterweight to CEO power. The prevailing US governance position on separation has made a policy election that the former concern—allowing CEOs to do their job—should carry more weight than the latter—providing a counterweight to CEO power.

For a sense of the current state of the US debate on the separation of the roles of chairman and CEO and the role of a lead or presiding director consider the following extract.

■ B. Behan, 'Splitting the Chairman and CEO Roles' (2008) *BusinessWeek.com*

U.S. boards typically combine the roles of chairman and chief executive officer, a majority practice among the **Standard & Poor's 1500 composite index** even today. Among the companies that do so, it is also common to appoint an outside independent director to serve as lead director. In Britain, where boards historically have had fewer independent directors than their American counterparts, a different practice arose: that of appointing an outside, independent director as non-executive chair. The question of whether U.S. companies should adopt the British model of separating chairman and CEO roles surfaces every time a corporate crisis erupts in America…

Institutional Shareholder Services' latest survey, released in September 2007, noted that 36% of U.S. institutional investors favored the separation, although 50% found appointment of a lead director entirely satisfactory when the chairman and CEO roles are combined. Does separating the roles really provide better governance, or is it simply window-dressing for shareholders with little impact on board effectiveness? Before deciding what's best for your board, here are some practical implications to consider:

In 2004, the National Association of Corporate Directors (NACD) convened a blue ribbon commission comprised of 50 experienced board members, CEOs, and institutional investors to study the issue. Among the commission's findings:

- One-third had a strong preference for separating the chairman and CEO roles, expressing concerns about the leader of the board (as chairman) also being the employee of the board (as CEO), and advocated the model of a non-executive chair as a best practice;

- One-third had strong reservations about separating the roles and advocated maintaining the current practice of combining them but appointing an outside, independent director as lead director;
- One-third felt it made little difference if independent board leadership was provided by a lead director or a non-executive chair. In this group's view, it was the effectiveness of the individual who provided leadership that mattered, and whether that person carried the title of non-executive chair or lead director didn't matter in the least.

The NACD endorsed the last view above as 'best practice.'

Recent surveys show that more than 70% of the Fortune 1000 now have lead directors. While some U.S. boards have appointed non-executive chairs, this practice has been adopted almost routinely at companies that have been through crises such as Tyco, Marsh & McLennan, AIG, Fannie Mae, and Walt Disney, which tout the separation of the roles as proof of a renewed commitment to good corporate governance.

5 Other Corporate Governance Code recommendations to enhance the monitoring function

The UK's approach to the primary composition and regulation themes have been addressed earlier. There are, however, two other recommendations in the Code which are designed to enhance the non-executive directors' monitoring and delegation function. The first is the recommendation that the chairman and the non-executive directors should meet without the executive directors being present.[97] The Code does not specify how often or how regularly these meetings should take place. The idea of these meetings is clear: non-executive directors may feel more comfortable raising concerns about the executive directors or asking questions that they may feel the executive directors will view as silly or stupid, when the executive directors are not present. However, if the chairman is not independent or, although originally independent, through his close working relationship with the executive directors his independence is diminished, then non-executive meetings with the chairman may not enable the non-executive directors to freely express their views. Non-executive director meetings without the chairman would, therefore, in addition, be beneficial. Indeed, the Code does recommend such meetings, although its recommendations in this regard are somewhat tentative. Provision A.4.2 provides that:

> Led by the senior independent director, the non-executive directors should meet without the chairman present at least annually to appraise the chairman's performance... and on such other occasions as are deemed appropriate.

The leadership role of the senior independent director in this regard is not specified in the Code. It is fair to assume that the senior independent director would: take responsibility for calling such meetings periodically; call such meetings on the request of any other non-executive directors; set the agenda for the meetings; and chair the meetings.

The role of a senior non-executive director was contemplated by the original Cadbury Committee recommendations. However, such a senior non-executive member—as with a lead or presiding director in the US—was viewed as necessary where the roles of CEO and chairman were combined. Following recommendations made by the Higgs Review, the Corporate Governance Code now recommends that there should be a senior independent director whether or not the roles of CEO and chairman are combined.

The Code envisages three roles for the Senior Independent Director. First, the Code provides that the Senior Independent Director should act as a 'sounding board' for the

---

[97] UK Corporate Governance Code, A.4.2.

chairman.[98] What appears to be envisaged here, as outlined more clearly in the FRC's *Guidance of Board Effectiveness*, is that the Senior Independent Director provides a supporting role to the chairman, in carrying out her responsibilities as chairman and also stepping in to resolve any disputes between the chairman and the CEO.[99] Secondly, as we have seen in relation to non-executive meetings, the senior independent director role facilitates the monitoring and delegation function by giving one director responsibility to lead the non-executive team. Note, however, that this role overlaps somewhat with the Code's view of the chairman's function which, amongst others, is to facilitate the effective contribution of the non-executive directors. Perhaps for this reason, the Code is very tentative in setting out the senior independent director's role providing *only* that independent non-executive sessions, which exclude the chairman, should be 'led' by the senior independent director. Thirdly, the Code provides that the senior independent director should be a conduit from shareholders to the board if communication between the CEO and/or the chairman fails to resolve an issue or 'is inappropriate', for example, where the shareholder wishes to discuss the possible removal of the CEO or chairman.

6 The Code and women on boards

Amendments to the 2010 Corporate Governance Code introduced a reference to diversity in the Code for the first time. Whilst the current regulatory debate focuses only on gender diversity, the Code refers to diversity more generally. In Supporting Principle B.2 the Code now provides that:

> The search for board candidates should be conducted, and appointments made, on merit, against objective criteria and with due regard for the benefits of diversity on the board, including gender.

Lord Davies' Review of *Women on Boards*, which we considered previously, was published in 2011. The Review did not recommend the introduction of mandatory quotas for the number of women on boards. Such quotas have been adopted in other jurisdictions.[100] Instead, Lord Davies recommended a 'business-led approach' in which companies themselves respond to his recommendation to increase the representation of women on boards to 25% by 2015. Lord Davies also recommended that the Corporate Governance Code should be amended to recommend that listed companies establish a policy on board room gender diversity. The FRC will implement this later recommendation in a forthcoming 2012 amendment to Provision B.2.4 of the Code, to provide that (the new language is in italics):

> A separate section of the annual report should describe the work of the nomination committee, including the process it has used in relation to board appointments. *This section should include a description of the board's policy on gender diversity in the boardroom, including any measurable objectives that it has set for implementing the policy, and progress on achieving the objectives.* An explanation should be given if neither an external search consultancy nor open advertising has been used in the appointment of a chairman or a non-executive director.

The FRC has made no proposal to include a 25% 2015 target in the Corporate Governance Code. The Government has accepted Lord Davies' 'business-led' approach instead of the imposition of quotas. However, the early signs are that only a minority of companies are

---

[98] UK Corporate Governance Code, A.4.1.

[99] FRC, *Guidance on Board Effectiveness* (FRC, 2011), 1.09–1.10.

[100] Norway have mandatory quotas of 40%. France and Spain also have such quotas. See LEX Column, 'Women on Boards' *Financial Times* (29 December 2011). On the Norwegian experience with gender quotas see 'Getting Women into Boardrooms, by Law' (27 January, 2010) *New York Times*.

taking his call to arms seriously. A 'progress report' published in October 2011 found that only 33 of the FTSE 100 companies had set gender targets for their boards.[101] A failure of companies to respond clearly risks the legislative imposition of quotas. Note also that this issue is on the current agenda of the European Commission who included gender board representation in its recent Green Paper on corporate governance. It seems distinctly possible that, in spite of the UK's business-led approach, the European Union may impose gender representation quotas on all EU Member State listed companies, and that those quotas may well be higher than Lord Davies' 25% target.[102]

Questions

1. What are the functions that we expect non-executive directors to perform?

2. In the 1990s, Calpers, a US pension fund, adopted a policy that its 'ideal board' would consist of all non-executive directors apart from the CEO. Is this, in your view, a good policy?

3. Should all non-executive directors be independent? Are there advantages of having outsiders that may not fulfill the Corporate Governance Code's independence criteria?

4. How independent should a non-executive director be? Do you think the UK Code's broader definition of independence is preferable to the New York Stock Exchange's definition of independence? What, if anything, would you alter in the UK definition?

5. Should the chairman of the board or the CEO be able to sit on the nomination and remuneration committee?

6. Do you think that the Corporate Governance Code's financial expertise requirements for audit committee members are strong enough? What, if anything, would be problematic about adopting the New York Stock Exchange's stronger qualification requirements?

7. Should there be other committees of non-executive directors apart from the nomination and remuneration committees? If so, what should they be?

8. Does the Corporate Governance Code strike the correct balance between the listed company board's management function and its delegation and monitoring function?

9. Should the roles of chairman and CEO be split? Would a US-style lead or presiding director with a combined CEO/chairman be a better solution for UK listed companies?

10. Does it make sense to have a senior independent director for a company that has a separate non-executive chairman?

11. Does the Corporate Governance Code provide for too many cooks that creates a significant risk of spoiling the broth of shareholder value?

12. Do you think the business-led approach to greater female representation on boards is likely to be successful? If Lord Davies is of the view that there are sufficient qualified women to make up 25% of UK boards by 2015, what good reasons, if any, are there for not imposing a quota?

III THE RELATIONSHIP BETWEEN BOARD COMPOSITION REGULATION AND COMPANY PERFORMANCE

As we have seen, for a unitary board composition regulation should ensure that the board can fulfil its dual management and delegation and monitoring mandates. The delegation and monitoring function is of course designed to make the company work well: to ensure that managers generate value with the company's resources and that they

---

[101] 'Boards prove slow to promote women' *Financial Times* (11 October 2011).

[102] See The EU Corporate Governance Framework (Green Paper) (COM, 2011, 164) para 1.1.3; European Commission, 'Gender Imbalance in Corporate Boards in the EU: Questions for Public consultation (5 March 2012)

do not use their power and authority to benefit themselves. A concern which we have raised at several points in this chapter is that board composition and structure regulation must not lose sight of the objective of value generation. We have noted some specific concerns in this regard. For example, in theory, enhancing the independence of the board vis à vis management and other mechanisms of reducing CEO power enhances the board's ability to act to replace underperforming management; however, as we have also noted in detail, composition regulation raises some concerns about the effectiveness of a board with a significant component of independent non-executive directors: will such a board be able to make informed business decisions when asked to do so, or provide good counsel and advice to management; will a separate CEO and non-executive chairman result in a less clearly formed and implemented business strategy?

However, thus far our analysis has consisted only of raising the theoretical pros and cons of specific composition and structure rules. It is very important, therefore, for our assessment of whether composition and structure regulation makes a positive contribution to UK companies to determine empirically whether or not composition and structure regulation enhances or destroys value or simply makes no overall value contribution. To determine this we must turn for assistance to the work of financial economists who try to assess whether there is a positive or negative value correlation[103] with certain types of composition rules, such as the number of non-executive directors or a CEO/chairman separation requirement. That value correlation may be measured by the change in the share price following the adoption of a particular composition rule by a regulator or the company, or could be measured by changes in companies' accounting performance, for example, certain measures of profitability for a period of time following the adoption of the composition rule.

The available UK evidence to determine whether UK composition regulation makes a positive or negative contribution to the value of UK companies is somewhat scarce. However, there is some empirical evidence that the introduction of corporate governance guidelines by the Cadbury Committee is associated with better value creation. In a recent study of the value effects of the Cadbury Committee recommendations, Dayha and McConnell found evidence that firms that adopted the recommended governance practices on average generated more value.

■ J. Dayha and J. McConnell, 'Board Composition, Board Performance and the Cadbury Committee Recommendation' (2007) *Journal of Financial and Quantitative Analysis* 535

During the 1990s and beyond, the global economy has witnessed widespread calls for more outside directors on corporate boards. A presumption that underlies this movement is that boards with more outside directors will lead to better board decisions and, as a result, better corporate performance... In this study, we examine changes in performance directly, but we began with that same level of scepticism. Somewhat surprisingly, we find that UK firms that moved to three outside directors in conformance with the Cadbury Committee recommendation show an improvement in operating performance both absolutely and relative to various peer group benchmarks[104] from before to after moving to three outside directors. We also find that firms that

---

[103] A correlation in statistics is a relationship between variables: one variable moves in response to the change of another variable. A useful basic definition is as follows: 'degree of relationship between two sets of information. If one set of data increases at the same time as the other, the relationship is said to be positive or direct. If one set of data increases as the other decreases, the relationship is negative or inverse' *The Free Dictionary*, http://encyclopedia.farlex.com/.

[104] A 'peer group benchmark' is a set of similar companies that had not moved to three non-executive directors as recommended by the Cadbury Committee.

move to three outside directors have a statistically significant[105] [share] price increase at the time of announcement of this decision. The results strongly suggest that adding outside directors led to improved performance by UK firms and increased value for shareholders. Even, then, however, most UK firms had less than a majority of outside directors—on average, outside directors comprised 44% of UK firms' directors. Thus, one question that our study raises is whether there is an optimal number or fraction of outside directors that may be less than 50% for UK firms.

As we have seen in our analysis in this chapter, the Corporate Governance Code now recommends that at least half of a board's membership consists of independent non-executive directors. The original Cadbury recommendation of three non-executives, two of whom had to be independent, is the subject of the Dayha and McConnell study. Accordingly, whilst Dayha and McConnell's evidence is positive in terms of value creation, it is not clear that we can extrapolate that evidence to the modern day Corporate Governance Code. In the US there is a richer body of work looking at the relationship between value creation and the number of non-executive directors. This work is arguably[106] relevant for the modern day Corporate Governance Code as US boards have had for some time a majority of non-executive directors. The results of this US work are mixed, but overall it suggests that there is no clear evidence that the presence of a majority of non-executive directors correlates with better performance.[107] In an important study Bhagat and Black looked at the long-term performance data of almost 1,000 US companies and found that:[108]

Low-profitability firms respond by increasing board independence. But this strategy doesn't work. Firms with more independent boards don't achieve improved profitability. This suggests that the conventional wisdom stressing the importance of board independence lacks empirical support, and could detract from other, perhaps more effective strategies for addressing poor firm performance.

This US empirical evidence raises the question, as Dayha and McConnell note, whether, although there are some performance benefits to be obtained from having non-executive directors on the board, too many non-executive directors may have value-negative consequences, for example, a deterioration in the effectiveness of the board's managerial and advisory function, which outweigh those benefits. This in turn raises a question of whether UK composition regulation has taken a good idea too far. Much more evidence is needed before we can feel assured about such a conclusion.

As previously noted, an important reason why the presence of non-executive directors may make a positive contribution to value is that their presence increases the likelihood that underperforming managers will be removed. There is some support for this view

---

[105] For our purposes 'statistically significant' is large enough that it is unlikely (usually less than 5%) that it is just a chance result.

[106] Any attempt to extrapolate findings from the US to the UK must be treated with caution. As we have already seen in Chapter 6 the context of corporate law within which US composition regulation operates is very different to that of the UK and therefore limited weight must be given to US evidence on the effects of one similar aspect of composition regulation.

[107] D.R. Dalton, C.M. Daily, A.E. Ellstrand and J.L. Johnson, 'Meta-Analytic Reviews Of Board Composition, Leadership Structure, And Financial Performance' (1999) 19 *Strategic Management Journal* 269 reviewing the various studies in question and finding no correlation between outside directors and positive performance.

[108] B. Bhagat and B. Black, 'The Non-Correlation Between Board Independence and Long-Term Firm Performance' (2002) *Journal of Corporation Law*. Note, however, that the outside non-executive directors which form part of this study may not have all complied with strict independence criteria, as independence criteria for US listed firms set forth in the NYSE's Listing Manual during the time of the study only applied to the non-executive directors that sat on the audit committee.

from work carried out by Dayha, McConnell, and Travlos in relation to the changes introduced by the Cadbury Committee:

■ **J. Dayha, J. McConnell and N. Travlos, 'The Cadbury Committee, Corporate Performance, and Top Management Turnover' (2002) 57 *Journal of Finance* 461**

We initiated this study with a degree of scepticism...We were...sceptical as to whether the observed changes in board composition would lead to changes in corporate decision making or to a change in the relationship between corporate performance and top management turnover. Part of our scepticism may stem from the mixed results of prior studies on board composition and management turnover. For example, for 367 publicly traded US companies, Weisbach[109] determines that CEO turnover is more highly negatively correlated with performance in firms with outsider-dominated boards. Contrarily, for 270 publicly traded Japanese companies, Kang and Shivdasani[110] find that the sensitivity of CEO turnover to performance is unrelated to the fraction of outside directors. Finally, Franks, Mayer and Renneboog[111] examine CEO turnover for a sample of poorly performing U.K. firms for the period 1988 through 1993. They are unable to draw definitive conclusions as to whether or not CEO turnover is more sensitive to performance when the board comprises more outside directors. The other part of our scepticism largely stems from our general expectation that, prior to Cadbury, market forces were likely to have propelled boards toward efficient structures. Thus, we are surprised to observe a significant increase in management turnover following Cadbury adoption, to find an increase in the sensitivity of management turnover to corporate performance following Cadbury adoption, and, especially, to find that the increase in sensitivity of turnover to performance is due to an increase in outside board members. These results are consistent with, and support, the argument that the Cadbury recommendations have improved the quality of board oversight in the United Kingdom.

With regard to the performance effect of separating the CEO and chairman, the evidence from the US and the UK is that separation does not have any positive performance impact nor,[112] perhaps more surprisingly, does it appear to increase the likelihood of CEO turnover.[113] Interestingly, however, recent US research suggests that the extent of CEO power vis à vis other executive directors does affect the variability of firm profitability—both up and down. That is, companies with more powerful CEOs have a disproportionate weighting in the companies that outperform but also in the companies that underperform. The suggested reason for this is that where a group of executives rather than the CEO alone make the decisions, the decisions are likely to filter out the more risky alternatives because of the difficulty of getting agreement amongst all the executives. The more risky decisions taken by more powerful CEOs will have more variability in terms of payoff. To test for the effect of CEO power on performance, the authors of this research use several indicators of power that we have considered in

---

[109] M.S. Weisbach, 'Outside Directors and CEO Turnover' (1988) 20 *Journal of Financial Economics* 431.

[110] J.-K. Kang and A. Shivdasani, 'Firm Performance, Corporate Governance, and Top Executive Turnover in Japan' (1995) *Journal of Financial Economics* 38.

[111] J. Franks, C. Mayer and L. Renneboog, 'Who Disciplines Managers in Poorly Performing Companies' (2001) 10 *Journal of Financial Intermediation* 209.

[112] N. Vafeas and E. Theodorou, 'The Relationship Between Board Structure and the UK' (1998) 30 *British Accounting Review* 383.

[113] The UK empirical evidence in this regard is very sparse: J. Dayha, J. McConnell and N. Travlos, 'The Cadbury Committee, Corporate Performance, and Top Management Turnover' (2002) 57 *Journal of Finance* 461 noting that splitting the responsibilities of the CEO and Chairman between two individuals appears to have had no effect on the rate of CEO turnover. There is, however, some recent evidence from the US of a positive correlation between separation of CEO and chairman roles and CEO turnover: see V. Goyal and C. Park, 'Board Leadership Structure and CEO Turnover' (2002) 8 *Journal of Corporate Finance* 49.

this chapter including: whether or not the CEO and chairman roles are separated; the number of executive directors on the board; and whether he is the founder of the firm. The authors of this research conclude that all these indicators of CEO power affect the variability of performance—up and down—but the strongest factor in this regard is the separation of the roles of CEO and chairman. They conclude as follows:

■ **R. Adams, H. Almeida and D. Ferriera, 'Powerful CEOs and their Impact on Corporate Performance' (2005) 18** *Review of Financial Studies* **1403**

> It is important to stress that our interpretation of these results does not depend on the existence of an agency problem. Even if managers are benevolent, corporate decisions may be good or bad because managers have different opinions. This raises the question of whether the concentration of power in the hands of the CEO is good. The governance literature argues that it is not, and advocates the separation of the CEO and Chairman of the Board positions. Although this is not the main focus of this article, we find no evidence that firms with powerful CEOs have on average worse performances than other firms. Instead, our results suggest that firms with powerful CEOs are those with the worst, but also with the best performances. Thus, one important implication of our findings is that any policy recommendations for the design of governance structures should not be based on the consideration of isolated cases of extreme performances. In addition, our results point out one potential cost of diluting CEO power: although performance will be less variable, the probability of spectacular performance will be lower.

Although this evidence is based on US company data and therefore does not necessarily apply to the UK context, for this author it makes intuitive sense for the UK as well. If this evidence is correct, and if it applies to the UK, it reaffirms the importance of the fact that UK composition and structure regulation is optional if a company has a good reason not to comply with it. If, for example, the shareholders have a higher risk profile or the industry in which the business operates is a business that requires greater risk-taking to survive then electing not to comply with the Corporate Governance Code's recommendation to separate the roles of chairman and CEO may make good sense.

As we have seen, the idea that companies should adjust their governance arrangements to fit them not to fit a norm of best practice underpins the Corporate Governance Code: companies should comply or explain.[114] However, if, as we saw earlier, market conditions constrain in practice a company's ability to not comply with the recommendation and explain non-compliance, then corporate value creation in the UK will suffer if an alternative arrangement such as a joint CEO/chairman is preferable for a firm but is not selected because of compliance pressure. As we saw in the context of the Marks and Spencer Plc's executive chairman debate, such compliance pressure clearly exists in the UK. If such compliance pressures cannot be mitigated then an important and open question for UK composition and structure regulation is whether it would be better in relation to some rules to go back to the pre-1990s position and have no rule at all.

 Online Resource Centre
http://www.oxfordtextbooks.co.uk/orc/kershaw2e/

Visit the Online Resource Centre for additional resources and information available for this chapter, including web links and an interactive flashcard glossary.

---

[114] See S. Arcot and V. Bruno, *One Size Does not Fit All, After All: Evidence from Corporate Governance* (Working Paper: See ORC for link to this): 'Our analysis provides support for the principle that in corporate governance regulation one-size-does-not-fit-all. We find that companies that depart from best practice because of genuine circumstances outperform all others. On the contrary, mere adherence to general accepted principles of good corporate governance is not necessarily associated with superior performance.'

CHAPTER EIGHT

REGULATING DIRECTORS' REMUNERATION

I INTRODUCTION

1 The objectives of remuneration

Every employer has an ideal of how she would like her employees to behave. It is a simple ideal consisting of two elements: in her working hours for the employee to do her best; to do her utmost to perform the functions given to her within the constraints of her applicable intellectual, educational, and physical capabilities; in her working hours to act in the interests of her employer not in her own interests—not to take excessive breaks; not to arrive late and finish early; not to work slower than she could work because she went out too late the night before; not to make personal phone calls or treat the office stationery cupboard as her own stationery cupboard. Every employer recognizes that every employee has a capability constraint. So whilst it is important for the employer that the 'ideal employee' maximizes her efforts within her capability constraint, it is equally important for the employer that she finds a person who—when maximizing—can perform all the functions that must be performed by the job/the position in question. No matter how hard a person tries and how loyal that person is, if she does not have the skill set to perform the job, the job will not get done.

The problem for an employer then is twofold: how to attract the person with the right skills to do the job properly and then, once employed, how to get that employee to behave like an 'ideal type employee'. In this regard there are several tools available to the employer to get the chosen employee to behave like an ideal employee. One way would be to try to instill in the employee the expectations of the employer from the first day and regularly thereafter: to appeal to the employee's sense of duty and obligation. Another way is to make it clear to the employee that if she does not perform close enough to the 'ideal-type employee' then she will lose her job. Another way is to offer carrots instead of sticks. For employees carrots take two forms—remuneration and promotion: more salary; a bonus on hitting certain targets or promotion to a more senior level which will also bring with it more salary and higher possible bonuses etc. For an employer all these factors will be part of her design of the best—the optimal—set of carrots and sticks to generate behaviour that approximates to 'ideal employee behaviour'. For each one of the available sticks and carrots the question for the employer is how to design that carrot and stick to generate 'ideal employee behaviour'. The design will vary depending on the job and the firm.

At this conceptual level of the role of remuneration in attracting the person with the talent and skills to do the job and getting that person to behave like an 'ideal employee' once in the job, a company's senior management—the executive directors—are no different than any other employees. Companies want to attract managers who can deploy the company's resources to generate the most value from those resources. Once in the job, remuneration should incentivize the manager to do his utmost to use his skills and experience to maximize the value that can be generated from the company's resources and not to use his power and those resources in ways that benefit himself. That is, remuneration for executive directors must be sufficiently attractive to:

- first, attract managers who have the skills and the talent to maximize the available value from the company's resources;
- secondly, to ensure that managers when in the job do everything within their capability constraints to maximize the value available from the company's resources; and
- thirdly, which follows from the second requirement, to ensure that the power and authority given to senior management is not abused, either directly or indirectly, to benefit themselves at the company's expense. That is, remuneration should as far as is possible align managers' and shareholders' interests so that a manager acting in the company's interests is also acting in his own interests.

2 The executive remuneration problem

The board appoints senior management and as part of that process will enter into a service contract with managers which will contain an agreed remuneration package. The Model Articles for Public Companies, for example, provides that the board of directors may delegate their powers on 'such conditions...as they think fit'.[1] Yet, as we have seen, executive directors wield considerable power, particularly in a widely-held company. If the executive directors wield significant influence on the board, then if the board is responsible for awarding their remuneration it follows that they wield significant influence in the setting of their own salaries and benefits. If they influence the setting of their own pay then it is highly probable that, acting in their own financial interests, they will pay themselves more than the market rate. As J. K. Galbraith put it: 'the salary of the Chief Executive Officer...is frequently in the nature of a warm personal gesture by the individual to himself'.[2] High levels of executive pay from this view come to look like an agency cost in and of themselves. Indeed, the 'market rate' itself may be infected with managerial agency costs. Even where a board of directors sets executive pay without any self-serving influence from management they will, quite reasonably, look to see what other CEOs in similarly situated companies earn. However, if those 'other company CEO pay-levels' are a product of, amongst others, executive director self-interested influence then the reference point of 'what other CEOs are paid' is a distorted one.

For the outsider it is difficult to know whether executive directors' pay and benefit levels reflect an attempt to use salaries to attract talent and to incentivize that talent or whether they represent an abuse of managerial power. In this regard, regulators need to be cognizant of the fact that running large companies is an exceptionally demanding and difficult job; that to do the job well requires a skill set and character traits that most of us do not possess and *cannot* learn—just as most of us cannot learn how to be professional sportsmen—and a commitment to one's working life and a willingness to sacrifice one's personal life that most of us—perhaps wisely—would not be willing to make. To recruit and retain individuals with such skill sets and levels of commitment is difficult and, necessarily, very costly. However, given the potential influence of executive directors over the pay-setting process, hidden within the costs of recruiting and retaining such individuals may well be managerial agency costs; and the claim that the required talent is rare and expensive is always available as a cover for such managerial agency costs. This problem becomes particularly acute when executive pay is increasing rapidly which, as we shall see, has been the case in the UK over the past decade. If pay increases are explained by companies' search for talent and attempts to incentivize that talent then regulators have no need to concern themselves with or interfere in the pay-setting process. However, if such factors cannot account for pay and benefits increases

---

[1] Model Articles for Public Companies, article 5.
[2] J.K. Galbraith, 'What Comes After General Motors' (2 November 1974) *The New Republic*.

then logically such increases are explained by either executive director influence or some other flaw in the pay-setting process and we need to consider what regulatory tools could be deployed to control such inappropriate influence by executive directors.[3]

Given the clear *potential* for abuse where a board of directors on which managers sit sets the pay of those managers, one might readily conclude that regulatory steps to reduce the potential for abuse should be taken in any event even if we cannot be sure that high or increasing pay levels are not simply the pay required to attract and incentivize talent: better, a regulator might say, safe than sorry. A caveat, however, needs to be registered in this regard. Such a 'better safe than sorry' approach is fine provided that regulation does not interfere with a company's ability to pay executive directors what they need to pay them to recruit the right people, to incentivize those people to do the job, and to retain those people. If regulation does interfere with the recruitment and retention process the cost to UK companies could be considerable. The value for the company that could be lost by having sub-optimal management talent or sub-optimal incentives for those managers will far exceed any agency costs hidden in most executive pay packages.

II THE TYPES AND TRAJECTORY OF REMUNERATION FOR EXECUTIVE DIRECTORS

1 Types of executive pay and benefits

There are two key components of remuneration for executive directors of UK companies: salaries, and performance-based remuneration. Salaries provide executives with regular and guaranteed payments. However, salaries alone may not encourage a manager to maximize his effort for the benefit of the company. If a manager is paid with a salary alone and knows that if he works at 80% of his capacity he will still receive his salary and will keep his job, then he has no incentive to work at 100% of his capacity. If he does give 100% effort, where he is paid by salary alone his remuneration will not change to take account of the additional value that his efforts have generated for the company. That extra 20% of time and effort at work away from his family or the golf course will benefit the company but not himself. His personal incentives are, therefore, not aligned with those of the shareholders. To encourage the manager to give that extra 20% of effort, he needs to be personally rewarded for any benefits that the extra 20% of effort brings to the company. That is, there needs to be a *performance-related* component of executive pay to maximize the executive's efforts: if increased effort generates value for the company his remuneration should increase accordingly.

Performance-related pay, therefore, goes some way to aligning managers' and shareholders' incentives. This is particularly the case in relation to indirect agency costs such as shirking—not working hard enough—but also in relation to managerial agency costs incurred through hubris, investment policy, and empire building. If pay is connected to performance then managers are less likely to make bad investments for self-interested reasons—because although running a larger company as a result of those bad investments may make managers feel more important it will also make them poorer. However, whilst performance-based remuneration goes some way to aligning incentives and can, therefore, reduce managerial agency costs it is only a partial solution to the managerial agency cost problem. In relation to other types of more direct agency cost—such as corporate opportunities and self-dealing—performance-related pay alone will not be sufficient to control such costs as the pay-off for managers who self-deal

---

[3] For a more detailed account of the factors that may—in addition to the abuse of managerial power explanation—make a contribution to explaining executive director pay levels see R. Thomas, 'Explaining the International CEO Pay Gap: Board Capture or Market Driven' (2003) 57 *Vanderbilt Law Review* 1171, an extract from which is set forth in section II.2 of this chapter.

or personally exploit the corporate opportunity may exceed what they would gain in performance-related pay had the company entered into the contract on arm's length terms or exploited the opportunity itself.[4]

There are three types of performance-related pay: performance cash bonuses on hitting specified targets related to profitability or share price; grants of share options; and grants of actual shares on hitting specified targets. Performance cash bonuses incentivize good performance by encouraging the manager to do everything necessary to hit those targets. Performance grants of shares work in this way as well. Performance grants of shares also ensure that, provided targets are attained, the manager builds up a significant shareholding stake in the company so that his personal wealth is connected to the company's share price. Typically it will not be possible for the shares granted to the manager to be sold for several years (usually three years) after they are issued.

The targets selected as the trigger-points for receiving the cash or share bonuses will typically involve one or a combination of the following financial targets:

- accounting targets—for example growth in certain measures of profitability such as **EBIT** or **EBITDA** as measured against the number of issued shares—this is referred to as earnings per share or EPS;
- share price targets which measure the overall growth in the company's share price over a given period of time; or
- a measure known as **total shareholder return** which determines the return to shareholders over a period of time by aggregating the increase in the share price over this time and the value of any dividends paid during this period.

However, performance targets for companies may be more nuanced than simply financial and accounting targets. Today it is common for cash bonus performance targets to include business objectives[5] and non-direct financial factors such as customer and employee satisfaction targets, and the company's record on risk management, health and safety, employee relations and environmental and community issues.[6]

Share options granted to managers give those managers the option to buy a certain number of shares in the company at a specified price, known as the exercise price. The exercise price will typically be the price of the company's shares at the time the share option is granted to the executive director. The share options create a performance incentive for the executive directors because if the price of the company's shares rises above the exercise price then the manager makes a profit: he could exercise his options at the exercise price and sell the purchased shares at the higher market price. Typically share options will provide that the options to buy the shares cannot be exercised for a period of time known as the vesting period, which, for UK companies, is typically three years after the grant of the options. This ensures that the manager has incentives to generate value for a longer period of time and to ensure that the share price stays above the exercise price for this period. The granting of share options may also be linked to the types of performance criteria referred to earlier.

The central problem with performance-based remuneration is that whilst a manager should be compensated for the increase in company value *that his efforts* create, he should not be compensated for any increase in company value that has nothing to do with his efforts. If an oil company's share price increases by 25% because of an increase in the price of oil, not because of the CEO's efforts, should he be rewarded with a cash or share bonus or be allowed to exercise his options? Of course, in practice it is rather difficult to know

---

[4] On self-dealing and corporate opportunities see Chapters 13 and 14 respectively.

[5] See PwC, *Executive Compensation: Review of the Year 2009*, 70 observing that 'the use of shared non-financial measures focusing on the specific business goals for the year as well as individual performance goals continues to gain in popularity'.

[6] *Ibid*, 63.

whether an increase in value is the product of the CEO's efforts or external factors such as the price of oil and the general economic well-being of the company's markets. One way of attempting to identify the contribution made by the manager is to compare the selected accounting or share price target with other companies that operate in the same industry as the company in question: the company's *peer group*. With this approach to assessing performance, if the share price increases by 25% but peer group company share prices increase on average by 20% then the CEO's efforts have made the 5% difference and his bonus should be determined by reference to the 5% figure not the 25% figure; if peer group company share prices increase on average by 40% then the CEO should get no bonus.

However, in setting the performance target and the connection to peer-group performance, companies need to be careful that they do not discourage managers from maximizing performance. Consider, for example, a company which may not have performed as well as its peer group—let's say 5% less share price growth—but without the exceptional efforts of the CEO the performance of the company would have been significantly worse—let us say 15% less. In such circumstances, the CEO has generated 10% of value but a bonus arrangement linked to peer-group performance will provide him with no bonus. If this is the case the CEO's pay arrangements provide him with no incentive to generate that 10% of value. Slavish adherence to peer-group targets may in some companies, therefore, incentivize sub-optimal performance by executive directors. Furthermore, in selecting a peer group a company needs to be wary of the risk profile of that peer group. If selected peer group companies take excessive risks to generate short-term returns at the risk of their long-term survival then managers will either be forced to replicate high-risk strategies or accept that they will underperform this peer group and receive no performance-related pay. Consider in this regard banks that selected comparator banks which had highly risky business models such as Lehman Brothers, HBOS, RBS, or Northern Rock as their peer group companies.

Whilst performance-related pay—calculated relative to a peer group or absolutely—clearly has the potential to incentivize managers to generate value, we must be aware of the risk that taking performance-related pay too far may, as odd as this may sound, have negative performance effects. We see this when we consider the question of how much, if any, remuneration should a director who is removed from office receive for loss of office when the company has failed to hit performance targets during his tenure. Should there be any *rewards for failure*? Through the lens of performance-related pay it would be perverse, and contrary to the policy underpinning performance-related pay, to reward a failing, leaving director. Such a remuneration arrangement would incentivize an executive director to underperform in the knowledge that he could walk away in any event with a remuneration package. Clearly this is correct if the rewards following failure are too large; however, it does not follow that the rewards for failure should be zero or even insubstantial.

As we shall consider in greater detail when we look at directors' duties in Chapters 9–14, managers make decisions that necessarily involve risk. Risky decisions, although they may be good decisions, necessarily contain some probability of failure; some probability, for example, that an investment will be lost or have a negative value by incurring losses for the company in excess of the original investment. Shareholders want managers to take business decisions that may involve some risk of failure but have, for the company, a positive **expected value**. A director who worries about losing his job if the decision turns out badly may not take the types of risky decisions that the company should be taking. He may become too risk-averse, preferring options that are less risky—more likely to have a positive outcome—but which have a lower expected value than the rejected, riskier options. As we saw in Chapter 6, the formal exposure to being removed from office for a UK director is high given the mandatory, simple majority shareholder removal right provided by section 168 of the Companies Act 2006.[7] As we

---

[7] Removal of an executive director from office will result in his dismissal as a senior manager either automatically or as a result of board action shortly thereafter. See Chapter 6.

noted, this generates some concern that directors may act in a more risk-averse fashion. This risk-averse sensibility is likely to be more pronounced if a director knows that if the decisions turn out badly then not only will he be removed from his position with his reputation sullied but that he will leave with no or a limited remuneration package to soften the blow. That is, putting in place some rewards for failure that cushion the blow of removal may encourage directors to take the more risky—*but positive expected value*—projects that shareholders would want the company's managers to take when thinking ex-ante about how they would like the managers of the company to behave.

There are four ways in which remuneration can be used to compensate removed executive directors. First, a contract of employment that following termination might provide the director with a claim for breach of contract for remuneration for the remaining period of the contract[8] or the unexpired notice period. An executive director with a contract with three years to run or which requires three years' notice would receive three years' of pay on being removed.[9] Secondly, there may be a fixed severance lump-sum payment. Thirdly, there may be the immediate vesting of any options that have been granted. Fourthly, payments into the executive director's pension fund may enable him to draw the pension on losing his job even when he is significantly below normal retirement age.[10] If the risk-taking concern is legitimate, then companies in organizing their remuneration arrangements for executive directors need to ensure that any remuneration following failure is not so large that it incentivizes underperformance by managers and yet gives them a sufficient cushion to incentivize appropriate risk-taking. It is clearly a very difficult regulatory tightrope to walk.

2 The structure and trajectory of executive pay for listed companies

Traditionally salary has been the most important component of UK listed company executive remuneration arrangements. However, share options also have a long pedigree and have been commonly used since the 1980s. In the 1990s, following public and political concerns about rising executive pay, the Confederation of British Industry (CBI) set up the Greenbury Committee to review UK executive pay practices. The Greenbury Report registered certain concerns regarding stock-option grants, in particular the fact that, as noted previously, they often reward directors for fortuitous increases in share price. The report encouraged companies to consider other types of *long-term incentive plans* which 'typically reward directors with a predetermined number of shares or cash amounts, rather than share options, if certain challenging performance criteria are fulfilled'.[11] The report also encouraged companies to ensure that any share option grants had longer-term incentives by ensuring they did not vest for a minimum of three years. These recommendations are now embedded in the UK Corporate Governance Code 2010, the relevant provisions of which provide as follows:

> A significant proportion of executive directors' remuneration should be structured so as to link rewards to corporate and individual performance[12]...The performance-related elements of executive directors' remuneration should be stretching and designed to promote the long-term success of the company[13]...

---

[8] Some executive contracts may be rolling contracts that never expire as the length of the contract is renewed each day. A rolling one-year contract will always have one year to run.

[9] *Southern Foundaries v Shirlaw* [1939] 2 All ER 113. If an executive director has no service contract or that contract does not set forth a contract term and a notice period, and the articles of the company provide for the termination of the managerial position on the removal from office, then termination of the management position does not amount to a breach of contract: *Read v Astoria Garage (Streatham) Ltd* [1952] 1 All ER 922.

[10] On leaving his position as CEO of the Royal Bank of Scotland, Sir Fred Goodwin, aged 50, drew a pension of approximately £693,000 a year. 'Goodwin stands firm on 16m RBS pension' *Financial Times* (26 February 2009).

[11] Greenbury Report, para 6.31.   [12] UK Corporate Governance Code, D1 Main Principle.

[13] *Ibid* D1, Supporting Principle.

The remuneration committee should consider whether the directors should be eligible for benefits under long-term incentive schemes. Traditional share option schemes should be weighed against other kinds of long-term incentive scheme...In normal circumstances shares or other forms of deferred remuneration should not vest, and options should not be exercisable, in less than three years. Directors should be encouraged to hold their shares for a further period after vesting or exercise, subject to the need to finance any costs of acquisition and associated tax liabilities[14]...

Payouts or grants under all incentive schemes, including new grants under existing share option schemes, should be subject to challenging performance criteria reflecting the company's objectives, including non-financial performance metrics where appropriate.[15]

The effects of this guidance on executive pay practices was notable resulting in a significant increase in the use of long-term incentive plans, colloquially known as LTIPs, and a decrease in the use of share options. LTIPs typically provide for grants of shares which are contingent on hitting certain performance targets. The most typical performance targets involve growth in earnings per share (EPS) or what is known as 'relative total shareholder return' which measures the total shareholder return from the gain in the share price as well as any dividends paid by the company as compared to a chosen peer group of companies.

There are three central themes in the trajectory of UK executive remuneration arrangements over the past 20 years: first, overall remuneration has increased markedly and at a far quicker rate than remuneration levels for other company employees; secondly, in the past 10 years the percentage of performance-related pay making up overall pay levels has increased notably; thirdly, remuneration for leaving directors that have failed to hit performance targets ('rewards for failure') has decreased which, in particular, is due to a decrease in the typical notice period for executive service contracts. Research by Conyon and Sadlers in both 1997 and 2003 provides useful data on CEO pay in this regard.[16] Table 8.1 details the average pay of CEOs of UK companies and the breakdown of pay into its component parts of salary, options, LTIPS and bonus in both 1997 and 2003.

Table 8.1 *Average pay of CEOs of UK companies and the breakdown of pay into its component parts*

| | Sample | Average Total Pay (£000s) | Median Total Pay (£000s) | Average Composition of Pay | | | | |
				Base Salary	Annual Bonus	Option Grant	LTIP Shares	Other Pay
United Kingdom								
Largest 200 firms: 1997	187	£955	£768	52.38	17.50	9.60	16.29	4.23
Largest 200 firms: 2003	176	£1,691	£1,290	40.56	22.04	11.34	20.07	5.99
Percentage change		76.95%	67.92%	−22.57%	25.95%	18.17%	23.19%	41.60%

[14] *Ibid* Schedule A; paras 2 and 3.

[15] *Ibid* Schedule A; para 5. Note that the introduction to non-financial metrics is a new addition to the 2010 Code.

[16] M. Conyon and G. Sadler, 'How Does UK and US CEO Pay Measure Up' (2005, Working Paper on file with the author).

These statistics detail a significant 77% increase in average CEO pay over a six-year period, but a decline in this period of 22.5% in base salary and significant increases in all the performance-based components of pay: bonus; option grants; and LTIPs. More recent, post-2003 developments show a marked decline in the number of companies making use of share options. In 2003, 90% of FTSE 100 companies used share options; by 2007 this had been reduced to 40%.[17] However, post-2003, apart from option grants, all components of executive pay—base salary, bonus, and LTIP grants—have increased. In this regard consider Figures 8.1, 8.2, 8.3, and 8.4, taken from PwC's Executive Remuneration report for 2009 relating to changes in base pay, bonus, and LTIPs:

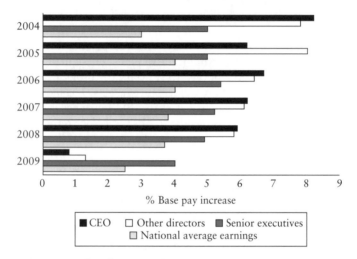

Figure 8.1 *FTSE 100 median base pay increase*
Source: Annual reports, PwC-Monks database

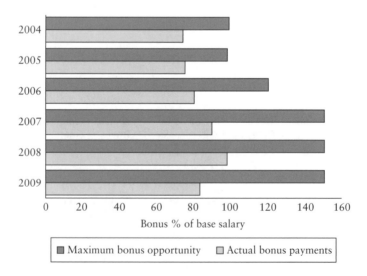

Figure 8.2 *Annual bonus trends—median FTSE 100 CEO*
Source: Annual reports, PwC-Monks database, IVIS

[17] PwC, *Executive Compensation: FTSE 100 Review of the Year 2007*, 7. Note that the PwC, *Executive Compensation: Review of the Year 2009*, 64 observes that the decline in the use of share options 'has slowed since the dramatic falls in the middle of the decade'. See also S. Pepper, *Senior Executive Reward: Key Models and Practices* (Gower, 2001).

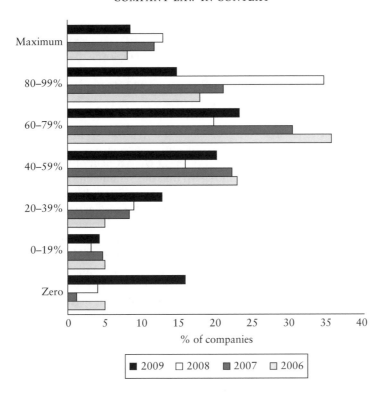

Figure 8.3 *Distribution of Annual Bonus Payouts (as a % of maximum)*

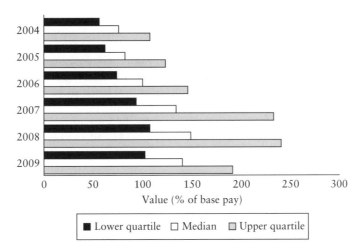

Figure 8.4 *Long-term incentive grants (economic values) FTSE 100 CEOs*
Source: Annual reports, PwC-Monks database, IVIS

We see clearly from this data that, apart from in 2009, overall pay levels have been increasing year on year at a significant rate, at a rate of increase far in excess of the inflation rate and average pay increases for other UK employees during this period of time.[18] It should be noted that 2009 was a year in which the UK economy suffered a

---

[18] During 2000–2009 the UK's inflation rate varied between an annual low of 0.7% in 2001 to a maximum of 5% in September 2008 (www.watsonwyatt.com/europe/pubs/statistics/render2.asp?ID=1 😊).

post-financial crisis recession. By way of contrast, in 2010, CEO pay of FTSE 100 companies was reported to have risen by 43%.[19] As of 2010, UK average executive director pay was 120 times higher than the pay of an average employee in the UK,[20] an increase from 80 times in 2002.[21] The High Pay Commission[22] observed that in 2011 BP's CEO earned 63 times the average worker, whereas in 1980 the figure was 16.5.[23] In relation to Barclays Bank, the Commission reports that the respective figures are 75 and 14.5 times, and that between 1980 and 2011 the pay of Barclays' CEO has increased by 4,899.4%.[24] Importantly, executive pay growth has not simply outstripped the pay growth of the average worker, but has significantly exceeded stock market returns when compared to the stock market as a whole. A recent Department of Business consultation paper on executive pay observes in this regard that the 'remuneration of FTSE 100 CEOs rose annually by 13.6% on average between 1999 and 2010. By comparison, an average annual increase of 1.7% in the FTSE index was observed across the same period'.[25] However, we need to take care with these broad brush performance comparisons. This period looks at market movements between the stock market's peak during the 1990s' technology stock bubble, which burst in 2000, with the post-credit crisis stock market. Furthermore, as we observed earlier, although one will find individual companies who underperform compared to their CEO's average pay inflation, we do not know what role, if any, the extra effort exerted by the CEO resulted in better performance than would otherwise have occurred.

With regard to length of executive director service contracts during this period we have seen widespread adoption of one-year service contract periods, as is recommended by the UK Corporate Governance Code.[26] Institutional investors have been very active in ensuring compliance with this recommendation.[27]

The crucial question for UK regulators is what explains this notable increase in executive pay. Is it explained by the market forces of supply and demand for managerial labour: the difficulties in recruiting and retaining individuals that have the necessary skill sets to do the job properly? Alternatively, is it explained by abuse of managerial influence in the pay-setting process—managers effectively giving themselves a pay rise—or some other flaw in the pay-setting process? The answer to this question is, somewhat frustratingly, that we do not know. Many scholars, regulators, and governments, driven by a sense of 'outrage' about both the recent pace of executive wage inflation as well a sense of 'outrage' about the actual levels of pay—even for successful CEOs—have readily reached the conclusion that the primary explanatory factor is abuse of managerial power in a context in which—because of rational apathy and collective action problems—those managers are not held to account either by shareholders or by boards who have failed to ensure that companies get value for money from their executives.

[19] B. Gavron and C. Tugendhat, 'We have to tackle the issue of executive pay' *Financial Times* (8 December 2011).

[20] P. Moxey, 'Time for boards to take sensitive line on executive directors' pay' *Financial Times* (28 November 2006).

[21] B. Groom, 'Executive Pay: The Trickle-Up Effect' *Financial Times* (27 July 2003).

[22] The High Pay Commission is not a Government body and its report was not commissioned by the Government. It was established by Compass, a pressure group for 'the Democratic Left', with the support of the Joseph Rowntree Charitable Trust.

[23] The High Pay Commission, *Cheques with Balances: Why Tackling High Pay is in the National Interest* (High Pay Commission, 2011) available at: http://highpaycommission.co.uk/wp-content/uploads/2011/11/HPC_final_report_WEB.pdf 🌐.

[24] During which period the High Pay Commission reports that average wages increased by 400% (at 7).

[25] Department of Business, Executive Remuneration: Discussion Paper (2011) at 11.

[26] UK Corporate Governance Code, D.1.5.

[27] See, for example, the institutional shareholders' position in relation to Tesco's CEO's two-year contract in 2003: M. Dickson, 'Tesco and the winds of political correctness' *Financial Times* (13 June 2003).

However, we must be wary of simply dismissing market-based accounts of pay inflation and pay levels. In this regard consider the factors outlined by Professor Thomas in the following extract, who is concerned with the factors that explain the significantly higher levels of pay for US executive directors as compared to those elsewhere in the world, including the UK. These factors are, however, equally relevant to answering the question of whether pay inflation in the UK is explained by the search for talent or the unchecked abuse of managerial power.

■ R. Thomas, 'Explaining the International CEO Pay-Gap: Board Capture or Market Driven' (2004) 57 *Vanderbilt Law Review* 1171

One of the most puzzling aspects of executive remuneration is the pay gap that exists between American and foreign Chief Executive Officers (CEOs). US CEOs are paid vastly more than their foreign counterparts: they have higher base salaries, they receive larger bonuses, they get more stock options, and they are given bigger chunks of company restricted stock. Commentators and the financial press have been quick to claim that such differences can be explained by 'Board Capture,' a theory that claims powerful American executives take advantage of weak domestic boards of directors and passive, dispersed shareholders to overpay themselves exorbitantly.

According to Board Capture theorists…CEOs orchestrate the appointments of their obedient subordinates as inside directors and of friendly, passive outside directors. The net result is a board comprised of compliant directors and a Remuneration Committee[28] that lacks the aggressive hard-nosed negotiators needed to keep executive pay in check. To make matters worse, the Remuneration Committee's advisors, usually paid consultants from a handful of well-known firms, have conflicts of interest that preclude them from giving truly disinterested advice. They tell directors to rely upon industry surveys of pay levels that have the (un)intended consequence of constantly ratcheting executive pay levels upward. American CEO pay levels have skyrocketed, they claim, as a result of this process…

In the wake of Enron, Global Crossing, and the host of other financial scandals, and the anecdotal evidence surrounding the abuse of corporate perks and remuneration schemes that has surfaced in their wake, Board Capture Theory has caught the public's attention. Executive remuneration has been painted as the symbol of out-of-control greed in corporate America. People here and abroad want to believe that American CEOs have been playing a one-sided game, and have been winning without really having to work hard for their pay. Board Capture Theory provides an argument supporting these claims.

This Article…is critical of the Board Capture explanation and offers several more plausible market-based theories that explain this phenomenon…This Article offers [four][29] alternative theories that justify higher pay for American CEOs than for foreign top executives. It argues that each one of these theories—Marginal Revenue Product Theory, Tournament Theory, Opportunity Cost Theory…and Risk Adjustment Theory—present better explanations for the international CEO pay gap than Board Capture Theory.

The Article starts with the Marginal Revenue Product Theory, which rests on the economic concept that each factor of production, including managerial labor, should be paid the amount of its contribution to the value of the firm; that is, its marginal revenue product. This theory claims that American CEOs should be paid more, on average, than foreign CEOs because American CEOs contribute more to their firms' value…

The second theory, the Tournament Theory, explains the international pay gap as a product of the workings of corporations' internal labor markets. In these markets, top executives' pay is the prize that is awarded to the winner of the internal labor market tournament. The tournament to

---

[28] 'Compensation committee' is the US term for remuneration committee.

[29] A fifth theory, bargaining theory, which relates to the use of takeover defences has been deleted from this extract due to its lack of relevance in the UK, as takeover defences cannot be deployed in the UK without shareholder approval—See Rule 21 of the UK Takeover Code and Chapter 11.

win these prized positions is analogized to a single elimination tournament in sports like tennis, where the winner is given by far the largest sum of prize money. The bigger the tournament is, the bigger the prize...

The third theory is based on the economic concept of **opportunity costs**. Opportunity costs in this context can be thought of as the amount that would be paid to a CEO in her best alternative job. The Opportunity Cost Theory recognizes that CEOs and other top executives are able to jump ship from their own firms and move to other companies, hoping to get better jobs and higher pay. In order to keep managerial talent in place, firms must pay their best executives an amount at least equal to their opportunity costs, or they will leave and go elsewhere...

The opening up of financial markets since the early 1980s has given...CEOs better access to capital markets for financing their own businesses, raising the value of their alternative opportunities. This occurred first through the use of the **leveraged buyout** (LBOs and **MBOs**) as a method of financing a new firm, then with the tremendous growth in venture capital financing for start-ups, and later on (at least for a period of years) when the technology boom made available massive amounts of capital to finance 'dot com' companies. Today, LBOs have returned to popularity, and are once again fueling the demand for top executives. Established American businesses that wish to compete for managerial talent are forced to offer their executives larger pay packages to keep them from being lured away by the newcomers.

The [fourth] theory, Risk Adjustment Theory, points out that...CEOs receive more of their pay in the form of stock options [and other forms of performance-based remuneration], and probably hold more of their wealth in company stock, than do foreign CEOs. Holding large amounts of options to buy their firm's stock and being forced to hold unbalanced personal investment portfolios create large risks for American CEOs. Their lack of diversification can be very costly to them, and they justifiably seek to be compensated for these risks. In other words, companies are forced to pay them more in order to get them to place all of their eggs in the firm's basket...

Although all of the theories may be right to some extent, so that executive pay is determined both for economic reasons and by American executives' power to obtain a disproportionate share of their firm's rents, more research needs to be done to understand the dynamics of this market before governments rush in and intervene.

Each of these market-based factors not only *may* explain why US CEOs are more highly paid than their non-US counterparts, but more importantly for our purposes may also make a contribution to explaining increasing and very high UK executive director salaries. To what extent they make a contribution in practice we would need to know: whether UK executive marginal product contribution has been increasing in recent years; whether, as in professional sports, the market for executive talent has become more like a tournament in the UK; whether the employment options for managers outside of listed companies have expanded as a result of **leveraged buyouts** by **private equity** firms; and whether UK CEOs feel like they take more personal risk in the company as a result of the increasing levels of performance-related pay. We do not have the time to explore these issues in depth in this book. However, it is fair to say that on the current rather limited state of UK research[30] we simply do not know. Importantly, this also means that the UK regulators do not know either.

---

[30] See, for example, M.J. Conyon, 'Executive Compensation and Consultants and CEO Pay' (2011) 64 *Vanderbilt Law Review* 399; B. Main et al, 'The Remuneration Committee and Strategic Resource Management' (2008) 16 *Corporate Governance: An International Review* 225; Buck, A. Bruce, B. Main and H. Udueni, 'Long Term Incentive Plans, Executive Pay and UK Company Performance' (2003) 40 *Journal of Management Studies* 1709; M.J. Conyon, S. Peck and G. Sadler, 'Corporate Tournaments and Executive Compensation: Evidence from the UK' (2001) 22 *Strategic Management Journal* 805; M.J. Conyon, S. Peck and G. Sadler, 'The Structure of Executive Compensation Contracts: UK Evidence' (2000) 33 *Long Range Planning* 478; M.J. Conyon, 'Corporate Governance and Executive Compensation' (1997) 15 *International Journal of Industrial Organization* 493.

III LEGAL STRATEGIES TO ENSURE THAT PAY IS NOT A MANAGERIAL AGENCY COST

As we have seen, a unitary board of directors consists of executive directors and non-executive directors. The board is typically authorized to delegate power to senior management and to set the terms of that delegation, including pay. Accordingly, the board is authorized to agree remuneration arrangements for the executive directors who themselves serve on the board. It would not be surprising, given such a dynamic, to find that the structure of executive pay and increasing pay levels contained a managerial agency cost component. In spite of the existence of market-based explanations of UK executive pay discussed earlier, UK regulators have in recent years viewed these increases primarily through the lens of managerial abuse of power coupled with the failure of shareholders to hold managers accountable. This has resulted in several waves of regulation over the past two decades. As of writing, the post-crisis regulatory and public mood is one of 'lost patience' with executive pay. As a recent PwC report on executive pay observes 'the public...see executive pay as nothing other than a gravy train—pay regardless of performance rather than pay for performance'.[31] We can expect this public view to continue to drive current political and regulatory responses and can expect an additional wave of regulation over the course of 2012–13.

To date UK regulation has responded to the view that pay inflation is explained by managerial abuse of power and the lack of shareholder-driven accountability in three ways. First, through composition and structure regulation it attempts to reduce executive influence over the pay-setting process by transferring board authority over pay to a remuneration committee consisting of independent non-executive directors. Secondly, in part because of government dissatisfaction with the apparent ineffectiveness of independent remuneration committees, in 2002 the Government introduced a further regulatory strategy in the form of mandatory extensive disclosure of the details of directors' remuneration arrangements—known as the *Directors Remuneration Report*—coupled with a shareholder non-binding advisory vote on the report as a means of enabling the shareholders' voice to be heard on the remuneration issue. The third strategy deployed by UK law is more direct and rigid than board process and disclosure regulation. This involves rules that require shareholder approval for certain types of remuneration arrangement. These approaches are discussed in turn in this chapter.

To date the UK has not completely prohibited any type of remuneration or imposed any form of cap on the extent of remuneration. Whilst the threat of such more extensive regulation looms over executive pay arrangements and, at times, this threat is explicitly deployed by governments, in reality the likelihood of such regulatory intervention is low. Whilst a prohibition or cap would indeed prevent the incurrence of agency costs, the rigidity of such mechanisms would run the risk that companies could not attract the talent needed to run the company.

1 The regulation of conflicts of interest and executive directors' pay

We shall see in Chapter 13 that company law adopts several strategies for addressing situations in which directors enter into agreements with the company—which we refer to as self-dealing. The common law default rule was that such contracts were void in the absence of shareholder approval. Companies typically amended the default rule to require disclosure of the director's interest in the transaction and to provide for a vote only of the disinterested directors in relation to the transaction. As we shall see in

---

[31] PwC, *Executive Compensation: FTSE 100 Review of the Year 2009*, 6.

Chapter 13, section 177 of the Companies Act 2006 has now made board disclosure the default approach. Any contract of service or agreement to pay an executive director remuneration is of course a self-dealing contract. However, section 177 excludes from the disclosure requirement any contract of service that has been considered by the board or a committee of the board previously. The details of this provision do not, therefore, concern us in relation to executive remuneration conflicts of interest.

2 Remuneration committees

The UK Corporate Governance Code recommends that the authority to set pay arrangements is transferred to a remuneration committee staffed with three independent non-executive directors.[32] The Code also gives companies the option of allowing the chairman of the board to be a member of the remuneration committee provided that he was independent at the time of his appointment and does not chair the committee. In theory, management influence over the setting of their own pay is thereby reduced. These structure and composition recommendations provide, *in theory*, for an arm's length negotiator with management in relation to executive pay issues. The remuneration committee assesses the requirements of the role in question and obtains information on market rates for the position and then it negotiates with management to obtain a good deal for the company: a deal that correctly incentivizes management but does not pay more than is necessary.

Whilst the Corporate Governance Code's recommendations aim to create an arm's length pay-setting process uninfluenced by management, several commentators have expressed doubts about the ability of independent remuneration committees to function in this ideal fashion. These commentators argue, first, that in practice management will continue to exert influence over the pay-setting process; and, second, that the make-up of the independent committee and the dynamics of the pay-setting process results in a bias towards higher executive pay.

In relation to management influence, we need to note first that the chairman of the board will often be a member of the remuneration committee. Whilst the chairman of the board may have been independent when appointed, he will work closely with management and may well over time develop close bonds of affinity and loyalty with the management team. In relation to the independent directors, as noted in Chapter 7, even though these directors may have been nominated through the independent nomination committee process, management is likely to have played an important role in advising the committee on the nomination recommendation. Even formally independent directors may, therefore, feel an element of gratitude to management in relation to the appointment. Bebchuk, Fried, and Walker note in this regard that:[33]

> It is well known that individuals working within a group feel pressure to placate group members, often at the expense of interests that are not directly represented at the table. The relationship between the CEO and the board is also likely to produce additional dynamics specific to that particular setting. Main, O'Reilly, and Wade[34] have found that directors are influenced by notions of reciprocity, authority, and similarity in their deliberations concerning executive remuneration.[35] Specifically, they find that remuneration committee chairmen who are appointed after the CEO takes office tend to reciprocate by awarding higher CEO remuneration.

---

[32] UK Corporate Governance Code (2010), D.2.1; extracted at p 264.

[33] L. Bebchuk, J. Fried and D. Walker, 'Managerial Power and Rent Extraction in the Design of Executive Compensation' (2002) 69 *University of Chicago Law Review* 751.

[34] B. Main, C. O'Reilly and J. Wade, 'The CEO, the Board of Directors and Executive Compensation: Economic and Social Perspectives' (1993) 11 *Industrial and Corporate Change* 293.

[35] In the extracts from Bebchuk et al, *ibid*, the word 'compensation' is replaced by the UK term 'remuneration'.

Upward pay pressure may also be generated by the fact that many wholly independent remuneration committee members will also be CEOs of other companies. CEOs may be subject to what Bebchuk, Fried, and Walker refer to as 'self-serving dissonance':

> It has been suggested that a CEO benefits when a well-paid CEO of another firm sits on the remuneration committee. If so, this phenomenon could be viewed as pure self-interest: by approving high remuneration for the evaluated CEO, the outside CEO increases the remuneration baseline. Alternatively, it may be seen as a form of cognitive dissonance wherein the outside CEO internally justifies his high pay and that of the subject CEO by viewing the remuneration data in the most favourable light.

As the members of the remuneration committee are unlikely to be experts on market pay rates for executives, it is important that they obtain data on the pay of managers in similar positions. Often this will involve instructing an external pay consultant to provide them with this information. The Corporate Governance Code recommends that any such consultant should be appointed by the remuneration committee, which, in theory, ensures that such consultants view the remuneration committee and not management as their client.[36] However, several doubts have been raised about the effectiveness and independence from management of such consultants. Whilst appointed by the remuneration committee the remuneration consultants may provide other consulting services to the company which are within management's gift and may, accordingly, not have a clear sense that their client is the independent remuneration committee rather than management. These concerns have led to the recent formation of the Remuneration Consultants Group,[37] whose sole aim is the maintenance of a voluntary code of conduct for remuneration consultants advising UK listed companies. The Code addresses, in notably scant detail, issues such as the avoidance of conflicts of interest and the provision of services with due care.[38] It is difficult to imagine that a Code of this nature, which is limited in detail and is subject to no enforcement mechanism, will have any greater effect on consultants' management and avoidance of conflicts of interest than the (existing) fear of actual government regulation itself. Such regulation could provide, for example, that consultants should have no other business relationships with the company.

One concern about the use of remuneration consultants is that they simply feed a ratcheting-up process whereby the excessive pay arrangements for managers in Company A are used to support excessive pay arrangements in Company B.[39] The Corporate Governance Code warns remuneration committees about this 'ratcheting' danger:

> The remuneration committee should judge where to position their company relative to other companies. But they should use such comparisons with caution, in view of the risk of an upward ratchet of remuneration levels with no corresponding improvement in performance.[40]

If remuneration committees, directed by their consultants, are too focused on what other companies do and simply adopt industrial and market practice 'with a little extra' to please or attract management, whilst the individual remuneration decisions of companies

---

[36] Corporate Governance Code (2010), Supporting Principle D.2.

[37] The Group was formed following a recommendation in the Walker Review of the corporate governance of banks and other financial industry entities (2009) available at: http://webarchive.nationalarchives.gov.uk/ + /http://www.hm-treasury.gov.uk/d/walker_review_261109.pdf. ☺

[38] Voluntary Code of Conduct in relation to Executive Remuneration Consulting in the United Kingdom, Fundamental Principles.

[39] A. Hill, 'Fewer Experts, Lower Pay' *Financial Times* (30 October 2007) arguing that remuneration committees should take pay consultants' reports 'with a large pinch of salt'. F. Guerrera, 'Investors warn on the use of pay consultants' *Financial Times* (2 November 2006). For a strong rebuttal of this position see the PWC, *Executive Compensation: Review of the Year 2009* at 46–7.

[40] UK Corporate Governance Code (2010), D1 Supporting Principle.

may avoid public scrutiny, over time UK managers pay will rise.[41] Such rises will not reflect performance or, in any significant respect, agency costs, but will paradoxically be the product of informed decision-making coupled with the fear of investor and public approbation. In this regard, Professor Brian Main has recently argued that such 'market mimicking' is the primary driver of pay inflation:[42]

> The remuneration committee has available to it abundant information on what and how rival companies are paying their directors.[43] It also finds itself at the centre of a highly visible and, at times, contentious process of determining directors' remuneration. Caught between providing the directors of the company with remuneration arrangements that leave them satisfied in the light of what they see rival companies doing, and being accountable to shareholders at the next AGM, the remuneration committee tends to revert to an isomorphism of practice and mimics what others are seen to be doing. But owing to the essentially Prisoners' Dilemma[44] aspect of such decisions, they err on the side of generosity. In a playing out of the law of unintended consequences, directors' remuneration in large UK companies is set to continue to drift upwards in the near future.

In addition to structuring the pay-setting process, the Corporate Governance Code also provides more specific guidance for remuneration committees on the actual form of the pay arrangements. This includes, for example, the recommendations that: pay arrangements should be subject to challenging performance criteria;[45] service contracts should not exceed one year;[46] consideration should be given to the part payment of the annual bonus in shares;[47] only salary should be pensionable;[48] and any options or grants of shares should be phased rather than awarded in one block and should not vest or be exercisable in less than three years.[49]

3 Disclosure and shareholder voice

In 1995 the Greenbury Report recommended that UK companies provide disclosure in their annual report about the company's remuneration policy and provide details of the remuneration arrangements for each individual director. The Greenbury Report recommended significant levels of disclosure about the different components of pay and the relationship between pay and performance.[50] These recommendations were incorporated into the Corporate Governance Code's predecessor, the Combined Code.

The idea behind such disclosure is a familiar one: disclosure makes it easier for shareholders to have an informed view on the company's executive pay arrangements and to judge whether such arrangements reflect an abuse of managerial power or are arrangements appropriately tailored to attract the best managers and maximize the efforts of those managers.[51] Disclosure reduces the costs for shareholders of gathering information about pay and thereby facilitates shareholder action. It also facilitates media

---

[41] Detailing the pressures for remuneration committee members to conform see B. Main, C. Jackson, J. Pymm and V. Wright, 'The Remuneration Committee and Strategic Human Resource Management' (2008) 16 *Corporate Governance: An International Review* 225.

[42] B.G.M. Main, 'Executive Pay—A Career Perspective' Hume Occasional Paper No 89 (The David Hume Institute, 2011).

[43] See section III.3 in this chapter on disclosure of remuneration information.

[44] In part because the remuneration committees often make their decisions without knowing what other companies will decide in the current year. See further Main n 42 at 9.

[45] UK Corporate Governance Code (2010), D1 Main Principle.

[46] UK Corporate Governance Code (2010), D.1.5.

[47] UK Corporate Governance Code (2010), Schedule A, para 1.

[48] UK Corporate Governance Code (2010), Schedule A, para 8.

[49] UK Corporate Governance Code (2010), Schedule A, paras 3 and 6.

[50] Greenbury Report, Recommendations, Section B.

[51] For a more detailed general discussion of disclosure see Web Chapter A.

coverage of pay arrangements enabling societal objections to excessive rewards—the outrage factor[52]—to play a role in controlling pay arrangements.

In the UK, neither an enhanced role for remuneration committees nor increased disclosure by companies resulted in a decrease in executive pay inflation. As we have seen, executive pay has increased markedly over the past decade. Interestingly, in the view of some market participants and commentators, increased disclosure has not dampened pay inflation, rather it has accelerated it. A report by Clarke, Conyon, and Peck in 1999 found that half of the chairmen of UK companies thought that pay disclosure had resulted in an increase in pay levels.[53] The reason for this was that it has contributed to the ratcheting effect, discussed earlier, whereby managers expect to be paid, and remuneration committees consider it reasonable and, from a retention and public relations perspective, safer to pay as well as or just slightly better than executives at other companies.

The previous Labour Government's view of the continued increase in executive pay levels was that the remuneration committee and disclosure approach was not, as suggested by Clarke, Conyon, and Peck, a contributory factor in executive pay inflation, rather that the existing regulatory approach was too weak to address pay inflation effectively. In particular, the Government at the time expressed concern about the failure of institutional investors to act to control what the Government and the media viewed as pay excesses.[54] Although initially expressing a preference for a market-based solution the Government showed the market place the 'red card'[55] in relation to pay regulation and introduced secondary legislation in the form of the Directors' Remuneration Regulations 2002 which amended the Companies Act 1985. These provisions are now in Part 15 of the Companies Act 2006 and Schedule 8 of 'The Large and Medium Sized Companies and Groups (Accounts and Reports) Regulations 2008'.

As a result of these reforms remuneration disclosure is no longer an optional comply-or-explain obligation; it is now a mandatory requirement for listed companies.[56] This disclosure must now be set out in a Directors' Remuneration Report that is approved by the board of directors.[57] The Regulations require significant disclosure regarding remuneration policy as well as the specific details of the nature and extent of each individual director's remuneration including salaries,[58] share options,[59] long-term incentive plans,[60] pension,[61] and any remuneration that would be paid following loss of office.[62] For a sense of the extent of the disclosure that is required in the Directors' Remuneration Report consider the following provision of Schedule 8 of the 2008 Regulations.

---

[52] Bebchuk et al, note 34.

[53] M.J. Conyon, R.N. Clarke and S.I. Peck, 'Corporate Governance and Directors' Remuneration: Views from the Top' (1998) 9 *Business Strategy Review* 21.

[54] See, for example, Vodafone-Airtouch's payment of £9 million of bonus payments to three directors to reward them in relation to their efforts in Vodafone's acquisition of Mannesman. See 'Vodafone Finds Little Reward in a Bonus' *Financial Times* (15 July 2000).

[55] The *Financial Times* reported the Government 1999 position as follows: 'Following a stream of disclosures of multi-million pound pay schemes for executives at the UK's biggest companies, Stephen Byers, the trade and industry secretary, has decided the government needs to make clear its disapproval. "Business has been shown the yellow card, a warning that we do not like what is going on," said one of his colleagues. "The question is when we show the red card." ' (R. Preston and D. Wighton, 'Byers seeks to halt big rises in boardroom pay' *Financial Times* (16 February 1999).)

[56] This requirement is now set out in section 420 of the 2006 Act. Failure to comply with the obligation is a criminal offence. The regulations apply to 'quoted companies' (Regulation 11). A quoted company is defined in section 385(2) CA 2006 Act and includes a UK company with a listing on the LSE's main market, in an European Economic Area state or on the New York Stock Exchange or is admitted for trading on Nasdaq.

[57] Section 422 CA 2006.

[58] Paragraph 6 Schedule 8 The Large and Medium Sized Companies and Groups (Accounts and Reports) Regulations 2008/410.

[59] Paragraphs 8 and 9 *ibid*.   [60] Paragraphs 11 and 12 *ibid*.

[61] Paragraph 13 *ibid*.   [62] Paragraphs 6(1)(b) and 15 *ibid*.

■ The Large and Medium Sized Companies and Groups (Accounts and Reports) Regulations 2008/410 Schedule 8

3. *Statement of company's policy on directors' remuneration*

(1) The directors' remuneration report must contain a statement of the company's policy on directors' remuneration for the following financial year and for financial years subsequent to that.

(2) The policy statement must include—

(a) for each director, a detailed summary of any performance conditions to which any entitlement of the director

    (i)   to share options, or

    (ii) under a long-term incentive scheme, is subject;

(b) an explanation as to why any such performance conditions were chosen;

(c) a summary of the methods to be used in assessing whether any such performance conditions are met and an explanation as to why those methods were chosen;

(d) if any such performance condition involves any comparison with factors external to the company

    (i)   a summary of the factors to be used in making each such comparison, and

    (ii) if any of the factors relates to the performance of another company, of two or more other companies or of an index on which the securities of a company or companies are listed, the identity of that company, of each of those companies or of the index;

(e) a description of, and an explanation for, any significant amendment proposed to be made to the terms and conditions of any entitlement of a director to share options or under a long term incentive scheme; and

(f) if any entitlement of a director to share options, or under a long-term incentive scheme, is not subject to performance conditions, an explanation as to why that is the case.

(3) The policy statement must, in respect of each director's terms and conditions relating to remuneration, explain the relative importance of those elements which are, and those which are not, related to performance.

(4) The policy statement must summarise, and explain, the company's policy on—

(a) the duration of contracts with directors, and

(b) notice periods, and termination payments, under such contracts.

As the directors' remuneration report is prepared under the control of management and the board there is a risk that board conflicts of interest may distort the disclosure process. Accordingly, the Directors' Remuneration Regulations 2002 introduced an element of third-party verification of the remuneration report in the form of a requirement that the company's auditors attest that the aspects of the remuneration report which set out the specific details of directors' remuneration are consistent with the company's accounting records and have been properly prepared in accordance with the Act.[63]

As already noted, one of the primary drivers which led to the introduction of the Directors' Remuneration Regulations 2002 was the Government's position at the time that institutional shareholders were not making use of the information about pay disclosed to them by acting to control the excesses of executive pay. The response provided by the Directors' Remuneration Regulations 2002 was to provide for a mandatory shareholder vote to approve of Directors' Remuneration Reports. This requirement is now set

---

[63] Section 497 CA 2006.

out in section 439 of the 2006 Act. However, whilst a shareholder vote is required, the vote itself is only an advisory vote. This means that even if the shareholders reject the remuneration report, the vote has no direct consequence for the validity of any arrangements that have been agreed with directors, and it does not require the board to take any action in relation to any proposed remuneration arrangements.

By providing for an advisory vote the Act provides a focal point for shareholder voice. As we have noted on several occasions, shareholders in companies that are widely-held, even those with a substantial institutional investor presence, are subject to different forms of rational apathy and collective action problems that disincentivize them from acting. Whilst a required advisory vote does not dissolve these disincentives, it does provide shareholders who wish to express their voice with a focal point around which objections can coalesce and a focal point which encourages the financial press to pay attention. In some scholars' view this facilitates what is referred to as the 'outrage' factor—expressions of 'outrage' that pay contravenes both societal and shareholder value expectations.[64]

One might ask why the Government elected to make the vote an advisory rather than a binding vote; after all a binding vote would have enhanced shareholder power in this regard. The answer appears to be that an advisory vote, whilst enhancing shareholder power, does not excessively interfere with the board's ability to negotiate pay arrangements with its executives. In relation to the hire of a new executive in particular, if any agreement reached was subject to a shareholder veto, it could undermine the company's ability to recruit that person.

It does mean, however, that in theory the board of directors could ignore an advisory vote that rejected the directors' remuneration report. In practice this has not happened. On the contrary, boards of directors have been very sensitive and responsive to negative sentiment expressed by shareholders and the press in the run-up to the advisory vote and have responded immediately in the few instances where the shareholders have rejected the directors remuneration report. Indeed, recent empirical work on the effectiveness of the advisory shareholder vote has found that it operates as an effective way of ensuring compliance with the recommendations set out in the Corporate Governance Code.[65] The advisory vote appears to have galvanized institutional shareholder activism in relation to a range of pay issues, most importantly relating to remuneration upon termination. This was seen most clearly in relation to rejection of the GlaxoSmithKline Plc's 2002 directors' remuneration report. In this regard the institutional investors were concerned about what the media described as the CEO's platinum golden parachute—that is, very favourable remuneration on the termination of the CEO's employment. In this regard consider the following editorial opinion of the *Financial Times*.

■ **'Parachute holed: GSK must respond to shareholder concerns on executive pay'** *Financial Times* **(20 May 2003)**

Jean-Pierre Garnier's platinum parachute is in tatters after GlaxoSmithKline's annual meeting yesterday. Shareholders mounted a serious rebellion against the company's executive remuneration policy, and in particular the severance package in the chief executive's contract. Although the vote is not binding, the GSK board can no longer ignore the opposition to the policy.

This is not the first setback for the board. In November, it was forced to withdraw proposals for a new remuneration package for Mr Garnier that investors saw as too generous, overly

---

[64] K. Sheehan, 'Is the Outrage Constraint an Effective Constraint on Executive Remuneration? Evidence from the UK and Preliminary Results from Australia' (2007) available at http://papers.ssrn.com/sol3/papers.cfm?abstract_id=974965 ◔; and 'K. Sheehan, Say on Pay and the Outrage Constraint' (2010) available at SSRN: http://ssrn.com/abstract=1679622 ◔.

[65] See Sheehan *ibid*.

complicated and badly timed. This time, shareholders rebelled over several aspects of the 'platinum parachute' Mr Garnier would be entitled to if he lost his job.

One is that he is entitled to two years' notice. It is almost eight years since the Greenbury report recommended a maximum 12 months' notice for executives—a period that still allows failed executives to leave with big sums in compensation.

Second, Mr Garnier would receive two years' pay and bonuses. The bonuses would be calculated as if he had hit his targets, and would thus be 100 per cent of basic salary. He would therefore walk away with four times his basic pay of $1.5m (£920,000)—a generous reward for failure if that were the cause of his departure.

Next, he would be eligible for share entitlements under the plans for US executives of the group for a further year. If he left after the share price had plummeted and his successor managed to restore it, he would benefit.

Fourth, his pension would be topped up with another three years of contributions. And when it came to paying the pension, the amount to be paid would be boosted by treating Mr Garnier and his wife as three years older than their actual ages.

In his letter to shareholders, Sir Christopher Hogg, GSK's chairman, warned that global companies must remain competitive in the remuneration they offer to top executives. The application of UK 'cultural attitudes' in companies that are big in the US could leave them vulnerable in a country where traditionally pay has been higher than in Europe.

There is nothing new in this, however. US executives in many British companies routinely earn more than their UK counterparts, and it is not unusual for some to earn more than British-based board members. And as the Financial Times said at the time of last year's storm over Mr Garnier's pay package, there is nothing wrong with high pay—so long as it is linked to outstanding performance.

Rightly, investors will no longer stomach generous payments for failure—wherever executives are based. The debate is not about how much they are paid, but what they are paid when they have failed. GSK investors have sent an important message to the company's board and to the wider corporate world.

The activism and media coverage surrounding GlaxoSmithKline's advisory vote in 2003 appears to have been something of a watershed resulting in the subsequent widespread adoption of one-year contracts for executive directors[66] and a reduction in other forms of remuneration following termination.[67]

In the post-credit crisis environment, although it remains rare for companies to suffer a defeat in the remuneration report advisory vote, institutional shareholders have clearly become more assertive in relation to remuneration arrangements that they consider to be unacceptable. Notable examples from this period include a 59% vote against Shell Plc's 2009 Remuneration Report and an 80% vote against RBS's 2009 Remuneration Report.[68] Shareholder outrage in these cases suggests that where pay arrangements step outside of standard practice institutional shareholders will express dissent and may vote against the remuneration report. In Shell's case, for example, the LTIP was only to pay out

---

[66] *Ibid*. Although note that 80% of FTSE 350 companies had already adopted one-year contracts prior to the introduction of the advisory shareholder vote.

[67] See S. Thompson, 'The Impact of Corporate Governance Reforms on the Remuneration of Executives in the UK' (2005) 13 *Corporate Governance: An International Review* 19 noting that 'perhaps the biggest stimulus to the reduction of over-generous compensation packages has come with the amendment of the Companies Act...requiring the shareholders' approval of compensation packages at the company AGM'.

[68] 'Investors Rebel over Shell Executive Pay' *Financial Times* (19 May 2009). Other companies have also been subject to institutional shareholder pressure on pay. For example, in both 2009 and 2010 Tesco was subject to strong negative votes—see 'Investors censure Tesco on pay plans' *Financial Times* (2 July 2010).

if Shell came in the top three of its comparator group on a total shareholder return basis. Shell came fourth instead of third by a narrow margin and the board elected to use the discretion that had been granted to them to award a reduced bonus instead of no bonus.[69] On its own terms this decision does not appear to be egregious or unreasonable: the difference between third and fourth place was marginal, and the shareholders in approving the LTIP had granted the remuneration committee discretion.[70] But without close attention to the detail of the LTIP and the bonus award it appeared unusual and inappropriate: the managers received a bonus that they were not entitled to. The Shell example suggests that institutional shareholders, cognizant of the political and media pressures on them to control executive pay, will pounce on and disapprove of anything that is, or can be presented by the media as being, unusual in a pay arrangement. This clearly reinforces pressure on remuneration committee members to closely mimic arrangements in other companies which have not generated media or institutional shareholder disapproval.

4 Executive remuneration arrangements subject to shareholder approval

We have seen that in relation to listed companies shareholders have an advisory non-binding vote on whether to accept or reject the directors' remuneration report. In addition, in relation to certain aspects of a director's remuneration, UK company law provides for a binding shareholder approval requirement.

In relation to all companies, whether listed or unlisted, public or private, pursuant to section 188 of the Companies Act 2006 the company cannot award an executive director a contract for longer than two years that has no notice period, or a longer contract that does not have a notice period of two years or less, without obtaining shareholder approval.[71] If any such longer contract or notice period is awarded the contract is still enforceable but a term or notice period of two years will be implied by law into the contract.[72] The Corporate Governance Code recommends that notice or contract periods should be set at one year or less.[73] As noted in the previous section, the effect of this recommendation in conjunction with institutional investor pressure has led to observance of this one-year requirement in the vast majority of companies. For listed companies, therefore, section 188 is of limited import.

The 2006 Act also requires shareholder approval for any payments made to directors in connection with their retirement or loss of office.[74] This requirement, however, does not apply to and does not affect any entitlement any executive director has pursuant to her contract of employment.[75] Accordingly, these provisions prevent supine boards awarding leaving executive directors additional—ex gratia—payments to which such

---

[69] See Shell Plc's 2009 Directors' Remuneration Report available at: www.annualreportandform20f. shell.com/2009/directorsremunerationreport.php. 🌐

[70] See the letter to shareholders from the chair of Shell's Remuneration Committee available at: www-static.shell.com/static/investor/downloads/shareholder/agm/2009/letter_sir_peter_ job_06052009.pdf. 🌐

[71] In *Wright v Atlas Wright (Europe) Ltd* [1999] 2 BCLC 301 the court held that the *Re Duomatic Ltd* [1969] 1 All ER 161 principle was applicable in relation to shareholder approval for service contracts beyond the—at the time—five-year period. Accordingly, such consent can be given by the informal approval of all the shareholders. On the *Re Duomatic* principle, see Chapter 3.

[72] Section 189 CA 2006, but in addition a term will be implied providing for termination upon the giving of reasonable notice (section 189(b)).

[73] UK Corporate Governance Code (2010), D.1.5.

[74] Sections 215–222 CA 2006. Pursuant to section 222 CA 2006 any payments made in contravention of the shareholder approval requirement are held on trust for the company by the recipient director and any director who authorized the payment is jointly and severally liable to the company for any loss which results.

[75] Section 220(1)(a)–(c) CA 2006.

executive directors have no legal entitlement in connection with their retirement or loss of office. Importantly, however, this restriction on ex gratia payments without shareholder approval does not apply to the award of pensions in respect of past services provided by the directors,[76] which in fact provides significant scope for companies to award ex gratia benefits to retiring or leaving directors.[77]

For premium listed companies, the UKLA's Listing Rules impose additional shareholder approval requirements in relation to certain aspects of directors' remuneration arrangements. Listing Rule 9.4.1 requires shareholder approval of directors' share option schemes[78] and long-term incentives plans prior to their adoption by the company. Such approval is not required, however, if in 'unusual circumstances'[79] the LTIP is required to recruit or retain a particular individual. This exception ensures that a potential managerial recruit or an existing manager who the company needs to retain is not deterred from agreeing to accept the company's offer for fear that the shareholders will not approve the LTIP. Such shareholders would, of course, continue to have the opportunity to cast their vote for or against the directors' remuneration report—which would include details of the LTIP—at the next annual general meeting following the appointment.

In addition to the shareholder approval requirements for LTIPs, Listing Rule 9.4.4 provides that separate shareholder approval is required for the issue of 'discounted share options' where such options are not issued to all, or substantially all, of the company's employees. Discounted share options are options whose exercise price is lower than the company's share price on the day or the day before the option was issued or lower than the average price of the company's shares over the 30-day period prior to the issue of the share. Options are designed to encourage directors to work to improve the company's future performance, whereas an option that is granted at below the existing market price immediately transfers value to the executive without any further effort— it is, in finance jargon, already *in the money*. Accordingly, regulators view such discounted options with suspicion and require shareholder approval for any such options. In contrast to the option scheme and LTIP shareholder approval requirement there is no 'unusual circumstances' recruitment or retention exception.[80]

5 Has UK executive pay regulation been successful?

As we have seen, during the period in which we have seen several regulatory initiatives in the field of executive pay overall executive pay levels in the UK have been increasing at rates far higher than the pay inflation of ordinary employees. However, levels of pay in themselves tell us little about the success or failure of these initiatives. In terms of their key objectives, a case can be made that these regulatory initiatives have been successful. The Corporate Governance Code's recommendation to introduce challenging performance-based elements of executive pay, together with the directors' remuneration reports' detailed disclosure on these performance conditions, has led to a significant

---

[76] Section 220(1)(d) CA 2006.

[77] For example, RBS Plc increased the 'pension pot' of Sir Fred Goodwin, former CEO of RBS, by £8.1 million when he left the company in 2008 (see 'Vilification of Goodwin fuelled further by retirement pot' *Financial Times* (27 February 2009)).

[78] Rule 9.4.1 refers to employee share option schemes as defined in section 1162 of the 2006 Act. Normally grants of options pursuant to the Act require shareholder approval (authority to grant— section 549 CA 2006) and waiver of pre-emption rights, if a non pre-emptive grant (section 561 CA 2006 see further Chapter 17); however, such authorization and waiver requirements do not apply to 'employee share option schemes' as defined by the Act (sections 549, 566 CA 2006). The Listing Rules insert such an approval requirement for listed companies.

[79] LR 9.4.2. The term 'unusual circumstances' is not defined.

[80] An exception is provided in the context of a takeover or reconstruction where the options replace existing options which were held by the director in the company that it had taken over or one of its subsidiaries (LR 9.4.5(2)).

increase in performance-based pay, particularly in the form of LTIPs and performance bonuses, and a decline in the use of options. The concern that directors should not be rewarded for failure has resulted in a marked decrease in remuneration for leaving directors where the company has not reached the specified performance objectives: in the vast majority of cases, such directors will leave with only one year's pay and their pension entitlement.

If pay increases unconnected to performance *conditions* and remuneration levels for 'failed' directors are a reliable proxy for managerial agency costs then the UK's regulatory approach has been effective in ensuring that these costs are controlled. Yet, as we have seen, although there has been a marked shift to performance based pay actual pay to executive of FTSE 100 companies as a whole has outstripped corporate performance over the past decade.[81] Furthermore, paradoxically, although executive pay is increasing there remains real doubt about whether performance-based pay arrangements are effectively incentivizing managers. This is the case particularly in relation to LTIPs and remuneration paid to failed directors.

As noted earlier, the Corporate Governance Code recommends that LTIPs be subject to challenging performance criteria and that in this regard such criteria should make reference to peer-group companies. The objective of such performance comparisons is to ensure that management is rewarded only for their own efforts, not through the good fortune of external market events such as the price of oil or a favourable economy. LTIPs in the UK typically use *relative total shareholder return*, which measures the company's total return to shareholders as compared to a group of peer-group companies. Increasingly, however, dissatisfaction is being expressed about the complexity of LTIPs and particularly about ability of *relative total shareholder return* to identify value creation in the firm. A survey of pay practices by the accounting firm PricewaterhouseCoopers (PwC) in 2009 concluded that:

> Generally management feel that incentives have become too complex and prescriptive, and are not aligned to the business strategy or within their control. As a result, they do not believe incentives drive performance or change behaviours and many perceive incentives simply to be a lottery…Long-term incentives can be considered too complex by executives, largely out of their control or unachievable almost as soon as they are granted. They therefore provide limited incentive effect until the few months before they vest.[82]

One reason for this managerial loss of faith in LTIPs is the inability of relative shareholder return to capture actual value creation within the company. Another is the complexity that is necessary to capture *relative total shareholder return* often makes the incentive arrangements so opaque that it is not clear to the managers what they have to do to obtain the LTIP payouts. If a manager cannot understand the consequences of an incentive package then the package will not influence managerial behaviour. In this regard, in a recent interview-based empirical survey of remuneration committee members, one remuneration committee chair observed:[83]

> This motivational business is 'phooey'. People do the best job they can. Our LTIP is based on the total shareholder return of a comparator group. You've no idea until the end of three years what the outcome will be. So what can you do? People just do their best.

Accordingly, whilst linking executive remuneration to relative performance conditions mitigates a concern that directors will be remunerated for developments outside of

---

[81] On the caveats about such broad brush performance comparisons see p 288 in this chapter.
[82] PWC, *Executive Compensation: Review of the Year 2009*, 6.
[83] B. Main, C. Jackson, J. Pymm and V. Wright, 'The Remuneration Committee and Strategic Human Resource Management' (2008) 16 *Corporate Governance: An International Review* 225 at 230.

their control, in the UK there is an increasing sense that performance conditionality is, paradoxically, undermining using pay as a way of encouraging executive directors to maximize their efforts. That is, the core aspect of executive remuneration's connection between pay and performance is not working. Companies have followed the Corporate Governance Code's recommendation to link pay to performance but the result appears to be more pay without effective long-term incentives. Today we see some companies responding to these concerns. Whilst relative total shareholder return remains the primary basis for calculating whether awards of shares are made to executives under a long-term incentive plan, increasingly some companies are using other accounting measures both connected and unconnected to peer-group performance and either in addition to or instead of relative total shareholder return.[84]

In relation to remuneration paid to directors who leave the company having failed to reach performance targets—rewards for failure—the decrease to what is in most cases one year's salary and the existing pension entitlement is widely viewed as a success.[85] However, as we noted in the introduction to this chapter, directors need to have a cushion for failure in order to incentivize them to take the risks shareholders would want them to take. Whilst clearly it is a regulatory high-wire act to ensure that the rewards for leaving directors incentivize such risk-taking whilst at the same time ensuring that they do not contain a component of managerial agency costs, it is by no means clear that the UK's balance is the correct one. Comparisons with the approach taken abroad to the maximum length of service contracts are instructive in this regard. The German comply-or-explain code recommends that severance pay should not exceed more than two years' remuneration based on remuneration received in the previous financial year.[86] In the US, severance pay levels are significantly higher. Executive service contracts typically provide for salary remuneration of between one to three years on termination with two years being the most common and three years the second most common.[87] In addition it is not uncommon to provide that unvested options vest upon removal. Typically in the US such unvested options will not be subject to performance-based conditions. This has led to several enormous severance payments for leaving directors. For example, Robert Nardelli of Home Depo Inc reportedly left the company with an effective severance package of $210 million, $20 million of which was cash severance pay.[88] As we see in more detail in Chapter 12 on the director's duty of care, the former president of Walt Disney Inc, Michael Ovitz, reportedly left the company with a pay-off of $140 million for one year's allegedly poor work.[89] Whilst with such extreme examples the conclusion that managerial influence or incompetence

[84] PwC, *Executive Compensation: Review of the Year 2009*, 5.

[85] To the extent that options have not vested they will not typically vest on removal if performance conditions have not been reached. Options that have already vested will be exercisable. LTIPs are performance-based which means as failing directors have not reached the performance targets they will not provide for pay-outs for the leaving director; this also applies for performance bonuses. Hence in most cases failing directors will leave with one year's salary and their pensions.

[86] German Corporate Governance Code, paragraph 4.2.3. The German Corporate Governance Code is a mandatory comply-or-explain code by virtue of section 161 of the German Stock Corporation Law.

[87] S. Schwab and R. Thomas, 'An Empirical Analysis of CEO Employment Contracts: What do CEO's Bargain For?' (2005) 63 *Washington & Lee Law Review* 231 noting that three years is the most common service contract period, with five years being the second most common period.

[88] The sum of $210 million reportedly contained 'cash severance of $20 million, unvested deferred stock awards of about $77 million and other payments'—'Home Depot shareholders sue to stop $210 million severance package for Nardelli' *International Herald Tribune* (11 January 2007). Note, however, that whilst Nardelli's tenure was not viewed as a success by many commentators, shareholders, and employees it was far from a failure in financial terms and, therefore, is not strictly speaking a reward for failure, more a reward for not enough success: see generally 'Home Depot Boots CEO Nardelli' *USA Today* (4 January 2007) noting that net revenue in the company increased by 129% during this period compared to 65% for the S&P 500.

[89] See Chapter 12.

have played a role in such pay arrangements seems inescapable, more importantly for our purposes is that we should note the extreme difference with the UK. Whilst in the US it is not unusual for 'failing managers' to leave with tens of millions, in the UK current executive pay arrangements mean that pay-offs for 'failing managers' are rarely greater than one year's salary. The important questions for regulators is whether this is sufficient to encourage optimal risk-taking in UK companies. Has the UK correctly regulated an excess driven by managerial power or has it tilted the regulatory scales too far in the direction of accountability?

6 The future of executive remuneration regulation

At the time of writing it is clear that further government regulation of executive pay will follow during the course of 2012.[90] The Government issued a consultation document in September 2011 in which it mooted several reform options. We consider the primary options here.[91]

The adopted solutions will obviously track the Government's understanding of the problem and its diagnosis of the cause of the problem. In the past although the size of pay packages created political discomfort, regulators and politicians identified the problem not in terms of absolute pay levels but the failure to link pay to performance and rewards for failure. Today, although there remains concern about the linkage between pay and actual performance, the real political and public concern is with the absolute and increasing pay levels: the public sense that in the significant and ongoing economic difficulties faced by the UK economy, and ordinary UK citizens, such pay levels and rises are unfair and reaffirm a sense held by ordinary people that our market economy is rigged. The regulatory paradox is that politicians need to connect to this public concern, but the regulatory tools that would address this problem, such as pay caps or fixed highest earner to lowest earner ratios, are not ones that any political party is willing to entertain. So we end up with more regulation from a regulatory tool box that is not devised to address the problem that has been identified, and indeed, as we noted earlier, may have actually created the problem by supporting a market-mimicking pay ratchet effect.

One of the reforms mooted by the Government, which at the time of writing the Government has now announced they will implement,[92] is to simplify the disclosure required in the Directors' Remuneration Report to make the disclosures more digestible and easier to follow for users.[93] Clearer and more transparent information is more useful information. However, if implemented, it seems unlikely that simplified disclosure would have any real impact in restraining pay inflation. Whilst it is true that shareholders complain about the complexity of reports, this is driven by the complexity of the pay arrangements. If, as we noted earlier, managers themselves struggle to understand the effect of the arrangements, then it is unclear that descriptions of the arrangements can be simplified and explained without being misleading. Nor, as we have already noted, is the UK pay problem associated with inadequate information. On the contrary a strong case can be made that remuneration disclosures appear to have fed a ratcheting/market-mimicking process that is one of the primary drivers of pay

---

[90] 'Cameron to tighten screw on top pay' *Financial Times* (3 January 2012).

[91] For consideration of all the reform options see: Department of Business: Executive Remuneration (September, 2011) available at: www.bis.gov.uk/assets/biscore/business-law/docs/e/11–1287-executive-remuneration-discussion-paper.pdf.

[92] These changes were announced during the final stages of the copy editing of the book. Information regarding how these changes will be implemented is not available at the time of writing. See www.bis.gov.uk/Consultations/executive-remuneration-discussion-paper for announcements and further updates on the proposed reforms.

[93] Note 92, at 17–19.

inflation. Accordingly, a solution that focuses on more or simpler disclosure would be a regulatory red herring.

A second option considered in the Department of Business's Discussion Paper is making shareholder advisory votes binding.[94] The Government has now announced that it will implement this measure.[95] The effect of this would be that if the shareholders do not vote in favour of the remuneration report then the pay arrangements cannot not be implemented. This reform proposal provides an excellent example of regulatory change driven by a pre-existing regulatory logic and not by an attempt to solve the identified problem—regulatory change produced by politicians who are desperate to show their constituents that they 'doing something' whilst hoping that the complexity of the solution will ensure that those constituents do not see that this is a regulatory waste of time. In this regard, note first, as discussed in section III.4 of this chapter, that important aspects of pay, namely option grants and the LTIP, are already subject to a binding shareholder vote. This leaves salary and short-term performance bonuses which are currently subject to an advisory vote only. Secondly, since the introduction of mandatory pay disclosure and advisory votes in 2002 pay inflation has risen dramatically, suggesting very clearly that increases in shareholder power are not correlated with decreases in pay. Shareholders have periodically used the advisory vote to publicly discipline managers but have rarely voted against a report. Nevertheless, boards appear to have been responsive to shareholder pressure coalescing around the annual advisory vote. Furthermore, there is no indication that shareholders feel that boards ignore them because the vote is not binding. Indeed there is a real risk that making the vote a binding vote will undermine shareholders' willingness to vote against management. All dissenting shareholders will be aware that there is a risk that their judgment is wrong. They are fully aware that the remuneration committee is better informed than them about the quality of the management and the risks of losing managers to competitors.[96] If the vote is a binding vote which ties management's hands then more shareholders may decide not to vote against, fearing that their negative view of the arrangements may be the product of an inadequate understanding of the situation. If this effect is realized then making the vote a binding vote may make it more difficult for shareholders to express dissent through the vote.

A third option is to tinker with the composition of remuneration committees. There are two possible regulatory changes in this regard. First, preventing executive directors of other companies from being the non-executive chair of the remuneration committee but *not* preventing them from serving on the committee. This change shares one of the concerns identified by Lucian Bebchuk et al in the previous section that where the remuneration committee consists of executive directors of other companies those non-executives may be more willing to grant larger pay rises, in part because they are aware that this may indirectly benefit themselves by pushing up the market standard. This problem may be particularly acute where such a director chairs the committee. The second possible change would involve including representatives or committee observers from non-traditional groups, such as employees.[97] It seems plausible that representation from ordinary employees may force the remuneration committee members to take seriously the pay differential between employees and managers within the firm. It may be a means of emphasizing concerns that many have about the 'fairness' of pay arrangements.

[94] *Ibid* at 21.
[95] These changes were announced during the final stages of the copy editing of the book. Information about how these changes will be implemented is not available at the time of writing. See www.bis.gov.uk/Consultations/executive-remuneration-discussion-paper ☻ for announcements and further updates on the proposed reforms. See also 'Cameron vows executive pay crackdown' *Financial Times* (9 January 2012).
[96] 'Shareholders reactions to board room pay' *Financial Times* (8 January 2012) quoting a spokesperson for the Investment Management Association observing that: 'Shareholders don't micromanage companies. That's for management.'
[97] *Ibid* 26–7.

However, it appears at the time of writing that this approach, whilst benefiting from the Labour Party's support, will not be implemented by the Government.[98]

A more effective way of addressing these fairness issues would be to provide a limit on the ratio of the highest to the average paid worker.[99] Such a rule, however, is both a blunt instrument and is likely to have many distortive effects, for example: the contracting out of lower paid elements of the business in order to raise the average wage; or the refusal to move production to a low labour cost overseas location. Note in regard to both of these possible changes that these changes are unlikely to affect one of the primary drivers of pay inflation, namely: the focus on paying your managers the same as managers are paid elsewhere in order to both keep your managers and avoid negative political, media, and institutional shareholder attention.

The final important option is to require simplified pay arrangements: to move away from LTIPs, bonuses, and share options, and instead to require a simple performance component.[100] For example: a salary and share options that are out of the money[101] and cannot be exercised for a long three- to five-year period of time; or a salary and a share bonus on hitting certain annual targets which cannot be sold for a three- to five-year restricted period of time. It seems clear that a simple salary and share option scheme with long-term holding requirements will incentivize managers to perform and enhance shareholder value in the long run. However, such arrangements would require the regulator to jettison the objective of identifying the actual value created by the manager as distinct from value generated by factors outside of the manager's control—such as a rise in the price of oil in an oil company. While such arrangements will incentivize value creation, it is also clear that such arrangements will, particularly in boom years, benefit managers who do not deserve it. A simplified system has to accept such outcomes as an unavoidable cost of the system. At the time of writing the Government's position on this reform option remains unclear.

Perhaps the truth of the matter is that although the excessive remuneration genie is out of the bottle, none of the existing regulatory approaches or the ones considered here are capable of putting the genie back into the bottle. The ones that would—mandatory limits or prohibitive tax rates on certain levels of pay—are not currently politically conceivable and strong arguments against them exist. It seems likely, therefore, that politicians will continue to bang tables about this issue and that the general public will continue to express outrage, but that pay will stay high and continue to rise no matter what regulatory interventions are forthcoming.

Questions

1. Is executive pay a solution to the managerial agency cost problem or is it part of the problem?

2. What is performance-related pay designed to do? How does it work? In what ways, if any, can it be counter-productive?

3. What factors may be relevant to explaining the marked increases in pay levels for executive directors over the past two decades?

4. How would you go about trying to work out whether executive pay inflation is part of the managerial agency problem?

---

[98] 'Cautious Cable leans towards wealth creation' *Financial Times* (23 January 2012).

[99] Note, however, that the disclosure of that ratio may also be a possible regulatory solution. At the time of writing it is a solution supported by the Labour Party but most likely not by the Coalition Government.

[100] *Ibid* at 35.

[101] The exercise price is above the market price of the share.

5. '£1 million is more than enough to compensate anyone for the loss of any job. Anything significantly higher is likely to be a managerial agency cost.' Discuss.

6. What mechanisms have been most effective in controlling executive pay setting in the UK?

7. Do you think it is possible for an independent remuneration committee to remain truly independent? If not, why not?

8. 'The continuing increase in executive pay in the UK reveals that the only way of really curbing pay abuse is to cap what any person can be paid, whether that person is an executive director or a footballer.' Discuss.

9. Is it possible that we do not pay our executive directors enough—whether successful or unsuccessful?

10. In your view, have the regulatory reforms put in place over the past two decades been a success or a failure?

11. How, if at all, should regulators respond to increasing executive pay inflation?

12. 'Institutional shareholders are part of the executive pay problem and should not be a part of the solution.' Discuss.

IV REMUNERATION FOR SERVICE AS A NON-EXECUTIVE DIRECTOR

Thus far in our analysis in this chapter we have considered the remuneration of executive directors. As we have seen, executive directors are also full-time managers and employees of the company. In contrast, non-executive directors are only part-timers who are not responsible for the day-to-day running of the company. As directors of the company, however, non-executive directors typically receive payment for performing their role as a director—these are sometimes referred to as directors' emoluments. Most companies' articles explicitly authorize the board to provide for payment to the directors for their services as directors.[102]

The terms, including pay, upon which non-executive directors are appointed are usually set forth in a letter of appointment, which typically does not create any rights to a term of notice or severance pay on the termination of the director's office.[103] However, some companies, for example, Marks and Spencer Plc, enter into agreements with the non-executive directors which set out the terms of office and may provide for a notice period. Marks and Spencer Plc currently provides for three-month notice periods for the non-executive directors and six months' notice for the senior independent director.[104] If a company has a separate non-executive chairman of the board, the chairman will usually have a contract with the company, which typically provides for a 12-month notice period.[105] As a reminder, these notice periods do not affect the ability of the shareholders acting in general meeting to remove the directors with immediate effect

---

[102] See, for example, The Model Article for Public Companies, article 23. Note that the articles provide for remuneration of directors generally and do not typically distinguish between non-executive and executive directors. Most companies do not make separate provision for executive directors for payment for their role as directors as distinct from their role as manager/employees—compensation for both functions is combined.

[103] See for example Vodafone Plc 20011 Directors' Remuneration Report (available at: www.vodafone.com/content/annualreport/annual_report11/governance/directors-remuneration.html ☺).

[104] See Marks and Spencer's 2011 Directors Remuneration Report at Board Appointments and Contracts (available at: http://annualreport.marksandspencer.com/governance/remuneration-report/unaudited.aspx ☺).

[105] See note 104 at 72; see also Marks and Spencer Plc 2008 Directors' Remuneration Report providing for a 12-month contract for the former non-executive chairman of the board.

pursuant to section 168 of the 2006 Act. However, it does mean that the non-executive directors will continue to be entitled to receive payment for the unexpired term of the notice period.

Given that non-executive directors do not work full time at the company, one would expect their remuneration to be commensurate with their—as compared to executive directors—reduced contribution to the company. Of course, the extent of each of the non-executive directors' work commitment will vary according to the function performed: chairman, senior non-executive director, committee member etc. One would expect non-executive directors emoluments to vary to take account of the variable workload of the different non-executive directors. If one compares base salary levels for executive directors with non-executive director emoluments these expectations are borne out. In 2011 for example, the base salary for Vodafone's CEO was £1,065,000, the Chairman £600,000, and the salaries of the non-executive directors were approximately £115,000.[106]

Whilst in regard to the level of remuneration we would expect to find, and do find, that non-executive directors receive significantly less overall remuneration than executive directors, a more difficult issue is whether non-executive directors should also be compensated with performance-based remuneration. The objective of ensuring that directors maximize their efforts to act in the company's interests and not in their own applies also to non-executive directors. As we discussed in Chapter 7, non-executive directors have an essential delegation and monitoring function and important—although limited—managerial and advisory functions. In theory, as with executive directors, performance-based remuneration could incentivize non-executive directors to perform these functions to the best of their abilities. However, for non-executive directors the connection between their performance of these functions and value generation is less direct and more opaque than it is in relation to executive directors.

Whilst non-executive directors make periodic and important management decisions and may be consulted and advise on the formulation of business strategy, they are not, as we have seen, the primary drivers of business strategy, nor are they involved in putting that strategy into operation. The scope for their direct efforts to generate value is, therefore, limited and incomparable to the value-generating potential of the company's executive officers. In this regard, it is questionable whether non-executive directors' efforts translate directly into value generation in the same way as executive directors' efforts translate into value generation. An increase in 50% in company profitability or the share price may therefore have little to do with the non-executive directors' efforts. This is true subject to one very significant caveat: the non-executive board bears the weight of responsibility in the appointment and removal of the executive directors. How demanding they are of senior management to generate value, how attentive they are to management performance, and how willing they are to replace underperforming management may profoundly affect value generation in the company. Giving non-executive directors a personal and significant stake in the performance of the company may, therefore, have a profound affect on the willingness of non-executive directors to be attentive, to be independent, and to act quickly to replace underperforming management.

However, providing non-executive directors with performance-related incentives comes with a set of additional problems. Acute conflicts are created when the board is responsible for setting executive pay. This is partly resolved in the UK by giving authority to set executive pay to a remuneration committee that is staffed with independent non-executive directors. To give authority to such a committee to set non-executive pay would generate a similar acute conflict. Non-executive pay is, therefore, typically set by the executive directors of the board. The Corporate Governance Code recommends

[106] Vodafone Plc 2011 Directors' Remuneration Report.

that the board should set non-executive pay[107] and that 'no director should be involved in setting his or her own remuneration'.[108] This conflict, however, has the potential to undermine the independence of the non-executives with regard to executive pay-setting as it generates a 'back-scratching risk': higher remuneration for non-executive directors will be rewarded by more generous pay for executive directors. These risks, however, are of limited concern where non-executive director pay is not linked to performance and is generally low. If non-executive directors receive only modest salaries—in relation to which there is a clear market standard—then concerns about conflicts and back-scratching, whilst not removed, are of a much lower order. However, if, taking account of the arguments set forth in the previous paragraph, non-executive directors are rewarded with higher performance-related remuneration, then these conflicts and back-scratching risks become very significant.

The second problem associated with giving non-executive directors performance-related remuneration arises from the effects that such incentive arrangements will have on one of the core monitoring functions which the Corporate Governance Code gives to non-executive directors, namely the monitoring of the processes by which the company produces its financial information. If non-executive directors are rewarded through performance-based pay linked directly or indirectly to accounting-based targets, their rewards are linked to the financial information that is produced by the company. The non-executive directors would then share the same skewed incentives to which the executive directors are subject: to present more favourably or even to distort the company's financial information; and to pressurize the auditors to accept management's preferred presentation. Performance-based remuneration for all non-executive directors would, therefore, undermine the independence and objectivity of the audit committee.

For these reasons, the Corporate Governance Code recommends that non-executive directors should not, save in exceptional circumstances, be granted options, and where options are granted that shareholder approval is obtained in advance and that the director keeps any shares she acquires by exercising the options for a period of at least a year after she leaves office.[109] Furthermore, the Code provides in its definition of independence that a director that receives options or other performance-related remuneration is not independent—unless the board determines that in spite of this factor the director is still independent.[110] That is, the Corporate Governance Code creates a presumption that such performance-related arrangements for non-executive directors compromise a director's independence. The vast majority of UK companies comply with this Code's independence provision and their non-executive directors are typically remunerated through salary alone. They will continue to receive this salary whether or not the company's performance is excellent, mediocre, or poor.

A third option that has not been explored in detail in the corporate governance debate, but has been adopted by a few companies,[111] would be to have two tiers of non-executive directors: one tier of non-executives who are incentivized by large performance-related remuneration arrangements, and a second tier of non-executives who are remunerated only with salary. The non-executive directors with performance-related packages would be incentivized to be very demanding of management and to organize the non-executive board to replace management if the expected level of suc-

---

[107] Corporate Governance Code (2010), Provision D.2.3. This provision also notes that where required by the articles the shareholders should set non-executive pay and where permitted by the articles the board may delegate this responsibility to a committee of which the CEO may be a member.

[108] *Ibid*, D2 Main Principle.

[109] Corporate Governance Code (2010), D.1.3.

[110] *Ibid* B.1.1, see p 258.

[111] For example, Cable & Wireless Plc, where the chairman as well as the senior managers were remunerated through high-powered incentives. 'C & W faces investor backlash' *Financial Times* (14 June 2007).

cess was not forthcoming. The salaried non-executives would perform the audit committee function and take control of the remuneration arrangements for both executive directors and the 'performance-related pay' non-executives. There are several potential explanations for why companies have not adopted these arrangements, including the barriers to them set out in the Corporate Governance Code and possibly also the 'outrage' objections for paying part-time monitors large amounts.

V REGULATING EXECUTIVE REMUNERATION ACROSS THE ATLANTIC

Executive remuneration—or compensation as it is referred to the US—is notably higher for leading US companies than it is for leading UK companies. US executives are paid more than their UK counterparts. The other notable difference as compared to the UK is that US executives receive a much greater proportion of their remuneration in performance-related pay; however, the form of this performance-related pay is typically bonuses and share options that are not linked to peer-group comparisons. Whilst the trans-Atlantic pay gap as well as the performance-related component has been shrinking in recent years it still remains. Compare UK and US pay amounts and structure in Table 8.2 from Conyon and Sadler:[112]

Table 8.2 *Comparison of UK and US executive pay amounts and structure*

	Sample	Average Total Pay (£000s)	Median Total Pay (£000s)	Base Salary	Annual Bonus	Option Grant	LTIP Shares	Other Pay
United Kingdom								
Largest 200 firms: 1997	187	£955	£768	52.38	17.50	9.60	16.29	4.23
Largest 200 firms: 2003	176	£1,691	£1,290	40.56	22.04	11.34	20.07	5.99
Percentage change		76.95%	67.92%	−22.57%	25.95%	18.17%	23.19%	41.60%
United States								
Execucomp firms: 1997	1664	£2,679	£1,346	33.80	20.23	32.25	3.83	9.88
Execucomp firms: 2003	1495	£2,830	£1,549	31.32	19.61	32.35	2.98	13.74
Percentage change		5.64%	15.08%	−7.32%	−3.08%	0.30%	−22.39%	39.05%

More recent data suggests that the process of convergence continues and that when one takes account of the size of companies and the industry in which companies operate as well as of the risks associated with performance-related pay—namely that the performance targets may not be realized—other jurisdictions including the UK are moving closer to US pay levels. Consider the graph in Figure 8.5 from a recent US survey.[113]

[112] M. Conyon and G. Sadler, 'How Does UK and US CEO Pay Measure Up' (2005, Working Paper on file with the author).
[113] N.G. Fernandes, M. Ferreira, P.P. Matos, K.J. Murphy, 'Are US CEOS Paid More? New International Evidence' ECGI—Finance Working Paper No 255/2009 (available at: http://papers.ssrn.com/sol3/papers.cfm?abstract_id=1341639 🌐).

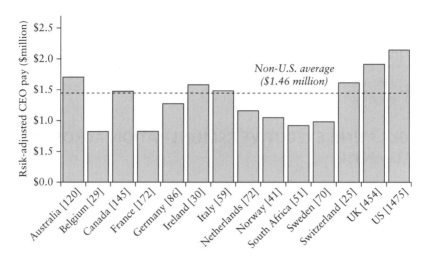

Figure 8.5 *Predicted level of risk-adjusted 2006 CEO pay for firms with $1 billion in revenues*

Over the past two decades public and political 'outrage' in relation to US executive pay levels has repeatedly grabbed the headlines.[114] The 2007–2009 credit crisis provides the latest instalment in this regard, resulting in several headline-grabbing stories about executive pay excess even in relation to companies that entered bankruptcy during the course of the crisis.[115] Here, however, is not the correct place for an in-depth inquiry into the causes of US pay levels or the causes of the trans-Atlantic pay differences of which there are many, both benign—such as the factors referred to in the extract from Randall Thomas set forth previously—and malign—such as self-interested managerial abuse of power and the failure of board oversight.[116]

Here we want to consider briefly US regulation of executive remuneration for comparative purposes: to consider how a jurisdiction with even greater pay excesses has approached the pay issue. However, the comparison needs to be treated very carefully. There are, as we shall see, available correlations between the lighter touch regulation in the US and higher overall pay levels as well as higher rewards for failure. However, the marked increase in remuneration is something that has only occurred in the past 15 to 20 years, although the light-touch regulation has a longer pedigree. In the UK, on the other hand, whilst rewards for failure have declined and the connection between pay and performance (in the pay arrangements themselves) has been strengthened, pay levels have increased markedly during the period when more intrusive regulation has been introduced. Furthermore, we have registered some concerns that UK regulation may inhibit the optimal recruitment, incentivization, and retention of executive directors. Whilst we cannot explore all of these comparative pay issues here, bear in mind that correlation may, but need not necessarily, mean causation.

The two primary regulatory strategies deployed by US regulators to address remuneration are: first, public disclosure of the details of the remuneration paid to executive directors; and, secondly, the setting of remuneration through 'compensation committees'

---

[114] See note 64.

[115] A. Clark and E. Schor 'Your company is bankrupt, you keep $480m. Is that fair?' *Guardian* (7 October 2008), detailing the executive pay of the failed investment bank, Lehman Brothers. In this regard see also the Congressional hearings with the former CEO of Lehman Brothers, Richard Fuld (www.youtube.com/watch?v=0GGV3GGHD2Q ●).

[116] Bebchuk et al, note 34.

staffed with independent directors. In 2011, in response to the pay excesses revealed in the credit crisis, Congress introduced a third regulatory strategy by legislating for advisory shareholder vote rules, referred to generically in the US as 'say on pay' rules.

The disclosure requirements are set out in Regulation S-K issued pursuant to the Securities Exchange Act of 1934. Regulation S-K requires that considerable detail of the remuneration paid to each executive director is set out in the company's annual report, which is referred to as the company's 10-K filing.[117] It is fair to say that this disclosure is extensive in nature, more so even than the considerable disclosure required in the UK to be set out in the directors' remuneration report. Note in particular the recent introduction of a requirement to disclose the ratio of CEO pay to median employee pay in publicly traded companies.[118]

In relation to the compensation committee, whilst the requirements for listed companies, such as those set out in the NYSE's Listing Manual, are mandatory requirements, the nature of the regulation is significantly more 'hands-off' than the UK recommendations set out in the Corporate Governance Code. Similar to the UK, the NYSE's composition rules require a committee of independent members;[119] however, in contrast to the UK, the rules provide virtually no substantive guidance on the structure or nature of the remuneration to be provided. In the commentary to the rule it states only that 'in determining the long-term incentive component of CEO compensation, the committee should consider the listed company's performance and relative shareholder return, the value of similar incentive awards to CEOs at comparable companies, and the awards given to the listed company's CEO in past years'.[120]

Section 951 of the Dodd-Frank Wall Street Reform and Consumer Protection Act,[121] the major US Federal legislative response to the credit crisis, provided for—and requires the US Securities and Exchange Commission (the US Federal Capital Markets Regulator, the 'SEC') to introduce rules relating to—a non-binding vote on executive remuneration. The SEC rules came into force in April 2011. The Dodd-Frank Act and the SEC rules provide that an advisory vote must be held at least every three years and that shareholders may elect to hold such votes on more regular annual or bi-annual basis.[122] Initial experience with the say on pay rules suggest that the advisory vote provides a welcome means for shareholders to signal disapproval of pay arrangements. As of July 2011 four companies had their remuneration arrangements rejected.[123] It is, of course, too early to say what effect these rules will have on US pay structures and levels.

In the US there is no limit on the length of service contracts absolutely or subject to shareholder approval.[124] Pursuant to the NYSE Listing Manual companies listed on the NYSE must obtain shareholder approval for 'equity compensation plans' which would include plans providing for option grants or grants of actual shares.[125] There are,

---

[117] See Item 402 of Regulation S-K (www.law.uc.edu/CCL/regS-K/SK402.html 🌐). The disclosures were recently subject to significant amendments: see Securities Act Release No 8732a (www.sec.gov/rules/final/2006/33-8732a.pdf 🌐) and Securities Act Release No. 8765 (www.sec.gov/rules/final/2006/33-8765.pdf 🌐). See also Section 953 of the Dodd Frank Wall Street Reform and Consumer Protection Act.

[118] Section 953(b) provides that the SEC shall promulgate rules to effect this requirement. At the time of writing these rules have not yet come into force.

[119] On the NYSE's definition of independence see p xxx.

[120] NYSE Listing Manual Rule 303A.05, Commentary.

[121] Inserting section 14A of the Securities Exchange Act of 1934.

[122] Securities and Exchange Commission, Release Nos 33–9178; 34–63768. The shareholder vote to determine the regularity of the advisory vote must be held at least once every six years.

[123] 'US Shareholders grab chance for "say on pay"' *Financial Times* (5 July 2011).

[124] To the author's knowledge no State provides such restrictions in its corporations code, although a review of every State has not been carried out.

[125] NYSE Listing Manual, Rule 303A.08. An equity compensation plan is defined as a plan or other arrangement that provides for the delivery of equity securities (either newly issued or treasury shares) of the listed company to any employee, director, or other service provider as compensation for services.

however, significant exceptions to the shareholder approval requirement, in particular, such approval is not required when hiring a new manager.[126] More recently as a result of the US bailout of US banks some substantive limits were placed on the remuneration of US banks taking government financial assistance.[127] However, even in the face of yet another round of 'pay outrage' arising from this credit crisis the US legislature retains a strong preference for leaving the pay process to the market subject to the composition, disclosure, and say on pay regulations.[128]

 Online Resource Centre
http://www.oxfordtextbooks.co.uk/orc/kershaw2e/

Visit the Online Resource Centre for additional resources and information available for this chapter, including web links and an interactive flashcard glossary.

---

[126] See Exceptions to NYSE Listing Manual, Rule 303A.08.

[127] The limitations involved, amongst others, a ban on severance payments in these institutions as well as the scope to claw back bonuses that were paid based on inaccurate accounts. See 'CEO Pay Takes a Hit on in Bailout Plan' *USA Today* (10 October 2008).

[128] *Ibid*, quoting a US compensation consultant as follows: 'It's highly unlikely that lawmakers will try to extend curbs on financial CEO compensation to other industries. "Congress should nudge the free market, not bludgeon it".'

CHAPTER NINE

INTRODUCTION TO DIRECTORS' DUTIES

I RULES VERSUS PRINCIPLES

The next six chapters of the book focus on the duties which company law imposes on directors of companies. A duty is an obligation to conduct yourself in a particular way or not to conduct yourself in a particular way. Such obligations could take a specific or general form. A men's clothing company could, for example, impose on its employees an obligation not to wear bright red trousers to work or its directors could be prevented from buying gold-plated waste paper baskets. Fact-specific obligations of this nature (which are referred to by some commentators as *rule-based regulation*) suffer from two problems. First, they cover only a limited number of circumstances. There may, for instance, be colour combinations that are just as 'offensive' to the company's fashion sense—perhaps bright red and green striped trousers—but are not strictly speaking red trousers. These trousers are not covered by the rule. For every new colour-specific rule there will be a colour combination which is outside of the rule, but perhaps just as 'offensive' to the company's followers of fashion. The second problem with this type of approach to regulating behaviour is that such rules are inflexible as the world around us changes. Red trousers may break the laws of fashion today but tomorrow it may be green trousers or blue trousers. A discovery of massive gold reserves in Wales could render the price of gold cheaper than the price of steel, rendering gold waste paper baskets cheaper than steel ones. Obligations set in more general terms, such as 'no coloured trousers', or more generally 'no bright and offensive clothing', may be more effective as we meet an uncertain future, particularly when it may be difficult to change the obligations quickly in response to such events. Such general obligations are sometimes referred to as standard-based or *principles-based* approaches to regulation.

All regulatory techniques whether rule-based regulations or principles-based regulations come with pros and cons. If a company selected a principles-based approach to clothing such as 'no bright and offensive clothing', the clear advantage of such a standard is that it is capable of adjusting to changes in the 'dos' and 'don'ts' of the fashion world. However, the term 'offensive' is very general and unclear. This uncertainty creates three problems. First, if the company's primary concern is to prevent bright red trousers being worn, then a specific rule referring to bright red trousers may be more effective than a general standard. Will a 'no bright and offensive clothing standard' give some scope for rebellious employees to argue that bright red is not offensive? Secondly, company managers will find themselves spending time trying to define what is meant by 'offensive', providing employees with guidance and arguing with those rebellious colleagues about why green trousers are acceptable but red and green trousers 'offensive'. A general statement may, therefore, be more flexible, but more costly to police. Thirdly, the uncertainty associated with such a general obligation might also have unintended negative side effects. Perhaps employees, fearful of being in breach of the rule because it is not clear what it actually prohibits, elect to wear nothing but black, bringing an atmosphere of doom and gloom to the company.

The choice of regulatory technique will vary depending on the context in which the rule applies and according to the nature of the problem which it is intended to regulate. Where a particular type of behaviour is an unqualified bad thing and under no circumstances could benefit society, and where a general standard gives scope for that behaviour to continue, then we may wish to select a rule that *specifically* prohibits just that behaviour. Where a type of behaviour can, depending on the context, be either detrimental to society or beneficial for society, we may wish to use a standard that may be able to navigate between the good and the bad, prohibiting such behaviour where it damages society but allowing it where it benefits society. The choice of rules-based versus principles-based regulation may also depend on how quickly the context in which it applies changes and how quickly the person setting the rules can change the rules to adjust to the changing context. If red trousers are 'offensive' on Monday but *de rigueur* on Wednesday then the person setting the rules needs to be able to act quickly and without cost to adjust to the tides of fashion.

The context in which companies operate is a rapidly changing environment in which it may be very difficult to predict the types of problems and opportunities that companies face in the future. It may, therefore, be very difficult for the regulator—the person setting the rules, which in the context of a company could be the legislature or the shareholder body—to ensure that rules-based regulation can be adapted quickly to changes in external circumstances and unanticipated events. Government may be slow to identify problems and the legislative process slow to respond. Shareholders in close companies may be able to react quickly but shareholders in widely-held companies are likely, due to rational apathy problems, to be passive in the face of change. Of course, directors are well positioned to be proactive and lead shareholders towards required regulatory changes; however, they are less likely to be proactive if a change in the rules is necessary to ensure that they do not abuse their power. Furthermore, with regard to regulating director behaviour, specific rules are poorly suited to regulating activities that have the potential to produce agency costs but *may* be necessary or beneficial for the company. If you prohibit the activity you may damage the company. For example, every company needs a waste paper basket; perhaps an expensive and stylish waste paper basket is necessary for the company's main conference room where it holds meetings with its most important clients. But a gold-plated waste paper basket for the chief executive officer's company flat is an agency cost. A contract with the chief executive officer's wife to provide advisory services involves a risk that agency costs will be incurred by overpaying his wife or employing her when she is not qualified to provide those services. But if she is the leading advisor in her field, employing her at her normal market rate may benefit the company. Rules that prohibit such transactions would throw the 'baby out with the bathwater'. On the other hand, general legal duties, in theory, allow the agency costs to be drained away whilst allowing such beneficial transactions to continue.

Additional reading on the relative merits of rules and principles

J. Black, Forms and Paradoxes of Principles-Based Regulation' (2008) *Capital Markets Law Journal* 425.

L. Kaplow, 'Rules vs Standards: an Economic Analysis' (1992) 42 *Duke Law Review* 557.

D. Kershaw, 'Evading Enron: Taking Principles Too Seriously in Accounting Regulation' (2005) 68 *Modern Law Review* 594, 605–8.

F. Schauer, *Playing By The Rules: A Philosophical Examination of Rule Based Decision Making in Law and Life* (Clarendon Press, 1991).

II DESIGNING BEHAVIOURAL EXPECTATIONS

Directors' duties, analysed in this chapter and Chapters 10–14 are, in the main, general principles-based regulations which set out behavioural expectations for directors. Failure to meet these expectations may, as we shall see, result in liability for the directors.

These duties, therefore, operate both as statements of behavioural expectation—*how we expect directors to behave*—and as sticks or deterrents to encourage directors to meet such expectations.

How should we go about determining what these behavioural expectations of company directors *should be*? Perhaps the starting point is to ask what would you expect of somebody who was entrusted to act on your behalf to manage your money? How would you state your general behavioural expectations of that person?

Assignment 1

You transfer your whole savings of £100,000 to Mr Maverick, an investment manager, to hold on trust for your benefit and to invest those funds to generate the maximum possible return. In your contract with Mr Maverick there is an empty space for you to specify **three** (and only three) expectations of him (in principles-based terms) in the management and investment of your money. Fill in the space with your three expectations.

As you will see shortly, the behavioural expectations we have of directors are similar to the expectations that many of you (as principal) will have had of Mr Maverick (as agent). They may also be similar in nature to the expectations partners may have of their fellow partners; or the expectations the beneficiaries of a trust fund may have of the trustees of the fund. Law recognizes the similarity between these different actors—directors; agents; partners and trustees—by giving them a shared title. They are referred to as 'fiduciaries' and the relationship with the 'principal' (the company, partner, beneficiaries) is a fiduciary relationship. However, we should be wary of this shared term. There may be similarities in these relationships and similarities in the nature of the obligations to which these fiduciaries are subject; however, one would expect the nature of these obligations to adjust to the different contexts in which the different fiduciaries operate. The context of managing a computer manufacturing company such as in our Bob's Electronics case study is very different from administering a children's trust fund.

Assignment 2

Instead of transferring £100,000 to Mr Maverick to invest your money on your behalf, Bob the 100% shareholder of Bob's Electronics Ltd persuades you to buy a 25% share in the company for £100,000. Bob is no longer the manager of the business having appointed Markus as CEO and sole director last year.

Would the nature of the three behavioural expectations that you would have of Markus the CEO change in any way from the expectations you set for Mr Maverick?

What are the reasons for the choice and form of your three behavioural expectations?

Try to do this assignment before reading on. In my experience of teaching company law, the topic of directors' duties is easier to follow and becomes more interesting when you can compare the law to your own regulatory solutions, and compare the policy elections made by the law with the policy choices that underpin your three behavioural expectations.

III INTRODUCTION TO THE KEY DUTIES OWED BY DIRECTORS

At the most abstract and general level, UK company law imposes on directors the duties to be *loyal to the company* and *to be competent* when acting as a director.

A director of a company is required to be loyal to the company. When exercising corporate powers loyalty requires that the director use those powers to further the company's interests—to benefit the company. The obligation to be loyal, however, extends beyond requiring that when one actually acts *as a director* that one is loyal. Once one becomes a director, a director's personal actions—such as entering into personal contracts or making an investment with his own funds—may be relevant to or affect the company and its interests. The duty to be loyal, therefore, extends beyond acting in the company's interests when 'at work' and formally exercising corporate powers or performing one's role as a director. The obligation to be loyal to the company may place constraints on personal actions by the director when those actions relate to, or conflict with, the interests of the company.

In the case of *Item Software (UK) Ltd v Fassihi*[1] Arden LJ spoke generally about the nature of the duty of loyalty in English law.

> This duty of loyalty is the 'time-honoured' rule: per Goulding J in *Mutual Life Insurance Co of New York v Rank Organisation Ltd* [1985] BCLC 11 at 21. The duty is expressed in these very general terms, but that is one of its strengths: it focuses on principle not on the particular words which judges or the legislature have used in any particular case or context. It is dynamic and capable of application in cases where it has not previously been applied but the principle or rationale of the rule applies. It reflects the flexible quality of the doctrines of equity. As Lord Templeman once put it 'Equity is not a computer. Equity operates on conscience...' (see *Winkworth v Edward Baron Development Co Ltd* [1987] BCLC 193 at 197, [1986] 1 WLR 1512 at 1516). Professor Robert C Clark has described the fundamental nature of the duty of loyalty in these terms:
>
> > 'The most general formulation of corporate law's attempted solution to the problem of managerial accountability is *the fiduciary duty of loyalty:* the corporation's directors...owe a duty of undivided loyalty to their corporations, and they may not so use corporate assets, or deal with the corporation, as to benefit themselves at the expense of the corporation and its shareholders. *The overwhelming majority of particular rules, doctrines, and cases in corporate law are simply an explication of this duty or of the procedural rules and institutional arrangements involved in implementing it.* The history of corporate law is largely the history of the development of operational content for the duty of loyalty. Even many cases that appear to be about dull formalities or rules of the road in fact involve disputes arising out of alleged managerial disloyalty...Most importantly, this general fiduciary duty of loyalty is a residual concept that can include factual situations that no one has foreseen and categorized. The general duty permits, and in fact has led to, a continuous evolution in corporate law.' (See *Corporate Law* (1986) pp 34 and 141.) [Emphasis in the original]
>
> Although Professor Clark was writing about the duty of loyalty in the United States, his observations seem to me to express qualities of the duty of loyalty applying equally to the law of England and Wales.

Arden LJ refers to the duty of loyalty as having a 'fundamental nature': it underpins more specific obligations which instantiate (put into effect) its 'fundamental nature' in different regulated contexts. It is *fundamental* because loyalty is an inextricable aspect of the original instruction—namely *to act on behalf of* the instructing person or the person who the instructing person tells you to act on behalf of. Students who analyse *Assignment 1* in this chapter often do not identify the expectation of loyalty and the reason for this is often that it is just too obvious—'of course he has to be loyal to my interests that is the very reason for instructing him'.

Most importantly for our analysis of company law, there are two key instantiations of this general obligation of loyalty, which are also referred to as *duties* although strictly speaking they are *sub-duties* of the core duty of loyalty. The first of which, until recent reforms set out in the Companies Act 2006, was known as the *duty to act in good faith in the best interests of the company*. This is now known as the *duty to promote the success of the company*. We shall consider this duty in the next chapter. The second is *the duty to avoid conflicts of interest*. At common law this duty regulates direct conflicts

---

[1] [2004] EWCA Civ 1244.

of interest between the directors' personal interests and the company's interests—areas where directors may incur what we referred to in Chapter 5 as direct agency costs, such as self-dealing and the taking of corporate opportunities. Pursuant to the Companies Act 2006 this explicit duty to avoid conflicts of interests now applies only to the taking of opportunities although, as we shall see, the regulation of self-dealing as set out in the Act is a clear product of this no-conflict obligation. The regulation of conflicts of interest will be addressed in Chapters 13 and 14.

In addition to loyalty, UK company law demands a degree of competence from directors. When acting as a director—when using corporate powers or performing one's role as a director—we might say, colloquially, that we expect the director 'to do a good job': we expect her to be competent; we expect her to take care when acting, as we expect anyone else, whether she is a plumber, a teacher or a judge, to take care to do a good job. This degree of competence required of directors is articulated most clearly through the *duty of care, skill and diligence*. We will consider the nature of this obligation to be competent in Chapter 12. However, as we shall also see in the next chapter when we consider the loyalty obligation imposed on directors to promote the company's interests when exercising corporate power, director competence is not regulated solely through the duty of care. As we shall see, the courts introduce standards of competence for corporate decisions and actions when reviewing whether directors have complied with this loyalty obligation.

IV THE SOURCES OF DIRECTORS' DUTIES

Until the Companies Act 2006, directors' duties of loyalty and care were set out in case law. One problem with relying on case law alone to define these duties is that it is more difficult to explain to directors, many of whom have no legal training, the nature of the duties they owe to the companies they serve. From a director's perspective it is preferable to have the duties set out in one authoritative document which is clearly drafted using modern language, rather than having to read a long memo from the company's law firm that refers to several cases whose exposition of the law may be, for a non-lawyer, difficult to grasp—even with the assistance of the company's legal advisors. A second problem with relying on case law as the source of directors' duties is that, due to the nature and the evolution of the common law, at any one point in time there will be certain gaps in the law as well as ambiguities and unresolved tensions between existing cases. The common law, as we shall see, has not always been wholly clear as to the nature of the obligations which directors' duties impose. A third problem is that case law may be slow to adjust to the changing circumstances in which business takes place and in which directors do their job. Codification is an opportunity to modernize the law. Accordingly, codification of directors' duties had three strong arguments in its favour: clarity of source and exposition for directors; an opportunity to fill in identified gaps and resolve identified ambiguities and tensions in the law; and an opportunity to reform the law and to bring it up to date with modern business conditions and practice.

Codification of the law of directors' duties brings with it, however, certain difficulties that one needs to consider in assessing whether codification is a good idea and whether, once undertaken, it is effective. Gap-filling and modernization sound eminently reasonable; even straightforward. However, the gaps, ambiguities, and inconsistencies which codification aims to resolve may be the product of competing and incommensurable underlying positions of policy and principle, both of which are operable in different cases and both of which have good arguments in their favour. Where the courts have made clearer policy elections, the legislature and its review bodies may discover that the traditional view may have much to be said for it and that alternative positions viewed as modern, perhaps in part because they have not been deployed or are deployed in other jurisdictions, may on closer inspection have potentially negative side-effects or at least present risks that deter the legislature from venturing beyond the security of the status quo. Accordingly, the legislature and its review bodies may find that they are no more capable of resolving these tensions, filling in these gaps, or modernizing the law than the courts have been.

If gap filling and modernization are found to be too difficult, controversial or unnecessary then codification is at most an accessible *restatement of the law*: a clearer exposition of the law for the directors whose behaviour it regulates. However, providing a clear restatement of the case law may not be as straightforward as one might expect. Where the law is complex or uncertain any attempt to *restate* the law runs the risk, as we shall see, of inadvertently *reforming* the law. If a company has a rule which says 'employees cannot wear coloured trousers' does a restatement of the rule to say 'employees cannot wear trousers which are coloured' change the rule in any way? If you think that on balance it does not, does it at least create scope to argue that it does?

Prior to the Companies Act 2006 there was an extensive reform debate which assessed and balanced the arguments for and against codification.[2] The Company Law Review recommended that the law of directors' duties be codified. The basis for this recommendation is set out in the following extract.

■ Company Law Review Steering Group: Final Report, Ch 3 'The Modern Company: Internal Governance and External Regulation'

The case for and against providing a clear restatement of directors' duties has been examined by the Law Commissions and has been set out by us in *Developing the Framework* and *Completing the Structure*. We continue to recommend such a legislative statement. We do so for three main reasons:

- it will provide greater clarity on what is expected of directors and make the law more accessible. We believe that this will in turn help to improve standards of governance…

- it will enable defects in the present law to be corrected in important areas where it no longer corresponds to accepted norms of modern business practice: this is particularly so in relation to the duties of conflicted directors and the powers of the company in respect of such conflicts (we deal with this in more detail below); and

- it is a key element in addressing the question of 'scope'—i.e. in whose interests should companies be run—in a way which reflects modern business needs and wider expectations of responsible business behaviour.

…

The need for clear, accessible and authoritative guidance for directors on which they may safely rely, on the basis that it will bind the courts and thus be consistently applied, combined with the need to clarify the law in the areas of uncertainty and to make good the defects, makes us all the more convinced that the case for a legislative restatement of directors' duties, or codification, is well founded.

The Government accepted the Company Law Review's codification recommendation. Sections 170–181 of the Companies Act 2006 codify the common law duties owed by directors of all companies, *whether public or private*. For the first time in English law

---

[2] Codification of directors' duties was considered by both a joint report of the Law Commission and the Scottish Law Commission, *Company Directors: Regulating Conflicts of Directors and Formulating a Statement of Duties* (Law Com No 261; Scot Law Com No 173) and the Company Law Review Steering Committee, *Developing the Framework*, 3.12–3.85 / *Completing the Structure*, ch 3.

since the introduction of the vehicle of the company form with separate legal personality, when a director asks his legal advisor what are the duties she owes as a director of the company the advisor will, in the first instance at least, show the director sections 170–181 of the Companies Act 2006. The Act makes it clear that these provisions replace the common law rules on directors' duties:

■ Section 170(3) CA 2006

(3) The general duties are based on certain common law rules and equitable principles as they apply in relation to directors and have effect in place of those rules and principles as regards the duties owed to a company by a director.

Note that although the Acts' provisions 'have effect in place' of the common law rules and equitable principles, as they are 'based on' those rules and principles it is clear that the Act's codification of directors' duties does not wipe the slate of the existing case law clean. Furthermore, section 170(4) clarifies that the pre-2006 case law continues to be applicable in interpreting these provisions.

■ Section 170(4) CA 2006

(4) The general duties shall be interpreted and applied in the same way as common law rules or equitable principles, and regard shall be had to the corresponding common law rules and equitable principles in interpreting and applying the general duties.

Accordingly, the pre-2006 cases remain of central importance to understanding directors' duties under the 2006 Act. Where the Act does not clearly change the existing law, we need to understand the prior case law in order to understand the corresponding legislative provisions. And, of course, in order to understand where, if at all, the law has been changed by the 2006 Act we need to understand the prior case law. Accordingly, the analysis of each duty in this book will commence with an examination of the pre-2006 position before proceeding to analyse the corresponding codification and its implications and effects.

V WHO OWES THE DUTIES?

The question for this section may strike the reader as odd. These duties are, after all, 'directors' duties'. They apply obviously, therefore, to directors! They apply to directors who have been correctly appointed in accordance with the appointment rules set out in a company's articles of association.[3] They apply to directors regardless of whether such directors are executive directors, who work full time at the company, or non-executive directors who do not. As we saw in Chapter 7, the increasing importance of the role of the non-executive director is a relatively recent phenomenon. Fully aware of this change in the composition of UK boards, in enacting the Companies Act 2006 the legislature has not sought to distinguish between these two types of director. Section 170(1) clarifies that the duties 'are owed by a director of the company to the company'. The Companies Act 2006 does not define the term director. It provides only that ' "director" includes any person occupying the position of director, by whatever name called'.[4]

---

[3] Respectively, articles 16 and 19 in the Draft Model Articles for Private and Public Companies.
[4] Section 250 CA 2006.

To what extent do these duties apply to persons who have not been formally appointed as directors? To what extent, if at all, do these duties apply to individuals who, with the directors' and/or shareholders' acquiescence, act as if they were directors; or to individuals or corporate persons who, through their active control and influence over formally appointed directors, in effect wield the power of a directorship? Do these duties, for example, apply to senior management who have not been appointed as directors?[5] Taking our case study as an example, assume Bob decides to retire from the day-to-day operational management of Bob's Electronics Ltd and to appoint Markus as CEO of the company but not as a director—Bob decides to remain as the sole director. Would Markus owe directors' duties to the company although not formally a director? Would it make a difference if Markus, with Bob's approval, called himself the managing director and acted as if he was a director? In the alternative, assume that Bob retires both from an operational role and as a director, appointing Markus as sole CEO and sole director of the company. Bob, however, is incapable of sitting on the sidelines and, following Markus's appointment, keeps interfering with the operational side of the business and regularly tells Markus what to do. Is Bob in such a situation subject to directors' duties? The answer to these questions are dependent on whether Markus[6] or Bob in these hypotheticals are 'de-facto' or 'shadow directors'.

1 De facto directors

1.1 Guidelines for identifying de facto directors

A *de facto director* is a person who the law treats as a director although she has not been formally appointed as a director. In the recent Supreme Court decision of *Re Paycheck Services 3 Ltd*[7] Lord Collins observes that the term 'de-facto director' was traditionally used to address situations in which there was a purported but defective appointment of a person as a director and where such person then proceeded to act as a director.[8] According to Lord Collins, as a result of a 'striking judicial innovation' in *Re Lo-Line Electric Motors Ltd*[9] and *Re Hydrodam (Corby) Ltd*[10] the term 'de-facto' director has come to be applied to persons in relation to whom there had been no purported or defective appointment but where a person merely purports to act as, or performs the functions of, a director.[11]

The courts have not provided a definition of a de facto director but rather have offered guidance on the factors which may be relevant to determining whether a person is a de facto director. In *Re Paycheck* several members of the Supreme Court approved of Millett J's definition in *Re Hydrodam (Corby) Ltd*:

> A de facto director is a person who assumes to act as a director. He is held out as a director of the company, and claims and purports to be a director, although never actually or validly appointed as such. To establish that a person was a de facto director of a company it is necessary to plead and prove that he undertook functions in relation to the company which could properly be discharged only by a director. It is not sufficient to show that he was concerned in the management of the company's affairs or undertook tasks in relation to its business which can properly be performed by a manager below board level.

---

[5] There is some authority that managers can owe types of duty (which are distinct from directors' duties and a function of their managerial role), for example a duty to disclose the misconduct of subordinate employees—*Sybron Corporation v Rochem* [1984] Ch 112.

[6] See *Fayers Legal Services Ltd v Day* [2001] All ER (D) 121 linking the determination of the application of a fiduciary duty to a manager to the analysis of whether the manager was a de facto director.

[7] [2011] 1 BCLC 141.

[8] See, for example, *Murray v Bush* (1873) LR 6 HL 37; *Mahoney v East Holyford Mining Co* (1875) LR 7 HL 869; *Morris v Kanssen* [1946] 1 ALL ER 586. See also section 161 CA 2006.

[9] [1988] BCLC 698.   [10] [1994] BCC 161.   [11] *Ibid.*

Millett J identifies three factors of relevance: first, is there an assumption by the person of the directorial role, suggesting an active and voluntary undertaking by the person to act as the company's director; secondly, was there a holding out *by the company*— which could be by the directors or the shareholders—that the person is a director; and thirdly, are the functions performed by that person functions that can only be carried out by directors and not merely functions that could be performed by senior managers with delegated authority. In *Secretary of State for Trade and Industry v Tjolle*[12] Jacobs J observed further that:

> I think what is involved is very much a question of degree. The court takes into account all the relevant factors. Those factors include at least whether or not there was a holding out by the company of the individual as a director, whether the individual used the title, whether the individual had proper information (e.g. management accounts) on which to base decisions, and whether the individual has to make major decisions and so on. Taking all these factors into account, one asks 'was this individual part of the corporate governing structure?', answering it as a kind of jury question. In deciding this, one bears very much in mind why one is asking the question.

For Jacobs J the central question is whether the person was 'part of the governing structure' of the company.[13] In addition, consistent with Millett J's judgment in *Hydrodam*, the court also considered whether the director was held out as a director by the company. In *Re Kaytech International plc*[14] Robert Walker LJ stressed that the courts in these cases were not 'enumerating tests which must all be satisfied if de facto directorship is to be established'. Nevertheless, he observed that the 'crucial issue is whether the individual in question has assumed the status and functions of a company director'.[15]

The focus on the assumption of status and function in *Hydrodam* and *Re Kaytech* were affirmed by their Lordships in *Re Paycheck*.[16] Although the Supreme Court was divided (a split 3–2 decision, with Lord Walker in the dissent), there is significant overlap between the majority and minority judgments both as regards the focus on assumption and as regards how courts should determine whether person has in fact assumed the role of a director. Lord Collins observes that: 'the basis of liability is the assumption of responsibility.'[17] Lord Hope DP, for the majority, observes that: 'one must look at what the person actually did to see whether he assumed those responsibilities in relation to the subject companies.'[18] Lord Walker (dissenting) also affirms that 'assumption' is the key consideration (as he did in *Re Kaytech*) but observes that it is used 'in a neutral sense, simply drawing attention to what the individual actually did'.[19]

If 'assumption' is a function of action, then the 'assumption' factor is effectively subsumed into the question of whether the person in question actually played a role in the governing structure of the company and actually exercised power as if he was a director.[20]

1.2 Corporate directors as de facto directors

In *Re Paycheck* the question for the court is whether the person who controls and acts on behalf of a corporate director of the subject company could be, or necessarily

---

[12] [1998] BCC 282.

[13] See also *Fayers Legal Services Ltd v Day* [2001] All ER (D) 121 focusing on the question of taking part in the governing structure.   [14] [1989] BCC 390.

[15] In spite of Walker LJ's protestations subsequent courts have referred to his approach as a 'test'—see Lord Hope DP in *Re Paycheck* [2011] 1 BCLC 141.

[16] *Ibid*.   [17] *Ibid* [96].   [18] [2011] 1 BCLC 141.

[19] Both Lord Hope and Lord Walker cite Lewison J in *Re Mea Corporation Ltd* [2006] EWHC 1846 (Ch), where he observed that 'in considering whether a person "assumes to act as a director" what is important is not what he calls himself, but what he did'.

[20] *Ibid per* Lord Walker at [115] 'if what he does amounts to taking all important decisions affecting the relevant company, and seeing that they are carried out, he is acting as a director of the company'.

is, a de facto director of that company.[21] In contrast to the corporate laws of most Anglo-American and Commonwealth jurisdictions, which require all directors to be real persons,[22] UK company law allows directors of a company to be real persons or corporate persons. The Companies Act 2006 requires that at least one director is a natural person and, by implication, provides that other directors could be corporate persons.[23] Prior to the 2006 Act there was no requirement that any director be a natural person.[24] So, for example, Bob from our case study could set up a separate company, Bob-The-Director Ltd, the shares in which are owned solely by him, and that company could then be appointed to the board of Bob's Electronics Ltd. When board meetings of Bob's Electronics Ltd are held a real person, designated by Bob-The-Director Ltd, would attend the meeting and vote at the meeting not in his personal capacity but as Bob-The-Director Ltd. While this may strike the uninitiated as quite bizarre, there are arguably some governance advantages of having a corporate director. Imagine that Bob-The-Director Ltd holds a majority of shares in Bobs Electronics Ltd and that Bob-The-Director Ltd is owned not by Bob alone but by Bob, Alison, and Helen. Bob, Alison, and Helen may all wish to play a role in the governance of Bob's Electronics but they decide that it is either inappropriate, or they have not got the time, for each of them to serve as members of the board. Appointing the corporate director would allow them to designate each of them in turn to represent Bob-The-Director Ltd at different meetings. It allows them to change the representative without having to go through the formal director removal and appointment process. It also enables them all to play a role in Bob's Electronics Ltd's board decisions by determining collectively, in advance of the meeting, how Bob-The-Director Ltd will vote.

However, the corporate director also, in theory, enables the avoidance of directors duties. Although Bob, Alison, and Helen play a role in controlling and directing Bob's Electronics Ltd through the corporate director, if their decisions—directing how the delegate should vote—result in a breach of duty by the corporate director, they themselves are not directly liable for that breach of duty. In many instances, of course, other legal rules may impose liability on Bob, Alison, and Helen. For example, a breach of the duty of loyalty by the corporate director in which Bob, Alison, or Helen benefit personally may well involve secondary liability for Bob, Alison, or Helen for dishonest assistance in the breach of fiduciary duty.[25] And of course, any damages for breach of duty may be enforced against the corporate director provided it is solvent; and in many instances—as will become clearer when you read the subsequent chapters—a breach of duty by the corporate director in the subject company is likely to be a breach of the duty of the directors of the corporate director.[26] Accordingly the extent to which a natural person can avoid directors' duties by using a corporate directorship should not be overstated. But it clearly makes it more difficult.

In *Re Paycheck*, a company in liquidation sued Mr Holland pursuant to section 212 of the Insolvency Act 1986[27] for breach of duty as a de facto director. Mr Holland was

---

[21] Note that *Re Hydrodam* also involved the question of whether corporate directors were de facto directors.

[22] See, for example, section 141(b) Delaware General Corporation Law; section 201B Australian Corporations Act 2001.

[23] Section 155 CA 2006.

[24] *Re Bulawayo Market and Offices Co Ltd* [1907] 2 Ch 458.

[25] See generally, P.S. Davies, 'Accessory Liability for Assisting Torts' (2011) 70 *Cambridge Law Journal* 368.

[26] However, enforcement of those duties may be more problematic—see further Chapter 15. In many instances the corporate director will have no function other than being a corporate director. If it does not have resources to pay for the breach then the subject company is likely to be the primary creditor of the corporate director enabling the subject company to take control of the corporate director.

[27] Section 212 Insolvency Act 1986 allows a liquidator or official receiver or creditor to apply for the court to examine the conduct of an officer of the company, including in relation to breach of duty or misfeasance, and to award a remedy in relation to such wrongdoing.

a 50% owner and designated representative of a corporate director[28] of multiple companies, including the claimant company, that were indebted to Her Majesty's Revenue and Customs (HMRC) due to a failed tax avoidance arrangement used by these companies. This failed avoidance scheme was designed to attract a lower rate of corporation tax and dividends were incorrectly paid on the basis that no additional tax would be payable. The majority of the Supreme Court held that he was not a de facto director simply by reason of controlling the corporate director and being the designated attendee of that director. Consider the following extracts from the judgment.

■ *Re Paycheck Services 3 Ltd* [2011] 1 BCLC 141

Lord Hope DP (in the majority together with Lord Collins and Lord Saville)
HMRC must plead and prove against Mr Holland that he was a de facto director of the composite companies. How is this to be done?...As Millett J said in *Re Hydrodam (Corby) Ltd* (at 182), the liability is imposed on those who were in a position to prevent damage to creditors by taking proper steps to protect their interests. As he put it, those who assume to act as directors and who thereby exercise the powers and discharge the functions of a director, whether validly appointed or not, must accept the responsibilities of the office. So one must look at what the person actually did to see whether he assumed those responsibilities in relation to the subject company.

The problem that is presented by this case, however, is that Mr Holland was doing no more than discharging his duties as the director of the corporate director of the composite companies. Everything that he did was done under that umbrella. Mr Green QC for HMRC was unable to point to anything that he did which could not be said to have been done by him in his capacity as a director of the corporate director. When asked what it was that lay outside his performance of that role, he said that it was simply the quality of his acts. He did everything. He was the decision maker, and he was the person who gave effect to those decisions. In *Re Hydrodam (Corby) Ltd* at 184 Millett J rejected the proposition that, where a body corporate is a director of a company, whether it be de jure, de facto or shadow director,[29] its own directors must ipso facto be shadow directors of the subject company. He said that attendance at board meetings and voting with others did not, *without more*, constitute him a director of any company of which his company is a director [emphasis added]. That would not be a fair description of what Mr Holland did in this case...

The 'without more' requirement that Millett J had in mind would not be satisfied by evidence that the individual director of the body corporate was actually giving instructions in that capacity to the subject company and the subject company was accustomed to act in accordance with those directions. That would not be enough to prove that the individual director assumed a role in the management of the subject company which imposed responsibility on him for misuse of the subject company's assets.

The facts of this case do not precisely match those in *Re Hydrodam (Corby) Ltd*. But I think, with respect, that Rimer LJ put his finger on the way the question in this case should be answered. In para [67] of his judgment he referred to the 'principle' that emerges from Millett J's judgment...He rejected the argument that the mere fact that an individual has been acting as a director of the corporate director can, or may, result in his also becoming a director of the subject company. In para [68] he expressed the principle that he had in mind in these words:

> '...The relevant act in relation to the affairs of the subject company is an act directed by the corporate director, not one directed by the latter company's individual board members. That may be regarded as a distinction of some technicality. But so long as we have a system of company law which recognises the difference between a company and its directors, it is a distinction which must be recognised and respected.'

---

[28] The corporate director was the sole director of each of these companies, as was permitted under the pre-2006 Act legal position.
[29] We consider shadow directors in section 2 of this chapter.

This was, I think, the point that Mr Knox was seeking to make when he referred to the speeches in *Salomon v A Salomon & Co Ltd* [1897] AC 22. As Lord Davey said (at 54), the intention of the legislature must be collected from the language of its enactments. One can properly say, as Lord Macnaghten did about the company and its subscribers (at 51), that a company is at law a different person from its directors and that it is the intention of the enactment that this distinction should be recognised. I do not think that one can overcome this distinction by pointing, as Mr Green seeks to do, simply to the quality of the acts done by the director and asking whether he was the guiding spirit of the subject company or had a real influence over its affairs. As a test, that would create far too much uncertainty…So long as the relevant acts are done by the individual entirely within the ambit of the discharge of his duties and responsibilities as a director of the corporate director, it is to that capacity that his acts must be attributed.

Lord Walker (dissenting)

'Something more'

The theme that 'something more' is required has been repeated in later cases, including the judgment of Rimer LJ in this case. Rimer LJ did not take from *Re Hydrodam (Corby) Ltd* (and I entirely agree) 'that the requisite more would be satisfied merely by the active participation of the board member in the making of board decisions by the corporate director in relation to the actions of the subject company.'

In a section of his judgment headed 'Mr Holland's case' (there is no parallel section considering the appellant's case) Lord Hope observes (at [41]), 'the facts of this case do not precisely match those in *Re Hydrodam (Corby) Ltd'*. That is, with respect, a considerable understatement. In *Re Hydrodam (Corby) Ltd*, as already noted, each of the individuals in question was one of about eight persons who made up the board of directors of Eagle, of which Hydrodam was a sub-sub-subsidiary. The pleaded case was that the Eagle directors were 'collectively responsible'. Being a de facto director is a matter of what the individual himself does on his own initiative, not simply as part of a process of collective decision-making.

Mr Holland was…the founder and guiding spirit of the whole Paycheck empire. With the concurrence of his wife (whose responsibilities were no more than secretarial) he was the only active director of both Paycheck Directors [the corporate director] and Paycheck Secretarial; he was the original holder of all the A shares which carried voting control of the composite companies…He took the decision (after receiving the advice of leading counsel at the consultation on 18 August 2004) that composite companies should continue trading, and should continue to pay dividends without reserving for higher rate corporation tax [which was subsequently found to be payable and which the company did not have the resources to pay].

If those facts did not amount to the 'something more' referred to in the authorities, it is hard to imagine circumstances that would do so. The repeated assertion that everything that Mr Holland did was done in his capacity as a director of Paycheck Directors, and was within his authority as a director of that company, is no doubt not 'pure sham' but it is, in my view, the most arid formalism. In my view Mr Holland was acting both as a de jure director of Paycheck Directors and as a de facto director of the composite companies. A de facto director is not formally invested with office, but if what he actually does amounts to taking all important decisions affecting the relevant company, and seeing that they are carried out, he is acting as a director of that company. It makes no difference that he is also acting as the only active de jure director of a corporate director of the company…

The Standard Chartered case

Mr Green QC, for HMRC, relied strongly on the decision of the House of Lords in *Standard Chartered Bank v Pakistan National Shipping Corp* [2002] UKHL 43. In that case Mr Mehra had made fraudulent misrepresentations on behalf of a company called Oakprime, of which he was a director. The Court of Appeal accepted the argument that he was not personally liable for deceit because he had been acting solely on behalf of Oakprime. The House of Lords trenchantly exposed the fallacy of this reasoning…[30]

Mr Knox QC, for Mr Holland, summarily dismissed this case as irrelevant on the ground that it was a claim in deceit. So it was, and there has never been any pleading or finding of dishonesty against Mr Holland. Nevertheless there is to my mind a significant parallel between liability for deceit and the unqualified statutory prohibition in s 263 of the 1985 Act on payment of a dividend otherwise than out of available profits. Contravention of this prohibition is a statutory wrong giving rise to strict liability, and anyone who is in a position to contravene it is likely to be in a fiduciary position (see further below). Mr Holland was the human cause of (and apart from his wife's secretarial assistance, the only human being who took any part in) the payment of unlawful dividends. They were, as Rimer LJ said (at [112]) payments which should never have been made. Mr Holland is liable for the payments because he deliberately made them. His liability has nothing to do with limited liability of shareholders, or with *Salomon v A Salomon & Co Ltd* [1897] AC 22, [1895–9] All ER Rep 33.

It is clear that the Companies Act 2006 allows a company to have a corporate director. It is equally clear that the corporate director owes duties to the company on which it serves as a director. The question here is in what circumstances a person who controls the decisions and actions of the corporate director—and thereby determines how a vote is cast in the board meeting—and who also represents the corporate director at the board meetings of the subject company is also a de facto director subject to directors' duties. Once again *Salomon v Salomon* and the notion that the company is a separate legal person casts a shadow of confusion over company law. However, as Lord Walker correctly points out, the case has nothing to do—or at least should have nothing to do—with *Salomon v Salomon*. The fact that the controller of the corporate director could be found to be a de facto director does not disregard the corporate entity. Just as finding a director personally liable in deceit[31] when he was acting in the course of his directorship does not ignore the separate legal personality of the company—his liability is a function of the tort of deceit—here the answer to the question who is a de facto director is determined *by the legal rules that determine who is a de facto director*. The fact that the answer to that question may encroach on what were perceived to be benefits of incorporation does not mean that the separate legal personality is disregarded. The majority is not correct when they suggest that to find the controller of the corporate director a de facto director when he has always acted in the parameters of that role would necessarily be contrary to the principle set forth in *Salomon v Salomon*.

The disagreement then between the majority and the minority rests not on the respect, or lack thereof, for the separate legal personality of the company, but on the rules that determine when a person is a de facto director. Yet, as discussed previously in section V 1.1, both Lord Hope and Lord Walker appear to agree on the core requirement: the assumption of responsibility by the person as evidenced by what he 'actually did'. In this corporate director context, what the majority—following Millett J in *Hydrodam*—mean by this is that the person in question must have actually acted in a way that indicates that he assumes personal responsibility; acted in a way that is distinctive from his actions taken in the role of the representative of the corporate director. That is, there must be *something more* than merely performing the role of the representative of the corporate director or participating in the corporate director's corporate organs (shareholder or board meetings); his actions must indicate that he assumes the role of the director in a personal capacity. It is very difficult to imagine what such actions would involve, or indeed any actions that could satisfy the requirement of 'something

---

[30] For extracts and consideration of this case see Chapter 4, pp 144–46.
[31] See Chapter 4.

more' apart from an explicit verbal assumption of such personal responsibility. This is closely analogous to the approach set forth in *Williams v Natural Life Health Foods Ltd*[32] where the House of Lords held that in order for the director to be personally liable in tort the director must have acted in a way that resulted in him assuming personal responsibility for the actions that caused loss to the claimant. In both contexts the likelihood of a personal assumption is very low.

In contrast, when Lord Walker says what matters is what the person 'actually did', he means quite simply that you are a de facto director if you alone are responsible for the vote cast in the board meeting of the subject company. He observes that: 'if what he actually does amounts to taking all important decisions affecting the relevant company, and seeing that they are carried out, he is acting as a director of that company'. Lord Clarke (also dissenting) observed in this regard that 'the real purpose of [the de facto director concept] is to identify those, other than professional advisers, with real influence in the corporate affairs of the company'.[33] The conceptual basis underpinning liability is, therefore, very different for the dissenting judges. For the majority, 'the basis of liability is the assumption of responsibility'.[34] For the dissent, directors' duties apply to those persons who *in fact* exercise real influence over the exercise of corporate power. With respect, it is submitted that the clarity of this approach is somewhat obfuscated by Lord Walker's acceptance of, and engagement with, the 'assumption/something more' framework, which is wholly unnecessary for the approach which he formulates. It seems likely that his Lordship was constrained in this regard by the fact that he himself articulated this 'test' in *Re Kaytech*.[35]

There is clearly much to commend such an approach which focuses on the exercise of or influence over corporate power. In this author's view, it is regrettable that the majority did not adopt it. It would ensure that directors' duties do what they are supposed to do: impose behavioural obligations on those who exercise, or who are responsible for the exercise of, corporate power. The path created by the requirement for assumption of responsibility appears to have distracted their Lordships from this core function.

2 Shadow directors

2.1 Who is a shadow director?

Section 170(5) provides that: 'The general duties apply to shadow directors where, and to the extent that, the corresponding common law rules or equitable principles so apply'. A shadow director is defined in section 251 of the Companies Act 2006 as: 'a person in accordance with whose directions or instructions the directors of the company are accustomed to act'.

In *Hydrodam (Corby) Ltd*,[36] Millet J (as he then was) provided a helpful and authoritative account of how to determine whether a person is a shadow director in the context of section 214 of the Insolvency Act 1986 (which also applies to shadow directors):

> A shadow director, by contrast, does not claim or purport to act as a director. On the contrary, he claims not to be a director. He lurks in the shadows,[37] sheltering behind others who, he claims, are the only directors of the company to the exclusion of himself. He is not held out as a director

---

[32] [1998] 2 All ER 577.

[33] At [127] echoing Morritt LJ in *Secretary of State for Trade and Industry v Deverell* [2002] 2 BCLC 133, [35].

[34] *Per* Lord Collins [96].   [35] [1989] BCC 390.   [36] [1994] BCC 161.

[37] Whilst the imagery of 'lurking in the shadows' is helpful, as Lord Walker points out in *Re Paycheck* [2011] 1 BCLC 141, a shadow director need not be hidden from view: 'he may be the chief executive of a group of companies who openly gives direction to the board of a subsidiary company on which he does not sit'.

by the company. To establish that a defendant is a shadow director of a company it is necessary to allege and prove: (1) who are the directors of the company, whether de facto or de jure; (2), that the defendant directed those directors how to act in relation to the company or that he was one of the persons who did so; (3) that those directors acted in accordance with such directions; and (4) that they were accustomed so to act. What is needed is first, a board of directors claiming and purporting to act as such; and secondly, a pattern of behaviour in which the board did not exercise any discretion or judgment of its own, but acted in accordance with the directions of others.

The phase 'accustomed to act' used by Millet J suggests that what is needed is more than a one-off event in which the actual director suspends her own judgment. Hence Millett J's suggestions that what is required is 'a pattern of behaviour' of implementing another person's (the shadow director's) instructions. However, establishing such a 'pattern of behaviour' does not require showing that the de jure directors in question never exercise their own discretion and judgment. In *Secretary of State for Trade and Industry v Deverell*, in relation to an action brought pursuant to the Company Directors Disqualification Act 1986, Morritt LJ observed that 'it is not necessary that [the] influence [of the shadow director] should be exercised over the whole field of its corporate activities'.[38]

It is common for company law lawyers to use epithets, such as 'puppet' and 'puppeteer' to convey the meaning of the term 'shadow director'. However, in *Deverell* Morritt LJ warns us that such epithets may make it more difficult to view a person as a shadow director than the law actually requires:[39]

Thus to describe the board as the cat's paw, puppet or dancer to the tune of the shadow director implies a degree of control both of quality and extent over the corporate field in excess of what the statutory definition requires. What is needed is that the board is accustomed to act on the directions or instructions of the shadow director.

A range of individuals and corporate bodies could, depending on the circumstances of each case, be found to be shadow directors. Obvious candidates would include active majority shareholders, directors of parent companies, or banks that take a more active role in the company when the company is struggling. Generally, the courts have been relatively conservative in actually finding persons to be shadow directors. In *Re PFTZM Ltd (in liquidation)*,[40] for example, a finance company held weekly management meetings with a failing company to whom they had lent money and, in addition, monies paid to the company were required to be paid into an account held in the name of the finance company. The court found that there was no prima facie case that the finance company was a shadow director, as they were merely trying to protect their position as creditors.

In *Hydrodam* the company in liquidation had a corporate director that was part of a multi-layered corporate structure with several subsidiaries between it and the ultimate parent. The liquidator claimed that two directors of the ultimate parent (of a board of nine members) were shadow directors, although it was unclear that they had been involved in any decision related to the corporate director. The question was whether they were shadow directors merely by reason of being directors of the ultimate parent. Millett J,

---

[38] *Secretary of State for Trade and Industry v Deverell* [2000] BCLC 133 also observing that: 'if, as the judge concluded, the directors usually took the advice of [the purported shadow director], it is irrelevant that on the occasions when he did not give advice the board did exercise its own discretion' [59]; and 'such directions and instructions do not have to extend over all or most of the corporate activities of the company' [36].

[39] Indirectly critiquing Harman J *Re Unisoft Group Ltd (No 3)* [1994] 1 BCLC 609 for using these terms.

[40] [1995] 2 BCLC 354.

applying the test that was central to the Supreme Court's analysis in *Re Paycheck*,[41] held that 'without more' a director of a corporate director was not a shadow director of the company. He observed that had the corporate director been used to taking instructions from the ultimate parent then the ultimate parent not its individual directors would be a shadow director. Following the approach taken in *Re Paycheck*, it seems probable in a corporate director context that the 'something more' required to find that a director of a corporate director is a shadow director would, similar to the Supreme Court's majority approach in *Re Paycheck*, require some act that indicates that the director of the corporate director is acting in his personal capacity not his corporate capacity.

If this is correct, a strong argument—which builds on the dissent in *Re Paycheck*—can be made that this is an unnecessarily narrow reading of the statutory definition of a shadow director. Clearly the definition could be read in the same way that the dissenting Law Lords approached the de facto director question: a person, or persons, who *in fact* exercise real influence over the exercise of corporate power through the de jure directors that do their bidding are shadow directors of the company. If a real person exercises corporate power through the vehicle of a corporate director, such an approach could result in a finding that the real person is a shadow director. If another company is placed between the corporate director (a corporate director's parent) and the real controlling person, then that could result in *both* the parent company and the actual real person being shadow directors. Such an approach does not disregard the separate legal personality of the company: the finding that such a real person (or the parent) is a shadow director is simply a function of a purposive interpretation of the definition of a shadow director.[42]

Finally we need to consider the relationship between a de facto director and a shadow director. Could a person be deemed to be both a de facto director and a shadow director? In *Hydrodam* the liquidator claimed that corporate directors of the subject company could be deemed to be de facto or shadow directors. Millett J took exception to this claim that there was any overlap between these two categories. He observed that:

> In my judgment an allegation that a defendant acted as de facto or shadow director, without distinguishing between the two, is embarrassing. It suggests—and counsel's submissions to me support the inference—that the liquidator takes the view that de facto or shadow directors are very similar, that their roles overlap, and that it may not be possible to determine in any given case whether a particular person was a de facto or a shadow director. I do not accept that at all. The terms do not overlap. They are alternatives, and in most and perhaps all cases are mutually exclusive.

However, in *Re Paycheck*[43] two of their Lordships, Lords Collins and Clarke, rejected this view. Lord Clarke observed that 'there is no conceptual difficulty in holding that a person can be both a shadow director and a de facto director'.

2.2 What duties do shadow directors owe?

Now that we understand what a shadow director is, in what circumstances are they required to comply with directors' duties? Section 170(5) refers us to the corresponding common law rules. However, to date there is only one reported case which addresses this issue in detail, an extract from which is included here.

---

[41] Note that in *Re Paycheck* the question of whether Mr Holland was a shadow director was not in issue because section 212 of the Insolvency Act 1986, pursuant to which the action was brought, applies to de facto but not shadow directors.

[42] See *Secretary of State for Trade and Industry v Deverell* [2000] BCLC 133 observing that 'the definition of a shadow director is to be construed in the normal way to give effect to the parliamentary intention ascertainable from the mischief to be dealt with'.

[43] [2011] 1 BCLC 141.

■ *Ultraframe (UK) Ltd v Fielding* [2005] EWHC 1638

Lewison J

Do shadow directors owe directors' duties to the company?

The statutory definition of 'shadow director' has been enacted for specific purposes of company legislation. These include many prohibitions relating to transactions between companies and their directors; duties of disclosure and liability for wrongful trading[44] or to the making of disqualification orders.[45] There is no specific statutory provision that says that a shadow director owes the same duties to a company as a *de jure* or *de facto* director. [Defendant counsel] submitted that a shadow director owes no fiduciary duties to a company in relation to which he is a shadow director. He said that the term 'shadow director' is a limited statutory concept, not a concept of the general law. From its statutory use, it is clear that the expression is used for far narrower purposes than the definition of a 'director', even where that definition is extended. If the intention of Parliament had been to equate 'shadow directors' with 'directors' *for all statutory purposes*, this could have been simply achieved by extending the definition of 'director' to include a 'shadow director'. This was not done. If Parliament had intended to impose all directors' duties on shadow directors, this would have been easy to achieve by the simple expedient of providing that a shadow director owes the same duties to a company as a director. Parliament has done this, for example, in section 417 (1) of the Financial Services and Markets Act 2000. Instead, in the Companies Act 1985 Parliament has specified those duties which apply to shadow directors, while remaining silent on others...

With one exception, there is no authority on the point. The one exception is *Yukong Line of Korea Ltd v. Rendsburg Corp Investments of Liberia Inc* [1998] 1 WLR 294 in which Toulson J said:

> 'As to an unlawful means conspiracy, Mr. Yamvrias undoubtedly owed a fiduciary duty to Rendsburg. Although he was not formally a director, he was a "shadow director" and controlled the company's activities.'

Toulson J did not explain the reasons that led him to the conclusion that a shadow director 'undoubtedly' owes fiduciary duties to the company. Indeed at least one distinguished academic commentator has expressed the opposite view (Pennington: *Company Law* (1995) p. 712).[46] The findings of fact that Toulson J made more naturally lead to the conclusion that Mr Yamvrias was a *de facto* rather than a shadow director. It seems to me, therefore, that I must be cautious before accepting that a shadow director 'undoubtedly' owes fiduciary duties to the company of which he is a shadow director. The instructions that a shadow director gives (and which the *de jure* directors act upon) may be quite inimical to the company's interests. It would be odd if, in those circumstances, a person who has no direct relationship with the company and who consistently gives instructions inimical to its interests were nevertheless held to have undertaken a duty of loyalty to the company; and to have agreed to subordinate his own interest to those of the company. Moreover the wider the interpretation of the statutory definition, the less easy it becomes to impose upon one who falls within the definition the full range of fiduciary duties imposed upon a *de jure* or *de facto* director. I am not persuaded that the mere fact that a person falls within the statutory definition of 'shadow director' is enough to impose upon him the same fiduciary duties to the relevant company as are owed by a *de jure* or *de facto* director.

In truth, it seems to me that the use of labels such as 'shadow director', which is a statutory definition, may serve only to obscure the real question. The real question is not what is the proper label to attach? It is: in what circumstances will equity impose fiduciary obligations on a person with regard to property belonging to another? Somewhat depressingly, *Snell's Equity* (31st ed. 7–07) says:

> 'Identifying the kind of circumstances that justify the imposition of fiduciary duties is made difficult by the fact that the courts have consistently declined to provide a definition, or even a uniform

---

[44] See Chapter 18.
[45] See footnotes 37–39 of Chapter 12 and section V of Chapter 18.
[46] R.R. Pennington, *Pennington's Company Law* (7th edn, Butterworths, 1995).

description, of a fiduciary relationship, preferring to preserve flexibility in the concept. Numerous academic commentators have offered suggestions, but none has garnered universal support. The fiduciary relationship is a concept in search of a principle.

There is, however, growing judicial support for the view that a fiduciary is someone who has undertaken to act for or on behalf of another in a particular matter in circumstances which give rise to a relation of trust and confidence. The concept encaptures a situation where one person is in a relationship with another which gives rise to a legitimate expectation, which equity will recognise that the fiduciary will not utilise his or her position in such a way which is adverse to the interests of the principal.'

The formulation in the second of these paragraphs is taken from the judgment of Millett LJ in *Bristol & West BS v. Mothew* [1998] Ch 1 and the opinion of the Privy Council in *Arklow Investments Ltd v. Maclean* [2000] 1 WLR 594. [Defendant counsel] thus submitted that the key component of a fiduciary duty is the obligation of loyalty. I must, therefore, he said look for facts which support the inference that the company was in a relation of trust and confidence with the putative fiduciary. The relation must be a direct one between the putative fiduciary and the person on whose behalf he acts…

The indirect influence exerted by a paradigm shadow director who does not directly deal with or claim the right to deal directly with the company's assets will not usually, in my judgment, be enough to impose fiduciary duties upon him; although he will, of course be subject to those statutory duties and disabilities that the Companies Act creates. The case is the stronger where the shadow director has been acting throughout in furtherance of his own, rather than the company's, interests. However, on the facts of a particular case, the activities of a shadow director may go beyond the mere exertion of indirect influence.

For example, [if a person who is not a de jure director becomes a signatory to a company's bank account]…By voluntarily becoming the sole signatory on that account, [such a person] took it upon himself to assume control of an asset belonging to another. That voluntary assumption must, in my judgment, carry with it a duty to use the asset for the benefit of the person to whom it belongs. That duty is properly called a fiduciary duty. However, it is important to recognise that this fact alone does not mean that wider fiduciary duties are imposed upon [that person].

For Lewison J whilst the circumstances of a particular case may result in a shadow director being subject to particular fiduciary duties, directors' duties will not automatically apply to the shadow director simply by reason of being a shadow director. The basis for this decision is that the imposition of directors' duties requires the voluntary assumption on the part of the person in question of obligations of trust and confidence. Section 170(5) of the Act does not alter this position rather it defers to the existing case law.

The idea of the shadow director was captured by Millett J in *Hydrodam* when he described them as lurking in the shadows. Clearly, actors who lurk in the shadows and influence the exercise of power by the actual power holders are highly unlikely to voluntarily assume a relationship of trust and confidence. The reason they lurk in the shadows is consciously to avoid to be seen to be exercising power on behalf of another; to avoid being the object of another person's trust and confidence. The decision in *Ultraframe* connecting the duties actually owed by a shadow director to a voluntary assumption of responsibility appears, therefore, to be contrary to the very idea of a shadow director. As a consequence, there remains some doubt about whether *Ultraframe* is correct in this regard. Dan Prentice and Jenny Payne have argued, correctly in this author's view, that 'the full panoply of directors duties' should be imposed by the law on shadow directors regardless of assumption.[47]

---

[47] D. Prentice and J. Payne, 'Directors' Fiduciary Duties' (2006) 122 *LQR* 558. A limited body of case law would support the position that a person will be treated as a fiduciary where they influence the exercise of corporate power—regardless of whether they have voluntarily assumed to act on behalf of another—see *Erlanger v New Sombrero Phosphate Co* [1874–80] All ER Rep 271.

VI TO WHOM ARE THE DUTIES OWED?

As we have seen, directors are the agents of the company. *In law* neither the company nor the board of directors is an agent of a 'principal' shareholder. It follows clearly, therefore, that the duties directors owe are owed to the company that they serve. These duties are *not* owed to shareholders, individually or collectively, or to any other constituency or group that has a relationship with the company. As we have seen, section 170(1) of the 2006 Act codifies this position: 'duties are owed by a director of a company *to the company*'.

This does not mean, of course, that in specific circumstances the relationship between a director and a shareholder or the shareholder body could not result in a duty-type relationship between director and shareholder or any other constituency. However, such duties are founded in the special circumstances of such relationships and are distinct from the generally applicable directors' duties discussed in the remainder of this chapter and Chapters 10–14.

■ *Peskin v Anderson* [2000] All ER (D) 2278

The Royal Automobile Club Limited (the RACL) club was a limited company formed for the purposes of furthering the interests of motorists. The company owned the well-known RAC car breakdown business. Pursuant to the provisions of RACL's articles of association, profits from the business could not be distributed to members but had to be used for furthering the interests of motorists. Following an approach by a company called Cendant, RACL decided to sell the RAC business and to change its articles of association to allow a distribution of some of the proceeds of the sale to members (a process sometimes referred to as de-mutualization). The former members of the RACL sued the directors of RACL for breach of fiduciary duty which they claimed was *owed to the members*. They argued that had they known that the directors were in negotiations to sell the RAC business then they would have remained members and that the directors had breached a duty owed to them *as members* to disclose the existence of the negotiations to sell the RAC business.

Mummery LJ

The fiduciary duties owed to the company arise from the legal relationship between the directors and the company directed and controlled by them. The fiduciary duties owed to the shareholders do not arise from that legal relationship. They are dependent on establishing a special factual relationship between the directors and the shareholders in the particular case. Events may take place which bring the directors of the company into direct and close contact with the shareholders in a manner capable of generating fiduciary obligations, such as a duty of disclosure of material facts to the shareholders...

These duties may arise in special circumstances which replicate the salient features of well established categories of fiduciary relationships. Fiduciary relationships, such as agency, involve duties of trust, confidence and loyalty. Those duties are, in general, attracted by and attached to a person who undertakes, or who, depending on all the circumstances, is treated as having assumed, responsibility to act on behalf of, or for the benefit of, another person. That other person may have entrusted or, depending on all the circumstances, may be treated as having entrusted, the care of his property, affairs, transactions or interests to him. There are, for example, instances of the directors of a company making direct approaches to, and dealing with, the shareholders in relation to a specific transaction and holding themselves out as agents for them in connection with the acquisition or disposal of shares or making material representations to them; or failing to make material disclosure to them of insider information in the context of negotiations for a take-over of the company's business; or supplying to them specific information and advice on which they have relied. These events are capable of constituting special circumstances and of generating fiduciary obligations, especially in those cases in which the directors, for their own benefit, seek to use their position and special inside knowledge acquired by them to take improper or unfair advantage of the shareholders.

...

The special facts from which it is contended that this fiduciary duty to the members emerges are that knowledge of the proposal by the directors was inside information of which the directors had exclusive possession; that they had acquired the information by virtue of their office; that the information provided knowledge to the directors of the potential financial value of membership of…RACL, which was not known to the members; that that knowledge was, contrary to their expectations, that their membership (which could not have been sold or transferred) could have any value; that, by resigning membership, the claimants had given up any right to participate in the substantial assets of RACL; and that they had done so in ignorance of the directors' plans to allow members to benefit from a distribution.

I agree with the judge that these factors are insufficient to found a claim for the existence and breach of a fiduciary duty to disclose to the claimants the proposals and plans for de-mutualisation. There was nothing special in the factual relationship between the directors and the members in this case to give rise to a fiduciary duty of disclosure. In particular there were no relevant dealings, negotiations, communications or other contact directly between the directors and the members; the actions of the directors had not caused the members to retire when they did; and, probably most important of all, prior to March 1998 there was nothing sufficiently concrete and specific, either in existence or in contemplation, for the directors to disclose to the members.

The Court of Appeal in *Peskin v Anderson* clearly affirms that directors' duties are owed to the company and not to any of a company's constituencies.[48] To the extent that directors owe fiduciary duties to other groups they arise idiosyncratically from the 'special circumstances' of the case which 'replicate the salient features of' fiduciary relationships.[49] The Court of Appeal suggests, in the final paragraph of this extract, that at a minimum this will require direct contact or communication between the director and the shareholder. Typically, therefore, the scope for such duties to arise is greater in the context of close companies, where direct contact is more common, than it is in widely-held companies.

One context in which direct communication between the board and shareholders takes place in listed companies is where directors provide shareholders with their opinion on the nature and merits of a takeover bid for their shares in the company.[50] The courts have resisted any attempt to formalize or to label any duty owed to shareholders—whether viewed as a fiduciary or other type of duty—as a result of such communication. They have, however, held that where directors advise shareholders it should be in good

---

[48] For an earlier authority in this regard see *Percival v Wright* [1902] 2 Ch 421. See also *Chez Nico (Restaurants) Ltd* [1991] BCC 736.

[49] For commonwealth cases finding a duty arising out of such special circumstances, see the New Zealand case of *Coleman v Myers* [1977] 2 NZLR 225 and the Court of Appeal of New South Wales' decision in *Brunninghausen v Glavanics* [1999] 46 NSWLR 538.

[50] Pursuant to Rule 25.1 of the Takeover Code, for example, the board of the target company (the company whose shares the buyer wishes to purchase) must 'circulate to the company's shareholders its opinion of the offer'.

faith and should not be misleading. Consider in this regard Lord Cullen's comments on this issue in *Dawson International Plc v Coats Paton Plc*:[51]

> Directors have but one master, the company…If on the other hand directors take it on themselves to give advice to current shareholders [then] clearly…they have a duty to advise in good faith and not fraudulently, and not to mislead whether deliberately or carelessly. If they fail to do so the affected shareholders may have a remedy, including the recovery of what is truly the personal loss sustained by them as a result. However, these cases do not, in my view, demonstrate a pre-existing fiduciary duty to the shareholders but a potential liability arising out of their words or actions which can be based on ordinary principles of law. This, I may say, appears to be a more satisfactory way of expressing the position of directors in this context than by talking of a so-called secondary fiduciary duty to the shareholders.

In summary, therefore, whilst the cases make clear that duties between directors and shareholders may arise, they are the product of special circumstances. Outside of these special circumstances, which will be of limited further concern to us in this book,[52] a director's duties are owed only to his 'master': the company.

 Online Resource Centre
http://www.oxfordtextbooks.co.uk/orc/kershaw2e/

Visit the Online Resource Centre for additional resources and information available for this chapter, including web links and an interactive flashcard glossary.

---

[51] [1989] BCLC 233; see also *Heron International Ltd v Lord Grade; Associated Communications Corp Plc* [1983] BCLC 244.

[52] One context in which such duties to shareholders raise issues of concern to us in this book is in the context of the rule on reflective loss, considered in Chapter 15.

CHAPTER TEN

REGULATING DISCRETION I: ACTING IN THE COMPANY'S INTERESTS

When directors make decisions there are two types of expectation we might have of them. The first would be an expectation in relation to the nature of the decision or action taken: we might expect, for example, that directors make good or reasonable decisions that further the company's interests or, alternatively, a decision that they think is in the company's interests. When reviewing that decision a court would ask: did the actual decision correspond to the standard for decisions—the expectation—that we set for the director. Separate from the nature and quality of the actual decision or action itself, we might also have an expectation of the director relating to the way in which he went about making the decision: we might require him to be careful or to take a certain degree of care when making the decision. The expectation we have of the director in regard to the care he takes in making decisions is a separate expectation than the expectation we have of the quality of the actual decision itself. English law separates these expectations into two separate duties: *the duty to promote the success of the company* (previously, the duty to act in good faith in the best interests of the company); and *the duty of care, skill, and diligence.*

The former duty to promote the company's best interests is traditionally, as it was presented in Chapter 9, presented as a branch or sub-duty of the duty of loyalty. This is correct: to demand loyalty is to demand that when corporate power is exercised by directors it is used to promote the interests of the company, not to promote the director's or someone else's interests. However, the duty to act in the company's interests, which we address in this chapter, is not only an expectation of loyalty, it sets forth the standard according to which courts review the actual action or decision taken by the director. One might say, therefore, that this duty regulates the exercise of discretion by directors; it provides the law's standard of competence in relation to the quality of the decision or action *as distinct from* the process that led up to the decision or action, which is regulated by the duty of care.[1]

---

[1] This is not a wholly uncontroversial position, and not one in relation to which one finds a clear statement of English law. It is, however, as will be set out in the following chapters, the most coherent explanation of how the law functions. There is some support for this position in cases that address business judgments only through the lens of the duty to promote the success of the company (e.g., *Regentcrest plc v Cohen* [2001] 2 BCLC 80); but equally some cases, wrongly in this author's view, have applied the duty of care to the business judgment itself (*Roberts v Frohlich* [2011] 2 BCLC 625). Care also needs to be taken in relation to this point in not assuming that the cases on section 214 Insolvency Act 1986 apply to directors' duties regulation of business decisions. Section 214(4) explicitly applies a reasonable average director standard to business judgments, which is not the case in relation to section 174 CA 2006.

I THE PRE-2006 ACT COMMON LAW DUTY TO ACT IN GOOD FAITH IN THE BEST INTERESTS OF THE COMPANY

A loyal director when exercising the powers that have been conferred upon him by the articles of association is expected to use those powers to benefit the company. In *Re Smith & Fawcett*,[2] where the court considered the directors' refusal to register a share transfer to the beneficiary of a deceased member, Lord Greene set forth the common law position as follows:

> The principles to be applied in cases where the articles of a company confer a discretion on directors...are, for the present purposes, free from doubt. They must exercise their discretion bona fide in what they consider—not what a court may consider—is in the interests of the company, and not for any collateral purpose.

Two questions arise from this statement *of the duty to act in good faith in the best interests of the company*. The first question is: what are the company's interests? Thus far in the analysis set out in this book we have assumed for simplicity's sake that the interests of the shareholders and the company are synonymous. But is this correct as a matter of law? The second question is: how does one determine whether a particular decision taken by a director has in fact been taken in what *he considers* to be the best interests of the company and not with some other interests in mind, what Lord Greene refers to as a 'collateral purpose'? This section will address these two issues in turn.

1 What are the company's interests at common law?

1.1 Does the company have its own interests?

The common law duty as set out by Lord Greene provides that directors when exercising their discretion must act in *the company's* interests. But what are the company's interests? Every real person has multiple interests and goals that may range from money and fast cars to free time and lots of sleep. Each real person is the arbiter of what interests she prioritizes—which interests count more than the others: time at work earning money and becoming a partner versus time at home with the children and less money to buy fast cars. A company is also a person, albeit a legal not a real person. As a legal person, does a company have its *own* interests or is it necessary to define the company's interests according to the interests of other groups with whom the company has relationships such as the shareholders, employees, or creditors (we will refer to such groups generally—including shareholders—as the company's constituencies)?

Many of you may respond that as a company is not a real person how could it possibly have its own interests distinct from those of its constituencies? Others may argue that the company, once it comes into existence, generates something akin to a real personality with real interests. The company may, for example, have a distinctive culture that forms the behaviour and personalities of real people who work there; there may be a distinctive 'idea' of the company held by its employees; it may have a distinctive image projected onto those who engage with it from the outside. For example, the London School of Economics (LSE), the author's employer, is a company[3] with separate legal personality. For the people who work and study at the LSE there is a sense that the LSE has an identity; that it stands for certain ideals or goals, whether they be intellectual goals—to produce high quality scholarship—or pedagogical goals—to produce high

---

[2] [1942] Ch 304.   [3] The London School of Economics is a company limited by guarantee.

quality teaching. There is something that we, as students or employees, feel is distinctive and alive about the institution of the LSE. However, is it possible to distil what this is into a coherent idea of 'company or organizational interests'; or does any statement of 'company interest' necessarily refer to the interests of one or more of the groups with whom the company has relationships? The two interests of the LSE just mentioned are not distinct from these groups: the Government in funding higher education at the LSE and elsewhere is interested in high quality scholarship; students are interested in good teaching.

In this regard, Professor Ferran notes that 'theories of the company in which the company is viewed as a real person [capable of having its own interests] have had a limited influence on the development of Anglo-American/Commonwealth company and corporations law but it is noticeable that in continental Europe...the idea of corporate interests being defined by reference to the business entity is not seen as problematic'.[4] In France, for example, she notes that a company's interests are viewed as distinct from the interests of the company's constituencies.[5] English company law does not, however, attempt to identify corporate interests that are distinguishable from the interests of its constituencies.[6]

1.2 The company's interests as shareholders' interests

Companies engaged in business for profit have several constituencies: members of the company who are the **residual interest holders** of the company; creditors who are owed sums of money by the company; employees who have contractual relations with the company to provide their services; customers who buy the company's products and services; and suppliers who provide supplies to make those products. At common law the interests of a company have long been understood to mean the interests of its members. However, the authority for this proposition in relation to a company limited by shares is somewhat sparse. In *Gaiman v National Association for Mental Health*,[7] a case dealing with a company limited by guarantee that carried out charitable activities, Megarry J held that:

> The question, then, is whether that powers [have been exercised by the board] in the best interests of the [company]. The [company] is, of course, an artificial legal entity, and it is not very easy to determine what is in the best interests of the [company] without paying due regard to the members of the [company]. The interests of some particular section or sections of the [company] cannot be equated with those of the [company], and I accept the interests of both present and future members of the [company], as a whole, as being a helpful expression of a human equivalent.

Megarry J cited *Greenhalgh v Arderne Cinemas Ltd*[8] in support of this holding. In *Greenhalgh*,[9] a case dealing not with the exercise of board authority but the question of

---

[4] E. Ferran, *Company Law and Corporate Governance* (OUP, 1999), 134.

[5] See further M. Viénot, 'Rapport sur le Conseil d'Administration des Sociétés Cotées' (1995) 8 *Revue de Droit des Affaires Internationales* 935.

[6] Making this point see Nourse LJ in the Court of Appeal's judgment in *Brady v Brady* [1988] BCLC 20: 'the interests of a company, an artificial person, cannot be distinguished from the interests of the persons who are interested in it. Who are those persons? Where a company is both going and solvent, first and foremost come the shareholders, present and no doubt future as well.' Note in *Dawson International Plc v Coats Paton Plc* [1989] BCLC 233 Lord Cullen distinguished between the interests of the company from the interests of 'current shareholders'. However, there is nothing in the opinion to suggest that Lord Cullen had in mind a distinct corporate interest distinct from the interests of current and future shareholders.

[7] [1970] 2 All ER 362.   [8] [1950] Ch 286, 291.   [9] [1950] 2 All ER 1120.

whether a shareholder resolution was passed in the 'best interests of the company as a whole',[10] Lord Evershed MR held that:

> The phrase, 'the company as a whole' does not (at any rate in such a case as the present) mean the company as a commercial entity as distinct from the corporators. It means the corporators as a general body. That is to say, you may take the case of an individual hypothetical member and ask whether what is proposed is, in the honest opinion of those who voted in its favour, for that person's benefit.

In the case of a commercial company, the interests of the members will usually be in increasing the value of their shareholding.[11] For most companies, therefore, acting in the 'company's interests' means acting to promote shareholder value. It is clear that at common law the interests of other constituencies could, however, be taken into account provided that so doing furthered the interests of shareholders.[12]

It is important to note that the common law provides a **default** understanding of what a company's interests are. That is, *in the absence of contrary intention* set out in the company's articles, the company's interests will be the interests of present and future members as a whole. But the company *could* elect to define its interests differently in its articles: to be run in the interests of other constituencies or a combination of constituencies.[13]

Lord Evershed MR in *Greenhalgh* refers only to the corporators, by which he means the shareholders' interests. Megarry J in *Gaiman* refers to both existing and future shareholders. It seems like an odd idea for the board to have to take into account the interests of someone who is not yet but will become a member. So what is intended by the reference to future members? Most sensibly, it suggests that the board must not only have regard to the interests of the current value of the company's shares but also the long-term value of the company. Directors comply with the duty if they make decisions that do not maximize the value of the shares today but will maximize that value over a longer time frame. The reference to the future gives the board more flexibility to formulate and implement a long-term value strategy.

If a *company's interests* are the shareholder's interests as a whole what happens if individual shareholders' interests diverge? For example, different shareholders may have different preferences as to whether a company issues dividends or reinvests the available funds itself. The variation in such shareholder interests may depend on factors such as individual shareholders' tax status and the types of investment opportunities available to them personally. Megarry J in *Gaiman* refers to the members' interests 'as a whole'. If interests conflict or vary the words 'as a whole' suggest that the board is entrusted with maximizing overall shareholder interests, which may involve balancing and choosing between the different shareholder interests.

---

[10] For a more detailed discussion of this case and of this duty imposed on the general meeting see Chapter 16.

[11] See also the dicta from *Brady v Brady* in note 6.

[12] Bowen LJ said in *Hutton v West Cork Railway Company* (1883) LR 23 Ch D 654, 673, 'The law does not say that there are to be no cakes and ale, but there are to be no cakes and ale except such as are required for the benefit of the company.' Cakes and ale was the metaphor for paying severance to employees following the sale of the business although they had no legal claim to severance. Bowen LJ observed that 'when one is applying the general test whether what has been done is incident to the business of the company, we have this further matter to recollect—what the business of this company is.' As the company had no business (as it had sold its business) apart from 'presiding at its own funeral' there could be no benefit for the company in making such payments. The decision was reversed by statute: see section 187 Insolvency Act 1986 and section 247 Companies Act 2006.

[13] See *Re Horsely & Weight Ltd* [1982] Ch 442.

Actions taken in the company's interests but contrary to some of the shareholders' interests were considered in *Mutual Life Insurance Co of New York v Rank Organization Ltd*[14] and *Re BSB Holdings Ltd (No 2)*.

■ *Re BSB Holdings Ltd (No 2)* [1996] 1 BCLC 155

Arden J

The duty of directors vis-à-vis different groups of shareholders whose shares carry the same rights and rank equally as regards distribution was considered in *Mutual Life Insurance Co of New York v Rank Organisation Ltd*. In that case the directors of Rank had given shareholders, other than those who were North American nationals or residents, the right to subscribe for new shares of the same class. The evidence showed that North Americans had been excluded in order to avoid the requirements of registration with the Securities and Exchange Commission in the United States and with comparable commissions in Canada. The directors had accepted advice from its **merchant bankers**, in turn based on earlier investigation by accountants, that such registration would not be in the interests of Rank. The plaintiffs who were North Americans and owned shares in Rank claimed that Rank had acted in breach of the membership contract contained in the articles. They contended that their shares entitled them to equal treatment without discrimination one from another…

Goulding J held that it was abundantly clear that the directors had acted in the best interests of Rank. He continued:

> 'I turn to the remaining test which I have proposed, namely, that of fairness between different share-holders. It must be borne in mind that in my view the equality of individual shareholders in point of right, does not always require an identity of treatment…After reflection on all that counsel for the plaintiffs said in argument I remain of opinion that the North American shareholders were fairly treated on the occasion of the offer for sale, notwithstanding their exclusion from participation along with their compatriots who were not already shareholders. Such exclusion did not in any way affect the existence of a shareholder's shares nor the rights attached to them. Moreover, the reason why North American shareholders were excluded was because of a difficulty resulting only from their own personal situation. It was not the fault of Rank that they were nationals or residents of countries whose laws impose onerous obligations.'

…where the proposed act under consideration has different effects on different groups of shareholders in a company, it is difficult to apply the test that what is done must be done in the interests of the members generally…The duty as formulated by Goulding J more accurately records what must be done to strike the right balance between conflicting sections of interest. It is in my judgment an accurate statement of the duty to which directors are subject in that situation. The duty is stated in very general terms; its content cannot be exhaustively defined but must depend on the facts of a particular case.

Accordingly, the common law provides that when acting in the company's interests, directors must treat shareholders *fairly* but the effects and the beneficial consequences of decisions may legitimately vary as between shareholders.

1.3 The 'interests' of other constituencies

As we have seen, the common law has traditionally associated the company's interests with those of the shareholders. Subject to one exception, it has not equated the company's interests with the interests of non-shareholder constituencies. This exception is in relation to creditors where the company is approaching insolvency or is insolvent: that

---

[14] [1985] BCLC 11.

is, it cannot pay its debts as they become due. In this situation creditors' interests join or replace the interests of shareholders as the company's interests. We address in detail the case law on directors' duties and creditors in Chapter 18 'Company law and creditor protection'.

The Companies Act 1980 introduced a requirement for directors to consider the interests of the company's employees. This provision was subsequently restated in section 309(1) of the Companies Act 1985, which provided as follows:

> The matters to which the directors of a company are to have regard in the performance of their functions include the interests of the company's employees, in general, as well as the interests of its members.

An important question with regard to this provision is whether it says anything about *in whose interests* decisions should be made. Arguably it does not, as the provision merely requires that *regard* be had to the interests of employees in the performance of a director's functions. In this reading, this provision is less about the company's interests and more about regulating the process that directors go through when making a decision. However, the connection of employee interests to directors' functions allows for the interpretation that employee interests can become company interests. Such a reading then begs the following question: are employee and member interests of equal importance when directors carry out their functions, or are the interests of employees subordinate to those of the members—that is the interests of employees must be considered to the extent that such consideration benefits members? If anything, the wording of the provision suggests the former not the latter interpretation. Commentators were generally of the opinion that section 309 was not intended to radically alter the common law position and that to the extent that section 309 has anything to say about company interests the appropriate reading was that employees' interests are subordinate to those of the shareholder body.[15] Importantly, section 309 did not confer on employees any right to enforce this provision.

Section 309 only refers to employees and members and not to any other company constituency. Prior to the 2006 Act (see section III of this chapter) there was no other statutory provision apart from section 309 requiring directors to have regard to the interests of other such constituencies.

2 Evaluating directors' actions

Lord Greene's statement of the common law in *Smith & Fawcett* makes it clear that the arbiter of whether a director's exercise of corporate power is taken in the best interests of the company is the director herself. It is what *she* in fact considered to be in the company's interests when she took the decision. The duty to act in good faith in the best interests of the company is, therefore, a subjective duty: to do what the *actual director* thinks is in the company's best interests. Any decision made or action taken by the director is subject to this standard of review: did she subjectively think it was in the company's interests. If what the director believed was in the company's interests would be, from most third-parties' point of view, ridiculous and absurd, so long as she actually considered the action to be in the company's best interests she is *not* in breach of this duty. As we see from the following quote of Jonathan Crow QC, the law does not demand that a decision is reasonable only that the director believed that it was in the company's interests.

---

[15] Cf *Fulham Football Club v Cabra Estates plc* [1992] BCC 863.

■ *Extrasure Travel Insurances Ltd v Scattergood* [2003] 1 BCLC 598

Jonathan Crow QC (sitting as Deputy High Court Judge)
The fact that his alleged belief was unreasonable may provide evidence that it was not in fact honestly held at the time: but if, having considered all the evidence, it appears that the director did honestly believe that he was acting in the best interests of the company, then he is not in breach of his fiduciary duty merely because that belief appears to the trial judge to be unreasonable, or because his actions happen, in the event, to cause injury to the company.

Although the rule looks to the subjective belief of the acting director, does this mean that the court when reviewing a decision to see whether it complies with the duty is reduced simply to asking the director whether she thought the decision was in the company's interests when it was made. If so, then the duty would only be a statement of behavioural expectation as all directors would say 'yes' and the standard would not operate in any way as a deterrent for misbehaving directors who may be tempted to further other, perhaps their own, interests when exercising corporate powers. This, however, is not the approach taken by the courts. A level of review and deterrence is involved. The director is the arbiter of whether a decision is in the best interests of the company *at the time the decision is made*. The court's role is to review whether the director really thought the decision was taken in furtherance of those interests at the time the decision was made. The problem for a court is, of course, how to do this. No one else can know someone else's mind and reliable evidence of belief, aside from the decision itself, may not be available. In this regard consider the following case.

■ *Regentcrest plc v Cohen* [2001] 2 BCLC 80

Regentcrest Plc was a property development company. Mr Richardson, together with his brother, was the owner of Regentcrest at the time of the disputed action in question, although Regentcrest Plc had previously been a listed company. At the end of the 1980s Regentcrest purchased the shares in a company called Greenground Ltd, which was owned by other directors of Regentcrest, Mr Scott and Mr Farley, and by a former director of Regentcrest, Mr Cohen. Regentcrest paid £4.25 million for the shares. The only asset which Greenground Ltd owned was a piece of development land in Altrincham, Manchester. The agreement to purchase the shares in Greenground Ltd contained a purchase price adjustment clause which provided that if, within the two years from the date of purchase of the shares, the value of the land in Altrincham had decreased there would be a decrease in the purchase price which would require a partial repayment by the sellers. This provision was known as the 'claw-back provision'. At the end of the 1980s the property market in the UK collapsed creating difficulties for Regentcrest and resulting in a decline in the value of Greenground's development property in the amount of approximately £1.5 million.

By 1990, Regentcrest was in serious financial difficulties. In an attempt to keep Regentcrest afloat the Richardson Brothers injected £5 million of their own funds into the company between June and August of 1990. On 5 September 1990 the Board of Regentcrest convened to consider what action should be taken in relation to the claim under the clawback provision. The directors at this time were the two Richardson Brothers, but also Mr Scott and Mr Farley. Mr Scott and Mr Farley took no part in the meeting's proceedings and did not vote. The Richardson Brothers, however, voted to waive the claim in exchange for receiving the services of Mr Farley, Mr Scott, and Mr Cohen for three years without remuneration.

On 17 September 1990 a petition was presented to wind up Regentcrest and on 21 November 1990 a compulsory winding-up order was made. An action was brought by Regentcrest's liquidator on behalf of the company claiming that Mr Richardson, as a director of the company, had breached his duty to act in good faith in the best interests of the company.

Jonathan Parker J

The duty imposed on directors to act *bona fide* in the interests of the company is a subjective one…The question is not whether, viewed objectively by the court, the particular act or omission which is challenged was in fact in the interests of the company; still less is the question whether the court, had it been in the position of the director at the relevant time, might have acted differently. Rather, the question is whether the director honestly believed that his act or omission was in the interests of the company. The issue is as to the director's state of mind. No doubt, where it is clear that the act or omission under challenge resulted in substantial detriment to the company, the director will have a harder task persuading the court that he honestly believed it to be in the company's interest; but that does not detract from the subjective nature of the test.

[The judge cited *In re Smith & Fawcett* and also cited the judgment of Millett LJ in *Bristol & West Building Society v Mothew (t/a Stapley & Co)* [1998] Ch 1, [1996] 4 All ER 698, who held that:]

'The various obligations of a fiduciary merely reflect different aspects of his core duties of loyalty and fidelity. Breach of fiduciary obligation, therefore, connotes disloyalty or infidelity. Mere incompetence is not enough. A servant who loyally does his incompetent best for his master is not unfaithful and is not guilty of a breach of fiduciary duty.'

…

Each of Mr Don Richardson and Mr Roy Richardson gave unequivocal evidence that in agreeing to the waiver of the clawback claim on 5 September 1990 he honestly believed that he was acting in the interests of Regentcrest; and each denied that his reason for so doing was to protect the vendors [of Greenground Ltd] in the event of a liquidation. Thus, when [counsel for Regentcrest] put this latter proposition to him in cross-examination, Mr Roy Richardson replied:

'The reason the deal was done was to ensure that Regentcrest succeeded. There was no fear of a liquidator looking afterwards at whatever…Regentcrest had got to succeed; that was the prime target, the prime object of everybody, me and the other directors.'

…

If that evidence of the Richardson brothers is accepted it must follow that, applying the appropriate test (see above) the claim of breach of fiduciary duty fails. For Regentcrest, it is contended that that evidence should be rejected. It is not suggested (nor could it be) that the Richardson brothers derived any personal benefit from the waiver; rather, it is contended that the true conclusion on the evidence as a whole is that in waiving the clawback claim the Richardson brothers were motivated simply by a desire to protect the vendors, and in particular Mr Scott and Mr Farley, against the risk of the clawback claim being pursued in the (by then inevitable) event of a liquidation of Regentcrest. In particular, Regentcrest contends: that by September 1990 Regentcrest was no longer a viable enterprise, as the Richardson brothers must have appreciated; that prior to 5 September 1990 the Richardson brothers had decided not to provide any further support for Regentcrest, with the consequence that, as they fully realised, Regentcrest no longer had a future and liquidation was inevitable; and that there were no 'good commercial reasons' for the waiver…

In considering the evidence in the context of Regentcrest's contentions, I bear in mind the danger of applying hindsight. There can be no doubt that the Summer of 1990 was an extremely fraught period so far as Regentcrest and the Regentcrest Group was concerned. Mr Roy Richardson, with the help of Mr Scott, Mr Farley, was personally engaged on a number of fronts. Not only was he attempting to minimise expenditure and keep pressing creditors at bay; he was also engaged in an almost constant process of negotiating with the banks in an attempt to give Regentcrest a breathing space. It is all too easy to analyse the course of the struggle for the survival of Regentcrest after the event, and to pick over specific decisions taken at the time, without making proper allowance for the exigencies of the moment. It seems to me that the dangers of so doing are particularly great in the instant case, given the atmosphere of crisis which existed in Regentcrest in early September 1990.

Bearing that in mind, I turn to the evidence. I start with the issue of the viability of Regentcrest, in September 1990, as an ongoing enterprise meriting investor support. I [note] the differing views of the two experts on this issue. Mr Holden makes the (to my mind) somewhat sweeping judgment that Regentcrest's financial state was by then 'not sufficient to justify shareholder investment', whereas Mr Smith offers the more cautious view that in the absence of indications that ongoing support (ie. support by the Richardson brothers) would be withdrawn, it would have been reasonable to believe that Regentcrest had a future…

I have no hesitation in preferring Mr Smith's conclusion to that of Mr Holden. Mr Holden's conclusion does not appear…to take account of the fact that by September 1990 the Richardson brothers had put some £5 million of their own money into Regentcrest. By contrast, in concluding that in the circumstances it would have been *reasonable to believe* that Regentcrest had a future *'in the absence of evidence to indicate that ongoing support would be withdrawn'* Mr Smith makes due allowance for these factors. I agree with that conclusion. [Emphasis added]

So one returns to the question whether, as at 5 September 1990, the Richardson brothers were still willing to provide further support for Regentcrest or whether they had by then decided to leave Regentcrest to its fate…[I find that] as at 5 September 1990 the Richardson brothers had not walked away from Regentcrest. As at that date they remained willing to support Regentcrest, and Mr Roy Richardson was still working, together with Messrs Scott [and] Farley to try to ensure its survival as a going concern. I further find that although they all recognised, as at 5 September 1990, that despite all their efforts Regentcrest might nevertheless fail, they genuinely believed that there was at the very least a real chance that Mr Roy Richardson's negotiations with the banks would bear fruit and that Regentcrest would survive the current crisis and be able to carry on trading.

Against that background, I turn next to the board meeting on 5 September 1990…[and] the evidence concerning the 'good commercial reasons' relied on by the Richardson brothers as persuading them to agree to the waiver of the clawback claim on the terms proposed by Mr Farley. Three main reasons were identified by the Richardson brothers in evidence. First, the need to retain the services of Mr Scott and Mr Farley, with the concomitant benefit of their knowledge and experience in seeking to realise the various properties in the Regentcrest Group's property portfolio, and (in the case of Mr Cohen) the desirability of retaining his services in relation to the Altrincham Site, about which he was thought to have a good deal of useful local knowledge; secondly, the need to preserve a united board in the face of pressure from the banks and other creditors; thirdly, the fact that it was (to put it at its lowest) questionable to what extent the vendors would be able to satisfy any judgment; and fourthly the fact that the vendors had made it clear (through Mr Farley) that they would not submit to judgment on the clawback claim but would defend the claim on whatever grounds might be open to them—in other words, they were not going to go quietly.

In assessing the 'commerciality' of the reasons put forward by the Richardson brothers I have to eschew hindsight and to place myself so far as possible in their shoes as at 5 September 1990. Viewed from that perspective, and bearing in mind that the concern of the board at that time was (as I have found) to try to achieve the survival of Regentcrest, there was a clear commercial benefit to Regentcrest in retaining the services of Messrs Scott and Farley free of charge on a formal basis for a specified period. True it is that they were already working for Regentcrest free of charge, and that they had not at any time indicated that they were considering leaving Regentcrest; but that is not to say that that situation would have continued unchanged had the Richardson brothers decided to pursue the clawback claim against them. Moreover, the maintenance of a united board in the face of bank and creditor pressure was plainly a very important consideration. I have no difficulty in accepting that the prospect of a split board, with two of the directors (or, as they would no doubt become, former directors) being sued by the company, could well have proved to be the last straw so far as banks and creditors were concerned, leading to the collapse of the ongoing negotiations and the attempts to save Regentcrest...

I am satisfied...that the decisive consideration in the minds of the Richardson brothers in agreeing to waive the clawback claim was the need to maintain a united board, and not to create a situation in which two of the directors were being sued by Regentcrest and were contesting the claim. No sensible businessman welcomes litigation, and in the fraught situation which obtained on 5 September 1990 the prospect of Regentcrest suing two of its directors must have given rise to the gravest misgivings on the part of anyone concerned (as the Richardson brothers then were) in trying to save Regentcrest. Thus, the need to avoid litigation against two of Regentcrest's directors was, I find, a weighty consideration, and one which *could reasonably have led a businessman in the position of the Richardson brothers on 5 September 1990 to conclude that the waiver of the claim on the terms proposed was in the interests of Regentcrest*, notwithstanding that the information before the board as to the vendors' ability to meet any judgment was far from complete. As to that, it is in my judgment wholly unrealistic to have expected Mr Roy Richardson at that stage to have initiated a detailed investigation into the personal financial circumstances of the vendors. [Emphasis added]

In my judgment, therefore, the circumstantial evidence to which I have referred does not, when considered in context, suggest that (contrary to the evidence which each of them has given) the Richardson brothers did not honestly believe that the waiver of the clawback claim was in the interests of Regentcrest, and that their only reason for agreeing to the waiver was to protect Mr Scott and Mr Farley against a liquidator seeking to pursue the claim against them. On the contrary, in my judgment the evidence as a whole supports the conclusion that as at 5 September 1990 the Richardson brothers were still prepared to support Regentcrest and were genuinely seeking to achieve its survival. Had that not been the case, it is impossible satisfactorily to explain Mr Roy Richardson's conduct in continuing thereafter to negotiate with the banks and in procuring the delisting of Regentcrest's shares. The notion that in so doing he was acting out some kind of charade in order to mask his true motives is simply not credible.

In the result, therefore, I have no hesitation in accepting the evidence of each of the Richardson brothers as to his reasons for agreeing to the waiver of the clawback claim, and I find that in voting in favour of the resolution for waiver each of them honestly believed that he was acting in the best interests of Regentcrest. It follows that the claim of breach of fiduciary duty on the part of Mr Richardson fails.

When reading the summary of the facts in this case most readers' initial reaction is to ask: how could it possibly be in the best interests of the company that has serious financial problems to waive a claim of £1.5 million? One readily concludes on these initial facts that the directors could not, therefore, have been acting in the company's interests and must have been thinking about their friends, Scott, Farley, and Cohen, who may have been liable to pay the 'clawback' claim once the liquidator took control of the company. The court, however, rejects this reading of the events.

The question for the court is: did the directors honestly believe that waiving the claim was in the company's interests? The directors, unsurprisingly, said they believed it was. But as is clear from the judgment this is only the beginning of the court's inquiry. The court must determine whether the directors *actually thought* it was in the company's interests at the time of the decision. To do this Jonathan Parker J considers not only evidence that goes to the question of what the Richardson brothers actually believed, but he also engages in a process of assessing the strength and credibility of the purported reasons for waiving the claim: the less plausible the reasons, the less credible is the defendant's claim to have acted on the basis of them.

In relation to the purported reasons for the decision the court identifies two concerns. First, was it possible to believe at the time the decision to waive the clawback claim was made that the company could survive and continue trading? If there was no possibility of survival then nothing could be gained in waiving the claim. Secondly, if survival was possible, what reasons would support waiving the claim: how would a waiver benefit the company given its financial predicament? Survival was possible, according to the court's preferred expert, if the Richardson brothers had continued to fund the company. Furthermore, the court was impressed by the fact that the support of Mr Scott and Mr Farley was necessary to maintain a unified board, which was essential if the company was to survive. Litigation to enforce the clawback claim would have destroyed that unity. This leads Jonathan Parker J to conclude that such considerations 'could *reasonably* have led *a businessman in the position of the Richardson brothers*...to conclude that the waiver of the claim...was in the interest of *Regentcrest*'.

Clear evidence of belief that a decision is in the company's best interests will be sufficient to demonstrate compliance with the duty and to overcome the fact that the decision was viewed by the court as patently unreasonable.[16] However, in the absence of such conclusive evidence of belief the subjective duty to act in the best interests of the company contains an element of objectivity based on the strength of the reasons given by the director for believing that the decision was one that benefited the company. The legal question of relevance in the absence of conclusive evidence of belief is: how good does the reason given for taking the decision actually have to be to support a finding of compliance?

The language of reasonableness used by Jonathan Parker J could be read to suggest that duty-compliant decisions are those supported by reasons that a reasonable director would require to take the decision. This is not, it is submitted, correct. Reasons that a reasonable director would accept are clearly strong enough reasons to render the decision duty compliant; but the reason does *not* have to be one a hypothetical reasonable director would accept in order for it to be strong enough to render the decision duty-compliant. To convey the idea that the standard is below one of reasonableness the courts sometimes express it in the following terms: that no reasonable director could have taken the decision in question. A first instance judgment recently put it as follows: 'a breach [of duty] will have occurred if it is established that the relevant exercise of the power is one which could not be considered by any reasonable director to be in the interests of the company'.[17] One might argue that logically if a breach of duty is committed if no reasonable director could take the decision, then to be duty compliant the decision must be one a reasonable director would have taken. This is not what is intended. The idea underpinning this phraseology is, it is submitted, that the decision is plausible or rational; a standard that sets the hurdle below a reasonableness standard.[18]

In summary, *in theory* a director complies with the duty to act in good faith in the best interests of the company if she actually believes the action is in the company's interests—a director who makes a good faith decision on behalf of the company which, for example, is based upon her instincts that oil will be discovered under company land,

---

[16] *Extrasure Travel Insurances Ltd v Scattergood* [2003] 1 BCLC 598.

[17] *Per* Warren J in *Re Southern Counties Fresh Foods Ltd* [2008] All ER (D) 195. See also *Fraser v Oystertec Plc* [2004] BPIR 486: 'further, in order to succeed in a claim for breach of fiduciary duty as a director it must be shown, to the standard required for summary judgment, either that [the defendant] was acting dishonestly or that no reasonable director in his position could have believed the transaction was in the best interests of the company'.

[18] See *Shuttleworth v Cox Bros Ltd* [1926] All ER Rep 498 where the courts addressed the standard that *general meeting decision-making* should be subject to the standard that the action is taken 'bona fide for the benefit of the company as a whole' (see further Chapter 16), where Banks LJ treats the standard of a decision so unreasonable that no reasonable person would think it is in the company's interests as equivalent to whether a decision is *capable* of being in the company's interests.

complies in theory with the duty. *In practice*, however, the evidentiary difficulties of assessing a director's state of mind at the time of the decision lead the courts to look not only at what she actually believed, based upon relevant evidence, but also what a director *could have plausibly* believed.

3 Judging with hindsight

When the court reviewed the decision in *Regentcrest* the review took place with the knowledge that the company did not survive and that its failure followed very shortly after the Regentcrest's board decision to waive the clawback claim. However, when this decision was made by the board of Regentcrest its outcome—whether the decision to waive the claim *actually* benefited the company—was uncertain. When we judge past decisions with the knowledge of how things turn out, we overestimate (overweight) the likelihood of the actual outcome at the time the decision is made. Consider the following example.

> Assume at time T1 when a decision is made there is a 50% probability that the decision will result in successful outcome A and a 50% probability that the decision will result in failed outcome B. If at time T2 when the decision is reviewed failed outcome B has occurred, the reviewer of the decision is likely to overweight the probability of failure (for example, a 75% chance of the probability of failed outcome B) at the time the decision was made.

The effect that the knowledge of the outcome has when judging the decision that led to the outcome is known as hindsight bias. Its operation in practice has considerable support from experiments carried out by behavioural psychologists.

■ **B. Fischhoff, 'Debiasing' in D. Kahneman, P. Slovic and A. Tversky (eds),** *Judgment Under Uncertainty: Heuristics and Biases* **(CUP, 1982)[19]**

> In hindsight, people constantly exaggerate what could have been anticipated in foresight. They not only view what has happened as having been inevitable, but also view it as having appeared 'relatively inevitable' before it happened. People believe that others should have been able to anticipate events much better than was actually the case. They even misremember their own predictions so as to exaggerate in hindsight what they knew in foresight.

Let us consider the possible effect of hindsight bias in the context of the *Regentcrest* decision. Assume that at the time the directors made the decision to waive the claim in *Regentcrest* there was 10% probability of the company surviving, and that anything less than this would not have been viewed by the courts as a sufficiently realistic probability to accept that the directors actually *could have* believed that the company would survive. With hindsight bias, knowledge of failure would increase the assessment of the probability of failure at the time the decision was made and decrease the probability of survival below 10%, rendering the directors, in the court's ex-post view, in breach of their duties when in fact they were in compliance with their duties.

In *Regentcrest*, Jonathan Parker J is aware of the problem of hindsight bias. He refers to the 'danger of applying hindsight' and says that he must 'eschew hindsight'. One could not, given the outcome and his sensitive attention to the difficulties of making the board decision, accuse Jonathan Parker J of applying hindsight bias. However, we

---

[19] See also B. Fischhoff, 'Hindsight ≠ Foresight: The Effect of Outcome Knowledge on Judgment under Uncertainty' (1975) *Journal of Experimental Psychology: Human Perception and Performance* 288.

may still want to ask whether it is possible to review a decision without allowing the actual knowledge of the outcome to distort that review: can one really ignore what one knows, no matter how hard one tries? Perhaps some of us can do it better than others; some judges are better than others. The limited evidence of this issue from behavioural psychologists suggest that such hindsight 'de-biasing' is difficult to do and often unsuccessful.[20]

4 Why is the standard for evaluating directors' decisions so low?

One might ask why the pre-2006 Act common law duty to act in good faith in the best interests of the company is such a low standard: to act only in what the director thinks is in the best interests of the company. In our hypothetical case study of Bob's Electronics Ltd, for example, Bob, as shareholder, will surely expect Markus the CEO's decisions to be good decisions or reasonable decisions; the types of decisions a good manager would make. It would be relatively easy for the law to express such higher expectations: compliance with the duty to act in good faith in the best interests of the company could be measured not by what the actual director thinks but by what a reasonable average director would have done in such a situation. The explanation for the law's resistance to setting a higher standard is found in its, typically unstated, commitment to provide the board with the freedom to exercise the authority delegated to it in order to generate value. In this regard consider the following extract.

■ **W.T. Allen, J.E. Jacobs and L.B. Strine Jr.,[21] 'Realigning the Standard of Review of Director Due Care with Delaware Public Policy: A Critique of Van Gorkom and its Progeny as a Standard of Review Problem' (2002) 96** *North Western University Law Review* **449**

In cases involving comparatively simple decisions such as automobile accidents, there is often little difference between decisions that are bad and good decisions that turn out badly. In such cases, typically only one decision is reasonable in a given set of circumstances, so decisions that turn out badly almost invariably turn out to have been bad decisions. Thus, in the tort area, there is no unfairness in conflating the standard of conduct [what one expects of a person] ('reasonableness') with the standard of review [the standard according to which one reviews such person's actions] (whether the defendant acted reasonably).

But where the subject of legal challenge is a business decision, to conflate the two standards and apply a 'reasonableness' standard of review risks imposing liability upon directors unfairly. Unlike automobile accident cases, it may be hard for judges to differentiate bad business decisions from good business decisions that turn out badly. Business decisions are virtually always made with less than perfect information and thus decision makers are required to assess and assume some degree of risk. Suppose, for example, that a board must decide between either investing in an expensive but untried new technology, or foregoing the investment. Each alternative involves certain risks. Given uncertainty, the only way the board can rationally decide is by weighing the benefit of each alternative against the probability that the associated negative risk will—or will not—materialize.

---

[20] See B. Fischhoff, 'Perceived Informativeness of Facts' (1977) *Journal of Experimental Psychology: Human Perception and Performance* 349 where persons had the bias described to them and they were asked to avoid it in the experiments when making judgments but in many cases did not manage to do so.

[21] William Allen was a former Chancellor of the Delaware Chancery Court—the primary corporate law court of first instance in Delaware. Jack Jacobs is a former Vice-Chancellor of the Chancery Court and now a member of the Delaware Supreme Court. Leo Strine is currently a Chancellor of the Chancery Court.

Thus, if the board chooses one alternative based on its assessment that a negative result is improbable, but the negative result nonetheless occurs, the decision may (in hindsight) be 'wrong' but it is not 'bad,' because in any normal probability distribution some outcomes will inevitably fall on the 'unlucky' side. If, however, the standard of review is 'reasonableness', a fact finder might erroneously treat reasonable decisions that turned out badly as bad decisions, and unfairly find the directors liable for such decisions. There is empirical evidence that persons who know the outcome of a decision tend to exaggerate the extent to which that outcome 'could have been correctly predicted beforehand.' That tendency is known as 'hindsight bias.' That is one reason why the business judgment rule employs a standard of review [how directors' actions are reviewed] that is more lenient than the standard of conduct [what is expected of directors]: to give directors a large zone of protection to avoid an unfair imposition of liability on corporate boards when their decisions are attacked. [In Delaware *the business judgment* rule provides that provided that care was taken in making the decision—the decision-making process—and provided that there is no conflict of interest for the director, the courts will only require that the decision is a rational decision. As one might expect directors to take reasonable decisions, this is why it is sometimes said of Delaware corporate law that the standard of review of business decisions—rationality—differs from the standard of expectation—reasonableness.[22]]

In addition to fairness, policy considerations may also dictate the need for divergence between a standard of review and a standard of conduct [expectation]. Because the **expected value** of a risky business decision may be greater than that of a less risky decision, directors may be acting in the best interest of the shareholders when they choose the riskier alternative. A standard of review that imposes liability on a board of directors for making an "unreasonable" (as opposed to an 'irrational') decision could result in discouraging riskier yet socially desirable economic decisions, because [a reasonableness] standard of care will tend to make directors unduly risk averse. If a high-risk decision leads to a good outcome, only the corporation (but not the directors) would benefit, whereas a bad outcome could cause the directors to be held liable for the corporation's entire loss.

This observation gives rise to the related policy concern that the risk of liability, at least in the case of non-[executive] directors, could be highly disproportionate to the incentives for serving as a director. Liability for an imprudent decision could be in the millions, but outside directors rarely receive annual fees commensurate with liability risk of that magnitude. Absent a mechanism that would reduce the risk of ruinous liability, conflating the standards of conduct and of review would make it more difficult to attract qualified candidates as outside directors—a result that can only disserve the [shareholders'] best interests.

A third policy consideration is that intracorporate remedies may be socially preferable. Directors are elected, and can be removed, by shareholders. Where [shareholders] are able to change the board because of inadequate performance, there is less reason for courts to intervene and police whether the directors are behaving reasonably. And, if [shareholders] believe that their well-intentioned directors have acted unreasonably, their ex-post [after the event] regret that they should have elected a different board ex-ante [before the event] is not a worthy justification for holding a director liable in damages...

These justifications for deferential review of due care cases were collectively voiced by the Court of Chancery in *Gagliardi v. Trifoods, Int'l, Inc*:[23]

'Where there is a large, well-developed stock market] shareholders can [cheaply] diversify the risks of their corporate investments.[24] Thus, it is in their economic interest for the corporation to accept, in rank order, all positive net present value investment projects available to the corporation, starting with the highest risk-adjusted rate of return first. Shareholders don't want (or shouldn't rationally want) directors to be risk averse. Shareholders' investment interests, across the full range of their

---

[22] See Chapter 12 for a more detailed discussion of the business judgment rule in the United States.
[23] 683 A 2d 1049 (Del 1996).
[24] For a general discussion of the benefits for the company of having a diversified shareholder base see Chapter 1, section III.

diversifiable equity investments, will be maximized if corporate directors and managers honestly assess risk and reward and accept for the corporation the highest risk-adjusted returns available that are above the firm's cost of capital.'

But directors will tend to deviate from this rational acceptance of corporate risk if, in authorizing the corporation to undertake a risky investment, the directors must assume some degree of personal risk relating to ex post facto claims of derivative liability for any resulting corporate loss.

Corporate directors of public companies typically have a very small proportionate ownership interest in their corporations and little or no incentive compensation. Thus, they enjoy (as **residual owners**) only a very small proportion of any upside gains earned by the corporation on risky investment projects. If, however, corporate directors were to be found liable for a corporate loss from a risky project on the ground that the investment was too risky (foolishly risky! stupidly risky! egregiously risky!—you supply the adverb), their liability would be joint and several for the whole loss…Given the scale of operation and modern public corporations, this stupefying disjunction between risk and reward for corporate directors threatens undesirable effects. Given this disjunction, only a very small probability of director liability based on 'negligence,' 'inattention,' 'waste,' etc., could induce a board to avoid authorizing risky investment projects to any extent! Obviously, it is in the shareholders' economic interest to offer sufficient protection to directors from liability for negligence, etc., to allow directors to conclude that, as a practical matter, there is no risk that, if they act in good faith and meet minimal proceduralist standards of attention, they can face liability as a result of a business loss. [On procedure—the process of taking care under Delaware law—see Chapter 12 on the duty of care skill and diligence.]

Questions and discussion

1. Allen, Jacobs, and Strine argue that if the standard for reviewing the decision is too high then directors, fearful of liability, will not take the types of decisions that shareholders would want them to take: decisions that have positive **expected value** but necessarily involve some risk of failure. For Allen et al, a 'reasonableness' standard of review would be too high and could chill (that is, deter) risk taking. Do you think that in practice directors would really be concerned about a reasonableness standard? Would directors really object to being told they had to act reasonably? How would hindsight bias feature in a director's response to these questions?

2. Allen, Jacobs, and Strine object to the standard of 'reasonableness' as the standard of review for business decisions. How does one articulate a standard that is lower than 'reasonableness'? Such a standard in the leading corporate law jurisdiction of Delaware is said to be a rationality standard: that there is some rational basis for the decision. To what extent, if any, is Jonathan Parker J's assessment of the board's reasons for waiving the clawback claim in *Regentcrest* any different from such a rationality based approach? How do the UK courts articulate what is required when reviewing decisions when clear evidence of the director's state of mind is not available?

5 Evaluating the failure to consider the company's interests

The earlier discussion analyses how courts evaluate whether a director has complied with his duty to act in good faith in the best interests of the company. The duty requires that when he acts *he believes* the action to be in the best interests of the company. Necessarily, therefore, the duty requires that he exercise his judgment. If he agrees to vote as a director according to someone else's instructions, without exercising any judgment on the applicable issue himself, then clearly the action he takes is not what *he believes* to be in the best interests of the company and he would be in breach of duty.

Any agreement to exercise his discretion according to someone else's wishes would, therefore, be void and enforceable. Consider dicta from Lord Denning in this regard:

■ *Boulting v Association of Cinematograph, Television and Allied Technicians* [1963] 2 QB 606

> No stipulation is lawful by which he agrees to carry out his duties in accordance with the instructions of another rather than on his own conscientious judgment...Take a nominee director, that is, a director of a company who is nominated by a large shareholder to represent his interests. There is nothing wrong in it. It is done every day. Nothing wrong, that is, so long as the director is left free to exercise his best judgment in the interests of the company which he serves. But if he is put upon terms that he is bound to act in the affairs of the company in accordance with the directions of his patron, it is beyond doubt unlawful.[25]

The common law duty to act in good faith in the best interests of the company requires that when making a decision the director has given consideration to the company's interests and reaches a conclusion that such a decision is in the company's best interests. How does one review compliance with the duty, however, if the director when making a decision has not given any thought to whether it is actually in the company's interests? This does not mean that he thinks it is not in the company's interests—he might have thought it was in the company's interests had he given it consideration, but he did not give it such consideration. Although this may sound odd, in practice it may be a common occurrence. Many companies (subsidiary companies) are owned by other companies (the parent company) or have the same shareholders (sister companies). The subsidiary or sister company may be one company in a group of companies and, although each individual company is a separate legal entity to whom the directors of each such company owe their duties, in practice the directors of each company are likely to think about the well-being of the group of companies and make decisions in the interests of the group without necessarily having specific regard to whether the interests of the specific company, who the director acts on behalf of, differ from those of the group of companies. In this regard, consider the following case.

■ *Charterbridge Corporation Ltd v Lloyds Bank Ltd* [1969] 2 All ER 1185

Castleford Ltd, a land development company, was one of a group of companies owned by Mr and Mrs Pomeroy. The directors of Castleford caused the company to guarantee the indebtedness of another group company, Pomeroy Ltd and subsequently agreed to grant a legal charge over certain of its property to secure the guarantee. It was accepted

---

[25] See also *Kuwait Asia Bank EC v National Mutual Life Nominees Ltd* [1990] 3 All ER 404. See further *Re Neath Rigby Ltd* [2009] 2 BCLC 427 at [33] *per* Stanley Burnton LJ: 'an appointed director, without being in breach of his duties to the company, may take the interests of his nominator into account, provided that his decisions as a director are in what he genuinely considers to be the best interests of the company; but that is a very different thing from his being under a duty to his nominator by reason of his appointment by it.' Clearly, in practice, the subjective nature of the standard will provide significant room to do the nominating person's bidding if such a decision benefits from a plausible reason as to why the decision benefits the company, which itself may be legitimately connected to the nominating person's interests, if those interests dovetail with the company's interests. On the extent to which a nominee director can take account of the interests of the nominating person Australian cases have taken a more flexible approach. See: *Re News Corporation Ltd* (1987) 70 ALR 419 at 437 where Bowen CJ observed that: 'It is both realistic and not improper to expect that such directors will follow the interests of the company which appointed them subject to the qualification that they will not so act if of the view that their acts would not be in the interests of the company as a whole.' See also: *Re Broadcasting Station 2GB Pty Ltd* [1964–5] NSWR 1648.

that when doing so the directors of Castleford had had regard for the interests of the group as a whole and had not separately considered the interests of Castleford itself. The court considered whether the directors had complied with their duty to act in good faith in the best interests of the company.

> *Pennycuick J*
>
> As I have already found, the directors of Castleford looked to the benefit of the group as a whole and did not give separate consideration to the benefit of Castleford. Counsel for the plaintiff company contended that in the absence of separate consideration, they must, *ipso facto*, be treated as not having acted with a view to the benefit of Castleford. That is, I think, an unduly stringent test and would lead to really absurd results, ie, unless the directors of a company addressed their minds specifically to the interest of the company in connection with each particular transaction [the directors would be in breach of duty]. Counsel for the bank contended that it is sufficient that the directors of Castleford looked to the benefit of the group as a whole. Equally I reject that contention. Each company in the group is a separate legal entity and the directors of a particular company are not entitled to sacrifice the interest of that company. This becomes apparent when one considers the case where the particular company has separate creditors. The proper test, I think, in the absence of actual separate consideration, must be whether an intelligent and honest man in the position of a director of the company concerned, could, in the whole of the existing circumstances, have reasonably believed that the transaction was for the benefit of the company. If that is the proper test, I am satisfied that the answer here is in the affirmative.
>
> Castleford looked to Pomeroy for its own day to day management...[and] looked to Pomeroy to supply the experience, skill and contacts requisite for the development of [its projects] and to pay the outgoings involved in such development...the collapse of Pomeroy would have been a disaster for Castleford....I am satisfied that a director of Castleford, taking an objective view in the exclusive interest of Castleford at the date of the guarantee, could reasonably have concluded that the transaction was for the benefit of that company.

The *Charterbridge* case tells us that a director's failure to consider the company's interests when making a decision will not automatically result in her being in breach of the duty to act in good faith in the best interests of the company. But as the director has not given consideration to the company's interests the standard by which the court reviews the director's actions cannot be the subjective standard we analysed in *Regentcrest*. Necessarily, in such circumstances, an objective standard must be applied. The standard applied by Pennycuick J is whether an 'intelligent and honest man in the position of the director' would have 'reasonably believed' that agreeing to the guarantee was in the company's best interests. At common law a director who fails to give consideration to the company's interest when he acts will, therefore, be subject to an apparently more exacting standard of review than he would have been had he given due regard to those interests at the time the decision was made. However, in practice what this standard demands of the quality of the decision may well be similar to that required pursuant to the subjective duty to promote the success of the company: that is, a plausible account of why the decision promotes the company's interests. Compare Pennycuick J's conclusion that a director 'could reasonably have concluded that the transaction was for the benefit of the company' with Jonathan Parker J's conclusion in *Regentcrest* that the reasons given for action could 'reasonably have led a businessman...to conclude that [the decision] was in the interests of *Regentcrest.*'

It is clear from Pennycuick J's judgment that in a group of companies the directors of each company must act in their individual company's interests not in the interests of the group as a whole or in the interests of another member of that group.[26] Consideration

---

[26] See *Re Pantone Ltd Miller v Bain* [2001] All ER (D) 428 reaffirming *Charterbridge* in this regard.

of the company's interest in a group context does not, however, mean that the interests of the group are irrelevant to the company's interests. *Charterbridge* makes clear that it is often in a single company's interests to do things that benefit the group or a particular member of the group. Guaranteeing the debt of another group company may seem contrary to the company's interests as an obligation is incurred for which no direct or immediate consideration is received. However, if the well-being of the company is dependent on the financial well-being of the group, then giving the guarantee may be in the company's interest, broadly construed.

Questions and discussion

1. '*Charterbridge* is, as a matter of principle, incorrectly decided. The duty for a director is to act in what he thinks is in the best interests of the company. How can one possibly do this if those interests have not been considered? Failure to consider the company's interests when exercising corporate powers should be a straightforward example of breach of duty.' Discuss.

2. In relation to the discussion of question 1 note the following considerations. Would too strict a rule interfere with the efficient functioning of corporate groups or act only to catch out those that were careless but not blameworthy? Consider two responses to this question: first, showing due respect to the separate interests of the company is a minimal condition for the benefit of separate corporate personality and limited liability in the group context; and second, and more powerfully, it is not clear why the courts need to offer any protection to directors operating in the group context when the group of companies is perfectly capable of protecting themselves by defining their interests in their constitutional documents to explicitly take account of the group's interests.[27]

3. Is the language used by Pennycuick J to set out the applicable standard in this case any different than the language used by Jonathan Parker J in *Regentcrest*? Is it different enough to support the conclusion that the standard applicable to a director that fails to consider whether a decision is in the company's best interests is higher than the standard applicable to a director who does consider whether the decision is in the company's interests?

6 Restricting discretion in the best interests of the company

The common law duty to act in good faith in the best interests of the company is a continuing duty. A director's decision may be in the interests of the company at time T1 but if the circumstances change to render that decision at time T2 not in the best interests of the company then the director must change the decision to realign the decision with the company's interests. Of course the events between time T1 and time T2 may have altered the ability of the director to change that decision. Suppose the board agrees to sell a plot of land for £10 and the company enters into a contract to sell the property. If the property market then booms rendering the value of the land £50, whilst it may be in the company's interest not to transfer the land, the company is under a legal obligation to do so. Here an enforceable legal obligation owed to a third party restricts the boards' ability to change its decision.

This problem arises commonly in the context of merger and acquisition transactions (the sale of whole companies or substantial parts of the companies). Consider, for example, company A that wishes to sell a division or subsidiary (the 'asset'). Typically the agreement to sell the asset may have an option for the seller to cancel the agreement if another possible buyer offers to buy the asset for more money. However, to limit the

---

[27] See, for example, the articles of association of BHP Billiton Plc (www.bhpbilliton.com/home/aboutus/ourcompany/Pages/governance.aspx/article104 ⬤).

likelihood of this happening the buyer will insist that the seller agrees—in the purchase contract—not to search for other buyers, or restricts the types of information about the asset that the seller can provide to another possible buyer. This provision is known as a 'non-solicitation' or 'no-shop' provision.[28] This makes sense from the buyer's point of view: he is investing much time and money in the purchase process and does not want a third party to come along and purchase the asset instead. From the selling company's perspective it may also make sense: there may be few buyers in the market willing to pay this price, and agreeing to these provisions helps sell the asset. Agreeing to such a 'non-solicitation' provision means, however, that the board is agreeing to restrict its own discretion: it cannot at a later date before the transfer of the asset instruct an investment banker to look for other buyers; nor does it have unfettered discretion to provide information to other potential buyers who knock on the company's door expressing an interest in the asset.

Taking another example from the world of mergers and acquisitions, when a company agrees to sell an asset there are typically many conditions that need to be fulfilled before the asset can be sold. For example, if a company is selling its mobile telephone subsidiary, the terms of the subsidiary's mobile telephone licence may provide that the licence will lapse unless the proposed buyer of the company has been pre-approved by the telecommunications regulator. In this situation the help of the seller will be essential to obtain this approval. In the sale agreement the selling company will typically agree to use 'its best endeavours' or 'best efforts' or 'reasonable best efforts' to ensure that the approval of the licence transfer is obtained.[29] What happens, however, if, after entering into the agreement, it becomes clear that the sale is no longer in the selling company's best interests, perhaps because another party is willing to pay more. Is the selling company still bound to use its 'best endeavours' to get the deal done; is the board prevented from acting to stop the company from using its 'best endeavours'?

There are two questions for us in this regard. First, are such types of restriction enforceable? In particular, is there any reason to treat these types of restriction any differently than the enforceable obligation to sell land in the example just given? Secondly, whether or not such agreements are enforceable, is the board of directors in breach of the common law duty to act in good faith in the best interests of the company in agreeing to such a restriction?

■ *John Crowther Group plc v Carpets International plc* [1990] BCLC 460 (case decided in 1985)

Vinelott J

The applications which are now before me relate to a dispute which has arisen concerning the acquisition by the plaintiff, John Crowther Group plc, (Crowther) from the first defendant, Carpets International plc, (International) of the shares of a subsidiary in that company called Carpets International (UK) Ltd (UK).

Under the terms of an agreement dated 12 September...between International and Crowther, Crowther agreed to buy the shares of UK for £1 and also to pay to International £5m and to procure the issue to International of a further one and a quarter million fully paid ordinary shares of

---

[28] Note that following recent changes to the Takeover Code which governs takeovers of, amongst others, listed UK companies, such provisions, which are known generically as 'deal protections', may no longer be used (without the Panel's permission). Such terms remain available for companies that are not listed or publicly traded. See Rule 21.2 Takeover Code.

[29] Note that providing assistance in obtaining official authorizations such as a telecoms licence transfer does not fall within the Rule 21.2 Takeover Code prohibition—see Rule 21.2(b)(ii).

Crowther of 25p each in consideration of, in effect, the acquisition by Crowther of very considerable debts owed by UK to International, amounting to some £40m.

The transaction affected a substantial part of the business of International and, under [London]
Stock Exchange requirements, it had to be made conditional on approval of the shareholders of
International.[30] Accordingly one of the conditions which had to be satisfied was the passing at
a general meeting of International of a resolution approving the transaction before 14 October
1985. Clause 2(3) of the agreement reads as follows:

'The parties hereto shall use all reasonable endeavours to procure the satisfaction of the conditions
set out in Schedule 4, which apply to them, by the dates therein mentioned, in particular without
prejudice to the generality of the foregoing the vendors hereby irrevocably undertake (a) to use all
reasonable endeavours to post and to do nothing to prevent the posting of the **circular** to the shareholders of the vendors by 11 am on Friday 13 September containing a recommendation to such
shareholders to vote in favour of the ordinary resolution to approve the transaction; (b) to procure
that the aforesaid resolutions are properly proposed and put to the aforesaid meeting whatever
circumstances may exist at that time in relation to any offers as made for the share capital of the
company or its business or any part thereof by any third party; (c) not to adjourn the said meeting,
save as may be required either by law or pursuant to the articles of association of the vendors.'
[Emphasis added]

[During the course of the negotiations between Crowther and International a rival bidder,
PMA Textiles Ltd, (PMA) entered the field.] Some few days before the agreement was executed
International, through Kleinwort Benson, its [investment] bankers, agreed that it would cease to
negotiate with rival bidders. That was something insisted on by the chairman of Crowthers. He
also sought and obtained a formal undertaking by a United States shareholder, holding 41.3% of
the shares of International, that it would vote in favour of the resolution.

I have already mentioned the circular which had to be sent round to shareholders. In its original form it contained a statement that the directors of International and its merchant bankers
considered the term of the sale were fair and reasonable and continued:

'In the absence of a materially better offer being received (in which event, shareholders will be
informed forthwith) your directors recommend you to vote in favour of the resolution.'

That somewhat lukewarm recommendation did not appeal to Crowthers, who through their
[investment] bankers, required the first part, 'In the absence of a materially better offer being
received (in which event shareholders will be informed forthwith)' to be deleted. The circular
went out in that amended form...

On 26 September [International's investment bankers were informed that] PMA wanted to
make an offer of £7m, some one and a quarter million more than the offer made by Crowther,
but the whole in cash instead of £5m cash and the balance in shares. Thereafter...meetings took
place between representatives of PMA and International, in the course of which the offer was
incorporated in a formal agreement which was signed on 1 October. Moreover, on 1 October a
circular was sent out by International [to its shareholders] in terms approved by PMA's advisers.

The agreement with PMA is a perfectly straightforward agreement similar to the agreement
with Crowther, except of course that it is conditional on the first agreement not becoming
unconditional and is itself in turn conditional upon shareholder approval. In the circular to the
shareholders of International the board [give] assurances that PMA had the necessary financial
resources, go on to say that the consideration is materially higher than that payable under the
Crowther agreement, and they continue in these terms:

'In these circumstances your board consider that it would be appropriate to secure this offer by
entering into a conditional agreement with PMA which would only become effective if the Crowther

---

[30] This would be because the sale of the subsidiary amounted to a significant transaction under Rule
10 of the Listing Rules which we considered in Chapter 6.

> agreement did not proceed. In view of the materially higher consideration which would be received from PMA and the substantial identity of the other terms, your board is now recommending that the proposed disposal to Crowther should not proceed…'
>
> The case for Crowther, as I understand it, is that the undertaking in clause 2(3) of the agreement is not only to take steps to procure the passing of the resolution if the board think it reasonable that it should be passed but to take all steps reasonably available to procure the passing of the resolution whether the board think it in the interests of the company that the resolution approving the sale be passed or not.
>
> I think I should say (and this is, of course, an interlocutory hearing) that I am not persuaded that is a possible view. The terms of the agreement must clearly be read in the light of the fact known to all parties that directors owe a fiduciary duty to act in the interests of their company and to make full and honest disclosure to shareholders before they vote on such a resolution. It seems to me that it must have been understood by all that if the undertaking was to use reasonable endeavours to procure the passing of the resolution it was necessarily subject to anything which the directors had to do in pursuance of that fiduciary duty. Indeed, as counsel for International and the second to fourth defendants… pointed out, this is underlined by the fact that it is made clear in sub-paragraph (b) of clause 2(3) that the resolutions must be put whatever other offers may have been made at the time they are put, whereas there is no similar qualification of the covenant to use reasonable endeavours. That contrast is some indication that any obligation to use reasonable endeavours to procure the passing of the resolution ceases if an offer plainly more in the interests of the company is made before that resolution is passed.
>
> …
>
> It seems to me plain beyond question that directors are under a duty to disclose the facts to the shareholders. Indeed a resolution passed in ignorance of them would be worthless. If directors must disclose the facts, then it seems to me they must equally express their honest opinion as to what is in the interests of the company…

The court holds that the obligation accepted by the company to use *all reasonable endeavours* to post the shareholder circular containing a board recommendation for the Crowther proposal must have been 'understood by all' as being subject to the directors' fiduciary duty to act in the best interests of the company, and that if the interests of the company are no longer aligned with the Crowther proposal that the recommendation would no longer be required. Note, however, that the court finds support for this holding in the contractual language of the agreement: that the best endeavours clause contained no requirement to continue with the recommendation when other offers had been made. This contrasted with another part of this contract that required the resolution approving the sale to Crowthers to be proposed at the shareholder meeting even if other offers had been made. The court does not explicitly say that *had* the provision required a board recommendation even where other better offers had been made that such a provision would have been void as incompatible with the directors' duty to act in the best interests of the company. Consider, hypothetically, the situation if International had, to no avail, been trying to sell UK for a year and Crowthers, at the time of the agreement, appeared to be the only possible buyer. If Crowthers had insisted on a board recommendation even in the face of alternative and superior offers, would the directors under the holding in *John Crowther Group plc* have been in breach of their duty to act in the best interests of the company in accepting such a term? Would the company have been bound by it? In this regard, consider the following case.

■ *Fulham Football Club Ltd v Cabra Estates plc* [1992] BCC 863

The facts are summarized in the headnote to the case as follows:

This was an appeal by Cabra Estates plc ('Cabra') from judgments of Chadwick J granting declarations as to the scope and legality of certain covenants entered into by the [directors of the Fulham Football Club Ltd].

In 1989, a subsidiary of Cabra, 'Vicenza', which owned the club's ground applied to the local council as planning authority for planning permission to develop the ground for residential purposes. The council then made its own planning applications for an alternative development and issued a compulsory purchase order ('CPO') for the ground.

In January 1990, before the commencement of a public inquiry into the CPO and planning applications, the club, its shareholders and directors [who were the plaintiffs in this case as they were seeking declaratory relief] made an agreement in writing with Vicenza and Cabra concerning the future development of the ground, involving the payment of substantial sums of money to the club. On the same day the…directors entered into a letter of undertaking under seal covenanting to procure the club to support Vicenza's planning applications and not to object to them or any other planning applications, and not to support the CPO or any new CPO, nor to support the council's case at any CPO inquiry or planning inquiry. At the first inquiry the directors acted accordingly. The CPO was not confirmed and planning permission was refused to the council and Vicenza.

Vicenza then submitted fresh applications which the council refused and a further public inquiry was ordered to begin in June 1992. The plaintiff directors then informed Vicenza that as a result of changed circumstances, they intended to give such evidence at the inquiry as they considered to be in the best interests of the club. Vicenza argued that the directors were still bound to support Vicenza's application.

The directors argued…that they could not be bound by the undertakings so far as they conflicted with their fiduciary duties to the club as directors. The judge [rejected this argument] on the basis that the directors had assumed the obligations. Cabra appealed to the Court of Appeal.

Neill LJ

…

The opening words of…the letter of undertaking [given by the directors] are: 'We will use our powers and rights as directors and members of the company to procure…'

Before the judge it was argued by the [directors] that it was an implied term of the undertaking that the directors would not thereby be required to do anything that would be inconsistent with the fiduciary duties owed by them to the company. It was further argued that, whether or not any such term should be implied, as a matter of law a director of a company may not fetter the exercise of his fiduciary duties by contractual undertaking. Both these arguments were rejected by the judge but were revived before us by a respondent's notice.

It is trite law that directors are under a duty to act bona fide in the interests of their company. However, it does not follow from that proposition that directors can never make a contract by which they bind themselves to the future exercise of their powers in a particular manner, even though the contract taken as a whole is manifestly for the benefit of the company. Such a rule could well prevent companies from entering into contracts which were commercially beneficial to them.

The true rule was stated by the High Court of Australia in *Thorby v Goldberg* (1964) 112 CLR 597. The relevant part of the headnote reads:

'If, when a contract is negotiated on behalf of a company, the directors bona fide think it in the interests of the company as a whole that the transaction should be entered into and carried into effect they may bind themselves by the contract to do whatever is necessary to effectuate it.'

Kitto J stated the argument in that case in the following passage from his judgment...:

'They [the appellant defendants] say...that because it [the alleged contract] purports to bind the directors of a company as to the manner in which they shall exercise a discretion of a fiduciary nature it is void for illegality.'

He dealt with that argument [as follows:]

'The argument for illegality postulates that since the discretionary powers of directors are fiduciary, in the sense that every exercise of them is required to be in good faith for the benefit of the company as a whole, an agreement is contrary to the policy of the law and void if thereby the directors of a company purport to fetter their discretions in advance... There may be more answers than one to the argument, but I content, myself with one. There are many kinds of transactions in which the proper time for the exercise of the directors' discretion is the time of the negotiation of a contract, and not the time at which the contract is to be performed. A sale of land is a familiar example. Where all the members of a company desire to enter as a group into a transaction such as that in the present case, the transaction being one which requires action by the board of directors for its effectuation, it seems to me that the proper time for the directors to decide whether their proposed action will be in the interests of the company as a whole is the time when the transaction is being entered into, and not the time when their action under it is required. If at the former time they are bona fide of opinion that it is in the interests of the company that the transaction should be entered into and carried into effect, I see no reason in law why they should not bind themselves to do whatever under the transaction is to be done by the board. In my opinion the defendants' contention that the agreement is void for illegality should be rejected.'

McTiernan J and *Windeyer* agreed with *Kitto* J and *Owen* J supported this particular part of the judgment of Kitto J in the following passage...:

'For all that appears from the plea, the directors of the Company may, before the execution of the agreement, have given proper consideration to the desirability of entering into it and decided that it was in the best interests of the Company that it should be made. If so, it would be impossible to argue that they had, by executing the document, improperly fettered the future exercise of their discretion. In fact they would already have exercised it and, in the absence of an allegation that they had done so improperly, the suggested defence could not be sustained.'

In the present case the undertakings given by the directors were part of the contractual arrangements made on 28 January 1990 which conferred substantial benefits on the company. In those circumstances it cannot be said that the directors improperly fettered the future exercise of their discretion, nor is there any scope for the implication of any such term as is suggested by the plaintiffs.

We were referred to two English cases at first instance where in each the court held that an undertaking by directors to use their best endeavours to ensure that their shareholders should approve a particular deal by the company (in one case a purchase, in the other a sale) was unenforceable. The cases are *Rackham v Peek Foods Ltd [1990] BCLC 895* and *John Crowther Group plc v Carpets International plc [1990]* BCLC 460. In neither case was *Thorby v Goldberg* cited. It may be that these decisions can be justified on their particular facts, but they should not be read as laying down a general proposition that directors can never bind themselves as to the future exercise of their fiduciary powers. If they could be so read then they would be wrong.

Following the Court of Appeal's decision in *Fulham Football Club* it is clear that at common law to agree to restrict the board's future discretion is not necessarily a breach of the duty to act in good faith in the best interests of the company. This is wholly sensible: it may benefit the company today to restrict the board's future discretion.

II RETHINKING WHAT IS IN THE COMPANY'S INTERESTS

As we have seen, the common law has defined a company's interests, when solvent, as the interests of the present and future shareholders as a whole. In recent years the legal and practical presumption that the company should be run in the interests of shareholders has been the subject of a lively and controversial debate in the UK and elsewhere. In this section we set out and evaluate the central arguments in this debate.

There are certain intuitive explanations for the legal presumption and commonly held assumption that the company should be run in the shareholders' interests, for example: 'companies are in the business of making profit; shareholders invest in the business to make a profit'. 'Shareholders *own* the business and as the *owners* of the business are entitled to define its interests.' This section aims to analyse in detail these intuitions and to provide the student of company law with an introduction to the terrain of this debate: the arguments in favour of giving priority to shareholder interests and the case for and against reform to treat other constituencies' interests as equally worthy of consideration when directors exercise corporate power. Inevitably in a book of this nature there are some limitations on the extent to which we can give this debate the full consideration it deserves. For those of you who wish to pursue the debate in greater depth additional reading is suggested at the end of this section.

1 The interests of the company's 'owners'

If you own a car or a house you are legally entitled to use that car or house to pursue your own interests. That is, an 'owner' has the right to control the object that is owned and to determine whose interests or what interests the use of that object furthers. A car or house owner will be subject to certain types of regulation that may restrict how she can drive the car or use the house: she cannot drive the car dangerously or over the speed limit; a residential house owner cannot use the house as a supermarket without first obtaining planning permission to do so; playing loud music every night may result in an anti-social behaviour order. However, subject to these external regulations a car owner or a house owner can use the car or house to further the owner's interests. In addition to these control or use rights an 'owner' of property has a **residual interest** right: the right, if the car or the house was sold today, to whatever is left over after any persons with a prior claim over the proceeds of sale have been paid. If a house is sold, for example, the 'owner' is entitled to what proceeds are left once the mortgage has been repaid. In everyday usage, therefore, what we mean by an 'owner' is a person who has control rights and residual interest rights.[31]

Do companies have owners in the same way that houses and cars have owners? If owners are the persons who have control rights and residual interest rights then the persons with control rights and residual interest rights in the company are its owners. Recall Bob's Electronics, the sole trader. Bob owned every asset and was the sole residual claimant. There is no doubt that he 'owned the business'. Following incorporation, however, the business is not owned by Bob but by the company. Bob, however, as sole shareholder has sole control rights and sole residual interest rights in relation to the company's activities and assets. It is true that if he appoints Markus the CEO to run the company he delegates certain control rights to Markus, but as sole shareholder in an English company, as we saw in our analysis of the distribution of power, he can take back that control, and cannot give up his ability to take it back. Is there anything conceptually distinctive, therefore, about the owner of a house who decides to rent it out and appoint a letting agent to manage the rental process and Bob, as sole shareholder of the company, who appoints a manager to run the company? If not, and we decide that

---

[31] See H. Hansmann, *The Ownership of Enterprise* (Harvard, 1996).

we can fairly view him as the owner of the company then it seems reasonable to assume that, as owner, he can decide in whose interests the company is run just as a house owner can decide in whose interests a house is used.

In the case of a house owner, apart from external regulation such as use or noise regulation, the house owner does not have to consider other persons' or groups' interests when he uses his house. A good citizen may switch off the lights when he leaves a room; however, if the owner finds winter depressing and bright lights cheer him up then there is no requirement, at the time of writing at least, that he should not burn the lights night and day. Why should Bob the sole trader as the owner of Bob's Electronics or Bob the sole shareholder as the owner of Bob's Electronics Ltd be treated differently in this regard and, apart from external regulation to which the business is subject, be restricted from pursuing the interests which he, as owner, identifies? If we are going to impose a legally different understanding of interest on the company than that chosen by its owners, then we would need a good reason to do so. We now look at some of the possible reasons.

Thus far we see that the logic of ownership and interest in the context of the company form is very strong: shareholders as 'owners' get to determine company interests. Typically shareholders are interested in maximizing their returns on their investment. Of course they could choose a different goal unrelated to generating profit. However, unless stated otherwise we assume that the primary interest of shareholders is in the value of their investment in the company. Accordingly, it follows that the company's interests are in maximizing the returns for shareholders.

Commentators who argue that a company's interests should include non-shareholder interests are aware of the power of this logical connection between *ownership* and *company interest* and have sought to question whether shareholders, particularly in companies with widely-held ownership, are *really owners* at all. Consider the following extract.

■ **P. Ireland, 'Company Law and the Myth of Shareholder Ownership' (1999) 62 *Modern Law Review* 32**

[During the late 19th century] increasingly, investors moved from holding shares in one or a small number of companies in whose affairs they took an active interest to holding a diversified basket of securities…Professional managers were paid to run enterprises, and the great majority of shareholders were reduced to the status of functionless rentiers, receiving their income in the form (if not the level of interest)—that is, as a return on their capital accruing from the mere passage of time. As the transformation of shareholders 'from active participants to passive investors' was completed, shareholders were not only established (both in law and economic reality) as money capitalists standing outside the company and the production process, the company, the sole legal and equitable owner of the firm *industrial capital*, was itself 'depersonified…ceasing to be an association and…becoming an institution'…

These changes in the economic (and legal) nature of the company and shareholding had profound effects on the developing law relating to joint stock companies…[For example,] there was a move from seeing directors as subject to the direction and control of the company, meaning the shareholders in general meeting, to seeing them as a self standing organ of the company as a separate depersonified entity. This conceptual change was accompanied by a decline in the right of shareholders to intervene in the day to day running of companies and by a steady shift of power from general meeting to board.[32] As their 'ownership' rights were steadily eroded, shareholders 'surrendered a set of definite rights for a set of indefinite expectations…'[33]

---

[32] *Automatic Self-Cleansing Filter Syndicate Co Ltd v Cuninghame* [1906] 2 Ch 34 is referenced as support in this regard (see Chapter 6).

[33] Quote from A.A. Berle and G.C. Means, *The Modern Corporation and Private Property* (Harcourt Brace, 1932).

With corporate shareholders ever more 'passive and functionless'…the justifications for their residual 'ownership' rights became even harder to discern…And yet…company law…'continued to vest significant property rights in the shareholder as residual claimants'. It still does, clinging on to the vestiges of shareholder 'ownership' and retaining for shareholders their place at the centre of the governance stage…

[The author then discusses and compares the legal and economic nature of a share and a **debenture**.] As Gower acknowledges, the rigid theoretical separation between shareholders, with rights in the company as well as against it, and **debenture holders**, with rights against the company but never in the company itself, collapses in contemporary 'economic reality'. Sealy concurs:

'The Theoretical differences between being a creditor of the company and being a member are considerable from a legal point of view, but…the practical consequences for investors…are very similar…an investment in debentures or debenture stock is very similar to an investment in shares: both are securities in the corporate sector of the economy offering different kinds of risk and different kinds of return.'[34]

The reality is, of course, that both debenture holders and shareholders are money capitalists, external to companies and the production process itself. Disinterested and uninvolved in management, and, in any case, largely stripped (in law as well as in economic reality) of genuine corporate ownership rights, the shareholder is, as Berle and Means pointed out, 'not dissimilar in kind from the…lender of money'. While, therefore, the relationship between shareholder and company is not exactly one of lender and borrower—the share is not, as some have suggested, a kind of loan—neither is it in any meaningful sense one of owner to owned.

[Modern company law has failed] to take separate corporate personality seriously enough. [Consequently it has attempted] to straddle two essentially irreconcilable positions. On the one hand, through the doctrine of separate corporate personality in its modern form, company law expresses and reinforces not only the separate existence of the 'the company' but the erosion, *de jure and de facto*, of the shareholder's ownership rights…On the other hand, in other ways company law has failed to fully recognise the depersonification of the company and the reduction of the corporate shareholder to the status of rentier investor with an interest very similar to that of a debenture holder. It has tried instead to hang on to the (always rather artificial) characterisation of corporate shareholders as 'insiders', 'members' and 'owners', continuing to grant to them exclusive residual ownership rights—most crucially of course the right to vote in general meetings. It has done this notwithstanding the true economic nature of the share; notwithstanding the absence of any property nexus between shareholders and the company's assets; notwithstanding the radical externality of shareholders to 'the company' and their superfluousness to and disinterest in the process of production…notwithstanding the fact that company law itself has done much to demote them from the status of owners. In short, company law has not taken separate corporate personality *really* seriously in contexts where it would be entirely justified so to do. Fuelled by the ownership myth and the legal remnants that sustain it, it continues rather to treat company and shareholders as in crucial respects synonymous…Fiduciary duties, in particular, still rest on this 'out-of-date assumption' with English law holding that the duty of directors is to act 'in the best interests of the company', interpreted to mean in the best interests of the shareholder…

The 'mistaken analogy'[35] of shareholder ownership…continues to cast a long shadow over the governance debate, serving as the main justification for the anachronistic retention by shareholders of exclusive governance rights and for the claim that public companies should be run predominantly, if not exclusively, in their interest. It has also done much to shape the debates

[34] Quote in L.S. Sealy, *Cases and Materials in Company Law* (Butterworths, 1996), 420–1.
[35] Quoting J. Kay, 'The Stakeholder Corporation' in Gavin Kelly et al (eds), *Stakeholder Capitalism* (Macmillan, 1997).

about corporate governance, most importantly, perhaps, in causing the issue generally to be cast [as an] agency problem…

Many are now…urging that corporate personality be taken more seriously. The economist John Kay…calls for the adoption of a German 'stakeholding' conception of the company as 'a community in itself and an organisation in turn embedded in a community', in which directors are cast in the role of trustees of the corporate assets including its employees. We need, he says, 'an organic model of corporate behaviour which gives to the corporation life independent from its shareholders' and which recognises it as an end in itself'…The question remains however, how does one begin to give content to the idea of the independent corporate interest which underlies it.

For Professor Ireland company law has recognized the separate legal personality of the company but has not taken this to its logical conclusion: that the company's interests are determined by the company as a separate autonomous entity and are not necessarily the interests of the shareholder constituency. What Ireland views as the 'myth of shareholder ownership' is, he argues, an important factor in supporting this connection between company and shareholder interests. Ireland's argument, therefore, seeks to detach shareholders from the 'ownership' label.

For Professor Ireland, understanding shareholders as owners ceases to make sense when one moves from the close company to large companies with many shareholders. In widely-held companies shareholders do not pay attention to the running of the business: they do not in practice act like owners. He views the retention by shareholders of control through, for example, the right to vote, as a vestige of history—the product of a time when shareholders in close companies monitored company activities and exercised their rights. Furthermore he argues that formal shareholder control rights have been progressively weakened. He cites the *Automatic Self-Cleansing* case, which we discussed in Chapter 6, in support of this claim. Accordingly, for Ireland shareholders in widely-held companies do not act like owners and their control rights are hangovers from a previous era. They are, therefore, not the 'owners' of the company and, accordingly, a company's interests should not be understood as the shareholders' interests. Professor Ireland provides further support for his argument through the comparison of the legal and economic nature of a share and a loan (or **debenture**). He argues that they differ primarily in the level of the risk they involve. When the debenture and the share are juxtaposed in this way the question that is begged is: what is the justification for viewing one instrument (the share) as an ownership instrument and the other (a debenture) as merely a financial claim?

Questions and discussion

- One response to Professor Ireland's argument is that shareholders are not as inactive as he thinks. Large institutional shareholders such as pension funds and insurance companies do pay more attention than many commentators give them credit for. However, as we saw in our analysis in Chapter 5, severe doubts remain whether this makes them the type of informed and active shareholders that Ireland associates with ownership.[36]

- Another challenge to the argument arises from whether we think owners have to be active in order to remain owners. Is ownership defined by the fact of having control rights and exercising them or simply by the possibility of exercising those control rights? It is not clear that our contemporary understanding of ownership requires being

---

[36] Ireland addresses this argument in *The Myth of Shareholder Ownership* at 50.

informed and attentive. A person may let his car rot in the garage but it does not mean that he is no longer the owner of the car?

- We need to ask whether there are benefits for shareholders in having control rights that they rarely, or never, exercise. If so then this suggests that the remaining shareholder control rights are not the legal residue of a different era but rather regulation that is well suited to the modern company that is widely-held. Consider the following comments in this regard:

■ D. Kershaw, 'The End of History in Corporate Law: The Case of Employee Participation on Corporate Governance' (2002) 2 *Journal of Corporate Law Studies* 34

Although [rational apathy] and collective action problems may inhibit effective exercise of control over the board and management, crisis circumstances may arise which trigger or motivate shareholder action to control egregious activity or to take emergency action. In the individual firm context it is unlikely that such action is cost effective; however, it may be deemed cost effective particularly by institutions that feel that action to discipline manage-ment is appropriate as 'a matter of principle', or 'to set an example'. It may be rare, but proxy actions do and can remove ineffective and incompetent management. The vote, which allows participation in such a crisis, is clearly a safeguard, albeit an extremely attenuated one. The shareholders here participate in defining the boundaries of the space in which the board and management can act in ways that fail to maximize shareholder value... Related to [this] factor, is that although the board and management may fairly be understood as adrift from shareholder control, the fact that the theoretical rather than effective power of the vote belongs to shareholders means that management and the board will prioritise shareholder interests above those of other corporate constituencies. This is not a concern where crisis voting, the market [for corporate control] or [directors'] duties adequately con-trol managerial self interest, shirking and incompetence; however, it remains a concern for those board decisions protected from review by the **business judgment rule**,[37] or that are not sufficiently inefficient or self-interested to trigger a market mechanism or principled shareholder action. The fact that the directors and management do not rely (in theory) on any other constituency to keep their jobs provides equity investors with comfort that where markets, fiduciary duties and principled disgust do not reach, management will be looking towards shareholders' interests even if at times they may be acting in their own. By [giv-ing shareholders the right to appoint directors] the primary incentive structure within the boundaries of unsanctioned board decision making is limited to the interplay of managerial self-interest and shareholder value.

- Consider from our analysis thus far in the book whether, as Ireland suggests, company law has formally taken away power from the shareholder in a widely-held company. Do you think that *Automatic Self-Cleansing* stands for a permanent loss of share-holder power or a reaffirmation of shareholders as the ultimate source of corporate power?

- For Ireland, detaching shareholders from the 'myth of ownership' allows other interests to be given equal consideration as the company's interest. Following Kay he suggests that the company is an 'end in itself' and that we should look to an 'independent corporate interest'. Can such an independent corporate interest be articulated without regard or reference to the interests of the company's constituencies? If so, how would you do it?

---

[37] The business judgment rules refers here generically to the fact that business decisions are only subject to rationality review requiring only a plausible or rational reason for action.

2 Contract and company interests

■ F. Easterbrook and D. Fischel, *The Economic Structure of Corporate Law* (Harvard, 1991) 35

What is the goal of the corporation? Is it profit (and for whom)? Social welfare more broadly defined? Is there anything wrong with corporate charity? Should corporations try to maximize profit over the long run or the short run? Our response to such questions is: 'who cares?' If the New York Times is formed to publish a newspaper first and make a profit second, no one should be allowed to object. Those who came in at the beginning actually consented, and those who came in later bought stock at a price reflecting the corporation's tempered commitment to a profit objective. If a corporation is started with a promise to pay half of the profits to the employees rather than the equity investors, that too is simply a term of the contract. It will be an experiment. We might not expect the experiment to succeed, but such expectations by strangers to the bargain are no objection. Similarly, if a bank is formed with a declared purpose to prefer loans to minority-owned businesses, or to third-world nations, that is a matter for the venturers to settle among themselves. So too if a corporation, on building a plant, undertakes never to leave the community. Corporate ventures may select their preferred 'constituencies.'

The one thing on which a contractual framework focuses attention is surprise. If the venture at its formation is designed in the ordinary fashion—employees and debt investors holding rights to fixed payoffs and equity investors holding a residual claim to profits, which the other participants promise to maximize—that is a binding promise. If the firm suddenly acquires a newspaper and declares that it is no longer interested in profit, the equity investors have a legitimate complaint. It is a complaint for breach of contract, not for derogation from some ethereal ideal of corporate governance.

The role of corporate law here, as elsewhere, is to adopt a background term that prevails unless varied by contract. And the background term should be the one that is either picked by contract expressly when people get around to it or is the operational assumption of successful firms. For most firms the expectation is that the residual riskbearers have contracted for a promise to maximize long-run profits of the firm, which in turn maximizes the value of their stock. Other participants contract for fixed payouts—monthly interest, salaries, pensions, severance payments, and the like. This allocation of rights among the holders of fixed and variable claims serves an economic function. Riskbearers get a residual claim to profit; those who do not bear risk on the margin get fixed terms of trade.

One thing that cannot survive is a systematic effort to fool participants. If investments are attracted on the promise of efforts to maximize profits, then that plan must be executed; otherwise new money cannot be raised and the firm will fail. If investors should come to doubt the worth of promises made to them, investment in the economy as a whole would fall. Similarly, if a firm building a new plant undertakes to operate it only as long as it is profitable and then to lay off the employees and move away, an effort to change the terms later on (if the feared condition materializes) to lock the plant in place or compel severance payments would be a breach of the agreement. Fear of such opportunistic conduct ex-post would reduce the willingness of investors to put up new plants and hire new workers.

Notice that a contractual approach does not draw a sharp line between employees and contributors of capital. Employees may be investors in the sense that portions of their human capital are firm-specific—that is, adapted to the corporation's business and worth less in another job. Holding firm-specific human capital is a way of investing in the firm. The question is not whether employees and other 'constituencies' of the firm have entitlements or expectations—they do—but what those entitlements are. If employees negotiate for or accept a system of severance payments to protect their firm-specific human capital, they cannot turn around later and demand an additional device (such as a contract for a term of years) when business goes bad. Each investor must live with the structure of risks built into the firm. Equity claimants lose out to debt claimants when times are bad and are not thereby entitled to some additional compensation. It is all a matter of enforcing the contracts. And for any employee or investor other than the residual claimant, that means the explicit, negotiated contract.

The choice of maximand is still important if political society wishes to change corporate behaviour. Given wealth as a maximand, society may change corporate conduct by imposing monetary penalties. These reduce the venturers' wealth, so managers will attempt to avoid them. So, for example, a pollution tax would induce the firm to emit less. It would behave as if it had the interests of others at heart. Society thus takes advantage of the wealth-maximizing incentives built into the firm in order to alter its behavior at least cost. Nothing in our approach asks whether political society should attempt to make firms behave as if they have the welfare of nonparticipants in mind. We do not address optimal ways to deal with pollution, bribery, plant closings, and other decisions that have effects on people who may not participate in the corporate contract. Society must choose whether to conscript the firm's strength (its tendency to maximize wealth) by changing the prices it confronts, or by changing its structure so that it is less apt to maximize wealth. The latter choice will yield less of both good ends than the former.

For Easterbrook and Fischel the company is best understood as a set of or a **nexus of contracts** between different parties: shareholders; creditors; employees; customers, etc. Interestingly, with regard to the 'myth of ownership' argument set out in the extract from Professor Ireland, the concept of 'ownership' is not viewed by the *nexus of contracts approach* as a useful category in corporate legal analysis; or as a justification for prioritizing shareholder interests. For these scholars the fundamental lens for the analysis of a company's interests is not ownership but contract. Professor Bainbridge puts it as follows:[38]

Nexus of contracts theory visualizes the firm not as an entity, but as an aggregate of various inputs acting together to produce goods or services. Employees provide labour. Creditors provide debt capital. Shareholders initially provide equity capital and subsequently bear the risk of losses and monitor the performance of management. Management monitors the performance of employees and coordinates the activities of all the firm's inputs. The firm is seen as simply a legal fiction representing the complex set of contractual relationships between these inputs. In other words, the firm is treated not as a thing, but rather as a nexus or web of explicit and implicit contracts establishing rights and obligations among the various inputs making up the firm.

Because shareholders are simply one of the inputs bound together by this web of voluntary agreements, ownership is not a meaningful concept in nexus of contracts theory.

For proponents of the nexus theory of contracts, what is in a company's interests is quite simply set out in the contracts the company enters into. The company could, *in theory*, agree with either the shareholders, employees, or any other group that the company should be run in its interests or a combination of interests. For Easterbrook and Fischel there are two fundamental requirements: first, that the parties have the freedom to choose the terms of the contracts which they enter into; and second, that those contracts should be enforced once they have been entered into. In a free market they argue that these contracts between the company and the different corporate constituencies will be written in a way that maximizes the value of those contracts for the contracting parties and, accordingly, from the company's

[38] S. Bainbridge, 'In Defense Of The Shareholder Wealth Maximization Norm: A Reply To Professor Green' (1993) 50 *Washington and Lee Law Review* 1423.

perspective, maximizes the value of the company. If companies choose to agree to maximize the value of the shareholders' residual interests then the reason for that is that it maximizes the value of the company. This means that the company gets more in return for agreeing to run the company in the shareholders' interests than it would get for agreeing to run it in the employees' interests or in the interests of all constituencies. If that is what a company agrees with the shareholders then the shareholders pay for that benefit (in the price they pay for the share). To change what the company's interests are after this agreement is, therefore, to expropriate value from the shareholders.

Let us illustrate this through our case study of Bob's Electronics Plc. Bob, the founder of the business, decides to retire and to sell 90% of his shares to the public at large. Assume first that he is interested in maximizing the money he receives for selling his shares so that he can buy the biggest house on the hill. In such a case he will ensure that the shares are sold on the understanding that the aim of the company (its 'interests') is to maximize value for the shareholders. With 'company interests' defined in shareholder value terms, shareholders know that the company will aim to maximize the size of the shareholders' residual interests. Alternatively, he could sell shares in the company on the contractual understanding that Bob's Electronics Plc is a 'good citizen' company that puts the local community and its employees first— the company aims to generate profits but not at the expense of good community and employee relations. This *may not* prevent shareholders buying shares in the company; however, they are unlikely to pay as much for the shares, as they will be aware that in putting employees and the community first the size of their residual interest will be smaller.

In this regard consider further the following attempt to explain why companies adopt the shareholder value approach as a result of the contracting process between the company and both shareholder and non-shareholder constituencies.

■ S. Bainbridge, 'In Defense of the Shareholder Wealth Maximization Norm: A Reply to Professor Green' (1993) 50 *Washington and Lee Law Review* 1423

Shareholders have no meaningful voice in corporate decision-making…As a practical matter, of course, the sheer mechanics of undertaking collective action by thousands of shareholders preclude them from meaningfully affecting management decisions.

In effect, shareholders have but a single mechanism by which they can 'negotiate' with management: withholding capital. If shareholder interests are inadequately protected, they can refuse to invest. The nexus of contracts model, however, demonstrates that equity capital is but one of the inputs that a firm needs to succeed. Non-shareholder corporate constituencies can thus 'negotiate' with management in precisely the same fashion as do shareholders: by withholding their inputs. If the firm disregards employee interests, it will have greater difficulty finding workers. Similarly, if the firm disregards creditor interests, it will have greater difficulty attracting debt financing, and so on.

In fact, withholding one's inputs may often be a more effective tool for non-shareholder constituencies than it is for shareholders. Some firms go for years without seeking equity investments. If the management groups in these firms disregard shareholder interests, the shareholders have little recourse other than to sell out at prices that will reflect management's lack of concern for shareholder wealth. In contrast, few firms can survive for long without regular infusions of new employees and new debt financing. As a result, few management groups can prosper for long while ignoring non-shareholder interests.

In any case, non-shareholders have a variety of other mechanisms available with which to influence management decisions that shareholders lack. One mechanism is contract negotiations. Unlike shareholders, employees regularly bargain with employers both individually and collectively. So do creditors. Even local communities sometimes bargain with existing or prospective employers, offering firms tax abatements and other inducements in return for which they could and should extract promises about the firm's conduct. Those non-shareholder constituencies that enter voluntary relationships with the corporation thus can protect themselves...

Perhaps an even more important consideration is the ability many non-shareholder constituencies have to protect themselves through the political process. Public choice theory teaches that well-defined interest groups are able to benefit themselves at the expense of larger, loosely defined groups by extracting legal rules from lawmakers that appear to be general welfare laws but in fact redound mainly to the interest group's advantage. Absent a few self-appointed spokesmen, most of whom are either gadflies or promoting some service they sell, shareholders—especially individuals—have no meaningful political voice. In contrast, many non-shareholder constituencies are represented by cohesive, politically powerful interest groups. Consider the enormous political power wielded by unions...

In sum...non-shareholder constituencies have adequate mechanisms to protect themselves... To be sure, neither the contracting nor the political process is perfect, but each standing alone probably provides non-shareholder constituencies with...meaningful protection...More to the point, shareholders are more vulnerable to management misconduct than are non-shareholder constituencies, because shareholders lack meaningful access to many of the protective mechanisms of which non-shareholder constituencies may avail themselves.

Questions and discussion

1. Professor Bainbridge argues that the outcome of a contracting process that treats the company's interests as the shareholders' interests makes good sense because in the absence of such an agreement shareholders have limited means of protecting themselves. Non-shareholder groups, he argues, have more extensive means of protecting themselves: through contract and the political process. This means that shareholders will pay more to have the company run in their own interests than would other constituencies. Do you agree with his assessment that shareholders have more limited means to protect themselves?

2. Are you persuaded by Bainbridge's argument that a form of contracting process takes place between the company and all of its constituencies? Do all employees really 'regularly bargain with employers both individually and collectively'? Do they need to actually bargain for the contractarian's claim to hold?

3. Are you persuaded that non-shareholder constituency groups, such as employees, have greater access to the political process in the UK to protect their interests than shareholders?

The extracts from Easterbrook and Fischel, and Bainbridge suggest that left alone to contract without interference from the state shareholders would pay for the right to run the company in their interests. Other constituencies would protect their interests through contract: employees would refuse to provide their labour if insufficiently protected or would demand higher salaries or forms of job security.

Accordingly, if the state, through regulation of a 'company's interests', elects to change the terms of the agreements made by the company or to restrict the freedom that shareholders and companies have to set the terms of their relationship then we require a persuasive justification for such an intervention. The following subsection considers the most prominent justification for such an intervention.

3 Justifying state regulation of company interests: trusteeship and social responsibility

■ E. Merrick Dodd Jr., 'For Whom are Corporate Managers Trustees?' (1932) 45 *Harvard Law Review* 1145

An individual who carries on business for himself necessarily [as sole trader] enters into business relations with a large number of persons who become either his customers or his creditors. Under a legal system based on private ownership and freedom of contract, he has no duty to conduct his business to any extent for the benefit of such persons; he conducts it solely for his own private gain and owes to those with whom he deals only the duty of carrying out such bargains as he may make with them.

If the owner employs an agent or agents to assist him in carrying on business, the situation is only slightly changed. The enterprise is still conducted for the sole benefit of the owner; the customers and creditors have contract rights against him and not normally against the agent even when the agent is the person who actually transacts business with them. The agent himself shares in the receipts of the enterprise only to the extent provided by his agreement. He, however, on his part owes something more than a contract duty toward his principal. He is a fiduciary who must loyally serve his principal's interests…

Incorporate the enterprise, making the owners [share]holders and some of them or persons selected by them directors, and…our picture is substantially unchanged. The business is still a private enterprise existing for the profit of its owners, who are now the [share]holders…

It is undoubtedly the traditional view that a corporation is an association of [share]holders formed for their private gain and to be managed by its board of directors solely with that end in view. Directors and managers of modern large corporations are granted all sorts of novel powers by present-day corporation statutes and charters, and are free from any substantial supervision by [share]holders by reason of the difficulty which the modern stockholder has in discovering what is going on and taking effective measures even if he has discovered it. The fact that managers so empowered not infrequently act as though maximum stockholder profit was not the sole object of managerial activities has led some students of corporate problems, particularly Mr. A. A. Berle, to advocate an increased emphasis on the doctrine that managerial powers are held in trust for [share]holders as sole beneficiaries of the corporate enterprise.[39]

The present writer is thoroughly in sympathy with Mr. Berle's efforts to establish a legal control which will more effectually prevent corporate managers from diverting profit into their own pockets from those of stockholders, and agrees with many of the specific rules which the latter deduces from his trusteeship principle. [The present writer] nevertheless believes that it is undesirable, even with the laudable purpose of giving [share]holders much-needed protection against

---

[39] As the extract hints, this was part of an ongoing debate during the Great Depression between Dodd and Adolf A. Berle, co-author with Gardiner Means of *The Modern Corporation and Private Property* (Harcourt, Brace and World, 1932), who observed the growing separation of ownership from control in the 'modern' corporation. Berle's position was that directors should be made to act more firmly in shareholders' interests. But after a series of cases decided in favour of other constituencies (e.g. *AP Smith Manufacturing v Barlow*, 98 A 2d 581 (NJ 1953)) Berle accepted Dodd's position in A.A. Berle, *The 20th Century Capitalist Revolution* (Harcourt, Brace and World, 1954) 169: 'the argument has been settled (at least for the time being) squarely in favor of Professor Dodd's contention.' In the *Preface* to the second edition of *The Modern Corporation* (1967) xxiii, the authors observed that: 'Stockholders…are beneficiaries by position only…Justification for the stockholder's existence thus depends on increasing distribution within the American population. Ideally the stockholder's position will be impregnable only when every American family has its fragment of that position and of the wealth by which the opportunity to develop individuality becomes fully actualized.' For a more nuanced account of Berle and Dodd's positions see W.W. Bratton and M.L. Wachter, 'Shareholder Primacy Corporatist Origins: Adolf Berle and the Modern Corporation' (2008) 34 *Journal of Corporation Law* 99.

self-seeking managers, to give increased emphasis at the present time to the view that business corporations exist for the sole purpose of making profits for their stockholders. [I believe] that public opinion, which ultimately makes law, has made and is today making substantial strides in the direction of a view of the business corporation as *an economic institution which has a social service* as well as a profit-making function, that this view has already had some effect upon legal theory, and that it is likely to have a greatly increased effect upon the latter in the near future...

Our present economic system, under which our more important business enterprises are owned by investors who take no part in carrying them on—absentee owners who in many cases have not even seen the property from which they derive their profits—alters the situation materially. That stockholders who have no contact with business other than to derive dividends from it should become imbued with a professional spirit of public service is hardly thinkable. If incorporated business is to become professionalized, it is to the managers, not to the owners, that we must look for the accomplishment of this result. If we may believe what some of our business leaders and students of business tell us, there is in fact a growing feeling not only that business has responsibilities to the community but that our corporate managers who control business should voluntarily and without waiting for legal compulsion manage it in such a way as to fulfil those responsibilities. Thus, even before the present depression had set many business men thinking about the place of business in society, one of our leading business executives, Mr. Owen D. Young, had expressed himself as follows as to his conception of what a business executive's attitude should be:

'If there is one thing a lawyer is taught it is knowledge of trusteeship and the sacredness of that position. Very soon he saw rising a notion that managers were no longer attorneys for stockholders; they were becoming trustees of an institution. If you will pardon me for being personal, it makes a great difference in my attitude toward my job as an executive officer of the General Electric Company whether I am a trustee of the institution or an attorney for the investor. If I am a trustee, who are the beneficiaries of the trust? To whom do I owe my obligations? My conception of it is this: That there are three groups of people who have an interest in that institution. One is the group of fifty-odd thousand people who have put their capital in the company, namely, its stockholders. Another is a group of well toward one hundred thousand people who are putting their labour and their lives into the business of the company. The third group is of customers and the general public. Customers have a right to demand that a concern so large shall not only do its business honestly and properly, but, further, that it shall meet its public obligations and perform its public duties—in a word, vast as it is, that it should be a good citizen. Now, I conceive my trust first to be to see to it that the capital which is put into this concern is safe, honestly and wisely used, and paid a fair rate of return. Otherwise we cannot get capital. The worker will have no tools. Second, that the people who put their labour and lives into this concern get fair wages, continuity of employment, and a recognition of their right to their jobs where they have educated themselves to highly skilled and specialized work. Third, that the customers get a product which is as represented and that the price is such as is consistent with the obligations to the people who put their capital and labour in. Last, that the public has a concern functioning in the public interest and performing its duties as a great and good citizen should. I think what is right in business is influenced very largely by the growing sense of trusteeship which I have described. One no longer feels the obligation to take from labour for the benefit of capital, nor to take from the public for the benefit of both, but rather to administer wisely and fairly in the interest of all'...

The view that those who manage our business corporations should concern themselves with the interests of employees, consumers, and the general public, as well as of the stockholders, is thus advanced today by persons whose position in the business world is such as to give them great power of influencing both business opinion and public opinion generally. Little or no attempt seems to have been made, however, to consider how far such an attitude on the part of corporate managers is compatible with the legal duties which they owe the [share]holder-owners as the elected representatives of the latter.

No doubt it is to a large extent true that an attempt by business managers to take into consideration the welfare of employees and consumers (and under modern industrial conditions the two classes are largely the same) will in the long run increase the profits of stockholders…If the social responsibility of business means merely a more enlightened view as to the ultimate advantage of the stockholder-owners, then obviously corporate managers may accept such social responsibility without any departure from the traditional view that their function is to seek to obtain the maximum amount of profits for their [share]holders.

And yet one need not be unduly credulous to feel that there is more to this talk of social responsibility on the part of corporation managers than merely a more intelligent appreciation of what tends to the ultimate benefit of their stockholders. Modern large scale industry has given to the managers of our principal corporations enormous power over the welfare of wage earners and consumers, particularly the former. Power over the lives of others tends to create on the part of those most worthy to exercise it a sense of responsibility. The managers, who along with the subordinate employees are part of the group which is contributing to the success of the enterprise by day-to-day efforts, may easily come to feel as strong a community of interest with their fellow workers as with a group of investors whose only connection with the enterprise is that they or their predecessors in title invested money in it, perhaps in the rather remote past…

But we are not bound to treat the corporation as a mere aggregate of stockholders. The traditional view of our law is that a corporation is a distinct legal entity…We may, as many do, insist that it is a mere aggregate of stockholders; but there is another way of regarding it which has distinguished adherents. According to this concept any organized group, particularly if its organization is of a permanent character, is a factual unit, 'a body which from no fiction of law but from the very nature of things differs from the individuals of whom it is constituted.'

If the unity of the corporate body is real, then there is reality and not simply legal fiction in the proposition that the managers of the unit are fiduciaries for it and not merely for its individual members, that they are, in Mr. Young's phrase, trustees for an institution rather than attorneys for the stockholders. As previously stated, this entity approach will not substantially affect our results if we insist that the sole function for the entity is to seek maximum stockholder profit. But need we so assume…A sense of social responsibility toward employees, consumers, and the general public may thus come to be regarded as the appropriate attitude to be adopted by those who are engaged in business, with the result that those who own their own businesses and are free to do what they like may increasingly adopt such an attitude. Business ethics may thus tend to become in some degree those of a profession rather than of a trade…

The question with which this article is concerned is not whether the voluntary acceptance of social responsibility by corporate managers is workable, but whether experiments in that direction run counter to fundamental principles of the law of business corporations. The view that they do so rests upon two assumptions: that business is private property, and that the directors of an incorporated business are fiduciaries (directly if we disregard the corporate fiction, indirectly in any case) for the stockholder-owners. Business—which is the economic organization of society—is private property only in a qualified sense, and society may properly demand that it be carried on in such a way as to safeguard the interests of those who deal with it either as employees or consumers even if the proprietary rights of its owners are thereby curtailed. [Emphasis added]

Writing in 1932, for Professor Dodd it is the position and role in our society of the modern public company with widely-held shareholder ownership that creates the scope for a new approach to defining a company's interests and goals. What is it about the modern large company that changes things for Professor Dodd? There are two factors in particular: first, the inability of the small shareholder to hold managers to account which results, in practice, in large companies being effectively unaccountable to any group, including shareholders; and secondly, these companies exercise tremendous power and influence over all aspects of our lives, and with power comes responsibility to those whose lives you affect. Accordingly, Dodd argues that companies should perform a 'social service' and act as a good citizen.

As in the earlier extract from Ireland, Dodd also stresses the fact that the company is an entity; something that is real in many respects. He says with regard to the corporation that there is 'reality and not simply legal fiction'. The fact that shareholders, because of rational apathy and collective action problems, do not pay attention and hold the company to account reinforces this idea: the corporate entity is not anchored to any real form of accountability. For Dodd there is a connection between personhood and responsibility, what he refers to as 'social service'. As persons we can demand responsible behaviour of companies when they act, especially given the power that they wield and the influence that they have over the various facets of our lives—as employees, as customers, as shareholders, as suppliers. For Dodd, supported by the approach of leading businessmen of the time, to provide this social service, to be responsible, means allowing the various interests of different groups to be considered and balanced against each other when exercising corporate power. Mr Young, an executive officer of the renowned General Electric Company quoted in the extract, suggests that his obligation is 'to administer wisely and fairly in the interest of all'.

Professor Dodd refers to and is aware of the strength of shareholder value arguments based upon contract and property (ownership). The justifications for pushing these arguments to one side are not outlined in detail in the article; however, we can see that they are based on the idea that the public may override contractual and property-based claims in the public or society's interest. Developing this argument consider the following extract.

■ **J.E. Parkinson, *Corporate Power and Responsibility* (Oxford University Press, 1993)**

A well established approach denies that the public interest is the relevant standard, or at least the primary standard by which company law should be assessed. It sees companies as purely private organisations, existing for whatever purposes their members had in mind. There is no assumption that they should serve the public good though the approach recognises that their operations are, in fact, highly beneficial to society. From this perspective proposals to redefine corporate decisional criteria in the public interest are misplaced. External regulation, at least in the form that applies to all citizens equally, is legitimate, but state intervention beyond that constitutes an illicit curtailment of individual freedom. The point then is not that reforms will necessarily fail in their objective of furthering the public good (though this is normally supposed), but that the interference in company affairs for that purpose is morally impermissible. We intend to reject this approach, and instead to embrace Dahl's claim that 'every large corporation should be thought of as a social enterprise; that is as an entity whose existence and decisions can be justified only insofar as they serve public or social purposes'.[40] The reason large companies should be viewed as social enterprises relies, it is suggested on a political theory about the legitimacy of private power. The theory holds that the possession of social decision-making power[41] by companies is legitimate (that is, there are good reasons for regarding its possession as justified) only if this state of affairs is in the public interest. Since the public interest is the foundation of the legitimacy of companies, it follows that society is entitled to ensure that corporate power is exercised in a way that is consistent with that interest. To describe companies as social enterprises

---

[40] Robert A. Dahl, 'A Prelude to Corporate Reform' (1972) *Business & Society Review* 17, 18.

[41] For Parkinson social decision-making power refers to power to make decisions that have social consequences: 'private decisions that have public results' (J.E. Parkinson, *Corporate Power and Responsibility* (OUP, 1993), 10.

is to hold that the state is entitled to prescribe the terms on which corporate power may be possessed and exercised.

It should be stressed at the outset that maintaining that large companies are social enterprises involves no necessary finding that the root principle behind the current rules of company law, that companies exist to make profits for the benefit of shareholders, is unsatisfactory. It is quite possible that that arrangement is one that is most conducive to the public good. But the point is that making profits for shareholders must now be seen as a mechanism for promoting the public interest, and not as an end in itself. It follows…that the detailed rules of company law must be tested, not just to see how they serve the interests of shareholders, but also how well they serve the interests of society in having an efficient and productive economy…

It may be on the other hand, that profit maximisation within the law is too limited a formula for aligning corporate decision making with the public good. Without examining at this stage the measures that might be necessary to improve the responsiveness of companies to the interests of the various groups that make up 'the public', we should note that the social enterprise perspective supplies a justificatory foundation for the relevant programme of reform. That foundation is analytically stronger than one relying on the casual observation that since companies possess power, they must use that power 'responsibly'. Rather, because the public interest is taken to be the root of all corporate legitimacy, compliance with whatever 'social responsibility' demands is seen as a prerequisite, a defining condition, for the possession of power. It follows that changes to the legal framework that are deemed necessary to encourage or induce the required behaviour should be viewed as permissible even though a substantial curtailment of shareholder rights may be involved…Because the public interest is the foundation of corporate legitimacy, demands for responsibility need not be confined to the avoidance of obvious forms of social harm, such as might result from pollution, dangerous products or false advertising, but potentially embrace all exercises of social decision-making power by companies, for example in relation to plant closures or policy on research and development.

For Professor Parkinson the precondition for a company being able to make decisions that have consequences and effects for real people's lives is that they behave in ways that are socially responsible. Furthermore, it is the democratic political process that has the power to define what is socially responsible behaviour and in the public interest. Parkinson views this as a different justification for regulation than the 'with power comes responsibility' approach which we saw in the extract from Dodd. Corporate responsibility does not arise as a result of having power; rather the precondition to being allowed to have power is that you behave according to the public's definition of what is responsible. Whereas in this extract Parkinson leaves open what it means for a company to behave in a socially responsible way, it is clear that he considers that a multi-interest approach to the company's interest would be justified by this public understanding of the company.

This focus on the company as a quasi-public entity which we see in Dodd and Parkinson's work contrasts sharply with Easterbrook and Fischel's account of the company as a nexus—or what Dodd calls an 'aggregation'—of contracts. Reducing the company to a set of private contractual relations de-emphasizes its personhood. For Easterbrook and Fischel separate legal personality is a tool for combining various contractual relationships. If we view the company—whether large or small—as the product of private contracting we require a justification for interfering with the arrangements that these parties agree upon amongst themselves. On the other hand, if we view the large company as a quasi-public actor, we do not need to justify regulation: the ability to regulate the company in the public interest is a fundamental condition of allowing the company to exist at all. So we see that the way in which we view the company—as a power-wielding entity or as a bundle of contracts—will have a profound effect on our willingness, or resistance, to regulating *the company's interests*.

Questions

1. Do you find Professor Parkinson's distinction between his justification for regulation and the 'power requires responsibility' justification persuasive?

2. Which one of these views of the company (private contractual being versus quasi-public entity) do you find more persuasive and why?

3. Do you think these two viewpoints outlined in the extracts from Easterbrook and Fischel, and Dodd and Parkinson are capable of engaging or arguing with each other; or are they two different incommensurable viewpoints on the organization of our society and/or what a company is?

3.1 Objections to multiple-interest approaches to the company's interests

■ Milton Friedman, 'The social responsibility of business is to increase its profits' *The New York Times Magazine* (13 September 1970) 33

In a free enterprise, private property system, a corporate executive is the employee of the owners of the business. He has direct responsibilities to his employers. That responsibility is to conduct the business in accordance with their desires, which generally will be to make as much money as possible while conforming to the basic rules of society, both those embodied in law and those embodied in ethical custom…the manager is the agent of the individuals who own the corporation…and his primary responsibility is to them. Needless to say this does not mean it is easy to judge how well he is performing his task but at least the criterion of performance are straightforward, and the persons among whom a voluntary contractual arrangement exists are clearly defined…

What does it mean to say that the corporate executive has a 'social responsibility' in his capacity as businessman? If this statement is not pure rhetoric, it must mean that he is to act in some way that is not in the interests of his employers [the shareholders]. For example, that he is to refrain from increasing the price of the product in order to contribute to the social objective of preventing inflation, even though a price increase would be in the best interests of the corporation. Or is he to make expenditures on reducing pollution beyond the amount that is in the best interest of the corporation or that is required by law in order to contribute to the social objective of improving the environment. Or that, at the expense of corporate profits, he is to hire 'hard core' unemployed instead of better qualified available workmen to contribute to the social objective of reducing poverty.

In each of these cases, the corporate executive would be spending someone else's money for the general social interest. Insofar as his actions in accord with his 'social responsibility' reduce returns to [shareholders,] he is spending their money. In so far as his actions raise the price to customers he is spending the customer's money. Insofar as his actions lower the wages of some employees, he is spending their money.

The [shareholders] or the customers or the employees could separately spend their own money on the particular action if they wished to do so. The executive is exercising a distinct 'social responsibility' rather than serving as an agent of the [shareholders] or the customers or the employees only if he spends the money in a different way than they would have spent it.

But if he does this, he is in effect imposing taxes, on the one hand, and deciding how the tax proceeds shall be spent on the other.

The process raises political questions on two levels: principle and consequences. On the level of political principle, the imposition of taxes and the expenditure of tax proceeds are government functions. We have established elaborate constitutional, parliamentary and judicial provisions to control these functions to ensure that taxes are imposed so far as possible in accordance with the preferences and desires of the public—after all, 'taxation without representation' was one of the battle cries of the American revolution...

The whole justification for permitting the corporate executive to be selected by the [shareholders] is that the executive is an agent serving the interests of his principal. This justification disappears when the corporate executive imposes taxes and spends the proceeds for 'social' purposes. He becomes in effect a public employee, a civil servant, even though he remains in name an employee of the private enterprise. On grounds of political principle it is intolerable that such civil servants—in so far as their actions in the name of social responsibility are real and not just window dressing—should be selected as they are now. If they are civil servants they should be selected through a political process. If they are to impose taxes and make expenditures to foster 'social' objectives, then political machinery must be set up to guide the assessment of taxes and to determine through a political process the objectives to be served...

On the grounds of consequences, can the corporate executive in fact discharge his alleged 'social responsibilities'? On the one hand, suppose he could get away with spending the [shareholders'] or customers' or employees' money. How is he to know how to spend it? He is told that he must contribute to fighting inflation. How is he to know what action might contribute to that end? He is presumably an expert in running the company—in producing a product or selling it or financing it. But nothing about his selection makes him an expert on inflation. Will his holding down the price of his product reduce inflationary pressure? Or, by leaving more spending power in the hands of his consumers, simply divert it elsewhere? Or by forcing him to produce less because of the lower price, will it simply contribute to shortages? Even if he could answer these questions, how much cost is he justified in imposing on his [shareholders], customers and employees for this social purpose. What is his appropriate share and what its the share of others...

In a free society 'there is only one social responsibility of business—to use its resources and engage in activities designed to increase its profits so long as it stays in the rules of the game'.[42]

Some of Friedman's objections to Dodd's trusteeship model of the company can be dealt with quite easily. His objection that this trusteeship model involves illegitimate taxation is only valid if the legal rule or contractual agreement requires that the company's interests are the shareholders' interests. If the rule of law (and therefore the underlying term of the company–shareholder contract) allows directors to consider other interests—as the executive of the General Electric company suggests in Dodd's article—then there is no illegitimate taking where shareholders purchased shares upon this understanding. Of course, where the shareholders purchased the shares on the understanding that their interests would be the company's interests and subsequently other interests are then given equal treatment or priority as a result of autonomous managerial action or a change in the law then the 'taxation claim' is more persuasive.

There are, as Friedman makes clear, wealth distribution consequences of giving directors this decision-making freedom. If directors elect to keep a plant open to protect the interests of the employees and the local community when the plant is loss-making and could be profit-making if moved to a developing country, then wealth is transferred from shareholders, whose residual interest shrinks, and from customers when products could be cheaper to the local community and employees. If the company decides not to have a late night shift this may benefit the local community by reducing noise and traffic congestion late into the night, but shareholder value and employee job security may be

---

[42] Quoted from M. Friedman, *Capitalism and Freedom* (Chicago University Press, 1962).

reduced by the decision. Friedman raises the question whether we want these types of distributional decisions being made by unelected officials.

Friedman also raises the question whether managers are capable of making these decisions. Professor Friedman was a famous monetary economist who spent much of his academic life looking at the causes, and mechanisms of controlling, inflation. The complex relationship between a business decision and inflation is used in his article to question the ability of company directors to perform a social function, such as acting to hold down inflation. However, we may feel less persuaded by his argument if we consider the plant or late night shift decisions set out above. Here we might be more willing to accept that managers are capable of assessing the various interests involved. However, although they may be able to understand the interests involved, how should managers balance interests or trade off one interest against another? As Friedman puts it: 'what is his appropriate share and what is the share of others'? Here Friedman's objection is very difficult to answer, for unless we require directors to prioritize one or more interests in defining a company's interests then what criteria should directors apply in carrying out the balancing act? How does one, as Mr Young, quoted in the Dodd extract, suggests, 'administer wisely and fairly in the interest of all'? In the absence of specific criteria, with a multi-interest approach we are left to trust managers to balance appropriately.

Some commentators have argued that one problem with trusting managers to balance the interests of different groups is that it gives them more room to act in their own interests, more room to incur agency costs. Easterbrook and Fischel put this as follows:

> A manager told to serve two masters...has been freed of both and is answerable to neither. Faced with a demand from either group, the manager can appeal to the interest of the other. Agency costs rise and social wealth falls.

If directors, for example, use the company's funds to expand the business into low return projects, the directors could claim to be acting in the interests of employees or the community at large, when in fact the motivating factor for their actions is to expand the business so that they feel more important running a bigger business and will be able to increase their remuneration because they manage a bigger business. However, we should be wary of assuming a dramatic increase in agency costs as a result of a multiple-interest understanding of company interests. As we saw in our analysis of the common law duty to act in good faith in the best interests of the company, the standard of review is very low which in any event creates considerable scope for such indirect agency costs.

3.2 Social responsibility means maximizing shareholder value

If one accepts the view that the company as a legal person exercising considerable power has an obligation to act as a good citizen and to be socially responsible, *it does not follow*, as Professor Dodd assumes, that the best way of being responsible is to have a multiple-interest understanding of the company's interests whereby directors are required to balance these interests. A strong counter-argument in this regard is that all groups in society will be financially better off if the 'company's interests' are defined in terms of shareholder value. As Friedman argues, the socially responsible thing for companies to do is to maximize profits and shareholder value. Professors Hansmann and Kraakman have put this argument more recently as follows:[43]

---

[43] R. Kraakman and H. Hansmann, 'The End of History for Corporate Law' (2001) 89 *Georgetown Law Journal* 439.

All thoughtful people believe that corporate enterprise should be organized and operated to serve the interests of society as a whole, and that the interests of shareholders deserve no greater weight in this social calculus than do the interests of any other members of society. The point is simply that now, as a consequence of both logic and experience, there is convergence on a consensus that the best means to this end (that is, the pursuit of aggregate **social welfare**) is to make corporate managers strongly accountable to shareholder interests and, at least in direct terms, only to those interests. It follows that even the extreme proponents of the [trusteeship/ social responsibility theory] of the corporation can embrace the primacy of shareholder interests in good conscience.

There are several ways of making this connection between shareholder value and social wealth or welfare. In a book on company law we can only scratch the surface of these arguments. Importantly, to understand the argument that shareholder value maximization maximizes social wealth (the size of the nation's pie) one needs to take a broader view than simply looking at individual company examples.

One argument in this regard is that in a competitive market companies produce products until the costs of producing the next product are more than the revenue that will be received for that product. If the costs of production increase and the revenue for the product stays the same then fewer products will be produced. If costs can be reduced then more products can be produced by the company. Putting more of the product into the market will reduce the price of the product. Society will be better off because we can afford to consume more of that product—with the same income you can buy two loaves of bread instead of one. If a company elects to maximize shareholder wealth it reduces its costs of capital which reduces the costs of production. In a competitive market everyone is therefore better off. Whether our product markets are competitive enough to validate this argument is clearly open to debate. Furthermore, the objective of maximizing shareholder wealth within the company also, many would argue, drives innovation in the productive process—the invention of new technology and production methods—that again results in the production of more loaves.

Another argument is that by maximizing shareholders' returns we encourage investors to invest their wealth in value-creating projects. Such funded projects create jobs and pay taxes and stimulate local economies. If the approach to the company's interests reduced the returns to shareholders then shareholders may be less willing to invest, creating fewer jobs and reducing the taxes paid into the state's coffers. Furthermore, if companies do not follow the profit maximization norm they may be too slow to adjust to changing economic circumstances, putting their longer term survival at risk.

This broader view is necessary to understand and to accept the link between shareholder value and social wealth because when looking at particular companies we can certainly imagine difficult decisions that are made that maximize shareholder wealth but reduce social wealth. Consider the recent high-profile decision of Burberry Plc to relocate their production from Treorchy in Wales to Spain and China, citing the more expensive costs of production in Wales as the reason for the relocation. This resulted in the loss of 300 jobs in a town of approximately 8,000 people and a celebrity-driven campaign to change Burberry's management's mind. One could imagine[44] in this specific case that the direct costs of job losses, the detrimental effects on the local community, and the costs of relocation for workers who seek employment elsewhere could exceed the cost benefits that shareholders receive as a result of the decision. Furthermore, the benefits of new jobs do not accrue to the UK economy but rather in this case to the Chinese and Spanish economies. In this regard, consider the following extract from

---

[44] This is purely conjecture for the benefit of our analysis.

the *Financial Times* arguing strongly that such a narrow firm-specific view cannot be taken when thinking about the economic benefits of profit-motivated decisions in an economy that must adapt to changing circumstances.

■ T. Harford, 'Checks and balances: Burberry is switching jobs from Wales to China. Should the government intervene?' *Financial Times* (Weekend Magazine–The Undercover Economist) (3 March 2007)

My eye has been caught recently by the contrast between two stories the [*Financial Times*] has been covering. Burberry, the luxury goods manufacturer, is to close a factory near Treorchy, South Wales, and expand production in Spain and China where rents and salaries are lower. This decision has drawn condemnation from everyone from the local MP to Charlotte Church. In other news, Glasgow has been persuading companies such as JP Morgan to move jobs away from London. Two of Glasgow's attractions are said to be, well, lower rents and lower salaries.

One of these stories is widely regarded as good news, and the other as a disaster. But the motives of Burberry and JP Morgan seem very similar: they are profitable businesses, aiming to stay profitable. The effects look similar too. Some people in the poorer of the areas (China is poorer than Wales, Glasgow is poorer than London) will get better jobs. Some people in the richer areas will lose theirs. Prices will adjust too: the richer areas will become just a tiny bit more affordable. When the new jobs go to Glaswegians, all this appears to be acceptable, but when the new jobs go to foreigners it is regarded as appalling.

The queue of celebrities eager to hitch themselves to the Burberry backlash seem to have entirely missed the xenophobia inherent in their views, but that is the risk of allowing the debate on globalisation to be carried out by Charlotte Church and Sir Tom Jones. Yet more sensible observers also seem a little confused...

Yet the government has not acted, and were it deranged enough to try, the result would be predictably catastrophic for Glasgow. At the moment, what Glasgow offers to employers over London is value for money. It would be nice if Glaswegians earned London wages, and perhaps they will if the Clyde continues to boom. But that will not happen by imposing a minimum wage in Glasgow of £100 an hour. It is hard to see how a project to legislate China into prosperity would work much better.

It turns out that jobs are created and destroyed all the time—several thousand a day in the UK alone. The jobs that visibly move to foreign parts get all the attention, but jobs can also be lost to other parts of the same country. Industries can fall out of fashion; what now for hula hoops in a PlayStation world? Jobs can be wiped out by technological change; there is not much call for typists these days.

It is not particularly helpful to distinguish between jobs lost to Glasgow, China or Microsoft Word, especially not to the people who have lost them. The typists, the City analysts and the Welsh textile workers have all fallen victim to economic change. The real difference—and it is very real indeed—between the workers of Treorchy and those of the Square Mile is that London is well-equipped to cope with economic change and Treorchy is not. Neither Burberry nor Sir Tom can do much about that, but there is a reason why more people today live in big cities than ever before.

Questions and discussion

1. A multiple-interest approach to company interests does not require that shareholder interests are ignored, rather that they are balanced. If the economic case at Burberry suggested the plant could never be profit making, what decision would you take as a director of a company with *a multiple-interest approach* to company interests?

2. Sometimes the choices faced by directors are clear cut: change the location of the plant and increase profitability or keep the plant open and continue to incur losses. However, many

decisions will not be as clear cut: can the products produced at the factory be changed to improve profitability; would more flexible working practices, for example, accepting night shifts or weekend work, assist with profitability? The question for us is whether in uncertain decision-making contexts a multiple-interest model would encourage directors to search harder for solutions that could save jobs without sacrificing shareholder value? Put differently, does a shareholder value approach make it easier, for example, for managers to move production and ignore alterative value-neutral options?

4 Justifying regulation: could multiple interest trusteeship increase the size of the economic pie?

As we have seen thus far, a company that has a multiple-interest approach to the 'company's interests' will have a higher cost of equity capital. That is, shareholders will not pay as much for the shares than they would do if the company had a shareholder value approach to the 'company's interests'. The reason for this is clear: if the value of a share is a prediction of the value of the residual interest of the company then that value will be lower where the company is allowed to make decisions that are in the interests of other constituencies rather than shareholder value. If in the future the company keeps a loss-making plant open to protect employee interests then shareholder value will be reduced. Shareholders when pricing shares will take account of such possible future events. A company or a country that adopts a multiple-interest approach to 'company interests' will, therefore, be less competitive; sell fewer products and generate less value.[45]

There is, however, an important counter-argument to this costs of capital argument against a multiple-interest approach. This counter-argument is based around the idea that a multiple-interest approach to a company's interests will increase the productivity of employees. If an employee increases his productivity to make four widgets an hour instead of two, then the company has two more widgets to sell and will make more profit. Some proponents of a multiple-interest approach argue that by giving discretion to the board to consider equally the interests of employees alongside shareholders, employees will be encouraged to make firm-specific investments which will improve their productivity.

There are skills that an employee learns and develops that are transferable to other companies and other jobs; however, many skills are firm-specific in that they relate to the specific products, processes, and culture of a particular company. Such skills are worth little elsewhere, yet companies need to encourage their employees to develop these firm-specific skills (to make the investments of time, effort, and attention). Employees who make these investments will be more productive (metaphorically, will produce more widgets) than employees who do not make these investments.

There are different ways in which employees through their contracts with the company could be encouraged to make these firm-specific investments, for example: increasing salaries; giving them performance bonuses; and increasing their job security. Some commentators argue that a multiple-interest approach to company interests would encourage employees to make such firm-specific investments, benefiting both employees but also the shareholder constituency. Such employees would feel more secure knowing that the interests of shareholder value do not automatically trump their interests as employees: a multiple-interest approach to company interest does not guarantee that a loss-making plant will be kept open, but it increases the likelihood that it will be kept open or that an employee-friendly solution will be found. The leading proponents of this idea are Professors Blair and Stout in what they refer to as *the team production theory of corporate law*.

---

[45] This argument of course relies on the assumption of sufficiently competitive markets.

■ M. Blair and L. Stout, 'A Team Production Theory of Corporate Law' (1999)
85 *Virginia Law Review* 247

Shareholders benefit from granting directors discretion to favour other constituencies, because...shareholders' 'long-run interests' should be interpreted to mean the long-run interests of all the shareholders who hold, have held, or will hold stock in the firm, including those original investors who bought their shares when the firm first went public. Opportunistically exploiting the firm-specific investments of corporate stakeholders (say, violating employees' expectations of job security by moving the firm's manufacturing plants to Mexico) may well benefit, in both the short and the long run, those individuals who happen to hold shares in the corporation at the time the decision to move is made. If the firm's employees anticipated this sort of conduct ex ante, however, they might well have demanded higher wages—or been more reluctant to invest in firm-specific human capital—in earlier years...

Treating directors as trustees charged with serving interests above and beyond those of share-holders in fact can be in shareholders' 'long-run interests,' because a shareholder decision to yield control rights over the firm to directors ex ante—that is, when the corporate coalition is first formed—can induce other participants in the team production process to make the kind of firm-specific investments necessary to reap a surplus from team production in the first place. Thus, a broad interpretation of [a company's interest] that permits directors to sacrifice shareholders' interests to those of other corporate constituencies...ultimately serves [shareholder] interests as a class, as well as those of the other [constituencies] of the corporate coalition.

Questions and discussion

- As a student of this debate, it is very difficult to adopt a clear position on the costs to the company of a multiple-interest approach to 'company interests' versus a shareholder value approach. Is it true that a multiple-interest approach will make employees feel more secure? Is that security likely to make them more willing to make firm-specific investments than a higher salary or performance bonus? If it is cheaper for the company to encourage those investments by bonuses and salary increases than by adopting a multiple-interest trusteeship approach (resulting in a decrease in what shareholders will pay for the shares), then adopting a multiple-interest trusteeship model would make no sense from a value perspective. But can financial incentives operate as effective sub-stitutes for the feeling that as an employee—whatever your position in the corporate hierarchy—your interests matter as much as the interests of other constituencies when decisions are made? Are they an effective substitute for the productive effects of the feel-ing that could be generated by such an approach: that you are part of the company, not just an input into what the company produces?

- Assuming that a multiple-interest trusteeship model makes workers more willing to make firm-specific investments, whether this approach injures shareholders (and results in an increase in the company's cost of capital) depends on the extent to which the approach reduces, if at all, the value of the shareholders' residual interest. This depends on the answer to the following question: will the multiple-interest approach allow a distribution of wealth to non-shareholder groups that exceeds the increased wealth that is generated from the productivity gains associated with employee firm-specific invest-ments? This is very difficult to measure and is likely to vary between firm size and industry.

- If Blair and Stout are correct that a trusteeship model creates a win–win situation for shareholders as well as employees, then we need to ask why companies in the UK do not adopt such an approach—that is, as UK company law allows them to do, adjust the default presumption that company's interests mean shareholder value. If a multiple-interest approach really benefited the company and shareholders wouldn't they make such an election? Or would the 'constraining normality'[46] of company law tradition—doing what we have always done and what others do when we have neither the time nor the resources to consider the implications of doing things differently—prevent experimentation and departure from the standard position? If the consequences of experimentation are uncertain, company law's normality is unlikely to be challenged by companies themselves, even if for some companies Blair and Stout's trusteeship model does indeed represent a 'win–win'.

- If it is the case that social wealth increases through a multiple interest model, although shareholders themselves would not elect to adopt such a model, then the market is failing and state intervention would be justified to correct the market by introducing a multiple-interest approach in order to maximize social wealth. The problem any regulator has when faced with this theory is how to determine whether or not a multiple interest model would generate more or less social wealth. In the absence of a solid empirical basis for such a decision is it understandable that regulators would be hesitant to fix what is not clearly broken? If uncertainty results in regulators sitting on the fence and abstaining from reform, what could company law do to facilitate experimentation by companies instead of the radical move of changing the default rule to a multiple-interest model of the corporation?

Further reading

B. Cheffins, *Company Law: Theory, Structure and Operation* (Clarendon, 1997), ch 2.

R. Clark, *Corporate Law* (Little Brown & Company, 1986), ch 16.

M.A. Eisenberg, 'Corporate Law and Social Norms' (1999) 99 *Columbia Law Review* 1253.

A. Keay, '*Ascertaining the Corporate Objective: An Entity Maximisation and Sustainability Model*' (2008) 71 *Modern Law Review* 663.

J.R. Macey, 'An Economic Analysis of the Various Rationales for Making Shareholders the Exclusive Beneficiaries of Corporate Fiduciary Duties' (1991) 21 *Stetson Law Review* 23.

J.E. Parkinson, *Corporate Power and Responsibility* (Clarendon, 1993), chs 1, 9–12.

L. Stout, 'Bad and Not-so-Bad Arguments for Shareholder Primacy' (2002) 75 *Southern California Law Review* 1189.

O. Williamson, 'Corporate Governance' (1984) 93 *Yale Law Journal* 1197.

5 The UK reform debate on the company's interests

The reform process that preceded the Companies Act 2006 gave considerable attention to whether or not the common law approach to the 'company's interests' should be changed to require a broader more inclusive consideration of non-shareholder constituency interests when exercising corporate powers. The Company Law Steering Committee set out two different ways of taking into account non-shareholder interests. The first approach was referred to as the 'enlightened shareholder value approach'. This approach would not alter the priority given to shareholder value; however, it would require that consideration be given to the interests of, and relationships with, other constituencies, and would support corporate action to further those interests or support those relationships provided that in so doing the interests of shareholders are also advanced. For example, taking into account the interests of employees when exercising corporate power may make the employees feel more valued and possibly more secure in

---

[46] T. Veblen, *Why Economics is Not an Evolutionary Science*' in M. Lerner (eds), *The Portable Veblen* (Viking Press, 1948) noting that 'this constraining normality is of the spiritual kind. It is for the scientific purpose an imputation of spiritual coherence to the facts dealt with'.

their jobs. More content and secure employees are likely to work harder and to be more willing to make the necessary firm-specific investments of human capital and, therefore, will be more productive workers which, in turn, generates more shareholder value. Importantly, however, where consideration of non-shareholder interests conflicts with shareholder interests then an enlightened shareholder value approach requires that the decision be taken in the shareholders' interests. If the choice is between keeping a loss-making plant open to save jobs or shifting production to a developing country where it will not be loss-making, the decision is clear: the plant must be closed down.

One might ask whether an enlightened shareholder value approach is any different than an approach that simply focuses on shareholder value. If happy workers are more productive workers then any director acting in the shareholders' interests will act to make the workers happy to the extent that value is thereby generated. This was certainly Professor Dodd's view when, in the article extracted earlier, he wrote: 'if the social responsibility of business means merely a more *enlightened* view as to the ultimate advantage of the stockholder-owners, then obviously corporate managers may accept such social responsibility without any departure from the traditional view that their function is to seek to obtain the maximum amount of profits for their [share]holders' (emphasis added). The second alternative identified by the Company Law Review Steering Committee is the multiple-interest trusteeship model outlined earlier where no constituency interest takes priority and directors are required to act in ways that balance these interests. The Company Law Review called this approach a **pluralistic approach.** Following a review of the arguments and thorough public consultation the Review recommended rejecting pluralism in favour of the enlightened shareholder value approach. The reasons for the rejection of pluralism are set out here.

■ **Company Law Review Steering Committee,** *Modern Company Law for a Competitive Economy: The Strategic Framework* **(1999), ch 5.1**

The case for reformulating directors' duties to give effect to the pluralist approach is as follows. The present law, in making shareholders' interests ultimately overriding, may create, or reinforce, an environment in which relationships of trust are difficult to sustain…Since the duty of directors is ultimately to further the interests of shareholders, parties who might otherwise make firm-specific investments in a company (such as employees who acquire specialised skill or suppliers who invest in tooling necessary for a particular customer) will be reluctant to do so, because of the level of risk to which they are exposed. Such investments are risky because they cannot be transferred to other uses without significant loss of value, and are difficult to protect contractually because of their long-term nature and the problems involved in predicting and providing for future contingencies. The pluralist view asserts that present law (even when understood in an enlightened shareholder value form) fails to cater for these considerations, because such firm-specific investments are best regarded as assets of the company as a wealth generating entity distinct from its members. Its directors should be accountable for the stewardship of the company's assets and the maximisation of their value for the benefit of all contributors and not just its shareholders. Only against the background of a regime which permits or requires directors to treat non-member participants in that way can they be expected to undertake the necessary commitments…

There are a number of possible counter-arguments to such pluralist views. First, it may be argued that in practice a broad enlightened shareholder value approach would provide an *adequate* environment for the development of such relationships. It is not clear that the trade-offs of shareholders' interests against those of other participants which the pluralist approach envisages would be necessary in practice…

Second, it is not self-evident that the normal process of bargaining between suppliers and consumers of factors of production is incapable of generating appropriate safeguards or incentives for all sides…

Third, it may be argued that if there are deficiencies in this area they are best made good by changes in other areas of the law and public policy, or in best practice, rather than by making changes in company law, which might have unpredictable and damaging effects. Examples include…in the employment field, the possibilities include increased levels of consultation and information with, for example, provision of information about training policies to recognised unions and consultation in the workplace, perhaps based on partnership agreements. Such developments operate within, and consistently with, the present company law systems of control, accountability and responsibility. So they require no company law reform.

There is a fourth argument, that to change the present focus of directors on increasing the value of the business over time, subject to clear single channel accountability to members, in favour of some broader objective involving the trade off of interests of members and others (with whom the company is in some aspects in an adversarial bargaining relationship), would dangerously distract management into a political balancing style at the expense of economic growth and international competitiveness.

For the argument for pluralism to be accepted it needs to be maintained that the net benefit, in overall welfare terms, of encouraging firm-specific investment by the proposed legal means, after taking account of the necessary disadvantage to shareholders, outweighs these possible objections.

At the minimum, implementation of the pluralist view would require a reform of the law of directors' duties to *permit* them to further the interests of non-shareholder participants that is employees, customers and suppliers—even if this were to the detriment of shareholders. A possible variant would be a duty *requiring* them to promote the success of the company as a business enterprise in this way—ie with the interests of none of the participants, including the shareholders, being regarded as overriding…At the same time we also see difficulties in merely enabling directors to diverge from the enlightened shareholder value objective, since there would be no formal remedy for abuse of the powers conferred (though the provisions against the directors furthering their own interests would remain in place). Arguably this would create a dangerously broad and unaccountable discretion, unless sufficient additional safeguards can be devised.

Questions

1. Does the Company Law Review view arguments about good corporate responsible citizens as supporting the pluralistic position or did they only consider economic arguments?

2. Are you persuaded that the introduction of a pluralistic approach would lead to a 'broad and unaccountable' discretion for directors? Consider in this regard the extent to which the duty of good faith at common law and the duty to promote the success of the company under the 2006 Act are capable of holding director's to account. It is noteworthy that other jurisdictions have introduced such pluralistic approaches. Consider for example the New York Business Corporations Law.[47]

---

[47] Note also that in Germany although the Stock Corporation Act is silent on the question of corporate objective it is widely accepted that the management board should act in the interests of shareholder, employees and society at large. W. Hefermehl and G. Spindler in B. Kropff and J. Semler (eds), *Münchener Kommentar zum Aktiengesetz* (Munich: Beck, 2nd edn, 2004), vol 3, s 76/53. In this regard Gerner-Beuerle, Kershaw and Solinas observe that 'the [German] Stock Corporation Act 1937, s 70(1), contained an express provision to the effect that the management board shall manage the company "for the benefit of the undertaking and its employees and as the common good of the people and the Reich requires". Not only because of its political undertones, but also because the legislature believed that the social obligations of management were self-evident and that an explicit provision was, therefore, unnecessary, this formulation was left out when the Stock Corporation Act was reformed in 1965' (see C. Gerner-Beuerle, D. Kershaw and M. Solinas, 'Is the Board Neutrality Principle Rule

■ Section 717(b) New York Business Corporations Law

In taking action, including, without limitation, action which may involve or relate to a change or potential change in the control of the corporation, a director shall be entitled to consider, without limitation, (1) both the long-term and the short-term interests of the corporation and its shareholders and (2) the effects that the corporation's actions may have in the short-term or in the long-term upon any of the following:

(i) the prospects for potential growth, development, productivity and profitability of the corporation;

(ii) the corporation's current employees;

(iii) the corporation's retired employees and other beneficiaries receiving or entitled to receive retirement, welfare or similar benefits from or pursuant to any plan sponsored, or agreement entered into, by the corporation;

(iv) the corporation's customers and creditors; and

(v) the ability of the corporation to provide, as a going concern, goods, services, employment opportunities and employment benefits and otherwise to contribute to the communities in which it does business.

Nothing in this paragraph shall create any duties owed by any director to any person or entity to consider or afford any particular weight to any of the foregoing or abrogate any duty of the directors, either statutory or recognized by common law or court decisions…

3. How do you think a pluralistic approach would work in practice?

4. On a point scale of one to five (with one being priority consideration and five being no consideration) where would you place employee interests under a shareholder value approach, an enlightened shareholder value approach, and a pluralistic approach?

III THE COMPANIES ACT 2006

1 The duty to promote the success of the company

The Companies Act 2006 replaces the common law duty to act in good faith in the best interests of the company with the duty to promote the success of the company set out in section 172.

■ Section 172 CA 2006 Duty to promote the success of the company

(1) A director of a company must act in the way he considers, in good faith, would be most likely to promote the success of the company for the benefit of its members as a whole, and in doing so have regard (amongst other matters) to—

(a) the likely consequences of any decision in the long term,

(b) the interests of the company's employees,

(c) the need to foster the company's business relationships with suppliers, customers and others,

(d) the impact of the company's operations on the community and the environment,

Trivial? Amnesia about Corporate Law in European Takeover Regulation' (2011) *European Business Law Review* 559 (2011) at n 99.

    (e) the desirability of the company maintaining a reputation for high standards of business conduct, and

    (f) the need to act fairly as between members of the company.

(2) Where or to the extent that the purposes of the company consist of or include purposes other than the benefit of its members, subsection (1) has effect as if the reference to promoting the success of the company for the benefit of its members were to achieving those purposes.

(3) The duty imposed by this section has effect subject to any enactment or rule of law requiring directors, in certain circumstances, to consider or act in the interests of creditors of the company.

1.1 Key points to note on the duty to promote the success of the company

Note the following key observations in relation to this new duty to promote the success of the company:

- In contrast to the common law duty there is no longer a requirement to act in the 'company's best interests'. The provision requires the promotion of the success of the company but not in its own right as a separate legal person but for the benefit of the shareholder constituency.

- The duty refers to the success of the company. It does not say that the directors must act in ways that maximize the value of the company or the value of the shares in the company. Does 'success of the company', therefore, mean something different than value? Ministerial statements during the legislative process suggest that success means long-term shareholder value. Lord Goldsmith, for example, in the Grand Committee of the House of Lords stated that 'for a commercial company, success will usually mean long-term increase in value'.[48]

- The provision, following the recommendation of the Company Law Review, is widely viewed as adopting an enlightened shareholder value approach. The duty clearly establishes the priority of members' interests in requiring that directors act to promote the success of the company 'for the benefit of its members as a whole'. If enlightened shareholder value means that the directors may act to promote the interests of non-shareholder groups to the extent that so doing promotes the interests of shareholders, then section 172 does not explicitly confirm this. Of course, it is patently clear that under section 172, as under the common law, if promoting the interests of other constituencies promotes the interest of the shareholders then the decision or action is duty compliant. Section 172 does, however, explicitly require that regard be had to other interests groups when considering what promotes shareholder interests. The duty provides that in acting in what the director considers to be for the benefit of the members, regard must be had to the interests of the other groups listed in sub-paragraphs (a)–(f), which includes employees, the community and the environment. This 'regard list' in section 172 is less about what a 'company's interests' are and more about regulating the process of acting: that is, in the process of making a decision the director must consider the interests of the listed groups. From this viewpoint the regard list is a more precise articulation of the expectations arising from the duty of care. The duty of care is addressed in detail in Chapter 12.

- With regard to non-member interests note that the section provides that directors have regard 'amongst other matters' to the factors and constituencies mentioned in

[48] DTI, *Companies Act 2006—Duties of Company Directors, Ministerial Statements* (2007) (www.berr.gov.uk/ 🌐).

sub-paragraphs (a)–(f). This means that sub-paragraphs (a)–(f) do not provide an exhaustive list of factors or constituencies.

- Sub-paragraphs (a)–(f) do not refer to creditors. However, subsection (3) provides that the existing common law and statutory rules on when duties are owed to creditors remain in force. These duties are analysed in detail in Chapter 18.

- Importantly section 172(2) makes it clear that the priority given to members is a default priority. That is, if a company wishes to be run in the interests of another constituency or for other purposes then it can state those purposes in its constitutional documents and, for the purposes of section 172, those purposes or interests will replace the members' interests. Although this provision was primarily intended for non-profit-making and charitable companies, it would also be available to a commercial company that wished to take a multi-interest/pluralistic approach to company goals and interests.

- Section 172 provides that acting for the benefit of the members means all the members—the 'members as a whole'. Sub-paragraph (f) reaffirms this by noting the need to act fairly as between members. In this regard, the Act codifies the holding in *Mutual Life Insurance Co of New York v Rank Organization Ltd.*[49] Sub-paragraph (a) directs directors' attention to the effect of the decision in the long term. This emphasizes that acting in the shareholders' best interests requires looking to the long-term implications for the business of any decision.

- The duty to act in good faith in ways that promote the success of the company remains a subjective duty: to do what the individual director thinks will promote the success of the company for the benefit of the members. Accordingly, although the formulation of the duty has changed, the approach the courts will adopt when reviewing compliance with the duty will follow the courts' existing approach as illustrated in the *Regentcrest v Cohen* extract. However, the requirement to have regard to the factors and constituencies set out in sub-paragraphs (a)–(f) when determining what the director *thinks* will promote the success of the company for the benefit of the members is an objective, not a subjective, requirement. He is required, as directors were in relation to employees alone under section 309 of the Companies Act 1985, to consider these interests. In contrast to the primary duty the provision does not say to have regard to the factors and constituencies which 'he considers' would be relevant to the promotion of the success of the company. We need to ask, therefore, how courts will determine whether a director has complied with this part of the duty. It will not be enough for him to demonstrate that he considered the factors and constituencies that he thought were relevant to the decision. The *Explanatory Notes* to the Act suggest that the compliance with this duty will be tested in accordance with the duty of care set out in section 174.[50] This is consistent with the view that the regard list is part of the duty of care. We shall look at the duty of care in detail in Chapter 11. For now, simplifying matters, this requires that the regard a director should have to these factors will be the regard that a reasonably diligent director would have when making the decision.

1.2 To what extent does section 172 change the existing law?

The new duty to promote the success of the company clearly makes changes of form to the existing law. The duty refers directly to member interests rather than indirectly through the 'best interests of the company'.

---

[49] [1985] BCLC 11.
[50] Companies Act 2006: Explanatory Notes, para 328.

Does the requirement to have regard to the factors and constituencies set out in sub-paragraphs (a) and (c)–(f) amount to a change in the law? Sub-paragraph (f) is clearly a restatement of the position in *Mutual Life Insurance Co of New York v Rank Organization Ltd* and *Re BSB Holdings Ltd (No 2)*[51] previously set out. Whereas under section 309 of the 1985 Act directors were required to have regard to the employees there was no prior legislative requirement to have regard to the interests of the other constituencies mentioned in the paragraphs (c)–(e). Whether or not this amounts to a change in the law depends on whether the pre-2006 duty of care would have required regard to such factors when considering what was in the company's best interests. The short answer to this is that it would have required regard; however, the standard of care by which appropriate regard is measured has been altered by the 2006 Act. We will discuss this further in Chapter 12 when we address the duty of care in detail.

Following the publication of the Companies Bill, the business community and their legal advisors expressed considerable concern about the new duty to promote the success of the company. They did not view the new provision as a restatement of the existing law. Consider the following letter from one of London's leading corporate lawyers.

■ Letter from J. Palmer, Chairman of the City of London Law Society Company Law Sub-Committee, 'Bill's requirements threaten to make UK law incompatible with practical running of companies' *Financial Times* (9 May 2006)

Sir, I am writing to express serious concerns at the provisions of the Company Law Reform Bill[52] codifying directors' duties. In particular…the government has unfortunately not addressed the fundamental concerns raised by company law specialists and the business community. The proposed legislation continues to impose a mandatory process on all directors of UK companies in relation to each and every decision or action they take.

The mandatory process requirements in clause 156[53] of the Bill require that directors, in fulfilling their good faith duties to promote the success of the company for the benefit of members as a whole, have regard to six factors: these include not only the interests of employees, but also relationships with customers and suppliers, impact on the community and the environment and the desirability of the company maintaining a reputation for high standards of business conduct.

By imposing a mandatory process, the Bill will impose potentially expensive process requirements for companies. Furthermore, it threatens to make UK company law incompatible with the practical running of companies: who as a director would be confident that he would always have regard to the six listed factors as regards every decision or action he took, as opposed to just those that in good faith seem to him relevant? Certainly not the directors of most smaller companies whose lives the bill elsewhere helpfully seeks to ease.

---

[51] [1996] 1 BCLC 155.

[52] The predecessor bill to the Companies Bill was the Company Law Reform Bill.

[53] The draft duty to promote the success of the company was set out in clause 156 of the Company Law Reform Bill. This clause was marginally different from section 172 but not in any respect that alters the application of Mr Palmer's argument to section 172. Clause 156(1) and (3) provided that: '(1) A director of a company must act in the way he considers, in good faith, would be most likely to promote the success of the company for the benefit of its members as a whole. (3) In fulfilling the duty imposed by this section a director must (so far as reasonably practicable) have regard to (a) the likely consequences of any decision in the long term, (b) the interests of the company's employees, (c) the need to foster the company's business relationships with suppliers, customers and others, (d) the impact of the company's operations on the community and the environment, (e) the desirability of the company maintaining a reputation for high standards of business conduct, and (f) the need to act fairly as between members of the company.'

The Company Law Review's work leading up to the bill proposed a more balanced approach to the introduction of regard to these so-called enlightened shareholder-value principles, which the government has unfortunately not adopted. If these principles are to be introduced into UK company law, it must be on a basis that works in practice for directors acting honestly and in good faith.

If UK companies cease to be attractive vehicles for businessmen to use to conduct their activities, there is a real risk that over time those activities and new ventures will be shifted into more business-friendly corporate forms…

Questions and discussion

1. Mr Palmer suggests that the new duty will have a negative effect on the process of decision-making. Certainly one could imagine that the duty might slow decision-making down if directors are concerned to ensure that they have, and that the record shows that they have, had adequate regard to each of the listed interests. Careful directors may refuse to make hasty decisions without obtaining information on the effects of a decision on each of these constituencies and the impact such effects may have on long-term shareholder value. Sometimes decisions in business need to be made very quickly—will the new duty prevent such decisions being made? On the other hand, what the new duty does is to extend a requirement that directors previously had in relation to employees (section 309 of the 1985 Act) to other areas. There was no indication from practice prior to this reform that companies found that section 309 slowed down or inhibited decision-making. Why then would the factors and constituencies in (c)–(e) make any difference in this regard?

2. How would you have amended section 172 to satisfy Mr Palmer's concerns?

3. If section 172 is a clearer restatement of the common law position, to what extent if at all does this provision benefit non-shareholder constituencies? Will this provision alter the process of decision-making in ways that may, some of the time, be favourable to non-shareholder constituencies? If so, how will it do this?

2 The duty to exercise independent judgment

In relation to the common law duty of good faith to act in the best interests of the company, we noted that the duty required a director to do what he thinks is in the company's best interests and not to take directions and orders from anyone else. Furthermore, we considered the scope for directors to act today in ways that would restrain their scope to act in the future. Both of these considerations were viewed as explanations of what the fundamental duty to act in the company's interests required. The Companies Act, however, provides for a separate *duty to exercise independent judgment*.

■ **Section 173 CA 2006 Duty to exercise independent judgment**

(1) A director of a company must exercise independent judgment.

(2) This duty is not infringed by his acting—

(a) in accordance with an agreement duly entered into by the company that restricts the future exercise of discretion by its directors, or

(b) in a way authorised by the company's constitution.

It is not entirely clear why it was necessary to address these points in the codification. After all section 172 makes it clear that the director must do what *he and not what anyone else considers* to be in the best interests of the company and, as we have seen, the case law on restricting future discretion was both clear and reflected a basic logic that acting in the company's interest today may necessarily involve the incurrence of legal obligations that restrict future discretion. Furthermore, why do these rules require the status of an independent duty rather than simply an embellishment of the expectations of directors when they act in compliance with the duty to promote the success of the company (as they were understood at common law)? New duties have a tendency to generate new law. The duty to exercise independent judgment may take us into terrain not previously envisaged.

Whilst this duty may not have been legally necessary, however, it does satisfy one of the stated objectives of the codification, namely providing directors with a clear statement of their obligations.

Note that the codification in sections 172 or 173 does not address the situation where the director fails to exercise any judgment about whether a decision promotes the company's success. In such a case the common law standard articulated in *Charterbridge Corporation Ltd v Lloyds Bank Ltd*,[54] as adapted to the language of section 172, would continue to apply. In such circumstances, the court would ask whether an 'intelligent and honest man in the position of the director' would have reasonably believed that the action promoted the success of the company for the benefit of the members as a whole.

 Online Resource Centre
http://www.oxfordtextbooks.co.uk/orc/kershaw2e/

Visit the Online Resource Centre for additional resources and information available for this chapter, including web links and an interactive flashcard glossary.

---

[54] [1969] 2 All ER 1185.

CHAPTER ELEVEN

REGULATING DISCRETION II: USING CORPORATE POWERS FOR PROPER PURPOSES

I THE DEVELOPMENT OF THE IMPROPER PURPOSE DOCTRINE: FROM RULE TO PRINCIPLE

Alongside the common law duty to act in good faith in the best interests of the company, it has in recent years become commonplace to refer to the directors' duty to use corporate powers for their proper purpose. The idea behind this duty is that powers delegated to directors, such as the power to enter into contracts, to raise finance, to sell property, or to issue shares, must be used for the purposes for which they were granted to the board and not for any unapproved (improper) purpose. Importantly, as we shall see, a director may comply with the duty of good faith but still be in breach of the duty to use corporate powers for their proper purposes: a director may in good faith use the powers in what she thinks is in the best interests of the company, but still use those powers for an improper purpose. We consider this duty here—following our analysis of the duty to act in good faith in the best interests of the company—because both duties regulate the actual decision made or action taken by directors.

The idea of a 'duty' to exercise powers for their proper purposes—or as it sometimes is referred to *the proper (or improper) purpose doctrine*—is based on two contexts and two primary cases. The contexts are: first, the use of corporate powers by directors to prevent takeover bids for a company's shares; and, second, the use of corporate powers to undermine the shareholder franchise (the use and effectiveness of a vote). The two leading English cases are the first instance decision of *Hogg v Cramphorn* and the Privy Council case of *Howard Smith v Ampol Petroleum Ltd*. In these cases, directors faced with an unwanted offer to buy shares in the company—which the directors had *in good faith* decided were not in the company's best interests—used corporate powers, in particular the power to issue shares, to prevent the bid from being successful. Extracts from these cases are provided here.

■ *Hogg v Cramphorn Ltd* [1967] Ch 254

Cramphorn Ltd was a successful seed merchant company. Its chairman of the board and managing director was one Colonel Cramphorn. Colonel Cramphorn was approached by a Mr Baxter who made clear his intention to make an offer to the company's shareholders for all the shares in the company. Mr Baxter assured Cramphorn of his intention to expand the business; however, Cramphorn did not view the offer favourably. The offer was presented to the board of directors who decided to reject the offer, expressing particular concern about the effect the offer would have on the company's employees 'upon whose loyalty and enterprise the company is very dependent for its success and development'. The board, however, decided to take steps beyond the simple rejection of the offer. The board resolved to form and finance a trust fund to be set up on behalf of the company's employees. The trust had three trustees: Colonel Cramphorn, a partner from the company's auditor, and a company employee. The board further resolved to issue 5,707 shares with multiple voting rights of 10 votes per share to the trust fund which the trust would purchase with funds made available to it by the company. In addition, the company made an interest-free loan to the trust fund to provide the funds necessary to purchase a certain number of shares from shareholders that wished to sell at the price which Mr Baxter intended to offer. Mr Baxter, who had acquired through an associate a number of shares in the company, brought an action against the company and the three trustees, seeking a declaration that the setting up of the trust fund was void. Buckley J found that the weighted voting rights were not consistent with the authority set forth in the constitutional documents and continued.

Buckley J

I now turn to what has been the main matter of debate in this case, which is whether the allotment of the 5,707 shares was an improper use by the directors of their discretionary and fiduciary power...to decide to whom these unissued shares should be **allotted**. Counsel for the plaintiff has submitted that the allotment was made with the primary object of preventing Mr Baxter from obtaining control of the company and ousting the then existing board of directors and that the allotment was accordingly a breach of the directors' fiduciary duties and should be set aside on the authority of *Piercy v S Mills & Co Ltd* ([1918–19] All ER Rep).

It is common ground that the scheme of which this allotment formed part was formulated to meet the threat, as the directors regarded it, of Mr Baxter's offer. The trust deed would not have come into existence, nor would the 5,707 shares have been issued as they were, but for Mr Baxter's bid and the threat that it constituted to the established management of the company. It is also common ground that the directors were not actuated by any unworthy motives of personal advantage, but acted as they did in an honest belief that they were doing what was for the good of the company. Their honour is not in the least impugned, but it is said that the means which they adopted to attain their end were such as they could not properly adopt. I am satisfied that Mr Baxter's offer, when it became known to the company's staff, had an unsettling effect on them. I am also satisfied that the directors and the trustees of the trust deed genuinely considered that to give the staff through the trustees a sizeable, though indirect, voice in the affairs of the company would benefit both the staff and the company. I am sure that Col Cramphorn and also probably his fellow directors firmly believed that to keep the management of the company's affairs in the hands of the existing board would be more advantageous to the shareholders, the company's staff and its customers than if it were committed to a board selected by Mr Baxter. The steps which the board took were intended not only to ensure that, if Mr Baxter succeeded in obtaining a shareholding which, as matters stood, would have been a controlling shareholding, he should not secure control of the company but, also, and perhaps primarily, to discourage Mr Baxter from proceeding with his bid at all.

Counsel for the defendants has submitted that a trading company and its board of directors are fully entitled to take an interest in who becomes a member of the company and to arrange or influence matters in such a way that a particular person shall not become a member. In the present case, he says, that the board was entitled to try to kill Mr Baxter's bid, if in doing so they acted in good faith, having regard to what they believed to be the interests of the company, and if the means they employed were lawful. The establishment of an employees' trust was [within the powers of the company and] the board under the general delegation of powers to them...Counsel for the plaintiff does not dispute the right and power of the company or of the board on a company's behalf to establish in proper circumstances a trust of shares in the company for the benefit of employees...

Accepting, as I do, that the board acted in good faith and that they believed that the establishment of a trust would benefit the company and that avoidance of the acquisition of control by Mr Baxter would also benefit the company, I must still remember that an essential element of the scheme, and indeed its primary purpose, was to ensure control of the company by the directors and those whom they could confidently regard as their supporters. Was such a manipulation of the voting position a legitimate act on the part of the directors? Somewhat similar questions have been considered in the well-known cases of *Punt v Symons & Co Ltd* and *Piercy v S Mills & Co Ltd*. In *Punt v Symons* directors had issued shares with the object of creating a sufficient majority to enable them to pass a special resolution depriving other shareholders of special rights conferred on them by the company's articles. In *Piercy v Mills* directors had issued shares with the object of creating a sufficient majority to enable them to resist the election of three additional directors, whose appointment would have put the two existing directors in a minority on the board. In each case the directors were held to have acted improperly...

In the later case, Peterson J after citing *Fraser v Whalley*, *Gartside v Whalley* and *Punt v Symons*, said ([1918–19] All ER Rep):

'The basis of the decisions in these two cases I have referred to is that directors are not entitled to use their powers of issuing *shares merely for the purpose of maintaining their control or the control of themselves and their friends over the affairs of the company, or merely for the purpose of defeating the wishes of the existing majority of shareholders*. That is, however, exactly what has happened in the present case. With the merits of the dispute as between the directors and the plaintiff I have no concern whatever. The plaintiff and his friends held a majority of the shares of the company, and they were entitled, so long as that majority remained, to have their views prevail in accordance with the regulations of the company; and it was not, in my opinion, open to the directors, for the purpose of converting a minority in voting power into a voting majority, and solely for the purpose of defeating the wishes of the existing majority, to issue the shares which are in dispute in the present action.' [Emphasis added]

With those observations I respectfully agree. Unless a majority in a company is acting oppressively towards the minority, this court should not and will not itself interfere with the exercise by the majority of its constitutional rights or embark on an enquiry into the respective merits of the views held or policies favoured by the majority and the minority. Nor will this court permit directors to exercise powers, which have been delegated to them by the company in circumstances which put the directors in a fiduciary position when exercising those powers, in such a way as to interfere with the exercise by the majority of its constitutional rights, and in a case of this kind also, in my judgment, the court should not investigate the rival merits of the views or policies of the parties...

In *Piercy v Mills*, Peterson J said that he had no concern whatever with the merits of the dispute. It is not, in my judgment, open to the directors in such a case to say, 'We genuinely believe that what we seek to prevent the majority from doing will harm the company and, therefore our act in arming ourselves or our party with sufficient shares to outvote the majority is a conscientious exercise of our powers under the articles, which should not be interfered with.' Such a belief, even if well-founded, would be irrelevant. A majority of shareholders in general meeting is entitled to pursue what course it chooses within the company's powers, however wrong-headed it may appear to others, provided the majority do not unfairly oppress other members of the company. These considerations lead me to the conclusion that the issue of the 5,707 shares with the special voting rights which the directors purported to attach to them could not be justified by the view that the directors genuinely believed that it would benefit the company if they could command a majority of the votes in general meetings. The fact that, as I have held, the directors were mistaken in thinking that they could attach to these shares more than one vote each, is, I think, irrelevant. The power to issue the shares was a fiduciary power and if, as I think, it was exercised for an improper motive, the issue of these shares is liable to be set aside.

...Had the majority of the company in general meeting approved the issue of the 5,707 shares before it was made, even with the purported special voting rights attached (assuming that such rights could have been so attached conformably with the articles), I do not think that any member could have complained of the issue being made; for in these circumstances, the criticism that

the directors were, by the issue of the shares, attempting to deprive the majority of their constitutional rights would have ceased to have any force. It follows, in my opinion, that a majority in
a general meeting of the company at which no votes were cast in respect of the 5,707 shares
could ratify the issue of those shares. Before setting the allotment and issue of the 5,707 shares
aside, therefore, I propose to allow the company an opportunity to decide in general meeting
whether it approves or disapproves of the issue of these shares to the trustees. Counsel for the
defendants will undertake, on behalf of the trustees, not to vote at such a meeting in respect
of the 5,707 shares.

…

What then of the other preference shares bought by the trustees [pursuant to the interest
free loan made by the company to the trust]?…These purchases in my judgment, formed a further integral part—although a less important one than the issue of the 5,707 shares—of the same
scheme, for I cannot doubt that the reasons for procuring the trustees to offer to buy these
shares at 25s each were to forestall criticism by preference shareholders of the directors having burked an opportunity for them to dispose of their preference shares to Mr Baxter at the
admittedly advantageous price of 25s a share…The loan was not made with the single-minded
purpose, or even with the primary purpose, of benefiting the company otherwise than by securing that control of the directors or facilitating their securing that control. Accordingly, although
I do not question that the loan was made with honourable intentions, the making of it was not,
in my judgment, a conscientious exercise by the directors of their powers to make loans of the
company's funds for the purposes of the company's business or purposes reasonably incidental
thereto. The loan was, consequently, in my judgment, ultra vires the directors and invalid unless
sanctioned or ratified by the company in general meeting.

In setting up the trust fund, issuing the shares to the trust, and in putting the trust in
funds to enable it to purchase shares from shareholders who wished to sell their shares,
the directors were using powers delegated to them. The claimant's counsel accepted
that formally such powers could be used by the directors to form a trust; to fund it;
and to issue shares to it. In addition, the court unequivocally accepted that the directors believed that Mr Baxter's offer was bad for the company and that in taking these
actions the directors complied with their duty to act in good faith in the best interests
of the company: 'their honour is not in the least impugned'. The question for the court
was whether compliance with the duty of good faith was sufficient to halt any further
inquiry into the use by the directors of these corporate powers. The court held that it
was not the end of its inquiry.

Buckley J, following *Piercy & Mills*,[1] focused on the fact that the powers, although
formally available for the board to use, were being used to usurp the constitutional
settlement of powers in the company between the directors and the shareholder body.
The directors, the court held, could not use their powers for the *primary* purpose of
interfering with 'the exercise by the majority of [shareholders of their] constitutional
rights'. From the judgment there appear to be two constitutional rights which the court
has in mind: first, the right to exercise one's vote and for that vote to be effective and not
undermined by director action; second, the right to be able to accept or reject an offer
to buy one's shares uninhibited by actions taken by the directors to prevent that offer
from being made or preventing the shareholder from accepting the offer. Accordingly,
the court held that both the issue of the shares and the making of the loan to the trust
fund should be set aside.

The court stressed in holding that the use of these powers was unlawful that the reason
for the directors using them in this way was 'even if well-founded…irrelevant. A majority of shareholders in general meeting is entitled to pursue what course it chooses within
the company's powers, however wrong-headed it may appear to others'. The directors

[1] [1918–19] All ER Rep 313.

argued that the bid unsettled its loyal employees and that unsettled employees could be damaging to the business. In the context of unwanted (from the board's perspective) takeover bids, one can envisage several other types of reason the directors could put forward, for example, the shareholders do not understand the true worth of the business or the potential value in the company's long term strategy. Such reasons may be very well founded but, as the court in *Hogg v Cramphorn* stressed, they are irrelevant to the court's analysis.

So how do we articulate the holding of this case? The specific holding of the case is that corporate powers cannot be used to usurp the basic constitutional rights of shareholders: the right to vote and the right to accept or reject an offer for your shares. The court recognizes that the restriction imposed by this case relates to actions whose 'primary purpose' is to usurp these rights. Accordingly, unintended or non-primary interferences with these rights will not restrict the director's exercise of corporate powers. Furthermore, it is clear that these shareholder constitutional rights protected by *Hogg v Cramphorn* are **default rights**. The shareholders themselves are entitled to alter—and to give up—these constitutional rights. In relation to both the issue of the shares and the making of the loan, the court noted that the shareholders could have empowered (before or after taking the action—'sanctioned or ratified'—and, one presumes, before or after the making of the offer) the board to act in these ways for these purposes. From this viewpoint, the holding in this case instructs directors to refrain from intentional interference with these basic constitutional rights in the absence of a specific instruction from the shareholders to permit the board to do so.

The default settlement of power provided by the holding in this case fits with the balance of power in UK company law which we analysed in Chapter 6. In that chapter we saw that UK company law emphasizes shareholder primacy. We saw that the board is empowered by a delegation of authority from the shareholders. The holding in *Hogg v Cramphorn* provides that in the absence of clear contrary intention, the shareholders will not be deemed to have delegated authority to the board to interfere with these core rights, regardless of the board's bona fides or their reasons for taking the action.

■ *Howard Smith Ltd v Ampol Petroleum Ltd* [1974] AC 821 (Privy Council)

The company, whose actions were the subject of dispute, was an Australian company, RW Miller (Holdings) Ltd ('Millers'). Two of the company's shareholders, Ampol and Bulkships, owned 30% and 25% of the issued shares in the company respectively. On 15 June 1972 Ampol made an offer to buy all the remaining shares of Millers for $2.27 a share. A week later, on 22 June, a company called Howard Smith Ltd made an offer for the shares at a higher price of $2.50 a share (10% more than the Ampol offer). On 27 June Ampol and Bulkships issued a joint statement that they both intended to 'act jointly in relation to the future operation' of Millers and that they had both decided to reject any offer for their shares 'whether from Howard Smith Limited or from any other source'. Effectively this prevented Howard Smith from making its higher offer to the other shareholders because it had no desire to purchase only a minority 45% shareholding in the company. In response to the announcement by Ampol and Bulkships, on 6 July 1972 the board of Millers resolved, as they were authorized to do under Australian company law and Millers' articles of association, to issue a block of shares to Howard Smith which would, if they had managed to purchase the remaining 45% of the shares held by the other shareholders, have given them control of Millers. At this time Millers did have a financing need to fund the construction of tanker ships and the number of shares issued at $2.30 a share was calculated to satisfy this financing need. Ampol brought an action challenging the issue of shares and requesting the removal of Howard Smith from Millers' share register. Following the decision of the Supreme Court of New South Wales an appeal was made to the Privy Council.

Lord Wilberforce

Findings of Fact

The judge [Street J] found, as their Lordships think it right to make clear at once, that the *Millers'* directors were not motivated by any purpose of personal gain or advantage, or by any desire to retain their position on the board. The judge said: 'I discard the suggestion that the directors of Millers allotted these shares to Howard Smith in order to gain some private advantage for themselves by way of retention of their seats on the board or by obtaining a higher price for their personal shareholding. Personal considerations of this nature were not to the forefront so far as any of these directors was concerned, and in this respect their integrity emerges unscathed from this contest.'

He then proceeded to consider the main issue which...was to ascertain the substantial object the accomplishment of which formed the real ground of the board's action. The issue before him he considered to be whether the primary purpose of the majority of directors was to satisfy Millers' need for capital or whether their primary purpose was to destroy the majority holding of Ampol and Bulkships. It was suggested on behalf of the appellants that in stating the issue in these terms the judge did not give adequate recognition to the concern felt by the management team, and by Mr. Taylor in particular, that the future of Millers under the control of Ampol and Bulkships might be uncertain and that he should have considered whether the purpose of the majority directors in deciding to make the allotment to Howard Smith might not have been, at least in part, to secure the company's future as a going concern and to prevent its possible dismemberment. But their Lordships do not consider this criticism to be justified. The judge indeed accepted that during the period antecedent to the issue the Millers' directors felt a growing concern, even apprehension, as to what the intentions of Ampol, or of Ampol and Bulkships together, might be, but what he had to decide was what was the primary purpose of the directors in making the disputed allotment. This decision he had to make on the case as presented by the majority directors and on the evidence. It...was clear from what each of them said at the trial, that they did not themselves contend that they were motivated by any other considerations bearing upon the interest of Millers than concern to satisfy Millers' capital needs. It is equally clear that the minutes and partial verbatim account of the critical meeting of July 6, 1972, did not suggest that any other consideration was at that time acting upon their minds...

In order to assist him in deciding upon the alternative motivations contended for, the judge considered first, at some length, the objective question whether Millers was in fact in need of capital. This approach was criticised before their Lordships: it was argued that what mattered was not the actual financial condition of Millers, but what the majority directors bona fide considered that condition to be. Their Lordships accept that such a matter as the raising of finance is one of management, within the responsibility of the directors: they accept that it would be wrong for the court to substitute its opinion for that of the management, or indeed to question the correctness of the management's decision, on such a question, if bona fide arrived at. There is no appeal on merits from management decisions to courts of law: nor will courts of law assume to act as a kind of supervisory board over decisions within the powers of management honestly arrived at.

But accepting all of this, when a dispute arises whether directors of a company made a particular decision for one purpose or for another, or whether, there being more than one purpose, one or another purpose was the substantial or primary purpose, the court, in their Lordships' opinion, is entitled to look at the situation objectively in order to estimate how critical or pressing, or substantial or, per contra, insubstantial an alleged requirement may have been. If it finds that a particular requirement, though real, was not urgent, or critical, at the relevant time, it may have reason to doubt, or discount, the assertions of individuals that they acted solely in order to deal with it, particularly when the action they took was unusual or even extreme...

[Although Street J found that the company had a need for capital, there was no crisis in this regard.] After hearing and considering the evidence of [the directors of Millers], each asserting that his primary purpose in voting for the allotment on July 6, 1972 was to meet an urgent capital need of Millers, the judge found that he was unable to accept these assertions. He found that:

'…the primary purpose of the four directors in voting in favour of this allotment was to reduce the proportionate combined shareholding of Ampol and Bulkships in order to induce Howard Smith to proceed with its takeover offer. There was a majority bloc in the share register. Their intention was to destroy its character as a majority…[and] to procure the continuation by Howard Smith of the takeover offer made by that company.'

Their Lordships accept these findings.

The law

The directors, in deciding to issue shares…to Howard Smith, acted under clause 8 of the company's articles of association. This provides…that the shares shall be under the control of the directors, who may allot…to such persons on such terms and conditions and either at a premium or otherwise and at such time as the directors may think fit. Thus, and this is not disputed, the issue was clearly intra vires the directors. But, intra vires though the issue may have been, the directors' power under this article is a fiduciary power: and it remains the case that an exercise of such a power though formally valid, may be attacked on the ground that it was not exercised for the purpose for which it was granted. It is at this point that the contentions of the parties diverge. The extreme argument on one side is that, for validity, what is required is bona fide exercise of the power in the interests of the company: that once it is found that the directors were not motivated by self-interest—i.e. by a desire to retain their control of the company or their positions on the board—the matter is concluded in their favour and that the court will not inquire into the validity of their reasons for making the issue. All decided cases, it was submitted, where an exercise of such a power as this has been found invalid, are cases where directors are found to have acted through self-interest of this kind.

On the other side, the main argument is that the purpose for which the power is conferred is to enable capital to be raised for the company, and that once it is found that the issue was not made for that purpose, invalidity follows…

In their Lordships' opinion neither of the extreme positions can be maintained. It can be accepted, as one would only expect, that the majority of cases in which issues of shares are challenged in the courts are cases in which the vitiating element is the self-interest of the directors, or at least the purpose of the directors to preserve their own control of the management; see *Fraser v. Whalley* (1864) 2 Hem. & M. 10; *Punt v. Symons & Co. Ltd.* [1903] 2 Ch. 506; *Piercy v. S. Mills & Co. Ltd.* [1920] 1 Ch. 77; *Ngurli Ltd. v. McCann* (1953) 90 C.L.R. 425 and *Hogg v. Cramphorn Ltd.* [1967] Ch. 254, 267.

Further it is correct to say that where the self-interest of the directors is involved, they will not be permitted to assert that their action was bona fide thought to be, or was, in the interest of the company; pleas to this effect have invariably been rejected…

But it does not follow from this, as the appellants assert, that the absence of any element of self-interest is enough to make an issue valid. Self-interest is only one, though no doubt the commonest, instance of improper motive: and, before one can say that a fiduciary power has been exercised for the purpose for which it was conferred, a wider investigation may have to be made…On the other hand, taking the respondents' contention, it is, in their Lordships' opinion, too narrow an approach to say that the only valid purpose for which shares may be issued is to raise capital for the company. The discretion is not in terms limited in this way: the law should not impose such a limitation on directors' powers. To define in advance exact limits beyond which directors must not pass is, in their Lordships' view, impossible. This clearly cannot be done by enumeration, since the variety of situations facing directors of different types of company in different situations cannot be anticipated. No more, in their Lordships' view, can this be done by the use of a phrase—such as 'bona fide in the interest of the company as a whole,' or ' for some corporate purpose'…

In their Lordships' opinion it is necessary to start with a consideration of the power whose exercise is in question, in this case a power to issue shares. Having ascertained, on a fair view, the nature of this power, and having defined as can best be done in the light of modern conditions the, or some, limits within which it may be exercised, it is then necessary for the court, if a particular exercise of it is challenged, to examine the substantial purpose for which it was exercised, and to reach a conclusion whether that purpose was proper or not. In doing so it will necessarily give credit to the bona fide opinion of the directors, if such is found to exist, and will respect their judgment as to matters of management; having done this, the ultimate conclusion has to be as to the side of a fairly broad line on which the case falls.

[His Lordship then considered several English and commonwealth cases where the power to issue shares was legitimately used for purposes other than raising capital.]

Their Lordships were referred to the recent judgment of Berger J. in the Supreme Court of British Columbia, in *Teck Corporation Ltd. v. Millar* (1972) 33 D.L.R. (3d) 288. This was concerned with the affairs of Afton Mines Ltd. in which Teck Corporation Ltd., a resource conglomerate, had acquired a majority shareholding. Teck was indicating an intention to replace the board of directors of Afton with its own nominees with a view to causing Afton to enter into an agreement (called an 'ultimate deal') with itself for the exploitation by Teck of valuable mineral rights owned by Afton. Before this could be done, and in order to prevent it, the directors of Afton concluded an exploitation agreement with another company 'Canex'. One of its provisions, as is apparently common in this type of agreement in Canada, provided for the issue to Canex of a large number of shares in Afton, thus displacing Teck's majority. Berger J. found, at p. 328:

> 'their [sc. the directors'] purpose was to obtain the best agreement they could while…still in control. Their purpose was in that sense to defeat Teck. But, not to defeat Teck's attempt to obtain control, rather it was to foreclose Teck's opportunity of obtaining for itself the ultimate deal. That was…no improper purpose.'

His decision upholding the agreement with Canex on this basis appears to be in line with the English and Australian authorities to which reference has been made. By contrast, the present case…does not, on the findings of the trial judge, involve any considerations of management, within the proper sphere of the directors. The purpose found by the judge is simply and solely to dilute the majority voting power held by Ampol and Bulkships so as to enable a then minority of shareholders to sell their shares more advantageously. So far as authority goes, an issue of shares purely for the purpose of creating voting power has repeatedly been condemned: *Fraser v. Whalley*, 2 Hem. & M. 10; *Punt v. Symons & Co. Ltd.* [1903] 2 Ch. 506; *Piercy v. S. Mills & Co. Ltd.* [1920] 1 Ch. 177 ('merely for the purpose of defeating the wishes of the existing majority of shareholders') and *Hogg v. Cramphorn Ltd.* [1967] Ch. 254…And, though the reported decisions, naturally enough, are expressed in terms of their own facts, there are clear considerations of principle which support the trend they establish. The constitution of a limited company normally provides for directors, with powers of management, and shareholders, with defined voting powers having power to appoint the directors, and to take, in general meeting, by majority vote, decisions on matters not reserved for management. Just as it is established that directors, within their management powers, may take decisions against the wishes of the majority of shareholders, and indeed that the majority of shareholders cannot control them in the exercise of these powers while they remain in office (*Automatic Self-Cleansing Filter Syndicate Co. Ltd. v. Cuninghame* [1906] 2 Ch. 34), so it must be unconstitutional for directors to use their fiduciary powers over the shares in the company purely for the purpose of destroying an existing majority, or creating a new majority which did not previously exist. To do so is to interfere with that element of the company's constitution which is separate from and set against their powers. If there is added, moreover, to this immediate purpose, an ulterior purpose to enable an offer for shares to proceed which the existing majority was in a position to block, the departure from the legitimate use of the fiduciary power becomes not less, but all the greater. The right to dispose of shares at a given price is essentially an individual right to be exercised on individual decision and on which a majority, in the absence of oppression or similar impropriety, is entitled to prevail. Directors are of course entitled to offer advice, and bound to supply information, relevant to the making of such a decision, but to use their fiduciary power solely for the purpose of shifting the power

> to decide to whom and at what price shares are to be sold cannot be related to any purpose for which the power over the share capital was conferred upon them. That this is the position in law was in effect recognised by the majority directors themselves when they attempted to justify the issue as made primarily in order to obtain much needed capital for the company. And once this primary purpose was rejected, as it was by Street J., there is nothing legitimate left as a basis for their action, except honest behaviour. That is not, in itself, enough.
>
> Their Lordships therefore agree entirely with the conclusion of Street J. that the power to issue and allot shares was improperly exercised by the issue of shares to Howard Smith.

In Lord Wilberforce's initial discussion of the law applicable in *Howard Smith* he sets forth a general principle of apparently broader application than merely the use of corporate powers to interfere with the right to use one's vote or the right to accept an offer for one's shares. For Lord Wilberforce, the principle is that powers must be used only for purposes *'for which they were conferred'* or *'granted'*. This statement of principle has come to be known as the improper purpose doctrine or, for some commentators and cases, the duty to use powers for proper purposes.[2]

This statement of the law differs from the statement of the law in *Hogg v Cramphorn* where Buckley J did not set forth the law in such principled terms. Nevertheless, *Hogg v Cramphorn* as well as *Howard Smith* can be used to put meat on the bones of this general principle: the power to issue shares was not *conferred* by the shareholders for the *purpose* of interfering with their rights to vote or sell their shares. However, in stating the law in general principled terms one necessarily assumes that Lord Wilberforce considered that the obligation to use powers only for the purposes for which they were conferred would have application beyond this specific understanding. If so, then we need to be able to make sense of what is and what is not a purpose for which a power had been conferred when directors exercise powers *outside* of the voting and takeover context. Consider the following commentary on this point.

■ D. Kershaw, 'The Illusion of Importance: Reconsidering the UK's Takeover Defence Prohibition' (2007) 56 *ICLQ* 267

> There are two fundamental problems with this theory of [purpose-specific] power delegation in the corporate context. First, in contrast to the drafting of state constitutions the drafting and formation of a corporate constitution is not the product of minuted debate about the purpose and intention of specific rules. In regard to most delegated powers there is no record that can enlighten a discussion about the proper purposes for which a specific power can be used. Indeed, most companies' powers are not the product of debate but of borrowed boilerplate, whether in the form of [the model articles] or professionally tailored versions thereof. At most the intention could be said to provide the company with the powers it needs to run the business. Secondly, because the future is unpredictable the viability and effectiveness of a corporate contract is dependent on it being incomplete. No one can predict all the business problems and opportunities that will face the company in its future and the value-generating purposes for which the delegated powers may have to be used. Delegated corporate powers therefore do not contain

[2] There are very few cases that refer to *the duty* to use powers for their proper purposes or not to use them for improper purposes. See, for example, *Re BSB Holdings Ltd (No 2)* [1996] 1 BCLC 155. Note in this regard that the courts have viewed the enforcement of the improper purpose doctrine as the enforcement of member's contractual rights (personal rights) and not the enforcement of a duty derivatively: see *Re a company (Case No 005136 of 1986) (Re Sherborne Park Residents Co Ltd)* [1987] BCLC 82. As we shall see at p 404 this doctrine is now codified in the 2006 Act as a duty. On derivative actions see Chapter 15.

at any time, at the time they were granted or at any point thereafter, an immanent, exhaustive list of proper purposes. Accordingly, any attempt by courts to assess original intent, to impute or to supplement purposive constraints is misdirected and hopeless. The logical dead end of this theory of delegated power-specific proper purposes is quickly reached in *Howard Smith* when Lord Wilberforce acknowledges that identifying valid purposes 'clearly cannot be done by enumeration, since the variety of situations facing directors of different types of company in different situations cannot be anticipated'.

Although, as noted in this commentary, Lord Wilberforce acknowledges that one cannot 'enumerate' a list of specific purposes for particular powers, he does proceed to provide a rule of construction for judges when attempting to determine for which purposes corporate powers have been conferred. He directs the court to ascertain: 'on a fair view, the nature of this power, and [to define] as can best be done in the light of modern conditions the, or some, limits within which it may be exercised'. This is a rather general rule of construction that provides very limited guidance, and considerable discretion, for other judges applying this principle. There is a sense in Lord Wilberforce's judgment that he himself is unconvinced that the principle he has stated is workable. In stating the principle in terms of what is 'conferred' or 'granted' this directs us to an analysis of what has been conferred. However, when Lord Wilberforce addresses this analysis he seems less confident about the principle's workability: he states that such purposes cannot be enumerated and reliance is placed on the generalities of a 'fair view' and 'modern conditions'.

Following his general consideration of proper purposes, his Lordship then turns his attention to the facts of this case, at which point his judgment develops a much closer affiliation with Buckley J's approach in *Hogg v Cramphorn*. Lord Wilberforce refers to the normal constitutional balance of power between the board and the shareholder body. He holds that it is 'unconstitutional' to use the power to issue shares to create a new majority or to destroy an existing majority. In relation to the right to sell one's shares he holds that it is an individual choice in relation to which the majority of shareholders 'is entitled to prevail'—that is, entitled to determine whether control should be transferred.[3]

Note that Lord Wilberforce refers to the 'normal' constitutional settlement and refers to the *Automatic Self-Cleansing* case in support of this position. We considered *Automatic Self-Cleansing* in Chapter 6 where we saw the court assess the distribution of power under the company's articles of association. Remember that, although the court affirmed the distribution of power under Automatic's articles, it was clear from that case that it was open to the shareholders to change that balance of power through the articles. Accordingly, we see that the constitutional settlement that Lord

---

[3] In the post-*Howard Smith* cases the duty not to use powers for an improper purpose continues to be applied in the context of infringement on constitutional rights. The courts have reaffirmed *Hogg v Cramphorn* and *Howard Smith* in this regard. See, for example, *Lee Panavision Ltd v Lee Lighting Ltd* [1992] BCLC 22, where the board of Lee Lighting Ltd had entered into a management agreement that effectively restricted the shareholders' ability to change management by changing the board; Dillon LJ held that: 'the function of the directors is to manage, but the appointment of the directors who are to do the managing is constitutionally a function of the shareholders in general meeting. Therefore it must have been unconstitutional for the directors, knowing...that the shareholders were proposing as soon as they could to exercise their constitutional right to appoint new directors, to take all managerial powers away from any new directors who might be appointed.' Interestingly, the judgment in *Lee Panavision* relied clearly on *Howard Smith*; however, it does not refer to the principle, only to use powers for which they are conferred. The judgment is set forth in constitutional terms.

Wilberforce refers to here is a default constitutional settlement that the shareholders themselves could alter if they chose to.[4]

Importantly, as in *Hogg v Cramphorn*, *Howard Smith* makes it clear that the improper purpose doctrine only invalidates action whose primary or 'substantial' purpose is an improper purpose—in this case the objective of destroying the existing majority and creating a new one. Lord Wilberforce's dicta on the approach to the review of business judgments in this regard is often cited as evidence that English courts do not review business judgments. The courts will not, as Lord Wilberforce observes, act as a supervisory board over management decisions. However, as his judgment makes clear, they will investigate the purpose for which an action was taken where it is alleged that purpose was improper. In this case the board minutes of the meeting suggested that the primary purpose was to raise finance and the directors, as witnesses, testified that this was the case. Neither the Supreme Court of New South Wales nor the Privy Council accepted this submission. The context within which the decision was taken implied strongly that the actions were taken primarily to enable the Howard Smith bid by destroying the Ampol/Bulkships majority.

Questions

1. In what respects, if any, does the holding in *Hogg v Cramphorn* differ from the holding in *Howard Smith v Ampol Petroleum Ltd*?

2. Why is the rule set forth in these cases a default rule?

3. What do you think is the purpose and the benefit, if any, of setting out the holdings in *Hogg v Cramphorn* and *Howard Smith* in general principled terms—directors should use the powers only for the purposes for which they were conferred—versus a rules-based approach—you cannot use corporate powers to directly interfere with voting rights or the right to sell shares?

4. Do you agree that Lord Wilberforce is unconvinced by the workability of the principle in practice?

5. Do you agree with Kershaw on the unworkability of a rule designed around a purpose-specific power delegation of authority?

6. Do you find Lord Wilberforce's rule of construction for determining proper and improper purposes for a power helpful? How would you apply it, for example, to the power to enter into contracts?

7. How easy is it for courts to make an assessment of the primary and secondary purposes for which powers are used?

II CAN GOOD REASONS EVER MAKE AN IMPROPER PURPOSE PROPER?

We saw in *Hogg v Cramphorn* that the court rejected any attempt by Cramphorn Ltd to argue that the use of powers to interfere with the shareholders' constitutional rights was justified by the fact that the action was taken for reasons that benefited the company. The court made it clear that even though the reasons the board had for acting in this way may have been good ones, they were irrelevant to the court's analysis: if the use of the powers interfered with the shareholders' basic constitutional rights then the

---

[4] In *Re a company (Case No 005136 of 1986) (Re Sherborne Park Residents Co Ltd)* [1987] BCLC 82 in relation to an alleged use of the power to issue shares for an improper purpose, Hoffmann J having referred to *Howard Smith* observed that 'an abuse of these powers is an infringement of a member's contractual rights under the articles'.

use of the powers in this way was unlawful, no matter how good or pressing the reason for using the power in this way. In *Howard Smith*, Lord Wilberforce does not explicitly address the possibility that good reasons could allow interference with the constitutional balance of power. However, he is clearly aware that the directors had arguably good reasons for using the power to issue shares to issue a block of voting shares to Howard Smith—for example, facilitating a higher takeover bid—but these reasons do not have any bearing on his Lordship's understanding or application of the law. Several recent cases have suggested that the courts may have softened their position in this regard. As a result of the cases considered below, there is now some uncertainty as to whether good reasons can render an ostensibly improper purpose a proper purpose.

■ *Criterion Properties plc v Stratford UK Properties Plc* [2002] EWHC 496 (Ch)

Stratford UK Properties Plc, a US company referred to in the case as Oaktree, and Criterion Properties plc (Criterion) were parties to a joint venture agreement for the purposes of investing in real property in the UK. The joint venture was carried out through a limited partnership in which both Oaktree and Criterion were members. The joint venture was governed by an investment and shareholders' agreement (the 'ISA'). The chairman of Criterion was a Mr Nordström. The managing director of Criterion was a Mr Glaser.

In March 2000 Oaktree and Criterion entered into a second supplementary agreement (the 'SSA') which amended the terms of the ISA. The objective of entering into the SSA was to deter a possible takeover by an investor that had been acquiring shares in Criterion (the 'Potential Bidder'). The SSA deterred this potential takeover bidder by putting in place what was called in the judgment a 'poison pill arrangement'. This poison pill[5] deterred the possible bidder because in the event that the bidder obtained control of Criterion the SSA gave Oaktree the right to be bought out of the joint venture by Criterion on very favourable terms. That is, the effect of the bidder successfully taking control of Criterion would be to significantly decrease the value of Criterion because under the terms of the SSA Criterion would have to pay Oaktree more than its share in the joint venture was worth. The buyout price was fixed at the greater of either the market value of Oaktree's interest in the joint venture or an amount which would guarantee Oaktree a 25% per annum return on its investment.

The poison pill arrangement was also triggered if Mr Nordström or Mr Glaser ceased to be directors or employees involved in the management of the business.

On 3 April 2001 Mr Glaser was dismissed. Oaktree then served notice on Criterion to exercise its option to be bought out in accordance with the terms of the SSA. Following which Criterion commenced proceedings for a summary judgment to set aside the SSA. Criterion argued that the purpose of entering into this agreement was an improper one and therefore should be set aside.

Hart J

[Counsel for Oaktree, arguing in favour of the validity of the agreement] submitted that the entry into the [poison pill arrangement] was a proper exercise by the Criterion board of its powers. In that connection, he referred me to some observations made by Sir Robert Megarry VC in *Cayne v Global Natural Resources Plc* in the following passage:

'...Most of what I have said is taken from *Howard Smith Ltd v Ampol Petroleum Limited* [1974] AC 821 (a case in which the sole purpose in issuing the shares was to alter the majority shareholding), and in

---

[5] Any one familiar with the use of poison pills in the US will be aware that the term 'poison pill' has a very specific meaning that differs from how it is used in this case. See generally, D. Kershaw, 'The Illusion of Importance: Reconsidering the UK's Takeover Defence Prohibition' (2007) 56 *ICLQ* 267.

Re Smith and Fawcett Ltd [1942] Ch 304. A particular application of these principles which has caused some difficulty is the case of directors who issue shares in order to maintain themselves in office in the honest belief that this is for the good of the company, and not for any unworthy motives of obtaining a personal advantage. In *Hogg v Cramphorn Limited* [1967] Ch 254 [1966] 3 All ER 420 it was held that this honest belief did not prevent the motive for issuing the shares from being an improper motive. At the same time, this principle must not be carried too far. If Company A and Company B are in business competition, and Company A acquires a large holding of shares in Company B with the object of running Company B down so as to lessen its competition, I would have thought that the directors of Company B might well come to the honest conclusion that it was contrary to the best interests of Company B to allow Company A to effect its purpose, and that in fact this would be so. If, then, the directors issue further shares in Company B in order to maintain their control of Company B for the purpose of defeating Company A's plans and continuing Company B in competition with Company A. I cannot see why that should not be a perfectly proper exercise of the fiduciary powers of the directors of Company B. The object is not to retain control as such, but to prevent Company B from being reduced to impotence and beggary, and the only means available to the directors for achieving this purpose is to retain control. This is quite different from directors seeking to retain control because they think that they are better directors than their rivals would be. I think that *Harlowe's Nominees Pty Ltd v Woodside (Lakes Entrance) Oil Company No Liability* (1968) 121 CLR 483, and *Teck Corporation Limited v Millar* (1972) 33 DLR 288, which were both cited with apparent approval in *Howard Smith v Ampol Petroleum Ltd* [1974] AC 821, [1974] 1 All ER 1126 go some way towards supporting such a restriction on the scope of *Hogg v Cramphorn Limited* [1967] Ch 254, [1966] 3 All ER 420, though I do not forget the way in which the *Teck* case was mentioned in the *Howard Smith...*'

[Counsel] also referred me to the judgment of Berger J in *Teck Corporation Ltd v Millar* [1972] 33 DLR (3d) 288 at 315 where he said:

'So how wide a latitude ought the directors to have? If a group is seeking to obtain control, must the directors ignore them? Or are they entitled to consider the consequences of such a group taking over? In *Savoy Corp Ltd v Development Underwriting Ltd* (1963) NSWR 138 at p.147 Jacobs J said: It would seem to me to be unreal in the light of the structure of modern companies and of modern business life to take the view that directors should in no way concern themselves with the infiltration of the company by persons or groups which they bona fide consider not to be seeking the best interests of the company. My own view is that the directors ought to be allowed to consider who is seeking control and why. If they believe that there will be *substantial damage* their powers to defeat those seeking a majority will not necessarily be categorised as improper.' [Emphasis added]

I would comment at this stage that the reasoning in those authorities was directed to a case where the exercise by the directors of their powers to raise capital was impugned on the grounds of improper motive. Where directors are raising capital, they are doing something which is prima facie for the benefit of the company as an economic unit. There clearly has to be a wide ranging investigation of all the facts and circumstances in such a case if there is an issue as to whether the exercise of the capital raising power was in fact motivated by an improper desire to deprive an existing majority of shareholders of their position as such. The present case is rather different since, if Criterion is right, the only possible consequence of the exercise of the power was to expose the company to the possibility of economic damage.

[Counsel's] submission on behalf of Criterion was that this was indeed the position. The inevitable consequence of the second supplementary agreement was contingently to transfer value from Criterion to Oaktree. If the second supplementary agreement was to achieve its object of deterring a predator from making a bid for Criterion, it was necessary that its provisions be tailored in such a way as to ensure that, if the trigger were ever to be pulled, the consequences for the predator would be so unappetising as to be indigestible. For that reason [the poison pill arrangement guaranteed Oaktree] a 25% per annum (compounded monthly) return on its investment in the partnership. This was all pure bounty so far as Oaktree was concerned, and pure detriment so far as Criterion was concerned. No matter how undesirable the presence [a takeover of the company] might be, it was in his submission impossible to see how it could justify this exercise of contingently 'giving away' Criterion's property.

Moreover, [counsel for Criterion submitted] that even if the limited purpose of preventing a take-over by the Claasen interests could have justified such a contingent gratuitous alienation of Criterion's property, the actual terms of the SSA went very much further. The trigger events extended to *any* change of control in Criterion, and to *any* circumstances in which either Mr Nordström or Mr Glaser ceased to be a director or an employee of Criterion or involved in its management. These provisions were self-evidently designed to entrench the status quo as regards the control of Criterion, both at shareholder level and at board level. Its practical effect was not merely (as in *Howard Smith v Ampol*) to interfere with the constitutional rights of an existing majority of shareholders but to interfere with the constitutional rights of the majority of shareholders at any time, since if such a majority were to exercise the power vested in them inalienably by statute (see s 303 of the Companies Act 1985)[6] to remove Mr Glaser or Mr Nordström as directors, they would potentially expose Criterion to a serious and wholly gratuitous liability...

Apart from a desire to avert the threat (which I take to have been real) that a controlling interest in Criterion [may have been purchased by the Potential Bidder], there cannot be said to be any commercial justification whatsoever for the SSA from Criterion's point of view...As it seems to me, I am left with the bare question of whether the granting of the [poison pill arrangement] could in any circumstances be justified by the desire to deter a predator whom the Criterion directors bona fide believed to be unsavoury. If the matter is simply one of degree, then I am inclined to agree with [Oaktree's counsel] that the matter would be one that would have to go to trial.[7] The issue would be whether reasonable directors could legitimately have concluded that the economic damage to the company which would result from the predator's acquisition of control justified the company in thus contingently alienating its assets. However, the logic of the SSA must be that the result of the calculation (had it been done) would have demonstrated that its effect on Criterion would in fact have been more damaging than the effect on Criterion of the acquisition of control by an unwanted predator. If that was not the effect of the agreement, it would fail to have the deterrent effect on the predator which it was professedly designed to have. On that analysis, I do not myself see how the exercise can begin to be justified as a proper exercise by the Criterion board of its powers...

If, prior to reading this judgment, you had been asked whether it was possible, without shareholder approval, to enter into an agreement whose primary purpose was to deter the making of a takeover offer, I think your answer would have been clear. Based on *Hogg v Cramphorn* and *Howard Smith* this would amount to an attempt to interfere with the Criterion shareholders' constitutional right to accept an offer for their shares. There is no issue here of primary or secondary purpose for the SSA as—in contrast to an issue of shares where the directors can claim they intended to raise capital—there is no other commercial justification for the SSA: the poison pill was designed specifically to stop the bid. Following *Hogg v Cramphorn* and *Howard Smith* the fact that the board of directors thought that the person who may make the takeover bid would damage the company would be irrelevant. The only question would be: had the shareholders approved of this action either before or after it was taken? If not, it would be unlawful.

Hart J's judgment, however, does not fit neatly within the structure of this analysis. The primary references in his judgment are to cases that challenge the *Hogg/Howard Smith* position that reasons for actions (the nature and gravity of the threat) are *irrelevant* if those actions interfere with constitutional rights. He quotes from

---

[6] Now section 168 CA 2006.
[7] The case involved an application by Criterion for a summary judgment.

Megarry VC's judgment in *Cayne v Global Natural Resources Plc*[8] who argues that the refusal to consider such reasons must not be taken too far and that the board must have authority to interfere with these constitutional rights where the threat is big enough. A company cannot, he suggests, be incapable of acting where it is at risk of 'being reduced to impotence and beggary'. Interestingly, one could argue that *Hogg v Cramphorn* and *Howard Smith v Ampol* offer a degree of flexibility that covers the types of pernicious shareholder behaviour described by Megarry VC. Both cases refer to the concept of 'oppression', the presence of which would justify board action. Consider, for example, Lord Wilberforce's observation that 'the right to dispose of shares at a given price is essentially an individual right to be exercised on individual decision and on which a majority, in the absence of oppression or similar impropriety, is entitled to prevail'.[9] The meaning and the parameters of this concept of oppression have not, however, been explored in subsequent case law.

Hart J finds that the poison pill arrangement interferes with the constitutional rights of the shareholders at all times, as it interfered with their right to be able to remove directors. Such a conclusion would have been sufficient for Buckley J in *Hogg v Cramphorn* and Lord Wilberforce in *Howard Smith* to halt the analysis and hold the arrangement unlawful. Hart J, however, continues. He holds that 'I am left with the bare question whether the granting of the [poison pill arrangement] could in any circumstances be justified by the desire to deter a predator whom the Criterion directors bona fide believe to be unsavoury'. He concludes that it could not be. However, had there been any doubt in this regard then the issue, he holds, would have been whether 'reasonable directors could legitimately have concluded that the economic damage to the company which would result from the predator's acquisition of control justified the company in thus contingently alienating its assets'. This holding directly conflicts with the holding in *Hogg v Cramphorn* and *Howard Smith* where such an assessment of the threat from the 'predator' are 'irrelevant' if the exercise of powers interferes with constitutional rights. Hart J's judgment, if accepted, would represent a new departure for English law. It would make 'reasons' for interfering with constitutional rights relevant to the court's review of the board's actions. Such reasons would, according to Hart J, be reviewed according to an objective, reasonable director standard: would a reasonable director find that the threat justified the infringement of constitutional rights.

Following the first instance judgment, Oaktree Appealed to the Court of Appeal.

■ Court of Appeal [2002] All ER (D) 280

Carnwath LJ

[Counsel for Criterion] accepts that it may, depending on the circumstances, be legitimate for the board to exercise its power to issue shares, in order to deter a takeover which would cause serious economic harm to the company. Examples, in relation to common law jurisdictions, can be found in *Siena Finance BV v Sea Containers Ltd* (1989) 39 WR 83 (Supreme Court of Bermuda); and *Re 347883 Alberta and Producers Pipeline Inc* (1991) 80 DLR (4th) 359 (Supreme Court of Saskatchewan)...

This agreement, he says, is wholly different, because it involved, not the issue of shares, but the gratuitous disposition of the company's assets...The SSA went far beyond anything which could be justified for the purpose of deterring an unwelcome predator. The buy-back provision could be triggered by any take-over, not only by a hostile predator, but even by one regarded as

---

[8] Lexis (unreported).

[9] Note also Buckley J's holding in *Hogg v Cramphorn* that 'a majority of shareholders in general meeting is entitled to pursue what course it chooses within the company's powers, however wrong-headed it may appear to others, provided the majority do not unfairly *oppress* other members of the company' (emphasis added).

wholly beneficial (or even by Oaktree itself). Furthermore, it could be triggered by the departure of Mr Nordström or Mr Glaser, even in circumstances which had nothing to do with a change of control, for example death or dismissal due to misconduct.

In my view, these submissions are compelling. Unlike the judge, I would not wish to rest this conclusion on the simple 'logic' that the poison-pill needed to be damaging to the company to achieve its effect. Had the agreement been so drafted as to be confined to the purpose of seeing off the particular predator, the present dispute would not have arisen. It is therefore unnecessary to decide to what extent 'poison pills', limited to that purpose, are permissible in English law. However, as Mr Steinfeld says, the agreement went far beyond that limited purpose. Even if one accepts the lawfulness of the purpose, and the power of the directors to use the mechanism of a 'contingent transfer' of assets to achieve it, it is very difficult to see how this particular agreement could be justified as a reasonable exercise of that power in the interests of the company.

Accordingly, I approach the second issue on the basis that, at least on the information presently available, the judge was correct to hold that the agreement was outside the powers of the directors of Criterion. I do so, not on the relatively limited basis on which he decided the matter, but taking account of the full effect of the agreement, including in particular the range of events (unrelated to the particular threat which then faced the company) which might trigger the buy-out right.

The Court of Appeal's judgment 'ducks' the issues generated by Hart J's judgment. They hold that it is not necessary to dispose of the case to decide whether such 'poison pills' limited to the purpose of deterring a takeover bidder would be lawful, because, even if they are, in this case it would not be a legal use of that power. The reason for this holding is that the poison pill was triggered by any change of control (one that was good for the company as well as one that was bad) as well as by the removal of the chairman or managing director in circumstances unrelated to a change of control. One might say that the court viewed the poison pill as a *disproportionate response to the threat posed*.[10] The court's judgment suggests that what would be proportionate would be determined by the court's assessment of whether such action would have been taken by a reasonable director.[11]

---

[10] See further section IV of this chapter on the relation between this approach and the Delaware approach to the exercise of corporate power in a takeover setting.

[11] The case was appealed to the House of Lords where it was dismissed: *Criterion Properties Plc v Stratford UK Properties LLC* [2006] BCLC 729. However, it was not dismissed through an analysis of the proper purpose doctrine. The court observed that the courts below had failed to consider properly whether or not the board of *Criterion* had actual or apparent authority to enter into the SSA. The court observed that section 40 CA 2006 would be relevant to this consideration (considered at pp 126–32 of Chapter 4). For the House of Lords the question of the enforceability of the 'poison pill' arrangement is a question answered by the law of agency: did the managers entering into the contract and/or Criterion's board of directors have actual or apparent authority to enter into the SSA containing the 'poison pill'. Lord Nicholls put it as follows: 'If a company (A) enters into an agreement with B under which B acquires benefit from A, A's ability to recover these benefits from B depends essentially on whether the agreement is binding on A. If the directors of A were acting for an improper purpose when they entered into the agreement, A's ability to have the agreement set aside depends upon the application of familiar principles of agency and company law'. As we saw in our analysis of *Hogg v Cramphorn* and *Howard Smith* the improper purpose doctrine is best understood as a default constitutional rule providing for the distribution of power between the board and the shareholder body. The doctrine says that in the absence of contrary shareholder intent (either *ex ante* or *ex post*) the board has not been delegated the power to use corporate power to interfere with fundamental constitutional rights. In this respect their Lordships' position could be read as an indirect affirmation of the constitutional power based approach of *Hogg* and *Howard Smith*. Perhaps one might be tempted to argue that the fact that their Lordships hold that the trial court needs to consider whether there is actual or apparent authority for the 'poison pill' provides indirect support for the availability of using corporate power in this way—because clearly their Lordships think that such arrangements *could* benefit from actual or apparent authority

This leaves the law in a rather uncertain state. The Court of Appeal suggests an approach to regulating director actions *if it is possible* in English law to use such a poison pill mechanism which intentionally interferes with the constitutional right to sell one's shares. However, the Court of Appeal declines to rule on the issue of whether proportionate poison pill arrangements designed only to deter a particular bidder are permissible or not. Yet, as we have seen, if *Hogg v Cramphorn* and *Howard Smith* are the leading cases, such an arrangement is clearly unlawful. The fact that the Court of Appeal leaves it unaddressed suggests a possible change in the legal wind.

Even if future courts were to accept the approach adopted by Hart J, it is unclear how much flexibility this would give boards of directors to use corporate power for defensive purposes. In this regard Gerner-Beuerle, Kershaw, and Solinas have argued that if *Criterion* does lead to a change in approach it is likely to be very strictly construed. They argue that it provides a framework: 'whose only UK judicial support is *Cayne* v *Natural Resources*. Accordingly, a reasonable director through the eyes of a UK court will require something close to impotence and beggary to justify defensive action'.[12]

Questions

1. In what respects does *Criterion* differ from *Howard Smith* and *Hogg v Cramphorn*?

2. Is it correct, or fair, to argue that the Court of Appeal 'ducks' the issue? What inference, if any, can be drawn from the Court of Appeal's approach?

3. If Gerner-Beuerle et al are correct that even if the approach suggested by *Criterion* is adopted it will be narrowly construed, can you imagine actions by a hostile bidder that you think could be described as reducing the company to 'impotence and beggary'?

III THE COMPANIES ACT 2006

We saw in Chapter 6 that the board of directors is empowered to act through a delegation of power from the shareholder body set forth in the articles of association. It follows, therefore, that directors of the company can only do what the articles authorize them to do. They breach the terms of their appointment if they exercise corporate powers in excess of the authorization set forth in the articles. This obligation to comply

and be enforceable. This is not correct. To see this we need to remind ourselves that it is possible for transactions to be enforceable even if they are in excess of the directors' powers.

Let us assume for the purpose of our analysis that the proper purpose doctrine is correctly articulated in *Hogg* and *Howard Smith*. It follows that the starting point is that in the absence of contrary intent the board of directors does not have the actual authority to enter into a poison pill arrangement. However, as Lord Scott observes, section 40 of the Companies Act 2006 may be applicable and could operate to confer actual authority on the board or an agent authorized by the board, or enable the board to make a representation in relation to such agent for the purposes of apparent authority. It does so by effectively dissolving the actual limitations on the board's actual authority. This would mean that where the board elected to enter into a 'poison pill' arrangement and authorized someone to enter into the transaction on the company's behalf then the transaction would be enforceable—on the basis of actual authority—provided that, pursuant to section 40, the third party in question could be shown to be dealing with the company and acting in good faith.

Accordingly, although the House of Lords judgment in *Criterion* focuses our attention on the relationship between authority to enter into a defensive transaction, its enforceability, and the proper purpose doctrine, the House of Lords' judgment does not tell us anything about whether the more flexible approach taken by Hart J in *Criterion* to whether or not the board has the power to put such arrangements in place (without shareholder approval) is good law.

[12] C. Gerner-Beuerle, D. Kershaw and M. Solinas, 'Is the Board Neutrality Rule Trivial? Amnesia about Corporate Law in European Takeover Regulation' (2011) *European Business Law Review* 559.

with the terms of that delegation is set out in the Companies Act 2006 as a duty to act in accordance with the constitution.

The logic of delegated board authority that requires compliance with the constitution is closely related to the way in which Lord Wilberforce articulated the improper purpose doctrine: you cannot use delegated powers for purposes other than the ones for which they are conferred. It is not surprising, therefore, that the Act finds a home for the improper purpose doctrine *as a duty*[13] in a general *duty to act within powers*.

■ Section 171 CA 2006 Duty to act within powers

A director of a company must—

(a) act in accordance with the company's constitution, and

(b) only exercise powers for the purposes for which they are conferred.

Questions and discussion

1. The Act appears to codify the approach taken in *Howard Smith v Ampol*. As we noted in our analysis, there are two aspects of Lord Wilberforce's judgment: the first, the provision of a general rule of construction for determining which powers are conferred; the second, which has a greater affinity with *Hogg v Cramphorn*, which says a power must not be used in a way that impinges on shareholders' core constitutional rights unless the shareholders have agreed to this. Which one of these approaches is codified by the Act?

2. The duty is the product of cases which address two contexts: the use by boards of directors of corporate powers in order to manipulate or interfere with shareholder voting; and the use of powers to manipulate the outcome of bids for a company's shares. We asked whether the general principled language set forth in Lord Wilberforce's judgment in *Howard Smith* was necessary and what was intended by it. The Act adopts this general principled approach. A duty set forth in such general terms may necessarily have application in contexts other than the ones in which it was formed. Can we envisage what these contexts might be?

3. If the use of Lord Wilberforce's language in section 171(b) represents the legislature's approval of the *Howard Smith* judgment, what are the implications of the codification, if any, for the *Criterion* 'reasons for acting' debate set out earlier?

4. At common law, was there ever a *duty* to use powers for their proper purposes or was there simply a default rule about the distribution of power in a UK company? If one views the improper purpose doctrine as a default constitutional rule distributing power between the board and the shareholder body rather than a director's duty then it would be enforced by shareholders as a breach of their personal rights[14] rather than the bringing of a derivative action[15] to enforce the rights of the company.[16] In viewing the use of corporate powers for an improper purpose as a breach of duty, does this foreclose shareholders bringing a more straightforward claim that their personal rights have been infringed by the action in question? Arguably it does not. The fact that there is in section 171(a) a duty to act in accordance with the company's constitution does not prevent a shareholder whose personal rights (as distinguished from an internal irregularity) have been infringed from bringing a personal action. Similarly, whilst the use of corporate power to interfere with the constitutional rights of the shareholder would amount to a

---

[13] See footnote 2 on whether the proper purpose doctrine was understood as a 'duty' at common law.

[14] On the enforcement of personal rights by shareholders see Chapter 3.

[15] See Chapter 15 on derivative actions.

[16] See *Re a company (Case No 005136 of 1986) (Re Sherborne Park Residents Co Ltd)* [1987] BCLC 82 where the action brought in relation to an improper use of corporate powers was viewed as the enforcement of a shareholder's personal rights.

breach of duty, it would also amount to a breach of the shareholders personal rights that could be enforced personally. Of course, the authority supporting personal enforcement is prior to the 2006 Act and prior to understanding the proper purpose doctrine in 'director's duty' terms. The courts may therefore require derivative enforcement. In this regard, note that if a personal action is allowed any damages that are sought would clearly be reflective losses which would not be recoverable. We address reflective loss in Chapter 15.

5. Do you think the adoption of Lord Wilberforce's language represents a restatement or a reform of the existing law?

IV A US COMPARISON

It is interesting to observe that the Court of Appeal in part of its judgment in *Criterion*, which has not been extracted in this chapter, referred to a Canadian case, *Alberta Ltd v Producers Pipeline Inc,*[17] which included 'helpful quotations from articles describing the "typical poison pill" and the history of its use in America and Canada'. This is interesting because it suggests that US authorities may well have been referred to by counsel and may well have had some unspecified influence on the *Criterion* judgments. This is noteworthy because both Hart J's dictum on the approach that he would have taken—had the 'poison pill' been more closely tailored to the threat to the company of a takeover bid by the original predator—and the Court of Appeals suggested approach—*if poison pills are valid at all*—appear to have a close affinity with the structure of the approach taken by the Delaware courts in the US. There is a significant amount of Delaware case law addressing the use of corporate power to deter takeover bids.[18] Here we consider only the structure of the approach taken by the courts as evidenced by one of the leading and well-known cases: *Unocal Corporation v Mesa Petroleum*.

■ *Unocal Corporation v Mesa Petroleum* (Delaware Supreme Court) 493 A 2d 946 (Del 1985)

In this case the bidder, Mesa Petroleum, announced its intention to make a bid for a certain number of the shares in Unocal. Mesa was a well-known 'greenmailer'. 'Greenmailers' are companies who buy a stake in the target company and threaten to takeover the company in the hope that the company will buy-back their existing stake in the company at a premium price. Mesa's bid provided that they intended only to buy enough shares to give them majority control of the company's voting shares. In the US it is possible to make such a partial offer provided that the bidder buys a pro rata share of the shares tendered by the shareholders. Mesa announced that the takeover bid would be for cash at $54 a share. However, they also announced at the same time that, once they had majority voting control of the company, they would use their power as majority shareholder to effect what is colloquially known as a 'squeeze-out merger'. In this squeeze-out, the remaining shareholders would receive loan notes in exchange for their shares which would be subordinated in ranking to other creditors of the company. The precise mechanics of a Delaware squeeze-out merger need not concern us here. The bottom line is that shareholders who did not tender in the first offer would be subsequently forced to sell their remaining shares not in exchange for cash but for subordinated

---

[17] (1991) 80 DLR (4th) 359.

[18] See further: *City Capital Associates v Interco Inc* 551 A2d 787 (Del Ch 1988); *Paramount Communications Inc v Time Incorporated* 1989 WL 79880 (Del Ch 1989); *Paramount Communications Inc v Time Incorporated* 571 A2d 1140 (Del 1990); *Unitrin Inc v American General Corp* 651 A2d 1361 (Del 1995); *Carmody v Toll Brothers, Inc* 723 A2d 1180 (Del Ch 1998); *Air Products and Chemical Inc v Airgas, Inc*, CA No 5249-CC (Del Ch Feb, 15, 2011).

promissory notes. This type of offer is known as a *front-loaded two-tier offer*. The effect of the offer is to force all shareholders to accept the first offer for fear of being left with subordinated loan notes in the subsequent squeeze-out merger. As a shareholder, even if you think the $54 is a poor price you will sell your shares in order to at least share in the cash consideration. Note that in the UK it is not possible to make such an offer as the UK's Takeover Code requires that an offer is made for all the shares in the company.[19]

The directors considered the offer to be a poor offer and were concerned that the structure of the offer was coercive and unfair. Accordingly, they devised the following defence to ward off Mesa Petroleum. They authorized a contingent and partial buy-back of the shares. If Mesa purchased a majority of the voting shares the company undertook to buy the remaining shares from the shareholders at $72 a share to be paid for with senior promissory notes. However, Mesa would not be allowed to participate in this offer. The effect of this offer was that as everyone would prefer to have $72 in **senior debt** rather than $54 in **subordinated debt**, no one was willing to tender in the Mesa offer. Mesa brought an action against the directors arguing that the steps they had taken were in breach of their duties to the company.

From a UK perspective the directors had used their corporate powers to thwart the exercise by the shareholders of their constitutional right to decide whether or not to accept an offer. The directors had, however, done so for what they considered to be very good reasons.

Justice Moore

The board has a large reservoir of authority upon which to draw. Its duties and responsibilities proceed from the inherent powers conferred by [section 141(a) of the Delaware General Corporation Law (DGCL)], respecting management of the corporation's 'business and affairs'.[20] Additionally, the powers here being exercised derive from [section 160(a) DGCL], conferring broad authority upon a corporation to deal in its own stock. From this it is now well established that in the acquisition of its shares a Delaware corporation may deal selectively with its stockholders, provided the directors have not acted out of a sole or primary purpose to entrench themselves in office.

Finally, the board's power to act derives from its fundamental duty and obligation to protect the corporate enterprise, which includes stockholders, from harm reasonably perceived, irrespective of its source...Thus, we are satisfied that in the broad context of corporate governance, including issues of fundamental corporate change, a board of directors is not a passive instrumentality.

Given the foregoing principles, we turn to the standards by which director action is to be measured. In *Pogostin v. Rice*, Del.Supr., 480 A.2d 619 (1984), we held that the business judgment rule, including the standards by which director conduct is judged, is applicable in the context of a takeover. The business judgment rule is a 'presumption that in making a business decision the directors of a corporation acted on an informed basis, in good faith and in the honest belief that the action taken was in the best interests of the company' *Aronson v. Lewis*, Del.Supr., 473 A.2d 805, 812 (1984). A hallmark of the business judgment rule is that a court will not substitute its judgment for that of the board if the latter's decision can be 'attributed to any rational business purpose.' *Sinclair Oil Corp. v. Levien*, Del.Supr., 280 A.2d 717, 720 (1971).

[The business judgment rule is addressed in Chapter 12. In essence the rule provides for a very low level review of the decision itself/the exercise of corporate powers—referred to as rationality review provided that the directors have complied with the duty of care regarding the decision-making process and the duty of loyalty. In this case there was no duty of loyalty or duty of care problem. So the question is whether the exercise of power—to put in place the contingent selective buy-back of shares—should be subject to a more onerous level of review.]

---

[19] See Rules 9 and 10 of the Takeover Code.
[20] Section 141(a) DGCL is discussed in detail in Chapter 6.

When a board addresses a pending takeover bid it has an obligation to determine whether the offer is in the best interests of the corporation and its shareholders. In that respect a board's duty is no different from any other responsibility it shoulders, and its decisions should be no less entitled to the respect they otherwise would be accorded in the realm of business judgment...There are, however, certain caveats to a proper exercise of this function. Because of the omnipresent spectre that a board may be acting primarily in its own interests, rather than those of the corporation and its shareholders, there is an enhanced duty which calls for judicial examination at the threshold before the protections of the business judgment rule may be conferred.

This Court has long recognized that we must bear in mind the inherent danger in the purchase of shares with corporate funds to remove a threat to corporate policy when a threat to control is involved. The directors are of necessity confronted with a conflict of interest, and an objective decision is difficult. In the face of this inherent conflict directors must show that they had reasonable grounds for believing that a danger to corporate policy and effectiveness existed because of another person's stock ownership. However, they satisfy that burden 'by showing good faith and reasonable investigation...' (*Cheff v. Mathes*, 199 A.2d at 554–55). Furthermore, such proof is materially enhanced, as here, by the approval of a board comprised of a majority of outside independent directors who have acted in accordance with the foregoing standards...The standard of proof established in *Cheff v. Mathes*...is designed to ensure that a defensive measure to thwart or impede a takeover is indeed motivated by a good faith concern for the welfare of the corporation and its stockholders, which in all circumstances must be free of any fraud or other misconduct...However, this does not end the inquiry.

A further aspect is the element of balance. If a defensive measure is to come within the ambit of the business judgment rule, it must be reasonable in relation to the threat posed. This entails an analysis by the directors of the nature of the takeover bid and its effect on the corporate enterprise. Examples of such concerns may include: inadequacy of the price offered, nature and timing of the offer, questions of illegality, the impact on 'constituencies' other than shareholders (i.e., creditors, customers, employees, and perhaps even the community generally), the risk of nonconsummation, and the quality of securities being offered in the exchange...Here, the threat posed was viewed by the Unocal board as a grossly inadequate two-tier coercive tender offer coupled with the threat of greenmail.

Specifically, the Unocal directors had concluded that the value of Unocal was substantially above the $54 per share offered in cash at the front end. Furthermore, they determined that the subordinated securities to be exchanged in Mesa's announced squeeze out of the remaining shareholders in the 'back-end' merger were **'junk bonds'** worth far less than $54. It is now well recognized that such offers are a classic coercive measure designed to stampede shareholders into tendering at the first tier, even if the price is inadequate, out of fear of what they will receive at the back end of the transaction. Wholly beyond the coercive aspect of an inadequate two-tier tender offer, the threat was posed by a corporate raider with a national reputation as a 'greenmailer'.

In adopting the selective exchange offer, the board stated that its objective was either to defeat the inadequate Mesa offer or, should the offer still succeed, provide the 49% of its stockholders, who would otherwise be forced to accept 'junk bonds', with $72 worth of senior debt. We find that both purposes are valid.

However, such efforts would have been thwarted by Mesa's participation in the exchange offer. First, if Mesa could tender its shares, Unocal would effectively be subsidizing the former's continuing effort to buy Unocal stock at $54 per share. Second, Mesa could not, by definition, fit within the class of shareholders being protected from its own coercive and inadequate tender offer.

Thus, we are satisfied that the selective exchange offer is reasonably related to the threats posed. It is consistent with the principle that 'the minority stockholder shall receive the substantial equivalent in value of what he had before.'

The Delaware Supreme Court applies proportionality review to the corporate action taken by the Unocal board to ward off the takeover bid. This involves a two-step process: first, asking the board to specify the nature of the threat posed by the takeover bid; and second, an investigation by the court to determine whether the exercise of corporate power was a proportionate response to address the specified threat to the company: it must be 'reasonable in relation to the threat posed'. If it is a reasonable response then the courts will apply the normal business judgment level review, which simply involves asking whether there is a rational basis for the decision. This approach is very similar to the approach which Hart J held that he would have taken had the Criterion 'poison pill' not been so disproportionate. The proportionality approach also resonates with how the Court of Appeal in *Criterion* addressed the issue. However, whilst these two approaches share a structural affinity they are, it is submitted, substantively very different.[21] A central question for UK courts *if* the *Criterion* approach finds fertile soil is: what types of threat would reasonably justify a defensive response? For Megarry VC in *Cayne v Global Natural Resources Plc*, which was an important case for Hart J, the directors would not have to stand by whilst the company was reduced to 'impotence and beggary', which suggests a very high threat threshold. The Delaware courts take a more flexible view of what could amount to a threat, referring to a broad range of options including inadequacy of price and the effects on the takeover on other constituencies. It is submitted that any UK development of the threat-proportionality test would be far more demanding of the nature of the threat required before permitting a defensive exercise of corporate power.

More importantly, the comparison with the Delaware court's approach allows us to see, in this author's view, that the threat-proportionality approach to the exercise of corporate power is a poor fit with English company law. In *Unocal* the Delaware Supreme Court justifies the additional level of review set out in the case on the basis that, although there is no actual breach of the duty of loyalty, takeover transactions create an 'omnipresent spectre' that the board may in fact be acting in its own interests in order to protect their jobs, which they could lose if the takeover is successful. The starting point for the Delaware courts is that the board may not be acting loyally; an additional level of review is required to ensure that this is not the case. This approach, as we shall see in Chapters 13 and 14 when we consider self-dealing and corporate opportunities regulation, is consistent with the Delaware court's approach to judicial review, which is to ensure that *in fact* the directors are behaving loyally. As we shall see in Chapters 13 and 14, such an approach to determine loyalty *in fact* has been rejected by the UK courts.

Furthermore, the UK's constitutional rights approach and the Delaware courts threat-proportionality approach are arguably logical extensions of the core balance of power elections which we discussed in Chapter 6: shareholder primacy in the UK and director primacy in the US.[22] In a shareholder primacy jurisdiction whilst shareholders may delegate power to the directors to manage the company, it makes sense that their core rights to vote and receive takeover offers are not relinquished without expressly doing so. In a director primacy jurisdiction, on the other hand, the shareholders' rights do not give up authority to the board, the board has original and undelegated authority, and the shareholders do not retain such fundamental constitutional rights to the same

---

[21] See also J. Armour and D.A. Skeel Jr., 'Who Writes the Rules for Hostile Takeovers, and Why? The Peculiar Divergence of US and UK Takeover Regulation' (2007) 95(6) *Georgetown Law Journal* 1727–94.

[22] See further Chapter 6.

extent.[23] If this is correct, it offers further support for the view that Hart J's suggested approach in *Criterion* and any implicit support for his view in the Court of Appeal's judgment is a mistake.

 Online Resource Centre
http://www.oxfordtextbooks.co.uk/orc/kershaw2e/

Visit the Online Resource Centre for additional resources and information available for this chapter, including web links and an interactive flashcard glossary.

---

[23] Cf *Blasius Industries v Atlas Corp.* 564 A2d 651 (Del 1988); *Codec Corporation v Lunkenheimer Company* 230 A2d 769 (Del Ch 1967); *Canada Southern Oils Ltd v Manabi Exploration Co* 96 A2d 810 (Del Ch 1953).

CHAPTER TWELVE

COMPETENCE AND THE DUTY OF CARE

I INTRODUCTION

1 Directors' decision-making activity and function

In Chapters 10 and 11 we looked at how company law regulates the decisions directors make: a director must make decisions that she considers will promote the success of the company and the exercise of corporate power must be for a proper purpose. In this chapter we look at the expectations English company law has regarding the care she takes when acting as a director.

To understand what it means to take care when acting as a director it is helpful to remind ourselves of what directors do—their role and function. There are different types of activity undertaken by directors. Most importantly directors make decisions as members of the board of directors. Those decisions include, for example: decisions about entering into contracts to sell property or to take a loan; deciding who the board should nominate as a director or appoint as an executive officer; agreeing executive directors' remuneration arrangements; or allowing the directors to exploit an identified business opportunity in their personal capacity. Directors, typically executive directors, will also exercise powers delegated to them to act in specified ways on behalf of the company or to implement board decisions. Executive directors may, for example, have delegated power to enter into contracts for the purchase and sale of goods and services as part of the day-to-day operation of the business; or they may have delegated power to negotiate and sign documents which implement, on behalf of the company, a decision made by the board such as to sell a major asset.

As we considered in detail in Chapter 7, directors also have non-decision-making functions such as (for non-executive directors) monitoring the performance and activities of executive directors and ensuring that the information the company produces about itself is reliable and not misleading. Of course, ultimately these non-decision-making activities service or support the directors' decision-making function: in order to *decide* whether to prolong or terminate a CEO's contract you need to pay attention to her performance. Reliable information, for example, about how much profit the company has made during the CEO's tenure is essential to any such assessment.

The activities that occupy a director's time will vary depending on the nature and size of the company. The directors of a smaller company may well be involved in many of the day-to-day management decisions. Boards of directors of large listed companies containing a mix of executive and non-executive directors may perform a very different role to the directors of small, close companies. The board of directors of listed companies will meet only periodically, perhaps less than once a month, and only for a few hours. Such directors' roles will be to make major decisions—such as approving the long-term business plan, the issue of new shares or the incurrence of significant debt—and to appoint, monitor and, where necessary, remove management.

In short, any attempt to impose a general behavioural expectation of how much care a director should take when acting will need to be sufficiently flexible to cover a wide range of decision-making and activity contexts; a wide range of different companies; and different types of directorship.

2 What does taking care involve in a company context?

What it means to take care obviously varies depending on the activity being performed by a director and the context within which she performs that activity. If a director signs a cheque on behalf of a company whether the appropriate degree of care was taken may relate to the value of the cheque as compared to the value of the company as well as whether the director knew or inquired about what the cheque was to pay for. If a director signs a contract on behalf of the company, whether she has exercised the authority delegated to her with due care will relate to factors such as the significance of the contract for the company and the director's knowledge about the contents and implications for the company of the contract.

Let us consider in more detail what is involved in taking care when the board makes a decision. In some areas of life and legal regulation the action you take is decisive in determining whether you took care. If you crash your car into a stationary car the very fact of the crash creates a strong presumption that you did not take care; that you were negligent and, therefore, liable to compensate the owner of the stationary car. Business decisions are very different in this regard. When the board of directors makes a business decision the outcome of the decision will often be unknown and the directors making the decision will be aware that there is some risk that the outcome will not be favourable. A decision, for example, to invest the company's funds in a new product line will involve a certain probability of success but also a certain probability of failure. Accordingly, the outcome of a business decision (whether or not, metaphorically speaking, it 'crashes') does not tell us whether or not the directors took care in making the decision. Consider further the following hypothetical.

Hypothetical A

Consider our case study company Bob's Electronics Plc with a board of two directors: Markus the CEO and Suzanne, a non-executive director and where Bob is the majority shareholder. Consider a situation where a third party has made an offer to purchase the company's build-to-order laptop division. Several factors will be relevant to the determination of whether the offer should be accepted—whether in the directors' view it promotes the success of the company. These would include—among other possible questions:

- What is the company's valuation of the division?
- What do the company's financial advisors think the division is worth?
- What would the impact on the value and the functioning of the remainder of the business be if this division is sold?
- Would more value be generated by selling the company's business as a whole?
- What would the effect of the sale be on the company's employees who work in the laptop division as well as those who do not?

Answers to these questions will take some time to produce and will be quite complex to digest. For example, valuations of the business assets often involve various assumptions such as the future economic condition of the industry or of the domestic economy. An assessment of the valuation requires an understanding of how realistic these assumptions are.

We might say, therefore, that there are three attributes of taking care in relation to this decision: first, obtaining the relevant information; secondly, an ability to understand this information; and thirdly, taking time to consider this information before making the decision.

Assume that Suzanne is new to the job: she was appointed last week and is yet to attend a board meeting. She was appointed as she is Bob's bridge partner and he trusts her. She has, however, no idea whatsoever about the business of build-to-order computers. Taking care for her, therefore, would appear to require requesting the sorts of information just mentioned and taking time to analyse and consider such information. For Suzanne care will necessarily involve a process that she goes through in order to make a decision: from questions and information requests, to analysis and time for thought. For a court assessing whether she has complied with a legal standard of care, one would expect that such a record of process would be available.

Markus the CEO as a long-serving senior manager may already have this information to hand, at the forefront of his mind. If so, taking care for him would not require asking for, or taking time to think about, such information because he has already digested and thought about such information. Accordingly, he can make his decision regarding the offer very quickly. If Markus is in such a position of knowledge and understanding about the business and the offer to purchase the laptop division then there will be no record of a process that he went through to reach his decision.

This analysis of what it means to take care for Suzanne assumes that she is capable of asking the right questions and requesting the information necessary to make a good decision, and that she is capable of understanding the information once it is provided. If she has experience in the world of business and finance then such an assumption may be well founded. But what if Suzanne is a well-respected artist with zero experience of business and finance? No matter how hard she tries to take care, she may ask the wrong questions, consider the wrong information, and have difficulty understanding the information that is pertinent to the decision whether or not to sell the asset. But if she tries her hardest and gives the job her best, will she have failed to provide the level of care that a director should take when making this decision?

With regard to what is involved in taking care when making decisions consider the facts in the following extract from what is probably the most well-known case on the duty of care in the United States. The court's holding in this case will be considered later in section V.3. The facts are considered separately here as they provide an interesting and useful way for any student of company law to think about what is involved in, and what we might expect of, a director taking care when she makes a decision on behalf of the company.

■ *Smith v Van Gorkom* 488 A 2d 858 (Del 1985)

Justice Horsey

Trans Union was a publicly-traded, diversified holding company,[1] the principal earnings of which were generated by its railcar leasing business. During the period here involved, the Company had a cash flow of hundreds of millions of dollars annually. However, the Company had difficulty in generating sufficient taxable income to offset increasingly large investment tax credits [credits that reduced the company's taxable income]. [The reason for this was although the company was generating a lot of cash this did not result in taxable income because of **depreciation** allowances on the railcars that they owned that reduced taxable income.]...

In July 1980, Trans Union Management prepared the annual revision of the Company's Five Year Forecast. This report was presented to the Board of Directors at its July, 1980 meeting. The report projected an annual income growth of about 20%. The report also concluded that Trans

---

[1] A holding company is a company that typically does not itself have any operational activities. Its only or primary function is to hold shares in other operational subsidiaries.

Union would have about $195 million in spare cash between 1980 and 1985, 'with the surplus growing rapidly from 1982 onward.' The report referred to the [company's inability to generate sufficient taxable income to make full use of the investment tax credits] as a 'nagging problem'. The report then listed four alternative uses of the projected 1982–1985 [cash] surplus: (1) [a share] repurchase;[2] (2) dividend increases; (3) a major acquisition program; and (4) combinations of the above. The sale of Trans Union was not among the alternatives…

On August 27, 1980, Van Gorkom [Trans Union's Chairman and Chief Executive Officer] met with Senior Management of Trans Union. Van Gorkom reported on his…desire to find a solution to the tax credit problem more permanent than a continued program of acquisitions. Various alternatives were suggested and discussed preliminarily, including the sale of Trans Union to a company with a large amount of taxable income.[3]

Donald Romans, Chief Financial Officer of Trans Union,[4] stated that his department had done a 'very brief bit of work on the possibility of a **leveraged buy-out**.' This work had been prompted by a media article which Romans had seen regarding a leveraged buy-out by management. The work consisted of a 'preliminary study' of the cash which could be generated by the Company if it participated in a leveraged buy-out.[5] As Romans stated, this analysis 'was [a] first and rough cut at seeing whether a cash flow would support what might be considered a high price for this type of transaction.'

On September 5, at another Senior Management meeting which Van Gorkom attended, Romans again brought up the idea of a leveraged buy-out as a 'possible strategic alternative' to the Company's acquisition program. Romans and Bruce S. Chelberg, President and Chief Operating Officer of Trans Union, had been working on the matter in preparation for the meeting. According to Romans: They did not 'come up' with a price for the Company. They merely 'ran the numbers' at $50 a share and at $60 a share with the 'rough form' of their cash figures at the time. Their 'figures indicated that $50 would be very easy to do but $60 would be very difficult to do under those figures.' This work did not purport to establish a fair price for either the Company or 100% of the stock. It was intended to determine the cash flow needed to service the debt that would 'probably' be incurred in a leveraged buy-out, based on 'rough calculations' without 'any benefit of experts to identify what the limits were to that, and so forth.' These computations were not considered extensive and no conclusion was reached.

At this meeting, Van Gorkom stated that he would be willing to take $55 per share for his own 75,000 shares. He vetoed the suggestion of a leveraged buy-out by Management, however, as involving a potential conflict of interest for Management. Van Gorkom, a certified public accountant and lawyer, had been an officer of Trans Union for 24 years, its Chief Executive Officer for more than 17 years, and Chairman of its Board for 2 years. It is noteworthy in this connection that he was then approaching 65 years of age and mandatory retirement.

For several days following the September 5 meeting, Van Gorkom pondered the idea of a sale. He had participated in many acquisitions as a manager and director of Trans Union and as a director of other companies. He was familiar with acquisition procedures, valuation methods, and negotiations; and he privately considered the pros and cons of whether Trans Union should seek a privately or publicly-held purchaser.

Van Gorkom decided to meet with Jay A. Pritzker, a well-known corporate takeover specialist and a social acquaintance. However, rather than approaching Pritzker simply to determine his

---

[2] Otherwise known as a 'share buy-back': a repurchase by the company of its own shares. Regarding the UK's regulation of share buy backs see Chapter 17.

[3] From the perspective of a company with a lot of taxable income the investment tax credits are an asset as they reduce the amount of tax they would have to pay. If the purchasing company merged with Trans Union those tax credits would become the purchasing company's tax credits.

[4] In the UK the chief financial officer is often referred to as the finance director.

[5] In a leveraged buy-out the buyer borrows heavily to buy the **target company**. The target's cashflow is then used to repay the loan (on the problems of doing this in the UK see section V in Chapter 17 on financial assistance). Accordingly the price the buyer is willing to pay relates to how much debt the target company's cashflow could repay.

interest in acquiring Trans Union, Van Gorkom assembled a proposed per share price for sale of the Company and a financing structure by which to accomplish the sale. Van Gorkom did so without consulting either his Board or any members of Senior Management except one: Carl Peterson, Trans Union's [Chief Accountant]. Telling Peterson that he wanted no other person on his staff to know what he was doing, but without telling him why, Van Gorkom directed Peterson to calculate the feasibility of a leveraged buy-out at an assumed price per share of $55. Apart from the Company's historic stock market price, and Van Gorkom's long association with Trans Union, the record is devoid of any competent evidence that $55 represented the per share intrinsic value of the Company…

Van Gorkom then reviewed with Pritzker his calculations based upon his proposed price of $55 per share. Although Pritzker mentioned $50 as a more attractive figure, no other price was mentioned. However, Van Gorkom stated that to be sure that $55 was the best price obtainable, Trans Union should be free to accept any better offer. Pritzker demurred, stating that his organization would serve as a 'stalking horse'[6] for an 'auction contest' only if Trans Union would permit Pritzker to buy 1,750,000 shares of Trans Union stock at market price which Pritzker could then sell to any higher bidder.[7] After further discussion on this point, Pritzker told Van Gorkom that he would give him a more definite reaction soon.

On Monday, September 15, Pritzker advised Van Gorkom that he was interested in the $55 cash-out merger[8] proposal and requested more information on Trans Union. Van Gorkom agreed to meet privately with Pritzker, accompanied by Peterson [the Chief Accountant], Chelberg [the Chief Operating Officer] and Michael Carpenter, Trans Union's consultant from the Boston Consulting Group. The meetings took place on September 16 and 17. Van Gorkom was 'astounded that events were moving with such amazing rapidity.'

On Thursday, September 18, Van Gorkom met again with Pritzker. At that time, Van Gorkom knew that Pritzker intended to make a cash-out merger offer at Van Gorkom's proposed $55 per share. Pritzker instructed his attorney, a merger and acquisition specialist, to begin drafting merger documents. There was no further discussion of the $55 price. However, the number of shares of Trans Union's [shares] to be offered to Pritzker was negotiated down to one million shares; the price was set at $38–75 cents above the per share price at the close of the market on September 19. At this point Pritzker insisted that the Trans Union Board act on his merger proposal within the next three days, stating to Van Gorkom: 'we have to have a decision by no later than Sunday [evening, September 21] before the opening of the [London] stock exchange on Monday morning'…

On Friday, September 19, Van Gorkom called a special meeting of the Trans Union Board for noon the following day. He also called a meeting of the Company's Senior Management to convene at 11:00 a.m., prior to the meeting of the Board. No one, except Chelberg and Peterson, was

---

[6] A stalking horse here is a person who by offering to buy the company encourages other third parties to try to buy the company.

[7] Arrangements such as these are known as 'break-fees' or 'lock-ups' in corporate legal circles. They can be in cash or in shares and typically are calculated as a proportion of the value of the company (in the UK following recent changes to the Takeover Code such fees are, subject to limited exceptions, no longer available for companies subject to the Takeover Code (see Rule 21.2 Takeover Code)). In the US a break fee in the region of 2–3% of the target company's value is not unusual. In this case value would be transferred to Pritzker as he buys shares at current market price ($38) and, assuming he has failed to buy the company, another bidder would buy the shares from him at $55. It may strike the reader encountering a 'break-fee' for the first time as very odd for a company to agree to transfer value to a potential buyer who fails in his attempt to buy the company. The reasoning behind agreeing to such fees is that potential buyers spend time and money in trying to buy a company. In addition, for investors such as Pritzker whose business is the purchase of companies, their reputation is damaged if they try and fail to buy a company: other companies may be less willing to do business with them if they have a reputation for announcing but failing to complete purchases. Accordingly, Pritzker could legitimately argue that he would only go ahead with the deal if he receives a break-fee.

[8] For the purposes of understanding these facts a cash-out merger means that the existing shareholders in Trans Union exchange their shares for cash.

told the purpose of the meetings. Van Gorkom did not invite Trans Union's investment banker, Salomon Brothers…to attend.

Of those present at the Senior Management meeting on September 20, only Chelberg and Peterson had prior knowledge of Pritzker's offer. Van Gorkom disclosed the offer and described its terms, but he furnished no copies of the proposed Merger Agreement. Romans announced that his department had done a second study which showed that, for a leveraged buy-out, the price range for Trans Union stock was between $55 and $65 per share. Van Gorkom neither saw the study nor asked Romans to make it available for the Board meeting.

Senior Management's reaction to the Pritzker proposal was completely negative. No member of Management, except Chelberg and Peterson, supported the proposal. Romans [the Chief Financial Officer] objected to the price as being too low…

Ten directors served on the Trans Union Board, five inside (defendants Bonser, O'Boyle, Browder, Chelberg, and Van Gorkom) and five outside (defendants Wallis, Johnson, Lanterman, Morgan and Reneker). All directors were present at the meeting, except O'Boyle who was ill. Of the outside directors, four were corporate chief executive officers and one was the former Dean of the University of Chicago Business School. None was an investment banker or trained financial analyst. All members of the Board were well informed about the Company and its operations as a going concern. They were familiar with the current financial condition of the Company, as well as operating and earnings projections reported in the recent Five Year Forecast. The Board generally received regular and detailed reports and was kept abreast of the accumulated investment tax credit and accelerated depreciation problem.

Van Gorkom began the special meeting of the Board with a twenty-minute oral presentation. Copies of the proposed Merger Agreement were delivered too late for study before or during the meeting.[9] He reviewed the Company's [investment tax credit] and depreciation problems and the efforts theretofore made to solve them. He discussed his initial meeting with Pritzker and his motivation in arranging that meeting. Van Gorkom did not disclose to the Board, however, the methodology by which he alone had arrived at the $55 figure, or the fact that he first proposed the $55 price in his negotiations with Pritzker.

Van Gorkom outlined the terms of the Pritzker offer as follows: Pritzker would pay $55 in cash for all outstanding shares of Trans Union…for a period of 90 days, Trans Union could receive, but could not actively solicit, competing offers; the offer had to be acted on by the next evening, Sunday, September 21; Trans Union could only furnish to competing bidders published information, and not proprietary information; the offer was subject to Pritzker obtaining the necessary financing[10] by October 10, 1980; if the financing contingency were met or waived by Pritzker, Trans Union was required to sell to Pritzker one million newly-issued shares of Trans Union at $38 per share.

Van Gorkom took the position that putting Trans Union 'up for auction' through a 90-day market test would validate a decision by the Board that $55 was a fair price.[11] He told the Board that the 'free market will have an opportunity to judge whether $55 is a fair price.' Van Gorkom framed the decision before the Board not as whether $55 per share was the highest price that could be obtained, but as whether the $55 price was a fair price that the [share]holders should be given the opportunity to accept or reject.

---

[9] 'The record is not clear as to the terms of the Merger Agreement. The Agreement, as originally presented to the Board on September 20, was never produced by defendants despite demands by the plaintiffs. Nor is it clear that the directors were given an opportunity to study the Merger Agreement before voting on it. All that can be said is that [the company's outside legal advisor] had the Agreement before him during the meeting.'

[10] Necessary finance here means the loans required to purchase the shares at the $55 price.

[11] The price is tested by the market because in theory another bidder willing to pay more could still purchase the company during this period.

Attorney Brennan advised the members of the Board that they might be sued if they failed to accept the offer and that a fairness opinion[12] was not required as a matter of law. Romans attended the meeting as chief financial officer of the Company. He told the Board that he had not been involved in the negotiations with Pritzker and knew nothing about the merger proposal until the morning of the meeting; that his studies did not indicate either a fair price for the stock or a valuation of the Company; that he did not see his role as directly addressing the fairness issue; and that he and his people 'were trying to search for ways to justify a price in connection with such a [leveraged buy-out] transaction, rather than to say what the shares are worth.' Romans testified:

'I told the Board that the study ran the numbers at 50 and 60, and then the subsequent study at 55 and 65, and that was not the same thing as saying that I have a valuation of the company at X dollars. But it was a way—a first step towards—reaching that conclusion.'

Romans told the Board that, in his opinion, $55 was 'in the range of a fair price,' but 'at the beginning of the range.' Chelberg, Trans Union's President [and Chief Financial Officer], supported Van Gorkom's presentation and representations...

The Board meeting of September 20 lasted about two hours. Based solely upon Van Gorkom's oral presentation, Chelberg's supporting representations, Romans' oral statement, [outside counsel's] legal advice, and their knowledge of the market history of the Company's stock, the directors approved the proposed Merger Agreement. However, the Board later claimed to have attached two conditions to its acceptance: (1) that Trans Union reserved the right to accept any better offer that was made during the market test period; and (2) that Trans Union could share its proprietary information with any other potential bidders. While the Board now claims to have reserved the right to accept any better offer received after the announcement of the Pritzker agreement (even though the minutes of the meeting do not reflect this), it is undisputed that the Board did not reserve the right to actively solicit alternate offers.

The Merger Agreement was executed by Van Gorkom during the evening of September 20 at a formal social event that he hosted for the opening of the Chicago Lyric Opera. Neither he nor any other director read the agreement prior to its signing and delivery to Pritzker.

[After the deal was publicly announced, following internal dissent from Trans Union senior management about the terms of the offer, Van Gorkom went back to Pritzker to renegotiate the terms of the 'market check'—that is the terms upon which Trans Union could search for a better offer and talk to other potential buyers. As a result, the merger agreement was amended to allow Trans Union to actively solicit other bidders (which under the original agreement they were not allowed to do). The agreement provided that it could be terminated if Trans Union received a superior and, apart from any shareholder approvals, unconditional offer.]

Questions

1. Do you think that the directors took enough care in relation to the decision to approve the merger?

2. What facts from the case would you refer to in order to support an argument that sufficient care was or was not taken by the Trans Union directors? Consider such factors as:

   - the experience and background of the directors;
   - the questions that they asked when presented with information about the merger;
   - the fact that Pritzker was paying a substantial premium over the current Trans Union share price ($55 compared to $38.75);

---

[12] A 'fairness opinion' is an opinion of a third party—such as an investment bank—that the value offered for the shares is a 'fair value'. See generally, S.M. Davidoff, 'Fairness Opinions' (2006) 55 *American University Law Review* 1557.

- the questions that you might think should have been asked given the statements made by members of the management team (Romans, for example, said that the price of $55 was only at the beginning of the range);
- the additional information, if any, that the board members should have requested;
- the directors' existing knowledge of the company and its problems;
- the fact that the directors did not review any draft of the merger agreement;
- the time spent considering the decision;
- the fact that no third-party advisor was asked to give an opinion on whether the $55 valuation was a fair price to pay for the company;
- the fact that the price was subject to a 'market check' whereby a third party could still bid for and purchase the company;
- the effectiveness of the market check: the terms upon which the company could search for or be receptive to another possible purchaser.

3. Are any of the factors noted in 2 relevant to the executive directors such as Van Gorkom or Romans, or are they only relevant to the non-executive directors?

4. Do you think the way in which Van Gorkom behaved suggested that he felt monitored and supervised by the board of directors/subject to their authority?

3 The structure and design of a duty of care

A duty of care, whether it is in the law of torts or in the law of directors' duties, sets out a standard or a benchmark of care which the person in question, whether a driver or a director, is expected to take. The standard of care is *necessarily an objective standard*: it provides a standard by which the care that the person actually took is measured; the *standard* itself *does not* depend on what the person actually did or thought.

The fundamental problem when designing a duty of care in any context is how to set the objective standard. Imagine a continuum from *no care* to *complete care* (an imaginary level of care that could not be exceeded). A regulator's problem is where to situate the benchmark of care along this continuum and how to articulate or identify this benchmark. We are very familiar, for example, with the law of negligence which requires that when you drive your car, for example, you act with 'reasonable care'. In order to determine what amounts to reasonable care when driving the law deploys an imaginary person who is placed *hypothetically* in the *actual* circumstance of the *actual* person. The law asks how would this imaginary person have acted in these circumstances? The way in which the imaginary person would have acted sets the legal benchmark of care. If the real person took less care than the imaginary person would have taken, the real person is negligent. In the law of negligence this imaginary person is an imaginary *average or ordinary person* referred to as the 'reasonable man'; the 'man on the Clapham Omnibus' or the 'ordinarily prudent person'. In the law of torts the standard of care is determined by focusing on what the *average careful person* would have done.[13]

In some areas of life, for example crossing the road, all adults participate and, accordingly, the imaginary person who determines what amounts to reasonable care is the average or ordinary person; a person without any exceptional faculties. In different areas of life setting the standard of care by reference to an ordinary or average person may not make any sense. If we ask what is the level of care owed by a surgeon, the man on the Clapham Omnibus may not be a surgeon. The level of care for surgeons makes more sense, therefore, if it is set by an imaginary average surgeon. Similarly when we think about the reasonable everyday driver, such a driver

---

[13] S. Deakin, A. Johnston and B. Markesinis, *Markesinis and Deakin's Tort Law* (5th edn, OUP, 2003), 170.

is an average qualified driver. In these examples, most readers would view the possibility of a surgical standard of care that took account of non-surgeons or a driver
standard of care that took account of unqualified drivers as absurd. As we shall see,
such an approach may not seem quite so absurd in the context of a director's duty
of care. Importantly for the time being, however, these examples highlight for us the
point that the attributes of the imaginary person (qualified or unqualified/skilled or
unskilled) who is used to set the standard of care profoundly affects the amount of
care that the law expects a person to take.

We see in this somewhat crude analysis that the law of negligence sets the standard
of care as 'reasonable care' which means the level of care that would, hypothetically,
be provided by an average person qualified to operate in the relevant walk of life,
whether it be surgery or driving a car. We need to remind ourselves, however, that
'reasonable care' is a regulatory choice to set the level of care at a point on the continuum from *no care to complete care*. The law could, therefore, select a level of care
below reasonable care. Putting it differently, it is possible that the law could provide
that a person has taken the required *legal* degree of care even though that person
has not taken 'reasonable care': the care an imaginary average person operating in
that context would have taken. Some jurisdictions deploy the term *gross negligence*
to identify such a lower standard of care. If negligence amounts to a failure to take
reasonable care then the term gross negligence suggests a level of care less than
reasonable care; in the context of a director's duty of care, a level of care somewhat
below the care that an imaginary average director would take. Such terms are very
difficult to pin down and English courts have been resistant to using them.[14] They
remain, however, as we shall see later, an important tool in other jurisdictions' regulation of the care required of directors.

It may strike the reader as odd that any regulator would consider setting a standard of care, such as gross negligence, that is below the care which your average or
ordinary person would take. However, when thinking about the design of a standard
of care for directors we need to remind ourselves that a duty provides two functions: first, it sets an expectation of behaviour for the directors: how we ideally would
like to see them behave; and, secondly, it provides a liability standard according to
which directors may be personally liable to the company if the directors breach this
standard. As we saw in Chapter 10 when looking at the common law duty to act in
the best interests of the company, there is a tension between these two functions where
only one standard serves both functions. This tension applies to the duty of care as
well. If we set the standard too high in order to set out high care expectations then
directors who are fearful of being held liable may either refuse to serve on boards
or prefer low risk decisions if they do so. High care standards may chill risk-taking
or deter board service if directors worry that decisions that turn out badly—even
though they actually complied with the standard of care—will be viewed by judges
to be non-compliant because the judges' knowledge of the failed outcome distorts

---

[14] Several of the earlier cases on the duty of care deployed the concept of gross negligence or crassa
negligentia. See, for example, *Overend v Guerney* (1872) LR 5 HL 480; *Lagunas Nitrate Company
v Lagunas Syndicate* [1899] 2 Ch 392. Subsequent cases expressed reservations about the usefulness of this term: *In re City Equitable Fire* [1925] Ch 407. Note also in relation to the regulation of
incompetence through the 'unfitness' ground for disqualifying directors pursuant to the Company
Directors Disqualification Act 1986 (discussed further at nn 37–39 and in more detail in Chapter 18)
that the term 'gross negligence' is sometimes used as the applicable standard for the disqualification
determination—see n 39 in this regard.

their assessment of whether care was taken.[15] But if we set the standard too low to take account of these concerns the standard of expectation may actually encourage directors to take insufficient care. A low care standard designed to take account of the risk-taking and board service concerns would not reflect our care expectations of directors, which would be much higher. One option to resolve this tension would be to have different standards for the two functions: a high standard to express our care expectations, and a lower standard for liability. This is not, as we shall see, the approach that has been taken by English law.

Assignment 1

You are the regulator who has to set the standard of care for directors. Draft the standard of care that the law expects directors to meet when performing their functions. This standard of care will also be a liability standard.

II THE DUTY OF CARE AT COMMON LAW

We saw in the introduction to directors' duties in Chapter 9 that the codification of directors' duties in the Companies Act 2006 is 'based on' the existing common law rules and that, although they replace those rules, the codified directors' duties 'shall be interpreted and applied in the same way as' those pre-existing common law rules.[16] As we shall see, however, the common law position on the duty of care owed by directors was in a state of flux prior to the enactment of the new legislation. The codification of the duty of care in section 174 of the Companies Act 2006 adopted a relatively recent change of approach taken by the courts in first instance judgments. This change of approach, however, did not give due regard to and was not consistent with the weight of authority on the duty of care. We shall see that section 174 of the Act reforms the law rather than restates the law 'based on' the existing common law position. Accordingly, we divide our analysis of the duty of care at common law into two sections: *the common law position prior to the 1990s*; and *the evolution of the common law position in the 1990s*.

1 The common law position prior to the 1990s

▪ *In re Brazilian Rubber Plantations and Estates Limited* [1911] 1 Ch 425

The Brazilian Rubber Plantations Company was incorporated in order to purchase a rubber plantation in Brazil from a syndicate that owned the plantation. The company issued shares to the public to raise the finance to purchase the plantation. The **prospectus** issued in relation to the share issue contained statements that were untrue as regards the

---

[15] For more detailed analysis of standards and the chilling of risk and hindsight bias see pp 345–48. One might argue that the hindsight bias problem is less significant in relation to the assessment of process care violations than it is in relation to business judgments. With a business judgment the decision that is reviewed ex-post had an uncertain outcome at the time it was made; the decision-making process does not have an uncertain outcome and can be assessed more easily ex-post according to good practice process guidelines which apply across time. However, the hindsight problem does not disappear in relation to process because there is an intuitive appeal in connecting incompetent decisions to incompetent process. If an ex-post reviewer is more receptive to interpreting the process record as lacking care if the actual decision is viewed as incompetent, then hindsight bias affects the assessment not only of the decision but of the process that led to the decision.

[16] Section 170(3) and (4) CA 2006.

size of the plantation, the number of trees on the plantation, and the expected amount of rubber that the plantation could produce. For example, the prospectus claimed that the plantation consisted of 12,500 acres but it only consisted of 2,500, and estimated rubber production at 900,000 lbs when in the year before sale it had only been 6,000 lbs. These statements were taken from a report furnished to the directors by a member of the selling syndicate who was the original owner of an option to purchase the plantation and who had never been 'anywhere near the property, and had made up the report in London from some correct but scanty data supplied by [the original owners of the plantation] and his own imagination'. Although 'the report was fraudulent...the directors believed it to be an honest report and adopted it without inquiry'. However, before the company had paid all of the purchase money, the directors received a cable from a manager who was sent by the company to Brazil, reporting that certain of the statements contained in the original report and, therefore, the prospectus were not true. However, the cable also contained a code word which meant 'very satisfactory'; nor did the cable advise 'the directors to throw up the contract, and indeed advised them to hasten the transfer'. The directors continued with purchase and payment. Before considering the judgment note the following, almost comical, information about the qualities and experience of the Brazilian Rubber Plantations Company board.

'The directors of the company, Sir Arthur Aylmer, Bart., Henry William Tugwell, Edward Barber, and Edward Henry Hancock, were all induced to become directors by Harbord or persons acting with him in the promotion of the company. Sir Arthur Aylmer was absolutely ignorant of business. He only consented to act because he was told the office would give him a little pleasant employment without his incurring any responsibility. H. W. Tugwell was partner in a firm of bankers in a good position in Bath; he was seventy-five years of age and very deaf; he was induced to join the board by representations made to him in January, 1906. Barber was a rubber broker and was told that all he would have to do would be to give an opinion as to the value of rubber when it arrived in England. Hancock was a man of business who said he was induced to join by seeing the names of Tugwell and Barber, whom he considered good men.'

Neville J

A director's duty has been laid down as requiring him to act with such care as is reasonably to be expected from him, having regard to his knowledge and experience. He is, I think, not bound to bring any special qualifications to his office. He may undertake the management of a rubber company in complete ignorance of everything connected with rubber, without incurring responsibility for the mistakes which may result from such ignorance; while if he is acquainted with the rubber business he must give the company the advantage of his knowledge when transacting the company's business. He is not, I think, bound to take any definite part in the conduct of the company's business, but so far as he does undertake it he must use reasonable care in its despatch.

   Such reasonable care must, I think, be measured by the care an ordinary man might be expected to take in the same circumstances on his own behalf. He is clearly, I think, not responsible for damages occasioned by errors of judgment...In this case, therefore, I must consider whether the directors acted without reasonable prudence in adopting the contract on the information which they possessed. I entirely concur in the view that this must not be tested by considering what the Court itself would think reasonable. The gravamen of the charge of negligence is based upon the absence of an independent report or opinion. Now, in my opinion, men in general take a very different view of the importance of independent testimony from that obtaining in the Courts. Business men have very frequently to act on information derived from interested persons. In so doing the wise men amongst them no doubt make an allowance for exaggeration, but exaggeration and fraud are not the same thing. If the report had been merely exaggerated, there was no fear of the company making a bad bargain; there was ample margin to allow for exaggeration.

The directors did make inquiries, but they were from persons whom, it is said, they ought to have known to be interested. One of them, Webb [a leading London solicitor at the time], was a person in a position entitling his opinion and word to great weight, and though reflection would have shown the directors that he could not have been instructed to act on behalf of the company by persons independent of the promoters, I think the directors were not to be blamed for placing considerable reliance upon his assurances [the directors were apparently not aware that the information provided by Webb was based on information provided by the promoters of the syndicate]...Upon the whole I come to the conclusion that the directors believed that the contract was a beneficial one for the company, and that, notwithstanding the discrepancy in prices and the absence of an independent report, this conclusion was not arrived at by negligence on their part as directors...

Neville J's judgment in *In re Brazilian Rubber Plantations* is well known first, for its statement that you can be a director of a rubber company without knowing anything about rubber, and, second, that you can accept office as a director of a company but you do not have to turn up for board meetings. This position perhaps reflected the view held by many during this period that shareholders appointed directors and, therefore, that they themselves must take responsibility if they employed the ignorant or the incapable, as well as the view that being a non-executive director of a company was an honour bestowed on people and which in practice need not involve any substantive obligations. It restates the position set out in *In re Cardiff Savings Bank; the Re Marquis of Bute's Case*[17] where the President of the Cardiff Savings Bank was appointed at the age of six months old, turned up to only one meeting as an adult, but was not found liable for breach of duty following the failure of the bank. Jessel MR held that 'neglect or omission to attend meetings is not, in my opinion, the same thing as neglect or omission of a duty which ought to be performed at those meetings'. This position is sometimes referred to as the 'intermittent' theory of directors' duties.[18]

However, the *Brazilian Plantations* judgment has a harder edge in relation to the duty of care. Note first, that the court says *if* you turn up to meetings you must exercise 'reasonable care'. The court provides that this reasonable care is to be measured by what 'an ordinary man might be expected to take in the same circumstances on his own behalf'. That is, the benchmark of care is measured by the actions a hypothetical average person would have taken when making a decision which directly affected his own wealth. The court also makes it clear that in assessing whether reasonable care has been taken regard should be had to the directors' actual knowledge and experience. If the director is ignorant of the rubber business this would obviously be relevant. However, it is clear from Neville J's approach that being ignorant of the business would not (if you choose to get involved as a director) reduce the benchmark of care to zero. Consider this from your own perspective: if you were contemplating an investment in the rubber business, but know nothing about rubber, how careful would you be/what types of question would you ask before making the investment?

Neville J's judgment is really rather confusing. Whilst generally viewed as a very light of touch approach to directors' duties, in fact the standard of an ordinary man acting on his own behalf is potentially a very onerous standard; and one that seems at odds with the nature of a non-executive position, the part-time nature of which necessarily means that one is unlikely to be able to give to the company's business the time and attention that an owner would give it. These standards are developed further in the following case.

---

[17] [1892] Ch 100.
[18] J. Lowry and A. Digman, *Company Law* (3rd edn, OUP, 2006), 325.

■ *In re City Equitable Fire* [1925] Ch 407

The facts are stated in the judgment.

Romer J

On June 27, 1916, Gerrard Lee Bevan became a director of the City Equitable Fire Insurance Company, Ltd. The company at that time was carrying on successfully the business of reinsurance of fire and marine risks, and was in a sound financial condition. On February 14, 1922, an order was made for the winding up of the company by the Court. A searching investigation of the affairs of the company was then made, and this investigation disclosed a shortage in the funds of which the company should have been possessed of over £1,200,000. This deplorable state of affairs was in no way due to the company's trading operations as a reinsurance company. From the year 1916 onwards to February 28, 1921, which is the date of the company's last published balance sheet, there was a steady and most remarkable increase in the premium income of the company...In each of the years 1919, 1920 and 1921 there was a large and progressive trading profit. The collapse of the company was not, therefore, due to its reinsurance business. It was entirely due to the following causes. Various industrial investments of the company, of which the net cost to the company had been £701,739, have realized or are estimated to realize £202,373, representing a loss of close upon £500,000. Over £445,000 of the company's funds had been applied in acquiring an interest in certain lands in Brazil, and this interest is estimated at the present time to be worth about £100,000 only. No less a sum than £110,000 had found its way into the hands of the company's manager...and none of that money is recoverable. A sum of £385,000 odd was due from Ellis & Co., the company's brokers, of which firm Bevan was the senior partner, and against this indebtedness the company held collateral security that has realized under £31,000...Bevan himself had misappropriated other moneys of the company amounting to nearly £7000 and some £9000 had been lent by Bevan or Ellis & Co to a company known as the Saskatoon Grain Company without any authority whatever. Little, if anything, will ever be recovered in respect of these two sums. Nearly the whole of these enormous losses were brought about through Bevan's instrumentality, and a large part of them by his deliberate fraud.

For that fraud he has been tried, and convicted, and is now suffering the just penalty. But the question not unnaturally arises as to whether, during the period covered by Bevan's nefarious activities, the other directors...of the company were properly discharging the duties that they owed to the [company]. The Official Receiver, as the liquidator of the company, alleges that they were not...Whilst admitting, and rightly admitting, that they have acted honestly throughout, he claims that they have been guilty of such negligence as to render themselves liable to the company in damages. Whether they are, or are not so liable, is the question that I have to determine...But before investigating the facts it will be convenient to consider the law applicable to the case...

In order, therefore, to ascertain the duties that a person appointed to the board of an established company undertakes to perform, it is necessary to consider not only the nature of the company's business, but also the manner in which the work of the company is in fact distributed between the directors and the other officials of the company, provided always that this distribution is a reasonable one in the circumstances, and is not inconsistent with any express provisions of the articles of association. In discharging the duties of his position thus ascertained a director must, of course, act honestly; but he must also exercise some degree of both skill and diligence. To the question of what is the particular degree of skill and diligence required of him, the authorities do not, I think, give any very clear answer...The care that he is bound to take has been described by Neville J. in...[*In re Brazilian Plantations*] as 'reasonable care' to be measured by the care an ordinary man might be expected to take in the circumstances on his own behalf. In saying this Neville J. was only following what was laid down in *Overend & Gurney Co. v. Gibb* as being the proper test to apply, namely: 'Whether or not the directors exceeded the powers entrusted to them, or whether if they did not so exceed their powers they were cognisant of circumstances of such a character, so plain, so manifest, and so simple of appreciation, that no men with any ordinary degree of prudence, acting on their own behalf, would have entered into such a transaction as they entered into?'

There are, in addition, one or two other general propositions that seem to be warranted by the reported cases: a director need not exhibit in the performance of his duties a greater degree of skill than may reasonably be expected from a person of his knowledge and experience. (1) A director of a life insurance company, for instance, does not guarantee that he has the skill of an actuary or of a physician. In the words of Lindley M.R.: 'If directors act within their powers, if they act with such care as is reasonably to be expected from them, having regard to their knowledge and experience, and if they act honestly for the benefit of the company they represent, they discharge both their equitable as well as their legal duty to the company': see *Lagunas Nitrate Co. v. Lagunas Syndicate*. It is perhaps only another way of stating the same proposition to say that directors are not liable for mere errors of judgment. (2) A director is not bound to give continuous attention to the affairs of his company. His duties are of an intermittent nature to be performed at periodical board meetings, and at meetings of any committee of the board upon which he happens to be placed. He is not, however, bound to attend all such meetings, though he ought to attend whenever, in the circumstances, he is reasonably able to do so...

These are the general principles that I shall endeavour to apply in considering the question whether the directors of this company have been guilty of negligence.

[Applying this standard the court found that several directors had breached their duty of care; however, the articles of association of the company contained a provision relieving directors for liability for negligence—such provisions, as we shall see later in the chapter (pp 450–451) are no longer enforceable.]

In Re City Equitable Fire is a pivotal case in the evolution of the duty of care in English law. Prior the 1990s it was widely viewed and cited as the leading case. It is pivotal because it offers two alternative directions for the duty of care, the first of which simply restates the position in *Brazilian Plantations*: the level of care required is *reasonable care which is measured by the care an ordinary man might be expected to take in the circumstances on his own behalf.* Romer J correctly attributes this position to the earlier House of Lords case of *Overend v Guerney*.[19] In *Overend v Guerney* Lord Hatherley LC held:

I should like to say one word as regards the case of *Turquand* and *Marshall*, which was cited by Sir *Roundell Palmer* yesterday, and referred to by Mr. *Cotton* this morning [*Turquand v Marshall* was an earlier case presided over by Hatherley LC]. I certainly never intended to lay down the strong proposition that a person acting for another as his agent is not bound to use *all the ordinary prudence that can be properly and legitimately expected from any person in the conduct of the affairs of the world, namely, the same amount of prudence which, in the same circumstances, he would exercise on his own behalf.* What I did intend to state in that case was, that I could not measure —and I think it would be a very fatal error in the verdict of any Court of Justice to attempt to measure—the amount of prudence that ought to be exercised by the amount of prudence which the judge himself might think, under similar circumstances, he should have exercised. I think it extremely likely that many a judge, or many a person versed by long experience in the affairs of mankind, as conducted in the mercantile world, will know that there is a great deal more trust, a great deal more speculation, and a great deal more readiness to confide in the probabilities of things, with regard to success in mercantile transactions, than there is on the part of those whose habits of life are entirely of a different character. It would be extremely wrong to import into the consideration of the case of a person acting as a mercantile agent in the purchase of a business concern, those principles of extreme caution which might dictate the course of one who is not at all inclined to invest his property in any ventures of such a hazardous character…Men were chosen by the company as their directors, to act on their behalf in the same manner as they would have acted on their own behalf as men of the world, and accustomed to business, and accustomed to speculation, and having a knowledge of business of this character. [Emphasis added]

Lord Hatherley states that the standard of care is the ordinary man acting on his own behalf although he warns the judiciary not to set the standard of care as the care that a risk-averse judge or lawyer would take in the circumstances in question. Lord Hatherley's ordinary man is therefore *an ordinary man* operating in the business world—a person who is willing to take risks in the face of uncertainty and to act based upon probabilities, even when more information and inquiry would reduce uncertainty. His analysis of the required level of care contains a plea to judges—who personally may be less used to taking risks in the face of uncertainty—to ensure that they do not put themselves in the shoes of the director; rather they must imagine an ordinary person acting in the business world on his own behalf. Nevertheless, even making allowance for the practices of the business world, the standard of what an ordinary man acting on his own behalf would do is potentially a demanding one. The possibility of losing one's money focuses the mind, even of the unskilled and inexperienced risk-taker.

Although Lord Hatherley does not directly consider the skill set of the 'ordinary man', his plea to other judges to take account of the context of business arguably suggests that the hypothetical person of the *ordinary man acting on his own behalf standard* is the ordinary man of business: an average business person. However, in *Brazilian Plantations* and *In re City Equitable Fire*, as well as some earlier cases,[20] the courts stress that the expectation that the law has of a director are formed by that director's actual 'knowledge and experience'. Both *Brazilian Plantations* and *In re City Equitable Life* consider the skills and experience of the director separately from the statement of the ordinary man acting on his own behalf standard of care. For Neville J a director's duty 'is to act with such care as is reasonably to be expected of him, having regard to his knowledge and experience'; he then proceeds to refer to the level of care as 'reasonable care' which is determined through reference to the ordinary man acting on his own behalf. Romer J states the *ordinary man acting on his own behalf* standard of care and then proceeds to state 'one or two other general propositions'. These include, most importantly, 'that a director need not exhibit in the performance of his duties a greater degree of skill than may reasonably be expected from a person of his knowledge and experience'.

The question for students of the pre-2006 directors' duty of care is: what is the interrelationship between the standard of care of the ordinary man acting on his own behalf and Romer J's general proposition about the skills of the director? What has tended to happen in much contemporary commentary is that the objective standard has tended to fade into the background as commentators focused on the general proposition about the directors' skills, which was often referred to as the 'subjective standard'.[21] That is, commentators referred to the duty of care by reference only to the general proposition about what can reasonably be expected in light of the skills and experience of

[20] *Lagunas Nitrate Company v Lagunas Syndicate* [1899] 2 Ch 392.

[21] Note, however, that the objective standard has not been wholly forgotten in the modern case law. See *Lexi Holdings (in administration) v Lugman* [2008] EWHC 1639 where Briggs J, having set forth the modern standard articulated in *D'Jan*, which we consider later in the chapter, observed that: 'to that analysis may be added the principle, established for example in *Re City Equitable Fire Insurance Company Limited* that, because of the essentially fiduciary nature of the office, a director is expected to apply to the management and custodianship of the company's property that same degree of care as she might reasonably be expected to apply in the management and custodianship of her own property'. Interestingly, Briggs J seems to infer that this principle continues to be applicable post-2006 Act.

the director.[22] For these commentators the standard of care was a reasonable director imbued only with the actual knowledge and experience of the actual director. Consider for example the following statement from the Law Commission:

■ The Law Commission and the Scottish Law Commission, *Company Directors: Regulating Conflicts of Interest and Formulating a Statement of Duties* (Law Com No 261)

> One option for a statutory statement of a director's duty of care was for a director to owe a duty to his company to exercise the care, diligence and skill that would be exercised by a reasonable person having his knowledge and experience. This is effectively the traditional view of the standard of care. (*In re City Equitable Fire* was cited in support of this proposition about the traditional view.)

Naturally this led to the impression that there was no floor or baseline of care required of a director who was wholly incapable: with no skills and experience. This subjective standard was often referred to as the standard of the 'amiable lunatic': you cannot expect very much of a reasonable lunatic. Of course, if the director in question was highly skilled then the standard of care would be a high one. Nevertheless, this impression that the law provided no baseline—no minimum—standard of care was instrumental in driving calls for reform. However, the analysis of the cases set out above questions such an understanding of the earlier cases. The cases did provide such a baseline: the ordinary man acting on his own behalf. In this regard, consider also the following commentary from Professor Hicks.

■ Andrew Hicks, 'Directors' Liabilities for Management Errors' (1994) 110 *Law Quarterly Review* 390

> City Equitable has perhaps been misrepresented by writers over-stressing the quaint subjective standard of the 'amiable lunatic'. If the lengthy judgment rather than the headnote is actually read, substantial objective elements are clearly apparent. Romer J. accepted as the primary test that of Neville J. in *Re Brazilian Rubber Plantations and Estates Ltd.* The necessary standard is that of ' "reasonable care" to be measured by the care an ordinary man ought to be expected to take in the circumstances on his own behalf', (i.e., running his own business affairs). Romer J.'s well known three propositions were expressed to be 'in addition' to this basic objective test. The first proposition is the subjective one that 'a director need not exhibit in the performance of his duties a greater degree of skill than may reasonably be expected from a person of his knowledge or experience'. This has been taken to mean that if the members appoint a half-wit as a director, he may only be judged by what one can reasonably expect of a half-wit. However the next sentence of the judgment qualifies the subjective test with the words 'A director of a life insurance company, for instance, does not guarantee that he has the skill of an actuary or of a physician'. This example indicates that the subjective test of skill does not allow the standard of care to be reduced to the level of the half-wit. Romer J. was setting out a dual standard, first the minimum and irreducible objective standard of the reasonable care of the ordinary man acting on his own behalf; and secondly, the subjective test that relieves him if he does not have highly specialised expertise. Romer J.'s subjective test is not intended to reduce the standard of care below that of the reasonable ordinary businessman. It relieves the director if he is not an actuary or a physician or an expert in offshore tax avoidance, but presumably holds him to that higher standard if he was appointed as having that expertise. This interpretation is wholly borne out by Romer J.'s

---

[22] See, for example, P. Davies, *Gower and Davies' Modern Principles of Company Law* (7th edn, Sweet & Maxwell, 2003), 389.

treatment of the actual allegations of negligence which, throughout the judgment, he deals with on the assumption of objective irreducible standards of proper management. Such a conclusion suggests that City Equitable has been widely misread.

There are three ways of interpreting the interaction of the *ordinary man acting on his own behalf* standard and Romer J's general proposition about a director's degree of skill and his actual knowledge and experience. They are as follows:

- The first reading set out by Professor Hick in this extract suggests that the ordinary man standard sets a baseline of the reasonable ordinary business person and that the general proposition makes it clear that if you do not have specific skills and experience you will not be held to a higher standard of someone who has those skills.

- The second option is to view the attributes of the *ordinary man acting on his own behalf* as qualified by the attributes of the actual director—his knowledge and experience. Importantly, however, as noted, this does not reduce the standard to one of *no care* if the director has no knowledge and experience as uninformed and unskilled people *acting on their own behalf* may be expected to take considerable care. For this author, this second reading appears to have the benefits of both logic and fidelity to the test used by the cases.

- A third option is that the standard of the ordinary man acting on his own behalf and the general proposition about the degree of skill refer to two separate duties; a duty of care and a duty of skill. Indeed, with regard to the *ordinary man acting on his own behalf* standard Romer J refers to the amount of 'care' the law expects the director to take. However, when he considers the 'knowledge and experience of the directors' he refers to 'skill' rather than 'care'. This view does not receive support from the case itself where Romer J uses the terms 'care' and 'skill' and 'diligence' interchangeably. Romer J answers the question: 'what is the particular degree of skill and diligence required of him' by referring to the standard of care of the ordinary man acting on his own behalf. Neville J in *Brazilian Plantations* refers to the *duty of care* when he uses the same phrase adopted by Romer J about what can be 'reasonably expected from him, having regard to his knowledge and experience'. The terms skill and care are interchangeable for Romer J and are concerned with the same issue: how careful does the law expect directors to be when they act; the knowledge and experience of the director is deemed relevant to determining the level of care. In this regard consider the following case.

■ *Dorchester Finance v Stebbing* [1989] BCLC 498 (1977 case reported in 1989)

Dorchester Finance Co Ltd (Dorchester) was incorporated in 1966 and carried on the business as a money lender and had a money lenders licence pursuant to the Moneylenders Act 1900. Dorchester carried out very little business until it was taken over by Robert Fielding Ltd (Fielding) in 1972. Thereafter, Dorchester was able to draw on the cash reserves of Fielding to fund its activities. The company had three directors: Stebbing, Hamilton, and Parsons. Stebbing was involved in the operational aspects of the money-lending business; Hamilton and Parsons were non-executive directors. The company required two signatures on any cheques. Hamilton and Parsons signed blank cheques. Using these blank cheques Stebbings lent money to several companies and individuals, several of which were controlled by or connected to him. No security was taken in relation to the majority of the loans and several of the loans failed resulting in considerable losses for Dorchester. The company brought an action against the directors for breach of their duty of care and skill. The court was asked to consider whether in signing the blank cheques the directors were in breach of their duty of care.

Foster J

For the plaintiffs three main submissions were made in regard to the duties of the directors. a) A director is required to exhibit in performance of his duties such a degree of skill as may reasonably be expected from a person with his knowledge and experience. b) A director is required to take in the performance of his duties such care as an ordinary man might be expected to take on his own behalf. c) A director must exercise any power vested in him as such honesty, in good faith and in the interests of the company and reliance was placed on *Re City Equitable Fire Insurance Co Ltd* [1925] Ch 407, [1924] All ER Rep 485, *Re Sharpe* [1892] 1 Ch 154, and *Re Smith & Fawcett Ltd* [1942] 1 All ER 542, [1942] Ch 304...

I accept the plaintiffs' three submissions as accurately stating the law applicable, and counsel for the first defendant conceded that I could take into account the fact that of the three directors two are chartered accountants and the third has considerable experience of accountancy.

Hamilton's evidence

Although he has no qualifications as an accountant he said that he trained as one and worked for some 14 years for the Ministry of Health on the audit of the books of regional hospital boards, and as a deputy finance officer of a regional hospital board controlling 12 hospitals. He then worked as a trust officer with Lloyds Bank and was responsible for some £9m worth of investments. Later he went to Jersey and became secretary and later general manager of a merchant bank there. In 1970 he started his own business there, through a company called Offshore Management Ltd. There were other companies which he formed which all became subsidiaries of Interaid Investment Consultants Ltd, which on 31 May 1972 became a wholly-owned subsidiary of Fielding. He freely admitted in his statement that he was negligent in certain particulars but wished to explain the circumstances. He said that he was fully employed in Jersey and during the period from 1 June 1972 to 31 December 1973 he visited the offices of Dorchester on 49 occasions only. He admitted that he signed blank cheques as a director of Dorchester but could not remember how many. However, five cheques dated in August and September 1973 were produced to him and he admitted signing them in blank. In his statement he says this:

'As they required the additional signature of either Mr Stebbing or Mr Parsons, both chartered accountants, the former being chairman, the latter, from 1 April 1973, managing director of the [Dorchester's ultimate parent company], both of whom had substantial personal interests in seeing that [the parent company] prospered, I considered this to be a reasonable thing to do.'

He also relied on the fact that the accounts for the years ending 31 July 1972 and 1973 had received an unqualified certificate from the auditors. Apart from the signing of the blank cheques, he did not consider that he had acted in an improper manner as a non-executive director of Dorchester...But he admitted that there had never been a board meeting of the directors of Dorchester, that he did not know whether Dorchester kept proper books of account or not, and he was not involved in the purpose of the various loans made by Dorchester. In his own words, 'I let Mr Stebbing have absolute control. He could dispose of money as he liked.'

Parsons' evidence

He became a chartered accountant in 1958 and in June 1967 became a partner with Stebbing and Mr Armstrong in the accountancy firm of Stebbing & Co. He was a director of Dorchester from 21 April 1972 until 21 February...[He] now carries on practice as a chartered accountant from his home address in Surrey. In his statement he says this:

'As I was very rarely at head office, a secretary would sometimes ask me to sign cheques in blank so that payments could be made whilst I was away and this I willingly did, assuming that they were used to pay expenses.'

When shown the five cheques, he admitted that when he added his signature on all five in addition to Mr Hamilton's signature the cheques were still blank. In his statement he further says: 'I think that a non-executive Director is entitled to rely on the auditors as I see no point in having auditors in the first place', and adds:

> 'My Directorship of Dorchester, like Mr Hamilton's was purely non-executive. No board meetings were ever held, as is the case in the vast majority of wholly-owned subsidiaries in groups in this country. Under the circumstances I have outlined, I do not believe I have acted negligently.'

He admitted knowing that it was the intention of Dorchester to use the cash of Fielding but had no knowledge of the loans made by Dorchester and never took part in its business at all...

Conclusion

For a chartered accountant and an experienced accountant to put forward the proposition that a non-executive director has no duties to perform I find quite alarming...The signing of blank cheques by Hamilton and Parsons was in my judgment negligent, as it allowed Stebbing to do as he pleased. Apart from that they not only failed to exhibit the necessary skill and care in the performance of their duties as directors, but also failed to perform any duty at all as directors of Dorchester.

   In the absence of any oral evidence by Stebbing, the documents must speak for themselves. They show clearly that Stebbing as a director of Dorchester failed to exercise any skill or care in the performance of his duty as a director and that he knowingly and recklessly misapplied the assets of Dorchester to the extent of nearly £400,000. His negligence can only be described as gross negligence and he also is liable for damages.

Foster J appears to view the two duties of skill and care separately. This does not, however, indicate a development of the case law in the direction of two separate duties. Foster J's statement of the law is faithful to *In re City Equitable Fire* which, as we have seen, deploys the terms 'skill' and 'care' interchangeably.

Note also the courts holding that the directors 'failed to perform any duty'. In *Brazilian Plantations* we saw the court articulate the intermittent theory of directors' duties: the duties apply only if you turn up to the board meetings. In *Dorchester Finance* the court's holding makes it clear that once a director is appointed doing nothing is no longer a defence to an alleged breach of the duty of care. This view is reinforced by Lord Woolf MR in *Re Westmid Packing Services Ltd*,[23] a case brought under the Company Directors' Disqualification Act 1986,[24] where his Lordship held that 'it is of the greatest importance that any individual who undertakes the statutory and fiduciary obligations of being a company director should realize that these are *inescapable* personal responsibilities' (emphasis added). See further in this regard the abstract from *Re Barings Plc and others (No 5), Secretary of State for Trade and Industry v Baker*.[25]

Assignment 2

Based upon the cases previously set out draft a codification of the duty of care in English law.

Questions

1. What is a duty of care designed to do?

2. Does a duty of care regulate the decision that is reached or the process involved in reaching the decision?

3. Is the author of this book correct when he says the duty of care is necessarily an objective standard?

4. Do you think the duty of care set out in the cases provides for a weak or a strong standard of care?

---

[23] [1998] 2 All ER 124.   [24] See nn 37–39.
[25] [1999] 1 BCLC 433 (p 437). See also *Bishopsgate Investment Management Ltd (in liq) v Maxwell (No 2)* [1993] BCLC 1282.

5. Professor Ferran argues that 'the problem with a duty formulated in the *Re City Equitable* decision is simple and obvious: incompetence is its own defence'.[26] Do you agree?

6. Do you think the standard of care set out in *Brazilian Plantation* and *Re City Equitable Fire* is the same as that set out by Lord Hatherley in *Overend & Guerney*?

7. What do you think is the best way of making sense of the relationship between the ordinary man acting on his own behalf standard and Romer J's general proposition about the knowledge and experience of the actual director?

2 The evolution of the common law position in the 1990s

Section 214 of the Insolvency Act 1986 introduced into UK law the offence of *wrongful trading*. Section 214 is a creditor protection provision designed to ensure that directors consider creditors' interests as a company approaches insolvency. We will address this provision in detail in Chapter 18. In order to determine whether a director has complied with section 214 and, therefore, to determine whether or not committed an offence of wrongful trading, the Act provides that the director's actions must not fall below what would be expected of a *reasonably diligent director*. The Insolvency Act 1986 specifies the attributes such a *reasonably diligent director* is deemed to have in objective and subjective terms. Pursuant to section 214(4), the *reasonably diligent director* is deemed to have both:

(1) the general knowledge, skill, and experience that may reasonably be expected of a person carrying out the same functions as are carried out by that director in relation to the company; *and*

(2) the general knowledge, skill, and experience that that director has.

It is clear from the legislative history of section 214 that it was never intended that this standard should have any effect on the general duty of care which is the subject of analysis in this chapter. Nevertheless, the existence of this standard emboldened the judiciary, in particular Lord Hoffmann, to consider whether the general duty of care should be stated in terms similar to those set out in the wrongful trading provision.

■ *Re D'Jan of London Limited* [1993] BCC 646 (Hoffmann LJ sitting in the Chancery Division; Companies Court)

Hoffmann LJ
The liquidator alleges that the respondent Mr D'Jan was negligent in completing and signing a proposal form for fire insurance with the Guardian Royal Exchange Assurances plc. As a result, the insurers repudiated liability for a fire at the company's premises in Cornwall which had destroyed stock said to be worth some £174,000. The company is insolvent, having a deficiency as regards unsecured creditors of about £500,000. The liquidator therefore brings these proceedings for the benefit of the unsecured creditors.

Mr D'Jan signed the insurance proposal on 18 September 1986. It was headed 'Business insurances proposal'. Mr D'Jan signed on the front page, under the words:

'I declare that to the best of my knowledge and belief all the statements and particulars made with regard to this proposal are true and I agree that this proposal shall be the basis of a contract of insurance to be expressed in the usual terms of the policy issued by Guardian Royal Exchange Assurances plc.'

On the same page the form required certain information to be filled in and also asked three specific questions, including:

'7. Have you or any director or partner...been director of any company which went into liquidation...?'

---

[26] E. Ferran, *Company Law and Corporate Finance* (OUP, 2009), 213.

The question was answered 'No'. Mr D'Jan admits that this was wrong. In the previous year, a company called Harleyshield Ltd, of which Mr D'Jan was a director, had gone into insolvent liquidation. And there had been a couple of other insolvencies about five years earlier. The liquidator says that Mr D'Jan gave a wrong answer to another question as well, but as this involves construing the rather obscure language in which the question is phrased and as Mr Russen, who appeared for Mr D'Jan, realistically accepts that the wrong answer to question 7 was enough to entitle the insurers to repudiate, I need not say more about the other question.

Mr D'Jan says he realises—perhaps more clearly now than he did at the time—the importance of giving correct answers on insurance proposals. But he says that he did not fill in the form himself or read it before he signed. It was filled in by his insurance broker, Tarik Shenyuz, who had been handling his personal and corporate insurance affairs for about five years. Mr D'Jan says that Mr Shenyuz had demonstrated his competence by obtaining good rates and recommending him to loss adjusters who had obtained satisfactory settlements on his claims. So he trusted Mr Shenyuz to fill in the form correctly.

Mr Shenyuz flatly contradicted this account of how the form came to be signed. He says that he simply delivered the form to Mr D'Jan's premises and took it away again, acting as no more than a messenger between the company and the firm of insurance brokers in Surrey for whom he was at the time acting as subagent. He says that Mr D'Jan's accountant Mr Ekrem was well versed in insurance matters and that the company would have needed no help in filling out the form.

Both Mr D'Jan and Mr Shenyuz are highly intelligent men who gave their evidence with confidence and the conflict is not easy to resolve. But I prefer the evidence of Mr D'Jan. He did not strike me as a man who would fill in his own forms. I think he would have wanted Mr Shenyuz to earn his commission by attending to these matters and I accept that he signed in the expectation that Mr Shenyuz would have completed the form correctly.

Nevertheless I think that in failing even to read the form, Mr D'Jan was negligent. Mr Russen said that the standard of care which directors owe to their companies is not very exacting and signing forms without reading them is something a busy director might reasonably do. I accept that in real life, this often happens. But that does not mean that it is not negligent. People often take risks in circumstances in which it was not necessary or reasonable to do so. If the risk materialises, they may have to pay a penalty. I do not say that a director must always read the whole of every document which he signs. If he signs an agreement running to 60 pages of turgid legal prose on the assurance of his solicitor that it accurately reflects the board's instructions, he may well be excused from reading it all himself. But this was an extremely simple document asking a few questions which Mr D'Jan was the best person to answer. By signing the form, he accepted that he was the person who should take responsibility for its contents. In my view, the duty of care owed by a director at common law is accurately stated in sec. 214(4) of the Insolvency Act 1986...

Both on the objective test [214(4)(a)] and, having seen Mr D'Jan, on the subjective test [214(4) (b)], I think that he did not show reasonable diligence when he signed the form. He was therefore in breach of his duty to the company...

It follows that Mr D'Jan is in principle liable to compensate the company for his breach of duty. But sec. 727 of the Companies Act 1985[27] gives the court a discretionary power to relieve a director wholly or in part from liability for breaches of duty, including negligence, if the court considers that he acted honestly and reasonably and ought fairly to be excused. It may seem odd that a person found to have been guilty of negligence, which involves failing to take reasonable care, can ever satisfy a court that he acted reasonably. Nevertheless, the section clearly contemplates that he may do so and it follows that conduct may be reasonable for the purposes of sec. 727 despite amounting to lack of reasonable care at common law...

It is relevant to the exercise of the discretion under sec. 727. It may be reasonable to take a risk in relation to your own money which would be unreasonable in relation to someone else's.

---

[27] This is now section 1157 Companies Act 2006. This section is considered in Part IV of this chapter.

And although for the purposes of the law of negligence the company is a separate entity to which Mr D'Jan owes a duty of care which cannot vary according to the number of shares he owns, I think that the economic realities of the case can be taken into account in exercising the discretion under sec. 727. His breach of duty in failing to read the form before signing was not gross. It was the kind of thing which could happen to any busy man, although, as I have said, this is not enough to excuse it. But I think it is also relevant that in 1986, with the company solvent and indeed prosperous, the only persons whose interests he was foreseeably putting at risk by not reading the form were himself and his wife. Mr D'Jan certainly acted honestly. For the purposes of sec. 727 I think he acted reasonably and I think he ought fairly to be excused for some, though not all, of the liability which he would otherwise have incurred. Mr D'Jan has proved as an unsecured creditor in the sum of £102,913. He has been paid an interim dividend of 40p in the pound and the liquidator has paid a further dividend of 20p but withheld payment to Mr D'Jan pending the resolution of these proceedings. In my view, having been responsible for the additional shortfall in respect of unsecured creditors, I do not think that he should be allowed any further participation in competition with ordinary trade creditors. On the other hand, I do not think it would be fair to ask him to return what he has received or make a further contribution out of his own pocket to the company's assets. I therefore declare that Mr D'Jan is liable to compensate the company for the loss caused by his breach of duty in an amount not exceeding any unpaid dividends to which he would otherwise be entitled as an unsecured creditor.

Lord Hoffmann holds that the duty of care at common law is correctly stated in section 214(4) of the Insolvency Act 1986. Importantly, he is not saying that section 214 addresses the general duty of care; rather he is saying that the general duty of care is identical to the formulation in section 214(4). He does not, however, offer any authority or legislative history in support of this proposition.[28] He does not refer to any authority or discuss whether or not such earlier authority is consistent with this holding. Note that subsequent case law has followed this approach.[29]

Assignment 3

You are asked to write a judgment showing that Hoffmann LJ's holding that the duty of care at common law is consistent with a duty of care set out in the terms of section 214(4) of the Insolvency Act 1986. Prepare your best case to support such a position. Do not read the questions and discussion below before completing this assignment.

Questions and discussion

- Following your work for Assignment 3, do you think that Hoffmann LJ's decision in *Re D'Jan* is consistent with the previous cases discussed in this chapter? If the pre-*D'Jan* standard of care was simply the reasonable man imbued with the *actual* knowledge and experience of the *actual* director, then clearly *Re D'Jan* represents a departure as, following the section 214 articulation of the standard, the hypothetical director would be imbued with at least the knowledge, skill, and experience attributes of an average director. That is, the test set forth in *Re D'Jan* sets a baseline benchmark of

---

[28] Hoffmann J (as he then was) made a similar holding in *Norman v Theodore Goddard* [1992] BCC 14. In that case some of the previous authorities were referred to, however, only in relation to their findings of fact. As in *Re D'Jan*, Hoffmann J did not consider in detail whether such a position is consistent with earlier authorities.

[29] *Equitable Life Assurance Society v Bowley* [2003] EWHC 2263.

the reasonable care that would have been taken by a hypothetical average director. If, however, we reject that 'subjective' articulation of the pre-*D'Jan* standard as a clear misreading of the cases and take as a point of comparison the *ordinary man acting on his own behalf* standard then the analysis becomes more difficult. The *D'Jan* standard is clearly a departure, in form at least, from the *ordinary man* approach as it relies on the reasonable director acting as a director. However, if, as has been argued by this author, the *ordinary man acting on his own behalf* standard represents a demanding, objective standard of care then it is very difficult to say whether the approach in *Re D'Jan* represents a departure from the pre-1990 standard. Indeed from Professor Hicks' point of view the pre-1990 case law provided for a baseline reasonable ordinary business person standard and for a higher standard if a 'person was appointed as having [additional] expertise'.

- Is Professor Hicks reading section 214 into the pre-1990 case law? Do the cases support his reading?

- Applying the law in *Re D'Jan* do you think it was unreasonable for Mr D'Jan not to fill out the form himself?

- If Hoffmann LJ had applied the standard of the ordinary man acting on his own behalf, do you think the outcome would have been different?

- Hoffmann LJ's imaginary director, which determines the benchmark of care by which the actual director's actions are measured, consists of both the average reasonable director and, where the actual director has additional skills, knowledge, and experience, this imaginary director is also imbued with such additional skills, knowledge, and experience. Where the actual director does not have the skills, knowledge, and experience of the average director the legal expectation of care is likely to be higher than the actual director is capable of providing. From one point of view this is surely a good thing: such a duty of care deters individuals who do not have, or doubt that they have, the skill set necessary to do the job well. Are there, however, any negative effects for companies with regard to attracting talent to serve on the board? Would, for example, a successful retired Formula 1 driver with no business experience be capable of complying with this standard if asked to serve on the board of a Formula 1 company? Are there good reasons for a Formula 1 company to recruit the retired driver to the board?

- A common justification for considering the actual director's knowledge and experience in determining the standard of care was that shareholders only had themselves to blame if they appointed someone with limited knowledge and experience. Why do you think that this justification was viewed as inadequate?

- Several years after the decision in *Re D'Jan* Lord Hoffmann, giving the Fourth Annual Leonard Sainer Lecture, suggested that he had some misgivings about tightening the duty of care standard and, therefore, indirectly, about *Re D'Jan* itself—to the extent that we view it as a tightening of the standard ([1997] 18 *The Company Lawyer* 194). He noted that 'it seems to me by no means clear that corporate efficiency would be improved by tightening up the *Brazilian Rubber Plantations* standard...It would if anything be likely to discourage people from accepting office. The position of a non-executive director pitted against the executives with their superior access to information and familiarity with corporate culture is, when push comes to shove, difficult enough at the best of times. I do not think that the standard of people accepting such positions would be improved by the thought that they were likely to be sued for damages for failing to take sufficient action. On the contrary, I think it would be likely to make non-executives, as a self-defensive move, less trusting and more likely to intervene than they are at present which may well be a wasteful addition to the costs of corporate decision making.' Do you agree with Lord Hoffmann's sentiments in this regard?

3 Monitoring and reliance on management and employees

3.1 What does monitoring entail?

As discussed in Chapter 7, boards of both small and large companies necessarily delegate power to full-time management, who in turn delegate power to junior management and employees. Directors subject to a duty of care must take the requisite degree of care in the delegation of this power. But what is involved in taking such care? There are three elements of the directors' role in this regard that we need to consider.

- First, what does the duty of care require of directors in relation to the risks that arise as a result of the delegation and diffusion of power throughout the company? Corporate activity necessarily entails risks; without such risks there is unlikely to be any return. However, risks taken need to be commensurate with returns: a company that produces computers can never provide a 100% guarantee that its computers will never injure anyone, but it needs to ensure that it does not cut corners with the safety of the product. If it does so, it may be able to sell computers more cheaply in the short run but is likely in the long run to develop a reputation for unsafe and unreliable computers which could destroy the company. An oil company that cuts corners with health and safety—or fails to comply with health and safety regulation—on its drilling platforms may, if this results in employee injuries or oil spills, find itself subject to huge damage claims as well as a reputation as a polluter that could cause customers to buy petrol from its competitors. A salesman in a financial services firm may mislead customers in order to increase sales and the commissions from those sales; but in doing so the firm breaches regulations on treating customers fairly[30] and exposes the firm to reputational damage.

    In large companies neither boards nor senior management can manage these risks on a day to day basis—these risks are an unavoidable part of the delegation and diffusion of corporate power from the board. The question for a board of directors—both non-executive and executive directors—is whether the company has adequate systems and controls in place through which corporate power is exercised and the company's business is carried out in order to manage these risks effectively; or at least to reduce the probability that serious risks will materialize. Such systems are referred to as 'internal control systems' and consist of internal procedures and processes that: ensure compliance with regulation and company policies; provide a means of assessing and reporting on the risks affecting the company's operations; and provide for the production of reliable information about the company's operations and activities.

    The duty of care will apply to the consideration given by directors to the need for, and the design and implementation of, such systems and controls. Indeed, one of the most important decisions a board will make is to approve the company's internal control systems and to ensure that the effectiveness of such systems are kept under review. In the United States, where litigation for breach of duty is more prevalent than in the UK, recent high profile events, including the ongoing financial crisis and the BP Deepwater Horizon disaster, have generated many duty of care claims that focus, amongst others, on the board of directors' failings to put in place effective internal controls to ensure compliance with regulations and the management of serious risks.[31] For example, a recent action brought against Citibank, one of the US's largest banks, claims that the directors failed 'to assure that adequate and proper corporate information and reporting systems existed that would have enabled them to be fully

---

[30] See generally, *Treating Customers Fairly—Towards Fair Outcomes for Consumers* (FSA, 2006).
[31] *In re BP Shareholder Derivative Action* (Shareholder Derivative Complaint) (United States District Court Southern District of Texas Court Case No. 4:10-cv-03447 (available at: www.blbglaw.com/cases/00160_data/BPDefendantsReply 👈)).

informed regarding Citibank's risk to the subprime mortgage market'.[32] Whilst, as
we shall see later in this chapter, the legal regime in the United States is very different
from that in the UK, the application of the duty of care to internal control failings
which the US cases highlight is also very relevant for UK companies.

As different companies face different risks and different regulatory regimes, a
system of controls must be designed for that company. To understand whether such
internal controls are fit for purpose will require a deep operational understanding of
the company's business. Whilst we may expect executive directors to have such an
understanding and to take an active role in the design and implementation of such
controls, can we realistically expect much of part time non-executive directors, even
those directors with industry expertise? Can we expect much more of those directors
than simply ensuring that the company has a system of controls and that there are
procedures in place to review the effectiveness of such controls? Can we expect anything more than is recommended by Provision C.2.1 of the UK Corporate Governance
Code, which provides that:

> The board should, at least annually, conduct a review of the effectiveness of the group's system of
> internal controls and should report to shareholders that they have done so. The review should cover
> all material controls, including financial, operational and compliance controls and risk management
> systems.

- Secondly, directors who delegate power must monitor the exercise of that power by
  senior management. But what is required of the board in this regard in order to comply
  with their duty of care? Are they required to do anything more than review the performance of the senior management and look towards replacing them if dissatisfied?
  When it comes to the monitoring of delegated power by the executive directors clearly
  the board is reliant on the non-executive directors. But how much actual monitoring
  and attention can the duty of care expect of part-time directors who attend board
  meetings no more, on average, than once a month?

- Thirdly, to what extent can directors rely on what they are told by executive directors
  and managers and to what extent can they rely on information that is the product of
  internal control systems that they themselves have considered and approved? Does
  a director comply with his duty of care if, in the absence of any suspicion or red
  flags, he simply accepts the validity of such information and does not inquire any
  further?

3.2 A duty to monitor?

In the context of the duty of care there are a limited number of cases that address possible violations of care as a result of the board's failure to monitor senior management or
the exercise of delegated corporate power more broadly within the company. This limited body of case law means that, although we can identify the standards applicable in
the monitoring context, the role of the duty of care in regulating the monitoring issues
identified in section 3.1 has been subject to only limited analysis in the UK.

The early case law imposed very low expectations on directors in relation to their
monitoring of delegated authority. The leading early case in this regard was *In re City
Equitable Fire*, where Romer J clarified that in the absence of grounds to suspect the
honesty of an executive director or official, the board could rely upon him to perform
his functions and rely upon the information provided by that person without examining
for himself the reliability of the information.

---

[32] *In re Citigroup Inc Shareholder Derivative Litigation* 964 A2d 106 (Del Ch 2009). See also *In re
Goldman Sachs Group Inc Shareholder Litigation* WL 4826104 (Del Ch 2011). For a more detailed
consideration of the *Citigroup* case see pp 470–72.

■ *In re City Equitable Fire* [1925] Ch 407

The facts have been set out in the earlier extract.

> *Romer J*
>
> In respect of all duties that, having regard to the exigencies of business, and the articles of asso-
> ciation, may properly be left to some other official, a director is, in the absence of grounds for
> suspicion, justified in trusting that official to perform such duties honestly. In the judgment of the
> Court of Appeal in *In re National Bank of Wales, Ltd*,[33] the following passage occurs in relation to a
> director who had been deceived by the manager, and managing director, as to matters within their
> own particular sphere of activity: 'Was it his duty to test the accuracy or completeness of what he
> was told by the general manager and the managing director? This is a question on which opinions
> may differ, but we are not prepared to say that he failed in his legal duty. Business cannot be car-
> ried on upon principles of distrust. Men in responsible positions must be trusted by those above
> them, as well as by those below them, until there is reason to distrust them. We agree that care
> and prudence do not involve distrust; but for a director acting honestly himself to be held legally
> liable for negligence, in trusting the officers under him not to conceal from him what they ought
> to report to him, appears to us to be laying too heavy a burden on honest business men.' That case
> went to the House of Lords, and is reported there under the name of *Dovey v. Cory*.[34] Lord Davey,
> in the course of his speech to the House, made the following observations: 'I think the respondent
> was bound to give his attention to and exercise his judgment as a man of business on the matters
> which were brought before the board at the meetings which he attended, and it is not proved that
> he did not do so. But I think he was entitled to rely upon the judgment, information and advice, of
> the chairman and general manager, as to whose integrity, skill and competence he had no reason
> for suspicion. I agree with what was said by Sir George Jessel in *Hallmark's Case*,[35] and by Chitty J.
> in *In re Denham & Co.*,[36] that directors are not bound to examine entries in the company's books.
> It was the duty of the general manager and (possibly) of the chairman to go carefully through the
> returns from the branches, and to bring before the board any matter requiring their consideration;
> but the respondent was not, in my opinion, guilty of negligence in not examining them for himself,
> notwithstanding that they were laid on the table of the board for reference.

This passage from Romer J makes a clear distinction between the role of executive and
non-executive directors. The non-executive directors attend board meetings where they
consider the issues and information laid before them. They are, in the absence of suspicion, allowed to rely on the 'information and advice' of executive directors and senior
management and they are not expected, in the absence of suspicion, to question the
validity and reliability of the information laid before them. Through the lens of this
case the non-executive director has a very limited role which involves: (a) delegating
board power to executive management; (b) making other decisions put before them in
board meetings; and (c) periodically assessing the performance of the executive directors
and using this assessment to make a determination about extending or terminating the
managers' tenure. Apart from these functions, in the absence of red flags—which would
require further questioning and engagement—the non-executive director is not required
to monitor the exercise of delegated authority by management. In the absence of red
flags, should losses result from the manager's incompetent or self-serving exercise of
authority, the non-executive director would not be liable for breach of the duty of care.

As we saw in Chapter 7, corporate governance regulation in the United Kingdom
has increasingly emphasized the role and importance of the non-executive director
in monitoring non-executive directors and managing the acute conflicts generated by
having senior managers as board members. This regulation has generated an understanding of the role of the non-executive director that is inconsistent with the view

---

[33] [1899] 2 Ch 629.   [34] [1901] AC 407.   [35] (1878) 9 Ch D 329.   [36] 25 Ch D 752.

of the non-executive role in *Re City Equitable Fire*. The common law is not static and has, arguably, adjusted to take account of this development. In the more recent and important case of *Re Barings plc and others (No 5), Secretary of State for Trade and Industry v Baker* the High Court considered the law's expectations of competence in relation to monitoring and internal controls in the context of an application by the Secretary of State for Trade and Industry to obtain disqualification against former directors of Barings Plc pursuant to the Company Directors Disqualification Act 1986[37]—on the grounds that the directors were 'unfit to be concerned in the management of the company'.[38] Whilst compliance with the duty of care is not directly in issue in this case, the court holds that the duties owed by the directors in question are relevant to the determination of whether the director was 'unfit' for the purposes of the Company Directors Disqualification Act and, accordingly, the court considers at length the duty of care as it relates to reliance, monitoring, and supervision.[39]

---

[37] The Company Directors Disqualification Act 1986 (CDDA) is considered in detail in section V of Chapter 18. An application brought to the court to make a disqualification order can only be brought by the Secretary of State for Business Enterprise and Regulatory Reform (formerly the Secretary of State for Trade and Industry). These actions are brought by the Insolvency Service as an executive branch of the Department for Business Enterprise and Regulatory Reform. Disqualification on the grounds of unfitness will result in a disqualification period ranging from a mandatory period of two years to a maximum period of 15 years (section 6(4) CDDA 1986). On disqualification periods see *Sevenoaks Stationers (Retail) Ltd* [1991] BCLC 325.

[38] Section 6 CDDA 1986. An application for disqualification is the 'unfitness' ground in section 6 CDDA 1986 can only be brought once the company is insolvent, defined by the CDDA to mean when the company is in liquidation, administration, or receivership.

[39] As the unfitness ground for director disqualification is tied to company insolvency, many of the 'unfitness' disqualification cases address how the directors' pre-insolvency competence and behaviour affected creditors' interests. Accordingly, this book gives closer attention to the disqualification regime in section V of Chapter 18 on 'Company law and creditor protection'. However, as the *Barings* case demonstrates, the 'unfitness' disqualification regime operates alongside directors' duties to impose standards of competence, breach of which do not result in liability for the director but in disqualification from being able to serve as a director for a period of time. Indeed, as is clear from *Barings* the two regimes interact along the plane of incompetence: on the one hand, we draw on this case for the purposes of understanding the nature of the duty of care; but the case itself draws on duty of care cases in determining what levels of incompetence amount to 'unfitness'. In this regard, in *Barings* Jonathan Parker J holds that the 'court will assess the competence or otherwise of the respondent in the context of and by reference to the role in the management of the company which was in fact assigned to him or which he in fact assumed...where the respondent was an executive director the court will assess his conduct by reference to his duties and responsibilities in that capacity'. More generally, although the two regimes interact they are not identical. In relation to general expectations of competence for a director to be 'unfit to be concerned with the management of the company' the courts typically require levels of incompetence that go beyond behaviour that would amount to a breach of the duty of care (either at common law or pursuant to section 174 of the Companies Act 2006). In this regard, Browne-Wilkinson in *Re Lo-Line Electric Motors Ltd* observed that 'ordinary commercial misjudgment is in itself not sufficient to justify disqualification. In the normal case, the conduct complained of must display a lack of commercial probity, although I have no doubt that in an *extreme case* of *gross negligence* or *total incompetence* disqualification could be appropriate' (emphasis added). However, this position was qualified by the Court of Appeal in *Sevenoaks Stationers (Retail) Ltd* [1991] BCLC 325 where Dillon LJ observed that '[the director's] trouble is not dishonesty, but incompetence or negligence in a very marked degree and that is enough to render him unfit; I do not think it is necessary for incompetence to be "total", as suggested by the Vice-Chancellor in *Re Lo-Line Electric Motors Ltd*...to render a director unfit to take part in the management of a company'. See also *Re Structural Concrete Ltd* applying *Sevenoaks*, where Blackburne J in finding that the directors were not 'unfit' observed that the behaviour in question did not 'cross the threshold of even a marked degree of incompetence or negligence, let alone a very marked degree' [2000] All ER (D) 848. In this regard, in *Re Barings*, Jonathan Parker J made the following observation: 'various expressions have been used by the courts in this connection, including "total incompetence"...incompetence "in a very marked degree" and "really gross incompetence" (see *Re Dawson Print Group Ltd* [1987] BCLC 601 per Hoffmann J). Whatever words one chooses to use, the substantive point is that the burden on the Secretary of State in establishing unfitness based on incompetence is a heavy one.' More recently, in this regard see: *Secretary of State for Trade and Industry v Swan* [2005] All ER (D) 102 (Apr); and *Official Receiver v Watson* [2008] All ER (D) 188 (Jan).

■ *Re Barings plc and others (No 5), Secretary of State for Trade and Industry v Baker* [1999] 1 BCLC 433

This case is one of several cases which arose from the fraudulent securities trading activities of a trader who was employed by what was, at the time, one of the UK's most renowned investment banks, Barings. The trader, Mr Nick Leeson, engaged in trading activities on the Singapore and Japanese stock exchanges. Mr Leeson was in charge of one of Barings' subsidiary companies responsible for carrying out the trading activities in Asian securities markets. He was responsible for making the actual trades (known as front office work) but also for recording the details and consequences of the trades in the company's accounts and records (known as back office work). Mr Leeson was viewed by the bank as one of its star traders until it was revealed abruptly that his trading activities had been making significant losses that he had hidden using fictitious internal accounts. The losses were so significant which they resulted in the destruction of the bank which was ultimately sold to the Dutch Bank ING for £1. Law suits were brought against three *executive* directors of the Barings' group companies under the Company Directors Disqualification Act 1986 on the basis that pursuant to section 6 of the Act their behaviour, in failing to adequately supervise Leeson and put in place systems of control that could have placed checks and limitations on his activities, demonstrated that they were 'unfit to be concerned in the management of a company'.

Jonathan Parker J summarized the executive directors failings as follows:

'From the factual background set out above, however, three basic facts emerge, namely:

(i) From the time when he started trading on SIMEX in July 1992 until the collapse in February 1995, Leeson was left in full control of both the front and the back offices at BFS: his roles were never segregated. This was allowed to occur despite the fact that in October 1994 the Internal Audit Report specifically recommended that his roles be segregated.

(ii) From (at the latest) early 1994 until the collapse, Leeson made unsubstantiated requests for funding on an increasingly massive scale, all of which requests were met and funds paid over to [him] without any proper investigation and without any attempt to reconcile the amounts requested with the underlying positions.

(iii) The failures of internal management controls within the Barings Group which allowed Leeson to operate as he did, and which thus led directly to the collapse, were accurately described by Mr Peter Baring as "crass" and "absolute".'

Jonathan Parker J

The Duties of Directors

'[E]ach individual director owes duties to the company to inform himself about its affairs and to join with his co-directors in supervising and controlling them' (see *Re Westmid Packing Services Ltd* [1998] 2 BCLC 646 at 653... This does not mean, of course, that directors cannot delegate. Subject to the articles of association of the company, a board of directors may delegate specific tasks and functions. Indeed, some degree of delegation is almost always essential if the company's business is to be carried on efficiently: to that extent there is a clear public interest in delegation by those charged with the responsibility for the management of a business...

But just as the duty of an individual director as formulated by the Court of Appeal in *Re Westmid Packing Services Ltd* does not mean that he may not delegate, neither does it mean that, having delegated a particular function, he is no longer under any duty in relation to the discharge of that function, notwithstanding that the person to whom the function has been delegated may appear both trustworthy and capable of discharging the function.

As Sir Richard Scott V-C said when making a disqualification order against [another Barings' director]:

'Overall responsibility is not delegable. All that is delegable is the discharge of particular functions. The degree of personal blameworthiness that may attach to the individual with the overall responsibility, on account of a failure by those to whom he has delegated particular tasks, must depend on the facts of each particular case. Sometimes there may be a question whether the delegation has been made to the appropriate person; sometimes there may be a question of whether the individual with overall responsibility should have checked how his subordinates were discharging their delegated functions. Sometimes the system itself, in which the failures have taken place, is an inadequate system for which the person with overall responsibility must take some blame.'

It is not in dispute in the instant case that where delegation has taken place the board (and the individual directors) will remain responsible for the delegated function or functions and will retain a residual duty of supervision and control. As Sir Richard Scott V-C made clear in the passage quoted above, the precise extent of that residual duty will depend on the facts of each particular case, as will the question whether it has been breached. These are matters which are in dispute in the instant case. It is the Secretary of State's case (denied by the respondents) that each of the respondents was incompetent in failing to discharge his individual duties as a director.

Directors' duties of skill, care and diligence have been exhaustively analysed by the Supreme Court of New South Wales in *Daniels v Anderson* (1995) 16 ACSR 607. Of particular materiality in the instant case is the following passage in the judgment (at 668):

'A person who accepts the office of director of a particular company undertakes the responsibility of ensuring that he or she understands the nature of the duty a director is called upon to perform. That duty will vary according to the size and business of the particular company and the experience or skills that the director held himself or herself out to have in support of appointment to the office. None of this is novel. It turns upon the natural expectations and reliance placed by shareholders on the experience and skill of a particular director...The duty includes that of acting collectively to manage the company.'

I respectfully adopt those observations as representing what I understand to be the law of England in this respect.

Where there is an issue as to the extent of a director's duties and responsibilities in any particular case, the level of reward which he is entitled to receive or which he may reasonably have expected to receive from the company may be a relevant factor in resolving that issue. It is not that the fitness or otherwise of a respondent depends on how much he is paid. The point is that the higher the level of reward, the greater the responsibilities which may reasonably be expected (prima facie, at least) to go with it. As Sir Richard Scott V-C said when making a disqualification order in respect of Mr Maclean (see *Re Barings plc, Secretary of State for Trade and Industry v Baker* [1998] BCC 583 at 586):

'[Counsel for the respondent] made the point that if an efficient system is in place, or if the individual in question has good reason for believing there to be an efficient system in place, the delegation within the system of functions to be discharged in accordance with the system by others cannot be the subject of serious criticism if, in the event, the persons to whom responsibilities are delegated fail properly to discharge their duties. That may be so up to a point in theory, but the higher the office within an organisation that is held by an individual, the greater the responsibilities that fall upon him. It is right that that should be so, because status within an organisation carries with it commensurate rewards. These rewards are matched by the weight of responsibilities that the office carries with it, and those responsibilities require diligent attention from time to time to the question whether the system that has been put in place and over which the individual is presiding is operating efficiently, and whether individuals to whom duties, in accordance with the system, have been delegated are discharging those duties efficiently.'

In summary, the following general propositions can, in my judgment, be derived from the authorities to which I was referred in relation to the duties of directors:[40]

(i) Directors have, both collectively and individually, a continuing duty to acquire and maintain a sufficient knowledge and understanding of the company's business to enable them properly to discharge their duties as directors.

(ii) Whilst directors are entitled (subject to the articles of association of the company) to delegate particular functions to those below them in the management chain, and to trust their competence and integrity to a reasonable extent, the exercise of the power of delegation does not absolve a director from the duty to supervise the discharge of the delegated functions.

(iii) No rule of universal application can be formulated as to the duty referred to in (ii) above. The extent of the duty, and the question whether it has been discharged, must depend on the facts of each particular case, including the director's role in the management of the company.

[The executive directors in this case were in fact found to be unfit to be concerned with the management of the company. Their actions amounted in Jonathan Parker J's view to serious infringements of the duty of care. The facts surrounding this holding are extremely detailed and complex—the judgment comes to 146 pages—in relation to both of the financial subject matter and Barings' corporate and management structure. I have extracted examples of the judge's holding on the issues of continuing supervision and the risk management systems in relation to two of the directors in question. For those of you who wish to engage with the full judgment you will see, for simplicity's sake, that these extracts have been purified of the Barings' corporate structure.]

[On Continuing Supervision: Mr Tuckey]

In assessing the conduct of Mr Tuckey (and of the other respondents) there is in this case a particular risk of applying the wisdom of hindsight. The collapse of Barings was a commercial catastrophe of epic proportions, and that fact alone makes it, perhaps, easier in the instant case than in others to fall into the error of looking at what happened prior to the collapse in the light of the collapse itself. That is not the correct approach. I have to put aside completely the wisdom of hindsight and judge the conduct of the respondents in the context of the circumstances which existed at the time…

Mr Tuckey was a director of [Barings] and its management committee (MANCO).[41] He was thus the senior executive of [Barings], and as such he had ultimate responsibility for the management of [Barings] (including Leeson's switching business [which involved trades that attempted to exploit the price differences of the same security on two different stock exchanges—principally SIMEX (the Singaporean exchange) and Japanese exchanges—which generated losses that resulted in Barling's collapse].

In his affidavit evidence, Mr Tuckey explained the genesis of the management structure in the following terms:

'[T]he only system of management which can possibly work is one which permits a high degree of delegation and de-centralisation. Such a system operated at Barings where the senior people had worked together for many years, had long experience and, wherever possible, delegated responsibility downwards: hence the existence of various committees with devolved responsibility from MANCO to those who had direct executive responsibility…'

---

[40] *Re Brazilian Rubber Plantations and Estates Ltd* [1911] 1 Ch 425, *Re City Equitable Fire Insurance* [1925] Ch 407, [1924] All ER Rep 485, *Re Norman Holding Co Ltd* [1991] BCLC 1, *Re D'Jan of London Ltd, Copp v D'Jan* [1994] 1 BCLC 561, *Bishopsgate Investment Management Ltd (in liq) v Maxwell (No 2)* [1993] BCLC 1282, *Martin v Webb* 110 US 7, *Briggs v Spaulding* 141 US 132, *Rankin v Cooper* 149 F 1010, *Atherton v Anderson* 99 F 2nd 883 and *Federal Deposit Insurance Corp v Bierman* 2 Fed Rep (3rd Series) 1424.

[41] Please note that this is not an accurate description—the several companies involved in the Barings Group are included under the heading Barings for simplicity's sake.

In the course of his oral evidence, Mr Tuckey repeatedly stressed the degree of trust which was reposed in senior colleagues in Barings. The following passage from Mr Tuckey's evidence under cross-examination is an example of this:

'…[I]t was not our practice with senior colleagues to interrogate them as to what steps they had actually taken to bring themselves to a state of confidence and satisfaction. This process of trust among colleagues evolves over many years. It was not necessary to sit down and put your colleagues through a sort of cross-examination when you have asked them to do something. Business just does not work like that. Certainly Barings did not. Our culture was particularly inconsistent with that…These were a group of people who [had] worked together for many years and who knew their responsibilities, and when they carried out those responsibilities and expressed confidence in…the business they were running, that was accepted by me and other senior colleagues.'…

[In] my judgment…the nature of the management structure adopted within Barings…[cannot] serve to limit or restrict the duties of those charged with the management of [Barings], at any level. The perceived commercial need for a 'flat' management structure, as Mr Tuckey described it, does not involve—nor, in my judgment, should it involve—any lesser degree of vigilance or diligence on the part of senior management in the performance of their managerial duties. Similarly, in my judgment, the mere fact that functions have been delegated to trusted colleagues whose capabilities are known and respected—in other words, the mere fact that the delegation was a proper one—does not relieve the delegator of the duty to supervise and monitor the discharge of those functions…

It is not suggested that MANCO was under a duty to 'second-guess' the decisions of Mr Norris or Mr Barnett, or to carry out itself functions delegated to them, and Mr Tuckey himself can have been in no different position. At the same time, as I have already observed, the mere fact of (proper) delegation did not relieve MANCO or Mr Tuckey as its chairman of the residual duty to supervise and monitor the discharge of delegated functions. It is not possible to formulate precisely the extent of that duty in a way which will apply to every situation, since differing situations will call for differing levels of action or reaction. What can be said is that Mr Tuckey, as the senior executive within [Barings], was not entitled simply to leave the management of [Barings] to his colleagues—however able and trustworthy they were. As chairman of [Barings] and chairman of MANCO, Mr Tuckey was at all times under a duty to take an active part in the management of [Barings], and that in turn meant that he was under a continuing duty to inform himself about [Barings'] affairs to the extent necessary to enable him properly to discharge that duty.

I conclude that…Mr Tuckey's breaches of duty involved not so much discrete failures of management as a general failure to manage: they amount not so much to bad management as to *non*-management. As such, they demonstrate what I regard as a high degree of incompetence on Mr Tuckey's part.

[On Risk and Internal Controls: Mr Baker]

It was Mr Baker's clear responsibility to ensure that Leeson was not breaching his risk limits [on his trading activities]: ie the intra-day or the overnight limit. So far as Leeson's intra-day limits are concerned, it is apparent from the primary documentation [that his trades were] massively in excess of Leeson's intra-day limits…so far as Leeson's overnight limit is concerned (ie the requirement that the switching books should be fully matched, or 'flat', overnight) the fact that the internal Barings statements on which transactions are recorded (known as 'contac statements') contain a number of fictitious transactions (ie, transactions which were not conducted on SIMEX and which accordingly do not appear in SIMEX's records) establishes that the switching books cannot have been kept fully matched overnight.

The information which [Barings] was receiving from Leeson did not enable [Barings] to monitor Leeson's compliance with his intra-day limits…The only way in which those limits could have been monitored would have been by means of a detailed examination of the traders' records…[An internal audit recommended the implementation of internal regulations to monitor Leeson's trading activities]. It was Mr Baker's responsibility to ensure that the steps recommended by the Internal Audit Report were taken: he wholly failed to do so.

Furthermore, Mr Baker was at all material times well aware that on the information available to [them they were] unable to monitor Leeson's compliance with risk limits. [A junior employee] told him as much in a telephone conversation between them on 26 January 1995, but I have no doubt that this news came as no surprise to Mr Baker. Mr Baker was in no better position... in this respect... On the information available to him he could not have monitored Leeson's risk limits if he had wanted to...

In short, there was no effective system in place for the monitoring of Leeson's risk limits, and Mr Baker took no steps to introduce one. [This was one of several reasons for a determination that Mr Baker was in 'serious' breach of duty].

There are three key statements of the law in this case extract. The first is that directors are under a continuing obligation to ensure that they have a 'sufficient knowledge and understanding of the company'. Confirming the holding in *Dorchester Finance*, as one might expect in a modern day company, you can no longer accept an appointment as a director and then do nothing. Secondly, Jonathan Parker J goes beyond the holding in *Re City Equitable Fire* that, in the absence of 'grounds for suspicion' that the individuals to whom responsibilities were delegated could not be trusted, the board would not be held personally responsible for failing to monitor the delegatee's actions. Jonathan Parker J holds that a director may delegate and trust the competence and integrity of the delegatee to a reasonable extent; however, delegation does not absolve the directors from a continuing care obligation of supervision in relation to those officers and employees to whom responsibilities have been delegated, as well as a continuing obligation to ensure that the necessary control structures are in place in the company to effect such supervision. Indeed, if the control system is inadequate this itself may amount to a breach of the duty of care. The standard in this regard is not articulated but it seems clear that the standard would be whether a reasonable director (as modified per *Re D'Jan*) would consider the control system adequate or whether steps had been taken that such a reasonable director would take to ensure that an adequate control system was in place. Thirdly, the judgment recognizes that the supervisory and internal control care obligations may vary depending on the nature and function of the director in question. He observes that 'it is not possible to formulate precisely the extent of that duty in a way which will apply to every situation, since differing situations will call for differing levels of action or reaction.' In this regard, Jonathan Parker J makes a distinction between directors according to the rewards they receive for their services. This difference will in most cases map onto the distinction between executive directors (who are highly rewarded) and non-executive directors (whose director's emoluments will in most cases not be the director's primary source of income).

The point here, however, is not that there are different standards of care applied to these different directors but rather that when applying the standard what will be expected of a reasonable part-time director is not going to be as demanding as what will be expected of a reasonable full-time director. This view was confirmed in *Equitable Life Assurance Society v Bowley*[42] where Langley J held the three-stage test articulated by Jonathan Parker J would also apply to non-executive directors. He observed that 'there is a considerable measure of agreement about the duty owed in law by a non-executive director to a company. In expression it does not differ from the duty owed by an executive director but in application it may and usually will do so.'[43]

For the non-executive director Langley J's holding is not particularly helpful. She wants to know in a greater degree of granularity what the duty of care expects of her in relation to: how well informed she needs to be; how carefully she must monitor management;

[42] [2003] EWHC 2263.
[43] Langley J then cited *Re D'Jan* approvingly. See also *Bishopsgate Investment Management Ltd (in liq) v Maxwell (No 2)* [1993] BCLC 1282.

how reliant she can be on the information produced by management; and how closely she needs to be involved in the design, implementation, and review of the company's internal controls. Clearly under the *D'Jan* standard the law's expectation will adjust to take account of her knowledge and experience if it exceeds an average director's knowledge and experience. But to have a sense of the law's expectations of her she needs to know what the law would expect of an average non-executive director in these contexts. The limited amount of UK case law in this regard means that the law as it stands provides only limited guidance. Some guidance is arguably available from recent Australian duty of care case law, which, as we saw from the extract in *Barings*, UK courts have shown a willingness to draw upon for guidance. The duty of care in Australia is an objective reasonable director standard akin to the first prong of the *D'Jan* standard and therefore this case law is arguably relevant for understanding the current UK standard as applied to the monitoring context. In this regard consider the following extract from the Federal Court of Australia case of *Australian Securities and Investment Commission (ASIC) v Healey*.[44]

■ *ASIC v Healey* (2011) 278 ALR 618 Federal Court of Australia

The directors of the Centro Group companies, a listed investment company, approved the accounts of several group entities. The approved accounts were found to be inaccurate in several material respects. In particular, in the Centro Properties Group accounts AU$1.5 billion of short-term current liabilities were classified as non-current liabilities and AU$ 1.75 billion of guarantees given by an associated company were not disclosed. ASIC brought an action for breach of the statutory duty of care (set forth in section 180 of the Australian Corporations Act) against eight directors, seven of whom were non-executive directors and only one of whom had an accounting qualification. The company had an audit committee and its accounts were audited by PwC, one of the 'big four' global audit companies. The judge found that 'each director knew of the current interest bearing liabilities and the guarantees'. Although the issue of classification of liabilities under the accounting standards was not without ambiguity—resulting from a recent change in the accounting rules—the judge concluded that 'each director was aware or should have been aware of the relevant accounting principles'. The directors were found to be in breach of duty. Note, however, that in a subsequent ruling on damages the court imposed no financial penalty on the non-executive directors apart from a proportion of the costs.[45]

Middleton J

The directors are intelligent, experienced and conscientious people. There has been no suggestion that each director did not honestly carry out his responsibilities as a director. However, I have found, in the specific circumstances the subject of this proceeding, that the directors failed to take all reasonable steps required of them, and acted in the performance of their duties as directors without exercising the degree of care and diligence the law requires of them.

The 2007 annual reports of Centro Properties Group (CNP) and Centro Retail Group (CER) failed to disclose significant matters…This proceeding is not about a mere technical oversight. The information not disclosed was a matter of significance to the assessment of the risks facing CNP and CER. Giving that information to shareholders and, for a listed company, the market, is one of the fundamental purposes of the requirements of the Act that financial statements and reports must be prepared and published. The importance of the financial statements is one of the fundamental reasons why the directors are required to approve them and resolve that they give a true and fair view.

---

[44] Note that one of the reasons why the duty of care case law is more developed in Australia is that ASIC, the Australian capital markets regulator, is empowered to bring actions against directors for breach of duty. An excellent analysis of this case and its relevance for UK law is provided in J. Lowry, 'The Irreducible Core of the Duty of Care Skill and Diligence: *Australian Securities and Investment Commission v Healey*' (2012) 75 *MLR* 249.   [45] *ASIC v Healey (No. 2)* [2011] FCA 1003.

The significant matters not disclosed were well known to the directors, or if not well known to them, were matters that should have been well known to them. In the light of the significance of the matters that they knew, they could not have, nor should they have, certified the truth and fairness of the financial statements, and published the annual reports in the absence of the disclosure of those significant matters. If they had understood and applied their minds to the financial statements and recognised the importance of their task, each director would have questioned each of the matters not disclosed. Each director, in reviewing financial statements, needed to inquire further into the matters revealed by those statements.

The central question in the proceeding has been whether directors of substantial publicly listed entities are required to apply their own minds to, and carry out a careful review of, the proposed financial statements and the proposed directors' report, to determine that the information they contain is consistent with the director's knowledge of the company's affairs, and that they do not omit material matters known to them or material matters that should be known to them.

A director is an essential component of corporate governance. Each director is placed at the apex of the structure of direction and management of a company. The higher office that is held by a person, the greater the responsibility that falls upon him or her. The role of a director is significant as their actions may have a profound effect on the community, and not just share-holders, employees and creditors.

This proceeding involves taking responsibility for documents effectively signed off by, approved, or adopted by the directors. What is required is that such documents, before they are adopted by the directors, be read, understood and focused upon by each director with the knowledge each director has or should have by virtue of his or her position as a director. I do not consider this requirement overburdens a director, or as argued before me, would cause the boardrooms of Australia to empty overnight. Directors are generally well remunerated and hold positions of pres-tige, and the office of director will continue to attract competent, diligent and intelligent people.

The case law indicates that there is a core, irreducible requirement of directors to be involved in the management of the company and to take all reasonable steps to be in a position to guide and monitor. There is a responsibility to read, understand and focus upon the contents of those reports which the law imposes a responsibility upon each director to approve or adopt.

All directors must carefully read and understand financial statements before they form the opinions which are to be expressed in the declaration required by [the Corporations Act]. Such a reading and understanding would require the director to consider whether the financial state-ments were consistent with his or her own knowledge of the company's financial position. This accumulated knowledge arises from a number of responsibilities a director has in carrying out the role and function of a director. These include the following: a director should acquire at least a rudimentary understanding of the business of the corporation and become familiar with the fun-damentals of the business in which the corporation is engaged; a director should keep informed about the activities of the corporation; while not required to have a detailed awareness of day-to-day activities, a director should monitor the corporate affairs and policies; a director should main-tain familiarity with the financial status of the corporation by a regular review and understanding of financial statements; a director, while not an auditor, should still have a questioning mind.

A board should be established which enjoys the varied wisdom, experience and expertise of persons drawn from different commercial backgrounds. Even so, a director, whatever his or her background, has a duty greater than that of simply representing a particular field of experience or expertise. A director is not relieved of the duty to pay attention to the company's affairs which might reasonably be expected to attract inquiry, even outside the area of the director's expertise.

The words of Pollock J in the case of *Francis v United Jersey Bank* (1981) 432 A 2d 814 (*Francis*), quoted with approval by Clarke and Sheller JJA in *Daniels v Anderson* (1995) 37 NSWLR 438; 16 ACSR 607 (*Daniels*), make it clear that more than a mere 'going through the paces' is required for directors. As Pollock J noted, a director is not an ornament, but an essential component of corporate governance.

Nothing I decide in this case should indicate that directors are required to have infinite knowl-edge or ability. Directors are entitled to delegate to others the preparation of books and accounts and the carrying on of the day-to-day affairs of the company. What each director is expected to do is to take a diligent and intelligent interest in the information available to him or her, to understand that information, and apply an inquiring mind to the responsibilities placed upon him or her. Such a responsibility arises in this proceeding in adopting and approving the financial statements. Because of their nature and importance, the directors must understand and focus upon the content of financial statements, and if necessary, make further inquiries if matters revealed in these financial statements call for such inquiries.

No less is required by the objective duty of skill, competence and diligence in the understanding of the financial statements that are to be disclosed to the public as adopted and approved by the directors.

No one suggests that a director should not personally read and consider the financial statements before that director approves or adopts such financial statements. A reading of the financial statements by the directors is not merely undertaken for the purposes of correcting typographical or grammatical errors or even immaterial errors of arithmetic. The reading of financial statements by a director is for a higher and more important purpose: to ensure, as far as possible and reasonable, that the information included therein is accurate. The scrutiny by the directors of the financial statements involves understanding their content. The director should then bring the information known or available to him or her in the normal discharge of the director's responsibilities to the task of focusing upon the financial statements. These are the minimal steps a person in the position of any director would and should take before participating in the approval or adoption of the financial statements and their own directors' reports.

The omissions in the financial statements the subject of this proceeding were matters that could have been seen as apparent without difficulty upon a focusing by each director, and upon a careful and diligent consideration of the financial statements. As I have said, the directors were intelligent and experienced men in the corporate world. Despite the efforts of the legal representatives for the directors in contending otherwise, the basic concepts and financial literacy required by the directors to be in a position to properly question the apparent errors in the financial statements were not complicated.

The defendant directors asserted in their defence that they were entitled to rely on the fact the accounts had been audited. In asserting this claim they relied on the first instance holding in *AWA v Daniels*[46] where Rogers CJ held, echoing *Re City Equitable Fire*, that: 'in relation to auditors, if directors appoint a person of good repute and competence to audit the accounts, absent real grounds for suspecting that the auditor is wrong, the directors will have discharged their duty to the corporation'. Middleton J was unpersuaded by this submission, citing in support the New South Wales Court of Appeal's doubts in *AWA v Daniels* about the 'reliance exception', and the subsequent case of *Vines v ASIC* where the court observed that:[47]

The degree of an officer's permissible reliance on others will turn on similar considerations as those that determine the overall standard of care for an individual director. They focus particularly on the characteristics of the company, the skills and experience of the officer concerned and the delegate, and the reasonably anticipated risks entailed in so doing. What is expected here is a level of scrutiny as befits supervision, not the detailed direct involvement that is associated with operational responsibility. Where there is no cause for suspicion *nor circumstances demanding critical and detailed attention*, it is reasonable for an officer to rely on advice, without independently verifying the information or scrutinizing the data or circumstances upon which that advice is based (emphasis supplied).

Note also that in determining what the law expected of the directors in performing their role, following an earlier decision of the Supreme Court of New South Wales

[46] (1992) 7 ACSR 759.   [47] (2007) 73 NSWLR 471.

in *ASIC v Rich*[48], Middleton J drew upon general materials that addressed corporate governance best practice. In *ASIC v Rich* these included: a 1973 report from
the British Confederation of Industry on *The Responsibilities of the British Public
Company*; observations in a book on corporate governance by Sir Adrian Cadbury;[49]
and the Higgs' *Review of the Role and Effectiveness of Non-Executive Directors*.[50]
With regard to this material, in *ASIC v Rich* Austin J observed that:

> ASIC's evidence does not purport to establish, directly, that Mr Greaves [the director] had spe-
> cific duties on particular occasions. It seeks to establish his 'responsibilities' by reference to
> usual practice. Much of the literature of corporate governance is in the form of exhortations
> and voluntary codes of conduct, not suitable to constitute legal duties. It is sometimes vague
> and less than compelling, and must always be used with caution. Nevertheless, in my opinion
> this literature is relevant to the ascertainment of the responsibilities to which Mr Greaves was
> subject during [the relevant period]…It should be remembered, however, that the court's role,
> in determining liability of a defendant for his conduct as company chairman, is to articulate and
> apply a standard of care that reflects contemporary community expectations.

The court in *Healey* relied in particular on materials produced by the Australian
Institute of Company Directors on financial reports and audit which set forth guidelines and expectations of directors in relation to financial statements. The guidelines
include the recommendation that directors consider whether: 'there [are] any matters
included in the financial statements that could be viewed as misleading or confusing?
Are any of the directors aware of anything, from their personal knowledge or warnings
from outside sources, which should be considered before signing?'[51] This recommendation, Middleton J observed: 'reflect[s] my own view of what is required of the directors
in this proceeding, and what is required by the Act and the case law.' Through the duty
of care these best practice guidelines became Australian company law.

Questions and discussion

- With regard to internal controls *Barings* is arguably an easy case. The executive directors
  in question appeared to have completely disregarded the need for any effective internal
  controls, even when an internal audit had recommended that they be implemented. It
  is difficult therefore to draw any conclusions from this case about the expectations that
  the law imposes on directors in relation to such controls. Clearly, as the case stresses,
  the standard of care will adjust to the director in question—her function, knowledge,
  experience, and exposure to the actual operation and effectiveness of those controls.
  In relation to non-executive directors, although the case makes it clear that delegation
  does not absolve directors of continuing responsibility, it is submitted that in relation to
  internal controls in order to be duty compliant non-executives will only be required to
  consider the need for them if they are not already in place and, as recommended by the
  UK Corporate Governance Code, to review their effectiveness annually.

- Although *Barings* clarifies that the director cannot simply delegate and then step back
  and do nothing, it does not alter the position set forth in *Re City Equitable Fire* that in
  the absence of suspicion the non-executive directors of a company are justified in relying
  on the information produced by management and do not have to personally investigate
  its accuracy and reliability. What is clear after *Barings* is that all directors must maintain their knowledge and understanding of the company as a reasonable director would
  do. The failure to have such an adequate understanding could of course mean that the

---

[48] (2003) 44 ACSR 431.
[49] Sir Adrian Cadbury, *A Company Chairman* (Director Books, 2nd edn, 1995).
[50] On the role of Sir Adrian Cadbury and Derek Higgs in the formation of the UK Corporate
Governance Code see Chapter 7.
[51] 'How to Review a Company's Financial Reports' (The Australian Institute of Company
Directors, 2006).

under-informed director's suspicions are not raised by particular events or information, when they would have been raised had the director maintained a reasonable level of knowledge and understanding about the business. Such directors—whose suspicions were not raised—would be in breach of duty.

- Applying the UK position (set forth in the previous bullet) to the facts in *ASIC v Healey* would the directors have been found liable? It is submitted that they would not. The English position appears closer to Rogers CJ's position set forth previously. Furthermore, following *Rich* and *Healey's* reliance on corporate governance documentation, nor does the position taken in *Healey* appear to accord with the understanding of the non-executive's role as set forth in the UK Corporate Governance Code. The Code requires that non-executive directors should 'satisfy themselves of the integrity of financial information'.[52] This, it is submitted, is achieved by ensuring that the procedures are in place to produce reliable financial information and a reliable audit. This could include: the existence of an audit committee; the appointment of an independent auditor; and the existence of communication channels (whistleblowing procedures) to ensure that non-executives can be made aware of problems by employees on a confidential basis. If the Code's understanding of the non-executive director's function were to be incorporated into the UK duty of care, it would not require the directors to correct mistakes made (intentionally or otherwise) in the financial statements, even those that in theory the non-executive directors' knowledge of the company's activities should have made them aware of. It is suspicion about the reliability of the experts responsible for producing information in accordance with accounting regulation that matters. In the absence of any such suspicion, breach of duty under UK company law would not arise from the failure to correct inaccuracies in the financial statements, but only from failure to consider, and review the adequacy of, the procedures and controls for the production of financial information. A reasonable part-time non-executive director could not be expected to perform the role of a final verifier of the financial statements if the best practice guidance from the Corporate Governance Code does not envisage him playing such a role.

- Is it appropriate to legalize best practice guidance set forth in either 'comply or explain' codes or in documents produced by trade associations such as the Confederation of British Industry or Institute for Chartered Accountants in England and Wales? If such guidance sets forth best practice, is it appropriate to absorb it into a duty of care which does not aspire to the very best of practice but to 'average practice'? In contrast to optional governance codes and industry best practice, the duty of care is not simply an expectation of behaviour, it is also a liability standard and, as we observed at several junctures in the book, if that standard is set too high then directors concerned about the effects of hindsight bias may either act in an excessively risk-averse fashion or refuse to act at all. Mr Justice Middleton may be correct that as a result of his ruling 'the board-rooms of Australia' will not 'empty overnight', but one would certainly expect them to be far less attractive places to be.

- With regard to the usefulness of these corporate governance materials, is it possible to make a distinction between, on the one hand, understanding of the role of the directors set forth in the 'best practice' materials and, on the other, the actual 'best practice' behaviour expected of directors when they perform the role? The former would be relevant and useful for the duty of care; the latter should not be. This would allow us to make productive use of such governance materials without falling foul of the critique in the previous bullet point? According to the distinction, the use in bullet point three of the Corporate Governance Code's understanding of the role of the non-executive director in relation to financial statements allows us to focus on the activity to which the duty of care applies—namely process and procedures for the production of financial information, which would satisfy the director of their 'integrity'. But this borrowing does not tell us anything about the actual expectation of behaviour in performing that role—what a reasonable director should actually do to, in this example, satisfy himself about those processes and procedures. By way of contrast,

[52] UK Corporate Governance Code, A4, Supporting Principle.

ASIC v Healey's use of the borrowing does fall foul of the critique in bullet point four—the materials it relies on specify an expectation of actual behaviour rather than the mere identification of a role.

- In relation to industry guidance, if such guidance is at risk of being 'legalized' by the duty of care, will it discourage the production of such documentation or the lowering of the expectation of care contained within such guidance?

- What are the benefits of holding the directors to account for failing to identify these accounting failings? Does it seem likely that the increased attention that Australian directors will now give the audited financial statements will result in an increase in the quality of those financial statements? Many accounting irregularities are rarely visible from the face of those documents, and most directors—without accounting expertise— are unlikely to able to identify even the most blatant of accounting errors. However, increased liability exposure for the board as a whole is certainly likely to lead to greater pressure placed upon auditors and management to take a careful and conservative approach to accounting.

- Will this judgment lead to an overweighting on the board of Australian companies of accountants? Is that a good thing?

- 'The upside of the judgment in *ASIC v Healey* is insignificant the downside is not'. Discuss.

III THE DUTY OF CARE AND THE COMPANIES ACT 2006

Hoffmann LJ's judgment in *Re D'Jan* was widely viewed as a favourable development. It quickly came to be seen as a 'modern approach'[53] that appropriately increased the care expectations of directors of the existing law which was viewed as too lax. Commentators did not on the whole share Lord Hoffmann's subsequently articulated misgivings, quoted earlier, about tightening the standard. Consider the following summary of a Law Commission consultation on the director's duty of care. Remember the words 'subjective' and 'objective' here are used to refer to the attributes of the imaginary director who sets the benchmark of care—does he have the attributes of the existing director (subjective) or of an average director carrying out a similar role (objective)? A dual objective/subjective standard would combine both attributes, as does section 214(4) of the Insolvency Act 1986.

■ **The Law Commission and The Scottish Law Commission,** *Company Directors: Regulating Conflicts Of Interests And Formulating A Statement Of Duties* **(1999) (Law Com No 261)**

Summary of Respondents Views

There was little support amongst respondents for a subjective test. One respondent said that this would be appropriate for an owner-manager whose role as a director would be secondary to his role as an owner. It was pointed out, though, that this would not be acceptable for a director of a plc and that it would be undesirable to draw a distinction between the two types of companies.

Indeed most respondents thought that a subjective test would produce too low a standard for modern business. It was considered that in the absence of a formal assessment of a person's fitness to become a director, the public interest demanded that directors should be subject to at least an objective standard. This might afford some protection to shareholders and creditors. (It was noted, however, that many executive directors owe duties under their contracts of

---

[53] See, for example, P. Davies, *Gower and Davies Principles of Modern Company Law* (7th edn, Sweet & Maxwell, 2003), 434; E. Ferran, *Company Law and Corporate Finance* (OUP, 1999), 216. Company Law Review Steering Committee, *Developing the Framework*, para 3.66.

employment that impose objective standards.) Instead the vast majority of respondents favoured the dual objective/subjective test. This included the Institute of Directors. Many agreed with our view that this was the current common law position. The dual test was widely regarded as the best way to account for the differing levels of knowledge and experience possessed by directors. Some respondents suggested that our illustrative clause needed to be more carefully drafted to ensure that it took into account both the functions to be performed by the individual director and the size and type of company. We agree that this is important.

A number of respondents argued that the test should be the same as that in section 214(4) of the Insolvency Act 1986. This was thought to be a workable formula. If a different standard were introduced, there would be two overlapping yet distinct duties in the same area. However, some respondents considered that there was no incoherence in a different duty arising on impending insolvency: a director would then owe duties to creditors in addition to those owed to the company.

There was little support for a purely objective test. It was thought that a director with special skills should be expected to use them. An objective test would be too low for skilled directors. Those who supported this option did so largely because they were concerned about the position of non-executive directors. It was thought that a dual objective/subjective test would discourage non-executive directors from taking up office or taking risks.

Recommendation

The Commissions provisionally supported codification of the dual objective/subjective standard. Respondents clearly supported setting this dual test out in statute. It is important that regard should be had to the functions of the particular directors and the circumstances of the particular company.

The Company Law Review endorsed, and the Government accepted, the recommendation. Section 174 of the Companies Act 2006 now sets out the duty of care as follows:

■ Section 174 CA 2006 Duty to exercise reasonable care, skill and diligence

(1) A director of a company must exercise reasonable care, skill and diligence.

(2) This means the care, skill and diligence that would be exercised by a reasonably diligent person with—

    (a) the general knowledge, skill and experience that may reasonably be expected of a person carrying out the functions carried out by the director in relation to the company, and

    (b) the general knowledge, skill and experience that the director has.

In relation to section 174 note the following points:

- Although the section refers to 'care, skill and diligence' there is only one duty provided here which is applicable to all activities undertaken by the director in his function as director. There are not separate duties of care, skill, and diligence. The three words refer to same expectation of care and competence. Traditionally this duty would simply have been referred to as the duty of care. We saw in our analysis of *Re City Equitable Fire* that unintended confusion was introduced by Romer J as he used the terms 'skill' and 'care' interchangeably. The common law did not provide for separate duties and, in accordance with section 170(4) which requires consistent interpretation with prior case law, section 174 does not change this.

- The benchmark of care is determined by a reasonable director who is imbued with the skills that you would expect such a director in that director's position to have;

the courts will ask the question what skills, knowledge, and experience would your average director have. However, if the director is more skilled and has more knowledge and experience than the average director then the imaginary director who sets the benchmark of expected care will also be imbued with those skills, knowledge, and experience. The court will then ask what care would a reasonable director with those skills, knowledge, and experience have taken in acting or making a decision.

• In the language of the Law Commission's analysis set out here, the duty of care set out in section 174 provides a dual objective/subjective test. Which means that the attributes of the hypothetical director who sets the benchmark of care include, as noted, the attributes of the average director carrying out that function and, where the director has a level of skill, knowledge, and experience above that level, such additional skill, knowledge, and experience.

• Does the effect of this provision mean that a person who has attributes that would be useful for a company but who does not have the business skills, knowledge, and experience of an average director is unlikely to serve as a director because he will be unable to comply with the provision? Would, for example, a Formula 1 racing driver with no business experience or acumen be effectively excluded from serving on the board of a racing car company even though his knowledge of the racing business would be hugely beneficial to the company? The answer to this question appears to depend on the flexibility of the word 'function' in section 174. Clearly directors have different functions. Some are executive directors, others are non-executive directors who are not involved in the operational aspects of the company's business. Some non-executive directors will receive specific roles such as serving on the audit committee or acting as the senior independent director. The duty of care in determining the expectations the law has of directors adjusts for these different functions. However, could we take this further to say that certain directors are appointed with a very narrow function related to the business—in our racing car example this could include overseeing the development of the Formula 1 car and racing strategy.[54] If his function could be so narrowed then the imaginary director setting the care standard for that director would be a person with only the functions of car development and racing strategy. It seems unlikely that the courts would approach the issue in this way because as a director the racing car driver will have an equal vote on all issues; that is, his function is necessarily to act as a director on all issues that the board considers. It seems likely, therefore, that the duty of care set out in section 174 would *effectively* preclude the appointment of the racing car driver in our example to the board. Of course, it would not preclude his appointment as a consultant to the firm in relation to car development and racing strategy.

Assignment 4

Reread the facts of the Delaware case of *Smith v Van Gorkom* extracted in section I.2.

(1) Applying section 174 of the Companies Act 2006 to those facts would you find the board of directors in breach of the duty of care when it approved the transaction? If so would you find the board liable to compensate the company for its losses?

(2) If you find the board liable, what losses would the board be liable for?

(3) In your application of section 174 to the *Van Gorkom* facts do you think that there is a hindsight problem? Are you capable of controlling that problem?

---

[54] Some support for this view may be available from *Bishopsgate Investment Management Ltd (in liq) v Maxwell (No 2)* [1993] BCLC 1282 where Hoffmann LJ, as he then was, observed that 'the existence of a duty to participate must depend upon how the particular company's business is organised and the part which the director could reasonably have been expected to play'.

IV INDEMNIFYING DIRECTORS FOR BREACH OF DUTY

1 Company waivers, indemnities, and insurance

Our analysis both in this chapter and in previous chapters has identified a tension between, on the one hand, the desire to use duties to express high expectations of directors when making decisions and monitoring management, and to use liability for breaching these expectations as a stick with which to encourage directors to act accordingly; and, on the other hand, the concern that if high expectations are also used as standards by which liability could be imposed on directors then this may have the unintended effect of chilling risk-taking by directors or deterring people from becoming directors in the first place. Thus far the only tool that we have analysed to negotiate this tension is the duty itself: we could lower the standard to take account of these concerns or we could separate the standards of expectation and of liability which would provide for high expectations but low liability exposure. In the UK we have seen that company law does not make a distinction in this regard and that our legal expectation of the care directors should take is the standard according to which the care actually taken will be judged and liability imposed. We have also seen that the contemporary standard is a demanding one.

The extent to which the standard of care raises these policy concerns about chilling risk and encouraging people to serve as directors is clearly a function of the broader context in which the standards are enforced and the consequences for breach are distributed. If the standard of liability is very demanding but the probability that the standard will be enforced against the director is very low, then the probability that the director will be found liable for breach of duty is also very low, in which case, the high standard will not chill risk-taking or deter people from becoming directors. In Chapter 15 we shall look at the probability that breaches of directors' duties will be enforced against directors. In this section we shall look at the consequences of effective enforcement, namely: who pays for the breach of the directors' duties?

There are four ways in which company law could enable companies themselves to provide directors with comfort that they will not be personally exposed to liability for their actions or inactions. The first would be to allow companies to alter the duty to which directors are subject; that is, to render duties default obligations that could be amended by a company's constitution and could, if shareholders elected to do so, be weakened for a particular company's directors. The second way would be to keep duties as mandatory rules but waive the company's right to claim any compensation or damages for breach of duty. The effect of this option is to render the relevant duty a mere statement of expectation with no liability consequences for the directors if they should breach the duty. The third option would be to allow the company to indemnify the director for the costs of defending any action for breach of duty and/or any amounts paid if the director was to lose the action. With regard to the second part of the indemnification option, this would, functionally, have the same effect as a waiver of liability as the company would not sue the director derivatively or otherwise if the company itself would have to pay any award. The fourth option is for the company to pay for insurance that would pay any amounts owed by the directors resulting from breach of duty litigation—this type of insurance is known as directors and officers insurance or, more typically, D&O insurance.

The duties owed by directors pursuant to the Companies Act 2006 are mandatory rules that cannot be derogated from. Although action that would amount to a breach of certain duties can be authorized or a breach ratified (see Chapter 15) the nature of the duties themselves cannot be altered by any means, including altering the corporate constitution. Although, with regard to section 171(b) we saw that what amounts to a 'proper purpose' for which powers have been conferred may be altered by shareholder action, the duty itself to use powers in accordance with such purposes is mandatory. In relation to section 174, although the behavioural standard generated by section 174 may vary depending on the director in question, his role and function, and the nature of the company, the standard itself is mandatory and cannot be departed from.

For a considerable period of time, however, English company law did allow companies either to waive liability for breach of certain obligations or provide indemnification for such breaches. Nor was it unusual for companies to provide for the waiver or indemnification of liability.[55] Indeed in one of the central pre-1990 cases, *In re City Equitable Fire*, two of the directors were found to be in breach of their duty of care but not liable to pay any damages because of the following provision set out in the company's articles of association:

> The directors, auditors, secretary and other officers for the time being of the company, and the trustees (if any) for the time being acting in relation to any of the affairs of the company, and every of them, and every of their heirs, executors and administrators, shall be indemnified and secured harmless out of the assets and profits of the company from and against all actions, costs, charges, losses, damages and expenses which they or any of them their or any of their heirs, executors or administrators shall or may incur or sustain by or by reason of any act done, concurred in or omitted in or about the execution of their duty, or supposed duty, in their respective offices or trusts, except such (if any) as they shall incur or sustain by or through their own wilful neglect or default respectively.

In part as a result of this case the Companies Act 1929, implementing recommendations of the Greene Committee,[56] provided that any attempts to waive liability or to allow companies to indemnify directors for breach of duty were void. Liability waivers or exemptions continue, without qualification, to be void. Subject to certain limited exceptions, attempts by the company to indemnify directors for breach of duty, such as the City Equitable Fire Insurance Company provision, are also void. The relevant provision is section 232 of the Companies Act 2006 Act.

■ Section 232 CA 2006 Provisions protecting directors from liability

(1) Any provision that purports to exempt a director of a company (to any extent) from any liability that would otherwise attach to him in connection with any negligence, default, breach of duty or breach of trust in relation to the company is void.

(2) Any provision by which a company directly or indirectly provides an indemnity (to any extent) for a director of the company, or of an associated company, against any liability attaching to him in connection with any negligence, default, breach of duty or breach of trust in relation to the company of which he is a director is void, except as permitted by—

  (a) section 233 (provision of insurance),

  (b) section 234 (qualifying third party indemnity provision), or

  (c) section 235 (qualifying pension scheme indemnity provision).

(3) This section applies to any provision, whether contained in a company's articles or in any contract with the company or otherwise.

---

[55] *Report of The Company Law Amendment Committee* (1926) Cmnd 2657 (Greene Committee) observed at [46] that 'another form of article which has become common in recent years goes even farther and exempts directors in every case except that of actual dishonesty...We consider that this type of article gives an unjustifiable protection to directors. Under it a director may with impunity be guilty of the grossest negligence provided that he does not consciously do anything which he recognises to be improper'.

[56] *Report of the Company Law Amendment Committee* (1926) (Cmnd 2657, 1926).

> (4) Nothing in this section prevents a company's articles from making such provision as has pre-
> viously been lawful for dealing with conflicts of interest.

The rule in English company law is that neither waivers of, nor indemnification for, liability arising from a breach of duty is possible by any means, including a contract with the director or amending the company's constitution. Any such provision or agreement is void and unenforceable. A company may, pursuant to sections 232(2) and 233 CA 2006, take out directors and officers liability insurance on behalf of the directors to cover any liability incurred for breach of duty. Furthermore, the company may make funds available to directors to defend against legal proceedings, including breach of duty claims; however, such advances must be repaid if the director is found liable.[57] Importantly, such advances are exempted from the restrictions on making loans to directors, which typically require shareholder approval (see Chapter 13). This very limited scope for UK companies to provide directors with relief against liability exposure for breach of duty should be compared with the more flexible regime found in most US states which allow for liability waivers in relation to care violations (see section V of this chapter).

The directors and officers insurance paid for by the company will typically cover both breach of duty claims and certain third-party litigation. Our concern here is in relation to breach of duty. In this regard, commentators have noted that the policies often mirror the language of section 232(1) in relation to the potential liabilities covered by the insurance. Colin Baxter has noted, for example, that 'protection is given where any director or officer is the target of a claim based on any actual or alleged breach of duty, breach of trust or neglect, plus errors, omissions, misstatements and breaches of warranty of authority'. However, he notes further that 'insurers will have nothing to do with dishonesty or other intentional misconduct or the making of improper personal profits'.[58] Typically D&O insurance will also provide cover for the costs of defending legal proceedings. In the UK D&O insurance has in recent years become increasingly popular. It remains the case, however, that not all companies take out such coverage for their directors.[59]

2 Court discretion to grant liability relief

Although it is no longer possible to waive liability for breach of duty, the Companies Acts have long provided the courts with a discretion to provide liability relief to directors who are found to be in breach of duty.[60] This provision is now set forth in section 1157 of the Companies Act 2006.

■ Section 1157 CA 2006 Power of court to grant relief in certain cases

> (1) If in proceedings for negligence, default, breach of duty or breach of trust against—
>
> (a) an officer of a company, or
>
> (b) a person employed by a company as auditor (whether he is or is not an officer of the company), it appears to the court hearing the case that the officer or person is or may be liable but that he acted honestly and reasonably, and that having regard to all the circumstances of the case (including those connected with his appointment) he ought

---

[57] Section 205 CA 2006.
[58] C. Baxter, 'Demystifying D&O Insurance' (1995) 15 *Oxford Journal of Legal Studies* 537.
[59] A. Felsted, 'The danger of being an executive in the UK' *Financial Times* (17 October 2006).
[60] This provision was first set forth in section 32 of the Companies Act 1907.

COMPANY LAW IN CONTEXT

> fairly to be excused, the court may relieve him, either wholly or in part, from his liability on such terms as it thinks fit.
>
> (2) If any such officer or person has reason to apprehend that a claim will or might be made against him in respect of negligence, default, breach of duty or breach of trust—
>
>   (a) he may apply to the court for relief, and
>
>   (b) the court has the same power to relieve him as it would have had if it had been a court before which proceedings against him for negligence, default, breach of duty or breach of trust had been brought.

Section 1157(1) provides the court with a discretion to relieve the director of liability where she has been found in breach of duty. Subsection (2) gives directors the right to apply to court for such relief prior to an action being brought. Section 1157 does not provide the courts with a general discretion to relieve directors of liability for breach of duty. In order to grant relief the court must be satisfied that three factors have been established. First, that the director acted honestly; secondly that he acted reasonably; and, thirdly, that in light of all the circumstances of the case he 'ought fairly' to be relieved of liability. The burden of proof lies with the directors to prove on the balance of probabilities that they acted reasonably and that they ought fairly to be relieved of liability. The court will typically presume the directors acted honestly unless the contrary is proved by the claimant (the company or the shareholder suing derivatively).[61]

With regard to director negligence and the breach of the duty of care, this section presents something of a conundrum. If a director has breached his duty of care then in English law, whether before or after 1990 or before or after the implementation of the 2006 Act, he necessarily has behaved unreasonably.[62] In which case, how could a director have behaved unreasonably for the purpose of the duty violation but reasonably for the purpose of section 1157?

One way of making sense of section 1157 is that the 'reasonableness standard' in section 1157 is a much lower benchmark than the reasonableness standard for the duty of care. This is suggested in *Re D'Jan* when Hoffmann LJ (as he then was) in granting relief pursuant to section 1157's predecessor provision (section 727 of the Companies Act 1985) held that although Mr D'Jan was negligent his negligence was not 'gross' and for the purposes of section 1157 he acted reasonably: 'it was the kind of thing which could happen to any busy man, although, as I have said, this is not enough to excuse it'. Subsequent cases have followed Hoffmann J's approach. In considering this anomaly Evans-Lombe J in *Barings plc v Coopers & Lybrand*,[63] an auditor negligence case in which the auditor requested liability relief pursuant to section 1157's predecessor, held that 'they may have acted reasonably for the purposes of the section even though I have found them to have acted negligently, if they acted in good faith and their negligence was technical or minor in character, and not "pervasive and compelling".'

One might argue that by granting relief for breach of the duty of care where the negligence is not 'gross' or 'pervasive and compelling' the standard of liability is separated from the standard of expectation, and that the standard of liability is not the standard set out in section 174, rather section 174 is only a statement of what one expects. This observation would be correct if courts automatically granted complete liability relief on the establishment that the directors in question did not behave unreasonably for the

---

[61] *Re Kirby Coaches Ltd* [1991] BCC 130, per Hoffmann J.

[62] As we have seen so far in this chapter, what amounts to unreasonable behaviour may of course have varied depending on the approach taken by the courts to the attributes of the hypothetical person setting the benchmark of care.

[63] [2003] EWHC 1319 (Ch).

purposes of section 1157. Section 1157 clearly lowers the standard of liability below the duty of care set out in section 174. However, the extent to which it does so is not only dependent on the meaning of 'reasonableness' in section 1157 but also upon the court's determination of whether, given honesty and reasonableness, it is fair to relieve the director of liability. Furthermore, the court has a discretion to relieve liability 'wholly or in part' and, as we saw in *Re D'Jan*, even if all the section 1157 criteria are satisfied, the courts may grant only partial relief.

In relation to the exercise of this fairness discretion commentators have noted that any attempt to identify the principles underlying the exercise of fairness discretion is unlikely to be successful. Edmunds and Lowry note that 'it is not possible to define clear categories of breach that will always be excused. Nor is it safe to speculate on the circumstances surrounding either the conduct giving rise to the breach or the particular defendant that will necessarily trigger its exercise.'[64] One consideration worth flagging, however, is the court's consideration of the 'economic realities' surrounding the breach when exercising their discretion. In this regard, in *Re D'Jan* Hoffmann LJ gave weight to the fact that D'Jan was the controlling shareholder and had everything to lose from an insurance policy that was void due to information inaccuracies. In *Barings plc v Coopers & Lybrand* Evans-Lombe J also held, following *Re D'Jan*, that the economic realities of the case were relevant to the exercise of the section 1157 discretion.[65]

Questions

1. If you were considering an offer to accept a position as a director would section 1157 give you adequate comfort to enable you (a) to accept the job and (b) not to alter your approach to risk taking when making decisions on behalf of the company?

2. If your answer to question (1) is 'no', would D&O insurance give you such comfort?[66]

3. Do you think the current regulatory settlement relating to liability waivers and indemnities involves significant risk that people will be deterred from serving as UK directors? What factors, in particular, could alter your assessment?

4. Should English law return to the situation prior to the Companies Act 1929 when companies could provide directors with full indemnities for breach of duty?

5. Why should shareholders be denied the option of providing their directors with the comfort of a full liability waiver or indemnity?

6. To what extent, if any, does section 1157 alter the standard according to which liability can be imposed on directors for care violations?

7. Do you think the concepts of 'gross negligence' or 'pervasive and compelling' negligence are clear enough to distinguish them from ordinary negligence? What alternative ways could you envisage for expressing such a lower standard?

8. Should English law have separate standards of expectation and liability in relation to care? What do you think the advantages and the disadvantages of such an approach would be?

---

[64] R. Edmunds and J. Lowry, 'The Continuing Value of Relief for Director's Breach of Duty' (2003) 66 *Modern Law Review* 195, 213.

[65] More recently see *Green v Walkling* [2007] All ER (D) 299.

[66] Note in this regard that D&O insurance is a contractual insurance policy—any doubt that the claim falls within the terms of that policy may be used by the insurance company to claim that they are not liable under the policy. See 'Directors' liability insurance' *Financial Times* (22 June 2009) observing that: 'insurers are increasingly willing to challenge the validity of policies when claims hit'.

V THE DUTY OF CARE IN US COMPARATIVE PERSPECTIVE

1 The standard of care

In certain US jurisdictions the duty of care is, as in the UK under the Companies Act 2006, set out in the corporate statute. Consider, for example, the New York Business Corporation Law:

■ **New York Business Corporation Law**

§ 717. Duty of directors

(a) A director shall perform his duties as a director, including his duties as a member of any committee of the board upon which he may serve, in good faith and with that degree of care which an ordinarily prudent person in a like position would use under similar circumstances.

In Delaware, the duty of care is a common law duty and is not set out in the Delaware General Corporation Law. Case law provides, similarly to the New York Statute, that the Delaware duty of care requires:

That directors of a Delaware corporation 'use that amount of care which ordinarily careful and prudent men would use in similar circumstances,' and 'consider all material information reasonably available' in making business decisions.[67]

Section 717 of the New York code sets the standard of care through reference to an ordinarily prudent person in like position, that is an ordinarily prudent director: the standard of care an average director would be expected to take. Delaware case law, rather than the Delaware Code, also sets the care standard by reference to the ordinarily careful and prudent person. These standards are objective 'average director' expectations and to that extent they appear very similar to the UK's duty of care. They do not, however, raise the standard of care for the more skilled and experienced directors, as is the case under section 174 of the Companies Act 2006.

Although the approaches of the UK, Delaware, and New York appear to have much in common, there are in fact two very significant differences. First, in contrast to the UK—where the duty to promote the success of the company provides the legal expectation and the basis for review of decisions and the duty of care, skill, and diligence provides the expectation and basis for review of the process involved in reaching a decision—the duty of care in the US applies to decisions themselves and the process involved in reaching the decision. Accordingly, the standards of care set out above demand both ordinarily prudent decisions and an ordinarily prudent decision-making process.[68] Although an expectation of ordinarily prudent process is similar to the UK's standard of the care of a reasonably diligent director, the expectation of ordinarily prudent decisions is much higher than the UK's subjective expectation in relation to the duty to promote the success of the company—to do what he or she *thinks* promotes the success of the company.

The second difference is that Delaware and New York corporate law on the duty of care makes a distinction between the standard of care *expected of* a director, which has been set out for New York and Delaware, and the standard by which the actions taken by directors *are reviewed*. That is, the standard of care for the purposes of reviewing director actions—which could theoretically result in liability—is different to the standard of

---

[67] *In re Walt Disney Derivative Litigation (Chancery Court)* 825 A 2d 275 (2003).
[68] See M. Eisenberg, *Corporations and Other Business Organizations* (Foundation Press, 2000).

care which sets out what is expected of directors when they act. The standard of care as expectation only is set out above. Failure to make a decision that an ordinarily prudent director would have made, to act as an ordinarily prudent director would act, or engage in a process that an ordinarily prudent director would have taken, will not result in liability for the director. Such a failure has no legal consequence for the director. What does have a consequence is the failure to comply with the standard of review. This is, as we shall see, a much lower standard than the expectation of care set out above. The rationale for this difference is that this enables the law to maintain high expectations of the standard of care whilst ensuring that the duty of care does not deter people from accepting a position as a director or chill risk-taking by those directors because they are concerned about liability resulting from judges reviewing their decision with hindsight. The analysis set out in the extract from Allen, Jacobs and Strine (pp 346–348) explains this second rationale. It would be worthwhile revisiting that extract before continuing.

2 The standard of review for business decisions

The *standard of review* for business decisions in Delaware[69] is articulated though a legal concept known as the business judgment rule. Consider the following summary of the business judgment rule from a recent case.

■ *In re Walt Disney Co. Derivative Litigation* 907 A 2d 693 (Del Ch 2005)

Chancellor Chandler
Delaware law is clear that the business and affairs of a corporation are managed by or under the direction of its board of directors. The business judgment rule serves to protect and promote the role of the board as the ultimate manager of the corporation. Because courts are ill equipped to engage in post hoc substantive review of business decisions, the business judgment rule 'operates to preclude a court from imposing itself unreasonably on the business and affairs of a corporation.'

The business judgment rule is not actually a substantive rule of law, but instead it is a presumption that 'in making a business decision the directors of a corporation acted on an informed basis,…and in the honest belief that the action taken was in the best interests of the company [and its shareholders].' This presumption applies when there is no evidence of 'fraud, bad faith, or self-dealing in the usual sense of personal profit or betterment' on the part of the directors. In the absence of this evidence, the board's decision will be upheld unless it cannot be 'attributed to any rational business purpose.'

[In support of this proposition Chancellor Chandler cites in a footnote former Chancellor Allen in *Gagliardi v TriFoods Int'l Inc.*[70] who observed that: 'Corporate directors of public companies typically have a very small proportionate ownership interest in their corporations and little or no incentive compensation. Thus, they enjoy (as residual owners) only a very small proportion of any "upside" gains earned by the corporation on risky investment projects. If, however, corporate directors were to be found liable for a corporate loss from a risky project on the ground that the investment was too risky (foolishly risky! stupidly risky! egregiously risky—you supply the adverb), their liability would be joint and several for the whole loss (with I suppose a right of contribution). Given the scale of operation of modern public corporations, this stupefying disjunction between risk and reward for corporate directors threatens undesirable effects. Given this disjunction, only a very small probability of director liability based on "negligence", "inattention", "waste", etc. could induce a board to avoid authorizing risky investment projects

---

[69] Here our analysis focuses on Delaware not New York. For a recent New York case applying the business judgment rules see *Hellman v Hellman*, No 2005/09695 (NY Sup Ct, 12 March 2008).
[70] 683 A2d 1049, 1052 (DelCh1996).

to any extent! Obviously, it is in the shareholders' economic interest to offer sufficient protection to directors from liability for negligence, etc., to allow directors to conclude that, as a
practical matter, there is no risk that, if they act in good faith and meet minimalist proceduralist
standards of attention, they can face liability as a result of a business loss.']

This presumption can be rebutted by a showing that the board violated one of its fiduciary
duties in connection with the challenged transaction. In that event, the burden shifts to the
director defendants to demonstrate that the challenged transaction was 'entirely fair' to the corporation and its shareholders.

[Note: fiduciary duties under Delaware corporate law include the duty of loyalty but also, in
contrast to the UK, the duty of care.]

We see from this extract that the business judgment rule is a presumption that the directors made an informed decision that was honestly believed to be in the best interests of
the company. If the business judgment rule's presumption is not rebutted then the courts
will subject business decisions only to rationality review—whether there is a rational
basis for the decision. If the presumption is rebutted—either because the director is
not deemed to have been informed, was acting in bad faith not in the interests of the
company, or he was conflicted—then the courts will engage in what is known as *entire
fairness review* to determine whether the decision in question and the resulting transaction was entirely fair to the company. This would include an analysis by the court of
whether the price was fair. One can present this rule in a different, perhaps for a student
of English company law, more accessible, way—a way offered by the final paragraph in
the extract. Making an informed decision requires an assessment of whether the director has taken sufficient care in the decision-making process; acting in good faith in the
best interests of the company requires compliance with the duty of loyalty. Accordingly,
if the board of directors complies with the duties of care and loyalty, the decision itself
will only be subject to rationality review.

3 The standard of review in relation to the decision-making process

The standard for determining whether a decision is informed—whether the director has
complied with the duty of care in relation to the decision-making process—is not the
standard of care (or expectation) outlined earlier, which would require a determination
of whether the director's decision-making process complied with the benchmark of the
decision-making process that would have been undertaken by an ordinarily prudent
person. Rather the standard is what is known as a *gross negligence* standard. Consider
the following case which involves Delaware's most famous application of the gross negligence standard.

■ *Smith v Van Gorkom* 488 A 2d 858

The facts of the case are set out on pp 412–16 above.

Justice Horsey (for the majority)
A director's duty to exercise an informed business judgment is in the nature of a duty of care...The
standard of care applicable to a director's duty of care has also been recently restated by this
Court. In *Aronson* [v *Lewis* 473 A2d at 812], we stated:

'While the Delaware cases use a variety of terms to describe the applicable standard of care, our
analysis satisfies us that under the business judgment rule director liability is predicated upon concepts of gross negligence.'

We again confirm that view. We think the concept of gross negligence is also the proper standard for determining whether a business judgment reached by a board of directors was an informed one…

-A-

On the record before us, we must conclude that the Board of Directors did not reach an informed business judgment on September 20, 1980 in voting to "sell" the Company for $55 per share pursuant to the Pritzker cash-out merger proposal. Our reasons, in summary, are as follows:

The directors (1) did not adequately inform themselves as to Van Gorkom's role in forcing the 'sale' of the Company and in establishing the per share purchase price; (2) were uninformed as to the intrinsic value of the Company; and (3) given these circumstances, at a minimum, were grossly negligent in approving the 'sale' of the Company upon two hours' consideration, without prior notice, and without the exigency of a crisis or emergency.

As has been noted, the Board based its September 20 decision to approve the cash-out merger primarily on Van Gorkom's representations. None of the directors, other than Van Gorkom and Chelberg, had any prior knowledge that the purpose of the meeting was to propose a cash-out merger of Trans Union. No members of Senior Management were present, other than Chelberg, Romans and Peterson; and the latter two had only learned of the proposed sale an hour earlier. Both general counsel Moore and former general counsel Browder attended the meeting, but were equally uninformed as to the purpose of the meeting and the documents to be acted upon.

Without any documents before them concerning the proposed transaction, the members of the Board were required to rely entirely upon Van Gorkom's 20-minute oral presentation of the proposal. No written summary of the terms of the merger was presented; the directors were given no documentation to support the adequacy of $55 price per share for sale of the Company; and the Board had before it nothing more than Van Gorkom's statement of his understanding of the substance of an agreement which he admittedly had never read, nor which any member of the Board had ever seen…

The defendants rely on the following factors to sustain the Trial Court's finding that the Board's decision was an informed one: (1) the magnitude of the premium or spread between the $55 Pritzker offering price and Trans Union's current market price of $38 per share; (2) the amendment of the Agreement as submitted on September 20 to permit the Board to accept any better offer during the 'market test' period; [and] (3) the collective experience and expertise of the Board's 'inside' and 'outside' directors…We discuss each of these grounds *seriatim:*

(1)

A substantial premium may provide one reason to recommend a merger, but in the absence of other sound valuation information, the fact of a premium alone does not provide an adequate basis upon which to assess the fairness of an offering price. Here, the judgment reached as to the adequacy of the premium was based on a comparison between the historically depressed Trans Union market price and the amount of the Pritzker offer. Using market price as a basis for concluding that the premium adequately reflected the true value of the Company was a clearly faulty, indeed fallacious, premise, as the defendants' own evidence demonstrates.

The record is clear that before September 20, Van Gorkom and other members of Trans Union's Board knew that the market had consistently undervalued the worth of Trans Union's stock, despite steady increases in the Company's operating income in the seven years preceding the merger. The Board related this occurrence in large part to Trans Union's inability to use its [Investment Tax Credits] as previously noted. Van Gorkom testified that he did not believe the market price accurately reflected Trans Union's true worth; and several of the directors testified that, as a general rule, most chief executives think that the market undervalues their companies' stock. Yet, on September 20, Trans Union's Board apparently believed that the market stock price accurately reflected the value of the Company for the purpose of determining the adequacy of the premium for its sale…

The parties do not dispute that a publicly-traded stock price is solely a measure of the value of a minority position and, thus, market price represents only the value of a single share. Nevertheless, on September 20, the Board assessed the adequacy of the premium over market, offered by Pritzker, solely by comparing it with Trans Union's current and historical stock price...[71]

Indeed, as of September 20, the Board had no other information on which to base a determination of the intrinsic value of Trans Union as a going concern. As of September 20, the Board had made no evaluation of the Company designed to value the entire enterprise, nor had the Board ever previously considered selling the Company or consenting to a buy-out merger. Thus, the adequacy of a premium is indeterminate unless it is assessed in terms of other competent and sound valuation information that reflects the value of the particular business.

Despite the foregoing facts and circumstances, there was no call by the Board, either on September 20 or thereafter, for any valuation study or documentation of the $55 price per share as a measure of the fair value of the Company in a cash-out context. It is undisputed that the major asset of Trans Union was its cash flow. Yet, at no time did the Board call for a valuation study taking into account that highly significant element of the Company's assets.

We do not imply that an outside valuation study is essential to support an informed business judgment; nor do we state that fairness opinions by independent investment bankers are required as a matter of law. Often insiders familiar with the business of a going concern are in a better position than are outsiders to gather relevant information; and under appropriate circumstances, such directors may be fully protected in relying in good faith upon the valuation reports of their management...

Here, the record establishes that the Board did not request its Chief Financial Officer, Romans, to make any valuation study or review of the proposal to determine the adequacy of $55 per share for sale of the Company. On the record before us: The Board rested on Romans' elicited response that the $55 figure was within a 'fair price range' within the context of a leveraged buy-out. No director sought any further information from Romans. No director asked him why he put $55 at the bottom of his range. No director asked Romans for any details as to his study, the reason why it had been undertaken or its depth. No director asked to see the study; and no director asked Romans whether Trans Union's finance department could do a fairness study within the remaining 36-hour period available under the Pritzker offer...

Had the Board, or any member, made an inquiry of Romans, he presumably would have responded as he testified: that his calculations were rough and preliminary; and, that the study was not designed to determine the fair value of the Company, but rather to assess the feasibility of a leveraged buy-out financed by the Company's projected cash flow, making certain assumptions as to the purchaser's borrowing needs. Romans would have presumably also informed the Board of his view, and the widespread view of Senior Management, that the timing of the offer was wrong and the offer inadequate...

None of the directors, Management or outside, were investment bankers or financial analysts. Yet the Board did not consider recessing the meeting until a later hour that day (or requesting an extension of Pritzker's Sunday evening deadline) to give it time to elicit more information as to the sufficiency of the offer, either from inside Management (in particular Romans) or from Trans Union's own investment banker, Salomon Brothers, whose Chicago specialist in merger and acquisitions was known to the Board and familiar with Trans Union's affairs.

Thus, the record compels the conclusion that on September 20 the Board lacked valuation information adequate to reach an informed business judgment as to the fairness of $55 per share for sale of the Company.

(2)

This brings us to the post-September 20 'market test' upon which the defendants ultimately rely to confirm the reasonableness of their September 20 decision to accept the Pritzker proposal. In

---

[71] The court observes here that 'control' of the company has a value which one would expect a bidder to pay for through a premium to the market price which does not incorporate the value of control.

this connection, the directors present a two-part argument: (a) that by making a 'market test' of Pritzker's $55 per share offer a condition of their September 20 decision to accept his offer, they cannot be found to have acted impulsively or in an uninformed manner on September 20; and (b) that the adequacy of the $17 premium for sale of the Company was conclusively established over the following 90 to 120 days by the most reliable evidence available—the marketplace. Thus, the defendants impliedly contend that the 'market test' eliminated the need for the Board to perform any other form of fairness test either on September 20, or thereafter.

Again, the facts of record do not support the defendants' argument. There is no evidence: (a) that the Merger Agreement was effectively amended to give the Board freedom to put Trans Union up for auction sale to the highest bidder; or (b) that a public auction was in fact permitted to occur. The minutes of the Board meeting make no reference to any of this. Indeed, the record compels the conclusion that the directors had no rational basis for expecting that a market test was attainable, given the terms of the Agreement as executed during the evening of September 20. We rely upon the following facts which are essentially uncontradicted:

...

Van Gorkom states that the Agreement as submitted incorporated the ingredients for a market test by authorizing Trans Union to receive competing offers over the next 90-day period. However, he concedes that the Agreement barred Trans Union from actively soliciting such offers and from furnishing to interested parties any information about the Company other than that already in the public domain...

The defendant directors assert that they 'insisted' upon including two amendments to the Agreement, thereby permitting a market test: (1) to give Trans Union the right to accept a better offer; and (2) to reserve to Trans Union the right to distribute proprietary information on the Company to alternative bidders. Yet, the defendants concede that they did not seek to amend the Agreement to permit Trans Union to solicit competing offers...

(3)

The directors' unfounded reliance on both the premium and the market test as the basis for accepting the Pritzker proposal undermines the defendants' remaining contention that the Board's collective experience and sophistication was a sufficient basis for finding that it reached its September 20 decision with informed, reasonable deliberation. [see the following dissent for details of the board's experience.]

...

We conclude that Trans Union's Board was grossly negligent in that it failed to act with informed reasonable deliberation in agreeing to the Pritzker merger proposal on September 20.

Justice McNeilly (dissenting)

The majority opinion reads like an advocate's closing address to a hostile jury. And I say that not lightly. Throughout the opinion great emphasis is directed only to the negative, with nothing more than lip service granted the positive aspects of this case. In my opinion Chancellor Marvel (retired) should have been affirmed...Because of my diametrical opposition to all evidentiary conclusions of the majority, I respectfully dissent...

The majority has spoken and has effectively said that Trans Union's Directors have been the victims of a 'fast shuffle' by Van Gorkom and Pritzker. That is the beginning of the majority's comedy of errors. The first and most important error made is the majority's assessment of the directors' knowledge of the affairs of Trans Union and their combined ability to act in this situation under the protection of the business judgment rule.

Trans Union's Board of Directors consisted of ten men, five of whom were 'inside' directors and five of whom were 'outside' directors...At the time the merger was proposed the inside five directors had collectively been employed by the Company for 116 years and had 68 years of combined experience as directors. The 'outside' directors were A.W. Wallis, William B. Johnson, Joseph B. Lanterman, Graham J. Morgan and Robert W. Reneker. With the exception of Wallis, these were all chief executive officers of Chicago based corporations that were at least as large as Trans Union. The five 'outside' directors had 78 years of combined experience as chief executive officers, and 53 years cumulative service as Trans Union directors…

Directors of this calibre are not ordinarily taken in by a 'fast shuffle'. I submit they were not taken into this multi-million dollar corporate transaction without being fully informed and aware of the state of the art as it pertained to the entire corporate panorama of Trans Union. True, even directors such as these, with their business acumen, interest and expertise, can go astray. I do not believe that to be the case here. These men knew Trans Union like the back of their hands and were more than well qualified to make on the spot informed business judgments concerning the affairs of Trans Union including a 100% sale of the corporation. Lest we forget, the corporate world of then and now operates on what is so aptly referred to as 'the fast track'. These men were at the time an integral part of that world, all professional business men, not intellectual figureheads…

I have no quarrel with the majority's analysis of the business judgment rule. It is the application of that rule to these facts which is wrong. An overview of the entire record, rather than the limited view of bits and pieces which the majority has exploded like popcorn, convinces me that the directors made an informed business judgment which was buttressed by their test of the market.

At the time of the September 20 meeting the 10 members of Trans Union's Board of Directors were highly qualified and well informed about the affairs and prospects of Trans Union. These directors were acutely aware of the historical problems facing Trans Union which were caused by the tax laws. They had discussed these problems *ad nauseam*. In fact, within two months of the September 20 meeting the board had reviewed and discussed an outside study of the company done by The Boston Consulting Group and an internal five year forecast prepared by management. At the September 20 meeting Van Gorkom presented the Pritzker offer, and the board then heard from James Brennan, the company's counsel in this matter, who discussed the legal documents. Following this, the Board directed that certain changes be made in the merger documents. These changes made it clear that the Board was free to accept a better offer than Pritzker's if one was made. The above facts reveal that the Board did not act in a grossly negligent manner in informing themselves of the relevant and available facts before passing on the merger. To the contrary, this record reveals that the directors acted with the utmost care in informing themselves of the relevant and available facts before passing on the merger.

I respectfully dissent.

The majority of the Supreme Court of Delaware found the Trans Union directors to have acted with gross negligence and, accordingly, their decision to enter into the merger and to call a shareholder meeting to approve the merger did not get the benefit of the business judgment rule. The court remanded the case back to the lower Court of Chancery to carry out an entire fairness review of the transaction, which involved the court determining whether the merger consideration amounted to 'fair consideration'. The case was subsequently settled for a reported £23.5 million. It was reported that £10 million was covered by the directors' D&O insurance policy and the remainder was paid by Pritzker.[72]

The case generated a storm of protest from business groups and legal academic and practitioner circles. Many commentators argued that although the court held that the standard of review for determining whether the directors were informed was gross negligence, in fact the court applied a higher reasonableness standard of review. The Delaware legislature swiftly responded to concerns that this ruling could lead to an

---

[72] Choper et al, *Cases and Materials on Corporations* (Foundation Press, 2004), 98 note 27 citing B. Manning, 'Reflections and Practical Tips on Life in the Boardroom After Van Gorkom' (1985) 41 *Business Lawyer* 1.

exodus of companies to other states by amending the Delaware General Corporation Law to allow companies to amend their certificate of incorporation (the core constitutional document) to provide their directors with a waiver of liability for breaches of the duty of care but not for intentional misconduct or breaches of the duty of loyalty.[73]

■ Section 102(b)(7) Delaware General Corporation Law

(b) In addition to the matters required to be set out in the certificate of incorporation by subsection (a) of this section, the certificate of incorporation may also contain any or all of the following matters:

(7) A provision eliminating or limiting the personal liability of a director to the corporation or its stockholders for monetary damages for breach of fiduciary duty as a director, provided that such provision shall not eliminate or limit the liability of a director: (i) For any breach of the director's duty of loyalty to the corporation or its stockholders; (ii) for acts or omissions not in good faith or which involve intentional misconduct or a knowing violation of law; (iii) under [section 174] of this title [unlawful payment of dividends]; or (iv) for any transaction from which the director derived an improper personal benefit. No such provision shall eliminate or limit the liability of a director for any act or omission occurring prior to the date when such provision becomes effective...

For companies who have adopted such a liability waiver the duty of care becomes, in effect, a pure expression of expectation because even if the directors do not comply with the gross negligence standard of review—that is, they are in breach of their duty of care—the director will incur no liability. A considerable majority of Delaware companies subsequently amended their certificate of incorporation to provide for such waivers.[74]

Questions and discussion

- What does gross negligence mean after *Van Gorkom*?
- Do you think that the Trans Union directors would have been liable for breach of their duty of care applying a reasonable average director standard? Are you persuaded that the price premium, the directors' knowledge of the industry and the market check (particularly after it was amended to allow the active solicitation of other buyers) were insufficient for a *reasonable average director* to conclude that the merger was in the best interests of the company?
- In practice, valuing companies is an extremely difficult process which typically results in considerable variation in what one expert thinks is a fair value and what another expert thinks is a fair value. The court in *Van Gorkom* makes much of the fact that the company did not obtain a **fairness opinion** from an investment bank which would have provided the company with the bank's opinion as to whether a price of $55 per share was fair. Indeed as a result of *Van Gorkom* it has become the norm in US takeover practice, rarely departed from, that target companies obtain fairness opinions from their investment banks. However, there is considerable scepticism in the market place about

---

[73] For a more nuanced account of the adoption of section 102(b)(7) see J.R. Brown and S. Gopalan, 'Opting Only In: Contractarians, Waiver of Liability Provisions, and the Race to the Bottom' (2008), University of Denver Legal Studies Research Paper No 08-02; available at SSRN: http://ssrn.com/abstract=1087404 ●.

[74] See M. Bradley and C. A. Schipani, 'The Relevance of the Duty of Care Standard in Corporate Governance' (1989) 75 *Iowa Law Review* 1, 62 detailing that 94% of Delaware companies adopted the liability waivers.

the usefulness of these opinions. Many would argue that a company will always be able to find an advisor—paid by the company—who will tell it that the price that has been agreed upon is or is not within a range of fair values, depending on the board's preferred position—to accept or reject the offer. It seems highly plausible that had Trans Union asked for such an opinion it could have obtained one that said that a price of $55 was fair. If the presence of such an opinion would have changed the court's view on whether there had been a breach of duty, yet such an opinion would not have changed the outcome for the shareholders—in terms of the price received—does this suggest that when it comes to reviewing the care taken by directors the Delaware courts focus too much on the appearance of care and not the reality of care? On fairness opinions see S. Davidoff, 'Fairness Opinions' (2006) 55 *American University Law Review* 1557. Of course one might argue that given that the 'reality' of the care actually taken is very difficult to assess it makes sense for courts to identify procedural preconditions to obtaining a favourable court determination. By requiring companies to follow such good practice steps, the courts increase the likelihood that directors of all companies will take the expected level of care.

- It is very difficult for a court to determine whether care has been taken when the directors in question have considerable experience and knowledge about the company. One of the reasons for this is that someone who is well informed about the subject matter of the decision is capable of making a good and informed decision quickly and without the need to ask additional questions. In contrast, a person who has less experience and knowledge will not be in a position to make the decision without requesting more information and taking time to think about issues that he may not have directed his attention to previously. With well-informed directors, factors such as the speed of the decision and the record of questions asked may tell us very little about the care taken by experienced directors. Do you think the majority give sufficient deference to the directors' experience in *Van Gorkom*?

- Do you think that the concern that director liability will chill risk-taking and deter people from accepting directorships justifies a complete waiver of liability for duty of care violations; even egregious care failings?

The Supreme Court in *Smith v Van Gorkom* applied the standard of gross negligence to determine whether the directors had breached their duty of care. The court did not, however, attempt to define what is meant by the term 'gross negligence'. We are left to determine this by looking at the facts of the case with the knowledge that these facts amounted to gross negligence. To answer the question 'what does gross negligence mean in Delaware law?', we find ourselves comparing it to the reasonableness standard: does this behaviour fall below, or significantly below, the behaviour we would expect of an imaginary average director acting in these circumstances? Indeed, it is very difficult to articulate clearly a standard of care that is below such an average director benchmark. Perhaps for this reason Romer J in *In re City Equitable Fire* noted in relation to prior English cases that had deployed the term gross negligence:[75] 'for myself, I confess to feeling some difficulty in understanding the difference between negligence and gross negligence, except in so far as the expressions are used for the purpose of drawing a distinction between the duty that is owed in one case and the duty that is owed in another'. Subsequent Delaware cases have, however, provided greater definitional clarity as to what gross negligence means and, in addition, have brought the meaning of gross negligence *in application* more into line with what one might expect from the adjective 'gross'.

---

[75] See, for example, *Overend v Guerney* (1872) LR 5 HL 480; *Lagunas Nitrate Company v Lagunas Syndicate* [1899] 2 Ch 392.

■ *In Re Walt Disney Derivative Litigation* 907 A 2d 693 (Del Ch 2005)

The Walt Disney case surrounds the appointment of one of Hollywood's leading tal-ent agents, Mr Michael Ovitz, to a position as executive president and director. As the founder of one of Hollywood's premier talent agencies—Creative Artist Agency (CAA)—Mr Ovitz generated an annual income of approximately $20 million. In the summer of 1995, the CEO of Walt Disney, Mr Michael Eisner, approached Ovitz with regard to appointing him as executive president and negotiations commenced regarding the terms of Ovitz's remuneration (compensation) arrangements. The board of directors as a whole never considered whether or not to attempt to recruit Ovitz, although several members of the board were aware of the approach. The negotiations were led by Irwin Russell, the chairman of Walt Disney's compensation committee, in close consultation with Eisner. The other members of the compensation committee, however, were not informed of the negotiations until they were well advanced.

Given Ovitz's significant existing compensation from CAA it was clear to all that the compensation negotiations would be difficult. Ovitz insisted on participation on the 'upside' together with 'downside protection'. That is, he insisted on increased remuner-ation if things went well but a significant exit package if they did not. Nevertheless, the parties managed to reach an initial agreement on terms, the key provisions of which were: (1) a five-year contract term without the ability to give notice except for gross negligence or malfeasance; (2) a $1 million base salary; and (3) two tranches of share options, the first of which vested at different periods within the first five years, the second of which would be provided if the contract was extended.

In relation to downside risk, in the event that Ovitz's contract was terminated by the company—in the absence of gross negligence or malfeasance and prior to expiry of the five-year term—he would be entitled to: (1) the remaining salary for the five-year term; (2) a payment of $7.5 million a year for each remaining year to compensate him for unaccrued bonus; (3) the first tranche of options would vest immediately which would mean he could exercise them at that point of time; and (4) a $10 million cash-out payment to compensate him for not receiving the second tranche of options. It was estimated that the total package was worth approximately $24 million a year. The court noted that 'according to Russell, Ovitz was an "exceptional corporate executive" who was a "highly successful and unique entrepreneur." Nevertheless, Russell cautioned that Ovitz's [package] was at the top level for any corporate officer and significantly above that of the CEO and that the number of stock options granted...was far beyond the standards applied within Disney and corporate America "and will raise very strong criticism." '

Once the terms of the basic agreement had been fleshed out, the company appointed a renowned compensation consultant, Graef Crystal. Crystal expressed concern that the package provided Ovitz with the best of both worlds—'low risk and high return'. This report was not provided to the whole board or the compensation committee. At the same time as the compensation consultant was appointed, another member of Disney's com-pensation committee, Mr Raymond Watson, was brought into the negotiation process.

On 14 August 1995, Ovitz and Eisner signed a letter agreement providing for Ovitz's appointment on the agreed terms (the Ovitz Employment Agreement or OEA). The agreement was subject to approval of the whole board and the compensation commit-tee. On the same day Eisner arranged for the company to make a press release announc-ing the appointment of Ovitz. Importantly, however, although OEA had been reached and the press release made, the compensation committee had not formally met to dis-cuss the appointment or its terms.

The compensation committee consisted of Russell, Watson, Sidney Poitier (the actor and director), and a fourth member, Ignacio Lozano. The compensation committee met to discuss Ovitz's compensation agreement for the first time over a month later on

26 September. The meeting lasted for one hour. But in addition to discussing the OEA the committee also discussed the following issues in that hour: (1) the compensation packages for other Disney employees; (2) 121 grants of stock options; (3) the employment agreement for an executive of CapCities/ABC, a Disney subsidiary; and (4) Russell's compensation for leading the negotiations on the Ovitz's employment agreement. The compensation consultant did not attend the meeting nor was his report distributed at the meeting. At the end of this meeting the compensation committee voted to approve the OEA. Subsequent to the compensation committee meeting the full board met and approved the OEA.

Although Ovitz made a good initial impression, within a year he had lost Eisner's confidence and was viewed as a poor fit for the company. Quickly Eisner came to the conclusion that Ovitz's contract would have to be terminated. Although there was some dispute about this issue, for our analysis of this case we shall assume that there was no basis for a termination of the contract on the grounds that Ovitz had been grossly negligent. Ovitz received the vast majority of the termination compensation detailed above which was reported to be $130 million. $130 million for one year's work.

A derivative action was brought by certain shareholders of the company claiming, amongst others, breach of the duty of care.

Chancellor Chandler

Unlike ideals of corporate governance, a fiduciary's duties do not change over time. How we understand those duties may evolve and become refined, but the duties themselves have not changed, except to the extent that fulfilling a fiduciary duty requires obedience to other positive law. This Court strongly encourages directors and officers to employ best practices, as those practices are understood at the time a corporate decision is taken. But Delaware law does not—indeed, the common law cannot—hold fiduciaries liable for a failure to comply with the aspirational ideal of best practices, any more than a common-law court deciding a medical malpractice dispute can impose a standard of liability based on ideal—rather than competent or standard—medical treatment practices, lest the average medical practitioner be found inevitably derelict.

Fiduciaries are held by the common law to a high standard in fulfilling their stewardship over the assets of others, a standard that (depending on the circumstances) may not be the same as that contemplated by ideal corporate governance. Yet therein lies perhaps the greatest strength of Delaware's corporation law. Fiduciaries who act faithfully and honestly on behalf of those whose interests they represent are indeed granted wide latitude in their efforts to maximize shareholders' investment. Times may change, but fiduciary duties do not. Indeed, other institutions may develop, pronounce and urge adherence to ideals of corporate best practices. But the development of aspirational ideals, however worthy as goals for human behavior, should not work to distort the legal requirements by which human behavior is actually measured...

Both parties agree that liability must be predicated upon a finding of gross negligence...In the duty of care context with respect to corporate fiduciaries, gross negligence has been defined as a '" reckless indifference to or a deliberate disregard of the whole body of stockholders" or actions which are "without the bounds of reason."' Because duty of care violations are actionable only if the directors acted with gross negligence, and because in most instances money damages are unavailable to a plaintiff who could theoretically prove a duty of care violation, duty of care violations are rarely found...

In the area of director action, plaintiffs must prove by a preponderance of the evidence that the presumption of the business judgment rule does not apply either because the directors breached their fiduciary duties...

Eisner

The decision to hire Ovitz and enter into the OEA is one of business judgment, to which the presumptions of the business judgment rule apply. In order to prevail, therefore, plaintiffs must demonstrate by a preponderance of the evidence that Eisner was either grossly negligent or acted in bad faith in connection with Ovitz's hiring and the approval of the OEA.

As I mentioned earlier, Eisner was very much aware of what was going on as the situation developed. In the limited instances where he was not the primary source of information relating to Ovitz, Russell kept Eisner informed of negotiations with Ovitz. Eisner knew Ovitz; he was familiar with the career Ovitz had built at CAA and he knew that the Company was in need of a senior executive, especially in light of the upcoming CapCities/ABC merger. In light of this knowledge, I cannot find that plaintiffs have demonstrated by a preponderance of the evidence that Eisner failed to inform himself of all material information reasonably available or that he acted in a grossly negligent manner.

Notwithstanding the foregoing, Eisner's actions in connection with Ovitz's hiring should not serve as a model for fellow executives and fiduciaries to follow. His lapses were many. He failed to keep the board as informed as he should have. He stretched the outer boundaries of his authority as CEO by acting without specific board direction or involvement. He prematurely issued a press release that placed significant pressure on the board to accept Ovitz and approve his compensation package in accordance with the press release. To my mind, these actions fall far short of what shareholders expect and demand from those entrusted with a fiduciary position. Eisner's failure to better involve the board in the process of Ovitz's hiring, usurping that role for himself, although not in violation of law, does not comport with how fiduciaries of Delaware corporations are expected to act.

Despite all of the legitimate criticisms that may be leveled at Eisner, especially at having enthroned himself as the omnipotent and infallible monarch of his personal Magic Kingdom, I nonetheless conclude, after carefully considering and weighing all the evidence, that Eisner's actions were taken in good faith. That is, Eisner's actions were taken with the subjective belief that those actions were in the best interests of the Company—he believed that his taking charge and acting swiftly and decisively to hire Ovitz would serve the best interests of the Company notwithstanding the high cost of Ovitz's hiring and notwithstanding that two experienced executives who had arguably been passed over for the position (Litvack and Bollenbach) were not completely supportive. Those actions do not represent a knowing violation of law or evidence a conscious and intentional disregard of duty. In conclusion, Eisner acted in good faith and did not breach his fiduciary duty of care because he was not grossly negligent.

[The court considered all of the compensation committee members individually. As Poitier and Lozano played a minimal role in the negotiation of the employment agreement and yet approved it in a short meeting, they appeared particularly exposed to a breach of duty claim. We therefore focus on the court's view of their behaviour.]

Poitier and Lozano

Poitier and Lozano were the remaining members of the compensation committee that considered the economic terms of the OEA. It is not disputed that they were far less involved in the genesis of the OEA than were Russell, and to a lesser extent, Watson. The question in dispute is whether their level of involvement in the OEA was so low as to constitute gross negligence and, therefore, a breach of their fiduciary duty of care, or whether their actions evidence a lack of good faith. As will be shown, I conclude that neither of these men acted in a grossly negligent manner or in bad faith.

Poitier is a man celebrated for his work both within and outside the entertainment industry. Poitier was elected to the Company's board of directors in 1994, and attended his first board meeting during January of 1995. Lozano was the publisher of the nation's largest Spanish language daily newspaper, is the former chairman of the board of that entity, and also served as the United States' ambassador to El Salvador. Lozano had a long tenure on the Company's board of directors, serving from the early 1980s until 2001. Lozano also has experience on the compensation committees of other corporations.

There is no question that Poitier and Lozano's involvement in the process of Ovitz's hiring came very late in the game. As found above, Poitier received a call from Russell on August 13 (and another the next day), during which they discussed the terms of the proposed OLA. Lozano spoke with Watson regarding this same subject. It appears that neither Poitier nor Lozano had any further involvement with the hiring process, apart from these phone calls, until the September 26, 1995 compensation committee meeting.

At that meeting, both Poitier and Lozano received the term sheet that explained the key terms of Ovitz's contract, and they were present for and participated in the discussion that occurred. Both then voted to approve the terms of the OEA, and both credibly testified that they believed they possessed sufficient information at that time to make an informed decision. Plaintiffs largely point to two perceived inadequacies in this meeting (and in Poitier and Lozano's business judgment), first, that insufficient time was spent reviewing the terms of Ovitz's contract and, second, that Poitier and Lozano were not provided with sufficient documentation, including Crystal's correspondence, Watson's calculations, and a draft of the OEA. These arguments understandably hearken back to *Van Gorkom*, where the Supreme Court condemned the Trans Union board for agreeing to a material transaction after a board meeting of about two hours and without so much as a term sheet of the transaction as contemplated. Although the parallels between *Van Gorkom* and this case at first appear striking, a more careful consideration will reveal several important distinctions between the two.

First and foremost, the nature of the transaction in *Van Gorkom* is fundamentally different, and orders of magnitude more important, than the transaction at issue here. In *Van Gorkom*, the Trans Union board was called into a special meeting on less than a day's notice, without notice of the reason for the meeting, to consider a merger agreement that would result in the sale of the entire company…[In the Walt Disney case] the board meeting was not called on short notice, and the directors were well aware that Ovitz's hiring would be discussed at the meeting as a result of the August 14 press release more than a month before. Furthermore, analyzing the transactions in terms of monetary value, and even accepting plaintiffs' experts' bloated valuations for comparison purposes, it is beyond question that the $734 million sale of Trans Union was material and significantly larger than the financial ramifications to the Company of Ovitz's hiring.

Second, the Trans Union board met for about two hours to discuss and deliberate on this monumental transaction in the life of Trans Union. A precise amount of time for the length of the compensation committee meeting, and more specifically, the length of the discussion regarding the OEA, is difficult to establish. The minutes of the compensation committee's meeting and the full board's meeting indicate that the compensation committee meeting convened at 9 am, and that the full board's meeting convened at 10 am, leaving no more than an hour for the compensation committee to meet. Lozano, although he had little recollection of the meeting, believed that the compensation committee meeting ran long—until 10:30 a.m. As I found above, the meeting lasted about an hour. Russell testified that the discussion of the OEA took about 25–30 minutes, significantly more time than the brief discussion reflected in the minutes would seem to indicate. Lozano believed that the committee spent 'perhaps four times as much time on Mr. Ovitz's contract than we did on Mr. Russell's compensation.'

I am persuaded by Russell and Lozano's recollection that the OEA was discussed for a not insignificant length of time. Is that length of time markedly less than the attention given by the Trans Union board to the merger agreement they were statutorily charged with approving or rejecting? Yes. Is that difference probative on the issue of whether the compensation committee adequately discussed the OEA? Not in the least. When the Trans Union board met for those two hours, it was the very first time any of those directors had discussed a sale of the company. Here, all the members of the committee were aware in advance that Ovitz's hiring would be discussed, and the members of the committee had also previously had more than minimal informal discussions amongst themselves as to the *bona fides* of the OEA before the meeting ever occurred. Furthermore, as mentioned above, the nature and scope of the transactions are fundamentally different.

Third, the Trans Union board had absolutely no documentation before it when it considered the merger agreement. The board was completely reliant on the misleading and uninformed presentations given by Trans Union's officers (Van Gorkom and Romans). In contrast, the compensation committee was provided with a term sheet of the key terms of the OEA and a presentation was made by Russell (assisted by Watson), who had personal knowledge of the relevant information by virtue of his negotiations with Ovitz and discussions with Crystal. Additionally, the testimony and documentary evidence support this conclusion. It is true that the compensation committee did not review and discuss the then-existing draft of the full text of the OEA. This, however, is not required. Nor is it necessary for an expert to make a formal presentation at the committee meeting in order for the board to rely on that expert's analysis, although that certainly would have been the better course of action. Furthermore, the Company's compensation committee reasonably and wisely left the task of negotiating and drafting the actual text of the OEA in the hands of the Company's counsel.

Fourth, Trans Union's senior management completely opposed the merger. In contrast, the Company's senior management generally saw Ovitz's hiring as a boon for the Company... In sum, although Poitier and Lozano did very little in connection with Ovitz's hiring and the compensation committee's approval of the OEA, they did not breach their fiduciary duties. I conclude that they were informed by Russell and Watson of all *material* information reasonably available, even though they were not privy to every conversation or document exchanged amongst Russell, Watson, Crystal and Ovitz's representatives.

Viewed objectively, the compensation committee was asked to make a decision knowing that: 1) Ovitz was a third party with whom Russell negotiated at arms' length; 2) regardless of whether Ovitz truly was 'the most powerful man in Hollywood,' he was a highly-regarded industry figure; 3) Ovitz was widely believed to possess skills and experience that would be very valuable to the Company, especially in light of the CapCities/ABC acquisition, [the death of the company's former president], and Eisner's medical problems; 4) in order to accept the Company's presidency, Ovitz was leaving and giving up his very successful business, which would lead a reasonable person to believe that he would likely be highly successful in similar pursuits elsewhere in the industry; 5) the CEO and others in senior management were supporting the hiring; and 6) the potential compensation was not economically material to the Company.

Poitier and Lozano did not intentionally disregard a duty to act, nor did they bury their heads in the sand knowing a decision had to be made. They acted in a manner that they believed was in the best interests of the corporation. Delaware law does not require (nor does it prohibit) directors to take as active a role as Russell and Watson took in connection with Ovitz's hiring. There is no question that in comparison to those two, the actions of Poitier and Lozano may appear casual or uninformed, but I conclude that they did not breach their fiduciary duties and that they acted in good faith in connection with Ovitz's hiring.

Questions and discussion

- In the *Walt Disney* case the Chancery Court held, and the Supreme Court subsequently affirmed, that 'in the duty of care context with respect to corporate fiduciaries, gross negligence has been defined as a "reckless indifference to or a deliberate disregard of the whole body of stockholders" or actions which are "without the bounds of reason" '.[76] This provides us with a definition of gross negligence that is clearly distinct from a reasonable average director standard. Note in particular the reference to actions that are 'without the bounds of reason'. This aspect of the gross negligence standard effectively dissolves duty of care review into the reasons for the decision. If there are rational reasons for the decision or action taken then the care review standard is satisfied. Note

---

[76] *Tomczak v Morton Thiokol, Inc*, 1990 WL 42607, at 12 (Del Ch, 5 April 1990) (quoting *Allaun v Consol Oil Co*, 147 A 257, 261 (Del Ch 1929).

that in the extract the court completes its analysis with a review of the reasons why the compensation committee could rationally have taken the decision it took.

- The bare facts of the *Walt Disney* case are shocking. For one year's work Mr Ovitz received a compensation package of $130 million.[77] For Eisner he clearly thought he was acting in the company's best interests and was wholly informed about the transaction in question. His role and behaviour, however, appeared to undermine the effective functioning of the board. He initiated and fully negotiated the OEA without any role for the full compensation committee or the board. Through the post-signing press release on 14 August he made the agreement look like a fait accompli, thereby undermining the board's ability to make an undistorted decision. Yet the court felt this did not amount to gross negligence or bad faith. Do you agree?

- One way of understanding *Van Gorkom* is that the Delaware Supreme Court were concerned that the board failed to exercise any effective supervision over an imperial CEO. Is *Walt Disney* any different in this respect?

- The court compares the time taken by the compensation committee for the decision, the information that they had available and the materiality of the decision with these aspects of the *Van Gorkom* decision. This comparison is effective in many respects. The decision in *Van Gorkom* was far more significant for Trans Union than the decision as to whether or not to hire Ovitz was for Walt Disney. However, is the court comparing apples with apples? The compensation committee has a very specific function. The decision to hire any senior officer is material to the compensation committee if not to the business as a whole. For the compensation committee it is difficult to imagine a more material decision—apart perhaps from hiring a new CEO. From this perspective, do you think the court makes a persuasive case that *Walt Disney* is factually distinct from *Van Gorkom*? If the answer is 'no', then what appears to be happening here is the court reasserting the idea of a gross negligence standard as being in fact significantly lower than a negligence standard—as indeed the definition set out in the case would suggest. The court tries to distinguish *Van Gorkom* on the facts, however, they are applying a different standard to the one applied in *Van Gorkom*. Following *Walt Disney* any concern that the gross negligence standard was really a negligence standard by another name was laid to rest.

- Would the directors sitting on the compensation committee have been found in breach of a UK duty of care, skill, and diligence?

- Why is it necessary to have a low standard of care such as the gross negligence standard articulated in *Walt Disney* when Delaware companies can waive liability for care violations in accordance with section 102(b)(7)? Does section 102(b)(7) remove any basis for claiming that the gross negligence care standard is justified by risk-chilling and director service policy concerns?

- The UK's standard of review under section 174 of the Companies Act 2006 is clearly a higher standard of review than the gross negligence care standard in Delaware. Furthermore, the pre-2006 Act standard of review was also much higher than the Delaware standard—whether one looks at the ordinary man acting on his own behalf standard or the subjective standard where the director was in fact skilled and experienced. Nor, as we have seen, does UK law allow companies to provide UK directors with the liability comfort that a liability waiver under section 102(b)(7) may provide Delaware directors. What implications does this difference have for the claims that higher review care standards chill risk-taking and deter board service? Is it possible that UK directors are more risk averse than Delaware directors because of the different care standard? There is certainly no empirical support for this claim. Is it the case then that it is harder to find people to serve on UK company boards than on Delaware boards? Again there is no empirical support for this claim. One point worth considering

---

[77] At the time of his departure this was worth approximately £85 million.

in this regard, however, and explored in greater detail in Chapter 15, is that although UK standards of review are high, the probability of being sued has always been very low because of the very restrictive rules for UK companies on the ability of individual shareholders to bring actions on behalf of the company to enforce a breach of a director's duty (so-called derivative actions). That is, the standards may be high but as the probability of enforcement has traditionally been low the standards did not give directors cause for concern. As we shall see in Chapter 15, changes to the rules on when a derivative action can be brought, introduced by the 2006 Act, *may* make it easier to bring litigation against directors. This may, if these policy concerns are well founded, be cause for concern for UK companies.

- Note the court's rejection of the incorporation of the ideals of corporate governance into the duty of care and compare that position to the position we saw in the Australian cases of *ASIC v Rich* and *ASIC v Healey*.

4 The standard of review and board monitoring

As we discussed in Part II of this chapter, in addition to a decision-making function, a central aspect of the role of a board of directors in large companies is a monitoring function: monitoring and assessing the performance of executive management and the company's performance as a whole. Clearly, the care that directors take in carrying out this monitoring function is central to the effective functioning of the board. A central aspect of this monitoring function is ensuring that the company has the necessary systems in place to ensure that the information on which the board relies is accurate and comprehensive and that employees are subject to the necessary checks and supervision to ensure that they act in accordance with the law and corporate policies when doing their job and when producing this information. Arguably, any ex-post (after the fact) review of whether directors have taken adequate care to ensure that such systems are in place and are effective is not subject to as great a concern about the relationship between hindsight bias and the risk and uncertainty involved in business judgments which, as we have seen, is the policy driver of the low standard of care in relation to business judgments and the care taken in making those judgments.[78] Does this mean we find a more demanding standard in Delaware in relation to monitoring? Consider in this regard the following Delaware case on monitoring and the duty of care.

■ *In re Citigroup Inc Shareholder Derivative Litigation*
964 A.2d 106 (Del. Ch. 2009)

Citigroup is a major US bank that suffered many billions of dollars of losses in the recent credit crunch as a result of poor investments in the subprime securities market. The subprime securities market relates to complex debt instruments created from pools of mortgages made to low income families, a significant number of which were not repaid. This case involves a derivative suit brought by shareholders of Citigroup claiming that the directors had breached their duty of care by: (a) failing to monitor effectively the risk profile of the bank prior to the crisis which resulted in huge exposures to these subprime securities; and (b) by failing to put in place effective controls to manage risk-taking by the bank. As an aside, it is worth noting in this regard that the former CEO of Citigroup, Chuck Prince, is known for his infamous observation shortly before the crisis that 'as long as the music is still playing you have to get up and dance'!

---

[78] See footnote 15. Clearly, however, if hindsight bias results in a good decision being perceived to a poor decision, and if judges are more likely to associate poor decisions with care failings, then hindsight bias may also affect the assessment of the compliance of the monitoring function with the duty of care.

Chancellor Chandler

Plaintiffs allege that defendants are liable to the Company for breach of fiduciary duty for (1) failing to adequately oversee and manage Citigroup's exposure to the problems in the sub-prime mortgage market, even in the face of alleged 'red flags' and (2) failing to ensure that the Company's financial reporting and other disclosures were thorough and accurate. As will be more fully explained below, the "red flags" alleged in the eighty-six page Complaint are generally statements from public documents that reflect worsening conditions in the financial markets, including the subprime and credit markets, and the effects those worsening conditions had on market participants, including Citigroup's peers. By way of example only, plaintiffs' 'red flags' include the following:

- *May 27, 2005:* Economist Paul Krugman of the *New York Times* said he saw 'signs that America's housing market, like the stock market at the end of the last decade, is approaching the final, feverish stages of a speculative bubble.'

- *May 2006:* Ameriquest Mortgage, one of the United States' leading wholesale subprime lenders, announced the closing of each of its 229 retail offices and reduction of 3,800 employees...

Plaintiffs' argument is based on a theory of director liability famously articulated by former Chancellor Allen [in *Caremark*].[79] In *Caremark*, the plaintiffs alleged that the directors were liable because they should have known that certain officers and employees were violating the federal Anti-Referral Payments Law. In analyzing these claims, the Court began, appropriately, by reviewing the duty of care and the protections of the business judgment rule.

With regard to director liability standards, the Court distinguished between (1) 'a board decision that results in a loss because that decision was ill advised or "negligent"' and (2) 'an unconsidered failure of the board to act in circumstances in which due attention would, arguably, have prevented the loss.' In the former class of cases, director action is analyzed under the business judgment rule, which prevents judicial second guessing of the decision if the directors employed a rational process and considered all material information reasonably available—a standard measured by concepts of gross negligence. In the latter class of cases, where directors are alleged to be liable for a failure to monitor liability creating activities, the *Caremark* Court...stated that while directors could be liable for a failure to monitor, 'only a sustained or systematic failure of the board to exercise oversight—such as an utter failure to attempt to assure a reasonable information and reporting system exists—will establish the lack of good faith that is a necessary condition to liability'.

In *Stone v. Ritter*,[80] the Delaware Supreme Court approved the *Caremark* standard for director oversight liability...The *Stone* Court explained:

'*Caremark* articulates the necessary conditions predicate for director oversight liability: (a) the directors utterly failed to implement any reporting or information system or controls; *or* (b) having implemented such a system or controls, consciously failed to monitor or oversee its operations thus disabling themselves from being informed of risks or problems requiring their attention.'

The test is rooted in concepts of bad faith; indeed, a showing of bad faith is a *necessary condition* to director oversight liability.

Plaintiffs' theory of how the director defendants will face personal liability is a bit of a twist on the traditional *Caremark* claim. In a typical *Caremark* case, plaintiffs argue that the defendants are liable for damages that arise from a failure to properly monitor or oversee employee misconduct or violations of law. For example, in *Caremark* the board allegedly failed to monitor employee actions in violation of the federal Anti-Referral Payments Law; in *Stone*, the directors were charged with a failure of oversight that resulted in liability for the company because of employee violations of the Federal Bank Secrecy Act.

[79] *In re Caremark Int'l Inc Derivative Litigation*, 698 A2d 959 (Del Ch 1996).
[80] 911 A2d at 370.

In contrast, plaintiffs' *Caremark* claims are based on defendants' alleged failure to properly monitor Citigroup's *business risk*, specifically its exposure to the subprime mortgage market. In their answering brief, plaintiffs allege that the director defendants are personally liable under *Caremark* for failing to 'make a good faith attempt to follow the procedures put in place or fail[ing] to assure that adequate and proper corporate information and reporting systems existed that would enable them to be fully informed regarding Citigroup's risk to the subprime mortgage market.' Plaintiffs point to so-called 'red flags' that should have put defendants on notice of the problems in the subprime mortgage market and further allege that the board should have been especially conscious of these red flags because a majority of the directors (1) served on the Citigroup board during its previous Enron related conduct and (2) were members of the ARM [audit and risk management] Committee and considered financial experts…

[The] plaintiffs in this case have failed to state a *Caremark* claim…that the directors did not fulfill their oversight obligations by failing to monitor the business risk of the company. The allegations in the Complaint amount essentially to a claim that Citigroup suffered large losses and that there were certain warning signs that could or should have put defendants on notice of the business risks related to Citigroup's investments in subprime assets. Plaintiffs then conclude that because defendants failed to prevent the Company's losses associated with certain business risks, they must have consciously ignored these warning signs or knowingly failed to monitor the Company's risk in accordance with their fiduciary duties. Such conclusory allegations, however, are not sufficient to state a claim for failure of oversight…

Plaintiffs do not contest that Citigroup had procedures and controls in place that were designed to monitor risk. Plaintiffs admit that Citigroup established the ARM Committee and in 2004 amended the ARM Committee charter to include the fact that one of the purposes of the ARM Committee was to assist the board in fulfilling its oversight responsibility relating to policy standards and guidelines for risk assessment and risk management…According to plaintiffs' own allegations, the ARM Committee met eleven times in 2006 and twelve times in 2007.

Plaintiffs nevertheless argue that the director defendants breached their duty of oversight either because the oversight mechanisms were not adequate or because the director defendants did not make a good faith effort to comply with the established oversight procedures. To support this claim, the Complaint alleges numerous facts that plaintiffs argue should have put the director defendants on notice of the impending problems in the subprime mortgage market and Citigroup's exposure thereto. [These facts were listed and included, for example, 'the steady decline of the housing market and the impact the collapsing bubble would have on mortgages and subprime backed securities since as early as 2005'].

However, to establish director oversight liability plaintiffs would ultimately have to prove bad faith conduct by the director defendants…The warning signs alleged by plaintiffs are not evidence that the directors consciously disregarded their duties or otherwise acted in bad faith; at most they evidence that the directors made bad business decisions. The 'red flags' in the Complaint amount to little more than portions of public documents that reflected the worsening conditions in the subprime mortgage market and in the economy generally…That the director defendants knew of signs of a deterioration in the subprime mortgage market, or even signs suggesting that conditions could decline further, is not sufficient to show that the directors were or should have been aware of any wrongdoing at the Company or were consciously disregarding a duty somehow to prevent Citigroup from suffering losses…

Instead of alleging facts that could demonstrate bad faith on the part of the directors, by presenting the Court with the so called 'red flags,' plaintiffs are inviting the Court to engage in the exact kind of judicial second guessing that is proscribed by the business judgment rule. In any business decision that turns out poorly there will likely be signs that one could point to and argue are evidence that the decision was wrong. Indeed, it is tempting in a case with such staggering losses for one to think that they could have made the 'right' decision if they had been in the directors' position. This temptation, however, is one of the reasons for the presumption against an objective review of business decisions by judges, a presumption that is no less applicable when the losses to the Company are large.

Questions and discussion

- The standard of liability for breach of duty of care for monitoring failures (oversight liability) is that the directors' actions in failing to monitor amount to bad faith. Such bad faith is established by: (*per Caremark*) a 'sustained or systematic failure by the board to exercise oversight' which would involve an '*utter failure* to attempt to assure a reasonable information and reporting system exists' (emphasis added); or (*per Stone v Ritter*) a conscious failure to monitor. Only a truly egregious disregard for the interests of the company and the shareholders could result in liability for the directors for failure to monitor or to put in place adequate internal controls. In relation to internal controls this effectively means there can be no liability exposure if a system of controls is in place, no matter how inadequate.

- The court firmly rejects the idea that red flags such as the ones in this case can result in a breach of a duty of care. The court in the broader judgment is keen to point out that the board's response to these red flags are in themselves business judgments about how to carry out business in the market place as it stands. Chuck Prince may have been vilified for his comments about having to continue dancing while the music is playing, but his comment represents merely a business judgment about how to do banking in an overheated market. There is a rational basis for this position, even if now we think it sounds ridiculous. The court is keen to make it clear that finding a breach of duty for a monitoring failure in relation to such flags encroaches on the cardinal precepts of the business judgment rule.

- The court is very aware of how with hindsight it is easy to associate disastrous consequences with monitoring failures. The low 'good faith' standard ensures that such hindsight-influenced judgments do not result in liability for directors in relation to anything other than egregious failings. Do you think that hindsight bias is a problem at all, or as a big a concern, in relation to monitoring, as it is in relation to business judgments?

- If this Delaware standard had been applied in *Barings* would the court's judgment have been any different. It is submitted that it would not, as in *Barings* there was indeed an '*utter failure* to attempt to assure a reasonable information and reporting system exists'. Clearly, however, that does not mean that UK directors are only exposed to oversight liability for breach of duty in such circumstances. They could be liable if a reasonable director carrying out the function of the director in question would have exercised greater oversight/demanded more effective controls. However, for the reasons outlined in Part II, it is submitted that in relation to non-executive directors UK law is unlikely to expect much more of directors than Delaware: they must ensure that internal controls have been put in place and kept under review. The duty of care in the UK will, of course, be much more demanding of the executive directors.

- How do *ASIC v Healey* and *Citigroup* differ in their view of the relationship between corporate law and directors? Which do you prefer and why?

VI DOES THE UK HAVE A BUSINESS JUDGMENT RULE?

We have seen in our analysis of the Delaware business judgment rule that the Delaware courts will apply rationality review to business judgments provided that the directors have complied with their duty of care and their duty of loyalty. As rationality review is such a low standard—that a rational reason can be given for the decision—compliance with the duty of care and the duty of loyalty means, in effect, that the business judgments will not be subject to court review. English company law does not structure the legal regulation of business judgments as clearly as this. It does not, formally at least, have a business judgment rule in these terms. It is often correctly stated, however, that English courts do not review business judgments. In support of this claim the following dicta from Lord Wilberforce in *Howard Smith v Ampol Petroleum Ltd*[81] is often cited:

> It would be wrong for the court to substitute its opinion for that of the management, or indeed to question the correctness of the management's decision, on such a question, if bona fide arrived at. There is no appeal on merits from management decisions to courts of law: nor will courts of law assume to act as a kind of supervisory board over decisions within the powers of management honestly arrived at.

The facts of the *Walt Disney* case provide a useful fact pattern to consider how and in what circumstances English courts will review business judgments. First of all let us consider the duty to promote the success of the company as applied to the facts of *Walt Disney*. As we saw in Chapter 10, when making a decision or exercising discretion English law expects of a director that the decision is one which *he considers* promotes the success of the company for the benefit of the members. We saw in *Regentcrest plc v Cohen*[82] that, although the duty is a subjective one, in determining what the director *actually thought* the courts may make reference to objective considerations such as the plausibility or rationality of the reasons given for taking the decision. With regard to the two non-executive Walt Disney board members sitting on the compensation committee, a UK court would ask if they thought that granting the remuneration package would promote the success of the company. The court would first consider available evidence of such belief. In the absence of clear evidence of belief such a consideration could involve in effect a level of review of the business decision: were the reasons for granting such compensation plausible enough for the court to accept that the directors actually thought it would promote the success of the company? Do you think that a UK court would find that the reasons given in the second to last paragraph of the *Walt Disney* extract would be plausible enough to support a finding that the directors would be compliant with section 172? In this author's view they would.

Let us now consider the relationship between the duty of care and court review of business decisions. The care or the absence thereof that a director takes in relation to a business decision is distinct from the quality of the decision itself. A director can behave negligently but still reach, fortuitously, a good decision. A judicial determination of a breach of the duty of care necessarily, therefore, results in a review of the decision in order to determine whether the company has suffered a loss and whether the directors are liable to make good that loss. If the nature of the decision is such that had the requisite degree of care been taken the decision would or could have been taken in any event, then the company suffers no loss as a result of the breach of the duty of care. Accordingly, where there has been a breach of the duty of care, the actual decision itself must be reviewed according to a specified benchmark such as whether the decision is one a reasonable director would have taken. The logic of the Delaware business judgment rule makes this clear—if the directors are found to have breached the gross negligence standard of review then the decision that resulted is reviewed according to the entire fairness standard, which includes an analysis of whether the company received or paid a fair price, that is, a determination of whether they suffered any loss by over- or under-paying. In *Smith v Van Gorkom* the finding of gross negligence resulted in an

---

[81] [1974] AC 821.   [82] [2001] 2 BCLC 80.

award of damages determined in relation to the merger price. In *Walt Disney*, had there been a finding of breach of the standard of review, then the question for the Delaware courts would have been how much did the $130 million compensation package exceed a market package for Ovitz given his skills and background? The UK courts would ask similar questions if the directors were found to be in breach of section 174 of the Companies Act 2006. Most likely, in such circumstances, they would determine loss by determining whether the actual decision was one that a reasonable director, with the section 174 skill set, would have taken.

Accordingly, in both the UK and Delaware the structure of the approach taken to reviewing business decisions that result from a duty of care (decision-making process) violation is very similar. The question of importance is what in each jurisdiction is the standard of care which operates as the gatekeeper to that business judgment review, and it is here that we see significant substantive differences between the UK and Delaware. In Delaware there is a much more aggressive gatekeeper preventing court review, namely the gross negligence standard. In the UK the standard of care is considerably higher: the objective/subjective reasonably diligent person standard.

 Online Resource Centre
http://www.oxfordtextbooks.co.uk/orc/kershaw2e/

Visit the Online Resource Centre for additional resources and information available for this chapter, including web links and an interactive flashcard glossary.

CHAPTER THIRTEEN

REGULATING CONFLICTS I: SELF-DEALING

I INTRODUCTION

Directors have personal interests, desires, aspirations, and ambitions. In certain circumstances those personal interests and concerns may come directly into conflict with the interests or the success of the company. This potential for conflict is, of course, the root of the managerial agency problem. Actual conflicts between personal and company interests do not, unfortunately, come in a neat package. Some conflicts result in a direct increase in the director's personal wealth. Other conflicts are less apparent, for example: decisions that do not promote the success of the company but may benefit a friend or a third party or a charitable or political institution with which the director is affiliated; decisions made ostensibly in the company's interests but really designed to protect the director's job and the benefits the job brings; or where a director elects to satisfy his preference for leisure rather than do the job that he is being paid to do. To varying degrees the duties we have considered in Chapters 10 to 12 address these more indirect conflicts. This chapter and the Chapter 14 are primarily concerned with the regulation of direct conflicts of interest where monetary personal benefit for the director translates into direct loss (direct agency costs) for the company. In particular Chapters 13 and 14 are concerned with two specific types of direct conflict, respectively. The first, addressed in this chapter, involves a transaction in which the director is on both sides of a contract: as an individual on one side and a director of the company on the other. The second, addressed in the Chapter 14, involves the exploitation by the director—directly himself or indirectly through a corporate vehicle—of new business opportunities the company itself would be interested in exploiting. The latter part of the next chapter will also consider the regulation of specific conflicts that are less direct, namely, the acceptance by the director of a directorship with a direct competitor of the company and the acceptance by directors of gifts and bribes by third parties.

II STRATEGIES FOR REGULATING SELF-DEALING

1 Introduction

Consider the following hypothetical transaction and subsequent assignment. Please do not read further until you have given the assignment questions set out here your due attention and thought.

Hypothetical A

Consider Bob's Electronics Ltd owned by Bob (50%), Alison—who is Bob's wife—(25%) and Helen (25%), who are all directors of the company. Bob is the CEO and sole executive director. The company has recently experienced an increase in the number of customers who are not paying on time or not paying at all. This has generated a short-term cashflow problem. The company has an urgent need for additional working capital finance to finance this short-term cashflow deficit. In addition, the company's laptop models are looking increasing dated. The company needs to finance a complete redesign of its laptop portfolio. However, given its current cash position it will need to raise finance to carry out this redesign.

The board of directors resolves to do two things to satisfy this financing need. First of all it agrees to sell to Bob (in his personal capacity) the land on which the company's computer assembly warehouse is situated and then to lease back the warehouse from Bob. The board also resolves to obtain a working capital loan which Bob will provide.

Assignment

1. Identify the specific risks for the company of agreeing to enter into these transactions.

2. What are the benefits to the company, if any, of entering into these transactions with Bob rather than with a third party such as a bank?

3. Would your answers to questions 1 and 2 change if Bob's Electronics was a listed public limited company?

4. What regulatory responses would you consider, if any, to address the risks you identify in question 1?

5. Would those regulatory responses vary depending on whether Bob's Electronics is a Ltd or a Plc?

A transaction such as this where Bob is on both sides of the transaction is colloquially known as *a self-dealing transaction*: Bob is dealing with/transacting with himself—on the one side in his personal capacity on the other as a representative of the company. The conflict between the company's interests and Bob's personal interests is acute in all of these transactions: the company could sell the warehouse property at a value below market value; it could agree to lease back the warehouse at an above market rent; it could pay an above market interest rate for the loan from Bob. In each of these instances the company would be transferring value directly into Bob's pocket. Had it instead negotiated transactions with third parties at market rates the company would be worth more.

2 Regulatory strategies

2.1 Prohibition

One option for addressing such conflicts would be to prohibit any transactions between the company and the director or any person associated with or related to the director. Such a regulatory response would clearly result in the reduction of scope for managers to act in their own interests and, therefore, a reduction in potential managerial agency costs. However, such an approach has potential negative consequences for the company. It may, for example, be possible to enter into the sale and lease-back transaction with an independent third party; however, Bob's Electronics needs to obtain the finance quickly and such a third party will take time to analyse the company, to consider the risks associated with the purchase and lease-back transaction, and to negotiate the price it is willing to pay. Furthermore, with a third-party transaction Bob and the company's employees may be distracted from their jobs as they are required to gather information to support the third party's analysis of the transaction, and such a third-party transaction may involve more legal costs for Bob's Electronics as its lawyers will need to address concerns that a third party would legitimately have but a knowledgeable insider, such as Bob, would not. Accordingly, if Bob pays a market price for the warehouse and demands a market rent then the company benefits in terms of both the time taken to complete the transaction as well as reduced transaction costs. Indeed it may be worthwhile for the company to sell Bob the property somewhat below market value and/or pay Bob above market rent to get these benefits of time and transaction costs. It may also be the case that no third party would be willing to enter into the sale and lease-back transaction or to lend the company the working capital.

Accordingly, to prohibit self-dealing transactions may deny the company the option of raising the finance in the most cost-effective way or indeed may deny the company the only way of raising the funds. For a regulator deciding how to regulate these transactions, the key question is: how important are the problems identified in the previous paragraph that would be generated by prohibiting self-dealing transactions when balanced against the need to hold directors to account and to ensure that they do not act in ways that benefit themselves at the expense of the company? The answer to this question will vary depending on the nature of the self-dealing transaction in question. If the potential for abuse and the incurrence of agency costs is high but the potential benefit to the company from the transaction type is low then prohibition may be the most effective option. For example, whilst we can see the benefits from Bob lending money to the company in terms of the time required to access the funds and the time and costs associated with the bank considering the risks of doing business with Bob's Electronics, what, if anything, would the benefits to Bob's Electronics be of lending money *to* Bob. Of course we can imagine such benefits if we try hard enough—Bob is willing to pay a high interest rate (which means, of course, he is likely to be a risky person to lend to); Bob needs the funds to allow him to buy a house near to the company's warehouse in order to devote more time to the business. However, these circumstances are likely to be unusual and overall the risk of agency costs arising from lending to Bob at too low an interest rate may well exceed the rarer benefits for the company of such a transaction that we might be able to imagine. This may make loans to directors from the company a good candidate for a self-dealing transaction type that should be dealt with by prohibition. Indeed this was in effect the regulatory approach in the UK *prior to* the 2006 Act (loans are considered in depth at section IV.4).

Where the strategy of prohibition is not adopted then what is the appropriate regulatory tool to ensure that only the transactions that benefit the company are entered into and are enforceable? There are three options in this regard: first, disclosure of the nature of the conflict; secondly, disclosure coupled with a conflict approval mechanism through the board or the shareholder body; and thirdly, exposure to ex-post substantive review of the transaction by a regulator or a court to determine whether the terms of the transaction were fair to the company and, therefore, do not contravene the director's duty of loyalty to the company.

2.2 Disclosure

Requiring disclosure of the nature of the director's conflict could operate in two ways: ex-ante (before the transaction) and/or ex-post (after the transaction). Ex-ante board disclosure would require that the board of directors were made aware of the conflict arising from a transaction which the board of directors were considering entering into—or a transaction type that the board had previously authorized a director or employee to enter into. This would enable the board to scrutinize the transaction prior to entering into it to ensure that it benefited the company and not merely the conflicted director. Such a disclosure requirement is a prerequisite to allowing the board to function properly to ensure that directors are aware of the conflict when, for example, the conflicted director argues in favour of, or lobbies them to vote for, the transaction.

Where the board has already authorized someone to enter into this type of transaction, disclosure gives the board an opportunity to qualify such authorization to prevent the transaction going ahead.

Whereas this disclosure requirement would typically be a precondition to the validity of the transaction, disclosure may also be used after entering into the transaction both to the shareholder body and the market place in order to incentivize the board and the conflicted director to ensure that the terms are fair to the company. Disclosure of the terms of the transaction makes shareholders aware of the transactions and enables them to reach their own conclusions as to whether they benefit the company. If sufficiently unhappy about these transactions shareholders could, in theory, act to remove the directors, conflicted and disinterested alike. Of course collective action and rational apathy problems may mean that widely-held shareholders act in only the most egregious of circumstances. In relation to larger companies, ex-post disclosure to the market place also allows the community of investors to draw their own conclusions about the nature of these transactions and, to the extent that they are viewed as suspect, reduce their valuation of the company to take account of these events, their likely future occurrence, and the quality of the existing board of directors. Such market judgments could also generate reputational damage for directors, reducing the value of their services in the market place for managerial labour. This applies most obviously to the conflicted directors but also to the disinterested directors who—in the market's view—will have failed to prevent the transaction from taking place. The extent to which ex-post disclosure enables shareholders and the investment community to draw informed conclusions will, of course, depend on the nature and extent of such disclosure.

2.3 Ex-ante approval mechanisms

A second regulatory strategy is to require that one of the company's organs approves the self-dealing transaction. Here the regulatory question is: which of the company's organs is best placed to ensure that any self-dealing transaction benefits the company and not the director. The analysis here adopts the structure of the analysis in Chapter 6 where we considered which was the appropriate body to decide whether or not the company should enter into a significant transaction. The criteria of relevance identified in that chapter were (1) which body is more capable of making the decision; (2) which body has the correct incentives to pay attention and make an informed decision; and (3) which body is less conflicted. The arguments made in the section on significant transactions[1] are relevant here and will not be repeated in as much detail.

The board of directors is likely to be the most informed and capable decision-maker, understanding the benefits of the transaction for the company and having the most nuanced sense of the appropriate market price for the transaction. However, if the board as a whole is required to grant approval—where the self-dealing director participates and votes—there would be significant concerns about whether the decision is taken in the company's best interests. Such concern will vary depending on the number of conflicted directors. Consider, for example, *Hypothetical A* where Bob and Alison, who are married, would be able to grant the approval for the transactions. One option to address these concerns would be to give the decision to the non-conflicted/disinterested members of the board. Such directors would be informed and would have concerns that their reputations will be damaged if they agree to a transaction that does not benefit the company. However, concerns about the real independence of such disinterested directors will remain especially where the self-dealing director is an influential executive director in relation to whom the disinterested director feels dependent or indebted. If the disinterested directors are the non-executive directors then in most instances they

---

[1] See pp 206–207 Chapter 6.

will not have a significant financial stake in the company to counterbalance any implicit pressure to do the self-dealing director's bidding.

An alternative approach to approval would be to require ex-ante approval of the shareholder body. In small companies, such as Bob's Electronics Ltd in Hypothetical *A*, simply giving the decision to the shareholder body does not deal with the independence problems identified at board level. Bob and Alison (Bob's wife) are conflicted and have a majority position at both the board and shareholder meetings. Accordingly, one response would be to give the decision to the disinterested shareholders—in the hypothetical, to Helen. Given Helen's financial stake in the company she is incentivized to make a decision that enhances company value; nor is she exposed to the pressures that may compromise a disinterested director vote, which we previously identified. Of course in larger widely-held companies where there is no dominant shareholder there will be less concern that the interested shareholders could affect the vote. However, even in such companies one needs to remember that where there are rationally apathetic shareholders who may elect not to vote, a less than majority stake in the company could effectively control the vote. If the interested director only has a 15% stake in the company but only 29% of the shareholder vote on average then approval will be assured for the director. Accordingly, even in widely-held companies there remain good independence reasons to give the approval vote to the disinterested shareholders. Nevertheless, from a regulator's perspective one needs to remind oneself that whilst independence may be assured with a disinterested shareholder approval mechanism, there are, in relation to a widely-held shareholder body, significant decision-making capability, and incentive concerns.

In widely-held companies, even if we have doubts about the ability of sophisticated shareholders to make a good informed decision about whether a self-dealing transaction benefits the company, it may be the case that the public effects of requiring shareholder approval ensures that such transactions benefit the company in any event. This consideration is similar to the one previously mentioned in relation to ex-post disclosure, namely that directors, interested and disinterested alike, will be concerned about the personal reputational impact of market disapproval of the self-dealing transaction. Importantly, however, in contrast to a general ex-post disclosure obligation, disclosure linked with shareholder approval encourages investors to pay attention to the transaction and provides investors with a readily available signal to this market in reputational capital that directors have performed badly—namely disapproval or even a significant vote in favour of disapproval. That is, linking disclosure with shareholder approval is likely to make reputational sanctions a more effective mechanism for ensuring that self-dealing transactions benefit the company. It is also worth noting that for large widely-held companies the costs associated with holding a meeting and obtaining approval may deter self-dealing transactions that do not generate significant benefits for the company, unless the timing of the annual general meeting coincides with the timing of the transaction and can be used to obtain the requisite approvals.

2.4 Ex-post review

A third regulatory option is to subject any self-dealing transaction to *ex-post* review by a regulator or a court to determine whether the transaction is fair to the company. This would involve the regulator or court in a determination of whether the transaction is fair to the company or *in fact* benefits the company. In relation to the sale of an asset or the leasing of a building as in *Hypothetical A* this would involve a determination of whether the purchase price or the rent paid was a market price or rent. To the extent it was not it would involve a determination of whether the benefits provided through the self-dealing transaction—such as those of time and transaction costs—compensated the company for the below market purchase price or the above market rent. If we take courts as the body who carried out this *ex*-post review, with regard to the criteria identified above to determine the appropriate body to approve the self-dealing transaction it is clear that the courts are totally independent from the self-dealing directors. But what about the court's capacity to determine a fair price? Certainly a sophisticated commercial judiciary, such as the judges who sit in the High Courts' Companies Court, are capable of obtaining and understanding expert evidence on the market value of an asset or contract. There may, however, be evidence and information related to the fairness determination that is in the control of or has been consciously moulded, even distorted, by the interested director. This may place certain limitations on the capacity of the courts to assess fairness. However, such limitations on the evidence would also apply to the disclosures made to the shareholder body through a shareholder approval mechanism.

In considering the effectiveness of this approach, we need to ask what the likely effect would be on the occurrence of self-dealing transactions that generate agency costs of a regulatory approach that relied purely on ex-post fairness review? A rational, self-serving director would, when considering whether to enter into a self-dealing transaction that benefited him at the company's expense, consider the likelihood that (1) the transaction would be brought before and assessed by the court; (2) the likelihood that he would lose that case; and (3) the likelihood that he would be able to reach a settlement with the company to stop the law suit for less than the personal profit generated by the self-dealing transaction. If the likelihood that the transaction will be considered by the court and held to be unfair to the company is 99.9% but there is a 100% likelihood the director will be able to settle the case for 90% of the proceeds because of the claimants risk-aversion in relation to the 0.1%, then it still makes sense for the director to enter into the transaction. In practice in all jurisdictions the likelihood of court review is significantly less than 99.9%. Of course, as with disclosure and shareholder approval a director will also take into account the reputational impact of a public court process. There is, therefore, a strong case that if an ex-post fairness review by courts is the only mechanism for regulating self-dealing transactions then the potential for agency costs arising from self-dealing transactions that are detrimental to the company is higher than it would be under an ex-ante disclosure and shareholder approval approach.

III SELF-DEALING AND THE COMMON LAW: THE DUTY OF LOYALTY

Contemporary self-dealing regulation in the UK relies upon ex-ante board disclosure, ex-ante disclosure and shareholder approval as well as the ex-post effects of disclosure. It does not, as we shall see, rely upon ex-post fairness review by courts.[2] The applicable mechanisms vary depending on the value of the self-dealing transaction in question and whether the company is a listed company. Today, the regulation of self-dealing transactions is set out in detail in the Companies Act 2006 and the UKLA listing rules. In effect these rules have displaced the traditional common law approach based upon the duty of loyalty, although in certain, but not all, respects have replicated the common law approach.

1 The common law

In *Item Software (UK) Ltd v Fassihi*,[3] citing Professor Robert Clark of the Harvard Law School, Arden LJ refers to the *fundamental nature* of the duty of loyalty. But what does loyalty demand of directors where they enter into relationships in their personal capacity

---

[2] Although there is scope for such review pursuant to what is known as the unfair prejudice remedy set out in section 994 of the 2006 Act dealt with in Chapter 16.

[3] [2004] EWCA Civ.

with the company. Logically one would think that even if the relationship presents a theoretical opportunity for the director to exploit his authority to benefit himself *if he does not do so* then his loyalty is not compromised. If a self-dealing transaction benefits him personally but benefits the company as much, or even more, than a similar transaction with a third party would have done then the director's loyalty *in fact* is unimpeachable. If the duty of loyalty was to take such an approach and demand loyalty *in fact* then the courts would be required in matters brought before them to engage in fairness review to determine *in fact* whether the transaction represented the best deal possible for the company. Of course, as noted, such an approach creates a greater incentive for the bad director to 'chance his hand': to take the benefit of the self-dealing transaction at the expense of the company in the expectation that the transaction will not be challenged or, if it is, that it can be settled for less than his profit. A logical approach to loyalty *in fact or reality* may therefore encourage less loyalty on the part of directors. The UK's duty of loyalty has not placed such demands upon courts. Instead, concerned to deter disloyalty on the part of directors and doubtful about the courts' ability to assess fairness effectively, the common law imposed *in effect* a prohibition on self-dealing transactions subject to ex-ante shareholder approval or ex-post shareholder ratification. The leading case on the common law duty of loyalty both generally and in relation to self-dealing transactions is the House of Lords' judgment in *Aberdeen Railway v Blaikie Brothers*.

■ *Aberdeen Railway v Blaikie Brothers* (1854) Macq HL 461

Mr Blaikie was director and chairman of Aberdeen Railway. He was also the managing partner of a partnership that was in the business of manufacturing, amongst other things, iron railway chairs, in which the rails lie and are fixed to the ground. Aberdeen Railway contracted to purchase from Blaikie Brothers iron railway chairs. Several consignments of the chairs were delivered. However, prior to final delivery of the chairs Aberdeen Railway repudiated the contract. Blaikie Bros sued, requesting specific performance or damages. In response Aberdeen Railway argued that the contract was voidable at the election of Aberdeen Railway because the contract was a self-dealing contract. The House of Lords held in favour of Aberdeen Railway.

Lord Cranworth LC

This, therefore, brings us to the general question, whether a director of a railway company is or is not precluded from dealing on behalf of the company with himself or with a firm in which he is a partner. The directors are a body to whom is delegated the duty of managing the general affairs of the company. A corporate body can only act by agents, and it is, of course, the duty of those agents so to act as best to promote the interests of the corporation whose affairs they are conducting. Such an agent has duties to discharge of a fiduciary character towards his principal, and it is a rule of universal application that no one having such duties to discharge shall be allowed to enter into engagements in which he has or can have a personal interest conflicting or which possibly may conflict with the interests of those whom he is bound to protect. So strictly is this principle adhered to that no question is allowed to be raised as to the fairness or unfairness of a contract so entered into. It obviously is, or may be, impossible to demonstrate how far in any particular case the terms of such a contract have been the best for the **cestui que trust** [the beneficiary of the trust] which it was possible to obtain. It may sometimes happen that the terms on which a trustee has dealt or attempted to deal with the estate or interests of those for whom he is a trustee have been as good as could have been obtained from any other person; they may even at the time have been better. But still so inflexible is the rule that no inquiry on that subject is permitted.

The English authorities on this subject are numerous and uniform. The principle was acted on by Lord King in *Keech v Sandford*[4] and by Lord Hardwicke, in *Whelpdale v Cookson*[5] and the whole subject was considered by Lord Eldon on a great variety of occasions. It is sufficient to refer to what fell from that very able and learned judge in *Ex parte James*.[6] It is true that the questions have generally arisen on agreements for purchases or leases of land, and not, as here, on a contract of a mercantile character. But this can make no difference in principle. The inability to contract depends not on the subject-matter of the agreement, but on the fiduciary character of the contracting party, and I cannot entertain a doubt of its being applicable to the case of a party who is acting as manager of a mercantile or trading business for the benefit of others no less than to that of an agent or trustee employed in selling land.

Was, then, Mr Blaikie so acting in the case now before us? If he was, did he, while so acting, contract, on behalf of those for whom he was acting, with himself? Both these questions must obviously be answered in the affirmative. Mr Blaikie was not only a director, but, if that was necessary, the chairman of the directors. In that character it was his bounden duty to make the best bargains he could for the benefit of the company. While he filled that character...he entered into a contract on behalf of the company with his own firm for the purchase of a large quantity of chairs at a certain stipulated price. His duty to the company imposed on him the obligation of obtaining these iron chairs at the lowest possible price. His personal interest would lead him in an entirely opposite direction—would induce him to fix the price as high as possible. This is the very evil against which the rule in question is directed; and I see nothing whatever to prevent its application here. I observe that Lord Fullerton [in the lower court—the Scottish Court of Session] seemed to doubt whether the rule would apply where the party whose act or contract is called in question, is only one of a body of directors not a sole trustee or manager. But, with all deference, this appears to me to make no difference. It was Mr Blaikie's duty to give to his co-directors, and through them to the company, the full benefit of all the knowledge and skill which he could bring to bear on the subject. He was bound to assist them in getting the articles contracted for at the cheapest possible rate. As far as related to the advice he should give them, he put his interest in conflict with his duty, and whether he was the sole director, or only one of many, can make no difference in principle. The same observation applies to the fact, that he was not the sole person trading with the company. He was one of the firm of Blaikie Brothers with whom the contract was made, and so was interested in driving as hard a bargain with the company as he could induce them to make...In truth, the doctrine rests on such obvious principles of good sense, that it is difficult to suppose that there can be any system of law in which it would not be found.[7]

For there *in fact/in reality* to be a conflict of interest between the director and his company then a benefit obtained by the director in a self-dealing transaction such as the one described in *Aberdeen Railway v Blaikie* must be to the detriment of the company. This would clearly be apparent if Aberdeen Railway had paid above market price for the railway chairs or if a superior chair had been available from a third party at the same or a lower price; but there is no conflict *in fact* if Aberdeen Railway would have willingly bought the same quality of railway chair from a third-party supplier at the same or a higher price. However, the court in *Aberdeen Railway v Blaikie* is not concerned with the ultimate outcome of the transaction. They note that 'no question is allowed to be raised as to the fairness or unfairness of the contract'. Vaughan Williams LJ's summary of *Aberdeen Railway* in *Costa Rica Railway Company, Limited v Forwood*,[8] which also involved a self-dealing transaction, reinforces this position of the role of fairness in the regulation of self-dealing transactions.

---

[4] (1726) Sel Cas Ch 61.   [5] (1747) 1 Ves Sen 9.   [6] [1803–13] All ER Rep 78.
[7] See further: *Broughton v Broughton* (1855) 5 De GM & G 160.   [8] [1901] 1 Ch 746.

> As I understand, the rule is a rule to protect directors, trustees, and others against the fallibility of human nature by providing that, if they do choose to enter into contracts in cases in which they have or may have a conflicting interest, the law will denude them of all profits they may make thereby, and will do so notwithstanding the fact that there may not seem to be any reason of fairness why the profits should go into the pockets of their cestui que trust, and although the profits may be such that their cestui que trust could not have earned them all.[9]

The court's reasoning for rejecting fairness review is that such review will be in many cases 'impossible'. Lord Cranworth notes that 'it obviously is, or may be, impossible to demonstrate how far in any particular case the terms of such a contract have been the best for the cestui que trust which it was possible to obtain'. For Lord Cranworth the courts are not capable of re-creating an imaginary bargaining process with an imaginary arm's length third party to determine a 'fair contract terms' benchmark with which to compare the actual terms of the self-dealing transaction. This view reflects the oft-cited views of Lord Eldon when considering the no-conflicts principle in the trusts context in *Ex parte James*, which is cited by Lord Cranworth, holding that 'the purchase is not permitted in any case, however honest the circumstances, the general interests of justice requiring it to be destroyed in every instance *as no court is equal to the examination and ascertainment of the truth in much the greater number of cases*' (emphasis added).[10]

The courts are concerned, therefore, with the potential for conflict inherent in the self-dealing dynamic; the fact that the interests *could* conflict: could Blaikie really drive the best bargain for Aberdeen Railway when he would have benefited as a partner of Blaikie Brothers from transaction terms that are not as good as the hardest bargain that could be struck? Nor, importantly, did it matter that Blaikie was only one of several directors who may—it is unclear from the case—have been in modern terms independent directors. The very fact of the possibility of conflict inherent in the self-dealing transaction is sufficient to render the contract voidable[11] and unenforceable by Blaikie Brothers. The court therefore imposes a prohibition on self-dealing transactions. In the terms used by the House of Lords, directors are 'precluded' from entering into such transactions. Subsequent courts, as we see in the cases considered in this chapter, often stated the rule in more straightforward terms: directors cannot make a profit by virtue of their position as directors and any such profit must be accounted for to the company.

What is not clear from the judgment in *Aberdeen Railway* is whether shareholders could alter this rule to provide either ex-ante approval or ex-post ratification by shareholders or indeed to provide ex-ante some other type of approval mechanism involving board approval or disclosure. Reading *Aberdeen Railway* alone, the duty of loyalty imposes a mandatory prohibition on such self-dealing transactions. However, the trust authorities upon which Lord Cranworth relies clearly contemplate that the beneficiary of the trust (the *cestui que trust*) may consent to a transaction involving the trustee and trust property.[12] By analogy, therefore, it was clear that the shareholder body could

---

[9] See also *Boston Deep Sea Fishing and Ice Co Ltd v Ansell* (1888) 39 Ch D 339.

[10] *Ex Parte James* [1803–13] All ER Rep 78 at 82.

[11] In this author's view the authorities support the position that self-dealing transactions are voidable for want of authority—see D. Kershaw, 'The Path of Fiduciary Law' (2012) *New York University Journal of Law and Business* (forthcoming) available at http://papers.ssrn.com/sol3/papers.cfm?abstract_id=1874763 at 28–9 and note 119. Some commentators have put forward the view that self-dealing transactions are void—see, for example, J. Edelman, 'The Fiduciary Self-Dealing Rule' in J. Glister and P. Ridge (eds), *Fault Lines in Equity* (Hart Publishing, forthcoming); see also M. Conaglen *Fiduciary Loyalty* (Hart Publishing, 2010) at 77–9 taking issue with the position articulated by Edelman.

[12] For example, Lord Eldon in *Ex Parte James* [1803–13] All ER Rep 75, 85 recognizes that the equitable rule is subject to the consent of the cestui que trust. See also *Benson v Heathorn* 1 Y&CCC 325 (1842).

consent to such a self-dealing transaction. Indeed, it is worth noting that without such flexibility even an executive director service contract would be unenforceable.

Companies responded to the strictures placed upon dealings with directors by this rule by amending their articles to allow such dealings with directors. Typically such rules provided for ex-ante disclosure to the board of the director's interest in the transaction and disallowed the interested director from voting on the transaction. The question for the courts following *Aberdeen Railway v Blaikie* was whether such amendments to the company's constitution were consistent with this strict rule of equity. The courts took a flexible, pragmatic approach to this question, interpreting articles that implicitly contemplated self-dealing transactions—without explicitly authorizing them—as being sufficient to render the transactions enforceable and to allow the interested director to keep the profits. In this regard consider the following case.

■ *Imperial Mercantile Credit Association v Coleman* (1871) LR 6 Ch App 558

Mr Coleman was a director of the Imperial Mercantile Credit Association, a financial investment company. Mr Coleman was also a partner in a firm that acted as brokers for placing debt and equity securities with investors. Mr Coleman was instructed to place the whole of securities to be issued by the London, Chatham and Dover Railway Company. His commission for placing the debt securities (the **debentures**) was 5%—that is, he purchased the debentures at 95% of their face value which was £356,300. Mr Coleman then approached the Imperial Mercantile Credit Association with regard to a sale to them of the debentures at a discount of 1½% of their face value. That is, Coleman intended to purchase them at 95% and sell them to Imperial at 98½%. A committee of the board of Imperial, of which Coleman was not a member, was set up to consider the purchase and the committee recommended to the board that they be purchased at the 1½% discount. This recommendation was accepted by the board. The articles of Imperial contained the following provision (article 83) designed to alter the strict rule of equity set out in *Aberdeen Railway*. The provision was as follows:

> 'The office of a director shall be vacated if he contracts with the company, or is concerned in or participate in the profits of any contract with the company, or participate in the profits of any work done for the company, without declaring his interest at the meeting of the directors at which such contract is determined on or work ordered, if his interest then exists, or in any other case, at the first meeting of the directors after the acquisition of his interest; and no director so interested shall vote at any meeting or on any committee of the directors on any question relating to such contracts or work.'

The court held that Mr Coleman had disclosed his interest. Subsequently to purchasing the debentures the debentures decreased considerably in value forcing Imperial into liquidation. The liquidator of the company brought an action against Coleman claiming an accounting for the profits made in breach of the strict equitable rule set out above. At first instance, Mallins VC held in favour of the liquidator. The court rejected the argument that the provision in the articles allowed Coleman to keep the profit. Mallins VC held that:

> 'That the co-directors knew or suspected that he was setting some greater advantage by the transaction than the ordinary broker's commission, I think highly probable; but no such knowledge on their part could absolve him from his duty to the shareholders. I do not, therefore, find anything in the transaction to relieve Mr. Coleman from the ordinary obligations of a director towards the company whose interests are committed to his charge. When he proposed that the company should take these debentures at 98½ per cent., he knew that he would procure them

at 95. Was he justified in charging a larger price to the company, and putting the difference in his own pocket? I am of opinion that he was not. It is of the highest importance that it should be distinctly understood that it is the duty of directors of companies to use their best exertions for the benefit of those whose interests are committed to their charge, and that they are bound to disregard their own private interests whenever a regard to them conflicts with the proper discharge of such duty.'

Coleman appealed to the Court of Appeal.

Lord Hatherley LC

This is a case in which the official liquidator of the Imperial Mercantile Credit Association, in the name of the company, has filed a bill in order to have it declared that a certain sum of money received by the Defendant..., who was a director of the company, is answerable to the company on the general principle that a person holding a fiduciary position with regard to a company cannot obtain for himself a benefit derived from the employment of the funds of the company in any matter in which he, the director, may happen to be engaged. The principle is so firmly established that I should be extremely sorry to say anything which would in the slightest decree impeach it; but the application of the principle is not always so easy in the various complicated arrangements which take place with regard to mercantile transactions, and especially with regard to the enormous transactions in which companies of this kind are in the habit of engaging. The Vice-Chancellor has thought it to be a case plainly and clearly within that principle. The whole history has, therefore, to be examined most carefully, to see what was the condition of the parties when the contract was entered into...

The matter would be much more simple if the regulations [the articles of association] of the association were in the ordinary form, if nothing whatever were said about directors interested or not interested, and if it were left to the ordinary operation of the rules of this Court, which lay down firmly that no director of a company can, in the absence of any stipulation to the contrary, be allowed to be a partaker in any benefit whatever from any contract which requires the sanction of a board of which he is a member. The reasons are given fully by the Vice-Chancellor Knight Bruce in *Benson v Heathorn* (Y. & C. Ch. 326), cited by the learned Vice-Chancellor in his judgment, and amount to this—that the company have a right to the services of their directors, whom they remunerate by considerable payments; they have a right to their entire services, they have a right to the voice of every director, and to the advice of every director in giving his opinion upon matters which are brought before the board for consideration; and that the general rule that no trustee can derive any benefit from dealing with those funds of which he is a trustee applies with still greater force to the state of things in which the interest of the trustee deprives the company of the benefit of his advice and assistance.

However, the question then remains, whether the company cannot stipulate that this is a benefit of which they do not desire to avail themselves, and if they are competent so to stipulate, whether they may not think that in large financial matters of this description it is better to have directors who may advance the interests of the company by their connection, and by the part which they themselves take in large money dealings, than to have persons who would have no share in such transactions as those in which the company is concerned.

It is not for me to say which was the wiser or better course of the two, nor do I think that this Court professes to lay down rules for the guidance of men who are adult, and can manage and deal with their own interests. It would be a violent assumption if any thing of that kind were attempted. It must be left to such persons to form their own contracts and engagements, and this Court has only to sit here and construe them, and also to lay down certain general rules for the protection of persons who may not have been aware of what the consequences would be of intrusting their property to the management of others where nothing is expressed as to the implied arrangement. In this case it does appear to me that there was a distinct contemplation of directors being interested in the concerns of the company, and acting and voting when the matter came before the board of directors, and that the shareholders took such precautions as they thought necessary:- (His Lordship then read the 83rd clause [of the articles of association set out in the facts of the case]). Is it possible to read that clause and find any mode by which it could be maintained that the company meant to exclude a director from his office in case he should have an interest in a contract, or to exclude any contract being made in which any director should be interested? It seems to me to be perfectly impossible. The whole clause would be idle. They have taken the matter into their own hands, and have said: 'We do not mind a director who has an interest, but all that we provide is this—that he shall fairly state that interest at the time when the matter is under discussion. He shall not vote on the matter himself, and if he acquires an interest after the matter has been discussed, and after he has voted upon it, or whether he has voted upon it or not, if after the matter is discussed he acquires an interest which he does not disclose he shall be forthwith disqualified.' That is the rule which they have laid down, and by that rule, as I apprehend, the conduct of [Mr Coleman] must be tested in this case…

It is upon that account that I have regarded this case with very great anxiety, because I would not be supposed for one moment to throw out a word that could tend to lead any trustee into the notion that he may deal with the persons for whom he is a trustee, or for whom he is a trustee with others, in any manner which will give him a benefit or put money into his own pocket. But that, like any other rule of the Court, is open to contract between the parties, for it is not a principle the benefit of which parties cannot waive by express and direct contract for the sake of other advantages which they suppose they derive…

The rules of the company seem to prescribe a mode of proceeding by which they exempted this particular case from the operation of the general rule of the Court of Equity, and it appears to me that Mr. Coleman sufficiently complied with that rule when he made it clear to all the persons (and they all admit that he made it clear) that he had an interest as a broker which placed him in exact hostility to the others…

I cannot say how much anxiety and labour it has cost me to examine minutely this case. I do not differ from the learned Vice-Chancellor in the slightest degree with regard to any of the principles of law which he laid down. I accept as guiding and enlightening the Court, and as having laid down the safe and sound rules of action in a case of this kind, every one of the authorities which the Vice-Chancellor referred to in his judgment; and the only conclusion which I come to, differing from him, is this, that in construing those articles I look upon this as a contract to which the rule of equity is not applicable in the particular case of this company; and I think—if it was fairly made known to the directors that their interests were antagonistic—that the circumstance that the commission was 5 per cent., instead [1½%]… That being so, of course I can only dismiss the bill.[13]

As Lord Hatherley notes on two separate occasions in the judgment, he is anxious about his holding. His anxiety stems from his holding that this central rule of equity—that a fiduciary cannot place himself in a position of conflict or potential conflict with his charge (the company/the principal/the beneficiary); that a fiduciary cannot profit from his position as a fiduciary—is subject to contractual variation through the corporate contract—the articles of association. The judgment is exceptionally deferential to the capacity of the shareholder body to decide for themselves whether it is beneficial to the company to allow directors to enter into self-dealing transactions and to keep the profits from such transactions if they comply with a procedure which does not involve shareholder approval. He notes that 'I [do not] think that this Court professes to lay down

---

[13] Note that the House of Lords ((1873) LR 6 HL 189) reversed the Court of Appeal's decision, but on the basis that the director's disclosure was insufficient to comply with the provision in the articles. It did not challenge Lord Hatherley's conclusion regarding the permissibility of contractual variation. Lord Hatherley's judgment in *Imperial Mercantile* was subsequently affirmed by the Court of Appeal in *Costa Rica Railway Company, Limited v Forwood* [1901] 1 Ch 746. See also *Transvaal Land Ltd v New Belgium* [1914–15] All ER Rep 987.

rules for the guidance of men who are adult, and can manage and deal with their own interests'. Lord Hatherley is very sensitive to the potential trade-offs which we identified in our analysis of *Hypothetical A*: there may be benefits from self-dealing transactions that outweigh, from the shareholders' perspective, the concern that the actual transactions may be infected with conflicts and be detrimental to the company. These risks can be mitigated by disclosure and voting rules such as those set out in article 83 of Imperial Mercantile's articles, and although risks remain this is, for Lord Hatherley, a choice for the shareholders, with their understanding of the company's business and activities, to make. It is not for the courts to take away from informed participants the right to assess these risks and make a regulatory choice tailored to such an assessment.

Importantly, to get the benefits of this approval mechanism requires compliance with all aspects of the approval mechanism. In *Imperial*, compliance under article 83 of the company's articles involved disclosure and abstention by the interested director from voting. These conditions were set out in one article. However, where these conditions are set out in several articles the courts held that compliance with all articles would be required to displace the strict rule of equity and to enable the director to keep the benefit of the transaction. This was stated explicitly in *Costa Rica Railway Company v Forwood*[14] where there were separate disclosure and voting articles. Rigby LJ held that:

> [Article 80 provides that:] 'No director shall vote on any question in which he has a personal interest apart from the members at large.' That is a very general clause: it is not so specific as that which follows, but it is not without importance. That appears to me to shew that a director in this company is not precluded from having interests which may not be in common with the members at large; but if he has such interests, he must not vote; and I take it that, if he did vote, he would be bound by the general equity which charges a fiduciary agent with the concealed profits that he makes.

Accordingly, where the articles contain separate ex-ante board disclosure and disinterested voting provisions (as was the case under the version of Table A issued pursuant to the 1985 Act: see section III.2 of this chapter), the common law position requires compliance with both the ex-ante disclosure and disinterested voting provisions. An interested director who disclosed but voted would not be allowed to keep the benefit of the transaction in the absence of shareholder approval.

Discussion points

- It was clear that under the common law position as stated in *Imperial Mercantile* shareholders *could* provide in the company's articles that disclosure alone without a disinterested board vote would suffice to approve a self-dealing transaction. In *Boulting v Association of Cinematograph, Television and Allied Technicians*,[15] Upjohn LJ noted that the 'articles may validly permit directors to be present at board meetings and even to vote when proposed contracts in which they are interested are being discussed'. Indeed, at common law, following Lord Hatherley's approach, the shareholders could have provided a blanket waiver of liability in relation to self-dealing transactions. Such an approach would, however, no longer be consistent with the Companies Act's prohibition on exempting directors for liability for breach of duty which is discussed further in section IV.1.1.

- It is worth making a note at this juncture of two factors. First, the transaction in issue in *Imperial Mercantile* was a very significant transaction for the company in terms of value. Indeed the loss in value of the debentures was apparently the primary cause of the company's bankruptcy. However, the value of the transaction had no bearing on the

---

[14] [1901] 1 Ch 746.   [15] [1963] 2 QB 606, 636.

willingness of the court to accept that the articles could alter the approval procedure for the transaction. Secondly, Lord Hatherley's judgment clearly envisages a small close company where the shareholders are capable of making a decision about whether or not it benefits the company to allow self-dealing transactions to go ahead through an alternative approval procedure. Indeed, this view makes particular sense in this case where the existing Table A articles (under the Companies Act 1862) did not provide for such a procedure and required amendment to provide for the procedure set out in article 83 of the Imperial Mercantile's articles. That is, a conscious choice was made to amend the articles.[16]

- A question for us to consider is whether this approach to regulating self-dealing trans- actions should change when: first, the shareholder body increases in size, becomes rationally apathetic and does not play an active role in producing and updating the company's articles; and, second, where such articles become the norm (in legal pro- fession jargon—'boilerplate') rather than thought-through amendments having had regard to the pros and cons for a particular company in a particular industry of facili- tating self-dealing transactions.

- Law and economics (contractarian) scholars would respond to the above bullet point by arguing that it is a mistake to suggest that boilerplate terms and the existence of ration- ally apathetic shareholders in widely-held companies means that there is no contractual process similar to the one that was so central to Lord Hatherley's judgment. These scholars would argue that a contractual process takes place through the valuation of such provisions in the articles by sophisticated investors. Managers are incentivized to offer terms that maximize the value of the company because if the terms they offer destroy value in the company then the company's share price will drop, managers' share options will be worth less, their bonuses will be lower, and the company more exposed to a takeover because of the lower share price. It is widely assumed that sophisticated investors are capable of paying, and actually pay, attention to such provisions in the articles; however, the empirical data supporting this assumption in relation to legal rules is very sparse and anecdotal. Even assuming that investors do pay attention and can value such rules, in relation to self-dealing approval provisions there is further reason for scepticism about the effectiveness of such a contractarian process, namely that it is not clear that directors' incentives all run in the direction proposed by con- tractarian scholars. Self-dealing transactions that destroy value for the company may benefit managers significantly. Accordingly, although there may be risks for managers in having provisions in the articles that make it easier for managers to enter into self- dealing transactions, it is not clear that these outweigh the benefits to directors of such transactions. If this is correct then the contractarian supports for Lord Hatherley's judgment in *Imperial Mercantile* may not be present where such provisions are standard boilerplate provisions and the company is widely-held.[17]

2 Opting out of shareholder approval and Table A

It is interesting to note that whilst it was common practice for companies to include articles such as those considered in *Imperial Mercantile Credit Association* that allowed for approval through ex-ante board disclosure, Table A articles of association were not amended to fully and *explicitly* reflect this approach until the amended Table A articles issued pursuant to the Companies Act 1985. The very first Table A articles issued under the Joint Stock Companies Act 1856 (which were actually known as Table B) contained

---

[16] It is interesting to note that the Joint Stock Company Act of 1844, the first Companies Act to provide for incorporation by registration, provided in the Act a section addressing self-dealing which, consistently with the trust law position, it prohibited subject to shareholder approval (see section 29 Joint Stock Companies Act 1844). This provision disappeared from the subsequent Act in 1856.

[17] L. Bebchuk, 'Federalism and the Corporation: The Desirable Limits on State Competition in Corporate Law' (1992) 105 *Harvard Law Review* 1437, 1462.

a requirement that a director should vacate his office 'if he is concerned in or participates in the profits of any contract with the company'.[18] The provision was not removed until the version of Table A promulgated under the Companies Act 1948. However, even in 1856 Table A articles provided for an exception to this requirement to vacate his office:

> That no director shall vacate his office by reason of his being a shareholder in any incorporated company which has entered into contracts with or done any work for the company of which he is director; nevertheless he shall not vote in respect of such contract or work; and if he does so vote his vote shall not be counted, and he shall incur a penalty not exceeding twenty pounds.[19]

In *Costa Rica Railway Company v Forwood*[20] the Court of Appeal held that this provision enabled a director of the subject company to keep profits from a transaction with another company in which he was a major shareholder. The Table A articles issued pursuant to Companies Act 1985 finally made it explicit in English company law's default articles that ex-ante disclosure of the interest in the transaction was sufficient to enable the director to keep the benefit of the transaction. Table A provided a separate provision requiring that directors could not vote as directors if interested in the transaction.

■ Table A (Issued pursuant to the Companies Act 1985)

Article 85

Subject to the provisions of the Act, and provided that he has disclosed to the directors the nature and extent of any material interest of his, a director notwithstanding his office—

(a) may be a party to, or otherwise interested in, any transaction or arrangement with the company or in which the company is otherwise interested;

(b) may be a director or other officer of, or employed by, or a party to any transaction or arrangement with, or otherwise interested in, any body corporate promoted by the company or in which the company is otherwise interested; and

(c) shall not, by reason of his office, be accountable to the company for any benefit which he derives from any such office or employment or from any such transaction or arrangement or from any interest in any such body corporate and no such transaction or arrangement shall be liable to be avoided on the ground of any such interest or benefit.

Article 86

For the purposes of regulation 85—

(a) a general notice given to the directors that a director is to be regarded as having an interest of the nature and extent specified in the notice in any transaction or arrangement in which a specified person or class of persons is interested shall be deemed to be a disclosure that the director has an interest in any such transaction of the nature and extent so specified; and

(b) an interest of which a director has no knowledge and of which it is unreasonable to expect him to have knowledge shall not be treated as an interest of his.

Article 94

Save as otherwise provided by the articles, a director shall not vote at a meeting of directors or of a committee of directors on any resolution concerning a matter in which he has, directly or indirectly, an interest or duty which is material and which conflicts or may conflict with the interests of the company

---

[18] Joint Stock Companies Act 1856, Table B, article 47.
[19] *Ibid.*   [20] [1901] 1 Ch 746.

It is possible to read Table A, article 85 as simply requiring ex-ante board disclosure by the interested director. This is incorrect. Following the holding in *Costa Rica Railways* and as Table A combines ex-ante board disclosure and disinterested director approval (although in separate articles) both requirements had to be fulfilled in order for a director to be able to keep any benefit of a self-dealing transaction.

IV SELF-DEALING REGULATION UNDER THE COMPANIES ACT 2006

1 Ex-ante board disclosure

The Companies Act 2006 reverses the common law's default position of prohibition subject to shareholder approval or an alternative approval mechanism such as Table A's board disclosure and disinterested board approval. Section 177, together with section 180, of the Companies Act adopts, subject to certain amendments set out below, the approach taken in Articles 85 and 86 of the 1985 Act's Table A articles. The effect of this is to make ex-ante board disclosure the default approval mechanism for self-dealing transactions (subject to the substantial property transaction rules discussed in section IV.3 of this chapter). Before looking at the requirements of section 177 in detail let us first consider the background to including this provision in the Act's codification of directors' duties.

1.1 Background to reform

The common law position that the articles could derogate from the strict rule that prohibited self-dealing transactions subject to shareholder approval was well established by the late nineteenth century. However, as we addressed in our analysis of the duty of care, following the *In re City Equitable Fire*[21] case Parliament passed the Companies Act 1929 which introduced a provision preventing companies from agreeing to 'exempt' or 'provide an indemnity' to directors from liability for breach of duty.[22] This provision clearly applies to any exemption or indemnity in relation to the duty set out in *Aberdeen Railway* that a director should not put himself in a position where his personal interests conflict, or may possibly conflict, with the company's interests. However, the introduction of this provision had no effect on companies' continued use of provisions in their articles such as the provision we encountered in *Imperial Mercantile*, nor did it affect the amendment of Table A in the 1948 and 1985 versions to align Table A with market practice in this regard.

However, the use of director disclosure approval procedures was widely perceived to create an ostensible conflict in the companies legislation, albeit one between the Act and the Table A articles which were issued by secondary legislation pursuant to the Act. Commentators who saw a conflict asked how could the Act prohibit exemptions and indemnities but provide for an ex-ante disclosure mechanism which in effect results in the dis-application of the duty. It was clear to all that a provision in the articles providing that directors could enter into any self-dealing transaction without having to take any steps at all (disclosure of interests or obtain approvals) would be prohibited. However, the problem was to what extent was the disclosure system provided for in Table A distinctive from such a general waiver and was it correct to view it as something different than an 'exemption' from the application of the duty so that the prohibition on exemptions and waivers did not apply.

---

[21] [1925] Ch 407.   [22] Now set out in section 232 CA 2006. See p 451.

One argument against the proposition that a legislative conflict existed at all is to view the combination of ex-ante disclosure and disinterested director approval as a delegation of approval authority from the shareholders and not, therefore, an *exemption* or an indemnity. Section 232 does not interfere with the shareholders' ability to ratify a breach and we can view ex-ante board disclosure approval as an ex-ante delegation of this ratification authority. This approach was rejected in *Movitex Ltd v Bulfield* by Vinelott J who elected to explain the legislative conflict by arguing that the basis that the director was not subject to a duty not to enter into self-dealing transactions but subject to a disability preventing him from entering into them. As a disability it was not subject to the prohibition on exemptions and indemnities for breach of duty. The Companies Act 2006 clearly resolves this legislative conflict. However, it is not clear that this discussion is completely consigned to the legal history books as a precursor to section 177. A question still remains about whether in accordance with the 2006 Act the articles of association can provide for a non-shareholder approval process different from that set out in section 177. Whether it can is in part a function of this discussion. We will revisit this question once we have outlined the precise nature of the disclosure obligation pursuant to section 177.

1.2 The disclosure requirement pursuant to section 177

■ Section 177 CA 2006 Duty to declare interest in proposed transaction or arrangement

(1) If a director of a company is in any way, directly or indirectly, interested in a proposed transaction or arrangement with the company, he must declare the nature and extent of that interest to the other directors.

(2) The declaration may (but need not) be made—

  (a) at a meeting of the directors, or

  (b) by notice to the directors in accordance with—

    (i) section 184 (notice in writing), or

    (ii) section 185 (general notice).

(3) If a declaration of interest under this section proves to be, or becomes, inaccurate or incomplete, a further declaration must be made.

(4) Any declaration required by this section must be made before the company enters into the transaction or arrangement.

(5) This section does not require a declaration of an interest of which the director is not aware or where the director is not aware of the transaction or arrangement in question.

  For this purpose a director is treated as being aware of matters of which he ought reasonably to be aware.

(6) A director need not declare an interest—

  (a) if it cannot reasonably be regarded as likely to give rise to a conflict of interest;

  (b) if, or to the extent that, the other directors are already aware of it (and for this purpose the other directors are treated as aware of anything of which they ought reasonably to be aware); or

  (c) if, or to the extent that, it concerns terms of his service contract that have been or are to be considered—

(i) by a meeting of the directors, or

(ii) by a committee of the directors appointed for the purpose under the company's constitution.

■ Section 180 CA 2006 Consent, approval or authorisation by members

(1) In a case where—

...

(b) section 177 (duty to declare interest in proposed transaction or arrangement) is complied with, the transaction or arrangement is not liable to be set aside by virtue of any common law rule or equitable principle requiring the consent or approval of the members of the company. This is without prejudice to any enactment, or provision of the company's constitution, requiring such consent or approval.

Section 177 imposes on directors a disclosure obligation in relation to any *proposed* transaction in which a director has a direct or indirect interest. She must disclose the nature and the extent of her interest in the proposed transaction unless the transaction involves her service contract that has been, or will be, considered by the board or one of its committees. The question of what amounts to an 'indirect interest' is not defined by the Act. Clearly this would include a shareholding in another company which enters into a transaction with the company. The term 'interest' would appear broad enough to pick up legal and beneficial ownership of the shares but also derivative rights such as options to buy the shares.[23] What is less clear is whether 'indirect interests' would also include family members and, if so, which family members. Perhaps in this regard the courts may take guidance from the concept of 'connected person' which is used in relation to the *substantial property transaction* regime addressed in section IV.3 of this chapter.[24]

Pursuant to section 180, the effect of complying with the disclosure obligation is that the director can keep the benefit of the transaction. Failure to comply with this disclosure obligation does not subject the director to any sanction apart from the fact that the transaction could be set aside and the director would have to account to the company for any profits made pursuant to the applicable common law rules and equitable principles. The disclosure of the interest can be made in person at a board meeting or in writing, including by email (section 184) and, as with article 86 of Table A, the director may make a general notice as regards his interest in any other company with whom the company does business (section 185). The disclosure must be made to the 'other directors', which means all the directors of the company. Whilst the disclosure may be made at a meeting or in writing, it will not be sufficient to disclose an interest to an individual director or committee of directors, even a committee or individual director with authority to enter into the transaction in question.[25]

---

[23] In relation to the Act's treatment of 'interests in shares' in relation to the *substantial property transaction regime* discussed in section IV.3 of this chapter, see Schedule 1 of the 2006 Act.

[24] Note that any transaction entered into between the company and a director's wife, for example, does not involve a breach of the no-conflicts rule at common law. That rule applies to the director as a result of his position as a fiduciary. However, the transaction would still be liable to be set aside if the wife was found to have dishonestly assisted the director in the breach of the fiduciary duty.

[25] *Guinness Plc v Saunders* [1988] 2 All ER 940. Note that this case was interpreting the predecessor to section 182 considered later (section 317 of the Companies Act 1985) which explicitly required the declaration to be made 'at the meeting of the directors'. Nevertheless it is clear that the omission of that wording is intended to provide companies with more flexibility regarding the means of disclosure

In several respects the disclosure requirements of section 177 differ from the approach many existing companies have adopted under Table A. In particular, the Act imposes a clear updating obligation on directors should the nature of their interest become inaccurate or incomplete following the initial declaration. This also applies with regard to a general notice of interest in a particular company should the extent of the director's interest change.[26] Subsection (5) relieves the director of an obligation to disclose where she was not aware of, and ought not to have been aware of, her interest in the transaction or aware of the transaction itself. Accordingly, a director who is relieved of the obligation to disclose by subsection (5) complies with section 177 for the purposes of section 180.

Furthermore, the Act provides that no such disclosure is required where the interest in the transaction 'cannot reasonably be regarded as likely to give rise to a conflict of interest'. This wording stems from a development of the no-conflicts principle in the context of corporate opportunities which we will address in the next chapter. An identical provision is set out in section 175(4)(a) which addresses corporate opportunities. The case law on conflicts and self-dealing transactions has not, however, previously deployed language of this nature. This generates some uncertainty about the meaning and effect of this provision. One obvious interpretation might cover *de minimis* transactions (from the director's not the company's perspective), for example, the director's purchase of an outdated computer from the company for £100 or where the director has a 1% shareholding (an indirect interest) in a company with whom the subject company contracts. Indeed article 85 of Table A contained a materiality threshold—that is only material disclosures needed to be made, although materiality was not defined. Materiality clearly is concerned with excluding *de minimis* transactions from the disclosure obligation. Accordingly, in electing not to use the word 'material' this provision suggests that the Act exempts a broader range of transactions than just *de minimis* transactions. This clearly creates scope for more radical incursions into the UK's traditional approach to self-dealing transactions and could lead UK courts down a path they have thus far been hesitant to take. How, for example, would the courts approach a claim that there is no reasonable possibility of conflict in a transaction where the director purchases an asset from the company because the director paid above market value for the asset? To assess this the courts would have to determine what in fact was the fair market value for the asset, something which, as we saw in *Aberdeen Railway v Blaikie*, the courts have resisted doing.

1.3 Is there a continuing role for disinterested directors?

The approval of self-dealing transactions through section 177 ex-ante disclosure does not contemplate a role for disinterested directors. In theory a company could allow interested directors to vote on interested transactions following disclosure. Indeed, many companies will provide for interested director voting, particularly small companies where there is only one director and the director and sole shareholder are the same person. Of course, many companies will continue to have a disinterested director provision in their articles, as will all those companies who continue to have Table A articles or are formed with Model Articles for either private or public companies

and is not intended to reduce the number of directors to whom disclosure should be made to less than the whole board.

[26] Arguably Table A also imposed an updating obligation, albeit indirectly. With regard to group disclosure (article 86(a)) the disclosure was deemed to be effective as a disclosure to the 'extent so specified'; that is, the disclosure only protected the director from a subsequent accounting to the extent of the originally specified conflict and not from a greater conflict arising, for example, from an increased shareholding in the third-party company that was not subsequently disclosed.

(articles 14 and 16 respectively).[27] Under the common law rules where the articles prevented an interested director from voting this requirement became part of the self-dealing approval process: that is, self-dealing transactions that were fully disclosed but where the interested director voted would be subject to the strict rule prohibiting the transaction unless shareholder approval was obtained. If shareholder approval had not been obtained then in such circumstances the director could be forced to account to the company for any profits made pursuant to the transaction. Under sections 177 and 180, even if the company's articles contain provisions such as those set out in the Model Articles prohibiting interested director voting, if ex-ante disclosure is made effectively *but* the interested director votes to approve the transaction in question, this will not affect the ability of the director to enforce the contract and take the benefit of the self-dealing transaction. Voting in relation to the transaction by the interested director would, of course, amount to a breach of duty pursuant to section 171(a) of the Companies Act 2006 which requires directors to observe the terms of the constitution. However, there is a distinction of effect worth noting here. Where the claim against the director is based on breach of section 171(a), the director would not be held liable to account for the profit from the transaction and would only be liable if the company could show that the director's breach of duty caused loss to the company.[28] Under the common law, where the disinterested vote requirement in the articles was viewed as part of the approval mechanism, if it was not observed then the director would have to account for any profit arising from the transaction *regardless* of whether the transaction caused any loss to the company.[29]

1.4 Is section 177 a safe harbour or a mandatory approval rule?

It is clear that section 177 is a mandatory rule, requiring disclosure of a director's interests in a proposed transaction. However, is the procedure set out in section 177 the only way that the Companies Act 2006 now allows for *non-shareholder* approval of self-dealing transactions? For example, what if the articles of Bob's Electronics Plc provided (as did the articles of Imperial Mercantile Credit Association considered earlier) that in addition to pre-transaction disclosure, post-transaction disclosure would suffice. So, for example, Bob as an executive director is authorized to enter into transactions for less than £100,000 without obtaining specific board approval. On behalf of the

[27] Note that the Model Articles contain an exception that allows a director to vote where the interest cannot reasonably be regarded as likely to give rise to a conflict of interest (articles 14(3)(b) and 16(3)(b) of the Model Articles for Private and Public Companies respectively). Note that this replaces the voting prohibition in Table A article 94 which prohibited directors from voting only where he had an interest that was 'material'.

[28] This assumes, following Matthew Conaglen, that 'the duty to perform the task undertaken' is not a fiduciary duty (M. Conaglen, *Fiduciary Loyalty: Protecting the Due Performance of Non-Fiduciary Duties* (Hart Publishing, 2010)). As Millett LJ (as he then was) observes in *Bristol West Building Society v Mothew* [1996] 4 All ER 698, 710 'not every breach of duty by a fiduciary is breach of fiduciary duty'. If this duty is not a fiduciary duty then its breach will not benefit from equitable remedies available for breach of fiduciary duty.

[29] However, whether in practice the profit can be distinguished from a loss depends on whether profit is determined by reference to the market value of the transaction or anything in excess of a cost basis for the self-dealing director. If a transaction is entered into to sell a £100 asset to a director for £80 then the loss to the company is £20 and the profit for the company is £20. However, if the director sells an asset for £100 that he produced for a cost of £80 but has a market value of $100 there is no loss to the company. Whether an equitable remedy of accounting allows the company to claim this £20 depends on whether profit is determined by reference to a cost or market value basis. This is a point that has not been explored in the UK company law case law. But see *Great Luxembourg Railway v Magnay* (1858) 25 Beav 586 where the court observed that 'when it is said that he cannot make a profit from the transaction, it is not meant that he is not to have the proper value of the property taken by the company'. US case law addressing this issue concluded that the self-dealing director was entitled to what was fair, which included, for example, what the property was 'reasonably worth'—*Gardner v Butler* (1878) 40 NJL 568.

company, he enters into a transaction to sell a company asset to Suzanne, a new director of the company. The transaction is completed before any disclosure is made to the
whole board. At the next board meeting Suzanne, in compliance with the articles of the
company, discloses her interest in the completed transaction. She is clearly in breach
of section 177, but can she still keep the profit from the transaction in the absence of
shareholder ratification?

Section 180 of the 2006 Act provides that if a director complies with section 177 then
'the transaction or arrangement is not liable to be set aside by virtue of any common law
rule or equitable principle requiring the consent or approval of the members of the company'. Section 180 then proceeds to make it clear that this position is a default position
that could be altered by the company's constitution; that is, the company's constitution
could still require shareholder approval following compliance with section 177.

Leaving aside issues relating to section 232 of the 2006 Act (the prohibition of
waivers and indemnities for directors' duties) it seems clear that the common law
would have allowed such an ex-post disclosure provision in the above example to displace the default equitable rule requiring shareholder approval. Accordingly, in such
circumstances failure to comply with section 177 would not mean that the transaction 'would be liable to be set aside by virtue of any common law rule or equitable
principle'. On the contrary, the common law would support such an ex-post board
disclosure approval rule. This creates a clear anomaly: the Act requires disclosure
through section 177 but the only sanction for failure to comply is that the common
law continues to apply. But if the common law allows the alternative approval mechanism then section 177 may, at least in the case described, be left as a mandatory rule
without any sanction.

Viewing section 177 as the sole non-shareholder approval mechanism could be supported by section 232 of the 2006 Act. It is clear that compliance with section 177
provides for the *approval* of a self-dealing transaction and that section 232 prohibiting exemptions or waivers for breach of duty is thereby not contravened. Both the
provisions now exist together in the Act, whereas Table A articles 85 and 86 were the
product of secondary legislation issued pursuant to the Act. However, the potential
legislative conflict identified between the prohibition on exemptions or waivers for
breach of duty and ex-ante disclosure approval mechanisms in Table A did not prevent them co-existing for nearly 80 years providing some support for the idea that
alternative approval mechanisms in the articles are consistent with section 232. If
this analysis is correct then what sections 177 and 180 do is create a 'safe harbour'
rather than an exclusive approval mechanism: a regulatory way of using the board
to ensure that self-dealing transactions are enforceable, but leaving it open to companies to experiment with different approaches. Any companies who experiment
with such mechanisms do, however, run the risk that with section 177 firmly in
place courts will be less receptive to the arguments in favour of the consistency of
such alternative provisions with section 232 put forward by this author here and in
Movitex Ltd v Bulfield.[30]

2 Mandatory ex-post disclosure

In addition to the requirement to provide ex-ante disclosure to the board of the nature
and extent of a director's interest in a self-dealing transaction, section 182 of the
Companies Act 2006 requires disclosure to the board of the nature and extent of the
director's interests, *once* the transaction has been entered into.

---

[30] [1988] BCLC 104.

■ Section 182 CA 2006 Declaration of interest in existing transaction or arrangement

(1) Where a director of a company is in any way, directly or indirectly, interested in a transaction or arrangement that has been entered into by the company, he must declare the nature and extent of the interest to the other directors in accordance with this section. This section does not apply if or to the extent that the interest has been declared under section 177 (duty to declare interest in proposed transaction or arrangement).

(2) The declaration must be made—

    (a) at a meeting of the directors, or

    (b) by notice in writing (see section 184), or

    (c) by general notice (see section 185).

(3) If a declaration of interest under this section proves to be, or becomes, inaccurate or incomplete, a further declaration must be made.

(4) Any declaration required by this section must be made as soon as is reasonably practicable. Failure to comply with this requirement does not affect the underlying duty to make the declaration.

(5) This section does not require a declaration of an interest of which the director is not aware or where the director *is* not aware of the transaction or arrangement in question. For this purpose a director is treated as being aware of matters of which he ought reasonably to be aware.

(6) A director need not declare an interest under this section—

    (a) if it cannot reasonably be regarded as likely to give rise to a conflict of interest;

    (b) if, or to the extent that, the other directors are already aware of it (and for this purpose the other directors are treated as aware of anything of which they ought reasonably to be aware); or

    (c) if, or to the extent that, it concerns terms of his service contract that have been or are to be considered—

        (i) by a meeting of the directors, or

        (ii) by a committee of the directors appointed for the purpose under the company's constitution.

Apart from the ex-post rather than ex-ante timing of the disclosure, the nature of the disclosure obligation is identical to the one set out in section 177. So what is the point of section 182? The first thing to note is that section 177 combined with section 180 addresses the enforceability of the transaction and the ability of the director to keep any profits arising from the transaction. If there is no ex-ante disclosure in accordance with section 177 and no other approval mechanisms provided for in the articles of association then, in the absence of shareholder approval for the transaction, the director will be liable to account to the company for the profits of the transaction. However, even if a director is liable to account, section 182 still imposes on him an obligation to disclose. This obligation is backed by criminal sanctions.[31] That is, failure to disclose before the company enters into the transaction could result in the director being liable to account; failure to disclose after the event could result in a criminal record and liability to pay a fine of, currently, up to £5,000. Regarding the nature of

---

[31] Section 183 CA 2006.

the disclosure obligation please refer to the discussion of the disclosure requirement under section 177. Note that the disclosure obligation in Section 182 does not apply if disclosure has been made pursuant to section 177. Note also that the disclosure obligation pursuant to section 182 applies also to shadow directors[32] whereas section 177 does not apply to shadow directors.[33]

The predecessor to section 182 was section 317 of the Companies Act 1985. In contrast to section 182, section 317 required disclosure in relation to proposed and existing transactions. However, it is important to note that section 177 is not a partial successor to section 317. Failure to comply with section 177 does not attract criminal sanctions.

Prior to the 2006 Act, the overlap between the nature of the disclosure obligation in section 317 and that set out in articles 85 and 86 generated a degree of uncertainty about the relationship between compliance with section 317 and the enforceability of the self-dealing transaction. Several cases held that failure to comply with section 317 attracted civil as well as the criminal sanctions set out in the 1985 Act. The civil consequences were that the transaction was deemed to be voidable.[34] Nevertheless, the weight of authority rested with the proposition that breach of section 317 had no effect on the validity of the contract.[35] This debate can, however, be consigned to the history books given how clearly section 177 addresses issues of contractual validity and section 182 provides for criminal sanctions.[36]

3 Shareholder approval and substantial property transactions

Having spent so much time on the board disclosure mechanisms and board voting, many of you will be somewhat surprised to discover that the sphere in which the above regulation operates is subject to significant value parameters. Where the value of a transaction exceeds the lower of £100,000 or 10% of the company's value, the Companies Act 2006, as did the 1985 Act before it,[37] insists upon shareholder approval. The Act in effect reinstates the common law requirement for shareholder approval of the transaction but does not, as does the common law, allow companies to contract out of this requirement. Transactions subject to this regime are called *substantial property transactions*. The approval requirements are currently set out in sections 190–196 of the Companies Act 2006. You will have noted that section 180 considered earlier is without prejudice to any enactment providing for shareholder approval. That is, sections 190–196 pre-empt section 180. Importantly, however,

---

[32] Section 187 CA 2006. On shadow directors and the applicability of fiduciary duties to shadow directors see Chapter 9.

[33] The general duties, which include section 177, only apply to shadow directors to the extent that the existing common law rules apply and as there is no common law ex-ante disclosure requirement (such requirements where they existed were constitutional amendments to the common law rule of shareholder approval) unless a contemporary court states otherwise there is no common law disclosure obligation for shadow directors and therefore section 177 does not apply to shadow directors.

[34] See *Re MDA Investment Management Ltd; Whalley v Doney* [2004] 1 BCLC 217 holding that 'the only consequence of non-disclosure which section 317 spells out is that a director who fails to comply with the section is liable to a fine. However, there are other consequences. One is that the contract which the director should have disclosed to the board but did not is voidable at the instance of the company unless it is too late to restore the parties substantially to the previous position' (*per* Park J). See also *Hely-Hutchinson v Brayhead Ltd* [1967] 3 All ER 98 (*per* Lord Denning).

[35] *Hely-Hutchinson v Brayhead Ltd* (*per* Lord Pearson) and Lord Goff who observed in *Guinness v Saunders* [1990] 2 AC 663 that 'on this basis I cannot see that a breach of section 317...had itself any effect upon the [self-dealing] contract'.

[36] Note, however, that if section 317 is viewed as having civil as well as criminal sanctions then it is possible to view section 177 as a partial predecessor to section 317. If one takes Lord Goff's view of the consequences of section 317, as does this author, then section 182 alone is the successor provision to section 317 of the 1985 Act.

[37] The substantial property transaction regime was first introduced by the Companies Act 1980.

these provisions do not affect the continuing requirements to provide ex-ante and ex-post disclosure pursuant to sections 177 and 182.

■ Section 190 CA 2006 Substantial property transactions: requirement of members' approval

(1) A company may not enter into an arrangement under which—

    (a) a director of the company or of its holding company, or a person connected with such a director, acquires or is to acquire from the company (directly or indirectly) a substantial non-cash asset, or

    (b) the company acquires or is to acquire a substantial non-cash asset (directly or indirectly) from such a director or a person so connected,

    Unless the arrangement has been approved by a resolution of the members of the company or is conditional on such approval being obtained.

    For the meaning of 'substantial non-cash asset' see section 191.

(2) If the director or connected person is a director of the company's holding company or a person connected with such a director, the arrangement must also have been approved by a resolution of the members of the holding company or be conditional on such approval being obtained.

(3) A company shall not be subject to any liability by reason of a failure to obtain approval required by this section.

(4) No approval is required under this section on the part of the members of a body corporate that—

    (a) is not a UK-registered company, or

    (b) is a wholly-owned subsidiary of another body corporate.

(5) For the purposes of this section—

    (a) an arrangement involving more than one non-cash asset, or

    (b) an arrangement that is one of a series involving non-cash assets, shall be treated as if they involved a non-cash asset of a value equal to the aggregate value of all the non-cash assets involved in the arrangement or, as the case may be, the series.

(6) This section does not apply to a transaction so far as it relates—

    (a) to anything to which a director of a company is entitled under his service contract, or

    (b) to payment for loss of office as defined in section 215 (payments requiring members' approval).

■ Section 191 CA 2006 Meaning of 'substantial'

(1) This section explains what is meant in section 190 (requirement of approval for substantial property transactions) by a 'substantial' non-cash asset.

(2) An asset is a substantial asset in relation to a company if its value—

    (a) exceeds 10% of the company's asset value and is more than £5,000, or

    (b) exceeds £100,000.

(3) For this purpose a company's 'asset value' at any time is—

    (a) the value of the company's net assets determined by reference to its most recent statutory accounts, or

(b) if no statutory accounts have been prepared, the amount of the company's called-up share capital.

(4) A company's 'statutory accounts' means its annual accounts prepared in accordance with Part 15, and its 'most recent' statutory accounts means those in relation to which the time for sending them out to members (see section 424) is most recent.

(5) Whether an asset is a substantial asset shall be determined as at the time the arrangement is entered into.

■ Section 195 CA 2006 Property transactions: civil consequences of contravention

(1) This section applies where a company enters into an arrangement in contravention of section 190 (requirement of members' approval for substantial property transactions).

(2) The arrangement, and any transaction entered into in pursuance of the arrangement (whether by the company or any other person), is voidable at the instance of the company, unless—

(a) restitution of any money or other asset that was the subject matter of the arrangement or transaction is no longer possible,

(b) the company has been indemnified in pursuance of this section by any other persons for the loss or damage suffered by it, or

(c) rights acquired in good faith, for value and without actual notice of the contravention by a person who is not a party to the arrangement or transaction would be affected by the avoidance.

(3) Whether or not the arrangement or any such transaction has been avoided, each of the persons specified in subsection (4) is liable—

(a) to account to the company for any gain that he has made directly or indirectly by the arrangement or transaction, and

(b) (jointly and severally with any other person so liable under this section) to indemnify the company for any loss or damage resulting from the arrangement or transaction.

(4) The persons so liable are—

(a) any director of the company or of its holding company with whom the company entered into the arrangement in contravention of section 190,

(b) any person with whom the company entered into the arrangement in contravention of that section who is connected with a director of the company or of its holding company,

(c) the director of the company or of its holding company with whom any such person is connected, and

(d) any other director of the company who authorised the arrangement or any transaction entered into in pursuance of such an arrangement...

■ Section 252 CA 2006 Persons connected with a director

(1) This section defines what is meant by references in this Part to a person being 'connected' with a director of a company (or a director being 'connected' with a person).

(2) The following persons (and only those persons) are connected with a director of a company—

(a) members of the director's family (see section 253);

(b) a body corporate with which the director is connected (as defined in section 254);

(c) a person acting in his capacity as trustee of a trust—

(i) the beneficiaries of which include the director or a person who by virtue of paragraph (a) or (b) is connected with him, or

(ii) the terms of which confer a power on the trustees that may be exercised for the benefit of the director or any such person, other than a trust for the purposes of an employees' share scheme or a pension scheme;

(d) a person acting in his capacity as partner—

(i) of the director, or

(ii) of a person who, by virtue of paragraph (a), (b) or (c), is connected with that director;

(e) a firm that is a legal person under the law by which it is governed and in which—

(i) the director is a partner,

(ii) a partner is a person who, by virtue of paragraph (a), (b) or (c) is connected with the director, or

(iii) a partner is a firm in which the director is a partner or in which there is a partner who, by virtue of paragraph (a), (b) or (c), is connected with the director.

■ Section 254 CA 2006 Director 'connected with' a body corporate

(1) This section defines what is meant by references in this Part to a director being 'connected with' a body corporate.

(2) A director is connected with a body corporate if, but only if, he and the persons connected with him together—

(a) are interested in shares comprised in the equity share capital of that body corporate of a nominal value equal to at least 20% of that share capital, or

(b) are entitled to exercise or control the exercise of more than 20% of the voting power at any general meeting of that body.

(3) The rules set out in Schedule 1 (references to interest in shares or debentures) apply for the purposes of this section.

(4) References in this section to voting power the exercise of which is controlled by a director include voting power whose exercise is controlled by a body corporate controlled by him.

The first point to note about the substantial property transaction rules is that they only apply to the transfer of ' "substantial" non-cash assets'. The rules do not apply if the transactions fall below the value thresholds set out in the definition of 'substantial' in section 191 and they *do not* apply if the transaction involves something other than a 'non-cash asset'. 'Non-cash asset' is defined by section 1163 to mean 'any property or interest in property other than cash'. The courts have interpreted this definition flexibly. In *Ultraframe v Fielding*,[38] Lewison J held that a non-cash asset could include a lease and a licence to exploit design rights. It is clear, however, that self-dealing transactions can fall outside the scope of the definition of non-cash asset. In *Ultraframe* the court held that the licence amounted to a non-cash asset because it was a licence to exploit property, namely, the design rights. The court also held that debentures would not amount to a non-cash asset as the amounts owed to the company could be monetized. Another example of a self-dealing transaction that would not involve a 'non-cash asset'

---

[38] [2005] All ER (D) 397.

would be an agreement to provide services—for example, consulting services or professional services. An agreement to provide services does not involve property or an interest in property and is not, therefore, a substantial property transaction even though such arrangements could clearly be worth more than £100,000. Accordingly, the substantial property transaction regime *does not* pre-empt the ex-ante board disclosure approach in relation to all transactions worth more than £100,000 or 10% of company value *but only* in relation to those transactions which involve the transfer of property or an interest in property.

It is difficult to find a plausible rationale to explain why the law makes this distinction between different types of self-dealing transaction. One could submit that property and rights in property are subject to greater valuation uncertainty than say the provision of services or the making of loans where market rates as a comparison are more readily available. It is, however, a weak policy basis upon which to rest this regulatory distinction.

If the transaction in question involves a substantial non-cash asset and is with a director of the company, a director of the subject company's holding company,[39] or a person connected with the director then the transaction must be approved by the shareholders in general meeting[40]—unless the company is a wholly owned subsidiary of another company, in which case shareholder approval is not required.[41] The definition of connected persons is very broad and addresses family members, partners, and other corporate bodies in which the director (together with other connected persons) has a 20% or greater share interest.[42] Accordingly, companies with whom the company does business that are less than 20% owned by the director do not fall within this regime.

With regard to the shareholder approval required pursuant to section 190 there are two points to note. First, the conflicted directors or the persons connected with the director can vote their shares to approve the transaction. The section does not require a disinterested shareholder vote. The rule set out in section 239 (discussed in Chapter 15), which prevents directors who are in breach of duty from voting their shares to ratify the breach, does not apply to substantial property transactions. Secondly, the principle in *Re Duomatic Ltd*[43] applies allowing for informal approval of all shareholders to substitute for formal approval in general meeting.[44]

If shareholder approval is not obtained the transaction is voidable by the company unless avoidance is no longer possible where, for example, a bona fide purchaser for value has purchased the asset, or where the company has been fully indemnified for its loss. Whether or not the transaction has been avoided the interested director or the connected person is liable to the company for any damage suffered by the company.[45] Importantly, not only is the interested director or connected person liable for the company's loss but so is any disinterested director who authorized the transaction (section 195(3) and (4)).

---

[39] If the transaction is with the director of the company's holding company (or a person connected with that director) then the transaction must also be approved by the members of the holding company (section 190(2) CA 2006).

[40] Section 190(1)(b) Companies Act 2006.

[41] Section 190(4)(b) Companies Act 2006. Although if such a director is a director of the holding company then holding company member approval would still be required—see note 39.

[42] Schedule 1 of the Companies Act 2006 contains a detailed set of rules designed to ensure that a broader set of 'interests' in shares are captured other than being the registered member, including for example, options to purchase shares and rights to direct the voting of shares owned by a third party.

[43] [1969] 1 All ER 161: see Chapter 3.

[44] *NBH Ltd v Hoare* [2006] 2 BCLC 649. On the principle in *Re Duomatic* see Chapter 3.

[45] See, for example, *Re Duckwari plc (No 3)* [1999] 1 BCLC 168 where the director was held liable for the loss in value of the non-cash asset purchased by the company and subsequently sold.

4 Loans to directors

In our analysis of the potential costs and benefits of self-dealing transactions at the beginning of this chapter we noted that the potential benefits of self-dealing transactions may vary depending on the subject-matter of the transaction. In our *Hypothetical A* whilst there were clearly benefits in terms of the savings of time and transaction costs of getting a loan on market terms from Bob we found it more difficult to envisage the benefits to Bob's Electronics of giving a loan to Bob. We noted, therefore, that loans *to* directors could be a self-dealing category suitable for a straightforward prohibition— which is not subject to approval by any company body. Following public concerns about loans made by companies to directors in the late 1970s, the Companies Act 1980 introduced, subject to minor exceptions, a blanket ban on company loans to directors. The Companies Act 2006, adopting the recommendation of the Company Law Review,[46] makes a significant alteration to this ban by allowing such loans to be made if they are approved by the shareholders in general meeting.

The provisions of the 2006 Act dealing with loans to directors pre-empt sections 177 and 180. These provisions are set out in sections 197–214 of the 2006 Act. Subject to the exceptions detailed in the next paragraph, the provisions prohibit the making of any loan or guarantee by a company to one of its directors, or one of the directors of its holding company.[47] In addition, the provisions prohibit the making of 'quasi-loans'[48] and entering into 'credit transactions' on behalf of company directors and directors of the company's holding company.[49] A quasi-loan covers situations where the company pays, or agrees to pay, an amount on behalf of the director, for example if the director falls behind on his car payments or his mortgage payments and the company pays them for him.[50] Credit transactions cover hire purchase and lease transactions, such as where the company enters into a hire purchase contract on behalf of the director.[51] To ensure that companies do not creatively avoid these rules by arranging for a third party to make the loans or quasi-loans, the Act prohibits these third-party arrangements which it labels 'related arrangements'.[52] The Act also extends the prohibitions to connected persons as defined in section 252 of the Act (see section IV.3 of this chapter).[53]

These prohibitions are subject to three key exceptions. First, loans, quasi-loans, credit transactions on behalf of directors, and related arrangements are allowed if the shareholders acting in general meeting authorize them. Interested shareholders (that is the directors who are receiving the loans) are not excluded from voting.[54] Secondly, the prohibition does not cover making available funds to directors to cover business expenditure—although it caps this exemption at £50,000 in relation to one transaction and related transactions.[55] Thirdly, there is a *de minimis* exception: loans and quasi-loans for less than £10,000 and credit transactions for less than £15,000 do not require shareholder approval.[56] The Act also provides for an exception in relation to the funding of litigation expenses discussed in detail in Chapter 12.[57]

The consequences of breaching these rules is that the transaction is voidable by the company; any monies lent or assets obtained as a result of the transaction must be transferred to the company unless this is no longer possible, for example a bona fide third party for value has acquired the asset. The director or connected person who received a

---

[46] Company Law Review Steering Committee, *Modern Company Law for a Competitive Economy: Completing the Structure*, para 4.21.

[47] Section 197 CA 2006.   [48] Section 198 CA 2006.   [49] Section 201 CA 2006.

[50] Section 199 CA 2006   [51] Section 202 CA 2006.   [52] Section 203 CA 2006.

[53] Sections 200; 201(2) CA 2006.

[54] If the director is a director of the company's holding company the members of the holding company must also approve of the transaction (section 197(2) CA 2006).

[55] Section 204 CA 2006.   [56] Section 207 CA 2006.   [57] Sections 205–206 CA 2006.

loan, quasi loan, or benefited from a credit transaction is liable to indemnify the company for any loss it suffers as is any disinterested director who authorized the transaction.[58]

V SELF-DEALING REGULATION BEYOND THE COMPANIES ACT

1 Additional self-dealing regulation for listed companies

Any UK company traded on the London Stock Exchange's **Main Market** is subject to the additional corporate regulation set out in the **UKLA** Listing Rules. As discussed in Chapter 6, the Listing Rules make a distinction between companies that have a premium listing and those with a standard listing, which are subject to fewer of the Listing Rules. Listing Rule 11[59] sets forth disclosure and shareholder approval[60] requirements in relation to transactions which it labels 'related party transactions'.[61] This rule only applies to companies with a premium listing.[62]

Listing Rule 11 defines a 'related party'[63] to include a person who in the last 12 months was a director, shadow director, or associate[64] of such director. 'Associate' is defined to include close relatives and companies in which the director, together with his other family members, has the right to exercise 30% of the voting rights or a right to appoint a majority of the directors. Accordingly, where the director's interest in a company is less than 30% this regime does not apply. The definition of 'related party' also extends to substantial shareholders and we shall revisit the application of these rules to such shareholders in Chapter 16 on 'Minority shareholder protection'. The rules apply to any related party transaction that is not a transaction in the 'ordinary course of business' and not a 'small transaction',[65] which is defined as less than 0.25% of the value of the company.[66]

Pursuant to Listing Rule 11.1.7, in relation to any related party transaction the company is required, first, to send a circular to shareholders providing them with information about the related party transaction and, second, to obtain shareholder approval for the transaction. Importantly, in relation to the shareholder vote the company must take steps to ensure that the interested director does not vote and that he takes 'all reasonable steps' to ensure that his associates with shares in the company do not vote their shares.[67] It should also be noted that Listing Rules 13.3 and 13.6 set out in detail the information to be provided to the shareholders in the circular about the transaction. These disclosure requirements generate additional substantive obligations. Most importantly, the board is required to make a statement that the transaction is fair and reasonable and that they have been so advised by an independent advisor—effectively requiring the appointment of an independent advisor in relation to the transaction.[68]

---

[58] Section 213 CA 2006.

[59] http://fsahandbook.info/FSA/ 🌐.

[60] On the interaction of disclosure, shareholder approval, and market mechanisms such as non-executive reputational capital see section II.2.3 of this chapter.

[61] These rules also apply if the listed company's subsidiary enters into a related party transaction—LR. 11.1.3.

[62] LR 11.1.1.   [63] LR 11.1.4.

[64] See Listing Rule Definitions, http://fsahandbook.info/FSA/ 🌐.

[65] Defined in Rule 11 Annex 1.1.

[66] Several tests (the Class tests) for calculating value are provided in the Listing Rules based on different value parameters such as gross assets and profits—LR 10 Annex 1.

[67] LR 11.1.8.   [68] LR 13.6.1(5).

2 Ex-post disclosure and accounting regulation

For companies that are required to produce audited accounts, their accounts must be compiled in accordance with the applicable accounting standards and auditors must certify compliance with these standards.[69] Accounting standards are the rules and principles that determine how to record a company's assets, liabilities, and transactions in its financial statements (the **balance sheet** and the **profit and loss account**). The nature of the audit and the nature and source of accounting standards is dealt with in detail in Web Chapter A. The applicable accounting standards are produced by the UK's Accounting Standards Board and the International Accounting Standards Board (IASB). The standards produced by the Accounting Standards Board are known as *Financial Reporting Standards*. However, listed UK Plcs must produce their group accounts in accordance with *International Financial Reporting Standards* (IFRS) issued by the IASB and adopted by the European Union.[70] Both the IASB and ASB have produced an accounting standard addressing related party transactions which covers self-dealing transactions with directors: IAS 24 *Related Party Disclosures* and FRS 8: *Related Party Disclosures*, respectively. Key provisions from IAS 24 are set out here.

The primary objective of IAS 24 is to enable the users of financial statements to understand the effect of related party transactions on the financial statements. The provision of detailed information on self-dealing transactions also assists shareholders and the market place in monitoring and assessing self-serving board behaviour.

■ IAS 24: Related Party Disclosures (November 2009, IASB)

Objective
The objective of this standard is to ensure that an entity's financial statements contain the disclosures necessary to draw attention to the possibility that its financial position and profit or loss may have been affected by the existence of related parties and by transactions and outstanding balances with such parties.

Definition of Related Party
A *related party* is a person or entity that is related to the entity that is preparing its financial statements (in this Standard referred to as the 'reporting entity').

(a) A person or a close member of that person's family is related to a reporting entity if that person:

    (i)   has control or joint control over the reporting entity;

    (ii) has significant influence over the reporting entity; or

    (iii) is a member of the key management personnel of the reporting entity or of a parent of the reporting entity.

(b) An entity is related to a reporting entity if any of the following conditions applies:

    (i)   The entity and the reporting entity are members of the same group (which means that each parent, subsidiary and fellow subsidiary is related to the others).

---

[69] Strictly speaking the company must produce, and the auditors must certify, that the accounts set forth a true and fair view of the company's financial position. However, in order to provide a true and fair view, in most instances, compliance with the accounting standards will be required. On the true and fair view and the relationship between company law and accounting standards see Web Chapter A.

[70] For a discussion of the option for UK companies to use IFRS for all their accounts not just their group accounts see Web Chapter A. International Accounting Standards were produced by the IASB's predecessor body, the International Accounting Standards Committee, and have been adopted by the IASB. We refer in this book to both IFRS and IASs as IFRSs.

(ii) One entity is an associate or joint venture of the other entity (or an associate or joint venture of a member of a group of which the other entity is a member).

(iii) Both entities are joint ventures of the same third party.

(iv) One entity is a joint venture of a third entity and the other entity is an associate of the third entity.

(v) The entity is a post-employment benefit plan for the benefit of employees of either the reporting entity or an entity related to the reporting entity. If the reporting entity is itself such a plan, the sponsoring employers are also related to the reporting entity.

(vi) The entity is controlled or jointly controlled by a person identified in (a).

(vii) A person identified in (a)(i) has significant influence over the entity or is a member of the key management personnel of the entity (or of a parent of the entity).

Definition of Related Party Transaction
A related party transaction is a transfer of resources, services, or obligations between a reporting entity and a related party, regardless of whether a price is charged…

Disclosure Requirements
If an entity has had related party transactions during the periods covered by the financial statements, it shall disclose the nature of the related party relationship as well as information about those transactions and outstanding balances, including commitments, necessary for users to understand the potential effect of the relationship on the financial statements.

Examples of transactions that require disclosure
- Purchases or sales of goods (finished or unfinished).
- Purchases or sales of property and other assets.
- Rendering or receiving of services.
- Leases.
- Transfers of research and development.
- Transfers under licence agreements.
- Transfers under finance arrangements (including loans and equity contributions in cash or in kind).
- Provision of guarantees or collateral.
- Commitments to do something if a particular event occurs or does not occur in the future, including executory contracts (recognised and unrecognised); and
- Settlement of liabilities on behalf of the entity or by the entity on behalf of another party.

[Disclosures that related party transactions were made on terms equivalent to those that prevail in arm's length transactions should be made only if such terms can be substantiated.]

Whilst IAS 24 is aimed broadly at related party transactions, we see clearly that it covers self-dealing transactions with any director through the related party category 'key management personnel', which is defined as those individuals who have 'authority and responsibility for planning, directing and controlling the activities of an entity, directly or indirectly, including any director (whether executive or otherwise) of that entity.'[71] This category could, depending on the circumstances, also include members of senior management that do not sit on the board. It also covers indirect

---

[71] IAS 24 Rule 9.

self-dealing transactions with companies 'controlled'[72] or 'significantly influenced' by 'key management personnel'.[73] Clearly, as you will see from the definition of 'related party', it covers a much broader range of transactions than self-dealing transactions. We shall revisit some of these other transactions when we look at minority share-holder protection in Chapter 16. As an example of related party disclosures in relation to director self-dealing transactions consider the following extract from Tottenham Hotspur Plc's 2005 annual report.

■ **Tottenham Hotspur Plc**

Notes to the Accounts

27. Related party transactions
Companies of which [Director A] is a Director, were invoiced £300 (2004: £72,225) plus VAT for corporate hospitality services during the year. [Director A] is an Executive Director of the Group.

A sum of £nil (2004: £15,000) was invoiced to Tottenham Hotspur plc relating to professional services supplied by Final Developments Limited during the period. [Director A] is a Director of Final Developments Limited. No balances were outstanding at the Balance Sheet date.

Except for the balances disclosed above, there were no other balances outstanding at the Balance Sheet date in 2005 or 2004. All of these transactions were at arm's length.

As we consider in further detail in Web Chapter A, whereas the accounts themselves are prepared by the company, they are subsequently verified by independent third-party auditors, such as PricewaterhouseCoopers or KPMG, to assess their accuracy and compliance with the accounting standards such as IAS 24. The role of the independent auditor both increases the likelihood that self-dealing transactions will be correctly disclosed in accordance with the applicable accounting standard and also provides for third-party oversight of the terms of the identified self-dealing transactions.

As we discuss in detail in Web Chapter A, auditors do not check every company transaction; rather they test and sample from a range of transactions.[74] Where management do not themselves reveal the self-dealing transaction, auditors cannot guarantee that their sampling will identify them. However, the audit standards that apply to auditors require that they put in place robust procedures to attempt to identify any undisclosed related party transactions. This makes it difficult for management to intentionally hide such transactions from view. Indeed a single audit standard is dedicated to related party procedures: *ISA 550 (UK and Ireland): Related Parties*. Once identified *ISA 550* requires the auditor to 'obtain sufficient appropriate audit evidence as to whether these transactions have been properly recorded' and to corroborate 'the explanation of the purpose of the transaction and, if necessary, confirming that the transaction is bona fide'.[75] For example, if Bob, a director of Bob's Electronics Plc, sold his house to Bob's Electronics for twice its market value, which is £1m, then Bob's Electronics Ltd would pay £2m in cash to Bob. Bob and the directors who approved the transaction would prefer to record the house as an asset worth £2m; if they do so then the shareholders may not be unduly concerned, as the company on the face of the accounts would not appear to have dissipated its assets to Bob. However, the auditors of the company's accounts will not take such a valuation of the house at face value. In order to give their stamp of approval of

---

[72] Control is defined as 'the power to govern the financial and operating policies of an entity so as to obtain benefits from its activities' *ibid*.

[73] Significant influence is defined as follows: 'significant influence is the power to participate in the financial and operating policy decisions of an entity, but not control over those policies' *ibid*.

[74] See *ISA 530 (UK and Ireland): Audit Sampling and Other Means of Testing*.

[75] *ISA 550: Related Parties* [14].

the value of the asset recorded in the company's balance sheet they will insist on some objective evidence that the house is worth £2m. If it is only worth £1m then the auditors will only certify the accounts if it is recorded in the accounts as £1m. Directors who engage in self-dealing transactions may, therefore, because of accounting disclosures on related party transactions and the audit process, be forced to reveal to shareholders any questionable self-dealing activities.[76] Accordingly, linking self-dealing disclosure to the audit process makes it harder for directors to hide from the shareholders and the market place any agency costs generated by the self-dealing transaction.

Students who look at any random sample of FTSE 100 companies' financial statements for related party transaction disclosure pursuant to IAS 24 and FRS 8 will find that self-dealing transactions that are not *de minimis* are very rare, suggesting that it is rarely necessary for public companies to enter into self-dealing transactions and that directors' authority is not abused in this regard. This in turn suggests that UK regulation—including both Listing Rule 11 and *ex-post* disclosure regulation—effectively deters self-dealing agency costs. What it does not tell us is whether it also deters beneficial transactions that were deterred by the monetary costs of approval and the fear of possible reputational costs of disclosure and shareholder approval.

VI UK SELF-DEALING REGULATION IN COMPARATIVE US PERSPECTIVE

It is worth pausing to consider the rather different evolution of the regulation of self-dealing in the US as compared to the evolution of UK regulation. In the following extract from Professor Marsh we see that the corporate law of most US states had a familiar starting point for UK corporate lawyers. This is perhaps hardly surprising given our shared common law heritage and the influence, as you will see from the article, of leading UK equity jurists on US law. However, from a shared starting point US state corporate law took a very different path from UK company law, resulting in a regulatory approach that relies predominantly on fairness review by the courts, even if the self-dealing transactions have been approved by disinterested directors and/or the shareholder body.

■ **H. Marsh, 'Are Directors Trustees: Conflicts of Interest and Corporate Morality' (1966) 22 *Business Lawyer* 35**

The phrase 'conflict of interest' is very old in the law. In the United States as early as 1846 Mr. Justice Wayne stated:

'The general rule stands upon our great moral obligation to refrain from placing ourselves in relations which ordinarily excite a conflict between self-interest and integrity...In this *conflict of interest* the law wisely interposes. It acts not on the possibility that, in some cases, the sense of that duty may prevail over the motives of self-interest, but it provides against the probability in many cases, and the danger in all cases, that the dictates of self-interest will exercise a predominant influence, and supersede that of duty.'

...

---

[76] One needs to be careful not to overstate the extent to which auditors can operate as a check on self-serving self-dealing. In practice an asset sold or purchased by the company may be subject to a broad range of valuations. If the transaction falls within the value range the auditor is unlikely to question it even though they suspect that the company would have obtained a better deal had it been subject to a real arm's length bargaining process.

There have been several different rules adopted by courts and legislatures to deal with this problem of conflict of interest, which correspond roughly with successive periods in the legal history of this country. Therefore in the discussion immediately following, I propose to consider the principles which have been advanced at one time or another, in more or less chronological order, even though the earlier ones have been largely if not completely abandoned.

I. Types of Legal Regulations

(a) Prohibition

In 1880 it could have been stated with confidence that in the United States the general rule was that any contract between a director and his corporation was voidable at the instance of the corporation or its shareholders, without regard to the fairness or unfairness of the transaction. This rule was stated in powerful terms by a number of highly regarded courts and judges in cases which arose generally out of the railroad frauds of the 1860's and 1870's.

In *Wardell v. Union Pacific R.R. Co.* Mr. Justice Field stated that:

'It is among the rudiments of the law that the same person cannot act for himself and at the same time, with respect to the same matter, as agent for another, whose interests are conflicting....The two positions impose different obligations, and their union would at once raise a conflict between interest and duty; and "Constituted as humanity is, in the majority of cases duty would be overborne in the struggle."...Hence, all arrangements by directors of a railroad company, to secure an undue advantage to themselves at its expense, by the formation of a new company as an auxiliary to the original one, with an understanding that they or some of them shall take stock in it, and then, that valuable contracts shall be given to it, in the profits of which they, as stockholders in the new company, are to share, are so many unlawful devices to enrich themselves to the detriment of the stockholders and creditors of the original company, and will be condemned whenever properly brought before the courts for consideration.'

Under this rule it mattered not the slightest that there was a majority of so-called disinterested directors who approved the contract. The courts stated that the corporation was entitled to the unprejudiced judgment and advice of all of its directors and therefore it did no good to say that the interested director did not participate in the making of the contract on behalf of the corporation: '...the very words in which he asserts his right declare his wrong; he ought to have participated...' Furthermore, the courts said that it was impossible to measure the influence which one director might have over his associates, even though ostensibly abstaining from participation in the discussion or vote: '...a corporation, in order to defeat a contract entered into by directors, in which one or more of them had a private interest, is not bound to show that the influence of the director or directors having the private interest determined the action of the board. The law cannot accurately measure the influence of a trustee with his associates, nor will it enter into the inquiry...'

...

This principle, absolutely inhibiting contracts between a corporation and its directors or any of them, appeared to be impregnable in 1880. It was stated in ringing terms by virtually every decided case, with arguments which seemed irrefutable, and it was sanctioned by age. As Justice Davies stated:

'To hold otherwise, would be to overturn principles of equity which have been regarded as well settled since the days of Lord Keeper Bridgman, in the 22nd of Charles second, to the present time— principles enunciated and enforced by Hardwicke, Thurlow, Loughborough, Eldon, Cranworth, Story and Kent, and which the highest courts in our country have declared to be founded on immutable truth and justice, and to stand upon our great moral obligation to refrain from placing ourselves in relations which excite a conflict between self interest and integrity.'

Thirty years later this principle was dead.

(b) Approval by a disinterested majority of the board

It could have been stated with reasonable confidence in 1910 that the general rule was that a contract between a director and his corporation was valid if it was approved by a disinterested majority of his fellow directors and was not found to be unfair or fraudulent by the court if challenged; but that a contract in which a majority of the board was interested was voidable at the instance of the corporation or its shareholders without regard to any question of fairness.

One searches in vain in the decided cases for a reasoned defense of this change in legal philosophy, or for the slightest attempt to refute the powerful arguments which had been made in support of the previous rule. Did the courts discover in the last quarter of the Nineteenth Century that greed was no longer a factor in human conduct? If so, they did not share the basis of this discovery with the public; nor did they humbly admit their error when confronted with the next wave of corporate frauds arising out of the era of the formation of the 'trusts' during the 1890's and early 1900's.

...

But in no case is there any discussion or attempted refutation of the reasons previously given by the courts as to why it is impossible, in such a situation, for any director to be disinterested. Some courts seem simply to admit that the practice has grown too widespread for them to cope with. In *South Side Trust Co. v. Washington Tin Plate Co.* the Supreme Court of Pennsylvania said: 'The interests of corporations are sometimes so interwoven that it is desirable to have joint representatives in their respective managements, and at any rate it is a not uncommon and [therefore?] not unlawful practice' (sic).

...

(c) Judicial review of the fairness of the transaction

By 1960 it could be said with some assurance that the general rule was that no transaction of a corporation with any or all of its directors was automatically voidable at the suit of a shareholder, whether there was a disinterested majority of the board or not; but that the courts would review such a contract and subject it to rigid and careful scrutiny, and would invalidate the contract if it was found to be unfair to the corporation.

...

The law can be caught in the process of change in some instances, as for example in Illinois in 1960 in the case of *Shlensky v. South Parkway Building Corp.* That decision specifically discussed and overruled previous Illinois decisions requiring approval by a disinterested majority of the board, and adopted the modern rule that 'transactions between corporations with common directors may be avoided only *if unfair,* and that the directors who would sustain the challenged transaction have the burden of overcoming the presumption against the validity of the transaction by showing its fairness.'

...

Effect of charter or by-law provisions.

...

Such clauses are typically drafted in the broadest imaginable terms and purport to exonerate the directors from all liability for conflict of interest in the absence of fraud and to validate all such transactions. The first such clause I ever drafted as a young associate for a law firm was for a small company which was going public. I took the standard office form and broadened it to some extent to show my zeal, and inserted it in the proposed charter amendment. For other reasons it was essential that we get a 100% vote of a rather substantial number of shareholders, among whom was a small insurance company. We received a communication from this insurance company wanting to know just what transactions of this sort the majority shareholder had in mind and what his purpose was in trying to insert this clause in the charter. In this case, at least, the clause did *induxit suspicionem*. We quieted their fears by writing them a letter stating truthfully that we had inserted the clause without even the knowledge of the majority shareholder just to 'modernize' the charter, and that he was not planning any such transactions. But the question, what did we think we were doing, has reoccurred to me intermittently over the intervening 15 years. The only satisfactory answer that I have ever been able to produce is that we were trying to make it easier for the first crook who got control of this corporation.

Statutory sanction. Even if there is no character or by-law provision and the decisions in the particular State have not clearly adopted the modern rule, there still may be a statute which authorizes all such transactions involving conflict of interest, subject only to a fairness test. Most of these statutes have been copied from or modelled upon California Corporations Code § 820. Such statutes have been adopted in recent years by Nevada, New York, North Carolina and South Carolina. These statutes purport to validate any transaction by a corporation with a director or another corporation in which the director is interested if (a) it is approved by a disinterested majority of the board, with the interested director eligible to be counted as a part of the quorum; *or* (b) it is approved by a majority of the shareholders; *or* (c) it is 'just and reasonable' as to the corporation. While literally under such a statute a transaction which was unjust and unreasonable would be immune from attack if it had been approved by a disinterested majority of the directors or by the shareholders, there is a California decision which indicates that the courts will in any event review the transaction for fairness (whatever the statute says). So the entire statute could just as well have been compressed into the final clause.

...

The final conclusion is that under statute, judicial decision or charter provision, it would be a rarity today to find a transaction involving interested directors which was not permitted by the law, subject only to possible invalidation for unfairness.

As this summary of the development of US state corporate law's regulation shows, state corporate law has evolved from a strict approach to self-dealing regulation that provided a prohibition on these transactions which was not, as is the case at UK common law, capable of being approved of by the shareholder body, to the position that allows directors to keep the benefit of such transactions provided that they are fair to the company. Although written in 1966 the position in Delaware today is accurately summed-up in Professor Marsh's conclusion.

US courts, therefore, have put themselves at the heart of self-dealing regulation by being willing to determine whether *in fact* the duty of loyalty has been compromised—which it has not been if the transaction is fair to the company. In contrast to UK courts, US courts have not resisted judicial analysis of transactional fairness and have not doubted their ability to engage in such review. But what exactly does such review involve? In this regard the Delaware Court of Chancery recently observed in *Valeant Pharmaceuticals International v Jerney* 921 A 2d 732 (Del 2007):

Directors who stand on both sides of a transaction have 'the burden of establishing its entire fairness, sufficient to pass the test of careful scrutiny by the courts.'[77] Entire fairness can be proved only where the directors 'demonstrate their utmost good faith and the most scrupulous inherent fairness of the bargain.'[78] Entire fairness has two components: fair dealing and fair price. The two components of the entire fairness concept are not independent, but rather the fair dealing prong informs the court as to the fairness of the price obtained through that process. The court does not focus on the components individually, but determines entire fairness based on all aspects of the entire transaction. Fair dealing addresses the 'questions of when the transaction was timed, how it was initiated, structured, negotiated, disclosed to the directors, and how the approvals of the directors and the stockholders were obtained.'[79] Fair price assures the transaction was substantively fair by examining 'the economic and financial considerations.'[80]

---

[77] *Weinberger v UOP, Inc, 457 A2d 701, 710 (Del 1983).*   [78] *Ibid.*
[79] *Ibid.*   [80] *Ibid.*

Questions and discussion

- According to Professor Marsh in the mid-1880s US courts in New York and New Jersey in the cases cited by Professor Marsh were rejecting the idea that disinterested directors could perform a regulatory function. At approximately the same period in 1871 Lord Hatherley in *Imperial Mercantile Credit Association v Coleman*[81] accepted the shareholders' contractual right to deploy disclosure and disinterested director approval in relation to very significant self-dealing transactions. In light of the UK's approach, consider the US courts' explicit doubts about the disinterested director mechanism. According to Marsh, US courts note that it is 'impossible to measure the influence which one director may have over his associates' and that 'the law cannot accurately measure the influence of a trustee with his associates'. In effect, UK company law has heeded this advice as it has moved to restrict significantly the scope of application of ex-ante board disclosure and approval, replacing it, in the various guises considered above, with shareholder approval. But it is worth bearing these judicial warnings in mind as we consider the next section of this chapter where we will see the Companies Act 2006 deploying the disinterested director approval mechanism in relation to corporate opportunities.

- Why do you think UK courts did not raise the policy concerns about disinterested directors that were so clearly at the forefront of the US judiciaries' mind?

- As documented by Professor Marsh, between 1880 and 1910 the US courts move away from a strict rule providing for the automatic voidability of any self-dealing transaction towards a rule combining disinterested director approval and fairness review. Professor Marsh notes that the judgments are devoid of any explanation for this shift in approach. Typically the explanations given for this shift in regulatory approach are economic ones. For example, the law needed to adjust to provide companies with greater scope to engage in beneficial self-dealing transactions; or these rules are the product of the federal structure of US corporate law which allows US states to compete with each other for incorporations resulting in a managerially-friendly race to the bottom (see Chapter 6 section 6.1) and managerially-friendly self-dealing rules. Recent scholarship takes issue with the idea that law simply capitulated to these economic drivers. It argues that the different paths taken by US and UK law from the same starting point are explained by very different understandings of what the company was in the UK and the US in the late 19th century. In the former, an incorporated partnership which involved the state conferring certain benefits on what was the existing product of private activity; in the latter an entity brought into being by state action. The conception of the UK company allowed companies and shareholders to contract around the strict rules of equity in order adapt law to enable benign self-dealing. By way of contrast, such contractual solutions were not available in the US which resulted in US courts exploring other solutions—within the law—to enable benign self-dealing. See further, D. Kershaw, 'The Path of Corporate Fiduciary Law' (2012) *New York University Journal of Law and Business* (forthcoming).

- It is sometimes claimed that the UK courts' aversion to fairness review was the product of a different era in terms of the courts' ability to gather and process information that goes to fair value.[82] From this view, modern, more sophisticated judges are capable of engaging questions of transactional fairness. Interestingly, however, as we see from the extract, early US courts were not afraid of engaging in fairness review. Do you think the reasons given by Lords Cranworth and Eldon are weighty enough reasons for the courts to elect not to deploy fairness review? Do you think modern courts are capable of

---

[81] (1871) LR 6 Ch App 588.

[82] J. Lowry and R. Edmunds, 'The No-Conflict–No-Profit Rules and the Corporate Fiduciary: Challenging the Orthodoxy of Absolutism' (2000) *Journal of Business Law* 122, 127; L. Sealy, *Company Law and Commercial Reality* (1984), 39.

engaging in fairness review of self-dealing transactions? What, if anything, has changed to make modern courts more capable in this regard than the courts in the nineteenth century?

- If in your view UK courts should engage in fairness review of self-dealing transactions, what factors would the courts look to in order to carry out fairness review, or, as the Delaware courts put it, to 'examine the economic and financial considerations' surrounding the transaction?

Additional reading

R. Clark, *Corporate Law* (Little, Brown: 1987), chapter 16.

R. Cooter and B. Freedman, 'The Fiduciary Relationship: Its Economic Character and Legal Consequences' (1991) 66 *New York University Law Review* 1045.

Z. Goshen, 'The Efficiency of Controlling Corporate Self-Dealing: Theory Meets Reality' (2003) 91 *California Law Review* 393.

D. Kershaw, 'The Path of Corporate Fiduciary Law' (2012) *New York University Journal of Law and Business* (forthcoming).

 Online Resource Centre
http://www.oxfordtextbooks.co.uk/orc/kershaw2e/

Visit the Online Resource Centre for additional resources and information available for this chapter, including web links and an interactive flashcard glossary.

CHAPTER FOURTEEN

REGULATING CONFLICTS II: CORPORATE OPPORTUNITIES

I INTRODUCTION

In this chapter we examine how UK company law regulates the conflict that is generated when a director of a company identifies a new business opportunity *whilst* a director of the company and exploits that opportunity in his personal capacity whilst remaining a director *or* following his resignation. The problem here is straightforward: if the director exploits an opportunity that the company itself could have exploited and would have been interested in exploiting then the company loses a potentially significant revenue opportunity. If this is an opportunity that a loyal director would have referred to the company and would have assisted the company in exploiting, then direct agency costs are incurred by the company if a disloyal director or ex-director exploits the opportunity himself. These agency costs could, depending on the nature of the opportunity, be very significant.

From a regulatory perspective we could state the problem in the following terms: which business opportunities does the duty of loyalty prevent a director or ex-director from personally exploiting without obtaining the company's approval to do so; or, put alternatively: to whom *as between the director (or ex-director) and the company* does the law allocate the right to exploit new business opportunities? If the right is allocated to the company then it follows that the company would have to consent to the director (or ex-director) exploiting the opportunity in his personal capacity if the company elects not to. If that right is allocated to the director or ex-director then no approval would be necessary.

1 An opportunities hypothetical

To identify some of the difficulties which company law faces in trying to address these problems consider the following Bob's Electronics hypothetical. As always, this works best if you think about the hypothetical before proceeding to read about how UK company law addresses this problem.

Hypothetical A

Bob is the chief executive officer and director of Bob's Electronic Plc. The business has been running for five years now but is finding it increasingly difficult to compete with the major players in the industry. Last year the company made a loss of £100,000. If business conditions and Bob's Electronics' performance do not improve then the directors are aware that the company will be in liquidation within a further two years.

There are three other directors of the company, Sylvia, Jeff, and Ken. Last week Ken was having a drink on his own at his private members club when he overheard a conversation between two members of the club who Ken had never met before. The two members of the club were discussing two business opportunities which they described as 'sure winners'. The two opportunities both involved new start-up companies that had been formed to develop business ideas. Both were looking for substantial equity investment. The first opportunity involved the development of a hand-held phone/personal digital assistant that produced a workable hologram keyboard (hereinafter, the 'hologram PDA opportunity'). The second opportunity related to the development of macrobiotic organic baby food where the food is sourced from an area not greater than 50 miles from the shops in which it is sold (hereinafter, the organic baby food opportunity).

Questions

1. Which of these opportunities, if any, would be of interest to Bob's Electronics Plc?
2. What does the previous question mean by 'being of interest'? What alternative understandings of 'company interest' could we identify here?
3. What reasons can you identify to argue that Bob's Electronics has no interest in either opportunity?
4. What difference, if any, does it make that Ken heard about these opportunities in his spare time?
5. Should Ken be allowed to exploit either of these opportunities without having to get approval from either the board of directors or the shareholder body?
6. If approval is needed, then which approval mechanism is best suited to providing approval: the disinterested directors or the shareholder body?
7. Would it make any difference to your analysis if Ken resigned before making investments in these opportunities?

In our analysis of self-dealing regulation in the Chapter 13 we saw that the common law took a strict approach which involved a prohibition on directors profiting from self-dealing transactions in the absence of shareholder approval. This followed as a result of the fact that directors could not put themselves in a position in which their personal interests conflicted, 'or which possibly may conflict',[1] with the company's interests. If a company has elected to enter into a transaction then it is self-evident that the transaction implicates the company's interests: the subject matter of the transaction is clearly of 'interest' to the company; if the terms of the deal are detrimental to the company its interests are undermined. Accordingly, in self-dealing transactions the very fact that the director is on both sides of the transaction means that there is necessarily a conflict, or at least the possibility of conflict, between the company's interests and the director's personal interests.

In the context of new business opportunities the question of whether a conflict or the potential for a conflict exists—whether a director's loyalty is in issue—is much more difficult than it is in the context of self-dealing. To determine whether we think there is a conflict or the potential for conflict we must determine first whether the opportunity falls within what we understand to be the 'company's interests'.

In *Hypothetical A* you were asked to consider whether Bob's Electronics would be interested in these opportunities: whether the nature of these opportunities fell within what we might understand Bob's Electronics' interests to be. There are three different ways in which we could think about or identify a company's interests. The first, an answer to which is not available from *Hypothetical A*, is to look at the company's constitution and to see whether in fact its objects are restricted or whether there is an explicit statement of company interests. If Bob's Electronics' constitution explicitly

---

[1] *Aberdeen Railway v Blaikie Brothers* (1854) Macq HL 461.

provides that it may only engage in the business of the manufacture, sale, and delivery of computers then we could argue that it is clear that the company would have no *interest* in the organic baby food opportunity, but, given the close relationship between PDAs and computers, that it would be interested in the hologram PDA opportunity. We may say, of course, depending on the precise wording of such an objects clause, that PDAs even with keyboards are not computers and, therefore, that the PDA opportunity is also outside of the company's interests. However, in practice it would be highly probable that either Bob's Electronics has a very broad and extensive objects clause or it has taken advantage of the introduction in the 2006 Act of the unrestricted objects clause.[2] An unrestricted or broadly drafted objects clause would place any opportunity within the 'company's interest' from the perspective of the company's constitution. Accordingly, if a regulator decided to define 'company interests' through reliance on the corporate constitution then the effect would be that for the vast majority of companies any opportunity of any nature whatsoever would fall within the 'company's interests' and that by personally exploiting any opportunity a director's personal interests would potentially conflict with the company's interests.

A second way of thinking about the company's interests would be to say that as commercial companies, like Bob's Electronics Plc, are in the business of making profits, any profit-making opportunity is of interest to the company. One might draw support for this position from section 172 of the 2006 Act which, as we saw in Chapter 10, requires that directors promote the success of the company and that success in a commercial company is understood in shareholder value terms. Applying this to *Hypothetical A*, Bob's Electronics would be interested in both opportunities and if Ken exploited either opportunity personally then he would be putting himself in a position in which his personal interests conflict with the interests of the company.

A third way of understanding the 'company's interests' is not to look at what the constitution says that the company can do through its objects clause, but to look at what the company actually does in practice and then to ask the question: is there a connection or link between what the company actually does—together with the ways in which one would expect what it does to develop and evolve—and the opportunity itself? We could try to paraphrase this idea by asking: does the opportunity fit within the company's 'line of', or 'area of', or 'scope of' its existing and intended future business? Many students who engage with *Hypothetical A* identify this concern in the following terms: 'why would a build-to-order computer company be interested in an organic baby food project'. Those same students, however, intuitively view the hologram PDA opportunity as something that relates to what Bob's Electronics already does.

Having established the range of ways in which we might think about 'company interest' in *Hypothetical A*, our inquiry into 'company interest' is not, however, at an end. A further question then follows, which is alluded to in the *Hypothetical*: 'yes, there may be a theoretical case that the company's interests cover either the hologram PDA opportunity alone, or even a case that it covers both opportunities, but does such a theoretical possibility necessarily mean that there is in fact a conflict or possible conflict?' Instead of thinking about this theoretically—does the opportunity fall within a theory of company interest—could we think about this practically? A practical approach would focus on the reality of conflict: is there a *real* potential conflict here; *in reality*, is this something the company is interested in, or do certain real-life facts get in the way to qualify or dissolve the apparent theoretical company interest and, therefore, the apparent conflict?

One such potential fact from *Hypothetical A* would be Bob's Electronics' financial difficulties—is the company really in a position to finance an investment in a new

---

[2] See Chapter 4.

opportunity? If the company does not have the financial capacity to engage in the transaction then how, one could argue, could it be interested in the transaction and how could there be any conflict of interest? In this book we shall refer to such factual claims that the company could not in fact have taken the opportunity in any event as capability facts. The capability facts raised by this *Hypothetical* are only examples of a much larger range of potential capability facts. We will see others in the cases that follow. In this regard consider the following questions:

- What problems does the court face in determining whether Bob's Electronics Plc had the financial capacity or not to exploit one or both of the opportunities?
- Do you think the court is capable of making such a determination?
- To what extent are the concerns that the courts identified in relation to determining whether self-dealing transactions are fair relevant here? Are they more or less pronounced here?
- Are the concerns that you identify here weighty enough to reject 'financial capacity' as a relevant factor for determining whether or not there is a possibility of conflict?

As these questions suggest, the problem of relying on *capability facts* in the context of regulating corporate opportunities is the difficulty for judges of being able to answer questions such as—could the company afford to pursue this transaction? Determining whether the company could have raised the necessary finance given its financial condition at the time the opportunity was identified may be dependent on information that is in the hands of the conflicted director and the people with whom the director has regular dealings and relationships. Some of the information and the views of disinterested directors and other potential witnesses may have been unintentionally or, indeed, intentionally moulded or distorted by the conflicted director. Accordingly, it may be very difficult for the courts to identify the accurate and reliable information. On the other hand, the court has access to market experts who could give well-informed opinions about whether the finance would have been available given the company's financial predicament. Clearly there are difficulties with the financial capacity evaluation, but are these problems large enough for regulators to say that we will not entertain such arguments—to say that such *capability facts* are not relevant to the determination of conflict?

Another fact that could be relevant to the determination of conflict in the *Hypothetical* is that the director discovered this opportunity in his spare time, not while he was at work. One argument that you may have raised when thinking about the *Hypothetical* is that whilst the company would be interested in this transaction in theory, there is *in fact* no conflict as this opportunity has no connection to the company: when the director takes off his suit, the argument runs, he is his own person, not the company's person and, therefore, taking this opportunity involves no conflict with his position as a 'director'. There is no difference here, the argument might run, between Ken and any other person who has nothing to do with the company but might have been sitting in the same bar as Ken and have overheard the club members talking about the opportunities. In this regard consider the following questions:

- What are the concerns generated if Ken is not allowed to exploit the opportunity even though it is correct that the company is not financially capable of exploiting the opportunity?
- When companies appoint directors do they appoint them only for the hours in which they work?
- Does your answer vary depending on whether the director is an executive director or a non-executive director?

- What would be the effect on individuals' willingness to serve as directors if all the opportunities they identified in their spare time had to be referred to the company?

2 Strictness versus flexibility/deterrence versus fairness

The above questions about the meaning of the company's interests, capability facts, and a director's professional and personal capacity are concerned with the same core problem—to what extent does the rule on prohibiting conflicts and potential conflicts allocate new opportunities identified by the directors to the company? A broad reading of company interest, such as the profit-making opportunity reading coupled with a rejection of the legal relevance of capability facts, results in a de facto allocation of all opportunities to the company; that is a prohibition on the exploitation of opportunities by directors without the requisite approvals from the company. Such a broad rule—or as it is sometimes referred to in the debate *strict rule*—raises policy questions about fairness to the directors and the effect that such rules might have on the willingness of directors to serve on boards of directors. It seems unfair to prevent a director from exploiting an opportunity, or to require him to account for profits he makes by exploiting the opportunity, when the opportunity is in a completely unrelated business area or the company was clearly not in a position to exploit the opportunity. Furthermore, such apparent unfairness may well reduce the pool of experienced and talented individuals willing to serve on UK company boards. In addition, if this approach prevents directors from exploiting opportunities and yet the company elects not to exploit the opportunity itself this could mean that the UK economy misses out on the economic benefits of exploiting opportunities because of its company law. From the perspective of these policy concerns, the law should only allocate opportunities to the company which fall within its existing area of business and only where it is actually capable of exploiting the opportunity. All other opportunities should be available to directors without having to go through any approval process.

However, such a flexible approach to regulation creates more scope for agency costs; more scope for bad directors to 'chance their hand' and take an opportunity for themselves even when they know that there is a strong case that the opportunity is within the scope of the company's business and that it is capable of exploiting it. The nature of a flexible approach allows directors to deploy weak counter-arguments that the opportunity is not in the company's future business area or that its capacity to exploit the opportunity was restricted. If he is never caught he gets to keep all the profits; if he is caught and sued the existence of these counter-arguments may be enough to persuade the claimant company to accept a settlement allowing him to keep some of the profits. Such additional room for the bad director to manoeuvre may also encourage him to mould the factual record in advance of taking the opportunity—for example, to encourage the company to move in an alternative direction away from the area of business in which the opportunity has been identified or to minute and overstate financial concerns. In contrast, a strict approach to opportunities regulation increases the likelihood that if a director is caught then he will have to pay the profits he has made to the company because a strict approach prevents him from making arguments about the scope of the company's business area or its ability to exploit the opportunity. This will deter many directors who know that making money from an opportunity involves a lot of time and effort, and if they are caught and have to return the proceeds then it is wasted time and effort. Of course, some directors will continue to 'chance their hand' under a strict regime; but there will be fewer of them.

We find in UK company law a rich body of cases and commentary that struggle with these issues and an attempt, by the Companies Act 2006, to codify a tricky and uncertain common law settlement. As we shall see, the codification process does little to resolve the outstanding uncertainty. We turn first to the case law.

II OPPORTUNITIES AND THE COMMON LAW

The regulation of opportunities is now set out in section 175 of the Companies Act 2006. Following the structure of the other chapters on directors' duties, we will analyse the common law's regulation of the opportunities problem and then consider its codification in the 2006 Act.

The terrain of the common law's regulation of the opportunities problem is marked out by two House of Lords judgments: *Regal (Hastings) v Gulliver* and *Boardman v Phipps*. These two cases are often said to provide two different approaches to opportunities regulation: the no-profits rule and the no-conflicts principle, respectively. In fact, on closer inspection we will see that both approaches are present in both cases and that the former approach, the no-profits rule, is the product of, and its parameters are determined by, the no-conflicts principle. We address each of these cases in turn.

1 *Regal (Hastings) v Gulliver*

■ *Regal (Hastings) Ltd v Gulliver* [1942] 1 All ER 378

Regal (Hastings) Ltd owned a cinema in Hastings. Regal were interested in acquiring long-term leases on two other cinemas in Hastings. At the same time as negotiating for the purchase of the two additional cinema leases, the company was also engaged in negotiations with a third-party purchaser for the sale of the whole business, including the new cinema leases. Regal formed a subsidiary company, Amalgamated Ltd, to purchase the two cinema leases. However, the landlord of the two cinema leases was concerned about the creditworthiness of Amalgamated. Initially, the directors of Regal responded to this concern by offering to personally guarantee the rent themselves. However, at a later date some of the directors retracted this offer. To satisfy the landlord's concerns it was agreed that the subsidiary company should be capitalized with £5,000 of equity. However, the directors agreed that Regal itself was only capable of providing £2,000 of equity. The directors, together with the solicitor of the company, agreed to provide the remainder in their personal capacity. The transaction to acquire the two cinema leases was completed shortly thereafter. It is worth emphasizing that at the time it was agreed that the directors would make these equity investments in Amalgamated, Regal had received a specific offer for the sale of the whole company (including Amalgamated's assets). This offer subsequently fell through but a revised offer was completed shortly thereafter involving the sale of all the shares in both Regal and Amalgamated. Following the completion of this transaction Regal, now under new ownership with new directors, brought an action against the former directors of Regal to recover the profits they made as a result of buying and selling their shares in Amalgamated.

> **Viscount Sankey**
> It must be taken, therefore, that the respondents acted *bona fide* and without fraud.
> In the Court of Appeal, Lord Greene MR said:
>
> > 'If the directors in coming to the conclusion that they could not put up more than £2,000 of the company's money had been acting in bad faith, and if that restriction of the company's money had been done for the dishonest purpose of securing for themselves profit which not only could but which

ought to have been procured for their company, I apprehend that not only could they not hold that profit for themselves if the contemplated transaction had been carried out, but they could not have held that profit for themselves even if that transaction was abandoned and another profitable transaction was carried through in which they did in fact realise a profit through the shares…but once they have admittedly *bona fide* come to the decision to which they came in this case, it seems to me that their obligation to refrain from acquiring these shares came to an end. In fact, looking at it as a matter of business, if that was by the evidence from a business point of view, then there was only one way left of raising the money, and that was putting it up themselves…That being so, the only way in which these directors could secure that benefit for the company was by putting up the money themselves. Once that decision is held to be a *bona fide* one and fraud drops out of the case, it seems to me there is only one conclusion, namely, that the appeal must be dismissed with costs.'

It seems therefore that the absence of fraud was the reason of the decision. In the result, the Court of Appeal dismissed the appeal and from their decision the present appeal is brought…

In my view, the respondents were in a fiduciary position and their liability to account does not depend upon proof of *mala fides*. The general rule of equity is that no one who has duties of a fiduciary nature to perform is allowed to enter into engagements in which he has or can have a personal interest conflicting with the interests of those whom he is bound to protect. If he holds any property so acquired as trustee, he is bound to account for it to his *cestui que trust*. The earlier cases are concerned with trusts of specific property: *Keech v Sandford*, per Lord King LC. The rule, however, applies to agents, as, for example, solicitors and directors, when acting in a fiduciary capacity. The headnote to *Ex p James*, reads as follows:

'Purchase of a bankrupt's estate by the solicitor to the commission set aside. The Lord Chancellor would not permit him to bid upon the resale, discharging himself from the character of solicitor, without the previous consent of the persons interested, freely given, upon full information.'

…

In *Aberdeen Ry Co v Blaikie*, the headnote reads:

'The director of a railway company is a trustee, and, as such, is precluded from dealing, on behalf of the company, with himself, or with a firm of which he is partner.'

At p 471, Lord Cranworth LC said:

'A corporate body can only act by agents, and it is of course the duty of those agents so to act as best to promote the interests of the corporation whose affairs they are conducting. Such agents have duties to discharge of a fiduciary nature towards their principal. And it is a rule of universal application that no one having such duties to discharge shall be allowed to enter into engagements in which he has, or can have, a personal interest conflicting, or which possibly may conflict, with the interests of those whom he is bound to protect.'

It is not, however, necessary to discuss all the cases cited, because the respondents admitted the generality of the rule as contended for by the appellants, but were concerned rather to confess and avoid it. Their contention was that, in this case, upon a true perspective of the facts, they were under no equity to account for the profits which they made…No doubt there may be exceptions to the general rule, as, for example, where a purchase is entered into after the trustee has divested himself of his trust sufficiently long before the purchase to avoid the possibility of his making use of special information acquired by him as trustee (see the remarks of Lord Eldon, in *Ex p James* at p 352) or where he purchases with full knowledge and consent of his *cestui que trust*. [There is] no exception to the general rule that a solicitor or director, if acting in a fiduciary capacity, is liable to account for the profits made by him from knowledge acquired when so acting…

At all material times they were directors and in a fiduciary position, and they used and acted upon their exclusive knowledge acquired as such directors. They framed resolutions by which they made a profit for themselves. They sought no authority from the company to do so, and, by reason of their position and actions, they made large profits for which, in my view, they are liable to account to the company…

Lord Russell of Killowen (with whom the remaining three Law Lords expressed their agreement)

The case has, I think, been complicated and obscured by the presentation of it before the trial judge. If a case of wilful misconduct or fraud on the part of the respondents had been made out, liability to make good to Regal any damage which it had thereby suffered could, no doubt, have been established; and efforts were apparently made at the trial, by cross-examination and otherwise, to found such a case. It is, however, due to the respondents to make it clear at the outset that this attempt failed. The case was not so presented to us here. We have to consider the question of the respondents' liability on the footing that, in taking up these shares in Amalgamated, they acted with *bona fides*, intending to act in the interest of Regal.

Nevertheless, they may be liable to account for the profits which they have made, if, while standing in a fiduciary relationship to Regal, they have by reason and in course of that fiduciary relationship made a profit. This aspect of the case was undoubtedly raised before the trial judge, but, in so far as he deals with it in his judgment, he deals with it on a wrong basis.

My Lords, with all respect I think there is a misapprehension here. The rule of equity which insists on those, who by use of a fiduciary position make a profit, being liable to account for that profit, in no way depends on fraud, or absence of *bona fides*; or upon such questions or considerations as whether the profit would or should otherwise have gone to the plaintiff, or whether the profiteer was under a duty to obtain the source of the profit for the plaintiff, or whether he took a risk or acted as he did for the benefit of the plaintiff, or whether the plaintiff has in fact been damaged or benefited by his action. The liability arises from the mere fact of a profit having, in the stated circumstances, been made. The profiteer, however honest and well-intentioned, cannot escape the risk of being called upon to account.

The leading case of *Keech v Sandford* is an illustration of the strictness of this rule of equity in this regard, and of how far the rule is independent of these outside considerations. A lease of the profits of a market had been devised to a trustee for the benefit of an infant. A renewal on behalf of the infant was refused. It was absolutely unobtainable. The trustee, finding that it was impossible to get a renewal for the benefit of the infant, took a lease for his own benefit. Though his duty to obtain it for the infant was incapable of performance, nevertheless he was ordered to assign the lease to the infant, upon the bare ground that, if a trustee on the refusal to renew might have a lease for himself, few renewals would be made for the benefit of *cestuis que trust*. Lord King LC said, at p 62:

'This may seem hard, that the trustee is the only person of all mankind who might not have the lease: but it is very proper that the rule should be strictly pursued, and not in the least relaxed…'

…

One other case in equity may be referred to in this connection, viz, *Ex p James*, decided by Lord Eldon LC. That was a case of a purchase of a bankrupt's estate by the solicitor to the commission, and Lord Eldon LC, refers to the doctrine thus, at p 345:

'This doctrine as to purchases by trustees, assignees, and persons having a confidential character, stands much more upon general principles than upon the circumstances of any individual case. It rests upon this: that the purchase is not permitted in any case however honest the circumstances; the general interests of justice requiring it to be destroyed in every instance; as no court is equal to the examination and ascertainment of the truth in much the greater number of cases.'

Let me now consider whether the essential matters, which the plaintiff must prove, have been established in the present case. As to the profit being in fact made there can be no doubt. The shares were acquired at par and were sold three weeks later at a profit of £2 16s 1d per share.

Did such of the first five respondents as acquired these very profitable shares acquire them by reason and in course of their office of directors of Regal? In my opinion, when the facts are examined and appreciated, the answer can only be that they did. The actual allotment no doubt had to be made by themselves…in their capacity as directors of Amalgamated; but this was merely an executive act, necessitated by the alteration of the scheme for the acquisition of the lease of the two cinemas for the sole benefit of Regal and its shareholders through Regal's shareholding in Amalgamated. That scheme could only be altered by or with the consent of the Regal board. Consider what in fact took place on 2 October 1935. The position immediately before that day is stated in [solicitor's] letter of 26 September 1935. The directors were willing to guarantee the rent until the subscribed capital of Amalgamated reached £5,000. Regal was to control Amalgamated and own the whole of its share capital, with the consequence that the Regal shareholders would receive their proportion of the sale price of the two new cinemas. The respondents then meet on 2 October 1935. They have before them an offer to purchase the Regal cinema for £77,500, and the lease of the two cinemas for £15,000. The offer is accepted. The draft lease is approved and a resolution for its sealing is passed in anticipation of completion in five days. Some of those present, however, shy at giving guarantees, and accordingly the scheme is changed by the Regal directors in a vital respect. It is agreed that a guarantee shall be avoided by the six respondents bringing the subscribed capital up to £5,000. I will consider the evidence and the minute in a moment. The result of this change of scheme (which only the Regal directors could bring about) may not have been appreciated by them at the time; but its effect upon their company and its shareholders was striking. In the first place, Regal would no longer control Amalgamated, or own the whole of its share capital. The action of its directors had deprived it (acting through its shareholders in general meeting) of the power to acquire the shares. In the second place, the Regal shareholders would only receive a largely reduced proportion of the sale price of the two cinemas. The Regal directors…would receive the moneys of which the Regal shareholders were thus deprived…

My Lords, I have no hesitation in coming to the conclusion, upon the facts of this case, that these shares, when acquired by the directors, were acquired by reason, and only by reason of the fact that they were directors of Regal, and in the course of their execution of that office.

In the result, I am of opinion that the directors standing in a fiduciary relationship to Regal in regard to the exercise of their powers as directors, and having obtained these shares by reason and only by reason of the fact that they were directors of Regal and in the course of the execution of that office, are accountable for the profits which they have made out of them. The equitable rule laid down in *Keech v Sandford* and *Ex p James*, and similar authorities applies to them in full force. It was contended that these cases were distinguishable by reason of the fact that it was impossible for Regal to get the shares owing to lack of funds, and that the directors in taking the shares were really acting as members of the public. I cannot accept this argument. It was impossible for the *cestui que trust* in *Keech v Sandford* to obtain the lease, nevertheless the trustee was accountable. The suggestion that the directors were applying simply as members of the public is a travesty of the facts. They could, had they wished, have protected themselves by a resolution (either antecedent or subsequent) of the Regal shareholders in general meeting. In default of such approval, the liability to account must remain. The result is that, in my opinion, each of the respondents…is liable to account for the profit which he made on the sale of his 500 shares in Amalgamated.

…

One final observation I desire to make. In his judgment Lord Greene MR stated that a decision adverse to the directors in the present case involved the proposition that, if directors *bona fide* decide not to invest their company's funds in some proposed investment, a director who thereafter embarks his own money therein is accountable for any profits which he may derive therefrom. As to this, I can only say that to my mind the facts of this hypothetical case bear but little resemblance to the story with which we have had to deal.

1.1 The no-profits rule

As we see from Viscount Sankey's judgment, Lord Greene MR in the Court of Appeal held that the question of whether the directors could keep the profits was to be determined by asking whether the directors acted in bad or good faith. As a fiduciary, to act in good faith is to act in a way that you believe furthers your charge, whether that be the beneficiaries to a trust, a principal, or a company. That is, good faith requires subjective loyalty: to do what the directors think furthers the company's interests. In this case, for Lord Greene their good faith is reinforced by the fact that as the company could not raise the £5,000 equity investment in Amalgamated alone, the directors by making equity investments themselves allowed the company to make a handsome profit, where without their involvement the company would have made nothing.

The House of Lords are unanimous in their rejection of Lord Greene's proposition that good faith alone is the applicable standard in this case. Lord Russell holds that liability 'in no way depends on fraud, or the absence of bona fides; or upon such questions or considerations as whether the profit would or should have gone to the [company]'. Lord Wright, whose judgment has not been extracted, puts it more forcefully. He observed that:

> [In] both in law and equity, it has been held that, if a person in a fiduciary relationship makes a secret profit out of the relationship, the court will not inquire whether the other person is damnified or has lost a profit which otherwise he would have got. The fact is in itself a fundamental breach of the fiduciary relationship. Nor can the court adequately investigate the matter in most cases.

The House of Lords reassert the strict common law position that we saw in the context of self-dealing as articulated in *Aberdeen Railway v Blaikie Brothers*.[3] However, the approach taken by Viscount Sankey to legally analyse the case differs from the approach taken by Lord Russell. Viscount Sankey starts his analysis of the law with the 'general rule of equity', familiar to us from the previous chapter, that a fiduciary cannot put himself in a position in which interests conflict with those of the company. Indeed he cites the important passage on conflicts from Lord Cranworth in *Aberdeen Railway v Blaikie*. When Viscount Sankey analyses the case he focuses on the fact that it was because of the positions the directors held and that through their actions the opportunity became available to them and a profit was made. Accordingly, they were liable to account to the company. Viscount Sankey does not then reconnect his analysis to the general no-conflicts principle but it is clear that by acting in ways that created the opportunity for the directors, and by acting on the knowledge of the opportunity to make a profit, they put themselves in a position in which their personal interests possibly conflicted with the company's interests.

Lord Russell's judgment, however, does not mention the general no-conflicts principle. For Lord Russell the rule applied to these facts is the rule drawn from the trusts case of *Keech v Sanford*[4] that a fiduciary cannot make a profit *by reason* and *in the course of* his office. That is, if a director makes a profit by relying on information about an opportunity which he became aware as a result of—by reason of—his position as a director and he exploits that information whilst a director then he is liable to account to the company for that profit regardless of his bona fides and regardless of the fact that in making a profit he also made a profit for the company. This rule is known as the *no-profits rule*. This begs two important questions relating to the status of the no-profits rule in the regulation of corporate opportunities. First, what is the relationship between the no-profits rule applied by Lord Russell and the no-conflicts principle applied by Viscount Sankey? Is the no-profits rule a stand-alone rule—applicable even

---

[3] (1854) Macq HL 461.   [4] (1726) Sel Cas Ch 61.

if the no-conflicts rule is inapplicable; indeed is the no-profits rule the common law's approach to opportunities regulation? Alternatively, is the no-profits rule a sub-rule of the no-conflict principle set out in Viscount Sankey's judgment, which means that it only applies where there is a conflict or the possibility of conflict. These questions are developed further in our discussion of *Boardman v Phipps*. To get a sense of the implications of these questions consider their application to *Hypothetical A*.

Hypothetical A continued

- If the no-profits rule is English law's only approach to opportunities regulation, then in *Hypothetical A* Ken would be allowed to exploit both the hologram PDA opportunity and the organic baby food opportunity in his personal capacity as he did not find out about the opportunities *by reason* of his directorship: he overheard people talking about the opportunities in his spare time.

- *Altering the fact pattern* in *Hypothetical A*, if Ken found out about the organic baby food opportunity in a board meeting, rather than at his private members club, and applying the no-conflicts principle there is deemed to be no conflict—because, let us assume there is no conflict as the company would not be interested in baby food projects—would the no-profits rule still apply? If the no-profits rule is a stand-alone rule, which is the sense one gets from Lord Russell's judgment, then the only question we have to ask is whether the profit was made *by reason* and *in the course of* the directorship. In this example, Ken would, therefore, be liable to account. However, if the no-profits rule is a sub-rule of the no-conflicts rules, as is suggested by Viscount Sankey's judgment, then as there is no conflict Ken would not be required to account to the company for those profits.

1.2 Capability facts and financial capacity

One could view the decision in *Regal (Hastings)* as a very harsh one for the directors. Arguably, the directors allowed the company to make a profit by enabling Amalgamated to enter into the additional two cinema leases. Without the directors' personal investment there would have been no transaction and no profit for anyone, including Regal; with them everyone, including Regal, made a profit. Although their Lordships affirmed the good faith of the directors, they were unwilling to take into account the purported financial incapacity of the company which would have prevented it completing the cinema lease transaction alone. The Law Lords are unwilling to make this a legally relevant issue at all.

Lord Wright articulates the policy of the court for refusing to inquire further in this regard: 'nor can the court adequately investigate the matter in most cases'. That is, in Lord Wright's view, it is very difficult for a court to determine whether in fact the company *could not* have raised the finance itself when much of the evidence on which such a determination is made is in the control of the conflicted directors. Interestingly, on the basis of the facts presented in the judgment, one might have reservations about the directors' claims about the financial incapacity of the company. Was it really the case that the company could not have raised funds at a time they were negotiating to sell both Regal and Amalgamated at a profit? Would a short-term loan not have been available in the market place to bridge the short period between purchase of the cinema leases and the sale of the business? One senses from Lord Russell's judgment that he also had his doubts. Importantly, however, any such doubts are not the reason for the rejection of the *relevance* of the financial incapacity claim. *Regal (Hastings)* clearly stands for the proposition that even if the financial capacity claim had been wholly accurate and unimpeachable it would have made no difference to the court's holding: financial capability facts are legally irrelevant. In *Regal (Hastings)* the House of Lords puts the deterrence of wrongdoing and a policy concern about the court's ability to assess financial capacity claims above issues of fairness to the parties.

2 *Boardman v Phipps*

Boardman v Phipps is a trusts law case. However, it is the leading case not only for trustee fiduciaries but also for director fiduciaries. In several instances in this book we have seen examples of borrowing from trusts law. It is rare, however, to find that the leading case is a trusts law case. It is worth reminding ourselves that directors are not trustees and are not automatically subject to the rules that govern trustees.[5] The similar roles of directors and trustees—being responsible for assets that belong to others (in this case, the company)—results in cross-subject-matter borrowing of legal rules. Importantly, however, we need to understand that to borrow is a decision that *company law as a system of law* makes. In borrowing these rules and principles, as we shall see, company law makes them its own and tailors them to the context of company law.

■ *Boardman v Phipps* [1967] 2 AC 46

The estate of Mr C.W. Phipps was left in trust to his wife, his three sons, and his daughter, Mrs Noble. The trustees to the trust were Mrs Noble, a Mr Fox, who was the family accountant, and C.W. Phipps' wife who at the time of the matters addressed in the case was senile and played no active part in the trust. One of the assets of the trust was a 27% holding (8,000 shares) in the shares of a textile company, Lester & Harris Ltd. The trust also had a substantial holding in another textile company, Phipps & Son Ltd.

Mr Boardman was a solicitor who advised the trust. In this capacity he received a letter asking whether the trust would be interested in selling its shares in Lester & Harris Ltd. On behalf of the trust, Boardman declined the offer. This inquiry did, however, result in Boardman paying greater attention to Lester & Harris, which Boardman viewed as underperforming. Boardman together with one of the beneficiaries, Mr Thomas Phipps (hereinafter 'Phipps'), attended the annual general meeting of Lester & Harris with a proxy from the trust. They had hoped to elect Tom Phipps to the board of Lester & Harris, but were unsuccessful. On returning from the general meeting Mr Boardman met with Mr Fox, the trustee, and suggested to him that the only way in which the real value of the trust's shareholding in Lester & Harris could be realized was to obtain control of the company. This exchange between Boardman and Fox was reported in Viscount Dilhorne's judgment as follows:

> 'Mr. Boardman in his evidence said that Mr. Fox's reaction was to say that "he did not consider that a take-over bid for shares in a private company was something that he as a trustee or the trust should take any part in." Mr. Fox when giving evidence was asked: "Was there ever any question, so far as you were concerned, of the trustees buying all the outstanding shares?" His answer was: "I would not consider the trustees buying those shares under any circumstances." He was then asked: "Did you consider the matter and reject it?" to which his reply was: "I considered the matter and rejected it."'

Indeed, the trust could not have taken steps to have bought the shares without the approval of the court. In this regard Viscount Dilhorne notes that:

> 'The trust could not in fact have bought the shares without the sanction of the court and whether the court would have sanctioned this speculation at a time when on the death of his widow, then

---

[5] See *Re Forest of Dean Coal Mining Co* (1878) 10 ChD 450.

> in failing health, Mr. C. W. Phipps' estate would have become divisible among the beneficiaries of his will and when the proposed investment was in a private company which was not doing well, and the trust had no money available for investment, may well be open to doubt.'

Boardman and Phipps decided then to take steps to acquire the shares in Lester & Harris themselves. They informed both trustees of their intention to do so. When asked whether Mr Fox had given consent to them doing this Mr Fox replied:

> 'I do not know that they asked my consent. I was only too glad. Here was I holding 8,000 shares, a minority interest in a company where the directors were unfriendly, and, having had experience in other cases of the weakness of the Companies Act with regard to minority shareholders, as soon as I could see the prospect of getting friendly directors and friendly shareholders I was only too glad.'

It is noteworthy in this regard, although the Law Lords do not make anything of it in their judgment, that Mr Fox was subsequently employed in his personal capacity as an accountant for Boardman and Phipps as part of their **due diligence** into the purchase of the shares.

The negotiations through which Boardman and Phipps tried to obtain a majority position in Lester & Harris were long and protracted. Their Lordships were satisfied that the trustees were aware that these negotiations took place in Boardman and Phipps' personal capacity. However, it is clear that at times during the negotiations Boardman and Phipps used their position as representatives of the trust to obtain information about the company (for example, on the timing of the annual general meeting) and to enhance their bargaining position with the company's directors (for example, that if progress was not made on the sale negotiations that the trust should be represented on the board and that the trust might resort to legal action to obtain such representation).

As a result of the additional information obtained by Boardman and Phipps about the value of the company they increased their offer and obtained control of the company. The major assets of the company were subsequently disposed of and a considerable profit was made by Boardman, Phipps, and the trust (as minority shareholder). Subsequent to these events one of the beneficiaries to the trust brought an action claiming that Boardman and Phipps were fiduciaries to the trust and were in breach of their fiduciary duties in acquiring the shares and making a profit in their personal capacity. Note that the precise legal status of Boardman and Phipps, in particular, was a little unclear, but the court accepted that they were fiduciaries as they acted as self-appointed agents for the trust.[6]

Boardman and Phipps were found to be in breach of their fiduciary duty by Wilberforce J at first instance and by the Court of Appeal. An appeal was made to the House of Lords. The House of Lords judgment in *Boardman v Phipps* is an exceptionally complex and difficult judgment. It is a majority decision with three Law Lords—Lords Cohen, Hodson, and Guest—holding that Boardman and Phipps had breached their duty and two Law Lords—Lord Upjohn and Viscount Dilhorne—holding that they did not.

Lord Cohen

The ratio decidendi of the trial judge is conveniently summed up in the following passage from the judgment in the Court of Appeal of Pearson L.J., where he said:

> '...the defendants were acting with the authority of the trustees and were making ample and effective use of their position as representing the trustees and wielding the power of the trustees, who were substantial minority shareholders, to extract from the directors of the company a great deal

---

[6] See generally, T. Akkouh and C. Webb, *Trusts Law* (2nd edn, Palgrave Macmillan, 2011).

of information as to the assets and resources of the company; and…this information enabled the defendants to appreciate the true potential value of the company's shares and to decide that a purchase of the shares held by the director's group at the price offered would be a very promising venture. The defendants made their very large profit, not only by their own skill and persistence and risk-taking, but also by making use of their position as agents for the trustees. The principles stated in *Regal (Hastings) Ltd. v. Gulliver* are applicable in this case.'

…

In the case before your Lordships it seems to me clear that the appellants throughout were obtaining information from the company for the purpose stated by Wilberforce J. but it does not necessarily follow that the appellants were thereby debarred from acquiring shares in the company for themselves. They were bound to give the information to the trustees but they could not exclude it from their own minds. As Wilberforce J. said, the mere use of any knowledge or opportunity which comes to the trustee or agent in the course of his trusteeship or agency does not necessarily make him liable to account. In the present case had the company been a public company and had the appellants bought the shares on the market, they would not, I think, have been accountable. But the company is a private company and not only the information but the opportunity to purchase these shares came to them through the introduction which Mr. Fox gave them to the board of the company and in the second phase when the discussions related to the proposed split-up of the company's undertaking it was solely on behalf of the trustees that Mr. Boardman was purporting to negotiate with the board of the company. The question is this: when in the third phase the negotiations turned to the purchase of the shares at £4 10s. a share, were the appellants debarred by their fiduciary position from purchasing on their own behalf the 21,986 shares in the company without the informed consent of the trustees and the beneficiaries?

Wilberforce J. and, in the Court of Appeal, both Lord Denning M.R. and Pearson L.J. based their decision in favour of the respondent on the decision of your Lordships' House in *Regal (Hastings) Ltd. v. Gulliver.* I turn, therefore, to consider that case. Mr. Walton relied upon a number of passages in the judgments of the learned Lords who heard the appeal: in particular on (1) a passage in the speech of Lord Russell of Killowen where he says:

'The rule of equity which insists on those, who by use of a fiduciary position make a profit, being liable to account for that profit, in no way depends on fraud, or absence of bona fides, or upon such questions or considerations as whether the profit would or should otherwise have gone to the plaintiff, or whether the profiteer was under a duty to obtain the source of the profit for the plaintiff, or whether he took a risk or acted as he did for the benefit of the plaintiff, or whether the plaintiff has in fact been damaged or benefited by his action. The liability arises from the mere fact of a profit having, in the stated circumstances, been made.'

…

[Counsel for Boardman and Phipps] argued that the present case is distinguishable. He puts his argument thus. The question you ask is whether the information could have been used by the principal for the purpose for which it was used by his agents? If the answer to that question is no, the information was not used in the course of their duty as agents. In the present case the information could never have been used by the trustees for the purpose of purchasing shares in the company; therefore purchase of shares was outside the scope of the appellant's agency and they are not accountable.

This is an attractive argument, but it does not seem to me to give due weight to the fact that the appellants obtained both the information which satisfied them that the purchase of the shares would be a good investment and the opportunity of acquiring them as a result of acting for certain purposes on behalf of the trustees. Information is, of course, not property in the strict sense of that word and, as I have already stated, it does not necessarily follow that because an agent acquired information and opportunity while acting in a fiduciary capacity he is accountable to his principals for any profit that comes his way as the result of the use he makes of that information and opportunity. His liability to account must depend on the facts of the case. In the present case much of the information came the appellants' way when Mr. Boardman was acting on behalf of the trustees on the instructions of Mr. Fox and the opportunity of bidding for the shares came because he purported for all purposes except for making the bid to be acting on behalf of the owners of the 8,000 shares in the company. In these circumstances it seems to me that the principle of the *Regal* case applies and that the courts below came to the right conclusion.

That is enough to dispose of the case but I would add that an agent is, in my opinion, liable to account for profits he makes out of trust property[7] if there is a possibility of conflict between his interest and his duty to his principal. Mr. Boardman and Tom Phipps were not general agents of the trustees but they were their agents for certain limited purposes. The information they had obtained and the opportunity to purchase the 21,986 shares afforded them by their relations with the directors of the company—an opportunity they got as the result of their introduction to the directors by Mr. Fox—were not property in the strict sense but that information and that opportunity they owed to their representing themselves as agents for the holders of the 8,000 shares held by the trustees. In these circumstances they could not, I think, use that information and that opportunity to purchase the shares for themselves if there was any possibility that the trustees might wish to acquire them for the trust. Mr. Boardman was the solicitor whom the trustees were in the habit of consulting if they wanted legal advice. Granted that he would not be bound to advise on any point unless he is consulted, he would still be the person they would consult if they wanted advice. He would clearly have advised them that they had no power to invest in shares of the company without the sanction of the court. In the first phase he would also have had to advise on the evidence then available that the court would be unlikely to give such sanction: but the appellants learnt much more during the second phase. It may well be that even in the third phase the answer of the court would have been the same but, in my opinion, Mr. Boardman would not have been able to give unprejudiced advice if he had been consulted by the trustees and was at the same time negotiating for the purchase of the shares on behalf of himself and Tom Phipps. In other words, there was, in my opinion, at the crucial date (March, 1959), a possibility of a conflict between his interest and his duty.

…That fiduciary position was of such a nature that (as the trust fund was distributable) the appellants could not purchase the shares on their own behalf without the informed consent of the beneficiaries: it is now admitted that they did not obtain that consent. They are therefore, in my opinion, accountable to the respondent for his share of the net profits they derived from the transaction.

I desire to repeat that the integrity of the appellants is not in doubt…As the last paragraph of his judgment clearly shows, the trial judge evidently shared this view. He directed an inquiry as to what sum is proper to be allowed to the appellants or either of them in respect of his work and skill in obtaining the said shares and the profits in respect thereof. The trial judge concluded by expressing the opinion that payment should be on a liberal scale. With that observation I respectfully agree.

In the result I agree in substance with the judgments of Wilberforce J. and of Lord Denning M.R. and Pearson L.J. in the Court of Appeal, and I would dismiss the appeal.

Lord Hodson

Regal (Hastings) Ltd. v. Gulliver differs from this case mainly in that the directors took up shares and made a profit thereby, it having been originally intended that the company should buy these shares. Here there was no such intention on the part of the trustees. There is no indication that they either had the money or would have been ready to apply to the court for sanction enabling them to do so. On the contrary, Mr. Fox, the active trustee and an accountant who concerned himself with the details of the trust property, was not prepared to agree to the trustees buying the shares and encouraged the appellants to make the purchase. This does not

---

[7] The term 'trust property' here should be read as information acquired whilst acting as a fiduciary.

affect the position. As *Keech v. Sandford* shows, the inability of the trust to purchase makes no difference to the liability of the appellants, if liability otherwise exists. The distinction on the facts as to intention to purchase shares between this case and *Regal (Hastings) Ltd. v. Gulliver* is not relevant. The company (Regal) had not the money to apply for the shares upon which the profit was made. The directors took the opportunity which they had presented to them to buy the shares with their own money and were held accountable. Mr. Fox's refusal as one of the trustees to take any part in the matter on behalf of the trust, so far as he was concerned, can make no difference. Nothing short of fully informed consent which the learned judge found not to have been obtained could enable the appellants in the position which they occupied having taken the opportunity provided by that position to make a profit for themselves...

The appellants obtained knowledge by reason of their fiduciary position and they cannot escape liability by saying that they were acting for themselves and not as agents of the trustees. Whether or not the trust or the beneficiaries in their stead could have taken advantage of the information is immaterial, as the authorities clearly show. No doubt it was but a remote possibility that Mr. Boardman would ever be asked by the trustees to advise on the desirability of an application to the court in order that the trustees might avail themselves of the information obtained. Nevertheless, even if the possibility of conflict is present between personal interest and the fiduciary position the rule of equity must be applied. This appears from the observations of Lord Cranworth L.C. in *Aberdeen Railway Co. v. Blaikie*...

I agree with the decision of the learned judge and with that of the Court of Appeal which, in my opinion, involves a finding that there was a potential conflict between Boardman's position as solicitor to the trustees and his own interest in applying for the shares. He was in a fiduciary position... For these reasons in my opinion the appeal should be dismissed; but I should add that I am in agreement with the learned judge that payment should be allowed on a liberal scale in respect of the work and skill employed in obtaining the shares and the profits therefrom.

Lord Upjohn (dissenting)

Rules of equity have to be applied to such a great diversity of circumstances that they can be stated only in the most general terms and applied with particular attention to the exact circumstances of each case. The relevant rule for the decision of this case is the fundamental rule of equity that a person in a fiduciary capacity must not make a profit out of his trust which is part of the wider rule that a trustee must not place himself in a position where his duty and his interest may conflict. I believe the rule is best stated in *Bray v. Ford* [1896] A.C. 44 by Lord Herschell, who plainly recognised its limitations:

> 'It is an inflexible rule of a Court of Equity that a person in a fiduciary position, such as the respondent's, is not, unless otherwise expressly provided, entitled to make a profit; he is not allowed to put himself in a position where his interest and duty conflict. It does not appear to me that this rule is, as has been said, founded upon principles of morality. I regard it rather as based on the consideration that, human nature being what it is, there is danger, in such circumstances, of the person holding a fiduciary position being swayed by interest rather than by duty, and thus prejudicing those whom he was bound to protect. It has, therefore, been deemed expedient to lay down this positive rule. But I am satisfied that it might be departed from in many cases, without any breach of morality, without any wrong being inflicted, and without any consciousness of wrong-doing. Indeed, it is obvious that it might sometimes be to the advantage of the beneficiaries that their trustee should act for them professionally rather than a stranger, even though the trustee were paid for his services.'

It is perhaps stated most highly against trustees or directors in the celebrated speech of Lord Cranworth L.C. in Aberdeen Railway v. Blaikie, [136 1 Macq. 461] where he said:

> 'And it is a rule of universal application, that no one, having such duties to discharge, shall be allowed to enter into engagements in which he has, or can have, a personal interest conflicting, or which possibly may conflict, with the interests of those whom he is bound to protect.'

The phrase 'possibly may conflict' requires consideration. In my view it means that the reasonable man looking at the relevant facts and circumstances of the particular case would think that there was a real sensible possibility of conflict; not that you could imagine some situation arising which might, in some conceivable possibility in events not contemplated as real sensible possibilities by any reasonable person, result in a conflict.

Your Lordships were referred at length to the decision of this House in *Regal (Hastings) Ltd. v. Gulliver*. That is a helpful case for its restatement of the well-known principles but the case itself bears no relation to the one before your Lordships…There has been much discussion in the courts below and in this House upon the observations of their Lordships in the *Regal* case. But in my view, their Lordships were not attempting to lay down any new view on the law applicable and indeed could not do so for the law was already so well settled. The whole of the law is laid down in the fundamental principle exemplified in Lord Cranworth's statement I have already quoted. But it is applicable, like so many equitable principles which may affect a conscience, however innocent, to such a diversity of different cases that the observations of judges and even in your Lordships' House in cases where this great principle is being applied must be regarded as applicable only to the particular facts of the particular case in question and not regarded as a new and slightly different formulation of the legal principle so well settled. Therefore, as the facts in Regal to which alone their Lordships' remarks were directed were so remote from the facts in this case I do not propose to examine the *Regal* case further…

My Lords, the judgments of Wilberforce J and Lord Denning MR and Pearson LJ proceeded upon the footing that by acting as self-appointed agents the appellants placed themselves in a fiduciary capacity to the trustees and became accountable accordingly…But as I have already pointed out it seems to me that this question whether this assumption of office leads to the conclusion that the appellants were accountable requires a closer analysis than it has received in the lower courts.

This analysis requires detailed consideration:

[1] Once it is established that there is [a fiduciary] relationship, that relationship must be examined to see what duties are thereby imposed upon the agent, to see what is the scope and ambit of the duties charged upon him.

[2] Having defined the scope of those duties one must see whether he has committed some breach thereof and by placing himself within the scope and ambit of those duties in a position where his duty and interest may possibly conflict. It is only at this stage that any question of accountability arises.

[3] Finally, having established accountability it only goes so far as to render the agent accountable for profits made within the scope and ambit of his duty. With these general observations on the applicable principles of law let me apply them to the facts of this case…

The appellants went to the meeting with the object of persuading the shareholders to appoint Tom [Phipps] a director, admittedly they were acting on behalf of the trustees at that meeting. It is the basis of the respondent's case that this placed the appellants in a fiduciary relationship which they never after lost or, as it was argued, it 'triggered off a chain of events' and gave them the opportunity of acquiring knowledge so that they thereafter became accountable to the trustees. From this it must logically follow that in acquiring the…shares they became constructive trustees for the trust.

My Lords, I must emphatically disagree. The appellants went to the meeting for a limited purpose (the election of Tom as a director) which failed. Then the appellants' agency came to an end. They had no further duties to perform. The discussions which followed showed conclusively that the trustees would not consider a purchase of further shares…I can see nothing to prevent the appellants from making an offer for shares for themselves, or for that matter, I cannot see that Mr. Boardman would have been acting improperly in advising some other client to make an offer for shares (other than the 8,000) in the company.

In the circumstances, the appellants' duties having come to an end, they owed no duty and there was no conflict of interest and duty, they were in no way dealing in trust property. Further, of course, they had the blessing of two trustees in their conduct in trying to buy further shares…

Consider a simple example. Blackacre is trust property and next to it is Whiteacre; but there is no question of the trustees being interested in a possible purchase of Whiteacre as being convenient to be held with Blackacre. Is a trustee to be precluded from purchasing Whiteacre for himself because he may have learnt something about Whiteacre while acting as a trustee of Blackacre? I can understand the owner of Whiteacre being annoyed but surely not the beneficial owners of Blackacre, they have no interest in Whiteacre and their trustees have no duties to perform in respect thereof.

...

I cannot see that they have, from start to finish, in the circumstances of this case, placed themselves in a position where there was any possibility of a conflict between their duty and interest...

I have dealt with the problems that arise in this case at considerable length but it could, in my opinion, be dealt with quite shortly.

In Barnes v. Addy [9 Ch.App. 244, 251] Lord Selborne L.C. said:

> 'It is equally important to maintain the doctrine of trusts which is established in this court, and not to strain it by unreasonable construction beyond its due and proper limits. There would be no better mode of undermining the sound doctrines of equity than to make unreasonable and inequitable applications of them.'

That, in my judgment, is applicable to this case. The trustees were not willing to buy more shares in the company. The active trustees were very willing that the appellants should do so themselves for the benefit of their large minority holding. The trustees, so to speak, lent their name to the appellants in the course of prolonged and difficult negotiations and, of course, the appellants thereby learnt much which would have otherwise been denied to them. The negotiations were in the end brilliantly successful.

And how successful Tom was in his reorganisation of the company is apparent to all. They ought to be very grateful. In the long run the appellants have bought for themselves at entirely their own risk with their own money shares which the trustees never contemplated buying and they did so in circumstances fully known and approved of by the trustees.

To extend the doctrines of equity to make the appellants accountable in such circumstances is, in my judgment, to make unreasonable and unequitable applications of such doctrines.

I would allow the appeal and dismiss the action.

2.1 No-profit versus no-conflict

There are two different regulatory lenses through which the Law Lords in *Boardman v Phipps* address the problem in this case. The first lens involves the application of the no-profit rule as set out in *Regal (Hastings)*: a fiduciary cannot make a profit by reason of and in the course of his fiduciary relationship. The second lens, which is adopted most clearly by Lord Upjohn, but which we also see in Lord Hodson and Lord Cohen's judgments, is the *no-conflict* lens which involves asking the question whether by purchasing the shares the fiduciaries' personal interests conflicted, or possibly conflicted, with the trust's interests.

Lord Upjohn in his judgment takes a step back from the statement of the law in *Regal (Hastings)*. He argues firmly that the no-profit rule set out in *Regal (Hastings)* is but one application of the general equitable no-conflicts principle. Thus in *Regal*, by taking the opportunity to invest in Amalgamated, the directors of Regal placed themselves in a position where their interests possibly conflicted with those of the company. As we have seen, this was more clearly stated in Viscount Sankey's judgment in *Regal*. For Lord Upjohn the statement of the law in *Regal* is a product of, and therefore subject to, the no-conflicts principle; that is, the no-conflicts principle needs to be considered when applying the holding in *Regal* in order to determine whether the fiduciary is liable to account. One cannot simply apply the rule that a director cannot make a profit by reason of and in the course of his directorship as if this rule was the sole reference point for the analysis. For Lord Upjohn if it is the case that a director makes a profit by reason and in the course of his directorship you still need to ask: does this put him in a position in which his personal interests may possibly conflict with the company's interests?

Lord Upjohn appears to be of the view that part of the reason that the majority reach, in his view, the wrong holding is that they apply *Regal (Hastings)* as if it was the statement of the law rather than simply an example of the application of the law (the no-conflicts principle). However, this is clearly not the case. Lord Cohen, having applied the holding in *Regal*, goes onto indicate that the holding is subject to the no-conflicts principle. Had there been no possibility of conflict, then for Lord Cohen, Boardman and Phipps would not have had to account for the profit. A similar appreciation of the role of the no-conflicts principle is found in the judgments of Lord Hodson (majority) and Viscount Dilhorne (in dissent). Lord Cohen seems aware of the danger of treating the no-profits rule as a stand-alone rule. Taken literally this would mean that any profit made from information acquired by the directors by reason of the directorship would be for the account of the company. Lord Cohen holds that it does not 'necessarily follow' that any profit made from any such information is for the account of the company. Directors are liable to account for any profit when acting on the information when doing so results in a conflict, or possible conflict, of interest.

Accordingly, it appears that the other Law Lords shared Lord Upjohn's view that the no-conflicts principle is the fundamental rule of law in this context; and the no-profits rule in *Regal* is an example of its application which we must be careful to apply in a con-versational relationship[8] with the no-conflicts principle. Nevertheless, the status of the no-profit rule with regard to the no-conflict rule has continued to attract debate, with both case law and commentary expressing support for the position that it is a stand-alone sister-rule of the no-conflicts principle rather than an example of the application of the no-conflicts principle. Recently, for example, in *Ultraframe (UK) Ltd v Fielding*[9] Lewison J referred to the no-conflicts principle and the no-profits rule as 'two strands of fiduciary duty' and observed that 'these two strands have been conveniently labeled the "no conflict rule" and the "no profit rule"; and must be considered separately'. In this author's view Lord Upjohn's position is wholly correct. In this regard consider the following extract.

■ **D. Kershaw, 'How the Law Thinks About Corporate Opportunities'
(2005) 25 *Legal Studies* 533**

There is English and commonwealth authority for the position that the no-profit rule should be viewed as separate and independent from the no-conflicts approach. Most recently in *Quarter Master (UK) Ltd v Pyke*, Paul Morgan QC categorised the no-profit rule separately from the no-conflicts principle, which he described as 'allied to but...separate from the no-profit rule'.[10] Morritt LJ in *Don King Productions Inc v Warren*[11] cited with approval the Australian case of *Chan*

---

[8] The term 'conversational' relationship is taken from F. Schauer, *Playing By The Rules: A Philosophical Examination of Rule Based Decision Making In Law and Life* (Clarendon Press, 1991). It means that when applying a rule you consider whether its application not only fits within the terms of the rule but also within the terms/spirit of the underlying principle, in this case the no-conflicts principle.

[9] [2005] EWHC 1638 (Ch). See *Re Allied Business and Financial Consultants Ltd*; *O'Donnell v Shanahan* [2009] EWCA Civ 751 presuming, without analysis that they are separate rules. See also *In Plus Group Ltd v Pyke* [2002] 2 BCLC 201 and *Wilkinson v West Coast Capital* [2005] EWHC 3009 (Ch).

[10] [2004] EWHC 1815.

[11] [2000] Ch 291 at 341. See also *Gencor ACP Ltd v Dalby* [2000] 2 BCLC 734; and *John Taylors v Masons* [2001] EWCA 2106.

v Zacharia in which Dean J identified the no-conflicts principle and the no-profits rule as separate themes which embodied 'one "fundamental" rule'.[12] Several commentators have expressed support for this position. Most recently Pearlie Koh has argued 'that it is perhaps more accurate to say that these are independent rules'.[13] It is submitted, however, that in English law the no-profit rule has not, as yet, become detached from the no-conflicts approach so that its final point of reference in determining its scope of application is the rule itself. The weight of authority provides that the no-profit rule operates within the parameters of the no-conflicts principle. The most familiar support for this position is Lord Upjohn's dicta in *Boardman v Phipps* where he stated that the House of Lords in *Regal (Hastings)* 'were not attempting to lay down any new view on the law applicable' and that 'law is laid down in the fundamental principle exemplified in Lord Cranworth's statement' of the no-conflicts principle in *Aberdeen v Blaike*. For this reason Lord Upjohn viewed *Regal (Hastings)* as 'an obvious case where the duty of the director and his interest conflicted'[14]...This article views the no-profit rule as a sub-rule of the no-conflicts principle; an obvious case of its application.[15] English law thinks through the no-conflicts approach and in so doing may deploy the no-profits rule. To treat the no-profit rule as a separate, independent rule is, it is submitted, to lose sight of the duty of loyalty, which, as Arden LJ recently held, is the 'fundamental duty to which a director is subject'. It is also the better reading of *Regal (Hastings)*. The shadow of potential conflict hangs over the decision in *Regal (Hastings)*. Questions about the director's conduct are begged: could the directors have been more forceful in their negotiations with the landlord; why couldn't bridging finance have been arranged on behalf of the company when there was a high likelihood of a swift exit strategy through the sale of the company? The no-profits rule articulated in *Regal (Hastings)* was forged in the context of potential conflict between the directors' and the company's interests. The House of Lords' articulation of the no-profit rule in *Regal (Hastings)* is an instantiation of the no-conflicts principle. To apply the rule in isolation from the principle risks its over-inclusive application in circumstances where the duty of loyalty would not be implicated. In this regard, commentators have noted, in support of the claim that the no-profit rule should be treated as an independent rule, that it is possible to imagine a hypothetical case where the facts do not involve a conflict of interests but do fall within the no-profit rule.[16] This is, of course, correct. Any rule which becomes, to use Frederick Schauer's useful terminology, entrenched: applicable in isolation from the principle it instantiates,[17] will

---

[12] (1984) 154 CLR 178 at 198.

[13] P. Koh, 'Once a Director, Always a Fiduciary' (2003) 62 *CLJ* 403 at 406. See also, R.P. Austin, 'Fiduciary Accountability for Business Opportunities' in P.D. Finn (ed), *Equity and Commercial Relationships* (The Law Book Company Ltd, 1987), 146–7.

[14] [1967] 2 AC at 124. See also *Bhullar v Bhullar* [2003] EWCA 424 extracted in section II.3 of this chapter in which Jonathan Parker LJ affirms Lord Upjohn's view in this regard; and *Industrial Development Corporation v Cooley* [1972] 1 WLR 443 extracting Lord Upjohn's view in this regard and observing that 'I think [counsel for the plaintiff] was right when he said in his reply that that is the basic rule from which all else has been founded. Certainly Viscount Sankey in the *Regal* case, at p. 137, so stated it and Lord Cranworth's well known statement has been repeated in innumerable cases of the highest authority.'

[15] Commentators who take this position include: B. Pettet, *Company Law* (2nd edn, Longman, 2005), 168, arguing that in *Regal* making a profit by reason *and* in the course of a directorship was 'sufficient for liability under the no-conflicts rule'; G. Moffat, *Trusts Law: Text and Materials* (3rd edn, Butterworths, 1999), 631, arguing that 'the primary duty is that a fiduciary may not have a conflict between his personal interest and that of his principal...*As a corollary of that principle*, the courts have developed the rule that the fiduciary will be liable to account to the "principal" for any unauthorised profit made by virtue as his position as fiduciary or through use of the principal's property' (emphasis added).

[16] Koh, note 13, at 406. See also Ellas J's judgment in *Nottingham University v Fischel* [2001] RPC 367 at 401 noting that the no-profit rule 'overlaps with, but is sometimes wider than, the strict no-conflict of duty and interest rule'.

[17] F. Schauer, *Playing By The Rules: A Philosophical Examination of Rule Based Decision Making In Law and Life* (Clarendon Press, 1991). Schauer contrasts two modes of decision-making. First, there is the conversational model where if a rule's application would diverge from its underlying principle (what Schauer calls a justification) the application is corrected to ensure it is compliant with the justification. In this case 'over inclusiveness would be but a temporary impediment' corrected by a

be applied in situations which are, vis-a-vis the principle, over- or under-inclusive. It is, however, circular to use an example of a rule's over-inclusive application to support its entrenchment. If there are circumstances where there is no possibility of conflict but the opportunity was identified by the director by reason and in the course of his directorship, then in such circumstances there is no threat to the duty of loyalty and no reason why the director should not be allowed to keep those profits.[18]

2.2 What is the nature of 'possible conflict'?

Although, as argued by this author, the Law Lords in *Boardman v Phipps* shared Lord Upjohn's view on the relationship between the no-profits rules and the no-conflicts principle, they differed significantly in relation to the application of the no-conflicts principle. The no-conflicts principle provides that a fiduciary is in breach of duty not only where there is an actual but where there is a possible conflict of interest. Their Lordships in *Boardman* disagreed on the extent to which they were willing to accept that real facts could alter the nature of a trust's or, by analogy, a company's interests, and thereby dissolve possible conflict.

For Lord Cohen, whilst he acknowledges the bona fides of Boardman and Phipps, Boardman and Phipps could not make use of the information they had acquired about the opportunity for personal gain when 'there was any possibility that the trustees might wish to acquire them for the trust'; that is where there is any possibility that the trust would be interested in acquiring the shares. Where the fiduciary's role is to advise the trust on whether to pursue an opportunity which could be of interest to the trust, if he takes the opportunity in his personal capacity he is placed in a situation in which his personal interests conflict or at least possibly conflict with the interests of the trust and his duty[19] to the trust and, accordingly, he is liable to account to the trust for any profit he makes. Mr Boardman, Lord Cohen observed, 'would not have been able to give unprejudiced advice'. This approach as applied to company directors means that there is a possible conflict of interest (and of interest and duty) where a director would be expected to advise the company on the taking of an opportunity which falls within the company's interests and he takes it for himself. In *Boardman*, the fact that two of the trustees testified that they would not have taken the opportunity and the fact that court approval would have been required, and may not have been granted, was for Lord Cohen insufficient to dissolve the possible conflict. For Lord Hodson, Mr Fox (the trustee)'s refusal to pursue the share purchase through the trust made 'no difference'. His Lordship observed further that: 'whether or not the trust or the beneficiaries in their stead could have taken advantage of the information is immaterial'.

This statement by Lord Hodson is a very important one. We will see when we look at the 2006 Act's codification of the no-conflicts rule that this statement is adopted more or less verbatim. It is important, therefore, to understand the statement within the context of the facts of this case as well as in the cases on which it draws. In *Keech v Sanford, Regal*

---

controlling principle (p 48). Second, there is the entrenchment model where the rule not its justification 'control[s] the decision even in those cases in which that generalization [the rule] failed to serve its underlying justification' (p 49). In this model, over- and under-inclusiveness are inevitable (p 35).

[18] More recently, see *Towers v Premier Waster Management Ltd* [2011] EWCA Civ 923 supporting Lord Upjohn's position (*per* Mummery LJ): 'the applicable duties are of a director's loyalty to the Company and the duty to observe the no conflict principle, which embrace a duty not to make a secret profit for himself.'

[19] Note that Lord Cohen and Lord Upjohn refer to the conflict of interest and duty, rather than a conflict of interests. This reference to conflict and duty is also used in *Bray v Ford* cited by Lord Upjohn in the extract. By taking the opportunity in this case the duty to avoid conflicts of interests was breached; but also by taking the opportunity a breach of the obligation to avoid a conflict of interests and duty arose—that is his personal interest and his duty to advise the trust on what to do about the possible opportunity. Of course this is somewhat circular, as the duty is to act in the interests of the trust or company, which brings us back to the question of what is in the company's interests.

(Hastings) and *Boardman v Phipps* strictly speaking it was not that the beneficiary in *Keech*, the company in *Regal (Hastings)*, or the trust in *Boardman* were subject to an absolute bar from taking the opportunity; rather it was that something was getting in the way of them taking the opportunity: the landlord's refusal in *Keech*; available finance in *Regal*; and the trustees' refusal to apply for court approval in *Boardman*. In each of these cases action by the fiduciary may have made a difference: persuading the landlord; obtaining finance; or actually making a strong case to the court, respectively. Whether the landlord could have been persuaded, the finance obtained, or the court persuaded are unknowns, but the conflicted fiduciary would have played a significant role in each of these regards. The role of the conflicted fiduciary renders these facts immaterial to the determination of the trust's, or the principal's or company's interests and therefore to the determination of whether the no-conflicts principle has been breached. However, it is not clear from the majority's position in *Boardman v Phipps* how far this 'immateriality' principle extends: would all such *capability facts* fall within the ambit of 'immateriality'? What about absolute bars to taking the opportunity, where the fiduciary could do nothing to change the fact that the company *could not* take the opportunity—such as a legislative bar on taking an opportunity? If we understand the 'immateriality principle' as articulated by the majority as dependent on a possible role for the conflicted director in changing the 'could not' into a 'could' then barriers such as legislative bars would not be immaterial.

Lord Upjohn's position on the extent of possible conflict is clearly distinct from the majority's position. He argues that the phrase 'possibly may conflict' requires further consideration. In his view it means that the reasonable man looking at the relevant facts and circumstances of the particular case would think that there was a real, sensible possibility of conflict; not that you 'could imagine some situation arising which might, in some conceivable possibility in events not contemplated as real, sensible possibilities by any reasonable person, result in a conflict'. The test articulated and applied by Lord Upjohn is more receptive than the majority of their Lordships to real facts that alter the nature of the trusts interests and dissolve an apparent potential conflict. The fact that the trustee testified that the trust was not interested in acquiring the shares and that court approval would have been required is sufficient for Lord Upjohn for there to be no real, sensible possibility of conflict with the trusts interests, even though Boardman as a fiduciary could have played a role in forming the trust's view in this regard. For Lord Upjohn whether or not the trust could have taken advantage of the opportunity is *not* immaterial. Indeed, those facts are the basis of his conclusion that there is no conflict.

Several commentators have argued that the refusal of the courts to be more flexible in relation to capability facts is based upon the evidentiary difficulties that eighteenth and nineteenth century courts had in assessing whether or not a capability fact is true and reliable and that modern courts with modern evidentiary techniques are now capable of making these assessments.[20] These commentators argue that the courts should, therefore, modernize their approach to capability facts by weighing the credibility and relevance of such facts and considering the extent to which they dissolve a 'possible conflict'.[21] Others, including this author, have argued that the court's concern is well founded and that assessing conflict is not a question of good technique, but rather a fundamental problem about the production of knowledge in situations of conflict. Consider the following extract in this regard.

---

[20] John Langbein observes that at the time courts developed rules on self-dealing and conflicts that 'Chancery had its own system of civil procedure which had become profoundly defective'. Citing William Holdsworth's *A History of English Law* (3rd edn, Sweet & Maxwell, 1944) he observes that 'in the early 19th century...the fact finding procedures of Chancery were as "futile...[as ever] existed in any mature legal system"' (J.H. Langbein, 'Questioning the Trust-law Duty of Loyalty: Sole Interest or Best Interest' (2005) 114 *Yale Law Journal* 929).

[21] See J. Lowry and R. Edmunds, 'The No-Conflict–No-Profit Rules and the Corporate Fiduciary: Challenging the Orthodoxy of Absolutism' (2000) *Journal of Business Law* 122, 127; L. Sealy, *Company Law and Commercial Reality* (Sweet & Maxwell, 1984), 39.

■ D. Kershaw, 'Lost in Translation: Corporate Opportunities in Comparative Perspective' (2005) 25 *Oxford Journal of Legal Studies* 603

This focus upon modern judicial technique misses the Law Lord's point. The evidentiary problem, as understood by the majority in *Regal (Hastings)* and *Boardman v Phipps*, is primarily an epistemological not a technical problem. Modern techniques have not and will not solve the epistemological problem that facts and evidence are deeply malleable and that honest and trustworthy witnesses' perceptions and recollections of events and of their own and others' actions may have been formed by the interrelationship of, amongst others, non-aligned interests, friendship, professional trust and personal pride. As noted above, in *Boardman v Phipps* although the active trustee testified that he would not have made a court application to allow the trust to purchase the shares, neither he nor the court could be sure that his decision and his subsequent justification thereof were not formed by the fiduciaries' personal rather than the trust's interests. In many corporate opportunity situations [capability] is not available for determination as its factual foundation is inaccessible. Consider for example, the financial incapacity claim. Determining what a company's sources of finance are requires information about, amongst others: the history of the company's financial relationships; the existing and potential finance contacts that directors and officers of the company may have; the willingness, at the time the opportunity became available, of the market to finance such a project; and current interest rates and spreads. Much of this information may not be forthcoming at all as it may be under the control of fiduciaries with compromised incentives. However, even to the extent that the information is made available and that uncompromised directors testify as to the non-availability of funds, the assessment of financial capacity remains highly speculative: were all avenues explored; how much creativity was brought to bear in the search for finance; was the refusal of third parties to finance the transaction in any way influenced by the presentation of the transaction by the compromised directors; did uncompromised directors form their opinions through interactions with the conflicted directors or through interactions with third parties whose attitude to the transaction had been formed through information provided by and prior interactions with the conflicted directors? Inevitably, given such a limited and unavoidably suspect factual record, determining the credibility of a financial incapacity claim becomes speculative and indeterminate. Accordingly, a flexible rule's willingness to consider [capability] facts does not reveal modern advances in evidence gathering and judicial technique, rather a policy choice which discounts epistemological concerns about the availability and production of evidence.

The author may, however, be overstating the problem here, or at least overstating how distinctive the judicial engagement with capability facts may be from what judges do all the time. Indeed, if any of you choose to read the full facts of the cases which are extracted in this chapter, you will see the courts engaging in difficult evidentiary determinations in other contexts in conditions of considerable uncertainty.[22]

2.3 Accounting for profits and the scope for an equitable allowance

As we have seen in *Regal (Hastings)* and in *Boardman v Phipps* the consequence for a fiduciary of being found to have breached the no-conflicts principle is that any profits made as a result of the breach must be paid to the company: the fiduciary must account for the profits made. The rationale for the imposition of this remedy is to deter directors from taking opportunities without obtaining the requisite consents, as failure to do so could result in the loss of all profits the directors' hard work

---

[22] See *Holder v Holder* [1968] 1 Ch 353, where Danckwerts LJ and Sachs LJ expressed similar reservations.

may have generated. It is, therefore, surprising to read at the end of Lord Cohen and Lord Hodson's judgments that Boardman and Phipps should be compensated for their efforts 'on a liberal scale'; that is compensated for the services rendered beyond the direct expenditure they incurred in effecting the share purchase transaction.[23] This discretion to make a *quantum meruit* award is referred to in this context as an 'equitable allowance'.

This holding in *Boardman v Phipps* has generated some uncertainty as to whether the courts have a discretion to grant an equitable allowance to all fiduciaries, in particular to directors and, if so, as to the criteria which determine its availability. The House of Lords had the opportunity to consider this issue in the context of company directors in *Guinness Plc v Saunders*, which arose out of an infamous takeover by Guinness Plc of Distillers Plc. In this case, Mr Ward, who was a director of Guinness Plc, was heavily involved in the deal process and he was awarded a £5.2 million payment by Guinness's remuneration committee for his efforts. The payment was, however, subject to the successful completion of the takeover offer. Following completion the monies were paid to Mr Ward but subsequently reclaimed in an action brought by the company. The House of Lords held that the payment was void for want of authority as only the board, not the remuneration committee acting alone, had the authority to award the payment. The House of Lords then proceeded to address the issue of equitable allowance. In this regard consider the following extract from Lord Goff's judgment.

■ *Guinness Plc v Saunders* [1990] 2 WLR 324

Lord Goff

The leading authorities on the doctrine have been rehearsed in the opinion of my noble and learned friend, Lord Templeman. These indeed demonstrate that the directors of a company, like other fiduciaries, must not put themselves in a position where there is a conflict between their personal interests and their duties as fiduciaries, and are for that reason precluded from contracting with the company for their services except in circumstances authorised by the articles of association...

Plainly, it would be inconsistent with this long-established principle to award remuneration in such circumstances as of right on the basis of a quantum meruit claim. But the principle does not altogether exclude the possibility that an equitable allowance might be made in respect of services rendered. That such an allowance may be made to a trustee for work performed by him for the benefit of the trust, even though he was not in the circumstances entitled to remuneration under the terms of the trust deed, is now well established. In *Phipps v. Boardman* [1964] 1 WLR 993, the solicitor to a trust and one of the beneficiaries were held accountable to another beneficiary for a proportion of the profits made by them from the sale of shares bought by them with the aid of information gained by the solicitor when acting for the trust. Wilberforce J. directed that, when accounting for such profits, not merely should a deduction be made for expenditure which was necessary to enable the profit to be realised, but also a liberal allowance or credit should be made for their work and skill...

It will be observed that the decision to make the allowance was founded upon the simple proposition that 'it would be inequitable now for the beneficiaries to step in and take the profit without paying for the skill and labour which has produced it.'... The inequity was found in the simple proposition that the beneficiaries were taking the profit although, if Mr. Boardman (the solicitor) had not done the work, they would have had to employ an expert to do the work for them in order to earn that profit.

The decision has to be reconciled with the fundamental principle that a trustee is not entitled to remuneration for services rendered by him to the trust except as expressly provided in the

---

[23] The House of Lords hereby affirmed Wilberforce J's holding in this regard.

trust deed. Strictly speaking, it is irreconcilable with the rule as so stated. It seems to me therefore that it can only be reconciled with it to the extent that the exercise of the equitable jurisdiction does not conflict with the policy underlying the rule. And, as I see it, such a conflict will only be avoided if the exercise of the jurisdiction is restricted to those cases where it cannot have the effect of encouraging trustees in any way to put themselves in a position where their interests conflict with their duties as trustees.

Not only was the equity underlying Mr. Boardman's claim in *Phipps v. Boardman* clear and, indeed, overwhelming; but the exercise of the jurisdiction to award an allowance in the unusual circumstances of that case could not provide any encouragement to trustees to put themselves in a position where their duties as trustees conflicted with their interests. The present case is, however, very different. Whether any such an allowance might ever be granted by a court of equity in the case of a director of a company, as opposed to a trustee, is a point which has yet to be decided; and I must reserve the question whether the jurisdiction could be exercised in such a case, which may be said to involve interference by the court in the administration of a company's affairs when the company is not being wound up. In any event, however, like my noble and learned friend, Lord Templeman, I cannot see any possibility of such jurisdiction being exercised in the present case. I proceed, of course, on the basis that Mr. Ward acted throughout in complete good faith. But the simple fact remains that, by agreeing to provide his services in return for a substantial fee the size of which was dependent upon the amount of a successful bid by Guinness, Mr. Ward was most plainly putting himself in a position in which his interests were in stark conflict with his duty as a director…I cannot think that this is a case in which a court of equity (assuming that it has jurisdiction to do so in the case of a director of a company) would order the repayment of the £5.2 million by Mr. Ward to Guinness subject to a condition that an equitable allowance be made to Mr. Ward for his services.

Lord Goff casts considerable doubt on the availability of an 'equitable allowance' discretion. He notes that its application to company directors is undecided but he is willing to proceed on the basis that it could be available. However, he views its availability as logically inconsistent with the strict no-conflicts rule. He holds that the discretion is available only if the inequity is 'overwhelming' and only where an equitable allowance would not undermine the deterrent effect of the strict rule. He holds that this was not the case in the 'unusual circumstances' of *Boardman v Phipps*. This is somewhat difficult to understand as clearly any equitable allowance granted to a fiduciary in breach of his duty softens the deterrent effect of the rule: the possibility of receiving some payment through an equitable allowance increases, however marginally, the incentive a director or trustee has to take an opportunity and breach his duty. Perhaps what is meant by Lord Goff here is that the unusual fiduciary position of Boardman and Phipps (fiduciary agents to the trust) means that it does not operate as any encouragement to the trustees or analogous fiduciaries to breach their duties. If that is the case, then on the basis of Lord Goff's judgment, the court's jurisdiction to grant an equitable allowance to a director or fiduciary would appear to be close to zero.

Commentators have critiqued this view of the availability of the equitable allowance discretion and the resulting reduced scope to treat the 'honest fiduciary' fairly.[24] Lower courts have not universally interpreted Lord Goff's judgment as reducing the scope for granting an equitable allowance in the corporate context as close to zero.[25] In

---

[24] Goff and Jones, *Law of Restitution* (6th edn, Sweet & Maxwell, 2002), 33-0118.
[25] *Crown Dilmun v Sutton* [2004] EWHC 52, *per* Peter Smith J expressing a willingness to grant an equitable allowance in the case. See also the Australian case of *Warman International Ltd v Dwyer* [1994–1995] 182 CLR 544. In the view of this author Lord Goff's judgment has, with respect, been subject to rather stark misunderstanding—see the trusts case of *Cobbetts LLP v Hodge* [2009] EWHC 786 (Ch) where it was observed, following reference to *Guinness v Saunders*, that 'The court therefore has a wide discretion as to whether to grant such an allowance'.

Nottingham University v Fischel the High Court held that compensation for the 'full value' of the services rendered may infringe the principle enunciated by Lord Goff, but that this did not 'bar the way to any allowance being made'.[26] In other cases, however, the courts have indicated that Lord Goff's judgment imposes considerable constraints on the ability to make an equitable allowance.[27] It is submitted that this latter position is consistent with the weight of authority.

Questions

1. Are you persuaded by Lord Upjohn's view that the no-profit rule is an example of the application of the no-conflicts rule? If so, why do courts and commentators often still view them as independent rules?

2. Applying the majority's holding in *Boardman v Phipps*, which opportunities in *Hypothetical A* would Ken be allowed to exploit himself?

3. Would your answer differ applying Lord Upjohn's dissenting judgment?

4. In your view do you think financial capability claims such as those made in *Regal (Hastings)* should be relevant to whether or not a director is liable to account?

5. On the facts of *Boardman v Phipps* do you think that there was a 'possible conflict' and do you think there was a 'real, sensible' possibility of conflict? How does a 'real, sensible' possible conflict differ from a 'possible conflict'?

6. Do any of the cases we have considered so far provide an answer to the question of how we should understand what a 'company's interests' are for the purposes of determining whether or not there is a possible conflict?

7. Do you think that the majority's judgment applies rules of equity in an 'unreasonable and inequitable' fashion which risks undermining these rules, as Lord Upjohn in citing *Barnes v Addy* suggests?

8. To what extent do courts have a discretion to grant an equitable allowance to directors in breach of the no-conflicts principle? Is the courts' discretion to grant an equitable allowance an anomaly driven by the courts' desire to do some justice to the facts?

3 The no-conflicts approach and the company's interests

■ *Bhullar v Bhullar* [2003] EWCA Civ 424

This case involved a company called Bhullar Bros Ltd. The company was a retail grocery company that operated in the Huddersfield area. In addition to its several grocery stores, the company also owned one investment property in Huddersfield. This property had been let to UK Superbowl Ltd who ran a bowling alley on the property.

Bhullar Bros Ltd was owned by the families of the two founders, Mr Mohan and Mr Sohan, who were brothers. Each brother owned 50% of the ordinary shares. In addition to Mr Mohan and Mr Sohan, one of Mr Mohan's sons (Tim) and two of Mr Sohan's sons (Inderjit and Jatinderjit) were directors of the company.

Around 1998 relations between the two families broke down. As a result of the breakdown in relations Mr Mohan and Tim informed the other directors at a board meeting in May 1998 that they did not wish any additional properties to be purchased by the company. Thereafter, the two families commenced negotiations to divide the assets of the company between them, which, at the time of the hearing, had not been successful.

[26] [2000] All ER (D) 269.
[27] See *Quarter Master UK Ltd v Pyke* [2004] All ER (D) 257 following Lord Goff in *Guinness* and refusing to grant an equitable allowance.

Approximately a year later, Inderjit went bowling at UK Superbowl in his spare time. On leaving the bowling alley he noticed that the property adjacent to the bowling alley was for sale. The car park for the bowling alley was situated on this property. Inderjit made an offer to purchase the property which was accepted. The property was purchased shortly thereafter through a company called Silvercrest Ltd which was jointly owned by Inderjit and Jatinderjit. The two brothers did not inform Bhullar Bros Ltd about the opportunity before purchasing the property themselves. Shortly thereafter the Mohan family brought an action[28] alleging that Inderjit and Jatinderjit were in breach of their fiduciary duties to the company.

Before reading Jonathan Parker LJ's judgment consider the following extract from the cross-examination of Inderjit:

'Q. There was no doubt in your mind, was there, that it would have been a worthwhile acquisition for the company, is that right?

A. No, because Tim and his dad [Mohan] had already ruled out any acquisitions of any further...

Q. It may be that the company did not want it, but would it not have been worthwhile the company having it?

A. Yes.

...

Q. What made you think it was necessary to go and get legal advice before acquiring the property?

A. I did not go to get the legal advice, I simply went to tell John that this is the case, my subject to contract has been accepted, you know: "Can you do the legalities on it, and do you see any problems with it?". You know—any conflict of interest in any shape or form...

...

Q. ...Did you go to get advice or not?

A. I went to give John Norcliffe the document for the offers etc. That's when I got the advice, and the completion took place several weeks afterwards. So yes, I did get the advice before, but I did not go specifically to get the advice.

...

Q. What was it you wanted legal advice about?

A. I just wanted to make sure there was no conflict of interest.

Q. What made you think there might be a conflict of interest?

A. Because the property was adjacent to our property.

Q. It was obvious to you, was it not, that there might be a conflict of interest about you acquiring that property instead of the company. Yes?

A. I believe there was no conflict of interest because I found the property in my private time. I had taken two or three days off, and therefore I didn't owe the company anything during my time off. And on top of which, Tim and Mohan had specifically said that they didn't really want anything to do with us after that. They wanted to split completely, separate the businesses, and not buy anything new or any other new business ventures or anything like that, they just wanted to separate.

Q. Did you regard yourself as not being a director during your time off?

A. No, I did not.

Q. You regarded yourself as being a director all of the time?

[28] The action brought by the Mohan family was a petition for relief under section 459 of the Companies Act 1985, now section 994 of the Companies Act 2006.

A. I am on call all the time in case there's staff problems or anything, yes I did. All the time…

Q. And you saw this property and thought about buying it for yourself, is that right?

A. Yes, I did…Because I did not find out [about] it while I was at work, or any information whatsoever. No information whatsoever came to me because of my position within the company.

Q. You did not mention to Mohan or Tim that you were thinking about buying the property did you?

A. No I did not.

Q. Why not?

A. Because at that time I did not feel that I needed to, once the company solicitor had told me that I could go ahead and that there was no conflict of interest, and that I thought I would tell them later on, in my good time.

Q. But they did not even have to be asked about whether this property next door to company property should be bought by the company?

A. Not in my view, because they had specifically said they didn't want anything to do with us. They didn't want to buy anything new, they didn't want to start any new business, nothing whatsoever. So I automatically took it that they're only going to say "We're not interested".'

Jonathan Parker LJ

The relevant rule, which Lord Cranworth LC in *Aberdeen Railway Co v Blaikie Bros* described as being 'of universal application', and which Lord Herschell in *Bray v Ford* [1896] AC 44 described as 'inflexible', is that (to use Lord Cranworth's formulation) no fiduciary 'shall be allowed to enter into engagements in which he has, or can have, a personal interest conflicting, or which may possibly conflict, with the interests of those whom he is bound to protect'.

In a case such as the present, where a fiduciary has exploited a commercial opportunity for his own benefit, the relevant question…is simply whether the fiduciary's exploitation of the opportunity is such as to attract the application of the rule. As Lord Upjohn made clear in *Phipps v Boardman*, flexibility of application is of the essence of the rule. Thus…he said:

> 'Rules of equity have to be applied to such a great diversity of circumstances that they can be stated only in the most general terms and applied with particular attention to the exact circumstances of each case.'

Later in his speech Lord Upjohn gave this warning against attempting to reformulate the rule by reference to the facts of particular cases…As it seems to me, the rule is essentially a simple one, albeit that it may in some cases be difficult to apply. The only qualification which is required to Lord Cranworth's formulation of it is that which was supplied by Lord Upjohn in *Phipps v Boardman*, where he said this:

> 'The phrase "possibly may conflict" requires consideration. In my view it means that the reasonable man looking at the relevant facts and circumstances of the particular case would think that there was a real sensible possibility of conflict; not that you could imagine some situation arising which might, in some conceivable possibility in events not contemplated as real sensible possibilities by any reasonable person, result in a conflict.'

The strictness of the rule, and the flexibility of its application, was stressed by Lord Wilberforce in the Privy Council decision in *New Zealand Netherlands Society 'Oranje' Inc v Kuys*,[29] where he said:

> 'The obligation not to profit from a position of trust, or, as it is sometimes relevant to put it, not to allow a conflict to arise between interest and duty, is one of strictness. The strength, and indeed the

---

[29] [1973] 2 All ER 1222.

severity, of the rule has recently been emphasised by the House of Lords in *Phipps v Boardman*… It retains its vigour in all jurisdictions where the principles of equity are applied. Naturally it has different applications in different contexts. It applies, in principle, whether the case is one of a trust, express or implied, of partnership, of directorship of a limited company, of principal and agent, or master and servant, but the precise scope of it must be moulded according to the nature of the relationship.'

[Counsel for the respondent directors relied] on Viscount Dilhorne's references to *Regal (Hastings) v Gulliver* when concluding (dissenting, with Lord Upjohn, from the majority of their Lordships) that, on the facts of *Phipps v Boardman*, the appellants were not accountable for the profits they had made. Thus, referring to the *Regal* case, Viscount Dilhorne said (at pp.88–89):

'Lord Russell of Killowen in the *Regal* case held that the directors had acquired the shares "by reason, and only by reason of the fact that they were directors of Regal, and in the course of their execution of that office." Lord Macmillan said that the directors were accountable for any profit which they made if it was by reason and in virtue of their office. Lord Wright said that an agent must account for profits secretly acquired "in the course of his agency," and Lord Porter said that "one occupying a position of trust must not make a profit which he can acquire only by use of his fiduciary position, or, if he does, he must account for the profit so made.'

…

As to the *Regal* case, Lord Upjohn said that in his view their Lordships in that case were not attempting to lay down any new view on the applicable law, and (he continued): '…indeed could not do so for the law was already so well settled.'

In so far as reference to authority is of assistance in applying the rule to the facts of any particular case, the authority which (of those cited to us) is nearest on its facts to those of the instant case is the decision of Roskill J in *Industrial Development Consultants Ltd v Cooley*.[30] In that case, a commercial opportunity was offered to the defendant, who was at the time the managing director of the plaintiff company, in his private capacity. The defendant subsequently obtained his release by the company in order to exploit that opportunity for his own benefit. Had the company known that he had been offered that opportunity, it would not have agreed to release him. He was held accountable for the benefits he had received by exploiting the opportunity. The opportunity was not one which the company could itself have exploited.

Roskill J, after quoting extensively from Lord Upjohn's speech in *Phipps v Boardman*, observed (plainly correctly, if I may respectfully say so) that although Lord Upjohn dissented (with Viscount Dilhorne) in the result, there was no difference between any of their Lordships as to the applicable principles, but only as to the application of those principles to the facts of the case. Turning to the facts, Roskill J said (at p.451):

'The first matter that has to be considered is whether or not the defendant was in a fiduciary relationship with his principals, the plaintiffs. [Counsel for the defendant] argued that he was not because he received this information which was communicated to him privately. With respect, I think that argument is wrong. The defendant had one capacity and one capacity only in which he was carrying on business at that time. That capacity was as managing director of the plaintiffs. Information which came to him while he was managing director and which was of concern to the plaintiffs and was relevant for the plaintiffs to know, was information which it was his duty to pass on to the plaintiffs because between himself and the plaintiffs a fiduciary relationship existed…'

Roskill J went on to hold that the defendant had: '…embarked upon a deliberate policy and course of conduct which put his personal interest…in direct conflict with his pre-existing and continuing duty as managing director of [the company].' He continued, referring to *Keech v Sandford* (1726) Sel Cas t. King 61: 'That is something which for over 200 years the courts have forbidden.'

---

[30] [1972] 1 WLR 443.

He went on to stress the rigidity with which the rule had since been applied. As confirmation of this, he cited the following well-known passage from the judgment of James LJ in *Parker v McKenna* (1874) 10 Ch App 96:

> 'I do not think it is necessary, but it appears to me very important, that we should concur in laying down again and again the general principle that in this Court no agent in the course of his agency, in the matter of his agency, can be allowed to make any profit without the knowledge and consent of his principal; that that rule is an inflexible rule, and must be applied inexorably by this Court, which is not entitled, in my judgment, to receive evidence, or suggestion, or argument as to whether the principal did or did not suffer any injury in fact by reason of the dealing of the agent; for the safety of mankind requires that no agent shall be able to put his principal to the danger of such an inquiry as that.'

I turn, then, to the facts of the instant case. Like the defendant in *Industrial Development Consultants Ltd v Cooley*, the appellants in the instant case had, at the material time, one capacity and one capacity only in which they were carrying on business, namely as directors of the company. In that capacity, they were in a fiduciary relationship with the company. At the material time, the company was still trading, albeit that negotiations (ultimately unsuccessful) for a division of its assets and business were on foot. As Inderjit accepted in cross-examination, it would have been 'worthwhile' for the company to have acquired the property. Although the reasons why it would have been 'worthwhile' were not explored in evidence, it seems obvious that the opportunity to acquire the property would have been commercially attractive to the company, given its proximity to Springbank Works. Whether the company could or would have taken that opportunity, had it been made aware of it, is not to the point: the existence of the opportunity was information which it was relevant for the company to know, and it follows that the appellants were under a duty to communicate it to the company. The anxiety which the appellants plainly felt as to the propriety of purchasing the property through Silvercrest without first disclosing their intentions to their co-directors—anxiety which led Inderjit to seek legal advice from the company's solicitor—is, in my view, eloquent of the existence of a possible conflict of duty and interest.

I therefore agree with the judge when he said...that 'reasonable men looking at the facts would think there was a real sensible possibility of conflict'.

I would dismiss this appeal.

Jonathan Parker LJ makes it very clear that *Boardman v Phipps* is the leading authority in the context of corporate opportunities. Interestingly, however, the judgment he relies upon is Lord Upjohn's dissent in that case. In two respects Jonathan Parker LJ reaffirms Lord Upjohn's view of the law. First, he rejects attempts by respondent counsel to rely solely on *Regal (Hastings)* and the no-profit rule as a basis for relieving the respondent directors from liability to account. Although the argument is not fully fleshed-out in the judgment we are already familiar with its contours. The respondent's counsel focuses on the fact that as per Lord Russell, Lord Wright, Lord Porter, and Lord McMillan in *Regal*, the directors made a profit 'by reason' of their directorship; in the scope of their agency. As in this case Inderjit discovered the real estate opportunity in his free time it is argued that it was not a profit made by reason of his directorship. Jonathan Parker LJ rejects this argument and following Lord Upjohn holds that *Regal* represents one application of the long-standing no-conflicts principle. Secondly, Jonathan Parker LJ follows Roskill J in *Industrial Development Corporation v Cooley* in holding that Lord Upjohn's 'real, sensible possibility of conflict test' represents the applicable law. Agreeing with Roskill J, he holds that the majority in *Boardman v Phipps* agreed on the law but not on its application to the facts.

Jonathan Parker LJ does not explicitly attempt to clarify the nature of/the meaning of 'company interests' in the context of the no-conflicts principle. Nevertheless there is much 'legal food for thought' in this judgment. He holds that there is possible conflict because the opportunity to buy the property would have been 'worthwhile' and observes that 'although the reasons why it would have been "worthwhile" were not explored in evidence, it seems obvious that the opportunity to acquire the property would have been commercially attractive to the company, given its proximity to Springbank Works'. The question for us is whether these notions of 'worthwhile' and 'commercially attractive' in this judgment contain an understanding of 'company interest' that means any profit-making opportunity would be in the company's interests or do they, on the other hand, contain an idea of 'company interests' constrained by what the company already does: a business area or line of business constraint. In this regard consider the following two commentaries.

■ D.D. Prentice and J. Payne, 'The Corporate Opportunity Doctrine' (2004) 120 *LQR* 198

> There is a niggling incompleteness about Bhullar…He does not articulate a clear definition of what does constitute a corporate opportunity. On the facts in Bhullar, the test is probably that the opportunity must be one that falls within the company's line of business and that this has to be expansively interpreted to cover not only what the company is interested in, but what it could be interested in. It would be in keeping with the approach in Bhullar to treat anything of economic value to the company as potentially within the company's line of business, and therefore a corporate opportunity. This entails that the company's objects clause does not determine the scope of its commercial interest.

■ D. Kershaw, 'Does it Matter how the Law Thinks about Corporate Opportunities' (2005) 25 *Legal Studies* 533

> At first glance the notion of 'commercially attractive' seems to correspond to the broad positive **net-present value** understanding of 'interest'. However, the court found that the real estate opportunity was commercially attractive as the real estate was adjacent the company's only investment property. It has been argued that this suggests an understanding of 'company interest' that includes opportunities that are geographically proximate to the corporate premises. It is suggested, however, that geographical proximity is relevant only because of the relationship between the nature of the opportunity and the company's ancillary real estate investment activities. That is, underlying the court's focus on geography is the idea that the adjacent property could enhance the value of its existing activities, which in this case involved a real estate investment. In fact the adjacent property was already being used in part to provide car-parking facilities to the lessee of the investment property. It is submitted that if the opportunity had simply been adjacent to the company's headquarters then it would not have been 'commercially attractive' to the company and there would have [been] no possible conflict of interest. [Unless, of course, the company, had been interested in expanding its headquarters].

You will recall from our analysis of *Boardman v Phipps* that in stating and applying the 'real, sensible possibility of conflict test' Lord Upjohn took a different view of *capability facts* than the majority of their Lordships. The fact that the trustees in *Boardman* did not want to pursue the opportunity and that court approval would have been required were not *immaterial* for *his* assessment of the trust's interests which could possibly conflict with the personal interests of Mr Boardman and Mr Phipps. Lord Upjohn's approach involved, therefore, a more receptive approach to capability facts. He did not accept Lord Hodson's immateriality principle as applied by the majority.

The differences between Lord Hodson and Lord Upjohn were not differences of application, they were differences of law. Indeed, Lord Upjohn's use of the words 'real' and 'sensible' appear to be formed by his view that the fact that the trustees did not want to take the opportunity, and that court approval would have been required to do so, were relevant to the conflict determination. The majority, however, were interested not in the reality of conflict as formed by these facts but the possibility of conflict without regard to these facts. It is, therefore, somewhat difficult to accept the proposition stated in *IDC v Cooley* and affirmed by Jonathan Parker LJ in *Bhullar* that the majority and the minority agreed on the law but not on its application to the facts. It is *not* clear that the majority in *Boardman v Phipps* would have accepted the 'real, sensible, possibility of conflict' test; however, had they done so it *is* clear that *as a matter of law* the majority and Lord Upjohn had different views on what facts would be taken into account to determine whether there is a 'real, sensible possibility of conflict'.

In *Bhullar* there are two factors which we might consider as capability facts. The first is the fact that the board had in effect determined that the company no longer had any interest in acquiring additional real estate properties. The second potential capability fact is that the company was deadlocked and in the process of trying to wind itself up; that is, it was approaching the end of its life, making it very unlikely that the directors of the company would agree that it should carry out any further business. Jonathan Parker LJ does not subject these factors to any analysis but his conclusion that there is a real, sensible possibility of conflict clearly appears to reject their relevance. They appear to be, to use Lord Hodson's vocabulary in *Boardman*, 'immaterial' to the determination of conflict.

We might ask whether Lord Upjohn would have been more receptive to these claims? It seems unlikely. In *Boardman v Phipps* the trustees testified that they had expressed no interest in purchasing the shares even though they were aware of the opportunity. As the trust had no interest in the shares there was, for Lord Upjohn, no possibility of conflict. In *Bhullar*, although the board was deadlocked and had rejected any future acquisitions prior to the opportunity arising, it was not given an opportunity to reconsider its view in light of this property opportunity becoming available. Accordingly, the legal implications of adopting Lord Upjohn's statement of the no-conflicts rule are not tested by *Bhullar* precisely because Lord Upjohn would not have gone so far as to have accepted the available capability facts in *Bhullar* as qualifying the possible conflict. For Lord Upjohn the capability facts in *Bhullar* would only have become relevant once the board of Bhullar Bros Ltd had been made aware of the opportunity by Inderjit and Jatinderjit.

This raises the question of whether disclosure to the board would have been sufficient to have allowed Inderjit and Jatinderjit to have taken the opportunity; put differently did the breach of duty arise from the failure to disclose or simply the taking of the opportunity. Jonathan Parker LJ observes in reaching his holding that 'the existence of the opportunity was information that it was relevant for the company to know and it follows that the appellants were under a duty to communicate it to the company'.[31] To explore this question we need to alter the facts in *Bhullar*. Let us assume that Inderjit and Jatinderjit disclosed the opportunity to the board and that the board unanimously, with only disinterested directors voting, rejected the opportunity,[32] *or* that because of the composition of the board even with only a disinterested director vote the board

---

[31] Note that in *Item Software v Fassihi* [2005] 2 BCLC 91 at [40–41] Lady Justice Arden clarified that the reference to a duty to communicate was not a reference to a separate duty but rather the duty to disclose here was an aspect of the director's duty of loyalty.

[32] Note that if the company had Table A articles (which is not disclosed in the case) then there would have been no deadlock in relation to a vote to consider whether the opportunity should have been taken, as Inderjit and Jatinderjit, who were both directors, would have not have been able to vote.

was deadlocked. On these hypothetical facts, which are closer to those in *Boardman v Phipps*, would a reasonable person consider that there is a real, sensible possibility of conflict? Following the majority in *Boardman*, even though there has been disclosure and a disinterested director vote/deadlock there remains a concern that the decision to reject the opportunity/maintain deadlock could have been tainted by Inderjit and Jatinderjit's interest in buying the property themselves and the self-interested influence they exerted—in the same way as the majority in *Boardman* were concerned about the potentially prejudiced advice of Mr Boardman. The fact of board rejection/deadlock would not therefore qualify the nature of the company's interest for the purpose of the no-conflict rules. For the majority in *Boardman*, disclosure by Inderjit and Jatinderjit would not have been sufficient to enable them to take the opportunity.[33]

For Lord Upjohn's approach, however, the fact that the clearly disinterested members of the board were informed of and rejected the opportunity/were in deadlock would be sufficient to qualify the company's interests in regard to this opportunity and to dissolve any possible conflict. The question for us, and a question that is *not* clearly answered by *Bhullar v Bhullar*, is whether in adopting Lord Upjohn's 'real, sensible possibility of conflict' test the courts are also more willing to be more flexible where there has been disclosure to board and board rejection of the opportunity. Jonathan Parker LJ's adoption of Lord Upjohn's test and his reference to the duty to communicate suggests that they are. But this position is not, it is submitted, consistent with the House of Lords' majority position in *Boardman*. However, it is also worth noting that allowing directors to personally exploit opportunities following board rejection of the opportunity seems consistent with the final paragraph in Lord Russell's judgment in *Regal (Hastings)* extracted and considered previously,[34] although this paragraph is clearly obiter dicta.

Finally, it is important to note that although the respondents discovered the opportunity in their spare time, following Roskill J in *IDC v Cooley*, Jonathan Parker LJ rejects the argument that the no-conflicts principle only applies during office hours. He holds that the defendants had only one capacity at the time they purchased the property and that was as directors. If 'company interest' is to be qualified, therefore, it is not through a distinction between the business activities of the directors in company time and their private time. For the purposes of the no-conflicts rule, it is irrelevant whether a director discovers the opportunity in his spare time through activities or happenstance that have zero connection to her role as director.

Questions and discussion

- If, on the hypothetical adjustment to the facts of *Bhullar*, a disinterested yet mutually antagonistic and (normally) deadlocked board had voted to reject the opportunity, what possible conflict could there possibly be? It seems wholly unrealistic that the directors who rejected to the opportunity could possibly have been influenced by directors to whom they feel deeply antagonistic. But would a holding which took account of this observation provide an example of extreme facts making bad law? We would clearly be more concerned about possible influence over board members who are not in such an antagonistic relationship. But can courts get involved in assessing personal relations amongst board members and their propensity to be influenced arising from those relationships?

---

[33] Note that in *Peso Silver Mines v Cropper* (1966) SCR 673, the Canadian Supreme Court held that board rejection of the opportunity enabled the director to keep the profits of personally exploiting the opportunity—even where the managing director in question who subsequently participated in the opportunity had voted to reject the opportunity.

[34] See p 522.

- What if, again altering the facts, Inderjit and Jatinderjit had disclosed the opportunity to the board but had claimed that they were not interested in the opportunity? They would then have been allowed to vote (they would not have been disqualified by Table A) and their votes would have counted towards rejection. Following rejection they acquired the opportunity as they thought 'well if the company doesn't want it we might as well buy it'. For those of you who are persuaded that board disclosure and disinterested board rejection of the opportunity considered above are sufficient, would board rejection here be sufficient? Assume that there is no evidence that Inderjit and Jatinderjit are lying about their original lack of interest. Does this example, support the majority in *Boardman's* view that the court's cannot get into questions of the nature and extent of a fiduciary's self-serving influence; its possible existence alone is sufficient?

- Prentice and Payne argue that the judgment in *Bhullar* stands for the proposition that the company's objects clause does not 'determine the scope of its commercial interest'.[35] Do you think that the judgment in *Bhullar v Bhullar* supports this reading? Does it exclude the possibility of using the objects clause in this way?

- Which reading of 'company interest'—area of business versus any profit-making opportunity—do you think best explains the judgment in *Bhullar v Bhullar*?

- Once you have given thought to the previous two bullet points on determining the 'company's interests' consider the following two cases: *Wilkinson v West Coast Capital* and *O'Donnell v Shanahan* (CA).

■ *Wilkinson v West Coast Capital* [2005] EWHC 3009 (Ch)

In this case several investors purchased a company, NGS, that was a holding company for an operating company (TGS), which ran a retail chain known as 'The Gadget Shop'. The ownership structure of NGS was as follows: 40% of the shares were owned by Mr Wilkinson (the petitioner) and his associates; 10% by the founder of the company; 25% were owned by a **private equity** partnership (West Coast Capital, WCC), in which Sir Tom Hunter ('Sir Tom') and Mr McMahon were the only partners; and 25% of the shares were owned by Mr Gorman who became the chief executive officer of NGS. Sir Tom and Mr Gorman were long-standing business associates. Mr Gorman and Mr McMahon were directors of NGS. It was alleged that Sir Tom was a de facto director of NGS.

When the shares were purchased all the shareholders in NGS entered into a shareholders agreement. This shareholders agreement contained an undertaking that 'unless the shareholders holding in excess of 65% of the issued shares otherwise agree in writing the shareholders shall exercise their power in relation to the company so as to ensure that...the company does not acquire or invest in another company or business or incorporate any subsidiary'. This gave both Wilkinson and his associates, as well as WCC and Gorman together, the ability to stop NGS from making any further acquisitions.

Several months following the purchase of NGS, NGS was approached by a separate company called Birthdays Ltd, a greeting cards company, regarding a possible cooperation with the Gadget Shop to cross-sell each other's products. A cross-selling trial was subsequently piloted. At the same time Sir Tom became aware, from sources completely unconnected to NGS, that Birthdays' original **venture capital** investors were looking to exit their investment. At this time Sir Tom and his business partners did not take the matter any further. However, some time later, at the bidding of Mr Gorman, Gorman and WCC commenced negotiations to purchase the company. As these negotiations progressed Sir Tom, on behalf of WCC, and Mr Gorman, informed the other shareholders of NGS of the Birthdays' opportunity and the fact that they were in the process of negotiating to purchase the company. One of the options at this time was for NGS

---

[35] D.D. Prentice and J. Payne, 'The Corporate Opportunity Doctrine' (2004) 120 *LQR* 198.

to purchase the company. However, Sir Tom was only willing to do this if WCC and Gorman funded the purchase of Birthdays and Wilkinson and his associates accepted a reduced shareholding in NGS. As relations between the investors had become very poor, it was felt by Sir Tom that if they were to purchase Birthdays through NGS, WCC and Gorman would need greater control over NGS than they currently had. No agreement was reached and shortly thereafter WCC and Gorman purchased Birthdays through an independent company called New Gifts Ltd.

Sir Tom, Gorman, and McMahon all testified that had there been any legal barrier to their acquiring Birthdays they would not have purchased the company through NGS given its current shareholder structure. Warren J accepted this evidence.

The Gadget Shop business was not successful and subsequently went into administration. Wilkinson brought a section 994 petition[36] on the basis that the directors of the company had breached their fiduciary duties in exploiting the Birthdays opportunity themselves.

Warren J

[Mr Wilkinson's complaint is as follows:] even if the directors learnt of the opportunity, and of the relevant information to permit them to formulate their offer [for Birthdays], quite independently of their capacity as directors of NGS, nonetheless they were in a position of conflict in relation to the acquisition of Birthdays and should not have acquired it for themselves.

In considering that complaint, [Counsel for Mr Gorman argued], correctly I think, that one must have regard…[to the] question of the scope of NGS's business. In that context, he relies on the decision of the Court of Appeal in *Aas v Benham* [1891] 2 Ch 244…and on certain passages of the judgments in *Boardman v Phipps*.[37]

Aas v Benham was a partnership case; the defendant was a partner in a ship-broking firm which hoped to act in negotiations between the Spanish and Portuguese Governments and ship builders. He had also been approached for advice by a shipbuilding company. He realised as a result of information he learnt while in Spain on behalf of the ship-broking firm that it would be advantageous for the ship-building company to reconstitute itself as a builder of warships and to acquire for this purpose a yard which he had discovered was available in Bilbao. He used that information to help write a prospectus for the ship-building company's reconstruction, and made profits for himself as a result of the reconstruction.

[Counsel for Mr Gorman] relies on the following passage from the judgment of Lindley LJ:

'As regards the use by a partner of information obtained by him in the course of the transaction of partnership business, or by reason of his connection with the firm, the principle is that if he avails himself of it for any purpose which is within the scope of the partnership business, or of any competing business, the profits of which belong to the firm, he must account to the firm for any benefits which he may have derived from such information, but there is no principle or authority which entitles a firm to benefits derived by a partner from the use of information for purposes which are wholly without the scope of the firm's business, nor does the language of Cotton LJ in *Dean v MacDowell* warrant any such notion. By 'information which the partnership is entitled to' is meant information which can be used for the purposes of the partnership. It is not the source of the information, but the use to which it is applied, which is important in such matters. To hold that a partner can never derive any personal benefit from information which he obtains as a partner would be manifestly absurd.'

However, more pertinent to the actual decision is a passage earlier:

---

[36] See Chapter 16.

[37] Lords Hodson, Guest, and Viscount Dilhorne referred approvingly to *Aas v Benham* in their judgments. See D. Kershaw, 'Does it Matter How the Law Thinks About Corporate Opportunities' on the use of *Aas v Benham* by their Lordships in *Boardman v Phipps* and the relevance of the approach taken in *Aas v Benham* for English opportunities regulation.

'The answer, however, to this claim is short and conclusive. It was no part of the business of [the firm] to promote or reconstruct companies, nor to advise them how to improve the management of them, All such matters were quite foreign to the business of [the firm]…He never was in fact acting for his firm in this matter, nor did his partners ever suppose he was, or treat him as so acting…'

In these circumstances, the defendant was held not liable to account to his partners in the ship-broking firm. Since it was no part of that firm's business to advise on corporate reconstructions or to build ships, the partner had no fiduciary duty to his partners which prevented him making use of the information as he did, even though he had learnt it while on the firm's business. The use he made of the information was outside the scope of his fiduciary duty. [Counsel for Mr Gorman] submits that exactly the same approach should be applied in the case of a company and the duties owed to it by a director.

Aas v Benham was considered in *Boardman v Phipps* [1967] 2 AC 46 (the facts of which are well-known) where there was no suggestion that it was wrongly decided. Lord Hodson, for instance, mentioned the case with apparent approval…

So *Aas v Benham* is an illustration of the importance of defining the scope of the duty before being able to decide whether a person is in breach of it and in particular whether the 'no con-flict' rule or the 'no profit' rule applies.[38] In that case, the position was that Mr Benham's duty as a partner did not require him to treat the information and opportunity which he obtained and learned as acquired by him in his capacity as partner since that information and opportunity fell outside the scope of the partnership business…

[Counsel for Mr Gorman] says that there is nothing in the company law authorities 'which in any way detracts from the principle in *Aas v Benham*.' I am not sure that there is anything which warrants the epithet 'principle' which can be derived from *Aas v Benham*. However, what it does establish, or reflect as existing law, is that the scope of the duty of a partner is circumscribed by the partnership agreement; and that the mere use of information or an opportunity obtained and acquired while acting in his fiduciary capacity does not necessarily mean that the partner cannot use that information or take advantage of that opportunity on his own account. The case possibly establishes, or re-affirms, a *negative* proposition, viz that there is no principle which entitles a firm to benefits derived from the use of information for purposes which are wholly outside the scope of the firm's activities.

In applying that negative principle, one must act with care because the firm's activities may not be limited by the formal partnership agreement. For instance, if Mr Benham had been man-dated, with a view to a possible extension of the firm's business, by his partners to investigate, on behalf of the firm, a possible investment in ship-building opportunities while in Spain and Portugal conducting business on behalf of the firm, the relevant activities might thereby have been extended to shipbuilding. Whilst the partners could not, in fact, have extended the scope of the business without Mr Benham's consent as a partner, and even though he might, on his return to England, refuse to agree to such an extension, it does not necessarily follow that he would have been entirely outside the constraints of the 'no conflict' and 'no profit' rules. Certainly, *Aas v Benham* is not authority for the proposition that he would have been free to act in his own interests in those circumstances.

Turning, now, to [Counsel for Mr Gorman's] comments on the company law authorities, I start with *Regal (Hastings) v Gulliver*…It is clear [from *Regal*] that the fact that a company might have been practically unable to take up an opportunity does not exonerate a director who takes it for himself. That is a hard rule: but it is a clear rule. So it seems to me that one needs to approach with caution the situation where the inability arises, or is said to arise, not from a practical inabil-ity but from a structural restriction comparable to that in *Aas v Benham*. The argument, in that sort of situation, is that, since there are constitutional restrictions on what the company can

---

[38] Note that Warren J adopts the position, following Lewison J in *Ultraframe v Fielding*, that the no-conflicts rule and the no-profit rule are independent rules.

do, an activity within the scope of that restriction cannot be an activity within the scope of the company's affairs...

[Counsel for Mr Gorman] accepts that, once a conflict has arisen and a profit has been made, it is no defence for the director to allege that the company could not *as a matter of fact* have acquired the opportunity itself, for example because the company could not afford to pursue the opportunity (as in *Regal (Hastings) Ltd v Gulliver*) or because the third party would not have wanted to deal with the company (as in *Industrial Development Consultants Ltd v Cooley*). But he submits that none of the cases is concerned with the situation where, as in *Aas v Benham* there was a legal impediment to the company taking up the opportunity; he says that, where there is a legal impediment of this sort, there is no relevant conflict of interest. On the facts on the present case there was, he submits, a legal impediment to the acquisition of Birthdays by NGS and there-fore no relevant conflict of interest in the acquisition by WCC and Mr Gorman.

By legal impediment, I understand [counsel for Mr Gorman] to be focusing essentially on con-stitutional documents such a partnership agreements, Articles of Association and shareholders agreements. A contractual restraint arising under an agreement with a third party (such an anti-competition covenant given on the sale of a business) would, I apprehend, more properly be regarded as a practical impediment although a statutory prohibition would certainly fall to be treated as a legal impediment. But even a legal bar (save a statutory prohibition and, perhaps, a true restriction on the powers of a company in its objects clause) in the sense used by [counsel for Mr Gorman] is not conclusive as to the scope of the activities of a company or partnership.

However, what I think is important in the present case is not so much the effect of a legal impediment on the duty of directors generally; but rather the impact of the director himself being able, in a non-fiduciary capacity, [namely as a direct or indirect shareholder] to prevent the company of which he is a director from obtaining the benefit of the opportunity. I doubt very much that a legal impediment requiring shareholder consent to certain matters impacts to any great extent on the duties of a director who is not a shareholder. It does not follow from the fact that a particular acquisition requires shareholder consent that a director is freed from any duty which would otherwise arise to bring an opportunity of acquisition to the attention of the board and the shareholders. In contrast, the ability of a shareholder, who also happens to be a director, to block certain action on the part of the company may be of great importance in the context of his duties to account under the 'no conflict' and 'no profit' rules.

Let me take an example. Consider a company (call it X) carrying on a particular business. Suppose X has three equal shareholders A, B and C, each of whom is a director; and suppose that it has one additional, non-shareholder, director D. Suppose that the Memorandum and Articles of Association restrict X's business to its current business but so that activities can be diversified (either directly or through a corporate acquisition) with the consent of 66% of the shareholders.

Suppose, then, that an opportunity to acquire a company (call it Y) whose business is outside the scope of X's existing business becomes generally known. There would be nothing, I think, to prevent A and B acquiring Y for themselves even if the board of X considered that it would be a good thing for X to acquire Y. In these circumstances, there is of course a conflict between the personal interests of A and B on the one hand and their duties, as directors, to X on the other hand. But it is not a conflict to which the 'no conflicts' rule has any application because A and B are entitled, as shareholders, to block the acquisition by X. There is, I consider, no duty on them to use their votes as shareholders to approve the acquisition (and this is so, in my judgment, even though it may be in the interests of X to make it and even though they are directors). There is no risk (such as that which caused concern in *Keech v Sandford*) which needs to be guarded against and no occasion for the intervention of equity...

The position would be the same, I consider, if the opportunity had come to the attention of A and B other than in their capacities as directors. It would be open, I think, for them to keep that opportunity for themselves. At most, detecting a possible advantage to X in acquiring Y, it may be their duty, acting in the interests of X, to bring the opportunity to the attention of the board. But having done that, they could not be compelled to agree to the actual acquisition by X of Y.

Being able, acting perfectly properly, to block such an acquisition, there is, as before, no relevant conflict of interest; and, in this case, there would clearly be no use of a corporate opportunity were A and B to acquire Y for themselves…

Now suppose that the opportunity has, instead, come to the notice of X and its board in circumstances where that opportunity is clearly that of X exclusively (eg because the owner of Y approaches D in his capacity as a director with an offer to sell to X). The board and the shareholders decide that it might be in the interests of X to effect the acquisition of Y because its business, whilst outside the scope of its own business, presents synergies with that business. Actual acquisition of Y will require the consent of A, B and C once the merits of the acquisition have been investigated. Suppose that the vendor of Y provides confidential information to the board to enable X to make an offer. At this stage,… if D were to attempt to divert [the opportunity], both the 'no conflict' rule and the 'no profit' rule would apply if he in fact acquired the target business/company and made a profit. It would not be open to D to claim, as against X or A, B and C, that the scope of X's business, and therefore his duty, was restricted by the scope of X's current business and that he could therefore obtain Y for himself. Nor would he escape the rules if X were unable to make the acquisition because it could not raise the finance: the case would fall squarely within the principles established in *Regal (Hastings) Ltd v Gulliver*.

[Earlier in the judgment dicta from Warren J, when considering Upjohn J's 'real, sensible possibility of conflict' test, observed that: 'a company with a wide objects clause could, in theory, diversify its business in limitless ways if the necessary funding were available'. But a director of a company selling fashion clothing for women could hardly be in breach of the 'no conflict' rule if he took a stake in a company distributing farm machinery, even if the company did have such a wide objects clause. There would simply be no 'real, sensible possibility' of conflict. In contrast, if the board of the fashion clothing company had been actively considering diversification into the distribution of farm machinery, there would be a real, sensible possibility of conflict in a director taking a stake in such a company.]

Next suppose that the board, having looked carefully at the potential acquisition, decides, for commercial reasons, not to proceed. It is a very difficult question whether this would take D out of either or both the 'no conflict' and 'no profit' rules. *Aas v Benham* certainly does not provide an answer. That D can do so with the informed consent of the company in general meeting is clear; that he cannot do so without it is not clear.

Whatever the position of D, however, the position of any two of the other shareholders, say A and B, acting together may be different. As before, where the opportunity is generally known, there is, I consider, no duty on them to use their votes as shareholders to approve the acquisition; they remain able to block it.

Applying these principles to the present case, there has, in my judgment, been no breach by Mr Gorman or Mr McMahon (or indeed by Sir Tom even if he is a *de facto* director) of the 'no conflicts' rule. On my findings of fact, there was no agreement that NGS should acquire Birthdays so that they were, as shareholders, able to block the acquisition. There is no question, on my findings, of the board being able to proceed with the acquisition in the face of the provisions of the shareholders' agreement to which NGS itself was a party.

Warren J appears to accept counsel's submission that the holding in *Aas v Benham* is good authority for the negative proposition that a firm or company is *not* entitled to benefits arising from the use of information which is outside the company's scope of business activities. Translating this into the no-conflicts principle would mean that if a director acts personally on information about an opportunity—whether obtained in company or his personal time—but the opportunity is outside of the scope of the company's activities then there is no conflict as the company has no interest in opportunities outside the scope of the company's activities. However, Warren J struggles valiantly to determine exactly how a company's scope of business restricts its 'interests' *for the purposes of the no-conflicts rule.* In this regard Warren J's judgment provides us with guidance in two respects: first, in relation to the objects clause; and, second, in relation to the company's business area.

In relation to the objects clause the guidance is perhaps a little confusing. The judgment appears to suggest that if there is a bar in the constitution to carrying out certain business activities then this will restrict the company's interests. He observes that 'even a legal bar (save a statutory prohibition and, perhaps, a true restriction on the powers of a company in its objects clause) in the sense used by [counsel for Mr Gorman] is not conclusive as to the scope of the activities of a company or partnership'. He does not define a 'true restriction', although one would imagine it would be something to the effect of 'the company can only engage in the business of selling Gadgets'. However, *per* Warren J other restrictions in the constitution such as, as in this case, that the company cannot purchase other businesses without the consent of a specific percentage of the shareholders would not limit the company's interests. Nor would, according to the hypothetical example given in the judgment, a specific restriction on diversifying the business interests without obtaining, in the hypothetical's example, 66% of the shareholders' votes. However, these types of restriction will, according to Warren J, restrict the 'company's interests' (for the purposes of the no-conflicts rule) if the directors who wish to personally exploit the opportunity are also shareholders with sufficient votes to prevent the approval for the purchase or diversification to be given. The problem here is that it is unclear how a 'true restriction' on the company's objects, which could typically be amended by a 75% shareholder vote, is any different than the example Warren J gives of a diversification prohibition subject to super-majority shareholder approval. The better view of the judgment, therefore, is that only where the directors as shareholders could block the vote—to amend the constitution or grant the specified approval—would the constitution operate as a restriction on 'company interests' for the purposes of the no-conflicts rule.

This part of the judgment is also helpful in our understanding of which capability facts are in fact 'immaterial' in the conflict determination once the subject company's interests have been established and there is an apparent conflict of interests. Warren J makes a useful distinction between a 'practical inability', such as limited available finance, and a 'structural restriction'. With regard to the latter he clearly accepts that a statutory bar on taking an opportunity would not be *immaterial* to a conflict determination. This, it is submitted, is consistent with the understanding previously outlined that the courts have treated those capability facts as immaterial where there is a significant potential role for the director to play in changing or removing the factual barrier to taking the opportunity.

The second respect in which the judgment provides us guidance is on the relationship between the company's existing activities and the meaning of 'company interests' for the purpose of the no-conflicts rule. In the dicta extracted from the earlier part of the judgment he observes that a fashion company would not be interested in a farm machinery distribution company, *unless* the fashion company had, prior to the opportunity becoming available, indicated an interest in branching out into the farm machinery distribution business! This tells us that business activities that are utterly distinct from the company's existing activities do not fall within the company's interests for the purpose of the no-conflicts rule unless the company has expressed a prior interest in expanding into that area. However, the judgment does not tell us how different (or how similar) the business activities have to be to fall outside of (or within) the 'company's interests'. Some further guidance is suggested by Warren J in his discussion of the hypothetical where it appears that opportunities that fall outside the company's actual scope of business and yet still 'present synergies with that business' would still fall within the 'company's interests'.

The *American Heritage Dictionary* defines 'synergy' helpfully as 'the interaction of two or more agents or forces so that their combined effect is greater than the sum of their individual effects'. The idea in the business context is that the two businesses together are worth more than the sum of their parts. There are several possible reasons for this: cross-selling opportunities—for example: people who buy cards for different occasions may be more likely to buy gadgets; if both businesses source from the same supplier they may get better prices with their combined muscle; and the two businesses together could require fewer administrative staff and lower office costs. The problem here is that the concept of 'synergies' is very elastic—there may be synergies between very different companies. Indeed we could identify some synergies from the merger of an oil company and an organic baby food company— staffing and product distribution may be examples. The concept of 'synergies' does not itself, therefore, answer whether one business area is sufficiently connected to the company's existing activities to fall within 'its interests' for the purpose of the no-conflicts rule. On this issue we can, at best, speculate. If the position in *Wilkinson* is good law, it appears that the 'company's interests' is determined not just by what it does but also activities that logically fit together with what it does, even though such other activities may be distinct from what it does. So a men's fashion company's interests would include opportunities in any type of clothing business—high fashion, low cost clothing, women's clothes, or children's clothes. It may also extend into fashion accessories, shoes etc., but it would not include selling food or drinks or fur- niture unless the board of the company had made a decision to explore such options. It is very difficult to draw a clear line conceptually and must be left to the courts to address on a case-by-case basis.

In summary, therefore, the judgment in *Wilkinson v West Coast Capital* affirms the view of *Bhullar v Bhullar* that there are business area constraints on the meaning of a 'company's interests' for the purposes of the no-conflicts rule. It also partially affirms Prentice and Payne's view: constitutional constraints on a 'company's interests' do not impose restrictions on 'company interests' *unless* the director taking the opportunity has sufficient shares to block a change to the constitution to broaden its interests.

Several of the issues raised in Warren J's judgment were recently addressed in the Court of Appeal case of *O'Donnell v Shanahan*. Consider the extract of this case set forth here.

■ *Re Allied Business and Financial Consultants; O'Donnell v Shanahan* [2009] 2 BCLC 666

The defendants, Mr Shanahan and Mr Leonard, set up a company, Allied Business and Financial Consultants Ltd, with the claimant, Mrs O'Donnell in the late 1980s. Shanahan, Leonard, and O'Donnell were all directors of the company. The company had a broad objects clause allowing the company to carry on 'any trade or business which can, in the opinion of the board of directors, be advantageously carried on by the company'. However, the company was primarily involved in the provision of financial services to companies through, for example, arranging loans, mortgages, and insurance. In early 1999 Mr Shanahan was approached by a Mr Sulaiman who wished to sell a large commercial property—the 5th floor of a building called Aria House. Mr Shanahan approached one of his contacts, Mr Walsh, who agreed to purchase the property and commissioned reports on the property. Mr Walsh paid for these reports. The company's commission for arranging the deal was agreed at £30,000. However, the deal with Mr Walsh fell through. Following this Mr Shanahan and Mr Leonard approached a company client, Mr Holleran. Mr Holleran agreed to be involved in the purchase of the property together with his brother but only if Mr Shanahan and Mr Leonard agreed to take a 50% stake between them. They agreed to do so and all parties to the purchase agreed that the £30,000 commission payment to the company would not be payable. Neither Allied Business and Financial Consultants Ltd nor Mrs O'Donnell were involved in the purchase of the property; however, Mrs O'Donnell was aware of the involvement of Mr Shanahan and Mr Leonard. Indeed she received a payment of £9,000 from Shanahan and Leonard to compensate her for lost earnings resulting from the loss of the £30,000 commission. She was not, however, aware that the defendants had relied on the reports commissioned and paid for by Mr Walsh. Mrs O'Donnell brought a claim for breach of the no-profit rule and the no-conflicts duty by the defendants. At first instance, Richard Sheldon QC found that there was no breach of duty.

An important consideration in the decision of Richard Sheldon QC was that the opportunity was not in the company's scope or area of business. In reaching this conclusion Richard Sheldon QC relied on the partnership case of *AAS v Benham*, referred to in the abstract from *Wilkinson v West Coast Capital* extracted earlier. This case was also subject to detailed analysis by their Lordships in *Boardman v Phipps*, although not in the extracted section of the case we considered. Richard Sheldon QC considered the no-profit rule separately from the no-conflicts rules and, without analysis, Rimer LJ, giving the judgment of the Court of Appeal, followed his lead. Note also that although this case is heard after the coming into force of the 2006 Act, the Act was not applicable to the facts of this case which took place prior to 2006.[39]

Rimer LJ

Central to the judge's reasoning in rejecting the case under both the 'no conflict' and the 'no profit' rules was his finding that the acquisition by the respondents of their interest in Aria House was of a nature falling outside the scope of the company's business. That was the key to the judge's conclusion. The authority that so influenced the judge, and was central to the argument before us, was this court's decision in *Aas v Benham*[40] [where] Lindley LJ said:

'As regards the use by a partner of information obtained by him in the course of the transaction of partnership business...there is no principle or authority which entitles a firm to benefits derived by a partner from the use of information for purposes which are wholly without the scope of the firm's business...'

The judge's conclusion was that the principle underlying the decision in *Aas v Benham* was equally applicable to the determination of the scope of a director's fiduciary duties to his company. He held that it was necessary to have regard to the scope of the company's business not just in relation to the application of the 'no conflict' rule...but also in relation to that of the 'no profit' rule...Whilst he found that the opportunity to buy Aria House came to the attention of Mr Shanahan and Mr Leonard in their capacity as directors of the company, it was one that was outside the scope of the company's business and so their exploitation of it involved no breach of the 'no profit' rule.

The 'no profit' rule

Subject to the *Aas v Benham* 'scope of business' point, to which I will come, I would regard this as a plain case in which Mr Shanahan and Mr Leonard had (without the company's informed consent) adopted for their private benefit a business opportunity that came to them in their capacities as directors of the company with the consequence that they would in principle be accountable to the company for any profit derived from it...

---

[39] Schedule 4 para 47 of Commencement Order 5, Transitional Provisions and Savings Order 2007, SI 2007/3495 provides 'Section 175 of the Companies Act 2006 (duty to avoid conflicts of interest) applies where the situation described in subsection (1) of that section arises on or after 1st October 2008'.

[40] [1891] 2 Ch 244. See *Wilkinson v West Coats Capital* for a discussion of the facts of *Aas v Benham*.

Mr Sulaiman's engagement of the company (acting by Mr Shanahan) to find a purchaser of Aria House was the company's first venture into estate agency. That shows that by 1999 the categories of its activities were not closed. All that Mr Shanahan then learnt about Aria House and its virtue as an investment opportunity derived from information he obtained as a director of the company in seeking such a purchaser...In my judgment, this was obviously a case in which, once that opportunity arose, the respondents could not properly make use of the information they had so obtained in deciding to take up the opportunity for their own benefit...As the respondents did not offer the opportunity to the company, but took it up personally, they engaged in a transaction that rendered them liable to account under the 'no profit' rule.

The authorities relating to trustees' and directors' duties to account for profit earned in consequence of a breach of the 'no profit' rule are legion, they all appear to me to point to the same conclusion and none appears to qualify the liability to account by reference to whether the impugned transaction was (in the case of an alleged breach by a director) within or without the scope of the company's business. The principle of accountability by directors in breach of the rule derives from the strict rule affecting trustees, the leading case in the latter field being *Keech v Sandford*...It may be thought odd that a strict principle of that nature, which fathered the like principle of accountability applicable to directors, can enable a director to answer a claim under the 'no profit' rule by asserting that the impugned transaction was unimpeachable because it was not the kind of transaction the company ordinarily engaged in. That is to ignore the point that the rationale of the 'no conflict' and 'no profit' rules is to underpin the fiduciary's duty of undivided loyalty to his beneficiary. If an opportunity comes to him in his capacity as a fiduciary, his principal is entitled to know about it. The director cannot be left to make the decision as to whether he is allowed to help himself to its benefit.

The authorities relating to directors' accountability not only do not support the 'scope of business' exception in relation to the 'no profit' rule, they are contrary to it...

In *Parker v McKenna*,[41] the directors of a bank acquired for themselves, and made a profit on, certain shares the subject of a new issue that were not taken up by the bank's shareholders. James LJ said:

'It appears to me very important, that we should concur in laying down again and again the general principle that in this Court no agent in the course of his agency, in the matter of his agency, can be allowed to make any profit without the knowledge of his principal; that that rule is an inflexible rule...'

According to James LJ, therefore, nothing less than the 'safety of mankind' depends on the rigorous application of the 'no profit' rule. How, it might be asked, is it consistent with that for the profiteer to claim, as do the respondents, that the company would not have taken advantage of the acquisition opportunity because it was outside the scope of its business...

What of *Aas v Benham*? That was a decision of a strong court, binding upon us, and showing that, in the context of a commercial partnership, the strict duties of accountability in accordance with the principles of, for example, *Parker v McKenna* and *Regal (Hastings) Ltd v Gulliver* will not apply in a case in which partnership information has been used by the defendant partner for the purpose of a separate business of a nature beyond the scope of the partnership business.

Aas v Benham was not cited in *Regal (Hastings) Ltd v Gulliver*, but it was cited in *Boardman v Phipps*, a case involving a successful claim against the appellants that they were accountable to a trust on the basis that, as agents of the trustees, they had obtained information that they then used to buy shares for themselves. The appellants argued (inter alia) that their case was akin to *Aas v Benham* in that the purchase of the shares was 'wholly outside the scope of any agency undertaken for the trustees'. The test was said to be whether the information could have been used by the principal for the purpose for which it was used by the agent; and if the answer

[41] (1874) LR 10 Ch App 96.

was no, the information was not the principal's property. The counter-argument was that *Aas v Benham* was 'distinguishable as being a very special case for a partner is only in a fiduciary position in relation to matters within the ambit of the partnership business'.

Viscount Dilhorne, in the minority in the House of Lords, would have allowed the appellants' appeal. He did not question the statements of principle in *Regal (Hastings) Ltd v Gulliver* and held the appellants to be in a fiduciary relationship towards the trust. On the facts, however, he concluded that there was no possibility of a conflict between their interests and those of the trust and, after citing *Aas v Benham* with apparent approval, said that the acquisition of the shares was outside the scope of the trust and the appellants' agency... Lord Hodson, also in the majority, regarded the case as turning on the principle of accountability by a fiduciary explained in *Regal (Hastings) Ltd v Gulliver*. The appellants were in a fiduciary position and had used information obtained by them as agents for the trustees to take the opportunity to make the profit that they did. He referred to the reliance placed on *Aas v Benham*, the argument being that the purchase of the shares was outside the scope of the fiduciary relationship between the appellants and the trustees. He said of that argument:

> 'The case of partnership is special in the sense that a partner is the principal as well as the agent of the other partners and works in a defined area of business, so that it can normally be determined whether the particular transaction is within or without the scope of the partnership. It is otherwise in the case of a general trusteeship or fiduciary position such as was occupied by Mr. Boardman, the limits of which are not readily defined, and I cannot find that the decision in the case of *Aas v. Benham* assists the appellants...'

Coming to my conclusions on the 'no profit' case, in my judgment the answer to the reliance placed by the judge... on *Aas v Benham* is that it is of no relevance in considering the extent and application of the 'no profit' and 'no conflict' rules so far as they apply to fiduciaries such as trustees and directors... The point about *Aas v Benham* is that it concerned the fiduciary duties owed by a partner whose duties were circumscribed by the contract of partnership. The extent of Mr Benham's fiduciary duties was determined by the nature of the partnership business, which was expressly limited by the terms of the partnership agreement. The consequence was that if he used partnership information for any purpose that fell within the scope of the partnership business, he was required by the fiduciary obligations to which the contract subjected him to account to the firm for any profits so made; but his fiduciary obligations did not require him similarly to account to the firm for any profits made by the use of such information for a purpose that was beyond the scope of the business of the partnership. To those familiar with the wider obligations of accountability to which trustees and directors are subject, the decision in *Aas v Benham* may at first sight appear to reflect a surprisingly narrow approach. But the explanation is that a trustee's and director's fiduciary duties are not similarly circumscribed by the terms of a contract. That distinction was squarely recognised by Lord Hodson in *Boardman v Phipps*...

By contrast with Mr Benham's position, directors of companies occupy what Lord Hodson in *Boardman v Phipps* called a 'general trusteeship or fiduciary position'... In my judgment, the decision in *Aas v Benham* provides no assistance in determining the nature and reach of the 'no profit' rule so far as it applies to trustees and directors. In particular, in the present case, the scope of the company's business was in no manner relevantly circumscribed by its constitution: it was fully open to it to engage in property investment if the directors so chose...

The 'no conflict' rule

I can take the 'no conflict' rule more shortly... In my judgment... there was a breach of it. The respondents became engaged in the Aria House affair in their capacity as directors of the company whose function was, as agent for Mr Sulaiman, to find a purchaser. They found Mr Walsh and brokered a deal under which, on exchange of contracts, £30,000 vendor's commission was payable to the company by Mr Sulaiman.

When the Walsh deal fell through, the respondents, still as directors and acting on behalf of the company, were anxious to find a substitute purchaser, one who would ideally simply slip into Mr Walsh's shoes and buy on like terms…The respondents appear to me to have conducted themselves generally in relation to this matter with a marked lack of business scruple…As it seems to me, the simple point is that once the substitute Holleran arrangement was arrived at, the respondents were faced with the prospect that he was not prepared to agree to…to pay the company the £30,000 commission or any commission…The only loser was the company. Under the substitute deal that the respondents brokered, one in which they were now personal partici- pants, they also agreed with Mr Holleran that the company should no longer have its commis- sion. When contracts were exchanged on 26 May 1999, it did not get any commission. Nor was it to be entitled to any in the future.

That feature of the new deal appears to me to have placed the respondents in a conflict between their personal interests (to achieve a purchase in concert with Mr Holleran, who had made his position clear about the commission payment) and the company's interests (to receive a proper reward for brokering the substitute deal). The respondents simply sacri- ficed the company's interests and preferred their own. The company had not authorised them to do that. As directors their duty was to achieve a proper reward for the company for negotiating a sale of Aria House. In my judgment that feature alone of the substitute deal meant that the respondents were in a state of conflict of interest and duty when, through HRL, they entered into the purchase contract on 26 May 1999. It is nothing to the point that some time after the exchange of contracts they agreed to and did compensate Ms O'Donnell for losing out on her share of a £30,000 commission. That may have redressed the wrong she had so suffered and it is no doubt relevant to the respondents' claim that Ms O'Donnell acquiesced in their purchase. It did not, however, retrospectively prevent the acquisition by the respondents…of their interest in Aria House from being one entered into in breach of the 'no conflict' rule.

I therefore respectfully disagree with the judge on his conclusion that the 'no conflict' rule was not breached in this case.

O'Donnell v Shanahan creates multiple conceptual difficulties. The first is that the judgment makes a distinction between the no-profit rule and the no-conflicts princi- ple as separate rules. As argued previously, this is neither correct nor consistent with authority. As Lord Upjohn in *Boardman v Phipps* makes clear, the no-profit rule is a sub-rule of the duty to avoid conflicts of interest and of interest and duty. Where loyalty is not in issue, because the company has no interest in an opportunity, then the company has no claim on a profit made by reason of the director's directorship. Yet courts persist in making this 'separate rule' distinction. Fortunately, as we shall see, in the company law context the Companies Act 2006 settles this argument squarely in favour of Lord Upjohn's position. Accordingly, for the purpose of analysing the holding of this case we shall not treat the no-profit rule as a separate rule. The outer extent of its reach, there- fore, is determined by what is in the company's interest.

The second and central issue raised by this case is whether a company's interests are limited to what it currently does: the scope, area, or line of its business. In *Wilkinson v West Coast Capital* we saw that Warren J clearly thought that a company's inter- ests are limited in this way: how could a fashion company, he asked, be interested in farming machinery? We also argued that there may be some support for this posi- tion in *Bhullar*. The Court of Appeal in *O'Donnell* disagrees. It concludes that the no-profit rule is not limited by scope of business restrictions. Of central importance to the Court of Appeal's conclusion is its interpretation of the 19th-century Court of Appeal case, *Aas v Benham*, which held that in relation to corporate opportunities a partnership's interests are limited by the scope of its business. Rimer LJ in *O'Donnell* concludes that *Aas v Benham* is a partnership case and as such is of 'no relevance' to companies. The justification for this view is that the scope of a partnership's business is circumscribed by contract—by the partnership deed—but a company's is not. Rimer LJ observes that 'a director's fiduciary duties are not similarly circumscribed by the terms of a contract'.

For students of English company law this is a counter-intuitive conclusion. Although it is true that it is not possible to waive the application of director's duties through contract,[42] in multiple areas of our journey through directors' duties we have seen that the corporate contract does circumscribe the fiduciary duties of directors. For example: the duty to use powers for their proper purpose is a function of what the constitution determines is a proper purpose—the improper interference with constitutional rights can be made proper by the constitution; and the articles can amend the promotion objective of the company in section 172 of the Act to focus on a constituency other than the members.[43] This relationship between the corporate contract and director's duties suggests a much closer affinity between the company and the partnership than Rimer LJ allows for. If, contrary to Rimer LJ's position, fiduciary duties of directors are in fact circumscribed by the corporate contract, this suggests that the principle in *Aas v Benham* is indeed applicable to the determination of a 'company interests'.

For Rimer LJ, *Aas v Benham* provides that the scope of a partnership business is circumscribed by the partnership deed. *Mutatis mutandis* this would mean that the scope of a company's interests would be circumscribed by the company's objects clause. Clearly, in relation to most companies this would not represent any constraint because, as we discussed in Chapter 4, the objects clause is typically broadly drafted. But even for companies with a narrow objects clause it is unclear that allowing the objects clause to limit the company's interests in the opportunities context is consistent with prior authority. A company's objects can be changed—as can a partnership deed—but conflicted directors would be at the heart of any recommendation to change or not to change the objects to encompass the identified opportunity. That is, objects clause amendment/non-amendment is a capability fact that, for the majority in *Boardman*, would be immaterial. This means that although a director's fiduciary duties are indeed circumscribed in some respects by contract, when it comes to determining a 'company's interests' for the purposes of the no-conflicts rule they are not so circumscribed by such objects-facts because such facts are inadmissible capability facts. It follows that *if* this is what *Aas* meant by a partnership's scope of business then it is no longer good authority—in either the partnership or the corporate context— and Rimer LJ's decision that it is not applicable to companies is of no consequence.[44] But is this all that *Aas v Benham* has to teach us about the determination of a company's interests?

Rimer LJ argues that any such scope of business restrictions on the company's interests would undermine the prophylactic effect of the no-profit rule upon which the 'safety of mankind' depends! But recourse to the objective of deterrence does not get us very far. We need to ask what is being deterred? The answer, of course, is disloyal behaviour. But we cannot know what is disloyal unless we know what the interests are of the person or entity to whom the fiduciary must be loyal—the trust, the principal, the company. All such protected persons and entities have bounded interests, although clearly some may have broader interests than others. The only questions of relevance here are first, which

---

[42] Section 232 CA 2006. See further Chapter 12.   [43] Section 172(2) CA 2006.

[44] Note that, following *West Coast Capital*, such facts would be admissible if the barrier to changing the objects clause has nothing to do with the director—such as where a controlling shareholder makes it clear that he would never approve of the change because he intends to exploit the opportunity himself.

Aas v Benham explores, how to determine the scope of those interests, and second, whether this can be done without reliance on capability facts.

Lord Hodson observes in *Boardman* that in relation to a trust 'the limits are not readily defined' and hence his conclusion that Boardman and Phipps are in breach of duty as their interests conflicted with those of the trust. By way of contrast, the Court of Appeal in *Aas v Benham* finds that the scope of a partnership's business and interests are limited. For Lord Hodson, in his consideration of *Aas*, this was because a partnership carries on a 'particular business'. However, it is unclear from Lord Hodson's judgment whether this was because the business objects of the partnership could be restricted in the partnership deed or simply because, regardless of that deed, a partnership's actual business is readily identifiable.[45] It is noteworthy in this regard that in *Aas v Benham* the determination of the company's scope of business is not determined through a close inspection of the partnership deed; rather the court's determination appears to be more about what it does—its 'line of business'[46]—than what it can do according to the partnership deed. That is, *Aas v Benham* suggests that the interests of a partnership, and by analogy a company, are limited by the scope of its actual activities as distinct from what it can do according to its partnership deed or objects clause.

There are, as we have already discussed in *Wilkinson v West Coast Capital*, evidentiary and practical difficulties associated with determining a company's areas of business as well as whether a new opportunity is sufficiently closely related to that area of business. An approach that views the company's interests as anything of commercial interest clearly resolves any difficulty and deters fiduciaries from 'chancing their hand' in any grey zone of uncertainty about a company's interests. Furthermore, as we have seen in this chapter, the law in this area has elected to reject a flexible approach to capability facts that could alter the company's 'real' interests. However, we need to remember why the law rejects those facts and ask whether those reasons mean that the law should not engage with the relationship between company interest and its area of activities. The law rejects capability facts because the fiduciary is at the heart of the production of that fact—obtaining finance for the company; the board decision to reject an opportunity. He should be doing his utmost to overcome this capability barrier and we cannot see what he does to build this barrier himself. These concerns do not apply in relation to the company's areas of business where an objective assessment of this can be made by reference to the actual activity of the company uninfected by the fiduciary's actions.

However, regardless of these important doubts about the reasoning in *O'Donnell v Shanahan* and its consistency with prior authority, if you are asked whether the company's interests are restricted according to the company's area of business activities the better answer would, as a result of this case, currently be 'no'.[47] This means that directors of aerospace companies cannot take macrobiotic organic baby food opportunities. As we have seen, the no-conflicts rule applies whether in the office or at work, which means that a director of an aerospace company that discovers a micro-biotic food opportunity in his spare time cannot take that opportunity. One hopes that this case is not the end of this story.

[45] In *Boardman v Phipps* Lord Guest's use of *Aas v Benham*, not included in the extract, focused on the partnership deed. For a consideration of the role of *Aas v Benham* in *Boardman v Phipps*, see D. Kershaw, 'Does it Matter How the Law Thinks About Corporate Opportunities?' (2005) 25 *Legal Studies* 533, 550–551.

[46] A phrase also used in *Aas v Benham* [1891] 2 Ch 244 at 256.

[47] One could of course argue that *Bhullar*, also a Court of Appeal decision, recognizes line of business limitations and therefore that we have conflicting Court of Appeal decisions. This argument is definitely available; however, it is clear that *Bhullar* only addresses the issue indirectly, whereas *O'Donnell* addresses the issue head on, making it a more powerful authority in this regard. The area is clearly ripe for the Supreme Court.

4 Approval mechanisms at common law

We saw in Chapter 13 in relation to self-dealing and breaches of the no-conflicts rule that at common law the default rule was that ex-ante or ex-post shareholder approval was required in relation to such a breach in order to enable the conflicted director to keep the profit. We saw in the *Imperial Mercantile Credit Association*[48] case Lord Hatherley taking a strongly contractarian approach to conflicts regulation, accepting that a company's articles could provide for alternative approval mechanisms to shareholder approval. We also saw that many companies' articles displaced shareholder approval with board disclosure and disinterested director approval in relation to self-dealing conflicts. In this regard, Lord Hatherley noted that 'I [do not] think that this Court professes to lay down rules for the guidance of men who are adult, and can manage and deal with their own interests...It must be left to such persons to form their own contracts and engagements, and this Court has only to sit here and construe them.'

In the context of corporate opportunities the same common law rule requiring shareholder approval is applicable. As we saw in *Regal (Hastings)*, Lord Russell observes that the directors would have been allowed to keep the profit if they had obtained approval of the general meeting before or after having purchased the shares in Amalgamated. In the *Regal* case itself, it appears that the directors themselves may have had sufficient votes to obtain such approval.[49] However, as they had not obtained such approval, the directors were liable to account for the profit. It is interesting to note that we have not seen opportunities cases similar to those we saw in the self-dealing context which consider the validity of board approval mechanisms provided for by a company's constitution. This is unsurprising given the clear benefits that self-dealing transactions can provide for a company. Nevertheless, there is no reason why, and no authority to suggest otherwise, that the contractarian principles of the common law espoused in *Imperial Credit* would not also allow a company's constitution to provide for board disclosure and disinterested director approval.[50] Of course, as was the case in the self-dealing context, such mechanisms raise concerns regarding their compliance with section 232 of the 2006 Act (the prohibition on duty waivers and indemnities for breach of duty). However, to the extent the disclosure and disinterested director provisions for self-dealing transactions were compliant with section 232,[51] similar provisions for opportunities would also be valid.[52] Nevertheless, neither Table A nor most company articles provided for such general board disclosure and approval mechanisms in the opportunities context.[53] In the absence of such a provision in the constitution authorizing board approval for the taking of an opportunity, board approval alone would not suffice to enable the director to take the opportunity without being in breach of duty.[54]

---

[48] (1871) LR 6 Ch App 558. See pp 440–2.

[49] Cf *Cook v Deeks* [1916] 1 AC 554. On the question of whether at common law interested shareholders could grant approval for breach of duty see Chapter 16 on minority shareholder protection.

[50] Indeed part of Table A itself provided for such delegated approval in relation to *Regal (Hastings)* type opportunities: article 85 stating that directors could keep the benefit arising from any interest they had in a company promoted by the company, which would cover the situation which in *Regal (Hastings)* (see extract of article 85 at p 490).

[51] See discussion at pp 485–491.

[52] See Company Law Review Steering Committee, Final Report, para 3.22.

[53] Except as detailed in note 50.

[54] It should be noted that there is Privy Council authority to the effect that board approval is sufficient. This is the Privy Council's judgment in *Queensland Mines v Hudson* (1978) 18 ALR 1 where board approval was deemed to be sufficient. Interestingly, this judgment is based heavily upon *Boardman v Phipps* and at first glance, therefore, seems to present a significant conflict with the position set forth in *Regal*. Indeed in *Boardman*, Lords Guest and Hodson were of the opinion that fully informed trustee approval would have been sufficient but it was not obtained. The Court of Appeal in *Boardman* were also of this view. This, naturally, led the Privy Council to the view that board approval would suffice in the company context. However, the *Queensland* judgment is fundamentally flawed as it fails to take

5 Resignation of office in order to take the opportunity

5.1 The resignation problem

A director may resign her position as a director at any time and without having to give any reason. If a director resigns her position she is no longer a director and no longer a fiduciary from the moment that the resignation takes effect. It follows logically that if a director is no longer a fiduciary then she no longer owes fiduciary duties to the company; she is no longer subject to a duty of loyalty and no longer subject to the no-conflicts obligation or its sub-rule, the no-profit rule. Indeed, the no-profit rule as set out in *Regal (Hastings)* structures liability around the continuing directorship: a profit must be made by reason and *in the course of* the director's office.

In the context of opportunities regulation this logic creates a significant problem: if a director identifies an opportunity whether at work or in his spare time which, if he exploited himself, would put his personal interests in a possible conflict with the company's interests, if he resigned before exploiting the opportunity he could keep the profits. If the law took this approach it would seriously undermine the effectiveness of the duty of loyalty in the opportunities context. If opportunities which a company would expect a loyal director to refer to it can be 'taken' from the company simply by resignation then the scope for agency costs increases markedly: if the opportunity is worth £10 million and the law does not prevent personal exploitation post-resignation then, from the company's perspective, it loses £10 million.

How could the law respond to this problem and what, in turn, are the concerns that we may have about such a response? There are three possible options. The first two options involve a qualified extension of the no-conflicts rule beyond resignation. We could say, for instance, that the no-conflicts rule continues to apply just as it applies to existing directors as regards any opportunities which the director finds out about whilst a director—either in work or his personal time. Alternatively, the law could provide for a less restrictive extension of the no-conflicts rule by providing that it only applies if the motive for resignation is to take a specific opportunity (put differently, one might say that the act of resignation to take the opportunity is the breach of the still applicable no-conflicts rule). Thirdly, if the law decides that logically we cannot extend the application of a duty to a person who is no longer a fiduciary, then we might seek an alternative basis of liability. Intuitively, this basis would be one that focuses on the company's right to exploit that opportunity—an idea that—*as between the director who has resigned and the company*—the opportunity which she has exploited '*belongs to*' the company; that is the company has a right, as against the director, to decide whether to exploit the opportunity. The law could then specify the rules that determine whether the opportunity 'belongs' to the company rather than the former director.

In deciding how and upon what terms to regulate this resignation problem the law must take into account not only the concern that in the absence of regulation companies could be injured by actions of disloyal directors, but also the competing concern that too strict regulation of the resignation problem could interfere with the efficient operation of the market place by, for example, preventing former directors from setting up competing businesses; preventing opportunities that are identified from being exploited;

account of the peculiar nature of the fiduciary relationship in *Boardman v Phipps*—that is Boardman was not a trustee but an agent (and therefore fiduciary) of the trust. As he was allowed to exercise this role by the trustees the court is of the view that either trustee or beneficiary consent would suffice to allow Boardman to keep the profits (neither of which was obtained). However, it is clear that had Boardman been the trustee then only beneficiary approval would have sufficed. Accordingly, translating properly into the company context, *Boardman v Phipps* is authority for the proposition that only shareholder approval would suffice.

and preventing third parties from deciding who they want to do business with (the former director rather than his former company).

5.2 Post-resignation opportunities regulation

5.2.1 *Extending the reach of the no-conflicts principle*

UK company law has struggled with the post-resignation problem and in particular with whether the duty to avoid a possible conflict of interest extends beyond resignation. Recent authority confidently asserts that the duty does not[55] extend beyond resignation. Nevertheless, in the important case of *Industrial Development (IDC) v Cooley*,[56] the facts of which are set out in Jonathan Parker LJ's judgment in *Bhullar v Bhullar* extracted above, the court relied upon the no-conflicts rule where the director had resigned from his position as managing director of IDC before obtaining the opportunity to design buildings for the Eastern Gas Board. In his judgment holding that Cooley was liable to account, Roskill J focused on the fact that Cooley had taken significant steps towards obtaining the opportunity, including preparing documentation relating to the project, whilst he was still managing director of IDC. Roskill J also observed that the information about the opportunity that Cooley obtained whilst a director was information that the company would have liked to have possessed.[57] Furthermore, it was clear on the facts that Cooley had faked his own ill health *in order that* he could leave IDC's employ and take the opportunity for himself.

Whilst *IDC v Cooley* has been regularly cited in subsequent cases, no subsequent post-resignation case has relied on the no-conflicts principle alone.[58] However, as we shall see, the Companies Act 2006's codification of the no-conflicts rule now explicitly makes the duty applicable to former directors in relation to information and opportunities which they identified whilst directors. In this regard the approach taken in *IDC v Cooley* may become much more important. So what lessons might it contain about the application of the no-conflicts rule to former directors? There are three factors that are particularly important to its application: first, taking steps whilst a director to position oneself to obtain the opportunity; secondly, not disclosing to the company what you know about the opportunity prior to your resignation; and, thirdly, resigning with the intention of exploiting the opportunity. If this is correct, then this would allow a former director to exploit an opportunity where: he knew about an opportunity whilst a director; informed the company about the opportunity; and resigned for other reasons only later to consider the opportunity, or was dismissed for reasons unrelated to the opportunity.

5.2.2 *'Property' and the maturing business opportunity approach*

As noted previously, the courts have taken a different path in post-resignation cases to the one offered by Roskill J's judgment in *IDC v Cooley*. Instead of looking toward the continuing application of the no-conflicts duty they have taken the third option, which

---

[55] *Ultraframe v Fielding* [2005] All ER (D) 397; *Wilkinson v West Coast Capital* [2005] EWHC 3009 (Ch).

[56] [1972] 1 WLR 443.

[57] Some commentators interpreted *IDC v Cooley* as providing a separate director's duty to disclose information to the company that would be of interest to it, including the director's own misconduct. In *Item Software (UK) Ltd v Fassihi* [2005] 2 BCLC 91 the Court of Appeal rejected this position. The Court did, however, hold that the duty of loyalty would require a director to disclose his own misconduct.

[58] Indeed some courts have found the no-conflict approach in *IDC v Cooley* unhelpful. Warren J in *Wilkinson v West Coast Capital* [2005] EWHC 3009 (Ch) at [264], argues that whilst the basis of liability in *IDC v Cooley* was no-conflicts 'it might be easier, conceptually, to view it as an application of the "no profit" rule' (note Warren J views the no-profit rule as an independent rule that applies beyond resignation).

has been to focus on the rights of the company in relation to the opportunity. To do so they have developed what Lewison J in *Ultraframe* referred to as a 'proprietary basis for liability'.[59] Before we analyse this approach, it is important to grasp a central idea: the language of ownership and property is used by this approach—often sloppily[60]—but in no sense do the cases think that an opportunity *is property* in the same sense that a company warehouse, machine or vehicle is company property.[61] The key idea here is that if certain conditions are satisfied then the opportunity is—*only* as between the former director and the company—*as if it were* company property; *as if* it belonged to the company. Let us now turn to the rules that determine whether the opportunity is to be treated *as if it were* the property of the company and, therefore, not capable of exploitation by the former director.

This approach is known as the *maturing business opportunity* approach. It was originally developed in the Canadian Supreme Court case of *Canadian Aero v O'Malley*.[62] In this case Canadian Aero was a topographical mapping company that had for some time been trying to obtain a contract to map Guyana. Shortly before the contract was awarded two of Canadian Aero's directors resigned from the company to form a separate company which bid for and successfully obtained the Guyana mapping contract. Canadian Aero subsequently sued the former directors to obtain an accounting of the profits which they had made from the contract. Interestingly, as an example of the dangers of viewing the no-profits rule as a stand-alone rule, the court of first instance held that the directors were not liable, in part because they viewed the no-profits rule as only applicable where the directors took the opportunity 'in the course of their' office. Laskin J in the Canadian Supreme Court held that this view was narrowly conceived; but also held that the no-conflicts and no-profit frameworks were not the only basis of liability:

> What I would observe is that the principle, or, indeed, principles, as stated, grew out of older cases concerned with fiduciaries other than directors or managing officers of a modern corporation, and I do not therefore regard them as providing a rigid measure whose literal terms must be met in assessing succeeding cases. In my opinion, neither the conflict test, referred to by Viscount Sankey, nor the test of accountability for profits acquired by reason only of being directors and in the course of execution of the office, reflected in the passage quoted from Lord Russell of Killowen, should be considered as the exclusive touchstones of liability. In this, as in other branches of the law, new fact situations may require a reformulation of existing principle to maintain its vigour in the new setting.

The approach was, therefore, contextualized by Laskin J within a willingness to depart from equitable principles set out in English law. Following an examination of the opportunities regulation in several jurisdictions including, in addition to Canada, the UK, the US. and New Zealand he reached the following conclusion:

> An examination of the case law in this Court and in the Courts of other like jurisdictions on the fiduciary duties of directors and senior officers shows the pervasiveness of a strict ethic in this area of the law. In my opinion, this ethic disqualifies a director or senior officer from usurping for himself or diverting to another person or company with whom or with which he is associated a *maturing business opportunity which his company is actively pursuing*; he is also precluded from so

---

[59] *Ultraframe (UK) Ltd v Fielding* [2005] EWHC (ch) 1638 at [1344].

[60] Compare Lewison J in *Ultraframe*, ibid at [1344], where it is incorrectly observed that the opportunity 'is treated *as* the property of the company' with Collins J in *CMS Dolphin Ltd v Simonet* [2001] 2 BCLC 704 at [96] who correctly observes 'that the opportunity is to be treated *as if it were* property of the company' (emphasis added).

[61] On the use and misuse of the concept of property in the opportunities context see D. Kershaw, 'Does it Matter How the Law Thinks About Corporate Opportunities' (2005) 25 *Legal Studies* 533.

[62] [1974] SCR 592.

> acting even after his resignation where the resignation may fairly be said to have been prompted or influenced by a wish to acquire for himself the opportunity sought by the company, or where it was his position with the company rather than a fresh initiative that led him to the opportunity which he later acquired. [Emphasis added]

According to the approach set out by Laskin J, if the opportunity which the former director exploits is a maturing business opportunity which the company was actively pursuing prior to the director's resignation then the opportunity is to be treated as 'belonging' to the company. A director cannot take what 'belongs' to the company and if he does so he must return it or any of the profits he makes therefrom. For Laskin J this approach applied both to existing directors as well as to former directors. In relation to former directors, he held that *in addition* to the opportunity being a maturing business opportunity which the company was actively pursuing, they must have resigned to take the opportunity or the former director's position at the company must have led him to the opportunity. Laskin J viewed this approach as a partial extension of the directors' fiduciary duty following resignation. He did not, however, give specific guidance on what amounted to a maturing business opportunity. He noted only that:

> In holding that on the facts found by the trial judge, there was a breach of fiduciary duty by [the former directors] which survived their resignations I am not to be taken as laying down any rule of liability to be read as if it were a statute. The general standards of loyalty, good faith and avoidance of a conflict of duty and self-interest to which the conduct of a director or senior officer must conform, must be tested in each case by many factors which it would be reckless to attempt to enumerate exhaustively. Among them are the factor of position or office held, the nature of the corporate opportunity, its ripeness, its specificness and the director's or managerial officer's relation to it, the amount of knowledge possessed, the circumstances in which it was obtained and whether it was special or, indeed, even private, the factor of time in the continuation of fiduciary duty where the alleged breach occurs after termination of the relationship with the company, and the circumstances under which the relationship was terminated, that is whether by retirement or resignation or discharge.

This approach was first adopted by an English court in the High Court's decision in *Island Export Finance Ltd v Umunna*.[63] In this case the company carried out business in Africa. One of its ventures had involved the supply of telephone boxes to Cameroon. The managing director subsequently became dissatisfied with his position with the company and resigned. Subsequently through his own company he obtained further orders to provide telephone boxes to Cameroon. Hutchinson J adopted the maturing business approach which he viewed as being consistent with the principles set out in *Regal (Hastings)*. He found that the director was not liable to account. This approach has also been applied in several first instance cases since *Island Export Finance* including in *CMS Dolphin v Simonet*[64] where Collins J observed that:

> In my judgment the underlying basis of the liability of a director who exploits after his resignation a maturing business opportunity of the company is that the opportunity is to be treated as if it were property of the company in relation to which the director had fiduciary duties. By seeking to exploit the opportunity after resignation he is appropriating for himself that property.

---

[63] [1986] BCLC 460.
[64] [2001] 2 BCLC 704. See also: *Balston Ltd v Headline Filters Ltd* [1990] FSR 385; *Framlington Group plc v Anderson* [1995] 1 BCLC 475, 495–6; *Hunter Kane Ltd v Watkins* [2002] EWHC 186 (Ch); *British Midland Tool Ltd v Midland International Tooling Ltd* [2003] EWHC 466 (Ch); *Shepherds Investments Ltd v Walters* [2006] EWHC 836.

Serious questions were raised about the continuing applicability of the maturing business opportunity approach following Jonathan Parker J's decision in *Bhullar v Bhullar*. He observed that: 'but it does not follow that it is a prerequisite of the accountability of a fiduciary that there should have been some improper dealing with property "belonging" to the party to whom the fiduciary duty is owed, that is to say with trust property'. This has been interpreted as a rejection of the maturing business opportunity test,[65] or at least any attempt to apply it in a non-resignation context. However, the approach continues to have traction, as we see in the following Court of Appeal case.

■ *Foster Bryant Surveying Ltd v Bryant* [2007] EWCA Civ 200[66]

Foster Bryant Surveying Ltd was a company owned 60% by its founder Mr Foster and 40% by Mr Bryant. Both Foster and Bryant were chartered surveyors. The company had one primary client, Alliance, with whom it had an exclusivity agreement to obtain all of Alliance's surveying work for a limited period of time. Mr Bryant's wife also worked for the company. Following the failure to acquire additional clients Mr Foster became increasingly dissatisfied with Mr Bryant and his wife. This dissatisfaction culminated in Foster deciding to fire Mrs Bryant. On being informed of Foster's decision in this regard Bryant resigned his position with the company. The judge found that on resigning he had no intention of taking Alliance work away from Foster Bryant Surveying Ltd. However, Alliance were very satisfied with Bryant and Alliance *itself* proposed to provide him with work in the future following the expiry of the exclusivity agreement. Alliance also planned to continue to provide Foster with work; however, they stopped doing so following legal action taken by Foster against Alliance. Shortly thereafter Foster Bryant Surveying Ltd sued Bryant for breach of fiduciary duty. At first instance Bryant was found not to be in breach. The company appealed.

> *Rix LJ*
>
> At trial it *was* common ground between the parties that the synthesis of principles expounded by Mr Livesey QC, sitting as a deputy judge of the High Court, in *Hunter Kane Ltd v Watkins* [2002] EWHC 186 (Ch), [2003] All ER (D) 144 (Feb), which Mr Livesey had himself taken largely from the judgment of Mr Justice Lawrence Collins in *CMS Dolphin Ltd v Simonet* [2001] 2 BCLC 704 and the authorities there cited and discussed, accurately stated the law. In this court in *In Plus Group Ltd v Pyke* [2002] 2 BCLC 201 Brooke LJ described the *Simonet* analysis as 'valuable' (at paragraph 71). Mr Livesey said:
>
> '1. A director, *while* acting as such, has a fiduciary relationship with his company. That is he has an obligation to deal towards it with loyalty, good faith and avoidance of the conflict of duty and self-interest.
>
> 2. A requirement to avoid a conflict of duty and self-interest means that a director is precluded from obtaining for himself, either secretly or without the informed approval of the company, any property or business advantage either belonging to the company or for which it has been negotiating, especially where the director or officer is a participant in the negotiations.
>
> 3. A director's power to resign from office is not a fiduciary power. He is entitled to resign even if his resignation might have a disastrous effect on the business or reputation of the company.
>
> 4. A fiduciary relationship does not continue after the determination of the relationship which gives rise to it. After the relationship is determined the director is in general not under the continuing obligations which are the feature of the fiduciary relationship.

---

[65] D.D Prentice and J. Payne, at note 29.

[66] Note that although *Foster v Bryant* is a 2007 case it is a pre-2006 Act case as section 175 of the Act discussed in the following section applies only to fact patterns which occurred after October 2008: The Companies Act 2006 (Commencement No 5, Transitional Provisions and Savings) Order 2007.

5. Acts done by the directors while the contract of employment subsists but which are preparatory to competition after it terminates are *not necessarily* in themselves a breach of the implied term as to loyalty and fidelity.

6. Directors, no less than employees, acquire a general fund of skill, knowledge and expertise in the course of their work, which is plainly in the public interest that they should be free to exploit it in a new position. After ceasing the relationship by resignation or otherwise a director is in general (and subject of course to any terms of the contract of employment) not prohibited from using his general fund of skill and knowledge, the "stock in trade" of the knowledge he has acquired while a director, even including such things as business contacts and personal connections made as a result of his directorship.

7. A director is however precluded from acting in breach of the requirement at 2 above, even after his resignation where the resignation may fairly be said to have been prompted or influenced by a wish to acquire for himself any maturing business opportunities sought by the company and where it was his position with the company rather than a fresh initiative that led him to the opportunity which he later acquired.

8. In considering whether an act of a director breaches the preceding principle the factors to take into account will include the factor of position or office held, the nature of the corporate opportunity, its ripeness, its specificness and the director's relation to it, the amount of knowledge possessed, the circumstances in which it was obtained and whether it was special or indeed even private, the factor of time in the continuation of the fiduciary duty where the alleged breach occurs after termination of the relationship with the company and the circumstances under which the breach was terminated, that is whether by retirement or resignation or discharge.

9. The underlying basis of the liability of a director who exploits after his resignation a maturing business opportunity of the company is that the opportunity is to be treated as if it were the property of the company in relation to which the director had fiduciary duties. By seeking to exploit the opportunity after resignation he is appropriating to himself that property. He is just as accountable as a trustee who retires without properly accounting for trust property.

10. It follows that a director will not be in breach of the principle set out as point 7 above where either the company's hope of obtaining the contract was not a "maturing business opportunity" and it was not pursuing further business orders nor where the director's resignation was not itself prompted or influenced by a wish to acquire the business for himself.

11. As regards breach of confidence, although while the contract of employment subsists a director or other employee may not use confidential information to the detriment of his employer, after it ceases the director/employee may compete and may use know-how acquired in the course of his employment (as distinct from trade secrets—although the distinction is sometimes difficult to apply in practice).'

In the present proceedings the principles with which we are most concerned are 1, 2, 4, 5, 7, 8, 9 and 10.

...

In *CMS Dolphin Ltd v Simonet* [2001] 2 BCLC 704 the relevant jurisprudence was carefully considered by Lawrence Collins J, as he then was. The director there resigned (without any notice) in order to profit from the claimant company's business. Having made plans in advance of resignation, after his departure he immediately set up in competition, first in partnership and subsequently through a new company. He approached the claimant's staff and clients, to draw them both to him. Before long, the claimant had no staff and no clients. The director was found to be in breach of fiduciary duty and liable to account. By resigning, he had exploited the maturing business opportunities of the claimant, which were to be regarded as its property. The case made by the claimant and accepted by Lawrence Collins J was that the director had been prompted or influenced to resign by a wish to acquire for himself or his company the business opportunities which he had previously obtained or was actively pursuing with the claimant's clients and had now actually diverted to his own profit...Having referred to *Regal (Hastings) v Gulliver*, he said that the case before him concerned the question of how far the principle of that case, which concerned directors who were in office at the time of acquisition of the shares, extended to—

'a director who resigns his office to take advantage of a business opportunity of which he has knowledge as a result of his having been a director' (at paragraph 87).

Turning to *IDC v Cooley*, he underlined the fact that Roskill J had there emphasised Mr Cooley's breaches of fiduciary duty prior to his release from the company (at paragraph 90)...

'There must be some relevant connection or link between the resignation and the obtaining of the business.'

He concluded:

'95. In English law a director's power to resign from office is not a fiduciary power. A director is entitled to resign even if his resignation might have a disastrous effect on the business or reputation of the company. So also in English law, at least in general, a fiduciary obligation does not continue after the determination of the relationship which gives rise to it (see *A-G v Blake (Jonathan Cape Ltd, third party)* [1998] 1 All ER 833 at 841, [1998] Ch 439 at 453, varied on other grounds [2000] 4 All ER 385, [2001] 1 AC 268 (HL)). For the reasons given in *Island Export Finance Ltd v Umunna* a director may resign (subject, of course, to compliance with his contract of employment) and he is not thereafter precluded from using his general fund of skill and knowledge, or his personal connections, to compete.

96. In my judgment the underlying basis of the liability of a director who exploits after his resignation a maturing business opportunity of the company is that the opportunity is to be treated as if it were property of the company in relation to which the director had fiduciary duties.'

In my judgment, Lawrence Collins J was not saying that the fiduciary duty survived the end of the relationship as director, but that the lack of good faith with which the future exploitation was planned while still a director, and the resignation which was part of that dishonest plan, meant that there was already then a breach of fiduciary duty, which resulted in the liability to account for the profits which, albeit subsequently, but causally connected with that earlier fiduciary breach, were obtained from the diversion of the company's business property to the defendant's new enterprise.

...

The parties are content that Mr Livesey's summary of the law in *Hunter Kane v Watkins* (see at paragraph 7 above) accurately restates it. The jurisprudence which I have considered above demonstrates, I think, that the summary is perceptive and useful. For my part, however, I would find it difficult accurately to encapsulate the circumstances in which a retiring director may or may not be found to have breached his fiduciary duty. As has been frequently stated, the problem is highly fact sensitive. Perhaps for this reason, appeals have been rare in themselves, and, of all the cases put before us, only *Regal (Hastings) v Gulliver* (not a case about a retiring director) demonstrates success on appeal. There is no doubt that the twin principles, that a director must act towards his company with honesty, good faith, and loyalty and must avoid any conflict of interest, are firmly in place, and are exacting requirements, exactingly enforced. Whether, however, it remains true to say, as James LJ did in *Parker v McKenna* (cited in *Regal (Hastings) v Gulliver*) that the principles are (always) 'inflexible' and must be applied 'inexorably' may be in doubt, at any rate in this context. Such an inflexible rule, so inexorably applied might be thought to have to carry all before it, in every circumstance. Nevertheless, the jurisprudence has shown that, while the principles remain unamended, their application in different circumstances has required care and sensitivity both to the facts and to other principles, such as that of personal freedom to compete, where that does not intrude on the misuse of the company's property whether in the form of business opportunities or trade secrets.[67] For reasons such as these, there has been some flexibility, both in the reach and extent of the duties imposed and in the findings of liability or non-liability. The jurisprudence also demonstrates, to my mind, that in the present context of retiring directors, where the critical line between a defendant being or not being

---

[67] On the no-conflicts principle and directors competing with the company see section IV of this chapter.

a director becomes hard to police, the courts have adopted pragmatic solutions based on a common-sense and merits based approach.

In my judgment, that is a sound approach, and one which reflects the equitable principles at the root of these issues. Where directors are firmly in place and dealing with their company's property, it is understandable that the courts are reluctant to enquire into questions such as whether a conflict of interest has in fact caused loss…Where, however, directors retire, the circumstances in which they do so are so various, as the cases considered above illustrate, that the courts have developed merits based solutions. At one extreme (*In Plus Group v Pyke*)[68] the defendant is director in name only. At the other extreme, the director has planned his resignation having in mind the destruction of his company or at least the exploitation of its property in the form of business opportunities in which he is currently involved (*IDC, Canaero, Simonet, British Midland Tool*). In the middle are more nuanced cases which go both ways: in *Shepherds Investments v Walters*[69] the combination of disloyalty, active promotion of the planned business, and exploitation of a business opportunity, all while the directors remained in office, brought liability; in *Umunna, Balston,* and *Framlington,* however, where the resignations were unaccompanied by disloyalty, there was no liability.

…

All that Mr Bryant did was to agree to be retained by Alliance after his resignation became effective. He did nothing more. His resignation was not planned with an ulterior motive. He did not seek employment, or a retainer, or any business from Alliance. It was offered to him, it might be said pressed upon him. It seems to me that in his situation, where his resignation had already been tendered and was irrevocable, his acceptance of [Alliance's] proposal was no different from (at worst) setting in train preparations for potential competition after his resignation had become fully effective and he had ceased any relationship or employment with the company. On all the authorities, that would not have been enough to render him liable to account. He did not seek any particular business with Alliance. It was left to Alliance to decide what it might offer him. The financial proposal which he accepted was neutral as to any particular projects on which he might work, so that he would receive the same income whatever work he was given, even if he was given no work at all. The judge found as a fact that he did not seek to divert to himself any maturing business opportunity or even a possible business opportunity. It was rather a customer-led initiative to find a solution to the problem caused to that customer by the departure of the Bryants from the company.

Moreover, in considering the claim for loss and damage, the judge was unable to identify any existing projects which had actually been subsequently transferred to Mr Bryant or his new company…Therefore the resignation was innocent of any disloyalty or conflict of interest; the acceptance of an offer of future employment was likewise innocent; and there is no finding of any property or maturing business opportunity taken or exploited by Mr Bryant.

Interestingly, although the Court of Appeal cites the majority of the authorities that we have covered in this chapter—both pre- and post-resignation cases—the court does not cite Jonathan Parker LJ's judgment in *Bhullar* and does not apparently share his scepticism about approaching opportunities regulation through a proprietary framework. Indeed the court cites with approval several of the maturing business opportunity cases. Nevertheless, if we look closer at the Court of Appeal's judgment we see that it steps towards and then away from the maturing business opportunity approach. The court accepts the increased flexibility that is contained within, and which was the original objective of, the maturing business opportunity approach. The court explicitly holds

[68] *In Plus Group Ltd v Pyke* [2002] EWCA Civ 370 where the court held that as the director had been effectively excluded from performing his role as a director his duty had been effectively reduced to 'vanishing point'.
[69] [2006] EWHC 836.

that the strict approach in *Regal (Hastings)* does not 'inexorably' apply 'in this [resignation] context'.

However, although the Court of Appeal accepts the maturing business opportunity approach, it does not view the maturing business opportunity approach as the sole touchstone of liability in a former director context. If a former director resigns in order to take a maturing business opportunity that the company was actively pursuing then the Court of Appeal in *Foster Bryant* would hold the director liable to account. However, Rix LJ finds 'it difficult to accurately encapsulate the circumstances in which a retiring director may or may not be found to have breached his fiduciary duty'. That is, he is unwilling to reduce the equitable principle in a resignation context to the maturing business opportunity approach. Rather he approves of a 'common sense and merits based approach' of which, it can be implied, the maturing business opportunity approach is just one example. What is central for Rix LJ is the fact of disloyalty which the court must assess. In the application of the law to the facts in this case you will note that Rix LJ observed that 'the judge found as a fact that he did not seek to divert to himself any maturing business opportunity or even a possible business opportunity'. We may read from this that a disloyal former director may find himself liable to account in relation to potential as well as maturing business opportunities exploited after the resignation. In this regard, the decision ends up being closer to *IDC v Cooley* than *CMS Dolphin*.

III THE COMPANIES ACT 2006

The rules codifying common law opportunities regulation are set out in section 170(2) and section 175 of the Companies Act 2006. Section 176 deals with a specific case of bribes, however, as we shall see, some commentators, wrongly in the opinion of this author, have argued that section 176 codified the no-profit rule. Accordingly, in this section we will also consider section 176.

■ Section 170(2) CA 2006 Scope and nature of general duties

(2) A person who ceases to be a director continues to be subject—

  (a) to the duty in section 175 (duty to avoid conflicts of interest) as regards the exploitation of any property, information or opportunity of which he became aware at a time when he was a director, and

  (b) to the duty in section 176 (duty not to accept benefits from third parties) as regards things done or omitted by him before he ceased to be a director.

To that extent those duties apply to a former director as to a director, subject to any necessary adaptations.

■ Section 175 CA 2006 Duty to avoid conflicts of interest

(1) A director of a company must avoid a situation in which he has, or can have, a direct or indirect interest that conflicts, or possibly may conflict, with the interests of the company.

(2) This applies in particular to the exploitation of any property, information or opportunity (and it is immaterial whether the company could take advantage of the property, information or opportunity).

(3) This duty does not apply to a conflict of interest arising in relation to a transaction or arrangement with the company.

(4) This duty is not infringed—

(a) if the situation cannot reasonably be regarded as likely to give rise to a conflict of interest; or

(b) if the matter has been authorised by the directors.

(5) Authorisation may be given by the directors—

(a) where the company is a private company and nothing in the company's constitution invalidates such authorisation, by the matter being proposed to and authorised by the directors; or

(b) where the company is a public company and its constitution includes provision enabling the directors to authorise the matter, by the matter being proposed to and authorised by them in accordance with the constitution.

(6) The authorisation is effective only if—

(a) any requirement as to the quorum at the meeting at which the matter is considered is met without counting the director in question or any other interested director, and

(b) the matter was agreed to without their voting or would have been agreed to if their votes had not been counted.

(7) Any reference in this section to a conflict of interest includes a conflict of interest and duty and a conflict of duties.

■ Section 176 CA 2006 Duty not to accept benefits from third parties

(1) A director of a company must not accept a benefit from a third party conferred by reason of—

(a) his being a director, or

(b) his doing (or not doing) anything as director.

(2) A 'third party' means a person other than the company, an associated body corporate or a person acting on behalf of the company or an associated body corporate.

(3) Benefits received by a director from a person by whom his services (as a director or otherwise) are provided to the company are not regarded as conferred by a third party.

(4) This duty is not infringed if the acceptance of the benefit cannot reasonably be regarded as likely to give rise to a conflict of interest.

(5) Any reference in this section to a conflict of interest includes a conflict of interest and duty and a conflict of duties.

1 Section 175(1)

It is worth reminding ourselves that section 170 of the Act states that the duties set out in the Act are based upon and should be interpreted in accordance with the pre-existing common law. Nowhere in the statement of directors' duties is this clearer than in section 175(1). You will recall Lord Cranworth's statement of the no-conflicts principle in *Aberdeen Railway v Blaikie*, that no one having 'duties to discharge shall be allowed to enter into engagements in which he has or can have a personal interest conflicting or which possibly may conflict with the interests of those whom he is bound to protect'. The Act restates that principle almost word for word but applies it specifically to the use of company property, information, and opportunities. Section 175 *does not* apply to self-dealing transactions, the regulation of which was addressed in the previous chapter.[70] The only change of note in the wording of section 175(1) as compared to the common law principle is that section 175(1) makes it clear that the duty to avoid conflicts of interest applies not only to direct conflicts but also indirect conflicts, which would cover, for example, the exploitation of opportunities by companies in which the director had a shareholding.[71]

If the Act's restatement of the no-conflicts principle had been left to section 175(1) alone, then the Act would have made no difference whatsoever to the continued application of the common law principles which we have analysed in depth in section II of this chapter, at least in regard to existing rather than former directors (on former directors see section III.6). However, there are two other provisions in the section which provide further guidance on the application of the principle, namely section 175(2) and (4)(a). These provisions require careful analysis to understand whether or not section 175 alters the common law position set out earlier.

2 Section 175(2)

Section 175(2) clarifies that the no-conflict rule applies to the exploitation of any information, property, or opportunity. The pre-2006 case law did not attempt to define a corporate opportunity to which the no-conflict rule applied. What mattered was that the director in his personal capacity engaged in business activity as a result of information about an opportunity or information which generated an opportunity—to, for example, purchase shares or real estate, or to provide a service. The Act does not alter this common law position.

As we have seen in *Regal (Hastings)* and *Boardman v Phipps* the House of Lords has steadfastly refused to allow 'capability facts'—such as financial capacity; 'the trustees would have required court approval to take the opportunity'; 'the company was deadlocked and did not wish to take any further opportunities'—to alter the determination of conflict. Section 175(2) reaffirms the court's position on capability facts: 'it is immaterial whether the company could take advantage of the property, information or opportunity'. This provision is taken, more or less verbatim, from Lord Hodson's judgment in *Boardman v Phipps*. Perhaps this drafting is a little unfortunate although literally accurate. What is intended here, as was stated in Lord Hodson's formulation, is that it is immaterial whether *or not* the company could have taken advantage of the property, information or opportunity.

This provision is clearly 'based upon' the existing law and as such it must be understood through the lens of the existing common law. Reading this provision, any uncertainty about the role of capability facts generated by the court's recent use of Lord Upjohn's test from *Boardman v Phipps* appears to be settled firmly in favour of the majority position in *Boardman*. A literal reading of the subsection would include all capability facts including not only those which we have encountered in the cases previously considered but also any absolute bars on the taking of the opportunity such as legal prohibitions. However, read in light of the case law considered earlier it applies only to those facts where the conflicted director (as director)[72] could play a role—could make a difference—in removing the factual barrier to taking the opportunity. Legal prohibitions or restrictions where the role the director could play in removing it are insignificant would not, therefore, be 'immaterial' to the conflict determination.

---

[70] Section 175(3).

[71] On the corporate veil and taking an opportunity through a corporate vehicle in which other innocent third parties participate see *CMS Dolphin Ltd v Simonet* [2001] 2 BCLC 704.

[72] Not in any other capacity, such as shareholder—see *Wilkinson v West Coast Capital* [2005] EWHC 3009 Ch, at pp 547–53.

3 Section 175(4)(a)

Section 175(4)(a) of the Act provides that 'the duty is not infringed if the situation cannot reasonably be regarded as likely to give rise to a conflict of interest'. Readers encountering this language for the first time having read the earlier discussion of the common law would readily assume that this provision gives effect to Lord Upjohn's 'real, sensible possibility of conflict test'. In fact, the Company Law Reform Bill 2005, which subsequently became the Companies Bill 2006, initially adopted part of Lord Upjohn's terminology and provided in the then clause 175(4)(a) of the Bill that the duty would not be infringed where there was 'no real possibility of a conflict of interest'. The wording was subsequently amended. Lord Goldsmith in the reading of the Bill in the House of Lords noted the following in relation to the change in wording:

■ Hansard, 6 Feb 2006: Column GC293

Lord Goldsmith, Attorney General
Following consultation, the Government…adjusted the provision that now appears in subsection (4)(a) so as not to use the version in the March 2005 White Paper which referred to there being no real possibility of a conflict of interest, but to use instead the expression, 'if the situation cannot reasonably be regarded as likely to give rise to a conflict of interest'. This introduces the concept of reasonableness which makes the situation easier from the point of view of a director and avoids a very harsh test, although it is still a heavy duty and intended to be so.

What is interesting in Lord Goldsmith's statement is the suggestion that this provision was intended 'to make the situation easier' from the point of view of the director. That is, the provision was intended to make English opportunities regulation more flexible than it was under the common law's real, sensible possibility of conflict test. Accordingly, although the 'reasonable man's view of real, sensible possibility of conflict' and 'cannot reasonably be regarded as likely to give rise to a conflict of interest' look remarkably similar, in fact the latter was intended to be more flexible than the former as applied by the courts.

The first question for us in understanding section 175(4)(a) is whether the use of this terminology is intended to render English law more flexible than had been intended by Lord Upjohn when he set out his 'real, sensible possibility of conflict test'. Clearly, the closeness of this wording to Lord Upjohn's test coupled with the parliamentary statement that would, under the rule in *Pepper v Hart*,[73] be admissible as an interpretative aid, suggests that the section 175 changes the common law position by enabling courts to take account of capability facts. But this appears wholly contrary to section 175(2).

Looking at section 175(2) and section 175(4)(a) separately it appears that section 175 effectively codifies both the majority position and the dissenting position in *Boardman v Phipps*. How can we make sense of this legislative conflict? One reading would be to argue that section 175(2) is part of the statement of the duty and, as section 175(4)(a) provides for circumstances in which 'the duty is not infringed', that section 175(2) is subject to the reasonable likelihood of conflict qualification. This would, however, be a very strained reading of the section. How can one subsection pronounce certain factors 'immaterial' only for another to qualify its immateriality and to say, in effect, that they are material if they mean that the situation cannot reasonably be regarded as likely to give rise to a conflict. Such a reading must surely be wrong. A better reading is

---

[73] *Pepper (Inspector of Taxes) v Hart* [1993] 1 All ER 42. *Pepper v Hart* allows recourse to certain parliamentary material as an interpretative aid where the legislation is 'ambiguous or obscure or the literal meaning of which leads to an absurdity'.

that because of section 175(2), section 175(4)(a) does not refer to capability facts. But if section 175(4)(a) does not refer to capability facts what situations could it refer to?

3.1 Board rejection of the opportunity

We saw in section II.3 of this chapter that there is some support based on the adoption by recent courts of Lord Upjohn's test and on dicta from Lord Russell in *Regal* for the proposition that disclosure to and board rejection of an opportunity enables a director to keep the opportunity without obtaining the required approvals and that the underlying rationale for this was that such rejection rendered the opportunity no longer of interest to the company. However, it is clear that Lord Hodson in *Boardman* viewed the approval of the trustees as immaterial to the determination of conflict and as section 175(2) codifies his view in this regard this appears to be incorrect. For Lord Hodson, ex-ante rejection of the opportunity by the board falls within the principle underpinning the 'immateriality of capability facts': the director could play a significant role in overcoming the barrier—that is, obtaining board approval. However, one could envisage a literal reading of section 175(2) that could create room for the argument that disclosure and board rejection does not fall within this sub-section and is therefore material. Section 175(2) refers to whether the company 'could' take advantage of the opportunity. This clearly covers claims relating to, for example, financial capacity. However, board rejection does not relate to whether the company 'could' take the opportunity, rather it is a statement that the company does not 'want' the opportunity. This would render section 175(2) inapplicable to this issue and leave section 175(4)(b) freer rein in this regard to say: following rejection there is no reasonable possibility of conflict. This would be a literal reading of the statute not a view that is consistent with the prior case law.

3.2 Area of business restrictions

In our analysis of the common law we have seen that there is some authority for restricting the 'company's interests' so that it does not apply to *any* profit-making opportunity but only those within its area of business or which connect to or synergize with its area of business. Although the Court of Appeal in *O'Donnell v Shanahan* has rejected this view, this chapter has argued that this holding is not consistent with prior authority. Could the additional flexibility introduced by section 175(4)(a) support this 'business area' restriction on 'company interests', moving company law away from *O'Donnell* and towards *Aas v Benham*? There is nothing in the legislative record to suggest that this was intended by section 175(4)(a); however, one might argue that the increased flexibility suggested by the provision may embolden the courts to specify such restrictions on the concept of company interest for the purposes of section 175.

4 Approval mechanisms under the 2006 Act

Section 175(5) provides explicitly for a board approval mechanism where there is a conflict for a private company where nothing to the contrary is set out in the articles, and for a public company where board approval is explicitly provided for in the articles. As we noted previously, at common law it was open to shareholders to provide for a board approval mechanism in any event although there remained a residue of doubt about the compliance of such terms with what is now section 232 of the 2006 Act (the prohibition on waivers and indemnities for breach of duty). The substantive effect of section 175(5) is to change the default rule for private companies (they have to opt out of board approval) but maintain the common law position for public companies (they can opt in to board approval). This inclusion of this provision in the statute also ensures that there is no longer any question that the board approval mechanism complies with section 232 of the Act. In section 175(6), the Act provides that any such board approval must be disinterested board approval at a board meeting where the meeting is quorate without having to count the presence of the interested directors.

Comparing this position with the approval rules on self-dealing, it is interesting to note that company law favours director approval in the context of opportunities but, as a result of the substantial property transaction rules and Listing Rule 11, favours shareholder approval in relation to self-dealing transactions that are non-*de minimis*. We need to ask ourselves whether this makes sense from a policy perspective. Clearly opportunities that involve a conflict and are taken personally by directors will often be worth substantially more than £100,000 (the substantial property transaction threshold). In rarer cases they could be worth millions of pounds. Why do we trust disinterested directors to make the decisions in the context of opportunities, but we do not trust them in the context of self-dealing?

5 The status of the no-profit rule

We saw in section II that there has been considerable debate about the relationship between the no-profit rule set out in *Regal* and the no-conflicts principle: is the no-profit rule a sub-rule of the no-conflicts principle, subject to its parameters of application, or an independent stand-alone rule? This book argued that the better position was the former position and the Act seems to reinforce this view.[74] It does not refer directly to the no-profit rule. This does not of course mean the no-profit rule is not applicable and the holding in *Regal* is overruled, but it does mean that if a director makes a profit by reason and in the course of his directorship he is only liable to account for that profit if in making that profit there is possible conflict between the company's and the director's interest.

Having said that there remains a new source of controversy in this regard. Some commentators[75] have suggested that section 176 amounts to the codification of the no-profit rule and, indeed, concern was expressed in this regard in legislative debates.[76] Most commentators, correctly it is submitted, view section 176 as effectively a prohibition on bribes, codifying the common law prohibition stated most recently by the Privy Council in *Attorney-General for Hong Kong v Reid*.[77] Section 176 refers to benefits received by the director from third parties by reason of him being a director or doing something as a director. In *Regal* the directors made a profit by reason of their directorship, but the benefit—selling the shares at a profit—was not conferred by the third-party purchaser by reason of them being a director; rather the third party made a payment to the owner of the shares. Also note in this regard that the Act provides explicitly for shareholder approval only, which would make little sense, as compared to section 175(5), if section 176 was intended to enact the no-profit rule, but makes more sense if the provision is simply a prohibition on bribes: directors are less likely to accept benefits that may be, or may be perceived as, bribes if they have to ask shareholders rather than directors for approval.

6 Former directors

Section 170(2) provides for an important departure for the pre-2006 common law position, which provided that the no-conflict principle no longer applied to a former director. Pursuant to this section the duty to avoid conflicts of interest continues to

---

[74] Taking the Act into account and confirming this view see *Towers v Premier Waste Management Ltd* [2011] EWCA Civ 923 at [48] (*per* Mummery LJ): 'the applicable duties are of a director's loyalty to the Company and the duty to observe the no conflict principle, which embrace a duty not to make a secret profit for himself.'

[75] See *Oxford Annotated Companies Acts* (OUP, 2007), 10–36.

[76] *Per* Lord Wedderburn, Hansard, 9 February 2006, col GC332.   [77] [1994] 1 All ER 1.

apply to a former director as regards information, opportunity and property which he became aware of whilst he was a director. The subsection provides that sections 175 and 176 apply to the former directors 'subject to the necessary adaptations'. Such adaptations refer only to replacing 'director' with 'former director' where necessary.

The question for us is, how does this change the common law position identified earlier? One could argue that the maturing business opportunity test is the extension of the duty of loyalty to post-resignation problems. From this viewpoint, the maturing business opportunity test is the common law application of the no-conflicts rule. However, the maturing business opportunity approach adopted a different (proprietary lens) which was a function of the fact that the fiduciary relationship—and therefore the application of the no-conflicts principle—was understood to have come to an end. Accordingly, it would seem very difficult to argue that the maturing business opportunity test implemented the no-conflicts rule. However, at the time of writing the only case to address this issue has held that as section 175 is based on the prior common law position that the maturing business opportunity test, as modified by *Foster Bryant*, continues to apply.[78] For the reasons already mentioned, whether this is correct and will be applied by other courts remains subject to some doubt.

If the maturing business opportunity test is no longer applicable then what would an approach to post-resignation cases through the no-conflicts lens look like? The only pre-2006 case to address a resignation opportunities problem through the lens of the no-conflict approach was *IDC v Cooley*. It would seem, therefore, that if the common law is to guide us in our understanding of the codification of directors' duties that *IDC v Cooley* has to be the primary reference point for understanding the extension of the no-conflicts rule to former directors. In which case, as already noted, the rule would allow a former director to exploit an opportunity—whether discovered in business hours or private time—only if: the opportunity is disclosed to the board in full prior to resignation; no steps were taken prior to resignation to position the director to personally exploit the opportunity; *and* the reason the director resigned was not to personally exploit the opportunity or he was dismissed (without having procured his dismissal).

IV DIRECTORS COMPETING WITH THE COMPANY AND HOLDING DIRECTORSHIPS IN COMPETING COMPANIES

If a director of Company A decided to form Company B, of which he was the 100% shareholder, and which he intended to compete in the same industry as Company A, would he be placed in a position where his personal interests conflicted, or possibly conflicted, with those of Company A? As Company B would be pursuing the same customers, employees and opportunities as Company A the answer to this question must be 'yes': his personal interests are in Company B taking market share from Company A, which is clearly contrary to Company A's interests. As there is a conflict then one would expect that authorization would be required through the appropriate mechanism as per section 175(5) and (6) of the 2006 Act. If a non-executive director of Company A decided to serve as a non-executive director on the board of Company C, a direct competitor company, would the director's personal interests conflict with the interests of either Companies A or C? If the director's knowledge gained as a director of Company A about the market, customers, suppliers etc., is used to benefit Company C, as the director receives remuneration for providing his services to C—and as his position

---

[78] *Thermascan Limited v Norman* [2009] EWHC 3694 (Ch) at [14] where *per* David Donaldson QC 'the parties agreed that these provisions of the Companies Act 2006 do not alter the pre-existing law, which...was...discussed most recently in *Foster Bryant Surveying Ltd v Bryant*'.

and remuneration may be enhanced by using that information to C's benefit—again the answer must be 'yes': using this knowledge to C's benefit is in his personal interests but contrary to Company A's interests. His gain, however, in such circumstances as a result of this breach of duty may be extremely difficult to quantify as not all his remuneration is a function of the breach. To avoid any breach of duty to either company such a director must be scrupulous in avoiding any such use of knowledge without first obtaining the requisite authorization from the company where the knowledge was acquired. It also seems clear that for a director holding directorships in direct competitors, even setting to one side the problem of knowledge acquisition referred to in the previous example, there will arise many situations in which it is impossible to act in ways that are loyal to both companies: could the director play an active role for both companies A and C in attempting to obtain business from Customer D? Accordingly, taking directorships in competing businesses may involve not only a conflict of interests but also a conflict of the duties owed to both companies.

The examples and analysis set out in this chapter suggest that competing with the company is highly likely to involve a breach of duty. It is perhaps odd, therefore, that the common law position, until recent clarification, suggested that competing with the company or holding directorships in competing companies did not involve a breach of duty. The law is usefully summarized and clarified by Brooke LJ and Sedley LJ in *Plus Group Ltd v Pyke*, a case which involved a director of the company setting up a competing business where, following an illness, he had been effectively excluded by his fellow director from playing any role in the company.

■ *Plus Group Ltd v Pyke* [2002] EWCA Civ 370

Brooke LJ

There is no completely rigid rule that a director may not be involved in the business of a company which is in competition with another company of which he was a director. A rather startling illustration of this proposition can be seen in the case of *London and Mashonaland Exploration Co Ltd v New Mashonaland Exploration Co Ltd* [1891] WN 165. Lord Mayo was a director and chairman of the board of directors of the first company which was incorporated for the purpose which its name suggests. He never in fact acted as a director, or attended a board meeting, or agreed, either expressly or in the articles of association, not to become a director of any similar company. Four months later the second company was formed for the same purpose. The first company had had some success with a share prospectus advertising Lord Mayo's name as director and chairman, and it took umbrage when it saw its rival's prospectus with Lord Mayo's name at the head of its list of directors.

After summarising the facts, and adding that there was no contract, express or implied, obliging Lord Mayo to give his personal services to the plaintiff company and not to another company, Chitty J dismissed the plaintiffs' application for an injunction. He said that no case had been made out that Lord Mayo was about to disclose to the defendants any information that he had obtained confidentially in his character of chairman, and that an analogy sought to be drawn between the present case and partnership was incomplete.

This decision was applied with approval by Lord Blanesburgh in *Bell v Lever Brothers Ltd* [1932] AC 161, at p 193-6. He distinguished between contracts in which the director's own company was concerned and contracts by which the director was bound to some outside party. In relation to the latter class of contract he said that the company had no concern in the director's profit, and could not make him accountable for it unless it appeared—and this was the essential qualification—that in earning that profit he had made use either of the company's property or of some confidential information which had come to him as director of the company.

I have read in draft the judgment of Sedley LJ, and I need not repeat his description of the unease with which some modern text book writers have viewed the *Mashonaland* case.

Sedley LJ

London & Mashonaland Exploration Co Ltd v New Mashonaland Exploration Co Ltd., in its solitary briefly reported form [1891] WN 165, establishes that there is nothing inherently objectionable in the position of a company director (and chairman) who, without breaching any express restrictive agreement or disclosing any confidential information, becomes engaged, whether personally or as a director of another company, in the same line of business. The extempore judgment of Chitty J on what appears to have been an interlocutory motion for injunctive relief, was given the imprimatur of the House of Lords by Lord Blanesburgh in *Bell v Lever Brothers* [1932] AC 161, 195. The case had not, according to the report, been referred to by counsel on either side in argument; but Lord Blanesburgh, with whom Lord Atkin and Lord Thankerton agreed, explicitly endorsed the principle set out by Chitty J. This, therefore, is the law which binds us…

The problem is obvious if one thinks of how shareholders in X Ltd or X Plc, or for that matter its creditors, would regard a director who used his boardroom vote, perhaps crucially, in a way which helped a competitor, when the competitor was the director himself or another company of which he was also a director. Whatever the perceived commercial morality of such a situation, I do not consider that it is sanctioned by law. The fiduciary duty of a director to his company is uniform and universal. What vary infinitely are the elements of fact and degree which determine whether the duty has been breached. If Mr Pyke's solicitors' view of the law is as widely held as it seems to be, it needs to be revised. They wrote this:

'The authorities are quite clear that it is no breach of any fiduciary duty to be involved with a business either of the same kind or in competition with the company of which he is a director.'

Counsel have put before us what…leading modern textbooks say about this received view of the law. The authors' and editors' views range from the dubious to the sceptical…

Palmer's *Company Law*, para 8.534, says:

'The no-conflict rule might also be thought to prohibit a person from being a director of competing companies, but it is unclear whether this is in fact the law. In *London and Mashonaland Exploration Co v New Mashonaland Corporation Co* Chitty J refused to restrain a dummy director who had never acted as a director or attended a board meeting of the plaintiff company from acting as director of the competing defendant company. This decision was taken by Lord Blanesburgh LC in *Bell v Lever Bros Ltd,.* as authority for a dictum that a director is generally free to be director of a competing company. In *Scottish Co-operative Wholesale Society Ltd v Meyer*, however, Lord Denning thought that the directors of the textile company were in breach of duty by continuing their association with the co-operative society when that society set up its own rayon department. This latter view is more in line with the principle applied to employees (including senior managers holding full-time service contracts) and trustees proper.'

Gower's *Company Law*, 6th Edition, says at p 622:

'Competing with the company. One of the most obvious examples of a situation which might be expected to give rise to a conflict between a *director's* interests and his duties is where he carries on or is associated with a business competing with that of the company. Certainly a fiduciary without the consent of his beneficiaries is normally strictly precluded from competing with them and this is specifically stated in the analogous field of partnership law. Yet, strangely, it is by no means clear on the existing case law that a similar rule applies to directors of a company. Indeed, it is generally stated that it does not, and there appears to be a definite, if inadequately reported, decision that a director cannot be restrained from acting as a director of a rival company. And it has been said that "What he could do for a rival company he could, of course, do for himself." This view is becoming increasingly difficult to support. It has been held that the duty of fidelity flowing from the relationship of master and servant may preclude the servant from engaging, even in his spare time, in work for a competitor, notwithstanding that the servant's duty of fidelity imposes lesser obligations than the full duty of good faith owed by a director or other fiduciary agent. How, then, can it be that a director can compete whereas a subordinate employee cannot? Moreover it has been recognised that one who is a director of two rival concerns is walking a tight-rope and at risk if he fails to deal fairly with both.

In arguing that a director who carries on a business which competes with that of his company inevitably places himself in a position where his personal interest will conflict with his duty to the company, it is not being contended that he will necessarily have breached his fiduciary duty; he will not if the company has consented so long as he observes his subjective duty to the company by subordinating his interests to those of the company. Nor is it being suggested that there is anything objectionable in his holding other directorships so long as all the companies have consented if their businesses compete. But in both cases consent is unlikely if he is a full-time executive director or if the extent of the competition is substantial. And even if the consent is given the director is likely to be faced with constant difficulties in avoiding breaches of his subjective duty of good faith to the company or companies concerned. He may be able to subordinate his personal interests to those of a single company but it is less easy to reconcile conflicting duties to more than one company. Nor would a reformed rule be inconsistent with the modern emphasis on a more important role for non-executive directors, who are often executive directors of other companies. Even if executive directors are regarded as a good source of non-executive talent for other companies (which some would question), a reformed rule would simply require executive directors not to become non-executive or *competing* companies, which they are, in fact, rarely asked to become.'

If one bears in mind the high standard of probity which equity demands of fiduciaries, and the reliance which shareholders and creditors are entitled to place upon it, the *Mashonaland* principle is a very limited one. If, for example, the two Mashonaland Exploration companies had been preparing to tender for the same contract, I doubt whether Lord Mayo's position would have been tenable, at least in the absence of special arrangements to insulate either company from the conflict of his interests and duties, for I see no reason why the law should assume that any directorship is merely cosmetic. A directorship brings with it not only voting rights and emoluments but responsibilities of stewardship and honesty, and those who cannot discharge them should not become or remain directors.

All the foregoing concerns breach of fiduciary duty. From such a breach, appropriate remedies will follow. But both common sense and equity indicate that it is not necessary to wait for a breach giving rise to a remedy before the possibility of intervention arises.

The *London & Mashonaland* case and its affirmation by the House of Lords in *Bell v Lever Brothers* provides long-standing authority that it is possible for a director to compete with the company without being in breach of his fiduciary duty to avoid a conflict, or possible conflict, of interests. Sedley LJ, whilst recognizing that the court is bound by higher authority, is clearly very sceptical of the appropriateness of this position for a contemporary commercial setting. Accordingly, he narrowly construes the position in *London & Mashonaland*. In Sedley LJ's view whilst the law does not impose an automatic bar on competing with the company or the taking of directorships in competing companies it will swiftly intervene to prohibit the director from acting where it is impossible to act for the benefit of one company without breaching his duty to the other company, *unless* the director has obtained the requisite approvals pursuant to section 175(5) and (6). Accordingly, any director who finds himself a director of two competing companies and has not obtained the requisite approvals will find, in order to comply with his duties to either company, that he will continually need to recuse himself from acting for either company. This could disable him from acting effectively as a director at all for either company.

Section 175 does not alter the position set out in *Plus Group Ltd*, although section 175 clarifies the duty's application to the competing directorships problem by providing in section 175(7) that the reference to conflict of interest includes a conflict of duties.

V STRICTNESS VERSUS FLEXIBILITY IN US COMPARATIVE PERSPECTIVE

In our journey through the rather difficult terrain of English company law's regulation of the taking of corporate opportunities by directors in their personal capacity we have seen that English law takes a rather strict approach, which means that many opportunities which a director identifies cannot be exploited by him without the consent of the company. There is strong authority for the position that the company's interests are not limited to the company's existing business areas but apply to any profit-making opportunity. Furthermore, in large part, English company law has rejected attempts to rely on capability facts which, if true, qualify the reality of conflict.

We have seen two rationales to support both the rejection of the relevance of these facts and of the resulting focus on the possibility of conflict rather than of actual conflict. The first is a deterrence rationale: a broad rule preventing directors from making arguments about the reality of conflict may result in some instances in unfairness to individual directors but—from the broader perspective of ensuring that fiduciary obligations are not compromised—it decreases the likelihood that bad directors will 'chance their hand' and take an opportunity for themselves. The second rationale, which is related to the deterrence rationale, is the courts' long-standing concern about their ability to assess capability facts when much of the information needed to assess them may be in the control of the conflicted director and where other evidence may have been 'infected' by the conflicted director. These rationales continue to attract much support amongst commentators on opportunities regulation. Consider, for example, the following extract.

■ **R. Flanigan, 'The Strict Character of the Duty of Loyalty' (2006)**
New Zealand Law Review **209**

Abandoning the strict ethic...amounts to a decision to allow bargaining with a judge after the fact if a conflict or benefit is eventually discovered. The effect of a strict liability, in contrast, is to force bargaining with the relevant party (principal, settlor, employer) up front so the parties themselves will reach consensus and thereby avoid any issue over the propriety of the benefit. We can very well see what will happen if the liability is stripped of its strict quality. It will become apparent to fiduciaries that they will be better off taking a benefit without consent whenever they are uncertain that consent will be forthcoming. They may first conclude that it is unlikely the benefit will be detected. They may also conclude that they will have opportunities to affect the probability of that detection. Even if detection is likely, they will conclude that they remain better off with litigation. The settlement process may well leave them with a portion of the profit. If they eventually do appear before a judge, the issue will be whether it is reasonable in the circumstances for the fiduciary to retain the benefit. At that point, any manipulations or fabrications of the fiduciary will have their intended effect. The 'circumstances' will have the colouration the fiduciary arranged. Further, the fiduciary can appeal to what is 'fair'. Where, for example, there would be a windfall to the beneficiary, a judge might be inclined to allow the fiduciary to share in the benefit. Or where an opportunity was developed by the fiduciary, a judge may again think it fair to compensate that effort. Overall then, the effect will be to increase the probability that fiduciaries will act with conflicts and extract unauthorised gains. That will generally compromise or impair commitment [on the part of fiduciaries].[79]

---

[79] See also P. Koh, 'Once a Director, Always a Fiduciary' (2003) 62 *CLJ* 403 in support of a strict approach.

Whilst it is correct to view the UK approach to opportunities regulation as strict, we have also seen that UK company law has in several respects slightly softened its strict edges: not all capability facts are immaterial; and in the context of resignation the courts have been more flexible and pragmatic in several respects. UK law is strict but it certainly provides a nod in the direction of flexibility. Nevertheless, many commentators remain very critical of the strictness of the conflicts rule. They argue that the strict approach may discourage directors with an entrepreneurial frame of mind from becoming directors in the first place and that it may mean that certain opportunities get 'left on the shelf' unexploited by either the director in his personal capacity or the company. If this claim is correct then the economy as a whole is damaged by strict opportunities regulation. For these commentators, UK law's strict approach as applied to directors is a hangover from eighteenth and nineteenth century trust law that is inapt for a modern commercial world. For these commentators the existence of a much more flexible approach to opportunities regulation in Delaware provides the UK with at least proof that more flexible regulation can work and, at best, with a model for reform. Consider, for example, Professors Lowry and Edmunds' view:[80]

> The challenge is therefore how best to achieve the optimum balance between corporate entrepreneurialism on the one hand, and strict rules of protection on the other. It is our contention that the pragmatic flexibility inherent in the Delaware Supreme Court's approach to determining liability is facilitative. It is therefore better than its English law counterpart at holding the most appropriate balance between deterring directorial abuse and promoting the prevailing enterprise culture.

In this regard, consider the following extract from one of the Delaware cases on which Lowry and Edmunds rely.

■ *Broz v Cellular Information Systems* 673 A 2d 148 (Del 1996)

Broz was president and sole shareholder of RFB Cellular, Inc ('RFB'), a corporation providing cellular telephone services in the midwestern United States. He was also a non-executive director of Cellular Information Systems, Inc ('CIS'), a competitor of RFB. CIS was a distressed company, which had recently emerged from Chapter 11 bankruptcy[81] and, in order to raise finance, had embarked on a programme of selling its existing cellular licences. In his capacity as president of RFB, in May of 1994, Broz was approached by a firm called Mackinac with regard to the sale by Mackinac of a cellular licence in Michigan (referred to in the case as 'Michigan-2'). CIS was not approached by Mackinac in this regard. Broz took informal soundings from several members of CIS's board, including the chief executive officer, to find out whether CIS would have an interest in the purchase of the licence. He was informed that it would not. Ultimately, all members of the CIS board testified that *had* they been asked they would have expressed no interest in the transaction.

---

[80] J. Lowry and R. Edmunds, 'The Corporate Opportunity Doctrine: The Shifting Boundaries of the Duty and its Remedies' (1998) 61 *Modern Law Review* 515. See also G. Jones, 'Unjust Enrichment and the Fiduciary's Duty of Loyalty' (1968) 84 *LQR* 472; J. Lowry and R. Edmunds, 'The No-Conflict–No-Profit Rules and the Corporate Fiduciary: Challenging the Orthodoxy of Absolutism' (2000) *JBL* 122; J. Langbein, 'Questioning the Trust Law Duty of Loyalty: Sole Interest or Best Interest?' (2005) 114 *Yale Law Journal* 929.

[81] Chapter 11 bankruptcy is a board-controlled bankruptcy proceeding that enables the company's management to stay in control of the company whilst the company's debt is reorganized (Chapter 11 US Bankruptcy Code).

At the same time CIS was also negotiating with a competitor of CIS and RFB, PriCellular Commications, Inc ('PriCellular'), initially to sell certain of its licences to PriCellular and then, by June of 1994, to sell all of the CIS stock to a PriCellular acquisition vehicle. On 2 August 1994 PriCellular commenced a **tender offer** for all outstanding CIS shares having obtained sale undertakings from the directors in relation to their shares in late June of 1994.

Broz submitted an offer for the Michigan-2 licence in early August 1994, at which time PriCellular was also negotiating an option to purchase the same Michigan-2 cellular licence from Mackinac. Indeed in late September 1994, PriCellular reached an agreement on an option to purchase the licence. This option, however, provided a termination right if any third party exceeded the $6.7 million exercise price by at least $500,000. RFB outbid PriCellular and purchased the licence for $7.2 million on 14 November 1994.

PriCellular completed its tender offer for CIS nine days later, the closing having being delayed due to PriCellular's financing difficulties. Under new management, CIS brought an action against Broz claiming that in purchasing the cellular licence through RFB he had usurped an opportunity properly belonging to CIS.

Chief Justice Veasey

The doctrine of corporate opportunity represents but one species of the broad fiduciary duties assumed by a corporate director or officer. A corporate fiduciary agrees to place the interests of the corporation before his or her own in appropriate circumstances. In light of the diverse and often competing obligations faced by directors and officers, however, the corporate opportunity doctrine arose as a means of defining the parameters of fiduciary duty in instances of potential conflict. The classic statement of the doctrine is derived from the venerable case of *Guth v. Loft, Inc.*

The corporate opportunity doctrine, as delineated by *Guth* and its progeny, holds that a corporate officer or director may not take a business opportunity for his own if: (1) the corporation is financially able to exploit the opportunity; (2) the opportunity is within the corporation's line of business; (3) the corporation has an interest or expectancy in the opportunity; and (4) by taking the opportunity for his own, the corporate fiduciary will thereby be placed in a position inimicable to his duties to the corporation. The Court in *Guth* also derived a corollary which states that a director or officer *may* take a corporate opportunity if: (1) the opportunity is presented to the director or officer in his individual and not his corporate capacity; (2) the opportunity is not essential to the corporation; (3) the corporation holds no interest or expectancy in the opportunity; and (4) the director or officer has not wrongfully employed the resources of the corporation in pursuing or exploiting the opportunity.

Thus, the contours of this doctrine are well established. It is important to note, however, that the tests enunciated in *Guth* and subsequent cases provide guidelines to be considered by a reviewing court in balancing the equities of an individual case. No one factor is dispositive and all factors must be taken into account insofar as they are applicable. Cases involving a claim of usurpation of a corporate opportunity range over a multitude of factual settings. Hard and fast rules are not easily crafted to deal with such an array of complex situations. As this Court noted in *Johnston v. Greene*, Del.Supr., 121 A.2d 919 (1956), the determination of '[w]hether or not a director has appropriated for himself something that in fairness should belong to the corporation is a factual question to be decided by reasonable inference from objective facts.' (quoting *Guth*). In the instant case, we find that the facts do not support the conclusion that Broz misappropriated a corporate opportunity.

We note at the outset that Broz became aware of the Michigan-2 opportunity in his individual and not his corporate capacity. As the Court of Chancery found, 'Broz did not misuse proprietary information that came to him in a corporate capacity nor did he otherwise use any power he might have over the governance of the corporation to advance his own interests.' This fact is not the subject of serious dispute. In fact, it is clear from the record that Mackinac did not consider CIS a viable candidate for the acquisition of Michigan-2. Accordingly, Mackinac did not offer the property to CIS…The burden imposed upon Broz to show adherence to his fiduciary duties to CIS is thus lessened to some extent…Nevertheless, this fact is not dispositive. The determination of whether a particular fiduciary has usurped a corporate opportunity necessitates a careful examination of the circumstances, giving due credence to the factors enunciated in *Guth* and subsequent cases.

We turn now to an analysis of the factors relied on by the trial court. First, we find that CIS was not financially capable of exploiting the Michigan-2 opportunity. Although the Court of Chancery concluded otherwise, we hold that this finding was not supported by the evidence. The record shows that CIS was in a precarious financial position at the time Mackinac presented the Michigan-2 opportunity to Broz. Having recently emerged from lengthy and contentious bankruptcy proceedings, CIS was not in a position to commit capital to the acquisition of new assets. Further, the loan agreement entered into by CIS and its creditors severely limited the discretion of CIS as to the acquisition of new assets and substantially restricted the ability of CIS to incur new debt.

The Court of Chancery based its contrary finding on the fact that PriCellular had purchased an option to acquire CIS' bank debt. Thus, the court reasoned, PriCellular was in a position to exercise that option and then waive any unfavorable restrictions that would stand in the way of a CIS acquisition of Michigan-2. The trial court, however, disregarded the fact that PriCellular's own financial situation was not particularly stable. PriCellular was unable to finance the acquisition of CIS through conventional bank loans and was forced to use the more risky mechanism of a junk bond offering to raise the required capital. Thus, the court's statement that 'PriCellular had other sources of financing to permit the funding of that purchase' is clearly not free from dispute. Moreover, as discussed *infra*, the fact that PriCellular had available sources of financing is immaterial to the analysis. At the time that Broz was required to decide whether to accept the Michigan-2 opportunity, PriCellular had not yet acquired CIS, and any plans to do so were wholly speculative. Thus, contrary to the Court of Chancery's finding, Broz was not obligated to consider the contingency of a PriCellular acquisition of CIS and the related contingency of PriCellular thereafter waiving restrictions on the CIS bank debt. Broz was required to consider the facts only as they existed at the time he determined to accept the Mackinac offer and embark on his efforts to bring the transaction to fruition.

Second, while it may be said with some certainty that the Michigan-2 opportunity was within CIS' line of business, it is not equally clear that CIS had a cognizable interest or expectancy in the license.[82] Under the third factor laid down by this Court in *Guth*, for an opportunity to be deemed to belong to the fiduciary's corporation, the corporation must have an interest or expectancy in that opportunity. As this Court stated in *Johnston* '[f]or the corporation to have an actual or expectant interest in any specific property, there must be *some tie* between that property and the nature of the corporate business'. [Emphasis added] Despite the fact that the nature of the Michigan-2 opportunity was historically close to the core operations of CIS, changes were in process. At the time the opportunity was presented, CIS was actively engaged in the process of divesting its cellular license holdings. CIS' articulated business plan did not involve any new acquisitions.[83] Further, as indicated by the testimony of the entire CIS board, the Michigan-2

---

[82] The court noted in this regard: 'The language in the *Guth* opinion relating to "line of business" is less than clear: "Where a corporation is engaged in a certain business, and an opportunity is presented to it embracing an activity as to which it has fundamental knowledge, practical experience and *ability to pursue,* which, logically and naturally, is adaptable to its business *having regard for its financial position,* and *is consonant with its reasonable needs and aspirations for expansion,* it may properly be said that the opportunity is within the corporation's line of business."'

[83] The court noted in this regard: 'At trial, each of the members of the CIS board testified to his belief that CIS would not have been interested in the Michigan-2 opportunity at the time it was presented to Broz. The Court of Chancery chose to disregard this testimony, holding that "the after the fact testimony of directors to the effect that they would not have been interested in pursuing this transaction had

license would not have been of interest to CIS even absent CIS' financial difficulties and CIS' then current desire to liquidate its cellular license holdings. Thus, CIS had no interest or expectancy in the Michigan-2 opportunity...

Therefore, the totality of the circumstances indicates that Broz did not usurp an opportunity that properly belonged to CIS.

Presentation to the Board:

In concluding that Broz had usurped a corporate opportunity, the Court of Chancery placed great emphasis on the fact that Broz had not formally presented the matter to the CIS board. The court held that 'in such circumstances as existed at the latest after October 14, 1994 (date of PriCellular's option contract on Michigan 2 RSA) it was the obligation of Mr. Broz as a director of CIS to take the transaction to the CIS board for its formal action...' In so holding, the trial court erroneously grafted a new requirement onto the law of corporate opportunity, viz., the requirement of formal presentation under circumstances where the corporation does not have an interest, expectancy or financial ability.

The teaching of *Guth* and its progeny is that the director or officer must analyze the situation *ex ante* to determine whether the opportunity is one rightfully belonging to the corporation. If the director or officer believes, based on one of the factors articulated above, that the corporation is not entitled to the opportunity, then he may take it for himself. Of course, presenting the opportunity to the board creates a kind of 'safe harbor' for the director, which removes the specter of a *post hoc* judicial determination that the director or officer has improperly usurped a corporate opportunity. Thus, presentation avoids the possibility that an error in the fiduciary's assessment of the situation will create future liability for breach of fiduciary duty. It is not the law of Delaware that presentation to the board is a necessary prerequisite to a finding that a corporate opportunity has not been usurped.

Thus, we hold that Broz was not required to make formal presentation of the Michigan-2 opportunity to the CIS board prior to taking the opportunity for his own. In so holding, we necessarily conclude that the Court of Chancery erred in grafting the additional requirement of formal presentation onto Delaware's corporate opportunity jurisprudence...

Alignment of Interests Between CIS and PriCellular

In concluding that Broz usurped an opportunity properly belonging to CIS, the Court of Chancery held that '[f]or practical business reasons CIS' interests with respect to the Mackinac transaction came to merge with those of PriCellular, even before the closing of its tender offer for CIS stock.' Based on this fact, the trial court concluded that Broz was required to consider PriCellular's prospective, post-acquisition plans for CIS in determining whether to forego the opportunity or seize it for himself. Had Broz done this, the Court of Chancery determined that he would have concluded that CIS was entitled to the opportunity by virtue of the alignment of its interests with those of PriCellular.

We disagree. Broz was under no duty to consider the interests of PriCellular when he chose to purchase Michigan-2. As stated in *Guth*, a director's right to 'appropriate [an]...opportunity depends on the circumstances existing at the time it presented itself to him without regard to subsequent events.' At the time Broz purchased Michigan-2, PriCellular had not yet acquired CIS. Any plans to do so would still have been wholly speculative. Accordingly, Broz was not required to consider the contingent and uncertain plans of PriCellular in reaching his determination of how to proceed.

---

it been brought to the board, is not helpful to the defendant, in my opinion, because most of them did not know at that time of PriCellular's interest in the property and how it related to PriCellular's plan for CIS." We disagree with the court's assessment...The Court of Chancery also held that "this sort of after the fact testimony is a very thin substitute for an informed board decision made at a meeting in "real time" (*i.e.*, while the opportunity to act with effect continues). *Id.* While it is true that contemporaneous decision-making or unanimous written consent is required for board action, in our view, this testimony of the CIS board was probative and should not have been wholly discounted.'

Whether or not the CIS board would, at some time, have chosen to acquire Michigan-2 in order to make CIS a more attractive acquisition target for PriCellular or to enhance the synergy of any combined enterprise, is speculative. The trial court found this to be a plausible scenario and therefore found that, pursuant to the factors laid down in *Guth*, CIS had a valid interest or expectancy in the license. This speculative finding cuts against the statements made by CIS' Chief Executive and the entire CIS board of directors and ignores the fact that CIS still lacked the wherewithal to acquire Michigan-2, even if one takes into account the possible availability of PriCellular's financing. Thus, the fact of PriCellular's plans to acquire CIS is immaterial and does not change the analysis…

Conclusion

The corporate opportunity doctrine represents a judicially crafted effort to harmonize the competing demands placed on corporate fiduciaries in a modern business environment. The doctrine seeks to reduce the possibility of conflict between a director's duties to the corporation and interests unrelated to that role. In the instant case, Broz adhered to his obligations to CIS. We hold that the Court of Chancery erred as a matter of law in concluding that Broz had a duty formally to present the Michigan-2 opportunity to the CIS board. We also hold that the trial court erred in its application of the corporate opportunity doctrine under the unusual facts of this case, where CIS had no interest or financial ability to acquire the opportunity, but the impending acquisition of CIS by PriCellular would or could have caused a change in those circumstances.

The Delaware courts adopt a proprietary approach to corporate opportunities. Whilst the corporate opportunities doctrine is viewed as the product of the duty of loyalty and is, therefore, concerned with conflicts of interest, the determination of whether a director can take an opportunity for himself without obtaining company approval does not take place through a conflicts framework, such as the one we have seen in UK company law. Rather, similar to the UK's maturing business opportunity approach, the court applies a set of rules that determine whether the opportunity 'belongs' to the company. This approach applies regardless of whether the director has resigned at the time he takes the opportunity. If the opportunity does 'belong' to the company then the director cannot take the opportunity without obtaining disinterested *board* approval.

The rules used by the courts to determine whether the opportunity belongs to the company were originally set out in the case of *Guth v Loft*. In theory, the rules vary if the opportunity is discovered by the director in his company or personal time. If discovered in his capacity as a director then the court asks whether: (1) the opportunity is in the company's line of business; (2) whether the company can afford to take the opportunity; and (3) whether the company has an interest or expectancy in the opportunity. If the director discovers the opportunity in his personal time then the 'Guth corollary' applies and requires a determination of: (1) whether the opportunity is essential to the company; (2) whether the company has an interest or expectancy in the opportunity; and (3) whether the director used the resources of the company wrongfully in exploiting the opportunity. Interestingly, however, in *Broz* the court applies the normal *Guth* rules even though Broz did not become aware of the opportunity in company time.

The contrast between the position set out by *Broz v Cellular Information Systems* and the UK duty to avoid conflicts is stark. Most striking for the student of UK company law is the Delaware court's willing engagement with the company's financial capacity. The court investigates whether the company had the financial capacity to take the opportunity and, contrary to the lower court's finding, holds that it does not and, as a result of this finding, that the opportunity does not belong to the company. The court also readily allows board action to qualify what is in the company's 'interest or expectancy'. CIS's board decision to divest itself of licences meant it was no longer interested in new licence opportunities such as the Michigan-2 licence. This was the case even though it was in advanced negotiations to be purchased by PriCellular, which was clearly interested in the opportunity to purchase the Michigan-2 licence because they were separately bidding for it. Nowhere in this judgment does the court indicate any anxiety about being able to appropriately assess capability facts; nowhere in the judgment does the court express a view that the duty of loyalty in the context of opportunities is underpinned by a deterrence rationale.

The corporate opportunities doctrine as applied by the Delaware Supreme Court in *Broz* is, therefore, a very flexible approach that tries to determine whether *in fact* the director's duty of loyalty has been compromised: if the company did not have the financial wherewithal to exploit the opportunity there is no real conflict and the duty of loyalty is not compromised; similarly if the company is not interested in the opportunity loyalty is not implicated. The court's role is to do justice to the facts in the case; to determine whether 'in fairness' the opportunity belongs to the company. The court is the guardian of the duty of loyalty but will only discipline real breaches of the duty not hypothetical ones.

There are of course certain limited similarities with UK company law. In particular Delaware's focus on the company's line of business chimes with the strands of UK authority—rejected by *O'Donnell v Shanahan*—which understand a company's interests to be qualified by its scope or line of business. Are there any lessons for UK company law's possible future exploration of scope of business restrictions from Delaware law's understanding of 'the company's line of business'? As you will see from the definition in note 82, much of the Delaware definition of 'line of business' incorporates capability facts and is, therefore, incapable of assisting UK law. However, the aspect of the definition which notes that the opportunity must 'logically and naturally [be] adaptable to its business... [and] consonant with its reasonable needs and aspirations for expansion', offers a sensible and pragmatic approach to what is necessarily a difficult line-drawing exercise.

Questions and discussion

- What would have been the outcome if the fact pattern in *Broz* had been subject to section 175 of the Companies Act 2006? It seems clear that Broz would have been liable to transfer the Michigan-2 licence to CIS or to account for any profits he made as a result of purchasing the licence. The financial incapacity of CIS would have been 'immaterial' for a UK court. Whether the interest of the company would not have been qualified by a general board resolution not to buy new licence—or even a specific consideration and rejection of the opportunity (as distinct from board authorization for Broz to take the opportunity)—is unclear given the tension between section 175(2) and 175(4)(a). In this author's view the more likely position is that board rejection would be deemed to be immaterial to the determination of company interest. No additional flexibility would have been granted to Broz because the opportunity came to him in his personal capacity.

- Is there a risk that the Delaware approach is too director friendly? Do you think directors of US companies are more likely to take opportunities for themselves than are UK directors? Do you think that the Delaware approach creates greater scope for managerial agency costs?

- Having seen the Delaware Supreme Court assess financial capacity do you think that the UK courts' view on this is weakened or strengthened? Interestingly, the Delaware Chancery Court (generally viewed as the US's most sophisticated corporate court) concluded that the company *did* have the financial capacity because PriCellular could have assisted the company in this regard by exercising an option it held to purchase CIS's debts and then waiving covenants preventing CIS from raising more finance.

It is also worth noting in this regard the fact—referred to in the Chancery Court judgment—that CIS engaged in a different transaction to swap one of its licences for a licence elsewhere which PriCellular were interested in acquiring, which involved an additional payment (in the form of a loan note) direct to the third party from PriCellular in order to complete the licence swap. Nevertheless the Supreme Court took a static view of the company's financial position and held that it did not have the financial capacity.

- Do you think the Delaware Supreme Court was correct in holding that CIS had no 'interest or expectancy' in the opportunity? Consider the author's view on *Broz* in this regard:

■ D. Kershaw, 'Lost in Translation: Corporate Opportunities in Comparative Perspective' (2005) 25 *Oxford Journal of Legal Studies* 603

In *Johnston v Greene*, the Delaware Supreme Court interpreted *Guth's* application of the interest or expectancy test to require 'some tie between that property and the nature of the corporate business'. Whilst post-*Johnston* case law has not defined the extent of the connection required for 'some tie' to be established, the words do not suggest a high threshold. In *Johnston* itself there was no such tie as the opportunity had *no* direct or close relation to the company's business. In *Broz*, the Court cites *Johnston* in this regard but then proceeds to empty the concept of 'some tie' between opportunity and company of much of its constraining content. In reaching its decision that CIS had no interest or expectancy in the license opportunity, the Court acknowledged a link between the license and the history of CIS's business but placed greater weight on CIS's business plan which involved the divesture of its cellular licences. However, this business plan was put in place prior to the PriCellular tender offer. The Court froze the dynamic nature of business activity by ignoring how CIS's interests changed with the increasing likelihood of being acquired by PriCellular. Indeed the Court held that 'the fact of PriCellular's plans to acquire CIS is immaterial and does not change the analysis' as a director's right to engage in other business activities would be unduly restricted 'if these individuals were required to consider every future occurrence'. However, PriCellular's acquisition of CIS was not a highly contingent or unforeseeable future event. It was, subject to certain financing problems, a likely event at the time *Broz* approached the other CIS directors and when he made his initial bid, and almost a foregone conclusion at the time RFB made the $7.2 million bid. It is surprising, therefore, that the Delaware Supreme Court held that the company would not be interested in the license when it became clear that such license would be attractive to a likely acquiror. As with the line of business test, a company's interests are not static, but dynamic, changing as the company develops and expands or contracts. The 'nature of the corporate business' with which, according to *Johnston*, the opportunity must have 'some tie' evolves as a function of expected developments, such as the high likelihood of being acquired by another company. Interestingly, CIS appeared in other licence contexts to agree with this assessment as they had, prior to the completion of the tender offer, been adjusting their license related activities to take account of PriCellular's interests.

- Does this argument overstate the effects of a possible takeover by PriCellular? Whilst the likelihood of the takeover increased during the course of negotiations by Broz to obtain the licence it had not taken place when he purchased the licence. Takeovers sometimes collapse at the last minute. One might argue that a company's interests remain *its* interests not the interests of another company or group of companies until it merges with another company or becomes part of a group of companies.

- If you were a director would you be less willing to serve/more willing to serve if the applicable law regulating opportunities was UK company law or Delaware corporate law?

- The Delaware Supreme Court in *Broz* notes that the corporate opportunity doctrine takes account of the 'competing demands placed on corporate fiduciaries in a modern business environment'. Do you think compared to Delaware law UK law is the outdated product of a bygone age unsuitable for our modern business conditions?
- In light of the Delaware approach, do you think the deterrence argument as set out in the extract from Flanigan is still valid or overstated?
- The Delaware corporate opportunities doctrine takes account of the fact that a director identifies an opportunity in his personal capacity. This contrasts starkly with the no-conflicts principle's rejection of a distinction between opportunities discovered in a director's personal or professional capacity. Have the UK courts got it wrong? Should UK company law reconsider the position of directors who discover opportunities in their personal capacity such as was the case in *Bhullar v Bhullar*?

VI **SUMMARY**

This is an extremely long and difficult chapter, justifying a summary of its major themes. The central functional question for this chapter is: what are the legal rules determining when, if at all, an opportunity identified by director can be taken by him *without* requiring any approval from the company. This question is regulated in English law through the no-conflicts principle. This principle is now set forth in section 175(1) of the Act. Accordingly, section 175 is always going to be your starting point where a director has taken a corporate opportunity for himself. It is *not* your starting for self-dealing transactions. *Section 175(3) makes it clear that it does not apply to transactions*. It is important to remember that if this provision is not breached by the taking of an opportunity then the director can take it, keep the profits, and does not have to obtain any corporate approval—from the board or the shareholders (the approval mechanism depending on the company type and its articles). Approval to take an opportunity is only required where section 175 would be breached by the taking of the opportunity.

In applying section 175 you must allow the section to guide you. The question is whether the director's actions put him in a position in which his personal interests conflict or possibly conflict with the interests of the company. To answer this question we need to determine what are the 'company's interests': there is no conflict if the company is not interested in the opportunity. There are two difficult aspects to answering this question. The first—although dealt with secondly in the chapter—is how does one determine the types of opportunities that fall within the company's interests? Although this author has argued in favour of a company's interests being limited by its current business area, the courts have not accepted this. Although there is some uncertainty, the current position, as evidenced by the more recent Court of Appeal case of *O'Donnell v Shanahan*, appears to be that a company is interested in any profit-making business opportunity.

The second question is whether a company is really interested in an opportunity that it is as a practical matter incapable of taking. Are real life facts—'capability facts'—that indicate that the company cannot really take the opportunity relevant to the determination of the company's interests? Here the answer is less than straightforward: any capability fact in relation to which the defendant director himself could have played a role (as a director) in removing the barrier—such as raising finance it is claimed the company does not have—is not relevant. But any fact where the director—as a director—could not have played a role in removing it—for example, a statutory bar on certain actions or where shareholder approval is needed and the shareholders have made clear that they will not give it—is admissible and will alter the determination of company interest. This is what the Act means when it says that it is 'immaterial' whether the company could have taken the opportunity. This is what Lord Hodson, in the majority in *Boardman*, meant when he used this language.

A further difficulty arises from understanding the effect of section 175(4)(a) which says that the duty is not infringed where there is no reasonable likelihood of conflict. This suggests that the Act is reasserting Lord Upjohn's minority position in *Boardman*. Yet, as we have noted, the majority position is codified in section 175(2). What does this mean? It remains unclear, which means you have to consider two possibilities: first, whether, contrary to our analysis of section 175(2) it makes the law more open to capability facts—even where the director plays a central role in turning a 'could' into a 'could not'; *and/or* whether courts are likely to use this provision to depart from the position on 'scope of business' adopted in *O'Donnell v Shanahan*.

Finally, we have the post-resignation cases. The common law has produced two means of addressing opportunities exploited by resigning directors: the approach in *IDC v Cooley*; and the *maturing business opportunity approach*. The former is more consistent with the no-conflicts approach; the latter uses a different proprietary framework. The Act now extends the no-conflicts framework to opportunities and information identified whilst the director was a director. What then does this mean for the maturing business opportunity approach? In this author's view it should signal its demise and the approach adopted in *IDC* should be followed. This means that where a director fails to disclose to the board an opportunity (within the company's interest) that he identifies and then resigns to take that opportunity he will be in breach of the extended no-conflicts duty. However, it is not clear that the courts will accept the demise of the maturing business opportunity approach—they may just treat it as the post-resignation embodiment of the no-conflicts approach, in which case you need to understand how it works and you need to understand that after *Foster Bryant* the approach may not merely apply to a maturing business opportunity but to any possible opportunity. If that is correct then the substantive distance between this approach and the *IDC* approach is small. Why then, you might ask, do we need to bother with the conceptual baggage of the maturing business approach? Good question!

Additional reading

V. Brudney and R. Clark, 'A New Look at Corporate Opportunities' (1981) 94 *Harvard Law Review* 998.

F. Easterbrook and D. Fischel, 'Contract and Fiduciary Duty' (1993) 36 *Journal of Law and Economics* 425.

G. Jones, 'Unjust Enrichment and the Fiduciary's Duty of Loyalty' (1968) 84 *LQR* 471.

P. Koh, 'Once a Director, Always a Fiduciary' (2003) 62 *CLJ* 403.

J. Langbein, 'Questioning the Trust Law Duty of Loyalty: Sole Interest or Best Interest?' (2005) 114 *Yale Law Journal* 929.

J. Lowry and R. Edmunds, 'The No-Conflict–No-Profit Rules and the Corporate Fiduciary: Challenging the Orthodoxy of Absolutism' (2000) *JBL* 122.

 Online Resource Centre
http://www.oxfordtextbooks.co.uk/orc/kershaw2e/

Visit the Online Resource Centre for additional resources and information available for this chapter, including web links and an interactive flashcard glossary.

CHAPTER FIFTEEN

ENFORCING DIRECTORS' DUTIES

I INTRODUCTION

1 Only the company can enforce rights owed to the company

In Chapter 9, 'Introduction to directors' duties', one of our first observations about directors' duties was that the duties are owed by the directors to the company.[1] Directors may be appointed by shareholder vote but strictly speaking they are not appointed by the shareholders but by the shareholders in general meeting *acting as the company*. That is, directors are appointed by the company and, accordingly, owe duties to the company and *not* to the shareholder body. As we also saw in Chapter 9, whilst in certain special circumstances it is possible that *fiduciary-like* duties may be owed by directors to shareholders such duties must be distinguished from the 'directors' duties' considered in Chapters 9–14 which are the duties owed by directors to the company as a result of them accepting a position as a director.

It is a basic premise of any legal arrangement that only a person who has a legal right can enforce that right. The right to take legal action to obtain a remedy where a legal obligation has been breached belongs to the person who is the recipient of that legal obligation. Applied to the company, this basic logic means that it is the company, and only the company, who can enforce a breach of any duty the director owes to the company.[2] Accordingly, only the company can enforce a breach of the duties set out in sections 171–177 of the Companies Act 2006. Similarly, if because of certain special circumstances[3] a director owes a duty to any shareholders, only those shareholders, not the company, can enforce those rights. This basic idea that only the company can enforce duties owed to it is often referred to as the 'proper plaintiff rule' following the statement of this principle in the 1843 case of *Foss v Harbottle*. This proper plaintiff rule is often said to be one of the two rules set out in *Foss v Harbottle*. It is, however, nothing more than a statement of the legally obvious: only the right-holder can enforce its rights.

2 Which corporate body should make the decision to commence litigation against a director?

There are four options to consider when thinking about which corporate organ or persons should be given the power to commence litigation in relation to an alleged breach of a director's duty. The two obvious options would be to allow the litigation decision to be made by the board or by the general meeting. The two less obvious options would be to allow a shareholder or group of shareholders holding a certain number of shares

---

[1] Section 170(1) Companies Act 2006.

[2] *Prudential Assurance v Newman Industries Ltd* [1982] 1 All ER 354 observing in this regard that: 'this is sometimes referred to as the rule in *Foss v Harbottle* when applied to corporations, but it has a wider scope and is fundamental to any rational system of jurisprudence.'

[3] *Peskin v Anderson* [2000] All ER (D) 2278.

(say, 5%, 10%, or 20%) of the company's voting share capital to make the litigation decision, or to allow any one shareholder—regardless of the number of shares owned—to
make the litigation decision. Before considering in depth which organ or person is most
suitable to make the decision to litigate against a board member, it is helpful to consider
first which corporate body typically makes the decision to litigate against a third party.

Hypothetical A

If some of the microchips sold to our case study company, Bob's Electronics Ltd, were
faulty and the use of these chips resulted in many of its computers being returned and
considerable damage to the company's reputation for building reliable build-to-order
computers, then Bob's Electronics Ltd would have a contractual right of action against
the supplier. Few of us would question that the appropriate body to make such a litigation decision is the board of directors. Generally speaking, regardless of whether Bob's
Electronics Ltd is closely or widely held, executive directors will be best placed to understand the reason why the microchips were faulty and, following receipt of appropriate
legal advice, the board as a whole will be best placed to decide whether taking legal
action would promote the company's commercial success. Assuming that the board acts
competently and there is no issue of any conflict of interest (such as board members
having a connection with the supplier) then there is no reason why the shareholder body
would be better placed to make the decision than the board, and several reasons to
think that they would not be as well placed, for example the *learning-by-doing* advantages of the executive directors and possible rational apathy problems where the shareholder body is widely held.

Question: What factors would a board of directors take into account in deciding
whether to bring such litigation against the third party? Give this question some thought
before reading the remainder of this *Hypothetical.*

Many readers' initial reaction to this faulty components scenario is 'of course legal
action must be brought to compensate the company for lost business and reputational
damage'. However, this may not necessarily be the case. The decision whether or not
to bring litigation is a very complex balancing process for the board. Factors that the
board will consider would include: the likelihood of winning the litigation; the probable
award of damages if successful; and the legal costs involved in bringing the litigation.
However, there are a whole range of other extra-legal considerations which the board
must take into account; for example: does the company still want to continue to have
a business relationship with the supplier—can the required chips be sourced effectively
from elsewhere; how much time and effort from management and other employees will
be required to pursue this claim effectively; will such time and effort distract management and employees from running and developing the business. In light of such considerations, the board's answer may be that it is not in the company's interests to pursue
the litigation, even where there is a strong possibility of winning the litigation and
obtaining compensation for the injury suffered by the company.

Determining which body can make the litigation decision becomes more complex when
we move from third-party litigation to a decision whether to bring litigation against a
member of the board of directors for breach of duty. All the points made above regarding
the advantages of using the board to make the litigation decision, in theory, continue to
apply in relation to the breach of duty by board members: the board in many instances
will have a superior understanding of the company, its strategy and future direction; the
board will have a more informed understanding of the effect on the business of the dis-
tractions for management and employees which the litigation may generate; the board

will be better placed to understand whether a director took due care in making a decision; the board may be better placed to know whether a business opportunity fell within the company's current and future business area or whether a director resigned in order to take an opportunity. The shareholders—where they are not also directors—are clearly less well placed to understand these issues and to factor them into any litigation decision.

However, as we saw in both our consideration of who should make decisions on significant transactions for the company[4] and again in our consideration of which corporate body should make the approval decision in relation to self-dealing transactions or opportunities,[5] the determination of whether a corporate body is the best body to make a decision is a function not only of the decision-making capability of that body and its incentives to pay attention to the question at hand but also, importantly, a function of the conflicts faced by that decision-making body. In this context the apparent and strong advantages of the board making the litigation decision are significantly compromised by the board's conflicts.

If the board is allowed to make the litigation decision then to the extent that the members who have allegedly breached their duties vote on the board's decision on whether to bring litigation they are being asked to sue themselves. The board's conflicts would be reduced if only those directors who are not alleged to have breached their duties (the disinterested directors) make the litigation decision. However, even in relation to these directors we may harbour reservations about their true independence. There is a risk of reciprocal 'back scratching': 'this time I will help you out; I hope you'll do the same for me if I ever find myself in such a position'. There are acute concerns about disinterested director independence in relation to breaches of duty allegations. It is one thing to deny a fellow director a business opportunity or the benefit of a self-dealing transaction; but quite another to subject the director to the stress, worry, and possible personal financial exposure of litigation. The disinterested directors are being asked to sue their fellow members: people who they may consider friends as well as colleagues; people who they view as members of the team, with whom they share a sense of corporate camaraderie. We are all familiar with that sense of internal obligation which is generated by membership of a family, a sports team, or club. Such internal group obligations may be generated in the boardroom just as they can be generated on a sports field. Such obligations clearly conflict with the decision to take an independent litigation decision according to the criteria: does this litigation promote the commercial success of the company.

Nevertheless, it is important to note that, whilst we may view as very serious board conflicts that result in a refusal to take the litigation, we have fewer concerns in relation to a board decision to commence such litigation. So whilst these concerns about board decision-making in relation to the litigation decision mean that we may require alternative means of enabling the company to commence litigation against directors, we do not want to take away from the board the ability to positively resolve to take such litigation against a board member. However, the taking of a positive decision to commence litigation by the board does not dissolve all our concerns about the conflict that the board faces. A decision to commence litigation but a refusal to grant appropriate resources to the litigation—in terms of both legal representation as well as management and employee time and effort—may have the same effect as a decision to refuse to take litigation: that is, the directors will not be held accountable for their breaches of duty. Regulators need to be wary of board-controlled litigation where the board's direct and indirect conflicts undermine the successful pursuit of the litigation. In such cases the company could end up with the worst of all possible worlds: a low likelihood of success but the incurrence of significant legal and **opportunity costs**.

One response to these significant concerns about *either* treating a litigation decision against a director in the same way as we treat a litigation decision in relation to a

[4] See Chapter 6.   [5] See Chapter 13.

third party *or* continuing to rely on board decision-making subject to a disinterested director qualification, would be, *in addition to giving the board the right to bring such litigation*, to allow the shareholder body to commence and control the litigation or to direct the board to commence litigation. However, as we have seen in other contexts this regulatory option brings with it several, by now familiar, problems/downsides. First, in close companies, if the directors who have breached their duties control a majority of the shares of the company then the wrongdoing directors can easily close down the possibility of litigation by using their votes in the general meeting to reject litigation. Secondly, although in widely-held companies directors are unlikely to have such shareholder voting power, shareholder decision-making in such contexts is subject to two significant problems: first, the shareholders' ability to make a good decision given the considerable number of company-specific concerns that need to be taken into account; and, second, the shareholders' willingness to invest the necessary time and money in order to cast an informed vote and to persuade others to act accordingly (the rational apathy and collective action problem). To address these information and capability concerns the board could be required to provide the shareholders with detailed information or even a recommendation. The production of such information and any recommendation is, however, subject to the same independence concerns outlined earlier in relation to board decision-making. It seems likely, therefore, that rational apathy and collective action problems will lead in many instances to the rubber stamping by the general meeting of the preferred position of the board (whether explicitly stated through a recommendation or implicitly stated through the produced disclosure).

If giving the decision to the general shareholder body is likely, in most instances, to result in the rubber-stamping of board conflicts then we are still in search of a decision-maker that is more informed and capable of making the decision than a widely-held shareholder body but more independent than the board or a closely-held shareholder body where the directors who have allegedly breached their duties control the general meeting as shareholders. One possible decision-maker fitting these criteria would be a smaller group of shareholders ranging from one shareholder to a specified percentage of shareholders. Giving a single shareholder or a group of shareholders the right to make the litigation decision would not involve giving such shareholders the right to act *as the company* in relation to the litigation decision—as a resolution of the board of directors or a general meeting is *the act of the company*—rather such shareholders would be given the right to bring the action to enforce the company's rights on behalf of the company. Such an action is known as a derivative action. Such an action derives from the company's rights and it is designed to enforce the company's rights, but it does not arise as a result of a company decision to bring litigation. Shareholders who bring a derivative action are not enforcing their own rights; they are enforcing the company's rights. And if they are successful any award made is to compensate the company for its loss and is paid to the company, not to the shareholders bringing the litigation.

Rational apathy problems continue to afflict any such shareholder who is required to invest legal costs and time to bring such a derivative action: the costs of bringing the action (legal costs, time and opportunity costs) may exceed the financial benefit the shareholder obtains as a result of bringing the action. The extent of the legal costs in this regard could be mitigated through litigation costs rules (for example, company indemnification of legal expenses or **contingency fees**); however, such arrangements do not compensate the shareholder for her own time and her own opportunity costs.[6] Collective action costs, on the other hand, are dissolved if a single shareholder is allowed to bring such an action: the shareholder is not, in order to commence the

---

[6] See further section VI in this chapter.

action, required to convince her fellow shareholders that bringing the action promotes the company's interests. To the extent that the agreement of more than one shareholder is required to bring such an action—for example, 5%, 10%, or 20% of the shareholder body—collective action costs remain but are reduced and are a function of the level of the ownership threshold. Even at lower thresholds, depending on the make-up of the shareholder body, such collective action costs may in fact be prohibitive.

While giving single shareholders, or groups of shareholders, the right to bring derivative actions on behalf of the company resolves the problems of independence from the directors who are alleged to have breached their duties, it does not fully deal with the issue of whether such a derivative action will promote the commercial success of the company. There are two reasons for this. First, there is the possibility that if the right to bring a derivative action is given to a single shareholder, an action may be brought by a shareholder (who may, for example, own only one share) who does not have a real interest in the economic well-being of the company but brings the action to forward other 'non-company interests' that are more important to that shareholder. For example, an action may be brought claiming that the directors are in breach of section 172 for failing to have regard to the effect particular decisions had on company employees or on the environment; however, the action is brought not because there is a strong case that there has been a breach of section 172 but more with an eye to potential news headlines and the media pressure that this may generate to promote the shareholder's labour or environmental agenda. Such derivative actions are—borrowing from US derivative action terminology—often referred to as nuisance suits or strike suits. The second reason why derivative actions may not promote the success of the company is that the shareholders bringing the action may take a myopic view of the company's interests: simply that duties owed to it should be enforced. But, as we saw in our consideration of third-party litigation by the company, simply because there is a right that can be enforced—whether it is a third-party right or a breach of duty by the director—does not mean that it is necessarily in the company's interests to enforce that right. The overall costs of such litigation must be taken into account, as must its effect on the morale of its directors, management, and employees. Shareholders angry about apparent breaches of duty may not take, or indeed be capable of taking, these factors into account in their decision as to whether or not to bring a derivative action.

Accordingly, if litigation to enforce breach of directors' duty can be brought through a derivative action, we require a control mechanism to ensure that the litigation actually benefits the company. If we do not have such a control mechanism then a system of company law that allows derivative actions will produce too much litigation that does not benefit companies. If we view derivative actions as a response to the failings of board litigation decision-making—whether full board or disinterested directors—and the limitations of giving the litigation decision to the shareholder body—whether the general meeting as a whole or disinterested shareholders—then clearly neither the board nor the shareholder body could be the body that regulates the derivative action to ensure that only litigation which promotes the success of the company is brought. In such an instance another regulatory body is required to oversee the availability of the derivative suit and the only option available is a third-party regulator such as a court or an administrative body which, on the application of the shareholder who wishes to bring a derivative action, makes the determination as to whether the litigation promotes the success of the company. However, as in any area of law, solutions are never perfect; solutions themselves generate additional problems. Although the court may be the most independent of all the regulatory solutions we have considered, an important issue is whether the court is capable of making such a decision. The answer to this question, however, is deferred to section III of this chapter.

3 Choosing between the regulatory options

None of the regulatory solutions to the question of who should make the decision to enforce an alleged breach of duty is perfect: all come with pros and cons orbiting the independence/capability dichotomy. The regulatory settlement and the role for each of the mechanisms set forth above will depend, most importantly, on the regulator's assessment of the capability and independence of board and shareholder decision-making.

- If the regulator believes that the disinterested board decision-making mechanism is in most cases effective and independent—and that the problems identified with disinterested board decision-making are overstated—then such a regulator is unlikely to provide for a significant role for derivative actions because disinterested board decisions will be viewed as not significantly less independent than the derivative shareholder's decision to bring the action but significantly more informed about whether the litigation is in the company's interests. For such a regulator: derivative actions *would only be allowed* to the extent that the disinterested directors had not formally considered possible litigation or if there were no disinterested directors; and a derivative action *would be discontinued* if subsequent to the bringing of the derivative litigation the disinterested directors considered it and decided that the litigation would not promote the success of the company.

- If the regulator does not think that shareholder rational apathy and collective action problems are significant—or at least as significant as corporate legal academics often suggest they are—then decisions of the general meeting may be allowed to override a board decision not to commence litigation and derivative actions would be excluded. If rational apathy and collective problems are overstated then we can expect the shareholder body to act to bring litigation when the litigation would promote the success of the company. If the shareholder body does not do so then we can take it as given that such litigation does not promote the company's commercial success. From this viewpoint an informed shareholder vote on the litigation decision will be more likely to benefit the company than the decision of one shareholder and, provided wrongdoers cannot take part in the decision, there will be less concern about the independence of the decision than there would be with disinterested directors. In which case there is little need to provide for a derivative litigation option.

- If a regulator is sceptical about the effectiveness of disinterested board decision-making in this context and views shareholder rational apathy and collective action problems as significant in widely-held companies then the derivative action becomes of increasing importance and there is only one mechanism which is available to ensure that it is used in ways that benefit the company, namely, a court or an administrative body.

With this range of regulatory options in mind let us now consider the choices that UK company law has made in this regard both before and after the Companies Act 2006.

Questions

1. Are the problems of disinterested directors overstated? Would you be happy to rely on disinterested directors to make a decision as to whether or not to commence litigation against a fellow director? If not, why not?

2. Should shareholders as a body have the right to commence and control litigation, or to tell directors to commence litigation against directors? If so, what type of resolution— ordinary or special resolution—would be appropriate for such a shareholder decision?

3. Do you think that, given the problems of board and shareholder decision-making identified, a derivative action mechanism is required to ensure that directors observe their duties?

4. How would you regulate access to the derivative mechanism:

(a) How many shareholders, or percentage holding of voting shares, should be required, in your view, to bring an action?

(b) Should there be any mechanism to determine whether the action is in the company's interests?

(c) What would be required of the courts in order to perform that function? Are courts capable of performing that function?

II CONTROL OF THE LITIGATION DECISION BY THE BOARD OR THE GENERAL MEETING

It is clear that to the extent that a company's articles of association delegate to the board of directors general powers to direct and manage the company, such as those set out in Article 3 of the Model Articles for both public and private companies,[7] that such authority encompasses the authority to decide whether the company should commence litigation against any person, whether a third party or a member of the company's board of directors. In light of our analysis of the balance of decision-making power in a UK company in Chapter 6, any role for shareholders in the litigation decision would depend on whether a company's articles reserves power for the shareholder body to bring and control litigation or to instruct the board to commence litigation. Shareholders could design any such reserve litigation power as they wished; however, in the Model Articles, its forerunner Table A, and in most company's actual articles, litigation against directors falls within the general delegation of board power and shareholder instruction right articles and is not dealt with separately.

We saw in Chapter 6 that for a company with Model Articles the shareholders can instruct the board to take action by passing a special resolution provided that 'no such resolution invalidates anything which the directors have already done'. According to this provision the shareholder body can by special resolution instruct the board to commence litigation or instruct the board to stop litigation if they have already commenced it.[8]

However, there is a view amongst UK company law commentators that, notwithstanding the absence of a reserved shareholder litigation power or any instruction right in a company's articles, the general meeting has co-decision-making authority with the board to bring litigation against a director, or to instruct the board to bring litigation, by passing an ordinary resolution to that effect.[9] Such a view is clearly contrary to articles providing otherwise and to the cases we looked at in Chapter 6, which focused on enforcing the contractual division of power set out in the articles.[10] However, there is support for this view in the authorities and as well as in English law's approach to regulating board power in the context of acute conflicts.

The case of *Alexander Ward v Samyang* is often cited in support of the position that the shareholder body has an ordinary resolution decision or instruction right in relation to company litigation against a director. In this case proceedings were commenced in the company's name by shareholders not as a derivative action and not as a result of a shareholder resolution in general meeting. At the time the proceedings were commenced

---

[7] See Chapter 6.

[8] Article 4 of the Model Articles for both public and private companies. Note the fact that directors had decided not to commence litigation would not prevent the shareholders from instructing them to do so pursuant to this provision. Such a resolution would not be invalidating their the original board resolution, but rather require them to pass another resolution commencing the litigation. See further, Chapter 6.

[9] Gower and Davies, *Modern Principles of Company Law* (8th edn, Sweet & Maxwell 2008), 608.

[10] See, for example, *Automatic Self-Cleansing Filter Syndicate Ltd v Cuninghame* [1906] 2 Ch 34. See further Chapter 6.

the company had no directors. The company subsequently went bankrupt and the question for the House of Lords, on appeal from the Scottish Second Division of the Court of Session, was whether the proceedings were properly commenced in the first place and whether the liquidator acting on behalf of the company could ratify the proceedings if incorrectly commenced. The judgments of their Lordships clearly provide support for the proposition that proceedings that are commenced in the company's name but which are not properly authorized may be ratified by the company subsequently and continued. Their Lordships also concluded that the shareholders in general meeting have reserve authority to bring proceedings in the company's name in spite of the provisions in the articles providing only the board with corporate power.

■ *Alexander Ward v Samyang* [1975] 2 All ER 424

Second Division of the Court of Session, Lord Fraser
With regard to ratification of the raising of the action…there is no doubt that where proceedings are started in name of a company…without proper authority the company can as a general rule ratify the act of the person who started the proceedings and adopt the proceedings in accordance with the ordinary law of principal and agent—see *Danish Mercantile Co. Ltd. v. Beaumont* [1951] 1 Ch. 680, *Wylie v. Adam* (1836) 14 S. 430. Such ratification can be done by the liquidator of the company—*Danish Mercantile Co. Ltd*. The law of principal and agent on this matter was stated by Wright LJ in *Firth v. Staines* 1897 2 Q.B. 70 at p. 75 thus:—'I think the case must be decided upon the ordinary principles of the doctrine of ratification. To constitute a valid ratification three conditions must be satisfied: first, the agent whose act is sought to be ratified must have purported to act for the principal; secondly, at the time the act was done the agent must have had a competent principal; and, thirdly, at the time of the ratification the principal must be legally capable of doing the act himself.' In the present case the first and third of these conditions stated by Wright L.J. have clearly been satisfied and there is no dispute about that, but dispute has arisen with regard to the second condition.

The defenders contend that at the time when this action was raised the…company was not 'competent' to raise an action, that is to say, that it had no power to do so, because it had no directors. If that contention is well founded, it follows that the raising of the action by individuals could not subsequently be ratified by the company—see *Boston Deep Sea Fishing and Ice Co. Ltd. v. Farnham* [1957] 1 WLR 1051. The argument was that the…company had by its Articles of Association handed over the powers of management to its directors, that the decision whether to raise an action or not was part of the duties of managers, and that no organ of the company other than the Board of Directors was capable of making that decision. The argument was supported by reference to the line of authority which started with *Automatic Self Cleansing Filter Syndicate Ltd. v. Cuninghame* [1906] 2 Ch. 34. Art. 74 of the pursuers' Articles of Association, which is in substantially the same terms as Art. 80 of Table A to the Companies Act 1948, provides that 'the business of the company shall be managed by the directors, who shall pay all expenses incurred in the formation and registration of the company, and may exercise all such powers of the company as are not by the Ordinance that is the Hong Kong Ordinance equivalent to the British Companies Act or by these articles required to be exercised by the company in general meeting…' I agree that the effect of Art. 74 is to delegate to the directors power to manage the company. I agree also that, so long as that article stands without amendment, the shareholders cannot by resolution passed at a general meeting interfere with the directors or give directions to them as to how the company's affairs are to be managed, or over-rule any decision come to by the directors in the conduct of its business, even as regards matters not expressly delegated to the directors by the Articles. That is amply vouched by authority including Buckley on Companies Acts (13th ed.) p. 860, *Quinn & Axtens v. Salmon* [1909] 1 Ch. 311 1909 A.C. 442, *Shaw & Sons (Salford) Ltd. v. Shaw* [1935] 2 K.B. 113 per Greer L.J. at p. 134. From that starting point [counsel for the defendant] went on to argue that the effect was that the shareholders in general meeting were left with only very limited residual powers which were virtually confined to appointing new directors. He referred to a number of cases such as *Barren v. Potter* [1914] 1 Ch. 895 and *Foster* [1916] 1 Ch. 532 where there had been deadlock on the board of directors and where the company had been held entitled to resolve the deadlock by appointing additional directors. He submitted that any difficulty in the present case could have been resolved by the company's appointing directors…and that therefore it had no residual power to give instructions for the raising of an action itself. In my opinion that argument is erroneous. The line of authority starting with *Automatic Self Cleansing Filter Syndicate* and the law laid down there applies to cases where there is an internal dispute within a company, usually between the Board of Directors and the majority of the shareholders, and the cases decide that the majority of the shareholders cannot interfere with the Board of Directors. But in my opinion these cases have no application to a case such as the present where there were no directors at the material time. None of the cases to which we were referred had arisen in circumstances where there were no directors. The theory underlying all the cases is that the shareholders are parties to a contract with the company which is embodied in the company's Articles and which provides that the company is to be managed by the directors. It follows that interference by the shareholders would be in breach of that contract. All the shareholders can do is either to amend the Articles by special resolution or, when occasion offers, to refuse to re-elect or to dismiss the directors. Such a contract is quite intelligible. Shareholders might be well content to risk their money in a company which was to be managed by a Board of Directors but they might not be willing to risk it in a company whose management was to be subject to the interference or control of a general meeting of shareholders. In my opinion therefore the authorities on which this part of the defenders' argument was based are not in point here where the question arises, not within the company, between directors and shareholders, but between the company itself and an outside party. Outsiders such as the defenders, have in my opinion no concern with the contract between the company and its members which is contained in the Articles of Association. So far as the outsider is concerned it is res inter alias acta—see *Eley v. Positive* etc. Co. 1876 1 Exchequer Division 88 per Lord Cairns L.C. at p. 90. So long as the company does not exceed its powers, as defined in its memorandum of association, an outsider has no complaint.

If I am right so far, the result is that when this action was raised the company itself had power in a question with a third party to instruct the raising of actions, and it was therefore a competent principal which could subsequently ratify the action of individuals who raised proceedings in its name. There is no doubt in the present case that the liquidator has purported to ratify the raising of the action. Accordingly the defenders must fail.

House of Lords

Lord Hailsham

In my opinion, at the relevant time the company was fully competent…to raise proceedings in the Scottish courts. The company could have done so either by appointing directors, or, as I think, by authorizing proceedings in general meeting, which in the absence of an effective board, has a residual authority to use the company's powers. It had not taken, and did not take, the steps necessary to give authority to perform the necessary actions. But it was competent to have done so, and in my view it was therefore a competent principal within the meaning of the second of Wright J's three conditions. So far as regards the powers of general meeting in Gower's Modern Company Law it is stated (1969 edition, pp. 136, 137): 'It seems that if for some reason the board cannot or will not exercise the powers vested in them, the general meeting may do so. On this ground, action by the general meeting has been held effective where there was a deadlock on the board, where an effective quorum could not be obtained, where the directors are disqualified from voting, or, more obviously, where the directors have purported to borrow in excess of the amount authorized by the articles. Moreover, although the general meeting cannot restrain the directors from conducting actions in the name of the company, it still seems to be the law (as laid down in *Marshall's Valve Gear Co. v. Manning, Wardle & Co.*)[11] that the general meeting can commence proceedings on behalf of the company if the directors fail to do so.'

Lord Kilbrandon

I am not at all convinced that, the management of a company having been confided to the Directors, and the instructing of actions at law being an act of management, then, if the company has for the time no Directors, it cannot during that time take steps to recover its debts. I think...Article [74] probably means no more than this, that the Directors, and no-one else, are responsible for the management of the company, except in the matters specifically allotted to the company in general meeting. This is a term of the contract between the shareholders and the company. But it does not mean that no act of management, such as instructing the company's solicitor, can validly be performed without the personal and explicit authority of the Directors themselves. In any case I have even graver doubts whether the validity of the company's act, resting as it must on a construction of the contract with the shareholders, can in such a matter be challenged by someone whose only relationship with the company is one of indebtedness.

The question for the court in *Alexander Ward* is whether the liquidator is capable of ratifying proceedings that were commenced by a shareholder group in the name of the company without authorization. One of the criteria to be fulfilled in order to answer this question affirmatively is whether the company could have commenced proceedings itself. The defendants argued that it could not have done so as at the time proceedings were commenced the company had no directors and the company's articles delegated power to manage the company to the board and did not reserve power to the shareholders in general meeting to make this decision.

The House of Lords hold that the shareholders acting in the general meeting would be a competent body to commence litigation. Lord Hailsham's, and also Lord Kilbrandon's, judgment provides for an implied reservation of authority by the general meeting to commence litigation by *ordinary resolution*, regardless of whether the articles provide for a special resolution instruction right or no instruction right at all. Lord Hailsham quotes Gower and Davies which, citing *Marshall's Valve Company Ltd*, observes that it 'seems to be the law' that the general meeting can commence proceedings where the directors do not do so. Interestingly, *Marshall's Valve* itself is a case that highlights the tension between the reserve power position we see in this case and the approach, following *Automatic Self-Cleansing Filter Company v Cunninghame*,[12] that relies on the enforcement of a literal interpretation of the article's distribution of power between the board and the shareholder body. In *Marshall's Valve* a majority shareholder had commenced an action against a third party on behalf of the company to enforce patent rights that the majority of the board had refused to bring. Neville J, at first instance, held that the majority shareholder had the right to commence the litigation and suggested that to the extent that *Automatic* required otherwise that it was inconsistent with the pre-existing law, which, in Neville J's view, provided that: 'in the absence of any contract to the contrary the majority of the shareholders in a company have the ultimate control of its affairs, and are entitled to decide whether or not an action in the name of the company shall proceed'. Neville J's position is clearly inconsistent with the contractual approach adopted in *Automatic*.[13] But for Lord Hailsham's resurrection of *Marshall Valve*, it would be better viewed as unreliable authority.

---

[11] [1909] 1 Ch 267.   [12] See Chapter 6 at pp 201–02.

[13] Indeed this was the view of successful counsel in the Court of Appeal in *Salmon v Quin & Axtens Ltd* (see the Court of Appeal judgment at [1909] 1 Ch 311) and the view of Harman J in *Breckland Group Holdings Ltd v London & Suffolk Properties Ltd* [1988] 4 BCC 452 considered later. It is also noteworthy that Neville J in *Marshall Valve* also held in this case that on the interpretation of the

Lord Fraser in his Second Division judgment in *Alexander Ward* also considers the *Automatic Self-Cleansing* line of cases.[14] But he distinguishes this line of cases in two ways. First, in *Alexander Ward* there are no directors at all to exercise these powers; and, second, the *Automatic Self-Cleansing* line of cases are concerned with enforcing the company's articles where there is a dispute between the board and the shareholders regarding particular corporate action and could not, therefore, be relied upon in the context of a dispute between the company and a third party. For Lord Fraser, therefore, where the board and the shareholders disagree about an issue, which could include whether litigation should be brought against a member of the board, then the courts would be bound to follow the *Automatic Self-Cleansing* line of authority and enforce the distribution of power set forth in the articles.

Although Lord Fraser's observations appear to encompass litigation against directors, his judgment does not directly address the situation in which the dispute between the shareholders and the directors relates to litigation against the director. Earlier dicta from the Court of Appeal suggests that in relation to litigation against a director the shareholder body, acting by ordinary resolution, may act for the company. In *Danish Mercantile Co Ltd v Beaumont*[15] proceedings were started by the managing director who did not have authority to commence the proceedings. The question was whether the liquidator of the company had the authority to ratify the proceedings. The Court of Appeal held that ratification by the company was possible and in so doing approved of the following passage in *Buckley on the Companies Acts*:[16]

> If the case be one in which the company ought to be plaintiff, the fact that the seal is in the possession of the adverse party will not necessarily preclude the intending plaintiffs from using the company's name. Neither will it be necessary to obtain the resolution of a general meeting in favour of the action before the writ is issued. In many cases the delay might amount to a denial of justice. In a case of urgency, the intending plaintiffs may use the company's name at their peril, and subject to their being able to show that they have the support of the majority. In an action so constituted, the court may give interlocutory relief, taking care that a meeting be called at the earliest possible date to determine whether the action really has the support of the majority or not.

Following *Buckley*, the Court of Appeal observes that there is a reserve power for the general meeting to commence litigation against the directors regardless of the power distribution in the articles, but only where 'the seal is in the possession of the adverse party', which means that the directors who would be sued control the board decision-making process. This case is cited approvingly in *Alexander Ward* by Lord Fraser on the issue of ratification of litigation commenced without authority to do so. The Court of Appeal in *Danish Mercantile* did not consider at all the balance of power approach set forth in *Automatic Self-Cleansing*. However, the judgment can still be understood through the lens of the balance of power between the board and shareholder body. In situations of acute conflict the common law has often implied limitations on the formal distribution of power to the board set forth in the articles. In Chapter 11, for example, we saw that although a board may formally have the power to issue shares to interfere with a takeover offer or with the existing control structure in the general meeting, the

---

article distributing power to the board that the general meeting had the power to instruct the board to take action by ordinary resolution. This conclusion appears to be based, incorrectly, on interpreting the word 'regulation' in the articles to mean 'resolution'. As noted in Chapter 6, although there is some uncertainty surrounding the meaning of the term 'regulation' in this article, the better position—taken in *Automatic* and subsequent cases—was not that regulation meant resolution but rather that regulation referred to an 'article' in the company's articles of association. See further, p 202.

[14] These cases are considered in Chapter 6.   [15] [1951] Ch 680.
[16] *Buckley on the Companies Acts* (12th edn, Butterworths, 1949), 169.

courts have held that, in the absence of explicit shareholder approval to do so, boards do not have the power to take such actions.[17] We could understand the litigation decision against directors where the 'seal is in the possession of the adverse party' in the same way: given the acute nature of the conflict, the shareholder body is, in the absence of contrary intent in the articles, presumed to have retained *co*-decision-making authority over the litigation decision against directors.

Support for this 'shareholder reserve power' approach is also available from the common law rules determining when a single shareholder can bring a derivative action. As we shall see, the common law has traditionally taken a very restrictive view of the scope for derivative actions by individual shareholders and has justified this position on the basis that the litigation decision is one for the shareholder body to take and not a decision which an individual shareholder acting alone can take. That is, the basis for the common law's restrictive approach to derivative actions assumes that a majority vote in general meeting has the power to commence litigation.[18] Note, in this regard a slight difference between this derivative action assumption and the position set forth in *Danish Mercantile*. In the former, the general meeting retains the power in relation to litigation against directors in all situations. In the latter, the suggestion in *Danish Mercantile* is that the reserve power is only triggered when the wrongdoing directors are in control of the seal, that is, the power would not be triggered where disinterested directors make the litigation decision.

However, recent authority suggests that this issue remains unresolved and that the literal contractual approach based on *Automatic Self-Cleansing* retains a gravitational pull for some courts. In the High Court case of *Breckland Group Holdings Ltd v London & Suffolk Properties Ltd*[19] Harman J referred to, but did not follow, the position set out in *Danish Mercantile*. In this case a majority shareholder commenced unauthorized litigation in the company's name in circumstances where it appeared unlikely that the board would vote to take litigation proceedings against the company's managing director. Harman J placed the consideration of a shareholder litigation power clearly within the *Automatic Self-Cleansing* line of authorities. The question for the court was: 'can a general meeting…pass a resolution to adopt "material legal proceedings" when by the provisions of article 80 of the articles of association [the predecessor to Model articles 3 and 4, under the 1948 version of Table A] which govern this company such a matter is within the remit of the board?'[20] Following consideration and approval of the *Automatic Self-Cleansing* line of cases, Harman J concluded that 'thus, as it seems to me, there is little doubt that the law is that where matters are confided by articles such as article 80 to the conduct of the business by the directors, it is not a matter where the general meeting can intervene'.[21]

In summary we see that in relation to a decision to bring litigation against a director, there is an unresolved tension in English law between, on the one hand, an approach

---

[17] For a view that self-dealing transactions are voidable—even when entered into on the company's behalf by disinterested directors—due to an implied limitation of board authority see D. Kershaw, 'The Path of Fiduciary Law' (forthcoming, 2012) *New York University Journal of Law and Business*.

[18] Below, we consider the foundational derivative action case of *Foss v Harbottle* (1843) 2 Hare 462 where Wigram VC observed 'as I understand the Act [of incorporation] the proprietors [shareholders] so assembled have power, due notice being given for the purpose of the meeting, to originate proceeding for any purpose within the scope of the company's powers'. But note in this regard that this was based on the interpretation of this chartered company's act of incorporation.

[19] [1988] 4 BCC 452.

[20] Following our consideration of the balance of decision-making power in Chapter 6, we concluded that under the applicable version of Table A considered in the *Automatic Self-Cleansing* line of cases—as was the case with the 1948 version of Table A—this article did not provide for a shareholder instruction right.

[21] For an excellent discussion of this case see further Lord Wedderburn of Charlton, 'Control of Corporate Actions' (1989) 52 *Modern Law Review* 401.

that relies on a literal interpretation of the articles' distribution of power to the board and, on the other, an approach which implies a shareholder reservation of power into the articles which, read literally, only empower the board to make the litigation decision. The former approach is consistent with the approach to board power which we considered in Chapter 6 and is exemplified by *Automatic Self-Cleansing*, which enforces the terms of the constitution as agreed to by the parties. The latter approach, however, is also consistent with the English common law's resistance to reading the transfer of power to the board to cover situations in which the director's interests are directly in conflict with those of the shareholders.

III THE COMMON LAW'S REGULATION OF DERIVATIVE ACTIONS

The common law rules which, prior to the coming into force of the 2006 Act, determined when an individual shareholder could bring a derivative action on behalf of the company to enforce a breach of duty by the directors, have been viewed by many generations of company law students as one of the most difficult and confusing areas of company law. The good news then is that it is no longer necessary to know and understand in detail these rules because the Companies Act 2006 introduces a statutory derivative action—referred to by the Act as a 'derivative claim'—that, in effect, abolishes the common law rules on derivative actions.[22] It is useful, however, to have a general understanding of how these common law rules worked for two reasons: first, to place in historical context the introduction of the 2006 Act statutory derivative claim which we consider in detail in section IV of this chapter; and, secondly, if we view derivative actions as an important mechanism for holding directors to account given board conflicts and shareholder rational apathy, to understand the extent to which directors of UK companies have historically been exposed to litigation for breaches of duty.

The common law's approach to derivative actions is often referred to as the rule in *Foss v Harbottle*, a first instance case involving a derivative action brought by two shareholders of a chartered company alleging self-dealing on the part of the company's directors. There are, it is often said, two rules set out in *Foss v Harbottle*. The first is the rule referred to previously that the company is the proper plaintiff in an action relating to a wrong done to the company. The second rule in *Foss v Harbottle* addresses derivative actions brought by shareholders on behalf of the company and provides that *if* the shareholder body in general meeting can ratify the wrongful act committed against the company then individual shareholders cannot bring a derivative action on behalf of the company. Importantly, the rule *did not say* that no derivative action could be brought if the wrong *had been* ratified; rather it provides that no derivative action could be brought if the wrong *could be* ratified by the shareholders in general meeting. Both of these rules are underpinned by the idea that it is for the company and its organs to determine whether or not litigation against a director should be brought.

---

[22] Some doubt remains in this regard. We shall argue that in relation to multiple derivative actions—actions brought by members of a parent company in relation to wrongdoing by subsidiary directors—the common law remains in place. In relation to normal derivative actions the recent case of *Cinematic Finance Ltd v Ryder* [2010] All ER (D) 283, *per* Roth J appeared to hold that the proper plaintiff rule, discussed later, has not been abolished. This possibility raises a set of very interesting questions that have the potential to up-end our current assumptions about the Act. However, given the somewhat speculative nature of this possibility, it is in this author's view more appropriate in a book of this nature to proceed on the assumption that *in effect* the common law rules have been abolished. For an exploration of these issues see D. Kershaw 'The *Rule in Foss v Harbottle is Dead*; Long Live the *Rule in Foss v Harbottle*' (forthcoming, 2012).

■ *Foss v Harbottle* (1843) 2 Hare 462

Vice Chancellor Wigram

It was not, nor could it successfully be, argued that it was a matter of course for any individual members of a corporation thus to assume to themselves the right of suing in the name of the corporation. In law the corporation and the aggregate members of the corporation are not the same thing for purposes like this; and the only question can be whether the facts alleged in this case justify a departure from the rule which, *prima facie*, would require that the corporation should sue in its own name and in its corporate character, or in the name of someone whom the law has appointed to be its representative…

The first objection taken in the argument for the Defendants was that the individual members of the corporation cannot in any case sue in the form in which this bill is framed. During the argument I intimated an opinion, to which, upon further consideration, I fully adhere, that the rule was much too broadly stated on the part of the Defendants. I think there are cases in which a suit might properly be so framed. Corporations like this, of a private nature, are in truth little more than private partnerships; and in cases which may easily be suggested it would be too much to hold that a society of private persons associated together in under-takings, which, though certainly beneficial to the public, are nevertheless matters of private property, are to be deprived of their civil rights, *inter se*, because, in order to make their common objects more attainable, the Crown or the Legislature may have conferred upon them the benefit of a corporate character. If a case should arise of injury to a corporation by some of its members, for which no adequate remedy remained, except that of a suit by individual corporators in their private characters, and asking in such character the protection of those rights to which in their corporate character they were entitled, I cannot but think that…the claims of justice would be found superior to any difficulties arising out of technical rules respecting the mode in which corporations are required to sue.

But, on the other hand, it must not be without reasons of a very urgent character that established rules of law and practice are to be departed from, rules which, though in a sense technical, are founded on general principles of justice and convenience…

Whilst the supreme governing body, the proprietors at a special general meeting assembled, retain the power of exercising the functions conferred upon them by the Act of Incorporation, it cannot be competent to individual corporators to sue in the manner proposed by the Plaintiffs on the present record…

How then can this Court act in a suit constituted as this is, if it is to be assumed, for the purposes of the argument, that the powers of the body of proprietors are still in existence and may lawfully be exercised…Whilst the Court may be declaring the acts complained of to be void at the suit of the present Plaintiffs, who in fact may be the only proprietors who disapprove of them, the governing body of proprietors may defeat the decree by lawfully resolving upon the confirmation of the very acts which are the subject of the suit. The very fact that the governing body of proprietors assembled at the special general meeting may so bind even a reluctant minority is decisive to shew that the frame of this suit cannot be sustained whilst that body retains its functions. In order then that this suit may be sustained it must be shewn either that there is no such power as I have supposed remaining in the proprietors, or, at least, that all means have been resorted to and found ineffectual to set that body in motion.

For Wigram VC there are two bases for his decision to prevent the individual shareholders from bringing the action. The first is that the company through its organs is the proper plaintiff and only if those organs are prevented from acting would a derivative action be entertained. This could encompass both a practical barrier to holding a meeting and where the organs are disabled from acting in the company's interests because they are controlled by the wrongdoers. The second ground is that the general meeting—which he refers to as the 'governing body of proprietors'—could lawfully confirm 'the very acts which are the subject of the suit'. This process of confirming a wrong is what today we would refer to as 'ratification'. For Wigram VC it is inappropriate to allow an individual shareholder to bring suit and concern the court with the issues in question when the general meeting retains ultimate control over the outcome through the power to ratify the wrong committed by the director.[23]

The rule in *Foss v Harbottle* assumes that the appropriate body to decide whether litigation should be brought is the shareholders in general meeting and not individual shareholders acting alone. The case asserts the primacy of the shareholder body as a whole acting by majority rule. As most wrongs—including the types of breach of duty we have considered in Chapters 9–14—could be ratified, this rule leaves minimal scope for shareholders to commence derivative litigation. However, as you will see from the extract from *Foss v Harbottle*, Wigram VC's judgment contemplated—but did not specify circumstances in which—a derivative action could be brought to ensure that justice was served and not obstructed by technical rules. Over the years the courts developed a list of so-called 'exceptions to the rule in *Foss v Harbottle*' which specified circumstances in which individual shareholders would be allowed to bring a derivative action on behalf of the company. The rule in *Foss v Harbottle* and these so-called exceptions[24] are summarized by Jenkins LJ in *Edwards v Halliwell*.

■ *Edwards v Halliwell* [1950] 2 All ER 1064

Jenkins LJ

The rule in *Foss v Harbottle*, as I understand it, comes to no more than this. First, the proper plaintiff in an action in respect of a wrong alleged to be done to company or association of persons is *prima facie* the company or the association of persons itself. Secondly, where the alleged wrong is a transaction which might be made binding on the company or association and on all its members by a simple majority of the members, no individual member of the company is allowed to maintain an action in respect of that matter for the simple reason that, if a mere majority of the members of the company or association is in favour of what has been done, then *cadit quaestio*...[25] If, on the other hand, a simple majority of members of the company or association is against what has been done, then there is no valid reason why the company or association itself should not sue. In my judgment, it is implicit in the rule that the matter relied on as constituting the cause of action should be a cause of action properly belonging to the general body of corporators or members of the company or association as opposed to a cause of action which some individual member can assert in his own right.

The cases falling within the general ambit of the rule are subject to certain exceptions. It has been noted in the course of argument that in cases where the act complained of is wholly *ultra vires* the company or association the rule has no application because there is no question of the transaction being confirmed by any majority. It has been further pointed out that where what has been done amounts to what is generally called in these cases a fraud on the minority and the wrongdoers are themselves in control of the company, the rule is relaxed in favour of the aggrieved minority who are allowed to bring what is known as a minority shareholders' action on behalf of themselves and all others. The reason for this is that, if they were denied that right, their grievance could never reach the court because the wrongdoers themselves, being in control,

---

[23] At common law ratification requires a majority vote (ordinary resolution) of the shareholders in general meeting. At common law the interested shareholders could vote as shareholders to ratify their own breach as directors—*Northwest Transportation Co Ltd v Beatty* (1887) 12 App Cas 589. This has now been changed by section 239 of the Companies Act 2006 which prevents interested shareholders from voting to ratify a breach. For a more detailed discussion see Chapter 16.

[24] Commentators have observed that many of these 'exceptions' are not really exceptions at all, rather logical applications of the rule. See B. Pettet, *Company Law* (2nd edn, Longman, 2005). In this author's view this is wholly correct; however, it has become customary to present the rule through the lens of the exceptions and accordingly we follow this custom here.

[25] Latin for 'the question falls'.

would not allow the company to sue. Those exceptions are not directly in point in this case, but they show, especially the last one, that the rule is not an inflexible rule and it will be relaxed where necessary in the interests of justice.

There is a further exception which seems to me to touch this case directly. That is the exception noted by Romer J in *Cotter v National Union of Seamen*. He pointed out that the rule did not prevent an individual member from suing if the matter in respect of which he was suing was one which could validly be done or sanctioned, not by a simple majority of the members of the company or association, but only by some special majority, as, for instance, in the case of a limited company under the Companies Act, a special resolution duly passed as such. As Romer J pointed out, the reason for that exception is clear, because otherwise, if the rule were applied in its full rigour, a company which, by its directors, had broken its own regulations by doing something without a special resolution which could only be done validly by a special resolution could assert that it alone was the proper plaintiff in any consequent action and the effect would be to allow a company acting in breach of its articles to do *de facto* by ordinary resolution that which according to its own regulations could only be done by special resolution.

The contours of these exceptions is now a matter only of historical interest. We do not, therefore, consider them here in depth. A few additional comments, however, are warranted in relation to the fraud on the minority exception in order to understand the availability in practice of the derivative suit prior to the 2006 Act.

Of the three exceptions, the most important and the most difficult for the student of company law is the 'fraud on the minority' exception. This exception provides that in relation to certain types of wrong that qualified as 'fraud' *within the meaning of this exception*, if the wrongdoers—that is the directors who had breached their duties— also had control of the general meeting by reason of their votes as shareholders then a derivative action would be allowed. There were two criteria to be fulfilled in order to fall within this exception. The first was that the wrong—for example, the breach of duty—to be addressed through the derivative action was a wrong that fell within the category of 'fraud on the minority'. The second was the requirement of 'wrongdoer control' of the general meeting.

In relation to the question of which wrongs fell within the exception one must not be misled by the label 'fraud'. It is clear, as stated by Megarry VC in *Estmanco v GLC*,[26] that the types of wrong that fell within this category extended well beyond common law fraud.[27] However, the types of wrong that fell within the 'fraud on the minority' exception remained unclear. For Megarry VC in *Estmanco* the term referred to the 'abuse of process', a seemingly very broad understanding of the exception. In *Daniels v Daniels* self-serving negligence was held to fall within this exception.[28] As *Daniels v Daniels* indicates, to fall within this category of 'fraud' the breach of duty had to both damage the company and also benefit or enrich the director who was in breach. Where there was no personal benefit for the director the wrong would not fall within the 'fraud' category and no derivative action could be brought in relation to that wrong.[29] So, for example, negligence that did not involve a 'self-serving' element did not fall within the exception.[30]

---

[26] [1982] 1 WLR 2.

[27] Megarry VC in *Estmanco v Greater London Council* [1982] 1 All ER 437 observed that ' "fraud on a minority" seems to be being used as comprising not only fraud at common law but also fraud in the wider equitable sense of that term...It seems to me that the sum total represents a fraud on the minority in the sense in which "fraud" is used in that phrase, or alternatively represents such an abuse of power as to have the same effect.'

[28] [1978] Ch 406.

[29] See, however, Vinelott J in his first instance judgment in *Prudential Assurance Co Ltd v Newman Industries Co Ltd (No 2)* [1980] 2 All ER 841 suggested it covered any wrong.

[30] *Pavlides v Jensen* [1956] Ch 565.

The second element of the 'fraud on the minority' exception required that the director in breach of his duties (the 'wrongdoer') controlled[31] the general meeting. The courts thereby responded to the concern we noted in section I of this chapter, that if you are going to rely on the shareholder body as a whole to police when litigation can be brought against directors it will be ineffectual if you allow the directors in breach of their duties to exercise their votes as shareholders where they have sufficient votes to determine the outcome of the vote. Subsequent courts tightened the rules on this exception by requiring not only that the wrongdoers had control, but also that a majority of the disinterested minority shareholders would wish to take litigation. The courts did not, however, outline how such majority or the minority opinion would be determined or canvassed by a court in the absence of an actual vote.[32]

The wrongdoer control requirement meant that this exception was not available in relation to the vast majority of listed companies where directors, although they may own shares in the company, typically do not have either de jure or de facto control of the general meeting. Indeed the last reported derivative litigation involving a listed company was in 1982 in *Prudential Assurance Co Ltd v Newman Industries*. Accordingly, prior to the 2006 Act there was very limited scope to use the derivative action mechanism to enforce breaches of directors' duties in relation to closely-held companies and virtually no scope whatsoever in relation to listed companies.

Note also that if a derivative litigant could establish that the wrong in question fell within the 'fraud on the minority exception' this did not mean that the litigant would automatically be able to proceed with the litigation. Courts required a preliminary hearing[33] at which, in addition to establishing whether the claim fell within the fraud on the minority exception, the derivative litigant had to demonstrate that there was a prima facie case for breach of duty, that the action was brought in good faith[34] by the derivative litigant, and, more recently, that the action could objectively be construed as being in the corporate interest.[35]

There were two significant flaws in the *Foss v Harbottle* approach to derivative litigation. The first was that this approach to derivative actions was premised on the idea that the general meeting is an effective decision-making body—that where litigation would be in the best interests of the company, shareholders would see to it that litigation would be brought. Importantly, the common law's faith in the shareholder body's ability to make such a decision was formed in a period in which no one had given consideration to the rational apathy and collective action problems associated with widely-held companies and to the concern that if the shareholders fail to act as rational, informed decision-makers then formally empowering shareholders indirectly cedes control of the litigation decision to the board. An increasing awareness of the problems generated by the separation of ownership and control did not, however, result in a reassessment by the common law of its approach to derivative litigation.[36] The second flaw in the common law's approach was that whilst the 'fraud on the minority' exception recognized that if shareholder decision-making is infected by the interests of

---

[31] Control was understood by the courts to mean both de jure and de facto control—i.e. actually holding 50% of the votes but also where less than 50% of the votes enabled control *in fact*, because, for example, a significant percentage of shareholders never vote at all—*Prudential Assurance Co Ltd v Newman Industries Co Ltd (No 2)* [1982] 1 All ER 354.

[32] *Smith v Croft (No 2)* [1988] Ch 114.

[33] *Prudential Assurance Co Ltd v Newman Industries Co Ltd (No 2)* [1982] 1 All ER 354.

[34] *Barrett v Duckett* [1995] 1 BCLC 243.

[35] *Mumbray v Lapper* [2005] EWHC 1152 and *Airey v Cordell* [2006] EWHC 2728 *per* Warren J: 'the correct test for allowing the action to continue' involved asking whether the decision is one 'which a reasonable board could take'.

[36] *Prudential Assurance Co Ltd v Newman Industries Co Ltd (No 2)* [1982] 1 All ER 354; *Smith v Croft (No 2)* [1988] Ch 114.

the individuals who are alleged to have breached their duties then an exception to the restrictive rule should be made, it failed to make this exception available in relation to any wrong, rather only in relation to wrongs that fell in the unclear and misleading category of 'fraud'.

In 1998 the Law Commission published a report on *Shareholder Remedies* in which they considered the status of the derivative remedy in UK law. In essence, they concluded that UK law's reticence to allow access to the derivative action was wise but the approach was too 'complicated and unwieldy' and restrictive. They summarized their position as follows.

■ **Law Commission, *Shareholder Remedies* LC 246, para 6.4**

Our view was that the basic approach to the right to bring a derivative action was a sound one: an individual shareholder should only be able to bring such an action in exceptional circumstances…But we considered that the rule was complicated and unwieldy. It could only be found in case law, much of it decided many years ago; the meaning of terms such as 'wrongdoer control' were not clear; and there were situations which appeared to fall outside the fraud on the minority exception when it might be desirable for a member to be able to bring an action.

The Law Commission accordingly recommended the introduction of a statutory derivative remedy that would address the shortcomings of the common law. This recommendation was seconded by the Company Law Review's Final Report[37] and resulted in the introduction of a statutory derivative claim in sections 260–264 of the Companies Act 2006, to which we now turn our attention.[38]

IV DERIVATIVE ACTIONS UNDER THE COMPANIES ACT 2006

1 The new statutory derivative action mechanism

The introduction of the new statutory derivative claim in effect overrules the rule in *Foss v Harbottle*.[39] In several respects, discussed later in this chapter, it represents a profound change in UK company law. Since the coming into force of this Part of the Act in 2007[40] there have been several cases dealing with the new procedure which we address later. However, as one would expect given the infancy of this procedure, there remain many open and unaddressed questions about how these rules will be interpreted and applied. The provisions implementing the statutory derivative mechanism are set out in Part 11 of the Companies Act 2006 (Derivative claims and proceedings by members); sections 260–264.

---

[37] CLR, chapter 7, para 7.42.

[38] The substantive terms of the 2006 Act's Derivative Claim procedure differ from the procedure recommended by the Law Commission and the Company Law Review in some important respects.

[39] In *Iesini v Westrip Holdings Ltd* [2010] All ER (D) 10 at [73] Lewison J observed that 'the new code has replaced the common law derivative action'. See note 22 regarding residual doubt regarding this position. The common law rules on derivative actions continue to apply to breaches of duty committed by directors prior to the coming into force of Chapter 11 on 1 October 2007—see Explanatory Memorandum to The Companies Act 2006 (Commencement No 3, Consequential Amendments, Transitional Provisions And Savings) Order 2007, SI 2007/2194 (C 84), para 7.2.

[40] *Ibid.*

■ Section 260 CA 2006 Derivative claims

(1) This Chapter applies to proceedings in England and Wales or Northern Ireland by a member of a company—

(a) in respect of a cause of action vested in the company, and

(b) seeking relief on behalf of the company.

This is referred to in this Chapter as a 'derivative claim'.

(2) A derivative claim may only be brought—

(a) under this Chapter, or

(b) in pursuance of an order of the court in proceedings under section 994 (proceedings for protection of members against unfair prejudice).

(3) A derivative claim under this Chapter may be brought only in respect of a cause of action arising from an actual or proposed act or omission involving negligence, default, breach of duty or breach of trust by a director of the company.

The cause of action may be against the director or another person (or both).

(4) It is immaterial whether the cause of action arose before or after the person seeking to bring or continue the derivative claim became a member of the company.

(5) For the purposes of this Chapter—

(a) 'director' includes a former director;

(b) a shadow director is treated as a director; and

(c) references to a member of a company include a person who is not a member but to whom shares in the company have been transferred or transmitted by operation of law.

■ Section 261 CA 2006 Application for permission to continue derivative claim

(1) A member of a company who brings a derivative claim under this Chapter must apply to the court for permission (in Northern Ireland, leave) to continue it.

(2) If it appears to the court that the application and the evidence filed by the applicant in support of it do not disclose a prima facie case for giving permission (or leave), the court—

(a) must dismiss the application, and

(b) may make any consequential order it considers appropriate.

(3) If the application is not dismissed under subsection (2), the court—

(a) may give directions as to the evidence to be provided by the company, and

(b) may adjourn the proceedings to enable the evidence to be obtained.

(4) On hearing the application, the court may—

(a) give permission (or leave) to continue the claim on such terms as it thinks fit,

(b) refuse permission (or leave) and dismiss the claim, or

(c) adjourn the proceedings on the application and give such directions as it thinks fit.

■ Section 262 CA 2006 Application for permission to continue claim as a derivative claim

(1) This section applies where—

(a) a company has brought a claim, and

(b) the cause of action on which the claim is based could be pursued as a derivative claim under this Chapter.

(2) A member of the company may apply to the court for permission (in Northern Ireland, leave) to continue the claim as a derivative claim on the ground that—

   (a) the manner in which the company commenced or continued the claim amounts to an abuse of the process of the court,

   (b) the company has failed to prosecute the claim diligently, and

   (c) it is appropriate for the member to continue the claim as a derivative claim.

(3) If it appears to the court that the application and the evidence filed by the applicant in support of it do not disclose a prima facie case for giving permission (or leave), the court—

   (a) must dismiss the application, and

   (b) may make any consequential order it considers appropriate.

(4) If the application is not dismissed under subsection (3), the court—

   (a) may give directions as to the evidence to be provided by the company, and

   (b) may adjourn the proceedings to enable the evidence to be obtained.

(5) On hearing the application, the court may—

   (a) give permission (or leave) to continue the claim as a derivative claim on such terms as it thinks fit,

   (b) refuse permission (or leave) and dismiss the application, or

   (c) adjourn the proceedings on the application and give such directions as it thinks fit.

■ Section 263 CA 2006 Whether permission to be given

(1) The following provisions have effect where a member of a company applies for permission (in Northern Ireland, leave) under section 261 or 262.

(2) Permission (or leave) must be refused if the court is satisfied—

   (a) that a person acting in accordance with section 172 (duty to promote the success of the company) would not seek to continue the claim, or

   (b) where the cause of action arises from an act or omission that is yet to occur, that the act or omission has been authorised by the company, or

   (c) where the cause of action arises from an act or omission that has already occurred, that the act or omission—

       (i) was authorised by the company before it occurred, or

       (ii) has been ratified by the company since it occurred.

(3) In considering whether to give permission (or leave) the court must take into account, in particular—

   (a) whether the member is acting in good faith in seeking to continue the claim;

   (b) the importance that a person acting in accordance with section 172 (duty to promote the success of the company) would attach to continuing it;

   (c) where the cause of action results from an act or omission that is yet to occur, whether the act or omission could be, and in the circumstances would be likely to be—

       (i) authorised by the company before it occurs, or

       (ii) ratified by the company after it occurs;

   (d) where the cause of action arises from an act or omission that has already occurred, whether the act or omission could be, and in the circumstances would be likely to be, ratified by the company;

(e) whether the company has decided not to pursue the claim;

(f) whether the act or omission in respect of which the claim is brought gives rise to a cause of action that the member could pursue in his own right rather than on behalf of the company.

(4) In considering whether to give permission (or leave) the court shall have particular regard to any evidence before it as to the views of members of the company who have no personal interest, direct or indirect, in the matter.

(5) The Secretary of State may by regulations—

(a) amend subsection (2) so as to alter or add to the circumstances in which permission (or leave) is to be refused;

(b) amend subsection (3) so as to alter or add to the matters that the court is required to take into account in considering whether to give permission (or leave).

(6) Before making any such regulations the Secretary of State shall consult such persons as he considers appropriate.

(7) Regulations under this section are subject to affirmative resolution procedure.

2 Structure and ground rules of the derivative claim

The formal structure of the statutory derivative action—referred to in the Act as a 'derivative claim'—is very different to the structure of the approach set out in the rule in *Foss v Harbottle* and the exceptions to the rule. Whereas under the common law in order to bring a derivative action a shareholder would have to demonstrate that the action fell within one of the exceptions to the rule in *Foss v Harbottle*, under the Companies Act 2006 in relation to claims against directors for breach of duty a shareholder may clearly bring a derivative claim; however, she must then apply to the court for permission to continue with the claim.

Section 260(3) of the Act specifies that a derivative claim may be brought in respect of an 'actual or proposed act or omission involving negligence, default, breach of duty or breach of trust by a director of the company'. The Act provides for a broad range of wrongful conduct which can be the subject of a derivative claim including: any breach of the duties set out in sections 170–177 of the Act; any 'default' which would, for example, cover any civil claim against a director for failure to observe the statutory requirements of the 2006 Act such as the substantial property transaction rules;[41] and any breach of trust, which, as we shall see in Chapter 19, is the conceptual basis for holding a director liable for authorizing the payment of an illegal dividend. The Act's intention to cover all potential wrongs that could be committed by a director is manifest in the subsection's repetition of the same wrong, namely negligence. One wonders in what circumstances would a negligent act by a director not also be a breach of a director's duty to act with reasonable care, skill, and diligence?

The derivative claim mechanism is made available to shareholders not only in relation to wrongs that have been committed by the directors but also in relation to wrongs that have been proposed. The remedy for a derivative claim brought in relation to a proposed wrong would be an injunction to stop the proposal from being implemented. But what exactly amounts to a proposed wrong or breach? It would clearly include a proposed resolution on a board agenda that if passed would amount to a breach of duty. Another possibility is that the concept of proposed breach encompasses circumstances in which the board has resolved to take action that has not been implemented by the company. This could include, for example, a board resolution to enter into a contract in excess of

---

[41] Sections 190–195 CA 2006.

the authority given to the board by the constitution prior to entering into the contract (section 171(a)); a resolution to issue shares for the improper purpose of interfering with shareholders' constitutional rights (section171(b)) prior to issuing the shares; a self-dealing contract yet to be entered into where the board resolved to enter into the contract but the interested director failed to provide the required disclosure pursuant to section 177; or the declaration of an illegal dividend that has not been paid. However, the concept of 'proposed breach' does not, it is submitted, encompass circumstances in which a director may act individually in breach of his duty, for example where a director is considering taking an unauthorized corporate opportunity. One could not say that in such circumstances the director had made a *proposal* to breach his duty.

2.1 Who can bring a derivative claim?

A derivative claim may be brought only by a member[42] of the company and not by any other corporate constituency. The constituencies to whose interests section 172(1)[43] requires that directors shall have regard when acting to promote the success of the company for the benefit of the members do not have a right to bring a derivative claim. Nor do creditors have any right to bring a derivative claim even where, because the company is insolvent or where it is approaching insolvency, the directors owe a duty to promote the success of the company for the benefit of its creditors rather than the members as a whole.[44] However, note in this regard that the Act does not impose a threshold shareholder ownership requirement in order to be able to bring a derivative claim: being a member with one share would be sufficient.[45] Nor does the shareholder who brings the claim have to have been a shareholder at the time the wrong, which is the subject of the claim, was committed.[46] Accordingly, whilst no right to bring a derivative claim is given to any constituency other than members, the barriers to other constituencies bringing actions *as members* are very low and, therefore, there is significant scope for the commencement of nuisance suits. In this regard, commenting on a proposed amendment to the Companies Bill which would have altered the provision to require that

---

[42] A member is defined in section 112 of the 2006 Act as a person who is entered in the company's register of members. Pursuant to subsection 260(5) a person who is not formally a member but to whom shares have been transferred by operation of law—for example, where a person inherits shares—is also entitled to bring a derivative claim pursuant to this Part 11 of the Act.

[43] See Chapter 10.

[44] See Chapter 18. Note, however, that when the company is in the process of being wound up that section 212 Insolvency Act 1986 provides a summary procedure for creditors (section 212(3)) to apply for the court to examine the actions of the director and, at the court's discretion, order relief.

[45] The Companies Act 2006 does provide for such an ownership threshold derivative action mechanism in relation to the enforcement of the breach by directors of the rules on political donations by companies set out in Part 14 of the Act. Although contained in the Companies Act 2006 these rules are viewed more as public law rules regulating the integrity of the UK's political parties and our democratic process than they are rules regulating the governance and operation of the company, although clearly the rules restrict and regulate corporate actions. In short these rules require member approval to make a donation to a political party (see sections 366–368 CA 2006) and hold directors liable for the amount of the donation and damage caused to the company if a donation is made in contravention of the rules (section 369 CA 2006). In relation to these rules the Act provides for a specific derivative suit mechanism to enforce these rules. Note that this mechanism has *no* application to the enforcement of any other rule or duties. This mechanism provides that shareholders who individually, or in aggregate, have 5% in nominal value of the company's issued share capital or a group of at least 50 members may bring a derivative action to enforce a breach of these rules by the directors (sections 370–373 CA 2006). Note also that many civil law jurisdictions make use of such threshold derivative actions—see, for example, section 148 of the German Stock Corporation Act providing for a 1% threshold (coupled with court control).

[46] Section 260(4) CA 2006. This contrasts with other jurisdictions, for example Delaware, that require that the shareholder who brings the suit was a shareholder at the time the act which allegedly involves a breach of duty was committed—see J.H. Choper et al, *Cases and Material on Corporations* (Foundation Press, 2004).

shareholders bringing derivative claims must have been members at the time the cause of action arose, Lord Grabiner noted:

> The amendment is directed towards a legitimate concern—namely, the risk of proliferation of vexatious or near-vexatious litigation. It is said, rightly, that that would damage commercial activity. It is easy to think of some examples, which my noble friend Lady Goudie and other noble Lords have identified, such as the [vulture fund], working in cahoots with the rough equivalent of the ambulance-chasing solicitor, buying a few shares in a targeted company and then bringing a derivative claim, alleging that its rights as a minority shareholder have been abused by the controllers of the company.[47]

These concerns were rejected by the Government. Lord Goldsmith on behalf of the Government noted that:

> This is the present position under the common law derivative action—that is, it does not matter when you became a member…Of course, the claim has to be there. You cannot create it but, if it is there, it should not matter whether you became a member before or after it came into existence…Company law works on the basis that, when you acquire shares, you get all the bad and all the good that go with them and sometimes perhaps a bit of both.[48]

2.2 Who can a derivative claim be brought against?

The derivative claim mechanism provides shareholders with a mechanism of enforcing breaches of duty and obligation by directors, former directors, or shadow directors.[49] It does not give shareholders the right to bring suit on behalf of the company in relation to claims the company may have against third parties. All wrongs referred to in section 260(3) which may be the subject of a derivative action are qualified by the words 'by a director'. In this regard do not be misled by the wording at the end of subsection (3) which provides that a claim may be brought against 'a director or another person'. This 'another person' does not refer to a third party unconnected to a director, rather it covers legal or real persons who have assisted the director in the breach of his duty. For example, if a corporate opportunity is exploited not by the director personally but indirectly through a company in relation to which he is the sole shareholder, then a derivative claim may be brought against that company as well as the director.[50]

3 Permission to continue the derivative claim

Although the Act provides that a member is entitled to bring a derivative claim to enforce a breach of duty or other obligation owed by a director, the Act does not give a shareholder general permission to continue the claim. Section 261 of the Act requires that

---

[47] Hansard, 27 February 2006, col GC13. Lord Grabiner, however, rejected the amendment on other grounds.

[48] Hansard, 27 February 2006, col GC16.

[49] Section 260(5) CA 2006. However, the extent to which a derivative action may be brought against a shadow director is a function of whether the shadow director has breached a duty to the company and, as we saw in Chapter 9, it is unclear to what extent a shadow director would owe duties to the company.

[50] See further *Explanatory Notes to Companies Act 2006*, para 494 referring to the example of knowing receipt by a third party in the commission of breach of trust by the director. See also *Iesini v Westrip Holdings Ltd* [2010] All ER (D) 108 at [75] *per* Lewison J observing in this regard that: 'a claim against a person who had dishonestly assisted in a breach of fiduciary duty or who had knowingly received trust property would be paradigm examples'.

once the claim has been brought the shareholder must apply to the court for permission to continue the claim.

The Act provides for a two-step procedure. Pursuant to section 261(2), following the filing of the application to continue the claim, the court will consider whether the application and any papers filed with the application establishes a prima facie case *for permission*; that is, whether the filed documents alone establish a prima facie case for permission. Importantly, this is not a prima facie case that there has been a wrong committed but a prima facie case that permission should be granted. However, in the recent first instance judgment of *Iesini v Westrip Holdings Ltd* Lewison J held in this regard that a prima facie case for permission 'necessarily entails that there is a prima facie case that the company has a good cause of action and that the cause of action arises out of directors' default, breach of duty etc'.[51]

If, on the face of the application and the filed evidence, the court concludes that there is no such prima facie case for permission to continue the claim then the court must dismiss the application, thereby discontinuing the claim. If the court dismisses the application at this stage then the shareholder who brought the claim may request an oral hearing for the court to reconsider the decision.[52] If the court decides that on the basis of the application and the submitted evidence a prima facie case for permission to continue the claim has been established then the court will adjourn the application and allow the company to file evidence and to be heard at a hearing on the application.

Where the court determines in stage one that the shareholder claimant has established a prima facie case for permission, stage two of the permission process involves a hearing where the court determines whether or not permission should be granted to continue the claim. Section 263 sets out both situations in which the court *must* refuse permission to continue the claim as well as criteria for the court to consider where the Act does not *require* the court to refuse permission. Note, however, that the court may allow the stage one process to be side-stepped where the review of the permission to continue with the action is appropriately dealt with in a single hearing which is also considering other procedural issues in relation to other claims of action arising from the same facts.[53]

3.1 Situations in which the court must refuse permission to continue the derivative claim

Section 263(2)(a) provides that permission to continue a derivative claim *must* be refused if 'a person acting in accordance with section 172 would not seek to continue the claim'. In subsection (2)(b) and (c) the Act provides that if an act that is yet to be carried out has been authorized by the company or a committed act has been ratified by the company then permission to continue the claim *must* be refused. Let us address subsections 2(b) and (c) first and then address the impact of subsection (2)(a).

3.2 Actual ratification or authorization

Subsections 2(b) and (c) of the Act refer to the authorization or ratification of an act or omission that is the basis for the derivative claim. The term 'authorization' refers to obtaining requisite approvals in advance of the commission of the Act. Typically this will involve the approval of the shareholder body but would also include disinterested director authorization pursuant to section 175—the duty to avoid conflicts of interest.

---

[51] [2010] All ER (D) 108 at [78].

[52] See Rule 19.9A Civil Procedure Rules and Practice Direction Part 19C, supplementing Civil Procedure Rules Part 19.

[53] See *Franbar Holdings Ltd v Patel* [2008] EWHC 1534 (Ch) where William Trower QC considered a stage two hearing without any stage one application where other procedural applications—including a section 994 petition—relating to the same facts were being considered.

If authorization is obtained there is no infringement of the duty. Ratification involves retrospective approval in relation to acts that have already been committed—it requires the approval of shareholders in general meeting (discussed further later in this chapter). The retrospective ratification of any breach cures the breach. It follows, therefore, that any act that has been authorized or ratified cannot be the basis for a cause of action and, logically, that any derivative claim based on such an act is without foundation and must be discontinued.

In relation to the mechanics of the ratification of a breach of duty by the shareholders, the Act makes important changes to the common law position. At common law the wrongdoing director was not prevented from voting as a shareholder in relation to any ratification resolution.[54] Section 239 of the Act reverses this rule and provides that the votes of the wrongdoing director, or any person 'connected with him',[55] do not count in any ratification resolution of the general meeting and that the director and persons connected with him do not count as members for the purpose of written resolutions. Accordingly, wrongdoing directors cannot use their votes as shareholders to ratify a breach and prevent the bringing of a derivative action. Interestingly, however, the amendment to the common law rules on ratification in section 239 do not apply to pre-breach authorization. Accordingly the common law rules on the ability of interested shareholders to authorize actions that would amount to a breach of duty continue to apply.[56]

3.3 The court's business judgment

3.3.1 *Section 263(2)(a)*

Section 263(2)(a) provides that the court must refuse permission to continue a derivative claim if 'a person acting in accordance with section 172 (duty to promote the success of the company) would not seek to continue the claim'. That is, the court must ask whether 'a person' would determine that continuing the claim would not promote the success of the company for the benefit of the members as a whole having had regard to the factors and constituency interests set out in section 172(1)(a)–(f). The Act does not specify who this hypothetical person is. One would expect the court to ask whether a reasonable director acting in accordance with section 172 would *not* seek to continue the claim.

Through the lens of a hypothetical reasonable director the courts are being asked, in effect, to make their own business judgment about whether it makes sense for the company to continue the action commenced by the shareholder. The courts, therefore, become the filter mechanism for distinguishing between the potential good and bad— *from the company's perspective*—of derivative actions.

As we saw in our analysis of directors' duties, UK company law subjects business judgments to a very low level of review. In Chapter 10 we noted that there are good reasons for taking a deferential approach in relation to business judgments, in particular that ex-post review of those judgments may chill risk-taking by directors fearful that if the outcome of a decision is unsuccessful judges may, ex-post, equate lack of success with incompetence and impose liability. This could mean that directors make less risky but less profitable investment decisions. Importantly, this policy concern is not relevant to the court's decision as to whether derivative litigation should be allowed to continue. The court is not being asked to review the board's previous business judgment; the court

---

[54] *Northwest Transportation Co Ltd v Beatty* (1887) 12 App Cas 589. In this author's view the common law did impose some restraints in this regard, which are considered in detail in Chapter 16, section II.1.1.

[55] Connected person is defined in section 252. Section 239(3) excludes section 252(3) for the purpose of the meaning of 'connected person' in section 239. Section 252(3) excluded from the definition of connected person any person who is himself a director. On the meaning of connected person see p 502.

[56] See Chapter 16, section II.1.1.

is being asked to make—through the lens of the hypothetical director—its own *de novo* business judgment.

A central part of any business judgment about whether litigation will promote the success of the company is clearly an assessment of the strength of the underlying claim and an assessment of the damages or compensation that will be paid to the company if the claim is successful. This is what judges do for a living and clearly they will be far more adept about making such an assessment than most directors would be. Similarly, judges have considerable knowledge about the legal costs that the company may incur in the litigation. However, as we identified in our introductory discussion in this chapter, although these factors are clearly very important, the business decision as to whether to bring litigation does not turn simply on the legal strength of the case and the likely award of damages if successful. Other factors are also very important, in particular: the costs that will be incurred by the business as a result of its directors', managers', and employees' involvement with, and the distraction caused by, the litigation process; the effect on company morale of the litigation; and the reputational damage that may be incurred by the company as a result of the publicity and disclosure arising from the litigation. The courts will find these business factors more difficult to assess and, importantly, the court's assessment will necessarily have to rely on information provided by the board of directors—which, as we have already noted, may be of suspect neutrality. Nevertheless, they are factors that the court *must* take into account because a business judgment in relation to the litigation, as contrasted with a legal assessment of the claim, will not merely take into account the probability, and the costs, of success in court. If courts, as a result of any discomfort regarding the assessment of these less tangible business factors, retreat into an assessment only of the legal factors associated with the litigation, then the courts will fail to perform the role designated to them by the legislature of acting as the filter mechanism between the good and the bad of derivative actions.

How then have the courts engaged with this new[57] role. We start with *Franbar Holdings Ltd v Patel*, which was one of the first cases to consider in detail the role of the court's business judgment pursuant to section 263(2)(a).

■ *Franbar Holdings Ltd v Patel* [2008] EWHC 1534 (Ch)

William Trower QC (sitting as a deputy court judge)
The duty under s 172 is to act in the way that the director considers, in good faith, would be most likely to promote the success of the relevant company for the benefit of its members as a whole, having regard amongst other matters to a number of listed criteria. [Counsel for the defendant] has sought to persuade me that I can be satisfied that directors acting in accordance with s 172 would not seek to continue the claim because Franbar [the shareholder in the company bringing the derivative claim] has not established a sufficiently cogent case on the merits to lead a reasonable director to conclude that the continuation of the claim would be in the best interests of Medicentres [(UK) Ltd, the subject company]. In particular, he submits that the evidence [set out

---

[57] Note that this role is not completely new for the courts. Under the old *Foss v Harbottle* approach to derivative actions the courts required that the derivative litigant must obtain the court's leave to continue with the claim. Many of the considerations which were taken into account by the courts were similar to the factors listed in section 263. Although of very late vintage (2005) the courts had begun to ask whether the bringing of the action was indeed in the company's interests. In *Mumbray v Lapper* [2005] EWHC 1152 and *Airey v Cordell* [2006] EWHC 2728 in order to obtain leave to bring the action the court asked whether the litigation was in the company's interest. Warren J in *Airey v Cordell*, for example, held that 'the correct test for allowing the action to continue' involved asking whether the decision is one 'which a reasonable board could take'. This approach was, however, wholly undeveloped prior to the coming into force of the Companies Act 2006.

in the witness statements] is of such low quality that the hypothetical director would not seek to continue the claim on that ground alone...

Franbar contends to the contrary. It says that the allegations made are so serious and have caused such serious losses that the hypothetical director contemplated by s 263(2) would undoubtedly seek to continue the claim. For reasons I shall come to, I am not satisfied that this is correct, but my conclusion does not mean that I must refuse permission. The court is only required to refuse permission if it is satisfied that the hypothetical director would not seek to continue the claim.

In my judgment, this is one of those cases in which there is room for more than one view. Directors are often in the position of having to make what is no more than a partially informed decision on whether or not the institution of legal proceedings is appropriate, without having a very clear idea of how the proceedings will turn out. Some directors might wish to spend more time investigating and strengthening the company's case before issuing process, while others would wish to press on with proceedings straight away; in a case such as this one, both approaches would be entirely appropriate. It is my view that there is sufficient material for the hypothetical director to conclude that the conduct of [the company's] business by those in control of it had given rise to actionable breaches of duty...Even though [a hypothetical director] may take a healthily sceptical approach to [the company's] ability to prove the allegations at trial, it does not follow that the claim should not be continued on that ground alone.

The next question for the court is to exercise its discretion having regard to the statutory considerations set out in ss 263(3) and 263(4) of the Companies Act 2006.

From this extract the court appears to perform only one part of what one would expect a hypothetical director acting in accordance with section 172 to do, namely to consider whether the available evidence provides a legal claim that is strong enough to support commencing litigation. For William Trower QC the fact that a hypothetical director *could* conclude that there was an actionable case for breach of duty would be sufficient to avoid the application of section 263(2)(a) and the mandatory discontinuance of the action. This view was affirmed in *Iesini v Westrip Holdings*.

■ *Iesini v Westrip Holdings Ltd* [2010] All ER (D) 108

Lewison J

As many judges have pointed out (e.g. Warren J in *Airey v Cordell* [2007] BCC 785, 800[58] and Mr William Trower QC in *Franbar Holdings Ltd v Patel* [2009] 1 BCLC 1, 11) there are many cases in which some directors, acting in accordance with section 172, would think it worthwhile to continue a claim at least for the time being, while others, also acting in accordance with section 172, would reach the opposite conclusion. There are, of course, a number of factors that a director, acting in accordance with section 172, would consider in reaching his decision. They include: the size of the claim; the strength of the claim; the cost of the proceedings; the company's ability to fund the proceedings; the ability of the potential defendants to satisfy a judgment; the impact on the company if it lost the claim and had to pay not only its own costs but the defendant's as well; any disruption to the company's activities while the claim is pursued; whether the prosecution of the claim would damage the company in other ways (e.g. by losing the services of a valuable employee or alienating a key supplier or customer) and so on. The weighing of all

---

[58] Note that *Airey v Cordell* is a pre-2006 Act case in which Warren J emphasized that there are likely to be a range of reasonable director decisions and, therefore, this test should only result in permission to proceed being refused where 'no board acting reasonably could decide to take proceedings, for instance because it was wholly disproportionate and cost effective'. Clearly this pre-Act position has been extremely influential in the interpretation of section 263(2)(a).

these considerations is essentially a commercial decision, which the court is ill-equipped to take, except in a clear case.

In my judgment therefore (in agreement with Warren J and Mr Trower QC) section 263(2)(a) will apply only where the court is satisfied that no director acting in accordance with section 172 would seek to continue the claim. If some directors would, and others would not, seek to continue the claim the case is one for the application of section 263(3)(b). Many of the same considerations would apply to that paragraph too.

[The court proceeded to consider the legal basis for the action which it concluded was so weak that the action should be discontinued]

Following *Franbar* and *Iesini* it appears that where there is a plausible case for breach of duty which can be prosecuted without incurring excessive costs and which could result in a more than *de-minimis* payment to the company, then the action will not be discontinued pursuant to section 263(2)(a). It is only when the case is exceptionally weak or the potential award of damages immaterial and *de-minimis* that the court will discontinue on the basis of section 263(2)(a).[59] This means that, at this stage of the process, in most instances the courts will only take into account legal considerations and not business considerations: where the case is legally very weak the litigation will be discontinued; where there appears to be a case to answer the court will address the matter under their discretion to allow the claim to continue pursuant to section 263(3).[60]

The key question that follows from this approach is whether, for the purpose of section 263(2)(a), there is a standard of proof with regard to the strength of the case which needs to be discharged in order to be able to avoid mandatory discontinuation. Lewison J suggests that there is. He observes that as a prima facie case is required at stage one of the hearing, necessarily at stage two 'something more than a prima facie case is required'. This suggests a standard somewhere between a prima facie case and a civil burden of proof. Other courts, however, have held explicitly that the Act does not require any standard of proof. Roth J in *Stainer v Lee*[61] was of the view that section 263 does 'not prescribe a particular standard of proof'. Newey J in *Kleanthous v Paphitis*[62] agreed with Roth J and observed that 'the 2006 Act does not in terms provide that a claim must reach a specific threshold if it is to be allowed to continue'. *Stainer* and *Kleanthous* also acknowledge that although the strength of the case is a central consideration for a person applying section 172, even weaker cases may justify continued litigation 'if the amount of the potential recovery is very large'.[63]

Given the fact that the we remain in the very formative stages of applying section 263, we need to ask whether the approach to section 263(2)(a) taken by the courts to date is the correct one. With respect, it is submitted that there are good reasons to doubt that it is. This approach appears to provide no room for the consideration of business factors at this stage of the process, yet these factors could render a legally strong case very clearly not in the company's interests. Indeed, the importance of legal factors such as probable

---

[59] In *Iesini* at [102], for example, Lewison J concluded that: 'in my judgment this is a clear case. The strength of the claim against the board is so weak that I conclude that no director, acting in accordance with section 172, would seek to continue the claim against the directors'.

[60] Affirming this view see *Kiani v Cooper* [2010] 2 BCLC 42 at [35] where the section 263(2) question is reduced to the question of whether the derivative litigant had made out a 'case for breach of fiduciary duty', which in this case the claimant was deemed to have done so. See also *Kleanthous v Paphitis* [2011] EWHC 2287 applying the 'no director' approach and discontinuing a claim against one of the defendants as 'the claim against him seems particularly weak' but allowing the claims to be considered under section 263(3) (court discretion) in relation to the other defendants.

[61] [2010] EWHC 1539 at [29].   [62] [2011] EWHC 2287.

[63] *Stainer v Lee* [2010] EWHC at [29]. In this case the size of the claim was of central importance to the conclusion that it was not possible to say that 'no director' would consider the litigation in the company's interests.

damages can only really be assessed in the context of the business costs of pursuing the litigation. If these costs are limited then most litigation in relation to meritorious claims will be in the company's interests; but if the costs of managerial and employee time and distraction are considerable then it may be clear to any director that it is not in the company's interest to pursue even a significant sum of damages.

Section 263(2)(a) of the Act requires mandatory discontinuance if the court is 'satisfied' that *a person*—read average director—acting in accordance with section 172 would not seek to continue the claim. *Franbar* and *Iesini* suggest that as different directors may disagree about the appropriateness of bringing an action it is appropriate for the court to take a very deferential approach to section 263(2)(a)—if there is a case to answer the court proceeds to section 263's discretionary phase. But section 263(2)(a) refers to 'a person' and not to 'no person' and although it is clear that different directors may have different views on the section 172 question, what the Act requires of the court is to reach *a* view on the question of whether the litigation is in the company's interest. In all walks of the law we find standards that may be interpreted differently by different people, but that does not allow the courts to abdicate their responsibility for deciding whether a defendant has complied with the standard. Similarly in this context, the court is required to cut through the legal and business uncertainty and to reach a view on whether or not the litigation is in the interests of the company. If it concludes that it is not, the litigation must be discontinued; if it concludes that it is then the court must make its decision in accordance with section 263(3), considered below. If having attempted to reach a conclusion it finds that because of legal or business uncertainty a definitive position is unavailable, then again it must proceed to section 263(3) where it can take account of its business judgment assessment, and the uncertainty associated with it, amongst the other considerations listed in that sub-section. Although, as Lewison J makes clear, the courts may be uncomfortable with assessing the business factors that reaching such a view entails, this is the standard that the Companies Act 2006 asks the judiciary to apply. Surely the judiciary can't say 'we'd rather not because we are not very good at it'.

Whilst the making of these litigation business judgments is a novel experience for UK judges, which they appear to be resisting, other jurisdictions have long had experience of these types of judicial business judgments. In the US the rules on the availability of derivative actions are complex and will not concern us here. However, in one context the corporate law in several states allows courts to carry out their own business review about whether the derivative litigation should be allowed to continue.[64] The approach taken may well be instructive for UK courts as it offers an approach which prioritizes legal considerations and uses the value of the claim as compared to the value of the company to determine whether business considerations are relevant at all. In this regard consider the following case extract.

■ *Joy v North* 692 F 2d 880 (1982)[65]

Judge Winter (for the majority)
The difficulties courts face in evaluation of business decisions are considerably less in the case of [a *de novo* decision as to whether to allow the derivative litigation to continue]. The relevant

---

[64] The context in which Delaware courts may—at their option—carry out such a *de novo* review is where a conflicted board of directors appoints a special committee of independent directors and the committee following a review of the litigation elects to discontinue the derivative litigation: *Zapata Corp v Maldonado*, 430 A2d 779 (Del Supr 1979).

[65] *Joy v North* is a Federal Court of Appeals case applying Connecticut law.

decision—whether to continue litigation—is at hand and the danger of deceptive hindsight simply does not exist. Moreover, it can hardly be argued that terminating a lawsuit is an area in which courts have no special aptitude…

We emphasize that what we say here applies to cases involving allegations of direct economic injury to the corporation diminishing the value of the shareholders' investment as a consequence of fraud, mismanagement or self-dealing…In cases such as the present one, the burden is…to demonstrate that the action is more likely than not to be against the interests of the corporation…The weight to be given certain evidence is to be determined by conventional analysis, such as whether testimony is under oath and subject to cross-examination. Finally, the function of the court's review is to determine the balance of probabilities as to likely future benefit to the corporation, not to render a decision on the merits, fashion the appropriate legal principles or resolve issues of credibility. Where the legal rule is unclear and the likely evidence in conflict, the court need only weigh the uncertainties, not resolve them. The court's function is thus not unlike a lawyer's determining what a case is 'worth' for purposes of settlement.

Where the court determines that the likely recoverable damages discounted by the probability of a finding of liability are less than the costs to the corporation in continuing the action, it should dismiss the case. The costs which may properly be taken into account are attorney's fees and other out-of-pocket expenses related to the litigation and time spent by corporate personnel preparing for and participating in the trial…The existence or non-existence of insurance should not be considered in the calculation of costs, since premiums have previously been paid. The existence of insurance is relevant to the calculation of potential benefits.

Where, having completed the above analysis, the court finds a likely net return to the corporation which is not substantial in relation to shareholder equity, it may take into account two other items as costs. First, it may consider the impact of distraction of key personnel by continued litigation. Second, it may take into account potential lost profits which may result from the publicity of a trial.

Judicial scrutiny…should thus be limited to a comparison of the direct costs imposed upon the corporation by the litigation with the potential benefits. We are mindful that other less direct costs may be incurred, such as a negative impact on morale and upon the corporate image. Nevertheless, we believe that such factors, with the two exceptions noted, should not be taken into account. Quite apart from the elusiveness of attempting to predict such effects, they are quite likely to be directly related to the degree of wrongdoing, a spectacular fraud being generally more newsworthy and damaging to morale than a mistake in judgment as to the strength of consumer demand.

We do recognize two exceptions, however. First, where the likely net return is not substantial in relation to shareholder equity, the court can consider the degree to which key personnel may be distracted from corporate business by continuance of the litigation. We appreciate that litigation can disrupt the decision-making process and thereby impose unforeseen and undetected costs. These are not measurable and we limit consideration of them to cases where the likely return to the corporation is not great. Where that is the case and many of the key directors and officers will be heavily involved in the litigation, a court may take such potential costs into account.

Second, where the corporation deals with the general public and its level of business is dependent upon public identification and acceptance of the corporate product or service, we believe the court ought to take potential business lost as a consequence of a trial into account when the likely net return to the corporation is not substantial in relation to total shareholder equity. In such a case, there is less likelihood of a direct relationship between impact on business and degree of misconduct. Where the likely return to the corporation from the litigation is higher, however, we believe the uncertainty as to the kind of publicity which will attend a trial precludes consideration of that impact. Moreover, when potential lost profits are taken into account, the basis for calculating them must be something more solid than the conclusory opinions of alleged experts, *e.g.*, verifiable examples in similar firms.

Judge Winter's approach is designed to determine whether the litigation is in the best interests of the company, which is clearly similar to the English courts' obligation under section 263(2)(a) and 263(3)(b) of the 2006 Act to determine whether continuing the litigation promotes the success of the company. His approach to considering the factors which are relevant to this determination is to start with, and to place greater reliance upon, what lawyers do well: namely, to determine 'what a case is "worth" for the purposes of settlement'. If following such analysis the case is deemed to be of 'substantial' value to the company then it will be allowed to proceed without regard to other 'business factors' which may be relevant to the decision. If the claim is large enough then it is improbable that business factors could alter a determination that the litigation is in the company's interests. Whether a claim is 'substantial' is a relative determination: relative to shareholder equity. Judge Winter does not specify a threshold percentage which would amount to a substantial claim; it is clear, however, that large absolute claims may not be substantial in large companies.

If the claim is not 'substantial' relative to shareholder equity then certain other business factors will be taken into consideration but not factors such as corporate morale and image which are considered by Judge Winter to be too 'elusive'. In these 'non-substantial' cases the business factors that are taken into account are: the extent to which the litigation will distract key management personnel and disrupt decision-making; and lost business caused by the litigation. In relation to the latter factor, however, Judge Winter is looking for evidence that is more probative than 'the conclusory opinions of alleged experts'.

There is much to commend in this approach. It focuses first on what courts do best: assessing the strength and value of a claim and placing that assessment within the context of the nature and the value of the firm. The court is relieved from considering other business factors if the claim is substantial. This makes good sense because if the value of the claim is relatively significant then it is unlikely that business costs of the litigation would outweigh the claim's value. Where the claim is not substantial, business factors are relevant but the court recognises the limitations in its ability—or indeed anyone's ability—to assess the real but intangible business costs of litigation. Accordingly the court only considers a limited sub-set of the *more*-tangible business factors. This approach seems to offer English courts much food for thought.

3.3.2 *The length and extent of the hearing*

As we have seen, the strength of the case in many instances will be the only consideration in relation to section 263(2)(a). However, we need to remember that the derivative claim hearing is not designed to determine whether the director has in fact breached her duty only to determine whether the derivative litigation addressing the alleged breach of duty can continue. It would, therefore, be inappropriate to have a long hearing that amounted to a mini-trial. In this regard in *Iesini v Westrip Holdings Ltd*[66] Lewinson J has made the following observations.

> In *Fanmailuk.com v Cooper* [2008] EWHC 2198 (Ch) Mr Robert Englehart QC said that on an application under section 261 it would be 'quite wrong...to embark on anything like a mini-trial of the action'. No doubt that is correct; but on the other hand not only is something more than a prima facie case required, but the court will have to form a view on the strength of the claim in order properly to consider the requirements of section 263 (2)(a) and 263 (3)(b). Of course any view can only be provisional where the action has yet to be tried; but the court must, I think, do the best it can on the material before it.

[66] [2010] All ER (D) 108.

The hearing in *Iesini* involved 'several rounds of written evidence, skeleton arguments, the reading of seven lever arch files and some four days of legal argument'.[67] It is noteworthy that the difficulty in reaching a view on complex issues within a short time frame is likely to lead judges to be wary of saying that the case is so weak that no director would think that the action does not promote the success of the company.

3.4 Situations in which the court has a discretion to allow the derivative claim to be continued

If section 263(2) does not apply this does not mean that the derivative claimant has a right to continue the claim. Once the court has decided that it is *not required* to refuse permission to continue the claim, the court must then exercise its discretion to determine whether the claim can continue. Section 263(3) sets out a list of factors that the court *must* take into account in exercising this discretion. This list of factors is, in theory, a *non-exhaustive* set of guidelines; that is, it does not exclude other considerations that the court considers relevant. It is also a non-hierarchical list of considerations with, on the face of the statute, no one consideration taking precedence over the others. Let us consider each of the considerations in turn.

3.4.1 *Whether the member is acting in good faith in seeking to continue the claim*[68]

Good faith on its own means acting honestly and sincerely. One could of course sincerely and honestly believe that the corporate world is the source of all our contemporary problems and that any action that undermines this world is a good thing. Would such a person bringing a derivative suit be acting in good faith for the purpose of section 263(3)? Clearly they would not. In this context good faith is connected to the objective of the well-being of the company which, as we have seen, in UK company law means the interests of the present and future shareholder body and for commercial companies means the creation of long-term shareholder value. Accordingly, this good faith standard is a subjective standard requiring that the member honestly believes that continuing with the derivative claim *is in the best interests of the shareholder body as a whole*. At common law, even where a derivative claimant fell within one of the exceptions to the rule in *Foss v Harbottle*, the court would not allow the litigation to proceed where the shareholder was not bringing the action in good faith in the best interests of the company. In *Barrett v Duckett*[69] the court held that 'the shareholder will be allowed to sue on behalf of the company if he is bringing the action bona fide for the benefit of the company for wrongs to the company for which no other remedy is available. Conversely if the action is brought for an ulterior purpose or if another adequate remedy is available, the court will not allow the derivative action to proceed.' In *Franbar Holdings v Patel*, the court referred to *Barrett v Duckett* with approval. The question asked by the court was whether the derivative claimant had an 'ulterior motive'.

It is also clear that the good faith requirement means that the derivative litigant must come to the court with 'clean hands' just as they were required to do at common law. In the 1985 case of *Nurcombe v Nurcombe* Lawton LJ observed that the courts would not allow derivative litigation to proceed if 'conduct of a shareholder may be regarded by a court of equity as disqualifying him from appearing as plaintiff on the company's behalf' and that 'this will be the case, for example, if he participated in the wrong of

---

[67] *Ibid* at [98]. In this regard see *Kiani v Cooper* [2010] 2 BCLC 42 at [14], Proudman J observed: 'the parties curtailed their arguments because of time constraints but still took up a day of argument. It is difficult in such a case to form a sensible provisional view as to the strength of the evidence on each side. The court is well aware that at trial with proper cross-examination a very different picture may well emerge from that appearing on documentary evidence alone. However, to quote Lewison J, the court must do the best it can on the material before it'.

[68] Section 263(3)(a).   [69] [1995] 1 BCLC 243.

which he complains'.[70] In *Iesini v Westrip Holdings Ltd* the court followed this pre-2006 'clean hands' understanding of good faith. In this case the litigant complained that the current board of Westrip Holdings were in breach of their duties for failing to contest the rescission of a material contract; however, the litigant was a former director whose incompetence, along with the other directors, resulted in the rescission of the contract. The court held that the litigants' prior involvement would have amounted to bad faith for the purposes of section 263(3)(a) of the Act.[71]

3.4.2 The importance that a person acting in accordance with section 172 would attach to continuing the derivative claim[72]

We have seen that section 263(2) requires the court to determine whether a person acting in accordance with section 172 would *not* seek to continue the derivative claim and that, if the person would not do so, the court must discontinue the claim. In the context of section 263(2)(a), we have argued that business judgments could be central to the determination of whether the litigation promotes the company's interests but we also noted a reticence/refusal, expressed most clearly by Lewison J in *Iesini*, to engagement with business factors. The court, Lewison J observed, was 'ill-equipped' to take account of such factors. The question here is whether we see such continued resistance in relation to section 263(3)(b) as well.

There are, it is submitted, good reasons to expect greater openness to business factors in relation to this section than in relation to section 263(2)(a). If, applying section 263(2)(a), a court was to take business factors into account in holding that a person applying section 172 would conclude that bringing a meritorious claim was not in the company's interests, then those business factors as assessed by the court would be *the reason* for the discontinuance. That is, the court's business judgment alone would be exposed to critique. In contrast, in section 263(3)(b) the court's business judgment, and the consideration of business factors, is part of a discretionary mix of factors. These other discretionary factors provide cover to hesitant judicial engagement with business considerations. Furthermore, the court is not required to make a definitive business judgment—as is required by a literal reading of section 263(2)(a)—but rather only to assess 'the importance' that a director would attach to that judgment. This means that the court's assessment of the business factors does not feel—although it may be—like it is the sole or primary driver of the court's decision.

If courts do take account of business factors in section 263(3)(b) then does this mean that the above critique of the courts' emerging approach to section 263(2)(a) is of no consequence? In this author's view it does not. By deferring consideration of business factors to section 263(3)(b), it allows courts to prioritize the other section 263(3) considerations over the court's business judgment. This creates space for the courts to permit litigation that should have been stopped because the applicable business factors render the litigation not in the company's interests.

Let us now turn to what the courts actually do. Several cases, for example, *Franbar Holdings v Patel*, refer to the business considerations that are relevant to the section 263(3)(b) consideration. In *Franbar*, for example, the court made the following observations:

> In my judgment, the hypothetical director acting in accordance with s 172 would take into account a wide range of considerations when assessing the importance of continuing the claim. These would include such matters as the prospects of success of the claim, the ability of the company to make a recovery on any award of damages, the disruption which would be caused

---

[70] [1985] 1 WLR 370, 376.

[71] Note that in *Iesini* in relation this claim this finding was of no consequence as Lewison J had already concluded that the claimant could not continue pursuant to section 263(2)(a).

[72] Section 263(3)(b).

to the development of the company's business by having to concentrate on the proceedings, the costs of the proceedings and any damage to the company's reputation and business if the proceedings were to fail. A director will often be in the position of having to make what is no more than a partially informed decision on continuation without any very clear idea of how the proceedings might turn out.

However, observing that these factors are relevant is not the same thing as taking them into account. In the subsequent part of this judgment there is no indication that the judge attempts to actually assess these factors or incorporate them into the hypothetical decision. But perhaps this is just a function of the novelty of this role for judges and that time will result in a more constructive judicial engagement with such factors. The recent case of *Kleanthous v Paphitis*[73] supports this view. In this case, a director of the subject company, who was also the company's majority shareholder, was alleged to have expropriated a corporate opportunity. Newey J made the following observations.

■ *Kleanthous v Paphitis* [2011] EWHC 2287

Newey J

In *Wishart v Castlecroft Securities Ltd*,[74] Lord Reed said (at para 37):

'A hypothetical director acting in accordance with section 172, and considering whether to commence legal proceedings, could ordinarily be expected to have regard to a range of factors, including the amount at stake, the apparent strength of the case, the prospects of securing a satisfactory outcome without litigation, the prospects of successful execution of any judgment, the likely cost of the proceedings, the disruption caused to the company's business, and potential risks to reputation and business relationships.'

I have commented above on the size and strength of the claim, and I am not aware of any reason to think that a judgment would go unsatisfied. As regards costs, these could doubtless be very substantial, but the [company] would probably be in a position to bear them. So far as disruption to business, reputation and relationships is concerned, Mr Kyprianou [a director and Chief Executive Officer of the company who was not alleged to have breached his duty and who was, together with the finance director, Mr Lakin, a member of a two member board committee which was formed to consider whether the litigation should continue, which it concluded it should not]—has advanced a number of reasons for considering that the claim would be very damaging to the [company]. Mr Kyprianou summarised the views of himself and Mr Lakin in these terms in a witness statement:

'To sum up, Simon [Lakin] and I find it very difficult to contemplate a situation in which the Companies bring a fraud claim (or continue the Derivative Claim) against their major shareholders and the other Defendant Directors. However, we believe it would have a devastating effect on the Ryman business for the following reasons:

(a) the Companies are likely to lose four of their most experienced directors. This in turn is likely to damage the trading performance of the RGL Group, staff morale and the reputation of the Companies;

(b) replacing the Defendant Directors with candidates of similar skills and experience would be extremely difficult and, in the case of Theo Paphitis, impossible;

(c) damaging the reputation of Theo Paphitis would mean damaging the reputation of Ryman, as Theo Paphitis' name is very closely linked to the Ryman brand. The RGL Group would

---

[73] [2011] EWHC 2287.   [74] [2009] CSOH 20.

> no longer benefit from the considerable free publicity gained by its association with Theo Paphitis and the numerous business advantages that result from this association;
>
> (d) the impact on employees, customers, suppliers and other shareholders would be disastrous and would be likely to cause a significant deterioration in the RGL Group's performance and consequently its value; and
>
> (e) the litigation would provide a significant distraction to any remaining senior management.'
>
> Mr Keen understandably sought to minimise the significance of Mr Kyprianou's evidence, but to my mind there is much force in what Mr Kyprianou says.

This case shows us that English courts can and will take business considerations into account for the purposes of making the section 263(3)(b) business judgment. It suggests that a broad range of business factors may be relevant including: keeping important directors within the company; good relations with majority shareholders; and the effects on the company's reputation of reputational damage to its key directors and shareholders. The extent to which these business factor claims are subject to robust testing is unclear. From the judgment it does rather feel like the company's claims are taken at face value.

Indeed, the approach in this case, if it is followed by other courts, arguably offers a 'model' approach for getting the courts to accept the company's claims about the business costs of this litigation; namely: provide a committee of disinterested directors with the authority to consider whether the litigation should be continued, and authorize the committee to obtain its own independent legal and business professional advice. If this committee recommends that the company should not proceed with the litigation, then the committee should be required to give both legal and business reasons for its decision. As we have noted at several junctures in this book, there are good reasons to doubt the true independence of ostensibly disinterested directors who make a decision about litigation against fellow directors (particularly when such fellow directors are majority shareholders, and particularly when such directors are insiders). However, Newey J here seemed unperturbed by such concerns, although both directors were insiders and one director was closely connected with the defendant director.

3.4.3 Where the act that is the basis for the cause of action is yet to occur whether the act in question would be likely to be authorized by the company before it occurs or ratified afterwards/where the act has occurred whether it would be likely to be ratified by the company[75]

Pursuant to sections 263(3)(c) and (d) the court must take into account, as one of the factors under consideration, the likelihood of authorization or ratification of the wrong allegedly committed by the director. How then is the court to determine whether the breach in question would be authorized or ratified?[76] In relation to private companies, obtaining the views of a majority of the shareholder body may not be very difficult where there are only a handful of shareholders. In relation to widely-held listed companies with many shareholders it may be more difficult for the court to obtain such a sense of the majority view. However, even in relation to listed companies such a disinterested shareholder view may be available if the board can persuade enough of its institutional investors to state that they object to the litigation and would ratify or authorize the alleged breach if asked to do so in general meeting. However, many of those shareholders

---

[75] Section 263(3)(c) and (d).

[76] On the requirements for authorization and ratification at common law and under the 2006 Act see section 3.2 of this chapter and Chapter 16.

may be wary of siding with management for fear of the negative publicity which such a position may generate for them, particularly where there appears to be a media-friendly narrative of wrongdoing. Accordingly, to persuade 50% of the shareholder body in a listed company to express its support for discontinuing the derivative claim may be very difficult for widely-held listed companies. Furthermore, if the company presents evidence from some of its disinterested shareholders but fails to demonstrate majority support for ratification then the company runs the risk that such evidence may allow the court to infer that the majority would not vote for ratification.

3.4.4 Whether the company decides not to pursue the claim[77]

As we saw in section II of this chapter, typically a company's board of directors will be empowered to make the litigation decision against directors. In addition, we saw that, notwithstanding the distribution of power in the articles, one view of the common law position is that the shareholder body has reserve power, acting by ordinary resolution, to commence or instruct the board to commence litigation. Nevertheless, in most cases consideration, pursuant to section 263(3)(e), of 'whether the company has decided not to pursue the claim' will involve the court taking into account a decision by the board of directors not to take litigation against the directors in question. This provision allows the court to give some weight to the opinion of the board of directors about the benefits of bringing litigation. Such weight may vary depending on the quality of the board's actual decision-making process in relation to the litigation decision and the make-up of the directors who made that decision: were they interested or disinterested directors; were the disinterested directors independent of the defendant director; were the interested directors present at the meeting in which the decision was made?

In *Kleanthous v Paphitis*[78] with regard to this consideration Newey J gave particular weight to the views of a committee of disinterested directors—which was empowered by the board to seek professional advice and make the litigation decision—even though the independence of the committee of two directors, consisting of the CEO and the Finance Director, was challenged by the claimant because the CEO had multiple and long-standing business relations with the defendant director. Newey J observed that:

> I do not think I would be justified in ignoring the conclusions arrived at by the chief executive officer (Mr Kyprianou) and finance director (Mr Lakin) of the relevant companies. To the contrary, I accept Mr Todd's submission that I should attach considerable weight to those conclusions. Mr Kyprianou and Mr Lakin are better placed than I am to assess where the companies' commercial interests lie.

If the courts, following Newey J in *Kleanthous*, attribute 'considerable weight' to this factor and yet do not impose demanding expectations of the directors' independence, as distinct from their disinterestedness, then section 263(3)(e) is destined to become the most important of all the considerations in section 263(3), as it will make it very easy for companies to dismiss derivative litigation particularly where the wrongdoing director is a dominant force in the boardroom and/or the shareholder meeting. In such circumstances there is clearly a risk that the disinterested directors would do the wrongdoing director's bidding and elect not to pursue the litigation, even if the litigation would be in the company's interests. In *Kleanthous*, could one really expect an independent assessment of the litigation from a CEO in a company with a controlling shareholder who has long-standing business relations with that shareholder? In this regard it may be worthwhile revisiting the observations on board independence and the litigation decision set forth in the introduction to this chapter.

---

[77] Section 263(3)(e).   [78] [2011] EWHC 2287.

3.4.5 *Whether the act or omission in respect of which the claim is brought gives rise to a cause of action that the member could pursue in his own right rather than on behalf of the company*[79]

If the cause of action is not based on breach of duty or obligation owed by the director to the company then it is clear from section 260 that it cannot be brought as a derivative action. An action brought to enforce a shareholder's personal rights, for example, would not be brought derivatively. However, in some circumstances the director's actions may involve a breach of the director's duty owed to the company but also contravene a shareholder's personal right. For example, where there is a breach of the the articles or where the cause of action would also allow a director to bring a petition for relief under section 994 of the Companies Act 2006 (the unfair prejudice remedy which we consider in detail in Chapter 16). If the shareholder bringing the derivative action could bring an action in his own name relating to the facts in question, this may be taken into account by the court in reaching its determination as to whether the derivative claim should be permitted to continue. In *Franbar v Patel Holdings Ltd*, this factor was a central consideration in the court's decision not to permit the derivative claim to continue. In this regard consider the following extract.

■ *Franbar Holdings Ltd v Patel* [2008] EWHC 1534 (Ch)

William Trower QC (sitting as a deputy court judge)
The final relevant statutory factor is whether the act or omission in respect of which the claim is brought gives rise to a cause of action that Franbar could pursue in his own right rather than on behalf of Medicentres. This is a factor which has central significance in the present case, because [counsel for the claimant] accepted that the factual allegations which Franbar wishes to make in the derivative claim are allegations which give rise to causes of action that Franbar can pursue in its own right, and that it is already doing so through the medium of the s 994 [unfair prejudice] petition[80]...

The adequacy of the remedy available to the member in his own right is...a matter which will go into the balance when assessing the weight of this consideration on the facts of the case...In my view most, if not all, of the allegations of breach of duty to Medicentres (and certainly all those which are even arguably incapable of ratification) are likely to be relevant to Franbar's complaint of unfair prejudice. Furthermore, the losses which Medicentres might have sustained as a result of the breaches of duty pleaded in the derivative claim are relevant to the fair value of Franbar's shares and to the question of what factual assumptions should be made on the valuation to ensure that Franbar is put into the position that it would have been in but for the unfair prejudice which it will (on this hypothesis) have established. I can see no reason why Franbar should not be granted such relief on the unfair prejudice petition as may be necessary to ensure that the interest which it seeks to realise is valued on a basis which takes full account of the value of the complaints it wishes to pursue on behalf of Medicentres in the derivative claim.

In the end, it was clear that Franbar's real concern was that Casualty Plus [the controlling shareholder in Medicentres that it was argued had benefited from the company's activities] might not be in a position to pay a fair value for Franbar's shares in Medicentres...while a judgment against [the directors] is one which is more likely to be satisfied, or in any event gives Franbar an extra string to its bow. There is some foundation for this concern because it seems possible that Casualty Plus will have to raise additional capital to fund its purchase of Franbar's shares [the remedy sought pursuant to the section 994 petition] and may have difficulty in doing so.

---

[79] Section 263(3)(f).
[80] The unfair prejudice petition pursuant to section 994 CA 2006 is discussed in detail in Chapter 16.

> Franbar also submits that continuation and consolidation will be a cost effective and proportionate way of resolving all claims between the parties. It is said that this is a more efficient way of dealing with the dispute than leaving over the possibility that a derivative claim might have to be pursued in due course, once unfair prejudice has been established. I cannot rule out the possibility that a derivative claim may need to be pursued at a later stage, but I am bound to say that it seems to me most unlikely that this will be necessary. In this particular case, the availability (and indeed use) of both the section 994 petition...weigh in the balance against the grant of permission to continue the derivative action.

It seems clear from this case that any permission to continue a derivative claim which is to be consolidated with a section 994 petition will, in all likelihood, result in the permission being refused. This does not exclude the possibility of revisiting the permission at a later date when the section 994 petition has run its course, if at that later date a court would view it as appropriate to allow the derivative claim to continue. However, where a derivative claim is brought *without* also bringing a section 994 petition, even though such a petition is theoretically available, it seems that the mere availability of such a remedy will not lead to the refusal of permission. In *Stainer v Lee*, for example, Roth J observed that 'the theoretical availability to the applicant of proceedings by way of an unfair prejudice petition...[was] not a reason to refuse permission'.[81]

More favourable claimant cost rules apply to derivative claims than to section 994 petitions, which may lead a claimant to prefer a derivative claim than a section 994 action even if the claimants ultimate objective is a personal remedy (available from a section 994 action) not a corporate remedy. Although a derivative claim is only capable of generating a corporate remedy, control over the litigation would be a useful bargaining chip for the derivative claimant in negotiating a personal remedy from the defendant or the company.

In a derivative claim the court may, at its discretion, award an indemnity costs order that covers, at the company's expense, the costs of the litigation even if the derivative litigant loses (we consider these costs orders in detail in section VI of this chapter). Is the fact that the defendant brings a derivative claim and not a section 994 claim in order to benefit from the favourable costs rule a factor that the court may take into account pursuant to this section 263(3)(f)? Initial indications suggest that the courts think it appropriate to do so, particularly where there is an indication that the claimant is using the negotiating power generated by the derivative claim to obtain the sort of personal remedy—such as the purchase of his shares—that would be available pursuant to a successful section 994 petition. In *Iesini v Westrip Holdings Ltd* Lewison J held that these cost considerations coupled with the availability of a section 994 action would be a basis to deny permission to continue.

> The potential liability of the company for costs is, in my judgment, a proper consideration for the court in deciding whether to allow a derivative claim to proceed. In the present case the combination of that potential liability and the availability of an alternative remedy under section 994 would have led me to the conclusion that, on the facts as they now are...it would not have been appropriate to allow the derivative claim to proceed.

Newey J in *Kleanthous v Paphitis* agreed with Lewison J's position that simply taking a derivative action to benefit from an indemnification costs order where a section 994 petition was available, and possibly more appropriate, would be a relevant consideration for refusing permission. In this case there was evidence presented to the court that the claimant was interested in getting the defendant to buy his shares.

---

[81] See also *Wishart v Castlecroft Securities Ltd* [2009] CSOH 20.

We might ask whether this is the right place in which to take costs, and the costs motivations of the claimant, into account. Surely the motivations of the claimant could be taken into account in deciding whether or not to award a costs order once permission has been granted? The problem is, as we shall see, whether such an indemnification order should be made depends on whether the court deems the litigation to be in the company's interests. One of the reasons why Lewison J in *Iesini* feels compelled to take costs considerations into account here is that if permission is given then in his view the determination that the litigation is in the corporate interests has been made and a costs order is then automatic; in which case there is no real discretion as to whether or not to award an indemnification order. Accordingly, if the action, because of the remedy sought, would be a section 994 petition but for the availability of the indemnification costs order then the courts need to take this into account at this stage of the proceedings. Arguably, this problem would be more appropriately solved by allowing the courts to take such considerations into account in deciding whether or not to award an indemnification order, even if the litigation is deemed to be in the company's interests. We consider these costs rules in further detail later in this chapter.

3.4.6 *In considering whether to give permission (or leave) the court shall have particular regard to any evidence before it as to the views of members of the company who have no personal interest, direct or indirect, in the matter*

This consideration is set out in a separate subsection (section 263(4)) to the other considerations (section 263(3)(a)–(f)). It is clear, however, that this consideration relates to the court's exercise of its general discretion to permit the derivative action to continue because, as with subsection 263(3), subsection 263(4) refers to 'in considering whether to give permission'. It is not, however, clear how this consideration differs significantly from the considerations set out in subsection 263(3)(c)(ii) and (d) which require the court to consider whether the shareholders are likely to ratify the breach. As we noted earlier, section 239 now requires a majority vote of the disinterested shareholders to ratify a breach of duty. The court's canvassing of opinion on whether such disinterested shareholders would be likely to ratify the breach will surely reveal 'the views of members of the company who have no personal interest, direct or indirect, in the matter'. This factor will have independent significance where the court only considers whether a proposed breach would be authorized by the shareholders as, as previously noted, the disinterested shareholder requirement set forth in section 239 does not apply to pre-breach authorization.

3.4.7 *Other considerations—the shadow of wrongdoer control*

Section 263(3) provides a non-exclusive list of considerations for the court to take into account when making its decision. Other considerations, on a case-by-case basis, could, therefore, be relevant to the determination. We noted earlier that under the common law derivative action rules in order to be able bring a derivative action the claimant needed to show that the wrongdoing director controlled the general meeting. Nowhere in Chapter 11 is there any reference to a requirement to show wrongdoer control. This is widely understood to mean that the absence of wrongdoer control is no longer a barrier to the bringing of a derivative claim.[82] However, it would clearly be possible for the courts to take into account the presence or absence of wrongdoer control as a section 263(3) consideration in deciding whether to permit the derivative litigation. Indeed, one recent case suggests that the absence of wrongdoer control could be a strongly influential factor making the refusal of permission very likely. In *Stimpson v Southern Private Landlords Association*[83] the Court briefly considered the status of wrongdoer control.

---

[82] A residue of doubt remains about this position. This doubt is explored in D. Kershaw, 'The *Rule in Foss v Harbottle is Dead; Long Live the Rule in Foss v Harbottle*' (forthcoming, 2012).
[83] [2009] EWHC 2072 [46].

Judge Pelling QC in response to a submission that wrongdoer control was no longer relevant indicated that it would be a relevant consideration. For Judge Pelling QC the fact that there was no wrongdoer control in this case was 'at least a powerful [considera-tion] that negatives the giving of permission and may be overwhelming'.

The majority of cases to date have involved close private companies in which there was wrongdoer control. Judge Pelling's position has not, therefore, been tested. His judgment does, however, hold out the possibility that for listed UK companies, which are rarely controlled by their directors, the probability of derivative suit for breach of duty, as under the common law rules, is close to zero.

4 Turning company-initiated litigation into derivative litigation

In our analysis of the various corporate bodies that could be given authority to initiate litigation in section I of this chapter, we noted that one way in which a conflicted board could act to the benefit of the allegedly wrongdoing director would be to foreclose the possibility of derivative litigation by commencing litigation itself but not pursuing the litigation effectively by, for example, failing to give the litigation the required resources of time and money. If the company commences litigation, a derivative claim is no longer possible: the company is already taking action to enforce its rights.

Section 262 responds to this problem by allowing a shareholder to apply to the court to take control of the litigation by continuing the claim derivatively. It is clear, however, that the Act sets a very high bar for shareholders to be able to wrestle control of the claim from the company. Pursuant to section 262(2), the shareholder must demonstrate not only that the company has not been pursuing the claim diligently, but also that the way in which the claim has been carried out amounts to an 'abuse of process of the court'. In distinguishing diligent prosecution of the case from 'abuse of process' the Act provides that very significant failings by the company are necessary before a shareholder can take control over the litigation away from the company. In most cases, therefore, if the company commences litigation against a director then a shareholder who believes the case is being prosecuted half-heartedly or even incompetently will not be able to convert the action into a derivative claim.

Questions

1. In your view is there likely to be a significant increase in derivative litigation in the UK following the introduction of the new derivative claim?[84]

2. In what ways will an increase in litigation damage companies? In what ways will it benefit companies? Will the benefits outweigh the costs?

3. How should the courts go about determining what a hypothetical director would do when acting in accordance with section 172? Should they take into account business factors? If so what types of business factors are they capable of taking into account?

4. In your judgment do you think the courts will accept the mandate to make a business judgment with regard to the litigation rather than simply make a legal judgment as to the strength of the case?

5. Do you think the approach set out in *Joy v North* offers a useful way of organizing the court's approach to the *de novo* business judgment?

6. Would it have made more sense to have relied upon independent directors to make the decision as to whether or not derivative litigation should continue?

7. How should the courts determine what is the disinterested shareholder's view of the derivative claim in a widely-held company?

---

[84] See further in this regard, A. Reisberg, *Derivative Actions and Corporate Governance* (OUP, 2007), chapter 4.

V MULTIPLE DERIVATIVE CLAIMS

In groups of companies wrongs may be committed by directors of subsidiary companies which damage the group as a whole and, indirectly, the shareholders in the parent company. Although the shareholders in the parent company are not members of the subsidiary company the question we ask in this section is whether it is possible for a member of a parent company to bring a derivative action on behalf of the subsidiary company to enforce the wrong done to the subsidiary company? Such an action is typically referred to as a double or multiple derivative action, which contrasts with the *direct* derivative action which has been the focal point of this chapter, where the shareholder bringing the action is a member in the company that has been wronged. We could, of course imagine several further degrees of separation in a group of companies—wrongs done to subsidiaries of subsidiaries—to which the same question would apply. If we understand the right to bring a derivative action as a membership right then our answer to this question is likely to be 'no'. But if we understand the derivative action as a means of ensuring that justice is done in situations where the company is incapable of protecting itself, then we might be more receptive to this idea.

This question of whether multiple derivative actions can be brought has never been subject to reasoned analysis by an English court. In several cases multiple derivative actions have been brought and their legality assumed, but such actions were neither challenged nor analysed.[85] However, in the recent judgment of the Hong Kong Court of Final Appeal in *Waddington v Chan*,[86] the retired Law Lord, Lord Millett, addressed this issue directly. Lord Millett concluded that:

> [The] justification of the derivative action [wrongdoer control]…applies as well to the case where the wrongdoers, who through their control of the parent company also control its subsidiaries, defraud a subsidiary or sub-subsidiary as it is to the case where they defraud the parent company itself. In either case wrongdoer control precludes action by the company in which the cause of action is vested…The question is simply a question of the plaintiff's standing to sue…The court must ask itself whether the plaintiff has a legitimate interest in the relief claimed sufficient to justify him in bringing proceedings to obtain it. The answer in the case of person wishing to bring a multiple derivative action is plainly 'Yes'. Any depletion of a subsidiary's assets causes indirect loss to its parent company and its shareholders.

For Lord Millett, the direct derivative action is allowed by the common law only in the exceptional case where the wrongdoers' control of the company means that the wrongdoers will not be held to account by the company and justice will not be done. In Lord Millett's view this justification applies equally to the case where there is wrongdoer control of the subsidiary, which has suffered the wrong, and its parent company. The question then becomes: who has standing to ensure that justice is done? Lord Millett concludes that a parent shareholders' indirect loss resulting from the wrongdoing gives her a 'legitimate interest' and standing. Accordingly, in Lord Millett's view, at common law, where the wrongdoers control the parent's board of directors (the parent board votes the shares of the subsidiary) then a member of the parent company will have standing to bring a multiple derivative action to enforce the wrong done to the subsidiary company. Of course, as this is a Hong Kong case it is not a binding precedent on the English common law of derivative actions. However, as Lord Millett is one of the 20th century's most respected judges, his assessment of the English common law will be treated by UK courts as extremely influential.

---

[85] See, for example, *Wallersteiner v Moir (No 2)* [1975] 1 All ER 849; *Halle v Trax BW Ltd* [2000] BCC 1020; and *Airey v Cordell* [2006] EWHC 2728.
[86] *Waddington Ltd v Chan Chun Hoo Thomas* [2009] 2 BCLC 82.

As a result of the holding in *Waddington v Chan* commentators have considered whether a double or multiple derivative claim is available in the UK following the enactment of Chapter 11. Dan Prentice and Arad Reisberg have argued that it is not available.[87] The reason for this, they argue, is that section 260(2) of the Act provides that a derivative claim can only be brought under Chapter 11 of the Act and that section 260(1) defines a derivative claim as an action brought by a member of the company in relation to a cause of action vested in the company. Accordingly, as Chapter 11 does not provide for multiple derivative claims and as derivative claims can only be brought under the Act, Prentice and Reisberg conclude that a multiple derivative claim, even if available at common law, is no longer available.

More recently Daniel Lightman, in an unpublished presentation given at the Chancery Bar Association Seminar, argues compellingly that this not correct.[88] He argues that the Act simply has nothing to say about multiple derivative actions *at all*, either expressly or by implication, and, as the common law is presumed to remain in the absence of express or implied repeal,[89] whether multiple derivative actions are available depends on the common law alone. For Lightman the Act only regulates what it defines as a 'derivative claim', namely direct derivative actions. Beyond that the Act has nothing to say at all about other forms of derivative action. Interestingly in this regard, and arguably supportive of Lightman's position, is that the Act elects to use the new term 'derivative claim' and not 'derivative action'. It is also worth noting in this regard that the Law Commission in their review of *Shareholder Remedies* concluded that the question of the availability of multiple derivative actions was best left to the courts and that it should not be included in the statutory procedure.[90]

If multiple derivative actions are not excluded by the Act and if, following Lord Millett in *Waddington v Chan*, the common law recognizes such actions, then the *Rule in Foss v Harbottle* and its exceptions are not as dead as we had thought. Apologies are due to students of company law from those of us who had suggested that these rules were merely of historical interest! This would mean that direct derivative actions are dealt with by Chapter 11 and multiple derivative actions by the *Rule in Foss v Harbottle* and its exceptions. For multiple derivative actions this would mean the action could only be brought if the action fell with the fraud on the minority exception. Only wrongs that fell within the 'fraud category' discussed earlier could be enforced and only where there is wrongdoer control. Note in relation to wrongdoer control in multiple derivative actions that it would not be assessed by reference to the general meeting of the subsidiary but by reference to the board of the parent which, as they vote all the shares of the subsidiary, is effectively the general meeting.

---

[87] D. Prentice and A. Reisberg, 'Multiple Derivative Actions' (2009) 125 LQR 209; see also P. Koh, Derivative Actions Once Removed' (2010) *Journal of Business Law* 101, 106 reaching a similar conclusion.

[88] D. Lightman, 'Two Aspects of the Statutory Derivative Claim' (Chancery Bar Association Seminar, October 2010).

[89] In *R v Secretary of State for the Home Department, ex p Pierson* [1998] AC 539. Lord Browne-Wilkinson observed that: 'It is well established that Parliament does not legislate in a vacuum: statutes are drafted on the basis that the ordinary rules and principles of the common law will apply to the express statutory provisions Parliament is presumed not to have intended to change the common law unless it has clearly indicated such intention either expressly or by implication.'

[90] Law Commission, *Shareholder Remedies (Final Report)* para 6.110: 'We consider that the question of multiple derivative actions is best left to the courts to resolve, if necessary using the power under section 461(2)(c) of the Companies Act 1985 to bring a derivative action. Accordingly, we do not consider that there should be any express provision dealing with multiple derivative actions.'

VI FUNDING DERIVATIVE CLAIMS

1 The relationship between legal cost rules and the effectiveness of the derivative claim

The extent to which derivative claims are *in practice* an important mechanism for holding directors to account for their breach of duty is a function not only of the rules providing and limiting access to derivative claims, which we have considered, but also of the rules which determine who funds the legal costs of bringing the derivative claim and who is liable to pay the legal costs of the successful party: the successful party himself or the losing party.

We should remind ourselves that a derivative claim is an action taken on behalf of the company to enforce the company's rights. Accordingly, if successful, it is the company that benefits from any award of damages not the derivative claimant. Any benefit for the derivative claimant arising out of successful litigation is an indirect one: if the derivative claimant owns 2% of the company then the value of his shares increases by an amount equal to 2% of the award of damages. This means that if the rules on the distribution of costs of the litigation impose on derivative claimants any of the costs arising from the litigation (whether their own costs or the defendants costs) then it will quickly become uneconomical for individual shareholders to consider derivative litigation. To enable us to see this more clearly consider the following worked hypothetical.

Hypothetical B

Jane is a 2% shareholder in Bob's Electronics Plc which is now listed on the London Stock Exchange. She believes that Fabian, one of its directors, has taken a corporate opportunity for himself in breach of section 175 of the Companies Act 2006. The board has refused to bring an action against Fabian. Jane's lawyers believe that on the evidence available to them a court would grant permission to continue a derivative claim. Consider whether Jane, acting rationally to maximize her own personal wealth, would bring this action under the following different cost rules.

(a) If the court grants permission to continue the derivative litigation, the court will require the company to indemnify Jane for her legal costs and for any costs the court imposes on Jane if the claim is unsuccessful.

   – Clearly, with such an arrangement the costs of the litigation will not affect Jane's decision to bring the derivative claim. To the extent that any damages are paid the litigation will increase the value of Jane's shareholding (by 2% of the award). With such a *company indemnity costs rule*, taking only the direct costs and benefits of the litigation into account Jane will be strongly incentivized to bring the derivative claim. Of course there are other costs for Jane—apart from legal costs—in bringing the claim: the costs of Jane's time and effort required to successfully prosecute the claim. These non-legal **opportunity costs** will vary depending on what Jane does for a living—whether she is an active investor with a large portfolio or a retired law lecturer. However, if these costs are significant—because Jane misses out on other investment opportunities or her existing investments decline in value for want of her attention—then even with this company indemnity cost rule it may not make economic sense for Jane to bring the litigation.

(b) Jane has to fund the litigation herself. If the litigation is not successful she will be liable to pay only her own costs—that is, there is *no* 'loser-pays' costs rule.

- According to her lawyer's estimates the costs of bringing the derivative claim will be approximately £100,000. If successful the losing director will not pay her costs as there is no loser-pays cost rule. Accordingly, she has a 100% chance that she will have to pay her own legal costs of £100,000. The probability of success is estimated by her lawyers to be 75% and if successful the director would have to account for the profits he has made from the opportunity, which are believed to be £5 million. As there is a 75% chance that success will generate £5 million the litigation has an **expected value** of £3.75 million for the company (not for Jane). For Jane, therefore, the litigation has a negative expected value of minus £25,000 (£75,000 (2% of £3.75 million) – £100,00). Acting as a rational economic agent Jane would not bring this derivative claim.

- Obviously the more significant the claim (in value terms), the more economical bringing the claim becomes. If the claim was for £10 million then the claim would have a positive expected value for Jane of £50,000 (£150,000 – £100,000). However, such a rule would render many substantial derivative claims, such as the £5 million claim, uneconomical.

- Even where the expected value of the claim for Jane is positive, bringing the claim may still not make sense for Jane if her non-legal opportunity costs outweigh these benefits.

- Even if the expected value of the claim is positive, as it is with the £10m claim, and these non-legal opportunity costs are zero, Jane may be unwilling to bring the litigation because in the real world people are wary of risk and fear losses more than they value gains.[91] The £100,000 lawyer's bill will be enough to put off many shareholders even if the expected value of the claim for her personally is positive. For those shareholders, such as institutional shareholders, who may be more risk neutral over a £100,000 legal bill, their opportunity costs may be significant—for example, the costs of employees being distracted from their normal tasks by the litigation.

(c) If the derivative claim is unsuccessful Jane will be liable for the costs of the defendant director; if successful the losing director will pay her legal costs. This is known as a 'loser-pays' costs rule.

- As the claim has a 75% chance of being successful; Jane has 25% chance of losing. If she loses she has to pay her own legal costs and those of the defendant director, which in this case are more extensive than Jane's in the directors' aggressive attempt to win: they are £200,000. The expected value of the legal costs she will have to pay is therefore 25% of £300,000 which is £75,000. Accordingly, with this cost rule change for a £5 million claim the expected value of the claim for Jane is zero (£75,000 minus £75,000) and for the £10 million claim £75,000. From this example from the perspective of encouraging litigation this *loser-pays* rule appears to be a preferable rule than the rule in (b) above where the loser does not pay the winner's legal costs. However, this is true in relation to strong claims but not as the strength of the claim weakens: if the chances of winning are reduced to 50:50 then the expected value of the £5 million claim is minus £100,000 and minus £50,000 for the £10 million claim.

---

[91] See generally, A. Tversky and D. Kahneman, 'Advances in Prospect Theory: Cumulative Representation of Uncertainty' (1992) 5 *Journal of Risk and Uncertainty* 278.

2 Costs rules in derivative claims

Typically in the UK the losing litigant pays his own legal costs and the legal costs of the winning party; that is the UK has a loser-pays costs rule.[92] As is clear from this *hypothetical*, if the 'loser-pays' rule applied to a derivative claimant it would create a significant disincentive for shareholders to bring derivative claims: if the claim is successful the pay-off (for the shareholder) is a moderate indirect benefit through an increase in the value of their shares; if they lose they are saddled with significant legal costs. Although at common law English courts restricted the availability of the derivative action they were not unsympathetic to the problems created by the costs rules for claimants who, in accordance with the rule in *Foss v Harbottle* and its exceptions, were allowed to bring a derivative action. In this regard consider the following judgment by Lord Denning MR in *Wallersteiner v Moir*.

■ *Wallersteiner v Moir* (No 2) [1975] 2 WLR 389

Lord Denning MR

This case has brought to light a serious defect in the administration of justice. Mr. Moir is a shareholder in a public company. He discovered that Dr. Wallersteiner had been guilty of grave misconduct in the management of the company's affairs. He tried every known way to get an inquiry held...The only way in which he has been able to have his complaint investigated is by action in these courts and here he has come to the end of his tether. He has fought this case for over 10 years on his own. He has expended all his financial resources on it and all his time and labour. He has received contributions from other shareholders but these are now exhausted. He has recovered judgment for over £250,000 against Dr. Wallersteiner. It may be difficult to get the money out of Dr. Wallersteiner, but if it is obtained, not a penny of it will go into Mr. Moir's pocket. It will all go to benefit the [Company]...Yet the litigation is by no means finished...In this situation he appeals to this court for help in respect of the future costs of this litigation. If no help is forthcoming, all his efforts will have been in vain...Mr. Moir will have to give up the struggle exhausted in mind, body and estate.

We felt the force of these points. So keenly indeed that we asked the Law Society to help. They instructed Mr. Peter Webster as amicus curiae. He analysed the legal position in a most illuminating manner. We are much indebted to him. He took us through the three ways in which it was suggested that Mr. Moir could be protected: (1) indemnity from the company; (2) legal aid; and (3) contingency fee. As the discussion proceeded, it appeared very necessary to be clear as to the nature of Mr. Moir's counterclaim. He is a minority shareholder seeking to redress a wrong done to the company...

Indemnity

The minority shareholder [the derivative claimant], being an agent acting on behalf of the company, is entitled to be indemnified by the company against all costs and expenses reasonably incurred by him in the course of the agency. This indemnity does not arise out of a contract express or implied, but it arises on the plainest principles of equity...Seeing that, if the action succeeds, the whole benefit will go to the company, it is only just that the minority shareholder should be indemnified against the costs he incurs on its behalf. If the action succeeds, the wrong-doing director will be ordered to pay the costs: but if they are not recovered from him, they should be paid by the company...

But what if the action fails? Assuming that the minority shareholder had reasonable grounds for bringing the action—that it was a reasonable and prudent course to take in the interests of the company—he should not himself be liable to pay the costs of the other side, but the company

---

itself should be liable, because he was acting for it and not for himself. In addition, he should himself be indemnified by the company in respect of his own costs even if the action fails. It is a well known maxim of the law that he who would take the benefit of a venture if it succeeds ought also to bear the burden if it fails...

In order to be entitled to this indemnity, the minority shareholder soon after issuing his writ should apply for the sanction of the court...[The court] should simply ask himself: is there a reasonable case for the minority shareholder to bring at the expense (eventually) of the company? If there is, let it go ahead.

Contingency fee

English law has never sanctioned an agreement by which a lawyer is remunerated on the basis of a 'contingency fee,' that is that he gets paid the fee if he wins, but not if he loses. Such an agreement was illegal on the ground that it was the offence of champerty. In its origin champerty was a division of the proceeds (campi partitio). An agreement by which a lawyer, if he won, was to receive a share of the proceeds was pure champerty. Even if he was not to receive an actual share, but payment of a commission on a sum proportioned to the amount recovered—only if he won—it was also regarded as champerty... In most of the United States and Canada, an agreement for a contingency fee is permissible, not only in derivative actions, but in all cases where the client is poor and his chances of success uncertain. This is seen as a way in which justice can be done. Otherwise a poor man would be without redress in the courts. If the lawyer was only ready to act on the terms: 'Win or lose, you must pay my fees,' the client would have to go away sorrowful. But if the lawyer is ready to act on the terms: 'It will cost you nothing. If we win, I will get a percentage of the damages. If we lose I will charge you nothing,' the client is content. Nay, what is more, he is happy. Especially as in the United States the loser is not liable to pay the costs of the other side except to a very small extent. It is realised that the contingency fee has its disadvantages. It may stimulate a lawyer to take on unworthy claims, or to use unfair means to achieve success. But these disadvantages are believed to be outweighed by the advantage that legitimate claims are enforced which would otherwise have to be abandoned by reason of the poverty of the claimant. The courts themselves are in a position to control any abuses. They can limit the amount of the fee which the lawyer is allowed to charge.

These are powerful arguments, but I do not think they can or should prevail in England, at any rate, not in most cases...Although public policy is against contingency fees in general, the question remains whether a derivative action should be an exception. There are strong arguments that it should be. Let me take a typical case. Suppose there is good ground for thinking that those in control of a company have been plundering its assets for their own benefit. They should be brought to book. But how is it to be done and by whom? By raising it at a meeting of shareholders? Only to be voted down...At present there is nothing effective except an action by a minority shareholder. But can a minority shareholder be really expected to take it? He has nothing to gain, but much to lose. He feels strongly that a wrong has been done—and that it should be righted. But he does not feel able to undertake it himself. Faced with an estimate of the costs, he will say: 'I'm not going to throw away good money after bad.' Some wrongdoers know this and take advantage of it. They loot the company's funds knowing there is little risk of an action being brought against them.

What then is to be done? The remedy, as I see it, is to do as is done in the United States—to permit a solicitor to conduct a derivative action on the basis of a contingency fee. It should be subject to proper safeguards. The action should not be started except on an opinion by leading counsel that it is a reasonable action to bring in the interests of the company. The fee should be a generous sum—by a percentage or otherwise—so as to recompense the solicitor for his work—and also for the risk that he takes of getting nothing if he loses. The other side should be notified of it from the very beginning: and it should be subject to the approval of The Law Society and of the courts. With these safeguards I think that public policy should favour a contingency fee in derivative actions—for otherwise, in many cases, justice will not be done—and wrongdoers will get away with their spoils.

> I would allow Mr. Moir to arrange with his lawyers for them to conduct the future proceedings on the basis of a contingency fee, subject to the permission, first of the Council of the Law Society and next of the courts. But Buckley and Scarman L.JJ [sitting together with Lord Denning MR] do not think this is open to us. So he must be content with an indemnity from the [company].

2.1 Company indemnities

The granting of an indemnification order, such as provided in *Wallersteiner v Moir*, became known as a Wallersteiner v Moir order. The courts' discretion to grant a Wallersteiner v Moir order was codified thereafter in the Civil Procedure Rules. Today the rule is found in Civil Procedure Rule 19.9E which provides that:

> The court may order the company…for the benefit of which a derivative claim is brought to indemnify the claimant against liability for costs incurred in the permission application or in the derivative claim or both.[93]

The rules provide the courts with a discretion to grant the derivative claimant a costs indemnification. The question of relevance is when will they do so? Buckley LJ in *Wallersteiner v Moir* made the following observations in this regard:

> An agent is entitled to be indemnified by his principal against costs incurred in consequence of carrying out the instructions…It seems to me that in a minority shareholder's action, properly and reasonably brought and prosecuted, it would normally be right that the company should be ordered to pay the plaintiff's costs so far as he does not recover them from any other party. In all the instances mentioned the right of the party seeking indemnity to be indemnified must depend on whether he has acted reasonably in bringing or defending the action…Nevertheless, where a shareholder has in good faith and on reasonable grounds sued as plaintiff in a minority shareholder's action, the benefit of which, if successful, will accrue to the company and only indirectly to the plaintiff as a member of the company, and which it would have been reasonable for an independent board of directors to bring in the company's name, it would, I think, clearly be a proper exercise of judicial discretion to order the company to pay the plaintiff's costs. This would extend to the plaintiff's costs down to judgment, if it would have been reasonable for an independent board exercising the standard of care which a prudent business man would exercise in his own affairs to continue the action to judgment. If, however, an independent board exercising that standard of care would have discontinued the action at an earlier stage, it is probable that the Plaintiff should only be awarded his costs against the company down to that stage.

According to Buckley LJ the indemnification order is available only where an independent board—acting with the care that would be taken by an ordinary man in the exercise of his own affairs—would have brought the litigation.[94]

Given that under the new derivative claim mechanism the question of whether the litigation can be continued depends on whether 'a person' acting to promote the success of the company would take the litigation, it would appear that the question of relevance to determine whether an indemnification order can be granted has already been answered by giving permission for the claim to continue. That is, if the court concludes that a person acting to promote the success of the company would continue with the litigation then Buckley LJ's test has been satisfied. Lewison J in *Iesini v Westrip Holdings Ltd* observed in this regard that: 'once the court has reached the conclusion that the

---

[93] Rule 19.9 CRP as amended by the Civil Procedure (Amendment) Rule 2007, SI 2007/2204 (L 20).
[94] This approach was followed in *Smith v Croft* [1986] 2 All ER 551 and *Jaybird v Greenwood* [1986] BCLC 319. See also *Airey v Cordell* [2006] EWHC 2728 (Ch).

claim ought to proceed for the benefit of the company, it ought normally to order the company to indemnify the claimant against his costs'.[95] However, the courts are clearly aware of the dangers of depleting company resources when the strength of the claim, or whether it is in the company's interest to bring the claim, is unclear. As a result of this concern, courts may elect to impose limits on the indemnity order which will force the derivative claimant to return to court to request a further order once the case has progressed further and the strength of the case has become clearer. In *Stainer v Lee*, for example, the court granted an indemnity order with a ceiling of £40,000 with the option of applying for an extension of the order. In *Kiani v Cooper* the court granted an indemnity order but only as far as the completion of the disclosure of documents process in the litigation.[96]

A question remains as to whether the financial well-being of the derivative claimant is relevant to the court's decision as to whether or not to grant an indemnification order. Would such an order be available to a powerful institutional shareholder or a hedge fund? In this regard we need to determine whether the underlying rationale in *Wallersteiner v Moir* for making the indemnification order was the financial need of the claimant, who in the absence of financial support could not have continued with the litigation, or whether the rationale for making the order was to counterbalance the skewed incentives created by the fact that in a derivative claim a successful claimant does not receive any of the damages awarded but only benefits indirectly as a result of her shareholding in the company. Clearly, if we revisit the extract of Lord Denning's judgment in *Wallersteiner v Moir*, we can find evidence of both rationales. In addition, there is some, although limited, authority for both positions and both rationales. Both cases are first instance judgments from 1986. In *Smith v Croft*[97] Walton J made the following observations:

> The rationale for a *Wallersteiner v Moir* order is to ensure that the plaintiff in a minority shareholders' action should not be prevented from pursuing an obviously just case through lack of funds, or fear that he may, for some reason, fail at the end of the day and be at risk as to costs which he cannot possibly pay. It has to be acknowledged that the making of such an order may turn out to have imposed on the company a liability which ought never to have been imposed on it. Therefore, one should be very careful not to extend that liability…
>
> It therefore appears to me that in order to hold the balance as fairly as may be in the circumstances between plaintiffs and defendants, it will be incumbent on the plaintiffs applying for such an order to show that it is genuinely needed, ie that they do not have sufficient resources to finance the action in the mean time. If they have, I see no reason at all why this extra burden should be placed on the company.

However in *Jaybird v Greenwood*,[98] the High Court held that the financial status of the claimant was irrelevant pursuant to the holding in *Wallersteiner v Moir*:

> Counsel for the second respondent says, in regard to the exercise of what is accepted to be my discretion, that whereas in *Wallersteiner v Moir* Mr Moir had a minute interest in the companies and was a person who, it was quite apparent, had largely exhausted his resources in the steps he had taken…the plaintiff here is somebody who does not need protection and is not a party without means…As to this, I would simply say, as counsel for the plaintiff pointed out, that there is nothing in *Wallersteiner v Moir* to suggest that the application of the principle which underlay

[95] [2010] All ER (D) 108 at [125]. In *Stainer v Lee* [2010] EWHC 1539 (Ch) at 56 Roth J similarly observed that: 'I think [*Wallersteiner v Moir (No 2)*] is clear authority that a shareholder who receives the sanction of the court to proceed with a derivative action should normally be indemnified as to his reasonable costs by the company for the benefit of which the action would accrue.'
[96] [2010] 2 BCLC 427 at [49].   [97] [1986] 2 All ER 551.   [98] [1986] BCLC 319.

that case is in any way limited to impecunious plaintiffs. For my part, I see no reason whatsoever to deprive Jaybird, as to whose finances I have no information whatever, of the sort of protection which was granted to Mr Moir.

In this author's view the correct position is set out in *Jaybird v Greenwood*.[99] The stronger rationale for making indemnification orders available is not to address the weak financial position of some derivative claimants but to correct the skewed incentives created by allowing litigation by a claimant that does not directly benefit from the success of the claim. That is, in order to make the derivative mechanism of practical significance the costs disincentives to bringing a claim, identified earlier, need to be addressed as they affect all shareholders, regardless of their wealth.

If courts, following *Jaybird v Greenwood*, elect not to impose such personal wealth limits on the availability of Wallersteiner v Moir orders then such orders will follow as a matter of course following a ruling that the derivative litigation may continue. The effect of such orders is to remove any disincentive arising from legal costs to commence and prosecute a derivative claim. Of course disincentives will still arise for individual shareholders from their non-legal opportunity costs.

2.2 Contingency fees and conditional fees

In the extract from Lord Denning's judgment in *Wallersteiner v Moir*, he considers favourably the option of allowing a derivative claimant to agree a contingency fee with his lawyers. Indeed Lord Denning would have allowed this, but Scarman and Buckley LJ did not agree. The effect of allowing a contingency fee is as follows: lawyers take the cost risks associated with losing the litigation and, in exchange, if they are successful obtain a considerably enhanced fee. In the US where, as Lord Denning explains, contingency fees are available, in derivative litigation the law firm bringing the litigation, if successful, may receive up to 40% of the amount awarded to the company by the court, or agreed to be paid in any settlement with the directors. This is an amount far in excess of what they would have earned in fees had they billed on a normal hourly basis.

Furthermore, in the US the typical legal costs rule is that the winner and the loser pay their own costs but not the other party's costs. This enhances the attraction of a contingency fee arrangement to lawyers in the US: if they lose they forfeit only their own costs; if they win they will generate many times the fees that would have been raised on a normal hourly fee basis. Lawyers with these very high incentives to bring legal action have become a very important tool for holding directors to account. These lawyers are sometimes called entrepreneurial litigants because as they make money from derivative litigation they are strongly incentivized to seek out corporate wrongdoing themselves rather than wait for a shareholder-client to walk through the door of their offices. With such costs arrangements in place lawyers, rather than shareholders, become a proactive force in the enforcement of directors' duties. Arguably this results in over-zealous attempts to hold managers accountable, resulting in a considerable waste of managerial time and effort in dealing with derivative litigation.

In the UK contingency fee arrangements have not to-date been available to derivative claimants. Lawyers have, however, been able to take cases on a no-win/no-fee basis. Under such arrangements if they do win they are allowed to be paid a specific multiple of the costs, usually up to a maximum of twice the fees that would have been charged. These fee arrangements are known as conditional fee arrangements.[100] If they lose, the

---

[99] In *Iesini v Westrip Holdings Ltd* [2010] 2 BCLC 427 at [125] Lewison J agreed with the position set forth in *Jaybird v Greenwood* that 'an indemnity as to costs in a derivative claim is not limited to impecunious claimants'.

[100] See further A. Reisberg, 'Funding Derivative Actions: A Re-examination of Costs and Fees as Incentives to Commence Litigation' (2004) 4 *Journal of Corporate Law Studies* 345.

claimant is still liable to pay the defendant's costs according to the loser-pays rule. Conditional fee arrangements at best function to provide a way of funding the derivative claimant's own legal costs if an indemnification order is not made. However, in most cases, as already argued, an indemnification order will follow automatically if permission to continue the litigation is granted, in which case conditional fee arrangements will not be required in this regard.

Following a review of the funding of litigation by Lord Justice Jackson, in March 2011, the Government announced its intention to allow contingency fees in Civil Litigation up to a cap of 25% of the award of damages.[101] The Legal Aid, Sentencing and Punishment of Offenders Bill, which is going through Parliament at the time of writing, amends the Courts and Legal Services Act 1990 to allow contingency fees in civil litigation.[102] There is scope to argue that derivative actions would fall within these amended rules.[103] If contingency fees are made available for derivative litigation then, in contrast to conditional fee arrangements, this creates the scope for US-style entrepreneurial derivative litigation, which would lead to a more pronounced sense for directors of exposure to litigation for breach of duty than has been the case to date. UK lawyers, with high-powered incentives to bring litigation, would be the drivers of this litigation. These lawyers would not seek indemnity orders and would provide the shareholders they act on behalf of with a costs indemnity from an insurance company that would cover any costs awarded against the claimant should they lose.

Even if the new derivative claim rules are interpreted restrictively, if contingency fees are available in derivative litigation, one can expect a significant increase in claims. Often these claims will be brought only with a view to obtaining a settlement. Although in this book we have not had the opportunity to explore US derivative action rules, it is worth noting in this regard that in the United States the rules on when derivative litigation can be brought are very director-friendly.[104] In spite of these restrictive rules the contingency fee costs arrangements drive a significant amount of derivative litigation or at least attempts to bring such litigation.

If contingency fee arrangements in the context of derivative litigation are permitted pursuant to the courts and Legal Services Act 1996, then these changes could have a profound effect on the UK corporate landscape. As we saw in Chapter 12, a simple comparison of directors' duties in the UK and the US would find higher standards in the UK[105] but with a low probability of enforcement of those standards, and lower standards in the US but with a much higher probability of enforcement. The primary reason for the higher probability of enforcement in the US is not the derivative action rules but the costs rules. If the UK moves towards US costs rules whilst keeping its higher liability standards then we should be very concerned about the effects that this will have on boards' willingness to take risk and the willingness of business persons to serve on boards.[106]

---

[101] Reforming Civil Litigation Funding and Costs in England and Wales—Implementation of Lord Justice Jackson's Recommendations: The Government Response (Ministry of Justice, 2011) at [13].

[102] Clause 44, Damage-Based Agreements Legal Aid, Sentencing and Punishment of Offenders Bill (2012).

[103] Whether they are available would appear to turn on whether a contingency fee agreement (damage-based agreement) with the derivative claimant provides 'legal services' to the company. Strictly speaking such services are provided to the derivative litigant. However, the derivative litigant brings the action on behalf of, and if allowed to continue, for the benefit of the company. See section 58AA of the Courts and Legal Services Act 1990.

[104] See *Aronson v Lewis* 473 A2d 805 (Del Ch 1984).

[105] As was set out in Chapter 12, in this author's view the UK care standard is, and has always been high: today through section 174 of the Companies Act 2006 and the dual objective/subjective standard of the reasonably diligent director; and at common law either through the standard of the ordinary prudent person acting on his own behalf or the so-called 'subjective standard' of the reasonable director with the skills, knowledge, and experience of the actual director, where—as is in most instances the case in larger UK companies—the actual director has considerable knowledge, skill, and experience.

[106] On these policy concerns see Chapters 10 and 12.

Questions

1. Should indemnification orders be available to all derivative claimants who are given permission to continue with the litigation? Should wealthy claimants be given this assistance?

2. Is the availability of indemnification orders likely to result in too much derivative litigation in the UK?

3. Are you in favour of introducing US-style contingency fees for derivative litigation in the UK? What, in your view, would be the pros and cons of doing so?

4. Given concerns about how high standards of care may chill appropriate risk-taking by directors, is the reason why the UK has been able to maintain high standards of care because the probability of suit has traditionally been so low? If so does the fact that the new derivative claim and the introduction of contingency fees increases the probability of suit raise any alarm bells?

VI REFLECTIVE LOSS: ENFORCING THE PRIORITY OF THE COMPANY'S CLAIM

1 Introduction

Directors' duties are owed to the company; not to the shareholders. Although shareholders may experience financial loss as a result of the breach of the duty, this is not a loss that they can directly recover as *their* rights have not been infringed. However, as we saw in Chapter 9, although rare, it is possible that separate duties of a fiduciary nature can be generated as a result of special circumstances typically involving direct communication between the shareholders and directors.[107] The infringement of these duties is enforceable by the shareholders. In addition, as we saw in Chapter 3, shareholders may have other types of personal right that arise, for example from a breach of the constitution.

In those circumstances where corporate activity and director behaviour result in breaches of rights owed to shareholders, the activities in question will often give rise to a claim by the company as well as the shareholder. Any breach of the constitution, for example, is a breach of the director's duty set out in section 171(a) to observe the terms of the constitution. If directors have breached a duty to shareholders by providing the shareholders with misleading information, it is possible that such actions may also amount to a breach of the director's duty to promote the success of the company or her duty of care. The problem that arises in circumstances which involve both a breach of rights owed to the company *and* the shareholders is that the resulting loss suffered by the company and the shareholders may be the same loss: a loss suffered directly by the company and indirectly by the shareholders as a result of the diminution in the value of the shares. In such circumstances the wrongdoer cannot be required to compensate both the company and the shareholder as this would result in double recovery for the shareholder—directly and indirectly as a result of the increase in the shares' value. The question for the law in such circumstances is: who, *as between the company and the shareholder*, should have the right to enforce the claim?

In answering this question three policy considerations favour the company; one favours the shareholders. The first consideration favouring the company is that if a shareholder is allowed to sue, unless all other shareholders are joined in the action, his recovery will only relate to his loss. Once he has recovered, if the company subsequently sues that shareholder will benefit from double recovery unless the original award of damages

---

[107] See, for example, *Peskin v Anderson* [2000] All ER (D) 2278.

obtained in his personal capacity is returned or taken into account. Secondly, if the wrongdoer has limited funds—perhaps insufficient to compensate the company or all of the shareholders—allowing an individual shareholder to sue in her personal capacity results in an unfair distribution amongst the shareholders of the available compensation for the breach. If only the company is allowed to recover damages, then any amounts paid by the wrongdoing director will benefit all shareholders and creditors equally. Thirdly, there is a strong society-wide efficiency argument for allowing the company to enforce the breach through one, rather than several, actions. Of course this problem is mitigated if the shareholder suit takes place through a class action that covers all shareholders.

From the shareholders' perspective, one strong argument in favour of allowing them to take an action to recover their loss is that neither the board nor the shareholder body may—for the reasons discussed in section I of this chapter—initiate litigation against the directors to recover the company's loss. Allowing shareholders to claim for the loss in their personal capacities would incentivize shareholder action and result in greater accountability for directors. The strength of this argument, however, has been undermined by the Companies Act 2006's introduction of the statutory derivative claim, which, in theory, provides easier access to the derivative mechanism. From the shareholders' perspective her recovery will be the same whether the action is brought individually or enforced derivatively on behalf of the company; in the former the recovery is direct, in the later indirect. Furthermore, the cost incentives to bringing a derivative claim provided by the availability of indemnification orders arguably renders the derivative claim more attractive than a personal action. This would not, however, have been the case prior to the 2006 Act when access to the derivative mechanism was limited.

The policy debate in the post-2006 setting would clearly seem to favour giving priority to the company to enforce its rights. However, even if the law gives priority to the company to decide whether or not it wishes to pursue the litigation, the policy factors in favour of this are not apposite if the company explicitly and definitively decides it does not wish to pursue the litigation. It could do this, for example, by ratifying the breach of duty on which its claim would be based. In such circumstances the arguments against allowing shareholders to recover seem weaker, especially if such recovery was allowed only on a representative basis for the shareholder group as a whole. To refuse to enable shareholder recovery in such circumstances would not only elevate the company's priority in terms of recovery but elevate the company's right above the personal rights of the shareholders.

2 The reflective loss principle

Where shareholders and the company both have legal claims to recover the same loss, English law firmly gives priority to the company to recover this loss. This rule of law giving priority to the company is known as the *reflective loss* rule. An important statement of this rule was provided by the Court of Appeal in *Prudential Assurance v Newman Industries Ltd*.[108] This case involved self-dealing transactions in which the subject company, Newman Industries Ltd, allegedly overpaid for assets from a company which was one of Newman's shareholders and in which certain Newman directors also served on the board. These facts, if correct, were clearly the basis for breach of duty claims by Newman. The transactions were also subject to a shareholder approval requirement pursuant to the Listing Rules as they amounted to Class 1 transactions.[109] The circular distributed to shareholders in relation to the required approval was misleading. The shareholders claimed that the directors had breached a duty owed directly to them arising from the provision to them of the information in the

---

[108] [1982] Ch 204.
[109] Listing Rule 10—see Chapter 6 for a detailed discussion of these rules.

circular. However, the claimed losses were reflective of the company's loss. Consider the following extract in this regard.

■ *Prudential Assurance v Newman Industries Ltd* [1982] Ch 204

Cumming-Bruce, Templeman and Brightman LJJ took it in turns to read the following judgment of the court

[At first instance, Vinelott J upheld the claimants' personal claim.] He began with the proposition, which accorded with his findings, that Newman had been induced by fraud to approve an agreement under which Newman paid more (he thought about £445,000 more) than the value of the assets acquired and thus £445,000 more than it needed to pay; therefore Newman's indebtedness to its bankers immediately after the transaction (about £5m) was £445,000 more than it would have been but for the [self-dealing]; therefore the [self-dealing] caused a reduction in net profits, which must have affected the quoted price of Newman shares; therefore, the plaintiffs suffered some damage in consequence of the [self-dealing] and that was sufficient to complete the cause of action, the quantum of damages being left to an inquiry.

In our judgment the personal claim is misconceived. It is of course correct, as the judge found and [the directors of the company], in advising the shareholders to support the resolution approving the agreement, owed the shareholders a duty to give such advice in good faith and not fraudulently. It is also correct that if directors convene a meeting on the basis of a fraudulent circular, a shareholder will have a right of action to recover any loss which he has been personally caused in consequence of the fraudulent circular; this might include the expense of attending the meeting. But what he cannot do is to recover damages merely because the company in which he is interested has suffered damage. He cannot recover a sum equal to the diminution in the market value of his shares, or equal to the likely diminution in dividend, because such a 'loss' is merely a reflection of the loss suffered by the company. The shareholder does not suffer any personal loss. His only 'loss' is through the company, in the diminution in the value of the net assets of the company, in which he has (say) a 3 per cent shareholding. The plaintiff's shares are merely a right of participation in the company on the terms of the articles of association. The shares themselves, his right of participation, are not directly affected by the wrongdoing. The plaintiff still holds all the shares as his own absolutely unencumbered property. The deceit practised upon the plaintiff does not affect the shares; it merely enables the defendant to rob the company. A simple illustration will prove the logic of this approach. Suppose that the sole asset of a company is a cash box containing £100,000. The company has an issued share capital of 100 shares, of which 99 are held by the plaintiff. The plaintiff holds the key of the cash box. The defendant by a fraudulent misrepresentation persuades the plaintiff to part with the key. The defendant then robs the company of all its money. The effect of the fraud and the subsequent robbery, assuming that the defendant successfully flees with his plunder, is (i) to denude the company of all its assets; and (ii) to reduce the sale value of the plaintiffs' shares from a figure approaching £100,000 to nil. There are two wrongs, the deceit practised on the plaintiff and the robbery of the company. But the deceit on the plaintiff causes the plaintiff no loss which is separate and distinct from the loss to the company. The deceit was merely a step in the robbery. The plaintiff obviously cannot recover personally some £100,000 damages in addition to the £100,000 damages recoverable by the company.

Counsel for the Prudential sought to answer this objection by agreeing that there cannot be double recovery from the defendants, but suggesting that the personal action will lie if the company's remedy is for some reason not pursued. But how can the failure of the company to pursue its remedy against the robber entitle the shareholder to recover for himself? What happens if the robbery takes place in year 1, the shareholder sues in year 2, and the company makes up its mind in year 3 to pursue its remedy? Is the shareholder's action stayed, if still on foot? Supposing judgment has already been recovered by the shareholder and satisfied, what then?

> A personal action could have the most unexpected consequences. If a company with assets of £500m and an issued share capital of £50m were defrauded of £500,000 the effect on dividends and share prices would not be discernible. If a company with assets of £10m were defrauded, there would be no effect on share prices until the fraud was discovered; if it were first reported that the company had been defrauded of £500,000 and subsequently reported that the company had discovered oil in property acquired by the company as part of the fraud and later still reported that the initial loss to the company could not have exceeded £50,000, the effect on share prices would be bewildering and the effect on dividends would either be negligible or beneficial.

This view of reflective loss was confirmed by the House of Lords in *Johnson v Gore Wood & Co* where a personal action was brought by a shareholder in relation to a breach of duty by the third-party (not a director) that had already resulted in an agreed settlement with the company in which the claimant was a shareholder.

■ *Johnson v Gore Wood & Co* [2002] 2 AC 1

Lord Millett

A company is a legal entity separate and distinct from its shareholders. It has its own assets and liabilities and its own creditors. The company's property belongs to the company and not to its shareholders. If the company has a cause of action, this is a legal chose in action which represents part of its assets. Accordingly, where a company suffers loss as a result of an actionable wrong done to it, the cause of action is vested in the company and the company alone can sue. No action lies at the suit of a shareholder suing as such, though exceptionally he may be permitted to bring a derivative action in right of the company and recover damages on its behalf... Correspondingly, of course, a company's shares are the property of the shareholder and not of the company, and if he suffers loss as a result of an actionable wrong done to him, then prima facie he alone can sue and the company cannot. On the other hand, although a share is an identifiable piece of property which belongs to the shareholder and has an ascertainable value, it also represents a proportionate part of the company's net assets, and if these are depleted the diminution in its assets will be reflected in the diminution in the value of the shares. The correspondence may not be exact, especially in the case of a company whose shares are publicly traded, since their value depends on market sentiment. But in the case of a small private company like this company, the correspondence is exact.

This causes no difficulty where the company has a cause of action and the shareholder has none; or where the shareholder has a cause of action and the company has none... Where the company suffers loss as a result of a wrong to the shareholder but has no cause of action in respect of its loss, the shareholder can sue and recover damages for his own loss, whether of a capital or income nature, measured by the diminution in the value of his shareholding. He must, of course, show that he has an independent cause of action of his own and that he has suffered personal loss caused by the defendant's actionable wrong. Since the company itself has no cause of action in respect of its loss, its assets are not depleted by the recovery of damages by the shareholder.

The position is, however, different where the company suffers loss caused by the breach of a duty owed both to the company and to the shareholder. In such a case the shareholder's loss, in so far as this is measured by the diminution in value of his shareholding or the loss of dividends, merely reflects the loss suffered by the company in respect of which the company has its own cause of action. If the shareholder is allowed to recover in respect of such loss, then either there will be double recovery at the expense of the defendant or the shareholder will recover at the expense of the company and its creditors and other shareholders. Neither course can be permitted. This is a matter of principle; there is no discretion involved. Justice to the defendant requires the exclusion of one claim or the other; protection of the interests of the company's creditors requires that it is the company which is allowed to recover to the exclusion of the shareholder. These principles have been established in a number of cases, though they have not always been faithfully observed...

It is of course correct that the diminution in the value of the plaintiffs' shares was by definition a personal loss and not the company's loss, but that is not the point. The point is that it merely reflected the diminution of the company's assets. The test is not whether the company could have made a claim in respect of the loss in question; the question is whether, treating the company and the shareholder as one for this purpose, the shareholder's loss is franked by that of the company. If so, such reflected loss is recoverable by the company and not by the shareholders.

[Counsel] acknowledged that double recovery could not be permitted, but thought that the problem did not arise where the company had settled its claim. He considered that it would be sufficient to make an allowance for the amount paid to the liquidator. With respect, I cannot accept this either. As Hobhouse LJ observed in *Gerber Garment Technology Inc v Lectra Systems Ltd* [1997] RPC 443, 471, if the company chooses not to exercise its remedy, the loss to the shareholder is caused by the company's decision not to pursue its remedy and not by the defendant's wrongdoing. By a parity of reasoning, the same applies if the company settles for less than it might have done. Shareholders (and creditors) who are aggrieved by the liquidator's proposals are not without a remedy; they can have recourse to the Companies Court, or sue the liquidator for negligence.

If a shareholder's claimed loss is reflective of the company's loss then the breach of the shareholder's right cannot be relied upon by the shareholder to recover this loss. This is the case even if the company will not recover the loss because it has elected not to pursue it or it has agreed a settlement for less than the shareholder's loss. As Lord Millett observes, in such a situation the loss is caused to the shareholder not by the breach of the shareholder's right but by the company's decision not to enforce it. Lord Millett makes it clear, however, that where company and shareholder claims are based on the same facts but result in losses for the shareholder that are not reflective of the company's loss, such damages claims are recoverable by the shareholder. For example, if in a takeover bid the directors owed a duty to shareholders arising from communications between them about the offer and as a result of a breach of that duty shareholders were deprived of the opportunity of accepting a higher offer, then the shareholders suffer a direct loss arising from having missed the opportunity to sell the shares for a higher amount. Such a loss is not suffered by the company but only by the shareholders and would be recoverable.[110]

A final problem in this regard arises from situations in which both the rights of the company and shareholders have been breached and the shareholder's loss is reflective; however, due to the actions of the wrongdoer, the company is not capable of enforcing its rights. In such a situation can the shareholder recover in his personal capacity? In *Giles v Rhind*[111] this issue arose where a company had given a court undertaking not to pursue litigation following its inability to give security for costs. The company's poor finances were clearly a direct consequence of the defendant's actions. The claimant brought a personal action in this regard; however, the loss claimed was reflective loss. The Court of Appeal held that such loss was recoverable:

Even in relation to that part of the claim for diminution which could be said to be reflective of the company's loss, since, if the company had no cause of action to recover that loss the shareholder

---

[110] *Heron International Ltd v Lord Grade* [1983] BCLC 244; *Day v Cook* [2001] Lloyd's Rep PN 551.
[111] *Giles v Rhind* [2003] Ch 618.

could bring a claim, the same should be true of a situation in which the wrongdoer has disabled the company from pursuing that cause of action.

Subsequent courts have been careful to narrowly construe the holding in *Giles v Rhind*. In *Gardner v Parker*,[112] Neuberger LJ, in holding that the rule against reflective loss would not be disapplied, observed that: 'the court must be satisfied that the sort of circumstances described in *Giles v Rhind*…exist, before the fact that the company has abandoned, or settled on apparently generous terms, its claim against the defendant, justifies disapplying of the rule against reflective loss'. However, subsequent cases have applied the exception in *Giles v Rhind*. For example, in *Perry v Day*,[113] applying the exception, the court held that the defendant should not, quoting *Giles v Rhind*, be allowed to say: 'the company had a cause of action, which it is true I prevented it from bringing, but that fact alone means that I, the wrongdoer, do not have to pay anybody'.

However, in the Hong Kong Court of Final Appeal's decision in *Waddington v Chan*, Lord Millett posted a strong objection to the approach adopted by the Court of Appeal in *Giles v Rhind*.

■ *Waddington Ltd v Chan Chun Hoo Thomas* [2009] 2 BCLC 82

Lord Millett

It is impossible not to share the determination of the Court of Appeal [in *Giles v Rhind*] not to allow a defendant who has been guilty of such conduct to escape liability. But with respect, it could not be right to allow the shareholder to bring an action for its own benefit; this would entail recovery by the wrong party to the prejudice of the company and its creditors. It would produce precisely the result which I identified as unacceptable in *Johnson v Gore Wood & Co*; it would allow the plaintiff to obtain by a judgment of the court the very same extraction of value from the company at the expense of its creditors that it alleged the defendant had obtained by fraud. The Court of Appeal vouchsafed no explanation to justify this result, an explanation which might be thought to be particularly necessary given that the company was in administrative receivership.

Some way needed to be found in *Giles v Rhind* which would allow the company to recover damages despite the discontinuance of its own proceedings. If the company had not been in administrative receivership, the simplest course would have been to allow the shareholder to bring a derivative action. As it was, this course would not have been open, for the company was no longer under the control of the wrongdoer. But the court could have given the shareholder leave to apply to direct the administrative receiver to bring the action if the shareholder was willing to fund it. The discontinuance should not have been an obstacle to either course. There is no logic in allowing such an action where the wrongdoers are in a position to stifle any proceedings by the company, and disallowing it where they have succeeded in doing so.

The Court of Appeal may have assumed that the principle established in *Johnson v Gore Wood & Co* is not engaged where the company has lost the right to sue. But the House of Lords expressly applied the principle not only where the company had the right to sue but also where it had declined or failed to sue. There was nothing new in this. In *Prudential v Newman (No 2)* it had been submitted that a personal action at the suit of the shareholder will lie to recover reflective loss if the company's remedy is for some reason not pursued. The Court of Appeal countered the argument by posing the rhetorical question: 'How can the failure of the company to pursue its remedy against the robber entitle the shareholder to recover for himself?'.

---

[112] [2004] 2 BCLC 554.   [113] [2005] 2 BCLC 405.

[*Giles v Rhind*] has been followed in England at first instance in *Perry v Day* and referred to without enthusiasm by the Court of Appeal in *Day v Cook* and *Gardner v Parker*. But in all these cases the court was bound by the decision in *Giles v Rhind*. In my opinion *Giles v Rhind* and *Perry v Day* were wrongly decided and should not be followed in Hong Kong.

This decision is a decision of the Hong Kong Court of Final Appeal and therefore is not binding on UK courts. The Court of Appeal continues to be bound by the decision in *Giles v Rhind*.[114] However, Lord Millett's powerful and persuasive 'dissent' in *Waddington* suggests that *Giles v Rhind* is operating on borrowed time, at least until the issue reaches the Supreme Court.

 Online Resource Centre
http://www.oxfordtextbooks.co.uk/orc/kershaw2e/

Visit the Online Resource Centre for additional resources and information available for this chapter, including web links and an interactive flashcard glossary.

---

[114] For example: *Webster v Sanderson* [2009] EWCA Civ 830: 'this court will regard itself as bound by *Giles v Rhind*, whatever the Hong Kong Final Court of Appeal may have said in *Waddington v Chan Chun Hoo Thomas* [2008] HK CU 1381 about not following it in Hong Kong'.

CHAPTER SIXTEEN

MINORITY SHAREHOLDER PROTECTION

I INTRODUCTION

1 The controlling shareholder agency problem

Thus far in Part II of the book our primary focus has been on the legal mechanisms that hold directors to account; that ensure that they act in the interests of the company and not in their own interests. We have viewed the law on the appointment and removal of directors, directors' remuneration, board composition, and directors' duties and their enforcement as ways in which the managerial agency cost problem is controlled or mitigated.

The managerial agency problem, however, is not the only agency problem to afflict the corporate form. An economic agency problem arises where one party (the agent, in economic terms) is in a position to act in ways that detrimentally affects the welfare of another (the principal, in economic terms). In this chapter we are concerned with agency problems between shareholders.

In a widely-held company shareholders with a small percentage holding are not typically in a position to act in ways that detrimentally affect the welfare of other shareholders as they are incapable of wielding sufficient power alone and are often rationally apathetic regarding the exercise of any power. A shareholder's incentive to exercise power increases where she owns a significant shareholding which gives her control over the company. Control need not be de jure control—whereby a significant shareholder owns or can direct the votes of an actual majority of the voting shares—a significant shareholder may have de facto control with fewer than 50% of the shares if other smaller and rationally apathetic shareholders fail to vote at the general meeting.[1] Control could be exercised directly or indirectly: directly through control of any decisions made by the general meeting; or indirectly through influence over the board of directors that is a corollary of the controlling shareholder's ability to appoint and remove the board. Where controlling shareholders use their control and influence in ways that benefit themselves but which are detrimental to the minority shareholders' interests there is a *controlling shareholder agency problem*. In economic terms, the controlling shareholder is 'the agent' and the minority shareholders are 'the principal'. The benefits that controlling shareholders can extract by exerting power and influence for their own benefit are referred to in the literature as *controlling shareholder agency costs* or as the *private benefits of control*.

In practice, large UK companies are widely-held and, therefore, in the vast majority of such large companies there is no controlling shareholder that is in a position to

---

[1] If a shareholder holds 30% of the shares but only 25% of the other shareholders vote regularly then the 30% shareholder will control the general meeting. In practice a large shareholder holding significantly less than 50% of the voting shares will control the general meeting. See also the discussion of this issue in Chapter 5, where we observed that Marks and Spencer Plc's 2011 general meeting had a 59.5% voter turnout.

extract benefits for itself to the detriment of minority shareholders. Although, as we have seen in Chapter 5, amalgamating the voting power of only a handful of institutional shareholders may give those shareholders de facto control in many UK listed companies, in practice these shareholders rarely act together to exercise the power that their combined shareholdings give them.[2] The UK ownership context contrasts with the ownership arrangements for large companies in the majority of EU Member States and other non-Anglo-American jurisdictions, where typically there is a large controlling shareholder with de facto and often de jure control.[3]

In spite of the dominance of widely-held ownership arrangements in large UK companies, in the UK there is a significant controlling shareholder agency problem that requires regulation in two respects. First, *by number* most UK companies are **close**, private companies that have only a few shareholders and where one shareholder, or shareholders from the same family, will often have de jure or de facto control. Secondly, although widely-held companies in practice do not typically have controlling shareholder agency problems, if regulation does not address the theoretical threat of such agency costs the likelihood that an investor will buy a block of shares, to extract the benefits which control brings, increases.

Before looking at how UK company law regulates the potential abuse of power by controlling shareholders we need to put a little flesh on the bones of the idea of controlling shareholder agency costs. More specifically we require a more concrete understanding of the *potential* ways in which a controlling shareholder can act that will benefit herself but detrimentally affect the minority shareholders. Below are the primary examples of corporate action that *in theory* the controlling shareholder can either control directly or influence to her benefit and to the minority shareholders' detriment.

- *Using controlling shareholder voting power to alter the terms of the constitution.* As we have seen, a company's constitution can be changed by passing a special resolution—75% of the votes cast at general meeting.[4] Amendments that would raise minority shareholder concerns would include: changes to the balance of power between the board and the shareholder body, for example, altering the constitution to provide for an ordinary resolution instruction right; amending the rights attached to shares or a class of shares;[5] amending the terms upon which the shares could be transferred or the terms upon which a company may force the sale of a shareholder's shares.

- *Changing the understanding that minority shareholders have about their role in the running of the company.* A minority shareholder may agree to buy shares in a company on the understanding that he will have a particular role, or occupy a particular position, in the company. For example, in our case study company, Bob's Electronics Ltd, assume that Ian agrees to buy 20% of the shares in the company and it is agreed that he will act as a director of the company so long as he remains a shareholder in the company. This agreement could be formally documented by amending the constitution or could be set forth in a separate contract between Bob and Ian. However, regardless of what is agreed between the parties, or of what is set out in the corporate constitution, any director can be removed by an ordinary resolution passed at general meeting at any time and without the need to specify any reason.[6] Whether Ian's continuing role as a director of the company is a formal

---

[2] On the 'rational apathy' of institutional investors and the fund managers that act on their behalf see Chapter 5.

[3] See generally M. Faccio and L.H.P. Lang, 'The Ultimate Ownership of Western Corporations' (2002) 65 *Journal of Financial Economics* 365.

[4] See Chapter 3.

[5] On the meaning of a 'class of shares' and 'class rights' see Chapter 17.

[6] Section 168 CA 2006. See further Chapter 6.

agreement or an informal understanding, he cannot be sure that Bob will not exercise his voting power to remove him once he has made the investment.

- *Excessive director remuneration.* It is typical in small companies where all the shareholders also participate in the management of the company for the shareholder-managers to receive the profits generated by the company through their salaries as managers rather than through the receipt of dividends as shareholders. Where a shareholder in a small company is not a manager, but other shareholders are managers, if excessive remuneration is paid to those shareholder-managers this reduces the profits available to pay a dividend or to reinvest in the company's business and, therefore, reduces the return for minority shareholders on their investment. Controlling shareholders, on the other hand, are incentivized to pay themselves in excess of what their services are worth to the company. In a company with two shareholders owning 80% and 20% of the company respectively, where only the controlling shareholder is a manager, the payment of £1 in excessive remuneration to the controlling shareholder-manager results in a transfer of 20 pence from the minority shareholder to the controlling shareholder. This problem becomes particularly acute where a minority shareholder is, contrary to his expectation, removed as a manager of the company and thereby loses his salary.

- *Related party transactions: transactions between the company and parties connected or related to the controlling shareholder.* If a company has £1 million of cash from profits generated by the company but has no immediate use for that cash, shareholders would expect the company to dividend those funds to shareholders who would receive it according to their proportionate shareholding in the company. A controlling shareholder with a 60% shareholding would receive £600,000. However, if the controlling shareholder can use his influence to get the board to agree to buy one of his own assets worth £1 million for £2 million then the controlling shareholder obtains a benefit of £1 million and the minority shareholders receive nothing.

- *Altering the control relationships in the company/transferring value to the controlling shareholder through share issues.* Company law and corporate constitutions provide that minority shareholders who own, either alone or in aggregate, a certain number of shares have certain rights.[7] Furthermore, where the controlling shareholder owns less than 75% of the voting shares, minority shareholders will take comfort from the fact that certain actions which require a special resolution, for example changing the constitution, would require the support of some of the minority shareholders. If controlling shareholders can exercise their influence to force or cajole the board to issue new shares to the controller, or to parties connected to or associated with the controller, then existing minority shareholder power could be taken away as the share issue pushes minority ownership below the relevant ownership threshold. The concern for minority shareholders in this regard is compounded by the risk that the newly issued shares may be issued for less than they are worth, thereby transferring value from the minority shareholders to the majority shareholders.[8]

- *The forced sale of the minority shareholders' shares.* We have already noted above the concern that a controlling shareholder could alter the constitution to provide for

[7] For example, 5% of the voting shares have the right to call a shareholder meeting (sections 303–305 CA 2006); 5% of the voting shares have the right to require the company to circulate a statement about a meeting agenda item (section 338 CA 2006).

[8] For an explanation of how value is transferred see section I of Chapter 17 where the regulation of share issues is addressed in detail.

the forced sale of the minority shareholders' shares.[9] 'Squeeze out' from a company raises two concerns for the minority shareholder: first, that he is no longer able to participate in the growth of this company; and, second, that he may be forced to sell his shares for less than they are worth.

2 Regulating controlling shareholder actions

We saw in Chapters 9–14 that the law of directors' duties regulates the activities of directors in two ways. First, it regulates the directors' exercise of the power delegated to them by requiring that when they exercise corporate power they act to promote the success of the company and take the requisite degree of care when so doing. Secondly, it regulates actions the directors may take in their personal capacity to promote their personal interests where in so doing those personal interests may conflict with the company's interests. The analysis in this chapter of the regulation of controlling share-holder power follows a similar structure. We shall ask: first, to what extent are a controller's actions in general meeting subject to any regulation and restrictions; and, second, to what extent does the law regulate controlling shareholder activity that does not involve the direct exercise of corporate power but arguably conflicts with the company's interests.

2.1 Regulating the shareholder vote

In a corporate democracy, the general meeting is an organ of the company that exer-cises corporate power according to the distribution of power set out in the articles and the 2006 Act. The question for company law in this regard is: to what, if any, extent is the exercise of majority power that is formally consistent with the constitution subject to constraint and oversight? More specifically, to what, if any, extent should company law regulate shareholder voting in general meeting to ensure that any decisions of the general meeting further the corporate interest and not the interests of a particular share-holder or group of shareholders to the detriment of other shareholders?[10]

Strong arguments are available to oppose such oversight of general meeting decision-making. First, decisions by shareholders in general meeting are taken by many differ-ent individuals who naturally have different and opposing views about the merits of a proposed resolution; no court, no matter how Herculean, can hope to navigate through the minefield of such views to identify the view what *is* or *is not* in the company's inter-est. Secondly, one might ask why the courts should even attempt to protect minority shareholders from the exercise of voting power that is permitted by the constitution. In this regard consider, for example, the issue of a change in the company's articles. Whilst typically a provision in the articles can be changed with a vote of 75% of the votes cast at the general meeting, it has always been open to shareholders to provide for a higher threshold or indeed to render a particular provision unamendable without the approval of every shareholder.[11] Alternatively, the shareholders could enter into a

---

[9] However, terms in the corporate constitution that provide for the forced sale of shares are not the only ways in which minority shareholders can be 'squeezed out' of the company. Such a 'squeeze out' could also follow from a merger or amalgamation with another company or pursuant to statutory mechanisms providing for squeeze out following a takeover—see section 979 CA 2006. We do not consider this mechanism in this book.

[10] The 'company's interests' is understood to mean the interests of all the present and future members of the company (*Greenhalgh v Arderne Cinemas Ltd* [1950] Ch 286)—see further Chapter 10 consider-ing company interests in the context of the previous common law duty to act in good faith in the best interests of the company.

[11] Section 22 CA 2006. On the entrenchment of provisions in the articles to prevent amendment without 100% shareholder consent see Chapter 3.

separate shareholders agreement that would give the shareholder a claim for breach of contract if the controller attempted to change the constitution in ways that were contrary to the shareholders agreement.[12] A **contractarian** scholar would argue that the minority shareholder could have negotiated for such provisions in the constitution or in a separate shareholders agreement in order to protect themselves; and if they did not do so then they were not willing to pay for the protection that such provisions would have given them—that is, the price they paid for their minority shareholding incorporated some risk that a controlling shareholder would act to change the constitution in a way which is detrimental to minority shareholder interests. For a contractarian, the minority shareholder has no complaint if she did not negotiate[13] and pay for this protection, and the law should encourage shareholders to protect themselves by not providing them with protection if they fail to do so: *caveat emptor.*

Of course, many small minority shareholders are rarely so well advised; they buy shares in a company which has Model Articles and do not take, or cannot afford, legal advice on how the constitution could be altered to protect their position. Furthermore, it is not possible for a shareholder to foresee all the ways in which voting power may be used by the controlling shareholder to the detriment of the minority shareholder. An enforceable standard that decisions of the general meeting must further the company's interest would provide minority shareholders with a general degree of protection in relation to an uncertain future and which, following the contractarian view, the shareholders will pay for in the price they pay for the shares.

2.2 Controlling shareholder activity outside of the general meeting

As we saw in Chapters 13 and 14 company law regulates a director's personal activities where there is potential for conflict between her personal interests and the company's interests. A controlling shareholder is in a similar position to a director: able to exert her power to encourage the company to act in ways that benefit the shareholder personally by, for example, entering into non-arm's length transactions with the shareholder (a 'related-party transaction'), or providing the shareholder with information about new opportunities which the shareholder rather than the company then exploits. Here influence and power is exerted informally through conversations with board members which take place in the shadow of the controller's control over board appointments. The conflict between personal and company interests to which directors are subject is, therefore, largely replicated in the case of controlling shareholders. The question for us is: what legal strategies does the law deploy to regulate these activities? Importantly in this regard we will ask whether the law imposes duty-like obligations on controlling shareholders, or standards of fair dealing, that prevent the controlling shareholder behaving in ways that damage the company even where the shareholder is not formally involved in the exercise of corporate power.

In many instances where controlling shareholders exercise inappropriate influence on the board the resulting actions—related-party transactions or giving away opportunities—will involve a breach of duty by the directors. Accordingly, it is important to note that the availability of a derivative action mechanism to hold directors to account for breach of duty is an important aspect of regulating controlling shareholder activity. This is especially true if the controlling shareholder is also a director. However, it is also true where the director is not the controlling shareholder. If directors fear suit and personal liability they will not do the controlling shareholder's bidding, particularly when the directors themselves may not gain directly from the transactions in question.

---

[12] On shareholder agreements see Chapter 3.

[13] On the contractarian view of an informal negotiating process in widely-held companies see Chapter 3.

However, regulating the controlling shareholder separately from the directors may still be important for two reasons. First, it may not always be the case that action that benefits the controlling shareholder to the detriment of the minority involves a breach of the director's duty. Perhaps, for example, the director really thought the action in question promoted the success of the company. Secondly, if the corporate action in question results in a considerable transfer of value to the controlling shareholder, the director, who has not personally directly benefited, may not have a deep enough pocket to compensate the company.

II COMMON LAW REGULATION OF CONTROLLING SHAREHOLDERS

1 Common law limits on shareholder voting

There are two primary contexts in which courts have considered, and on rarer occasions imposed, limits on general meeting decision-making where the general meeting is controlled by a majority shareholder. These two contexts are: first, the ratification of a breach of a director's duty where the shareholder was interested in the transaction or action that led to the breach, typically because the shareholder is the conflicted director; secondly, amendments to a company's articles of association, in particular, where that amendment leads to the compulsory sale of a minority shareholder's shares. On the whole courts, whilst noting that general meeting decisions may be subject to certain restrictions, have rarely held general meeting actions to be invalid.

1.1 Shareholder votes to ratify breaches of duty: common law oppression

As we noted in Chapter 15, pursuant to section 239 of the Companies Act 2006, only a vote of the majority of disinterested shareholders can ratify a breach of duty by a director. This provision amended the common law rule that interested shareholders could vote in a general meeting decision to ratify a breach of duty. Nevertheless, as we see in the cases set out below, at common law the courts imposed some limits on the ability of conflicted controlling shareholders to ratify a breach. The leading case in this regard is the Privy Council case of *North West Transportation Company Limited v Beatty*. As we observed in Chapter 15, these common law rules continue to regulate pre-breach authorization by shareholders which is not subject to the disinterested shareholder requirement in section 239.

■ *North West Transportation Company Limited v Beatty* (1887) 12 App Cas 589

James Beatty was a director of the North West Transportation Company Limited. He also controlled a majority of the voting shares in the company. The company was a steamship company. Following the loss of one of its ships and the unsuitability of another the company required an additional vessel. It purchased this vessel—the *United Empire*—from Mr Beatty. The shareholders in general meeting ratified the purchase and any breach of Mr Beatty's duty involved in his sale of the ship to the company. Mr Beatty voted his shares in favour of the purchase. The question for the court was whether, given his conflict of interest as a director, he was allowed to vote his shares to ratify his own breach of duty. Note, with regard to the facts of the case that it is unclear to the court whether the shareholder resolution was an act of the company to buy the ship or a ratification of a breach of duty. For the purposes of our analysis, we shall view the resolution as the ratification of the breach of duty.

Sir Richard Baggallay (delivering their Lordships' judgment)

The general principles applicable to cases of this kind are well established. Unless some provision to the contrary is to be found in the charter or other instrument by which the company is incorporated, the resolution of a majority of the shareholders, duly convened, upon any question with which the company is legally competent to deal, is binding upon the minority, and consequently upon the company, and every shareholder has a perfect right to vote upon any such question, although he may have a personal interest in the subject-matter opposed to, or different from, the general or particular interests of the company.

On the other hand, a director of a company is precluded from dealing, on behalf of the company, with himself, and from entering into engagements in which he has a personal interest conflicting, or which possibly may conflict, with the interests of those whom he is bound by fiduciary duty to protect; and this rule is as applicable to the case of one of several directors as to a managing or sole director. Any such dealing or engagement may, however, be affirmed or adopted by the company, provided such affirmance or adoption is not brought about by unfair or improper means, and is not illegal or fraudulent or oppressive towards those shareholders who oppose it…

It is proved by uncontradicted evidence, and is indeed now substantially admitted, that at the date of the purchase the acquisition of another steamer to supply the place of the *Asia* was essential to the efficient conduct of the company's business; that the *United Empire* was well adapted for that purpose; that it was not within the power of the company to acquire any other steamer equally well adapted for its business; and that the price agreed to be paid for the steamer was not excessive or unreasonable.

Had there been no material facts in the case other than those above stated, there would have been, in the opinion of their Lordships, no reason for setting aside the sale of the steamer…There is, however, a further element for consideration, arising out of the following facts, which have been relied upon in the arguments on behalf of the plaintiff, as evidencing that the resolution of the 16th of February was brought about by unfair and improper means…[namely that] the majority of votes in favour of the [ratification by the shareholders] was due to the votes of the defendant J. H. Beatty…

On the 9th of April, 1886, the Supreme Court reversed the order of the Court of Appeal, and affirmed that of the Chancellor. It appears to have been the opinion of the judges of the Supreme Court that the case turned entirely on the fiduciary character of the defendant J. H. Beatty as a director: that, if the acts or transactions of an interested director were to be confirmed by the shareholders, it should be by an exercise of the impartial, independent, and intelligent judgment of disinterested shareholders and not by the votes of the interested director, who ought never to have departed from his duty; that the course pursued by the defendant J. H. Beatty was an oppressive proceeding on his part; and that, consequently, the vote of the shareholders, at the meeting of the 16th of February, 1883, was ineffectual…The nature of the transaction itself does not appear to have been taken into consideration by the judges in their decision of the case.

From this decision of the Supreme Court of Canada the appeal has been brought with which their Lordships have now to deal. The question involved is doubtless novel in its circumstances, and the decision important in its consequences; it would be very undesirable even to appear to relax the rules relating to dealings between trustees and their beneficiaries; on the other hand, great confusion would be introduced into the affairs of joint stock companies if the circumstances of shareholders, voting in that character at general meetings, were to be examined, and their votes practically nullified, if they also stood in some fiduciary relation to the company.

It is clear upon the authorities that the contract entered into by the directors on the 10th of February could not have been enforced against the company at the instance of the defendant J. H. Beatty, but it is equally clear that it was within the competency of the shareholders at the meeting of the 16th to adopt or reject it. In form and in terms they adopted it by a majority of votes, and the vote of the majority must prevail, unless the adoption was brought about by unfair or improper means.

The only unfairness or impropriety which, consistently with the admitted and established facts, could be suggested, arises out of the fact that the defendant J. H. Beatty possessed a voting power as a shareholder which enabled him, and those who thought with him, to…ratify and adopt a voidable contract, into which he, as a director, and his co-directors had entered, or to make a similar contract, which latter seems to have been what was intended to be done by the resolution passed on the 7th of February.

It may be quite right that, in such a case, the opposing minority should be able, in a suit like this, to challenge the transaction, and to shew that it is an improper one…but the constitution of the company enabled the defendant J. H. Beatty to acquire this voting power; there was no limit upon the number of shares which a shareholder might hold, and for every share so held he was entitled to a vote; the charter itself recognised the defendant as a holder of 200 shares, one-third of the aggregate number; he had a perfect right to acquire further shares, and to exercise his voting power in such a manner as to secure the election of directors whose views upon policy agreed with his own, and to support those views at any shareholders' meeting; the acquisition of the *United Empire* was a pure question of policy, as to which it might be expected that there would be differences of opinion, and upon which the voice of the majority ought to prevail; to reject the votes of the defendant…would be to give effect to the views of the minority, and to disregard those of the majority.

The judges of the Supreme Court appear to have regarded the exercise by the defendant J. H. Beatty of his voting power as of so oppressive a character as to invalidate the adoption of the [resolution]; their Lordships are unable to adopt this view; in their opinion the defendant was acting within his rights in voting as he did.

The judgment in *North West Transportation* strongly affirms that unless the constitution restricted the voting power of the shares held by the controlling shareholder, Mr Beatty, or restricted his ability to participate in a ratification decision, then he was entitled to vote his shares in favour of the purchase of the asset from him and to ratify any breach of duty.[14] However, in certain respects the judgment suggests that there are limits on the ability of interested shareholders to vote how they please. As we saw in our discussion of the regulation of self-dealing transactions, the common law's traditional view was that a self-dealing transaction was voidable unless ratified by the shareholders in general meeting.[15] This was the case regardless of the fairness of the transaction in question—whether it benefited the company or not. However, in this judgment the ability of a shareholder to vote his shares to ratify his breach as a director appears to be subject to some fairness-type considerations. There are two points to note in this regard. First, the court notes that such ratification cannot be 'illegal or fraudulent or oppressive towards those shareholders who oppose it' (the minority shareholders). What exactly amounts to oppression is unclear, but the distinction suggests something of a lesser order than illegality or fraud. Secondly, it is relevant for the court that there is evidence that the company needed the ship and that the price paid for the ship was not excessive or unreasonable. Because there was no question of impropriety regarding the suitability of the vessel for the company and the price paid, the issue became 'a pure question of policy' upon which business opinion can differ and in relation to which the court should not interfere. An open question from this case is: would evidence of impropriety or unfair terms amount to oppression that would prevent the exercise of the conflicted shareholder's votes?

[14] Affirmed by *Burland v Earle* [1902] AC 83 where the Privy Council observed that 'unless otherwise provided by the regulations of the company, a shareholder is not debarred from voting or using his voting power to carry a resolution by the circumstance of his having a particular interest in the subject matter of the vote'.

[15] See Chapter 13.

This 'oppression'-based restriction on the exercise of a controller's votes is developed in the Privy Council case of *Cook v Deeks*,[16] a case involving the taking of a corporate opportunity by directors of the claimant company. Here the directors of the plaintiff company negotiated with the counterparty to a contract apparently in the company's name until, once the negotiations had been finalized, they took the contract in their own name. Here the Privy Council considered whether the directors who were majority shareholders of the company could exercise their votes to ratify that breach of duty. The court held that they could not, because 'it appears quite certain that directors holding a majority of the votes would not be permitted to make a present to themselves. This would be to allow a majority to oppress the minority.'

Readers will recall from our discussion of shareholder approval of the taking of corporate opportunities in Chapter 14 that in *Regal (Hastings) v Gulliver*[17] the House of Lords held that the directors could have kept the personal profits they had made from the sale of their shares in Regal's subsidiary if the shareholders had ratified their breach of duty. Even though those same directors were majority shareholders in Regal, the House of Lords viewed interested shareholder ratification as legitimate. The distinction between *Regal* and *Cook v Deeks* is that there was no impropriety or bad faith on the part of the directors in *Regal*; no explicit attempt to damage the company to the detriment of the minority—to *oppress* the minority. Indeed, in *Regal* the court accepted that the director-shareholders had acted in good faith in a way that they thought benefited the company, as well as themselves.

Juxtaposing *Regal (Hastings)* next to *Cook v Deeks* suggests that if the actions were taken by the directors to benefit the company, even though they resulted in a breach of duty, then the breach is capable of ratification by conflicted shareholder-directors. However, if that action was not taken in the company's interests, or cannot be presented as being taken in the company's interest, then the action cannot be ratified by the conflicted shareholder director. Such a view, if correct, bears a close affinity to the approach taken by the courts in relation to general meeting decisions to amend the articles discussed later.

One final point in this regard requires consideration. In some commentators' view, *Cook v Deeks* stands for the proposition that some wrongs are not ratifiable and that this remains the case even following the introduction of section 239. Whether this is correct, however, is open to some doubt.[18] We have already seen that in *Cook v Deeks* the inability for the shareholder to ratify the wrong was a function of the fact that this would involve 'oppression' of the minority by the majority. If, therefore, the majority are prevented by section 239 from voting and oppressing the minority the basis for preventing ratification is removed.

1.2 Amending the articles of association: acting bona fide in the interests of the company

The Companies Acts have long provided that a company's articles can be amended by a special resolution in general meeting, unless the constitution itself provided for a higher threshold.[19] Where a controlling shareholder controls 75% of the votes cast at the general meeting such a shareholder can exercise her voting power to amend the articles without the agreement of the minority shareholders, even where the amendment

---

[16] [1916] 1 AC 554.   [17] [1942] 1 All ER 378.

[18] Apart from in relation to an ultra vires acts which it is not possible to ratify—*Ashbury Railway Carriage and Iron Company Limited v Rich* [1874–80] All ER Rep Ext 2219. Of course pursuant to section 39 CA 2006 this does not affect the validity and enforceability of the contract.

[19] Section 22 CA 2006. See further Chapter 3.

detrimentally affects the minority. Such amendments could include, amongst others: altering the minority shareholder's understanding of how the company may be run, what it can do, who can act on its behalf; or altering the balance of power in the company between the board and the shareholder body; or, more fundamentally, amending the constitution to enable the minority shareholders to be bought or squeezed out of the company.

The question for us in this section is: whether the general meeting's decision to amend the articles is subject to any further legal constraint apart from the requirement to obtain the required number of votes in favour of an amendment resolution. In this regard, let us consider first Lindley LJ's well-known judgment in *Allen v Gold Reefs of West Africa Ltd*.

■ *Allen v Gold Reefs of West Africa Ltd* [1900–03] All ER Rep 746

The articles of association of Gold Reefs of West Africa Ltd provided for a lien in favour of the company for any unpaid shares. If the owner of the shares did not pay any amount due on the shares upon demand to do so, the lien enabled the company to sell the shares to recover the amounts owed. The defendant, Mr Zuccani, who was deceased, had owned both paid-up shares and unpaid shares. To recover the amounts owed on the unpaid shares the company wanted to take a lien over the defendant's paid-up shares. However, the articles of association did not provide for a lien over paid-up shares in respect of any debts owed by the shareholder to the company. The company amended the articles to provide for such a lien over a shareholder's paid-up shares in respect of debts owed by the shareholder to the company. An action was brought challenging the general meeting's decision to amend the articles.

> **Sir Nathaniel Lindley MR**
> This is an appeal from a decision of Kekewich, J, granting an injunction restraining the defendants from enforcing a lien on some fully paid-up shares in the company and belonging to a deceased shareholder named Zuccani. The appeal is not only important to the parties to it, but it raises several questions of great general interest relating to the power of limited companies to alter their articles, and especially to their power to alter their articles so as to affect shares standing in the names of deceased shareholders...
>
> The articles of a company prescribe the regulations binding on its members. They have the effect of a contract; but the exact nature of this contract is even now very difficult to define. Be its nature what it may the company is empowered by the statute to alter the regulations contained in its articles from time to time by special resolutions (secs 50 and 51 [Companies Act 1862]); and any regulation or article purporting to deprive the company of this power is invalid on the ground that it is contrary to the statute: (*Walker v London Tramways Co*).[20] The power thus conferred on companies to alter the regulations contained in their articles is limited only by the provisions contained in the statute and the conditions contained in the company's memorandum of association. Wide, however, as the language of s 50 is the power conferred by it must, like all other powers, be exercised subject to those general principles of law and equity which are applicable to all powers conferred on majorities and enabling them to bind minorities. It must be exercised, not only in the manner required by law, but also bona fide for the benefit of the company as a whole, and it must not be exceeded. These conditions are always implied, and are seldom, if ever, expressed. But if they are complied with, I can discover no ground for judicially putting any other restrictions on the power conferred by the section than those contained in it. How shares shall be transferred, and whether the company shall have any lien on them, are clearly matters of regulation properly prescribed by a company's articles of association...

[20] (1879) 12 Ch D 705.

Speaking, therefore, generally, and without reference to any particular case, the section clearly authorises a limited company, formed with articles which confer no lien on fully paid-up shares and which allow them to be transferred without any fetter, to alter those articles by special resolution, and to impose a lien and restrictions on the registry of transfers of those shares by members indebted to the company. But then comes the question whether this can be done so as to impose a lien or restriction in respect of a debt contracted before and existing at the time when the articles are altered. Again, speaking generally, I am of opinion that the articles can be so altered, and that, if they are altered bona fide for the benefit of the company, they will be valid and binding as altered on the existing holders of paid-up shares, whether those holders are indebted or not indebted to the company when the alteration is made. But, as will be seen presently, it does not by any means follow that the altered article may not be inapplicable to some particular fully paid-up shareholder. He may have special rights against the company which do not invalidate the resolution to alter the articles, but which may exempt him from the operation of the articles as altered.

The conclusion thus arrived at is based on the language of s 50, which, as I have said already, the court, in my opinion, is not at liberty to restrict. This conclusion, moreover, is in conformity with such authorities as there are on the subject. *Andrews v Gas Meter Co* (2) is an authority that, under s 50 of the Companies Act, 1862, a company's articles can be altered so as to authorise the issue of preference shares taking priority over existing shares, although no power to issue preference shares was conferred by the memorandum of association or by the original articles. The answer to the argument that the company could not alter existing rights is that, within the limits set by the statute and the memorandum of association, the rights of shareholders in limited companies, so far as they depend only on the regulations of the company, are subject to alteration by s 50 of the Act…

It is easy to imagine cases in which even a member of a company may acquire by contract or otherwise special rights against the company which exclude him from the operation of a subsequently altered article…To exclude…the application of an altered article to particular shares, some clear and distinct agreement for that exclusion must be shown, or some circumstances must be proved conferring a legal or equitable right on the shareholder to be treated by the company differently from the other shareholders. [The court concluded that there was no such agreement in relation to Zuccani.]…

Zuccani bargained for fully paid-up shares, and he got them. The imposition of a lien on them did not render them less fully paid-up than they were before. They remained what they were. Zuccani did not bargain that the regulations relating to paid-up shares should never be altered, or that if altered his shares should be treated differently from other fully paid-up shares. I cannot see that the company broke its bargain with him in any way by altering its regulations or by enforcing the altered regulations as it did…No allottee of shares, whether a vendor or an ordinary applicant, can justly complain of injustice or even hardship if his rights under the original articles are modified to his disadvantage. Every allottee was told by the memorandum that his rights as a shareholder were subject to alteration, and no allottee acquired any rights except on these terms, unless, of course, some special bargain was made with him. If Zuccani had not been indebted to the company, could he have successfully maintained that the company had no power to alter the articles and so make his shares liable to a lien, and, consequently less marketable than before? I take it that it is clear that he could not. But I arrive at this conclusion only because the bargain with him has not been broken. Zuccani's indebtedness to the company confers on him or his executors no rights against it. But it is his indebtedness which creates the embarrassment from which they seek to escape. The fact that Zuccani's executors were the only persons practically affected at the time by the alterations made in the articles excites suspicion as to the bona fides of the company. But, although the executors were the only persons who were actually affected at the time, that was because Zuccani was the only holder of paid-up shares who at the time was in arrear of calls. The altered articles applied to all holders of fully-paid shares, and made no distinction between them. The directors cannot be charged with bad faith.

After carefully considering the whole case, and endeavouring in vain to discover rounds for holding that there was some special bargain differentiating Zuccani's shares from others, I have come to the conclusion that the appeal from the decision of the learned judge, so far as it relates to the lien created by the articles, must be allowed.

Romer LJ

A company such as this may undoubtedly by its articles of association provide for a lien on the shares of its shareholders in respect of any debts for the time being due from them to the company, and, if the original articles do not provide for the lien, the company may subsequently, by duly altering its articles, give itself such a lien; and the fact that the original articles did not provide for a lien would be in itself no ground justifying a shareholder who was indebted when the articles were altered in saying that he contracted the debt or that he took his shares in reliance on there being no lien, and that the new articles must not operate so as to make the lien thereby given extend to his existing debt. A shareholder must be taken to have known that the articles might be so altered as to give the lien…

Of course, by the above observations I have not been dealing with exceptional cases. I can imagine a case, for example, where by the memorandum of association certain provisions as to lien are made part of the constitution of the company which could not be affected by any alteration of the articles.[21] And special contracts might be made with particular classes of shareholders or individuals, or special obligations to them might be incurred by the company, and that even by virtue of the original articles alone, which would prevent the articles being altered as against them, or prevent the alteration being enforceable against them. But, putting aside such exceptional cases, the observations I have made as to the general law are in my opinion sound…

This being so, in my opinion Zuccani's shares became bound by the company's alteration of its articles, unless he can show some special bargain with the company or some special obligation incurred towards him by the company in respect of his fully paid-up shares. He fails to establish any such special bargain or obligation…

Something was said on behalf of the respondents as to want of good faith on the part of the company in altering its articles. I fail to see any want of good faith. In my opinion it is eminently fair for a company to provide by its articles as originally framed, or as altered by resolutions, that shareholders who are indebted to the company should not be permitted to dispose of their shares without paying their debts, and that the company should have a lien on the shares for the debts. In the ordinary case of a partnership no partner would be permitted to withdraw or sell his shares in the partnership venture without his debts to the partnership being first paid thereout and if the company in the present case had, as I think it had, the legal right to alter its articles so as to give it the lien it now claims, I cannot see why, in exercising that legal right, it should be accused of want of good faith. That the reason for the alteration was the very existence of the large debt due from Zuccani, and that the company had principally in mind this large debt when it made the alterations in the articles, is no ground for impeaching the action of the company. It appears to me that the shareholders were acting in the truest and best interests of the company in exercising the legal right to alter the articles so that the company might, as one result, obtain payment of the debt due from Zuccani. The shareholders were only bound to look to the interests of the company. They were not bound to consult or consider Zuccani's separate or private interests…

I have now dealt substantially with the points raised on behalf of the respondents, and in the result I can find no good or sufficient ground on which to hold that the lien given by the amended articles was not good against Zuccani's executors, and accordingly I think that the appeal on this point should be allowed.

---

[21] Prior to the Act 2006 provisions of the articles that were to be rendered unalterable by the normal special resolution procedure for amending articles had to be set forth in the memorandum and the memorandum had to specify that they were amendable only in accordance with the conditions set forth in the memorandum: section 17(2)(b) CA 1985.

Lindley MR holds that the exercise of powers conferred on the general meeting, such as altering the articles, is subject to an implied condition that it must be exercised 'bona fide for the benefit of the company as a whole'. Romer LJ also, although less explicitly, conditions the validity of the amendment to the articles on the good faith of the general meeting's decision. Strictly speaking this is a restriction placed on the general meeting's decision-making power. Clearly, however, if a controlling shareholder wields sufficient votes to control the general meeting this restriction restrains the ability of the controlling shareholder to vote how he chooses.

The judgment itself is a strongly contractarian judgment. For Lindley MR the plaintiff shareholder purchased shares in a company with articles which enabled those articles to be changed in ways that could affect the shares purchased, and unless he bargained not to be affected by particular changes then he has no complaint. The court takes a broad view of the types of agreement or understanding that could exclude Mr Zuccani from the effects of this amendment to the articles. In this regard, Romer LJ refers to 'special contracts' and 'special obligations'; Lindley MR refers to 'clear and distinct' agreements but also to 'some circumstances conferring a legal or equitable right'. The latter suggests that informal understandings may also enable a shareholder to claim that his rights as a shareholder are unaffected by shareholder action. From this perspective for Lindley LJ acting 'bona fide in the interests of the company' may mean, therefore, that the power of the vote may not be used to breach an agreement—whether written or informal—that the articles will not be changed in a particular way to the detriment of a particular shareholder.[22]

A second possible meaning of 'acting bona fide for the benefit of the company as a whole' that is suggested by Lindley MR's judgment is that this power cannot be used to *directly* discriminate between shareholders by an amendment to the constitution which explicitly provides one shareholder or a group of shareholders with superior rights to the others. In this regard, Lindley MR notes that although the change to the constitution in this case only affected Mr Zuccani and no other shareholder, the reason for this was not because the change did not apply to all shareholders but because Mr Zuccani was the only indebted shareholder in relation to arrears for his unpaid shares. That is, changes can be made to the constitution consistently with the bona fide obligation where they are intended to address particular problem shareholders, provided that such changes are formally applicable to all shareholders. Had the amendment provided only that paid-up shares held by Mr Zuccani would be subject to a lien this would not, therefore, have been a general meeting decision taken bona fide in the interests of the company. From this perspective the 'acting bona fide in the interests of the company' requirement requires only that any amendment provides for formal equality of treatment amongst shareholders.

Romer LJ considers good faith separately from the issue of a special contractual agreement or obligation not to amend the articles. His assessment of good faith appears to involve the consideration of whether such an amendment can be understood to be in the company's interests. In this regard, he considers it 'eminently fair' that the company's articles can be amended to provide for a lien on the shares held by shareholders in arrears. Importantly, it is not necessary that this was the *actual* reason why the shareholders in general meeting voted as they did; rather that such an explanation/reason is available to support what they did. From this perspective the requirement that the general meeting act in good faith in the interests of the company results in rationality review by the courts: can this decision be rationally explained as a decision that benefits the company as a whole. For the common law what benefits the company, or what is

---

[22] On informal agreements, compare this position to the approach taken by section 994 CA 2006 considered in section III of this chapter.

in the company's interests, is understood to be what benefits the present and future shareholders of the company.[23]

For the Court of Appeal in *Allen v Gold Reefs* the requirement to act 'bona fide for the benefit of the company as a whole' is easily discharged: the courts will not interfere with non-discriminatory decisions that benefit from a rational justification. However, extracted from the context in which it was deployed in *Allen v Gold Reefs*, the standard itself is *capable* of being interpreted as an invitation to the courts to assess whether, *in their opinion*, the general meeting's decision was *in fact* taken to further the company's interests or the interests of the controlling shareholder. This was clearly not how the court understood the standard in *Allen v Gold Reefs*. However, not all courts addressing the 'bona fide' standard have resisted this temptation. In *Brown v British Abrasive Wheel Co, Ltd*,[24] for example, the High Court invalidated the alteration of a company's articles providing for a right for the company to squeeze out shareholders holding 10% or less of the company's shares. The articles were altered following the refusal of the shareholders to sell the shares. The judgment does not raise any issue regarding the adequacy of the price to be paid for the shares. Astbury J held that:

> The question which I have to decide is whether this is an alteration which the majority should be allowed to press on an unwilling minority. It is said that this is an oppressive attempt to buy out the minority forcibly for the benefit of the holders of this large block of shares. The question is whether this proposition is contrary to natural justice. If the proposition is fair and just, in the interests of the company and the shareholders generally, the court cannot interfere, but if, on the other hand, it is oppressive and unfair the court should prevent it being carried out. There are two shareholders who hold forty-nine fiftieths of the capital, and the proposed alteration would place it in their decision as to whether they are to become the owners of all the shares they want. They attempted to buy up all the outstanding shares at par, and failed, and in my opinion this is a proposition to enable them to do forcibly what they were unable to do by agreement....
>
> The question here is whether the power of the company to make this proposed alteration, asked for by the holders of forty-nine fiftieths of the shares, is limited only by the statute and the provisions of the company's memorandum of association, or whether it is subject to those general principles of law and equity which are applicable to all powers conferred on majorities enabling them to bind minorities, and whether the alteration itself is for the benefit of the company as a whole. I find it difficult to follow how it can be just and equitable that a majority who failed to purchase the shares of others by agreement should be entitled to so exercise their votes as to take power to do so compulsorily, and I am of opinion that the proposed alteration is not for the benefit of anyone except the majority.

The holding in *Brown v British Abrasive Wheel* is based upon *what Astbury J considers* to be fair and equitable. It is, therefore, inconsistent with *Allen v Gold Reefs*. The correctness of this holding was, rightly in the view of this author, questioned shortly thereafter by the Court of Appeal in *Sidebottom v Kershaw, Leese and Company Ltd*.

---

[23] In the later case of *Greenhalgh v Arderne Cinemas Ltd* [1950] Ch 286 in this regard the Court of Appeal observed that '"the company as a whole" does not (at any rate in such a case as the present) mean the company as a commercial entity as distinct from the corporators. It means the corporators as a general body. That is to say, you may take the case of an individual hypothetical member and ask whether what is proposed is, in the honest opinion of those who voted in its favour, for that person's benefit.'

[24] [1918–19] All ER Rep 308. Note that the extract set forth here from [1918–19] All ER Rep 308 is significantly different—in form but not in outcome—and longer than the judgment provided in [1919] 1 Ch 290. The All ER Rep version is used as it is more comprehensive and coherent, although it should be noted that the Chancery report was the report referred to in the *Sidebottom v Kershaw* case addressed in this chapter.

■ *Sidebottom v Kershaw, Leese and Company Ltd* [1920] 1 Ch 154 (CA)

The defendant company amended its articles to provide that where any shareholder was in direct competition with the company the directors could give notice to that shareholder instructing him to transfer his shares to specified persons. The amended article specified that such a shareholder would receive 'fair value' for the shares. The article was originally adopted in light of concerns about the competitive activities of one of the company's shareholders, a Mr Bodden. The plaintiff shareholders who brought the action challenging the resolution amending the articles were also competitors of the company but were not in the contemplation of the company at the time the resolution was adopted. The question for the court was whether the amendment was valid.

Lord Sterndale MR

The directors of the defendant company did not introduce this alteration in the article with any view of using it against the plaintiff firm, but they did introduce it with the view of using it if necessary against Mr. Bodden. Now it does not seem to me to matter, as to the validity of this altered article, whether it was introduced with a view of using it against the plaintiff firm or not, except to this extent, that it might be that if it had been introduced specially for the purpose of using it against the plaintiffs' firm some question of bona fides might possibly have arisen, because it might have been argued that it was introduced to do them harm, and not to do the company good. That is the only way in which it seems to me to be relevant. The same seems to me to be the case with regard to the position of Mr. Bodden. If the alteration were proposed with the intention of injuring Mr. Bodden only, or getting Mr. Bodden out of the company only, without any reasonable ground, and not for the benefit of the company, then again there would be, as it seems to me, a lack of bona fides, and in that way and in that way only Mr. Bodden's position is of importance…The question is whether it is invalid. It introduces a new power which did not exist in the original articles at all—a power to buy out on the terms mentioned in the article any shareholder who was engaged in a competing business…

It is admitted that there is a prima facie right to put any thing into an altered article which might have been in the original articles, subject to some limitation, and the limitations have been variously stated; but in my opinion they all come down to the same thing, which is expressed by Lindley M.R. in [*Allen v Gold Reefs*], where he says: 'Speaking generally, I am of opinion that the articles can be so altered,' that was, altered as in that particular case, 'and that, if they are altered bona fide for the benefit of the company, they will be valid and binding as altered'. The limitation is also stated by Astbury J. in *Brown v. British Abrasive Wheel Co.*, to which I shall have to refer later on, and it is stated by Lord Wrenbury in the 9th edition of his book on the Companies Act, at p. 25, that 'Possibly the limitation on the power of altering the articles may turn out to be that the alteration must not be such as to sacrifice the interests of the minority to those of a majority without any reasonable prospect of advantage to the company as a whole.' As I have said, this has been expressed in various other terms in a number of cases. In *Brown v. British Abrasive Wheel Co.*, before Astbury J., it is called, I think, 'the ordinary principles of justice,'[25] and the learned judge [at first instance] says: 'The question therefore is whether the enforcement of the proposed alteration on the minority is within the ordinary principles of justice and whether it is for the benefit of the company as a whole.' The learned judge speaks there as if those two were different things. I respectfully doubt the accuracy of it, because I think it is more accurately expressed by the passage I have cited from the judgment of Lindley M.R.: 'If they are altered bona fide for the benefit of the company,' and that the two things are not different things, but if they are bona fide for the benefit of the company they are consonant with the ordinary principles of justice. Of course that is excluding any question of fraud or malice, which is excluded by

---

[25] Note that in *Brown v British Abrasive Wheel*, Astbury J refers to whether the majority's exercise of power is 'contrary to natural justice' rather than to 'ordinary justice', which is the term used in the Chancery report of the case: [1919] 1 Ch 290.

the words 'bona fide.' The learned Vice-Chancellor in this case adopted that passage from the judgment of Astbury J., and said that the enforcement of the proposed alteration must be within the ordinary principles of justice, and must be for the benefit of the company as a whole, but he also cited the passage from Lord Wrenbury's book, which seems to me to be more accurate, and to agree with the principle stated by Lindley M.R. Those, in my opinion, are the principles we have to apply to this case...

In my opinion, the whole of this case comes down to rather a narrow question of fact, which is this: when the directors of this company introduced this alteration giving power to buy up the shares of members who were in competing businesses did they do it bona fide for the benefit of the company or not? It seems to me quite clear that it may be very much to the benefit of the company to get rid of members who are in competing businesses...I think there can be no doubt that a member of a competing business or an owner of a competing business who is a member of the company has a much better chance of knowing what is going on in the business of the company, and of thereby helping his own competition with it, than if he were a non-member; and looking at it broadly, I cannot have any doubt that in a small private company like this the exclusion of members who are carrying on competing businesses may very well be of great benefit to the company. That seems to me to be precisely a point which ought to be decided by the voices of the business men who understand the business and understand the nature of competition, and whether such a position is or is not for the benefit of the company. I think, looking at the alteration broadly, that it is for the benefit of the company that they should not be obliged to have amongst them as members persons who are competing with them in business, and who may get knowledge from their membership which would enable them to compete better.

That brings me to the last point. It is said that that might be so were it not for the fact that the directors and the secretary have said, 'this is directed against Mr. Bodden,' and therefore it is not done bona fide for the benefit of the company, but it is done to get rid of Mr. Bodden. If it were directed against Mr. Bodden from any malicious motive I should agree with that—the thing would cease to be bona fide at once; but these alterations are not as a rule made without some circumstances having arisen to bring the necessity of the alteration to the minds of the directors. I do not read this as meaning anything more than this: 'It was the position of Mr. Bodden that made us appreciate the detriment that there might be to the company in having members competing with them in their business, and we passed this, and our intention was, if it became necessary, to use it in the case of Mr. Bodden; that is what we had in our minds at the time; but we also had in our minds that Mr. Bodden is not the only person who might compete, and therefore we passed this general article in order to enable us to apply it in any case where it was for the good of the company that it should be applied.' It is a question of fact. I come to the conclusion of fact to which I think the Vice-Chancellor came, that the directors were acting perfectly bona fide; that they were passing the resolution for the benefit of the company; but that no doubt the occasion of their passing it was because they realized in the person of Mr. Bodden that it was a bad thing to have members who were competing with them. [The amendment] was directed against every competing person, and Mr. Bodden was only the occasion of the passing of the alteration of the article; but I do not think that that is any objection to its validity...

For these reasons I think this is a valid article. I think the alteration was within the competence of the company, and therefore this appeal must be allowed with costs here and below.

Lord Sterndale places the law back on the rails laid by *Allen v Gold Reefs*. He reins in the lower court's temptation—in *Brown v British Abrasive Wheel* and the court of first instance in this case—to overstate the courts' jurisdiction to review the exercise of corporate power by the general meeting. The question for the court is not whether the action is compliant with principles of ordinary or natural justice, or whether it is, *in the court's view*, fair; rather the question is whether the action was taken bona fide for the benefit of the company. For Lord Sterndale, following Lord Wrenbury's explanation of this phrase, this means that the general meeting may act in ways that disadvantage some shareholders—in this case by making it possible that they could be forced to sell their shares—provided that in doing so there is some 'reasonable prospect of advantage to the company as a whole'; that is, some sensible explanation of why the action can benefit the company. His Lordship then proceeds to apply this understanding in holding that the amendment to the articles is valid.

In determining that the action to amend the articles in this case is bona fide for the benefit of the company, he notes that 'it may be very much to the benefit of the company to get rid of members who are in competing businesses' as the knowledge they could gain as shareholders of the company could enable them to compete against the company. However, his Lordship is not asking for the defendants to overcome any evidentiary burden to demonstrate that this is a legitimate reason; rather he is asking whether the explanation makes sense from the view of the company's interests. If it does, the courts will not inquire further or place any restrictions on the exercise of the general meeting's decision-making power. Furthermore, consistent with Lindley LJ's position outlined earlier, provided that this reason has general application to all shareholders the fact that the action was taken to address one shareholder—whose activities led to the identification of the problem—will *not* render the action *not* bona fide for the benefit of the company.

In *Dafen Tinplate Company Limited v Llanelly Steel Company*[26] the company amended the articles to provide for the forceable sale at fair value of shares where the general meeting directed such a sale. However, the amendment excluded one shareholder from the application of the amendment. The reason given for the exemption was that the exempted shareholder was not a customer of the company's products as were the other shareholders. The court invalidated the amendment holding that:

> While on the authorities as they stand at present it is possible to alter the articles in such a way as to confer this power, if it can be shown that the power is for the benefit of the company as a whole, I am of opinion that such a power cannot be supported if it is not established that the power is bona fide or genuinely for the company's benefit...
>
> The majority cannot alter the articles in such a way as to place one or more of the minority in a position of inferiority, as for instance, by attributing to his or their shares a smaller proportional share of the available profits than that which the others receive, nor can it in my view confer on one or more of its own number benefits or privileges in which other shareholders of the same class do not participate. It may be that the exclusion of some particular shareholder from the operation of an expropriation clause can in some cases be justified by showing that the exclusion is for the benefit of the company as a whole. On that point I do not express any opinion, but assuming this to be so, I am not able to find any adequate reason in this case for saying that the exemption of [one shareholder] from the operation of the new article is or was for the benefit of the company.

This holding is best viewed as consistent with the Court of Appeal's judgment in *Sidebottom v Kershaw*: for the exercise of corporate power by the general meeting to be bona fide in the company's interests, the action must be supported by a reason that explains why the action benefits the company: a rational account of why the action benefits the company. Explicitly discriminating between shareholders in the articles may *in theory*, the court observes, benefit from such a reason but, as we see in *Dafen Tinplate*, such a reason is likely to be hard to find. *Dafen Tinplate* has, however, been interpreted as imposing a much more demanding standard on the review of general meeting decisions, namely, satisfying the court that the exercise of power by the general meeting *does in fact* benefit the company. This is perhaps suggested by the court's choice of words: requiring that it be '*established*' that the exercise of general meeting power does

[26] [1920] 2 Ch 124.

'genuinely' benefit the company. To the extent that this is the holding in *Dafen Tinplate* it is incorrect, as the Court of Appeal in the following case makes very clear.

■ *Shuttleworth v Cox Bros Ltd* [1926] All ER Rep 498

Three partners of a business transferred the business into a private limited company. The articles of the company provided that the three partners be appointed directors of the company for life unless they were unable to act as a director for reasons of ill health. At the time of this case the strong mandatory removal right we see set out in section 169 of the Companies Act 2006 was not in place. This removal right was first introduced in the Companies Act 1948. Following some apparent irregularities the plaintiff director and shareholder was removed as a manager. Some time later the company in general meeting amended the articles to provide that a director could be removed if a majority of the other directors gave notice to remove that director. Several months later the plaintiff was removed as director. The plaintiff brought an action challenging the amendment to the articles of association.

> *Banks LJ*
>
> The plaintiff's complaint in his statement of claim was that the amendment of the article was a breach of the contract to be implied from the articles of association, and 'that the said proposed article is not bona fide for the benefit of the company as a whole.' He was, therefore, challenging the validity of the resolution.
>
> The first thing one has to decide is this, in reference to the decision of Lindley, MR: is he there dealing with two quite separate things, first, bona fides—that is to say, the state of mind of the persons whose act is complained of—and, secondly, apart altogether from their state of mind, the question whether, in the opinion of the court, what the shareholders have done is for the benefit of the company. I think that that view of the test has been negatived in this court in *Sidebottom v Kershaw, Leese & Co, Ltd*. I think that there all the members of the court, Lord Sterndale, Mr, Warrington, LJ, And Eve, J, negatived that suggestion as to the meaning of the words used by Lindley, MR. One has, therefore, to deal with the test formulated by Lindley, MR, in this way. [The question is whether] these shareholders acted bona fide in the interests of the company as a whole? You may consider the question of bona fides from the point of view of whether they were actuated by an improper motive, or malice and so forth; and you may come to a conclusion which governs the whole case upon the question of their good faith or want of good faith. But assuming good faith in the sense of no wrong motive, what is to be the test that the court, sitting, as it were, as a Court of Appeal from the action of the shareholders, is to apply in reference to that part of the test which deals with the action being, in the opinion of the shareholders, for the benefit of the company? It may be that the action is so outrageous that it throws a light upon the bona fides of the persons who were responsible for it, but, short of being outrageous, it seems to me that it may be so unreasonable that no reasonable men could arrive at such a conclusion, and the court is entitled, I think, to apply the same test to the action of the shareholders as it does to a verdict of a jury, and say that the court will not allow a decision of shareholders to stand which is so unreasonable that no reasonable people could possibly arrive at that conclusion. The case may be still stronger, and one may be able to apply another common law test, and that is, whether or not, upon the facts, the action of the shareholders is capable of being treated as for the benefit of the company. I think these are both tests which the court may properly apply to the action of the shareholders, and I think that *Sidebottom v Kershaw, Leese & Co Ltd* indicates that that is the line which the court ought to take. I respectfully disagree with the view which seems to me to be the view of Peterson, J, in *Dafen Tinplate Co, Ltd v Llanelly Steel Co (1907) Ltd* that it is for the court to treat the matter as though they were the sole judges in the matter, apart altogether from the action of the shareholders which the court is called upon to deal with.

In the present case it seems to me, applying the test which I have endeavoured to indicate, that it is quite impossible to say that, given good faith, which I think is abundantly proved here, the action of these gentlemen could be said to be either incapable of being for the benefit of the company or so unreasonable that no reasonable men could consider it was for the benefit of the company, and it is quite insufficient to say that it is action which works extremely hardly upon the minority, the plaintiff, or that it is action which was specially directed against him, because the more outrageous the conduct of a plaintiff the more certain it is that the action of the share-holders, acting entirely bona fide and for the benefit of the company, will be directed against that person, and directed against that person because of his outrageous conduct and because it is necessary to protect the company against that conduct. In these circumstances, I think that this appeal fails, and that the plaintiff has failed to show either want of good faith or that the action of these gentlemen was not for the benefit of the company.

Scrutton LJ

But if I understand the argument which was put forward by counsel for the plaintiff, based upon an expression of Peterson, J's, in *Dafen Tinplate Co, Ltd v Llanelly Steel Co* it was this. It does not matter whether the directors thought that this alteration was for the benefit of the company; the question is whether the court thinks it was for the benefit of the company…and the court, on the materials before it, ought to think that it was not genuinely for the benefit of the company, and, therefore, reject both the honest opinion of the [shareholders]…and say that the alteration was invalid. To adopt any view of that sort would be to make the court manager of the affairs of innumerable companies instead of the directors to whom the shareholders have entrusted that right of management. I think, with respect to Peterson J, and counsel for the plaintiff, that that view is based on a misunderstanding of the expression used by Lindley, MR, in *Allen v Gold Reefs of West Africa, Ltd*…

The material language there is 'exercised…bona fide for the benefit of the company.' I do not read that as two separate ingredients: (i) You must find it to be bona fide, and (ii) whether bona fide or not, you must find that it is in fact in your, the court's, opinion for the benefit of the company. I read it as being that the [shareholders] must act honestly having regard to, and endeavouring to effect, the benefit of the company as a whole. [We must distinguish between] the acts of people who, acting honestly, consider the thing that they ought to consider, namely, the benefit of the company as a whole, and endeavour to decide what will be for the benefit of the company as a whole, with the acts of those who approach the matter, not from that point of view, but from the point of view of considering what will be for the benefit of the majority of the company or themselves as distinguished from the people against whom they are legislating. From that point of view, provided there are grounds on which reasonable people could come to a decision, considering the matters I have indicated only, it does not seem to me to matter at all whether the court would not have come to the same conclusion. It is not the court which manages the affairs of the company; it is the shareholders through the directors whom they appoint; and so long as the shareholders act honestly and endeavour to consider only the matters they should legitimately consider, namely, the interests of the company as a whole and such action as will promote those interests, it seems to me quite immaterial that the court would come to a different conclusion. The absence of any reasonable ground for a decision that a certain action is conducive to the benefit of the company may be, first of all, a ground for finding lack of good faith, because it may be said that there were no grounds on which honest people could have come to this decision and you may infer bad faith; but, secondly, given honesty, the fact that the company has come to a decision for which there are no reasonable grounds may show that they have not considered the matters that they ought to have considered. On both those grounds you may set a decision aside, but, in my view, if they act honestly, and if the decision is such that honest and reasonable people might come to, the fact that the court would have come to a different decision is no ground whatever for the court interfering.

The Court of Appeal in *Shuttleworth* makes it very clear that the bona fide standard does not require that the court determine whether or not the general meeting's decision *does in fact* benefit the company as a whole, rather, *per* Banks LJ, it requires *either* that the decision is *capable* of being for the company's benefit—that a rational reason is available to explain why it benefits the company—*or* that the decision is not so 'unreasonable that no reasonable people could possibly arrive at that conclusion'. These two approaches are treated effectively as substitutes.

Scrutton LJ's judgment is also worthy of closer scrutiny. Note his focus on the honesty of the shareholders—did such shareholders consider the interests of the company and vote in what they honestly considered to be for the company's benefit. This will remind readers of the directors' common law subjective duty to act in good faith in the interests of the company and the statutory subjective duty to promote the success of the company. But note further, that Scrutton LJ tests acting honestly for the benefit of the company by reference to available reasons for the decision—what he refers to as reasonable grounds for the decision, the absence of which indicates either bad faith or the failure to consider what would benefit the company. In the subsequent Court of Appeal case of *Greenhalgh v Arderne Cinemas*,[27] the court similarly expresses the bona fide standard in subjective shareholder terms. In this case the articles were amended to permit sales of shares to third parties where such sales had previously been subject to restrictions. Evershed MR held that:

> Certain principles, I think, can be safely stated as emerging from [the] authorities. In the first place, I think it is now plain that 'bona fide for the benefit of the company as a whole' means not two things but one thing. It means that the shareholder must proceed upon what, in his honest opinion, is for the benefit of the company as a whole.

More recent cases typically refer to this *Greenhalgh* holding as a statement of what acting bona fide for the benefit of the company means. To connect this statement of the standard to the earlier authority we should understand this standard in the same way as it was understood by Scrutton LJ: as requiring 'reasonable grounds' *capable* of explaining why the decision is in the company's interests; an account of why the decision involves 'a reasonable prospect of advantage to the company as a whole'. As with the subjective duty for directors to promote the success of the company, the difficulty in determining what any person 'honestly believes' typically requires recourse to whether such a belief is capable of being construed as benefiting the company.[28]

Note, however, that the articulation of the standard in subjective terms does represent a subtle change in the nature of the standard to act bona fide for the benefit of the company as a whole. As articulated in *Allen v Gold Reefs* it was the power to change the articles that had to be exercised by the general meeting bona fide for the benefit of the company as a whole. The requirement was imposed on the body exercising the corporate power, namely the general meeting. It was not an obligation imposed on each shareholder individually when exercising his vote. By contrast, in *Shuttleworth* and *Greenhalgh* the obligation is applied to the shareholder exercising their vote. Importantly, however, the nature of the court's review is unaltered.[29]

---

[27] [1951] Ch 286.

[28] Consider the similarity of this approach to the approach taken in *Regentcrest v Cohen* [2001] 2 BCLC 80 to determining whether a director had acted bona fide in the best interests of the company. See further Chapter 10.

[29] This shift in 'who' owes the duty does have substantive consequences. See *re Holders Investment Trust Ltd* [1971] 2 All ER 289 where the decision of a class vote was invalidated as the majority class shareholder did not consider the interests of the class when exercising the vote—the application of this case to a non-class vote setting is unclear. The shift in the later decisions towards a subjective shareholder standard enabled this judgment in *Holders Investment Trust*. Previously the courts had

The level of court review resulting from the *bona fide for the benefit of the company as a whole* standard is a relatively low one. In most instances a good reason explaining a general meeting decision will be available to comply with the standard. It will, however, be difficult in practice to identify a coherent, rational reason that explains explicit discrimination between shareholders in the amendment to the articles. Where an amendment to the articles provides for explicit discrimination between shareholders it is likely to be invalidated. This view is supported by the Court of Appeal in *Greenhalgh v Arderne Cinemas*. Evershed MR held as follows in this regard:

> I think that the [obligation to act bona fide in the company's interests can] in practice, be more accurately and precisely stated by looking at the converse and by saying that a special resolution of this kind would be liable to be impeached if the effect of it were to discriminate between the majority shareholders and the minority shareholders, so as to give to the former an advantage of which the latter were deprived. When the cases are examined in which the resolution has been successfully attacked, it is on that ground.

To be clear, the discrimination that is likely to result in the invalidation of general meeting action is explicit, direct discrimination. This is not to be mistaken for action that may detrimentally affect a particular shareholder or shareholder group. Clearly, in *Allen v Gold Reefs*, *Sidebottom v Kershaw* and *Shuttleworth* some shareholders felt that their interests had been detrimentally affected. This distinction is brought into sharper relief by the recent Privy Council case of *Citco Banking Corporation NV v Pusser's Ltd*[30] where the general meeting of Pusser's Ltd (a British Virgin Island's company) resolved to issue a new class of Class B shares carrying 50 votes a share, where the existing Class A shares carried one vote a share, and to convert some of the Class A shares held by the largest shareholder in the company—who had control over 28% of the shares—into Class B shares. This shareholder was also the executive chairman of the company. These actions gave the chairman/shareholder clear control over the company. The reason given for the action taken was that potential equity investors in the company were only willing to invest if this shareholder had control over the company. In this case, therefore, the general meeting took action to create a new class of shares and to transfer some of these shares to the largest shareholder in the company. The action taken by the general meeting clearly benefited the controlling shareholder. However, in the Privy Council's view the reason given for the action was sufficient to render it bona fide in the company's interests. Lord Hoffmann, having considered the case extracted earlier, observed:

> These were cases in which the amendment operated to the particular disadvantage of a minority of shareholders: Mr Zuccani's estate in *Allen's* case and the director whose removal was proposed in *Shuttleworth's* case. But the same principle must apply when an amendment which the shareholders bona fide consider to be for the benefit of the company as a whole also operates to the particular advantage of some shareholders.
>
> The [British Virgin Islands] Court of Appeal, reversing the [judgment of the lower court held] that [the first instance judge] should...have applied the test laid down in *Shuttleworth's* case, namely, whether reasonable shareholders could have considered that the amendment was for the benefit of the company.[31] The Court of Appeal considered that it would have been reasonable for

just asked whether the decision of the *general meeting* was capable of being construed as being in the company's interests. If it was, the actual thought process of the shareholders was not relevant.

[30] [2007] UKPC 13. See also, *Rights & Issues Investment Trust Ltd v Stylo Shoes Ltd* [1965] Ch 250.

[31] With respect, in this author's view this is not the correct, or is at least a potentially misleading, way of presenting the test. It is a very fine distinction but the standard set out in the authorities is not an objective reasonable shareholder standard, it is lower than this—even though Scrutton LJ refers to reasonable grounds—it is whether a reason is available that makes sense of the decision; that rationally

> shareholders to have accepted in good faith the arguments put forward by Mr Tobias as to why the amendment would be in the interests of the company…It was not necessary for [chairman/shareholder] and the company to prove to the judge that the arguments were justified by the facts. Their Lordships consider that this reasoning is correct.

This statement is wholly consistent with the way this chapter has interpreted the meaning of acting bona fide for the benefit of the company as a whole. In this regard, note that the reasons given for the action taken by the general meeting did not have to be 'justified by the facts'.

2 Regulation of controlling shareholder activities where they do not exercise corporate power

In section II.1 of this chapter we considered the common law constraints on the exercise of power by the general meeting and, therefore, the restraints on the exercise by controlling shareholders of their voting power. However, controlling shareholders can act in ways that influence corporate action to their benefit without explicitly exercising corporate power. A clear example of such activity would involve encouraging the board to enter into non-arm's-length related-party transactions with the controlling shareholder. Accordingly, our question of relevance in this section II.2 is: in what ways, if any, has the common law imposed upon controlling shareholders obligations to act in ways that do not damage the company's interest *where* the actions in question do not involve any explicit exercise of voting power by the controlling shareholder but only the exercise of pressure and influence over the company?

If you cast your mind back to our discussion of directors' duties you will remember that at common law there were two core sub-duties of the duty of loyalty: to act bona fide in the best interests of the company and the obligation not to place a director's personal interests in a position where they possibly conflict with the company's interests. In light of our discussion it might, therefore, seem logical that controlling shareholders would also be subject to an obligation not to allow personal interests to conflict with corporate interests. Indeed, many of you will have been impressed by the substantive similarity of the common law directors' duty to act in good faith in the best interests of the company and the general meeting *bona fide duty*—we see this similarity in its articulation in *Greenhalgh* as a subjective standard but also in the approach by the courts in both contexts which is to ask: are there reasons that plausibly explain the action in question in terms of the company's interests?

English law, it is said, *does not* impose on controlling shareholders fiduciary duties of loyalty to the company in relation to voting or otherwise, although the authorities in this regard are rather sparse and although the duty in the interests of the company as a whole bears a close affinity to one of the directors' fiduciary duties.[32] This view that the controlling shareholder is not a fiduciary makes sense given the way English law understands how one becomes a fiduciary. In *Bristol & West Building Society v Mothew*[33] Millet LJ set out this understanding as follows:

> A fiduciary is someone who has undertaken to act for or on behalf of another in a particular matter in circumstances which give rise to a relationship of trust and confidence. The distinguishing

explains the decision. If courts follow the reasonable shareholder instruction it is likely that some courts will be more aggressive than the authorities require.

[32] *Estmanco (Kilner House) Ltd v Greater London Council* [1982] 1 All ER 437; *Phillips v Manufacturers' Securities Ltd* (1917) 86 LJ Ch 305 (CA) holding that the shareholder is not subject to a fiduciary duty in relation to the exercise of his vote.

[33] [1997] 2 WLR 436.

> obligation of a fiduciary is the obligation of loyalty. The principal is entitled to the single-minded loyalty of his fiduciary. This core liability has several facets. A fiduciary must act in good faith; he must not make a profit out of his trust; he must not place himself in a position where his duty and his interest may conflict; he may not act for his own benefit or the benefit of a third person without the informed consent of his principal.

This understanding of how one becomes a fiduciary involves the acceptance by the person in question that he has accepted a charge to act on behalf of another. Clearly a controlling shareholder could become a fiduciary if he accepted such a charge, but he is not in English law a fiduciary just because he is a controlling or majority shareholder and, therefore, does not *by reason of being* a controlling shareholder owe a duty of loyalty that could regulate his actions that detrimentally affect the company.

Some scope to apply duties to controlling shareholders arises from the concept of the 'shadow director'. The Companies Act 2006 provides that directors' duties are owed by directors to the company; however, it also holds out the possibility that shadow directors *may* owe duties to the company 'where, and to the extent that, the common law and equitable principles so apply'. The term 'shadow director' is defined in section 250 of the 2006 Act as 'a person in accordance with whose directions or instructions the directors of the company are accustomed to act'. Courts have generally to date viewed this as a very high hurdle. A controlling shareholder would qualify as a shadow director only where there is a pattern of behaviour in which the directors do 'not exercise any discretion or judgment of [their] own' but rather follow the controlling shareholder's instruction.[34] Many very active controlling shareholders would not qualify as shadow directors pursuant to this understanding. Furthermore, following the judgment of Lewinson J in *Ultraframe v Fielding*[35] shadow directors will only be subject to any duties[36] if the court finds that the controlling shareholder 'has undertaken to act for or on behalf of another in a particular matter in circumstances which give rise to a relation of trust and confidence'; that is, only where he is in a fiduciary relationship with the company.

English law in the field of shadow directors and the duties to which they are subject is undeveloped. Clearly there is scope for developments in this area of the law to apply constraints on controlling shareholder activity. If, for example, a controlling shareholder is found to be a shadow director subject to section 175 of the 2006 Act, such a controlling shareholder/shadow director would then be subject to the Act's constraints on taking corporate opportunities. However, most importantly, we should note that the role of shadow directors and duties is designed to prevent a person from being able to *effectively* act as a director whilst avoiding the obligations imposed on directors. It is designed to ensure the integrity and effectiveness of the role of duties in regulating the activities of the individuals responsible for managing and directing the company. The shadow director innovation is not, therefore, designed to regulate the activities of majority shareholders as shareholders, only their actions as *effective* directors.

English law's understanding of when a person is a fiduciary contrasts with other common law, but also civil law jurisdictions where controlling shareholders are, in certain circumstances, treated as fiduciaries subject to a duty of loyalty.[37] Most US states' corporate law views controlling shareholders as fiduciaries.[38] A leading and well-known Californian case is instructive in this regard:

---

[34] *Hydrodam (Corby) Ltd* [1994] 2 BCLC 180 *per* Millet J. See further Chapter 9.

[35] For a detailed discussion of *Ultraframe* see Chapter 9.

[36] Section 170(5) refers to the common law to determine whether duties are applicable to directors.

[37] Generally on *Treuhandspflicten* in Germany and Austria see S. Kalss and F. Linder, *Minderheitsrechte- und Einzelrechte von Aktionären* (Manz, 2006).

[38] Delaware courts have on many occasions made it clear that controlling shareholders are subject to fiduciary duties; see, for example, *Kahn v Lynch Communication Systems, Inc,* 638 A2d 1110 (1994); *Thorpe v Cerbco Inc* 676 A2d 436 (1995).

■ *Jones v HF Ahmanson & Company* 1 Cal 3d 93 (1969)

Traynor J

Defendants take the position that as shareholders they owe no fiduciary obligation to other shareholders, absent reliance on inside information, use of corporate assets, or fraud. This view has long been repudiated in California. The Courts of Appeal have often recognized that majority shareholders, either singly or acting in concert to accomplish a joint purpose, have a fiduciary responsibility to the minority and to the corporation to use their ability to control the corporation in a fair, just, and equitable manner. Majority shareholders may not use their power to control corporate activities to benefit themselves alone or in a manner detrimental to the minority. Any use to which they put the corporation or their power to control the corporation must benefit all shareholders proportionately and must not conflict with the proper conduct of the corporation's business.

The extensive reach of the duty of controlling shareholders and directors to the corporation and its other shareholders was described by the Court of Appeal in *Remillard Brick Co. v. Remillard-Dandini Co.*,[39] where, quoting from the opinion of the United States Supreme Court in *Pepper v. Litton*,[40] the court held: ' "A director is a fiduciary... So is a dominant or controlling stockholder or group of stockholders... Their powers are powers of trust... Their dealings with the corporation are subjected to rigorous scrutiny and where any of their contracts or engagements with the corporation is challenged the burden is on the director or stockholder not only to prove the good faith of the transaction but also to show its inherent fairness from the viewpoint of the corporation and those interested therein... The essence of the test is whether or not under all the circumstances the transaction carries the earmarks of an arm's length bargain. If it does not, equity will set it aside." Referring directly to the duties of a director the court stated...: "He who is in such a fiduciary position cannot serve himself first and his *cestuis* second. He cannot manipulate the affairs of his corporation to their detriment and in disregard of the standards of common decency and honesty. He cannot by the intervention of a corporate entity violate the ancient precept against serving two masters. He cannot by the use of the corporate device avail himself of privileges normally permitted outsiders in a race of creditors. He cannot utilize his inside information and his strategic position for his own preferment. He cannot violate rules of fair play by doing indirectly through the corporation what he could not do directly. He cannot use his power for his personal advantage and to the detriment of the stockholders and creditors no matter how absolute in terms that power may be and no matter how meticulous he is to satisfy technical requirements. For that power is at all times subject to the equitable limitation that it may not be exercised for the aggrandizement, preference, or advantage of the fiduciary to the exclusion or detriment of the *cestuis*. Where there is a violation of these principles, equity will undo the wrong or intervene to prevent its consummation." This is the law of California.' In *Remillard* the Court of Appeal clearly indicated that the fiduciary obligations of directors and shareholders are neither limited to specific statutory duties and avoidance of fraudulent practices.

For the Californian Court of Appeal the fiduciary obligations arise—for both directors and controlling shareholders—from the power that they wield. That power, which is subject to the fiduciary duty of loyalty, is not limited to the formal exercise of voting in general meeting but also to the effects of the power dynamics in a company that, for example, encourage the board to enter into non-market related-party transactions or enable an opportunity to be exploited by the controller that it would have been in the company's interest to exploit.

Whilst the UK has not taken this path of imposing duties of loyalty on controlling shareholders, in the context of the exercise of voting power in the general meeting, the

---

[39] 109 Cal App 2d 405.   [40] 308 US 295.

failure to label controlling shareholders 'fiduciaries' is really of only semantic relevance. Both directors and controlling shareholders are in effect subject to a light-of-touch restraint that any decision that they make be *explainable* as being in the corporate interest. Outside of the voting context, do we also see a similar type of regulation to which controlling shareholders are subject, even if we do not describe that regulation in terms of fiduciary duties? The answer to this question is 'not really but possibly'!

There is a limited amount of early and undeveloped authority which suggests that if a controlling shareholder exercises his influence to transfer value to the controlling shareholder to the detriment of the minority shareholders, the minority shareholder may bring suit and the courts have the jurisdiction to intervene to hold the controlling shareholders to account.[41] This authority is found in the 1873 Court of Appeal case of *Menier v Hooper's Telegraph Works*. This approach has not been further developed by the courts and is unlikely to be in the future because the statutory remedies we address in the next section mean that in large part it is not necessary. However, it is interesting for our purposes as it reveals the reservoir of equitable principles that can be brought to bear by courts in addressing controlling shareholder agency problems.

■ Menier v Hooper's Telegraph Company (1874) LR 9 Ch App 350

Menier and the Hooper's Telegraph Company (Hooper's) were shareholders in the European and South American Telegraph Company (EST), a company that had been set up to obtain the concession to put in place telecommunications cables between Brazil and Portugal and to lay those cables. Hooper's owned 3,000 shares and Menier 2,000 shares of a total of 5,325 allotted shares. The intention was for Hooper's to manufacture the cable and to sell it to EST.

Apparently, EST did not obtain the concession to lay the cable but this was obtained by a former director of the company, Baron de Maua. EST brought suit against the Baron and although unsuccessful at first instance there was the possibility of appeal. It seems that EST's only valuable asset was the potential damages from the litigation.

Hooper's decided not to pursue the litigation as did the board of directors of EST which Hooper's had nominated and appointed. However, at the same time, Hooper's had struck an agreement with the Baron to manufacture the cable for the Portugal–Brazil concession. That is, it effectively obtained a side-payment for using its influence with EST to stop the litigation. Note, however, it appears that no general meeting decision was taken not to appeal: 'Hooper's Company procured the abandonment of the suit against the Baron de Maua and the winding-up of the European Company through the influence which they had as holders of 3000 shares in the European Company and through the influence of the directors nominated by them.'

The minority shareholder, Menier, brought suit claiming that in relation to the profits made by Hooper's through its agreement with the Baron, that Hooper's be treated as holding those profits as trustee on behalf of EST. The court of first instance held in favour of Menier. The Court of Appeal affirmed the first instance judgment.

> **James LJ**
>
> I am of opinion that the order of the Vice-Chancellor in this case is quite right.
>
> The case made by the bill is very shortly this: The Defendants, who have a majority of shares in the company, have made an arrangement by which they have dealt with matters affecting the whole company, the interest in which belongs to the minority as well as to the majority. They have dealt with them in consideration of their obtaining for themselves certain advantages.

---

[41] In addition see the case law on the fiduciary obligations of promoters. Most importantly in this regard see *Erlanger v New Sombrero Phosphate Co* [1874–80] All ER Rep 271.

Hooper's Company have obtained certain advantages by dealing with something which was the property of the whole company. The minority of the shareholders say in effect that the majority has divided the assets of the company, more or less, between themselves, to the exclusion of the minority...

Assuming the case to be as alleged by the bill, then the majority have put something into their pockets at the expense of the minority. If so, it appears to me that the minority have a right to have their share of the benefits ascertained for them in the best way in which the Court can do it, and given to them.

Mellish LJ

I am entirely of the same opinion.

It so happens that *Hooper's Company* are the majority in this company, and a suit by this company was pending which might or might not turn out advantageous to this company. The Plaintiff says that *Hooper's Company* being the majority, have procured that suit to be settled upon terms favourable to themselves, they getting a consideration for settling it in the shape of a profitable bargain for the laying of a cable. I am of opinion that although it may be quite true that the shareholders of a company may vote as they please, and for the purpose of their own interests, yet that the majority of shareholders cannot sell the assets of the company and keep the consideration, but must allow the minority to have their share of any consideration which may come to them.

The principle underlying this judgment is that majority shareholders cannot wield their influence in the company to transfer value to them to the detriment of the minority. Here, through Hooper's power and influence in the company, they stopped the litigation against EST's former director, Baron de Maua, whilst apparently using the threat of continuing with the litigation as a bargaining chip to obtain a beneficial agreement with the Baron. For explanatory purposes, if the **expected value** of the litigation was worth £100 then, given their respective shareholdings, that is worth approximately £60 to Hooper's and £40 to Menier; however, if Hooper's extract a deal from the Baron worth more than £60 it makes sense to use its influence to stop the litigation. The principle underlying the holding in this case clearly has traction in other contexts— for example where influence is deployed to make the company enter into non-market related-party transactions with the controlling shareholder—or where directors ensure that the controlling shareholder receives first option on any opportunities identified by or brought to the directors. This principle looks very similar to a negative duty imposed on controlling shareholders not to exercise their power to influence the company to act in ways that benefit the controlling shareholder to the detriment of the company and, therefore, the minority.[42]

Questions

1. At common law were there any limitations on the ability of directors to exercise their votes as shareholders to ratify their own breach of duty?

2. In your view was it necessary to reform to the common law rule by enacting section 239 of the Companies Act 2006 to prevent any director-shareholders or persons connected to them from voting?

3. What does it mean to say that the general meeting must exercise power bona fide for the benefit of the company as a whole? In what different ways have the courts articulated the meaning of this phrase?

---

[42] Compare this, for example, to the German Stock Corporation Law's imposition of liability on any person who exercises his influence over a member of the management board or the supervisory board and this results in damage to the company or the shareholders (section 117 German Stock Corporation Act).

4. How, if at all, does this obligation differ from the obligation placed on directors by the common law to act in the best interests of the company?

5. Should controlling shareholders be fiduciaries subject to a duty of loyalty to prevent them from influencing the board from acting in ways that are detrimental to the company?

6. Would you impose duties on controlling shareholders similar to those imposed on directors in section 177 (duty to disclose transactions) and section 175 (duty to avoid conflicts of interest)? Would the imposition of these duties arise simply as a result of the controlling shareholders control position or as a result of the influence they exert over the board?

III STATUTORY REGULATION OF CONTROLLING SHAREHOLDER POWER

As we have seen, the common law does not operate to protect expectations minority shareholders may have that the articles will not be changed in a way that is detrimental to their interests unless the shareholder has negotiated for such protection by entrenching particular provisions. Provided that the exercise of power by the general meeting is both compliant with the constitution and is capable of being construed as benefiting the company, the common law places no further restraint on the exercise of that power.

In many small close companies the shareholders will have an understanding amongst themselves that they will all play a role in the management of the company so long as they remain shareholders and so long as they wish to do so. However, as we saw in *Shuttleworth*, in applying the *bona fide for the benefit of the company* standard, the court did not intervene to prevent the majority from: changing the terms of the constitution which had provided for life-long tenure for the claimant as a director; and then removing him as director. From *Shuttleworth* it is clear that the *bona fide* standard does not protect such an agreement or expectation whether set out in the articles[43] or in any other written or informal agreement.[44]

Statutory innovations, and importantly the court's interpretation of those innovations, have softened the common law's hard contractarian edges. Most importantly in this regard was the introduction in the Companies Act 1980 of what is known as the 'unfair prejudice remedy'. The remedy is now set out in section 994 of the Companies Act 2006, but many in practice continue to refer to it by its Companies Act 1985 section number as a '459 petition'. The unfair prejudice remedy and its application to the exercise of corporate power through the general meeting must be understood in the context of two other statutory provisions. The first is the courts' power to provide for the winding up of the company where it is just and equitable to do so. This power is now set forth in section 122(g) of the Insolvency Act 1986. As we shall see below, the courts' approach to the exercise of this power has had a significant influence on the courts' approach to the unfair prejudice remedy. The second, and no longer in force, statutory innovation was introduced by section 210 of the Companies Act 1948 following the recommendation of the Cohen Committee[45] which considered company law reform in

---

[43] Remember that at the time of the *Shuttleworth* case English company law did not provide for a mandatory removal right as is found today in section 168 CA 2006.

[44] Note that there was a suggestion in *Allen v Gold Reefs* that informal agreements may be protected as 'special contracts' although there is no sense of that position in the later case of *Shuttleworth*. Cf *Clemens v Clemens* [1976] 2 All ER 268 suggesting that the exercise of majority power is subject to 'equitable considerations', a phrase taken from *Ebrahimi v Westbourne Galleries Ltd* [1972] 2 All ER 492 which, as we shall see, is used to provide some protection for precisely such informal agreements.

[45] *Report of the Committee on Company Law Amendment* (Cohen Committee) (1945).

the 1940s. This 'oppression remedy' provided for a remedy where the activities of the company amounted to oppression of a 'part of' the company's shareholders. In application, the courts interpreted this provision rather restrictively creating several technical[46] and substantive[47] hurdles to its operation. The Jenkins Committee on Company Law which considered company law reform in 1962 recommended reform of the oppression remedy to address these technical and substantive limitations by, amongst others, recommending that the concept of 'oppression' be replaced by 'unfair prejudice'.

Whilst the unfair prejudice remedy is the most important statutory innovation for protecting minority shareholders in the history of English company law, we start our analysis with the role played by the just and equitable winding-up remedy in placing limits on the exercise by controlling shareholders of corporate power. The reason for this is that the approach taken by the courts to the just and equitable winding-up remedy is an essential building block for understanding the operation of the unfair prejudice remedy.

1 Just and equitable winding-up

The power of the court to order the winding up of a company where it deems it just and equitable to do so has a pedigree dating back to the Joint Stock Companies Winding-Up Act 1848. Subsequent to this Act the provision was placed in the Companies Acts. Today the provision is set out in section 122(g) of the Insolvency Act 1986 and provides as follows:

> A company may be wound-up by the court if the court is of the opinion that it is just and equitable that the company should be wound-up.

There are several situations in which the courts will exercise their just and equitable winding-up jurisdiction, a common example of which is when a company is in deadlock due to disagreement between shareholders each owning 50% of the shares.[48] Our concern here is not to consider the just and equitable jurisdiction generally but to consider the ways in which the just and equitable winding-up remedy limits the exercise of corporate power by a controlling shareholder.

The bases upon which courts will exercise this just and equitable jurisdiction to wind up the company were considered in detail in the leading and influential House of Lords case of *Ebrahimi v Westbourne Galleries Ltd.*

---

[46] See generally, K.W. Wedderburn, 'Oppression of Minorities' (1966) 29 *Modern Law Review* 321; H. Rajek, 'The Oppression of Minority Shareholders' (1972) 35 *Modern Law Review* 156. The remedy was only available to the extent that oppression affected the member qua member and not qua any other corporate role: *Re Bellador Silk Ltd* [1966] 2 WLR 288; the remedy was unavailable if oppression had driven the company into insolvency giving the member no financial interest in the company: *Re Lundie Brother Ltd* [1965] 1 WLR 1051.

[47] It was not wholly clear from the authorities whether the oppression remedy was only available in relation to actions that of themselves were illegal—such as a fraud or a breach of duty. That is, it did not create an independent basis of oppression that went beyond existing wrongs in relation to which shareholders could bring suit. The authorities provide support for this view but also provide some support that oppression may provide some—although limited—stand-alone grounds for action. In this regard, see *Scottish Co-Operative Wholesale Society Ltd v Meyer* [1959] AC 324. The Jenkins Committee on Company Law (Cmnd 1749) thought that the remedy should be available in situations other than where there was an independent basis of illegality and recommended, therefore, that the concept of oppression be replaced with unfair prejudice.

[48] *Re Yenidje Tobacco Co Ltd* [1916] 2 Ch 426. Other examples or a basis upon which to petition for a just and equitable winding up include: lack of probity: *Loch v John Blackwood Ltd* [1924] AC 783; and loss of substratum: *Re Suburban Hotel Co* (1867) 2 Ch App 737.

■ *Ebrahimi v Westbourne Galleries Ltd* [1973] AC 360

The petitioner and the respondent, Mr Nazar, set up a carpet dealership business in 1945. Initially, the business was carried out as a partnership. In 1958 a company, Westbourne Galleries, was formed to take over the business. Initially 500 ordinary shares were issued to both the petitioner and Mr Nazar. Shortly after the formation of the company both the petitioner and Mr Nazar transferred 100 shares to Mr Nazar's son George. This resulted in the petitioner, Mr Nazar, and George owning 40%, 40%, and 20% of the company's issued shares, respectively. All three men were directors of the company, which prospered over the subsequent years. All profits to the company were paid to the directors through directors' remuneration. At no point was a dividend paid. However, in 1969, combining their votes, Mr Nazar and George voted in general meeting to remove the petitioner as a director. The petitioner petitioned the court for a just and equitable winding up of the company. At first instance the petition was granted. The respondents appealed.

The Court of Appeal granted the appeal: Russell LJ

In our judgment, in a case of a quasi-partnership company such as the present, the exercise by a majority in general meeting of the power under the articles or the statute to remove a director from his office, and consequently to exclude him from participation in the management and conduct of the business of the company does not form a ground for holding that it is just and equitable that the company be wound up, unless it be shown that the power was not exercised bona fide in the interests of the company, or that the grounds for exercising the power were such that no reasonable man could think that the removal was in the interest of the company.

Applying those principles to the present case it appears to us clear that the winding up order should, on the facts, not have been made. Quite apart from the question of onus, Nazar deposed in terms that in his opinion the removal of the petitioner from office and consequently from participation in the management of the business was in the interests of the company and its business; George deposed that his own view was that the removal was justified and in the best interests of the company; and they were not challenged on those statements in cross-examination.

The petitioner appealed to the House of Lords.

House of Lords: Lord Wilberforce

My Lords, the petition was brought under s 222(*f*) of the Companies Act 1948 [the predecessor to section 122(g) Insolvency Act 1986], which enables a winding-up order to be made if 'the court is of opinion that it is just and equitable that the company should be wound up'.

[His Lordship considered the authorities addressing the application of the just and equitable winding-up jurisdiction.]

My Lords, in my opinion these authorities represent a sound and rational development of the law which should be endorsed. The foundation of it all lies in the words 'just and equitable' and, if there is any respect in which some of the cases may be open to criticism, it is that the courts may sometimes have been too timorous in giving them full force. The words are a recognition of the fact that a limited company is more than a mere judicial entity, with a personality in law of its own: that there is room in company law for recognition of the fact that behind it, or amongst it, there are individuals, with rights, expectations and obligations inter se which are not necessarily submerged in the company structure. That structure is defined by the Companies Act 1948 and by the articles of association by which shareholders agree to be bound. In most companies and in most contexts, this definition is sufficient and exhaustive, equally so whether the company is large or small. The 'just and equitable' provision does not, as the respondents suggest, entitle one party to disregard the obligation he assumes by entering a company, nor the court to dispense him from it. It does, as equity always does, enable the court to subject the exercise of legal rights to equitable considerations; considerations, that is, of a personal character arising between one individual and another, which may make it unjust, or inequitable, to insist on legal rights, or to exercise them in a particular way.

It would be impossible, and wholly undesirable, to define the circumstances in which these considerations may arise. Certainly the fact that a company is a small one, or a private company, is not enough. There are very many of these where the association is a purely commercial one, of which it can safely be said that the basis of association is adequately and exhaustively laid down in the articles. The superimposition of equitable considerations requires something more, which typically may include one, or probably more, of the following elements: (i) an association formed or continued on the basis of a personal relationship, involving mutual confidence—this element will often be found where a pre-existing partnership has been converted into a limited company; (ii) an agreement, or understanding, that all, or some (for there may be 'sleeping' members), of the shareholders shall participate in the conduct of the business; (iii) restriction on the transfer of the members' interest in the company—so that if confidence is lost, or one member is removed from management, he cannot take out his stake and go elsewhere.

It is these, and analogous, factors which may bring into play the just and equitable clause, and they do so directly, through the force of the words themselves. To refer [to the companies involved in these cases], as so many of the cases do, to 'quasi-partnerships' or 'in substance partnerships' may be convenient but may also be confusing. It may be convenient because it is the law of partnership which has developed the conceptions of probity, good faith and mutual confidence, and the remedies where these are absent, which become relevant once such factors as I have mentioned are found to exist: the words 'just and equitable' sum these up in the law of partnership itself. And in many, but not necessarily all, cases there has been a pre-existing partnership the obligations of which it is reasonable to suppose continue to underlie the new company structure. But the expressions may be confusing if they obscure, or deny, the fact that the parties (possibly former partners) are now co-members in a company, who have accepted, in law, new obligations. A company, however small, however domestic, is a company not a partnership or even a quasi-partnership and it is through the just and equitable clause that obligations, common to partnership relations, may come in.

My Lords, this is an expulsion case, and I must briefly justify the application in such cases of the just and equitable clause. The question is, as always, whether it is equitable to allow one (or two) to make use of his legal rights to the prejudice of his associate(s). The law of companies recognises the right, in many ways, to remove a director from the board. Section 184 of the Companies Act 1948[49] confers this right on the company in general meeting whatever the articles may say…And quite apart from removal powers, there are normally provisions for retirement of directors by rotation so that their re-election can be opposed and defeated by a majority, or even by a casting vote. In all these ways a particular director-member may find himself no longer a director, through removal, or non-re-election: this situation he must normally accept, unless he undertakes the burden of proving fraud or mala fides. The just and equitable provision nevertheless comes to his assistance if he can point to, and prove, some special underlying obligation of his fellow member(s) in good faith, or confidence, that so long as the business continues he shall be entitled to management participation, an obligation so basic that if broken, the conclusion must be that the association must be dissolved. And the principles on which he may do so are those worked out by the courts in partnership cases where there has been exclusion from management (see *Const v Harris* (1824) Tur. & Rus. 496, 525) even where under the partnership agreement there is a power of expulsion (see *Blisset v Daniel* (1853) 10 Hare 493 and Lindley on Partnership).

I come to the facts of this case. It is apparent enough that a potential basis for a winding-up order under the just and equitable clause existed. The appellant after a long association in partnership, during which he had an equal share in the management, joined in the formation of the company. The inference must be indisputable that he, and Mr Nazar, did so on the basis that

---

[49] The predecessor provision to section 168 CA 2006.

the character of the association would, as a matter of personal relation and good faith, remain the same. He was removed from his directorship under a power valid in law. Did he establish a case which, if he had remained in a partnership with a term providing for expulsion, would have justified an order for dissolution? This was the essential question for the judge. Plowman J—the first instance judge in this case—dealt with the issue in a brief paragraph in which he said ([1970] 3 All ER at 384):

> '…while no doubt the petitioner was lawfully removed, in the sense that he ceased in law to be a director, it does not follow that in removing him the respondents did not do him a wrong. In my judgment, they did do him a wrong, in the sense that it was an abuse of power and a breach of good faith which partners owe to each other to exclude one of them from all participation in the business on which they have embarked on the basis that all should participate in its management. The main justification put forward for removing him was that he was perpetually complaining, but the faults were not all on one side and, in my judgment, this is no sufficient justification. For these reasons, in my judgment, the petitioner therefore has made out a case for a winding-up order.'

Reading this in the context of the judgment as a whole, which had dealt with the specific complaints of one side against the other, I take it as a finding that the respondents were not entitled, in justice and equity, to make use of their legal powers of expulsion and that…the only just and equitable course was to dissolve the association. To my mind, two factors strongly support this. First, Mr Nazar made it perfectly clear that he did not regard the appellant as a partner; but did regard him as an employee. But there was no possible doubt as to the appellant's status throughout, so that Mr Nazar's refusal to recognise it amounted, in effect, to a repudiation of the relationship. Secondly, the appellant, through ceasing to be a director, lost his right to share in the profits through directors' remuneration, retaining only the chance of receiving dividends as a minority shareholder. True that an assurance was given in evidence that the previous practice (of not paying dividends) would not be continued, but the fact remains that the appellant was henceforth at the mercy of the Messrs Nazar as to what he should receive out of the profits and when. He was, moreover, unable to dispose of his interest without the consent of the Nazars. All these matters lead only to the conclusion that the right course was to dissolve the association by winding-up.

I must deal with one final point which was much relied on by the Court of Appeal. It was said that the removal was, according to the evidence of Mr Nazar, bona fide in the interests of the company, that the appellant had not shown the contrary, that he ought to do so or to demonstrate that no reasonable man could think that his removal was in the company's interest. This formula, 'bona fide in the interests of the company' is one that is relevant in certain contexts of company law and I do not doubt that in many cases decisions have to be left to majorities or directors to take which the courts must assume had this basis. It may, on the other hand, become little more than an alibi for a refusal to consider the merits of the case, and in a situation such as this it seems to have little meaning other than 'in the interests of the majority'. Mr Nazar may well have persuaded himself, quite genuinely, that the company would be better off without the appellant but if the appellant disputed this, or thought the same with reference to Mr Nazar, what prevails is simply the majority view. To confine the application of the just and equitable clause to proved cases of mala fides would be to negative the generality of the words. It is because I do not accept this that I feel myself obliged to differ from the Court of Appeal.

I would allow the appeal.

The result of the holding in *Ebrahimi* is that, *where companies are deemed to be quasi-partnerships*, the ability of shareholders to exercise power at the general meeting is not—as the Court of Appeal in this case held—limited to compliance with the company's articles, the Companies Act and the requirement that the power be exercised 'bona fide for the benefit of the company as a whole'. It is also limited by 'equitable considerations' which impose constraints on the exercise of general meeting power to ensure compliance with any informal obligations and understandings between the shareholders/quasi-partners about how the business will be run and managed.

Importantly, these constraints upon the exercise of the general meeting's formally available powers apply *only* to the types of company that qualify as 'quasi-partnerships' *and* only where an informal understanding exists between the shareholder/quasi-partners in such companies. Simply because a company is a quasi-partnership does not automatically give a shareholder a right to petition for a just and equitable winding-up if he is removed from management by his fellow shareholders. To have such a right there must have been an informal understanding between the shareholders that the petitioner would not be removed from management.[50]

Through the just and equitable jurisdiction, these equitable considerations do not protect these informal understandings by explicitly prohibiting the exercise of corporate power to alter these understandings; rather they give the affected shareholder the right to petition to end the life of the company—to wind-up the company—if such informal understandings are breached. Note, however, that the court is not offering a complete guarantee that these informal understandings will be protected through the Damoclean sword of a just and equitable winding up. The first instance court's judgment, quoted favourably by Lord Wilberforce, contemplates behaviour that could justify ending the petitioner's role in the company. However, in this case the claims made by the respondents about the petitioner's conduct were not 'sufficient' to allow them to terminate his management role.[51]

The term *quasi-partnership* is *not* a formal legal category of company as is a 'private limited company' or a 'public limited company'. The term 'quasi-partnership' is not a term used anywhere in the Companies Act 2006. Rather it is a legal concept that describes specific types of relationships in a company. It is a concept that looks through the corporate veil and looks at the nature of the roles played by the owners in the company. It does not pierce or disregard the veil, as the legal form of the company is not disregarded. However, the quasi-partnership concept does look beyond the legal reality created by incorporation and ask whether *in fact* the shareholders behave and understand their relationship with each other in partnership-like terms. Accordingly, as Lord Wilberforce emphasizes, a company is not a quasi-partnership simply because it is a small private company. Lord Wilberforce provides three criteria of relevance that assist in determining whether a company is a *quasi-partnership*. Not all of these factors need to be present. One may be enough, although Lord Wilberforce suggests, somewhat unclearly, that 'probably more' than one is required. The criteria are: first whether the company is an association based on personal relationships and mutual confidence amongst those persons; second, whether there is an understanding or agreement that some of the shareholders will participate in the management of the company; and, third, whether the articles contain restrictions on the transfer of shares—such restrictions will typically involve a requirement to obtain the consent of the other shareholders before selling to a third party or a requirement to offer the shares to existing shareholders before being allowed to sell them to a third party.

---

[50] *Tay Bok Choon v Tahansan Sdn Bhd* [1987] BCLC 472 (Privy Council), per Lord Templeman: 'In this company there were only four shareholders, they held an equal number of shares, they were all directors and no one shareholder could transfer his shares without the consent of at least two of the others. These facts may go some way to establish that the relationship between the shareholders shared some of the attributes of a partnership. But in the absence of any further indications or oral assurances the petitioner would not discharge the burden of proving that the other shareholders were not entitled to use their voting powers in the company to oust the petitioner without due cause and in the interests of the company and were under an obligation to continue to appoint the petitioner as a director of the company.'

[51] See *Tay Bok Choon v Tahansan Sdn Bhd* [1987] BCLC 472 where the Privy Council confirmed the winding-up remedy following breach of the informal management participation understanding but noted that removal from management/the board may have been possible for a 'good reason'.

Clearly, as in *Ebrahimi*, the situation is somewhat easier for the courts if a business starts out as a partnership and then transfers the business into a private limited company with no change in the management roles of the partner-shareholders in the business. The situation is more difficult where the business itself commences as a company, and more difficult still where the company starts life with one manager-shareholder and subsequently issues shares to one or more of the company's managers or employees. The question whether such companies can be *quasi-partnerships* was considered in the following case.

■ *Strahan v Wilcox* [2006] EWCA Civ 13

In this case a company was formed by the respondent, Mr Wilcox, who at a later date appointed Mr Strahan as managing director of the company. Mr Strahan subsequently purchased a 5% stake in the company and had an option to purchase further shares in the company. At a later date Mr Strahan was dismissed from the company. He petitioned the court for a remedy under section 459 of the Companies Act 1985 (now section 994 of the Companies Act 2006), which, as we shall see, in some circumstances also requires the determination of whether a company is a 'quasi-partnership'. The court held that the company was a quasi-partnership. The focus here is to consider how the court approached the question of whether the company was a 'quasi-partnership'.

> *Arden LJ*
>
> This appeal concerns a situation that often arises in a closely-held company. The sole or principal shareholder of the company brings in a person ('the new participant') to help him run the company. The new participant is given an executive role. The parties get on well, and the principal shareholder gives him or sells him an equity stake. Then, after some time, the parties fall out and the principal shareholder causes the dismissal of the new participant. He and the principal shareholder part company...
>
> The question whether the relationship between shareholders [in such circumstances] constitutes a 'quasi-partnership' is relatively easy to answer if the company's business was previously run by a partnership in which the shareholders were the partners. It is indeed common for partnerships to be converted into companies for tax or other reasons. It is also relatively easy to establish whether a relationship between shareholders constitutes a 'quasi-partnership' when a company was formed by a group of persons who are well known to each other and the incorporation of the company was with a view to them all working together in the company to exploit some business concept which they have. It is much less easy to determine whether a company is a 'quasi-partnership' in a case such as this. Mr Strahan did not know Mr Wilcock when the company was formed. He joined the company as an employee. It was only subsequently that he acquired some of its shares from Mr Wilcock and became a director. However, it is clear on the authorities that a relationship of 'quasi-partnership' may be acquired after the formation of the company. Lord Wilberforce specifically refers to an association 'formed or continued' on the basis of a personal relationship.
>
> The question then is: in what circumstances should the courts determine that such a company constitutes a 'quasi-partnership'?...Logically, the appropriate question is whether, if the company had been formed (viz incorporated) at the time the company is alleged to have become a 'quasi-partnership' (that is, in this case, at the time when Mr Strahan acquired his shares), the company would have qualified as a 'quasi-partnership', applying the guidance set out by Lord Wilberforce. Thus, it is important to ask whether at that point in time the company would have been formed on the basis of a personal relationship involving mutual confidence. It would also be appropriate to ask whether, under the arrangements agreed between the parties, all the parties, other than those who were to be 'sleeping' members, would be entitled to participate in the conduct of the business. Likewise it would be appropriate to ask whether there was a restriction

on the transfer of the members' interests in the company. That last requirement is in fact met by the articles of association in the present case, which restrict the transfer of shares. With limited exceptions, the directors can refuse to register the transfer of shares. The articles would therefore enable the directors to prevent Mr Strahan from transferring his shares to a third party.

Accordingly, to determine whether a company that has evolved from a one-person company to a multi-person company is a 'quasi-partnership', the courts will apply Lord Wilberforce's criteria at the time the company is alleged to have become a quasi-partnership, which *in this case* was at the time the employee became a member. In the leading 'unfair prejudice' case of *O'Neill v Phillips*,[52]—considered in detail later in this chapter—which involved a similar evolution of the company, the quasi-partnership did not arise at the time the employee became a member but at a later date as his role in the company became more substantial and he used his personal assets to support the company. Accordingly, a company becomes a 'quasi-partnership' at the time when one or 'probably more' of the *Ebrahimi* criteria are fulfilled and is not tested by reference to any specific events such as incorporation or the issue of shares to the petitioner.

Whilst the equitable considerations that a court may take into account in exercising its just and equitable winding-up jurisdiction in theory impose limits on the exercise of general meeting power, in practice it is worth noting that the only available remedy of winding-up undermines the protection. Winding up the company means in effect that the assets are sold off, creditors repaid and what remains—the residual interest—is paid to shareholders according to their proportionate shareholding. Such a process, how-ever, can result in value destruction if, for example, it is not possible to sell the business as a whole or if buyers are not found for the assets. The potential loss of value—for minority and controlling shareholders alike—that could be generated by winding up a successful going concern means that in many instances whilst minority shareholders may threaten a just and equitable winding-up petition they will be hesitant to 'pull the trigger'. Nevertheless, the threat of a well-founded action may operate as an important bargaining chip to protect the minority shareholders' position.

2 The unfair prejudice remedy

The unfair prejudice remedy is set out in section 994 of the Companies Act 2006.

■ Section 994 CA 2006 Petition by company member

(1) A member of a company may apply to the court by petition for an order under this Part on the ground—

    (a) that the company's affairs are being or have been conducted in a manner that is unfairly prejudicial to the interests of members generally or of some part of its members (includ-ing at least himself),[53] or

    (b) that an actual or proposed act or omission of the company (including an act or omission on its behalf) is or would be so prejudicial.

---

[52] [1999] 2 BCLC 1. See further section III.2 in this chapter.

[53] The Companies Act 1989 amended the original unfair prejudice remedy which provided only that the conduct of the company's affairs be 'unfairly prejudicial to the interests of some part of the mem-bers' (Schedule 19, paragraph 11 Companies Act 1989). This amendment followed the holding in *Re a Company (No 00370 of 1987), ex p Glossop* [1988] BCLC 570 that the remedy was unavailable where conduct affected all the members.

> (2) The provisions of this Part apply to a person who is not a member of a company but to whom shares in the company have been transferred or transmitted by operation of law as they apply to a member of a company.

Section 994 provides a potentially expansive remedy for minority shareholders faced with what they view as the unfair actions or proposed actions of the controlling shareholders but also, potentially, more generally a remedy for any shareholder that is aggrieved by the conduct of the company's affairs even where there are no controlling shareholders. To the extent that the conduct in question is deemed to be unfairly prejudicial to the members' interests the court may, pursuant to section 996 (which is considered in detail in section V of this chapter), make any order that it thinks fit. The most common type of order for the court to make in this regard has been an order for the company or the controlling shareholder to buy the shares of the petitioner.

The two key concepts which the provision uses to set out the remedy are: *the conduct of the company's affairs* and *unfair prejudice to members' interests*. None of 'company's affairs', 'unfair prejudice' or 'members' interests' are defined by the 2006 Act. Read literally, these concepts offer considerable scope for the judiciary to intervene in a company's activities and to craft remedies—of the types the court thinks appropriate—for members whose interests are detrimentally affected by such activity. We consider, in turn, how the courts have interpreted these concepts. Our primary focus in this section is the extent to which the unfair prejudice remedy acts as a constraint on the exercise of corporate power by controlling shareholders.

2.1 Conducting the company's affairs

Conduct of the company's affairs would cover any action taken by or on behalf of the company, by the board, the general meeting or any person with delegated authority. Actions taken by the company's organs, for example, to change the articles or remove a director in a general meeting controlled by a controlling shareholder, clearly fall within section 994's understanding of conduct of the company's affairs. However, the courts have taken a broad view of the conduct of the affairs of the company, and have held that actions that do not involve action taken by the company may amount to the conduct of the affairs of the company. In *Re Phoneer Ltd*,[54] for example, the attempt by the senior manager of the company to renegotiate his remuneration arrangements and then to withdraw from his management role amounted to a breach of the terms on which the shareholders had agreed the affairs of the company would be conducted.

A more difficult question is whether the phrase 'company's affairs' includes actions and activities that take place beyond the strict legal borders of the company's separate legal personality. Does, for example, the conduct of the company's affairs include the stand-alone conduct of a controlling shareholder or parent company; and, vice versa, does the conduct of a subsidiary's activities count as the conduct of the parent's affairs. The courts have answered these questions affirmatively and have interpreted the term 'affairs' very broadly in this regard. The leading case in this regard is *Re Citybranch Group Ltd v Rackind*[55] where Sir Martin Nourse, giving the judgment of the Court of Appeal, held that 'I would hold that the affairs of a subsidiary can also be the affairs of its holding company, especially where, as here, the directors of the holding company, which necessarily controls the affairs of the subsidiary, also represent a majority of the

---

[54] [2002] 2 BCLC 241.
[55] [2004] 4 All ER 735. In reaching his judgment Sir Martin Nourse relied heavily on the Australian cases of *Re Norvabron Pty Ltd (No 2)* (1986) 11 ACLR 279 and *Re Dernacourt Investments Pty Ltd, Baker Davis Supply Co Pty Ltd v Dernacourt Investments Pty Ltd* (1990) 2 ACSR 553.

directors of the subsidiary.' In this case the affairs of a 100% owned subsidiary, whose directors were also the directors of the parent company, were held to be the affairs of the parent. Whether the affairs of a parent are the affairs of the subsidiary, or vice versa, will always be a fact-dependent determination.[56] Important, but not determinative, considerations in this regard will be existence and exercise of control by the parent[57] over the subsidiary and the make-up of the parent and subsidiary boards.

2.2 Unfair prejudice to members' interests

As noted earlier, the 'unfair prejudice' remedy's predecessor was the oppression remedy set out in section 210 of the Companies Act 1948 which provided certain remedies where 'the affairs of the company are being conducted in a manner oppressive to some part of the members'. The introduction of the 'unfair prejudice' remedy was intended to address the technical and substantive limitations of the oppression remedy. In this regard, Lord Hoffmann has observed that '"unfairly prejudicial" is deliberately imprecise language which was chosen by Parliament because its earlier attempt in s 210 of the Companies Act 1948 to provide a similar remedy had been too restrictively construed'.[58] Harman J in *Re a Company* observed that 'unfair prejudice' 'plainly requires allegations of conduct of a much lesser weight' than was required by the oppression remedy.[59] The unfair prejudice remedy, therefore, was designed to give courts greater scope to protect minority shareholders.

The courts have not, however, treated the unfair prejudice remedy as an invitation to review corporate action according to the judiciary's view of what is fair to a company's shareholders. Rather, the courts have legally categorized the ways in which the remedy may be used. The most important of these categories draws on the developments in relation to the *just and equitable winding-up* jurisdiction, discussed previously, where, as we saw, the courts have imposed limitations on the exercise of corporate power to protect certain extra-legal understandings. The genesis and development of this aspect of the unfair prejudice remedy is found in several of Lord Hoffmann's judgments. The first of these is *Re a Company*[60] in 1986 where he made the following observations:

> Counsel for the company submitted that the section must be limited to conduct which is unfairly prejudicial to the interests of the members as members. It cannot extend to conduct which is prejudicial to other interests of persons who happen to be members.
>
> In principle I accept this proposition, as did Lord Grantchester QC in *Re a company* [1983] 2 All ER 36. But its application must take into account that the interests of a member are not necessarily limited to his strict legal rights under the constitution of the company. The use of the word 'unfairly' in s 459, like the use of the words 'just and equitable' in s 517(1)(g), enables the court to have regard to wider equitable considerations. As Lord Wilberforce said of the latter words in *Ebrahimi v Westbourne Galleries* they are a recognition of the fact that:
>
> > '...a limited company is more than a mere legal entity, with a personality in law of its own: that there is room in company law for recognition of the fact that behind it, or amongst it, there are

---

[56] See *Re Neath Rugby Ltd* [2007] EWHC 2999 (Ch) *per* Lewison J: 'there is no absolute rule that the affairs of one company cannot count as the affairs of another; but the question is fact-sensitive. In looking at the facts, the court must look at the business realities and must not adopt a narrow, legalistic view.'

[57] See also *Nicholas v Soundcraft Electronics Ltd* [1993] BCLC 360 where the failure of a 75% controlling shareholder to continue, as agreed, to support the subsidiary amounted to the affairs of the company. Lewison J in *Re Neath Rugby Ltd* [2007] EWHC 2999 at [213] observes that 'the essential features of the facts of [Soundcraft], to my mind, was that Soundcraft Electronics was intervening in the internal affairs of Soundcraft Magnetics'. See also *Re Grandactual Ltd* [2006] BCC 85.

[58] *Re Saul D Harrison Plc* [1995] 1 BCLC 14.

[59] [1985] BCLC 80.   [60] [1986] BCLC 376.

individuals, with rights, expectations and obligations inter se which are not necessarily submerged in the company structure.'

Thus in the case of the managing director of a large public company who is also the owner of a small holding in the company's shares, it is easy to see the distinction between his interests as a managing director employed under a service contract and his interests as a member. In the case of a small private company in which two or three members have invested their capital by subscribing for shares on the footing that dividends are unlikely but that each will earn his living by working for the company as a director, the distinction may be more elusive. The member's interests as a member who has ventured his capital in the company's business may include a legitimate expectation that he will continue to be employed as a director and his dismissal from that office and exclusion from the management of the company may therefore be unfairly preju- dicial to his interests as a member.

Hoffmann J (as he then was) accepts that the unfair prejudice remedy addresses corpor- ate conduct that affects the interests of a person as a member not in any other capacity of that person—for example, as employee or creditor.[61] However, a 'member's interests' must not be narrowly construed and it is clear for Hoffmann J that any detriment to a person's non-member interests may affect his interests as a member.

For Hoffmann J the use by the legislature of the term 'unfair' opens the door to equit- able considerations that may restrict the exercise of corporate power which subverts an understanding amongst the shareholders, for example, about the continuing role of the shareholders in the running of the business. Shareholders may, he observes, have certain 'legitimate expectations' arising from these understandings which will be protected by the unfair prejudice remedy. A 'member's interests', therefore, extends beyond their formal legal rights to these 'legitimate expectations'. The application of the unfair preju- dice remedy to these understandings and expectations will be referred to in this section as the 'equitable considerations' category.

It is important to note here that to the extent the unfair prejudice remedy enforces the same equitable considerations which were of concern in *Ebrahimi*, the unfair prejudice remedy offers less drastic remedial solutions—such as buying out the petitioner—than a winding-up petition. Mummery J (as he then was) in *In re A Company (No. 00314 of 1989), ex p Estate Acquisition and Development Ltd*[62] put this point as follows:

[With the unfair prejudice remedy] the court is not…faced with a death sentence decision dependent on establishing just and equitable grounds for such a decision. The court is more in the position of a medical practitioner presented with a patient who is alleged to be suffering from one or more ailments which can be treated by an appropriate remedy applied during the course of the continuing life of the company.

The meaning of a member's 'legitimate expectations' was developed further in the Court of Appeal case of *Re Saul D Harrison & Sons Ltd*. The facts of this case involved a peti- tioner who claimed that the subject company's business model did not justify the con- tinued operation of the business and that to continue the business unfairly prejudiced the petitioner's interests. The case, therefore, did not invoke the equitable considera- tions category through the use of corporate power to breach informal understandings. Nevertheless, Hoffmann LJ made important observations about the unfair prejudice remedy generally as well as about this equitable considerations category.

---

[61] See, for example, *Re J E Cade & Son Ltd* [1992] BCLC 213 where the petition was 'pursuing his interests as a freeholder of the farm and not his interests as a member of the company'; see also *Re Haden Bill Electrical Ltd* [1995] 2 BCLC 280.

[62] [1991] BCLC 154.

■ *Re Saul D Harrison & Sons Ltd* [1995] 1 BCLC 14

Hoffmann LJ

[Counsel for the] petitioner, said that the only test of unfairness was whether a reasonable bystander would think that the conduct in question was unfair. This is correct, so far as it goes, and has some support in the cases. Its merit is to emphasise that the court is applying an objective standard of fairness. But I do not think that it is the most illuminating way of putting the matter. For one thing, the standard of fairness must necessarily be laid down by the court. In explaining how the court sets about deciding what is fair in the context of company management, I do not think that it helps a great deal to add the reasonable company watcher to the already substantial cast of imaginary characters which the law uses to personify its standards of justice in different situations. An appeal to the views of an imaginary third party makes the concept seem more vague than it really is. It is more useful to examine the factors which the law actually takes into account in setting the standard.

In deciding what is fair or unfair for the purposes of s 459, it is important to have in mind that fairness is being used in the context of a commercial relationship. The articles of association are just what their name implies: the contractual terms which govern the relationships of the shareholders with the company and each other. They determine the powers of the board and the company in general meeting and everyone who becomes a member of a company is taken to have agreed to them. Since keeping promises and honouring agreements is probably the most important element of commercial fairness, the starting point in any case under s 459 will be to ask whether the conduct of which the shareholder complains was in accordance with the articles of association...

Although one begins with the articles and the powers of the board, a finding that conduct was not in accordance with the articles does not necessarily mean that it was unfair, still less that the court will exercise its discretion to grant relief...In choosing the term 'unfairly prejudicial', the Jenkins Committee (para 204) equated it with Lord Cooper's understanding of 'oppression' in *Elder v Elder and Watson* 1952 SC 49:

> 'a visible departure from the standards of fair dealing and a violation of the conditions of fair play on which every shareholder who entrusts his money to a company is entitled to rely'.

So trivial or technical infringements of the articles were not intended to give rise to petitions under s 459.

Not only may conduct be technically unlawful without being unfair: it can also be unfair without being unlawful. In a commercial context, this may at first seem surprising. How can it be unfair to act in accordance with what the parties have agreed? As a general rule, it is not. But there are cases in which the letter of the articles does not fully reflect the understandings upon which the shareholders are associated. Lord Wilberforce drew attention to such cases in *Ebrahimi v Westbourne Galleries Ltd*, which discusses what seems to me the identical concept of injustice or unfairness which can form the basis of a just and equitable winding up...

Thus the personal relationship between a shareholder and those who control the company may entitle him to say that it would in certain circumstances be unfair for them to exercise a power conferred by the articles upon the board or the company in general meeting. I have in the past ventured to borrow from public law the term 'legitimate expectation' to describe the correlative 'right' in the shareholder to which such a relationship may give rise. It often arises out of a fundamental understanding between the shareholders which formed the basis of their association but was not put into contractual form, such as an assumption that each of the parties who has ventured his capital will also participate in the management of the company and receive the return on his investment in the form of salary rather than dividend...But in *Ebrahimi v Westbourne Galleries Ltd* Lord Wilberforce went on to say:

> 'It would be impossible, and wholly undesirable, to define the circumstances in which these considerations may arise. Certainly the fact that the company is a small one, or a private company, is not

enough. There are very many of these where the association is a purely commercial one, of which it can safely be said that the basis of association is adequately and exhaustively laid down in the articles. The superimposition of equitable considerations requires something more...'

Thus in the absence of 'something more', there is no basis for a legitimate expectation that the board and the company in general meeting will not exercise whatever powers they are given by the articles of association.

There are two general points about the unfair prejudice remedy to take from this passage. The first is that the courts should not determine whether the unfair prejudice remedy is available by reference to a hypothetical reasonable person—i.e. would that person consider that the company's conduct unfairly prejudiced the member's interests? Several lower instance judgments had taken this approach.[63] Rather Hoffmann LJ refers us to specific factors that determine whether the remedy is available. This is important as it withdraws from the courts a general fairness review power and refers them to the specific legal rules that determine whether the remedy is available in relation to different types of corporate conduct. One group of such rules is in relation to the equitable considerations category. The second general observation from *Saul D Harrison* is that whilst the unfair prejudice remedy is in theory available to enforce breaches of the shareholders' legal rights—for example, a breach of the constitution—such breaches may not be unfair for the purposes of section 994 if the breach is not substantial.[64]

The second part of this passage addresses the equitable considerations/legitimate expectations category developed by Hoffmann J in *Re a Company*. There are two key points to note in this regard. First, the context in which these equitable considerations are applicable is not as clearly specified as it was by Lord Wilberforce in *Ebrahimi*. Lord Wilberforce clearly restricted its application to 'quasi-partnerships' and specified criteria for those 'quasi partnerships' whereas Hoffmann LJ's judgment does not explicitly restrict the protection of 'legitimate expectations' to quasi-partnership companies. He refers only to the 'personal relationship' between the petitioner-shareholder and the controller. However, subsequent cases, including Lord Hoffmann's judgment in *O'Neill v Phillips* (considered later), make it clear that this equitable considerations/legitimate expectations category is only applicable to quasi-partnership companies.[65] Secondly, Hoffmann LJ suggests that the category of using corporate power to breach informal contract-like understandings is a subset of a broader category of 'legitimate expectations' or rights that arise out of a relationship. He observes that the expectations and rights '*often*'—and therefore not exclusively—arise out of an 'understanding...which formed the basis of their association'. Accordingly, the judgment implicitly sets out the 'legitimate expectations' category as an umbrella category of which the *Ebrahimi* quasi-partnership restrictions are a sub-category. As we will see in the following case such a view of the 'legitimate expectations' category generates, to Lord Hoffmann's regret, its own problematic dynamic.

[63] Doubt is thereby cast on the cases that deployed this approach: see, for example, *Re R A Noble & Sons (Clothing) Ltd* [1983] BCLC 273 (objective reasonable bystander approach); *Re Macro (Ipswich) Ltd* [1994] 2 BCLC 354 (assessing unfair prejudice on an 'objective basis').

[64] See also *Rock (Nominees) Ltd v RCO (Holdings) plc (in liq)* [2004] 1 BCLC 439; *Re McCarthy Surfacing Limited* [2009] 1 BCLC 622 *per* Michael Furness QC: 'Prejudice must be substantial, not merely technical or trivial in nature (*Re Saul D Harrison & Sons plc*). Technical breaches of fiduciary duties, or the company's constitution, will not constitute prejudice if the outcome would have been no different if the directors had scrupulously observed their duties, or the constitution.'

[65] See *Re Blue Arrow plc* [1987] BCLC 585.

■ *O'Neill v Phillips*

Pectel Limited was an asbestos-stripping company that, as of 1983, was solely owned by Mr Phillips. In the same year, Mr O'Neill started working for Pectel as a manual labourer. He quickly progressed in the company and by 1985 was appointed director of the company and given 25% of the shares. At the end of that year Mr Phillips stepped aside from the day-to-day management of the company leaving Mr O'Neill as the sole, and effectively managing, director. It was understood by both parties that Mr O'Neill would receive half the profits of the company whilst performing this role. The company prospered in the late 1980s and Mr Neill received his half-share of the profits in the form of salary, dividends and additional shares. In this period Mr O'Neill also personally guaranteed Pectel Ltd's bank account and mortgaged his house to secure this guarantee.

At the end of the 1980s discussions commenced between Mr Phillips and Mr O'Neill with a view to Mr O'Neill obtaining 50% of the shares in the company. There was evidence that Mr Phillips had indicated to Mr O'Neill and third parties that this would happen. In this regard solicitors were instructed, documentation drafted and the negotiations proceeded to a point where agreement in principle was reached. The in-principle agreement was that when the net-asset value of the company reached £500,000 Mr O'Neill would receive a 50% shareholding, and those shares would be granted 50% of the voting rights when the company's net-asset value reached £1 million. However, no documentation was signed. In this regard, Mr Phillips testified as follows:

> 'Question: So that if a rich man had come at the end of January 1991 and offered you a million pounds for the company as a whole, lock, stock and barrel, Mr O'Neill would have reasonably expected to have got half of that, would he not?
> Answer: Correct, yes.'

The negotiations did not proceed any further because in the early 1990s Mr Phillips became concerned about Mr O'Neill's ability to manage the company. Mr Phillips reinstated himself as managing director of the company and gave Mr O'Neill the option of running the UK or German part of the business under Mr Phillips' overall management. Mr O'Neill elected to run the German side of the business. Furthermore, Mr Phillips informed Mr O'Neill that, as he was no longer the managing director of the company, he was no longer entitled to 50% of the profits, only his salary and 25% dividend.

Thereafter, relations between the parties continued to deteriorate resulting in Mr O'Neill filing an unfair prejudice petition which claimed that Mr O'Neill's interests as a member had been unfairly prejudiced by the termination of the 50% profit-sharing arrangement and the failure to make Mr O'Neill a 50% shareholder in the company.

The court of first instance rejected the petition. The court held that Mr Phillips had not committed himself irrevocably to making Mr O'Neill a 50% shareholder and that the 50% profit-sharing arrangement, as well as the negotiations relating to issue of additional shares, were part of Mr O'Neill's remuneration and incentives as a manager of the company and their termination did not, therefore, affect Mr O'Neill's interests as a member—as required by the unfair prejudice remedy—rather his interests as a manager. Mr O'Neill appealed.

> **Court of Appeal (overturning the first instance judgment) [1998] BCC 405: Nourse LJ**
> I am, with respect to the judge, unable to accept his assessment of the position. On 29 January 1985, less than two years after he had started to work for the company, Mr O'Neill became both a member and a director of it. It is true that he did not subscribe for his shares and did not bring any capital into the company. But that is immaterial. From the end of January 1985, or at any rate from May of that year when the understanding as to an equal sharing of profits was come to, the

company represented an association continued on the basis of a personal relationship involving mutual confidence between Mr Phillips and Mr O'Neill, with an understanding that Mr O'Neill should participate in the conduct of the business and restrictions on share transfers. All three typical elements of a quasi-partnership were present. At all times thereafter Mr O'Neill had a legitimate expectation that he would receive 50% of the profits. By the beginning of 1991 he had a legitimate expectation, subject to meeting the £500,000 and £1,000,000 targets respectively, that he would receive 50% of its voting shares.

On this analysis, taking the broad view which is appropriate, I conclude that the unfair prejudice, if such it was, can only have been to Mr O'Neill's interests as [a] member of the company. Certainly, if one were to ask in what other capacity [his] interests were prejudiced, no answer could be given. Test it in this way. Suppose that the relationship between Mr O'Neill and Mr Phillips had in reality been one of partnership and that Mr Phillips had acted in such a way as to force Mr O'Neill out of the business. The interests prejudiced could only have been his interests as a partner.

[Mr Phillips appealed.]

House of Lords [1999] 2 BCLC 1: Lord Hoffmann

1. 'Unfairly Prejudicial'
In s.459 Parliament has chosen fairness as the criterion by which the court must decide whether it has jurisdiction to grant relief. It is clear from the legislative history (which I discussed in *In re Saul D. Harrison & Sons plc* [1995] 1 BCLC 14, 17–20) that it chose this concept to free the court from technical considerations of legal right and to confer a wide power to do what appeared just and equitable. But this does not mean that the court can do whatever the individual judge happens to think fair. The concept of fairness must be applied judicially and the content which it is given by the courts must be based upon rational principles. As Warner J. said in *In re J. E. Cade & Son Ltd.* [1992] BCLC 213, 227:

> 'The court…has a very wide discretion, but it does not sit under a palm tree.'

Although fairness is a notion which can be applied to all kinds of activities, its content will depend upon the context in which it is being used. Conduct which is perfectly fair between competing businessmen may not be fair between members of a family. In some sports it may require, at best, observance of the rules, in others ('it's not cricket') it may be unfair in some circumstances to take advantage of them. All is said to be fair in love and war. So the context and background are very important.

In the case of s.459, the background has the following two features. First, a company is an association of persons for an economic purpose, usually entered into with legal advice and some degree of formality. The terms of the association are contained in the articles of association and sometimes in collateral agreements between the shareholders. Thus the manner in which the affairs of the company may be conducted is closely regulated by rules to which the shareholders have agreed. Secondly, company law has developed seamlessly from the law of partnership, which was treated by equity, like the Roman *societas*, as a contract of good faith. One of the traditional roles of equity, as a separate jurisdiction, was to restrain the exercise of strict legal rights in certain relationships in which it considered that this would be contrary to good faith. These principles have, with appropriate modification, been carried over into company law.

The first of these two features leads to the conclusion that a member of a company will not ordinarily be entitled to complain of unfairness unless there has been some breach of the terms on which he agreed that the affairs of the company should be conducted. But the second leads to the conclusion that there will be cases in which equitable considerations make it unfair for those conducting the affairs of the company to rely upon their strict legal powers. Thus unfairness may consist in a breach of the rules or in using the rules in a manner which equity would regard as contrary to good faith.

This approach to the concept of unfairness in s.459 runs parallel to that which your Lordships' House, in *In re Westbourne Galleries Ltd.* [1973] AC 360, [1972] 2 All ER 492 adopted in giving content to the concept of 'just and equitable' as a ground for winding up...

I would apply the same reasoning to the concept of unfairness in s.459... In my view, a balance has to be struck between the breadth of the discretion given to the court and the principle of legal certainty. Petitions under s.459 are often lengthy and expensive. It is highly desirable that lawyers should be able to advise their clients whether or not a petition is likely to succeed. Lord Wilberforce... said that it would be impossible 'and wholly undesirable' to define the circumstances in which the application of equitable principles might make it unjust, or inequitable (or unfair) for a party to insist on legal rights or to exercise them in particular way. This of course is right. But that does not mean that there are no principles by which those circumstances may be identified. The way in which such equitable principles operate is tolerably well settled and in my view it would be wrong to abandon them in favour of some wholly indefinite notion of fairness...

The parallel is not in the conduct which the court will treat as justifying a particular remedy but in the principles upon which it decides that the conduct is unjust, inequitable or unfair... I agree with Jonathan Parker J when he said in *In re Astec (BSR) plc* [1998] 2 BCLC 556, 588:

'in order to give rise to an equitable constraint based on "legitimate expectation" what is required is a personal relationship or personal dealings of some kind between the party seeking to exercise the legal right and the party seeking to restrain such exercise, such as will affect the conscience of the former.'

This is putting the matter in very traditional language, reflecting in the word 'conscience' the ecclesiastical origins of the long-departed Court of Chancery. As I have said, I have no difficulty with this formulation. But I think that one useful cross-check in a case like this is to ask whether the exercise of the power in question would be contrary to what the parties, by words or conduct, have actually agreed. Would it conflict with the promises which they appear to have exchanged?... In a quasi-partnership company, they will usually be found in the understandings between the members at the time they entered into association. But there may be later promises, by words or conduct, which it would be unfair to allow a member to ignore. Nor is it necessary that such promises should be independently enforceable as a matter of contract. A promise may be binding as a matter of justice and equity although for one reason or another (for example, because in favour of a third party) it would not be enforceable in law.

I do not suggest that exercising rights in breach of some promise or undertaking is the only form of conduct which will be regarded as unfair for the purposes of s.459. For example, there may be some event which puts an end to the basis upon which the parties entered into association with each other, making it unfair that one shareholder should insist upon the continuance of the association. The analogy of contractual frustration suggests itself. The unfairness may arise not from what the parties have positively agreed but from a majority using its legal powers to maintain the association in circumstances to which the minority can reasonably say it did not agree: non haec in foedera veni. It is well recognised that in such a case there would be power to wind up the company on the just and equitable ground (see *Virdi v Abbey Leisure Ltd.* [1990] BCLC 342) and it seems to me that, in the absence of a winding up, it could equally be said to come within s.459. But this form of unfairness is also based upon established equitable principles and it does not arise in this case.

2. Legitimate expectations

In *In re Saul D. Harrison & Sons plc* [1995] 1 BCLC 14, 19, I used the term 'legitimate expectation,' borrowed from public law, as a label for the 'correlative right' to which a relationship between company members may give rise in a case when, on equitable principles, it would be regarded as unfair for a majority to exercise a power conferred upon them by the articles to the prejudice of another member. I gave as an example the standard case in which shareholders have entered into association upon the understanding that each of them who has ventured his capital will also participate in the management of the company. In such a case it will usually be considered unjust, inequitable or unfair for a majority to use their voting power to exclude a member from participation in the management without giving him the opportunity to remove his capital upon reasonable terms. The aggrieved member could be said to have had a 'legitimate expectation' that he would be able to participate in the management or withdraw from the company.

It was probably a mistake to use this term, as it usually is when one introduces a new label to describe a concept which is already sufficiently defined in other terms. In saying that it was 'correlative' to the equitable restraint, I meant that it could exist only when equitable principles of the kind I have been describing would make it unfair for a party to exercise rights under the articles. It is a consequence, not a cause, of the equitable restraint. The concept of a legitimate expectation should not be allowed to lead a life of its own, capable of giving rise to equitable restraints in circumstances to which the traditional equitable principles have no application. That is what seems to have happened in this case.

3. Was Mr Phillips unfair?

The Court of Appeal found that by 1991 the company had the characteristics identified by Lord Wilberforce in *Ebrahimi v Westbourne Galleries Ltd* [1973] AC 360 as commonly giving rise to equitable restraints upon the exercise of powers under the articles...I agree. It follows that it would have been unfair of Mr Phillips to use his voting powers under the articles to remove Mr O'Neill from participation in the conduct of the business without giving him the opportunity to sell his interest in the company at a fair price. Although it does not matter, I should say that I do not think that this was the position when Mr O'Neill first acquired his shares in 1985...Mr O'Neill was simply an employee who happened to have been given some shares. But over the following years the relationship changed. Mr O'Neill invested his own profits in the company by leaving some on loan account and agreeing to part being capitalised as shares. He worked to build up the company's business. He guaranteed its bank account and mortgaged his house in support...

The difficulty for Mr O'Neill is that Mr Phillips did not remove him from participation in the management of the business. After the meeting on 4 November 1991 he remained a director and continued to earn his salary as manager of the business in Germany. The Court of Appeal held that he had been constructively removed by the behaviour of Mr Phillips in the matter of equality of profits and shareholdings. So the question then becomes whether Mr Phillips acted unfairly in respect of these matters.

To take the shareholdings first, the Court of Appeal said that Mr O'Neill had a legitimate expectation of being allotted more shares when the targets were met. No doubt he did have such an expectation before 4 November and no doubt it was legitimate, or reasonable, in the sense that it reasonably appeared likely to happen. Mr Phillips had agreed in principle, subject to the execution of a suitable document. But this is where I think that the Court of Appeal may have been misled by the expression 'legitimate expectation'. The real question is whether in fairness or equity Mr O'Neill had a right to the shares. On this point, one runs up against what seems to me the insuperable obstacle of the judge's finding that Mr Phillips never agreed to give them. He made no promise on the point. From which it seems to me to follow that there is no basis, consistent with established principles of equity, for a court to hold that Mr Phillips was behaving unfairly in withdrawing from the negotiation. This would not be restraining the exercise of legal rights. It would be imposing upon Mr Phillips an obligation to which he never agreed. Where, as here, parties enter into negotiations with a view to a transfer of shares on professional advice and subject to a condition that they are not to be bound until a formal document has been executed, I do not think it is possible to say that an obligation has arisen in fairness or equity at an earlier stage.

The same reasoning applies to the sharing of profits. The judge found as a fact that Mr Phillips made no unconditional promise about the sharing of profits. He had said informally that he would share the profits equally while Mr O'Neill managed the company and he himself did not have to be involved in day-to-day business. He deliberately retained control of the company and with it, as the judge said, the right to redraw Mr O'Neill's responsibilities. This he did without objection in August 1991. The consequence was that he came back to running the business and Mr O'Neill was no longer managing director. He had made no promise to share the profits equally in such circumstances and it was therefore not inequitable or unfair for him to refuse to carry on doing so…

It follows in my opinion that there was no basis for the Court of Appeal's finding that Mr O'Neill had been driven out of the company. He may have decided that he had lost confidence in Mr Phillips and that he could no longer work with him. After Christmas 1992 Mr Phillips said that he recognised that Mr O'Neill had come to this conclusion and that there was no way in which he could put their relationship together again. But Mr O'Neill's decision was not the result of anything wrong or unfair which Mr Phillips had done.

The first general point to note about the judgment is Lord Hoffmann's emphasis that the unfair prejudice remedy does not allow judges to do what they view as fair; to do justice to the facts. Citing Warner J he notes that judges do not sit under a palm tree. For Lord Hoffmann the application of the unfair prejudice remedy must be based upon rational principles, which in this context means the rules and principles of what, following *Ebrahimi*, we have called the equitable considerations category or, following Lord Hoffmann's previous unfair prejudice judgments, we might call the 'legitimate expectations' category. However, in this judgment Lord Hoffmann backtracks on the concept of 'legitimate expectations'.

The phrase 'legitimate expectations' has an appealing simplicity. For a student of company law the notion of 'legitimate expectation' makes it easier to grasp the idea that non-written understandings may be protected from breach. But the term 'legitimate expectation' encourages us to focus on the petitioner's viewpoint—what did *he* legitimately expect from the relationship. It enables the courts to move beyond the bi- or multilateral focus on what both, or all, parties agreed to, and to protect the understandings and expectations of one shareholder, that were not shared by the other shareholders. For Lord Hoffmann the term 'legitimate expectation' misled the Court of Appeal and resulted in them underestimating the extent of the promise-like nature of the informal understanding: they focused too heavily on Mr O'Neill's expectation and not on the nature of any informal bargain. This is why Lord Hoffmann guides lower courts by focusing on a 'useful cross-check' of what the parties by words or conduct have agreed—what promises have they exchanged. It is noteworthy that, arguably, this understanding of the term legitimate expectation was encouraged not just by the term itself but also by Hoffmann LJ's position in *Saul Harrison* which suggests that the term means more than just the *Ebrahimi* understanding of equitable considerations.

There is also a sense that the user-friendliness of the term 'legitimate expectation' distorts what the equitable considerations category of the unfair prejudice remedy actually does: it *does not* simply protect or enforce an informal agreement; rather it provides a remedy where *in a quasi-partnership* corporate power *is exercised* to breach that informal agreement. The 50% shareholding issue in the case allows us to see this more clearly. In relation to the shares, they had not been issued; to issue them would have required the exercise of corporate power. In relation to the share issue, therefore, there was no exercise of corporate power to be restrained; no board or shareholder resolution that invalidated an existing informal promise that Mr O'Neill could acquire the shares. Even if Lord Hoffmann had accepted, *which he did not*, that there was an informal promise-like understanding to issue the shares of equivalent standing to an informal understanding in a quasi-partnership that the petitioner have a continuing involvement in management, there had in this case been no exercise of corporate power which could be restrained by the unfair prejudice remedy. Whilst it is true that the wording of the unfair prejudice remedy refers not just to corporate conduct but also to 'proposed act or omission(s)' the equitable considerations category is *only* applicable to restrain the actual exercise of power.[66]

IV THE UNFAIR PREJUDICE REMEDY BEYOND THE EQUITABLE CONSIDERATIONS CATEGORY

1 The move towards independent illegality

Prior to Lord Hoffmann's judgments in *Saul Harrison* and *O'Neill v Phillips* in addition to the developing equitable consideration/legitimate expectations category the courts had developed a more general approach to applying the unfair prejudice remedy. This involved applying the remedy as an objective standard. The leading statement of this approach was provided by Slade J in an unreported case of *Re Bovey Hotel Ventures Ltd* (31 July 1981, unreported):

> I do not think it necessary or appropriate in this judgment to attempt any comprehensive exposition of the situations which may give rise to the court's jurisdiction under [section 994]. Broadly however, I would say this. Without prejudice to the generality of the wording of the section, which may cover many other situations, a member of a company will be able to bring himself within the section if he can show that the value of his shareholding in the company has been seriously diminished or at least seriously jeopardised by reason of a course of conduct on the part of those persons who have had de facto control of the company which has been unfair to the member concerned. The test of unfairness must, I think, be an objective, not a subjective one. In other words it is not necessary for the petitioner to show that the persons who have had de facto control of the company have acted as they did in the conscious knowledge that this was unfair to the petitioner or that they were acting in bad faith; the test, I think, is whether a reasonable bystander observing the consequences of their conduct would regard it as having unfairly prejudiced the petitioner's interests.

The test of unfair prejudice as determined by the reasonable bystander was followed in several cases prior to *Saul Harrison* and *O'Neill v Phillips*.[67] This test is true to a literal reading of the statute. The test has the considerable advantage of policing all controlling shareholder activity that, objectively, unfairly diminishes the value of the minority shareholder shareholding. This approach regulates all aspects of controlling shareholder activity, whether through the exercise of direct voting power in the general meeting or the informal exercise of power.[68] However, in application it generates a considerable degree of uncertainty because the judge is empowered—through the reasonable bystander framework—to 'do fairness' to the facts.

In *Saul Harrison* Hoffmann LJ gently rejected the 'reasonable bystander' approach to the remedy.[69] In his judgment in *O'Neill v Phillips* Lord Hoffmann stresses that

---

[66] See *Re Guidezone Ltd* [2000] 2 BCLC 321 where Jonathan Parker J, interpreting Lord Hoffmann's judgment in *O'Neill v Phillips*, appears to suggest that the unfair prejudice equitable consideration category could intervene to enforce an informal promise in the absence of the exercise of power where the minority has relied on the promise (the judgment is more equivocal than the headnote in this regard). To the extent that this was intended by Jonathan Parker J it is respectfully submitted that it is incorrect. This category of the unfair prejudice remedy is only available according to Lord Hoffmann's judgment where power is used in contravention of an informal agreement.

[67] See, for example, *Re R A Noble & Sons (Clothing) Ltd* [1983] BCLC 273.

[68] For an example of its application to value transfers to controlling shareholders see *Re Little Olympian Each-Ways Ltd (No 3)* [1995] 1 BCLC 636.

[69] The test has been referred to and applied in a few post-*Saul Harrison* and *O'Neill v Phillips* cases. Whether the use of this approach is consistent with existing authority is doubtful. See, for example,

section 994 does not provide courts with a general jurisdiction to do fairness to relationships between the company and shareholders. Judges, he reminds us, do not sit under a palm tree. Whilst in *Saul Harrison* Hoffmann LJ noted that corporate conduct 'can also be unfair without being unlawful' this statement appears to be true only for the equitable considerations category considered previously. For Lord Hoffmann, in both *Saul Harrison* and *O'Neill v Phillips*, the equitable considerations category is the only exception to a general rule that breach of right or duty is required to successfully bring a petition for unfair prejudice. In *Saul Harrison*, for example, he observes that:

> Thus it seems to me that in this case one can be a good deal more precise than to ask in general terms…whether a bystander would think that the board had been unfair. As there are no grounds for saying that it would be unfair for the board to act in accordance with the bargain between the petitioner and the company [that is, the equitable considerations category], the very minimum required to make out a case of unfairness is that the powers of management have been used for an unlawful purpose or the articles otherwise infringed.

The Law Commission, in their 1997 report on *Shareholder Remedies*,[70] criticized this view of the remedy and suggested that the approach was contrary to the Jenkins Committee's objective in proposing the remedy, which was to make a remedy available to shareholders where there had been no breach of right. Indeed one of the reasons the Jenkins Committee proposed the change of terminology from oppression to unfair prejudice was because of the concern that the courts had crafted an understanding of 'oppression' which required an independent illegal event in order for the remedy to be available. In *O'Neill v Phillips* Lord Hoffmann rejects this criticism and elevates the value of legal certainty over fairness:

> The Law Commission, in its report on Shareholder Remedies expresses some concern that defining the content of the unfairness concept in the way I have suggested might unduly limit its scope and that 'conduct which would appear to be deserving of a remedy may be left unremedied.' In my view, a balance has to be struck between the breadth of the discretion given to the court and the principle of legal certainty… The way in which such equitable principles operate is tolerably well settled and in my view it would be wrong to abandon them in favour of some wholly indefinite notion of fairness.

Furthermore, echoing his position in *Saul Harrison*, he observes that shareholders will not ordinarily be able to complain of unfairness where there has been no 'breach of the terms on which he agreed that the affairs of the company should be conducted'. Such terms would include: the articles; any shareholder agreements or informal promise-like understandings; and any obligations imposed on corporate participants such as directors' duties or the bona fide obligation to which general meeting decisions are subject.[71] More recently in *Irvine v Irvine (No 1)* Blackburne J has noted that 'unfairness contemplates breach of an agreement, or of a duty or of a legitimate expectation. For an expectation to be a legitimate expectation it must arise out of the relationship between the parties in the

---

Fisher v Cadman [2006] 1 BCLC 499; *Re Regional Airports Ltd* [1999] 2 BCLC 30. Note that in *Gamlestaden Fastigheter AB v Baltic Partners Ltd* [2007] All ER (D) 222 the Privy Council referred approvingly to *Re Little Olympian Each-Ways Ltd (No 3)* which deployed the reasonable bystander approach, although their Lordships did not refer to the 'reasonable bystander' approach.

[70] Law Commission, *Shareholder Remedies* (Law Com No 246) (Cm 3769, 1997), para 4.11.

[71] Clarifying that unfair prejudice can arise from breach of duty see *Re BSB Holdings Ltd (No 2)* [1996] 1 BCLC 155. Cases where the unfair prejudice remedy has been used to enforce a breach of duty include, for example, *O'Donnell v Shanahan* [2009] EWCA Civ 751; *Bhullar v Bullar* [2003] EWCA Civ 424 and *Cutland v Clark* [2003] 2 BCLC 393.

circumstances explained in *Ebrahimi v Westbourne Galleries Ltd*.'[72] Accordingly, outside of the equitable considerations category, Lord Hoffmann's position in *O'Neill v Phillips* subjects the availability of the unfair prejudice remedy to situations in which there is in effect an 'independent illegality'.

The fact that unfair prejudice may be suffered to a shareholder's interests as a result of a breach of directors duties provides a very important minority protection tool. Corporate action that damages a minority shareholder's interests, such as entering into non-arm's length related-party transaction with a controlling shareholder may well involve breaches of duty by the directors. For example, if no plausible explanation could be given for selling an asset to the controlling shareholder too cheaply it may be difficult for a director to convince a court that he really acted in a way which he considered promoted the success of the company or that, as is required by section 172, he did—as a reasonably diligent directors would have done[73]—have regard to the 'need to act fairly between members of the company'.[74] Importantly, it does not matter whether the controlling shareholder is a director for the 994 petition to act as a minority shareholder protection device in this regard, as the breach of duty by the director is sufficient to found the petition and to obtain a remedy. Given our discussion in Chapter 15 regarding the enforcement of directors' duties, this may seem surprising to the reader. However, note that although directors' duties are owed to the company, an unfair prejudice remedy is not enforcing the duty on behalf of the company, rather petitioning the court for a remedy because such a breach of duty affected their interests as members, by for example, reducing the value of the company. On the issue of whether the unfair prejudice remedy can function as a de facto derivative action mechanism see section V.3 in this chapter.

Finally in this regard, it is important to note that whilst the courts have restricted the application of the unfair prejudice remedy through the move towards an independent illegality requirement (outside of the equitable consideration category), in relation to what constitutes the members' interests for the purpose of the remedy the courts have continued to be very flexible. This was seen most clearly in the Privy Council case of *Gamlestaden Fastigheter AB v Baltic Partners Ltd*[75] where Lord Scott of Foscote, giving the court's judgment, granted a member relief pursuant to the Jersey unfair prejudice remedy—which is identical to the UK remedy—where the relief sought benefited the petitioner in his capacity as creditor. The case involved a joint venture company and the court stressed that where the petitioner is involved in a business in several different capacities, for example as member and creditor, the remedy may be available even where the relief benefits him in a non-member capacity.

2 Testing the boundaries of the independent illegality requirement

Outside of the equitable considerations category, following *O'Neill v Phillips*, the unfair prejudice remedy will not constrain controlling shareholder activity in the absence of a breach of the shareholders' or the company's legal right. However, it is clear that some

---

[72] [2007] 1 BCLC 349. See also: *Re McCarthy Surfacing Limited* [2009] 1 BCLC 622 *per* Michael Furness QC: 'the requirement for unfairness means it is not enough for the petitioners to show that they have been prejudiced in some way. That prejudice must have come about as a result of some wrongdoing; either the breach of an agreement, or the breach of some other duty owed to them as shareholders, or the frustration of some legitimate expectation on their part' (at [67]); *Holman v Adams Securities Limited* [2010] EWHC *per Edward Bartley Jones QC*: 'this is not a quasi-partnership company. Accordingly, if unfair prejudice is to be found it must lie in some abuse by the directors of the Company of their fiduciary powers and duties or in the conduct of the affairs of the Company in breach of its Articles of Association or Companies Acts requirements.'

[73] Compliance with the 'regard list' in section 172 is determined by reference to the care standard set forth in section 174. See further Chapters 10 and 12.

[74] Section 172(1)(f) CA 2006.   [75] [2007] All ER (D) 222.

forms of corporate action that do not involve a breach of the corporate constitution, a shareholders' agreement, or a director's duties, may damage the company in a way that many, including an objective reasonable bystander, would view as unfairly prejudicial to the minority shareholders' interests. We should not overstate the number of cases that fall through the cracks of the breach of legal right requirement; however, such cases can be envisioned. Three such examples are:

- Consider a non-market related-party transaction with a controlling shareholder that is duty compliant because the director had no personal conflict in the transaction and there is clear evidence that the director actually considered that the transaction would promote the success of the company, even though bystanders would treat that view as ridiculous.[76] Of course, one might argue, following *Menier v Hooper's Telegraph*, which we discussed earlier, that even in the absence of a breach of a director's duty that such a transaction is independently unlawful and therefore the unfair prejudice remedy is available as a remedy. However, as we saw in section II.2, the status of the principle in *Menier* is wholly undeveloped. If the common law does not regulate such a situation would the unfair prejudice remedy be able to step in?[77]

- Another example would be where excessive remuneration is paid to controlling shareholder-managers, diminishing the funds available for distribution to non-managerial shareholders but where the disinterested directors who made the remuneration decision actually believe that the manager's skills and efforts support such a remuneration policy.

- A third, and perhaps the best, example of corporate conduct that does not involve a breach of any right or duty yet affects the members' interests is not one that fits within the problem addressed in this chapter of controlling shareholder agency costs: this is the example of mismanagement and poor decision-making that does not involve a breach of the duty of care or of the duty to promote the success of the company. There is no question that incompetence damages the members' interests; but can conduct that is compliant with directors' duties but prejudicial to members' interests benefit from the unfair prejudice remedy?

It is submitted, somewhat speculatively, that the remedy would be made available in such *no breach of right or duty situations* where a transaction or dealing was clearly unfair to the minority shareholders whilst benefiting the controlling shareholder. In such situations the observations of Lord Hoffmann in *Saul Harrison* and *O'Neill v Phillips* would be treated as obiter. The remedy would not, however, extend to duty-compliant mismanagement. There are three reasons for this view. First, there is an important body of dicta stressing that the approaches of the courts to date have not closed off the ways in which the remedy could be used when faced with circumstances not previously considered. That is, the ways in which the courts have engaged the remedy to date do not provide an exhaustive and closed category of options. In this regard, Neill LJ in *Saul Harrison* observed that:

> It seems to me that it is already possible to collect from the cases decided under the 1948 Act and under the 1985 Act the following guidelines as to the correct approach to the concept of 'unfairly prejudicial' in s 459. The words 'unfairly prejudicial' are general words and they should

---

[76] Remember the duty to promote the success of the company is a subjective standard; so that if the director can show that he really believed it would promote the success of the company then he complies with that duty no matter how ridiculous his view. Of course, as we saw in Chapter 10, ridiculous decisions cast a shadow of doubt over whether the director truly believed it.

[77] To date where the courts have used the unfair prejudice remedy to consider self-dealing transactions there has typically also been a breach of a director's duty. For example, see *Rock Nominees Ltd v RCO (Holdings) Plc* [2003] 2 BCLC 493.

> be applied flexibly to meet the circumstances of the particular case. I have in mind the warning which Lord Wilberforce gave in *Ebrahimi v Westbourne Galleries Ltd* in relation to the words 'just and equitable': 'Illustrations may be used, but general words should remain general and not be reduced to the sum of particular instances.'

More recently in *Gamlestaden Fastigheter AB v Baltic Partners Ltd*[78] Lord Scott cited Arden J's dicta in *In re Macro Ipswich* favourably where she noted that 'the jurisdiction under s 459 has an elastic quality which enables the courts to mould the concepts of unfair prejudice according to the circumstances of the case'.[79]

Secondly, the courts, including Hoffmann LJ in *Saul Harrison*, have regularly referred to the fact that the Jenkins Committee viewed the unfair prejudice as 'a visible departure from the standards of fair dealing and a violation of the conditions of fair play on which every shareholder who entrusts his money to a company is entitled to rely'.[80] Non-arm's length related-party transactions and excessive remuneration would arguably be a 'visible departure from fair dealing'. Thirdly, cases specifically addressing the director remuneration issue have continued to address the issues through a general 'fairness of the compensation framework' rather than through a breach of duty or illegality framework,[81] a view that has continued to receive judicial support after *O'Neill v Phillips*.[82] For example, in *Re a company (No 004415 of 1996)* Scott VC held that:

> If the respondents are unable to justify by objective commercial criteria that the companies' dividend policy was a reasonable one and that the remuneration the P family directors were paid by the companies was within the bracket that executives carrying the sort of responsibility and discharging the sort of duties that they were carrying and discharging would expect to receive, the petitioners will, in my opinion, have succeeded in establishing their s 459 case.[83]

With regard to the availability of the unfair prejudice remedy for mismanagement, the issue was addressed in *Re Elgindata*,[84] where Warner J made the following observations.

> There is little authority on the extent to which negligent or incompetent management of a company's business may constitute conduct which is unfairly prejudicial to the interests of members for the purposes of s 459...
>
> I do not doubt that in an appropriate case it is open to the court to find that serious mismanagement of a company's business constitutes conduct that is unfairly prejudicial to the interests of minority shareholders. But...the court will normally be very reluctant to accept that managerial decisions can amount to unfairly prejudicial conduct.
>
> Two considerations seem to me to be relevant. First, there will be cases where there is disagreement between petitioners and respondents as to whether a particular managerial decision was, as a matter of commercial judgment, the right one to make, or as to whether a particular proposal relating to the conduct of the company's business is commercially sound...In my view, it is not for the court to resolve such disagreements on a petition under s 459. Not only is

---

[78] [2007] All ER (D) 222.   [79] [1994] 2 BCLC 354.

[80] This is how oppression pursuant to section 210 was viewed in *Elder v Elder* 1952 SC 49.

[81] This is not true of all dividend cases. See, for example, *Re McCarthy Surfacing Limited* [2009] 1 BCLC 622 where the failure to consider making a dividend was deemed to be in breach of duty and therefore unfairly prejudicial.

[82] See *Irvine v Irvine (No 1)* [2007] 1 BCLC 349 where Blackburne J refers to Scott VC's statement of the law with approval. See also, *Estill v Cowling Swift & Kitchin (a firm)* [2000] All ER (D) 69.

[83] [1997] 1 BCLC 479. Note in this regard that UK company law requires of business judgments that they are made in what the directors consider will promote the interests of the company. The law does not require reasonable decisions.

[84] [1991] BCLC 959.

> a judge ill-qualified to do so, but there can be no unfairness to the petitioners in those in control of the company's affairs taking a different view from theirs on such matters.
>
> Secondly…a shareholder acquires shares in a company knowing that their value will depend in some measure on the competence of the management. He takes the risk that management may prove not to be of the highest quality. *Short of a breach by a director of his duty of skill and care*…there is prima facie no unfairness to a shareholder in the quality of the management turning out to be poor. It occurred to me during the argument that one example of a case where the court might none the less find that there was unfair prejudice to minority shareholders would be one where the majority shareholders, for reasons of their own, persisted in retaining in charge of the management of the company's business a member of their family who was demonstrably incompetent. [Emphasis added]

For Warner J a breach of the duty of care is required to found an unfair prejudice petition based on managerial failings. Subsequent cases have, however, focused on the concept identified by Warner J of serious mismanagement rather than on breach of duty.[85] In *In re Macro Ipswich Ltd*,[86] for example, Arden J (as she then was) held that the respondent's activities amounted to sufficiently serious mismanagement to found a petition without determining whether the mismanagement in question amounted to a breach of duty. Whether, and to what extent, serious mismanagement differs from breach of duty of care or the duty to promote the success of the company is unclear from the cases. However, it is worth noting that in *In re Macro Ipswich* the multiple acts of mismanagement would appear to have supported a breach of duty of care claim. It is submitted, therefore, that the weight of authority supports the position that mismanagement and incompetence can support an unfair prejudice petition only when the acts of incompetence in question would support a finding that the directors breached their duty to promote the success of the company or their duty of care.[87]

Questions

1. What is a quasi-partnership? When does a company become a quasi-partnership?

2. In what ways does the just and equitable winding-up jurisdiction provide protection for minority shareholders? What are its limitations?

3. In what ways is the 'equitable considerations' category in relation to a 994 petition distinctive from the reliance upon equitable considerations to support the just and equitable winding-up of a company?

---

[85] Neill LJ in *Re Saul D Harrison & Sons plc* [1995] 1 BCLC 14 referring approvingly to *Re Elgindata* and observing that 'though it is open to the court to find that serious mismanagement of a company's business constitutes conduct that is unfairly prejudicial to the interests of the shareholders the court will normally be very reluctant to accept that managerial decisions can amount to unfairly prejudicial conduct'.

[86] [1994] 2 BCLC 354.

[87] Note, however, that courts do continue to refer to serious mismanagement as a basis for a 994 petition without presenting such mismanagement through the lens of breach of the duty of care. See *Oak Investment Partners XII, Limited Partnership v Boughtwood* [2009] 1 BCLC 453 *per* Phillip Sales J: 'it is agreed that mismanagement of the business affairs of a company could in principle amount to unfairly prejudicial conduct of those affairs for the purposes of s 994. In order to do so, however, the mismanagement must be serious, and the court will be astute not to "second guess' legitimate management decisions taken upon reasonable grounds at the time, albeit as events transpired they may not have been the best decisions in the interests of the company'. Note here that there is a suggestion that decisions that do not benefit from 'reasonable grounds' may be a basis for an unfair prejudice claim. Such a standard is clearly higher than the rationality standard effectively required by section 172 (in the absence of clear evidence of state of mind) and therefore would amount to a basis for unfair prejudice for behaviour that does not amount to breach of duty.

4. What are the criteria to determine when the equitable considerations category is available to a shareholder?

5. Why does Lord Hoffmann regret the use of the term 'legitimate expectations'?

6. In the absence of section 122(g) of the Insolvency Act 1986 or section 994 of the Companies Act 2006, do you think a modern court would take account of equitable considerations to address the circumstances in which informal promises were broken? How in your view would a modern court do this?

7. Outside of the equitable considerations category, in what circumstances can minority shareholders bring a section 994 petition to protect their interests?

V THE REMEDIES AVAILABLE THROUGH AN UNFAIR PREJUDICE PETITION

1 The available remedies

If the court accepts that the petitioner's interests as a member have been unfairly prejudiced by the conduct of the company's affairs, section 996 of the Act empowers the court to make any order it thinks fit.

■ Section 996 CA 2006 Powers of the court under this Part

(1) If the court is satisfied that a petition under this Part is well founded, it may make such order as it thinks fit for giving relief in respect of the matters complained of.

(2) Without prejudice to the generality of subsection (1), the court's order may—

    (a) regulate the conduct of the company's affairs in the future;

    (b) require the company—

        (i) to refrain from doing or continuing an act complained of, or

        (ii) to do an act that the petitioner has complained it has omitted to do;

    (c) authorize civil proceedings to be brought in the name and on behalf of the company by such person or persons and on such terms as the court may direct;

    (d) require the company not to make any, or any specified, alterations in its articles without the leave of the court;

    (e) provide for the purchase of the shares of any members of the company by other members or by the company itself and, in the case of a purchase by the company itself, the reduction of the company's capital accordingly.

Subsection (2) sets out a list of specific remedies available to the court. This is a non-exhaustive list that does not limit other types of remedy that the court can fashion if it thinks it is appropriate. The court may, therefore, if it thinks fit, order the payment of compensation to the petitioner.[88] However, the most common remedy is the buy-out

---

[88] Note that on current authority the reflective loss limitation on shareholders claiming damages in relation to the breach of a personal right does not apply to damages sought pursuant to section 994—*Atlasview v Brightview* [2004] All ER (D) 95 (Apr) where Jonathan Crow (Sitting as Deputy Court Judge) held that 'the "reflective loss argument" does not provide a bar to any of the relief sought in the Petition. The fact that the impugned conduct might give rise to a cause of action at the suit of the company does not mean that it is incapable also of giving rise to unfair prejudice: nor does it necessarily preclude the court from awarding financial compensation to the petitioners in satisfaction of their claim.' See the judgment of the Hong Kong Court of Final Apppeal in *Re Chime Corp Ltd* (2004) 7 HKCFAR 546 at [46]. On reflective loss see Chapter 15.

remedy referred to in subsection (2)(e). Where the controlling shareholder has acted in ways that a petitioner views as detrimental to its interests she may not simply want the court to stop such behaviour or compensate her for any injury she suffers, she would rather exit the company.

An important question for a court that accedes to a petitioner's request for a buy-out remedy is how her shareholding should be valued. In this regard the Court of Appeal in *Re Bird Precision Bellows Ltd*[89] held that the court has considerable discretion to determine the price to be paid and is not restricted in its valuation to the existing market valuation, to the extent that there is one, nor is it required to discount the price per share to take account of the fact that the petitioner's shareholding is a minority one, although it may do so if the court considers it fair to do so.[90] Oliver LJ held that:

> The whole framework of the section, and of such of the authorities as we have seen, which seem to me to support this, is to confer on the court a very wide discretion to do what is considered fair and equitable in all the circumstances of the case, in order to put right and cure for the future the unfair prejudice which the petitioner has suffered at the hands of the other shareholders of the company; and I find myself quite unable to accept that that discretion in some way stops short when it comes to the terms of the order for purchase in the manner in which the price is to be assessed...In my judgment the 'proper' price is the price which the court in its discretion determines to be proper having regard to all the circumstances of the case.

With regard to the valuation of the shares, a problem often arises as to what is the appropriate date on which to value the shares. If the actions that have been complained of have resulted in a significant diminution in value then the appropriate date would appear to be a date prior to the corporate conduct in question. However, if the unfairness has not only prejudiced the member's interests but subsequent events in the company itself or in the wider economy have resulted in a decrease or increase in the value of the shares, should the date of the valuation be the date on which the petition was filed or the date when the purchase order is made? These issues and the considerable body of case law surrounding them are not considered in depth here. They were considered by the Court of Appeal in *Profinance Trust SA v Gladstone*,[91] where Robert Walker LJ for the court summarized the position as follows:

> The starting point should in our view be the general proposition stated by Nourse J in *Re London School of Electronics* [1986] Ch 211, 224:
>
> > 'Prima facie an interest in a going concern ought to be valued at the date on which it is ordered to be purchased.'
>
> That is, as Nourse J said, subject to the overriding requirement that the valuation should be fair on the facts of the particular case.
>
> The general trend of authority over the last 15 years appears to us to support that as the starting point, while recognising that there are many cases in which fairness (to one side or the other)

---

[89] [1985] BCLC 493.

[90] See, for example, *Richards v Lundy* [2000] 1 BCLC 376 where the court elected for an intermediate discount between a pro rata valuation—which ignores the fact that the minority shareholder has no control—and a minority shareholding valuation—which discounts the pro rata valuation to take account of the absence of control—and held that there 'may be cases in which neither a pro rata valuation nor a minority shareholding valuation is fair, and I do not accept the submission that it would be "palm tree" justice to find a middle course'. In *re Elgindata* [1991] BCLC 959, Warner J held that in a quasi-partnership a pro rata valuation may be appropriate but that in other companies where the shareholding represents an investment only that there should be a discount to take account of the fact of the lack of control.

[91] [2001] EWCA Civ 1031.

requires the court to take another date. It would be wrong to try to enumerate all those cases but some of them can be illustrated by the authorities already referred to:

(i)   Where a company has been deprived of its business, an early valuation date (and compensating adjustments) may be required in fairness to the claimant (*Meyer*).[92]

(ii) Where a company has been reconstructed or its business has changed significantly, so that it has a new economic identity, an early valuation date may be required in fairness to one or both parties (*OC Transport*,[93] and to a lesser degree *London School of Electronics*). But an improper alteration in the issued share capital, unaccompanied by any change in the business, will not necessarily have that outcome (*DR Chemicals*).[94]

(iii) Where a minority shareholder has a petition on foot and there is a general fall in the market, the court may in fairness to the claimant have the shares valued at an early date, especially if it strongly disapproves of the majority shareholder's prejudicial conduct (*Cumana*).[95]

(iv) But a claimant is not entitled to what the deputy judge called a one-way bet, and the court will not direct an early valuation date simply to give the claimant the most advantageous exit from the company, especially where severe prejudice has not been made out (*Elgindata*).

(v)   All these points may be heavily influenced by the parties' conduct in making and accepting or rejecting offers either before or during the course of the proceedings (*O'Neill v Phillips*).

2 Encouraging out-of-court settlements: buy-out offers and unfair prejudice

Since the introduction of the unfair prejudice remedy in 1980 the courts have heard a considerable number of unfair prejudice petitions. These cases are often lengthy and fact-intensive. In *O'Neill v Phillips*, for example, the petition was filed in January 1992 and first instance judgment was not obtained until July 1995. As noted earlier, the outcome for a successful petition is often an order for the respondent to buy out the petitioner's shareholding. During the 1990s the judiciary came to the view that many of the cases that reached a full hearing could have been settled by the parties at an earlier date without the incurrence of legal fees and occupying court time.[96] In *O'Neill v Phillips* Lord Hoffmann responded to this concern by linking a pre-hearing fair offer to buy the petitioner's shares to the determination of whether the petitioner's member interests had been unfairly prejudiced.

■ *O'Neill v Phillips* [1999] 2 BCLC 1

Lord Hoffmann
I think that parties ought to be encouraged, where at all possible, to avoid the expense of money and spirit inevitably involved in such litigation by making an offer to purchase at an early stage…Unfairness does not lie in the exclusion alone but in exclusion without a reasonable offer. If the respondent to a petition has plainly made a reasonable offer, then the exclusion as such will not be unfairly prejudicial and he will be entitled to have the petition struck out. It is therefore very important that participants in such companies should be able to know what counts as a reasonable offer.

In the first place, the offer must be to purchase the shares at a fair value. This will ordinarily be a value representing an equivalent proportion of the total issued share capital, that is, without a

---

[92] *Scottish Co-operative Wholesale Society v Meyer* [1959] AC 324.
[93] *Re OC (Transport) Services* [1984] BCLC 251.
[94] *Re DR Chemicals* (1988) 5 BCC 39.   [95] *Re Cumana* [1986] BCLC 430.
[96] See *Re Unisoft Ltd (No 2)* [1994] BCC 766 where the judge noted that 994 petitions 'have become notorious to the judges of this court for their length, their unpredictability of management and for the enormous and appalling costs…'

discount for its being a minority holding. The Law Commission[97] has recommended a statutory presumption that in cases to which the presumption of unfairly prejudicial conduct applies, the fair value of the shares should be determined on a pro rata basis. This too reflects the existing practice. This is not to say that there may not be cases in which it will be fair to take a discounted value. But such cases will be based upon special circumstances and it will seldom be possible for the court to say that an offer to buy on a discounted basis is plainly reasonable, so that the petition should be struck out.

Secondly, the value, if not agreed, should be determined by a competent expert. The offer in this case to appoint an accountant agreed by the parties or in default nominated by the President of the Institute of Chartered Accountants satisfied this requirement. One would ordinarily expect the costs of the expert to be shared but he should have the power to decide that they should be borne in some different way.

Thirdly, the offer should be to have the value determined by the expert as an expert. I do not think that the offer should provide for the full machinery of arbitration or the half-way house of an expert who gives reasons. The objective should be economy and expedition, even if this carries the possibility of a rough edge for one side or the other...

Fourthly, the offer should, as in this case, provide for equality of arms between the parties. Both should have the same right of access to information about the company which bears upon the value of the shares and both should have the right to make submissions to the expert, though the form (written or oral) which these submissions may take should be left to the discretion of the expert himself.

Fifthly, there is the question of costs. In the present case, when the offer was made after nearly three years of litigation, it could not serve as an independent ground for dismissing the petition, on the assumption that it was otherwise well founded, without an offer of costs. But this does not mean that payment of costs need always be offered. If there is a breakdown in relations between the parties, the majority shareholder should be given a reasonable opportunity to make an offer (which may include time to explore the question of how to raise finance) before he becomes obliged to pay costs. As I have said, the unfairness does not usually consist merely in the fact of the breakdown but in failure to make a suitable offer. And the majority shareholder should have a reasonable time to make the offer before his conduct is treated as unfair. The mere fact that the petitioner has presented his petition before the offer does not mean that the respondent must offer to pay the costs if he was not given a reasonable time.

This approach represents a balanced way of guiding unhappy petitioners and respondents to reach a solution without incurring legal costs and occupying court time. It alters the bargaining position of both respondent and petitioner but does so fairly. As a result of this judicial guidance, a petitioner's ability to use the time and cost involved in an unfair prejudice remedy as a bargaining tool to extract a better offer is undermined. If they reject a fair buy-out offer from the respondent they may find themselves without a remedy, even if they would have been granted relief had no offer been made. Furthermore, if a petitioner moves too quickly to file a petition they will find that they have to pay their own legal costs if a fair offer is subsequently made within a reasonable timeframe. Whilst these guidelines benefit respondents, others do not. We see from these guidelines that a fair offer at this stage in the proceedings will typically involve a non-discounted pro-rata offer. Furthermore, once the reasonable time to make an offer has elapsed without making an offer, if the respondent subsequently makes an offer then, in order for the offer to dissolve the unfair prejudice, it must also include an offer in relation to the petitioner's legal costs.

It should be noted, however, that whilst courts have followed these guidelines some courts have stressed that they are not to be treated as if they were a statute and that

[97] Law Commission (paras 3.57–62).

the courts must be 'highly sensitive to the facts and circumstances of each case'.[98] One also needs to be aware that Lord Hoffmann's context in the extracted passage was the unfair prejudice suffered by a minority shareholder. Where there are two equal parties in a quasi-partnership company the courts need to be wary of the fact that unfair prejudice coupled with a 'reasonable offer' could be a means of wresting control from the innocent member.[99] As the High Court recently observed in *Harborne Road Nominees Ltd v Karvaski*: 'Lord Hoffmann's remarks were not intended to have the effect of establishing a mechanism for seizure and exclusion'. These concerns about 'seizure and exclusion', however, also resonate in the minority shareholder context. By linking the determination of unfair prejudice to a reasonable offer, there is a risk that section 994 can operate as a 'rogue's charter' in relation to minority shareholders where the 'reasonable offer' pressurizes the shareholder to sell out when he would prefer a remedy for the unfair prejudice which does not involve him exiting the company. For the same reason articulated in *Harborne Road*, where the petitioner does not seek a buy-out remedy then the determination of unfair prejudice should have nothing to do with the making of a reasonable offer.

3 Corporate remedies for breach of duty: the unfair prejudice remedy as a 'derivative action'

Section 994 provides the court with a discretion to grant any relief that it thinks fit. In most cases petitioners attempting to rely on the remedy are looking for a remedy that is personal to them: that allows them to exit the company or that compensates them individually for injury suffered. In many of the unfair prejudice cases that we have considered in this chapter the injury that has been suffered to the member is personal to him. This is the case, for example, where in a quasi-partnership his share of the profits was paid through his salary as manager and the controlling shareholder removes him as manager. However, other instances of unfair prejudice to a member's interests may involve not only unfair prejudice to the member but also a wrong to the company. This is the case, for example, where a director has breached his duties to the company. In such cases one available remedy would be to instruct the wrongdoing director to compensate the company for the injury suffered to the company and thereby, albeit indirectly, compensate the shareholder by increasing the value of the shares.

Such a remedy is clearly within the authority of the court pursuant to section 996. One counter-argument in this regard could be based on the fact that section 996(2) when setting forth specific examples of remedies available to the court refers in subsection (2)(c) to authorizing the bringing of proceedings in the company's name; that is, the court could, as a remedy for a successful unfair prejudice petition, authorize the bringing of a derivative claim to enforce the breach of duty. However, it is clear that subsection (2) provides a *non-exhaustive* list of remedies and does not prevent the court from fashioning other remedies that would address the unfair prejudice suffered to the member's interests. Corporate relief would clearly be an example of such a remedy.

Any such relief granted to the company as a result of a 994 petition in relation to a breach of a director's duty is, to be clear, relief granted by the court pursuant to sections 994 and 996. However, *the effect* of such relief is the *functional equivalent* of a successful derivative claim. As we saw in Chapter 15, pursuant to Part 11 of the Companies Act 2006, a derivative claim is a claim brought by a shareholder on behalf of the company to enforce duties owed by the director to the company. Importantly, we saw that whilst the rules in Part 11 appear to represent an easing—as compared to the common law rules—of the scope for shareholders to bring such actions, such actions

---

[98] *Harborne Road Nominees Ltd v Karvaski* [2011] EWHC 2214 (Ch) *per* Judge David Cooke.
[99] *Ibid.* See also *Re Neath Rugby Ltd* [2007] EWHC *per* Lewison J.

may only continue if the court grants permission to continue such claims. Generally speaking, the court will grant permission to continue the claim if satisfied that the litigation promotes the success of the company.[100] The objective of giving the courts this role in relation to derivative claims is to ensure that companies are not burdened with derivative litigation that it is not in the company's interests to pursue. However, whilst in theory a 994 petition can act as the *functional equivalent* of a derivative claim, its availability in relation to directors' duties and corporate relief is not subject to the court review safeguards to which derivative claims under Part 11 are subject.

An important question, therefore, is whether, given the regulation of derivative claims set out in Part 11 of the Act, section 994 is available where (1) the conduct of the company's affairs which is the basis for the petition is a breach of duty, *and* (2) where the relief that is sought pursuant to section 996 is corporate relief. In short, the pre-2006 Act answer is, perhaps somewhat surprisingly, yes. Although wholly consistent with the interpretation of section 459 of the 1985 Act, it was surprising as it presented courts and commentators with a paradox: on the one hand, courts had consistently reaffirmed the restrictions on bringing derivative actions under the rule in *Foss v Harbottle*, whilst, on the other hand, courts enabled the strict rule in *Foss* to be circumvented through a 994 petition. Initially, in response to this paradox, some courts suggested that whilst a 994 petition could be based on a breach of duty, the only relief that could be provided was personal not corporate relief. In *Re Charnley Davies Ltd (No 2)*, a case involving the unfair prejudice remedy against a liquidator which is set out in the Insolvency Act 1986,[101] the court observed that:

> 'the very same facts may well found either a derivative action or a section 459 petition. But that should not disguise the fact that the nature of the complaint and the appropriate relief is different in the two cases. Had the petitioners' true complaint been of the unlawfulness of the respondent's conduct, so that it would be met by an order for restitution, then a derivative action would have been appropriate and a section 459 petition would not.'

Subsequent cases, however, have not adopted this position; rather, they have accepted that the unfair prejudice remedy is available to obtain corporate relief for breach of duty. We are already familiar with cases in which the unfair prejudice remedy was used in this way. Most importantly, the Court of Appeal case of *Bhullar v Bhullar*[102] was an unfair prejudice petition based upon a breach of the common law duty that a director should not place his personal interests in a position where they possibly conflict with the interests of the company. In this case the court ordered that the respondents held the property they had acquired in breach of duty on trust for the company. The court in *Bhullar* did not, however, provide a reasoned analysis of the availability of corporate relief pursuant to a 994 petition; rather it just granted the relief. In *Clark v Cutland*,[103] also a 2003 Court of Appeal decision, the case commenced both as a derivative action and as an unfair prejudice petition claiming that a director was in breach of duty as a result of payments of unauthorized remuneration. The derivative action was subsequently consolidated into the unfair prejudice petition. The first instance judge granted corporate relief for the breach of duty and explicitly observed that the court could grant remedies pursuant to an unfair prejudice petition that it could have granted pursuant to a derivative action. The Court of Appeal affirmed.

The fact that courts have granted corporate relief in relation to 994 petitions does not, however, settle this debate. Whilst corporate relief was granted in both *Bhullar* and

---

[100] For a detailed analysis of the courts' determination to continue a derivative claim see Chapter 15.

[101] Set out in what was section 27 of the Insolvency Act 1986. This remedy, in amended form, is now found in Schedule B1 of the Insolvency Act 1986, para 74.

[102] [2003] EWCA Civ 424.

[103] [2003] 2 BCLC 393. See also *Anderson v Hogg* (2002) *The Times*, 22 January.

Cutland, the relationship between the 994 petition providing for corporate relief and the derivative action was not subject to reasoned consideration by the Court of Appeal in either case. Furthermore, as Professor Davies observes, both *Bhullar* and *Clark v Cutland* involved fact patterns that would have supported derivative actions under the *Foss* rules. Accordingly in these cases, the courts may have viewed it as a waste of time and money to require that the action be recommenced in a different—derivative—form.[104] The Hong Kong case of *Kung v Kou*, whilst not binding authority, is relevant in this regard as it takes a similar view. The case involved the application of the identical Hong Kong unfair prejudice remedy.

■ *Kung v Kou* [2004] HKCU 1453

In this extract for our purposes the Hong Kong statutory references have been replaced with the equivalent UK references.

Lord Scott of Foscote NPJ

Although...the court has jurisdiction, in the strict sense, to make the orders sought [pursuant to section 994] it would not, in my opinion, be proper for the court on this petition to entertain what would, in effect, [be an] action against the directors for their breach of duty in causing the loan to be made. If there is misconduct it can be established in a derivative action. If the court, on hearing the petition, thinks that a derivative action prosecuting this alleged misconduct should be brought, it can make an order to that effect under [section 996(2)(c)]. It could also, if persuaded it were a convenient course to adopt, order that the petition and the derivative action be tried together...

As a general rule, in my opinion, the court should not in a [994] petition make an order for payment to be made by a respondent director to the company unless the order corresponds with the order to which the company would have been entitled had the allegations in question been successfully prosecuted in an action by the company (or in a derivative action in the name of the company). In any other case, in my opinion, if the allegations against the director are proper to be relied on as evidence of unfairly prejudicial conduct, the appropriate relief to be sought would be an order under [section 996(2)(c)] for a derivative action to be brought for the recovery of the sum legally due. It would be proper for the company to express its views as to whether it would be in its interests for such an action to be brought.

The use of a [section 994] petition in order to circumvent the rule in *Foss v Harbottle* (1843) in a case where the nature of the complaint is misconduct rather than mismanagement is, in my opinion, an abuse of process...

The circumvention of the rule in *Foss v. Harbottle* by the inappropriate use of an unfair prejudice petition would be open to the same objections. In *Re Saul D Harrison & Sons plc*, Hoffmann LJ said that:

'Enabling the court in an *appropriate* case to outflank the rule in *Foss v. Harbottle* was one of the purposes of [section 994].' [Emphasis added by the court]

The outflanking would not, in my opinion, be appropriate unless the criterion were met.

Lord Scott's position is that unless the identical award would have been made pursuant to a derivative action legitimately brought then corporate relief would not be available pursuant to a 994 action. To allow otherwise would be an abuse of process.

---

[104] P. Davies, *Gower and Davies' Principles of Modern Company Law* (Sweet & Maxwell, 2008), 688. See also *Atlasview v Brightview* [2004] 2 BCLC 191 where Deputy Judge Crow argued that it would 'fly in the face of common sense' to decline unfair petition relief and require that a derivative action be brought instead.

This was the only way, in Lord Scott's view, of maintaining the integrity of the rule in *Foss v Harbottle*. In this author's view, however, whilst offering an attractive division of remedial authority for the derivative action and the 994 petition, prior to 2006 Act this view was inconsistent with the clear statutory authority to do otherwise. Whilst neither *Bhullar v Bhullar* nor *Clark v Cutland* provided a reasoned opinion as to the availability of corporate relief for breach of duty they were correctly decided regardless of whether or not the action could have been brought as a derivative claim pursuant to the rules in *Foss v Harbottle*.

Accordingly, for public and private companies alike, prior to the 2006 Act the unfair prejudice remedy could indeed function as the functional equivalent of a derivative suit. The fact that we saw so few cases in this regard, and no cases in relation to any widely-held company, is probably best explained by the fact that *Wallersteiner v Moir* orders[105] are not available for 994 petitions.[106] However, in this author's view there is a strong case that the situation has changed as a result of the 2006 Act. Before the 2006 Act the rules on derivative actions were common law rules in place at the time the unfair prejudice remedy was enacted in 1980. Now the 2006 Act contains in Part 11 statutory rules on the enforcement of directors' duties. Whilst the Act does not address the interrelationship between Part 11 of the Act and the 994 petition, there is a strong case that to bring a derivative action, whether pursuant to Part 11 or its functional equivalent through a 994 petition, requires a judicial determination, reached in accordance with section 263 of the Act, that the litigation can continue. In this regard, it is submitted that Part 11 pre-empts the general remedial discretion given to the courts by section 996(1). This means that a 994 petition which seeks corporate relief should only be allowed to continue if, had the claim been brought as a derivative claim, the court would grant permission to continue the claim. If this is correct, it is unlikely that we will see any 994 petitions seeking corporate relief for breach of duty as the remedy sought is the same under a derivative claim, but a *Wallersteiner v Moir* indemnification order would not be available as it may be for a derivative claim.

VI LISTED COMPANY-RELATED PARTY TRANSACTIONS

As we have seen, there are significant risks of controlling shareholder agency costs where the controlling shareholder or an entity controlled by the controlling shareholder enters into a transaction with the company—a 'related-party transaction'. The analysis of the potential pros and cons of these related-party transactions is similar to our analysis of the pros and cons of self-dealing transactions between directors and the company.[107] Whilst both self-dealing and related-party transactions may in theory be useful for and benefit the company, if the terms of the transaction are not market/arm's length terms then value is transferred from minority shareholders to majority shareholders.

As we saw in Chapter 13, directors of all companies are subject to a range of different regulation to address the problems generated by self-dealing transactions, including common law duties of loyalty, statutory disclosure, and shareholder approval obligations, as well as, for listed companies, disclosure and approval obligations pursuant to the listing rules. Related-party transactions are not, however, subject to the same range of regulation as are self-dealing transactions with directors. As we have seen, controlling shareholders

---

[105] See Chapter 15.

[106] Note, however, that costs may be awarded to a successful petitioner where corporate relief is granted (*Clark v Cutland* [2003] 2 BCLC 393); however, note that this means that the petitioner must bear the costs risk of losing which will be a substantial deterrent to bringing such an action: see further Chapter 15.

[107] Please see Chapter 13 section V for a more detailed consideration of these issues.

are not subject to fiduciary duties of loyalty that could police related-party transactions, although there is some very limited authority from *Menier v Hooper's Telegraph* to suggest that the common law would prevent the use of controlling shareholder influence over the company to channel value to controllers, and there is scope to argue that the unfair prejudice remedy may be available to police related-party transactions even in the absence of independent illegality. There is not, however, for either public or private companies any ex-ante disclosure obligation to the board or the shareholder body for related-party transactions with controlling shareholders, or any approval requirement. That is, there is no equivalent for controllers to the section 177 and 182 board disclosure obligations for self-dealing transactions nor any requirement to obtain shareholder approval for related-party transactions, as is required for self-dealing transactions pursuant to the substantial property transaction rules in sections 190–195 of the 2006.[108]

UK companies are, however, subject to additional regulation of related-party transactions in two respects. First, for all companies that are required to produce accounts in conformity with UK or international accounting rules, the accounting standards require that companies disclose in their annual accounts the existence and the terms of related-party transactions. This is ex-post disclosure. These accounting standards are set out in the IASB's *International Accounting Standard 24* and the Accounting Standards Board's *Financial Reporting Standard 8* which address related-party disclosures. Both standards require the same types of disclosure. This accounting standard was considered earlier in relation to director self-dealing, as directors who self-deal qualify as 'related parties' for the purposes of these disclosures. These accounting standards capture transactions between the company and controlling shareholders as their definition of a 'related-party' includes any person who controls or who exercises significant influence over the company. For a detailed discussion of the operation and effect of this ex-post financial statement disclosure please refer to Chapter 13 where we considered these issues in the context of self-dealing. The analysis and the issues raised in relation to self-dealing are directly applicable also to controlling shareholder related-party transactions.

The second aspect of the additional related-party regulation for UK companies is that UK companies with a premium listing[109] are required to comply with the related-party transaction rules set out in Listing Rule 11. Any 'substantial shareholder' qualifies as a 'related party' for the purpose of these listing rules.[110] A 'substantial shareholder' is defined by the Listing Rules as 'any person who is entitled to exercise or to control the exercise of 10% or more of the votes' to be cast in general meeting.[111] Again, as self-dealing directors qualify as 'related parties' for the purposes of the Listing Rules, we addressed the operation of this rule in depth when we considered the regulation of self-dealing transactions in Chapter 13. Please take a moment to re-read this section, as we will not repeat the level of detailed analysis of the Rule here. The Rule requires ex-ante (pre-transaction) disclosure and shareholder approval. Importantly, the disclosure requirements require in effect third-party verification of the fairness of the terms of the transaction[112] and the shareholders who must approve the transaction are the disinterested shareholders. That is, the controlling shareholders cannot vote their shares to approve a related-party transaction. One might respond that shareholders are apathetic and have poor incentives to pay attention; however, here the law facilitates minority shareholder involvement by providing them with disclosure and expert advice

---

[108] Note that section 182 does apply to shadow directors. See further Chapter 13 section IV.2.

[109] On the distinction between premium and standard listing see Chapter 6.

[110] LR 11.1.4(1).

[111] http://fsahandbook.info/FSA/glossary-html/handbook/Glossary/S?definition=G1839 ⊘.

[112] This is because the circular to shareholders in relation to the approval must state that the transaction is fair and reasonable and that they have been so advised by an independent advisor (see LR 13.3 and LR 13.6). See further Chapter 13.

on the related-party transactions and by enhancing their power by excluding the voting power of controlling shareholders. Accordingly, the costs of acting for the disinterested shareholders is low and the benefits—stopping non-market transactions—are tangible.

This provision is widely viewed as a very important deterrent to non-market related-party transactions and an important disincentive for any investor to become a controlling shareholder just because he believes that he can use his power as a controller to benefit himself. With regard to how the effectiveness of this provision is dependent on how it interacts with reputation concerns of the board please review the analysis of self-dealing transactions in Chapter 13.

VII MINORITY SHAREHOLDER PROTECTION BEYOND THIS CHAPTER

This chapter has focused on minority shareholder protection mechanisms: ways in which English company law responds to possible abuse of power and influence by controlling shareholders to benefit themselves. It is important, however, that you do not read this chapter and think that it has dealt with all aspects of UK company law that operate to limit the abuse of power by controlling shareholders. Many of the rules we have already considered in the earlier chapters of the book offer forms of minority shareholder protection, for example: the ability to bring a derivative claim where the abuse of controlling shareholder power results in a breach of a director's duty; or the ability of 5% of the shareholder body to requisition a shareholder meeting to provide an opportunity to publicly challenge the controlling shareholder and the company's supine board. Other areas of regulation which we will consider in subsequent chapters offer protection from specific types of behaviour that can expropriate value from minority shareholders. These include, in particular:

- rules requiring that new shares be offered to existing shareholders in proportion to their existing holdings to prevent further dilution of control or the issuing of shares to controllers for less than they are worth (see Chapter 17);
- rules providing a degree of protection for shareholders from changes in the rights attached to their shares (class rights: see Chapter 17).

These transactions and the rules regulating them could clearly fall into the category of minority shareholder protection and must be considered when we think broadly about how the UK protects minority shareholders.[113] However, for a book of this nature it is more appropriate and user-friendly to deal with these issues in other sections of the book.

 Online Resource Centre
http://www.oxfordtextbooks.co.uk/orc/kershaw2e/

Visit the Online Resource Centre for additional resources and information available for this chapter, including web links and an interactive flashcard glossary.

---

[113] Other areas of corporate regulation are also relevant to protecting minority shareholders. Most importantly in this regard is the mandatory bid rule set forth in Rule 9 of the UK Takeover Code. In the first edition of this book these takeover regulation issues were addressed in what was then Web Chapter A. This edition does not include this Web Chapter as this material will be addressed in a separate book—D. Kershaw, *Principles of Takeover Regulation* (OUP, forthcoming 2013).

PART III
CORPORATE FINANCE

CHAPTER SEVENTEEN

SHARES

I INTRODUCTION

1 Shares as financial contractual claims

Shares are financial instruments that provide their holders with a financial claim on the company. As we have seen shares do not give their holders any property right in the assets of the business—which are owned by the company.[1] We have labelled this financial claim a **residual interest claim**; it is *in effect* a claim to the value remaining if the company was wound up, the assets of the company were sold, and all other claims on the company were discharged. It is, necessarily, a claim that stands last in line behind all other claimants following the company's liquidation and it is a *variable* claim that varies from one day to the next as the business generates profits or losses. Of course, shareholders, particularly in larger companies, do not have to wait for the company to be wound up to receive a financial return from their shareholding. Companies generating profit or surplus will be entitled to issue a dividend provided that such dividends comply with the Companies Act 2006's rules on the issuing of dividends, which we address in Chapter 19. One might ask how can a residual claimant receive such a payment prior to liquidation; prior to the actual discharge of the company's liabilities? In this regard a dividend should be viewed as an interim or advance payment on the residual claim made out of a surplus that the company has generated which exceeds the claims other parties have on the company.

In contrast to the shareholders' residual interest right, debt or loan capital provides those who purchase a debt claim (by lending money to the company) with a right to receive contractually specified fixed payments at specific points in time: payments of principal—repayments of the amount lent to the company—and interest—payment of a specified percentage return on the amount lent to the company. As we have seen, whilst all debtholders are in front of shareholders in the liquidation repayment queue, different debtholders may occupy different positions in the repayment queue. A secured debtholder has a right to be repaid from all the proceeds of the sale of the secured asset. In addition, a debtholder may contractually agree to subordinate his claim below other debtholders—that is, not to be repaid until other debtholders have been repaid in full. Agreeing to such repayment subordination increases the debtholder's risk and one would expect such a debtholder to be paid a higher interest rate to reflect this increased risk. Indeed companies often have layers of debt that occupy different positions on this repayment hierarchy. A company could have senior debt A which ranks above senior debt B in the repayment hierarchy, which in turn ranks above subordinated debt A. There is no limit to the number of positions in this repayment hierarchy that contract can create.

Whilst debt may occupy different—contractually determined—positions in the liquidation repayment queue the understanding of 'the share' as a residual interest claim places shareholders clearly at the end of this queue. However, whilst it is correct that

---

[1] *Macaura v Northern Assurance Company* [1925] AC 619.

all companies will issue shares that provide the holders of those shares with a variable residual financial claim, the term 'share' is also used for financial claims that are *not* variable residual interest claims. If a share provides for a residual interest claim it is in UK company law parlance an **ordinary share**.[2] Thus far in this book when we have referred to shares we have been referring to *ordinary shares*. However, the term 'shares' is also used in relation to the sale of financial claims that sit—in the repayment queue—directly in front of the residual claims of the ordinary shareholders. These shares are generally known as **preference shares**, although each company may label such shares as it chooses.

There is no fixed content of a preference share; no fixed set of rights that a preference share must provide in order to qualify for the label 'preference share'. However, typically such shares are preferential to ordinary shares in two respects. First, *if there are profits available to be distributed*[3] *and the company declares a dividend*, holders of preference shares are entitled to be paid a fixed annual dividend before any dividend is paid to the ordinary shareholders. Such a fixed sum will normally be expressed as a certain percentage of the nominal value of the preference share. Such a preference is often cumulative, meaning that if a company has failed to pay the preference share dividend in years one and two it can only pay a dividend to ordinary shareholders in year three once the preference shareholders have received the specified dividend for years one, two, and three. Secondly, preference shareholders have a liquidation preference over ordinary shareholders which will on liquidation *typically* involve the payment of an amount of the **nominal value** of each share prior to any payment to the ordinary shareholders. Large companies often have several tiers of preference shares which rank in different positions on the liquidation and dividend payment hierarchy. Vodafone Plc, for example, has cumulative preferred shares that have liquidation and dividend preferences that rank above Vodafone's ordinary shares. Vodafone labels these shares 'fixed rate shares'. In this regard consider the rights attached to Vodafone's fixed rate shares.

▪ Vodafone Group Plc's Articles of Associations[4]

4 Right of Fixed Rate Shares to profits

4.1 If the Company has profits which are available for distribution and the directors resolve that these should be distributed, the holders of the Fixed Rate Shares are entitled, before the sholders of any other class of shares, to be paid in respect of each financial year or other accounting period of the Company a fixed *cumulative*[5] preferential dividend ('preferential dividend') at the rate of 7 per cent. per annum on the *nominal value* of the Fixed Rate Shares which is paid up or treated as paid up…

5 Right of Fixed Rate Shares to capital

5.1 If the Company is *wound up* (but in no other circumstances involving a repayment of capital or distribution of *assets* to shareholders whether by reduction of capital, *redeeming* or buying

---

[2] Ordinary shares are defined for the purposes of chapter 3 of Part 17 of the Act, dealing with the authority to allot shares and pre-emption rights, discussed later, as: 'shares other than shares that as respects dividends and capital carry a right to participate only up to a specified amount in a distribution' (section 560(2) CA 2006).

[3] On profits available for distribution see Chapter 19.

[4] See Vodafone Plc's articles of association at www.vodafone.com/content/index/investors/management/governance/articles_of_association.html ●.

[5] 'Cumulative' is defined in Vodafone's articles as: 'if a dividend which is cumulative cannot be paid in one year because the company does not have enough profits to cover the payment, the shareholder has the right to receive the dividend in a future year, when the company has enough profits to pay the dividend.'

back shares or otherwise), the holders of the Fixed Rate Shares will be entitled, before the holders of any other class of shares to:

- repayment of the amount paid up or treated as paid up on the *nominal value* of each Fixed Rate Share;

- the amount of any dividend which is due for payment on, or after, the date the *winding up* commenced which is payable for a period ending on or before that date. This applies even if the dividend has not been *declared* or earned;

- any *dividend arrears*[6] on any Fixed Rate Shares held by them. This applies even if the dividend has not been *declared* or earned; and

- a proportion of any dividend in respect of the financial year or other accounting period which began before the *winding up* commenced but ends after that date. The proportion will be the amount of the dividend that would otherwise have been payable for the period which ends on that date. This applies even if the dividend has not been *declared* or earned.

5.2 If there is a *winding up* to which Article 5.1 applies, and there is not enough to pay the amounts due on the Fixed Rate Shares, the holders of the Fixed Rate Shares will share what is available in proportion to the amounts to which they would otherwise be entitled…[Emphasis in the original].

The difference between the attributes of a preference share and debt claims, particularly debt that has agreed to be subordinated to other debt, is somewhat blurred. A preference share has a right to a specific percentage return, when a dividend is declared, which looks like a rate of interest; a preference share has a claim to a fixed payment on liquidation just as a debtholder who has not been paid would have a fixed claim on liquidation. We see from Vodafone's Fixed Rate Shares above that such a liquidation entitlement includes the nominal value of the preference share and any unpaid cumulative dividends. One could readily recharacterize these rights granted by these shares as a debt claim with a rate of interest of 7% interest with the right, at the company's option, to capitalize—that is, add to the principal amount of the loan—the interest payment. One important difference as compared to a debt claim, however, is that there is no specified repayment date for the principal prior to liquidation. Preferential claims typically provide for a fixed financial claim but one that can be deferred ad infinitum[7] provided the company does not enter liquidation.

This comparison of preference shares, ordinary shares and debt claims allows us to see that equity and debt are labels for different types of financial contracts and within each category of equity and debt different financial claims may be provided to different types of shares and debt. Shares, therefore, are a set of rights which are purchased by an investor. Each share that is issued with a specific set of rights that differ from the rights attached to other shares is known as a *class* of share.[8] These specific rights attached to each class of share will typically be set out in a company's constitution. The important point to note here is that the scope of rights conferred by a share is a function of the terms of the contract setting out those rights and *not* a function of any inherent rights associated with the ownership of 'a share', whether preferred or ordinary. Accordingly, to determine the rights granted to the shareholder one has to interpret this contract. In the example of Vodafone's Fixed Rate Shares above, one has

---

[6] Dividend arrears are defined in Vodafone's articles as: 'any *dividend arrears*. This includes any dividends on shares with *cumulative* rights which could not be paid, but which have been carried forward.'

[7] Provided they are not redeemable preference shares subject to specified redemption date. In this regard, see section IV.3.3 of this chapter.

[8] On class rights see section III of this chapter.

to interpret articles 4 and 5 of Vodafone's constitution. This contractual view has a long-standing pedigree in English law. Consider the following extracts in this regard:

■ *Borland's Trustee v Steel Brothers & Co. Limited* [1901] 1 Ch 279

Farewell J

A share is the interest of a shareholder in the company measured by a sum of money, for the purpose of liability in the first place, and of interest in the second, but also consisting of a series of mutual covenants entered into by all the shareholders inter se in accordance with s. 16 of the Companies Act, 1862.[9] The contract contained in the articles of association is one of the original incidents of the share. A share is not a sum of money settled in the way suggested, but is an interest measured by a sum of money and made up of various rights contained in the contract, including the right to a sum of money of a more or less amount.

■ *Scottish Insurance Corporation Limited v Wilsons & Clyde Coal Company Limited* [1949] AC 462

Lord Simonds

It is clear from the authorities, and would be clear without them, that, subject to any relevant provision of the general law, the rights inter se of preference and ordinary shareholders must depend on the terms of the instrument which contains the bargain that they have made with the company and each other. This means, that there is a question of construction to be determined and undesirable though it may be that fine distinctions should be drawn in commercial documents such as articles of association of a company, your Lordships cannot decide that the articles here under review have a particular meaning, because to somewhat similar articles in [prior cases] that meaning has been judicially attributed.[10]

2 Shares and control rights

Thus far in our analysis of the share we have focused on the nature of the financial claim provided by the ordinary or preferred share—does the share provide a residual interest financial claim or does it rank above a residual claim? As has been clear throughout this book, shares *typically* provide not only for a financial claim but also for control rights—the right to vote in specified circumstances. However, just as the nature of a financial claim provided by a share is a function not of any inherent attributes of 'the share' but rather a function of which rights the company decides to attach to a share—the rights purchased by the investor—so too are the control rights granted to shareholders a function of the control rights a company wishes to attach to the shares—the control rights it wishes to sell. No share, whether ordinary or preferred, necessarily has

---

[9] Now section 33 CA 2006.

[10] Cf *Birch v Cropper* (1889) 14 App Cas 525 in relation to which Lord Simonds in *Scottish Insurance* observed: 'Finally on this part of the case I ought to deal with an observation made by Lord Macnaghten in *Birch v. Cropper* upon which counsel for the appellants relied. "They," he said, "[the preference shareholders] must be treated as having all the rights of shareholders, except so far as they renounced these rights on their admission to the company." But, in my opinion, Lord Macnaghten can have meant nothing more than that the rights of the parties depended on the bargain that they had made and that the terms of the bargain must be ascertained by a consideration of the articles of association and any other relevant document, a task which I have endeavoured in this case to discharge'. See further: *In re William Metcalfe & Sons Ld* [1933] Ch 142; *Will v United Lankat Plantations Co Ld* [1914] AC 11; *Re Saltdean Estate Co Ltd* [1968] 1 WLR 1844.

to be provided with a right to vote on any issue or a specific issue; different shares can be granted different control rights. Whilst most companies will have ordinary shares with a single vote for each share held, it is not uncommon for companies to issue ordinary shares without voting rights. It is also possible, although not particularly common in UK companies,[11] to grant specific shares more than one vote per share. This is possible generally, for example, by giving such shareholders five votes or 100 votes per share or in relation to specific issues, for example removing a director[12] or entering into a new line of business.

Similarly, the company has a free hand to determine which, if any, control rights are attached to preference shares. It could grant such shares no voting rights, one vote per share, multiple voting rights, or contingent voting rights. Typically preference shares have contingent voting rights that provide that each preference share has no vote unless the preference dividend is not paid, at which point in time each share has one vote per share.

The Companies Act 2006 has nothing to say about the nature of control rights attached to shares although it does regularly refer to 'voting rights' in the company, for example in relation to the definition of an ordinary[13] or special resolution or the criteria for a shareholder requisitioned general meeting.[14] UK company law leaves the determination of the control rights to be attached to shares to contract: what the company wishes to sell and what an investor is willing to purchase. This contrasts with several European jurisdictions that explicitly prohibit certain types of voting arrangements, such as multiple voting shares.[15]

Whilst not all shares provide for voting rights, all companies have a class of shares that do have voting rights. An important question in understanding shares is: why are control rights provided to the holders of shares rather than the holders of debt or any other constituency, such as employees? The answers to and the arguments surrounding this question closely map the debate on the 'company's interests' which we analysed in depth in section II of Chapter 10. Arguably, however, the answer to the question posed here is of greater importance than the question of in whose interests the company should be run. Even if directors are given the legal freedom to make decisions in the interests of multiple constituencies and not only shareholder interests, the likelihood is that they will exercise their power and their discretion in the interests of those who appoint them. The arguments and extracts set out in Chapter 10 should be revisited in thinking about this question. In this regard note the following summary observations:

- The concept of ownership is unhelpful when thinking about why shareholders alone should be granted control rights. Ownership can be broken down into its constituent element rights of residual interest rights and control rights. To say

---

[11] For an empirical survey of multiple voting share and non-voting shares in the UK see Shearman & Sterling, *Report on the Proportionality Principle in the European Union* (http://ec.europa.eu/internal_market/ 😊), 77.

[12] As we saw in Chapter 6 in our consideration of section 168 and the House of Lords' decision in *Bushel v Faith* [1970] AC 1099, it is possible to give a shareholder extra votes in relation to a proposed resolution to remove him as a director.

[13] Section 282 CA 2006.

[14] Sections 303–305 CA 2006.

[15] Germany, for example, does not allow multiple voting but does allow preference shares without voting rights (sections 134, 139 German Stock Corporation Act). The European Commission recently facilitated a review process to consider whether the European Union should mandate one share one vote. The concern was that as multiple voting rights result in disproportionality between economic interests and control rights they can be used to extract controlling shareholder agency costs (on such costs see Chapter 16). The review concluded that the evidence as to whether or not multiple voting rights had a positive or detrimental impact was inconclusive. See http://ec.europa.eu/internal_market/😊.

that shareholders should have control rights because they are owners is, therefore, circular. We need to explain why they alone should have control rights.

- A strong economic argument, from society's macro-economic perspective, is that control should be given to the residual interest holder because that person has the incentives to take steps to maximize his residual interest, which maximizes the value of the company and maximizes social wealth as a whole. Consider, further, the discussion of this point at pp 373–75.

- Contractarians such as Easterbrook and Fishel argue that there is no a priori reason why shareholders as opposed to other corporate constituencies should have control rights. The reason that they typically have such rights is because they are willing to pay more for such rights than other constituencies—the amount they are willing to pay for those control rights benefits the company more, in most instances, than other constituencies would pay for them by, for example, debtholders reducing their interest rate, or employees reducing their salary demands. The reason why equity is willing to pay more than these other constituencies is that residual interest holders—who have a variable interest depending on the performance of the company—are particularly exposed to opportunistic behaviour by managers, acting in their own or others' interests, which reduces the size of the variable residual interest. Furthermore, there is, it is argued, no other contractual mechanism to protect a residual interest holder, whereas other constituencies have other protections or safeguards available to them. Debtholders, for example, are protected by their ranking in the liquidation repayment hierarchy. Consider further the discussion of this argument at pp 362–65.

- Arguably the above arguments are weaker in relation to large, widely-held companies whose shareholders are, as we have seen, often rationally apathetic and fail to exercise these control rights. Justifications based upon why shareholders are the appropriate constituency to exercise control rights or why they will pay more for those control rights are suspect if, in practice, shareholders fail to exercise those rights. An important response to these concerns is that even where shareholders are rationally apathetic, granting shareholders control rights creates a structure of control and a hierarchy of constituency interests that protects shareholder interests even where shareholders rarely formally exercise control. For a further development of this argument see the extract at page 361. Whether, in order to create such structures of control and interest hierarchies, it is necessary to grant exclusive control rights to shareholders has, however, been questioned by some commentators.[16]

- An important consideration in thinking about the justifications for giving control rights exclusively to shareholders is the fact that in many jurisdictions qualified control rights are given to employees as well as shareholders. For example in Austria, such rights are given to employees to appoint a third of the supervisory board members,[17] and in Germany, employees of large companies have the right to appoint half the members of the supervisory board.[18] The sharing of appointment rights between shareholders and employees is referred to as *co-determination*. As we have seen in Chapter 6 the supervisory board of German companies is not as powerful a governance body as the board of directors of a UK company.

---

[16] D. Kershaw, 'No End in Sight for the History of Corporate Law: The Case of Employee Participation in Corporate Governance' (2002) *Journal of Corporate Law Studies* 34.

[17] Paragraph 110 Austrian Work Constitution Law (*Arbeitsverfassungsgesetz*).

[18] Paragraph 7(2) German Co-determination Act (*Mitbestimmungsgesetz*). For a discussion of the efficiency attributes of co-determination see H. Hansmann, *The Ownership Of Enterprise* (Harvard University Press, 1996) and Kershaw, note 16.

Nevertheless, the supervisory board is responsible for the appointment and removal of the company's management board. Opponents of co-determination view it as the inefficient product of a post-World War II social democratic political settlement; a governance arrangement that does not maximize the value of the company.[19] Importantly, the continuing presence of co-determination in very successful German companies raises at least a significant element of doubt as to the correctness of the claim that granting control rights to shareholders alone is necessarily the most beneficial governance arrangement for corporations. Co-determination generates an element of doubt that should drive scholars of company law to be demanding of the persuasiveness of the rationales for sole shareholder control.

3 Choice of finance: equity versus debt; ordinary shares versus preferred shares

Companies, such as our case study company, need to finance the expansion of their business. As Bob's Electronics Ltd expands its operations it will need to build new assembly lines; expand its fleet of vehicles; or more fundamentally expand its product range by entering into other related businesses. It may be able to fund some of this expansion through the income generated by the successful operation of the business. However, to the extent that its income is insufficient to fund these investments, the company will have to source additional finance externally. In Chapter 1 we considered this problem in our *introduction to risk and return* from the viewpoint of a sole trader considering how to expand a nascent business. The same considerations as apply to a sole trader in deciding what types of financial instruments to use to raise finance apply to a larger company. From a shareholder's perspective using debt rather than a new issue of shares means that the shareholder's control of the company and their residual interest claim is not diluted. However, the downside of using debt is that it increases the risk of a company's bankruptcy, as debt is a fixed claim requiring repayments of principal and interest on the dates specified in the debt contract. Companies that have concerns about their ability to meet projected income at any point in the period during which the debt must be repaid may be advised to issue shares.

Preferred shares may, however, offer a middle ground in regard to these competing concerns of control dilution and bankruptcy risk. As noted, preferred shares do not typically have full voting rights. The preferred shares' voting rights typically come into effect if the company fails to pay the preferred dividend. This allows companies to raise equity finance—which has the distinct advantage over debt that it does not have to be repaid if the company fails to generate sufficient cash—but at the same time the controllers of the company do not have to relinquish or share control over the company with the preferred equity investors so long as the preferred dividend is paid.

In practice, the determination of whether it is preferable to raise external finance through debt or equity and through ordinary or preferred shares is a complex consideration involving, in addition to considerations of control dilution and the risk of bankruptcy, considerations such as the tax treatment of debt and equity;[20] the accounting implication of debt and equity;[21] and, importantly, the efficiency of the debt and equity markets—whether these markets are efficiently pricing debt and equity, which as recent

---

[19] See generally, M. Roe, 'Political Preconditions to Separating Ownership from Control' (2002) 53 *Stanford Law Journal* 539.

[20] R. Gilson and D.M. Schizer, 'Understanding Venture Capital Structure: A Tax Explanation for Convertible Preferred Stock' (February 2002), Columbia Law and Economics Working Paper No 199; available at SSRN: http://papers.ssrn.com/ 🌐.

[21] P. Pope and A. Puxty, 'What is Equity?' (1991) 54 *Modern Law Review* 889.

events demonstrate they often do not. If debt is cheap because the market place is not effectively pricing the risk of debt then at that point in time debt may be particularly attractive to a company; similarly if in management's view the equity markets are over-valuing the shares then it makes sense to raise finance by issuing more shares.[22]

II ISSUING SHARES

1 Who should make the decision to issue shares?

In Chapter 6 we considered the balance of power between the shareholder body and the board of directors. We saw that in UK company law whilst the board was typically empowered by the articles to exercise all the powers of the company, certain decisions were retained by the articles, or by mandatory company law rules, for the shareholders. We asked what the criteria were which determined when it was appropriate to give shareholders a veto or approval right in relation to a corporate decision. The factors which we considered to be particularly important to the granting of a shareholder decision-making role were: first, whether the decision in question could result in the incurrence of significant managerial agency costs; secondly, whether the value of the transaction was very large compared to the value of the company; and, thirdly, whether the transaction affected the shareholders directly as shareholders, as contrasted to a business decision that would have indirect value implications for the shareholders. The first question for us in this section, therefore, is whether the corporate decision to issue shares and to attach specific rights to those shares is a decision that, on the basis of these factors, should be subject to shareholder approval.

Decisions, for example, to expand the business or to make an investment for which new financing is required are clearly business decisions that are within the purview of the board of directors and senior management. The determination of the appropriate form of the required finance—whether debt or equity; and the type of debt or equity—is also fundamentally a business decision. Senior management should identify the cheapest and most suitable way of raising the required finance. From this perspective the decision to raise finance by issuing shares is a business decision that should be made by senior management and the board of directors. However, whilst the decision to issue shares is clearly a business decision, it is also a decision that directly affects the shareholders' interests *as shareholders*. It does so in two respects. First, the issue of shares risks diluting the existing shareholders' residual claim. The newly issued shares, therefore, must either be issued to the existing shareholders in proportion to their existing shares (known as a pre-emptive issue), or, if issued to a third party, the shares must be issued for an amount equal to at least the value of the existing shares, otherwise part of the existing shareholders' financial claim is expropriated and transferred to the new shareholder. To see this consider the following worked examples.

Hypothetical A

Bob's Electronics Ltd has five shareholders, Bob, Alison, Ian, Suzanne, and Helen. Bob is the CEO of the company and Bob and Alison are the only directors of the company.

---

[22] In an efficient marketplace and ignoring taxation and accountancy considerations a companies leverage—its debt compared to its equity—does not affect the value of the company. See M. Miller and F. Modigliani, 'The Cost of Capital, Corporation Finance and the Theory of Investment' (1958) 48 *American Economic Review* 261.

Each shareholder holds 10 shares (50 shares outstanding). The company needs to raise a substantial amount of finance to fund an ambitious expansion programme. One option proposed by Bob would be to issue an additional 50 shares. How much should those shares be issued for?

If those 50 shares are to be issued to Fabian then how much the new shares are issued for is of considerable importance to the existing shareholders. If the company is worth £10 million then each of the shares is worth £200,000. In order for the shares still to be worth £200,000 after the issue of new shares Fabian will need to pay £200,000 a share. After the shares are issued the company has issued 100 shares and has assets of £20 million: a business worth £10 million and £10 million of cash.

However, if, because Bob and Fabian are golf buddies and Fabian agrees to vote his shares with Bob, the shares are sold to Fabian for £150,000 a share, then after the share issue the company's shares are worth £175,000 (£10 million business plus £7.5 million for the new shares divided by 100). At this price the share issue has diluted the value of the existing shareholders' financial claims and transferred £2,500,000 value into Fabian's pocket.

If, on the other hand, instead of issuing the new shares to a third party such as Fabian, each of the existing shareholders will take an additional 10 shares then the question of how much the new shares should be issued for does not raise concerns for shareholders. If they purchase the shares for £150,000 the £2,500,000 of value transferred from the old to the new shareholders is transferred to themselves.

The second way in which a share issue affects shareholders as shareholders is if it diminishes the existing shareholders' control rights. If, in the *hypothetical*, all shares are voting shares and the new shares are issued to Fabian, then there is significant shift in control from a situation in which each shareholder exercised 20% of the voting rights to a control arrangement in which one new shareholder controls 50% of the voting rights. This problem would be exacerbated if the board was entitled to issue new shares with greater voting rights than the existing shares. Even if such an issue of shares represents an excellent deal for the company, and therefore the shareholders, in financial terms it may in the existing shareholders' view be detrimental to their interests because of their loss of control over the company. Of course, if the new shares are issued to the existing shareholders in proportion to their existing holdings then no change in control takes place; although each shareholder owns more shares after the new issue each shareholder still has 20% of the voting rights.

Accordingly, as the decision to issue shares affects the shareholders *as shareholders*, any issue of shares and the determination of the rights attached to shares qualifies as a decision type in relation to which a shareholder approval right may be appropriate. However, giving shareholders a role in the specific decision to issue shares is not unproblematic. Managers of companies may need to move quickly to raise finance from the investors that are willing to pay the best price for the company's shares. Any delay could in some instances result in the loss of the business opportunity which the new issue of shares is intended to finance. Indeed, a counterparty with several interested buyers may not be willing to wait for a buyer that needs to obtain shareholder approval to issue shares in order to raise finance to buy the asset. To the extent that either the requirement to obtain shareholder approval, or the rules that determine how shareholders grant or refuse approval, inhibits the raising of equity finance or the speed of the financing process, the company may be damaged.

2 The regulation of share issues in UK company law

2.1 Basic concepts and vocabulary

Since its inception company law has made a distinction between a company's share capital and the shares that the company has actually issued. Prior to the 2006 Act, a company was required to state its share capital in its memorandum of association, which was at the time one of the company's constitutional documents.[23] To make it clearer what was intended by this term 'share capital' commentators typically referred to it as the company's 'authorized share capital'. The company's 'authorized share capital' did not represent the number of shares that had been issued or the amount that had been paid for the company's shares, rather it determined the number of shares the company could issue. It did so by specifying an amount that was the company's 'share capital' and dividing that amount by shares given a nominal or a par value. So, for example, on its formation Marks and Spencer Group Plc had a share capital of 100 shares of £1 each. That is the company was empowered to issue 100 shares with a nominal value of £1 each. The nominal value of a share is a *nominal* amount. It bears no relationship to the value of the share, which may be sold to an investor for more than, but not less than,[24] this nominal value. The difference between the nominal value of the share and the amount paid for the share is referred to by the Act as the share premium.[25] Effectively Marks and Spencer Group Plc's authorized share capital of 100 £1 shares means that the company *is able to* issue 100 shares. It *does not* mean that it has done so. It *does not* mean that a shareholder has paid £100 for a share; or that the company has £100 of cash following the sale of any shares. Prior to 2006 a company's 'share capital' or its 'authorized share capital' represented a reservoir of created shares that could then be issued. This reservoir was created upon incorporation and could be increased by shareholder action; however, if all the company's authorized share capital had been issued the company was incapable of issuing more shares without increasing the company's authorized share capital by an ordinary resolution.[26]

The Companies Act 2006 no longer requires that a company's share capital be stated in its constitution. That is, the Companies Act 2006 abolishes the requirement for a company to have an authorized share capital. After the 2006 Act a company's power to issue shares is dependent solely on the constitution's authorization for the company to issue shares. Hence the Model Articles for public and private companies both provide:[27]

> Subject to the articles, but without prejudice to the rights attached to any existing share, the company may issue shares[28] with such rights or restrictions as may be determined by ordinary resolution.

Accordingly section 545 of the 2006 Act now provides that 'references in the Companies Acts to a company having a share capital are to a company that has power under its constitution to issue shares'. Of course existing companies may maintain the limitations provided by the authorized share capital concept and new companies could include such a requirement in their constitution if they chose to do so.

---

[23] Section 2(5)(a) CA 1985.

[24] Section 580 CA 2006. *Ooregum Gold Mining Co of India v Roper* [1892] AC 125.

[25] A sum equal to the share premium must be transferred to the share premium account (section 610 CA 2006). On the regulation of share premium as legal capital see Chapter 19.

[26] Section 121 Companies Act 1985 providing for an increase in share capital by ordinary resolution where authorized to do so by a company's articles.

[27] Articles 22 and 43 of the Model Articles for Private and Public Companies, respectively.

[28] This contrasts with Table A, article 2 which provided that 'any share may be issued with such rights or restrictions as the company may by ordinary resolution determine' which contemplates the prior existence of the share prior to issue.

A further distinction made by English company law is between *the issuing* of shares and *the allotment* of shares. The Act uses both terms but only defines 'allotment'. Section 558 provides that an allotment of shares takes place when a person obtains an unconditional right to be entered into the register of members. One may infer from this that an issue of shares takes place when the allottee is actually entered into the register of members. This view was confirmed by Lord Templeman in *National Westminster Bank plc and another v Inland Revenue Commissioners; Barclays Bank plc and another v Inland Revenue Commissioners*:[29]

> The 1985 Act preserves the distinction in English law between an enforceable contract for the issue of shares (which contract is constituted by an allotment) and the issue of shares which is completed by registration. Allotment confers a right to be registered. Registration confers title. Without registration, an applicant is not the holder of a share or a member of the company: the share has not been issued to him.
>
> The allotment of a share, followed by the registration of the shareholder followed by the furnishing of a share certificate may take place on the same day or on different days. In the present case shares were allotted on 12 March but the shares were not registered and therefore no share certificate could be furnished until 2 April. The shares were allotted on 12 March and issued on 2 April.
>
> No person can be a shareholder until he is registered. A person who is not a shareholder by registration cannot claim that the share has been issued to him, but only that the company is bound by contract to issue a share to him. A person who has been allotted shares is in as good a position in equity as a person to whom shares have been issued but that does not mean that there is no distinction between allotment and issue; an allotment creates an enforceable contract to issue and accept shares.

2.2 The distribution of the corporate power to allot, issue, and attach rights to shares

As we have seen from the extract from the Model Articles, the constitution of a company empowers the company to issue shares. The permission to issue shares is not granted to the board or to the shareholder body but rather to the company. As a company with model articles delegates to the board the ability to 'exercise all the powers of the company' the board is empowered to issue shares.[30] Accordingly, in a UK company the board has the power on behalf of the company to issue shares. Of course, as the Model Articles for both public and private companies provide for an instruction right, the shareholder body in a company with such articles could, by passing a special resolution, instruct the board to issue shares.[31] Note that the provision gives the board the power to issue, not to allot, shares. However, clearly the power to allot is contained within a power to issue as being a necessary precursor to the issuance of shares.

With regard to the rights attached to those shares, the Model Articles reserves the power to determine those rights to the shareholders, who must determine those rights by ordinary resolution.[32] Interestingly, many companies change this default position to provide for board power to determine the rights attached to shares provided that such rights are consistent with prior shareholder resolutions. Marks and Spencer Group Plc's articles, for example, provide as follows:

> Subject to the legislation, the company can issue shares with any rights or restrictions attached to them as long as this is not restricted by any rights attached to existing shares. These rights or

[29] [1994] 3 All ER 1.
[30] Article 3 of the Model Articles for Private and Public Companies.
[31] On shareholder instruction rights see Chapter 6.
[32] Articles 22 and 43 of the Model Articles for Private and Public Companies, respectively.

restrictions can be decided either by an ordinary resolution passed by the shareholders or by the directors as long as there is no conflict with any resolution passed by the shareholders.[33]

However, where the constitution of a company gives the board of directors both the power to issue shares and the power to determine the rights attached to shares, this does not mean that the shareholders have no decision-making authority in relation to the issue of shares. Prior to 1980 the only restriction on the power of the board to issue shares—other than restrictions set out in the constitution—was the requirement for the company to have enough shares in its pool of authorized share capital to issue new shares. In theory this represented a form of shareholder control over the issue of shares, but as most companies had a large reserve of authorized share capital, it provided for very limited shareholder control in practice. However, in order to implement the requirements of the European Union's Second Directive, English company law introduced much more significant shareholder control over share issues. Arguably, these controls rendered authorized share capital functionless and resulted in it being abolished.

There are two aspects of shareholder control over share issues set out in the Companies Act 2006: first, the requirement to obtain shareholder authorization to allot shares or rights to purchase shares; and, second, shareholder pre-emption rights—a right to buy a proportion of any new issue of shares equal to the shareholder's percentage holding of shares prior to the issue. We address each of these in turn.

2.3 Authority to allot shares

Sections 549–551 of the Companies Act 2006 set out the requirements for public and private companies in relation to shareholder approval to allot shares.[34] The provisions are set out here.

■ Section 549 Companies Act 2006 Exercise by directors of power to allot shares etc

(1) The directors of a company must not exercise any power of the company—

    (a) to allot shares in the company, or

    (b) to grant rights to subscribe for, or to convert any security into, shares in the company, except in accordance with section 550 (private company with single class of shares) or section 551 (authorization by company).

(2) Subsection (1) does not apply—

    (a) to the allotment of shares in pursuance of an employees' share scheme, or

    (b) to the grant of a right to subscribe for, or to convert any security into, shares so allotted.

(3) Subsection (1) does not apply to the allotment of shares pursuant to a right to subscribe for, or to convert any security into, shares in the company.

(4) A director who knowingly contravenes, or permits or authorizes a contravention of, this section commits an offence...

(5) A person guilty of an offence under this section is liable—

    (a) on conviction on indictment, to a fine;

    (b) on summary conviction, to a fine not exceeding the statutory maximum.

(6) Nothing in this section affects the validity of an allotment or other transaction.

---

[33] Marks & Spencer Group Plc Articles of Association, article 4A (as amended, 2010).
[34] Implementing article 25 of the Second Council Directive 77/91/EEC.

■ Section 550 Companies Act 2006 Power of directors to allot shares etc: private company with only one class of shares

Where a private company has only one class of shares, the directors may exercise any power of the company—

(a) to allot shares of that class, or

(b) to grant rights to subscribe for or to convert any security into such shares, except to the extent that they are prohibited from doing so by the company's articles.

■ Section 551 Companies Act 2006 Power of directors to allot shares etc: authorization by company

(1) The directors of a company may exercise a power of the company—

    (a) to allot shares in the company, or

    (b) to grant rights to subscribe for or to convert any security into shares in the company, if they are authorized to do so by the company's articles or by resolution of the company.

(2) Authorization may be given for a particular exercise of the power or for its exercise generally, and may be unconditional or subject to conditions.

(3) Authorization must—

    (a) state the maximum amount of shares that may be allotted under it, and

    (b) specify the date on which it will expire, which must be not more than five years from—

        (i) in the case of authorization contained in the company's articles at the time of its original incorporation, the date of that incorporation;

        (ii) in any other case, the date on which the resolution is passed by virtue of which the authorization is given.

(4) Authorization may—

    (a) be renewed or further renewed by resolution of the company for a further period not exceeding five years, and

    (b) be revoked or varied at any time by resolution of the company...

(8) A resolution of a company to give, vary, revoke or renew authorization under this section may be an ordinary resolution, even though it amends the company's articles...

The rules on the requirement to obtain authorization to allot shares apply to the allotment of any shares, including both ordinary shares and also any type of preferred shares. It also applies to the granting of any right to purchase any share type or to convert a security[35] (for example a debt claim) into shares.

The Act's requirement to obtain shareholder authorization prior to the board exercising its delegated power to allot shares is a mandatory rule in relation to public companies and private companies with more than one class of shares but does not apply to private companies with one class of shares. Such private companies could, of course, elect to adopt authorization to allot requirements by setting out provisions to that effect in the constitution.

---

[35] The term security is the umbrella term which refers to any financial instrument creating a financial claim on the company—hence one might refer to debt or equity securities. It is not to be confused with taking security in an asset to secure repayment of a loan.

The Second Directive only applies to public companies; making the authorization to allot provisions applicable to a private company with more than one class of shares goes beyond the Directive's requirements. The exclusion of private companies with only one class of share is a recognition that in close private companies the directors and the shareholders will often be the same individuals so that requiring separate shareholder approval would unnecessarily add to corporate bureaucracy. Private companies with more than one class of shares may well, on balance, be larger private companies where there is some degree of separation of ownership and managerial control and, in addition, the further issue of shares may raise issues of fairness between different classes of shares.[36] We address such issues of share-class conflict in section III of this chapter. Note that in relation to private companies with one class of share the 2006 Act reverses the default rule under the 1985 Act which applied authorization to allot requirements to private companies but gave them the option of opting out of the regime.[37]

The authorization to allot shares or to grant rights in shares, by for example issuing share options, may be provided in the company's articles of association or by an ordinary resolution. The authorization may be specific—authorizing a specific issue of shares—or general by providing the board with the power to allot shares up to a specified amount even though the board has not indicated any immediate need to issue such shares. A general authorization must still state the maximum number of shares that can be allotted. Any authorization given, whether by the articles or by ordinary resolution, is only effective for a five-year period, after which time a new authorization to allot would be required. Shareholders retain the right at any time to revoke the authorization and may attach any conditions to the authorization.[38] Considerable formal control is, therefore, given to the shareholders in relation to share issues. In large public companies, in practice the shareholders will be asked on a yearly rolling basis at the company's annual general meeting to provide general authorization to allot shares.[39] Consider for example, Vodafone Group Plc's explanation of its allotment resolution at its 2011 AGM.[40]

■ Resolution 20–Authority to Allot Shares

The authority in paragraph 20.1 will allow the directors to allot new shares and grant rights to subscribe for, or convert other securities into, shares up to a nominal value of US$1,955,207,296,

---

[36] The Company Law Review's primary recommendation was that the authorization to allot regime only apply to public companies but suggested that 'if this is not thought to offer sufficient protection, there may be a case for retaining the statutory requirement for shareholder authorization where the company has, or as a result of the issue would have, shares of more than one class' (*Developing the Framework*, para 7.30). The reasoning behind singling out private companies with one class of shares is not outlined in the Review documents.

[37] Section 80A allowing private companies to opt out of the regime by what was known under the 1985 Act as an 'elective resolution', which required the approval of all the members entitled to attend and vote at a general meeting (section 379A CA 1985).

[38] Section 551(2) and (4) CA 2006.

[39] The Association of British Insurers recommends that authority to allot should not typically exceed shares equal to one-third of the company's share capital, although following recent revisions such authority may be granted for shares equal to two-thirds of share capital should such shares be issued pursuant to a rights issue. The ABI recommends that if such authority to allot shares in excess of the routine one-third level is used, then all the directors of the company should stand for re-election at the next AGM: Association of British Insurers, *Directors' Powers To Allot Share Capital And Disapply Shareholders' Pre-Emption Rights* (2008) (www.ivis.co.uk/ ●). These changes were introduced following the problems that arose for banks as a result of the rights issue timetable—see A Report to the Chancellor of the Exchequer: by the Rights Issue Review Group (November 2008) (www.hm-treasury.gov.uk/ ●). On rights issues see p 728.

[40] See Vodafone Group Plc's 2011 Review of the Year and Notice of Annual General Meeting (available at www.vodafone.com/content/index/investors/share_debt/agm.html ●).

which is equivalent to approximately 33 per cent of the total issued ordinary share capital of the Company, exclusive of treasury shares, as at 18 May 2011...

There are no present plans to undertake a rights issue or to allot new shares other than to fulfil the Company's obligations under its executive and employee share plans. The directors consider it desirable to have the maximum flexibility permitted by corporate governance guidelines to respond to market developments and to enable allotments to take place to finance business opportunities as they arise...[41]

Finally in this regard, note that the requirement to obtain authorization to allot shares does not qualify the directors' power to issue shares or render the exercise of this power contingent on shareholder authorization. That power is a function of the distribution of power in a company's constitution. Sections 549–551 provide that if this power is exercised in the absence of such authorization the directors commit a criminal offence but the allotment remains valid.[42]

2.4 Pre-emption rights

Having obtained authorization to allot shares, the board of directors' ability to exercise the power to issue shares is *not* unrestricted. As we saw in *Hypothetical A*, the concerns shareholders may have about the expropriation of the value of their shares or the dilution of control rights are addressed if each shareholder is entitled to purchase a proportion of the newly issued shares equal to her existing percentage shareholding. Such a right is known as a pre-emption right. Whilst many English companies have long provided for pre-emption rights in their constitutions, particularly in small private companies, traditionally the Companies Acts did not require the provision of pre-emption rights.[43] However, as a result of the implementation of the Second Directive the Companies Act provides for mandatory—although waivable—pre-emption rights for shareholders in public companies and for the default application of pre-emption rights for private companies. The pre-emption right and its scope of application are set out in the following sections.

■ Section 561 Companies Act 2006 Existing shareholders' right of pre-emption

(1) A company must not allot equity securities to a person on any terms unless—

    (a) it has made an offer to each person who holds ordinary shares in the company to allot to him on the same or more favourable terms a proportion of those securities that is as nearly as practicable equal to the proportion in nominal value held by him of the ordinary share capital of the company, and

    (b) the period during which any such offer may be accepted has expired or the company has received notice of the acceptance or refusal of every offer so made.

    ...

(4) Shares held by the company as treasury shares are disregarded for the purposes of this section, so that—

---

[41] Note that pursuant to section 549(2) the authorization to allot requirement does not apply to shares issues to employee share schemes.

[42] Section 549(4)–(6) CA 2006.

[43] For an interesting view that this was a superior rule to jurisdictions which required pre-emption rights (as many US states did at the time, but interestingly, do not do so today) see L.C.B. Gower, 'Some Contrasts between British and American Corporation Law' (1956) 69 *Harvard Law Review* 1369.

(a) the company is not treated as a person who holds ordinary shares, and

(b) the shares are not treated as forming part of the ordinary share capital of the company.

(5) This section is subject to—

(a) sections 564 to 566 (exceptions to pre-emption right),

(b) sections 567 and 568 (exclusion of rights of pre-emption),

(c) sections 569 to 573 (disapplication of pre-emption rights), and

(d) section 576 (saving for certain older pre-emption procedures).

■ Section 564 Companies Act 2006 Exception to pre-emption right: bonus shares

Section 561(1) (existing shareholders' right of pre-emption) does not apply in relation to the allotment of bonus shares.

■ Section 565 Companies Act 2006 Exception to pre-emption right: issue for non-cash consideration

Section 561(1) (existing shareholders' right of pre-emption) does not apply to a particular allotment of equity securities if these are, or are to be, wholly or partly paid up otherwise than in cash.

■ Section 566 Companies Act 2006 Exception to pre-emption right: employees' share schemes

Section 561 (existing shareholders' right of pre-emption) does not apply to the allotment of equity securities that would, apart from any renunciation or assignment of the right to their allotment, be held under or allotted or transferred pursuant to an employees' share scheme.

The Act provides that before 'equity securities' can be allotted the holders of ordinary shares must have been offered the opportunity to buy a proportion of these shares equal to the existing proportion of ordinary shares which the shareholder already holds. The pre-emption rights set out in these sections only apply in relation to issues of 'equity securities' which the Act defines as ordinary shares or rights to subscribe for or to convert a security (such as a debt claim or a preferred share) into ordinary shares.[44] Accordingly, only the holders of ordinary shares benefit from pre-emption rights and ordinary shareholders only benefit from pre-emption rights in relation to a new issue of ordinary shares or rights to purchase those shares. Preferred shares can, therefore, be issued by the company non-pre-emptively. The pre-emption regime applies both to a new issue of ordinary shares and also to the sale of ordinary shares that are held by the company as treasury shares.[45] Treasury shares are shares that have been repurchased by the company but have not been cancelled.[46]

Pursuant to section 564 pre-emption rights do not apply to a bonus issue of shares or to shares issued under an employee share scheme. A bonus issue of shares in effect amounts to a dividend in shares not in cash. All shareholders entitled to receive the

---

[44] Section 560(1) CA 2006.   [45] Sections 560(3) and 573 CA 2006.
[46] See further section IV.3.2 in this chapter.

dividend will receive the bonus shares in proportion to their dividend entitlement. In relation to shares issued to an employee share scheme, such shares are used as remuneration and as mechanisms to incentivize performance on the part of employees. Obviously it would make no sense if such shares would have to be offered to existing shareholders first before they could be used to remunerate and incentivize employees.

Section 565 is worthy of closer attention. This section provides that the pre-emption rights do not apply to an issue of shares the payment for which involves any element of non-cash consideration. An issue of 10 million shares for £100 million and a chocolate bar would therefore be a legal non-pre-emptive issue. The underlying idea behind this exception is that pre-emption rights make sense where the shareholders themselves can provide the same assets as the third party provides in exchange for the shares. If a company wishes to issue shares to buy another company, or to buy a specific large asset such as a warehouse, the existing shareholders themselves cannot provide the target company or the warehouse as consideration. Of course, the company could issue the shares first and then pay for the asset in cash, but in some instances the seller of the asset may not be interested in cash. This exception clearly presents considerable scope to evade the pre-emption regime with relatively straightforward legal avoidance structures that involve an element of non-cash consideration. In practice, abuse of this provision does not take place. As discussed further later in this chapter, institutional shareholders in large listed companies in the UK have engaged in active policing of these rights. Furthermore, if authority to allot was granted and then the board abused their powers in this way, the next time authority to allot was required in relation to this company conditions could easily be imposed on any future allotment thus preventing any such further abuse.

The pre-emption regime is mandatory for public companies, although such companies may, as we shall see, disapply the application of the rules. In relation to private companies this pre-emption regime is applicable as a default rule. Such companies can opt out of the regime by including a provision in the articles excluding the application of section 561.[47] This option to opt out applies to all private companies and not just to those with one class of share.

For public companies and those private companies to whom the regime applies, the pre-emption rights may be disapplied by shareholder vote. Where the shareholders have provided a general authorization to allot, the shareholders may provide a general waiver of pre-emption rights in relation to those shares. This could be done by placing a provision in the articles to that effect or by special resolution.[48] Alternatively, the shareholders can disapply the pre-emption rights in relation to a specific allotment by special resolution.[49] Note, however, that where a proposal is put to the shareholders to disapply the pre-emption rights in relation to a specific allotment of shares, the Act requires that, first, the directors recommend the disapplication; and, second, the price to be paid by the third party for the shares is disclosed to the shareholders and that the directors provide a 'justification of that amount'.[50]

A private company is provided with an additional disapplication option. A private company with one class of shares may disapply the application of the pre-emption rights to any allotments by a special resolution.[51] The extent to which this provides such a private company with additional flexibility is unclear as the constitution can be amended by special resolution to opt out of the regime, as outlined earlier.

From the company's perspective, if shareholders have a right of pre-emption they need to decide quickly whether they wish to exercise this pre-emption right. If they do not wish to do so then the company is entitled to sell those shares to third parties on the same terms or, from the company's perspective, better terms. If the rules on pre-emption rights create excessive delay in the raising of finance, either from the shareholders themselves or

---

[47] Section 567 CA 2006.   [48] Section 570 CA 2006.   [49] Section 571 CA 2006.
[50] Section 571(5) and (6) CA 2006.   [51] Section 569 CA 2006.

from third parties, the company may be damaged if the delay results in a deterioration of the terms upon which it can allot its shares or if the asset which the finance is necessary to purchase is lost to another party. In this regard the Act provides for a pre-emption right timetable and procedure. The Act provides that the shareholder-offeree must have at least 14 days[52] within which to signal whether or not she wishes to accept the company's offer to allot shares. If she fails to respond within the offer period or rejects the offer then the shares may be sold to non-shareholders.[53] There is no requirement in the Act to offer those declined shares to the other shareholders before selling them to a third party. However, it is noteworthy that it is not unusual to see such provisions in the constitution of small companies, whose shareholders wish to exert more extensive control over who becomes a shareholder of the company.

If the directors authorize an allotment of shares in contravention of these pre-emption provisions the allotment of shares is unaffected but the directors who authorized or permitted the contravention are *jointly and severally* liable to compensate the shareholders for losses arising as a result of the contravention.[54]

2.5 Pre-emption rights in practice

Listed companies that wish to raise additional equity capital are required first to offer the new shares to their existing shareholders unless shareholders disapply the pre-emption rights. Where shareholders disapply pre-emption rights the issue of a block of shares to a third party is known as 'placing'. It is normal practice for listed companies to obtain, on a rolling annual basis, shareholder approval to disapply pre-emption rights in relation to a not insignificant number of shares, even where there are no specific plans to make a non pre-emptive allotment of shares. Consider for example, Vodafone Group Plc's explanation of its pre-emption right waiver resolution at its 2011 AGM:

Resolution 21

The purpose of paragraph 21.1 is to authorize the directors to allot new shares pursuant to the authority given by paragraph 20.1 of Resolution 20, or sell treasury shares, for cash (a) in connection with a pre-emptive offer or rights issue or (b) otherwise up to a nominal value of US$324,635,375, equivalent to 5 per cent of the total issued ordinary share capital of the Company as at 18 May 2011, in each case without the shares first being offered to existing shareholders in proportion to their existing holdings...

The Board considers the authority in Resolution 21 to be appropriate in order to allow the Company flexibility to finance business opportunities or to conduct a pre-emptive offer or rights issue without the need to comply with the requirements of the statutory pre-emption provisions.

The Board intends to adhere to the provisions in the Pre-Emption Group's Statement of Principles not to allot shares for cash on a non pre-emptive basis (other than pursuant to a rights issue or pre-emptive offer) in excess of an amount equal to 7.5 per cent of the total issued ordinary share capital of the Company within a rolling 3-year period without prior consultation with shareholders.

---

[52] Section 562(5) CA 2006. The period was reduced from 21 days to 14 days in 2009 (The Companies (Share Capital and Acquisition by Company of its Own Shares) Regulations 2009 (SI 2009/2022), **reg** 2) following the Government's acceptance of the recommendations of the *Report to the Chancellor of the Exchequer: by the Rights Issue Review Group* (November 2008). It was felt that the pre-emptive issue timetable for public companies created problems for banks when attempting to raise equity finance during the financial crisis in 2007–2009. See also D. Stewart, 'Pre-emption rights issues take far too long' *Financial Times* (12 April 2009).

[53] Sections 561(1)(b) CA 2006.

[54] Section 563(2) CA 2006. The Act provides for a two-year limitation period in this regard: section 563(3).

Note with regard to this resolution that Vodafone asserts that the requested shareholder approval is consistent with investor guidelines. These guidelines are those produced by a body called the Pre-Emption Group.[55] Institutional investors recognize that in some instances the company will need the flexibility to issue shares non-pre-emptively. However, institutional shareholders value the protection that pre-emption rights provide from value dilution and are keen to impose limits on such non pre-emptive issues. The Pre-Emption Group guidelines attempt to balance these competing concerns. The Guidelines provide both a set of best practice rules in relation to pre-emption disapplication, which the Pre-Emption Group expects companies to follow, and a set of guidelines on what it is reasonable for shareholders to accept when asked to disapply pre-emption rights.[56] Consider the following provisions from the Pre-Emption Group's Statement of Principles.

■ Pre-Emption Group: Statement of Principles (2008)

Routine Disapplications

7. In a significant number of situations a request for disapplication is likely to be considered non-controversial by shareholders. While this does not reduce the importance of effective dialogue and timely notification, routine requests are less likely to need in-depth discussion and shareholders will be more inclined in principle to support them.

8. Requests are more likely to be routine in nature when the company is seeking authority to issue non-pre-emptively no more than 5% of ordinary share capital in any one year.

9. This principle applies whatever the structure of the proposed issue. For example, an issue of shares which contains both a pre-emptive and non-pre-emptive element ('combination issues') would normally be considered routine provided that the non-preemptive element met the criteria specified for routine applications within these guidelines. This would include issues that comprised a placing of shares with a partial clawback by existing shareholders.

10. In the absence of (a) suitable advance consultation and explanation or (b) the matter having been specifically highlighted at the time at which the request for disapplication was made, companies should not issue more than 7.5% of the company's ordinary share capital for cash other than to existing shareholders in any rolling three year period.

11. Where a request is made for the disapplication of pre-emption rights in respect of a specific issue of shares, the price at which the shares are proposed to be issued will also be relevant...Companies should note that a discount of greater than 5% is not likely to be regarded as routine...

14. **These principles are intended to ease the granting of authority below those figures, not to rule out approvals above them. Requests which, if granted, would exceed these levels should be considered by shareholders on a case by case basis**. In these instances it is particularly important that there is early and effective dialogue, and that the company is able to communicate to shareholders the information they need in order to reach an informed decision. [Emphasis in the original]

According to these guidelines annual requests for pre-emption disapplication in relation to shares not amounting to more than 5% of a company's ordinary shares will be treated as routine and approved by institutional shareholders. This does not mean that

[55] The membership of the Group consists primarily of investment fund managers, insurance companies, pension funds, and banks, but also consists of representatives from business. Note that a connection to government rather than market regulation is generated through Financial Reporting Council representation on the Group: see www.pre-emptiongroup.org.uk/ ●.

[56] These rules are expected to be applied by companies listed on the LSE's **Main Market**. The Guidelines recognize that companies quoted on the Alternative Investment Market (AIM) may need greater flexibility in this regard. Many AIM companies are in a much earlier stage of their development than companies listed on the main market and will require greater flexibility when raising equity finance (see Principle 5 of the Pre-Emption Group's Statement of Principles).

the Pre-Emption Group accepts that the company can make full use of the disapplication each year. Companies should not issue more that 7.5% of the shares non-pre-emptively in any three-year rolling period.

We identified earlier two concerns for existing shareholders arising from a new issue of shares: value and control dilution. For most shareholders in widely-held companies, as their percentage holding is low and their ability to exercise control very limited, control dilution does not represent a significant concern. However, value dilution is a clear concern for all shareholders in close and widely-held companies alike. The Pre-Emption Group's guidelines provide dilution protection not only by limiting the extent of any non-pre-emptive issues but also by providing that, in relation to a pre-emption right waiver for a specific issue of shares,[57] a discount greater than 5% will not be regarded as routine; which means that shareholders should not, as a matter of course, approve such requests.

In relation to pre-emptive issues of shares by listed companies, there is additional terminology and regulation that we need to be aware of. A pre-emptive issue of shares in a premium listed company may take place through one of two procedures: either by a **rights issue**[58] or by an **open offer**.[59] A rights issue involves a pre-emptive offer to existing shareholders by means of what is known as a 'renounceable letter'. This 'renounceable letter' is a negotiable instrument. This means that if the shareholder does not herself wish to buy the shares she can sell the right to do so to a third party. The rights that are traded are known as 'nil-paid rights'—as nothing has been paid for them or paid to exercise them. This enables a shareholder to avoid significant value dilution without having to participate in the offer.[60] Rights issues are typically made at a significant discount to the existing market price of the shares in order to attract the company's existing shareholders to purchase the newly allotted shares.

An *open offer* is a pre-emptive offer of shares that is not made by a negotiable instrument such as a renounceable letter.[61] This means that if a shareholder does not wish to participate in the offer, or is unable to do so, then, depending on the terms of the offer, she may be subject to value dilution as she is unable to sell the right to participate to a third party. For this reason, to provide value dilution protection for non-participating shareholders, the Listing Rules provide that an open offer should not take place at a discount of greater than 10% to the market price at the time of the offer.[62]

An open offer is more attractive to the company where the company does not have sufficient authorization to allot the shares it intends to issue. In such circumstances the company cannot commence a rights issue immediately because the issue of the renounceable letter creates a tradable right to buy shares which itself requires *authorization to grant* pursuant to section 551(b) of the Act.[63] In such circumstances a rights issue would require an additional delay to obtain the required authorization to allot/grant. At a minimum this will take 14 days.[64] As an open offer does not create a tradable right to buy the share the pre-emption timetable can run in parallel with the authorization to allot/grant timetable.

---

[57] See text to notes 49–50.   [58] LRs 9.5.1–9.5.6.   [59] LRs 9.5.7 – 9.5.8B.

[60] There will, of course, typically be some dilution in order to attract the third party to purchase the nil-paid rights.

[61] LRs 9.5.7–9.5.8.   [62] LR 9.5.10.

[63] Note for this reason companies typically obtain additional authority to allot in the context of a rights offer. See note 39. See, for example, Resolution 20.2 of Vodafone Group Plc's Annual General Meeting providing additional authority to allot for a further 33% of the total issued ordinary share capital of the company (that is authorization of up to 66% in total)—available at www.vodafone.com/content/index/investors/share_debt/agm.html ●. This additional authorization is consistent with the Association of British Insurer's guidelines amended in response to the *Report to the Chancellor of the Exchequer: by the Rights Issue Review Group* (November 2008)—see ABI: *Director's Power to Allot Share Capital and Disapply Shareholders' Pre-Emption Rights* (ABI, 2008) available at: www.ivis.co.uk/PDF/1.1_Directors_powers_to_allot_shares.pdf ●.

[64] The notice period for a General Meeting is 14 days or, in the case of a public company's Annual General Meeting, 21 days (section 307 CA 2006).

2.6 Consideration paid for the shares

Shares are allotted by the company for an amount agreed between the company and the investor purchasing the shares. In relation to smaller companies the amount agreed to be paid for the shares will be the subject of a negotiation between the company, as seller, and the investor, as buyer. Where larger companies issue shares to a specific third party, in accordance with the pre-emption regime outlined previously, the price paid will also be the subject of a direct negotiation between the company and the investor. In contrast, where shares are issued to the public at large the company will make an offer to the investing public to buy the shares at a price set by the company. This price will of course reflect what the company and its advisors think will be attractive to the market place, having taken soundings from institutional investors.[65]

The price that is agreed to be paid for the shares may be more than the nominal value of the shares; but cannot be less than that value. They cannot be issued at a discount.[66] The company's legal capital, the regulation of which we consider in Chapter 19, is the sum of the aggregate nominal value of the issued shares (aggregate share capital) and the aggregate share premium (the aggregate amount paid for shares in excess of the nominal value).[67]

The amount that is agreed to be paid need not, subject to certain qualifications, be paid up. That is, the company and the investor may agree with the shareholders or a particular shareholder that either:[68] all amounts owed are paid at the time the share is issued, in which case those shares would be paid up or fully paid; that a part of the amount due is paid up with the remainder to be paid at a later date, in which case the shares would be partly paid up; or that the amount due shall be paid at a later date or when the company requests payment, in which case until any payment is made the shares will be unpaid. A company's constitution could require that all shares allotted by the company must be fully paid. The Model Articles for private companies require this.[69] In relation to a public company the Act requires that any shares allotted are paid up in the amount of at least one-quarter of the nominal value and wholly paid up in relation to any share premium.[70]

With regard to the means of payment, the Act provides that payment may be made in money or money's worth (in-kind consideration).[71] Money or cash consideration includes the discharge of an existing liability;[72] however, no shares can be issued to discharge a commission or amounts owed to a person as a result of the purchase by that person of the company's shares or that person having arranged for the sale of the company's shares.[73]

In relation to public companies, there are two exceptions to the rule that shares can be allotted for in-kind consideration. First, the subscribers to the memorandum of a public

---

[65] In the pricing of a public offer see Web Chapter B.

[66] Section 580 CA 2006; *Ooregum Gold Mining Co of India v Roper* [1892] AC 125.

[67] Section 610 CA 2006.   [68] Section 581 CA 2006.

[69] Model Articles for Private Companies Limited by Shares, article 21.

[70] Section 586 CA 2006. Failure to pay these required amounts will result in the shareholder being liable to pay interest at an 'appropriate rate' on the amounts that should have been paid up at the time of allotment (section 586(3)(b) CA 2006).

[71] Section 582 CA 2006. The Act specifies that money's worth includes goodwill and know how. If a company purchases all the assets of another company or business the value of that business may exceed the 'book value'—the value of its assets recorded in its accounts; that excess is goodwill, which may reflect the value of supplier and customer relationships, reputation, brand name etc. Neither goodwill or know-how are defined in the Act.

[72] What amounts to cash consideration is defined in section 583 CA 2006 and includes a release from a liability for a liquidated sum.

[73] Section 552 CA 2006. An exception to this rule is provided by section 553 CA 2006 which allows shares to be issued in payment of commissions, discounts or allowances not exceeding 10% of the value of the shares (or a lesser amount set out in the articles) provided that such payments are authorized by the constitution.

company—the founding shareholders of the company—must pay for the shares agreed to be taken pursuant to the memorandum in cash.[74] Secondly, public companies cannot accept as payment for shares the provision of future services,[75] although the discharge of a liability for services already incurred would be acceptable (cash) consideration.[76]

Apart from these exceptions for public companies, shares may be paid for in non-cash, in-kind consideration. As we saw in *Hypothetical A*, where shares are issued non-pre-emptively this creates a significant concern for shareholders regarding value dilution if the shares are issued to third parties for less than they are worth. This concern is mitigated by the mandatory provision of pre-emption rights for all companies, apart from private companies that opt out of the regime. These concerns are mitigated further for listed companies through the use of nil-paid negotiable rights in a rights issue as well as the Listing Rule's requirement that open offers, that do not benefit from the negotiable nil-paid rights, should not take place at a greater than 10% discount. Furthermore it would be open to shareholders to subject any authorization to allot to pricing restrictions if they considered it necessary to do so. The concern regarding value dilution is, however, heightened where the price for the shares is not paid in cash but in in-kind consideration such as shares in another company, real property or machinery. This presents a problem for two reasons. First, the protection shareholders receive from pre-emption rights is not available where payment for shares contains any element of in-kind consideration.[77] Secondly, whereas if shares are issued for cash it is easy for the shareholder to compare the price the shares have been issued for against what he thinks the shares are worth, the value of a non-cash asset—and therefore the actual price paid for the shares—is likely to be much more opaque and subject to a range of opinions as to its actual value. Although the board of directors may affix a value to the consideration received for the shares, that value, if inaccurate, could hide significant value dilution for the shareholders and it may be very difficult for shareholders to determine whether or not such dilution has taken place.

At common law, in the absence of any evidence of mala fides, the courts have typically taken a very deferential approach to the board's valuation of in-kind consideration paid for an allotment of shares. Consider in this regard *In re Wragg Ltd*, a case in which it was claimed by a liquidator of the claimant company that the in-kind consideration paid in relation to an issue of shares was worth less than the value attributed to it by the board and the allottees, who were the founders of the company.

■ *In re Wragg Limited* [1897] 1 Ch 796

Lindley LJ

I understand the law to be as follows…It is, however, obviously beyond the power of a limited company to release a shareholder from his obligation without payment in money or money's worth. It cannot give fully paid-up shares for nothing and preclude itself from requiring payment of them in money or money's worth…From this it follows that shares in limited companies cannot be issued at a discount. By our law the payment by a debtor to his creditor of a less sum than is due does not discharge the debt; and this technical doctrine has also been invoked in aid of the law which prevents the shares of a limited company from being issued at a discount. But this technical doctrine, though often sufficient to decide a particular case, will not suffice as a basis for the wider rule or principle that a company cannot effectually release a shareholder from his statutory obligation to pay in money or money's worth the amount of his shares. That shares cannot be issued at a discount was finally settled in the case of the *Ooregum Gold Mining Co. of*

[74] Section 584 CA 2006.
[75] Section 585 CA 2006. Note, however, that the agreement to provide services remains enforceable (section 591 CA 2006).
[76] Section 583 CA 2006.   [77] Section 565 CA 2006.

India v. Roper,[78] the judgments in which are strongly relied upon by the appellant in this case. It has, however, never yet been decided that a limited company cannot buy property or pay for services at any price it thinks proper, and pay for them in fully paid-up shares. Provided a limited company does so honestly and not colourably, and provided that it has not been so imposed upon as to be entitled to be relieved from its bargain, it appears to be settled by *Pell's Case*[79] and the others to which I have referred, of which *Anderson's Case*[80] is the most striking, that agreements by limited companies to pay for property or services in paid-up shares are valid and binding on the companies and their creditors...

These and other cases decided upon the [Companies] Act of 1867 shew (1) that since that Act, as before, shares must be paid for in money or money's worth; (2) that since that Act, as before, they may be paid for in money's worth; [3] that, even if there is such a contract, shares cannot be issued at a discount; [4] that if a company owes a person 100*l.*, the company cannot by paying him 200*l.* in shares of that nominal amount discharge him, even by a registered contract, from his obligation as a shareholder to pay up the other 100*l.* in respect of those shares. That would be issuing shares at a discount. The difference between such a transaction and paying for property or services in shares at a price put upon them by a vendor and agreed to by the company may not always be very apparent in practice. But the two transactions are essentially different, and whilst the one is ultra vires the other is intra vires. It is not law that persons cannot sell property to a limited company for fully paid-up shares and make a profit by the transaction. We must not allow ourselves to be misled by talking of value. The value paid to the company is measured by the price at which the company agrees to buy what it thinks it worth its while to acquire. Whilst the transaction is unimpeached, this is the only value to be considered.

Smith LJ

If... the consideration which the company has agreed to accept as representing in money's worth the nominal value of the shares be a consideration not clearly colourable nor illusory, then, in my judgment, the adequacy of the consideration cannot be impeached by a liquidator unless the contract can also be impeached; and I take it to be the law that it is not open to a liquidator, unless he is able to impeach the agreement, to go into the adequacy of the consideration to shew that the company have agreed to give an excessive value for what they have purchased.

For the Court of Appeal in *In re Wragg*, provided that the company acts 'honestly and not colourably' and provided that the value of the consideration received does not mean that the shares are issued at a discount to their aggregate nominal value, then the bargain that is struck by the company in relation to the issue of shares will not be investigated or disturbed by the court. Note, however, the slight distinction between Lindley LJ and Smith LJ in relation to what is 'colourable'. For Lindley LJ it is the company's actions that must not be colourable. For Smith LJ the consideration must not be 'colourable' or 'illusory'.

In the later Court of Appeal case of *In re Innes & Co. Limited*[81] Vaughan Williams LJ considered the adequacy of in-kind consideration in an action brought by the company's liquidator. Applying *In re Wragg* he concluded that there was nothing 'colourable' about the *transaction* and held that 'there is, in my judgment, nothing in that bargain to lead us to the conclusion that it was not in truth made by persons who were honestly acting in what they conceived to be the interests of the company'. This position suggests that the common law demands only that in determining the value of the in-kind consideration that the directors comply with their obligation to act bona fide in the best

---

[78] [1892] AC 125. [79] (1869) LR 8 Eq 222.
[80] (1876) 7 Ch D 75. [81] [1903] 2 Ch 254.

interests of the company.[82] Subsequent authority, however, suggests a qualification to this position. In *In Re White Star Line Limited*,[83] White Star made a call for payment of the amount of £750,990 due on shares issued to the Royal Mail Company. The call was paid for with 'creditor certificates' issued by the Royal Mail which, although they had a face value of the amount of the capital call, provided no guarantee of any payment and were understood by all parties concerned to be worth significantly less than the face value of the certificates. The liquidator brought an action claiming the payment of the amounts unpaid on the shares.

■ *In Re White Star Line Limited* [1938] Ch 458

Clauson LJ (*giving the judgment of the court*)
[The judgment considered the Court of Appeal's judgment in *In re Wragg*.] In view of the principles to be deduced from the authorities it is clear that a discharge by accord and satisfaction of the…debt resulting from a call must be subject to the qualification that the consideration which is given by way of satisfaction must not be a mere blind or clearly colourable or illusory, and that the question whether it is so or not is one of fact, and the language of Lindley LJ cannot, in our judgment, fairly be construed otherwise…

It was, however, strenuously argued before this Court that, unless and until the contract is impeached in an independent action for that purpose, any consideration which, on the face of the contract, is accepted by the company as money's worth, must be taken as money's worth until the contract is set aside. We are not prepared to hold that, if the facts are sufficiently plain, the Court is bound to insist on what, after all, in such a case is a mere technical requirement—namely, that the contract for payment in what is represented as money's worth should be impeached in an independent action…

By letter of March 25, 1937, the liquidator of the Royal Mail Co. admitted, for the purposes of the present proceedings, that the deferred certificates issued by the Royal Mail Co. under the scheme were at all material times worth less than their nominal or face value, and further by letter of May 3, 1937, that to the knowledge of Sir William McClintock, the liquidator of the Royal Mail Co., who was a director of the Royal Mail Co. from October 20, 1932, to the date of liquidation, the deferred certificates were at all material times worth less than their nominal or face value. There is also before the Court an affidavit by Mr. Charlton, who was…from 1930 a director of the White Star Co., to the effect that the certificates were at all material times…worth a great deal less than their nominal or face value. He adds that everyone with a knowledge of the affairs of the Royal Mail Co. realized…that it must be several years before the revenues of the Royal Mail Co. would be sufficient to permit any payment of interest on the certificates and the value of the certificates was, therefore, wholly speculative, and that the facts were well known to the directors of the White Star Co.

In our judgment it is possible to draw one inference only from these facts—namely, that the transaction was an acceptance by the White Star Co. of the deferred certificates, not as in any sense a payment for the £750,990 due for calls on the shares, but as the best that could be saved

---

[82] See also *Ooregum Gold Mining Co of India v Roper* 1892] AC 125 *per* Lord Watson: 'so long as the company honestly regards the consideration given as fairly representing the nominal value of the shares in cash, its estimate ought not to be critically examined'. See also *Stanton (Inspector of Taxes) v Drayton Commercial Investment Co Ltd* [1982] 2 All ER 942 observing that '[*In re Wragg* is] also clear authority for the proposition that, unless the agreement in furtherance of which the shares were issued for a consideration other than cash can be successfully impeached as, for example, colourable, the courts will not go behind it and consider whether or not it was commercially prudent, or whether a more advantageous bargain might have been made, *since to do so would be to question the honest commercial judgment of the directors of the company concerned in the ordinary management of that company's business*' (emphasis added).

[83] [1938] Ch 458.

out of the wreck of the Royal Mail Co.'s finances towards making some provision for compensation in the future for the failure of the Royal Mail Co. to provide a sum of £750,990, which they were unable in fact to pay. The transaction was in effect a release of the Royal Mail Co. from a liability which they could not meet at the time in consideration of a limited obligation undertaken by them which was and was understood by every one to be far less onerous than the obligation to pay £750,990. It is not, in our view, possible, as the authorities stand, to hold, on the facts, that such a transaction amounted to payment of £750,990…

If the view above expressed be correct, it must follow that the Royal Mail Co. is to be treated as the holder of shares on which £750,990 remains unpaid.

The Court of Appeal in *White Star Line* focuses on whether the consideration paid is colourable or illusory. The Court is not willing to accept that simply because the directors acted bona fide in the interests of the company that the courts will not review the consideration paid for the shares. The consideration cannot be 'a mere blind'. Where there is evidence 'sufficiently plain' to all parties concerned, including the directors of the company, that the consideration is not worth what it purports to be worth then the court will interfere and hold that the amounts outstanding on the shares remain unpaid. Arguably this holding is restricted to situations in which, although acting in the company's interests, the directors of the company are aware that the consideration is not worth what it purports to be worth.[84] However, the judgment itself does suggest that the court's jurisdiction may extend beyond these facts and permit court review of in-kind consideration where, even though the board is of the view that the consideration is worth what it purports to be worth, the evidence that it is not is 'sufficiently plain'. Such circumstances are, however, likely to be rare and in most instances where directors are of the view that the consideration is worth what they have valued it at, the courts will not review or interfere with this assessment.

Although the common law takes a deferential stance in relation to the valuation of in-kind consideration, additional valuation regulation for public companies only was introduced by the Companies Act 1980, which implemented the European Union's Second Company Law Directive.[85] These rules are now set out in Chapter 6; Part 17 of the Companies Act 2006. We will detail the operation of these rules only in outline. The rules provide that in-kind consideration can only be paid as consideration for shares where the in-kind consideration has been valued by an independent valuer,[86] which for larger companies would typically be one of the Big Four accounting firms,[87] although not usually the company's own auditor.[88]

---

[84] See, for example, the Australian case of *Pilmer v Duke Group Ltd (in liquidation)* [2001] 2 BCLC 773 holding that 'the actual decision in *Re White Star Line* may be understood as turning on the fact that both parties to the transaction knew that the consideration offered and received was not worth the sum attributed to it'.

[85] Sections 598–604 CA 2006 also contain provisions addressing the valuation of non-cash consideration paid by a person who is a subscriber to the memorandum in the two-year period starting with the issue of the trading certificate pursuant to section 761 CA 2006. The rules provide both for independent valuation of the in-kind consideration (section 599 and 600 CA 2006) but also for shareholder approval (by ordinary resolution) of the agreement providing for the payment of the in-kind consideration (section 601 CA 2006).

[86] Section 593 CA 2006.

[87] Section 1150 CA 2006 requiring that the valuation be carried out by a statutory auditor although providing the use of a non-auditor in specified circumstances (section 1150(2) CA 2006).

[88] Ethical standards issued by the Financial Reporting Council's Auditing Practices Board restrict the scope for the auditor to carry out valuation work for the audited company: Auditing Practices Board, *Ethical Standard 5 (Revised): Non-Audit Services Provided to Audit Clients* (APB, 2010), paras 76–8 in particular 77.

The valuation must be provided to the company within six months prior to the allotment[89] and must state that the basis of the company's valuation is reasonable and that the value of the in-kind consideration, plus any cash payable, is equal to the aggregate share capital and aggregate share premium that has been attributed to the shares to be allotted to the proposed allottee.[90] The valuation must be sent to the proposed allottee[91] and a copy must be filed with the Companies Registrar.[92] An allotment that takes place in violation of these rules remains valid, but the allottee is liable for the amount of the aggregate share capital and share premium represented by the shares if either: he did not receive a copy of the valuation; or he knew or ought to have known about the contravention of the Act's valuation requirements.[93] This independent valuation requirement for in-kind consideration does not apply, however, when the in-kind consideration is *in whole or part* shares in another company[94] or where the shares are issued as part of a merger in which the consideration for the shares is the transfer of *all* the assets and liabilities of another company.[95]

2.7 Registration; return of allotment and the statement of capital

As previously observed, company law distinguishes between an allotment and an issuance of shares. An allotment of shares gives the allottee an unconditional right to be entered on the register of members.[96] However, no share is issued and the allottee does not become a member of the company until the allottee is entered into the company's register of members. In this regard, the Act requires that the company register the allotment of shares as soon as practicable and in any event within two months from the date of allotment.[97] The Act also requires that the company issue a share certificate to the allottee within two months of the allotment unless the terms of allotment provided that the shares were not to be in certificated form.[98]

In addition to entering the allotment in the register of members, within one month of the allotment the company must deliver to the Companies Registrar a *return of allotment*.[99] This return contains a *statement of capital* which provides the Registrar, and, via Companies House, the public at large, information about: the number of shares allotted; the rights attached to those shares; the aggregate nominal value of the shares; and the amounts paid up or unpaid on the allotted shares.

III CLASS RIGHTS

1 Variation of class rights

As we have seen in this chapter, shares can be issued with different rights. Preference shares may be granted priority in relation to dividends or in relation to their position in the repayment queue on the company's liquidation. Shares may be issued with no

---

[89] Section 593 CA 2006.   [90] Section 596 CA 2006.
[91] Section 593(1)(c) CA 2006.   [92] Section 597 CA 2006.
[93] Section 593(3) CA 2006.   [94] Section 594 CA 2006.
[95] Section 595 CA 2006.   [96] Section 558 CA 2006.   [97] Section 554 CA 2006.
[98] Section 769 CA 2006. The shares of all Listed Companies are issued in uncertificated form to facilitate ease of share transfers. Uncertificated form means that share transfers do not involve the transfer of paper share certificates; rather transfer takes place through entries in the electronic register of shareholders known as the CREST system—to be eligible for listing, shares must be transferable in electronic form (LR 6.1.23). This book will not address the regulation of uncertificated shares and their transfers. For a leading account of this regulation see chapter 27 of P. Davies, *Gower & Davies' Principles of Modern Company Law* (8th edn, Sweet & Maxwell, 2008).
[99] Section 555 CA 2006.

voting rights, one vote per share, multiple voting rights, or contingent voting rights. The power to attach rights to shares is, as we saw in section II, typically granted to the shareholder body but often to the board as well, provided that the board's decisions in this regard are consistent with applicable shareholder resolutions. If a company issues shares with a set of rights that are different from the rights attached to other shares that it has issued, we refer to the shares that have identical rights as a *class* of shares. Subject to any restrictions set out in a company's constitution, there is no limit on the number of classes of shares that a company can issue.

As we have seen, following the allotment of any shares the company must deliver to the Companies Registrar a *return of allotment* which makes publicly available the details of the rights attached to the newly allotted shares. In addition, it is common practice, although it is not required by law, to include the details of the rights attached to the shares in a company's articles of association. As we saw in section I, the rights attached to Vodafone Group Plc's Fixed Rate Shares are set out in Vodafone's articles.

A company may, for legitimate reasons, wish to change the rights attached to its shares. For example, the board of directors may decide that the share structure of the company is too complex with too many classes of shares with too many different rights and may wish to restructure these rights to provide a simpler and more transparent share structure. However, from the perspective of the holders of a particular class of shares a proposal to change the rights attached to shares raises significant concerns. After all, the rights attached to those shares are what the shareholder paid for when he purchased those shares. The class holder would be very concerned if the shareholder body as a whole is empowered to make the decision as to whether or not to change the rights attached to classes of shares. In such a situation controlling shareholders could act ex-post (after the class shareholder has purchased the shares) to remove rights granted to the class of shares. Those concerns will be less acute where the class of shareholders as a whole has a veto over any changes in class rights, and will evaporate altogether if every class holder must individually consent to a change in those rights. Of course, the rights a class shareholder pays for include the set of rights that determine how, if at all, those rights can be changed ex-post. A rational shareholder will pay little for class rights that can be amended after the purchase of the shares by the shareholder body as a whole. Accordingly, offering 'amendment protection' to minority shareholders is important for a company concerned to maximize the price investors will pay for a newly issued class of shares.

Traditionally UK companies have provided protection for holders of classes of shares by providing, in the company's constitution, that the rights attached to the class of shares can only be amended with the consent of a separate meeting of the class of shareholders at which 75% of the class cast their vote in favour of the amendments. Such a mechanism provides some flexibility for the company to amend its share structure whilst providing considerable comfort for the class of shareholders that the proposed amendments are not detrimental to their interests. Consider, for example, the variation of Vodafone Group Plc's class of Fixed Rate Shares:

■ Vodafone Group Plc Articles of Association

7. Varying the rights of Fixed Rate Shares

The rights of the holders of the Fixed Rate Shares will be regarded as being varied or *abrogated* if any resolution is passed for the reduction of the amount of capital paid up on the Fixed Rate Shares but not for the repayment of the Fixed Rate Shares at *par*.

Accordingly, this can only take place if:

- holders of at least three quarters in *nominal value* of the Fixed Rate Shares agree in writing; or

> - a *special resolution* is passed at a separate class meeting by the holders of the Fixed Rate Shares approving the proposal,
>
>   in accordance with Article 40.

It would be open to a company to provide lesser or greater protection for holders of a class of shares. It could, for example, provide for ordinary resolution class meeting approval or a higher threshold than the special resolution threshold, even requiring unanimity.

The Companies Act 2006 provides that in relation to 'the variation of the rights attached to a class of shares' where a company's articles provide for a class rights amendment procedure that procedure is the applicable procedure. However, where a company's articles do not provide for such a procedure then the Act provides for a class rights amendment procedure similar to the procedure described previously.

■ Section 630 Companies Act 2006 Variation of class rights: companies having a share capital

> (1) This section is concerned with the variation of the rights attached to a class of shares in a company having a share capital.
>
> (2) Rights attached to a class of a company's shares may only be varied—
>
>   (a) in accordance with provision in the company's articles for the variation of those rights, or
>
>   (b) where the company's articles contain no such provision, if the holders of shares of that class consent to the variation in accordance with this section.
>
> (3) This is without prejudice to any other restrictions on the variation of the rights.
>
> (4) The consent required for the purposes of this section on the part of the holders of a class of a company's shares is—
>
>   (a) consent in writing from the holders of at least three-quarters in nominal value of the issued shares of that class (excluding any shares held as treasury shares), or
>
>   (b) a special resolution passed at a separate general meeting of the holders of that class sanctioning the variation.
>
> (5) Any amendment of a provision contained in a company's articles for the variation of the rights attached to a class of shares, or the insertion of any such provision into the articles, is itself to be treated as a variation of those rights.

Where the company's articles do not provide a variation procedure section 630 requires, in relation to a public or private company, that a variation of the rights attached to shares requires *either* consent in writing from three quarters of the holders of shares of that class *or* a special resolution passed in a meeting of the holders of that class of shares.

As the Act defers to the class amendment procedure set out in a company's constitution this creates an additional class rights problem. As that procedure is part of the articles it can be amended just as any other provision of the articles can be amended. Section 21 of the 2006 Act provides that the articles can be amended by special resolution unless a particular provision has been 'entrenched' by providing for a higher amendment threshold. A provision must be entrenched either at the time of formation or thereafter by obtaining the agreement of *all* the members to entrenchment.[100]

---

[100] Section 22 CA 2006.

In large, widely-held companies, with many thousands of members, obtaining unanimous approval is close to impossible. Accordingly, in large companies entrenchment of class rights amendment procedures is not practical. The Act responds logically to this problem by clarifying in section 630(5) that any attempt to change the class variation procedure set out in the constitution is itself to be treated as a variation of class rights, which means the procedure could not be changed without obtaining the approval of the class in accordance with the existing procedure set out in the constitution.

2 What rights are class rights?

Section 630 applies to a variation of 'rights attached to a class of shares'. Certain rights annexed to shares are part of the metaphorical genetic structure of those shares—without reference to those rights the share would be an empty vessel. Such rights include the nature of the financial claim created by the share in question as well as the number of votes per share annexed to those shares. Where a company issues shares with such different core rights then those shares represent a class of shares to which the class variation regulation clearly applies. A difficulty arises where rights are granted to a shareholder, or to a person who is a shareholder, which are neither specifically annexed to the shares nor granted to other shareholders. Those rights may be set out in the constitution or in a separate document. Such rights could include, for example, the right to appoint a director, or the right of first refusal if any other shareholder wishes to sell his shares. Do such rights, although not attached to the shares in the same way as voting rights or dividend preference rights, amount to 'rights attached to a class of shares' for the purpose of section 630? Are the shares held by the members who have been granted such rights a class of shares? If so, such rights could only be varied with the approval of the class, which in many instances will mean the consent of the one member who has been granted those rights. This issue was directly considered in the following case.

■ *Cumbrian Newspapers Group Ltd v Cumberland & Westmorland Herald Newspaper & Printing Co Ltd* [1986] BCLC 286

Scott J

The plaintiff company, Cumbrian Newspapers Group Ltd, is the holder of 10.67 per cent of the issued ordinary shares in the defendant company, Cumberland & Westmorland Herald Newspaper & Printing Co Ltd.

The plaintiff's shares were issued to it in 1968. At the same time, and as part of the arrangement under which the shares were issued, the defendant adopted articles of association under which, inter alia, the plaintiff was granted [certain rights. These rights were set out in: article 5—which granted the plaintiff by name rights in relation to certain unissued shares; article 7—which granted the plaintiff the right not to have a transfer of shares to the plaintiff refused by the directors; article 9—which granted rights of pre-emption to the plaintiff; and article 12—which granted the plaintiff the right to appoint a director so long as it held 10% of the defendant's issued ordinary shares. Scott J observed that the rights granted to the plaintiff were part of the commercial agreement between the plaintiff and defendant; involving the plaintiff agreeing to act as the defendant's advertising agent and also agreeing to close a newspaper which it owned which competed with the defendant's newspaper, the *Cumberland Herald*. Had these rights not been provided to the defendant as part of the deal Scott J held that the transaction would not have taken place.]

The board of directors of the defendants have made it known that they desire to convene an extraordinary general meeting of the shareholders of the defendant, and to put before the general meeting a special resolution designed to cancel the articles under which the plaintiff enjoys the special rights I have mentioned.

The plaintiff contends that the special rights which it enjoys under the articles in question are 'class rights' which cannot be varied or abrogated without its consent...

I turn to the critical question: are the plaintiff's rights [provided in the articles] rights attached to a class of shares?

Rights or benefits which may be contained in articles can be divided into three different categories. First, there are rights or benefits which are annexed to particular shares. Classic examples of rights of this character are dividend rights and rights to participate in surplus assets on a winding up. If articles provide that particular shares carry particular rights not enjoyed by the holders of other shares, it is easy to conclude that the rights are 'attached to a class of shares'... The plaintiff's rights under arts 5, 7, 9 and 12 cannot, however, be brought within this first category. The rights were not attached to any particular shares. In arts 5, 7 and 9, there is no reference to any current shareholding held by the plaintiff. The rights conferred on the plaintiff under art 12 are dependent on the plaintiff holding at least 10 per cent of the issued ordinary shares in the defendant. But the rights are not attached to any particular shares. Any ordinary shares in the defendant, if sufficient in number and held by the plaintiff, would entitle the plaintiff to exercise the rights.

A second category of rights or benefits which may be contained in articles (although it may be that neither 'rights' nor 'benefits' is an apt description), would cover rights or benefits conferred on individuals not in the capacity of members or shareholders of the company but, for ulterior reasons, connected with the administration of the company's affairs or the conduct of its business.

Eley v Positive Government Security Life Assurance Co Ltd (1875) 1 Ex D 20, was a case where the articles of the defendant company had included a provision that the plaintiff should be the company solicitor. The plaintiff sought to enforce that provision as a contract between himself and the company. He failed. The reasons why he failed are not here relevant, and I cite the case only to draw attention to an article which, on its terms, conferred a benefit on an individual but not in the capacity of member or shareholder of the company. It is, perhaps, obvious that rights or benefits in this category cannot be class rights. They cannot be described as 'rights attached to a class of shares'. The plaintiff in *Eley v Positive Government Security Life Assurance Co Ltd*, was not a shareholder at the time the articles were adopted. He became a shareholder some time thereafter. It is easy, therefore, to conclude that the article in question did not confer on him any right or benefit in his capacity as a member of the company. In a case where the individual had been issued with shares in the company at the same time and as part of the same broad arrangement under which the article in question had been adopted, the conclusion might not be so easy. But if, in all the circumstances, the right conclusion was still that the rights or benefits conferred by the article were not conferred on the beneficiary in the capacity of member or shareholder of the company, then the rights could not, in my view, be regarded as class rights. They would not be 'rights attached to any class of shares'...

[However,] the evidence in this case has clearly established that the adoption by the defendant of arts 5, 7, 9 and 12, was inextricably connected with the issue to the plaintiff... In my judgment, the plaintiff's rights under those articles do not fall within this second category.

That leaves the third category. This category would cover rights or benefits that, although not attached to any particular shares, were none the less conferred on the beneficiary in the capacity of member or shareholder of the company. The rights of the plaintiff under arts 5, 7, 9 and 12 fall, in my judgment, into this category. Other examples can be found in reported cases.

In *Bushell v Faith* [1969] 1 All ER 1002 articles of association included a provision that on a resolution at a general meeting for the removal of any director from office, any shares held by that director should carry the right to three votes. The purpose of this provision was to prevent directors being removed from office by a simple majority of the members of the company. The validity of the article was upheld by the Court of Appeal and by the House of Lords; the reasons do not, for present purposes, matter. But the rights conferred by the article in question fall, in my view, firmly in this third category. They were not attached to any particular shares. On the other hand, they were conferred on the director/beneficiaries in their capacity as shareholders. The article created, in effect, two classes of shareholders, namely shareholders who were for the time being directors, on the one hand, and shareholders who were not for the time being directors, on the other hand...

In the present case, the rights conferred on the plaintiff under arts 5, 7, 9 and 12 were, as I have held, conferred on the plaintiff as a member or shareholder of the defendant. The rights would not be enforceable by the plaintiff otherwise than as the owner of ordinary shares in the defendant. If the plaintiff were to divest itself of all its ordinary shares in the defendant, it would not then, in my view, be in a position to enforce the rights in the articles. But the rights were not attached to any particular share or shares. Enforcement by the plaintiff of the rights granted under arts 5, 7 and 9, would require no more than ownership by the plaintiff of at least some shares in the defendant. Enforcement by the plaintiff of the rights granted under art 12, require the plaintiff to hold at least 10 per cent of the issued shares in the defendant. But any shares would do. It follows, in my judgment, that the plaintiff's rights under the articles in question fall squarely within this third category.

The question for decision is whether rights in this third category are within the meaning of the phrase...'rights attached to a class of shares'...It would, in my opinion, be surprising and unsatisfactory if class rights contained in articles were to be at the mercy of a special resolution majority at a general meeting, unless they were rights attached to particular shares. If the articles of a particular company grant special rights to a special class of members, it would be odd to find that members not in that class could cancel the rights simply by means of a special resolution.

[Scott J considered the intention of the legislature in this regard. As many of his observations relate to provisions of the predecessor Companies Act 1985 not all of which have been re-enacted by the 2006 Act, these reasons are not extracted here.]

I conclude that [the term 'rights attached to a class of shares'] was intended by the legislature to cater for the variation or abrogation of any special rights given by the memorandum or articles of a company to any class of members, that is to say, not only rights falling into the first category I have described, but also rights falling into the third category...

In my judgment, a company which, by its articles, confers special rights on one or more of its members in the capacity of member or shareholder thereby constitutes the shares for the time being held by that member or members, a class of shares for the purposes of [the Act]. The rights are class rights.

I have already expressed the opinion that the rights conferred on the plaintiff under arts 5, 7, 9 and 12, were conferred on the plaintiff as member or shareholder of the defendant. It follows that, in my judgment, the shares in the defendant for the time being held by the plaintiff constitute a class of shares for the purpose of variation or abrogation of those rights.

Scott J identifies three categories of rights for consideration: rights annexed to shares; rights conferred on a member other than as member; and rights conferred on a member as member. The first and third categories qualify as 'rights attached to a class of shares' for the purpose of section 630 and are, therefore, rights to which the Act's class variation regulation applies. The first category of right includes the financial claim created by the share and, one presumes, the general voting rights attached to the shares.

In relation to the third category, the basis upon which one determines whether a right is conferred on a member in his capacity as member is not entirely clear given the range of rights in this case that were deemed to be class rights. Two considerations appear to be of particular importance for the court: first, that the right provides some protection for the member in relation to his interests as a shareholder or enables the member to protect those interests; and, secondly, that the rights granted were part of the bargain in relation to which the shares were issued.[101]

---

[101] For examples of cases where following *Cumbrian Newspapers* the courts refused to hold that there were class rights see *Re Blue Arrow* [1987] BCLC 585 and *Alvona Developments Ltd v Manhattan Loft Corp (AC) Ltd* [2006] BCC 119.

Arguably, the judgment is tainted by Scott J's intuition that if specific rights are given then they should not be amendable by the general meeting as a whole. He observes that 'it would be odd to find that members not in a class could cancel the rights simply by means of a special resolution'. However, a note of dissent could be registered. The statute refers to 'rights attached to shares'. The language used appears to refer to financial rights and voting rights, whatever their nature. Specific pre-emption rights or rights relating to the registration of shares, which were the subject of consideration in this case, are not 'rights attached to shares' and, although it would indeed be 'odd' to grant such rights and then not to protect them from general meeting amendment, the Companies Act provides a means to protect them from amendment, namely entrenchment. The use of class rights to address such rights appears to stretch the language of the provision.

3 Variation in rights versus detriment to class interests?

The procedure set out in section 630 of the Act applies to the variation in rights attached to shares; it does not apply to corporate action that may affect the class of shareholders without varying those rights. Whilst a new issue of shares with a different set of rights, or new shares with the same rights, may alter the position or affect the interests of the existing holders of the class of shares,[102] it does not vary their rights. For example, if additional ordinary shares are issued this may dilute the voting power of preference shares that have a right to vote, or whose contingent right to vote has been triggered. Clearly, however, this does not vary the rights of the preference shareholders.

Companies could elect to provide more extensive protection for a class of shareholders, for example, by giving them a right to a class vote where the rights attached to the shares are affected rather than varied, or indeed where *the interests* of that class are affected. *In White v Bristol Aeroplane Co Limited*,[103] for example, the Court of Appeal considered a provision in Bristol Aeroplane Co's articles which provided for a class vote where class 'rights or privileges attached to any class of shares' were 'affected, modified, varied, dealt with, or abrogated'. However, even in relation to such broader class rights provisions the courts have construed them narrowly to distinguish between detrimental effects on the class shareholders' position and variations to the rights attached to those shares. In *White v Bristol Aeroplane,* for example, a case involving the issue of additional shares that altered the control position of the preferred shareholders, the court stressed that the shareholders' rights and not their interests had to be affected or varied, and found that their rights were neither varied or affected, holding that the preference shareholders took 'their rights subject always to the normal incidence of the company's right to increase its capital'.[104]

---

[102] For a recent example see *Citco Banking Corporation NV v Pusser's Ltd* [2007] UKPC 13.

[103] [1953] Ch 65.

[104] Shortly thereafter in *Re John Smith's Tadcaster Brewery Co Ltd* [1953] 1 All ER 518 the Court of Appeal held in relation to a similar class rights provision that the capitalization of undistributed profits through a bonus issue of ordinary shares to existing ordinary shareholders did not affect or vary the rights of preference shareholders. See further *Greenhalgh v Arderne Cinemas Ltd* [1946] 1 All ER 512 where following the subdivision of a class of 10 shilling shares into 2 shilling shares all carrying one vote per share, Greenhalgh, the holder of the pre-existing 2 shilling shares lost control of the company. In this regard Lord Greene MR observed 'instead of Greenhalgh finding himself in a position of control, he finds himself in a position where the control has gone, and to that extent the rights…are affected, as a matter of business. As a matter of law, I am quite unable to hold that, as a result of the transaction, the rights are varied; they remain what they always were—a right to have one vote per share *pari passu* with the ordinary shares for the time being issued which include the new 2s ordinary shares resulting from the subdivision.' See also *Dimbula Valley (Ceylon) Tea Co Ltd v Laurie* [1961] Ch 353.

4 **Protecting minority class shareholders**

Most companies will provide for special resolution class meeting amendment procedures or, alternatively, the class will benefit from such procedures pursuant to section
630 of the Act. Such procedures provide a significant amount of protection for class
holders. A considerable majority of the holders of those shares must agree to those
amendments. Where class shareholders act in their own interests *as class shareholders*,
although class holders may disagree on the merits of the proposed changes, if 75% vote
in favour then the changes are unlikely to be detrimental to the class as a whole. A problem arises, however, where the class shareholders do not act in their interests as class
shareholders but rather in their other interests, perhaps as holders of a different class of
shares. Such a situation is particularly problematic where the shareholder acting in his
other *non-class* interests controls a 75% majority of the class shares. The law provides
protection for minority class shareholders in two ways: first, through the common law
duty for shareholders[105] to exercise their votes bona fide for the benefit of the company
as a whole; and secondly, through a statutory right to apply to court for a relief from a
vote in favour of the variation in class rights where the variation is *unfairly prejudicial*
to the minority class shareholders' interests.

We saw in Chapter 16 that votes cast in general meeting[106] must be exercised bona fide
for the benefit of the company as a whole. We saw that this standard evolved to require
that the shareholder, in good faith, believed that the action taken by the general meeting
benefited the company. We concluded from our analysis of this standard that it imposed
on controlling shareholders a requirement to exercise their voting power in a way that
does not directly discriminate between shareholders and can be rationally construed as
benefiting the company. Provided that shareholder action is not directly discriminatory
the obligation imposes a very deferential standard of review on general meeting decisions. Where a class vote takes place, the requirement to vote in a way that benefits the
company as a whole is inapposite. The changes to the class rights may indeed be viewed
as benefiting the company as a whole, but the purpose of a class vote is to enable the
class holders to protect their rights and they may elect to reject the amendments even if
the rejection is detrimental to the company. The courts have sensibly modified the bona
fide obligation in the context of class votes to require that the class meeting's decision is
bona fide in the interests of the class as a whole. The standard of review entailed by this
obligation is unaltered—it requires only that the decision is not discriminatory among
the class holders and can rationally be construed as being in the class interest, not that
in the court's view it actually is.

However, where class rights are altered to the detriment of the class and to the benefit
of a different class in which the majority class holder also has a significant stake, the
appearance of discrimination may lead the courts to carry out a less deferential review
of the class vote. Arguably, this was seen in *In Holders Investment Trust Ltd*,[107] a
case involving a reduction of capital[108] and the cancellation of a class of shares, where
trustees holding the majority of preference shares that were subject to the class vote
also held a significant proportion of the ordinary shares. The trustees had apparently
acted on the basis of advice relating to their overall holdings in the company. Megarry J
rejected the class vote as sanctioning the capital reduction, which meant that the burden

---

[105] In relation to this obligation see Chapter 16.
[106] Whether the obligation applies to the exercise of general meeting power or applies to shareholders
and the exercise of their votes see p 665.
[107] [1971] 2 All ER 289.
[108] On capital reductions see further Chapter 19, section IV.

of proof was placed on those supporting the reduction to prove to the court that it was fair in order for the court to confirm the reduction.[109] In this regard he held as follows:

> That exchange of letters seems to me to make it perfectly clear that the advice sought, the advice given [by the trustees], and the advice acted on, was all on the basis of what was for the benefit of the trusts as a whole, having regard to their large holdings of the equity capital [in the company]. From the point of view of equity, and disregarding company law, this is a perfectly proper basis: but that is not the question before me. I have to determine whether the supporting trustees voted for the reduction in the bona fide belief that they were acting in the interests of the general body of members of that class. From first to last I can see no evidence that the trustees ever applied their minds to what, under company law, was the right question, or that they ever had the bona fide belief that is requisite for the effectual sanction of the reduction...The result is therefore that on the issue of fairness the burden of proof devolves on those supporting the reduction to prove that it is fair. Unless this burden is proved, confirmation of the reduction will be refused. [Megarry J concluded that the reduction was unfair].

In addition to the protection provided by the common law *bona fide for the benefit of the class* obligation, section 633 of the Act provides shareholders representing 15% of the class of shares with a right to apply to the court to have the variation cancelled.[110] The court will exercise its discretion to cancel the variation where it is satisfied that 'having regard to all the circumstances of the case that the variation would *unfairly prejudice* the members of the class represented by the applicant'. The extent to which the provision is relied on in practice and the meaning given by the courts to 'unfairly prejudice' is somewhat unclear given the very few reported cases addressing this provision, or its predecessor provisions in prior Companies Acts.[111] Clearly, the provision provides minority class shareholders with some protection. However, where the controlling class shareholder owns more than 85% of the class of shares, minority class shareholders will only be able to rely on the common law obligation imposed on the controller to exercise the votes bona fide for the benefit of the class.

IV SHARE BUY-BACKS

1 Why would a company repurchase its own shares?

In Chapter 19 of this book we will consider how the regulation of legal capital affects the company's ability to make a dividend. A dividend is a distribution of value to shareholders that may be in cash or in kind. As we shall see in Chapter 19, companies can make a dividend to shareholders provided that the dividend does not amount to a return of legal capital. The ability of a company to pay dividends is important for two reasons: first, dividends are important to investors to satisfy their own liquidity needs, whether personal needs or institutional needs such as paying pensions and insurance claims; and, second, if the company does not have available to it investment opportunities which can generate an adequate return, shareholders would prefer to have the available cash returned to them and to invest it themselves. Dividends, however, are not the

---

[109] *Ibid* observing in relation to court confirmation for the capital reduction: 'the burden of proof depends on whether or not there is any such sanction. If there is, the court will confirm the reduction unless the opposition proves that it is unfair; if there is not, the court will confirm the reduction only if it is proved to be fair.'

[110] Section 634 CA 2006 provides a similar procedure for company's limited by guarantee.

[111] *In re Sound City (Films) Limited* [1947] Ch 169 addressing section 61 CA 1929 which did not contain the 'unfair prejudice' requirement; see also *Re Suburban and Provincial Stores Ltd* [1943] Ch 156.

only way of transferring value to shareholders. An alternative way of distributing value to shareholders is by buying back the company's own shares from its shareholders. But why would a company be interested in buying back its own shares, and if a company decides to buy back its own shares, why would shareholders care whether the shares are sold to the company or to other third parties?

In relation to small close companies, share buy-backs may be a useful way to provide one of the company's shareholders with an exit from the company where there is no market in the company's shares or where sales of such shares are subject to restrictions set out in the constitution. An alternative to a share buy-back would be for one or all of the remaining shareholders in the company to purchase the exiting shareholder's shares. However, it may be easier for the company to effect the purchase if it has access to funds to do so and where the other shareholders do not. In relation to listed companies, where there is an active market in the company's shares, shareholders can exit their investment in the market place. Why then would a listed company elect to buy back its own shares? In this regard, consider the following extracts:

■ C. Hughes, 'Dash to splash the cash: by using buy-backs companies are taking advantage of low interest rates and cheap borrowing to return money to investors' *Financial Times* (11 September 2006)

Companies are funnelling cash to investors like never before. But it is not just dividends that are going up. On both sides of the Atlantic, companies are also splashing out on their own shares to return cash burning a hole in their pockets...UK-listed companies spent £32 billion buying back their own stock last year—about 2 per cent of their total market capitalisations, according to Citigroup. But they have spent a further £41 billion on these so-called share buy-backs so far in 2006, and look set to have returned as much as 3.5 per cent of their total market capitalisations by the year-end.

This means UK-quoted companies—led by the likes of Diageo, Anglo American, BP, Hanson, HBOS and Tesco—will dish out roughly as much cash to investors via buy-backs as they pay in dividends this year. Buy-backs are also booming in the US, where Microsoft, Hewlett-Packard, AT&T, TimeWarner and Gap are setting the pace. Dresdner Kleinwort estimates that buy-backs will, in effect, boost the US market's dividend yield by some 3 per cent this year.

Why the dash to splash the cash using buy-backs? Partly, the reasons are technical. From a company's point of view, buy-backs are a cheap and flexible method of getting cash to shareholders without having to commit to do so indefinitely. When a company buys its shares for cancellation, its earnings per share are subsequently calculated on a lower base.[112] This drives EPS upward, even if profits are flat. Moreover, a policy of buy-backs rather than a hike in the regular dividend gives corporate flexibility. If capital is needed in a few months' time, the buy-back can be suspended and need not be repeated. A dividend cut, however, is often a corporate humiliation.

Equally, it is hard to renege on a promised one-off 'special dividend' once it is announced. Special dividends also tend to be expensive to administer. For shareholders, buy-backs may sometimes be preferable to increased dividends because the latter are taxed as income. Gains on shares sold in a buy-back can be offset against losses elsewhere. As for the current buy-back boom, stock market strategists say it is a cyclical phenomenon—up to a point. A buoyant economy has seen companies generate higher-than-normal earnings, and buy-backs offer a neat method of distributing these unusually large profits...

---

[112] Earnings per share or EPS is calculated by dividing a company's net income by the number of outstanding ordinary shares. The less shares are outstanding the higher earnings per share. If a buy-back reduces the number of outstanding shares it necessarily increases earnings per share.

From this extract we see that from a company's perspective share buy-backs have two advantages over making a dividend to shareholders. The first is that they allow cash to be returned to shareholders without creating an expectation that this return of cash in excess of the company's regular dividend will be a regular event and, if necessary, it is easier to withdraw a buy-back than it would be to withdraw a special dividend if company or market conditions change before the buy-back has taken place. If a listed company authorizes the buy-back this will typically take place over a period of time and can be stopped at any time without fanfare. The article suggests that by contrast cancelling an announced special dividend would be viewed as a humiliation. The second benefit from the company's perspective is that as a result of the buy-back the company's earnings per share (EPS) increases. As a higher earnings per share makes the company appear healthier the market place may look favourably upon it even though the company's actual earnings have not changed. With regard to the pros and cons of share buy-backs consider further the following extract:

■ R. Dobbs and W. Rehm, 'Are share buy-backs a good thing?' *Financial Times* (28 June 2006)

Over the past 18 months, companies around the world have announced more than Dollars 500bn of share buy-backs…Stock markets almost always react enthusiastically to news of a buy-back. Research shows that the share price of companies initiating small repurchase programs rise on average by 2 to 3 per cent on the day of an announcement. Larger buy-backs tend to deliver much bigger increases.

But companies and shareholders should not get too carried away by the prospect of buy-backs. Yes, they can create value through improved tax efficiency and by establishing better capital discipline for the business.

But, contrary to what many believe, they do not improve a company's underlying performance. Indeed, they can actually prejudice the long-term health of the company if they are chosen as an alternative to value-creating investments.

The idea, expressed by some commentators, that share buy-backs improve earnings per share, return on equity, return on capital employed, economic profit and fundamental intrinsic value is simply wrong. It is true that share buy-backs result in higher stated earnings per share—a target often used in performance-based compensation programmes. This is because the number of shares in issue falls proportionally further than the drop in earnings because cash has been returned to investors rather than generating interest. But there is no impact on the value of the company's operations. In fact, other influences apart, the increase in EPS is exactly offset by a reduction in the price–earnings ratio…

However, share buy-backs can still increase the value of companies—but for other reasons. Some of the increase in the value of a company that announces a share buy-back is attributable to the tax benefits of its new capital structure.

This is because holding excess cash raises the cost of capital: since interest income is taxable, a company that maintains large cash reserves puts investors at a disadvantage. But it is important to note that this tax effect is much smaller than the observed effect of buy-backs on share prices would warrant.

Markets respond positively to share buy-back announcements because they offer new information, or 'signals', about a company's future. One signal might be that management believes the stock to be undervalued, an interpretation generally confirmed if executives also purchase significant numbers of shares on their own account.

Another signal might be that management is confident it will not need the cash to cover future commitments such as interest payments and capital expenditures—perhaps because underlying operations are doing better than the market realises.

> Yet, in many cases, the most significant reason why investors respond positively is because they are relieved that managers are not going to spend a company's cash either on a rash or ill thought-out merger or acquisition or some other project with negative net present value. Such scepticism can be well-founded. In many industries, chief executives and their management teams have allocated cash reserves poorly and destroyed shareholder value...
>
> Rather than feeling relieved that their cash will not be wasted, some investors may feel disappointed that a company's executives seem to be admitting that it is unable to find worthwhile investment opportunities—one explanation perhaps of why the share prices of a few companies decline in the wake of an announcement. And, in businesses where boards link compensation to EPS, the markets may suspect that managers are promoting the short-term effects of a share buy-back for their own ends rather than investing the company's funds with a view to tending its long-term health. Value-minded executives should therefore resist pressure to conduct share buy-backs, if it means forgoing value-creating investments.

Dobbs and Rehm argue that some of the apparent benefits of share buy-backs are illusory. Increase in earnings per share is merely window dressing and does not reflect an increase in the company's intrinsic value. However, they observe that share buy-backs can have positive real effects on company value and that the decision to make a share buy-back may convey important information to the market place. Real intrinsic value improvements can be created by the tax benefits associated with the buy-back.[113] These involve no longer paying income tax on cash in the bank or being able to deduct interest payments from taxable income if extra debt is taken on to fund the share buy-back. With regard to information provided to the market place, the share buy-back may signal to the market place that in the managers' view the shares are undervalued and so it is a good time to buy back the shares. Importantly, however, Dobbs and Rehm stress that companies may buy back shares for bad reasons—for example, executive compensation targets based on earnings per share, or the fact that the managers do not know what to do with the funds at their disposal. In this regard, investors may like share buy-backs for disappointing reasons, namely their relief that managers will not waste the funds on projects that generate poor returns but increase the size of 'their' empire.

Note, that the two extracted articles were written at the peak of the recent bull market and prior to the crisis. As the economy has soured so too have commentators' views of the purported benefits of share buy-backs. In this regard consider the following extract from the former Director of the Confederation of British Industry:

■ R. Lambert, 'Buy-backs are often doomed to destroy value'
Financial Times (21 August 2011)

> Far from buying when prices are low and falling, companies in the US and the UK invariably step up buy-backs when their shares are selling at or close to the peak, and they do so on a large scale... In the UK... the high point for these transactions came as the market reached new heights in the second half of 2007 and share repurchases climbed to £18.6bn over that six-month period. Then came the market slump, and buy-backs at the low point in March 2009 amounted to just £32m. Share prices rallied again this spring, and the figure for repurchases in the second quarter of the year came to more than £4bn.

---

[113] On the relationship between debt and equity and company value see M. Miller and F. Modigliani, 'The Cost of Capital, Corporation Finance and the Theory of Investment' (1958) 48 *American Economic Review* 261 and M. Miller and F. Modigliani, 'Corporate income taxes and the cost of capital: a correction' (1963) 53 *American Economic Review* 433.

These figures imply value destruction on a large scale, an impression confirmed by analysis in the US, which shows that the implied returns over a period from buy-backs by big companies would have been laughed out of the boardroom if they had been proposed for investment in bricks and mortar or other more conventional projects.

So what explains this irrational behaviour? Institutional investors, many of whom have little interest in the company's long-term well-being, naturally welcome the chance to cash in their shares at high prices. Investment banks get fees from promoting buy-backs, which does not happen when companies pay out boring old dividends. So both these groups have an incentive to persuade company managers to play the game.

Of course companies should have no interest in buying shares at high prices. But managers' appetite for risk tends to rise in bull markets, and so do their cash balances as profits rise. That is why they can gear up[114] their balance sheet by buying in their equity while the good times last. Moreover, these transactions have the mechanical effect of increasing earnings per share—but not the overall profitability of the business—as the number of outstanding shares is reduced. This tends to make executives feel smarter, and richer too, if their compensation is tied to increases in their companies EPS as is sometimes still the case.

But there are losers from this process as well as winners. Long-term shareholders will always be worse off, unless the shares are bought at below their intrinsic value and their company can see no better way of using the money by investing in building value for the future. The public interest also suffers, as money that could have been used to create long term returns and jobs is frittered away in uneconomic transactions.

In this way, share buy-backs have an adverse impact on the long-term competitiveness of UK business, which means that they should be on the agenda of John Kay as he works on his review of UK equity markets for the government. The solutions are not difficult to find: Terry Smith, the straight-talking City of London pundit, has spelt them out. Among other things, he suggests that management should be required to justify buy-backs by reference to the price paid and the implied return on the investment, and to compare this with alternative uses of the cash. He also argues that the repurchased shares should be reflected as assets on the balance sheet, and the return on these assets should flow through the profit-and-loss account.

If Mr Lambert is correct then companies and long-term shareholders are being damaged by buy-backs as value is wasted by overpaying for shares, and the economy is damaged *if* corporate projects and investment are detrimentally effected due to the reduced financial firepower of the company. *If* this view is empirically correct then tailored regulation of share buy-backs, beyond the current state of regulation, which we consider later in the chapter, may be required. Note in this regard, that Mr Lambert suggests that such regulation may be on the radar of Professor John Kay who, on behalf of the Government, is carrying out a review on *UK Equity Markets and Long Term Decision Making*.[115] At the time of writing the Review's consultation period has ended but the Review's findings and recommendations are yet to be published.

2 Regulation of share buy-backs at common law

The common law has long viewed the purchase by a company of its own shares as unlawful. In 1887 in *Trevor v Whitworth*, a company had purchased shares from one of its shareholders who later made a claim in the company's liquidation proceeding

---

[114] Gearing is the UK term for leverage. To 'gear up' means to take on additional debt. Buy-backs are often funded through additional debt.

[115] See www.bis.gov.uk/Consultations/kay-review-call-for-evidence-uk-equity-markets ⚫.

for the balance of the amounts owed in relation to the buy-back. The House of Lords, overruling the Court of Appeal, held that the repurchase of shares by the company was prohibited and *ultra vires* the company.

■ *Trevor v Whitworth* (1887) 12 App Cas 409

Lord Herschell

I pass now to the main question in this case, which is one of great and general importance, whether the company had power to purchase the shares…Let me now invite your Lordships' attention to the facts of the present case. The company had purchased, prior to the date of the liquidation, no less than 4142 of its own shares; that is to say, considerably more than a fourth of the paid-up capital of the company had been either paid, or contracted to be paid, to shareholders, in consideration only of their ceasing to be so. I am quite unable to see how this expenditure was incurred in respect of or as incidental to any of the objects specified in the memorandum. And, if not, I have a difficulty in seeing how it can be justified. If the claim under consideration can be supported, the result would seem to be this, that the whole of the shareholders, with the exception of those holding seven individual shares, might now be claiming payment of the sums paid upon their shares as against the creditors, who had a right to look to the moneys subscribed as the source out of which the company's liabilities to them were to be met. And the stringent precautions to prevent the reduction of the capital of a limited company, without due notice and judicial sanction, would be idle if the company might purchase its own shares wholesale, and so effect the desired result. I do not think it was disputed that a company could not enter upon such a transaction for the purpose of reducing its capital, but it was suggested that it might do so if that were not the object, but it was considered for some other reason desirable in the interest of the company to do so. To the creditor, whose interests, I think, sects. 8 and 12 of the Companies Act were intended to protect, it makes no difference what the object of the purchase is. The result to him is the same. The shareholders receive back the moneys subscribed, and there passes into their pockets what before existed in the form of cash in the coffers of the company, or of buildings, machinery, or stock available to meet the demands of the creditors.

What was the reason which induced the company in the present case to purchase its shares? If it was that they might sell them again, this would be a trafficking in the shares, and clearly unauthorized. If it was to retain them, this would be to my mind an indirect method of reducing the capital of the company. The only suggestion of another motive (and it seems to me to be a suggestion unsupported by proof) is that this was intended to be a family company, and that the directors wanted to keep the shares as much as possible in the hands of those who were partners, or who were interested in the old firm, or of those persons whom the directors thought they would like to be amongst this small number of shareholders. I cannot think that the employment of the company's money in the purchase of shares for any such purpose was legitimate. The business of the company was that of manufacturers of flannel. In what sense was the expenditure of the company's money in this way incidental to the carrying on of such a business, or how could it secure the end of enabling the business to be more profitably or satisfactorily carried on? I can quite understand that the directors of a company may sometimes desire that the shareholders should not be numerous, and that they should be persons likely to leave them with a free hand to carry on their operations. But I think it would be most dangerous to countenance the view that, for reasons such as these, they could legitimately expend the moneys of the company to any extent they please in the purchase of its shares. No doubt if certain shareholders are disposed to hamper the proceedings of the company, and are willing to sell their shares, they may be bought out; but this must be done by persons, existing shareholders or others, who can be induced to purchase the shares, and not out of the funds of the company.

There are three primary drivers of this decision. First, that a repurchase of shares may be beyond the company's objects and, therefore, *ultra vires*. Secondly, even if it is not *ultra vires* the company's objects, as a repurchase of shares and the subsequent cancellation of shares results in a reduction of capital it is illegal as the Act provides only one means of reducing a company's share capital, namely by capital reduction following the statutory procedure. Thirdly, trafficking in the company's shares is prohibited. Lord Herschell does recognize the potential legitimate reason for a buy-back, namely, ensuring that the shares in the company are not sold to persons that the company would not want to own the shares. However, he views this justification as inadequate in light of the concerns noted above.

Of the three identified concerns the primary one is reduction of capital. For anyone reading this book in chapter order it is somewhat difficult to engage with this argument, as the regulation of legal capital is dealt with in Chapter 19. Legal capital at the time of this case was the aggregate nominal value of the company and capital regulation prevented a transfer of value to the shareholders which reduced the **shareholder equity** accounting entry below this legal capital amount. For current purposes, note that if the company had made sufficient profits the funds transferred to buy back the shares would not reduce capital, although capital would be reduced if the shares were then subsequently cancelled. If such shares were not cancelled and were retained by the company with a view to selling them again, then although capital would not be reduced the court's third concern would be triggered, namely that the purchase and sale of the company's shares by the company could result in a manipulation of the company's share price; this is what is intended by the reference to trafficking.

What is noteworthy then is that none of the House of Lords' objections necessarily lead to the court's conclusion of a general ban on the repurchase of shares: if a company explicitly authorized in its objects the repurchase of shares there is no *ultra vires* problem; if the shares are purchased out of profits and are not subsequently cancelled there would be no reduction in capital; and if the resale of those shares was prohibited there is no scope for company 'trafficking in its own shares'. Nevertheless, the common law imposed a clear and unequivocal ban on the repurchase by a company of its own shares.

3 Regulation of share buy-backs pursuant to the Companies Act 2006

The prohibition remained in place until the reforms introduced by the Companies Act 1980 which are now set out in Part 18 of the Companies Act 2006. Section 658 of the 2006 Act provides a qualified restatement of *Trevor v Whitworth* by requiring that 'a limited company must not acquire its own shares, whether by purchase, subscription or otherwise, except in accordance with the provisions of this Part'. There are two primary exceptions set out in Part 18 to this general prohibition, which we shall address in turn: general provisions on the buy-back of shares set out in sections 690–708 (Chapter 4) of the Act; and provisions providing for the issue and redemption of redeemable shares set out in sections 684–690 (Chapter 3) of the Act.

3.1 Purchase of the company's own shares

Chapter 4 of Part 18 of the Act provides that a public or a private company may purchase its own shares providing that it complies: first, with the rules relating to the financing of the purchase; and, second, with the rules relating to shareholder approval of the repurchase. The rules relating to the financing of the repurchase are designed to ensure that a company's legal capital is not reduced as a result of the repurchase unless the repurchase involves a permitted purchase out of capital for a private company in accordance with sections 709–723 (Chapter 5) of the 2006 Act. Where the repurchase is not a repurchase out of capital in accordance with Chapter 5 of Part 18 of the Act, then the repurchase must be financed out of distributable profits or a fresh issue of shares.[116] We will postpone our analysis of the reasons for and the effects of these financing provisions to section III.6 of Chapter 19 of this book.

To effect a share buy-back the Act requires the approval of the shareholder body. The nature of the required approval varies depending on the nature of the purchase. If the company intends to purchase shares on a stock exchange such as the **Main Market** of the London Stock Exchange there is no concern that the price that will be paid by the company will have been determined in part through influence exerted by the seller of the shares or as a result of relationships between senior management and the seller. The repurchase programme will be implemented through the company's broker buying shares in the market place from sellers whose identity is unknown to the broker. However, if the shares to be repurchased are not purchased on a stock exchange but through direct negotiations between the company and the selling shareholder then there is scope for the price paid to be in excess of an 'arm's length' price. In such a case, the shareholders who are not selling their shares will be concerned that the repurchase could contain a transfer in value from the company to the shareholder in excess of the actual value of the purchased shares.

The Companies Act 2006 is cognizant of this problem and distinguishes between 'market' and 'off-market' purchases. A 'market' purchase is one that takes place through a 'recognised investment exchange' such as the London Stock Exchange.[117] For such a purchase to be implemented the shareholders must give *prior* approval by ordinary resolution. The authority given may be general or refer specifically to particular classes of shares[118] and must specify the maximum number of shares to be purchased and the maximum and minimum price to be paid for these shares.[119] The resolution must also provide a time period at the end of which the shareholders' authorization will expire, and this cannot be a date later than five years after the resolution is past.[120]

If the purchase is an 'off-market' purchase the Act imposes more onerous shareholder approval requirements. The purchase must be approved by special resolution.[121] Prior to the shareholder meeting, or, in relation to a private company, a written resolution, the contract between the company and the selling shareholder[122] must be made available to the shareholders.[123] The Act provides for disinterested shareholder voting: the member who is selling shares which is the subject of the proposed authorization is not an 'eligible member' in relation to the vote.[124] The resolution is not effective if the selling shareholder votes on the authorization *and* the authorization would not have been granted if the selling shareholder had not voted in favour.[125] Once shareholder approval has been given the contract cannot be varied without first disclosing the details of the variation and obtaining renewed special resolution approval for the variation.[126]

Whilst shareholders will have concerns that the price paid for shares in an off-market purchase may be in excess of the value of the shares, they may be similarly concerned

---

[116] Section 692 CA 2006. Distributable profits are considered in detail in Chapter 19.

[117] Section 693(2) CA 2006.   [118] Section 701(2) CA 2006.

[119] Section 701(3) CA 2006.

[120] Section 701(5) CA 2006. This was extended to five years from 18 months by The Companies (Share Capital and Acquisition by Company of its Own Shares) Regulations 2009 (SI 2009/2022), reg 4(2).   [121] Section 694(2)(a) CA 2006.

[122] If there is no contract then a memorandum of the terms of the repurchase must be provided instead: section 696(2) CA 2006.

[123] In relation to the general meeting approval the contract must be made available at the at the company's registered office at least 15 days prior to the meeting, as well as at the meeting, and in relation to written resolution approval with the proposed resolution: section 696(2) CA 2006.

[124] Section 695 CA 2006.   [125] Section 695(3) CA 2006.

[126] Sections 697, 689, 699 CA 2006.

that directors should not exercise their powers to release a selling shareholder from a contract which represents a good deal for the company. This problem may arise, for example, where between entering into the contract and the completion of the share purchase, market conditions result in an increase in the value of the shares above the price at which the company has agreed to repurchase them. To protect shareholders in this regard the Companies Act 2006 requires special resolution approval of a release from a buy-back contract.[127]

Once the purchase has been implemented in accordance with these requirements, the company must deliver a return to the Companies Registrar detailing, among others, the number and nature of the shares that have been repurchased and the number of shares to be cancelled.[128]

In addition to the regulation of share buy-backs set out in the Companies Act 2006, listed companies with a premium listing[129] are subject to additional regulation of buy-backs set out in the Listing Rules. Where the Company wishes to repurchase more than 15% of a class of shares it must effect such repurchase through a tender offer at a fixed price to all shareholders of that class and purchase the shares pro rata from the shareholders who accepted the offer.[130] However, if the shares are purchased in a series of purchases, only the final purchase that results in crossing the 15% threshold in aggregate must be made by tender offer.[131] Where the company wishes to repurchase at a price above the current market price a pro-rata tender offer ensures equal access to the buy-back offer to all shareholders. Where the market repurchases are less than 15% of the shares of that class, although the offer does not have to be made by tender offer, the Listing Rules impose pricing regulation that prevents a purchase for more than 5% above the average price in the five days prior to the day the purchase is made.[132] This ensures that the company's repurchases do not artificially inflate the price of the shares and, as there is a limit on the amount paid above the market price, the fact that all shareholders do not have equal access to participate in the repurchase is less of a concern.

Two other aspects of the Listing Rules' regulation of share buy-backs are noteworthy. First, concerned to ensure that these buy-backs do not facilitate manipulation of the price of the shares due to inside information possessed by the company, the Listing Rules prohibit buy-backs during 'prohibited periods',[133] which include specific time periods prior to the publication of interim or end-of-year financial statements, but also at any time where inside information has not been made public. However, the company may repurchase shares during such a *prohibited period* if the repurchase is pursuant to a pre-announced repurchase programme which provides fixed dates and quantities to be repurchased or where the repurchase is carried out by an independent third party.[134] Finally, to the extent that the company has issued securities that are convertible into the class of shares being repurchased, or that provide a right to purchase those shares, the repurchase cannot take place unless approved by a special resolution of the holders of those securities.[135]

---

[127] Section 700 CA 2006. The disclosure and voting rules set out in sections 698 and 699 also apply to this release vote.

[128] Section 707 CA 2006. Company shares purchased by the company but not cancelled are known as 'treasury shares'.

[129] On the difference between a premium and standard listing see Chapter 6 pp 206–07.

[130] LR 12.4.2. The definition and terms of a tender offer are set out in the Listing Rules' Glossary of Definitions.

[131] LR 12.4.3.   [132] LR 12.4.1.

[133] LR 12.2.1. 'Prohibited period' is defined in para 1(e) of The Model Code (Listing Rule 9 Annex 1).

[134] LR 12.2.1(2).   [135] LRs 12.4.7–12.4.9.

3.2 Treasury shares

Treasury shares are shares that are repurchased by the company but are not cancelled and are held by the company for resale at a subsequent date. Traditionally in the UK it was not possible for companies to hold treasury shares and any repurchased shares had to be cancelled. This position was amended with regard to listed companies by secondary legislation in 2003.[136] The regulation of treasury shares is now set out in Chapter 6 of Part 18 of the 2006 Act.

The Act allows companies to repurchase and hold those shares rather than cancel those shares where the repurchased shares classify as 'qualifying shares'. In essence 'qualifying shares' are shares listed on the LSE **official list**, traded on AIM or listed or traded on another European Economic Area exchange.[137] Shares that are not qualifying shares cannot be held as treasury shares and are treated as cancelled following repurchase.[138]

Where the company has treasury shares the company is entered in the register of members as the member[139] in relation to those shares, but it may not exercise the votes attached to those shares.[140] The Act provides that shares held as treasury shares may be disposed of by the company;[141] however, it imposes two important restrictions in this regard. First, although no authority to allot those shares is required, ordinary treasury shares are subject to the Act's pre-emption regime,[142] discussed above. Secondly, treasury shares disposed of must be disposed of for cash consideration or transferred into an employee share ownership scheme.[143]

Finally, note that additional regulation of treasury shares is provided by the Listing Rules which provide that treasury shares may not be sold during a 'prohibited period'.[144]

3.3 Issue and redemption of redeemable shares

In addition to the repurchase regime, the Companies Act makes specific provision for the issuing of redeemable shares. To redeem an object is to take back ownership of it following compliance with specified conditions. If redeemable shares are issued the company can redeem them without having to comply with the Act's repurchase regulation detailed in section 3.1 of this chapter. When we discussed preference shares earlier, we noted that certain attributes of the shares appeared more akin to debt than equity. One important distinction in this respect was that although the preference share may have a preference in terms of dividend and in its position in the liquidation queue, it does not provide the shareholder with a right to receive the money back that he paid for the share on a specified date. A redeemable preference share with a specified

---

[136] The Companies (Acquisition of Own Shares) (Treasury Shares) Regulations 2003, SI 2003/1116.

[137] Section 724(2) CA 2006.

[138] Section 706(b) CA 2006. Prior to 2009 companies could only hold a maximum of 10% of repurchased shares as treasury shares. This limitation was removed by repealing section 725 of the Act (The Companies (Share Capital and Acquisition by Company of its Own Shares) Regulations 2009 (SI 2009/2022), reg 5(1)).

[139] Section 724(4) CA 2006.   [140] Section 726 CA 2006.

[141] Sections 724(3)(b), 727 CA 2006.

[142] Section 560(3) includes ordinary treasury shares within the definition of equity securities to which the pre-emption regime applies. Section 573 provides for disapplication in relation to treasury shares.

[143] Section 727(1) CA 2006. Cash consideration is defined in section 727(2) and includes the discharge of a liability. Section 728 CA 2006 requires that the company file a return with the Company's Registrar following disposal of the shares detailing, among others, the number of shares disposed of. If any shares are held as treasury shares but subsequently cancelled a return informing the Companies Registrar of the cancellation must be filed (Section 730 CA 2006: 28 days from cancellation).

[144] Listing Rule 12.6.2. See section IV.3.1 of this chapter.

redemption date does provide such a right, albeit qualified, in this regard, rendering such a redeemable preference share even more like debt.

The Act provides for the regulation of redeemable shares in Chapter 3 of Part 18 of the Act. Redeemable shares cannot be issued unless the company has issued non-redeemable shares.[145] A public company can only issue redeemable shares if authorized to do so by its articles, whereas a private company does not require such authorization.[146] The terms, conditions, and manner of redemption must be determined before allotment and will typically be determined by the board. To be able to do so the board must be authorized to set such terms either by the articles or by an ordinary resolution.[147] As with a repurchase of non-redeemable shares, the redeemable shares must be repurchased from either available distributable profits or from the proceeds of a fresh issue of shares.[148] Accordingly, whilst redeemable shares may provide for redemption on a specific date, as with a principal payment under a loan, if there are no available distributable profits from which the shares can be redeemed, the redemption will not take place. In this regard the Act specifically provides that the company is not liable for damages for its failure to redeem and that the courts will not order specific performance where the company does not have sufficient distributable profits to effect the redemption.[149] Shares that are redeemed must be cancelled and cannot be held as treasury shares.[150]

Once the redemption has been implemented in accordance with these requirements, the company must notify the Companies Registrar of the number and nature of the shares that have been redeemed.[151]

V FINANCIAL ASSISTANCE

1 Introduction

As we shall see in this section, the Companies Act 2006 prohibits a public company from providing financial assistance in relation to the acquisition of the company's shares or providing financial assistance to discharge a liability that a person incurs to buy those shares. However, from the perspective of the effective operation of the **market for corporate control** there may be good reasons for allowing a company to provide such financial assistance. Control entrepreneurs, such as **private equity** firms, purchase companies which in their view can be better run and managed by them or that can be restructured by them to realize the value potential of the company's assets. These control entrepreneurs, however, have limited funds and, in order to maximize the number of the companies they can purchase, they typically buy companies with both their 'own'[152] funds together with funds that they have borrowed. The money they borrow to purchase the shares is typically short-term expensive funding—sometimes referred to as bridge financing. Once the shares in the company have been repurchased the bridge finance needs to be replaced with longer-term, cheaper finance. Ideally, from the control

---

[145] Section 684(4) CA 2006.   [146] Section 684 CA 2006.   [147] Section 685 CA 2006.

[148] Section 687(2) CA 2006. Note that redeemable shares may also be purchased out of capital in accordance with the procedure set forth in Chapter 5 of Part 18 of the Act, discussed in detail in Chapter 19 of this book (section 687(1) CA 2006).

[149] Section 735(2) and (3) CA 2006. These provisions also apply to the repurchase of shares, although in practice they are less relevant to repurchases because of the typically shorter time period between deciding and agreeing to repurchase and carrying out the repurchase as compared to issuing redeemable shares and redemption.

[150] Section 688 CA 2006.   [151] Section 689 CA 2006.

[152] Private equity firms are investment vehicles that raise funding from investors, the reference here to their 'own' funds refers to the funds investors have invested in the private equity vehicle, which is usually a limited or limited liability partnership. On such partnerships see Chapter 1.

entrepreneur's perspective, the company's assets can be used to secure the new financing and the company's cashflow can be used to directly pay off the refinanced debt. Any prohibition, therefore, on the company providing finance to pay off the debt finance used to buy the company's shares or on using the company's assets to reduce the costs of such debt creates an obstacle to this type of control activity.

If such control activity is viewed as a positive[153] then we require a good regulatory rationale for removing one of the tools available to control entrepreneurs to facilitate transactions. In the UK, whilst we impose restrictions on the ability of a control entrepreneur to use a public company's assets to finance the purchase of its shares, it is not clear that there is a persuasive rationale for these restrictions. Whilst there are rationales that can be marshalled in its favour it is unclear, given other aspects of UK company law, that the financial assistance prohibition is necessary to achieve such goals. More importantly, any such rationales are weakened further by the fact that if the public company subject to the financial assistance prohibition converts into a private company there is, following reforms introduced by the Companies Act 2006,[154] no restriction at all on the provision of financial assistance, provided that it complies with regulation protecting legal capital addressed in detail in Chapter 19.[155] With regard to the available rationales consider the following extract.

■ **Eilis Ferran, 'Corporate Transactions and Financial Assistance: Shifting Policy Perceptions but Static Law' (2004)** *Cambridge Law Journal* **225**

Why do we ban financial assistance? According to Arden L.J. [in *Chaston v SWP Group plc*][156] the mischief is the use of target company resources to assist the acquisition of its shares. This is objectionable because 'this may prejudice the interests of the creditors of the target or its group and the interests of any shareholders who do not accept the offer to acquire their shares or to whom the offer is not made'. Looking at creditors' interests first, there are many corporate actions that are potentially prejudicial but which are not specifically banned by the companies legislation.[157] Why is financial assistance so very different? Moreover, since...the step that constitutes unlawful financial assistance may even be positively beneficial to the providing company [but still be unlawful]—detriment to creditors clearly does not fully explain or justify the scope of the ban as currently interpreted...

As for shareholders' interests, the quotation from Arden LJ's judgment above implies that the ban is intended to prevent discrimination between shareholders in acquisition or takeover situations. Protection against discrimination falls squarely within the general fiduciary duties of directors to use their powers in good faith and for proper purposes and to treat shareholders

---

[153] There is vigorous debate about whether private equity transactions make a positive contribution to the value of the company and the welfare of our society. The outcome of that debate remains very unclear. We are not in a position here to explore this debate in any detail. To facilitate our analysis we make the, somewhat controversial, assumption that such activity makes a long-run positive economic contribution. In this regard see, R.D. Harris et al, 'Assessing the Impact of Management Buyouts on Economic Efficiency: Plant-Level Evidence from the United Kingdom' (2005) 87 *The Review of Economics and Statistics* 148; S. Kaplan, 'The Effects of Management Buyouts on Operating Performance and Value' (1989) 24 *Journal of Financial Economics* 215.

[154] Previously under the Companies Act 1985 whilst the financial assistance prohibition applied to private companies the financial assistance could be 'whitewashed' through a combination of shareholder approval and a board solvency statement, see sections 155–158 CA 1985.

[155] Sections 97–101 CA 2006 provide for the conversion of a public company into a private company. Shareholder approval by special resolution is required. The Act grants rights of objection to shareholders who own 5% of the company's issued shares.

[156] [2002] EWCA Civ 1999. This case is considered in detail in section V.2.2 of this chapter.

[157] Paying a lawful dividend, for example, prejudices a creditor's, in particular a non-adjusting creditor's interests, to the extent the net-assets of the company are thereby diminished. On company law and creditor protection see Chapters 18 and 19.

fairly.[158] The general duty is reinforced (for public companies) by the provisions of the City Code on Takeovers and Mergers and by the statutory rights of minorities to be bought out at a proper price at the conclusion of a takeover. In some circumstances, it may also be possible to challenge allegedly discriminatory behaviour by the management of a target company and/or controlling shareholders under the Companies Act 1985, section 459 (unfairly prejudicial conduct). With such strong shareholder-orientated protection against abuse otherwise in place, why do we also need a specific and rigid ban on financial assistance which could, because of its breadth, catch harmless and possibly even beneficial (from the shareholder viewpoint) transactions as well as those that are objectionable? The prevailing view in the policy debate is simple: we don't.

For Professor Ferran there is neither a persuasive creditor protection nor shareholder protection function performed by banning the provision of financial assistance by the company to third parties to buy a public company's shares. This view is widely accepted in academic and regulatory circles. The prohibition remains because the Second Directive requires it.[159] As the prohibition remains, we must understand how it works.

2 The prohibition on the provision of financial assistance

2.1 The prohibition

The prohibition on the provision of financial assistance by a public company is set out in section 678 of the Companies Act 2006. If a company provides unlawful financial assistance both the company and every officer in default in regard to the provision of the assistance commits a criminal offence punishable by fine or imprisonment.[160] The transaction providing the unlawful assistance will be void[161] and the directors are likely to be found in breach of duty.[162]

Prior to the Companies Act 2006 the prohibition applied to both public and private companies.[163] Private companies, however, had available to them a 'whitewash procedure' that enabled the private company to 'whitewash' any financial assistance made out of 'distributable profits'[164] provided the assistance was supported by a special resolution and the directors certified the solvency of the company for the year after the assistance was to be given.[165] The Companies Act 2006 removed the application of the financial assistance prohibition to private companies.

■ **Section 678 Companies Act 2006 Assistance for acquisition of shares in public company**

(1) Where a person is acquiring or proposing to acquire shares in a public company, it is not lawful for that company, or a company that is a subsidiary of that company, to give financial

---

[158] See Chapters 9 and 10.

[159] On reforming the Second Directive's financial assistance rules see E. Ferran, 'Simplification of European Company Law on Financial Assistance' (2005) 6 *European Business Organisation Law Review* 93.

[160] Section 680 CA 2006.

[161] *Heald v O'Connor* [1971] 1 WLR 497. To the extent that the transaction providing the financial assistance can be separated from the other parts of the share purchase transaction the courts will only invalidate that part of the transaction providing financial assistance. If the different aspects of the transaction cannot be separated the whole transaction will be unenforceable. See, for example, *South Western Mineral Water Co Ltd v Ashmore* [1967] 2 All ER 953.

[162] Sections 171, and 174 CA 2006. The determination of breach will of course be fact dependent.

[163] Section 151 CA 1985.   [164] On 'distributable profits' see Chapter 19.

[165] Sections 155–158 CA 1985.

assistance directly or indirectly for the purpose of the acquisition before or at the same time as the acquisition takes place.

(2) Subsection (1) does not prohibit a company from giving financial assistance for the acquisition of shares in it or its holding company if—

    (a) the company's principal purpose in giving the assistance is not to give it for the purpose of any such acquisition, or

    (b) the giving of the assistance for that purpose is only an incidental part of some larger purpose of the company, and the assistance is given in good faith in the interests of the company.

(3) Where—

    (a) a person has acquired shares in a company, and

    (b) a liability has been incurred (by that or another person) for the purpose of the acquisition, it is not lawful for that company, or a company that is a subsidiary of that company, to give financial assistance directly or indirectly for the purpose of reducing or discharging the liability if, at the time the assistance is given, the company in which the shares were acquired is a public company.

(4) Subsection (3) does not prohibit a company from giving financial assistance if—

    (a) the company's principal purpose in giving the assistance is not to reduce or discharge any liability incurred by a person for the purpose of the acquisition of shares in the company or its holding company, or

    (b) the reduction or discharge of any such liability is only an incidental part of some larger purpose of the company, and the assistance is given in good faith in the interests of the company.

(5) This section has effect subject to sections 681 and 682 (unconditional and conditional exceptions to prohibition).

■ Section 683 Companies Act 2006 Definitions for this Chapter

...

(2) In this Chapter—

    (a) a reference to a person incurring a liability includes his changing his financial position by making an agreement or arrangement (whether enforceable or unenforceable, and whether made on his own account or with any other person) or by any other means, and

    (b) a reference to a company giving financial assistance for the purposes of reducing or discharging a liability incurred by a person for the purpose of the acquisition of shares includes its giving such assistance for the purpose of wholly or partly restoring his financial position to what it was before the acquisition took place.

The prohibitions on financial assistance are set out in section 678(1) and (3). Subsection (1) prohibits the provision of financial assistance by a public company or its subsidiary 'for the purpose' of the acquisition of the public company's (parent's) shares; subsection (3) prohibits the provision of financial assistance by a public company or its subsidiary to discharge a liability that was incurred by the purchaser in order to buy the shares. The prohibition applies to public companies and their subsidiaries, whether private or public, in relation to the provision of assistance to buy the public company shares. It does not apply to a private subsidiary of a public company in relation to the purchase of that subsidiary's shares. Whilst the general prohibition no longer applies to the purchase of shares in private companies the prohibition applies to the provision of financial assistance by a public company for the purchase of shares in its private company parent.[166] Note also that although the prohibition applies to subsidiaries of public companies providing assistance for the purchase of shares in the public company parent, the courts have held that the word 'subsidiary' refers to a UK company and, therefore, does not apply to financial assistance given by a foreign subsidiary.[167]

2.2 The meaning of 'financial assistance'

What then is 'financial assistance'? For the uninitiated the Act appears on first glance to provide an answer in section 677 whose header refers to 'the meaning of "financial assistance"'.

■ Section 677 Companies Act 2006 Meaning of 'financial assistance'

(1) In this Chapter 'financial assistance' means—

   (a) financial assistance given by way of gift,

   (b) financial assistance given—

      (i) by way of guarantee, security or indemnity (other than an indemnity in respect of the indemnifier's own neglect or default), or

      (ii) by way of release or waiver,

   (c) financial assistance given—

      (i) by way of a loan or any other agreement under which any of the obligations of the person giving the assistance are to be fulfilled at a time when in accordance with the agreement any obligation of another party to the agreement remains unfulfilled, or

      (ii) by way of the novation of, or the assignment (in Scotland, assignation) of rights arising under, a loan or such other agreement, or

   (d) any other financial assistance given by a company where—

      (i) the net assets of the company are reduced to a material extent by the giving of the assistance, or

      (ii) the company has no net assets.

Whilst it is not unreasonable to expect that a section entitled 'the meaning of "financial assistance"' would provide a definition of 'financial assistance', section 677 does not do so. Rather it provides a list of transaction types that are still qualified by the term 'financial assistance': 'financial assistance' given by way of gift, guarantee, indemnity etc. What section 677 does is to make it clear that the prohibition on financial assistance set out in sections 678 and 679 does not apply to all types of financial assistance but only

---

[166] Section 679 CA 2006.

[167] *Arab Bank plc v Merchantile Holdings Ltd* [1994] 1 BCLC 330. However, note that Millett J in *Arab Bank* held that if the parent financially assisted the foreign subsidiary in order to enable the subsidiary to give the assistance that would constitute an 'indirect provision of financial assistance by the English company': 'even if the section does not apply to foreign subsidiaries, the hiving down of an asset by an English company to such a subsidiary in order to enable it to be made available to finance a contemplated acquisition of shares of the English company would clearly contravene the section'. Note more recently that the Court of Appeal in *AMG Global Nominees (Private) Ltd v Africa Resources Ltd* [2008] EWCA Civ 1278 held that a parent's approval or instigation of its foreign subsidiary's financial assistance does not amount to the parent's indirect provision of financial assistance. Such approval or instigation does not, in contrast to the transfer of an asset or the assumption of a liability, amount to *financial* assistance.

to those types of financial assistance listed in section 677. Section 677 does not, and nor does any other provision of the Act, tell us what the term 'financial assistance' actually means. To understand the term we need to turn to the case law applying this provision. Consider first, in this regard, the leading case of *Chaston v SWP Group Plc*.

■ *Chaston v SWP Group Plc* [2003] 1 BCLC 675

The shares in DRC Polymer Products Ltd ('DRC') were owned by Dunstable Rubber Co Holdings Ltd ('DRCH') and by Mr Robert Chaston, who was also a director of DRC. The SWP Group Plc, a listed company, agreed to buy the shares in DRCH for £2.55 million to be paid in cash and loan stock. In order to do so approval was required of SWP's shareholders. To fund the acquisition SWP issued new shares in relation to which a **prospectus** was prepared. In order to obtain shareholder approval the company had to provide its shareholders with information about the proposed transaction, including financial information about the DRCH group of companies. The required information is known as a 'short form report'; however, in this case a more detailed 'long form report' was provided to SWP's shareholders. Note, in particular, that the information contained in the report was about the DRC group of companies but the report was required by SWP to obtain the approval of its shareholders.

The accounting work for the report was carried out by Deloitte & Touche and resulted in fees of approximately £20,000. These fees were paid for by DRC. In this regard the first instance judge held 'that none of this particular work would have to have been done were the shareholders of DRCH not negotiating a sale of their shares to SWP'. Following the acquisition SWP brought an action against Mr Chaston 'for damages for breach of fiduciary duty for having procured, or connived in, the grant by DRC…of financial assistance for the purpose of the acquisition by SWP of the shares in [DRCH]'. As it was not clear whether DRC had undertaken to pay the fees before the transaction or had simply paid them after the transaction, the case was dealt with as falling under both the prohibition on giving financial assistance for the purpose of buying shares (section 678(1)) and the prohibition on discharging a liability incurred to purchase the shares (section 678(3)). Note in this regard that the parties accepted that DRC's net assets were less than £100,000.

Arden LJ

[31] I start with the mischief to which [section 678][168] is directed. Section [678] is derived from s 45 of the Companies Act 1929 which was enacted as a result of the previously common practice of purchasing the shares of a company having a substantial cash balance or easily realisable assets and so arranging matters that the purchase money was lent by the company to the purchaser (see *Re VGM Holdings Ltd* [1942] 1 All ER 224 at 225–226). The prohibition was amended in 1948 and reformulated in 1981. The *Report of the Company Law Committee* (the Jenkins Committee) (Cmnd 1749, 1962) para 180, p 66 expressed the view that it was 'unwise' to attempt a precise definition of financial assistance. It is clear from the way in which [section 677 and 678] are drafted that it covers financial assistance in many forms apart from loans (see for example the wide wording of [section 683(2)]. The general mischief, however, remains the same, namely that the resources of the target company and its subsidiaries should not be used directly or indirectly to assist the purchaser financially to make the acquisition. This may prejudice the interests of the creditors of the target or its group, and the interests of any shareholders who do not accept the offer to acquire their shares or to whom the offer is not made.

---

[168] The financial assistance prohibition was previously set out in section 151 of the Companies Act 1985. All references to the Companies Act 1985 have been updated in this extract to refer to the corresponding provisions of the 2006 Act.

[32] Thus although [section 677] proscribes a number of forms of financial assistance, it does not define the words 'financial assistance'. It is clear from the authorities that what matters is the commercial substance of the transaction: 'The words [financial assistance] have no technical meaning and their frame of reference is the language of ordinary commerce' (per Hoffmann J in *Charterhouse v Tempest Diesels* [1986] BCLC 1 at 10, approved by the Court of Appeal in *Barclays Bank plc v British & Commonwealth Holdings plc* [1996] 1 BCLC 1 at 40). This approach was confirmed by Lord Hoffmann (with whom the other members of the House of Lords agreed) in a recent revenue case: *MacNiven (Inspector of Taxes) v Westmoreland Investments Ltd* [2001] STC 237 at 254. In the relevant passage, Lord Hoffmann usefully draws a distinction between the expression 'financial assistance', which conveys a commercial concept, and other words used in this group of sections which by contrast have a recognised legal meaning:

> 'The distinction between commercial and legal concepts has also been drawn in other areas of legislation. So, for example, the term "financial assistance" in [section 678] of the Companies Act [2006] has been construed as a commercial concept, involving an inquiry into the commercial realities of the transaction (see *Burton v Palmer* [1980] 2 NSWLR 878 at 889–890 and *Charterhouse Investment Trust Ltd v Tempest Diesels Ltd* [1986] BCLC 1). But the same is not necessarily true of other terms used in the same section, such as "indemnity". As Aldous LJ said in *Barclays Bank plc v British & Commonwealth Holdings plc* [1996] 1 BCLC 1 at 39: "It was submitted that as the words 'financial assistance' had no technical meaning and their frame of reference was the language of ordinary commerce, the word 'indemnity' should be similarly construed. The fallacy in that submission is clear. The words 'financial assistance' are not words which have any recognised legal significance whereas the word 'indemnity' does. It is used in the section as one of a number of words having a recognised legal meaning." I would only add by way of caution that although a word may have a "recognised legal meaning," the legislative context may show that it is in fact being used to refer to a broader commercial concept'...

[34] *Charterhouse v Tempest Diesels* was a decision on s 54 of the Companies Act 1948, which was in somewhat a different form [section 678]. Doubts arose as to whether s 54 applied to a transaction where only one of the purposes was to assist in the acquisition of shares and in addition as to whether financial assistance which did not diminish the company's net assets constituted 'financial assistance' for the purposes of this section...

[35] The Companies Act 1981 was consolidated with other companies legislation in the Companies Act 1985. In short, two changes were made by the 1981 Act (so far as relevant). First, Parliament limited the prohibition to certain forms of financial assistance. These include a residual category: see [section 677(1)(d)]. This provision incorporates, for companies with positive net assets, a 'de minimis' exception. The giving of any form of financial assistance not previously mentioned in [section 677(1)] is outside the categories of financial assistance for the purposes of [section 678] if it does not reduce actual net assets to a material extent...

[37] It is thus apparent that [sections 677–683] distinguish between various categories of transactions. First, there are the categories of financial assistance listed in [section 677(1)(a)–(c)] which are prohibited whether or not there is any diminution in net assets, unless [one of the exceptions in sections 678, 681, or 682] applies. Second, there is financial assistance of a kind not specifically mentioned in [section 677(1)(a)–(c)]. This does not contravene [section 678] provided the company has positive net assets and the reduction in actual net assets is immaterial... Third, there are those which although carried out for the purpose of an acquisition of shares and have financial implications do not constitute financial assistance for the purposes of [section 678]. This category includes lawful dividends: see [section 681(2)]. Fourth, there are transactions which although they constitute financial assistance within [section 677] are taken outside the prohibition in [section 678] by the principal purpose defences in [sections 678(2) and (4)]. Fifth, there are the transactions exempted by [section 682], such as the lending of money by a money-lending company in the ordinary course of its business.

[38] The first issue on this appeal is whether the incurring of liability to pay the fees to D & T or the payment of those fees constituted 'financial assistance' for the purpose of [section 678].

Although it does not clearly so appear, it would seem that the judge concluded that there was financial assistance in the circumstances of this case. It is clear from the *Charterhouse* case, as approved by this court in the *British & Commonwealth* case, that the test is one of commercial substance and reality. Looking simply at the facts, the judge found…that the payments were 'to facilitate the progress of the negotiations and to enable SWP to conclude its due diligence exercise: and having done so, then to make up its mind whether or not to acquire the shares in DRCH'. As a matter of commercial reality, the fees in question smoothed the path to the acquisition of shares. There was no provision in the agreement for any benefit to be given to the DRC group. What the DRC group was looking for was the spin-off benefits of the acquisition. The DRC group had financial difficulties and it would be joining a larger group which saw a future for it. However, the negotiations appear to have been solely concerned with the actual terms of the acquisition, for example, as to the giving of warranties by the selling shareholders.

[39] Mr Cunningham argues persuasively that we should take into account that [section 678] imposes criminal liability. That is so, but the effect is, as Hoffmann J said in the *Charterhouse* case, only that the language must not be strained as to include transactions not fairly within it. Moreover, the term 'financial assistance' is clearly established to be a commercial concept. Accordingly, the question whether financial assistance exists in any given case may be fact-sensitive and not one which can be answered simply by applying a legal definition. The question is whether from a commercial point of view the transaction impugned amounts to financial assistance. If the company's participation in the transaction meets that test, no straining of the statutory language occurs.

[40] Here as a commercial matter assistance was clearly given. D & T received payment for their services and both the purchaser and the vendors were relieved of any obligation to pay for this service themselves. Mr Cunningham submits that [section 677] should be restricted to assistance given to purchasers, alternatively to assistance given to vendors and purchasers. However, in so far as that point matters in this case there is no mandate in my judgment for reading any such limitation in that section. There is no reason why assistance which is paid to a subsidiary or associated company or other person nominated by one of the parties to the transaction should not be assistance contrary to the section. This again does not involve straining the language of the section to include transactions not fairly within it.

[41] Mr Cunningham also argues that financial assistance cannot be given without a detriment to the company being acquired. This argument was considered by the Court of Appeal in the *Belmont*[169] case and there rejected. That decision was later distinguished in the *Charterhouse* case. In my judgment, detriment is not necessarily required. The forms of financial assistance which contravene [section 678] are spelt out in [section 677(1)] (which was new in 1981). As Mr Todd demonstrated, there is no reason why for instance financial assistance given by way of loan should not be given on terms which are highly beneficial to the target company. The only situation in which detriment is essential is in [section 677(1)(d)] where financial assistance of a kind not previously specified is prohibited if (in the case of a company having positive net assets) it reduces the company's assets to a material extent…

[42] Mr Cunningham made a further submission that there was a distinction to be drawn between financial assistance given in advance of a transaction and financial assistance given in the course of a transaction. As to the former, this was not prohibited…In my judgment, this distinction is not justified by [section 678]. It prohibits financial assistance given 'directly or indirectly' and those words are sufficiently wide to cover 'pre-transactional' financial assistance. Moreover [section 678(1)] provides that a transaction can offend the section even though a person is only 'proposing' to acquire shares. In my judgment, the distinction which Mr Cunningham seeks to draw is not borne out by the authorities which he cites in support. The obiter passage from the *Charterhouse* case is concerned with the meaning of financial assistance; it was dealing with a composite transaction and is an application of the commercial concept of financial

---

[169] *Belmont Finance Corp Ltd v Williams Furniture Ltd (No 2)* [1980] 1 All ER 393.

assistance. It thus must be read against the particular facts of the case. It is not based on the bright line distinction which Mr Cunningham draws...

[45] In my judgment the financial assistance in the present case was clearly 'financial'. It makes no difference that the payment of the fees had no impact on the share price. As I see it, the policy of [section 678] extends beyond assistance given to enable the price for shares to be paid. There must be a link, and the link which the section requires is that the financial assistance must be 'for the purpose of' the acquisition. That is the issue which particularly concerned the judge and to which I now turn.

[51] Accordingly, in my judgment the judge was in error in his conclusion on [section 678] and the appeal must be allowed. [The assistance fell within the section 678(1)(d) material net-asset diminution category as although the payments were small (approximately £20,000) DRC's net-assets were only £100,000. Accordingly the payment amounted to unlawful financial assistance and none of the exceptions referred to here were applicable.]

Following *Chaston*, the term 'financial assistance' does not have a specific legal meaning that is distinct from how the term would be understood in commercial practice. That is, its legal meaning is derived from how it would be understood in commerce. One must ask whether, from a commercial point of view, there is any financial assistance. This determination is a necessary precursor to determining whether the financial assistance is financial assistance that falls within section 677 and then for determining whether it is given for the purposes of acquiring the shares, or discharging a liability incurred for the purpose of that acquisition.[170]

For there to be financial assistance from a commercial point of view the actions in question must provide the purchaser of the shares with some form of financial benefit or help.[171] As the term is a commercial concept it is important in any applicable case to determine whether in fact any *financial* benefit, aid or help was provided.[172] Many actions taken by the company may not *in reality* provide any financial assistance to the purchaser even though they may appear to be assisting the purchaser by making the company and the purchase of the shares more attractive to the purchaser.

Consider, for example, actions that are taken by the company in connection with, but prior to, the sale of the company, which could involve agreeing to transfer assets to the seller of the shares or making a dividend to the seller in advance of the sale. Such actions reduce the value of the company and the price that the purchaser has to pay for the shares. Such actions to restructure the company in advance of the sale of the shares *appear* to assist the purchaser in purchasing the shares—they may make the company more attractive to the purchaser. But such actions *do not* amount to financial assistance from a commercial perspective. To see this consider *Charterhouse Investment Trust Ltd v Tempest Diesels Ltd*,[173] a case relied on in *Chaston*. The question for the court

[170] In *Charterhouse Investment Trust Ltd v Tempest Diesels Ltd* [1986] BCLC 1 in relation to the financial assistance prohibition set out in the Companies Act 1948 Hoffmann J observed that 'there are two elements in the commission of an offence under s 54. The first is the giving of financial assistance and the second is that it should have been given "for the purposes of or in connection with", in this case, a purchase of shares. As Schreiner J said in a passage in *Gradwell (Pty) Ltd v Rostra Printers Ltd* 1959 (4) SA 419 at 425...: "Unless what was to be done would amount to giving of financial assistance within the meaning of the sub-section the purpose and the connection would not be important."'

[171] In *MT Realisations Ltd (in liquidation) v Digital Equipment Co Ltd* [2003] 2 BCLC 117, extracted below, the Court of Appeal favourably cited the Australian case of *Sterileair Pty Ltd v Papallo* (16 November 1998, unreported), where it was held that: '"assistance" involves something in the nature of aid or help. It cannot exist in a vacuum; it must be given to someone.'

[172] Assistance alone is insufficient is clear—see *AMG Global Nominees (Private) Ltd v Africa Resources Ltd* [2008] EWCA Civ 1278 where the parent's approval and instigation of its foreign subsidiaries financial assistance (see note 167) did not itself amount to indirect financial assistance.

[173] [1986] BCLC 1.

in *Charterhouse* was whether an agreement to transfer tax losses from the purchased company (Tempest) to its parent (seller) company prior to the transfer amounted to financial assistance. Here the claim was that these assets were valuable assets which if transferred to the parent seller resulted in assistance to the purchaser in purchasing the shares. Hoffmann J (as he then was) held that this did not amount to financial assistance from a commercial point of view, rather it was part of a restructuring process necessary to render Tempest sellable. If at time T1 the value of Tempest was £120 which included the value of the tax losses and the price of the shares for Tempest at time T1 is £12 per share, if at Time T2 following the transfer of the tax losses to the parent the company is worth £30 and the shares are worth £3 per share this looks like financial assistance to purchase the shares as the price for the shares has been reduced. But does this amount to financial assistance? It does not. If someone offers to sell you two cars for £10,000 but one car for £5,000, if you elect to purchase one car you have not been financially assisted in regard to that purchase, rather you have purchased something of lesser value than the two cars. In the example from *Tempest*, even if the transfer of assets had been gratuitous—for no consideration from the parent—this would not amount to financial assistance by lowering the share price because what was purchased was worth less because of that transfer. Transfers of assets by the subject company prior to selling the shares which result in a reduction in the value of the shares do not, therefore, amount to financial assistance. Simply because those actions are taken with a view to enabling the company to be sold—smoothing the path of the sale—does not render those actions financial assistance.

This position is affirmed by the case of *Anglo Petroleum v TFB (Mortgages) Ltd*[174] where, prior to the sale of the company, a restructuring of the company's debt to its parent seller for the purpose of facilitating the sale of the shares resulted in the company undertaking to pay back certain amounts after the acquisition. The case makes it clear that the seller of the shares was only willing to sell them if it received £15 million for the shares. The transaction was structured in a way that provided that the company agreed to pay £15 million to the parent, and the shares in the company were then sold to the purchaser for £1. The court held, correctly, that this did not amount to financial assistance and that 'just because it smoothed the path to the acquisition, it does not follow that it amounted to financial assistance'.[175] The agreed payment by the company simply reduced the value of the shares to £1; it did not assist in the purchase of those shares. Of course, there must be a legal basis for making the payment to the parent—in this case it arose from a restructuring of existing indebtedness.

For a demanding focus on whether in fact the purchaser has been financially assisted from a commercial point of view, consider the following Court of Appeal case decided shortly after *Chaston*.

■ *MT Realisations Ltd (in liquidation) v Digital Equipment Co Ltd* [2003] 2 BCLC 117

MT Realisations Ltd (MTR) was a member of the Digital Group of companies. It was loss making and insolvent and depended on financing from its parent company which amounted to £8 million. This loan was secured on MTR's assets. MTI was interested in purchasing the company. The initial terms of purchase involved MTI paying £6.5 million for the shares of MTR and Digital would agree to write off the £8 million loan to MTR. The terms of the agreement, however, subsequently changed and it was agreed that MTI would buy the shares in the company for £1 and purchase the rights arising

---

[174] *Anglo Petroleum Ltd and another v TFB (Mortgages) Ltd* [2008] 1 BCLC 185.
[175] *Armour Hick Northern Ltd v Armour Trust Ltd* [1980] 3 All ER 833.

from the £8 million loan to MTR for a discounted price of £6.5 million. This £6.5 million was to be paid in instalments. Following the purchase MTR continued to do business with the Digital group of companies.

MTI was unable to meet its debts and it was agreed that amounts owed to MTR by the Digital companies would not be paid rather would set off amounts owed by MTI to Digital for the purchase of the £6.5 million loan. MTR subsequently went into liquidation and the liquidator brought an action claiming that MTR's agreement that payments owed to it would be used to set off amounts owed by MTI was unlawful financial assistance. Laddie J, at first instance, held that this did not amount to financial assistance. The liquidator appealed.

Mummery LJ

[27] I have reached the same conclusion as Laddie J, though by a slightly different route. This is largely explicable by the fact that, as quite often happens, the arguments were deployed on the appeal with a different emphasis than in the court below.

[28] On the 'commercial realities of the transaction' approach to [section 678], as expounded by Hoffmann J in *Charterhouse Investment Trust Ltd v Tempest Diesels Ltd* [1986] BCLC 1 at p 10–11 (a case on s 54 Companies Act 1948) and followed in later cases, such as *Chaston v SWP Group plc* [2002] EWCA Civ 1999 no 'financial assistance' was, in my judgment, given by MTR to MTI 'for the purpose of' reducing or discharging a liability incurred for the purpose of the acquisition of shares in MTR.

[29] The legal analysis shortly stated as follows is sufficient to dispose of the appeal:…

(2) The breach of [section 678(3)] is said to have resulted from the agreement that sums due to MTR should be diverted to Digital UK, not for the benefit of MTR but to give financial assistance to MTI so that it could pay off the sum owed to Digital UK under the loan assignment. In order to appreciate the 'commercial realities of the transaction' it is necessary to examine more closely MTI's legal rights against MTR in respect of the inter-company indebtedness at the date of the rescheduling agreement…

(4) The legal position at the date of the rescheduling agreement was that MTI was…entitled to take steps to enforce its rights as a secured creditor against MTR in respect of sums due to MTR from Digital UK and its associated companies. By enforcing its security rights as chargee it would recover its legal entitlement, rather than be the recipient of 'financial assistance' from MTR as chargor and debtor. The overall net effect of the rescheduling agreement was simply to short-circuit the position. Instead of MTR receiving sums due to it from Digital UK and its associated companies and then paying them to its parent, MTI, in repayment of the inter-company loans, it was arranged that what was due for payment to MTR would instead be paid direct to Digital UK, to whom MTI owed the instalments of the purchase price under the loan assignment.

(5) Both as a matter of the 'commercial realities of the transaction' and of legal principle such an arrangement did not involve MTR in giving 'financial assistance' to MTI within the meaning of [section 678(3)]. Quite apart from the point that it did not have any negative impact on MTR's overall net balance sheet position, the relevance of which is disputed, there was no 'gift' by MTR to MTI. As MTI was in the position of a secured creditor of MTR, it was entitled to help itself by exercising its security rights over the book debts due to MTR from Digital UK and other companies in its group. As was said in the decision of the Federal Court of Australia in *Sterileair Pty Ltd v Papallo* (1998) 16 November, unreported:

'"Assistance" involves something in the nature of aid or help. It cannot exist in a vacuum; it must be given to someone.'

In this case nothing was given by MTR to MTI which it had not already acquired as its own resource by assignment from Digital UK in order to secure performance of the obligation to repay the inter-company loans due on demand from MTR to Digital UK. No financial assistance was being given to MTI by MTR out of its own free assets or resources.

We see in *MT Realisations* that although MTR allows amounts it is owed to be used to offset amounts owed by its parent in relation to a loan incurred to buy the shares,[176] this does not amount to financial assistance to discharge a liability incurred to buy the shares. The set off is not financial assistance given to MTI from a commercial point of view because those monies could have been obtained by a separate route as MTI was a first priority secured creditor over MTR's assets, including any amounts owed to it by the Digital companies. There was, therefore, no assistance at all; rather it was a more practical way of discharging MTI's liability to Digital.

Questions and discussion

1. What would have been the situation had MTI purchased the shares according to the first proposal? This would have involved a payment of £6.5 million for the shares in MTR, payable in instalments, together with a write off of the amounts owed by MTR to Digital. If, in those circumstances, MTR had subsequently allowed amounts owed to it by Digital to be used to set-off the amounts owed to Digital by MTI arising from the share purchase, would that have amounted to financial assistance? There is a strong case that it would: the amounts owed to MTR would be used to discharge a liability incurred by MTI to purchase the shares and, on these facts, MTI would not be a secured creditor, so the argument that the set off amounted merely to a practical short-cut would not be available. One interesting argument might be available in such a case: namely that if MTR was capable of distributing[177] the amounts required by MTI to discharge its liability to Digital then, as controller of the company, MTI could have forced MTR to distribute those funds to it. If that is the case, then one could argue in relation to this hypothetical fact pattern that there is no financial assistance rather only a short-cut to discharging the liability owed by MTI to Digital. The House of Lords judgment in *Brady v Brady*,[178] however, weighs against this position. In this case, defendant counsel argued that although there was financial assistance it was not unlawful as the amounts in question *could have* been distributed as a dividend to the parent and, had a distribution been made this would not have been financial assistance because, as will be discussed in section 2.4, distributions are exempt from the regime.[179] The House of Lords, however, held that as a distribution had not in fact been made the assistance did not, therefore, fall within the exception.[180] However, there is a nuance here that was not considered by the House of Lords. Here the argument would not be that it could have been a lawfully declared distribution that fell within the exception set out in the Act, rather that, as a dividend could have been made and as MTI had complete control over MTR, there was in fact no financial assistance in the first place.

2. Evelyn wishes to purchase the shares in Bob's Electronics Plc but she is concerned that when her purchase offer becomes public knowledge someone else may attempt to poach the company by paying more for the shares. She is concerned that if she announces her intention to purchase the company but fails to do so then: first, her reputation in the market place will be damaged making it harder to buy other companies; and, second, the transaction costs invested in trying to purchase the company will be completely wasted. Accordingly, she tells Bob, the CEO of Bob's Electronics Plc, that she will only agree to offer to buy the shares in the company if the company agrees to pay her an amount equal

---

[176] Assuming the share purchase and the loan purchase are treated as one. See further on this point paragraph 30 of Mummery LJ's judgment.

[177] On the rules governing distributions see Chapter 19.

[178] [1988] BCLC 579.   [179] Section 681 CA 2006.

[180] *Brady v Brady* [1988] BCLC 579. Lord Oliver held in relation to this argument that 'this is incontestable but the short answer to it is that it was not what was agreed between the parties and that it involves the consequence that, in the absence of a fresh Revenue clearance, which, it is common ground, has not been obtained, the individual shareholders in [company] will suffer tax on the dividends. It is unnecessary, therefore, to consider this point further.'

to 3% of the value of the company if another party actually purchases control of the company. Such a fee is sometimes referred to as a 'break fee'. Does the agreement to pay such a fee if the deal is not completed amount to financial assistance within the meaning of section 678?

3. Does this analysis of the meaning of 'financial assistance' cast doubt on whether *Chaston* is correctly decided? In *Chaston*, the amounts paid reduced the company's net assets and therefore the DRCH group's net assets. Had they not been paid by DRC, SWP would have reduced the price they were willing to pay for the shares to take account of the additional transaction costs. If the DRCH group was worth £100 without regard to transaction costs of the acquisition but the costs of buying the shares are £10 then SWP will only pay £90. Whether they pay £90 and the transaction costs themselves or £90 and DRCH or its subsidiary pays the transaction costs makes no difference to the value position after the transaction—(they pay £100 in total [90 + 10]) for a company that is worth £100 or £90 for a company that is worth £90 [100 − 10]). From a commercial point of view SWP is not financially assisted in buying the shares; there is no financial help or benefit.

2.3 Prohibited financial assistance

Once one has determined that the assistance amounts to 'financial assistance' from a commercial point of view, several further steps have to be taken to determine whether the assistance falls with the Act's financial assistance prohibition. First, one needs to determine whether the financial assistance falls within one of the 'financial assistance categories' set out in section 677(1)(a)–(c), for example financial assistance by way of loan, guarantee, assignment, or indemnity. In relation to these categories Arden LJ observes that there is no requirement that these types of assistance cause detriment to the company. A loan given to a third party to fund the purchase of the company's shares could be on market or better than market terms (from the company's perspective) but would still be financial assistance within the meaning of section 678.

If the assistance does not fall within categories (a)–(c) the next step is to determine whether the assistance falls within section 677(1)(d) which requires that the assistance results in a material diminution of the company's net assets. Materiality is not defined. We know from *Chaston* that a 20% reduction in net assets is material, however, financial assistance would most probably be material at a much lower percentage level than 20% of net assets and may well be material at very low percentage levels where in absolute terms it is significant. Would an amount of £1 billion be material in a £100 billion company? If the assistance falls within one of the section 677 categories then it is 'financial assistance' within the meaning of section 678(1) and (3) unless it falls within one of the exceptions in section 681, which we shall consider in further depth.

If the assistance is financial assistance for the purposes of the section 678 prohibition, the next question is whether it is given, directly or indirectly, *for the purpose of the acquisition*, or to reduce or discharge a liability incurred *for the purpose of the acquisition*. Arden LJ in *Chaston* affirms a broad reading of *for the purpose of the acquisition*. Anything that is financial assistance, falls within one of the section 677 categories, and smoothes the path of the acquisition, including any 'pre-transactional' assistance, falls within the prohibition. Arguably, however, a distinction should be made between, on the one hand, financial assistance that is connected with the purchase and, on the other hand, financial assistance *to purchase* the shares or to discharge the liability incurred *to purchase* the shares. This is an important distinction that, arguably, the court in *Chaston* does not take seriously enough.

The 2006 Act's financial assistance prohibitions in section 678(1) and (3) are identical to the 1985 Act prohibitions which were in issue in *Chaston*. However, the version of the prohibition prior to the 1985 Act, set out in section 54 of the Companies Act 1948, provided as follows:

> (1)…it shall not be lawful for a company to give, whether directly or indirectly, and whether by means of a loan, guarantee, the provision of security or otherwise, any financial assistance for the purpose of or in connection with a purchase or subscription made or to be made by any person of or for any shares in the company.

Note in particular that the prohibition relates to financial assistance provided 'for the purpose of *or in connection with*' the purchase of the shares. A clear inference from this change in the terms of the prohibition suggests that in relation to the current prohibition where assistance is deemed to be financial assistance but is *in connection with* rather than *for the purchase of* the shares or to discharge a liability incurred *for the purpose of the acquisition*, then it is not prohibited by sections 678 and 679. Some support for this is found in *Dyment v Boyden*[181] where payments that a company agreed to make under a lease to a former shareholder, that were part of restructuring arrangements that included the transfer of the shareholder's shares, did not amount to financial assistance to discharge a liability incurred to purchase the shares. Hart J held that 'while the company's entering into the lease can be said to have been "in connection with" (in the words of the old s 54) the acquisition of the shares, it cannot fairly be said to have been "for the purpose" of that acquisition'.[182]

These observations cast further doubt on whether *Chaston* is correctly decided. Even if the payment of the fees can be viewed as financial assistance—which is queried in question 3—it did not assist in the purchase of the shares, rather it was given 'in connection with' the purchase and, therefore, falls outside the scope of the prohibition. It is respectfully submitted, therefore, that *Chaston* is incorrectly decided.

2.4 Exceptions and exemptions

The Act provides a list of exemptions for certain types of action which, although they amount to financial assistance, are *not* financial assistance for the purposes of the prohibition in section 678. In addition the Act provides for a general exception from the application of the prohibition.

The exemptions are set out in sections 681 and 682.[183] Section 681 provides a list of corporate transactions that are not subject to the financial assistance prohibition. These include, among others, a distribution, a capital reduction, a share buy-back out of capital or a scheme of arrangement.[184] Section 682 provides for exemptions where the giving of financial assistance is by a company whose business is the lending of money or the assistance is given in relation to the company's share ownership scheme or to facilitate the purchase of shares by employees. Such assistance given by public companies pursuant to section 682 must not reduce its net assets and must be paid out of distributable profits, the calculation of which we discuss in Chapter 19.

The general exception is set out in section 678(2) in relation to financial assistance to acquire the shares and in section 678(4) in relation to financial assistance for the discharge of a liability incurred to purchase the shares. Each provision provides in theory for two exceptions, although, as we shall see, it is not clear that there is any exception left at all. The first exception is whether the 'principal purpose' of the transaction which provides the assistance is not to assist in the purchase of shares or the discharge of the liability incurred to purchase the shares. The second exception applies where the giving

---

[181] [2004] 2 BCLC 423.
[182] In this regard, see further E. Ferran, *Principles of Corporate Finance Law* (OUP, 2008), 291–3.
[183] Section 678(5) provides that the prohibition is subject to sections 681 and 682.
[184] See Chapter 19 with regard to distributions, reduction of capital, and share buy-backs.

of the assistance is 'an incidental part of some larger purpose of the company'. These provisions were considered in depth by the House of Lords in *Brady v Brady*.

■ *Brady v Brady* [1988] BCLC 579

This case involved a highly complex restructuring of a company, T. Brady & Sons Ltd and its subsidiaries, as a result of the falling out of the two brothers who owned the majority of shares in the company. The restructuring was designed to divide the company's assets between the two brothers. However, one of the steps of the restructuring process involved the payment of financial assistance to pay off a liability incurred to purchase the shares of the company giving the assistance. It was accepted that this involved financial assistance. The question for the court was whether the assistance fell within one of the exceptions in section 678(4).

Lord Oliver of Aylmerton

The appellants, however, rely on the provisions of [section 678(4)]…The appellants' case failed in the Court of Appeal because the assistance given by Brady was not, in the view of the majority (albeit for different reasons), in the interests of the company and therefore failed to satisfy [the requirement that the assistance is given in good faith in the interests of the company]. Both the trial judge and all three members of the Court of Appeal held, however, that para [4(b)] was satisfied, although Nourse LJ evidently felt some doubt on that question.

My Lords, I have found myself unable to share the views of the majority of the Court of Appeal [with the regard to the requirement of good faith]. The words 'in good faith in the interests of the company' form, I think, a single composite expression and postulate a requirement that those responsible for procuring the company to provide the assistance act in the genuine belief that it is being done in the company's interest. In the circumstances of this case, where failure to implement the final stage of the scheme for the division of the two sides of Brady's business is likely to lead back to the very management deadlock that it was designed to avoid and the probable liquidation of Brady as a result, the proposed transfer is not only something which is properly capable of being perceived by Brady's directors as calculated to advance Brady's corporate and commercial interests and the interests of its employees but is indeed, viewed objectively, in the company's interest. The corporators who sanctioned the transactions clearly considered that it was in their interests and in the interests of the company's business that it should continue in being under proper management unhampered by insoluble differences between the directors and I am not sure that I understand why [the Court of Appeal] considered that there was no evidence that the interests of the company's creditors had been considered and that this was fatal to the proposal…

Where I part company both from the trial judge and from the Court of Appeal is on the question of whether [paragraphs (4(a) and (b)] can, on any reasonable construction of the subsection, be said to have been satisfied. As O'Connor LJ observed, the section is not altogether easy to construe (see [1988] BCLC 20 at 25). It first appeared as part of s 42 of the Companies Act 1981 and it seems likely that it was introduced for the purpose of dispelling any doubts resulting from the query raised in *Belmont Finance Corp Ltd v Williams Furniture Ltd (No 2)* [1980] 1 All ER 393 whether a transaction entered into partly with a genuine view to the commercial interests of the company and partly with a view to putting a purchaser of shares in the company in funds to complete his purchase was in breach of s 54 of the Companies Act 1948. The ambit of the operation of the section is, however, far from easy to discern, for the word 'purpose' is capable of several different shades of meaning. This much is clear, [subsection (4) contemplates] two alternative situations. The first envisages a principal and, by implication, a subsidiary purpose. The inquiry here is whether the assistance given was principally in order to relieve the purchaser of shares in the company of his indebtedness resulting from the acquisition or whether it was principally for some other purpose, for instance the acquisition from the purchaser of some asset which the company requires for its business. That is the situation envisaged by Buckley LJ in the course of his judgment in the *Belmont Finance* case as giving rise to doubts. That is not this case, for the purpose of the assistance here was simply and solely to reduce the indebtedness [of the purchaser of the shares].

The alternative situation is where it is not suggested that the financial assistance was intended to achieve any other object than the reduction or discharge of the indebtedness but where that result (ie, the reduction or discharge) is merely incidental to some larger purpose of the company. Those last three words are important. What has to be sought is some larger overall corporate purpose in which the resultant reduction or discharge is merely incidental. The trial judge found Brady's larger purpose to be that of freeing itself from the deadlock and enabling it to function independently and this was echoed in the judgment of O'Connor LJ where he observed that the answer 'embraces avoiding liquidation, preserving its goodwill and the advantages of an established business' (see [1988] BCLC 20 at 26). Croom-Johnson LJ found the larger purpose in the reorganisation of the whole group. My Lords, I confess that I have not found the concept of a 'larger purpose' easy to grasp, but, if the paragraph is to be given any meaning that does not in effect provide a blank cheque for avoiding the effective application of [section 678] in every case, the concept must be narrower than that for which the appellants contend.

The matter can, perhaps most easily be tested by reference to [section 678(2)(b)], where the same formula is used. Here the words are 'or the giving of the assistance for that purpose [ie the acquisition of shares] is but an incidental part of some larger purpose of the company'. The words 'larger purpose' must here have the same meaning as the same words in [section 678(4)(b)]. In applying [678(2)(b)] one has, therefore, to look for some larger purpose in the giving of financial assistance than the mere purpose of the acquisition of the shares and to ask whether the giving of assistance is a mere incident of that purpose. My Lords, 'purpose' is, in some contexts, a word of wide content but in construing it in the context of the fasciculus of sections regulating the provision of finance by a company in connection with the purchase of its own shares there has always to be borne in mind the mischief against which [section 678] is aimed. In particular, if the section is not, effectively, to be deprived of any useful application, it is important to distinguish between a purpose and the reason why a purpose is formed. The ultimate reason for forming the purpose of financing an acquisition may, and in most cases probably will, be more important to those making the decision than the immediate transaction itself. But 'larger' is not the same thing as 'more important' nor is 'reason' the same as 'purpose'. If one postulates the case of a bidder for control of a public company financing his bid from the company's own funds, the obvious mischief at which the section is aimed, the immediate purpose which it is sought to achieve is that of completing the purchase and vesting control of the company in the bidder. The reasons why that course is considered desirable may be many and varied. The company may have fallen on hard times so that a change of management is considered necessary to avert disaster. It may merely be thought, and no doubt would be thought by the purchaser and the directors whom he nominates once he has control, that the business of the company will be more profitable under his management than it was heretofore. These may be excellent reasons but they cannot, in my judgment, constitute a 'larger purpose' of which the provision of assistance is merely an incident. The purpose and the only purpose of the financial assistance is and remains that of enabling the shares to be acquired and the financial or commercial advantages flowing from the acquisition, whilst they may form the reason for forming the purpose of providing assistance, are a by-product of it rather than an independent purpose of which the assistance can properly be considered to be an incident.

Now of course in the instant case the reason why the reorganisation was conceived in the first place was the damage being occasioned to the company and its shareholders by reason of the management deadlock, and the deadlock was the reason for the decision that the business should be split in two, so that the two branches could be conducted independently...or my part, I do not think that a larger purpose can be found in the benefits considered to be likely to flow or the disadvantages considered to be likely to be avoided by the acquisition which it was the

> purpose of the assistance to facilitate. The acquisition was not a mere incident of the scheme devised to break the deadlock. It was the essence of the scheme itself and the object which the scheme set out to achieve. In my judgment, therefore, [section 678(4)] is not satisfied and if the matter rested there the appeal ought to fail on that ground.

Lord Oliver clarifies that subsections 678(2) and (4) provide for two exceptions which have a common condition of application, namely that the assistance is given in good faith in the best interests of the company. Lord Oliver holds that this condition imposes a subjective standard that the directors genuinely believed that the assistance was given in the best interests of the company.

In relation to the first principal purpose exception, set out in subsections 678(2)(a) and (4)(a), Lord Oliver observes that the provision contemplates a principal and subsidiary purpose and was introduced to address a situation where the company purchases an asset from a person who then uses the funds to buy shares in the company. It is difficult to imagine any other situation in which this principal purpose exception would apply, particularly given Lord Oliver's distinction between reason and purpose, discussed in the next paragraph. However, if this is the only context in which it applies it appears that it is not necessary at all as the purchase of assets for value would not fall within any of the financial assistance categories set out in section 677.

The second exception is more difficult to apply. The words of the statute appear to exempt financial assistance where the assistance is given in order to achieve a broader company objective—a 'larger purpose', which, in *Brady*, counsel argued was 'freeing the company from deadlock'. Lord Oliver labels such objectives 'reasons' which he holds are distinct from purposes. Such 'reasons' are readily available and could include, for example, improving the management of the company, or facilitating an exit for the company's shareholders. The problem with equating 'larger purpose' with 'reasons' is, as Lord Oliver observes, that it would significantly undermine the scope of application of the financial assistance prohibition as such reasons are so readily available—a purchase of shares invariably takes place to further a corporate objective. Accordingly, Lord Oliver rejects such a reason-based understanding of larger purpose. Purposes, he holds, are different from reasons and having a good reason to provide financial assistance for the purchase cannot exempt the provision of financial assistance from the section 678 prohibition. However, whilst it is clear from *Brady v Brady* what a 'larger purpose' *is not*—it is not a reason—it is much less clear what would be an example of a 'larger purpose'. In fact, it is, at least for this author, difficult to imagine anything that could be a larger purpose that does not look like a reason. *Brady v Brady* therefore effectively deleted subsections 678(2)(b) and (4)(b) from the statute.

 Online Resource Centre
http://www.oxfordtextbooks.co.uk/orc/kershaw2e/

Visit the Online Resource Centre for additional resources and information available for this chapter, including web links and an interactive flashcard glossary.

PART IV
CREDITOR PROTECTION

CHAPTER EIGHTEEN

COMPANY LAW AND CREDITOR PROTECTION

I INTRODUCTION

In Chapter 1 we considered the rationales for limiting the liability of shareholders to what they agreed to pay for the allotted shares. We saw that the economic benefits of limited liability are considerable, although the nature and extent of the benefits vary according to the type of company and the ownership structure of the company. It would be worthwhile to revisit section III of Chapter 1 to review the available rationales before proceeding with the reading in this chapter.

By limiting the liability exposure of shareholders, the institution of limited liability results in a transfer of risks to other parties who have financial claims against the company: the company's creditors. Lending to Bob's Electronics Ltd rather than to Bob as sole trader increases creditors' risk exposure as Bob's personal assets are no longer available to satisfy creditors' claims. However, as we will see, the problems for creditors generated by limited liability are more complex than the simple increase in risk arising from a reduced asset pool to satisfy debt claims. The incentives generated by limited liability may alter the way in which the company does business: the types of investment made by the company and the risk profile of those investments and, therefore, the risks for creditors of doing business with the company. This chapter explores these problems. It asks: first, to what extent can, and to what extent should, we expect creditors to protect themselves from the problems that limited liability generates for creditors; and second, what role, if any, *should* company law play and what role does UK company law *actually play*, if any, in addressing these problems?

Before we consider the nature and extent of these problems, we must consider what we mean by the term 'creditor'. The first distinction that we must consider is the distinction between a voluntary creditor and an involuntary creditor. A voluntary creditor is a creditor who voluntarily agrees to provide credit to the company. A bank, for example, who agrees to lend a company £100 is a voluntary creditor. The bank agrees to provide £100 to the company in exchange for a fixed claim on the company, namely the agreement by the company to pay back the principal (the £100) plus interest at a specified rate on the principal amount. There are many examples of voluntary creditors in addition to the providers of bank finance: an employee who has worked for a month but is not paid until the end of the month is a voluntary creditor until paid; as we saw in *Salomon v Salomon*[1] suppliers who have not been paid for the goods which they deliver are trade creditors of the company. Involuntary creditors are those parties that do not voluntarily provide credit to the company. The prototypical involuntary creditor is the tort victim or product liability claimant. If a person purchases a computer from Bob's Electronics Ltd and the computer screen explodes when it is plugged in, causing damage to the customer's vision, then the customer will most likely have a claim for damages against

---

[1] [1897] AC 22. See Chapter 2.

Bob's Electronics Ltd. If the customer obtains an award of damages, until that award is paid the customer is an involuntary creditor of Bob's Electronics Ltd: the company owes an amount to the customer but obviously the customer did not ex-ante (prior to the event) agree to be injured.

A similar, but related, distinction is made between adjusting creditors and non-adjusting creditors. An adjusting creditor is a creditor that is capable of altering the terms on which the creditor provides credit to the company. A bank would be a prototypical adjusting creditor. The bank will assess the risk of doing business with the company, in particular the likelihood that the company could default and not pay back the loan, and will adjust the terms of the loan to take account of that risk, by for example, increasing the interest rate charged or decreasing the term of the loan (the time within which it has to be paid back). Whilst adjusting creditors are always voluntary creditors not all voluntary creditors are necessarily adjusting creditors. Whilst involuntary creditors are necessarily non-adjusting creditors, some voluntary creditors *may* also be non-adjusting: unpaid employees or small trade suppliers may be voluntary creditors but do they adjust the terms on which they agree to provide their services to take account of the risk of default/non-payment by the company?

II PROBLEMS GENERATED BY LIMITED LIABILITY

This section identifies the nature of the problems that limited liability generates for the different creditors of a company. By definition there is only a problem for a creditor if limited liability affects the creditor's position but the creditor does not, or is not able to, fully adjust to this changed position. If a creditor type cannot, or in practice does not, adjust to take account of the potential problems generated for creditors by limited liability then there may be a role for regulation to protect such creditors from these problems. This section is, therefore, concerned not only to identify the problems generated for creditors by the institution of limited liability but to understand the scope available, in theory and in practice, for creditors to protect themselves by adjusting to these problems.

1 Transferring risk from members to creditors

Any creditor lending any business or organization money, whether it is a sole trader, a company, or a government, has credit risk in relation to that loan; that is the risk that the loan and accompanying interest will not be repaid in full. As discussed in the extract from Professor Cheffins in Chapter 1, by limiting a member's liability to what she agrees to pay for the shares, risk is transferred from shareholders to other providers of finance to the firm, namely the firm's creditors. From this perspective the institution of limited liability increases credit risk. If a company's business fails to generate sufficient funds to repay all creditors then, in a situation where Bob's Electronics is a sole trader, creditors can make claim against Bob's personal assets to cushion their loss. At first glance taking away this option for creditors seems problematic: why should they be required to bear more of the losses arising from business failure? The House of Lords decision in *Salomon v Salomon*, discussed in detail in Chapter 2, has already directed us to the reason why this is reasonable, namely that creditors can adjust the terms on which they do business with the company to take account of this risk. We could say that they are paid by the company to bear this risk by, for example, the company agreeing to pay a higher interest rate.

There are three prerequisites for a creditor to be able to adjust to the credit risk associated with a business carried out through a company with limited member liability: first, the creditor must have the opportunity to negotiate the terms on which credit is provided; secondly, the creditor must have the sophistication to understand how an organizational form, like limited liability, alters the risk profile for the creditor; and, thirdly, the creditor must have the information about the nature and operation of the business required to make an informed assessment about the risk of non-payment. In relation to information about the company, we have seen that UK company law provides that certain information is made publicly available. Disclosure requirements include detailed information about: the fact that the business is carried out through a company; the company's financial position as detailed in its accounts; its membership; and security interests over its property. The regulation of disclosure by the company is dealt with in detail in Web Chapter A.

To the extent that a potential creditor is dissatisfied with the amount of information that is available publicly he could request additional private information from the company. Many creditors of the company, such as banks, will indeed request additional information about the company in making their assessment of credit risk. Banks clearly have the sophistication and opportunity to understand the risk involved in doing business with a company and they have the opportunity to insist on terms that protect their position. With Bob's Electronics Ltd, for example, they could request that Bob give a personal guarantee for any amounts not repaid by the company; that is, *in relation to their debt* such adjusting creditors can reinstate unlimited liability. There appears to be little concern about the distributional implications of limited member liability for such creditors. If the business fails and the company's funds are insufficient to pay them back in full then we are likely to find that the bank has protected itself through personal guarantees or was paid by the company to take account of such a risk (through a higher interest rate). If the bank did not do their homework properly and adjust the terms of the credit accordingly then they have no one to blame but themselves.

But what about other creditors such as the trade creditors in *Salomon v Salomon* or the providers of computer components to Bob's Electronics Ltd? Are such trade creditors also adjusting creditors? Often these trade creditors have lower value contractual relationships with many customers. One might question whether such creditors have the time or the resources to adjust their terms of trade to take account of the specific risks associated with specific companies. Investigating each company in detail is costly and time consuming. To understand the information, the trade creditor may have to employ experts who, in contrast to the bank, are not available within the firm. The time it takes to analyse the company may be better spent looking for new customers. This may mean that the trade creditors pay little attention to even the publicly available information about the company in question, let alone request additional private information. Lindley LJ in the Court of Appeal in *Salomon* made a similar point when he noted that in practice business persons do not read a register of security interests, which would have placed the trade creditors on notice of Mr Salomon's first priority secured debenture. This argument still holds weight with some commentators today. Professors Eidenmueller, Grunewald, and Noack, for example, have recently argued in relation to a company's legal capital[2] that: 'for many contractual partners—such as suppliers— the relatively small credit volume in relation to the individual enterprise means that obtaining all this information is not worthwhile... This involves time and expenditure that may be more than negligible.'[3]

---

[2] Legal capital is discussed in detail in Chapter 19.

[3] H. Eidenmueller, B. Grunewald and U. Noack, 'Minimum Capital in the System of Legal Capital' in M. Lutter (ed), *Legal Capital in Europe* (2006) European and Company Financial Law Review, Special Volume, 25.

There are, however, alternative means of adjustment. Some traders may include an industry-wide price premium to take account of possible bad debts in a particular industry. Alternatively legal techniques, such as reservation of title clauses, could be used if they are available given the nature of the product. This involves retaining ownership of the goods until they are paid for.[4] If such creditors do adjust then, as with sophisticated creditors such as banks, there seems to be little concern about the distributional implications of limited liability because these creditors have already taken into account the transfer of risk in their terms of trade.

The available empirical evidence, looking at what suppliers do in practice, suggests that trade creditors do not use the price of the goods to adjust the credit risk associated with a particular firm. Prices tend to be the same for all buyers.[5] This is not inconsistent with the argument that price may include an industry-wide premium for bad debts. There is, however, evidence that the willingness of creditors to give credit is affected by an assessment of the risk of the borrower.[6]

If a creditor could protect himself but 'elects' not to, the case for law to intervene to protect him seems less compelling. But what of those creditors who by definition are not capable of adjusting to the risks associated with doing business with the company, including the transfer of risk that is entailed by providing for limited member liability. This could include the prototypical involuntary creditor, the tort victim, but could also include, for example, former employees of a company who had reasonably assumed that their pension was secure only to discover that the company had not adequately funded the pension. For the involuntary creditor this transfer of risk goes uncompensated. If the company does not have sufficient funds to pay a claim one obviously cannot say that the involuntary creditor was paid to take account of this risk.

2 Limited liability and the opportunistic transfers of wealth from creditors to shareholders

Limited shareholder liability means that regardless of how risky the company's investments are, and regardless of the losses they generate, the most the shareholders can lose is the value of their equity investment. The riskier a company's investments the more likely it is that the shareholder will lose her investment. However, investments which involve significant risk of loss may make sense from a shareholder value perspective if the **expected value**[7] for the company of that investment is positive. If the company changes the risk profile of its investments this may also increase the risk associated with the company's debt by decreasing the likelihood of it being repaid in full. This is a problem for creditors because it is the shareholders who control the company and managers, who determine the investment profile of the company, are required to promote the interests of shareholders. Here, therefore, we see another example of an agency problem with the company as agent and the creditors, whose welfare can be detrimentally affected by the actions of the agent, as principal. The agency costs that are incurred by company decisions that enhance shareholder value at the expense of the value of the company's debt are referred to here as **financial agency costs**. In this regard consider the following extract.

---

[4] See generally R. Goode and L. Gulliver, *Legal Problems of Credit and Security* (4th edn, Sweet & Maxwell, 2008).

[5] J. Smith, 'Trade Credit and Information Asymmetry' (1987) *Journal of Finance* 863.

[6] M. Peterson and R. Rajan, 'Trade Credit: Theories and Evidence' (1997) *Review of Financial Studies* 661, 679.

[7] Expected value is the sum of the range of possible payoffs from the investment. If a £10 investment has 50% chance of earning £20 and 50% chance of earning £40 its expected value is 50% × 20 plus 50% × 40 which is 30 (10 plus 20).

■ J.H. Choper, J.C. Coffee, Jr and R.J. Gilson, *Cases and Materials on Corporations* (Aspen, 2004)

Suppose a [company] has assets of $1000, entirely invested in government bonds,[8] and a capital structure[9] of [$250 in equity and] $750 in debt. In this circumstance, the debt will be paid with certainty, and the value of the debt is $750 and the [shares] is $250. Now suppose the [company] is offered the opportunity to replace its investment in government bonds with a risky $1000 investment. This investment has an expected return of $1,100 composed of a 50% likelihood of a $2,200 return and a 50% likelihood of a zero return. This is a good investment for the shareholders. As set out in Table [1], if the transaction pays off, the shareholders...repay their debt, and are left with [shares] worth $1,450. If the transaction does not pay off, they default on the debt having lost their [shares'] $250 pre-transaction value. The debtholders do not fare so well. If the transaction pays off, the debtholders are repaid. If the transaction does not pay off, the debtholders lose the $750 pre-transaction value of the debt. On an expected value basis, the transaction *increases* [share] value from $250 to $725, but *decreases* the value of the debt from $750 to $375. The result of increasing the risk of the [company's] investment is a shift of $375 in value from the debtholders to the shareholders. Because the debtholders' returns are fixed, all of the potential gains from the transaction go to shareholders.[10] And because the shareholders cannot lose more than the pre-transaction value of their [shares],[11] debtholders bear most of the potential loss from the transaction.

Table [1]: The Effect of Risky Investment on the Value of [Shares] and Debt

	Before Risky Investment	After Risky Investment		
		Pays off	No Payoff	
[Shares] Value	$250	0.5($2200–£750) +	0.5($0) =	$725
		Pays off	No Payoff	
Debt Value	$750	0.5($750) +	0.5($0) =	$375
Firm Value	$1,000			$1,100

In the previous example, the expected value of the firm still increased as a result of the risky investment even though it also resulted in the transfer in value from debtholders to shareholders. This was because the risky investment that replaced the government bonds still had a positive expected value net of its cost. However, this need not be the case...An investment may increase the value of [the shares] even though it *decreases* the expected value of the [company]. Suppose

---

[8] Although the ongoing sovereign debt crisis has made us acutely aware of the credit risk associated with sovereigns (even the United States) it is still true today that one of safest investments you could make with your money is to invest in US government bonds, known as treasuries. A bond is a form of loan—simply a right to be repaid a certain amount. If you buy a US government bond, in effect you are lending the US Government the value of that bond and the US Government agrees to pay you that value at sometime in the future. This is a very low risk investment as the US economy is the largest in the world and it is very unlikely that the US Government will not be in a position to pay you back.

[9] 'Capital structure' is a term used to refer to how a company's investments are funded. Here the $1,000 investment in government bonds is funded by $250 of equity (shares) and $750 of debt, say from a bank.

[10] Remember creditors have a fixed claim to the return of the principal amount loaned and the interest. This contrasts with shareholders residuary interest that varies depending on how successful or unsuccessful the company is.

[11] Because they benefit from limited liability.

the [company], is more highly leveraged,[12] this time with assets of $800 all of which are invested in government bonds, and debt of $750. The [shares are] then worth $50. This time the risky investment costs $800, with a 20% likelihood of a return of $2,000 and an 80% likelihood of a return of 0. The investment has a net expected value of a negative $400, which reduces the value of the firm to $400. Nonetheless the investment is still attractive to shareholders. If the investment pays off, the shareholders...repay the debt, leaving a [share] value of $1,250. If the investment does not pay off, the shareholders lose their $50, and the debtholders lose $750. As shown in table [2] the result is transfer of $200 from debtholders to shareholders, and a $400 reduction in the value of the [company].

Table [2]: The Effect of Risky Investment with Negative Expected Value on the Value of [Shares] and Debt

	Before Risky Investment	After Risky Investment		
[Shares] Value	$50	Pays off 0.2($2000–£750)	No Payoff + 0.8($0) =	$250
Debt Value	$750	Pays off 0.2($750)	No Payoff + 0.8($0) =	$150
Firm Value	$1,000			$400

The problems identified by Choper et al relate to ex-post (after the provision of the debt) action by the company to change its investment policy. The sense from this extract is that shareholders can lure debt providers, such as banks, into providing loan finance for the company's activities and then, once the funds have been provided, opportunistically exploit the fact that the funds have been paid out. Of course sophisticated investors are very aware that this could happen and can take steps ex-ante (before the finance is provided) to prevent such opportunism. They could, for example, require that the company contractually bind itself to its current investment strategy or demand a higher interest rate to compensate them for this risk. Other creditors, such as trade creditors, could also use their crude adjustment mechanisms of: increasing prices for all customers; using reservation of title clauses; or, where they have some firm specific knowledge, not providing credit at all. As we have seen, it is a moot question, however, whether in practice they do so. Obviously, involuntary creditors who could also suffer at the hands of such opportunism are not in a position to take account of this risk ex-ante, prior to their injury.

3 Limited liability and incentive to invest in hazardous activities

Limited shareholder liability means that shareholders do not have to be concerned about possible losses arising from an investment that exceeds the value of the net assets of the business. Of course, the shareholders do not want the company to incur an overall loss because they will lose their investments. However, investments rarely provide certain returns with little to no risk of loss. An investment with the scope for a good return may also involve a small possibility of a disastrous loss in excess of the value of

---

[12] 'Highly leveraged' means that its investments are funded by a substantial amount of debt compared to equity. 'Leveraged' is a term used more typically in the US and is becoming more common in the UK. UK corporate finance persons have traditionally referred to gearing rather than leverage.

the investment or the company. *Because* of limited liability, in calculating the expected return for shareholders associated with such an investment the calculation can ignore such expected losses (the amount of the loss multiplied by the probability of its occurrence) to the extent they fall below the value of the company.

■ **D.W. Leebron, 'Limited Liability, Tort Victims and Creditors' (1991) 91 *Columbia Law Review* 1565**

Consider, for example, an investment in a high-technology, high-risk enterprise, such as biotechnology. The shares of the company are being offered to the public for $20 each. On the upside, the investor believes that in three years there is a 50% chance each share of the company will be worth $30, a 20% chance they will be worth $40, a 4% chance they will be worth $50, and a 1% chance they will be worth $60 or more. This latter 1% figure includes some chance (significantly less than 1%) that the shares will turn out to be a true bonanza, worth more than $100. On the other hand, there is 20% chance they will still be worth $20, a 4% chance they will only be worth $10, and a 1% chance they will be completely worthless. If shareholders enjoy limited liability, there is no chance that the shares will be worth less than zero—even though, for example, there may be a 0.1% chance that a dangerous organism will escape causing extensive injury and legally triggering mammoth corporate liability. If, however, there were no limitation on liability, the 1% chance of a zero return likely would be distributed over an amount from zero to a negative return representing the shareholder's wealth.[13] Thus, one effect of limiting shareholder liability is to increase the expected value of investments by replacing each potential negative value—a call on the shareholder's other wealth—by a value of zero[14]... Simplifying this example, if there were a 0.1% chance that the shareholder would have to pay $2,000 per share to meet corporate liabilities, and no other chance of a shareholder assessment, the expected future value of the shares would be $2 less under an unlimited liability regime. With limited liability, there are $2 of expected costs that are imposed on others and not reflected in the investor's decision-making.

Whether the effect of unlimited liability on investment decisions is significant depends on both the perceived probability of a call on the shareholder's wealth and the expected magnitude of that call. If an enterprise is financed solely with equity and debt that is explicitly nonrecourse to shareholders,[15] the probability and magnitude of a call on shareholder resources will depend primarily on the expected tort liability of the enterprise. For virtually all enterprises that are financially viable at the outset, such a call will be an event of very low probability.[16] Few

---

[13] Even with an unlimited member liability regime the shareholder's liability is not of course unlimited; it is limited to the wealth of that shareholder. So if a shareholder was subject to unlimited liability the expected value calculation of an investment would still be distorted. See further the comparison in the next note.

[14] Consider this example: an investment funded by equity alone of £100 has a 50% chance of a £260 return, a 40% chance of a return of £20, and a 10% chance of a negative £2,000 return (understood here as an additional cost of £200). The expected value of the investment is (50% × £260) + (40% × £20) + (10% × (-)£2,000) = £130 + £8 – £200 = (-)£62. However, if the investor benefits from limited liability he need not concern himself with negative value possibilities as he does not need to pay any more than what he agreed to pay for the shares (the original investment). From such a shareholder's perspective, therefore, the negative 200 is replaced by zero and the expected value calculation becomes £130 + £8 – £0 = £138. Now if this investor does not benefit from limited liability but is worth only £1700 of personal wealth then the most he can lose if the negative value possibility is realized in practice is £1,400. Accordingly, in the expected value calculation the figure of negative £2,000 is replaced with negative £1,400. This would result in an expected value calculation of £130 + £8 – £140 = (-)£2.

[15] Debt that is non-recourse to shareholders means debt that involves an agreement with the creditor that if the business assets are insufficient to pay back the debt then the creditor has no right to demand further payment from the shareholder, i.e. contractually agreed limited liability in relation to each creditor who agrees to such a provision. As mentioned earlier, this was common practice in the UK prior to the introduction of limited member liability.

[16] See the extract from Cheffins later in this section arguing that most companies will have the financial wherewithal or the insurance cover necessary to cover any such claim.

enterprises will be worthwhile investments if there is a significant chance the investment will be wiped out by tort liability. As the preceding example illustrates, events of such small probability have relatively little effect on the expected value of an investment, even if the magnitude of any call would be fairly large...

In summary, investments under a limited liability regime have greater expected value and are less risky to investors than investments under unlimited liability. Because of these two effects of the limitation of liability, a move from limited to unlimited liability would result at the margin in the abandonment of some investments previously deemed worthwhile by the investor. The efficiency implications of limited liability depend on two considerations. First, it must be deter- mined whether the limited liability of equity investors truly externalizes[17] costs by removing con- sideration of costs from investors' decisions. If the costs are taken into account by other actors, such as creditors or potential tort victims, then there may be no efficiency[18] consequences. If, on the other hand, costs are externalized, limited liability is likely to produce inefficient investment decisions. Second, the measure of the risk of an activity to an investor may or may not reflect the social risk. We must ask under which regime the risk to the investor represents a more accurate measure of social risk. If the investor faces less risk under limited liability than potential tort victims who cannot affect the enterprise, the venture will engage in overly risky activities from a societal point of view.

Limited liability may be inefficient because it allows enterprises to externalize costs and makes activities less risky to investors than to society as a whole. This is not to say that limited liability is necessarily inefficient. First, limiting the liability of shareholders may simply shift the costs to other actors who will take them into account and either unilaterally make efficient decisions, or be able to force the enterprise, despite its limited liability, to make socially efficient choices. The efficiency consequences of limiting liability thus differ with respect to contracted debtholders and potential tort victims. With respect to the debtholder, risk and potential loss have been sim- ply transferred from the equity holder to the debtholder. The debtholder will correspondingly reduce the expected value of his investment, and demand a greater expected return. No costs of the enterprise have been externalized as a result of shareholders' limited liability to debtholders— regardless of the source of the enterprise's losses. Furthermore, to the extent the allocation of costs is not optimal, the shareholder and debtholder can contract around the liability rule. When liability is limited with respect to third-party tort victims, the potential loss beyond the equity investment is simply not part of any actor's calculation and thus disappears as an element in the enterprise's investment evaluations. In this sense, costs of the enterprise are not internalized to any actor; an investment may be undertaken even though from society's point of view it is not worthwhile...The tort victim, or society at large, may be quite averse to the prospect of the cata- strophic loss. The purely rational [shareholder], however, will continue to regard the enterprise as being only moderately risky since the worst possible outcome is the loss of the investment.

These two aspects—the increase in the expected value of the investment and the decrease in the riskiness of the investment—are each of potential significance in assessing the impact of limited liability. While the failure of an enterprise to take the expected tort liability into account may have little effect on the future expected value of the enterprise, it might still significantly affect investment decisions in light of its effect on the perceived riskiness of the enterprise. If, however, there is an efficient insurance market for these risks and firms choose to insure, then the only effect of limited liability will be on the expected future value. In this case, the expected

---

[17] Externalizing costs means imposing those costs on others without their consent. If, in the example set out in the extract from Leebron's article, extensive injury is caused by the product and the value of the claims exceed the value of the business then the tort victims will have to bear those costs themselves as there is no one else to compensate them. Hence those costs are externalized on them.

[18] The term 'efficiency' is used in the company law literature in many different ways. Here an efficient investment means that the investment has a positive expected value when it reflects the full range of value outcomes both positive and negative.

future cost would become a certain insurance cost. However, it is doubtful whether firms able to externalize some losses through the device of limited liability would choose to insure fully.

However, judging the efficiency consequences of limited liability requires more than a theoretical examination of the benefits of unlimited liability. Even assuming that shareholders who would be held liable will cause managers to act efficiently in taking potential losses into account—an assumption made in this Article—there may be costs to unlimited liability that outweigh its benefits.

Professor Leebron argues that companies, in calculating the expected value of an investment opportunity, can ignore losses that *may* be generated by investments which exceed the value of the company. This is because shareholders who control a limited liability company are not liable for claims if the company does not have sufficient assets to satisfy them. Investments that contain a risk of wiping out the company obviously increase the risk of doing business with the company for all creditors. As Professor Leebron points out many creditors can adjust to this additional risk by altering the terms upon which they do business with the company. Involuntary creditors do not, by definition, adjust to take account of these risks.

Some of the adjustments required by adjusting creditors—for example, higher interest rates—will, however, benefit the involuntary creditor constituency where, by increasing the costs of the project, they force the company to view the expected value of the project in a way which is not distorted by the effects of limited liability. Here one might say that the involuntary creditors 'free-ride' on the protections negotiated by adjusting creditors. However, as we have noted previously, certain protections that adjusting creditors may bargain for—such as personal guarantees from shareholders—will protect the adjusting creditor but provide no free-riding benefits for non-adjusting creditors. Where the company is not required to take the potential costs imposed on involuntary creditors into account, companies are more likely to produce tort victims through their activities than would be the case under an unlimited liability regime.

Whether or not companies, when making decisions, fail to take account of the possible injuries and the extent of the injuries that could be caused to third parties will depend on the nature of the companies. In relation to large companies worth hundreds of millions if not billions of pounds it is very unlikely that any tort claim would be big enough to wipe out the company, which means that such costs are always taken into account in the investment decisions of those companies. Furthermore, such companies are likely to have substantial insurance cover for such claims. In the UK there is no mandatory requirement for companies to obtain product liability insurance. However, invariably companies do have substantial product liability insurance cover. Consider the following extract from Professor Cheffins in this regard.

■ B. Cheffins, *Company Law: Theory Structure and Operation* (OUP, 1997)

Limited liability's adverse impact on tort creditors is not likely to be as dramatic in practice as it appears to be in theory. Only a small fraction of tort victims ever seek any form of legal redress. When tort claims are pursued, the vast majority are settled out of court by the defendant's insurer. In both sets of circumstances the presence or absence of limited liability will be irrelevant to the victim.

Admittedly, situations can arise where victims are likely to sue and outside insurers are not obliged to cover the loss, at least fully. This can occur, for instance, with an accident in which many are killed or injured (e.g. a plane crash) or suffer adverse effects from using a defective product (e.g. drugs). Nevertheless, even with these types of 'mass tort', the limited liability which shareholders of a defendant company enjoy is unlikely to have a substantial impact on the amount available for recovery. A key consideration is that such occurrences rarely bankrupt companies. The tortfeasors in such instances are usually large enterprises, which means they will probably have substantial assets available to satisfy claims. As well, such companies often set up a 'captive' in-house insurer to provide cover for any losses not dealt with by outside insurance. Furthermore, to the extent that tort liability does push a large enterprise to the brink of financial collapse, management has every incentive to strike some form of compromise with the tort creditors. The impetus is that if one of the formal procedures available under English law for dealing with distressed companies…is invoked, the executives will have to step aside in favour of a licensed insolvency practitioner.

If one thinks about large companies that are adequately insured the problems for involuntary creditors identified in this section seem less pressing. However, it is possible for such large companies to protect their own assets from the negative value effects of hazardous investments. That is, with careful planning, large companies can organize their activities through thinly capitalized subsidiary companies. As we saw in Chapter 2, English company law shows considerable respect for the separate legal personality of parent and subsidiary companies and provides very limited scope for piercing the corporate veil between them. For a large, high-value company an investment that if taken by the parent company has a negative expected value may have a positive expected value if taken by a thinly capitalized subsidiary company. This, if not properly regulated, could result in an over-investment by business in hazardous industries or, which is the other side of the same coin, an under-investment by business in safety.

The case for regulation to protect involuntary creditors from the effects of enabling business activity to be carried out through the limited liability company is, therefore, a strong one. However, as the leading book on comparative corporate law, *The Anatomy of Corporate Law*, observes, in all European jurisdictions, the US and Japan involuntary creditors do not typically benefit from specific protections from these negative effects. The reason for this, the authors suggest, is that the cost of collective coordination and action by involuntary creditors in order to pressurize the legislature to take account of their interests is prohibitive.[19]

In the UK involuntary creditors are the beneficiaries of very few legal protections designed specifically for this group. As noted earlier there is no mandatory requirement to take product liability insurance. However, where the company does have such an insurance policy the Third Party (Rights Against Insurers) Act 1930 ensures that the insurance claim of an insolvent company is transferred to the creditor to prevent other creditors having any claim to the insurance proceeds. Another possible protective mechanism would be to give involuntary creditors priority in bankruptcy so that their claims would be satisfied prior to other creditors, including secured creditors. This is not the case currently in the UK and commentators consider it very unlikely that such a reform option is politically viable.[20] Some degree of protection may be provided in relation

---

[19] G. Hertig and H. Kanda, 'Creditor Protection' in Kraakman et al (eds), *The Anatomy of Corporate Law: A Comparative and Functional Approach* (OUP, 2004): 'to date…almost no specialized measures to protect involuntary creditors have been adopted anywhere'. They offer the following explanation for 'this lacuna': 'since tort victims do not know they will become victims, they have little incentive to lobby for corporate law reform before they are injured. After injury, however, it may be too late to lobby for reform because their damages are fixed, and they can no longer benefit from a change in the law.'

[20] Professor Ferran has noted in this regard that 'the historical evidence of insolvency law reform in the United Kingdom suggests that proposals along these lines are unlikely to receive a favourable welcome'—E. Ferran, 'Creditors' Interests and "Core" Company Law' (1999) *Company Lawyer* 314.

to groups of companies as a result of recent developments in tort law[21] considered in Chapter 4: where parent companies actively assume responsibility for risks arising from the subsidiary's activities that cause harm they may be subject to a duty of care, the breach of which would allow a involuntary creditor to bring an action against the parent company. However, as noted in chapter 4 there remain several doubts about: (i) the reach of these cases to involuntary creditors other than employees; (ii) whether higher courts will follow the lead of these cases;[22] and (iii) whether or not parent companies can take practical steps to prevent the duty from arising.

For a text on company law the first regulatory question raised by these negative effects for involuntary creditors of providing limited shareholder liability, and by the absence of any specific regulatory protections to address these effects, is whether we should reconsider the appropriateness of providing limited liability to shareholders *in relation to such involuntary creditor claims*.

III RECONSIDERING UNLIMITED LIABILITY FOR TORT VICTIMS

In Chapter 1 we considered the economic benefits of providing companies with limited member liability. We noted the benefits of encouraging entrepreneurial activity where entrepreneurs, like Bob from our case study, would not take the risk of starting or expanding a business when all the entrepreneur's personal wealth would be exposed to the business's creditors. We also considered how limited liability facilitated the transfer of shares and allowed investors to diversify their portfolios. Given the problems we have identified for involuntary creditors that arise, or are exacerbated by, business activity carried out through the limited liability company, we might want to ask what the implications would be for these economic benefits if we qualified limited member liability by making shareholders liable *only* for the unpaid debts of involuntary creditors. This would, of course, incentivize shareholders to ensure that the company does not make investments that do not take full account of the fact that those investments *could* result in injuries to third parties.

This theme has been the subject of a debate led by US law professors Leebron, Hansmann, and Kraakman. Leebron notes 'that almost every commentator has paused to note that limited liability cannot be satisfactorily justified for tort victims ("involuntary creditors") and then moved on as though there is nothing to do about this unfortunate wrinkle in the economic perfection of the law'.[23] Professors Hansmann and Kraakman argue that shareholders in both companies with few shareholders (close companies) and listed public companies should have pro rata unlimited liability in relation to tort creditors, that is, each shareholder will be liable for the losses in excess of company value in proportion to the number of shares held. According to this proposal, the shareholders would not be jointly and severally liable for the whole amount so that one wealthy shareholder with say 0.1% of the shares could be sued for the whole of the excess amount. They argue that by selecting pro rata unlimited liability instead of joint and several liability the economic benefits of limited member liability detailed earlier will not be placed in jeopardy.

---

[21] *Chandler v Cape* [2011] EWHC 951; [2012] EWCA Civ 525 (CA); *Newton-Sealey v ArmorGroup Services Ltd* [2008] EWHC 233.

[22] Particularly in relation to *Chandler v Cape* [2011] EWHC 951.

[23] D.W. Leebron, 'Limited Liability, Tort Victims and Creditors' (1991) 91 *Columbia Law Review* 1565.

Let us consider this argument first in relation to small private companies (close companies) where the rationale that limited liability encourages entrepreneurial activity is particularly relevant.

■ H. Hansmann and R. Kraakman, 'Toward Unlimited Shareholder Liability for Corporate Torts' (1991) *Yale Law Journal* 1879

Liability insurance is widely available for small businesses, and this vitiates an argument for limited liability based on shareholder risk aversion. Undoubtedly, some small corporations that are viable under limited liability would cease to be so under unlimited liability, since they could not buy adequate insurance and their shareholders would be unwilling to expose personal assets to the risks of a tort judgment. But there is no reason to assume that such small firms should exist—that is, that they have positive net social value. In fact, an important advantage of unlimited liability is precisely that it would force such firms—which are effectively being subsidized by their tort victims—out of business. When liability insurance is available, as it is for most businesses, the argument for unlimited liability is further strengthened.

Consider first the simple case in which perfect insurance is available—that is, insurance that has no loading costs[24] ... and gives rise to no moral hazard[25] (presumably because the insurer can monitor the insured's behaviour effectively). In this case, with unlimited liability, a shareholder having personal assets sufficient to cover any tort judgment will have an incentive to purchase full insurance. In turn, such insurance will give the shareholder efficient incentives[26] to internalize costs with respect to both level of care and magnitude of investment.

With limited [member] liability, on the other hand, the shareholder will often have an incentive either to purchase no insurance or to purchase insurance that is insufficient to cover the full range of losses that her corporation might cause. Liability insurance sold to businesses invariably has an upper limit on coverage, and it appears that most firms choose a relatively low coverage limit, suggesting that incomplete insurance is a common strategy. And, to the extent that a corporation is underinsured, its shareholder will once again have incentives to take insufficient care and to choose an inefficient scale for the firm.

In reality, of course, perfect insurance cannot be purchased. Loading costs account for roughly one-quarter of all premiums, and most liability insurance undoubtedly involves a degree of moral hazard. If these market imperfections were severe enough, many firms would not purchase full insurance even under a regime of unlimited liability.[27] Yet these imperfections may not be very serious for most businesses. Loading costs are probably not disproportional to the transaction costs of self-insurance or insolvency. That is, even without insurance, the average firm would probably incur expected costs of similar magnitude in the form of lawyers' fees to defend tort actions and costs associated with bankruptcy. In addition, writers of liability insurance for businesses claim to be able to control moral hazard by inspecting their insureds and employing experience ratings.[28] These considerations, together with the fact that even today, under limited liability, most businesses do purchase significant—albeit not fully adequate—amounts of liability insurance, suggest that insurance markets work reasonably well. Thus we have good reason to believe that a shift to unlimited liability would be less likely to greatly increase risk-bearing by shareholders of small corporations than to induce those shareholders to purchase adequate insurance.

---

[24] 'Loading costs' are the administrative costs of the insurance company of providing insurance.

[25] Moral hazard here means the incentive to engage in the insured activity (here causing personal injury to third parties) because as you are insured you do not bear the costs of that activity. Insurance companies can reduce moral hazard by monitoring the insured person or by including deductibles (that is, an amount for which the insured is personally liable) or through such mechanisms as no-claims bonuses.

[26] Such mechanisms would be deductibles or no-claims bonuses.

[27] They would not purchase such insurance because the cost of insurance—due to administrative costs and the cost associated with moral hazard—would be too high.

[28] An example of an 'experience rating' would be a no-claims bonus.

Now consider Hansmann and Kraakman's argument in relation to listed companies. According to our analysis in Chapter 1, limited liability enables the free transferability of shares by reducing shareholder–shareholder monitoring and enables the diversification of an investor's share portfolio, because with an unlimited liability regime the more shares you hold the greater the likelihood that your personal assets will be exposed.

■ **H. Hansmann and R. Kraakman, 'Toward Unlimited Shareholder Liability for Corporate Torts' (1991) *Yale Law Journal* 1879**

Limited liability gives the managers of publicly-traded corporations an incentive to assume too much risk, just as it does the shareholders of closely-held firms. However, the public corporation adds several novel elements to the comparison of liability regimes. In addition to a new class of hired managers, these include: (1) large numbers of passive shareholders; (2) a market for freely-trading [shares]; (3) substantial assets; and (4) potential tort liability that may not only exceed the firm's assets but that may not be fully insurable at any premium. The traditional view is that these elements—and especially the need to maintain an efficient market for shares—make unlimited liability even less appropriate for public firms than for closely-held firms...

There is no doubt that unlimited liability, as we have described it, would increase the cost of equity. Indeed, the purpose of unlimited liability is to make share prices reflect tort costs. Yet the literature suggests that, beyond internalizing tort losses, unlimited liability might generate additional costs by (1) impairing the market's capacity to diversify risk[29] and to value shares, (2) altering the identities and investment strategies of shareholders, and (3) inducing market participants to monitor excessively. The magnitude of these additional costs, however, turns chiefly on the choice between a joint and several or a pro rata liability rule. If shareholders faced joint and several personal liability...these costs might be very large. But, as Leebron persuasively argues, they should be much smaller if shareholder liability is...governed by a pro rata rule.

Diversified Portfolios and Market Prices
The claim that unlimited liability might distort share prices or prevent shareholders from diversifying risk is persuasive only under a joint and several liability rule...Although individual stocks would be riskier under such a rule, the additional risk would be no more difficult to diversify than the risk of tort liability is today. It would simply be larger in absolute terms, which would increase the number of stocks in an optimally diversified portfolio as well as the risk of taking a large position in a single firm...Risk-averse small investors with too little capital to diversify fully under an unlimited liability regime could shift their investments at very little cost to mutual funds or corporate debt. Moreover, the infrequency of catastrophic torts suggests that a pro rata rule would impose relatively small expected costs, even on undiversified investors, except when corporate activities are extremely risky—which is precisely when an unlimited liability regime is needed to prevent corporations from externalizing large costs. It is sometimes argued that, regardless of how remote the probability of a substantial judgment against them, the mere prospect of unlimited personal liability would cause many individual stockholders to abandon the equity markets entirely in favour of fixed-return securities [such as bonds], with the arguable consequence of impairing the liquidity of the markets.[30] But such behaviour seems as unlikely as it would be irrational. For example, under current [US] law, every time a person drives an automobile she exposes herself to unlimited tort liability. Yet nearly all adults regularly drive automobiles, and casual empiricism suggests that few individuals even feel it worthwhile to purchase liability insurance that has exceptionally high coverage limits.

---

[29] To remind yourself of why the diversification of an investor's share portfolio reduces the risks of the portfolio and, thereby, individual companies' cost of capital see Chapter 1 section III.

[30] 'Impairing the liquidity of the markets' means simply that there are fewer investors willing to buy shares which may make it harder to sell the shares.

Shareholder Investment Strategies

More subtle critics [have argued that] unlimited liability might encourage wealthy shareholders to 'overdiversify' by eschewing large stock positions, hence reducing the frequency of control transactions and depriving all shareholders of the services of sophisticated monitors…A pro rata rule clearly would increase a risk-averse investor's cost of accumulating a large holding in a risky corporation relative to the investor's cost of holding a diversified portfolio. On this dimension, unlimited liability poses a real question of the second best; at the margin, control blocks in risky firms would become less attractive and takeover premia[31] would decline under unlimited liability, with a consequent decrease in shareholder monitoring of the management of risky firms. This loss is arguably a real social cost. Nevertheless, it would probably be a small loss in comparison to the potential gains of inducing risky corporations to internalize their full expected tort liability. The cost would be restricted to unusually risky corporations and, even there, the magnitude of expected tort losses would presumably pale in most cases next to the prospects for ordinary business gain or loss associated with taking a control position in a public corporation. Finally…when determining the magnitude of tort damages to be assessed against a firm and its shareholders under unlimited liability, courts might appropriately consider the greater risk aversion of controlling shareholders with concentrated stock holdings and temper damage awards accordingly.

Excessive Monitoring Costs

A final claim often made in defence of the status quo is that unlimited liability would generate excessive monitoring of both management and shareholders by all participants in public corporations. This claim would be plausible if each shareholder were liable for all corporate debts as they would be under a joint and several rule: in that case, the risks borne by each individual shareholder or creditor would depend in part on fluctuations in the aggregate wealth of all shareholders.[32] All shareholders would then have a personal stake in knowing about the personal assets of other shareholders who entered or exited the firm. In contrast to shareholders in closely-held firms, moreover, shareholders in public firms could not hope to reallocate payouts among themselves to compensate for their disparate costs of risk-bearing.

Yet, this monitoring argument fails against a rule of pro rata liability for tort losses. Under such a rule, a shareholder's risk would depend only on the size of her own investment rather than on the wealth of other shareholders. Furthermore, contract creditors would not rely on the wealth of shareholders at all. Thus, the only effect of pro rata liability would be a marginal increase in shareholder incentives to monitor the enterprise's expected tort losses. Although this additional monitoring would not differ in kind from what shareholders already do, it would encourage managers to consider the full social costs of investment decisions. Additional monitoring would cost more on the margin, but it would be no more duplicative or socially wasteful than the attention that shareholders already devote to all other matters affecting the value of the firm. Indeed, tort risks might even be less costly to monitor than other business risks. A developed industry of expert monitors—liability insurers—already sells assessments of liability risk, with or without the benefit of insurance. These same firms might easily collectivize the costs of evaluating liability risks for the public market.

Hansmann and Kraakman argue that unlimited liability for tort claims incentivizes shareholders to ensure that a company's investment policy takes full account of the possible costs imposed on future tort victims. However, much of this book has focused on

---

[31] A takeover premium is the amount paid for a share in a takeover above the trading price of the share.

[32] Under a joint and several liability rule a wealthy shareholder with one share could find herself liable for all the excess debt and then have to pursue other shareholders (who may not have the resources to pay) for contribution. Hence the risks borne by each shareholder varies (both positively and negatively) according to the wealth of the other shareholders.

the fact that shareholders in public, widely-held companies may be passive rather than active in relation to monitoring management's behaviour. Whilst increasing shareholder liability exposure increases incentives to monitor, Hansmann and Kraakman argue, in the previous extract, that in widely-held companies it would only marginally increase the incentives to monitor. We need to ask, therefore, whether, in the absence of effective shareholder monitoring, providing unlimited pro rata shareholder liability would alter managers' behaviour so that they take account of such costs when making investment decisions on behalf of the company.

■ **H. Hansmann and R. Kraakman, 'Toward Unlimited Shareholder Liability for Corporate Torts' (1991)** *Yale Law Journal* **1879**

Management's Incentives to Take Care

Given that unlimited liability is feasible for public firms, we must still ask whether it can significantly improve their incentives to take care. In particular, will the managers of publicly-traded firms be responsive to the incentives created by unlimited liability? Unlike the shareholder-managers of closely-held firms and the corporate parents of subsidiary firms, who make corporate policy directly, the disparate shareholders of most public corporations seldom exercise direct control over corporate policy. Why, then, should we expect the managers of public corporations to respond to liability imposed on shareholders?

One answer is that a variety of market mechanisms press corporate managers to be responsive to shareholder welfare as this is reflected in share prices. If shareholders faced full liability for potential tort losses, share prices would incorporate available information about the full extent of these possible losses. Managers, in turn, would then have as much incentive to consider the full expected social costs of corporate torts as they now have to weigh all other costs to the firm that shareholders presently bear as a matter of course. Moreover, shareholders who faced contingent liability would presumably demand—and managers as well as outside analysts would presumably supply—far more information about the riskiness of corporate policies, precisely because this information would have greater importance in valuing shares. This additional information, especially when it came from market sources outside the firm, would further enhance management's incentive to consider the tort risks associated with its policies...

On the other hand, the problem may not be that managers will respond too little to expected liability costs but, conversely, that they will respond too much. As we have previously argued, shareholders can diversify tort risks under a regime of unlimited pro rata liability and, therefore, will prefer that public firms continue to invest as risk-neutral actors. Yet, even today, large public corporations insure heavily against tort liability under the existing limited liability regime. Although there are other possible explanations, such insurance may be evidence of managerial risk aversion. Managers cannot diversify their investment of firm-specific human capital in the corporation. Consequently, if managers expect large, uninsured tort losses to threaten their jobs, they may manage in a risk-averse manner in order to lower the probability of such losses—and, in particular, of losses that might induce bankruptcy. Managers who are risk averse in this fashion, it might be feared, would be overdeterred by unlimited liability.

It is, to be sure, theoretically possible that managers in hazardous industries are already over-deterred by the risk of bankruptcy induced by tort losses, even under the current regime of limited liability, so that a shift to unlimited liability would simply accentuate this problem. Yet, as a practical matter, this seems implausible. Many important classes of torts which create a risk of catastrophic loss that might bankrupt the firm ten or twenty years in the future seem unlikely to carry any weight in management's incentive calculus today beyond their effect on share prices. Consequently, even if managerial risk aversion might overdeter projects with volatile near-term payouts, it is unlikely to overdeter distant harms that may remain undiscovered until well after management's tenure is over. Further, with respect to both near-term and long-term risks, managerial decisionmaking is commonly shaped in important part by market-based performance incentives that work to align management's interests with those of shareholders.

With a system of pro rata unlimited liability, shareholders are liable only for their share of the excess according to the proportion of shares in the company they hold. Where a company only has one or a handful of shareholders the excess liability which the company cannot meet can easily be recovered from these shareholders at little cost. However, recovery becomes more burdensome in relation to companies with many hundreds if not thousands of shareholders. Some commentators have argued that the costs of recovery in relation to such companies may impede the effectiveness of the pro rata rule in practice.

■ D.W. Leebron, 'Limited Liability, Tort Victims and Creditors' (1991) 91 *Columbia Law Review* 1565

It should be recognized that for the publicly held corporation with numerous relatively small shareholders, unlimited liability may be pointless, at least under present administrative and judicial mechanisms. The transaction costs of collecting the pro rata shares against typical individual share-holders would in almost every case be so high that it would not be worth it. The uncertain applica-tion of the rule would create substantial uncertainty. In view of the transaction costs, the market would probably discount heavily the likelihood that additional assessments would be made.

Thus, only very large expected pro rata assessments would be incorporated into the share price for all shareholders. For smaller expected assessments, the pro rata rule would not function as a true pro rata rule, but would have differing effects depending on the number of shares held. Consider, for example, the case of a company with twenty million shares outstanding and a tort liability judgment that exceeds its available assets by $100 million. On a pro rata basis each share would be assessed five dollars. If we assume that the marginal cost of enforcement against any individual shareholder is $1000, enforcement will be worthwhile only for shareholders holding more than 200 shares. Thus, the pro rata rule, unlike the joint liability rule, will not discourage wealthy investors from investing in equities, but will encourage all to keep the amount invested in any single company small. This effect will increase the costs of assembling an efficient port-folio. One further consequence might be that extremely large mutual funds would cease to exist since they would likely be attractive targets for at least partial collections. This possible discour-agement of sophisticated investors might entail further consequences for the efficient function-ing of the markets. The absence of large mutual funds would also seriously erode the ability of the small investor to diversify adequately under a pro rata unlimited liability regime. An investor would have to weigh the advantages of adequate diversification against the possibility of avoid-ing exposure to unlimited liability through small direct stock holdings.

Importantly, in considering the applicability of this analysis to UK companies, account must be taken of the different rules on the payment of legal costs arising from litigation. Typically, in the US, the claimant pays the costs of the fees even if he is successful. In the UK legal costs are typically paid by the respondent if the claimant is successful.[33] This cost rule reduces the transaction costs of enforcement and undermines the strength of this counter-argument to an unlimited liability regime for widely-held UK companies.

Questions

1. Would unlimited pro rata liability affect your decision to invest in shares and, if so, why?

2. Do the arguments outlined here support pro rata unlimited liability for private/close companies with only a few shareholders?

---

[33] Civil Procedure Rules, Rule 44.3(2).

3. Why is imposing liability on shareholders for corporate torts preferable to simply requiring companies to insure for personal injury to customers and other third parties?

4. What do you consider the strength of these arguments to be in relation to parent–subsidiary companies?

5. In light of the arguments set out above, if you were a regulator would you take the risk of tampering with limited member liability? Would your answer differ depending on the type of company or the relationship between the company and the shareholder?

IV CREDITOR-REGARDING OBLIGATIONS

1 Introduction

As we saw in section II.2 of this chapter, management investment decisions which increase the company's risk profile may benefit shareholders by increasing the value of their shares but detrimentally affect creditors' interests by decreasing the value of their debt. This detrimental effect could take place at any time during the company's life, even if the company is solvent at the time the investment decision is made. However, we also saw that the incentive to act in this way increases as the shareholders' stake in the company decreases. It follows, therefore, that for companies which are insolvent, or in the vicinity of insolvency, this incentive for shareholders, or managers acting on behalf of shareholders, to expropriate value by altering the company's investment profile, increases.

Company law could attempt to regulate this financial agency problem either generally, that is at all times during a company's existence, or at specific times when this problem becomes particularly acute, for example when the company is in the vicinity of insolvency. To protect creditors at all times from this problem would involve imposing duties on directors to consider the interests of creditors when making investment decisions. That is, it would introduce into the realm of directors' duties a creditor-regarding obligation. Directors *could* be required at all times to take into account the interests of creditors as well as shareholders when making decisions. This would result in a significant qualification to the current duty imposed on directors to promote the success of the company *for the benefit of the members*.[34] It would result in directors seeking a middle ground between increasing the risk profile of the company by investing in positive expected value projects but not increasing the risk too much; to ensure that investment decisions do not extract too much value from creditors. Such a rule would inevitably result in the loss or rejection of opportunities to generate value. One could attempt to craft a regulatory middle ground that could require that investment decisions must not have a 'significant' or 'material' negative impact on creditors' interests. This too would, although to lesser extent, constrain a director's ability to take risky but positive expected value decisions.

Alternatively we could decide not to regulate this problem at all, in any situation. We could rely on the fact that sophisticated creditors would put in place protections to prevent such abuses where they were required. Although non-adjusting creditors could not negotiate for those protections, in many instances they will be able to free-ride on the protections negotiated by the sophisticated creditors. There will, of course, be situations where sophisticated creditors do not have the bargaining power to insist upon such protections or they may negotiate for other types of protection that do not allow for such free-riding, for example personal guarantees from the directors.

---

[34] See Chapter 10.

English law requires directors to act in the interests of creditors when making decisions *only* when the company is insolvent or is approaching insolvency. Insolvency, or the likelihood that the company will become insolvent, is the driver of English law's creditor-regarding obligations. In such situations **shareholder equity** may be very small, or non-existent, and the incentive for directors, acting on behalf of shareholders, to transfer value from creditors to shareholders through a high-risk investment strategy, is very strong. However, as we shall see, simply having a very small amount of equity in the company or having no equity in the company (where balance sheet assets are less than liabilities) does not mean that the directors are subject to these creditor-regarding obligations. If the company is cashflow solvent, that is it is generating enough cash to pay its debts as they become due, and there is no indication that this will change, then directors are not required to consider creditor interests when making investment decisions. In such circumstances they may, unless they are prohibited from doing so by contractual restrictions negotiated by adjusting creditors, freely alter the risk profile of the company's investments.

There are two primary mechanisms through which UK company law requires that directors have specific regard to creditors' interests: first, common law rules, which continue to apply after the 2006 Act, on when the duty to act in the company's interests require that the directors have to act in/promote the creditors' interests; and, secondly, the rules on wrongful trading set out in the Insolvency Act 1986. These rules provide some regulation of the financial agency cost problem that we have identified in this chapter. However, it is fair to say that, with regard to creditor protection, these mechanisms do more that this. In this section we will consider the creditor protection function of these mechanisms generally.

2 Directors' duties and creditor protection

In Chapters 9–14 of this book we studied directors' duties. We established that the duty to promote the success of the company in section 172(1) of the Companies Act 2006 requires directors to promote the success of the company for the benefit of its members. This section also requires the directors to have regard to a range of other constituencies' interests when acting to promote the success of the company. Interestingly, the 'regard list' does not include creditors. However, creditors are not left unconsidered by section 172. Indeed, section 172(3) provides that section 172(1) is 'subject to any enactment or rule of law requiring directors, in certain circumstances, to consider or act in the interests of creditors of the company'. The enactment of particular relevance here is section 214 of the Insolvency Act which we shall consider in the next section. Furthermore, in its reference to 'any . . . rule of law' section 173(3) directs us back to the common law position on directors' duties and creditors.

2.1 Creditor-regarding duties in insolvency

■ *West Mercia Safetywear Ltd (in liq) v Dodd* [1988] BCLC 250

Mr Dodd was the director of AJ Dodd & Co Ltd and its subsidiary company, West Mercia Safetywear Ltd. Mr Dodd had personally guaranteed the overdraft of AJ Dodd & Co Ltd. Both companies were in financial difficulties. In addition, West Mercia owed £30,000 to AJ Dodd. As director of West Mercia, Mr Dodd arranged for the repayment of £4,000 to AJ Dodd even though he knew that West Mercia was insolvent at the time. The court found that the objective of this transfer was to reduce AJ Dodd's overdraft which would reduce the amount owed by Mr Dodd under the personal guarantee. The liquidator of

West Mercia applied to court for an order that the amount be paid by Mr Dodd as the payment amounted to a misfeasance and breach of duty and trust.[35] The court of first instance found that there had been no breach of duty. The liquidator appealed.

> **Dillon LJ**
>
> We have been referred to quite a number of authorities on this topic. For my part I find helpful, and would approve, the statement of Street CJ in *Kinsela v Russell Kinsela Pty Ltd (in liq)* (1986) 4 NSWLR 722 at 730, where he said:
>
> > 'In a solvent company the proprietary interests of the shareholders entitle them as a general body to be regarded as the company when questions of the duty of directors arise. If, as a general body, they authorise or ratify a particular action of the directors, there can be no challenge to the validity of what the directors have done. But where a company is insolvent the interests of the creditors intrude. They become prospectively entitled, through the mechanism of liquidation, to displace the power of the shareholders and directors to deal with the company's assets. It is in a practical sense their assets and not the shareholders' assets that, through the medium of the company, are under the management of the directors pending either liquidation, return to solvency, or the imposition of some alternative administration.'
>
> In the present case, therefore, in my judgment Mr Dodd was guilty of breach of duty when, for his own purposes, he caused the £4,000 to be transferred in disregard of the interests of the general creditors of this insolvent company. Therefore the declaration sought in the notice of motion ought to be made as against Mr Dodd.

That creditors' interests should replace members' interests when the company becomes insolvent makes sense in terms of our earlier analysis of why shareholders, as residual interest holders, have a strong claim to benefit from control rights (as variable residual interest holders they have the best incentives to maximize the value pie).[36] Once the company is incapable of repaying its creditors, the creditors have a type of variable residual interest. They have an incentive to ensure that managers or the liquidator use the company's assets in such a way as to ensure that creditors receive as much as possible of what they are owed. Furthermore, as we have seen, to run the company in the interests of members whose financial stake in the company has been wiped out would encourage the taking of high-risk decisions that may generate some possibility of a return for shareholders but destroy expected value for creditors and the value of the company as a whole.

The *West Mercia Safetywear* case, as well as *Kinsella v Russell* on which it relies, refers generically to directors' duties rather than distinguishing between the different types of duty. This shift of focus from shareholders to creditors would affect several of the duties we addressed in Chapters 9–14.[37] In relation to the duty of care, the factors that a reasonable director would consider when making a decision, or the attention and weight given to such factors, may vary if the decision should promote the creditors', not the shareholders', interests. Translating this changed focus to the duty to promote the success of the company involves some technical difficulties. Prior to the 2006 Act

[35] The action was brought pursuant to section 212 Insolvency Act 1986 which provides a summary procedure available to a liquidator or creditor of a company during the company's winding up in relation to a director's misfeasance, breach of duty or trust.

[36] See Chapter 17. Remember that the duty is owed to the company. The question here is in whose interests should the company be run to satisfy that duty. Just as the duty is not owed to members individually when the company is solvent, it is not owed to creditors individually when the company is insolvent (*Yukong Line Ltd of Korea v Rendsburg Investments Corp of Liberia and others (No 2)* [1998] 4 All ER 82).

[37] This change of interests would not, however, alter the operation of section 177 CA 2006 (self-dealing disclosure) or section 175 CA 2006 (the avoidance of conflicts of interest).

this transfer of focus was straightforward. The duty was to act in good faith in the best interests of the company. Whilst solvent 'the company' meant shareholders' interests, but when the company became insolvent 'the company' meant creditors' interests. Section 172, the duty to promote the success of the company, does not, however, contain this flexibility. It explicitly provides that success of the company means for the benefit of the members. This leaves us with two substantively similar options: *either* the effect of section 173(3) is that upon insolvency section 172 ceases to be applicable and the duty becomes to act in the best interests of the creditors; *or* the duty upon insolvency becomes the *duty to promote the success of the company for the benefit of the creditors as a whole* having had regard to the list of factors set out in section 172(1)(a)–(f). It is submitted that the latter is the preferable approach.

This transfer of the beneficiary of the duty to promote the success of the company from members to creditors when the company is insolvent restricts the directors' scope to act in several respects. It prevents certain types of transfers to shareholders such as the transfer in *West Mercia* (although transfers are also specifically regulated by other legal mechanisms[38]). In addition it blocks the incurrence of financial agency costs through a change in the company's investment profile: it would be a breach of duty for the managers to take exceptionally risky investments that decreased the value of debtholders' claims in order to try to generate a return for the shareholders. However, this duty would allow risk-taking investments if such investments promote the interests of the creditor body. It would also require that, once insolvent, if the losses through continued trading will continue with little chance of turning around the company's fortunes then the company must cease trading. This duty is, of course, a subjective duty, which, as we considered in Chapter 10, in the absence of clear evidence of state of mind becomes a rationality standard. Nevertheless, in the context of an insolvent company this standard will have bite: where the company is insolvent it will be difficult for a director to find a rational reason for taking actions that remove assets from the creditors' reach or expropriate creditor value by taking greater risk.

Note also that although breaches of duty can be ratified by disinterested shareholders,[39] where the company is insolvent it would not make any sense to allow shareholders to ratify breaches of duty that detrimentally affect creditors. In this regard, in *Kinsela v Russell Kinsela*[40] the Court of Appeal for New South Wales—a judgment approved of in *West Mercia v Dodd*[41]—observed that: 'once it is accepted, as in my view it must be, that the directors' duty to a company as a whole extends in an insolvency context to not prejudicing the interests of creditors...the shareholders do not have the power or authority to absolve the directors from that breach.'

2.2 Creditor-regarding duties when approaching insolvency

Following *West Mercia Safetywear*, creditors' interests '*intrude*' into a company's interests on insolvency. But what about prior to insolvency? Where the company is not insolvent it is clear that directors' duty to promote the success of the company is for the benefit of the members not the creditors.[42] However, is there any point prior to or approaching insolvency when creditors' interests *creep in* rather than *intrude*? What about the situation where the company is solvent but it appears increasingly likely that the company will not escape looming failure and insolvency?

---

[38] On distributions see Chapter 19. On the regulation of preferences see V. Finch, *Corporate Insolvency Law: Perspectives and Principles* (2nd edn, CUP, 2009).

[39] Section 239 CA 2006.   [40] (1986) 4 NSWLR 722, NSW CA.

[41] Also cited with approval in *Bowthorpe Holdings Ltd v Hills* [2003] 1 BCLC 226.

[42] *Multinational Gas and Petrochemical Co v Multinational Gas and Petrochemical Services Ltd* [1983] BCLC 461.

There is some authority that the creditors' interest could intrude not only when the company is actually insolvent but is approaching insolvency. In *Colin Gwyer & Associates Ltd v Palmer*,[43] Mr Leslie Kosmin QC, sitting as a deputy High Court Judge, held that:

> Where a company is insolvent or of doubtful solvency or on the verge of insolvency and it is the creditors' money which is at risk the directors, when carrying out their duty to the company, must consider the interests of the creditors as paramount and take those into account when exercising their discretion.[44]

In *Re MDA Investment Management Ltd Whalley v Doney*,[45] relying on *West Mercia Safetywear*, Park J held that:

> When a company, whether technically insolvent or not, is in financial difficulties to the extent that its creditors are at risk, the duties which the directors owe to the company are extended so as to encompass the interests of the company's creditors as a whole, as well as those of the shareholders.

These cases, as they extend the zone within which directors' duties require regard to creditors' interests, struggle with two tensions: first, how to mark the boundaries of this zone beyond actual cashflow insolvency; and, secondly, once within the zone, what is the relationship between shareholder and creditor interests? In *Colin Gwyer* the court uses the language of the 'verge' of insolvency: a space where the likelihood that the company will become insolvent is very high. In *MDA Investment Management* the court clarifies that technical insolvency (where balance sheet asset value is less than balance sheet liabilities) is not the issue. For Park J the issue is whether financial difficulties place the creditors at risk.[46] In *Colin Gwyer* the effect of being in the zone of the 'verge of insolvency' is that creditors' interests become 'paramount'. In *MDA Investment Management* where financial difficulties place the creditors at risk the interest of creditors and shareholders appear to coexist, although the court does not provide further guidance on how this co-existence will operate in practice.

The Company Law Review put forward a draft statutory provision for Government consideration which would address both of these tensions. The proposition was rejected by the Government when finalizing the Companies Bill 2006. It is worth considering whether we think the proposal was clearer and more effective than the current common law position.

■ Company Law Review Steering Committee: Final Report, Annex C

> **Special duty where company more likely than not to be unable to meet its debts**
> At a time when a director of the company knows, or would know, but for a failure of his to exercise due care and skill, that it more likely than not that the company will at some point be unable to pay its debts as they fall due—
>
> (a) the [duty to promote the success of the company in section 172] will not apply to him; and

---

[43] [2002] EWHC 2748.

[44] Cited with approval in *Secretary of State for Business, Innovation and Skills v Doffman* [2010] EWHC 3175 (Ch) *per* Newey J.

[45] [2003] EWHC 2277. Referred to with approval in *Re Cityspan Ltd* [2007] All ER (D) 61 (Apr).

[46] Nourse LJ in *Brady v Brady* [1988] BCLC 20 observed in this regard that 'where the company is insolvent, or even doubtfully solvent, the interests of the company are in reality the interests of existing creditors alone'.

(b) he must, in the exercise of his powers, take such steps…as he believes will achieve a reasonable balance between:

   (i) reducing the risk that the company will be unable to pay its debts as they fall due; and

   (ii) promoting the success of the company for the benefit of its members as a whole.

As noted previously, the notion of 'verge of insolvency' contains within it an unspecified threshold of the probability of insolvency. The imagery of 'the verge' suggests a high probability. Certainly, to this author, the probability suggested by the word 'verge' is something well in excess of a 50% probability of insolvency. The Company Law Review's proposal provided for 'a more likely than not' probability of insolvency: anything in excess of a 50% probability. The effect of this provision, had it been enacted, would have been to expand the zone within which creditors' interests intrude. Note also that the nature of the duty is closer to the position set out in *MDA Insvestment Management* than it is to the position in *Colin Gwyer*: it provides for a balancing of creditor and shareholder interests rather than prioritizing creditors' interests.

Other jurisdictions have also struggled with the question of when, if at all, outside of insolvency creditors' interests should intrude. Consider the following case decided by the US State of Delaware's Chancery Court where this issue was considered in a complex case arising out of a leveraged buyout.

■ *Credit Lyonnais Bank Nederland, NV v Pathe Communications Corporation* [1991] WL 277613 (Del Ch)

Chancellor Allen

The possibility of insolvency can do curious things to incentives, exposing creditors to risks of opportunistic behaviour and creating complexities for directors. Consider, for example, a solvent corporation having a single asset, a judgment for $51 million against a solvent debtor. The judgment is on appeal and thus subject to modification or reversal. Assume that the only liabilities of the company are to bondholders in the amount of $12 million. Assume that the array of probable outcomes of the appeal is as follows:

	Expected Value
25% chance of affirmance ($51mm)	$12.75
70% chance of modification ($4mm)	$ 2.8
5% chance of reversal ($0)	$0
Expected Value of Judgment on Appeal	$15.55

Thus, the best evaluation is that the current value of the equity is $3.55 million. ($15.55 million expected value of judgment on appeal [minus] $12 million liability to bondholders). Now assume an offer to settle at $12.5 million (also consider one at $17.5 million). By what standard do the directors of the company evaluate the fairness of these offers? The creditors of this solvent company would be in favour of accepting either a $12.5 million offer or a $17.5 million offer. In either event they will avoid the 75% risk of insolvency and default. The [shareholders], however, will plainly be opposed to acceptance of a $12.5 million settlement (under which they get practically nothing). More importantly, they very well may be opposed to acceptance of the $17.5 million offer under which the residual value of the corporation would increase from $3.5 to $5.5 million. This is so because the litigation alternative, with its 25% probability of a $39 million outcome to them ($51 millon – $12 million = $39 million) has an expected value to the residual risk bearer of $9.75 million ($39 million x 25% chance of affirmance), substantially greater than the $5.5 million available to them in the settlement. While in fact the [shareholders'] preference would reflect their appetite for risk, it is possible (and with diversified shareholders likely) that shareholders would prefer rejection of both settlement offers.

But if we consider the community of interests that the corporation represents it seems apparent that one should in this hypothetical accept the best settlement offer available providing it is greater than $15.55 million, and one below that amount should be rejected. But that result will not be reached by a director who thinks he owes duties directly to shareholders only. It will be reached by directors who are capable of conceiving of the corporation as a legal and economic entity. Such directors will recognize that in managing the business affairs of a solvent corporation in the vicinity of insolvency, circumstances may arise when the right (both the efficient and the fair) course to follow for the corporation may diverge from the choice that the [shareholders] (or the creditors, or the employees, or any single group interested in the corporation) would make if given the opportunity to act.

Chancellor Allen describes the extended zone within which creditors' interests intrude as the 'vicinity of insolvency'. But for Chancellor Allen entering this 'vicinity' does not result in giving creditors' interests priority but rather requires that the interests of different groups, including, *but not limited to*, creditors and shareholders are balanced in making decisions. In the language of the UK reform debate surrounding the duty to promote the success of the company, when a company is in the vicinity of insolvency the duty, for Chancellor Allen, becomes a multiple interest/pluralistic standard.

Chancellor Allen's dicta on duties in the 'vicinity of insolvency' has attracted some criticism in the US which is worth considering in light of the UK developments outlined previously in *Colin Gwyer* and *MDA Investment Management*. Consider the following commentary:

■ Choper et al, *Cases and Material on Corporations* (Foundation Press, 2004)

Suppose the board of directors of a corporation that might be in the zone of insolvency must choose between two investments, buying government bonds and investing in a risky project that the board believes has a higher expected return even taking into account the increased risk. While there is not uncertainty concerning the return from the government bond, assessment of the return (and the risk) from the risky project depends on subjective evaluation...Which investment would you advise the board to take? Does discouraging risk taking in financially troubled companies also impose a social cost by increasing the likelihood of their failure? Might imposing a fiduciary obligation to the entity create a barrier to changing the corporation's previously unsuccessful strategy?

With regard to this criticism it is worth noting that the UK Government rejected the draft CLR proposal on the ground that it was inconsistent with a legal framework that is designed to assist in the rescue of struggling companies.[47]

Questions

1. What in your view is the rationale for making creditors' interests paramount in insolvency?

2. How should we define insolvency for this purpose: should it be balance sheet insolvency; cashflow insolvency or both?

---

[47] P. Davies, 'Directors' Creditor-Regarding Duties' (2006) 7 *European Business Organization Law Review* 301, 317.

3. How would you explain to a lay person the concepts of 'verge of' or 'in the vicinity of' insolvency?

4. What in your view is the rationale for extending creditor-regarding duties to a zone beyond insolvency?

5. In this zone should creditors' interests be 'paramount', as suggested in *Colin Gwyer*, or one of several interests to be balanced, as suggested in *MDA Investment Management*?

6. Do you agree with Choper et al's argument that such a duty could get in the way of turning around struggling companies?

3 Fraudulent trading

A company that has failed and can no longer continue as a going concern will be wound up and its assets sold to realize as much value as possible to pay back the creditors to the extent of those assets. A liquidator will be appointed either by the creditors in a *creditors voluntary winding up* or by the court in a *compulsory liquidation*.[48] The liquidator is given control over the company for the purpose of maximizing the value of the company's remaining assets. One route to increasing the size of the asset pie available to creditors is for the liquidator to take legal action to recover any amounts owed from the directors for any breach of duty or other legal obligation. The liquidator could cause the company to bring proceedings against directors for the breach of the duties set out in the previous section.[49] Importantly, UK law supplements these duties with provisions imposing personal director liability where directors have engaged in *fraudulent or wrongful trading*. The fraudulent trading provision has long been a part of UK company law, originally introduced in section 75 of the Companies Act 1928. It is currently set out in section 213 of the Insolvency Act 1986. The wrongful trading prohibition was first introduced in section 214 of the Insolvency Act 1986 and is considered in section iv.4 of this chapter.

■ Section 213 Insolvency Act 1986 Fraudulent trading

(1) If in the course of the winding up of a company it appears that any business of the company has been carried on with intent to defraud creditors of the company or creditors of any other person, or for any fraudulent purpose, the following has effect.

(2) The court, on the application of the liquidator may declare that any persons who were knowingly parties to the carrying on of the business in the manner above-mentioned are to be liable to make such contributions (if any) to the company's assets as the court thinks proper.

Section 213 of the Insolvency Act provides the liquidator (and only the liquidator) with the right to apply for a court order that the director[50] make a contribution to the company's assets where the directors acted with the 'intent to defraud creditors of the company'.[51] A literal reading of the words 'intent to defraud' suggests that the provision only bites in relation to egregiously dishonest behaviour. The leading cases relate to the fraudulent

---

[48] See generally V. Finch, *Corporate Insolvency Law: Perspectives and Principles* (2nd edn CUP, 2009).

[49] Section 212 Insolvency Act 1986 provides the liquidator with a summary procedure to enforce such breaches.

[50] Note that whilst our focus here is on creditor-regarding duties imposed on directors, section 213 applies to persons rather than directors and may therefore apply to other persons such as controlling shareholders. In this regard see *Morris v Bank of India* [2005] 2 BCLC 328.

[51] A parallel criminal fraudulent trading provision is set out in section 993 CA 2006.

trading prohibition set out in the Companies Act 1928. In *Re William C Leitch Bros Ltd*,[52] Maugham J held in relation to section 75 of the Companies Act 1929:

> In my opinion I must hold with regard to the meaning of the phrase carrying on business 'with intent to defraud creditors' that, if a company continues to carry on business and to incur debts at a time when there is to the knowledge of the directors no reasonable prospect of the creditors ever receiving payment of those debts, it is, in general, a proper inference that the company is carrying on business with intent to defraud.

In the following year, in *Re Patrick & Lyon Ltd*[53] Maugham J held:

> I will express the opinion that the words 'defraud' and 'fraudulent purpose,' where they appear in the section in question, are words which connote actual dishonesty involving, according to current notions of fair trading among commercial men, real moral blame. No judge, I think, has ever been willing to define 'fraud,' and I am attempting no definition. I am merely stating what, in my opinion, must be one of the elements of the word as used in this section.

More recently in *Bernasconi v Nicholas Bennett & Co*[54] Laddie J stressed that dishonesty was the central consideration in the application of section 213 and simply because the actions taken by the directors 'seriously, unfairly and impermissibly disadvantage creditors does not per se offend against the [dishonesty requirement]'.

Section 213 clearly has application where the company continues to trade and takes additional debt, for example trade debt, when the directors are fully aware that there is little prospect that those debtors will receive payment in full. However, proving such knowledge on the part of the directors is extremely difficult.[55] The claim that the directors, although blinkered, were trying to save the company by continuing to trade through the company's problems will always be a plausible defence.[56]

4 Wrongful trading

Section 214 provides creditor-regarding regulation of a director's actions prior to insolvency. The section is designed to deter directors from making decisions that detrimentally affect creditors at a time when it is clear that the company will not evade insolvent liquidation.

■ Section 214 Insolvency Act 1986 Wrongful trading

(1) Subject to subsection (3) below, if in the course of the winding up of a company it appears that subsection (2) of this section applies in relation to a person who is or has been a director of the company, the court, on the application of the liquidator, may declare that that person is to be liable to make such contribution (if any) to the company's assets as the court thinks proper.

(2) This subsection applies in relation to a person if—

---

[52] [1932] 2 Ch 71.   [53] [1933] Ch 786.   [54] [2000] BCC 921.

[55] Note that 'knowledge' would include 'blind eye knowledge': 'shutting one's eyes to the obvious' *per* Roth J in *Goldfarb (Liquidator of Overnight Ltd) v Higgins* [2010] EWHC 613. See also *Re BCCI* [2003] EWHC 1868 (Ch) *per* Paten J (as he then was): 'blind-eye knowledge requires, in my opinion, a suspicion that the relevant facts do exist and a deliberate decision to avoid confirming that they exist.'

[56] See Goldfarb *ibid* where two of the three respondents were found to have the requisite state of mind for liability under section 213; and *R v Grantham* [1984] 3 All ER 166 where the court found the defendants guilty of fraudulent trading in relation to credit given by a trade creditor.

(a) the company has gone into insolvent liquidation,

(b) at some time before the commencement of the winding up of the company, that person knew or ought to have concluded that there was no reasonable prospect that the company would avoid going into insolvent liquidation, and

(c) that person was a director of the company at that time;

but the court shall not make a declaration under this section in any case where the time mentioned in paragraph (b) above was before 28th April 1986.

(3) The court shall not make a declaration under this section with respect to any person if it is satisfied that after the condition specified in subsection (2)(b) was first satisfied in relation to him that person took every step with a view to minimising the potential loss to the company's creditors as (assuming him to have known that there was no reasonable prospect that the company would avoid going into insolvent liquidation) he ought to have taken.

(4) For the purposes of subsections (2) and (3), the facts which a director of a company ought to know or ascertain, the conclusions which he ought to reach and the steps which he ought to take are those which would be known or ascertained, or reached or taken, by a reasonably diligent person having both—

(a) the general knowledge, skill and experience that may reasonably be expected of a person carrying out the same functions as are carried out by that director in relation to the company, and

(b) the general knowledge, skill and experience that that director has.

(5) The reference in subsection (4) to the functions carried out in relation to a company by a director of the company includes any functions which he does not carry out but which have been entrusted to him.

(6) For the purposes of this section a company goes into insolvent liquidation if it goes into liquidation at a time when its assets are insufficient for the payment of its debts and other liabilities and the expenses of the winding up.

(7) In this section "director" includes a shadow director.

4.1 When does section 214 apply and how does it protect creditors?

The section works in a somewhat convoluted fashion. Pursuant to subsection (1), if a director falls within the three criteria set out in subsection (2) then the court may order him or her to make a contribution to the company's assets, *unless* he or she can demonstrate compliance with subsection (3).

The criteria in subsection (2) require first that the company has entered insolvent liquidation: that is, the company is insolvent and, as a result of a creditors' voluntary liquidation or a court-ordered compulsory liquidation, a liquidator has been appointed and the liquidator is in the process of winding up the company. What amounts to insolvency for section 214 is set out in subsection (6): the company's assets are insufficient for the payment of its debts. This appears to be a balance sheet test for insolvency (that is when assets are less than liabilities).[57] However, note the focus on 'payment' in subsection (6) which indicates the provision's concern is not with the accounting entries for assets and liabilities in a company's balance sheet but rather with the *actual* availability of assets to pay debts. Importantly, if the requirement was that assets be available to cover the payment of all liabilities, this would cover many healthy and cashflow solvent companies. A company may, for example, have a large bank loan as a liability which it can pay in accordance with the repayment schedule, but could not pay if repayment

---

[57] Davies, 'Directors' Creditor-Regarding Duties', note 47.

in full was demanded tomorrow. Courts interpreting the meaning of 'insolvent liquidation' for section 214 have required cashflow insolvency only, with balance sheet insolvency being insufficient to trigger the application of section 214.[58]

The second requirement of subsection (2) is that *'at some time'* prior to the insolvent liquidation a director of the company *at that point in time* knew or should have realized (*'ought to have concluded'*) that there was *'no reasonable prospect'* that the company would avoid insolvent liquidation. If the directors have actual knowledge that there was 'no reasonable prospect' of avoiding insolvent liquidation then they clearly fall within subsection (2). The more difficult determination is when they did not actually realize this but they ought to have realized this. The Insolvency Act 1986 provides that in their determination the court should ask whether a reasonably diligent person would have realized this. Similar to the duty of care and skill set out in section 174 of the Companies Act 2006, such a reasonably diligent person is deemed to have the knowledge, skill, and experience of a director in that position, plus any additional knowledge, skill, and experience that the actual director has.

4.2 When is there 'no reasonable prospect' of avoiding insolvent liquidation?

■ Re Hawkes Hill Publishing Co Ltd (in liquidation) Ward v Perks
[2007] All ER (D) 422

In this case a company was set up to produce a free golf magazine that would generate revenue through selling advertising in the magazine. The company was funded through a bank loan of £20,000. To secure the loan the bank took a security interest over the company's assets and personal guarantees from the company's two directors, who were also the company's only shareholders. The company experienced serious cashflow problems and quickly became insolvent. Eventually the company sold its magazine titles to another company for £20,000. In order to obtain a release of the bank's security for the sale the funds were paid to the bank. This also had the effect of releasing the two directors from liability under their guarantee. Following the sale the company went into insolvent liquidation and the liquidator applied to the court for a contribution from the directors pursuant to section 214.

> **Lewison J**
> It is important at the outset to be clear about the relevant question. The question is not whether the directors knew or ought to have known that the company was insolvent. The question is whether they knew or ought to have concluded that there was no reasonable prospect of avoiding insolvent liquidation. As Chadwick J pointed out in *Secretary of State for Trade and Industry v Gash* [1997] 1 BCLC 341:
>
> > 'The companies legislation does not impose on directors a statutory duty to ensure that their company does not trade while insolvent; nor does that legislation impose an obligation to ensure that the company does not trade at a loss. Those propositions need only to be stated to be recognised as self-evident. Directors may properly take the view that it is in the interests of the company and of its creditors that, although insolvent, the company should continue to trade out of its difficulties. They may properly take the view that it is in the interests of the company and its creditors that some loss-making trade should be accepted in anticipation of future profitability. They are not to be criticised if they give effect to such view.'
>
> ...

---

[58] *Re Purpoint* [1991] BCLC 491; *Re Rod Gunner Organization* [2004] BCLC 110.

So: what did the directors know in April 1998? And what, in addition to what they did know, ought they to have known?...By April 1998 the directors knew that the money that they had originally borrowed from the bank had been spent. They knew also that they had had to inject capital into the company to keep it going. I am therefore prepared to accept that they ought to have known (even if they did not actually know) that the company was balance sheet insolvent. I am also prepared to accept that they ought to have known (even if they did not actually know) that the company could not pay its debts as they fell due. In other words they ought to have known that the company was insolvent. Less than two years after April 1998 the company went into insolvent liquidation. But that is not enough to establish the liquidator's case...

However, there is a crucial stage in the analysis that is missing. Accepting as I do that the directors ought to have known that the company was insolvent, it still leaves open the question: did they know (or ought they to have concluded) that there was no reasonable prospect that the company would avoid an insolvent liquidation? The answer to this question does not depend on a snapshot of the company's financial position at any given time; it depends on rational expectations of what the future might hold. But directors are not clairvoyant and the fact that they fail to see what eventually comes to pass does not mean that they are guilty of wrongful trading.

So far as their actual knowledge is concerned, I am satisfied that they did not know or conclude that there was no reasonable prospect that the company could avoid going into insolvent liquidation.

Should they have concluded that the company had no reasonable prospect of avoiding insolvent liquidation? Mr Richmond pointed out, correctly, that:

i)   The company never made a profit during its short life;

ii) [The directors] had been compelled to make loans to the company in order to keep it going;

iii) Following the termination of the factoring agreement[59] the company's financial position was uncertain;

iv) The company's sales team, who had been employed in early 1998, were ineffective and not cost efficient;

v)   It was proving difficult to persuade golf clubs to take up advertising;

vi) The company could not afford to pay [the directors] any wages (apart from one relatively small payment);

vii) The directors did not keep as full financial records as they could have done.

However all these features, in my judgment, only lead to the conclusion that at the end of the first ten or eleven months of trading, the company was not yet solvent. It does not, to my mind, lead to the conclusion that the directors ought to have concluded that the company would never be solvent...There could have been (at least) two ways in which [the company could have increased its revenue]: first by increasing the proportion of advertising carried by the magazine, either by altering the balance between editorial and advertising within the existing size of the magazine, or by increasing the number of pages, or both; and second by increasing advertising rates once the magazine had proved its success with its readership. I do not therefore accept the proposition that the directors ought to have concluded, after less than a year's trading, that the magazine could never be profitable.

The court in *Re Hawkes* makes it very clear that simply being insolvent does not mean that there is no reasonable prospect of avoiding insolvent liquidation. Lewison J is concerned to give the directors a certain degree of latitude to make the decision about whether continuing to trade makes sense. Even though the company is insolvent and

[59] Factoring is an arrangement whereby you sell your debt claims to a third party. This improves the company's cashflow as, although you receive less cash than the face value of the debt, you do not have to wait for the actual debt to be paid.

may continue to make losses does not mean that there is 'no reasonable prospect' of avoiding insolvent liquidation. In *Re Hawkes* the court requires a plausible account of why it would be reasonable for a director to conclude that a return to solvency is a realistic possibility, which in this case was the expansion of future advertising revenues. The court appears to be satisfied with identifying possible ways in which revenue could plausibly have been increased—the available reasons why insolvent liquidation could have been avoided. Formally pursuant to section 214 the question for the court is whether a *reasonably diligent director* would have realized at that time that there was no possibility of avoiding insolvent liquidation. However, in application in *Re Hawkes* the court does not appear to require that any burden of proof in relation to such reasons be discharged beyond the fact that they appear plausible to the court.[60]

Not all courts considering a section 214 application by a liquidator have been as deferential to director decision-making as *Re Hawkes*. In *Re Brian D Pierson*, the court, whilst professing to be wary of both judging directors with hindsight and of the judiciary's commercial limitations, found the directors liable.

■ *Re Brian D Pierson* [2001] 1 BCLC 275

D Pierson Ltd was a company engaged in the construction and maintenance of golf courses. The company was successful for a period of time, although its fortunes declined following two projects where the contracting party failed to pay. The company continued to trade after these difficulties. In June 1994 the company's auditor noted a 'fundamental uncertainty' whether the company could continue as a going concern (this was not, however, what is known as a 'going concern qualification' of the accounts which would amount to an expression of the auditor's 'significant doubt' about the company's ability to continue as a going concern).[61] The company went into insolvent liquidation in January 1996. The liquidator, amongst others, applied for a contribution for wrongful trading for the period after June 1994. The court considered whether at that point in time the director, Mr Pierson, ought to have realized that there was no reasonable prospect of avoiding insolvent liquidation.

> **Hazel Williamson QC**
>
> Mr Pierson submitted that as at 13 June 1994, he could not reasonably be expected to have concluded that the company was heading inevitably for an insolvent liquidation, for several reasons. First, he urged that the court must have regard to the particular industry in which he was engaged and its nature, as he described, and I have recorded, above...He emphasised that his business had always been run, and had to be run, according to his 'gut feel' based on experience, and said that his decision to trade on was perfectly reasonable, based on his experienced view of the position at the time. He attributes the eventual downfall of the company mainly to the consequences of bad weather conditions in 1994 and 1995[62]—unduly hot dry summer weather and unduly inclement winter weather—causing extra cost, the need to repeat work and the withholding of payments.
>
> As regards what could be expected of him in appraising the position, he points out that he is not an accountant. He says that he relied on his trained staff to inform him of the facts. He would only look at the 'bottom line' of a set of accounts and would derive nothing more subtle than that from them without assistance. He says he had advisers in the shape of Mr Weeks and Mr Brunt, and was accustomed to confer with, certainly, the latter quite often.

---

[60] See also in this regard *Re Sherborne Ltd* [1995] BCC 40.

[61] International Standard on Auditing (UK and Ireland) 570 *Going Concern* (APB, 2009), para 30.

[62] The court accepted that these factors were relevant consideration in assessing the director's contribution.

He relies on the fact that the 1992/93 accounts were not qualified, and that there was no suggestion that the 1993/94 accounts were going to be qualified either, according to Touche Ross's working papers. No-one, neither his advisers, nor his former accountants, nor the bank, had suggested at or before the relevant time that the company ought to go into liquidation, or was in serious difficulty, and he submits that the relaxed tenor of Touche Ross's working papers for the 1993/94 accounts supports the view that the company was not obviously in terminal difficulty.

With regard to the trading position, he submits that he was entitled to rely on the fact that the company had a healthy order book at the time, and he refers to a letter written to the bank on 13 June 1994 by Paul Mould, enclosing the company's May management figures and a Contract Position Statement, this being information which the bank had requested on a monthly basis. On reading, this letter lists contract work in hand at about £1.7m, with a further £1.45m all but signed up, and a further £4.185m [of] more projects 'under negotiation'. In addition, he says that the signs in the press, and so forth, all pointed to the market's having recovered from the depressed state of 1992/93 and being ready to improve—an opportunity that the company was therefore poised to use to its advantage, not least because several of its competitors were foundering.

The question, I have to answer is whether a reasonable director in Mr Pierson's position and with the knowledge which was available to him, would, or ought, to have concluded, at or shortly after 13 June 1994 that there was no reasonable prospect that the company would avoid insolvent liquidation. Whilst the burden of proof is on the liquidator to prove his case, the combination of points which he makes is formidable. Nevertheless, I heed the injunction that it is easy to be wise with hindsight. I am also very conscious that the standard to be applied is that of the reasonably prudent businessman, a breed which is likely to be less temperamentally cautious than lawyers and accountants. I must therefore give proper respect to Mr Pierson's evidence as to how his industry operates, and his judgment based on experience, remembering also that he had operated this business, apparently successfully, for many years before its collapse. I am not dealing with an enterprise which never became properly established at all. Also, this is not the case of a company suffering losses continuously over several years. The loss in 1992 was exceptional, and at the material time, only one further complete and one almost complete year of further loss occurred.

Nevertheless, in my judgment, the liquidator's case is made out. I am satisfied that the directors of this company ought to have concluded at or about 13 June 1994, that there was no reasonable prospect that the company would then avoid an insolvent liquidation. The company's business had consistently had difficulties with maintaining current cash flow. It had had additional burdens placed upon it by the losses of resources, occasioned by [the bad debts from the two failed projects]…Its recent results suggested clearly that the basic core of its business was not capable of generating profits in those circumstances, let alone sufficient profits, quickly enough, to improve the cash flow position and restore the company's health. [The court continued to cast severe doubt on the value of bad debts from the two failed projects and on the directors' judgment in regard to assessment of the value of this debt]…

However, the audited accounts for 1992/93 revealed a modest loss and a small balance sheet insolvency, and, most importantly, they contained the warning of the 'fundamental uncertainty' paragraph. Mr Pierson emphasises that the auditors' opinion was 'not qualified in this respect'.[63] However, that was no excuse for ignoring the auditors' comment as being nothing serious. In my judgment receipt of that report was a warning, which ought to have brought about a careful and cool appraisal of the company's position. There is no evidence that any such analysis occurred…

With regard to the strength of the company's order book, the letter to the bank dated 13 June 1994 looks impressive, but was clearly written for presentation purposes, and includes only the positive side of the picture. I can see nothing to suggest that it showed such a change in the company's fortunes as to be regarded as stemming the decline which had set in and

---

[63] Such a qualification would be a 'going concern qualification'.

> justifying ignoring the 'fundamental uncertainty' and the worsening picture in the intervening 10 or 11 months. Moreover, I cannot place great weight on the justifiability of Mr Pierson's relying on his 'feel' that the business was improving, given that his judgments [of the value of the bad debt from the failed projects] were so obviously grossly optimistic.
>
> I find that, in practice, Mr Pierson simply hoped that, by carrying on as before, everything would come right, somehow. He gave no proper thought to whether that was a realistic possibility, given the additional burdens which had been placed on the company, and he failed to appreciate, as he should have done, his duty to persons with whom the company had already contracted and would contract in the ordinary course of its business.

Courts, when reviewing business decisions, often note that they need to be wary of the problem of hindsight and second-guessing business decisions. However, in practice it may be very difficult for a judge, like any other person, to separate knowledge from how events turned out when reviewing ex-post the decisions that lead to the end result.[64] Deference to the decision-maker's decision is an essential part of avoiding hindsight bias. We clearly see this deference in *Re Hawkes*. Such deference is less apparent in *Re Brian D Pierson*. The judge finds it difficult to be deferential when the director's judgment in relation to bad debts seemed so poor. There were clearly facts in the case that a deferential judge could have focused on to reject the liquidator's application: the absence of a formal **going-concern** qualification; a relatively healthy order book; a more general view of the upturn in the market place. The judge, however, rejected these arguments submitted by the director, and held, in effect, that they were not good enough grounds for there to be a 'realistic possibility' of avoiding insolvent liquidation.[65]

4.3 Taking steps to minimize creditor losses

If the court finds that the conditions in subsection (2) are applicable then the court may order the directors to make a contribution *unless*, pursuant to section 214(3), the court is satisfied that the directors took every step they ought to have taken to minimize loss to creditors. The court will judge whether sufficient steps have been taken according to the reasonably diligent director standard. In many instances such required steps will involve immediately entering into a liquidation proceeding. Note here that the reasonable director standard (the same standard as the standard set forth in section 174 of the 2006 Act) is applied to the quality of the decision itself—the steps actually taken. By way of contrast, section 174 does not require reasonable decisions, just that the quality of the decision-making process was one that a reasonable average director would have required. Outside of a section 214 application, the quality of the director's decision is regulated by the subjective standard set forth in section 172 of the 2006 Act.

Section 214, in conjunction with the creditor-regarding directors' duties discussed previously, creates a dilemma for directors of companies in financial difficulties. If one continues trading and incurring additional losses directors expose themselves to a possible section 214 application by a future liquidator on the basis that trading should have stopped at an earlier point in time. However, if there is a possibility that continued trading may result in a complete recovery then a director's duty to act in the interests of creditors as a whole may require continued trading. Consider in this regard the following example.

[64] For a more detailed analysis of hindsight bias see Chapter 10.
[65] See also *Earp v Stevenson* [2011] EWHC 1436 (Ch); *Roberts (as Liquidator of Onslow Ditching Ltd) v Frohlich* [2011] EWHC 257 (Ch).

Worked Example A

Assume that our case study company, Bob's Electronics Ltd, is balance sheet insolvent and will soon be cashflow insolvent. If it entered into a liquidation procedure now creditors would receive 20% of what they are owed. *If* losses continue to be made at this rate, in another year the creditors of the company (who will be greater in number and amount) will receive 5% of what they are owed. However, the directors consider that there is a *25% possibility* that: market conditions will improve and that within a year the company will be cashflow positive; and within two years all creditors will be repaid. What would creditors prefer: to continue trading or to stop trading and to wind up the company?

Consider creditor A who is owed £1,000. If the company is liquidated today she will receive £200, which she can take and invest elsewhere. Let us assume that she will receive a 10% rate of interest in her investment elsewhere. In two years' time that investment would be worth £242 (with compound interest).

If Bob's Electronics Ltd continues to trade (provided they can obtain the credit to do so) there is 75% possibility that in a year's time the company will be liquidated and she will receive 5% of £1,000 = £50. She would then invest that £50 for a year and at the end of Year 2 it would be worth £55. There is also a 25% possibility that in two years' time she will be paid in full (£1,000 owed today plus interest = £1,210 compounded) at the end of Year 2.

What, therefore, is the expected value of these two options in two years' time:

- Liquidation now: £242.
- Continuing to trade: £41.25 (75% × 55) + £302.50 (25% × £1,210) = £343.75

Question: if you were creditor A what would you want the company to do?

Let us assume that Bob's Electronics Ltd continues to trade but the directors' hopes do not come to fruition and the company enters insolvent liquidation a year later (time T2), with substantially more creditors and fewer assets than it had one year previously (time T1). If the liquidator brings an action claiming a wrongful trading contribution consider the following questions:

1. At time T1 would a reasonable director have concluded that there was 'no reasonable prospect of avoiding insolvent liquidation'?

2. If so, if the directors elected to continue trading, did they take all reasonable steps with a view to 'minimizing losses for creditors'?

   Think about these questions before reading on.

Analysis:

1. At time T1 there was 75% likelihood that the company would enter into insolvent liquidation in a year's time. Is a 25% of avoiding it a 'reasonable prospect of avoiding insolvent liquidation'? Does reasonable prospect require more than 50%. Remember that the Company Law Review in trying to codify directors' duties to creditors used 'more likely than not' language to determine when such duties would be triggered. A 'reasonable prospect', it is submitted, suggests less than 50%. But how much less is unclear. However, taking *Re Hawkes* as our guide the plausible existence of trading out of the company's problems may be sufficient.

2. Assuming that there is deemed to be at T1 no reasonable prospect of avoiding insolvent liquidation (that is, as 25% chance of survival is not sufficient), would

> the decision to continue trading amount to taking all steps that ought to be taken to minimize losses to creditors? Applying expected value analysis at time T1 the expected value of creditors' claims is greater by continuing to trade than by entering liquidation. Accordingly, losses are thereby minimized.

As this example demonstrates, continuing to trade may be a real and creditor-friendly option even when the directors decide that there is 'no reasonable prospect' of avoiding insolvent liquidation. However, whilst there is limited authority on this point, the court in *Re Pierson* suggests that such a strategy would not benefit from the 'all steps' defence.

■ *Re Brian D Pierson* [2001] 1 BCLC 275

Hazel Williamson QC

Mr Pierson has argued that if he ought to have appreciated that the company was heading for an insolvent liquidation, nevertheless, after the date on which the liquidator relies, he 'took every step with a view to minimising potential loss to the company's creditors that…he ought to have taken' within the meaning of s 214(3) of the Insolvency Act 1986, such that the defence afforded by that sub-section is available to him.

In my judgment Mr Pierson cannot make out that defence. There was no question, in mid-1994, of his taking any steps to 'minimise loss to the creditors'; the company simply continued trading in the same way as before. In my judgment this section is intended to apply to cases where, for example, directors take specific steps with a view to preserving or realising assets or claims for the benefit of creditors, even if they fail to achieve that result. *It does not cover the very act of wrongful trading itself, just because this would have been done with the intention of trying to make a profit.* [Emphasis added]

Question

1. Do you agree with Hazel Williamson QC's position that continued trading is not a possible option if the directors knew, or ought to have known, that there was no reasonable prospect that insolvent liquidation could be avoided? What are the costs and benefits of taking that position?

2. In what respects do the approaches taken in *Re Hawkes* and *Re Brian D Pierson* differ? What, in your view, is the preferable approach? Which approach correctly applies section 214?

3. What percentage probability should in the view of a reasonably diligent director represent a 'reasonable prospect of avoiding insolvent liquidation'?

4.4 Mediating between directors' duties and section 214 liability

At time T2 in *Worked Example A*, when the business is in liquidation it is very easy to draw the inference that a decision to continue trading, in the absence of any other creditor-regarding steps, did not involve the taking of steps that a reasonably diligent director would take to minimize losses to creditors. Directors are aware of this and may be concerned that courts reviewing events with hindsight may not view the directors' decision to continue trading as reasonable. This awareness could lead directors to stop trading and enter insolvent liquidation when it is not in the creditors' interest to do so. However, such a decision may not necessarily protect the directors from liability exposure because, as we have seen, in insolvency directors must act in the best interests of the creditors. Accordingly, ceasing trading for fear of section 214 liability could result in liability for breach of duty (section 172). Of course, as section 172 is a subjective standard, and as ceasing to operate is likely to benefit from a rational justification, in most cases it will be very difficult to establish breach of section 172. In this regard consider the following dicta from Park J in *Re Continental Assurance Company of London plc*:[66]

> An overall point which needs to be kept in mind throughout is that, whenever a company is in financial trouble and the directors have a difficult decision to make whether to close down and go into liquidation, or whether instead to trade on and hope to turn the corner, they can be in a real and unenviable dilemma. On the one hand, if they decide to trade on but things do not work out and the company, later rather sooner, goes into liquidation, they may find themselves in the situation of the Respondents in this case—being sued for wrongful trading. On the other hand, if the directors decide to close down immediately and cause the company to go into an early liquidation, although they are not at risk of being sued for wrongful trading, they are at risk of being criticised on other grounds. A decision to close down will almost certainly mean that the ensuing liquidation will be an insolvent one. Apart from anything else liquidations are expensive operations, and in addition debtors are commonly obstructive about paying their debts to a company which is in liquidation. Many creditors of the company from a time before the liquidation are likely to find that their debts do not get paid in full. They will complain bitterly that the directors shut down too soon; they will say that the directors ought to have had more courage and kept going. If they had done, so the complaining creditors will say, the company probably would have survived and all of its debts would have been paid. Ceasing to trade and liquidating too soon can be stigmatised as the cowards' way out.

4.5 Section 214 and financial agency costs

So far our analysis has focused on the decision by directors to decide whether to continue trading or cease trading and enter insolvent liquidation. We also need to consider how section 214 would, if at all, deter directors from transferring value from creditors to shareholders by altering the risk profile of the company. As we have seen, the incentive to do so rises exponentially when the company is insolvent or approaching insolvency. Consider the following example.

Worked Example B

Assume that our case study company, Bob's Electronics Ltd, is balance sheet insolvent with assets of £50,000 and liabilities of £200,000. Although it has cash reserves of £20,000 in the bank they are insufficient to pay the liabilities that will become due over the next year.

Bob and Margaret, the directors of the company, are aware that the company will soon be cashflow insolvent and that there is no reasonable prospect of avoiding insolvent liquidation.

Bob has a close friend, Fred, who is a successful entrepreneur. Fred feels sorry for Bob and to help him out comes to him with two small-scale investment opportunities in areas outside of Bob's Electronics Ltd business areas. They are as follows:

- a £20,000 investment that has a 50% chance of making £100,000 in a year's time and a 50% chance of making £10,000.
- a £20,000 investment that has a 3% chance of making £1,000,000 and a 97% chance of making £0.

---

[66] [2001] BPIR 733.

The first investment has an expected value of £55,000 (£50,000 + £5,000). This investment would be in the creditors' interests and should be made even though there is no prospect of avoiding insolvent liquidation. This investment has no effect on shareholder value which remains zero but decreases expected creditor losses by £35,000 (£55,000 minus the original £20,000).[67] Of course whether creditors would actually want the directors to take this risk and make the investment (and whether it actually would minimize their losses) would depend on the creditors' appetite for risky investments. However, as this amounts to a 175% expected return on the £20,000 investment it is highly probable that this is an investment that the creditors would approve of.

The second investment has an overall positive expected value of £30,000 (3% × £1,000,000). Shareholders would clearly prefer this option as it increases the expected value of their equity from zero to £24,900.[68] Creditors' expected value however decreases from £50,000 prior to the investment (the liquidation value of the assets) to £36,000.[69]

The first investment will not avoid insolvent liquidation, assuming that there is no chance that the existing business can survive. However, it results in a decrease in the expected losses to creditors and should not, pursuant to section 214(3), result in the directors making a contribution *even* if the investment only makes £10,000.

The second investment results in a 3% chance insolvent liquidation will *be avoided* which is unlikely to be viewed as a reasonable prospect of avoiding insolvent liquidation. The steps taken by making this investment result in increase in the expected losses to creditors and should result in the directors being required to make a contribution under section 214.

Accordingly, this example demonstrates that section 214 allows a change in investment strategy for the company even where the company has no prospect of avoiding insolvent liquidation. However, if such an increase in the risk profile results in a decrease in value of the creditors' claims, directors will be caught by section 214.

4.6 Who does section 214 apply to?

The wrongful trading prohibition applies to directors. In addition, pursuant to section 214(8) the prohibition applies to shadow directors. The term 'shadow directors' is defined in section 251 of the Insolvency Act 1986 as follows:

> 'shadow director', in relation to a company, means a person in accordance with whose directions or instructions the directors of the company are accustomed to act (but so that a person is not deemed a shadow director by reason only that the directors act on advice given by him in a professional capacity);

The meaning of the term 'shadow director' is discussed in section V of Chapter 9.

4.7 Nature and quantum of contribution for breach of section 214

The first point to note about any contribution from a director ordered by the court pursuant to section 214 is that it is not deemed to be the company's property prior to the

---

[67] Prior to the investment if Bob's Electronics Ltd were to be liquidated immediately the value of the debt is £50,000 (asset value which includes £20,000 cash). Following the investment the value of the debt is £30,000 (remaining assets after the investment) plus £55,000 (50% × £100,000 plus 50% of £10) = £85,000.

[68] 3% × (£1,000,000 plus £30,000 (remaining assets) minus £200,000).

[69] Prior to the investment if Bob's Electronics Ltd were to be liquidated immediately the value of the debt is £50,000 (asset value which includes £20,000 cash). Following the investment the debt is worth £30,000 (remaining assets after investment) plus the expected value of the investments *for the debt-holders* of £6,000 (3% × £200,000 + 97% × 0) = £36,000.

liquidation.[70] The importance of this point is that any security interest in the company's property granted prior to the liquidation does not apply to the contribution, which means such proceeds are made available to the company's unsecured creditors.

With regard to calculating the amount of the contribution, section 214(1) confers on the court a discretion to make such contribution 'as the court thinks proper'. In practice, as Professor Davies notes, 'the courts seem to have settled down with an approach whereby the maximum contribution is the diminution in the company's net asset position during the period of wrongful trading, with discounts being available from that theoretical maximum for directors who are not regarded as strongly blameworthy'.[71] Available authority suggests that, consistent with recent case law on damages for economic torts, such as the House of Lords decision in *South Australia Asset Management Company*,[72] the courts will take into account other causes of loss during the wrongful trading period, such as the 'bad' weather in *Re Brian D Pierson*.[73]

4.8 The effect of section 214 in practice: funding section 214 applications

Imagine a liquidator appointed to wind up a company who has grave concerns about directors' decisions prior to the company entering into insolvent liquidation. After taking legal advice he may consider that he has a good case, although recognizes that if the judiciary take a deferential approach to the business decisions made by the directors then the action may not be successful. Against her, and her advisors', assessment of the likelihood that a case will be successful she has to weigh the costs of the action should the action fail. These costs will diminish further the pool of assets available for the unsecured creditors. In practice, there are relatively few reported cases on section 214. This may be explained by the fact that liquidators are hesitant to put a portion of the available assets at risk to fund liquidation. Of course, the limited number of reported cases does not tell us how many actions are brought or threatened that result in the directors making an out-of-court contribution to the company.

V DIRECTORS' DISQUALIFICATION

The Company Directors Disqualification Act 1986 (CDDA) empowers the Secretary of State for Business Enterprise and Regulatory Reform to bring an action to disqualify directors from acting as directors for a period of time.[74] It also empowers the Secretary of State to accept a disqualification undertaking that a director will not act as a director for a period of time.[75]

The Act provides for multiple grounds upon which a disqualification order can be made including: committing an indictable offence in connection with the formation or management of a company;[76] persistent failure to comply with the disclosure obligations

---

[70] *Re Oasis Merchandising Services Ltd* [1995] 2 BCLC 493.

[71] Davies, 'Directors' Creditor-Regarding Duties' note 47, 325. See, for example, *Earp v Stevenson* [2011] EWHC 1436 (Ch) [62].   [72] [1997] AC 191.

[73] In *Re Brian D Pierson (Contractors) Ltd* [2001] 1 BCLC 275 Hazel Williamson QC held: 'I am not satisfied that the full extent of the worsening of the position of the company is to be attributed to the continued trading of the company. This is applying a "but for" test of causation. I accept, from Mr Pierson's evidence, that the eventual position of the company owed something to losses caused by the particularly bad weather conditions of 1994–95. Whilst the wrongful trading may have provided the opportunity for those losses, it could not be said to have caused them.' See also, *Re Continental Assurance Co of London plc* [2001] All England Official Transcripts, paras 379–80.

[74] Section 1 CDDA 1986.

[75] Section 1A CDDA 1986. On disqualification undertakings see R. Williams, *Disqualification Undertakings: Law, Policy and Practice* (Jordan Publishing, 2011).

[76] Section 2 CDDA 1986.

of the Companies Act;[77] conduct that makes the director 'unfit' to be concerned in the management of the company;[78] and the commission of fraudulent or wrongful trading.[79] Accordingly, in relation to section 214 of the Insolvency Act 1986, a disqualification order operates as an additional deterrent to a possible court order to make a contribution to the company. Importantly in this regard, a court that finds a director in breach of section 214 may make a disqualification order even in the absence of a disqualification application.[80]

Our concern here is specifically with the ground for the making of a disqualification order set out in section 6 of the Company Directors Disqualification Act 1986 and, in particular, the extent to which this ground imposes additional creditor-regarding obligations on company directors. Section 6 provides that a director may be disqualified from acting as a director for a period ranging from a mandatory minimum of two years to a maximum of 15 years,[81] where the director's conduct renders him unfit to be concerned in the management of the company. Importantly, this ground is only available as a basis for disqualification where the company is insolvent,[82] understood by this Act to mean that the company has entered a liquidation or administration or receivership process.[83]

The types of conduct that can amount to 'unfitness' are far wider in scope than actions that incur financial agency costs or damage creditors' interests. Indeed the CDDA refers to the court in Parts I and II of Schedule I[84] of the Act to a wide range of factors that are relevant to an unfitness determination including, amongst others, breach of duty, misapplication of property, and, of particular relevance for this chapter, the director's responsibility for the insolvency of the company.[85] The courts' general approach to determining unfitness was explained by Browne-Wilkinson VC in *Re Lo-Line Electric Motors Ltd* as follows:[86]

> What is the proper approach to deciding whether someone is unfit to be a director? The approach adopted in all the cases to which I have been referred is broadly the same. The primary purpose of the section is not to punish the individual but to protect the public against the future conduct of companies by persons whose past records as directors of insolvent companies have shown them to be a danger to creditors and others. Therefore, the power is not fundamentally penal. But, if the power to disqualify is exercised, disqualification does involve a substantial interference with the freedom of the individual. It follows that the rights of the individual must be fully protected. Ordinary commercial misjudgment is in itself not sufficient to justify disqualification. In the normal case, the conduct complained of must display a lack of commercial probity,

---

[77] Section 3 CDDA 1986.   [78] Section 6 CDDA 1986.
[79] Section 10 CDDA 1986.   [80] Section 10(1) CDDA 1986.
[81] Section 6(4) CDDA 1986. In *Re Sevenoaks Stationers (Retail) Ltd* [1991] BCLC 325 with regard to disqualification period Dillon LJ held that: 'I would for my part endorse the division of the potential 15-year disqualification period into three brackets...: (i) the top bracket of disqualification for periods over ten years should be reserved for particularly serious cases. These may include cases where a director who has already had one period of disqualification imposed on him falls to be disqualified yet again; (ii) the minimum bracket of two to five years' disqualification should be applied where, though disqualification is mandatory, the case is, relatively, not very serious; (iii) the middle bracket of disqualification for from six to ten years should apply for serious cases which do not merit the top bracket.'
[82] Section 6(1)(a) CDDA 1986.
[83] Section 6(2) CDDA 1986. On rescue procedures designed to save struggling companies as going concerns See V. Finch, *Corporate Insolvency Law: Perspectives and Principles* (2nd edn, CUP, 2009), Part III.
[84] Section 9 refers the court to Parts I and II of Schedule I in relation to an unfitness determination. Part I refers the court to factors that are relevant in all cases, Part II to factors that are relevant where the company is insolvent.
[85] For a discussion of the 'unfitness' ground and incompetence see note 39 of Chapter 12.
[86] [1988] BCLC 698.

although I have no doubt that in an extreme case of gross negligence or total incompetence disqualification could be appropriate.

The phrase 'lack of commercial probity' or, as it was described in some of the earlier cases, 'want of commercial morality'[87] suggests that a finding of unfitness may be based on conduct that falls below the standard of conduct we expect of directors. Actions taken by company directors when the company is insolvent or in the zone of insolvency which have a detrimental impact on the creditors' interests may form the basis of a finding of 'lack of commercial probity'. For example, in *Keypak Homecare Ltd*,[88] the directors of the company purchased significant amounts of stock for the business 'at a time when Keypak Homecare must have been to the knowledge of the directors in grave peril of going down' and then subsequently sold this stock to a new company, owned by the same directors, at what was described as a 'forced sale price'. Harman J held, in ordering the disqualification of the directors, that 'this was a course of conduct which any decent directors ought to have realized was a serious breach of commercial probity. It involved plainly an attempt to trade out on the back of their creditors.'

In this context of directors' conduct which has a detrimental impact on creditors, the grounds for an unfitness determination often track the existing creditor-regarding obligations considered in section IV of this chapter. Consider in this regard *Re CS Holdings Ltd*,[89] where a disqualification action was brought by the Secretary of State based on the fact that the director had failed to resign when, to no avail, he had taken steps to bring to the other directors' attention the steps that needed to be taken to address the company's difficulties as well as their possible obligations if the company was subsequently found to have been 'trading at the expense of certain creditors'. In holding that the failure to resign in such circumstances was insufficient for a finding of unfitness, Chadwick J made the following observations.

■ *Re CS Holdings Ltd* [1997] BCC 172

Chadwick J

The companies legislation does not impose on directors a statutory duty to ensure that their company does not trade while insolvent; nor does that legislation impose an obligation to ensure that the company does not trade at a loss. Those propositions need only to be stated to be recognised as self-evident. Directors may properly well take the view that it is in the interests of the company and of its creditors that, although insolvent, the company should continue to trade out of its difficulties. They may properly take the view that it is in the interests of the company and its creditors that some loss-making trade should be accepted in anticipation of future profitability. They are not to be criticized if they give effect to such view. But the legislation imposes on directors the risk that trading while insolvent may lead to personal liability. Section 214 imposes that liability where the director knew or ought to have concluded, that there was no reasonable prospect that the company would avoid going into insolvent liquidation.

If it is established, in proceedings under s. 6 of the 1986 Act, that a director has caused a company to trade when he knew, or ought to have known, that there was no reasonable prospect that the company would avoid going into insolvent liquidation, that director may well be held unfit to be concerned in the management of a company. But a director who, believing that there is no reasonable prospect of avoiding insolvency, protests against further trading and uses such

---

[87] *Re Dawson Print Group Ltd* [1987] BCLC 601, per Hoffmann J.

[88] [1997] BCC 172.

[89] Other courts have used less demanding language in this regard, for example in *Keypak Homecare Ltd* Harman J preferred 'lack of proper standards' [1997] BCC 172—although in application he referred to 'commercial probity'.

influence as he has to bring the trading to an end, is not in my view a person whose failure to resign his directorship must lead to a finding of unfitness. He is entitled to remain a member of a board to whose collective decisions he is continuing to contribute...

I am not to be taken as expressing the view that there may not be circumstances in which a director who has ceased to exercise any influence in the deliberations of the board will be at risk of being held unfit if he fails to resign. The duties of a director include, in my view, the duty to inform himself as to the company's affairs and the duty to make his views known to the other directors. If there comes a point at which his attendance at board meetings is purposeless because he must recognise that his co-directors take no account of his views and recommendations, then it may well be appropriate to ask why he continues to remain as a director. If he continues to remain as a director in those circumstances for no purpose other than to draw his director's fees or to preserve his status, a court might well come to the conclusion that he was so lacking in appreciation of a director's duties that he was unfit to be concerned in the management of a company.

We see in *CS Holdings* that the court links the unfitness determination to the approach and the language of section 214. If the directors continue to trade where there is no reasonable prospect of insolvency then not only may this amount to wrongful trading but it may also form the basis of an unfitness determination for the purposes of the disqualification regime. In this regard, in *Secretary of State for Trade and Industry v Van Hengel*[90] a disqualification application was brought on the basis that, amongst others, the company had continued to trade although the company was 'hopelessly insolvent'. Even though the company had significant losses, the court found that the continued trading did not support a finding of unfitness as, at the time in question, the company had begun to generate a small profit and there was a 'genuine prospect'[91] of an additional equity investment—which did not come to fruition. However, a clear picture of how deferential the courts will be to directors' decisions to continue to trade is not available in relation to disqualification on the ground of 'unfitness', as it was similarly not available in relation to section 214. In *Re Richborough Furniture Ltd*,[92] for example, in finding that continued trading justified a determination of unfitness, the court observed that although 'before 1985 it may have been seen as acceptable for directors to try to trade their way out of insolvency. That is no longer the case, as what is now section 214 of the Insolvency Act 1986 makes plain.'

Whilst with regard to the incurrence of financial agency and other creditor-*disregarding* behaviour, the unfitness ground for a disqualification order imposes similar substantive requirements to the creditor-regarding obligations set out in the common law and in section 214, the disqualification regime differs in an important respect, namely the resources available for enforcement. As we noted in section III, liquidators have made only limited use of section 214. One of the reasons for this is the costs associated with bringing the action which may further deplete the resources available to creditors if the action is unsuccessful. Similar constraints apply to liquidator actions to enforce breaches of directors' duty. A disqualification application, however, is not brought by the liquidator but by the Insolvency Service, an executive branch of the Department of Business and Regulatory Reform; a government body that has resources available to it to bring such disqualification applications. Indeed, typically over 1,000 disqualification orders are made each year.[93] Accordingly, whereas the low probability of section 214

---

[90] [1995] 1 BCLC 545.

[91] Compare the language of 'genuine prospect' with 'realistic prospect' in the context of section 214 in *Re Brian D Pierson* [2001] 1 BCLC 275 considered in section 4.3.

[92] [1996] 1 BCLC 507.

[93] See, for example, *Companies in 2005–2006* (The Stationery Office, 1996–2006).

or breach of duty actions being brought significantly undermines the deterrent effect of these creditor-regarding obligations, the disqualification regime would appear to operate as a more significant deterrent to avoid breaching of a very similar substantive standard. Not all commentators, however, agree that the disqualification regime represents a deterrent. In this regard consider the following extract.

■ R. Williams, 'Disqualifying Directors: A Remedy Worse than the Disease' (2007) 7 *Journal of Corporate Law Studies* 213

A survey carried out for the *Follow-up Report*,[94] which indicated that 64% of directors questioned felt that the disqualification regime was unsuccessful in deterring unfit conduct and that 65% felt it was not successful in protecting the public. Research carried out for Andrew Hicks's ACCA[95] report found that a similar number (two-thirds) of insolvency practitioners felt that the risk of disqualification did not influence directors' behaviour.

These findings are in keeping with apparently low awareness of the disqualification regime amongst directors. In the [National Audit Office's] first survey of attitudes towards disqualification (carried out at the time of its First Report) 58% of directors questioned claimed to be unaware of the legislation. A similar survey carried out for the *Follow-up Report* showed increased levels of ignorance, with 66% of directors then claiming no knowledge of the sanction. Baldwin's survey,[96] though not specifically testing awareness of disqualification, suggests little improvement in these figures, with only 38% of directors questioned there claiming that they were aware of 'company law' regulatory risks.

Empirical evidence does not therefore suggest that disqualification successfully deters unfit conduct, even more so because effective deterrence rests upon much more than mere knowledge of the existence of disqualification, or indeed any other sanction. At least as significant as awareness of the existence of a sanction is knowledge of the conduct that attracts the sanction. Put simply, if directors do not know what 'unfit' conduct is, they cannot be deterred from carrying it out. And, given the low awareness of the existence of disqualification, it seems unlikely that more than a few directors would be well acquainted with the specifics of unfit conduct. A director who wished to acquire such knowledge would be faced with the costly task of investigating numerous precedents concerning the nature of unfitness, as well as matters identified in the Act itself. This is not a task that business people, immersed in the day-to-day affairs of their enterprises, are likely to devote a considerable time to. Indeed, the post-insolvency focus of the disqualification regime makes ignorance of 'unfit acts' a perfectly rational state for most directors.

Post-insolvency disqualification, by its nature, is likely to be seen as remote from the day-to-day activities of directors and, as such, the incentive to comply with its standards is likely to be limited. This is compounded by the fact that it is only directors of companies that enter formal insolvency proceedings who come into contact with the disqualification system. Directors of companies that are simply dissolved and struck off the register fall completely outside of the system, the effect of which is stark in itself. In 2003–2004, for example, 154,300 companies were struck off the register and dissolved, whereas only 15,700 were subject to formal insolvency proceedings before being removed.[97] However, even in the event of formal insolvency proceedings, the chances of becoming subject to disqualification proceedings are low, resting, in the first instance, on an insolvency practitioner or official receiver finding sufficient evidence of unfit conduct to prompt him to make a substantive report of it to the Secretary of State and, in the

---

[94] The 'Follow-up Report' referred to in this extract is the official report on the operation of the Company Directors Disqualification regime carried out by the National Audit Office (NAO): National Audit Office, *Insolvency Service Executive Agency, Company Director Disqualification—A Follow-up Report* (House of Commons Papers, Session 1998–9, 424).

[95] The Association of Chartered Certified Accountants.

[96] R. Baldwin, 'The New Punitive Regulation' (2004) 67 *Modern Law Review* 351.

[97] *Companies in 2003–2004* (The Stationery Office, 1996–2006).

second, on the Secretary of State taking the report forward to formal proceedings. Neither link in the chain aids the deterrent effect of the sanction.

The discretion given to insolvency practitioners and official receivers in the reporting process is a significant weakness in the system. An obligation to report a director's conduct to the Secretary of State arises where an insolvency practitioner believes that there is sufficient evidence to indicate that a director's conduct makes him unfit to be concerned in the management of a company. The test is therefore simply a replication of the test in section 6(1) of the CDDA; however, this means that its application requires office holders to exercise the same value judgment about a director's conduct as the courts are expected to in judicial proceedings. It is therefore little wonder that successive inquires have found confusion and inconsistent reporting amongst insolvency practitioners and official receivers. Correct application of the 'test', if such a thing were possible, would require an encyclopaedic knowledge of disqualification precedents. To be sure, the *Follow-up Report* noted early successes of the Insolvency Service's efforts to increase the quality of office holders' reports, but it still showed significant variations between official receiver offices and discretion in the reporting process remains a potential weakness in disqualification. In 2002, for example, the Secretary of State received over 5,000 reports of unfit conduct, yet pursued only 1,561 to formal disqualification proceedings. The extent to which such a large number of reports were rejected due to poor quality is not known, but with over two-thirds of reports rejected significant doubt must still surround the extent to which office holders successfully discharge their duties under the CDDA. For directors, however, the lesson is clear: even where unfit conduct is reported the odds are firmly stacked against it resulting in a disqualification application.

Rational deterrence assumptions dictate that a director will weigh the expected costs and benefits of non-compliance with a behavioural rule before deciding whether to comply with it. A rational director who undertook such an exercise in relation to disqualification may well therefore conclude that non-compliance with, or remaining in complete ignore of, the tenets of the disqualification regime is the rational course of action. Put simply, the chances of falling within the current disqualification regime are slight, the uncertainty that surrounds the exercise of discretion by office holders great and the number of reports of unfit conduct pursued by the Secretary of State limited. Consider also evidence indicating low regard for personal sanctions and it is little wonder that surveys indicate that a majority of directors and insolvency practitioners feel that disqualification does not deter unfit conduct.

 Online Resource Centre
http://www.oxfordtextbooks.co.uk/orc/kershaw2e/

Visit the Online Resource Centre for additional resources and information available for this chapter, including web links and an interactive flashcard glossary.

CHAPTER NINETEEN

REGULATING LEGAL CAPITAL

I INTRODUCTION

This chapter considers the nature and regulation of legal capital. In particular we shall consider to what extent, if at all, legal capital and its regulation have a creditor protection function: to what extent, if at all, it can be viewed as a response to the problems, identified in Chapter 18, which limited shareholder liability generates for different creditor constituencies. To provide some introductory context in this regard consider the following hypothetical.

Hypothetical A

....

Bob, as CEO of Bob's Electronics Ltd, approaches a bank to obtain a loan to fund a portion of the £300,000 start-up costs for Bob's business idea. In considering whether to make the loan the bank will have two primary concerns: first, will the expected cash-flow return[1] of the project be sufficient to service the principal and interest payments under the loan; and, second, can the risk associated with the loan be reduced by either taking security interests in the company's assets, or a personal guarantee from Bob. Here, the first concern is our primary focus.

The company's business plan, which is presented to the bank, contains three projections: a *best case scenario*—if all goes as well as could be hoped; *a likely case scenario*—containing the most probable outcome; and *a worst case* scenario. The best case scenario projects that the business will generate an annual cash return of £50,000, the likely case £35,000, and the worst case only £10,000. Let us assume that the bank views the business plan and its range of projections as informed and reliable.

Bob proposes to borrow £200,000 from the bank at a 5% interest rate with the principal to be repaid over 10 annual instalments of £20,000 each. Yearly repayments will range from £30,000 in year one to £21,000 in the final year when only £20,000 of the principal is outstanding. The bank is likely to be concerned about this proposal: if the business performs worse than the likely case, the business will not generate enough cash to repay the principal and interest on the loan, particularly in the first few years. The bank is likely to be less concerned if the project is funded by more equity (Bob's own funds) and less debt from the bank. If the finance provided by the bank was reduced to £150,000 of the required £300,000, with the remainder being equity finance from Bob's personal funds, the bank would be more comfortable with making the loan. Now the annual repayments would range from £22,500 (£15,000 in principal and £7,500 in interest) in the first year to £15,750 in the final year. One could refer to this difference between likely cash return of £35,000 per year and debt repayment obligations of £15,750 to £22,500 as a cushion. Indeed in the financial world the amount of equity is sometimes referred to as an equity cushion.

The language of a cushion suggests something that is always there to soften a fall. This is misleading because the equity investment is not 'stashed away under the floorboards'

---

[1] For a definition of 'expected return' see the glossary.

to provide the creditors with protection if things do not go according to plan. The equity investment is, of course, invested into the business—to buy the assets required to operate the business. If Bob's Electronics is catastrophically unsuccessful and generates no cash then there will be nothing left to soften the fall for the creditors apart from the proceeds from the sale of the company's assets. In a sense, equity is a cushion because the more equity which funds a business the more room there is for the business to operate less successfully than had been projected and yet avoid becoming cashflow insolvent—being unable to pay its debts as they become due.

In *Hypothetical A* the equity finance from Bob's personal funds would be injected into the company by the purchase of shares allotted by the company to Bob. The amount of this equity finance is the company's 'legal capital'. The term 'legal capital' is not a term that is either defined by the Act or used in the cases we consider later. It is, however, a useful term to provide us with a clear reference point for the amount that is regulated by the rules we will consider below. We saw in Chapter 17 that although a share has a nominal value, a share may be issued for more, but not less, than the nominal value of the share. Any amount paid in excess of the nominal value is referred to as the share premium.[2] The term 'legal capital' is used therefore as an umbrella term referring to an amount represented by the sum of the company's share capital—the aggregate nominal value of the shares it has issued—and the aggregate share premium.

In *Hypothetical A* we saw the company raising equity and debt finance to fund the business. The finance raised by the company from Bob and from the bank is invested to buy the assets—warehouse; components; delivery vehicles etc.—that are required to build and sell computers. At the time Bob pays for the shares legal capital is a cash asset in the company's bank account; but this cash amount will, along with the loan capital provided by the bank, be quickly spent and transformed into the non-cash assets. If all goes well cash will subsequently be generated by deploying those assets to run a successful business. The legal capital amount is not, therefore, represented by cash in the bank or by any particular asset; legal capital is simply the historic amount, in pounds,[3] that was paid for the shares.

It is important to distinguish clearly between legal capital and the term 'equity', in particular everyday and accounting uses of this term. As we have seen, shares give their owners a variable residual financial claim on the company. This claim varies in size as the company succeeds and generates profits or fails and generates losses. Owners of businesses, whether sole traders or shareholders, often refer to the size of their residual interest as their equity in their business just as a house owner's residual interest in his house is often referred to as that house owner's equity. This understanding of 'equity' is reflected in the company's accounts in an entry called **shareholder equity**. If a company is successful and generates profits, as we shall see later in this chapter, the profits may either be retained in the company or paid out to shareholders as dividends. If the profits are retained and invested this increases the size of a shareholder's residual financial claim; in colloquial terms increases a shareholder's 'equity'. This accounting entry should not be confused with 'legal capital'. 'Shareholder equity' includes both the legal capital amount and any profits that are retained in the company, less any losses that are generated by the company.

[2] Section 610 Companies Act 2006.
[3] Whilst it is possible for a UK company to issue shares in other currencies, typically UK companies issue shares for pounds sterling (section 542(3) CA 2006).

II MINIMUM CAPITAL REQUIREMENTS

1 Do minimum capital requirements protect creditors?

From *Hypothetical A* we can see that the amount of legal capital as a proportion of the total funding for a business alters the level of risk for creditors. One way of protecting creditors, therefore, would be to regulate the amount of legal capital required in a company at the moment when it is formed and/or during its existence. Company law could require minimum initial equity investments on the formation of a company or could require minimum continuing shareholder equity (in the accounting understanding of the term) as the business progresses. Minimum initial capital would involve specifying a minimum amount of equity capital that must be purchased in order for the company to be formed or to carry on business. Minimum continuing shareholder equity would require additional equity investments to the extent that losses reduce shareholder equity below the minimum legal capital amount, if the company is to continue to trade. Both minimum equity amounts and continuing equity requirements could be provided for by specifying a specific monetary amount or by providing for a minimum ratio of the extent to which a company's assets are funded by equity or debt (a debt/equity ratio).

The primary problem with minimum equity capital amounts is that the extent to which they provide creditor protection is a function of the size of the company's investments. If Company A is set up to make a £500 investment and the minimum equity investment to form a company is £200 then the minimum requirement significantly decreases credit risk. However, in the context of the £300,000 required by Bob's Electronics Ltd in *Hypothetical A*, a minimum equity investment of £200 is irrelevant. However, if in an attempt to address this problem the law requires a higher minimum capital amount it may discourage individuals from using the corporate form and, in some instances, discourage them from exploiting wealth-generating ideas at all. An equity investment ratio (for example of 30%) addresses some of these difficulties by ensuring that the minimum equity capital amount adjusts to the size of the company's business. However, it may similarly operate to discourage use of the corporate form and dampen business activity. In this regard consider the following extracts.

■ **H. Eidenmueller, B. Grunewald and U. Noack, 'Minimum Capital in the System of Legal Capital' in M. Lutter (ed),** *Legal Capital in Europe* **(2006) European and Company Financial Law Review, Special Volume, 25**

Benefits of Minimum Capital

Whilst it is certainly correct that the minimum capital is wholly inadequate for larger enterprises, this does not, however, produce a decisive objection to the use of such a requirement for smaller enterprises. The same also applies to the accusation that the minimum capital reflects the initial capital equipment and is thus insignificant for creditors. If a minimum capital requirement prevents the formation of certain corporations with limited liability at all…then a filter effect can hardly be denied.

At first sight, another objection, by contrast seems to be more serious: potential contract partners are naturally also aware that an equity contribution by the founders can improve the average quality of the enterprise operated with limited liability. It is thus by no means clear why a compulsory statutory regulation should be necessary…A minimum capital requirement therefore only results in genuine economic advantages if it can be shown that this market mechanism fails, at least in part.

[The authors then raise the objections considered in Chapter 18 about the ability of involuntary creditors to adjust at all and information and time barriers to adjustment by small creditors. They then consider whether non-adjusting creditors can take advantage (free ride) on the creditor protections negotiated by sophisticated adjusting creditors such as banks.] A bank is naturally only interested in a secure position for itself. For this reason it will not primarily insist on high contributions by the founders to the company, but rather on the provision of loan security. The investment assets (purchased with the loan) but above all the material and personal security out of the shareholder's private assets, are suitable as such loan security... The compulsory minimum capital makes it more difficult to concentrate loss-risks in a corporation with limited liability, in order to pass them on to smaller contractual partners...

Costs of Minimum Capital

...

It cannot be excluded that the minimum capital requirement forces profitable enterprises to comply with an unreasonably high equity capital ratio or to waive the choice of a legal form with limited liability. Here we think in particular of certain service providers with low investment requirements. In some cases, the minimum capital can prevent the formation of a profitable enterprise. These are opportunity costs of [a minimum capital regime]. However, such a scenario probably only arises very infrequently, because [two] circumstances must coincide. First, it must be impossible for any of the founders [to pay the minimum equity capital amount]. Second, the entrepreneurial risk may be so great in the eyes of the founders that they prefer to abandon their project instead of accepting limited liability...

For a trenchant critique of the creditor protection function provided by minimum capital rules consider the following extract.

■ **J. Armour, 'Legal Capital: An Outdated Concept?' (2006) 7**
European Business Organization Law Review 5

As we have seen, a minimum capital requirement imposes an 'entry price' for limited liability. The effect of such a restriction is most likely to be felt on small firms. For such firms, which are typically owner-managed, limited liability is not used to reduce risk-bearing costs by permitting shareholders to diversify, as it is for listed companies.[4] Rather, the principal benefit brought by limited liability is probably the reduction in risk it offers to entrepreneurs. The willingness of marginal individuals[5] to engage in entrepreneurial activity does appear to be affected by the actual or perceived riskiness of such endeavour. For example, more lenient personal insolvency laws are associated with higher levels of self-employment, plausibly because by reducing the harshness of the consequences of failure, they make entrepreneurial activity more appealing to risk-averse individuals. A similar effect could be expected to be associated with the ease of obtaining limited liability. That is, inability to gain access to limited liability (because of lack of sufficient resources to meet a minimum capital requirement) might deter individuals from engaging in entrepreneurial activity. Consistently with this, one study finds a negative correlation between size of minimum capital requirements (scaled for GDP) and self-employment—a common proxy for entrepreneurship—in European countries during the 1990s.[6]

[4] On the role of limited liability in facilitating the transfer and diversification of shares see Chapter 1 section III.

[5] 'Marginal individuals' here refers to the individuals for whom a decrease or increase in risk that is provided by limited liability will affect their decision as to whether or not to make an investment or commence a project.

[6] W. Fan and M.J. White, 'Personal Bankruptcy and the Level of Entrepreneurial Activity' (2003) 46 *Journal of Law and Economics* 543.

To be sure, facilitating access to limited liability may be expected to result in would-be entrepreneurs coming forward with more marginal projects, in terms of quality. Whether or not these will be funded (in the absence of a minimum capital requirement) depends on the ability of private creditors to discriminate in terms of project quality... Moreover, there is nothing to stop an entrepreneur credibly signalling the quality of his or her project in the absence of a minimum capital requirement, either by committing personal funds to the corporate enterprise or by agreeing to stand guarantor for its debts. Thus, provided adjusting creditors are able to distinguish project quality, or require shareholders to give a personal guarantee (by way of signal), then a minimum capital requirement will impose a social cost, by preventing some entrepreneurial projects from being undertaken.

We have on the other hand hypothesised that a minimum capital regime may yield social benefits, through the amelioration of the position of non-adjusting creditors. Whilst adjusting creditors may be able to screen out the more marginal projects associated with ready access to limited liability, non-adjusting creditors cannot. The existence and extent of any benefits for such creditors through the imposition of a minimum capital regime therefore merits careful scrutiny...

Consider first tort victims. In economic terms, tortious liability is imposed on those conducting hazardous activity in order to encourage them to internalise the social costs of their actions. Yet the amount necessary to capitalise a business adequately so as to internalise the risks of hazardous activities will depend on the nature of the business, and a unitary minimum capital requirement is likely to be a very haphazard means of achieving this. Moreover, there are more precise means of achieving the same goal. One is to regulate hazardous activity and to require that firms carry insurance commensurate with their potential risk. The pricing of insurance premia would be a more precise internalisation mechanism than a 'fixed-rate' minimum capital requirement, not least because the insurance company would act as an ongoing monitor for the firm's activities...

Trade creditors are a third category of supposedly 'non-adjusting' claimant. It is argued by some that trade creditors' adjustment may only be partial, because of information and transaction costs relative to the amount at stake. Indeed, empirical studies confirm that trade creditors tend to offer the same terms to all 'borrowers' (that is, customers who purchase on credit).[7] Some suggest that the use of such a 'blended' term in the face of asymmetric information about borrower quality may result in good-quality borrowers being overcharged and poor-quality borrowers being undercharged, implying an inefficient 'subsidy'. Yet empirical studies also report that the amount of trade credit granted is a function of the borrower's creditworthiness and of the scope for misbehaviour by the debtor. This implies that trade creditors do in fact adjust [by adjusting the] amount of credit extended as opposed to variations in terms.

It appears, therefore, that it is hard to find a category of non-adjusting creditors for whom minimum capital rules offer useful protection.

Questions and discussion

1. Which creditors would benefit from a minimum capital regime? Why would they benefit?

2. Eidenmueller et al argue that free-riding—benefiting from the actions of others—by non-adjusting creditors on the adjustments of sophisticated creditors, such as banks, is not always possible as the protections which adjusting creditors bargain for are not capable of being shared with other creditors—such as personal guarantees. Do you agree?

3. Is a minimum capital regime more appropriate for a private company or a public company?

---

[7] Trade credit is typically offered on very similar terms within an industry: C.K. Ng, J.K. Smith and R.L. Smith, 'Evidence on the Determinants of Trade Credit Terms in Interfirm Trade' (1999) 54 *Journal of Finance* 1109.

4. Do you agree with Eidenmueller et al's argument that the extent to which a minimum capital regime deters the exploitation business is low? At what monetary level would you agree with them? At what monetary level would you disagree with them?

5. Is there any agreement between the positions of Eidenmueller et al and Armour? Does their disagreement pivot on their views as to which creditors adjust and which do not?

6. To the extent specific creditors do not adjust, are other regulatory techniques better tailored and more effective means of assisting the creditors?

7. There are no compulsory insurance obligations in the UK in relation to personal injury product liability claims, although many companies have such insurance (although insurance is required for motor vehicle accidents and workers compensation). Professor Ferran has noted, in regard to some of the alternative regulatory tools for protecting involuntary creditors including mandatory insurance, but also giving involuntary creditors priority in bankruptcy, that 'the historical evidence of insolvency law reform in the United Kingdom suggests that proposals along these lines are unlikely to receive a favourable welcome'.[8] If theoretically available alternatives would provide protection but are unlikely to be introduced does this alter your view on whether we should have minimum capital rules?

2 UK and European approaches to minimum capital

UK company law has traditionally not required a minimum capital amount to form a company. As a result of the implementation of the European Union's Second Company Law Directive,[9] public companies are now subject to minimum capital requirements. The Second Directive requires a minimum capital amount of €25,000.[10] However, the Companies Act 2006 provides that in order to trade a public company must have an allotted nominal share capital—aggregate nominal value of the allotted shares—of at least £50,000.[11] This requirement is set out in sections 761–763 the Companies Act 2006, which provide that a public company cannot commence trading activity until it has received a trading certificate from the Companies Registrar. This certificate is issued upon receipt by the Companies Registrar of a *statement of compliance* from the company that it has complied with the minimum allotted share capital amount. If a public company trades without the trading certificate section 767 provides that the directors of the company are jointly and severally liable to indemnify third parties who suffer any loss as a result of the company's failure to fulfil its obligations.

The Companies Act 2006 does not extend the minimum capital requirement to private companies. In the UK there is no minimum capital requirement for private companies. A company can be set up by issuing one £1 share to one member. This contrasts with many European jurisdictions where typically one sees minimum capital requirements for both public and for private companies. In France, for example, the minimum capital for a public company (a *société anonyme*, SA) is €37,000, unless the company is listed, in which case the minimum capital amount rises to €225,000. In France, following reforms in 2003, the minimum capital requirement for a private limited company (a *société à responsabilité limitée*, 'SARL') was abolished from a previous minimum amount of €7,500.[12] In Germany, the minimum capital amount for a public company (*Aktiengesellschaft*, AG) is €50,000 and for a private company (*Gesellschaft mit beschränkte Haftung*, GmbH) it is €25,000.[13]

---

[8] E. Ferran, 'Creditors' Interests and "Core" Company Law' (1999) *Company Lawyer* 314.

[9] Second Council Directive 71/91/EEC.   [10] *Ibid* article 6(1).

[11] Section 586 CA 2006 requires that for a public company at least one quarter of the nominal value and the whole of any share premium must be paid-up.

[12] See generally, I. Urbain-Parléani, 'Working Group on the Share Capital in Europe—French Answers to the Questionnaire' in M. Lutter (ed), *Legal Capital in Europe* (2006) European and Company Financial Law Review, Special Volume, 480.

[13] See section 7 German Stock Corporation Law (*Aktiengesetzt*) and section 5(1) German Limited Liability Company Act (*GmbH Gesetz*). One quarter of which must be paid-up.

The UK does not have any continuing shareholder equity requirements. There is no obligation to provide additional capital if a public company's net assets (assets minus liabilities) or shareholder equity falls below the minimum capital figure for a public company or below a certain percentage of its legal capital. Section 656 of the 2006 Act does, however, provide that if the net assets of the company fall to a level which is half of the company's 'called-up share capital' the board of directors must call a general meeting to consider whether any steps should be taken. Called-up share capital includes the aggregate nominal value of allotted shares that are paid up, called but unpaid, and any shares that are to be paid at a future specified date as set out, for example, in the articles.[14] Allotted share capital that is unpaid and not payable on any specified date is uncalled share capital.[15] Importantly, however, although the Act requires that a meeting be called in this event it does not require that any steps be taken to address the situation.

Questions

1. Even the proponents of minimum capital rules think they make more sense for smaller companies than larger ones. Does it make any sense, therefore, to have minimum capital rules for public companies but none for private companies?

2. Is £50,000 of equity capital significant for most public companies/most creditors?

3. Should listed companies be subject to separate and higher minimum capital amounts?

4. Why do you think the UK legislature elected to introduce a higher minimum amount than is actually required under EU law?

III DISTRIBUTIONS

1 Approaches to distribution regulation

Returning to the Bob's Electronics case study (set forth in *Hypothetical A*), assume that following the initial investment of £300,000 (£150,000 of equity capital invested by several shareholders and £150,000 of bank finance) the business is a great success, exceeding the *best case scenario's* projections. In fact the business generates £77,500 of **net profits** in year one after having paid principal and interest payments of £22,500. The question for the company is what should it do with these funds. It could reinvest them or return them to the shareholders. A return of these funds to the shareholders could take place in one of two ways: through a dividend or through a repurchase of shares (a share buy-back). A dividend is simply a distribution of value to shareholders for each share they hold. It is best understood as an interim payment on the shareholder's residual financial claim.

One might ask why a company should make or should be able to make a payment to its shareholders? Why are the funds simply not reinvested in the business? The first part of the answer to this question is that many shareholders require liquidity. For smaller companies dividends may be a mechanism of providing funds to shareholders who are in need of personal liquidity to fund their personal activities. However, liquidity may also be important for shareholders in larger companies, for example, **institutional shareholders** of listed companies such as pension funds or insurance companies, who may need cash to pay pension liabilities or insurance claims and would prefer not to sell the shares to generate those funds. If successful companies were not allowed to pay dividends and provide their shareholders with some liquidity, investing in companies would be far less

---

[14] Section 547 Companies Act 2006.   [15] *Ibid*.

attractive for many investors and this would make it more difficult and more expensive for companies to raise equity finance. A second reason to allow companies to make dividends is that the company itself may not have investment opportunities available to it that would allow it to make an adequate return from the excess cash and shareholders would prefer to invest the cash themselves rather than have the company do it on their behalf. If companies were not able to make a distribution of these funds to shareholders this could result in an inefficient use of wealth as the company invested the funds in projects that do not generate as much wealth as the projects which the shareholders would have funded if they had received the funds though a dividend.

The mechanics for issuing dividends are set out in a company's constitution. Article 70 of the *Model Articles of Association for Public Companies* provides, for example, that the company may declare a dividend by ordinary resolution *if* the board of directors have recommended that a dividend in that amount be paid. Under these articles, the shareholders in general meeting are not specifically empowered to require that the directors issue a dividend.[16] However, if a dividend is declared a debt in favour of the shareholders is created which they can enforce.[17] Article 70 also empowers the board of directors to issue interim dividends. Importantly, a dividend can be made in cash or can be made in kind, which includes the distribution of shares or other securities.[18] Bob's Electronics, for example, could in theory dividend a delivery van to Bob.

There are, therefore, good economic reasons to permit companies to make distributions to shareholders. However, from the creditors' perspective the ability of the company to make distributions to shareholders increases the risk associated with the credit provided to the company because distributions reduce the assets available to satisfy the creditors. To see this consider the following simple examples.

Example 1

If Bob's Electronics Ltd generates £100,000 of cash each year and has principal and interest payments of £90,000 each year, and invests the excess £10,000 in US treasury stock each year, then although from a cashflow perspective the bank loan appears relatively risky, each year that risk declines as the company's assets, available to repay the loan if the company's fortunes decline, increase. If after three years Bob's Electronics Ltd sells its £30,000 of treasury stocks and makes a cash dividend to the shareholders of the proceeds of sale, the risk that the bank loan will not be repaid in full increases.

Example 2

Bob forms Bob's Electronics Ltd and pays £100,000 for 10 shares. Bank A lends Bob £200,000 to invest in the Bob's Electronics project. Bob's Electronics Ltd has one bank account in which there is a balance of £300,000. Bob's Electronics Ltd's **balance sheet** records assets of £300,000 (the cash in the bank), a liability of £200,000 and shareholder equity of £100,000. However, prior to commencing the project, Bob, as director and manager, decides the project requires less initial finance than initially calculated and pays a dividend out to himself, as sole shareholder, of £50,000. From the bank's

---

[16] The shareholders in a company with Model Articles could instruct the board to declare a legal dividend pursuant to the general instruction right set out in article 4 of the Model Articles. See further Chapter 6.

[17] *Bond v Barrowhaematite Steel Company* [1902] 1 Ch 353; *Re Accrington Corporation Steam Tramways Company* [1909] 2 Ch 40.

[18] See, for example, article 76 of the Model Articles for Public Companies.

perspective the project which will generate the funds to repay the bank was a £300,000 project funded one-third by equity and two-thirds by debt. Now it is a £250,000 project funded 20% by equity and 80% by debt. This represents a substantial deterioration in the credit risk associated with the loan.

Regulation could, with the intention of protecting creditors, prohibit any distribution. One would have to ask, however, which creditors this would really protect? If voluntary adjusting creditors valued such protection they could insist contractually upon such a prohibition to prevent the distribution in either Example 1 or 2. Alternatively, in the absence of such a prohibition adjusting creditors could alter their required rate of interest to take account of the possibility of a distribution which detrimentally affected their position. To the extent that restrictions on distributions were negotiated for by adjusting creditors, other non-adjusting creditors may be able to free ride on these protections: that is, they obtain the benefits of the protections without having to negotiate for them. However, as Eidenmueller et al argue in the above extract on minimum capital regulation, the contractual protections negotiated for by adjusting creditors, for example personal guarantees, may not necessarily provide benefits for the non-adjusting creditors. It is clear, however, that a mandatory distribution prohibition imposed by law would provide protection for non-adjusting creditors who are incapable of insisting upon such contractual protections.

If one acknowledges that restrictions on distributions may provide some degree of creditor protection but at the same time one acknowledges that being able to make distributions provides demonstrable benefits to companies and investors, how should distribution regulation strike the appropriate balance between the interests of the company, shareholders and creditors, in particular non-adjusting creditors? Before looking in detail at how UK company law regulates distributions, let us consider the regulatory strategies available to strike this balance.

- *Distributions from surplus calculated by accounting formulae.* This regulatory strategy enables companies to make distributions provided that their activities have generated surplus or profit over a specified time period. There is no formal role for directors' discretion in determining this surplus, only in deciding whether or not to distribute all or any of the surplus. This available surplus is calculated through an accounting formula. Through this approach company law uses both accounting terms such as profits, assets or liabilities as well as legally defined terms such as 'share capital' and 'share premium' to determine when a distribution can be made. The accounting numbers that are inputted into the formula to determine available surplus are taken from the company's financial statements. This approach, therefore, results in the indirect incorporation into the distribution test of the accounting standards[19] that determine how a company should record the results of its activities: the profits that it generates; the liabilities that it incurs. Through this approach the applicable accounting standards become central to whether or not a company can make a dividend.

- *Board reliance and liability strategy.* This regulatory strategy relies upon the board of directors to balance the creditors' interest in ensuring that their debts are repaid in full with the interests of companies and their shareholders in being able to make a distribution. It does so by requiring that in order to make a distribution the directors certify that the company will be able to pay its debts when they arise for a specified period of time following the distribution: a solvency certification. As the interests of directors are more likely to be aligned with those of shareholders—as

[19] On accounting standards see Web Chapter A.

they may be substantial shareholders themselves and their job tenure depends on shareholder approval—this strategy typically imposes liability on directors for a negligent and inaccurate certification.

- *Third-party approval strategy.* This regulatory strategy relies upon an independent third party to ensure that creditor interests are protected. This strategy accepts the core premise of the *board reliance and liability strategy* that the important question, from the creditor's perspective, is whether the company will be able to continue to pay its debts following the distribution. However, this strategy is less trusting of potentially conflicted directors to make this decision. This strategy could involve, for example, the requirement to obtain court approval to make a distribution that would be granted where the court is satisfied that creditors' interests are not detrimentally affected by the distribution. Alternatively, this strategy could involve a requirement that an independent third party, for example the company's auditor, certify that the company will be able to pay its debts for a specified period of time following the distribution.

2 UK distribution regulation prior to 1980

As we have seen, the mechanics of how to make a dividend are set out in a company's articles of association. Regulation of the extent to which a company can make a distribution is currently today set out in Part 23 of the 2006 Act. Prior to the enactment of the Companies Act 1980, distribution regulation was left to the common law. The impetus to codify distribution regulation was provided by the European Union's Second Directive. However, as we shall see, the UK legislature went further than was required by the directive by providing statutory distribution regulation for private as well as public companies. Before analysing the current statutory provisions we will consider the pre-1980 common law position.

The pre-1980 distribution rules developed by case law is generally viewed as being both confusing and very light of touch.[20] It is, however, from the perspective of a student of company law, interesting in several respects, and thoughtful consideration of the approaches taken by the courts prior to 1980 enables us to have a better understanding of how contemporary distribution regulation functions as well as of the current reform debate. Commentators divide the pre-1980 cases into two periods, pre- and post-1889.[21] The extracts from *Flitcroft's Case* and *Lee v Neuchatel* that follow are the exemplary cases from both periods.

■ *In re Exchange Banking Company (Flitcroft's Case)* (1882) LR 21 Ch D 519

Jessel MR
The facts are these. The directors had for several years been in the habit of laying before the meetings of shareholders reports and balance-sheets which were substantially untrue, inasmuch as they included among the assets as good debts a number of debts which they knew to be bad. They thus made it appear that the business had produced profits when in fact it had produced none. The meetings acting on these reports declared dividends which the directors paid…

A limited company by its memorandum of association declares that its capital is to be applied for the purposes of the business. It cannot reduce its capital except in the manner and with the safeguards provided by statute, and looking at [the Act], it clearly is against the intention of the

---

[20] For a more detailed consideration of the early cases see D. Kershaw, 'The Decline of Legal Capital: An Exploration of the Consequences of Board Solvency Based Capital Reductions' in A. Reisberg and D. Prentice (eds), *Corporate Finance in the UK and US* (OUP, 2011).

[21] See B. Yamey, 'Aspects of the Law Relating to Company Dividends' (1941) *Modern Law Review* 273.

Legislature that any portion of the capital should be returned to the shareholders without the statutory conditions being complied with. A limited company cannot in any other way make a return of capital, the sanction of a general meeting can give no validity to such a proceeding, and even the sanction of every shareholder cannot bring within the powers of the company an act which is not within its powers. If, therefore, the shareholders had all been present at the meetings, and had all known the facts, and had all concurred in declaring the dividends, the payment of the dividends would not be effectually sanctioned. One reason is this—there is a statement that the capital shall be applied for the purposes of the business, and on the faith of that statement, which is sometimes said to be an implied contract with creditors, people dealing with the company give it credit. The creditor has no debtor but that impalpable thing the corporation, which has no property except the assets of the business. The creditor, therefore, I may say, gives credit to that capital, gives credit to the company on the faith of the representation that the capital shall be applied only for the purposes of the business, and he has therefore a right to say that the corporation shall keep its capital and not return it to the shareholders, though it may be a right which he cannot enforce otherwise than by a winding-up order. It follows then that if directors who are *quasi* trustees for the company improperly pay away the assets to the shareholders, they are liable to replace them…The order of the Vice-Chancellor will therefore be affirmed, but with this variation, that the directors in each case are to be declared jointly and severally liable and not only jointly liable.

There are two organizing tenets of Jessel MR's judgment. First, pursuant to the Companies Act 1862, which was applicable to this case, the capital invested by the company could not be returned to the shareholders. Importantly, under the Companies Act 1862 'capital' (or *legal capital*, as we shall refer to it) was only the aggregate nominal amount of the issued shares[22] rather than, as is the case under the 2006 Act, the aggregate share capital and the share premium. Secondly, dividends should be paid out of profits. Here the directors prepared accounts which overstated the profits because certain amounts due from third parties were unlikely to be paid (they were 'bad debts'). Let us consider how, from an accounting perspective, the dividends issued here would amount to a reduction of capital.

Worked Example A

Assume, for simplicity's sake, that the nominal value of the shares of the Exchange Banking Company was £10 and that the shareholders had purchased 100 shares for £10 each so the legal capital (referred to in the case as capital) of the company was £1,000. Assume also that all of these funds were invested in the company's projects. The company also has a loan of £1,000. The balance sheet recording assets, liabilities and shareholder equity would be as follows. Shareholder equity represents both the initial amount invested but also, as the company progresses, any losses incurred by the company and any profits made that are not distributed to the shareholders. At time *T1* when the debt and equity have been invested but trading has not commenced the balance sheet will be as follows:

Assets:	£2,000
Liabilities:	£1,000
Net assets:	£1,000
Shareholder equity:	£1,000

---

[22] There is some uncertainty as to what the courts meant by reference to capital. The better position, it is submitted, is that it was nominal issued share capital not nominal paid-up share capital: see Cotton and Lopes LJJ's judgments in *Lee v Neuchatel* (1889) LR 41 Ch D 1.

As this is a balance sheet necessarily Assets = Liabilities plus Shareholder equity. This equation could be represented as follows, which makes more sense of the 'accounting speak' that refers to 'both sides' of a balance sheet:

Assets	Liabilities
£2,000	£1,000
	Shareholder equity
	£1,000

Assume that, according to the balance sheet prepared by the directors of the Exchange Banking Company, the company had earned income in the amount of £1,000 and had expenses of £500 making a profit of £500. In the absence of a dividend this £500 of profit will have two effects on the balance sheet. First, there is a £500 increase in the Exchange Banking Company's assets and, second, a £500 increase in shareholder equity resulting in assets of £2,500 and liabilities plus shareholder equity of £2,500. If a dividend is then made of £500 both sides of the balance sheet return to £2,000, as assets are reduced by the payment of £500 and shareholder equity is reduced to £1,000.

In Web Chapter A we discuss how accrual accounting records income at the time the transaction is entered into, which may differ from the time when the actual payment is made. In this case Exchange Banking Company recorded an increase in income, and in assets, arising from transactions that created bad debts; that is although there was a transaction there was little likelihood that the amounts owed to the company under that transaction would be paid. In fact if the accounts had been correct the income that the company recorded and the company's assets would have been much lower. Let us assume it would only have been £600 resulting in a profit of £100. In the absence of any distribution the two sides of the balance sheet would have recorded £2,100. However, if a distribution is made on the basis of the false and inflated profit amount of £500, this means *in fact* that real assets are now £1,600 (£2,100 – £500) and shareholder equity should be recorded as £600 (£1,100 – £ 500). The effect, therefore, of making the dividend based on an inaccurate profit and loss account and balance sheet is to reduce the actual shareholder equity entry below the legal capital benchmark of £1,000 as a result of a payment to shareholders. *This is what is meant by a return of capital*. It is, of course, *not* the return of original equity funds or assets purchased with those funds.

How does the rule set out in *Flitcroft's Case* benefit creditors? For Jessel MR, a creditor is entitled to assume that monies invested by shareholders will be invested in the business and not returned to them. This obligation extends beyond the actual funds received by the company in exchange for issued shares which are expected to be used to purchase assets for the business, but also to the return of assets generated by the original investment that, *in accounting terms*, would amount to the shareholders' value stake in the business falling below the original legal capital threshold. In *Worked Example A* this clearly amounts to a benefit for all creditors. Where the profits are only £100 then the company cannot pay a £500 dividend to the shareholders even if the company has £500 of unutilized cash in the bank. It is a benefit for two reasons: first, it increases the asset base of the company, thereby decreasing the risk of insolvency and increasing the assets available to creditors if the company were to be wound up; and, secondly, by forcing shareholders to maintain a larger asset position in the company than they would have had if a larger dividend had been made, their incentives to expropriate value from creditors (financial agency costs) decreases.[23]

The extent to which a rule preventing the return of legal capital to shareholders provides protection to creditors varies according to how much the shareholders decide to invest in the company—the extent to which the business is funded by equity rather than debt—and the extent to which the equity investment is classified as legal capital. As noted previously, *at the time* of *Flitcroft's Case* the legal capital amount that could not be returned to shareholders was only what we refer to today as the company's 'share capital', that is the aggregate nominal value of the issued shares. In *Worked Example A*, if the company had decided instead to have nominal value shares of £1 and pay £10 for each share (that is, a £9 per share premium) then the dividend could have been made regardless of the fact that the profits were less than the dividend, because the £9 of share premium would not have been classified as legal capital and could be returned to shareholders.

■ *Lee v Neuchatel Asphalte Company* (1889) LR 41 Ch D 1

In this case the court was asked to decide whether the respondent company, a mining company, could pay a dividend when the profits from which the dividends were paid did not take account of the fact that the company's main asset, the mine, was declining in value as its mineral reserves were mined.

> #### Lindley LJ
> This company was formed in 1873, and…was formed for the purpose of working a concession, which may be called a lease, of some asphalt mines or mineral property in Switzerland. The original lease was afterwards extended, and the company may be treated as having been formed for the purpose of acquiring a lease which will run out in 1907. It is obvious with respect to such property, as with respect to various other properties of a like kind, mines and quarries and so on, every ton of stuff which you get out of that which you have bought with your capital may, from one point of view, be considered as embodying and containing a small portion of your capital, and that if you sell it and divide the proceeds you divide some portion of that which you have spent your capital in acquiring. It may be represented that that is a return of capital. All I can say is, if that is a return of capital it appears to me not to be such a return of capital as is prohibited by law.
>
> In order to make this out it is necessary to look through the Companies Acts. I have done so, and that not for the first time, and I cannot find any provision in the Acts which prohibits anything of the kind. The sections referring expressly to capital are very few. The two most important are the 8th and the 12th sections of the Act of 1862. The 8th section says that, when a company is registered as a company limited by shares, the memorandum of association must state the amount of capital with which the company proposes to be registered, divided into shares of a certain fixed amount. Then the 12th section says that the capital so referred to in the memorandum may be increased or converted into stock, but the conditions contained in the memorandum shall not be otherwise altered. That prohibits what is called a reduction of capital. Then under sect. 26, certain returns[24] are to be made, and in the returns so to be made must be specified among other things the amount of the capital and the number of shares into which it is divided, and the number of shares which have been issued and the number which have been forfeited, and the amount of calls made on each share and the total amount of calls received. In sects. 28 and 34 there is further provision that any alterations made in the capital pursuant to

---

[23] On expropriating value from creditors by changing the risk profile of the company see Chapter 18.

[24] 'Returns' here refers to providing information to the Companies Registrar. Today, for example, we still refer to the 'annual return' (see further Web Chapter A).

the Act are to be notified to the Registrar. Then in the Act of 1867 provision is made for reducing the capital, and that was amended in 1877 by being applied to a reduction of capital when part of the capital was lost.

What I have stated is the whole of the enactments relating to capital which are to be found in the Companies Acts. If you look further you find next to nothing about profits or dividends. There is nothing at all in the Acts about how dividends are to be paid, nor how profits are to be reckoned; all that is left, and very judiciously and properly left, to the commercial world. It is not a subject for an Act of Parliament to say how accounts are to be kept; what is to be put into a capital account, what into an income account, is left to men of business...

We are dealing with a lease for a limited number of years, which is a wasting property, and while it is wasting the capital spent in acquiring it is wasting. The [articles say] in so many words that although in every year the capital may be wasted by working out the mine so that at the end there may be nothing left, yet this company is formed on the principle that it shall not be obliged to replace year by year that which is so wasted. [The claimant] says that is contrary to law. Let us see whether that is made out.

Having stated shortly what are the provisions of the Acts of Parliament relating to this matter, I may safely say that the Companies Acts do not require the capital to be made up if lost. They contain no provision of the kind. There is not even any provision that if the capital is lost the company shall be wound up, and I think this omission is quite reasonable. The capital may be lost and yet the company may be a very thriving concern. As I pointed out in the course of the argument, and I repeat now, suppose a company is formed to start a daily newspaper; supposing it sinks £250,000 before the receipts[25] from sales and advertisements equal the current expenses, and supposing it then goes on, is it to be said that the company must come to a stop, or that it cannot divide profits until it has replaced its £250,000, which has been sunk in building up a property which if put up for sale would perhaps not yield £10,000? That is a business matter left to business men. If they think their prospects of success are considerable, so long as they pay their creditors, there is no reason why they should not go on and divide profits, so far as I can see, although every shilling of the capital may be lost...

Having shewn from the Acts (negatively, of course, because this is a negative proposition, and can only be proved by looking through the Acts) that the Acts do not require the capital to be made up if lost, I cannot find anything in them which precludes payment of dividends so long as the assets are of less value than the original capital. If they are so, it becomes a question of prudence for mercantile men whether they will wind up or not. I have already pointed out that the Act says nothing to make the loss of the capital a ground for winding up, and I have already pointed out that it says nothing about profits. The Act does not say that dividends are not to be paid out of capital, but there are general principles of law according to which the capital of a company can only be applied for the purposes mentioned in the memorandum of association. That is a fundamental principle of law, and if any of those purposes are expressly or impliedly forbidden by the statutes, the capital cannot be applied for those purposes even though there may be a clause in the memorandum that it shall...

Now we come to consider how the Companies Act is to be applied to the case of a wasting property. If a company is formed to acquire and work a property of a wasting nature, for example, a mine, a quarry, or a patent, the capital expended in acquiring the property may be regarded as sunk and gone, and if the company retains assets sufficient to pay its debts, it appears to me that there is nothing whatever in the Act to prevent any excess of money obtained by working the property over the cost of working it, from being divided amongst the shareholders, and this in my opinion is true, although some portion of the property itself is sold, and in some sense the capital is thereby diminished. If it is said that such a course involves payment of dividend out of capital, the answer is that the Act nowhere forbids such a payment as is here supposed...

---

[25] 'Receipts' are income from sales.

> If the working expenses exceed the current gains, you cannot divide your capital under the head of profits when there are no profits in any sense of the term, as was done, for example, in *Rance's Case*,[26] *In re Oxford Benefit Building and Investment Society*,[27] and *Leeds Estate, Building and Investment Company v. Shepherd*.[28] If those cases are studied, it would be seen, I think, with sufficient clearness that that is really what is meant. You must not have fictitious accounts. If your earnings are less than your current expenses, you must not cook your accounts so as to make it appear that you are earning a profit…
>
> As regards the mode of keeping accounts, there is no law prescribing how they shall be kept. There is nothing in the Acts to shew what is to go to capital account or what is to go to revenue account. We know perfectly well that business men very often differ in opinion about such things. It does not matter to the creditor out of what fund he gets paid, whether he gets paid out of capital or out of profit net or gross. All he cares about is that there is money to pay him with, and it is a mere matter of bookkeeping and internal arrangement out of what particular fund he shall be paid. Therefore you cannot say that the question of what ought to go into capital or revenue account is a matter that concerns the creditor…
>
> I hope I am not inadvertently, certainly I am not intentionally, laying down any rule which would lead people to do anything dishonest either to shareholders or creditors.

Lindley LJ's judgment makes it clear that dividends must be paid out of profits and that the accounts which set out the company's profits must not be 'fictitious'. This basic proposition is consistent with Jessel MR's holding in *Flitcroft's Case*. The difficulty arises in determining how one should calculate profits and the impact upon legal capital of the different available approaches to the calculation of profit. This case involves what is referred to as 'wasting asset'. It is easy to understand how a mine is a wasting asset. If the mine contains one million tons of coal then every time a ton of coal is mined the value of the mine, assuming it has no other available use, declines. Many other asset types are wasting assets: in the case study, Bob's Electronics Ltd's delivery vans depreciate in value the older they get and the more they are driven; the buildings where the computers are built may function well for building today's computers, but be obsolete for the computers of the next decade. The question for the Court of Appeal in *Lee v Neuchatel Asphalte* was whether the depreciation in value through the use (or the wasting) of the mining asset should be taken into account in calculating profit. The Court of Appeal held that it did not. Whereas the expenses of carrying out business did need to be taken into account, the depreciation of the mine did not. Lindley LJ recognized, however, that the effect of this 'may be represented…[as] a return of capital'. To understand this consider the following example.

Worked Example B

Assume Neuchatel Asphalte Company has £2,000 of assets funded by £1,000 of debt from a bank loan and £1,000 of equity. The bank debt is to be repaid in one instalment in 10 years' time plus an annual interest payment. The £1,000 is represented by 100 £10 shares. With these funds the company purchased the mining concession for £1,000 and purchased mining equipment for £1,000. The mine is estimated to have 1,000 tons of coal.

In Year 1 the mine sells 100 tons of coal for £500. Assume that this £500 was paid for in cash and that all expenses are paid from the cash generated in Year 1. In Year 1 expenses such as wages and utility bills amount to £100. If these are the only expenses

[26] (1870) Law Rep 6 Ch 104.   [27] (1886) 35 Ch D 502.   [28] (1887) 36 Ch D 787.

that are taken account of then profit is £400. One could present the balance sheet after Year 1 and prior to any dividend as follows:

Assets	Liabilities
£2,400	£1,000
(£2,000 + £400 cash)	
	Shareholder equity
	£1,400
	(£1,000 + £400)

Following *Lee v Neuchatel Asphalte* a dividend of £400 could be paid to shareholders, which would reduce asset value to £2,000 and shareholders equity to £1,000. The problem here, of course, is the fact that although the value of the mine is still represented in the accounts at £2,000, in fact (assuming market conditions for mines remain unaltered) it has declined in value because 100 of the mine's 1,000 tons of coal have been mined and sold; that is, its value has declined by 1/10th. Accountants at the time of *Lee v Neuchatel*, as they do today, typically took account of this decline in value by providing for a depreciation entry in the accounts.[29] If depreciation was taken into account then the loss of 1/10th in value (£100) would be treated as an expense in the profit and loss account (for simplicity's sake we ignore here depreciation on the equipment). Profits would then only have been £300. In this situation the balance sheet prior to any dividend would be as follows:

Assets	Liabilities
£2,300	£1,000
(£2,000 + £400 cash less £100 depreciation)	
	Shareholder equity
	£1,300
	(£1,000 + £300)

If the company ignores depreciation in calculating the profit and pays out £400 as a dividend the effect is, as compared to the second of the above balance sheets, to reduce shareholder equity to £900 (£100 below the legal capital entry of £1,000): the shareholder equity is £1,300 when one takes account of depreciation and, therefore, £900 following the payment of a £400 dividend. This is why the payment 'may be represented...[as] a return of capital'.

You can also see from this example that if one is required to take account of depreciation in the calculation of profits for the purposes of determining the available dividend this results in retaining additional assets in the company.

Lindley LJ holds that depreciation does not have to be taken account of for the purposes of the dividend calculation. This is the case even though at the time of the judgment it was common accounting practice to do so.[30] What appears to be an accounting

[29] For a more detailed discussion of depreciation see Web Chapter A.
[30] See B. Yamey, 'Aspects of the Law Relating to Company Dividends' (1941) *Modern Law Review* 273.

rules-based strategy in Lindley LJ's hands actually becomes a board reliance strategy as a result of the considerable accounting discretion he is willing to give the board of directors. He holds that 'it is not a subject for an Act of Parliament to say how accounts are to be kept; what is to be put into a capital account, what into an income account, *is left to men of business*'. Indeed he seems to view the determination of whether a dividend should be made as a matter on which neither the courts nor the legislature are qualified to opine; rather it should be left to 'men of business'. However, as we have seen, the selection of accounting policies has implications for creditor protection. In allowing a dividend to be issued according to a profit calculation that did not take account of depreciation, was Lindley LJ sacrificing the interests of creditors at the altar of the principle of non-interference in business matters?[31] Basil Yamey, in an excellent summary of the law prior to 1941, argued thus.[32] However, creditor protection remains a concern in Lindley LJ's judgment. Dividends could be made to the extent to which their payment did not impinge on the ability of the company to pay its debts. He holds that if *men of business* 'think their prospects of success are considerable, *so long as they pay their creditors*, there is no reason why they should not go on and divide profits, so far as I can see, although every shilling of the capital may be lost'. Indeed he goes so far as to suggest that the accounting niceties of dividend calculation are irrelevant to creditors as all they care about is whether they are going to get paid. As we shall see, Lindley LJ's analysis and approach arguably has much in common with the contemporary reform proposals.

Subsequent judgments, some of them from Lindley LJ, reaffirmed the approach taken in *Lee v Neuchatel*. In *Verner v General and Commercial Investment Trust*,[33] Lindley LJ held that 'lost capital did not have to be made good before dividends could be paid'. In this case a dividend was deemed payable because although the value of the company's assets (investments in securities) had declined substantially dividend payments from those investments were still generating income for the company. In *Ammonia Soda Co v Chamberlain*,[34] it was affirmed that a dividend could be made out of current year profits even when the company had suffered losses in previous years that exceeded the profits made in the current year. In *Lubbock v British Bank of South America*,[35] it was affirmed that a dividend could be paid out of an upward revaluation of company assets. Not in all cases, however, was Lindley LJ's general concern for creditors heeded. In *Lawrence v West Somerset Mineral Railway Company*[36] bondholders attempted to prevent the payment of a dividend in a company that had a finite income stream under a fixed-term contract. Although the payment of the dividend would clearly leave inadequate funds to repay creditors following the termination of the contract, as there were current profits the court approved the dividend.

In these cases one sees the courts attempting to grapple with the interrelationship between legal standards and accounting terminology and practices. These early cases dating from the late nineteenth century considered this interaction between law and accounting at a time when there were no generally applicable accounting standards[37] only the practices of the business and accounting communities. In the UK the long process towards creating generally applicable accounting standards did not really commence until the 1970s.[38] This absence of generally accepted accounting regulation enabled the courts in the pre-1980 cases to be more deferential to directors' determinations of the appropriate dividend payment.

---

[31] In a later judgment, *In re National Bank of Wales* (1899) 2 Ch 629, Lindley LJ held 'it may be safely said that what losses can properly be charged to capital, and what to income, is a matter for business men to determine'.

[32] Note 30.   [33] [1894] 2 Ch 239.   [34] [1918] 1 Ch 286.

[35] [1892] 2 Ch 198.   [36] (1918) 2 Ch 250.

[37] On accounting standards and UK GAAP see Web Chapter A.

[38] The standards issued by the Institute for Chartered Accountants in England and Wales's Accounting Standards Steering Committee which in 1976 became the Accounting Standards Committee.

3 Distribution regulation under the Companies Act 2006

Reform of common law distribution regulation was both required and encouraged by the European Union's Second Directive on Company Law.[39] 'Required' because the Second Directive provided directly for distribution regulation for public companies, and 'encouraged' as the Government at the time took the opportunity to reform the rules applicable to both private and public companies.

The preamble to the Second Directive provides 'that provisions should be adopted for maintaining the capital, which constitutes the creditor's security, in particular by prohibiting any reduction thereof by distribution to shareholders where the latter are not entitled to it'. The directive adopts a position on the relationship between capital maintenance and creditor protection similar to the position taken by Jessel MR in *Re Flitcroft's Case*. What is to be maintained, of course, is not the original capital investment which is invested in the purchase of assets to run the business, but rather the legal capital accounting entry. In the Second Directive the legal capital to be maintained is referred to as 'subscribed capital'. It is, however, unclear from the directive whether subscribed capital represents what is actually agreed to be paid for the shares (that is, aggregate share capital and share premium) or only aggregate share capital (the aggregate nominal value of the shares). In the UK we have adopted the former broader understanding but several EU jurisdictions, for example Spain and Italy, in implementing the Directive have taken the latter position and maintain only aggregate nominal capital (this, remember, was the position of the pre-1889 English law).[40]

Article 15 of the Directive provides for distribution regulation as follows:

1. (a) Except for cases of reductions of subscribed capital, no distribution to shareholders may be made when on the closing date of the last financial year the net assets as set out in the company's annual accounts are, or following such a distribution would become, lower than the amount of the subscribed capital plus those reserves which may not be distributed under the law or the statutes.

   (b) Where the uncalled part of the subscribed capital is not included in the assets shown in the balance sheet, this amount shall be deducted from the amount of subscribed capital referred to in paragraph (a).

   (c) The amount of a distribution to shareholders may not exceed the amount of the profits at the end of the last financial year plus any profits brought forward and sums drawn from reserves available for this purpose, less any losses brought forward and sums placed to reserve in accordance with the law or the statutes.

   ...

The distribution requirements of the Second Directive were first implemented by the Companies Act 1980. Today Part 23 of the Companies Act 2006 provides for the regulation of distributions for UK companies. Distributions are defined in section 829 to mean any 'distribution of a company's assets to its members, whether in cash or otherwise'. This includes, most importantly, dividends but also any share repurchase. Section 829 exempts from this definition any payment or reduction of liability through a reduction of capital or redemption of repurchase of shares out of capital (which we will examine in section IV of this chapter), as well as the issue of bonus shares[41] (which involves the issue of fully paid-up shares to existing members), and any payments to members during the course of the company's winding up.

---

[39] Second Council Directive of 13 December 1976 (77/91/EEC).
[40] J. Rickford et al, 'Reforming Capital' (2004) *European Business Law Review* 921, n 57. Rickford et al also observe that the view that a share premium does not fall within the meaning of 'subscribed capital' is shared by the European Commission.
[41] See note 42.

3.1 The accumulated profits test

Pursuant to section 830 of the 2006 Act public and private companies can only make a dividend *out of* profits available for distribution.

■ Section 830(2) CA 2006

A company's profits available for distribution are its accumulated, realised profits, so far as not previously utilised by distribution or capitalisation, less its accumulated, realised losses, so far as not previously written off in a reduction or reorganisation of capital duly made.

We shall refer to this test as the accumulated profits test. To determine whether, and the extent to which, a company can make a dividend, the company must first accumulate all its prior 'realized profits' and deduct from those profits any previous distributions that it has made or profits which it has capitalized.[42] From this accumulated profit number the company must then deduct all its accumulated realized losses as adjusted to take account of any write-offs of its liabilities resulting from a capital reduction (see section IV of this chapter). If this accumulated realized profits figure exceeds the accumulated losses figure then the company may issue a dividend to the extent of the excess. For example, if Bob's Electronics Ltd makes a profit in Year 1 of £50 it may pay a dividend of up to £50 at the end of Year 1. In fact it pays a dividend of £30. In Year 2 it makes a loss of £100 and in Year 3 a profit of £110. After Year 3 its accumulated realized profits are £50 + £110; however, it paid a dividend in Year 1 of £30. Its accumulated losses are £100. Accordingly, it can pay a dividend after year 3 of £30 ((50 − 30) + 110 − 100 = 30).

Under the pre-1980 position, set out in section III.2, the common law provided that distributions could only be made out of 'profits' but deferred to 'men of business' in the determination of what amounted to 'profits'. This, as we saw in *Lee v Neuchatel*, involved accepting the board's determination that depreciation of fixed assets did not need to be taken into account when calculating profit even when accounting practice of this period typically provided for depreciation. The Act reverses this deference. Pursuant to section 853(4) realized profits and losses are to be determined by the application of accounting principles generally accepted at the time the accounts are prepared.

Pursuant to section 836 the 'realised profits' and 'realised losses' are taken from, or calculated by reference to,[43] the 'relevant accounts' which in most cases will be the accounts for the previous financial year.[44] Section 837(2) of the Act requires that the 'relevant accounts' be prepared in accordance with the Act. If the 'relevant accounts' are

---

[42] Capitalization could, for example, take place if the company issues a bonus issue of shares to existing shareholders. If this involves the issue of 100 £10 shares then funds must be provided to the legal capital account in the amount of £1,000. This can be done by capitalizing £1,000 of profit. The effect would be the same if the company paid a dividend of £1,000 and that £1,000 was then used to buy 100 £10 shares for £10 each.

[43] One might, perhaps reasonably, assume that the profit or loss figures in a company's relevant accounts would be the same as the 'realised' profit and loss figures. However, this is not necessarily the case. In some cases the actual profit or loss entries in a company's annual profit and loss statement will require adjustment to determine the profits that are 'realised profits' and losses that are 'realised losses' for the purposes of distribution regulation. This is a very complicated process on which there is guidance issued by the accounting body the Institute for Chartered Accountants in England and Wales, the detail of which need not concern us here (ICAEW, Technical Release: 7/03 *Guidance on the Determination of Realised Profits and Losses in the Context of Distributions Under the Companies Act 1985* (2003)). See further in this regard the very interesting, although now somewhat out-of-date, analysis in R.D. Morris, 'Distributable Profit in Britain Since 1980: A Critical Appraisal' (1991) 27 *Abacus* 15.

[44] The Act also provides for the reliance on 'interim accounts'—section 836(2) CA 2006.

not prepared in accordance with the Act, for example, if they do not present a true and fair view of the company's financial position in relation to matters that are 'material'[45] for the distribution,[46] then those accounts cannot be relied on for the purposes of making a distribution.[47] If a distribution is made on the basis of those accounts the whole of the distribution is unlawful. This is the case even if, had the 'relevant accounts' been properly prepared, a portion of the distribution could have been paid. The courts have been very strict in insisting upon compliance with all the requirements related to the preparation of 'relevant accounts'.[48]

3.2 The 'net assets' test

Section 831 of the Companies Act 2006 provides that in order to make a distribution *public* companies must, in addition to complying with section 830's accumulated net profits test, comply with a second test which is colloquially, and somewhat misleadingly, referred to as 'the net assets test'.

■ Section 831 CA 2006 Net Asset Restriction on distributions by public companies

(1) A public company may only make a distribution—

   (a) if the amount of its net assets is not less than the aggregate of its called-up share capital and undistributable reserves, and

   (b) if, and to the extent that, the distribution does not reduce the amount of those assets to less than that aggregate.

(2) For this purpose a company's 'net assets' means the aggregate of the company's assets less the aggregate of its liabilities...

(4) A company's undistributable reserves are–

   (a) its share premium account;

   (b) its capital redemption reserve;

   (c) the amount by which its accumulated, unrealised profits (so far as not previously utilised by capitalisation) exceed its accumulated unrealised losses (so far as not previously written off in a reduction or reorganisation of capital duly made);

   (d) any other reserve that the company is prohibited from distributing

      (i) by any enactment (other than one contained in this Part), or

      (ii) by its articles

      ...

The effect of this 'net assets' test is to prevent a public company from making a distribution if its net assets (that is the value of its assets *recorded in its accounts*, such as real property, delivery vans and unused components, minus the value of its liabilities

---

[45] The Act provides in effect that 'matters that are not material' for determining the distribution can be ignored for the purposes of this Part 23 of the Act. The term 'material' appears to be being used in the sense of 'relevant' to the determination but clearly it would also enable a court to ignore accounting errors which are relevant to the determination but *de-minimis*. No case to date has addressed the interpretation of this provision.

[46] Section 393 CA 2006 requiring that a company's financial statements (balance sheet and profit and loss account) present a true and fair view of the company's financial position. As discussed in Web Chapter A, the true and fair view requirement requires, *in effect*, compliance with the accounting standards issued by the ASB and, where applicable, the IASB.

[47] Section 836(4) CA 2006.   [48] See further section III.7

recorded in its accounts, such as bank debt or trade debt) exceed legal capital. For section 831, legal capital is the aggregate of a company's 'called-up share capital and undistributable reserves'. With some allowance for simplification, legal capital, for the purposes of the 'net assets' test, is the amount paid, or agreed to be paid, for the company's issued shares: aggregate share capital plus aggregate share premium. The category of undistributable reserves, again with some allowance for simplification, is the Companies Act's way of ensuring that this basic legal capital equation is maintained. With regard to this complexity note the following points:

- Called-up share capital is defined in section 547 of the 2006 Act and includes aggregate nominal paid-up share capital and unpaid nominal share capital that has been called or is due to be paid on a specified date.

- 'Undistributable reserves' are defined in section 831(4). Typically in everyday conversation when we refer to a reserve, such as oil reserves or reserves of energy, we refer to something real that we can draw on when we need it. The first point to grasp about 'undistributable reserves' is, therefore, that the word 'reserves' is not used in this real sense, rather it is purely an accounting reserve.

- Section 831(4)(a) includes in the definition of 'undistributable reserves' any share premium.

- Section 831(4)(b) addresses the complexities that arise if either redeemable shares are redeemed or if issued shares are repurchased by the company pursuant to Part 18 of the 2006 Act, which we considered in detail in Chapter 17. If shares are redeemed or repurchased out of profits available for distribution then, unless the shares are held as **treasury shares** in accordance with the Act,[49] the shares are cancelled and the company's share capital is reduced by the aggregate nominal value of the shares redeemed[50] or repurchased.[51] The effect of this is to reduce the share capital of the company creating additional scope to make a distribution than a creditor would have understood was possible prior to the buy-back or redemption. To close this limited scope for an effective reduction in legal capital, the Act requires that an amount equal to the aggregate nominal value of the shares repurchased and cancelled or redeemed is added to a *capital redemption reserve*[52] which is an undistributable reserve. The legal capital amount is thereby unaffected by the share buy-back or redemption. As the share premium account is unaltered by a redemption or repurchase there is no need to make a corresponding entry in the capital redemption reserve to take account of this.

- Section 831(4)(c) effectively ensures that this test tracks the accumulated realized profits test by excluding unrealized profits. To the extent that unrealized profits have boosted the asset entry in the company's accounts, this provision effectively eliminates them from the balance sheet by classifying them as an undistributable reserve.

3.3 Comparing the effects of the accumulated profits test and the net assets test

The accumulated profits and net assets tests perform the same function: they protect the legal capital entry in the accounts. The application of both tests typically have the same outcome as regards the extent to which a company can make a legal distribution. To see this, consider the following worked example. Note that in practice divergence between the results of these two tests will occur in companies with more complex asset structures subject to complex accounting standards.[53] This complexity will not concern us here.

---

[49] Chapter 6, Part 18 CA 2006. See further Chapter 17.   [50] Section 688(b) CA 2006.
[51] Section 706(b) CA 2006.   [52] Section 733 CA 2006.
[53] For example, IAS 39 Financial Instruments, *Recognition and Measurement* (IASB, 2008).

Worked Example C

....

Neuchatel Asphalte Company has £2,000 of assets funded by £1,000 of debt from a bank and £1,000 of shareholder equity. The bank debt is to be repaid in one instalment in 10 years' time plus an annual interest payment. The £1,000 is represented by 100 £10 shares. With the funds the company purchased the mining concession for £1,000 and purchased mining equipment for £1,000. The mine is estimated to have 1,000 tons of coal.

In Year 1 the mine sells 100 tons of coal for £500. Assume that this £500 was paid in cash and that all expenses are paid from the cash generated in Year 1. In Year 1 expenses such as wages and utility bills amount to £100. Following applicable accounting standards the mine and the equipment are depreciated on a straight line basis over their lifespan of 10 years, i.e. £200 a year.[54] Profit, therefore, is £500 less £100 of expenses and less £200 of depreciation. One could present the balance sheet after Year 1 and prior to any dividend as follows:

Assets	Liabilities
£2,200	£1,000
(£2,000 + £400 (cash) – £200 depreciation)	*Shareholder equity*
	£1,000 (share capital)
	£200 (retained profit)

Applying the accumulated profits test, assuming that all the profits are realized profits then the profits available for distribution are £200. Applying the net assets test we see that assets are £2,200, liabilities are £1,000 and share capital (in this example there is no share premium) is £1,000 leaving profits available for distribution in the amount of £200. We see that the reason they are the same is that the company's assets increase according to the cash that they received from their customers (these amounts are income in the profit and loss account) but decrease to take account of the depreciation in value of the mine.

4 Creditor protection through post-1980 distribution regulation

Distributions can be recommended by directors and approved by the general meeting only to the extent that, applying the applicable distribution rules, the distribution falls within the amount allowed by those rules. Directors are not, according to these rules, explicitly required separately to consider the interests of creditors when making the dividends. Nevertheless, these provisions are widely thought to have a creditor protection function. In this section we consider to what extent in fact these provisions protect creditors and, if so, which creditors do they protect? Professor Armour, in the extract that follows, argues that benefits provided by the distribution regulation only benefit adjusting creditors.

[54] Financial Reporting Standard 15, *Tangible Fixed Assets* (ASB, 1999) paras 77–102. See further Web Chapter A for a more detailed discussion of accounting for depreciation.

■ **J. Armour, 'Legal Capital: An Outdated Concept?' (2006) 7**
European Business Organisation Law Review **5**

> A restriction on the return of capital to shareholders can be understood as protecting creditors against the risk of opportunistic behaviour by the shareholders. Distributions to shareholders reduce a company's net assets, making it more exposed to the risk of default. Creditors' interests can be harmed even if the company does not actually become insolvent. Such a transfer will still decrease the **expected value** of their claims, whilst commensurately enhancing the combined value of shareholders' private wealth and their stake in the firm. A restriction on distributions can prevent this from happening.
>
> However, for non-adjusting creditors, a restriction on the return of capital to shareholders is by itself of little assistance. This is because, if creditors do not adjust, the optimal level of capitalisation by shareholders is zero. Thus it is a truism that those carrying on hazardous enterprises—which are likely to result in tort claims—have a tendency to structure their affairs using thinly-capitalised subsidiaries.
>
> A distribution restriction can, however, be understood as protecting adjusting creditors against the risk of opportunistic behaviour by the shareholders. If lenders' loans were priced on the basis of pre-existing levels of net assets, then a transfer of assets to shareholders will decrease the expected value of creditors' claims, whilst commensurately enhancing the combined value of shareholders' private wealth and their stake in the firm. Creditors' interests will be harmed even if the company does not actually become insolvent, because by reducing a company's net assets, distributions make it more exposed to the risk of default. A restriction on distributions can prevent this sort of wealth transfer from happening.

Professor Armour's logic is compelling: how can distribution rules protect non-adjusting creditors if under UK company law it is possible to form a private company with an amount of legal capital that is close to zero and a public company with an amount that is for many companies, given the size of their operations, insignificant: 'for non-adjusting creditors, a restriction on the return of capital to shareholders is of little assistance...if creditors do not adjust, the optimal level of capitalisation by shareholders is zero'. Put another way: how can these rules protect non-adjusting creditors if what they prevent being distributed could be insignificantly above zero? In this regard, consider the following worked example.

Worked Example D

On the formation of Mine Ltd, Ben subscribes for 10 £1 shares and pays £100 per share. The share capital of this company is £10 and its share premium £990. Ben is the sole director of Mine Ltd. Mine Ltd borrows £1,000 from the bank. With the £2,000 from equity and debt financing, Mine Ltd buys the right to mine coal in a small area of Yorkshire and the equipment required to mine the coal.

Following the purchase of the assets, but prior to commencing business, Ben decides that he is in need of funds to purchase a house for himself. He requires £500 and, as director of Mine Ltd, decides to sell all the mining equipment for a price of £500 and in place of that equipment the company will lease equipment which will cost Mine Ltd £40 a year. However, although he wishes to pay the £500 of sale proceeds to himself as a dividend, this is not possible as it amounts to an unlawful dividend pursuant to both the accumulated profits test and the 'net assets' test.

Consider the effects in this regard of an alternative finance structure for the company. Mine Ltd is a private company which means Ben could have chosen to form the company and provide it with £1,000 of funds by purchasing one share for £10 and then providing the remaining £990 in the form of a loan. This alternative way of providing the £1,000 to the company clearly does not increase the scope for the company to make a distribution to Ben—there is virtually no legal capital to prevent being returned. Here the distribution rules provide no protection for any creditor—there is effectively nothing to prevent being returned to shareholders.

However, this second financing structure provides much greater scope to return assets to Ben but *not* in his capacity as a *shareholder* but in his capacity as a *creditor*. If the terms of the loan to Mine Ltd from Ben were drafted carefully, for example if the loan is payable on demand by Ben, this could give Ben, as director, the scope to make the £500 payment to Ben, as creditor.

We see from this example that the distribution rules can provide *all creditors*, including non-adjusting creditors, with some protection. However, as this example shows us, the extent of the protection for non-adjusting creditors is a matter of good fortune. Here the good fortune was that when Mine Ltd was formed Ben decided to contribute £1,000 of equity capital rather then use the second financing structure.

The protection that these rules give adjusting creditors, however, is not a matter of good fortune. Adjusting creditors adjust the terms of the credit to take account of the company's legal capital. If legal capital is effectively zero then an adjusting creditor, such as a bank, will take this into account in determining whether to lend, the interest rate it will charge and the types of security over company assets or even shareholders' personal assets that it will require in order to make the loan. The greater the equity as a proportion of the overall finance for the company's business the lower the risk for the bank. The distribution rules ensure that the bank's assessment of risk is not altered once they have made the loan by preventing the company from opportunistically making a distribution to the shareholders if such a value transfer results in the reduction in the legal capital entry; an effective repayment of their original equity investment in the company as distinct from a return on their investment. In *Worked Example D*, if Ben funds the company through an equity investment of £1,000 the bank can take this and the effects of the distribution rules into account in deciding on its terms for its loan. Similarly, if Ben proposes to use the second financing structure the bank can take this risk into account by requiring a higher rate of interest, or insisting that no payment will be made to Ben under the loan until the bank has been fully repaid, or by taking a personal guarantee from Ben.

Having digested this argument, consider the following extract arguing that the relationship between the UK distribution rules and accounting regulation provides a degree of variable but tailored protection for non-adjusting involuntary creditors:

■ D. Kershaw, 'Involuntary Creditors and the Case for Accounting Based Distribution Regulation' (2009) 2 *Journal of Business Law* 140

If any amounts *actually or potentially* owed by the company to involuntary creditors either decreases net-assets or increases accumulated realised losses, the extent to which the company may make a distribution will be reduced by the amount of the relevant involuntary creditor liability or loss entry. Whether this affects the ability of the company to make the distribution it wishes to make will depend on the size of the liability or loss entry and the value of existing assets and accumulated realized profits.

Pursuant to UK generally accepted accounting principles (UK GAAP) and international accounting standards (IAS), a company's financial statements in both the balance sheet and through the profit and loss account must take account of potential as well as actual liabilities. Currently the probability that a liability will have to be paid in the future determines how it is accounted for in the financial statements. Under current UK *Financial Reporting Standards*, as well as the applicable *International Accounting Standards* and *International Financial Reporting Standards*,[55] the treatment of a potential liability depends on whether it is dealt with as a *provision* or as a *contingent liability*, where a liability that must be provisioned being more probable than a contingent liability. If a liability is treated as a provision then the liability is reported on the balance sheet and flows through the profit and loss account. If the liability is deemed a contingent liability it is not recorded on the balance sheet or in the profit and loss account, however, a note to the financial statements will disclose information about such potential liability. The distribution rules note generally that provisions are to be taken account of in determining the amount of any distribution and specifically that provisions are treated as liabilities for the purpose of the net-assets test and realised losses for the accumulated profits test.

The UK accounting standard on provisions and contingent liabilities is set out in Financial Reporting Standard 12, *Provisions, Contingent Liabilities and Contingent Assets*. FRS 12 mirrors International Accounting Standard 37, *Provisions, Contingent Liabilities and Contingent Assets* which is applicable to the consolidated accounts of UK listed companies. According to FRS 12, a provision, which is defined as 'a liability that is of uncertain timing and amount', must be recognised when: a company has a 'present obligation' arising from a 'past event'; it is more likely than not that 'economic benefits' must be transferred by the company to settle the obligation; and where a 'reliable estimate' of the amount of the obligation can be made.

A present obligation includes both legal and constructive obligations. Legal obligations include those arising from contract, legislation or operation of law. Constructive obligations may arise, amongst others, from a pattern of past practice or the creation of an expectation in third parties. An involuntary creditor such as a person injured by company products or activities, with a product liability or tort claim, would be owed a *legal obligation* for the purposes of FRS 12. Clearly, in many instances, whether or not a company is liable for such person's injuries may be the subject of dispute. Any legal claim made by such person may well be subject to a vigorous defence by the company. In such contentious circumstances could one say that a 'present obligation' is owed? FRS 12 addresses this issue directly by using the example of a law suit. In such circumstances a present obligation is owed where 'taking account of all available evidence, *it is more likely than not* that a present obligation exists at the balance sheet date' [emphasis added]. FRS 12 notes that 'available evidence' would include expert opinion regarding the likely outcome of the litigation. Accordingly, even where the company's litigation and public posture adamantly denies any responsibility to an involuntary creditor, as far as the company's financial statements are concerned accounting standards force the company to take a more impartial view of its potential liability exposure.

The above example postulates a specific involuntary creditor who makes a claim against the company which the company refutes. However, a *present obligation* may arise from the company's past activities even where a specific person has not made a claim or has not even been identified at the time the financial statements are issued. In this regard FRS 12 notes that 'it is not necessary, however, to know the identity of the party to whom the obligation is owed—indeed the obligation may be to the public at large'. Accordingly, providing all other conditions are satisfied, FRS 12 may force a company to take account of potential liabilities to involuntary creditors, even when those creditors themselves are not aware, at the time the financial statements are issued, that they have been injured or who is responsible for the injury. GlaxoSmithKline, for example, provisions for 'unasserted claims' in relation to products that have a 'history of claims'...

---

[55] The standards issued by the International Accounting Standards Board (IASB) are *International Financial Reporting Standards*. The IASB has also adopted the standards issued by its predecessor the Board of International Accounting Standards Committee which are known as *International Accounting Standards* (IAS). See further Web Chapter A.

The amount of the potential liability that must be recorded as a provision must be the best estimate that can be made, which FRS 12 defines as the 'amount that an entity would rationally pay to settle the obligation at the balance sheet date or to transfer it to a third party at that time'. Accordingly, if the probability of a legal obligation and the probability of payment to settle that obligation are both greater than 50% then the net-assets of the company will be reduced by an amount equal to the best estimate of such payment. Such an amount will also be recorded as an expense in the company's profit and loss account, reducing any profit or increasing the loss in the current financial year. It is a realised loss for the purpose of calculating the distribution. This is the case even in relation to those creditors who are yet to realise that they have been injured or yet to realise who is responsible...[56]

The important question, however, is whether this link between the accounting rules on provisioning and distribution regulation actually protects involuntary creditors' interests by increasing the probability, or to the extent to which, they will be compensated. It is submitted that it does so in two distinct ways. First, where provisioning for the involuntary creditor liability results in a retention of funds, at least in the short to medium term, this reduces the probability of insolvency. Whilst it is true that the company may not be able to identify and exploit profitable opportunities with these funds, and that any investment could be wasted, until the point in time where the invested funds generate losses in excess of the value of the investment, the company's assets available to settle the involuntary debt exceed what would have been available had the distribution taken place. Second, shareholders have incentives after the incurrence of debt, including involuntary debt, to alter the risk profile of their investments by making riskier investments thereby decreasing the value of existing debt and increasing the value of the equity investment.[57] Whilst managers may not share the same incentives as shareholders in this regard, as Armour points out, the extent to which executive compensation arrangements improve the alignment of managerial and shareholder interests, the incentives for managers to expropriate value from debtholders also increases. These incentives to expropriate value increase as the funds the shareholders have invested in a company decrease, as they have less to lose and more to gain from riskier investments. As the value of their shares necessarily decreases by the amount of any received distribution, the extent to which provisioning for involuntary creditor debt prevents a distribution or part thereof, it reduces the shareholders' incentives to expropriate value from *existing* involuntary creditors.

Questions

1. Is Kershaw's argument trivial? Do you think the protection provided by the distribution rules for non-adjusting involuntary creditors is significant? Is it significant enough to justify the existence of these distribution rules if we accept that these rules provide no real benefit for adjusting creditors?

2. Are there other existing or plausible regulatory tools that are better suited and better tailored to protecting involuntary creditors?

---

[56] One might argue that, given the interpretative flexibility in relation to such accounting judgments, provisions are unlikely to reflect the true value of involuntary creditor claims. In theory the audit function should ensure that provisions reflect an objective and fair assessment of existing and potential liability. However, as this author has argued elsewhere, pressures on auditors to acquiesce to management's preferred accounting treatments may not be effectively counterbalanced by UK auditor independence regulation (D. Kershaw, 'Waiting for Enron: The Unstable Equilibrium of Auditor Independence Regulation' (2006) 33 *Journal of Law and Society* 388). To the extent that auditors are not robust in their confrontations with management regarding provisioning the benefits of accounting-based distribution regulation for involuntary creditors is undermined. Importantly the regulatory failure here is in the regulation of the audit function.

[57] On the risk profile of the company and the expropriation of value of debt see Chapter 18 section II.1.

3. 'Involuntary creditors are clearly losers from the winners and losers that are generated by the corporate form with limited member liability. Whilst the advantages identified by Kershaw may not always be very significant, something is better than nothing.' Discuss.

4. If Professor Armour is correct that distribution rules only protect adjusting creditors is it necessary to have such rules? Should these rules be default rules or mandatory rules?

5. If you were forming Mine Ltd and wanted to minimize any future limitations on transfers of assets from the company to you, what steps would you take?

5 Reforming the distribution rules

Over the past few years a vibrant debate has emerged regarding the appropriateness and effectiveness of current UK distribution regulation. Although the Government's ability to amend this regulation is, as far as public companies are concerned, constrained by the Second Directive, this reform debate is taking place both at an EU and UK level and is worthy of close attention.

5.1 The logic of reform if distribution rules protect only adjusting creditors

This far in our analysis of distribution regulation we have been asked: what is the nature of UK distribution regulation; which corporate constituency is it designed to protect; and who does it actually protect? The answer to these questions may affect our assessment of whether we think distribution regulation is effective and necessary. If one decides, along with Professor Armour, that the distribution rules only protect adjusting creditors then the case for mandatory distribution rules that must be complied with by all companies seems weak. The reason for this is that adjusting creditors could, by definition, adjust the terms on which they provide credit to a company to insist upon distribution restrictions. If such creditors are capable of adjusting does it make sense for corporate law to provide these rules; and, if so, should the rules be mandatory rules applicable to all companies or should they be default rules allowing companies to opt-out of or adjust the rules to suit their circumstances and their own assessment of whether their creditors would like the company to be subject to these rules or would prefer to craft their own?

■ **J. Armour, 'Legal Capital: An Outdated Concept?' (2006) 7**
***European Business Organisation Law Review* 5**

A prohibition on return of capital can...be understood as saving creditors the cost of writing such a term into their loan contracts—a sort of implied covenant. Whilst incorporators lack the freedom to say whether or not they want this framework to apply to their firm, they do have considerable flexibility in setting the conditions under which the maintenance of capital rules will restrict distributions. Their application will be determined by the size of a company's share capital and share premium account, which—in the absence of a minimum capital requirement—the shareholders are free to set.

However, restrictions of the sort these rules create might alternatively be generated through loan covenants. Thus the 'benefits' of the legislation are not the costs which the prohibited transactions would impose on creditors, but rather savings in contracting costs[58] which might otherwise be incurred.

Sophisticated (i.e., 'adjusting') creditors do in fact frequently include loan covenants that restrict debtors' ability to engage in transactions harmful to lenders' interests. Thus there are

---

[58] The costs of negotiating such a term if the law did not provide one—in mandatory or default terms.

potentially significant savings to be made through company law providing 'creditor terms' which restrict such transactions. Commercial parties could thereby be spared the costs of writing such terms themselves.

Nevertheless, it seems most unlikely that a distribution restriction that conditioned on legal capital would succeed in capturing these benefits. Whilst there may clearly be benefits to imposing dividend constraints based on net asset values, it is hard to understand why it would make sense to calibrate those restrictions by reference to historic contributions by shareholders, as opposed to the state of the balance sheet at the time the loan is advanced. The utility of capital as a yardstick will diminish over time, as the value of the company's assets bears less and less resemblance to the amount of the shareholders' capital claims. If this is the case, then any 'savings' in terms of drafting costs will tend to diminish as the age of the debtor company increases.

Moreover, it should be appreciated that the appropriateness of distribution restrictions—and hence the preferences of commercial parties—will differ depending on the debtor company. This point is relevant for consideration of both the benefits and costs of a mandatory rule: where a distribution rule is appropriate, it creates a benefit, and where inappropriate, a cost. In theory, a distribution restriction is likely to be particularly useful for companies which have a large proportion of their value tied up in growth opportunities. Where the exploitation of such opportunities must be financed with equity (as, for example, if they are based on 'soft' assets[59] upon which security cannot be taken).

...

The foregoing points imply that the costs of mandatory rules based on legal capital are likely to outweigh their benefits. One issue arising consequently is whether a case may nevertheless be made out for default rules…Distribution rules could be recast as frameworks to which companies opt in or opt out on formation.

If, as Professor Armour argues, these rules only protect adjusting creditors then, as those creditors could contract for such provisions, these rules only make sense if the provision of such an implied collective term saves adjusting creditors the costs of negotiating for such a provision. However, he argues that the way in which the current rules are drafted means that they are not likely to be valued by adjusting creditors. A bank making a decision to lend to an established company will, he argues, be interested in a dividend restriction that is linked not to the original amount paid by the shareholders for the shares but rather to actual shareholder equity account at the time the funds are lent, which could, if profits have been retained, be in excess of that legal capital amount. If adjusting creditors are the constituency for these rules, but they do not value them, then no costs will be saved in the state providing them. At best, the rules should be opt-in default rules that a company could adopt in its constitution if it felt that its creditors would value them: that is, if some companies believe it would save them contracting costs they can adopt the provision; those who believe it is unhelpful need not. For further consideration of the problems with default rules in this context see pp 21–22 of Professor Armour's article.

5.2 The costs of the distribution rules

The contours of this argument depend, of course, on accepting the proposition that these rules only protect adjusting creditors. If Kershaw is correct that other non-adjusting creditors receive variable benefits from these rules then we cannot determine whether these rules should be reformed by reference only to whether adjusting creditors benefit from or rely on these rules.

---

[59] For example, unpatented ideas or skills and knowledge of employees (human capital).

A separate argument in favour of reforming the distribution rules has been made by Professor Jonathan Rickford together with a panel of interdisciplinary experts. Following Armour, this group argues that the distribution rules provide limited benefits to their primary adjusting-creditor constituency. However, in addition to these limited benefits, the interdisciplinary group argues that the costs of the distribution rules are considerable. They argue that accounting rules prevent distributions and impose costs on companies in ways that bear no relationship to the core creditor concern, namely, the company's ability, in reality, to pay its current and future debts.

In this regard consider the following example. Many companies provide their employees with what are known as defined benefit pensions. This means that when an employee retires he will receive a pension of, for example, 50% of his final salary. During the course of an employee's employment both employer and employee make contributions to a pension fund. Those contributions and the investment returns from those contributions will fund the employee's pension. To the extent that such amounts are insufficient to cover the pension payment obligations the company is responsible to make payments to cover this shortfall. Recently it became apparent that many company pension funds were in substantial deficit which would result in additional significant payments being made by many companies over the course of several years. Whilst these additional payments represented a significant financial burden for these companies, in most cases it did not have any impact on their current viability or on their ability to pay all their debts now or in the foreseeable future. Around the time of these pension funding problems a new accounting standard came in to force that addressed the accounting of these liabilities: *Financial Reporting Standard 17, Retirement Benefits*.[60] The effect of this standard was to markedly increase the liability entry on a company's balance sheet. Whilst there was some dispute about the effect of pension liabilities on profit and loss calculations it is clear that it increases the liability entry and that it therefore has an impact on companies' ability to make distributions pursuant to the 'net assets' test.

■ **J. Rickford et al, 'Reforming Capital' (2004)** *European Business Law Review* **921**

Conclusion on Legal Consequences—A Need for Urgent Reform
It seems clear therefore that, as a matter of both domestic and European law, the inclusion in the balance sheet of the provisions for pension liabilities, as required by FRS 17…, will have the effect of reducing a public company's distributable profits to the relevant extent. Whether such a provision also reduces the earned surplus for the purposes of the net realised profits/accumulated profits test (which applies to all companies, public and private) seems somewhat more debatable. But we believe that it does…

Reform the Law or Reform the Standards?
It may be suggested that the *difficulties* identified here and in the preceding chapter could be resolved by the adoption of different accounting standards. This does not appear to be a realistic approach. The [International Accounting Standards Board (IASB)] adopts accounting standards to satisfy the needs of investors worldwide for the highest quality financial information. The difficulties considered in this report arise because of the inflexible adoption of that information to calibrate a rule which serves a different purpose, control of imprudent distributions. Predictably, this confusion of purposes leads to unsatisfactory results. It should also be recognized that company accounts convey information not only through the balance sheet and profit and loss account but also through the notes to the accounts, and increasingly through other statements.

---

[60] *FRS 17: Retirement Benefits* (ASB, 2006, as amended).

Yet it is only these two selective statements, which inevitably only summarise and provide a certain limited perspective on the overall financial picture, which are invoked to set the amount fit for distribution.

Nor are the accounting standards on…pensions the only ones which can be expected to give rise to such difficulties. Similar problems are already emerging in the areas of accounting for financial instruments and for deferred tax. The problem is systemic. The only viable solution appears to be for Europe to establish its company law on a basis better suited to achieve the policy results required.

But reverting to the main subject of this chapter, we regard the case for amending domestic and community law to remove the automatic effect of the newly required recognition of actuarial pension deficits on companies' capacity to make distributions as a strong and urgent one. So long as a company can safely be regarded as a going concern, the fact that it will have to make substantial payments over time to fund its pension scheme, just as it will have to fund its workforce for wages and to meet other ongoing liabilities, should not affect its immediate financial capacity. To require otherwise will damage companies, the capital markets and even the very employees whom pension funds are established to protect. In particular the application of traditional capital maintenance doctrine provides a further disincentive for the maintenance and establishment of defined benefit pension schemes, which alone provide employees with a secure prospect of income on retirement.

There is no suggestion here that appropriate prudential standards should not be applied to distribution transactions, nor that, where companies have pension scheme deficits, proper account of these should not be taken in deciding on distribution policies. But the automatic effect of the Second Directive and the implementing UK legislation, in attributing such deficits to distributable profits (or surpluses) is crude and inappropriate. Better means must be found to give creditors proportionate protection against insolvency risks, which is their only legitimate concern.

Accounting standards are not devised with the regulation of distributions in mind. They are devised in order to improve the quality of company financial statements so that those statements are useful for shareholders in understanding how well the company is being managed, and useful for other investors when considering whether to invest in, or lend to, the company. Rickford et al's argument is a compelling one: these standards although not designed for distribution regulation can have perverse effects on the application of distribution regulation. They may prevent dividends being made when the company is, from a financial perspective, perfectly capable of making such a dividend without detrimentally affecting its ability to satisfy its present and future obligations to creditors, *including* its future pension obligations. Rickford et al argue that this inability to make a dividend when it can afford to do so may damage the company. The reason for this is that where investors value regular dividends, for example for liquidity or tax reasons, they may be unwilling to invest in good companies that are affected by such accounting rules. The reduction in the number of potential investors for a company's shares could result in an increase in the costs of capital for that company: the price investors are willing to pay for its shares decreases.

The appropriate reform response suggested by Rickford et al is to reject distribution regulation that is based on formulae that refer to a company's financial statements and thereby incorporate accounting rules. They argue that the appropriate response is to move to a director-reliance strategy, similar to the one we saw previously, in somewhat underdeveloped form, in *Lee v Neuchatel*. Under the Rickford proposal a distribution could be made provided that the directors of the company certify its solvency following the distribution and for the reasonably foreseeable future thereafter.

■ J. Rickford et al, 'Reforming Capital' (2004) *European Business Law Review* 921

Since the basic interest of creditors in contexts where assets are to be returned to shareholders is a fair and proportionate protection against threats to solvency, the logical starting point is with the general rules which prohibit undue risks to solvency.

...

The best approach, focused on solvency, is that directors who pay or recommend distributions should have their special responsibilities in this context brought home to them. This can be achieved by a mandatory, transparent board level decision agenda, and a clear formal requirement to focus on the merits of the case, (ie the expectation of continuing solvency) creating the conditions for a clearly defined liability to arise where professional care is not properly taken. This suggests an explicit act, in the form of certification of solvency…But very important questions of detail arise as to the content and effect of the certificate…

Should such certificates be audited? This is not required for distributions in any existing system…Reliance on a solvency test of this kind, buttressed by the formality of certification, is consistent with the modern British trend in this field. Solvency certification is the main safeguard (though audit of the certificate is required) in the British Companies Act provisions on purchase of private companies' own shares out of capital. In the Company Law Review, the Steering Group also took the view, after careful consideration and wide consultation, that reductions of capital for private companies should be permitted on the basis of such a certificate, with no additional creditor protection and no audit certificate, and that this protection was adequate in cases of capital reductions combined with distributions of capital, which had the same effect as share buy-backs out of capital.[61] The principle is thus widely, though not unanimously, accepted in modern British thinking that transactions economically indistinguishable from normal distributions, so far as creditor protection is concerned, should be regulated by solvency certification, without more.

...

So, subject to such wider consultation, we would provisionally favour a solution as follows:

– the directors should provide and publish a certificate along the lines of the first part of the present Companies Act precedent. This however currently only gives an assurance that, in their opinion, immediately after the payment there would be no grounds on which a court could find that the company was unable to pay its debts. As with the present regime, prospective and contingent liabilities should be taken into account. However the limits implicit in this extension are technical and not ones which we would expect company directors in the normal course to recognize as representing a normal commercial test of viability; we believe that the assurance should go further, beyond the contingent and prospective liabilities as defined above, to encompass the normal trading prospects of the business and the need for cash to satisfy the liabilities which will occur in consequence. This immediately gives rise to the question whether future, prospective and contingent *assets* should by parity of reasoning also be considered. Commercial realism would suggest that they should. However a measure of prudence is clearly required. The prospect of a capital increase, for example, seems obviously too contingent and remote to be permitted to count. We believe that the answer here is that the directors should be required to reach the view that *for the reasonably foreseeable future, taking account of the company's expected prospects in the ordinary course of business, it can reasonably be expected to meet its liabilities*. Thus normal trading assets, including future and contingent ones, should be allowed to be taken into account, but not extraordinary transactions.

– To this should be added a requirement to certify, along the lines of the second part of the current certificate that, having regard to their intentions and the resources in their view likely

---

[61] This provision has now been implemented by the Companies Act 2006: see section IV of this chapter.

to be available, for the year immediately following the company will be able in the ordinary course of business to meet all its debts as they fall due as a going concern throughout that year. This provides a firm assurance of liquidity over what is normally the next trading cycle, based on a firm prediction of trading intentions and available resources. Here again all existing liabilities (including contingent and prospective ones) and any other liabilities which are expected to mature into obligations to pay money during the period should be included.

– …This does not mean that the company's accounts (taken as a whole, and not merely with exclusive focus on the two traditional statements) ought to be neglected. We therefore would propose that in making the certificate the directors should be required to take account of the company's accounts and annual report as a whole and that where the result is to declare that the company is solvent while on an application of the narrow balance sheet net assets test the result would be a deficit, they should explain why they take the favourable view. This will provide a measure of discipline.

– Civil liability on the certificate and for recipients of unlawful distributions should be based on fault. There should also be criminal liability and liability to disqualification for directors at fault, as under the present Act. The extent of the fault liability should be the normal one under the directors' duty of care, skill and diligence.

Questions

1. How does the solvency standard proposed by Rickford et al differ from Lindley LJ's required director regard for creditors set out in *Lee v Neuchatel*?

2. Can we rely on solvency certifications by directors to protect creditors' interests? What concerns might creditors have about relying on directors to make this determination? (See further section IV 2.1 for a related discussion.)

3. For what period of time should the directors be required to certify that the company will be able to pay its debts?

4. Should director certification be subject to verification by a third-party auditor? What are the costs and benefits of requiring such verification of a solvency statement?

5. 'By opening its doors to accounting regulation through the regulation of distributions, company law relies upon a set of accounting rules and practices which it doesn't really understand and the effects of which it has not properly considered. It does not make any sense for company law to rely upon a separate realm of regulation with different concerns and objectives.' Discuss.

6. Are non-adjusting creditors such as involuntary creditors indifferent to these proposed reforms?

With regard to question 6, consider the following extract:

■ **D. Kershaw, 'Involuntary Creditors and the Case for Accounting Based Distribution Regulation' (2009) 2 *Journal of Business Law* 140**

Consider a public pharmaceutical company with significant positive cash flow which is able to meet its debts when due and, subject to the problem set out below, expects to meet these debts when due for the foreseeable future. This company is, however, aware that certain of its now withdrawn pregnancy healthcare products may cause congenital liver problems for the children whose mothers took the product during their pregnancy. However, those affected are unlikely to experience any symptoms until they reach puberty. These *long-tail* claims may well destroy the company when they are made in 10 to 15 years time. Current provisioning rules would require that a provision is recorded on this year's balance sheet putting the company in technical insolvency and preventing any distribution. They do not, however, affect the company's current or medium term ability to pay its debts. Would a solvency certification approach allow a dividend?

Consider for example, the recently introduced solvency-based test for capital reductions for private companies. Pursuant to section 641 of the Companies Act 2006, a private company may reduce its share capital[62] by passing a special resolution approving the reduction which is supported by a solvency statement made by all the directors to the effect that the company can pay its debts at the time of the statement and as they fall due over the following year.[63] It is clear that, in the context of the above hypothetical where the latent liability exposure would not have any affect on the company's cash flow or solvency for 10 to 15 years, a solvency approach for distributions which requires a short-term, fixed time solvency statement would allow a distribution where the current rules would not. The introduction of such a solvency approach for distribution regulation would, therefore, represent a deterioration in the protection provided to involuntary creditors by the current distribution rules. The Interdisciplinary Group, however, propose a broader *principles-based* time frame that asks the directors to certify solvency in the *reasonably foreseeable future*. In theory, this would, along with the current distribution rules, restrict the distribution if a reasonable director would foresee no way of avoiding insolvency 10 or 15 years in the future.

The adoption of a principles-based approach to the time period to which the solvency certification applies increases the exposure that directors have to ex-post sanction resulting from a court process brought by a liquidator (*as compared to* their exposure under a fixed time period certification): will the court, who will assess the legality of the dividend with the knowledge that the company has failed, take a more expansive view of what was reasonably foreseeable at the time of the dividend? Will the court judge reasonableness with the hindsight of failure? This potential exposure could lead directors to take a risk averse position and refuse to give the solvency certification where there are possible and significant long-tail claims. In theory, this could render a solvency test more protective of involuntary creditors than the current rules (that require provisioning where the probability of payment is 50% or more) if risk averse directors refuse to pay dividends where the possibility of paying a future claim is less than 50%.

This incentive for directors to be conservative is, however, significantly mitigated in relation to long tail claims by three factors. First, although there may be serious concerns about long term solvency, it may, given the company's product line and research and development activity, be reasonable for a director to conclude that the company would be in a position to negotiate and settle future claims, even if at the time the claims are made in the future this turns out not to be the case. Such a solvency assessment is a business judgment and UK courts have typically treated such judgments deferentially.[64] Furthermore, a carefully crafted record supporting the assessment of reasonableness of the certification is likely to deter many a liquidator from deploying its limited funds on further litigation.

Second, directors making a distribution decision are faced with the immediate concern that unhappy shareholders may remove them versus a probability of future liability. Similarly, directors who are shareholders may be swayed with the incentive of immediate funds versus probabilistic future liability...

Third, the actual time frame within which directors have to think about solvency under a *reasonably foreseeable future test* may be curtailed by the limitation periods applicable to any action that could be brought against the director in relation to an unlawful dividend...the law of limitation periods reduces an open ended 'reasonably foreseeable future' solvency test to six years.[65] Accordingly, a solvency test, whether based on *either* a fixed-time period as in capital reductions under the Companies Act 2006 *or* based on solvency for the reasonably foreseeable future as proposed by the Interdisciplinary Group, could enable distributions to be made where there

---

[62] Pursuant to section 610(4) Companies Act 2006 for the purposes of the capital reduction procedures the 'share premium' is treated as part of the 'share capital'. We consider reductions of share capital in detail in section IV of this chapter.

[63] Section 643 Companies Act 2006.

[64] *Howard Smith v Ampol Petroleum Ltd* [1974] AC 821.

[65] For further detail on limitation period analysis see D. Kershaw, 'Involuntary Creditors and the Case for Accounting Based Distribution Regulation' (2009) 2 *Journal of Business Law* 140, 163.

exist substantial long-tail claims that the current regime would prohibit. The constituency of involuntary creditors, were they capable of acting collectively, would, therefore, object to these reform proposals.

The question you have to answer is whether you think that accounting-based distribution rules benefit any creditor constituency. If the answer is 'no' then there is no case for bothering companies with the costs of applying them and the costs incurred as a result of distribution restrictions imposed on companies whose creditworthiness would be unaffected by the distribution. If you think creditors obtain benefits from these rules then the question becomes: do these benefits outweigh the costs they impose and who bears the costs arising from their reform? If it is the case that reform along the solvency-based lines could reduce the costs incurred by companies through distribution regulation but maintain the existing level of creditor protections then we are in 'win–win' reform territory. If reform reduces the costs but the protections are also undermined then this is a more difficult regulatory decision. Overall society may benefit from reduced costs on companies but this may be at the expense of imposing additional costs on a vulnerable creditor group, such as involuntary creditors.

6 Distributable profits and share buy-backs and redemptions

Whilst distributions through dividends have been the primary focus of our analysis in this chapter, distributions of value to shareholders may also be made through a share buy-back or a redemption of shares.[66] A buy-back of shares that transfers value to a shareholder in order to purchase his shares reduces the company's net asset position and reduces the shareholder equity entry. To the extent that such a distribution reduces the shareholder equity entry below the legal capital amount it is an unlawful distribution.[67]

The Act specifically addresses the capital implications of share buy-backs in Chapter 4 and of share redemptions in Chapter 3 of Part 18 of the Act. The Act also provides that the repurchase of shares in a private company may be made out of capital if the procedures set out in Chapter 5 Part 18 of the Act are complied with.[68] We address these Chapter 5 provisions in section IV when we consider the reduction of legal capital.

If the repurchase of shares takes place in accordance with Chapter 4 Part 18 of the Act, discussed in detail in Chapter 17 of this book, then the shares must be paid for either from distributable profits[69] or from a fresh issue of shares made for the purposes of funding the repurchase.[70] The same requirement applies to the funding of a redemption of shares.[71] By allowing the repurchase or redemption to be funded by a fresh issue of shares the Act effectively allows for the substitution of legal capital.

Where the shares are repurchased at a premium over nominal value such a premium can only be paid for by distributable profits and not by a fresh issue of shares unless the shares were originally issued at a premium. In which case the proceeds of the new issue may be used to pay the premium to the extent of the *lesser* of either the original

---

[66] Section 829 CA 2006 excludes buy-backs out of capital or unrealized profits.

[67] As discussed in section III.3.2 (fourth bullet), if shares are cancelled following a share buy-back this would result in a reduction of share capital. This is addressed in the Companies Act 2006 by requiring the creation of a capital redemption reserve in the amount of such cancelled share capital.

[68] A buy-back out of capital in accordance with Chapter 5 Part 18 is not a 'distribution': section 829(2) CA 2006.

[69] In Part 18 distributable profits means 'profits out of which the company could lawfully make a distribution (within the meaning given by section 830) equal in value to the payment' (section 736 CA 2006).

[70] Section 692(2) CA 2006.   [71] Section 687(2) (redemption) 692(2) (repurchase) CA 2006.

aggregate premium on the shares repurchased or the amount in the share premium account.[72] The reason for this complexity is to ensure that the legal capital from the newly issued shares replaces the legal capital from the repurchased or redeemed shares and to ensure that, in using the funds from the new issue to buy back or redeem the shares, this does not result in an overall reduction in legal capital.

7 Liability for unlawful distributions

If a dividend is paid in contravention of distribution regulation the dividend is an unlawful dividend. What options would be open to the company to recover the actual amounts paid or amounts equal to that amount? There are two obvious candidates to obtain relief for the company: the shareholders who received the dividend payments and the directors who authorized the payment. This section considers shareholder and director liability in turn.

7.1 Shareholder recipient liability

Section 847(2) of the Companies Act 2006 imposes liability on the shareholder who at the time of the distribution 'knows or who has reasonable grounds for believing' that the distribution does not comply with the applicable distribution rules. Such shareholders are liable to pay to the company an amount equal to the amount which exceeds the distribution which the company could lawfully have made.[73] Accordingly, the Companies Act 2006 does not require a shareholder who receives the funds to repay them if he was not aware that the distribution was unlawful and had no reason to think it might be unlawful. In the recent Court of Appeal case of *It's A Wrap (UK) Ltd (in liquidation) v Gula*,[74] with regard to shareholder knowledge requirements of section 847(2) Chadwick LJ made the following observations.

> The obligation to repay a distribution, imposed on a member of a company by s [847(2)] of the Companies Act [2006], arises where two conditions are satisfied. The first is that the distribution has been made in contravention of…the Act. The second is that, at the time of the distribution, the member 'knows or has reasonable grounds for believing that it is so made'.
>
> The second of the two conditions can be established in one or other of two ways. First, by establishing that, at the time of the distribution, the member 'knows that [the distribution] is so made'. Second, by establishing that, at the time of the distribution, the member 'has reasonable grounds for believing that it is so made'. The phrase 'has reasonable grounds for believing that' plainly connotes some degree of knowledge or belief which falls short of actual knowledge. For the moment I will assume for convenience—but without intending to pre-empt further consideration of the true meaning of that phrase—that 'has reasonable grounds for believing' can be equated with some concept of constructive knowledge. So the condition is that the member has actual or constructive knowledge[75] that the distribution 'is so made'.

---

[72] Section 687(3)–(4) (redemption) 692(2)(b)–(3) (repurchase) CA 2006.

[73] For an example of a case where the shareholders were held to be liable for the unlawful dividend see *Precision Dippings Ltd v Precision Dippings Marketing Ltd* [1985] BCLC 385.

[74] [2006] EWCA Civ 544.

[75] Chadwick LJ defined constructive knowledge as 'knowledge which a person would have but for his negligence'. In *Bairstow v Queens Moat Houses Plc* [2001] EWCA Civ 712 Robert Walker LJ observed that 'the statutory remedy [under section 847] is…available only…against a shareholder with actual or constructive knowledge of the unlawfulness of the dividend'. Arden LJ in *It's A Wrap* takes a narrower view of the shareholder knowledge requirement based upon an analysis of article 16 of the Second Directive, which section 847 implements: 'What the company must prove is one of two matters: knowledge of the "irregularity" of the distributions made to the members or alternatively that the shareholders could not in view of the circumstances have been unaware of "that irregularity".' See further in this regard J. Payne, 'Recipient Liability for Unlawful Dividends' (2007) *LMCLQ* 7.

Note, however, the Court of Appeal in *It's a Wrap* clarified that the shareholder knowledge requirements for recipient liability under section 847(2) do not extend to simply not knowing that making a distribution where there are no distributable profits is unlawful under the Act where the shareholders were aware that there were no profits.

Some commentators have argued that, in linking shareholder liability to the shareholder's actual or constructive knowledge that the dividend is unlawful, the Act is overly narrow and shareholder friendly.

■ J. Payne, 'Unjust Enrichment, Trusts and Recipient Liability For Unlawful Dividends' (2003) 119 *Law Quarterly Review* 583

The requirement of knowledge in this context has meant that dividends are only likely to be recovered from parent companies and those within the management of the company. This seems overly narrow. Although the shareholders may not have compelled payment and may have no knowledge of its unlawfulness, they have nevertheless received a windfall for which they have given no consideration and which the company had no power to pay.

...

Why should lack of knowledge act as a complete bar to a claim against the recipient of an unlawful dividend? Perhaps the real reason why the innocent shareholders have so far avoided liability is because the primary focus to date has fallen on the directors. They are the most obvious targets for a company seeking to recoup the sums paid out. They have acted wrongfully and in breach of their duty to the company in making the payment on the company's behalf. They have a duty to compensate the company to the full extent of the company's loss.

In comparison, the recovery of money from the shareholders is less attractive for two reasons. The first is practical [the practicalities of recovery from many shareholders]. The second reason rests on the idea of comparative fault. The shareholders have not compelled the payment of the dividend, indeed they are unable to do so, and they may be entirely lacking knowledge of the unlawfulness of the payment. Although shareholders do normally authorise the payment of dividends, on the recommendation of the directors, this is merely a rubberstamping exercise. Shareholders therefore look less obvious and less attractive targets than the directors. Indeed the scarcity of cases dealing with recipient liability in this context is testament to the fact that generally the company will not need or wish to pursue the shareholders, unless the directors are unable to compensate the company and the shareholders have enticingly deep pockets.

However, the role of fault requires examination. The shareholders do something wrong, arguably, not by compelling the unlawful payment, or by knowing of the unlawfulness of the payment, but by retaining something which they had no right to receive...and in relation to which the company had no power to make the payment in the first place...However, the use of the word 'wrong' here is arguably inappropriate, because the shareholders' only wrong is the fact that they have been unjustly enriched.

Shareholder liability to repay unlawful distributions pursuant to section 847(1) supplements rather than replaces any liability imposed in this regard by the common law.[76] However, at common law the liability of shareholders to return such a dividend is based on effectively identical principles. The courts' approach to recipient liability for unlawful dividends borrows from trust law on unlawful payments of trust property, which required third-party notice or knowledge of illegality in order to recover the funds. In *Russell v Wakefield Waterworks* the Court of Appeal held that 'in this Court the money of the company is a trust fund, because it is applicable only to the special purposes of the company in the hands of the agents of the company, and it is in that sense

---

[76] Section 847(3) CA 2006 provides that section 847(1) 'is without prejudice to any obligation imposed apart from this section on a member of a company to repay a distribution unlawfully made to him'.

a trust fund applicable by them to those special purposes; and a person taking it from them *with notice* that it is being applied to other purposes cannot in this Court say that he is not a constructive trustee' (emphasis added).[77] In this regard, Jennifer Payne argues that developments in the law of restitution holds out that the possibility that the law could develop to treat unlawful dividends as part of the law of unjust enrichment which could result in requiring repayment by shareholders even where those shareholders had no knowledge, actual or constructive, of the fact the dividends have been paid unlawfully. To date, however, the courts have not taken this step.[78]

Questions

1. Does the law on shareholder recipient liability make sense? What compelling policy reasons are there that innocent shareholders should not have to return unlawfully paid dividends?
2. What exactly should shareholders know or ought to know for liability to attach? Would this require actual or constructive knowledge of defective 'relevant accounts' or would knowledge of the existence and operation of distribution regulation also be required?

7.2 Director liability for unlawful dividends

7.2.1 *The standard of liability*

Although the Act makes provision for shareholder recipient liability, determining when directors are liable for unlawful dividends is left to the common law. When considering director liability for illegal dividends we need to separate two factual situations: first, where the director is aware, or ought to have been aware, that the dividend payment exceeds the amount that would be allowed under the applicable distribution regulation; and, secondly, where the director reasonably relies upon the 'relevant accounts' to recommend a dividend but it later materializes that such accounts were inaccurate, by reason of negligence or fraud on the part of the company's officers or employees, but not by reason of the director's negligence. Approaches to director liability could either ignore this distinction and impose liability regardless of fault on the part of the director; or could restrict liability to the former case where the director is at fault. In which case we would need to determine the nature or degree of fault, such actual knowledge or want of reasonable care, that would result in her being held liable for the unlawful dividend.

Central to an understanding of director liability for unlawful dividends is an understanding of the conceptual legal basis for holding the director liable. One readily available framework for imposing liability would be through the lens of the duty of care, skill, and diligence. If, applying section 174 CA 2006, a director in approving a dividend has not acted with the care a reasonably diligent director would have taken in relation to the preparation of the accounts or the dividend determination then the director will be liable. The duty of care, however, cannot make sense of strict no-fault liability for an unlawful dividend. In fact the UK courts have not used the duty of care as the conceptual basis for director liability for unlawful dividends. Rather, they have

---

[77] (1875) LR 20 Eq 474. See also *Moxham v Grant* [1900] 1 QB 88 where the court considered the possibility of an equitable contribution from shareholders to directors held liable for the unlawful dividend where the shareholders had notice that the dividend was not lawful.

[78] Although note the dicta for Lord Nichols' judgment in *Criterion Properties plc v Stratford UK Properties LLC* [2006] 1 BCLC 729 suggesting strict liability on the basis of unjust enrichment following from receipt of funds pursuant to an agreement that has been set aside. For a discussion of these issues see N. Kiri, 'Recipient and Accessory Liability: Where do we Stand Now' (2006) *Journal of International Banking Law and Regulation* 611.

drawn on the law of trusts and viewed an unlawful dividend as analogous to a breach of trust. However, whilst the logic of this framework tends toward director liability regardless of fault, as you will see from the following extract the courts have combined the trust approach with a care standard.

In this regard, consider the first instance judgment of Bacon VC in *Flitcroft's Case* where the directors had been recommending dividends based upon financial statements which included debts of the company which the directors knew were 'bad debts' and were unlikely to be paid. In finding the directors liable for the unlawful dividends Bacon VC and Jessel MR made the following observations.

■ *In re Exchange Banking Company (Flitcroft's Case)* Ch D 519

Bacon VC

One must have regard to the position of directors of a joint stock company. It is said they are not trustees. Answering that objection in general, I should say they are trustees and nothing else. They have interests of their own, but they are trustees of the money which may be collected by subscriptions, and of all the property that may be acquired; they have the direction and management of that property, and at the same time they have incurred direct obligation to the persons who have so entrusted them with their money...A man going abroad says to another person: 'You take charge, possession, and management of all my property and account to me for it when I come back.' What do the subscribers to a joint stock company say? 'We select you as directors; we entrust you with all our moneys now paid, and all that we are liable to pay hereafter, and with the management of all our interests, and we look upon you to account to us for them;' and they do account at their general meetings, and by their balance sheets, and so on...that the relationship of trustee and *cestui que trust* subsists between the directors of joint stock companies and the shareholders, I do not entertain the slightest of doubt...

Having attended with the utmost care to the arguments which have been addressed to me, I repeat I can entertain no doubt, first, that the directors are, *in the most general sense*, trustees for the company.

Court of Appeal: Jessel MR

If directors who are *quasi* trustees for the company improperly pay away the assets to shareholders, they are liable to replace them...The order of the Vice-Chancellor will therefore be affirmed, but with this variation, that the directors in each case are to be declared jointly and severally liable and not only jointly liable.

In *Flitcroft's Case* the court treats the directors as trustees or quasi trustees.[79] The basis for the directors' joint and several liability is breach of trust. In this case the directors were clearly at fault: they were aware that the company had not in fact been making profits from which dividends were declared. However, in trusts law a trustee who is in breach of trust is liable to compensate the trust for lost funds regardless of fault.

Treating the director as a type of or quasi trustee with similar obligations to a trustee could lead to holding the director who authorizes a dividend liable in the amount of the illegal dividend[80] even in situations where he was not aware and could not have been aware that the dividend contravened the Act and resulted in an illegal reduction of capital. Such an approach would clearly encourage serving directors to take considerable care when determining the amount of the dividend and to ensure that the accounts provide a reliable basis for the dividend. It would also mean that,

[79] See also *Russell v Wakefield Waterworks Co* (1875) LR 20 Eq 474.
[80] On the extent of liability for unlawful dividends see section III.7.2.3 of this chapter.

because of the complexity of corporate life particularly in larger companies, even the most careful of directors could find themselves liable for errors that were undetectable at the time the dividend was made. Such risk exposure for directors would operate as a considerable disincentive to board service and a disincentive for a serving director to recommend that the general meeting declare a dividend: even a remote risk that the accounts are inaccurate would deter most directors from such a course. Of course any unfairness associated with, or risk aversion created by, this approach is mitigated through the discretion given to courts under section 1157 of the Companies Act 2006 to relieve the director of liability where 'he acted honestly and reasonably, and that having regard to all the circumstances of the case...he ought fairly to be excused'.[81]

However, in spite of the no-fault approach that logically follows from treating an unlawful dividend as analogous to a breach of trust, several English law authorities on director liability for unlawful dividends have required fault on the part of the directors. Consider the following judgment in this regard.

■ *In re Kingston Cotton Mill Company (No 2)* [1896] 1 Ch 331

In this case prior to becoming insolvent the directors of Kingston Cotton Mill Company had approved and paid dividends based upon balance sheets that contained accounting inaccuracies some of which the directors were aware of and others they were not as they relied on information provided by more junior management.

> ### Vaughan Williams J
> If I were free to decide this case according to my own judgment, [I should hold] that a director *is in no sense a trustee*. The [Companies] Act does not say that a director is a trustee. He is not the owner of the funds which he has to apply; and I should have thought that he might safely be treated as the paid manager and agent of the company, and might well be held not to be responsible for the misapplication of the funds of the company unless he, through want of care or fraud, misapplied those funds. If it is said that, if his responsibility were thus defined, he would not be responsible if, by the direction of the shareholders, he applied the funds to a purpose which the company could not authorize because it was a purpose ultra vires, my answer would be that, if he did so without carelessness or fraud, he ought not to be held liable, and that if he did so knowing that the purpose was ultra vires, or carelessly, he ought to be held responsible, *not because he is a trustee*, but because the ownership of the company is limited—i.e., is limited to the application of the funds to the statutory purposes—and his duty to the company as manager is not knowingly or carelessly to apply the funds to a purpose ultra vires of the company, even though he may have the authority of the shareholders; for a company does not seem to me in regard to questions of ultra vires, to be an aggregate of the shareholders, but a substantive legal entity. I do not think that anyone can doubt that thus to define the duties of a director is more in accordance with commercial necessity and the sense of the commercial community than it is to hold directors liable to refund dividends which they have misapplied without fraud or careless-ness, on the ground that legal principles compel lawyers to hold them liable in such a case as trustees or quasi-trustees. Nor is the view which I have suggested without high legal authority, for it seems to me that it is the basis of the decision of Chitty J. in *In re Denham & Co.*,[82] and of the dicta of James and Mellish LJ in *Rance's Case*[83] ...
>
> There is, however, a considerable bulk of authority to shew that directors are trustees for the company of such funds as are committed to their control in such sense that they will be liable for a misapplication of the funds which is ultra vires of the company, independently of any proof of fraud or actionable negligence by the directors. The authorities as to the liability of directors as

---

[81] Section 1157 is considered in detail in Chapter 12.
[82] (1883) 25 Ch D 752.   [83] (1870) Law Rep 6 Ch 104.

trustees seem to begin with the case of *In re National Funds Assurance Co.*,[84] followed by *Flitcroft's Case*, and more recently by *In re Oxford Benefit Building and Investment Society*, by *Leeds Estate Building and Investment Co. v. Shepherd*, and by *In re Faure Electric Accumulator Co*; but in not one of those cases can I find that directors were held liable unless the payments were made either with actual knowledge that the funds of the company were being misappropriated or with knowledge of the facts that established the misappropriation. Take, for example, *In re Faure Electric Accumulator Co.*,[85] in which Kay J expressly finds that no imputation whatever is to be made upon the honesty or honourable conduct of the directors, but proceeds to find them liable for having committed breaches of trust in making certain payments out of the money of the company which were ultra vires, the purpose for which the payment was made being known to the directors, although they were ignorant of its illegality, as, indeed, were many, if not a majority of the legal profession. On the whole, I have come to the conclusion that there is no such bulk of authority as binds me to hold that directors who pay away the funds of the company under an honest and reasonable belief in a state of facts which would justify the payments must be held liable to replace those funds because it turns out that on the true facts the payments were ultra vires. [Emphasis added]

In *Dovey v Cory*[86] the House of Lords considered a similar fact pattern involving dividend payments based upon inaccurate accounts which the defendant director, Mr Cory, had reasonably relied upon. Lord Davey in holding that the director was not liable referred to Sterling J's judgment in *Leeds Estate Building and Investment Co v Shepherd*,[87] a case relied upon by Vaughan Williams J in *In re Kingston Cotton Mills*, where it was held that:

Directors who are proved to have, in fact, paid a dividend out of capital fail to excuse themselves if they have not taken *reasonable care* to secure the preparation of estimates and statements of account, such as it was their duty to prepare and submit to the shareholders, and have declared the dividends complained of without having exercised thereon their judgment as mercantile men on the estimates and statements submitted to them... My Lords, I agree in this statement of the law... It is by this standard that the conduct of the [director] must be judged in this case. [Emphasis added]

Although Vaughan Williams J in *Kingston Cotton Mills* finds the trust analogy inapposite he recognizes the weight of authority in this regard. However, although the conceptual basis for liability may be breach of a quasi-trust,[88] his judgment and the House of Lords judgment in *Dovey v Covey* clarifies that the standard of liability is one based on reasonable care.

This view, it is submitted, *was* (and may still be) the correct view of English law of director liability for unlawful dividends. The recent Supreme Court decision in *Re Paycheck Services Ltd* has, however, muddied these waters. In *Re Paycheck*, both the Court of Appeal and the House of Lords made some important observations about director liability for unlawful dividends. However, both courts stressed that they were not definitive observations as the issue had not been fully argued before their Lordships.

---

[84] (1878) 10 Ch D 118.   [85] (1888) 40 Ch D 141.   [86] [1901] AC 477.

[87] *Leeds Estate Building Investment Company v Shepherd* (1887) 36 Ch D 787. See also *In re Oxford Benefit Building and Investment Society* (1886) 35 Ch D 502 in relation to which Sterling J summarized the holding as follows: 'directors who had omitted to lay before shareholders proper accounts of income and expenditure and balance sheets, and who act negligently or carelessly as regards the ascertaining of profits which they proposed to divide, were jointly and severally liable to repay the sums improperly paid out of capital by way of dividends.'

[88] For a more recent case reaffirming this view see *Bairstow v Queens Moat Houses Plc* [2001] EWCA Civ 712.

Nevertheless, their Lordships who expressed a view on this issue all shared the same tentative view:[89] that director liability for unlawful dividends is strict and is not dependent on fault.

■ *Re Paycheck; Revenue and Customs Commissioners v Holland* [2009] EWCA Civ 625 (CA)[90]

The facts of this case are set forth in Chapter 9 pp 322–23. The central question in this case was whether Mr Holland was a de facto director (discussed in detail in Chapter 9) and, if so, whether he was liable for the payment of unlawful dividends

> *Rimer LJ*
>
> Mr Holland's [the Defendant's] second ground of appeal asserts that his causing of the payment of the unlawful dividends as from 19 August 2004 did not subject him to any *strict* liability to make good to the composite companies the assets so misapplied; it asserts that he would only be answerable to a claim to make such restitution if he had acted negligently in breach of his common law duty of care to the companies or dishonestly in breach of his fiduciary duty to them. The further assertion was that as he paid all the dividends in the honest and reasonable belief that it was in the companies' interests to do so, he committed a breach of neither duty and so the claim must fail. Mr Knox [Counsel for Mr Holland] accepted that there are authorities indicating that directors are under an unqualified duty not to cause an unlawful and ultra vires payment of a dividend.[91]
>
> His submission, however, was that these were all cases in which the defaulting director had either acted dishonestly in causing the payment (and so had been in breach of fiduciary duty), or at least had no reasonable ground for causing it. He submitted also that, in so far as these authorities suggest that the liability is strict, they are inconsistent with another line of authorities to the effect that a director making a misapplication of company assets will only be liable to make restitution if he knew or ought reasonably to have known it was a misapplication.[92]
>
> Mr Knox submitted that the latter line of authorities reflects the correct principle. Mr Green [counsel for Revenue and Customs], in response, pointed out that the [section 1157] relief available by the time of this litigation dates only from the Companies Act 1907 (s 32) and so was not available when most of the cases in this line were decided. Now that statutory relief from liability is available in a proper case, he submitted that the court should prefer the view that a director who causes an ultra vires misapplication of company assets should in principle be strictly answerable to a claim to make good the misapplication, subject always to his right to make good, if he can, a claim to relief under section 1157.
>
> I regard Mr Green's submission as a compelling one but find it unnecessary to express a view on its correctness and do not do so. For one thing, we did not have the benefit of full oral argument on the two line of authorities.

---

[89] In the Supreme Court ([2011] 1 BCLC 141) Lord Hope's judgment addresses the issue; Lords Walker and Clarke agree with Rimer LJ's observations in the Court of Appeal [2009] EWCA Civ 625. Note that Lord Walker and Clarke simply say they agree with Rimer LJ 'on the other issues', of which there were several.

[90] I have elected to extract Rimer LJ's view in this regard as his position was followed by two of their three Lordships that addressed the issue in the Supreme Court.

[91] Counsel referred to *Re Exchange Banking Co, Flitcroft's Case* (1882) 21 Ch D 519, *Re Lands Allotment Co* [1894] 1 Ch 616 at 638; *Re Sharpe, Re Bennett, Masonic and General Life Assurance Co v Sharpe* [1892] 1 Ch 154; *Selangor United Rubber Estates Ltd v Cradock (a bankrupt) (No 3)* [1968] 2 All ER 1073 at 1092; *Belmont Finance Corp v Williams Furniture Ltd (No 2)* [1980] 1 All ER 393 at 404; *Bairstow v Queens Moat Houses plc* [2000] 1 BCLC 549 at 555; and *Re Loquitur Ltd, IRC v Richmond* [2003] EWHC 999 (Ch).

[92] Counsel referred to *Re County Marine Insurance Co, Rance's Case* (1870) 6 Ch App 104 at 118, 122; *Re Kingston Cotton Mill Co (No 2)* [1896] 1 Ch 331 at 345–8; *Dovey v Cory* [1901] AC 477; and *Re City Equitable Fire Insurance Co Ltd* [1925] Ch 407 at 426.

The underlying idea of Rimer LJ's position is that the fault-element set forth in *Dovey v Cory* and the other cases detailed here was introduced to temper the strictness of the trust rule and as—following the introduction of the court's liability discretion in 1907—this was no longer necessary, it enables the law to return to a purer breach of trust basis for liability.

With respect, it is submitted that this is incorrect and it is hoped that if a court addresses this with the benefit of full argument it would not follow this tentative position. There are several problems with this position. First, although clearly the ability/inability to provide liability relief would be relevant background consideration for the early cases when determining the liability standard, it was not the only (or even the primary) consideration. It does not follow, therefore, that the provision of discretion given to courts to relieve the directors of liability should alter the selected conceptual basis for liability. The fault basis for liability was the product of the interaction of trust rules with the very different context of the incorporated company. It was not a legal fudge that impurified the necessarily applicable trust rules; a fudge that could be cured following the introduction of the court's liability discretion. It represented an adaption of trust rules to the very different context of the incorporated company and the very different role of directors as compared to trustees. *In re Kingston Cotton Mill* provides an excellent example of a 19th-century court's acute awareness of the importance of this different context. When we compare *In re Exchange Banking* with *In re Kingston Cotton Mill* we see that how similar the court views the company-director relationship to the trust-trustee relationship is the driver of the different legal approaches: if they are the same then the same no-fault standard applies; if they are different this gives the courts room to explore a different approach (one that treats the making of a dividend decision like any other business decision). Secondly, it is incorrect to argue that liability relief was only available after the Companies Act 1907. It was available through the different and, arguably, more effective[93] form of liability waivers set forth in the articles, which were valid and enforceable until the Companies Act 1929 rendered them void.[94] Although clearly, where such provisions were not provided for in the articles liability relief prior to 1907 was unavailable. Thirdly, the availability of a court's discretion to waive liability does not fully address the problems associated with a no-fault rule. Although a director would have every expectation that if he is not at fault he would be relieved of liability, he may worry that although he took reasonable care in making the dividend decision, the mistakes made in issuing the dividend could result in a judge electing to impose some liability upon him. Furthermore, even for a director that feels comfortable with the liability protection given by section 1157, this section neither absolves him of the fact that, even though not at fault, he is found to have acted in breach of trust, nor does it relieve him of the damage to his reputation that the breach of trust finding generates.

7.2.2 Is director liability dependent on the company's solvency?

In *Flitcroft's Case* the company was insolvent and the action against the directors had been brought by the liquidator. A narrow reading of *Flitcroft's Case* would suggest that the directors are only exposed to liability where the company is insolvent. However, the courts have rejected such a narrow reading. In *Bairstow v Queens Moat Houses Plc* former directors of the company were sued in relation to breaches of the distribution rules that involved both distributions in excess of distributable profits and also distributions based on inaccurate accounts. Counsel for the respondent directors argued that the principle set out in *Flitcroft's Case* was applicable where the company was insolvent. The court, in rejecting this submission, made the following observations.

[93] More effective, because once included it is not dependent on court discretion.
[94] See Chapter 12 at p 451.

■ *Bairstow v Queens Moat Houses Plc* [2001] EWCA Civ 712

Robert Walker LJ

In my judgment the point must be decided by reference to principle rather than authority. Queens Moat's case is founded on the fundamental *proposition* (which was affirmed by the House of Lords in *Salomon v A Salomon & Co Ltd* [1897] AC 22 and which Cotton LJ had well in mind in *Flitcroft's Case*) that a corporation is a legal person separate from the persons who are from time to time its members (in the case of a company limited by shares, the shareholders). The basic rules about lawful and unlawful dividends, developed from the earliest days of company law and now elaborated in accordance with Community legislation, exist not only for the protection of creditors but also for the protection of shareholders. If directors cause a company to pay a dividend which is ultra vires and unlawful…the fact that the company is still solvent should not be a defence to a claim against the directors to make good the unlawful distribution. Against that [counsel for the respondent directors] pressed the court with the prospect of shareholders receiving an unmerited windfall, if the amounts of unlawful dividends which they have received in the past were now restored to Queens Moat by the former directors and were again to be distributed (this time lawfully) by way of dividend.

In considering this windfall objection it is no doubt right to ignore the fact that the appellants are in practice unlikely, in view of the very large sums involved and the costs orders already made against them, to be able to meet even a small part of any judgments against them. It is not so easy to ignore the fact that the present shareholders in Queens Moat are probably a very different body of investors than those who received the unlawful dividends ten years ago. Some of those early investors may have cut their losses by selling their shares at the bottom of the market. Some of the present investors may have been astute enough or lucky enough to have bought their shares at the bottom of the market. Some may even have formed a view, in deciding to invest in Queens Moat, as to the prospects of a successful recovery on the counterclaim…These considerations put some flesh on the *Salomon v Salomon* point. They are matters which the court cannot easily take into account, however strong its instinct to achieve a fair result and avoid anything which resembles double recovery. Nevertheless it may be assumed that some of the present shareholders did receive and benefit from unlawful dividends paid between 1991 and 1993.

Even in relation to those long-term investors the objection taken [by the respondent directors] is in my judgment misconceived. If there is any unfairness in the situation it does not arise from the so-called windfall which (if and so far as it occurs) will be a distribution lawfully made on the basis of properly prepared accounts for 2001 or some later accounting period. It will be made out of distributable profits which are disclosed in those accounts. Any unfairness would, on the contrary, arise from long-term investors not being required to account for the unlawful dividends which they received in the past. [The court then proceeded to consider the issue of whether directors could claim an equitable contribution from shareholders who had notice of the unlawful dividend and concluded that it might be possible to raise this point but it had in fact not been raised.] For all these reasons the windfall argument must in my judgment be rejected.

Questions

1. Should the law on director liability for unlawful dividends be fault based, for example, dependent on the failure to take reasonable care? If liability was not fault based do you think most directors will be comfortable that the court would exercise their discretion to relieve liability under section 1157 appropriately?

2. Is there any justification for the shareholder windfall referred to in *Bairstow v Queens Moat*?

3. Does it make sense to view directors as quasi-trustees?

4. Would the adoption of a solvency-certification approach to dividends alter the conceptual basis for illegal dividends—from quasi-trust to duty of care?

7.2.3 *The extent of the unlawful dividend*

It is clear from section 847 that shareholders who are liable to return funds pursuant to that section must return funds equal to the amount by which the dividend is unlawful. If, for example, Bob's Electronics Ltd had distributable profits of £100,000 and issues a £150,000 dividend to Bob who was aware that the dividend was £50,000 more than could be legally made, then he is liable to return £50,000 to the company. The directors of Bob's Electronics Ltd would also be exposed to liability on the breach of quasi-trust grounds previously outlined. Through the breach of trust lens the waste of 'trust' property (the extent of the unlawful dividend) would be the amount by which the dividend exceeded the legal dividend, in this case £50,000.

However, a problem arises in relation to the issue of dividends that are based on 'relevant accounts' that do not comply with the requirements of the Companies Act 2006, for example, they do not provide a true and fair view in relation to matters that are material for determining the distribution.[95] Section 836(4) together with section 836 provides that if the applicable 'relevant accounts' are not prepared in accordance with the Act then those accounts cannot be relied upon for the purpose of making a distribution. If a distribution is made based upon such flawed 'relevant accounts' the distribution is treated as if it contravened the Act. The Act does not say to the extent that the distribution is rendered unlawful it contravenes the Act; rather the Act says simply that the distribution, which appears to mean the whole distribution, contravenes the Act. This means that a board who *negligently* approve a distribution based on flawed accounts may find that they are liable for the whole distribution even though if the accounts had been prepared correctly a distribution, or part thereof, could still have been made. Consider the following example: assume that the accounts of Bob's Electronics Ltd had been prepared in such a way that based on those accounts the company had £150,000 of distributable profits, whereas in fact, properly prepared accounts would have reduced this amount to £100,000. If director liability is still fault based and the directors failed to take reasonable care in the preparation of those accounts and/or in the recommendation of the dividend then they will be liable for the whole of the unlawful dividend—£150,000 not £50,000—because pursuant to section 836(4) the whole of the distribution, not simply the £50,000 excess of what could have been distributed, is unlawful. If director liability, after *Re Paycheck*, is strict then they will be liable for the whole £150,000 regardless of fault. This approach was taken by the Court of Appeal in *Bairstow v Queens Moat Houses* where counsel for the respondent directors argued that although the accounts did not provide a true and fair view, had they done so a dividend could have been paid. Robert Walker LJ rejected this argument, holding that this 'submission was in my view bound to fail'. Whilst directors will be liable for the whole dividend not just the portion which was in excess of actual distributable profits, the courts have a discretion pursuant to section 1157 of the Act to relieve the directors of all or a portion of their liability exposure. This was affirmed by Lord Hope in *Re Paycheck Services Ltd* where, citing *Bairstow*, he observed 'where dividends have been paid unlawfully, the director's obligation is to account to the company for the full amount of those dividends'.[96]

---

[95] Section 837(3) and section 393 CA 2006 requiring that the accounts provide a true and fair view. See further Web Chapter A.

[96] [2011] 1 BCLC 141 at [49]. Rimer LJ in the Court of Appeal [2009] EWCA Civ 625 at [98], with whom Lord Walker and Lord Clarke in the Supreme Court agreed, also took this view.

IV REDUCING CAPITAL

Whilst distribution regulation which protects legal capital provides certain benefits to the company's creditors, it can create difficulties for companies. Companies may find that, although they have cash reserves that are not being invested in new projects, they are, due to the application of distribution regulation, unable to distribute this cash to their shareholders. A close company may have the cash available to buy back the shares of a retiring manager-shareholder but is unable to do so because it does not have sufficient distributable profits. A company may be generating cash today for which it has no identified projects but significant prior year losses means that it will not have accumulated net profits for distribution for several years to come. When companies do have projects to invest in, such significant prior year losses make it difficult for the company to attract new equity investors in the company who will be aware that they will have to wait several years before they can receive a dividend.

In order to distribute available cash to its shareholders, to buy out a retiring manager-shareholder or to place the company on a more attractive footing for new investors, the company would have to reduce its legal capital and to write off some of its realized losses from previous years. What is meant by reducing a company's capital is reducing the legal capital entry in a company's accounts. This could be implemented in several ways: a reduction in the nominal value of the issued shares; a cancellation of shares; a reduction in share premium account; or a cancellation of the requirement for shareholders to pay unpaid amounts on the shares (which in turn could reduce nominal value or share premium depending on the nominal/premium arrangements when the share was issued).

Hypothetical B

Bob's Electronics Ltd was formed with £1,000 of legal capital (share capital plus share premium); in its first 10 years of trading it made losses of £500. However, in Year 11 due to an improvement in the demand for computers it started making a profit of £50 a year. If it continues making a profit of £50 a year it will not be able to pay a dividend until Year 21. This will make it very difficult for Bob to attract other equity investors in the company. If Bob elects to use one of the mechanisms discussed below to reduce the company's capital the effect of the reduction is not to reduce any real monetary account, rather it is to reduce the legal capital entry in the accounts, which in this case is £1,000. If legal capital is reduced to say £500 then it would be possible for the company to pay dividends in Year 11. Applying the 'net assets' test, if net assets are £1,000 and legal capital £1,000 then no dividend can be made; however if assets are £1,000 and legal capital £500 then a dividend can be paid up to £500. With regard to the accumulated profits test reducing the legal capital accounting entry of itself makes no difference to the company's ability to pay dividends. However, a capital reduction in this example would also involve 'writing off', that is for the purpose of the accounts getting rid of, losses equivalent in value to the amount that capital is reduced, which in this case would create space for a dividend from Year 11 of the profits made in Year 11.

Reducing legal capital and writing off losses may make perfect sense for the company but, lest we forgot, distribution regulation's primary function is creditor protection. Whether it does so effectively is, as we considered in section III of this chapter, a matter of some debate; however, it is clear that the objective of this regulation is to protect creditors. It would make a nonsense of distribution regulation if the company could reduce its capital at will without being subject to creditor-regarding obligations that would provide creditors with equivalent protection.

The Companies Act 2006 provides mechanisms for public and private companies to reduce their legal capital whilst continuing to protect creditors. A more flexible regime applies to private companies than to public companies. There are calls for reform to provide public companies with similar flexibility; however, the UK legislature's hands are currently tied by the Second Directive in relation to public companies. Sections 641–653 of the 2006 Act which regulate capital reductions apply to 'share capital'. However, section 610(4) of the Act provides that for the purposes of capital reductions the share premium account shall be treated as part of share capital. In the analysis that follows we shall continue to refer to legal capital to make clear that the reduction may apply both to aggregate nominal value and/or share premium.

For private companies the Companies Act 2006 provides three alternative means of reducing its legal capital: reduction through a special resolution approving the reduction supported by a solvency statement from the company's directors; reduction through a share buy-back supported by a solvency statement from the directors certified by the company's auditors; and reduction through a special resolution approving the reduction coupled with court approval of the reduction. Public companies may only reduce their capital through the special resolution/court confirmation procedure, and it is with this procedure that our analysis commences.

1 Court confirmation capital reduction procedure

Pursuant to section 641 of the Act a public or a private company can reduce its capital by a two-step procedure that involves: first, shareholders passing a special resolution approving of the reduction; and, secondly, the company obtaining court confirmation for the reduction. In relation to the procedure for obtaining court confirmation the Act distinguishes between, on the one hand, reductions in capital that involve a real transfer in value from the company to the shareholders (as a result of a payment to shareholders or a cancellation of unpaid amounts on the shares) and, on the other hand, reductions that involve a legal capital reduction and write-off of prior losses but do not involve any payment to shareholders or cancellation of unpaid amounts at the time of the reduction and write-off.[97] The Act sets out a procedure to be followed in the case of reductions that involve a transfer in value to shareholders, but not where the reduction merely involves a write-off of prior losses. However, the Act's procedural requirements are more in the form of a strong steer or guidelines rather than a mandatory requirement. The courts may disapply the procedure in cases that involve reductions in real value[98] and apply it in cases that do not.[99]

Consider further *Hypothetical B* in this chapter. In this case at the end of Year 11 the company had accumulated losses of £450. If at the end of Year 11 the company effects a reduction of legal capital and write off of £500, this would then allow £50 to be distributed. If that £50 is distributed as part of the capital reduction then it falls within the creditor protection procedure. However, if the £50 is not distributed then it falls outside of the procedure, even though the company could distribute that £50 by interim dividend shortly thereafter. Even if the company does not have distributable profits following the reduction, the reduction clearly enables distributions to be made (if the company is profitable) much sooner than would have been the case without the reduction and, accordingly, detrimentally affects the existing creditors position as compared to the position prior to the reduction. In such a case the court could exercise its discretion to apply the procedure. In practice, what typically happens is that the court will not apply the creditor protection procedure where an undertaking is given by the company that the profits made available for distribution as a result of

---

[97] Section 645 CA 2006.   [98] Section 645(3) CA 2006.   [99] Section 645(4) CA 2006.

the reduction will not be distributed until all the creditors existing at the time of the reduction have been repaid.[100]

Where there is a possibility that any part of the losses being written off may be recovered after the reduction the court will typically require an undertaking that any amounts recovered after the reduction will not be treated as realized profits and will be allocated to an undistributable reserve. In some cases the courts have required that such recovered amounts are permanently not distributable, in others that the restriction applies only until all the creditors existing at the time of the reduction have been discharged. In *Re Jupiter House Investments (Cambridge) Ltd*[101] the court required an undertaking that the lost capital, if made good, would not be distributed at all in the future. In *Re Grosvenor Press Plc*[102] Norse J recognized that the effect of such an undertaking was to provide additional protection for both existing and future creditors. He felt that 'anyone who gives credit to or acquires shares in the company after the reduction takes effect is prima facie adequately protected by existing statutory safeguards' and held that such an undertaking was only required where there were 'special circumstances' justifying the protection of future creditors. He did not attempt to detail such special circumstances.

In cases where the creditor notification and consent procedure applies, creditors of the company have a right to object to the capital reduction if they can show that 'there is a real likelihood that the reduction would result in the company being unable to discharge his debt or claim when it fell due'.[103] The Act requires the court to compile a list of creditors who could object.[104] In this regard the court may require the publication of notices, for example in national newspapers, notifying creditors of the capital reduction and the compilation of the creditor list. Effectively either all the creditors on the list must consent to the reduction or the company must take steps to secure the debtors' claims.[105] Typically, because this process of compiling creditor lists and requesting consents is time consuming and costly, courts will dispense with the creditor list and consent process if the company can demonstrate that it has sufficient liquid assets,[106] such as cash and listed shares, or if the company can provide a bank guarantee to cover all claims existing at the time of the reduction should the company be unable to satisfy the

---

[100] Practical Law Company, *Reduction of Capital*, 8 (www.practicallawcompany.co.uk 🌐).

[101] [1985] 1 WLR 975.   [102] [1985] BCLC 286.

[103] Section 646(1) CA 2006. This provision requiring that the creditor establish that there is a real likelihood that the reduction will result in the company being able to discharge its debts was added by The Companies (Share Capital and Acquisition by Company of its Own Shares) Regulations 2009 (SI 2009/2022), reg 3(b) which implements the Simplification of the Capital Maintenance Directive (2006/68/EC) which amends the Second Directive (77/91/EEC). Clearly on the face of this provision it makes it more difficult for a creditor to object. However, it is unclear whether this provision will in practice alter the court practice which is detailed later in this chapter. Consider the observations of Lord Glennie in the Scottish Outer House in *Royal Scottish Assurance Plc* [2011] CSOH 2: 'The restriction brought in by the amendment of s.646(1)(b) on the category of creditors entitled to object has not resulted, in Scotland at least, in an alteration of that practice.' The only case so far to have addressed the meaning of 'real likelihood' in this section observed that 'the section obviously does not require a creditor to prove that a future event will happen: it is concerned to evaluate the chance of the event (the company's inability to discharge the debt because it has returned capital). It describes the chance as 'real likelihood', thereby requiring the objecting creditor to go some way up the probability scale, beyond the merely possible, but short of the probable' (*Re Liberty International Plc* [2010] 2 BCLC 665 at [20]).

[104] Section 646 CA 2006.   [105] Section 646(4) 2006 Act.

[106] Typically the figure is 10% above the debts existing at the time of the reduction (Practical Law Company, *Reduction of Capital* (www.practicallawcompany.co.uk 🌐), 6–7). See further the extract from *Martin Currie Ltd* that follows, which suggests the courts may take a more flexible view on the types of assets to be taken into consideration in deciding whether to dispense with the creditor list and consent procedures.

claims.[107] The guarantee will typically be in force for a 12-month period and possibly longer if the company has longer-term creditors that have not consented to the reduction.[108] Effectively what the courts are doing here is imposing an informal solvency standard, which requires evidence that current liquid assets are sufficient to pay existing debts and, in the absence of such evidence, a more creditworthy bank guarantee in the amount of such debts. The courts, however, do not always demand 100% coverage for all future obligations, for example payments under a long-term lease.[109] Furthermore, there are signs that the courts are taking a more flexible approach to the types of assets that the court will take into account in considering whether a company can meet its future debts. Whether such flexibility will continue to be apparent in light of the effects of the ongoing credit crisis is open to question. Consider the following recent Outer House Scottish case of *Re Martin Currie Ltd* that addressed a capital reduction that did not involve any payment to shareholders or cancellation of any unpaid amount. Consider both the court's approach to creditor protection as well as the types of asset that are relevant to assessing the solvency of the company.

■ *Re Martin Currie Ltd* [2006] CSOH 77

Lord Drummond Young

It is…the *practice* of this Court, in cases where a distributable reserve is created, to consider whether any creditors of the company require the protection given by section [646(1)–(5)] of the Companies Act [2006][110]: *Quayle Munro Ltd.*, 1993 SLT 723. In such cases, the court will normally dispense with the application of sections [646(1)–(5)] if the company's margin of solvency is such that no relevant creditor is likely to be prejudiced by the cancellation. In considering the margin of solvency, the normal practice of the court is to consider whether the company's readily realizable assets are sufficient to provide for both the amount owed to relevant creditors and the amount that the company would be entitled to return to its shareholders, with a reasonable margin of safety…

In my opinion it is important that, in their approach to the margin of solvency calculation, the court should have regard to commercial realities, and in particular to the changing circumstances of the commercial world…The normal rule is that, in considering a company's margin of solvency, the court will only have regard to readily realizable assets.[111] Nevertheless, I am of opinion that that rule may be subject to exceptions. As is emphasized by Buckley J. in *Re Lucania Temperance Billiard Halls (London) Ltd* and Lord President Clyde in *Anderson Brown & Co Ltd*,[112] the court has a discretion under section [645(3)]. I do not think that that discretion should be

---

[107] Consider the observations of Lord Glennie in this regard in *Royal Scottish Assurance Plc* [2011] CSOH 2: 'In general terms, it has become the practice of the Court of Session in Scotland and, as I understand it, also of the Companies Court in London, to dispense with settlement of a list of creditors if the court can be satisfied that there is no realistic possibility of any creditor being put at risk by the reduction or if one or more of certain accepted methods of creditor protection are adopted. The principal methods are: (a) obtaining the consent of creditors and, where only some of the creditors consent, subordinating the claims of consenting creditors to those of non-consenting creditors; (b) setting aside cash in a blocked account in an amount sufficient to discharge the claims of non-consenting creditors; (c) the provision by a bank or other third party with a sound credit covenant of a guarantee in an amount sufficient to cover the claims of non-consenting creditors; and (d) the giving of an appropriately worded undertaking, the effect of which is to ensure that any distribution consequent upon the reduction being confirmed by the court does not reduce the net assets of the company below a figure sufficient to ensure that the claims of non-consenting creditors will be paid as they fall due. No doubt other methods have been used from time to time.'

[108] Practical Law Company, *Reduction of Capital* (www.practicallawcompany.co.uk 🌐), 7.

[109] *In re Lucania Temperance Billiard Halls (London) Ltd* [1966] Ch 98.

[110] The case dealt with the 2006 Act's predecessor sections: section 136(3)–(5) CA 1985.

[111] For example, liquid assets such as cash and listed securities.   [112] 1965 SC 81.

rigidly constrained by a formulaic approach to the margin of solvency. *Ultimately, the critical question is whether there is any significant risk of prejudice to the company's existing creditors*, in the sense that those creditors may not have their debts paid in ordinary course. If it appears from the totality of the facts put before the court about the company and its business that no such risk exists, I am of opinion that the court may dispense with the requirements of section 646(1)–(5), even if the formula based on readily realizable assets is not satisfied. In considering the risk to creditors, a range of matters may be taken into account. These include the general financial strength of the company, measured by either earnings or the valuation of the company's shares. (These two are of course likely to be related). Also relevant is the likelihood or otherwise that a purchaser will be found for assets that do not fall into the readily realizable category. In this connection an important consideration is the growth in recent years of private equity funds.[113] This appears to have been prompted in large measure by what is perceived as the overregulation of public companies. Nevertheless, the result has been that large amounts of money are available to purchase shares in private companies. That inevitably has a major effect on the marketability of holdings such as those that the company has in its subsidiaries. In my opinion the courts must have regard to the existence of large private equity funds if their approach to company law is to reflect current commercial reality. [Emphasis added]

If the court is satisfied that creditors have either consented to the reduction or that their claims have been secured then the court will sanction the reduction. It has the discretion to confirm the reduction on the terms that the court thinks fit.[114]

Following receipt of the court order confirming the reduction, the company must deliver to Companies House a copy of the order together with a revised statement of capital detailing, amongst others: the number of shares, the nominal value of shares, the extent to which they are paid up, together with particulars of the rights attached to the shares or any class thereof.[115] The reduction takes effect as of delivery to Companies House, or, if required by the court, registration of the order and statement of capital by Companies House.[116]

2 Solvency statement and the board approval strategy

We saw earlier that the courts' focus in deciding whether or not to confirm a reduction is upon the solvency of the company. For those companies who are solvent and capable of paying their debts as they arise one could argue that the capital reduction procedure is a costly waste of time both for the company and for the courts. An alternative approach to the court approval strategy would be a board approval strategy or possibly a hybrid board/third-party approval process where the third party is not the court but an independent auditor.

2.1 Should boards rather than courts determine solvency?

A board approval strategy would require that we rely upon the board to decide whether the creditors' interests are detrimentally affected by the reduction in capital. The question for any regulator is whether there are any problems with board reliance in this context that make it preferable for the company and society to incur the costs of using the courts as the arbiters of solvency rather than the board. If we identify any such problems

---

[113] Private equity funds are investment vehicles that purchase both listed companies and turn them into privately held companies and private companies. The importance of private equity companies has grown dramatically in recent years.

[114] Section 648(1) CA 2006.   [115] Section 649 CA 2006.   [116] Section 649(3) CA 2006.

we need to consider whether those problems vary in gravity depending on whether the company is a private or a public company.

In the situations where the company is solvent and is capable of paying its existing and future debts (whether actual debts or contingent debts) then a board reliance strategy saves the company and society the costs of a court approval mechanism. The regulatory concern is whether we can trust the board where the company's future solvency is in question and when board members may have personal incentives to transfer value to shareholders through the reduction. In such circumstances we need to ask what the costs and benefits are to directors of inaccurately certifying the solvency of the company in order to effect the reduction and value transfer. We need to assess, on the one hand, to what extent the directors themselves will benefit from the capital reduction and, on the other hand, what the extent of the director's liability exposure is for an inaccurate solvency statement.

The extent to which directors will benefit personally from the capital reduction will vary depending on the payout (or potential future payout) to shareholders as a result of the reduction and the extent of each individual directors' shareholding in the company. The extent to which directors are liable as directors or as shareholders is set out in section III.7 of this chapter.

In a listed company, although the director may have a significant shareholding in the company, it is likely to be in the low single digits and often less than 1%. Although any distribution (or future distribution) to the director as a shareholder made possible by a capital reduction in such a company may amount to a significant sum of money to the director, as a proportion of the overall amount distributed by the company through the capital reduction in most instances it will be very small. On the other hand, the director could find himself jointly and severally liable for the *whole* distribution if he is found to have wrongly approved of a solvency statement either intentionally or negligently. The costs for the director of knowingly or negligently making an incorrect solvency statement are, therefore, significantly greater than the benefits of receiving the distribution.

Compare this situation with, for example, Bob's Electronics Ltd when Bob was the sole shareholder in the company. Here the benefits of making an inaccurate solvency statement and enabling a payment now or in the future to shareholders may outweigh the costs. On the one hand, the benefit is equal to the whole payment. On the other hand, the costs could amount to the whole of any distributed amount if he is, as shareholder or as director, found liable. However, there is always a possibility that the company will not go into liquidation—in which case no one will sue Bob—and even if it does go into liquidation the liquidator may elect not to sue because, after all, Bob will argue fiercely in court that the company was solvent at the time of the distribution. If there is a possibility that the liquidator will incur litigation costs and lose the case the liquidator may not take the action or settle for less than the unlawful dividend. We could say that the probability of Bob being caught (held liable) for the inaccurate solvency statement and any resulting payments is less than one (that is, less than 100%). Given the immediate benefits of receiving a distribution Bob, as director, is incentivized to sign off on the solvency statement when he should not do so. Accordingly, it looks likely that from the perspective of this basic cost/benefit analysis that for large companies with many shareholders the board approval strategy is likely to be more appropriate than it is for smaller companies. For smaller companies a court-based approval approach may be more appropriate.

One strategy that regulators could adopt to counteract these problematic incentives in smaller companies would be to require that a third-party arbiter other than a court approve of the director's solvency certification. Such a requirement would, of course, impose additional costs on small companies including those companies that do not have any solvency concerns at the time of the capital reduction.

2.2 Board solvency approval of capital reduction under the Companies Act 2006

Interestingly, in light of this cost/benefit analysis, the Companies Act 2006 introduced a board solvency certification procedure for private companies but not for public companies. The Company Law Review was critical of the court confirmation procedure which they viewed as unnecessary, particularly in cases where the company was in a good financial position.[117] It is likely that the Government would have adopted the solvency-certification approach for public companies as well; however, they were not able to do so because of the requirements of the Second Directive in relation to protecting creditors in capital reductions.[118] It does mean, however, that the law now offers a board approval strategy approach only to companies to which, if one accepts the cost/benefit analysis set out earlier, it is least suited.

Section 641(1)(a) of the 2006 Act provides that a private company can reduce its capital 'in any way'[119] provided that the shareholder body passes a special resolution which is supported by a solvency statement from the directors. The special resolution must be passed not later than 15 days after the making of the solvency statement. Section 643 sets out the requirements of the solvency statement.

■ Section 643 CA 2006 Solvency statement

(1) A solvency statement is a statement that each of the directors—

   (a) has formed the opinion, as regards the company's situation at the date of the statement, that there is no ground on which the company could then be found to be unable to pay (or otherwise discharge) its debts; and

   (b) has also formed the opinion—

      (i) if it is intended to commence the winding up of the company within twelve months of that date, that the company will be able to pay (or otherwise discharge) its debts in full within twelve months of the commencement of the winding up; or

      (ii) in any other case, that the company will be able to pay (or otherwise discharge) its debts as they fall due during the year immediately following that date.

(2) In forming those opinions, the directors must take into account all of the company's liabilities (including any contingent or prospective liabilities).

The section requires that each director make the solvency statement. Accordingly, board unanimity is required to effect a capital reduction through this procedure. The statement covers two types of debt obligation: first, in section 643(1)(a) the actual debts existing at the date of the statement; and, secondly, in section 643(b) the debts of the company that are expected to arise and may arise in the year following the date the statement is made,[120] or should the winding up of the company be commenced at some point in the year following the statement, 12 months from the date the winding up commences.[121] Both (a) and (b) are cashflow solvency tests—that is the company has the cash to pay the debts, they are not balance sheet solvency tests—that the company has assets which exceed its liabilities.[122]

---

[117] Company Law Review, *Modern Company Law for a Competitive Economy: The Strategic Framework*, para 5.4.5.

[118] Second Directive (77/91/EEC), article 32.   [119] Section 641(3) CA 2006.

[120] Section 643(1)(b)(ii) CA 2006.   [121] Section 643(1)(b)(i) CA 2006.

[122] In this regard note the observations made by this author elsewhere: 'It is clear that the second opinion required by section 643(1)(b) is a cash-flow solvency test as it refers to debts as they fall due. The first opinion refers only to the company being "unable to pay its debts". Of course the absence of the reference to "as they fall due" in the section 643(1)(a) opinion tells us nothing in this regard, as

Section 643(2) requires that the directors take into account prospective and contingent liabilities[123] in forming their opinions.[124] This creates some confusion. It has been submitted that subsection (2)(a) concerns debts that have accrued at the time of the statement, whereas subsection (2)(b) concerns debts that will arise over the next year. It is only in relation to (b) that taking account of prospective or contingent liabilities makes sense. If, in forming the opinion under subsection (2)(a), directors would have to take into account contingent liabilities, this would in effect be a forward-looking statement with no time limit. It would not make any sense to provide an unlimited future statement in (a) and then provide a one-year time period in (b). Accordingly, the better reading is that subsection (2) should be read as applying only to the opinion required in (b). If the reading suggested in this paragraph is correct then the time horizon for a

clearly an immediate cash-flow solvency opinion would not refer to debts as they fall due because it is concerned with debts at the time of the statement. Read literally the word "pay" implies cash rather than an excess of balance sheet assets over liabilities. However, it is noteworthy that the balance sheet insolvency test in section 123(2) of the Insolvency Act 1986 provides that a company is "deemed *unable to pay its debts*" where the value of the company's assets are less than its liabilities, suggesting that the term "unable to pay" could refer to either a balance sheet or cash-flow solvency test. Importantly, when compared with the balance sheet insolvency test in the Insolvency Act 1986 it should be noted that section 643(1) makes no reference to "assets" and "liabilities" which one would have expected had it been intended that section 643(1) was based on balance sheet solvency. Indeed, in other contexts the courts have interpreted insolvency tests that directly refer to "assets" and "liabilities" as cash-flow insolvency tests, suggesting that if the legislature intended a balance sheet solvency test for section 643(1)(a) then it should have left the decision maker in no doubt. Other aspects of the language used in section 643(1) (a) reinforce the view that the test is a cash-flow solvency test. First, the sense of payment in terms of immediate cash discharge is reinforced by the connection of 'unable to pay' to the date of the statement: "could *then* [referring to the date of the statement] be found to be unable to pay". Second, the provision provides that the opinion must state that "there is no ground" on which the company would be unable to pay. The ability to make a cash discharge of debts at the time of the statement can be assessed with some degree of certainty enabling the directors to certify that there is "no ground" on which payment cannot be made. In contrast, the significant number of accounting judgments that are part of any balance sheet would mean that it would very difficult for many, if not most, directors to certify that there is "no ground" on which, based on the balance sheet, the company would be unable to discharge all its liabilities, particularly when regard is to be had to contingent and prospective liabilities. A balance sheet approach to section 643(1)(a) would, therefore, render the solvency statement reduction approach unavailable for most companies' (D. Kershaw, 'The Decline of Legal Capital: An Exploration of the Consequences of Board Solvency Based Capital Reductions' in A. Resiberg and D.D. Prentice (eds), *Corporate Finance in The UK and EU* (OUP, 2011)).

[123] A prospective liability is a liability that is not yet payable but will be payable. Lawyers have tended to view the term 'contingent liability' as a liability that is contingent on the occurrence of a particular event. A widely cited definition of 'contingent liability' is Lord Reid's interpretation of the term in section 50 of the Finance Act 1940 as 'a liability which, by reason of something done by the person bound, will necessarily arise or come into being if one or more certain events occur or do not occur' (*Winter (exors of Sutherland (decd) v IRC* [1961] 3 All ER 855; more recently see *Re T&N Ltd (No 2)* [2005] EWHC 2870. In *In re British Equitable Bond And Mortgage Corporation, Limited* [1910] 1 Ch 574 counsel for the company observed that 'a prospective creditor is one who has a maturing claim which will inevitably by mere lapse of time ripen into a debt, but whose debt is not presently payable, the right to receive payment ensuring at a future date. A contingent creditor is one whose jus action against the company is contingent on some act done or omitted by a third party.' In accounting terms a contingent liability is a liability in relation to which there is a less than 50% chance of the company having to use its resources to settle the claim. See Financial Reporting Standard 12, *Provisions, Contingent Liabilities and Contingent Assets*. Prospective liability is not an accounting term of reference; such a liability is simply a liability.

[124] Note that it is this reference to prospective and contingent liabilities that provides the only good argument that the test in section 643(1)(a) is a balance sheet insolvency test. Why, after all, would contingent liabilities be relevant to the ability to pay off debts in cash as of the date of the statement? Surely such considerations would only be relevant to a balance sheet solvency test. Nevertheless, in this author's view, the balance of the arguments set forth in this note and in note 122 tend towards the view that section 643(1)(a) is a cashflow insolvency test. See further the discussion of the tests in section IV.2.3 of this chapter.

solvency statement in relation to a company that is not expected to enter a winding-up process in the next year is one year from the date of the solvency statement.

Any director who makes the statement without having 'reasonable grounds' for the opinion given in the solvency statement commits a criminal offence and, if convicted, is liable to a fine.[125] The effect of this provision is to apply a negligence standard to the *actual reasons*—as distinct from the decision-making process—for the giving of the solvency opinion and to criminalize that standard. The presence of criminal liability exposure represents, in theory, a distinctive deterrent to abusing the solvency statement approach to capital reductions. Whether it will operate as a deterrent in practice is another matter. Several considerations suggest that the impact may be muted. First, the burden of proof for establishing breach would be 'beyond reasonable doubt' rather than on the 'balance of probabilities'. The higher burden of proof will mitigate against actions being brought at all and the probability of success when brought. Secondly, criminal convictions for breach of the Companies Acts provisions are rare; and likely to be rarer in this case where business judgment is an inherent part of the offence. It seems unlikely, in this author's view, that actions will be brought or convictions obtained where there is plausible case that the director acted reasonably or simply believed the statement to be correct.[126] It is noteworthy, in this regard, that an identical standard[127] applied to the solvency statement made to whitewash financial assistance pursuant to sections 155–8 of the Companies Act 1985[128] did not result in any reported cases arising from prosecutions for breach of this standard. The one reported case to have addressed this 'whitewash standard' in any depth, *Re Bunting Electric Manufacturing Co Ltd*,[129] arises from an action brought by the Secretary of State for Trade and Industry seeking disqualification of a director pursuant to section 6 of the Company Directors Disqualification Act 1986. A noteworthy aspect of this case is that although the court held that the director did not have 'reasonable grounds' for making the solvency statement, in reaching its judgment the court focused upon both the subjective belief of the director and on the fact that 'there was no rational basis for [the statement]'.[130] Accordingly, as in most *actually* abusive reductions (where the directors do not actually believe there are reasonable grounds for giving the opinion) a plausible or rational basis for the action will be available, it is submitted that the probability of criminal conviction for directors who give inaccurate solvency opinions is close to zero.

The basis for civil liability for directors is not set forth explicitly in the Act. There are two bases for liability which closely track English law's regulation of any business decision by a company director. The solvency statement requires that the directors set forth their subjective opinions on the company's solvency. Accordingly, the first basis of liability is one based upon demonstrating that the directors did not in fact believe the opinion they gave. In this regard, one would expect the courts to engage in a process similar to the one undertaken where directors are alleged to have breached section 172 of the Act.[131] Indeed, it is quite likely that the claim itself would be framed as a breach of section 172 itself: giving a false solvency statement is clearly not acting in good faith to promote the success of the company. To determine liability in this absence of clear evidence of the directors' state of mind, courts would look to the plausibility or

[125] Section 643(4) CA 2006.

[126] English company law has shown in other contexts its willingness to lower the standard suggested by 'reasonableness' when it comes to the actual imposition of liability. See, for example, Lord Justice Hoffmann's (as he then was) interpretation of reasonableness in the context of section 1157 of the Companies Act 2006 as 'gross negligence' (*Re D'Jan* [1993] BCC 646), although it should be noted that section 1157 of itself suggests that the term may have a different meaning in this section.

[127] Section 156(7) CA 1985.

[128] On financial assistance see Chapter 17. Note that under the 2006 Act there is no longer a whitewash procedure, as the financial assistance prohibition no longer applies to private companies.

[129] [2006] 1 BCLC 550.   [130] *Ibid*, 588.   [131] See further Chapter 10.

rationality of the directors' opinions.[132] The second basis of liability would be based on the directors' failure to take reasonable care pursuant to section 174 of the Companies Act 2006, in the process which resulted in the giving of the opinions: did the directors consider and request the information that a reasonable director would have requested and considered in order to be able to give the solvency opinions?[133]

Within 15 days of the passing of the special resolution approving of the reduction of capital the company must deliver to Companies House a copy of the solvency statement together with a revised statement of capital, which provides details of the company's share capital following the reduction.[134] The Companies Registrar is required to register the delivered documents upon receipt.[135] The reduction takes effect upon registration.[136]

Questions

1. Do you think courts are capable of making an assessment of a company's future solvency?

2. Do you think that the introduction of the board-approved solvency approach for private companies is a good idea?

3. What do you view as the primary problems for a solvency approach?

4. If you were asked to consider any possible reforms of the existing capital reduction regime, would you recommend a board-approval solvency approach for public companies?

5. Do you think that legislature should have required that an independent auditor approve the director's solvency statement?

6. Does the imposition of criminal liability on directors who do not have 'reasonable grounds' for making the solvency statement make any difference?

7. Do you think the one-year time period in which directors have to consider the company's solvency when making a solvency statement is long enough? If not how long or short should it be?

8. If private companies can be formed with virtually zero share capital, why should we be concerned about whether a company can reduce its share capital or not?

9. The cost/benefit analysis of capital reductions under a board-approval solvency approach does not incorporate the effect of criminal liability for making a solvency statement without having reasonable grounds for doing so. Is this a flaw in the analysis? Do you think that criminal liability makes a significant difference in this regard? If so, how does it make this difference?

10. Although the distribution rules considered in section III continue to apply to private companies, are they now irrelevant following the introduction of the board-approved solvency approach for capital reductions?

2.3 Board-approval solvency approach to share repurchase out of capital

As noted previously the board-approval mechanism for capital reductions in private companies was introduced by the 2006 Act. However, the Companies Act 1985 did

---

[132] *Regentcrest v Cohen* [2001] 2 BCLC 80. Hoffmann LJ in *Re Saul D Harrison & Sons Plc* [1995] 1 BCLC 14.

[133] In *Re In a Flap Envelope Co Ltd* [2004] 1 BCLC 64 Jonathan Crow held that 'in order for a declaration to comply with s 155(6) [the solvency statement pursuant to the financial assistance whitewash procedure under the Companies Act 1985], the directors must have made sufficient inquiries into the financial affairs of the company to satisfy themselves that the statement required by s 156(2) can be honestly made.'

[134] Section 644(1)–(2) CA 2006.

[135] Section 644(3) CA 2006.   [136] Section 644(4) CA 2006.

provide a board-approval mechanism for companies to reduce their capital by repurchasing shares out of capital. In Chapter 17 we looked at the Companies Act's procedures for repurchasing shares. Here we are concerned only with the additional requirements where the repurchase results in a reduction in capital. In particular, we are interested in comparing these procedures with the new capital-reduction mechanism discussed earlier. Indeed, the Company Law Review which recommended a capital-reduction mechanism thought that the share repurchase out of capital should be abolished as it would no longer be necessary. However, the legislature chose to keep it.

The repurchase out of capital procedure *for private companies* is set out in sections 709–723 of the 2006 Act. Repurchase out of shares can be made if profits available for distribution have been exhausted[137] and the procedures set out in these sections are followed. The strategy that the repurchase out of capital provisions adopts is a hybrid board-approval/third-party confirmation approach. As with the capital-reduction procedure outlined in section 2.2, the approval requires a special resolution supported by a solvency statement. The resolution must be passed within a week following the statement (as compared to 15 days in the section 641 solvency statement capital-reduction procedure). The solvency statement must be made in accordance with the requirements of section 714.

■ Section 714 CA 2006 Directors Statement and Auditors Report

...

(2) The statement must specify the amount of the permissible capital payment for the shares in question.

(3) It must state that, having made full inquiry into the affairs and prospects of the company, the directors have formed the opinion—

  (a) as regards its initial situation immediately following the date on which the payment out of capital is proposed to be made, that there will be no grounds on which the company could then be found unable to pay its debts, and

  (b) as regards its prospects for the year immediately following that date, that having regard to—

    (i) their intentions with respect to the management of the company's business during that year, and

    (ii) the amount and character of the financial resources that will in their view be available to the company during the year, the company will be able to continue to carry on business as a going concern (and will accordingly be able to pay its debts as they fall due) throughout that year.

(4) In forming their opinion for the purposes of subsection (3)(a), the directors must take into account all of the company's liabilities (including any contingent or prospective liabilities).

Note first that the statement provides that the directors have formed the opinion. It does not, therefore, in contrast to section 643, appear to require unanimity. However, in other respects the statement required under section 714 appears to be more onerous than the statement required under section 643 considered earlier. It requires 'a full inquiry into the affairs and prospects of the company' whereas section 643 does not require such an inquiry. Both sections set the standard for criminal liability as being the absence of reasonable grounds for the statement.[138]

---

[137] Sections 710–712 CA 2006.   [138] Sections 715(1) and 643(4) CA 2006.

The first opinion given in relation to the share repurchase out of capital is the company's ability to pay its debts at the date when the payment out of capital is made, which contrasts to section 643(1)(a) which focuses on the date when the statement is made. The second opinion in section 714 focuses on the ability of the company to pay its debts in the year following payment similar to section 643(1)(b)(ii). Interestingly, section 714(4) requires that the directors take account of prospective and contingent liabilities but only in relation to the first section 714(3)(a) opinion. This seems to be at odds with the argument made by this book about the relationship between contingent and prospective liabilities and section 643(1)(a) and (b). It seems that this section takes it as given that the ability to pay debts as they arise in the future necessarily involves possible contingent and prospective debts for the year ahead.[139] But how does one take account of these debts when section 714(3)(a) focuses on the debts that must be paid as of a specific date. The difference it seems is that for section 714 there is a time delay between when the statement is made and when the opinion states the company will be able to pay its debts. The directors may make their statement in Week 1 but due to additional protections detailed later, they are not allowed to make the payment for a further five weeks. Section 714(4) requires the directors to take into account other debts that may accrue in that time period even if they are currently prospective or contingent.

In contrast to the section 641 solvency statement capital-reduction procedure the solvency statement is not sufficient to permit the repurchase out of capital. The Act builds in two additional protections. First, the Act requires the production of a report by the company's auditors which is attached to the board's solvency statement.

■ Section 714 CA 2006 Directors Statement and Auditors Report

...

(6) It must in addition have annexed to it a report addressed to the directors by the company's auditor stating that—

(a) he has inquired into the company's state of affairs,

(b) the amount specified in the statement as the permissible capital payment for the shares in question is in his view properly determined in accordance with sections 710 to 712, and

(c) he is not aware of anything to indicate that the opinion expressed by the directors in their statement as to any of the matters mentioned in subsection (3) above is unreasonable in all the circumstances.

The report does not certify the accuracy of the solvency statement, rather it contains a much weaker form of negative audit opinion: that the auditors are not aware of any facts that indicate that the directors' solvency statement is unreasonable. The second additional protection for creditors[140] provided by this procedure is a publicity and objection procedure. Section 719 requires notification to existing creditors by publishing a notice in a national newspaper within a week of the passing of the special resolution.[141] This is coupled with the ability of a creditor or a member to take court action to object to the repurchase out of capital within a five-week period from the date the special resolution approving the repurchase out of capital was passed.[142] The Act gives

---

[139] On the meaning of 'prospective' and 'contingent' liabilities see note 123.

[140] Section 721 CA 2006; this section of the Act also provides members with rights of objection.

[141] Section 719(2)(b) CA 2006. Alternatively the company can provide notice to each individual creditor (section 719(2)(b)).

[142] Section 721(1) CA 2006.

the court a broad discretion on such an application to confirm or cancel the resolution in such terms as it thinks fit.[143] During this five-week period the repurchase out of capital cannot be implemented.[144]

3 Classes of shares and capital reductions

A capital reduction that either involves the transfer of value to ordinary shareholders or facilitates future distributions to ordinary shareholders may affect the value of preference shares to the extent that such immediate or future payments decrease the probability that future preference share dividends will be paid or that preference shareholders will receive their agreed entitlement on a winding up. On the other hand, if preference shares are cancelled as a result of a capital reduction in a successful company then the preference shareholders' interests are detrimentally affected where they could have expected to receive dividends going forward, had they remained preference shareholders.[145] Accordingly, whilst the capital reduction procedures focus on creditor protection, a capital reduction in a company with more than one class of shares also raises questions of equal treatment between classes of shareholders. Note, however, that unless the company's articles state explicitly that a reduction of capital which involves a repayment and cancellation of a class of preference shares amounts to a variation of class rights, such a capital reduction will not *require* the separate approval of the class in accordance with applicable class variation procedure.[146]

In the context of court-confirmed capital reductions the courts have made it clear that in order to confirm the reduction, the reduction must provide for equitable or fair treatment of shareholders. Consider in this regard Harman J's observations in *Re Ratners Group Plc:*[147]

> The court has over the years established…three principles on which the court will require to be satisfied. Those principles are, first, that all shareholders are treated equitably in any reduction. That usually means that they are treated equally, but may mean that they are treated equally save as to some who have consented to their being treated unequally, so that counsel's word 'equitably' is the correct word, which I adopt and accept. The second principle to be applied is that the shareholders at the general meeting had the proposals properly explained to them so that they could exercise an informed judgment on them. And the third principle is that creditors of the company are safeguarded so that money cannot be applied in any way which would be detrimental to creditors.

More recently in *Re Ransomes Plc*[148] the Court of Appeal confirmed the first instance judge's finding that a reduction in the share premium account, which it was argued by the preference shareholders detrimentally affected their position by prejudicing their future entitlement to dividends, was substantively fair, which in this case meant 'that there was not in any meaningful sense any increased risk of holders of preference shares being prejudiced by non-payment of future dividends'.[149]

Note that where a capital reduction affects a class of shares but is supported by a class vote supporting the reduction, the burden of proof is placed on the parties opposing

---

[143] Section 721(3)–(4) CA 2006.   [144] Section 723 CA 2006.

[145] See *Re Saltdean Estate Co Ltd* [1968] 3 All ER 829 where the court confirmed the reduction in such a situation.

[146] See *Re Saltdean Estate Co Ltd* [1968] 3 All ER 829. For an example of a case where the articles provide that 'the reduction of the capital paid up on those shares' amounted to a variation of class rights see *Re Northern Engineering Industries plc* [1994] 2 BCLC 70. On class rights variation see Chapter 17.

[147] [1988] BCLC 685.   [148] [1999] 2 BCLC 591.

[149] See *Re Holders Investment Trust Ltd* [1971] 2 All ER 289 where the court held the capital reduction was not fair to preference shareholders.

the reduction to prove that it is not fair. Where there is no such class vote the burden is placed on those supporting the capital reduction to prove that it is fair.[150]

4 Will private companies continue to use the court-confirmation procedure or the share-repurchase procedure?

Does it make sense to continue to offer private companies either the court-confirmation or the share-repurchase out of capital procedures? Why, one might ask, would companies use these procedures when there is a more straightforward procedure under the board-approved solvency statement approach. One answer to this question would be: where the board takes a risk-averse position regarding its personal liability exposure. A capital reduction confirmed by a court involves very low liability exposure as the court effectively makes the solvency decision. A capital reduction pursuant to section 641 involves greater exposure for directors to creditor claims that the solvency statement was made negligently if the company fails to satisfy all debts within the required timeframe. Directors may be rightly concerned that courts judging with the hindsight of failure may see a negligent solvency statement when in fact the statement was accurate and made with due care.[151]

If the solvency-statement approach was the only reduction mechanism available then companies with risk-averse directors may not make use of a capital reduction even where a reduction would benefit the company. The court-confirmation approach provides a safety valve for litigation-wary directors. However, 'safety-value' argument does not explain why the repurchase out of capital mechanism is still available. Arguably, the requirement of a weak audit opinion reduces director litigation risk, but, of course, there is nothing to stop worried directors from voluntarily obtaining such a report under the board-approved capital-reduction approach. It is, therefore, rather difficult to understand why the share repurchase out of capital provisions are still included in the Companies Act 2006.

V STRUCTURING AROUND CAPITAL AND DISTRIBUTION REGULATION

1 Legal engineering

Consider the following scenario involving Bob's Electronics Ltd.

Hypothetical C

Bob is the sole shareholder and the managing director of Bob's Electronics Ltd. His wife Alison is the only other director. The company has legal capital of £1,000. The company pays Bob for his services an annual salary of £100. The company's net profit in Year 1 is £100 (this profit calculation takes into account the £100 payment to Bob, which is an expense for the company). The company has, therefore, £100 of distributable profit which it dividends to Bob. Bob, therefore, receives, £200 in total from the company in his two capacities: as managing director and as shareholder.

The board of directors (Bob and Alison) could, however, elect to pay Bob a more substantial salary for his services as managing director. If it elects to pay him £400,

---

[150] *Re Holders Investment Trust Ltd* [1971] 2 All ER 289.
[151] On the effects of hindsight bias see Chapter 12.

what is the outcome? First, the company will make a loss of £200 (it previously made a profit of £100 when his salary expense was £100). Secondly, as the company makes a loss it will have no distributable profits with which to make a dividend to Bob. Thirdly, in order to take account of this loss, Bob's Electronics Ltd's shareholder equity entry will be reduced by £200 to £800 (that is, £200 below legal capital). However, remember that distribution and capital reduction regulation only prevent reductions in the legal capital accounting entry *as a result of a transfer of assets to shareholders*. Equity capital can, of course, be lost in trading. The increased salary paid to Bob is part of the trading activities of the company—to trade Bob's Electronics Ltd has to employ skilled staff. From Bob's (as an individual) perspective he now has £400 in his pocket instead of £200 although this time the £400 is received in one capacity, namely as managing director.

One might argue that such arrangements in close companies are just the inevitable consequence of incorporation and separate legal personality that enables one real person to play several roles in the company. In Chapter 2 in *Lee v Lee Air Farming Ltd*[152] we saw that Mr Lee was the managing director, sole employee pilot, and sole shareholder. The issue here, however, is determining whether the payment made to Bob is in fact a payment for his services. If the market rate of pay for managing directors of small to medium-sized companies in the computer industry is between £100–£200, then is the payment of £400 really a payment for services provided to the company by Bob, or is it in fact a 'hidden' distribution to Bob in his capacity as shareholder? If this payment can be re-characterized as a distribution, then it is an illegal distribution of £200 in relation to which the company may be able to claim recovery from Bob as shareholder or manager.

Similarly other business relationships between Bob and the company that could be re-characterized as distributions where the terms of those relationships are not on market/arm's length terms. Consider, for example, a loan made by Bob to Bob's Electronics Ltd in excess of market interest rates or, for that matter, any self-dealing transaction on non-arm's length terms where the company does not have sufficient distributable profits in the amount of the value transferred in excess of what would be arm's length terms.

2 Substance over form in distribution regulation

Regulatory tools are available to liquidators of companies, and in some instances creditors themselves, to address such transactions. For example, the Insolvency Act 1986 directly regulates transfers of assets out of the company in exchange for lower value assets—transfers at an undervalue.[153] As we have seen in Chapter 18, directors may be liable for breach of duty for approving transactions which are detrimental to creditors when the company is insolvent or, possibly, in the vicinity of insolvency. Our concern here, however, is not with the regulatory techniques that offer creditors protection from such transactions; rather it is whether company law's prohibition on unlawful dividends can regulate such transactions. Do the courts take the form and structure of a corporate transaction, which may be explicitly devised to avoid the restrictions imposed by distribution and capital reduction regulation, at face value? Or do they attempt to look through the form of these arrangements to regulate their substance?[154]

---

[152] [1961] AC 12.

[153] Section 423(3) of the Insolvency Act 1986 allows a liquidator or a person who is a victim of a transaction at an undervalue to apply to the court for relief. The excessive pay and interest rate examples set out earlier in this chapter could fall within section 423(3)(c).

[154] For an excellent review of the authorities see E. Micheler, 'Disguised Returns of Capital—An Arm's Length Approach' [2010] CLJ 151.

■ *Re Halt Garage (1964) Ltd* [1982] 3 All ER 1016

In 1964 Mr and Mrs Charlesworth set up a garage business through a company Halt Garage (1964) Ltd. The business was initially very successful but declined in profitability after Mrs Charlesworth became seriously ill. At the end of 1967 the business had a turnover of £6,000. By 1971 the company went into voluntary liquidation. During the period 1968–1971 Mr Charlesworth worked full time for the business (although was absent for a period of time due to an accident) and was paid director's remuneration of £3,500. During this period Mrs Charlesworth did not provide any services to the company but was still paid annual director's remuneration of between £500–£1,500. The liquidator of the company brought an action claiming that these payments amounted to an illegal reduction of capital.

Oliver J

The real test must, I think, be whether the transaction in question was a genuine exercise of the power. The motive is more important than the label. Those who deal with a limited company do so on the basis that its affairs will be conducted in accordance with its constitution, one of the express incidents of which is that the directors may be paid remuneration. Subject to that, they are entitled to have the capital kept intact. They have to accept the shareholders' assessment of the scale of that remuneration, but they are entitled to assume that, whether liberal or illiberal, what is paid is genuinely remuneration and that the power is not used as a cloak for making payments out of capital to the shareholders as such...

Turning now to the facts of the instant case, it seems to me that the question which I have to determine is whether, on the evidence before me, I can say that the payments made to Mr Charlesworth and to Mrs Charlesworth were genuinely exercises of the company's power to pay remuneration...This was a business with a turnover of the order of £100,000 per annum and the director's remuneration for a full-time working director on a scale of £3,500 per annum does not, I am bound to say, appear to me to be over-generous or unreasonable...Once bona fides is conceded, there seems to me to be nothing unreasonable in his continuing, as the person with the responsibility, both legal and financial, for the running of the business, to draw remuneration on the same scale as that which had been established and accepted in the past and, according to Mr Gore's evidence, discussed with the company's accountants...In my judgment, the remuneration has to be looked at as a whole against the background of the company's practice that drawings were made weekly and that wages continued to be paid during sickness. Mr Charlesworth was a working director over the whole year and the fact that for part of the time, even a substantial part of the time, he was disabled from attending to the business cannot, I think, alter the quality of the payments made. He was throughout the man ultimately in charge...

I do not think that, in the absence of evidence that the payments made were patently excessive or unreasonable, the court can or should engage on a minute examination of whether it would have been more appropriate or beneficial to the company to fix the remuneration at £X rather than £Y, so long as it is satisfied that it was indeed drawn as remuneration. That is a matter left by the company's constitution to its members. In my judgment, a general meeting was competent to sanction the payments which he in fact drew and the claim in misfeasance against Mr Charlesworth under this head must fail.

I have felt considerably greater difficulty over the payments to Mrs Charlesworth...It was known from, at the latest, December 1967 onwards, that Mrs Charlesworth could never return to render any services in the actual conduct of the company's business, and she was never thereafter called on, nor was she ever expected, to fulfil any function save that of being a director and carrying out such minimal formal acts as the holding of that office entailed. Mr Charlesworth in his evidence admitted that the company derived no benefit at all from the payments made to her, save such as may be thought to flow from the fact that she held office. She was incurably ill and living at a distance of several hundred miles from the company's place of business. Yet in each of the years 1968–69 and 1969–70 she received a sum of some £1,500 and in the year 1970–71 something over £500…

I do not think that it can be said that a director of a company cannot be rewarded as such merely because he is not active in the company's business. The mere holding of office involves responsibility even in the absence of any substantial activity, and it is indeed in part to the mere holding of office that Mrs Charlesworth owes her position as a respondent in these proceedings. I can see nothing as a matter of construction of the article to disentitle the company, if the shareholders so resolve, from paying a reward attributable to the mere holding of the office of director, for being, as it were, a name on the notepaper and attending such meetings or signing such documents as are from time to time required. The director assumes the responsibility on the footing that he will receive whatever recompense the company in general meeting may think appropriate. In this case, however, counsel for the liquidator is entitled to submit that the sums paid to Mrs Charlesworth were so out of proportion to any possible value attributable to her holding of office that the court is entitled to treat them as not being genuine payments of remuneration at all but as dressed-up dividends out of capital, like the dressed-up payments of 'interest' in the *Ridge Securities* case.

The difficulty that I felt about this at first was that there is…no allegation of fraud or mala fides in relation to these payments. The liquidator's case has been argued throughout on the footing that they were payments of remuneration but were also payments which could not be sanctioned by a general meeting because it was not for the benefit of the company to resolve on payments on this scale. For the reasons which I have endeavoured to state, I think that in circumstances such as exist in this case, where payments are made under the authority of a general meeting acting pursuant to an express power, the matter falls to be tested by reference to the genuineness and honesty of the transaction rather than by reference to some abstract standard of benefit. I do not, however, think that bona fides (in the sense of absence of fraudulent intention) and genuineness are necessarily the same thing. It is not suggested here that there was any intent to defraud, but that cannot be conclusive. As Jessel MR remarked in *Re National Funds Assurance Co* (1878) 10 Ch D 118, to say that something is done bona fide is not the same thing as merely to say that the actor had no intention to commit a fraud. The real question is, were these payments genuinely director's remuneration? If your intention is to make a gift out of the capital of the company, you do not alter the nature of that by giving it another label and calling it 'remuneration'.

The cases show, I think, that the mere fact that the company is in low financial water does not prevent the payment of a proper director's remuneration even though it may be technically a gratuity. But equally, the court is not, in my judgment, precluded from examining the true nature of the payments merely because the members choose to call them remuneration…

I find it really impossible on the facts to hold that the whole of these sums, amounting to £1,500 per annum, drawn during the years 1968–69 and 1969–70, can be treated as genuine director's remuneration in any real sense of the term. They were, as it seems to me, simply a recognition that, as a co-proprietor of the business with her husband, she ought to be getting out of the business what she had had before and that 'director's remuneration' was a convenient label to attach to these sums and one which, it was thought, would enable them to be properly paid. The mere attachment of that label cannot, in my view, alter the fact that they were in truth, from 1 April 1968 onwards, paid out of capital, which, so far at any rate as they exceeded anything which could reasonably be called remuneration for acting as a director, the company had no power to sanction…

Counsel for the liquidator submits here, however, that the entirety of the payments to Mrs Charlesworth over the relevant period are recoverable because she should and could have been paid nothing at all since she was not actively working in the business at the garage. That I feel unable to accept. As I have said, a sum paid simply for the assumption of the responsibility of being a director is, in my view, properly described as remuneration. The difficulty must necessarily be to know where to draw the line between what could reasonably be described as

> a genuine reward for service and what could not. Remuneration does not cease to be remuneration because it is generous or even, perhaps, unwisely generous, but there is an obvious difficulty about fixing any point at which it can be said that a purported exercise of the power to pay ceases to be genuine. In the absence of any evidence of actual motive, the court must, I think, look at the matter objectively and apply the standard of reasonableness.

In *Re Halt Garage* Oliver J considers the basis upon which a transaction purporting to be one thing (in this case executive remuneration) can be re-characterized as a dividend. It is, he holds, motive not label which counts. However, where the actor's motives are illusive then the correct approach is an objective one which requires looking at the reasonableness of the compensation in order to determine whether the transaction is in fact something other than its label. In applying this approach, he eschews a 'minute examination' of such decisions 'in the absence of evidence that the payments made were patently excessive or unreasonable'. That is, the amount paid for the service or the product has to be demonstrably unreasonable in order for the courts to re-characterize. In Mr Charlesworth's case the court does not interfere with these payments. Mrs Charlesworth, on the other hand, due to her illness, did nothing apart from hold the position as director. Whilst the court accepts that some form of remuneration for accepting a position as director was reasonable, the amounts received by Mrs Charlesworth could not, in Oliver J's view, be genuinely understood as remuneration. Accordingly, these payments were re-characterized by the court as distributions out of capital.

Consider now the recent and important Supreme Court case of *Progress Property Company Ltd v Moorgarth Group Ltd*.

■ *Progress Property Company Ltd v Moorgarth Group Ltd* [2011] 2 BCLC 332

The facts in *Progress Property* are complex. For our purposes the issue in the case arose out of a transfer of the shares in Your More Store Ltd (YMS) from Progress Property Co Ltd (PPC) to another group company, Moorgarth Group Ltd (Moorgarth). The price for the shares transferred to Moorgarth by PPC was calculated under the mistaken impression that PPC had provided an indemnity of up to £4 million to Moorgarth in relation to another transaction. Accordingly, it was agreed that PPC would be released by Moorgarth from the indemnity and the share price to be paid by Moorgarth would be reduced by £4 million. All parties genuinely thought that this was the case. At the time of the transfer both companies were controlled by the same parent company. Following the transfer and the sale by Moorgarth's parent of the shares in PPC, it was subsequently discovered that PPC did not in fact owe the £4 million indemnity and that the shares had, therefore, been transferred at a significant undervalue. As Moorgarth's parent was the controlling shareholder in PPC at the time of the sale of the shares and as PPC did not have the distributable reserves to make a distribution in that amount, PPC claimed that the transaction at an undervalue was an unlawful disguised distribution. The first instance court rejected this submission, as did the Court of Appeal. PPC appealed to the Supreme Court.

Lord Walker SCJ (with whom their Lordships agreed)
A limited company not in liquidation cannot lawfully return capital to its shareholders except by way of a reduction of capital approved by the court. Profits may be distributed to shareholders (normally by way of dividend) but only out of distributable profits computed in accordance with the complicated provisions of the Companies Act 2006 (replacing similar provisions in the Companies Act 1985)...

PPC's case, as finally formulated at first instance, relied not on s 263 of the 1985 Act (now replaced by ss 829 and 830 of the 2006 Act) but on what Mummery LJ referred to (at [23]) as 'the common law rule':

'The common law rule devised for the protection of the creditors of a company is well settled: a distribution of a company's assets to a shareholder, except in accordance with specific statutory procedures, such as a winding up of the company, is a return of capital, which is unlawful and ultra vires the company.'

The rule is essentially a judge-made rule, almost as old as company law itself, derived from the fundamental principles embodied in the statutes by which Parliament has permitted companies to be incorporated with limited liability...

Whether a transaction infringes the common law rule is a matter of substance, not form. The label attached to the transaction by the parties is not decisive. That is a theme running through the authorities, including *Ridge Securities Ltd v IRC* [1964] 1 All ER 275, [1964] 1 WLR 479 and *Aveling Barford Ltd v Perion Ltd* [1989] BCLC 626...

The essential issue then, is how the sale by PPC of its shareholding in YMS is to be character-ized...The deputy judge did not ask himself (or answer) that precise question. But he did roundly reject the submission made on behalf of PPC that there is an unlawful return of capital 'when-ever the company has entered into a transaction with a shareholder which results in a transfer of value not covered by distributable profits, and regardless of the purpose of the transaction'. A relentlessly objective rule of that sort would be oppressive and unworkable. It would tend to cast doubt on any transaction between a company and a shareholder, even if negotiated at arm's length and in perfect good faith, whenever the company proved, with hindsight, to have got significantly the worse of the transaction.

In the Court of Appeal Mummery LJ developed the deputy judge's line of thought into a more rounded conclusion:

'In this case the deputy judge noted that it had been accepted by PPC that the sale was entered into in the belief on the part of the director, Mr Moore, that the agreed price was at market value. In those circumstances there was no knowledge or intention that the shares should be disposed of at an undervalue. There was no reason to doubt the genuineness of the transaction as a commercial sale of the YMS shares. This was so, even though it appeared that the sale price was calculated on the basis of the value of the properties that was misunderstood by all concerned.'

In seeking to undermine that conclusion Mr Collings QC (for PPC) argued strenuously that an objective approach is called for. The same general line is taken in a recent article by Dr Eva Micheler commenting on the Court of Appeal's decision, 'Disguised Returns of Capital—An Arm's Length Approach' [2010] CLJ 151. This interesting article refers to a number of cases not cited to this court or to the courts below, and argues for what the author calls an arm's length approach.

If there were a stark choice between a subjective and an objective approach, the least unsat-isfactory choice would be to opt for the latter. But in cases of this sort the court's real task is to inquire into the true purpose and substance of the impugned transaction. That calls for an inves-tigation of all the relevant facts, which sometimes include the state of mind of the human beings who are orchestrating the corporate activity.

Sometimes their states of mind are totally irrelevant. A distribution described as a dividend but actually paid out of capital is unlawful, however technical the error and however well-meaning the directors who paid it. The same is true of a payment which is on analysis the equivalent of a dividend, such as the unusual cases (mentioned by Dr Micheler) of *Re Walters' Deed of Guarantee, Walters' 'Palm' Toffee Ltd v Walters* [1933] Ch 321, [1933] All ER Rep 430 (claim by guarantor of preference dividends) and *Barclays Bank plc v British & Commonwealth Holdings plc* [1996] 1 BCLC 1 (claim for damages for contractual breach of scheme for redemption of shares). Where there is a challenge to the propriety of a director's remuneration the test is objective (*Re Halt Garage*), but probably subject in practice to what has been called, in a recent Scottish case, a 'margin of appreciation': see *Clydebank Football Club Ltd v Steedman* 2002 SLT 109 at [76] (discussed further below). If a controlling shareholder simply treats a company as his own property, as the domineering master-builder did in *Re George Newman & Co* [1895] 1 Ch 674, [1895–9] All ER Rep Ext 2160, his state of mind (and that of his fellow-directors) is irrelevant. It does not matter whether they were consciously in breach of duty, or just woefully ignorant of their duties. What they do is enough by itself to establish the unlawful character of the transaction.

The participants' subjective intentions are however sometimes relevant, and a distribution disguised as an arm's length commercial transaction is the paradigm example. If a company sells to a shareholder at a low value assets which are difficult to value precisely, but which are potentially very valuable, the transaction may call for close scrutiny, and the company's financial position, and the actual motives and intentions of the directors, will be highly relevant. There may be questions to be asked as to whether the company was under financial pressure compelling it to sell at an inopportune time, as to what advice was taken, how the market was tested, and how the terms of the deal were negotiated. If the conclusion is that it was a genuine arm's length transaction then it will stand, even if it may, with hindsight, appear to have been a bad bargain. If it was an improper attempt to extract value by the pretence of an arm's length sale, it will be held unlawful. But either conclusion will depend on a realistic assessment of all the relevant facts, not simply a retrospective valuation exercise in isolation from all other inquiries.

Pretence is often a badge of a bad conscience. Any attempt to dress up a transaction as something different from what it is is likely to provoke suspicion…The right approach is in my opinion well-illustrated by the careful judgment of Lord Hamilton in *Clydebank Football Club Ltd v Steedman* 2002 SLT 109. It is an example of the problems which can arise with football clubs owned by limited companies, where some small shareholders see the club as essentially a community enterprise, and other more commercially-minded shareholders are concerned with what they see as underused premises ripe for profitable redevelopment. The facts are complicated, and the main issue was on s 320 of the 1985 Act [substantial property transaction—now section 190 CA 2006]. But the judge also dealt with a claim under s 263 [now section 830 CA 2006] (unlawful distribution). He held that the sale of the club's derelict ground at Kilbowie Park, and another site originally purchased under an abortive plan for a new ground, was a genuine arm's length sale even though effected at a price £165,000 less than the value as eventually determined by the court after hearing expert evidence. Lord Hamilton said:

> '…It is also clear, in my view, that a mere arithmetical difference between the consideration given for the asset or assets and the figure or figures at which it or they are in subsequent proceedings valued retrospectively will not of itself mean that there has been a distribution. If the transaction is genuinely conceived of and effected as an exchange for value and the difference ultimately found does not reflect a payment "manifestly beyond any possible justifiable reward for that in respect of which allegedly it is paid", does not give rise to an exchange "at a gross undervalue" and is not otherwise unreasonably large, there will not to any extent be a "dressed up return of capital". In assessing the adequacy of the consideration, a margin of appreciation may properly be allowed.'

The words quoted by Lord Hamilton are from *Re Halt Garage* and the *Aveling Barford* case. Lord Hamilton said (at [79]):

> '…It is plain, in my view, that directors are liable only if it is established that in effecting the unlawful distribution they were in breach of their fiduciary duties (or possibly of contractual obligations, though that does not arise in the present case). Whether or not they were so in breach will involve consideration not only of whether or not the directors knew at the time that what they were doing was unlawful but also of their state of knowledge at that time of the material facts. In reviewing the then authorities Vaughan Williams J in [*Re Kingston Cotton Mill Co (No 2)* [1896] 1 Ch 331 at 347] said: "in no one of [the cases cited] can I find that directors were held liable unless the payments were made with actual knowledge that the funds of the company were being misappropriated or with knowledge of the facts that established the misappropriation". Although this case went to the Court of Appeal, this aspect of the decision was not quarrelled with (see [1896] 2 Ch 279)…'

> I agree with both those passages. In this case there are concurrent findings that the sale of YMS to Moorgarth was a genuine commercial sale. The contrary was not pleaded or put to Mr Moore in cross-examination. I would dismiss this appeal.

Although *Progress Properties* is difficult to parse, its core holding appears to be consistent with Oliver J's holding *Re Halt Garage*, namely that the starting point is the motive of the directors who enter into the transaction: did they intend to enter into the transaction to further the company's interests, or was the transaction merely a cover for transferring value to shareholders? Accordingly, even though a transaction at an undervalue transfers value to shareholders which—because of insufficient distributable profits—they were not entitled to have had transferred to them, if the parties genuinely intended to enter into that transaction on those terms then the transaction will not be re-characterized as a dividend. Accordingly, as PPC's director was of the view at the time of the sale that the price was part of a genuine commercial transaction, the transaction did not amount to an unlawful distribution. What is intended by the idea of 'genuine commercial transaction' is that the director of the subject company when he entered into the transaction considered its terms to be beneficial to the company. The fact that—due to information that comes to light following the entering into of the transaction—the terms turn out not to have been beneficial is irrelevant. In this regard, *Progress Properties* was an easy case as the claimant accepted that this was the view of PPC's director at the time he agreed to enter into the transaction.

Where the director's state of mind is disputed and not readily available to the court, what then is the basis for determining whether the transaction should be re-characterized? *Progress Properties* sets forth an approach, again consistent with Oliver J in *Re Halt*, that could be labelled a *deferential objective approach*: objective because the court is involved in a process of determining the actual value of the transaction; deferential as the court will allow considerable leeway in determining the range of possible values. That is, it is only when the terms of the transaction are 'manifestly beyond any justifiable reward' or patently unreasonable that the transaction will be re-characterized as a disguised distribution; the courts will give managers a significant 'margin of appreciation' in determining the value of a good or a service before invoking their power to re-characterize. Lord Walker recognizes that a more intrusive approach by courts to identify the actual value of any transaction would be 'oppressive and unworkable'. However, note that on the facts of this case there was indeed a manifest undervaluation when one removed the £4 million indemnity from the equation. Why then was it not re-characterized? The key point to remember is that this deferential objective approach is only triggered in the absence of clear evidence of intent, and in *Progress* such evidence was available. In most cases, however, it will not be and accordingly in most cases the deferential objective approach will be applicable.

 Online Resource Centre
http://www.oxfordtextbooks.co.uk/orc/kershaw2e/

Visit the Online Resource Centre for additional resources and information available for this chapter, including web links and an interactive flashcard glossary.

■ INDEX